Hillier's

Fundamentals of Motor Vehicle Technology

BOOK 1

Sixth Edition

Revised by
Calex UK

Nelson Thornes

This edition published in 2012 by:
Nelson Thornes Ltd
Delta Place
27 Bath Road
CHELTENHAM
GL53 7TH
United Kingdom

12 13 14 15 16 / 10 9 8 7 6 5 4 3 2 1

A catalogue record for this book is available from the British Library

ISBN 978 1 4085 1518 1

Cover photograph: Cla78/Fotolia

Page make-up by Greengate Publishing Services, Tonbridge, Kent

Printed and bound in Spain by GraphyCems

Contents

Preface

The first edition of this book was published in 1966 by V.A.W. Hillier. It was written in response to the need for a textbook covering the construction of motor vehicles and their components in a manner simple enough to be understood by young apprentices beginning their training as mechanics, and detailed enough to serve as a solid foundation for later work.

Now in its 6th edition and in full colour, *Hillier's Fundamentals of Motor Vehicle Technology 6th Edition Book 1* continues this tradition by providing up-to-date and straightforward information that spans the evolution of vehicle development from the 'horseless carriage' to the hybrid vehicles of today. Hillier's text has been carefully updated by an expert team of authors at Calex UK. It maintains its authoritative, yet simple style and is now accompanied by colour photographs and illustrations as well as key terms and feature boxes to enhance your reading experience. Key terms are shaded to allow easy identification of new terminology and feature boxes are included to highlight important concepts.

The structure of the book is easy to follow with seven chapters that clearly delineate the content, including a chapter on new vehicle technology and alternative fuels. In addition to the standard electrical systems, this book gives an overview of the advanced electronic control systems now used by today's motor vehicles, providing the knowledge required to progress to more advanced detail in *Hillier's Fundamentals of Automotive Technology 6th Edition Book 2*.

Keeping in tradition with its previous editions, the 6th edition is aimed at apprentices, trainees, practitioners, car enthusiasts and anyone curious about cars. It is structured thematically to cater for all audiences. However, for the first time, there is online material available to support apprentice mechanics and tutors with the resources aligned to the current Level 2 and 3 IMI specifications.

For more than 45 years Hillier's books have been assisting apprentices, enthusiasts and novices with the fundamentals of motor vehicle technology – this new edition will ensure that thousands more will benefit from this accessible manual.

Vehicle evolution, layout and structure

Ever since the first motor vehicle was produced, inventors, engineers, designers and scientists have strived to improve them using the latest technology and materials. As time has passed, we have seen and experienced many changes in design and development to give us today's motor vehicles. Learning from those early designs, and with today's manufacturing skills, vehicle manufacturers can now produce motor vehicles that use very strong but lightweight materials in their structure and drive train. Many innovative materials are also now used in vehicle manufacture, some of which are recyclable, which helps reduce costs and reduces the environmental impact of the industry.

As we now live in a world of electronic technology, the motor vehicle has become a designer's dream in providing systems that continue to improve the protection of its occupants, provide stability and economy and also take interior comfort to new levels of refinement. Packaged with this, we now have engines and transmissions that are high performance, environmentally friendly and economical to run, giving today's drivers an exciting all-round driving experience with a very high level of safety. The following sections outline the fundamentals in vehicle construction and design on which the reader can build their understanding of the latest developments.

1.1 Vehicle evolution

1.1.1 Early days

At a very early stage in human history people must have realised that the human body was severely limited in terms of the loads it could carry and the distance it could carry them. Furthermore, it is safe to assume that the physical exertion involved was no more to people's liking then than it is today.

Much progress was achieved through the domestication of suitable animals to enable heavier loads to be carried greater distances, often at greater speeds than people were capable of attaining. There was the added advantage that, as most of the effort was provided by the animal, the people could travel at their ease and in relative comfort.

At first, heavy loads were dragged upon sledges until an early and unknown engineer invented the wheel. This made it possible to construct crude carts upon which even heavier loads could be carried more easily. The one drawback to the use of wheeled vehicles was – and still is – the necessity of providing a reasonably smooth and hard surface upon which the wheels could run. The development of wheeled vehicles, therefore, is closely related to the development of roads.

As new materials and manufacturing methods were developed, it became possible to make improvements in vehicles, but as long as animals were the only form of motive power it was not possible to significantly increase loads and speeds. The development of the steam engine during the 18th and 19th centuries led to its application to the driving of vehicles, and though some of the early attempts were crude and not very successful, several extremely promising carriages were produced. These might have been developed into very practical vehicles had not restrictive legislation forced them off the roads. In any case, the steam engine proved less suited to road vehicles than it did to the railway. It was the successful development of the light, high-speed internal-combustion engine towards the end of the 19th century that really opened up the way to the power-driven road vehicle, and that made possible the development of the modern motor car, truck, bus and coach.

1.1.2 Development of layout

Motor vehicles were developed from horse-drawn carriages – they were, in fact, originally called 'horseless carriages' – and naturally owed something of their general form to those carriages. For instance, the system of four wheels arranged one at each end of two transverse axles so that their points of contact with the ground are at the corners of a rectangle (see Figure l.la) has been used on carts and wagons since time immemorial and is still by far the commonest arrangement. While three wheels are sufficient to give stability, they do not provide so much 'useful space' for a given amount of road space taken up (compare Figure l.la with Figure l.lb).

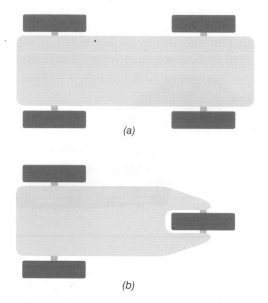

Figure 1.1 Wheel arrangements for simple vehicle layout

The horse was invariably put in front of the cart, to pull it rather than push it, to allow the animal to see where it was going and the driver to keep an eye on the horse. The driver steered the vehicle through shafts attached to a front axle, which could pivot about its centre, and when it came to replacing the horse by an engine, it was natural that front-wheel steering should be retained, at least for a while. It was not long, however, before vehicles with rear-wheel steering were tried, but it was soon found that rear-wheel steering had disadvantages that ruled it out for general use. For example, a vehicle steered by its rear wheels would steer to the right by deflecting its rear end to the left, making it impossible to drive away forwards from a position close to a wall or kerb (see Figure 1.2). A rear-wheel-steered car moving at any speed and coming alongside a wall, kerb, ditch or another vehicle could very easily find itself in a situation in which a collision could not be avoided.

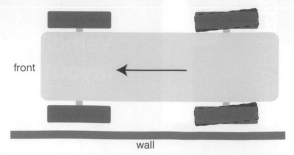

Figure 1.2 One inconvenience of rear-wheel steering

The swivelling axle arrangement is not very satisfactory for powered vehicles, partly because a good deal of space must be left for the axle and wheels to swivel. Also, if one wheel strikes an obstruction, such as a large stone, it is extremely difficult, without the leverage of the long shafts, to prevent the axle swivelling about its pivot, causing the vehicle to swerve off the road. An alternative arrangement, whereby the wheels were carried on stub axles free to pivot at the ends of a fixed axle, had already been used on some horse carriages, and this was soon adopted for motor vehicles.

When it came to using mechanical power to drive vehicles, it was natural that the power should be applied to the non-steerable wheels, since the problem of driving these is simpler than powering the driving wheels which have also to be swivelled for steering purposes. This explains why, in the past, rear-wheel drive was universally adopted. The increased load on the rear wheels when climbing hills or accelerating gives a better grip, making rear-wheel drive attractive. Front-wheel drive vehicles lose this advantage, so under these conditions the wheels spin more easily. However, this drawback, together with the extra complication of the drive arrangement to the steered wheels, is the price paid to achieve either extra space for the vehicle's occupants or a shorter vehicle.

Figure 1.3 shows that the width between the front wheels is restricted by the necessity for the wheels to swivel for steering purposes, but there is a space that might provide room for one seat. However, people seem to prefer to sit side by side, and, though there may be much to be said in favour of placing the driver by themselves in the extreme front of the vehicle, this arrangement is not popular. The engine can be made to fit into this space very conveniently and, although the earliest vehicles had their engines elsewhere, this position was adopted by almost all manufacturers from a very early stage.

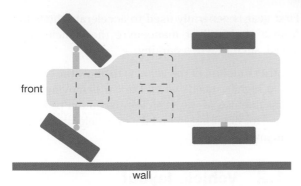

Figure 1.3 One reason for placing the engine at the front

1.1.3 Power sources

The most convenient source of power so far developed for driving road vehicles is the internal-combustion engine, which derives its power from the burning of fuel inside the engine itself. Alternative power units are the steam engine and the electric motor. The former requires a boiler to generate the steam, in addition to the engine itself, making the complete installation rather bulky. Also, there are heat losses in the boiler as well as in the engine, therefore it is less efficient than the internal-combustion engine. During temporary halts, the steam engine continues to consume fuel in order to maintain steam pressure, whereas the internal-combustion engine consumes fuel only when it is actually running.

An electric motor needs a supply of electrical energy to operate it. If this energy is to be carried on the vehicle, it must be in the form of batteries or accumulators. These are both heavy and bulky in relation to the amount of energy they can store, limiting the range, speed and load-carrying capacity of the vehicle. If an external supply of electrical energy is to be used, the vehicle must be connected to a distant power station by some means such as a system of wires, suspended at a safe height above the road, with which contact is made by suitable arms mounted on top of the vehicle and provided with some form of sliding connection to the wires. Such a system has obvious limitations.

Although both steam and electric vehicles have been tried, the internal-combustion engine has become almost universal. However, the development of more practical electric cars and of **hybrid** vehicles is gaining momentum because of the ecological advantages these types of vehicles offer.

Hybrid: a vehicle that can be powered by both electricity and an internal-combustion engine.

Torque converter: a device that transmits or multiplies the torque generated by an engine.

Internal-combustion engine

The internal-combustion engine has two characteristics that necessitate certain arrangements in the mechanism connecting the engine to the driving wheels.

Firstly, the engine cannot produce any driving effort when it is not running. When a steam engine is at rest, it is necessary merely to admit steam under pressure from the boiler, by opening a valve, and the engine will start to work immediately. An electric motor needs only to be switched on. An internal-combustion engine, on the other hand, must be driven by some external means before it will begin to run under its own power. Once the internal-combustion engine is running at speed and sufficient power is being produced, it has to be connected to the driving wheels of the vehicle by some arrangement that permits the running engine to be coupled smoothly and without shock to the initially stationary wheels.

In order to facilitate this, a manual gearbox and clutch arrangement was developed. The clutch is a device that allows the drive from the engine to be connected smoothly and progressively to the gearbox to propel the vehicle, and also disconnected to allow the vehicle to change gear or become stationary. More and more of today's vehicles are now fitted with automatic gearboxes to improve the drive engagement through a fluid- (oil) based drive using a **torque converter** or fluid flywheel.

Figure 1.4 Engine and gearbox arrangement

Secondly, the power developed by an engine depends upon the speed at which it runs. A small engine running at high speed can develop as much power as a larger engine running at low speed, and is to be preferred since it will be lighter and take up less space. Such small high-speed engines generally run four or five times faster than the road wheels, so a speed-reducing gear has to be included in the driving mechanism connecting the engine to the driving wheels. This forms part of the rear axle in a rear-wheel drive vehicle and usually part of the gearbox in a front-wheel drive vehicle.

There is a minimum speed below which the engine will not run. Most modern engines have a speed range from about 800 to 9000 revolutions per minute (rpm) or more. Therefore, if the maximum speed of a car is 241 kph (150 mph), its minimum speed will be about 10 kph (6 mph), unless the clutch is partly disconnected or slipped. In starting off from rest, the clutch cannot be fully engaged until the road speed has reached at least 13 kph (8 mph), during which time a great deal of heat will have been generated in the slipping clutch, which will damage it. This difficulty is overcome by providing additional gearing in the driving arrangements, which can be brought into use – either by the driver or automatically – to enable the car to move slowly with the clutch fully engaged and the engine running faster than its minimum speed. Several such speeds or gears are usually provided in a mechanism called the gearbox.

Gearbox

Modern vehicles with internal-combustion engines require a gearbox, providing a range of gear ratios to maintain engine power and speed to allow the vehicle to travel at appropriate road speeds relevant to the driver and environmental requirements.

The gearbox can be manual or automatic. The lowest forward gear (first gear) allows the engine to operate at peak power and torque, but produces low road speed. As one moves up the gears, the ratio allows the engine revolutions to remain fairly constant within the peak operating efficiency, while increasing road speed. Using a high gear will allow the vehicle to travel at higher road speeds, but lower engine speeds, resulting in increased fuel efficiency and lower emissions.

First gear is generally used to accelerate the vehicle from a standstill or manoeuvre the vehicle at low speed, such as when parking.

Another function of the gears is to allow the engine to run at higher speeds when the car is moving slowly, so making use of the vehicle's maximum power and torque for climbing steep hills or accelerating rapidly from low speeds.

1.2 Vehicle layout

1.2.1 Light vehicles

Vehicles classified in this category have a laden mass of less than 3 tonnes: this group is the main subject for this book. A wide range of different body shapes and sizes come into this light-vehicle category, ranging from two-seater cars to personnel carriers (minibuses) and small trucks. Multi-purpose vehicles (MPVs) and small commercial vehicles are also included. These make use of similar mechanical components to normal passenger cars but have bodies specifically constructed for individual purposes. This process of using the same basic components across a range of vehicles is called platform sharing and is common with a large number of manufacturers.

Figure 1.5 shows a simplified layout of the various basic components used on a vehicle. The layout of this vehicle, which is based on a minibus, is a comparatively simple construction. Here, you can see the location and study the function and purpose of each of the main components. Once this foundation has been established, it will be possible to appreciate the finer details of the more sophisticated systems in common use.

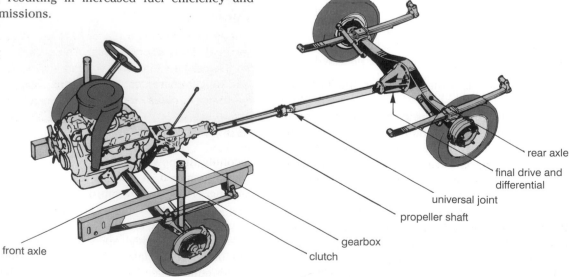

Figure 1.5 Layout of mechanical systems (simple front-engine, rear-wheel drive layout)

Wheels and tyres

Most light vehicles run on four wheels made from steel or aluminium. These wheels are fitted with hollow rubber tyres filled with air, under sufficient pressure to support the load they have to carry. The tyres provide grip to the road surface and absorb shocks caused by small road irregularities. Larger shocks are taken by suspension springs and these allow the wheels to move vertically in relation to the rest of the vehicle.

Front axle

The front axle supports the front of the vehicle and is also used for steering. In Figure 1.5 the axle is mounted on leaf-type springs, which form the flexible suspension system needed to absorb the road shocks. Each wheel is carried on a stub axle; this is pivoted to the extremity of the front axle by a **kingpin**. The two stub axles are linked together by steering arms, which are joined together by a track rod and connected to a linkage coupled to the driver's steering wheel.

Kingpin: a main or large bolt in a central vertical position, used as a pivot.

On most modern light vehicles, the one-piece axle beam has been superseded by a suspension arrangement that allows each front wheel to rise and fall with its own spring without affecting the other front wheel. This arrangement is called independent front suspension.

Rear axle

The rear axle carries the wheels and supports the weight of the rear of the vehicle. The axle type shown in Figure 1.5 is tubular in section and contains two axle shafts (half shafts), one for each side, to drive the road wheels.

On the vehicle centre line, the axle is enlarged to house the final drive. The final drive system contains a pair of gears that turn the drive through 90° and reduce the driving speed to that suitable for the size of the road wheels.

When the vehicle is turning a corner, the inner and outer road wheels travel at different speeds. When the two road wheels are both rigidly connected to one axle shaft, the greater distance covered by the outer wheel causes one or both wheels to slip on the road. In addition to causing excessive tyre wear, this action makes the vehicle difficult to steer in a path other than straight ahead. These problems are overcome by using a **differential**. Fitted adjacent to the final drive gears, this unit ensures that each road wheel can rotate at a speed that suits the cornering conditions. In addition, it arranges for each wheel to receive an equal driving effort irrespective of the speed of rotation of the wheel.

Differential: a set of gears that allow the driven wheels of a vehicle to revolve at different speeds when turning.

An alternative to the construction shown in Figure 1.5 is to mount the final drive and differential casing to the vehicle frame and arrange each wheel to be independently sprung. This independent rear-suspension arrangement uses a short drive shaft with a **universal joint** at each end to transmit the drive from the differential to the wheel (Figure 1.6).

Universal joint: a coupling that can transmit rotary power over a range of angles.

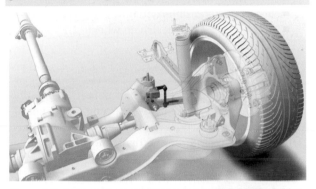

Figure 1.6 Independent suspension using separate final drive

Modern suspensions also use air-, gas- and oil-based systems, which are electronically controlled to enhance the handling and smoothness for today's driving demands. Lighter materials, such as aluminium, are used in the design and construction of many suspension components. Rubber compound suspension bushes are commonly used, but hydro bushes (rubber compound bushes with an internal chamber of oil) that improve stability and lower noise and vibration are also found.

Power unit

The normal source of power in motor vehicles is an internal-combustion engine. The petrol (gasoline) engine has been the most popular for its performance and weight characteristics, but **diesel (compression-ignition) engines** are an attractive alternative for their excellent fuel economy, which for high-mileage users offsets the higher initial cost and slightly reduced output. With advances in engine design, construction and electronic management control systems, diesel and petrol engines are becoming more equal in performance, depending on driver demands and drive cycle requirements.

Diesel (compression-ignition) engine: an engine that burns a light oil, which is ignited by the high temperature produced by compressing air to a very high pressure in the engine cylinders.

Transmission system

In the UK, the transmission system is understood to refer to the complete driveline between the engine and the road wheels. However, in many other countries the term 'transmission' refers to the gearbox unit and applies in particular to the type of arrangement used on a given vehicle (i.e. whether the selection of the gears has to be carried out manually by the driver or uses automatic means).

The complete transmission system includes:

- gearbox
- clutch
- propeller shaft
- final drive and differential
- drive shafts to each driven wheel
- universal joints.

Manual gearbox

The manual gearbox consists of sets of gears that amplify the output given by the engine to enable the driving force at the road wheels to be increased sufficiently to overcome the resistance to movement of the vehicle. The gearbox enables the engine speed to be kept within its working limits irrespective of the speed of the vehicle. It also allows a 'neutral' position where the engine can run without moving the vehicle.

Early manual gearboxes had four forward-moving gears and a reverse gear to drive the vehicle backwards. Modern gearboxes now consist of up to six forward-moving gears in manual gearboxes (up to eight in automatic gearboxes). This enhances the vehicle's overall performance and fuel efficiency. By having more gear ratios, the engine's power can be kept within the peak power band to improve acceleration and performance.

Automatic transmission

Automatic transmission systems relieve the driver of the task of gear selection, other than choosing the direction of travel and gear pattern needed to suit the general driving conditions. The automatic gearbox system allows the vehicle to be either moved off or brought to rest in a smooth manner, without the driver having to do anything except press the accelerator or brake pedal. Automatic gearboxes can have a selection of drive methods, ranging from a fluid flywheel or torque converter to conventional gear sets, similar to manual gearboxes but with electronic control of clutch and gear shift.

Early automatic transmissions had limited gear selection such as 'drive' for forwards, 'reverse' for backwards and 'park' and 'neutral' for stationary situations where no drive was transmitted to the road wheels. More modern automatic gearboxes have up

Figure 1.7 Automatic gearbox internals

to eight forward-moving gears to improve overall performance and fuel efficiency. The conventional reverse, park and neutral complete the automatic transmission assembly.

The inclusion of electronic control systems in modern vehicles gives the driver the option of an automatic gearbox that can also be driven manually. This option can be selected via the gear lever, a button or switch, or paddle shift levers on the steering column. This option has now made the automatic transmission more popular with drivers than the conventional manual gearbox.

Clutch

The gears in a manual gearbox have to be changed when appropriate to suit the varying driving conditions. This requires the driver to move a selector lever, which in turn either engages or disengages a pair of gears. This action should only be performed when the gears are not under load; therefore a clutch is fitted, which enables the driver to disconnect the engine from the gearbox in order that the gear can be changed.

Figure 1.8 Example of a clutch assembly fitted to a manual gearbox vehicle

A sudden connection of the drive from the engine to the transmission would cause a severe jolt and subsequent damage to the vehicle. The clutch is designed to avoid this; it allows the driver to accelerate the vehicle away from a stationary position gradually. Also, it enables the driver to disconnect the engine from the wheels temporarily when road conditions dictate such a need. Vehicle manufacturers have used many variations of clutch designs depending on the vehicle's driving demands. The conventional dry clutch is the most commonly used, with other options being wet clutch, multi-plate or centrifugal. Each variant of clutch has the same basic function of operation, but is used in different vehicle applications to suit the vehicle's requirements. Many mechanical systems are now electronically controlled using systems such as dual clutch and direct shift systems. These are discussed in the transmission section on page 346.

Propeller shaft

The propeller shaft is the long tubular shaft that links the gearbox to the final drive on rear-wheel drive vehicles. Normally, an open type arrangement is used in which the shaft is exposed. Most early designs of propeller shafts were of a one-piece tube design, but with modern design structures and driving demands the majority today are two- or even three-piece units. Some modern vehicles also have propeller shafts that are designed to collapse if the vehicle receives a severe impact to the rear from another vehicle. This design is intended to enhance vehicle deceleration, reduce driveline impact damage and improve passenger safety.

Universal joints

Universal joints are fitted to each end of the propeller shaft to enable the drive to be transmitted through a varying angle. This variation is due to the movement of the axle relative to the engine and gearbox. Even when the final drive is fixed to the frame and the wheels are independently sprung, the propeller shaft still needs universal joints to allow for the flexing of the frame structure that occurs when the vehicle is travelling over a bumpy surface. Although there is a great variation in modern driveline layouts available to vehicle manufacturers, the universal joint is still used with drive shafts to link from the transmission through to the road wheels. Other joint designs, such as constant velocity joints and rubber-compounded joints, are also used in the propeller and drive shaft construction.

Brakes

Vehicles are required by law to be fitted with an efficient braking system; this usually means having a brake attached to each wheel.

Two types of brake are used: drum and disc. Early vehicles used drum brakes at the front and rear, then moved towards disc brakes at the front and drums at the rear. Now most vehicles have disc brakes at the front and rear, as these are more effective.

A disc brake consists of an exposed disc, which is attached to, and rotates with, the road wheel and hub. A fixed calliper, mounted to the axle, prevents a friction pad on each side of the disc from rotating with the wheel when the disc is sandwiched by the pads during brake application. Braking is achieved by converting the energy of motion (**kinetic energy**) to heat energy, so exposure of the disc to the air stream for cooling is an important feature of this type of brake.

Kinetic energy: energy stored in a moving object.

Figure 1.9 Example of disc brake assembly

Drum brake systems have been in use for many years and are still seen on rear wheels. This is because they can also be used as a parking brake (handbrake) to keep the vehicle stationary when it is not in use.

This type has two brake shoes, which are lined with a friction material and secured to a back-plate fixed to the axle. The shoes are contained in a drum that is attached to the rotating hub. Retardation of the drum is achieved by moving the shoes outwards. This expansion is normally driven by a piston in a **hydraulic** cylinder.

Hydraulic: system powered by a fluid.

Light vehicles use a hydraulic system to operate the brakes. The insertion of a vacuum **servo** between the driver's foot pedal and the hydraulic actuating system boosts the force applied to the brakes; this minimises the effort that the driver has to apply.

Servo: supplementary power unit to provide added control.

Modern vehicles' braking systems are now electronically controlled by an electronic control unit (ECU). This system is known as an anti-lock braking system (ABS). The ABS controls braking force by controlling the hydraulic pressure of the braking system, so that the wheels do not lock during braking. This procedure, along with other monitored system inputs, greatly improves the vehicle's braking efficiency and safety.

Electrical equipment

Vehicle manufacturers are required by law to design their vehicles to meet current legislation and regulatory standards. Vehicle electrical systems, such as exterior lighting and brake lights are good examples. Early motor vehicle electrical systems were very basic in their functionality and monitoring control. Most vehicle systems were mechanically operated with only minimal electrical control in each of the systems operated. Modern motor vehicle electrical and electronic systems are now extremely sophisticated and wide-ranging.

An electric motor is used to rotate the engine, enabling it to start. Vehicles are required by law to be fitted with certain lights, for instance sidelights and headlights for use during darkness and in poor visibility. Many manufacturers now also fit daytime running lights for improved visibility. Indicator lights are required for the driver to signal when they are going to change direction, flashing orange on the side of the vehicle that is turning. Brake lights at the rear illuminate red when the brake is operated. Reversing light(s) at the rear illuminate white when reverse gear is selected, indicating to other road users that the vehicle is travelling, or about to travel, backwards.

Other functions that were once operated mechanically, such as windscreen wipers and washers, horns, heaters, audio systems, central locking and various other aids for the comfort and safety of the driver and passengers, are today operated by more complex electronic control systems.

Electrical and electronic equipment is powered by a battery, which is charged by a generator called an alternator, driven from the engine. The battery provides the main source of electrical energy when the engine is not running. Today's vehicles have ECUs to operate and monitor fuel, ignition and other functions. This allows for more accurate control, improved emission levels and fuel economy.

Manufacturers are now producing cars that run on electrical power either alone or alongside the engine. This move in technology has been driven by the need to reduce both the amount of emissions produced by vehicles and the amount of fossil fuels the world is using to power vehicles and aircraft.

Fundamentals of Motor Vehicle Technology 6th Edition Book 1 explains the basic principles of electricity and electrical circuit calculations. There is also an introduction to electrical components and a description of the operating principles of batteries, starter motors, alternators and their operating systems. Also included are other electrical circuits, such as lighting systems, auxiliary systems, heating, air conditioning, safety restraint systems and basic diagnostic routines. In addition to the standard electrical systems, this book gives an overview of the advanced electronic control systems now used by today's motor vehicles, providing the knowledge required to progress to more advanced detail in *Fundamentals of Automotive Technology 6th Edition Book 2*.

1.2.2 Cars

The layout shown in Figure 1.5 was similar to that used on cars up to about 1950. Since that time, various developments have considerably improved the overall performance of motor vehicles. This can be seen, for example, in body design where aerodynamic shapes have been developed to improve performance and efficiency.

There is much variation in vehicle layout design, for instance the location of the engine and the driving arrangement (i.e. the number and position of the driving wheels). These variations offer specific advantages.

Engine position

Front engine

Apart from tradition, there are a number of reasons for positioning the engine at the front of a car as shown in Figure 1.10. Engine cooling is simple to arrange and the large mass of an engine at the front of the car gives the driver protection in the event of a head-on collision. In addition, the cornering ability of a vehicle is normally better if the weight is concentrated at the front, over the steered wheels.

Figure 1.10 Front-engine arrangement

Rear engine

By placing the engine at the rear of the vehicle, it can be made as a unit that incorporates the clutch, gearbox and final drive assembly. With such an arrangement it is necessary to use some form of independent rear suspension.

Most rear-engine layouts have been confined to comparatively small cars because having the engine at the rear has an adverse effect on the handling of the car by making it 'tail-heavy'. It also takes up a good deal of space that would be used on a front-engine car for carrying luggage. Most of the space vacated by the engine at the front end can be used for luggage, but this space is usually less than that available at the rear. Although vertical engines of conventional form are occasionally used in rear-engine cars, a 'flat' engine, or a conventional engine laid on its side, offers the advantage of leaving some space for luggage above the engine.

One advantage attributed to a rear-engine layout is that it increases the load on the rear driving wheels, giving the tyres better traction.

Figure 1.11 shows a rear-engined car. Notice that the front seats are nearer the front wheels than a front-engined car, and the floor is quite flat.

Figure 1.11 Rear-engine arrangement

Central and mid-engine

These engine configurations generally apply to sports cars because the engine location gives a balanced load distribution and achieves both good handling and maximum traction from the driving wheels.

These advantages, while of great importance for special cars, are outweighed in the case of everyday cars by the fact that the engine takes up space that would normally be occupied by passengers.

The mid-engine layout shown in Figure 1.12 combines the engine and transmission components in one unit. The term 'mid-engine' is used because the engine is mounted in front of the rear axle line.

Figure 1.12 Mid-engine arrangement

Drive arrangements

Rear-wheel drive

The traditional layout shown in Figure 1.13 shows the engine situated with its output shaft set longitudinally. In this arrangement the rear wheels act as the driving wheels and the front wheels swivel to steer the vehicle. In the past, rear-wheel drive was a natural choice because of the difficulty of transmitting drive to a wheel that had to swivel for steering purposes.

Spacing out the main components in this layout makes each unit accessible, but a drawback is the intrusion of the transmission components into the passenger compartment. These create a large bulge in the region of the gearbox and a raised long bulge, called a tunnel, down the centre of the car floor for the accommodation of the propeller shaft.

Using the rear wheels to propel the car utilises the load transfer that takes place from the front to rear of the vehicle when the car is climbing a hill or accelerating. Good traction is obtained but when the wheels lose adhesion, the driving wheels move the rear of the car sideways or oversteer. This motion causes the car to 'drift' and requires considerable movement of the steering wheel if a straight path is to be maintained.

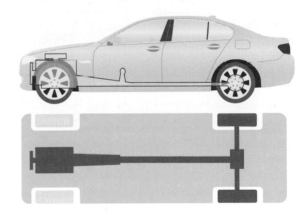

Figure 1.13 Rear-wheel drive arrangement

Front-wheel drive

The compactness of the front-wheel drive layout shown in Figure 1.14 has made it a very popular choice for cars. Originally introduced for small cars, the advantage associated with the engine being placed across the vehicle (i.e. mounted transversely) has spread the use of front-wheel drive to many larger cars. For space reasons the length of the engine is the limiting factor, but the increased use of V-type engines for larger power units has enabled many of these engines to be placed transversely. Accommodating all of the main components under the bonnet (hood) in one compartment gives maximum space within the car for the occupants. Also, the absence of floor bulges and the tunnel provides more room for the rear passengers.

Transverse mounting of the engine simplifies the transmission because the output shafts from the engine and gearbox move in a similar direction to the wheels. This avoids the need for a bevel-type final drive; instead a simple reduction gear, incorporating a differential, transmits the power by short drive shafts to the road wheels. Each drive shaft is fitted with an inner and outer universal joint. Since the outer joint must accommodate the steering action, it is specially designed to ensure that an even speed is obtained as it rotates. This avoids vibration even when the drive is being transmitted through a large angle.

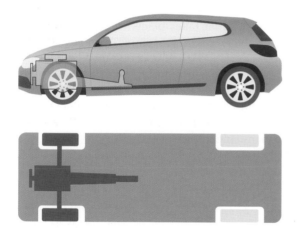

Figure 1.14 Front-wheel drive arrangement

Mounting the main units in one assembly sometimes makes it difficult to gain access to certain parts. In today's vehicles this problem has been largely overcome. Units such as the clutch can be easily removed for overhaul and, by making removal of the engine assembly simpler, the cost of many major repair tasks has been minimised.

One criticism of front-wheel drive is that the driving wheels can lose grip as they have to cope with delivering the power from the engine to the road along with steering the vehicle. Although this characteristic can be partly corrected by placing the engine well forward to increase the load on the driving wheels, the car is then liable to become 'nose-heavy'. The effect of this is to make the steering of the car more arduous. Cars are now usually fitted with power-assisted steering; this system uses hydraulic pressure generated by the engine to help the driver turn the steering wheel.

Using the front wheels for steering allows the driving force to act in the same direction as the wheel is

pointing. The front-wheel driving layout, together with the fact that the vehicle is being 'dragged' behind the front driving wheels, improves vehicle handling, especially in slippery conditions.

Four-wheel drive

The four-wheel drive arrangement shown in Figure 1.15 is safer than two-wheel drive because it distributes the drive to all four wheels. The sharing of the load between the four wheels during acceleration reduces the risks of wheel spin. Also, the positive drive to each wheel during braking minimises the possibility of wheel lock-up.

A further advantage of this layout is demonstrated when the vehicle is driven on slippery surfaces, such as snow and mud. When on an icy road or driving cross-country (off-road), a two-wheel drive vehicle soon becomes impossible to drive because the loss of grip of one of the driving wheels causes the wheel to spin. Since a normal differential always transmits an equal share of the power to both wheels, the small driving force applied to the non-spinning wheel is insufficient to propel the vehicle. On some modern vehicles the four-wheel drive system is electronically controlled. The system monitors the vehicle's requirements and determines whether it requires four-wheel drive or two-wheel drive to suit the driving conditions and reduces the fuel consumption on the drive cycle undertaken. This system also controls loss of traction, using the brakes through the ABS to improve traction further.

Figure 1.15 Four-wheel drive arrangement

Bodywork

The main purpose of the bodywork is to provide accommodation for the driver and passengers, along with suitable protection against wind, weather and collision. The degree of comfort provided will naturally depend upon the type of car and its cost.

The majority of mass-produced cars have a pressed-steel body, although lightweight aluminium is increasingly being used as a viable alternative. Where production is small scale, it is usual to construct the body by either hand-working aluminium alloy into shape, moulding glass-reinforced plastics (GRP/fibreglass) or using composite materials, such as carbon fibre. As body design technology continues to progress, manufacturers are keen to produce their vehicles with a sleek, aerodynamic, eye-catching look to entice customers to purchase. As we now live in a world where global demand on resources is great, manufacturers have to consider using many reusable materials when designing each new model range. Materials such as aluminium and magnesium are now commonly used in body construction, and advanced plastic compound materials are used in areas such as bumpers, sill panels and wheel arches. Depending on the body materials used, surfaces must be treated and painted. Primarily this is to give protection against rust or other corrosion, and secondly to improve the appearance. External trim, made of stainless steel, chromium-plated brass, plastics or rubber, embellishes the body and appeals to the eye by providing a contrast with the plain coloured surface. Figure 1.16 shows some of the body styles used for cars.

Most modern body styles have to be designed to meet stringent build and safety requirements. Body construction is designed to include safety crumple zones. These are areas specially designed to absorb impact and protect occupants in a collision. All vehicles have to pass a number of crash tests to be certificated prior to customer ownership. Many of today's vehicles use special high-strength steels, such as boron steel, to increase the strength of the passenger compartment or, as it is often called, the 'safety cell'. When repairing these types of vehicles, it is very important to make sure that you understand about the different metals used as they have different properties and require various different methods of joining.

Body styles

Saloon

Saloons are fully enclosed two- or four-door cars for four or more people. The common shape of body shell is based on three 'boxes'; the front box forms the engine compartment, the centre box the passenger capsule and the rear box a storage space, called a boot (trunk), for the luggage. The three boxes are blended together to give a pleasing appearance and are shaped to enable the car to move through the air with the minimum drag.

For safety purposes, the passenger capsule must be suitably strengthened to keep its shape following any collision with another object. Extra safety during front or rear impact can be obtained by designing the front and rear regions of the car to fold up in

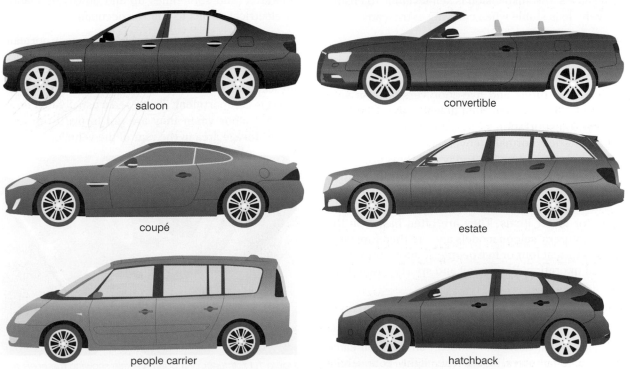

saloon

convertible

coupé

estate

people carrier

hatchback

Figure 1.16 Some of the body styles used for cars

a concertina fashion, creating impact zones. This absorbs the shock of impact and, although damage to these regions is more extensive, the passenger capsule remains intact.

Coupé

Coupés are generally two-door cars and can have a rigid roof or a foldaway metal roof. Usually they offer two seats for the driver and passenger, but can have two small seats in the rear. This latter type is called a '2+2'. This seat arrangement generally means that the rear seat accommodation is rather cramped for adults but is suitable for children or for occasional adult use.

Convertible

Convertibles are also known as cabriolets and drop-head coupés. They can be converted into an open car by either removing a rigid roof or lowering a fabric or foldable steel collapsible roof. Prior to the introduction of air conditioning, this type was widely used in hot countries.

Estate

Also known as a shooting-brake, station-wagon or sports wagon, the estate car has the roof extended to the rear to enlarge the internal capacity. Folding the rear seats down gives a large floor area for the carriage of luggage or goods. A tailgate (door at the rear) enables bulky or long objects to be loaded easily. Stronger suspension springs are generally fitted at the rear to support the extra load and, in some cases, the suspension is self-levelling to ensure the vehicle is stable when carrying extra loads.

Hatchback

Hatchbacks are halfway between a saloon and an estate car. Counting the tailgate as one door, they are made in three- and five-door versions. As with the estate, the rear seats fold down to give a flat floor for the transportation of luggage or other objects. A parcel shelf normally covers the luggage space. Hatchbacks are popular today as they provide a very flexible transport solution for most drivers due to the ease of access to the rear luggage space and the ability to fold the rear seats flat to make more room for larger items. They are often based on the manufacturers' saloon models and are therefore large enough to seat four or five people comfortably during normal operation. Both small and sporty hatchbacks also exist.

People carriers and minibuses

People carriers were commonly known as minibuses in their earliest designs. Minibus construction came from manufacturers using the light commercial van, and then modifying the vehicle by increasing

its visibility around the rear panelled areas and adding additional seating to provide up to 16 seats, including the driver. These vehicles are still widely used to transport people around with a good level of safety and comfort. However, with the demand for manufacturers to produce a more versatile range, the 'people carrier' was born. Most variants come from manufacturers modifying the body designs of their smaller car platforms to increase the passenger-carrying capacity to seven seats. Larger people carriers are generally designed from utility construction and give the passengers greater interior space and comfort. These types of vehicle are sometimes referred to as MPVs (multi-purpose vehicles) and they are very popular across a number of manufacturers due to their versatility.

Internal furnishings and fittings

The quality of interior fittings and fabrics depends on the amount that the customer is prepared to pay for the car. Today, the quality of the interior finish of cars is high so it is the level of luxury that separates the various models in a given range.

Most cars have individual bucket-type front seats. In the past, a single one-piece bench-type seat was used allowing three persons to be seated. Besides giving greater comfort and safety, the space between the bucket seats allows for the fitting of the gear lever (or selector), handbrake and other controls. Each seat is carried on rails or runners securely fixed to the floor, which allow the seats to be moved backwards and forwards (and sometimes up and down) by manual or electrical means to suit the occupants.

The rear seat for two or three passengers is normally a non-adjustable, bench-type seat with a centre armrest to improve comfort when only two people are carried. MPVs have extra rear seats in the rear luggage compartment. These seats usually fold down into the floor when they are not in use to provide more storage area in the rear of the vehicle.

Figure 1.17 Interior of modern vehicle showing materials and layout

All seating has to meet a high level of safety and incorporate seat belts, along with other safety devices such as airbags and seat belt pre-tensioners, which hold the passenger in the seat when an impact occurs. On modern vehicles, depending on the level of luxury, you will now find heating or cooling of seats, massage systems and seats pre-fitted with the fixings for child safety seats.

Seat belts

Seat belts must be provided by law for the driver and all passengers to minimise the risk of severe injury if the car is involved in a collision. These belts must be anchored to a substantial part of the vehicle structure in such a way that the anchorages will not be torn out when an accident occurs. The most popular type of belt used today has three mounting points, which connect with a diagonal shoulder strap and lap belt to restrain the occupant (Figure 1.18). An automatic inertia-controlled belt reel attachment is generally preferred because this type allows the occupant to move freely in the seat when the car is stationary or moving normally. When a ball in the mechanism senses that the deceleration (slowing down) of the car is rapid, it rolls forward and locks up a toothed wheel attached to the belt, resisting forward movement of the occupant. On modern vehicle systems the seat belt system is controlled by a control unit, which monitors the occupant's safety throughout a journey and will operate its safety functionality within milliseconds of a crash or impact situation occurring to protect the occupants and minimise the risk of injury. This involves the deployment of airbags and seat belt pre-tensioners that restrain the occupants in their seats to prevent them from being thrown forward by the impact. The airbag inflates, cushioning the passenger from an impact with any hard surface on the vehicle interior.

Carpets and interior trim

Fitment of a carpet to the floor and other metal body panels enhances the appearance and improves the noise level and comfort. A fabric or plastic material is used as a head lining for the roof and for facing other interior surfaces. Panels are fastened to the interior surface of the doors to cover the mechanism for door locking and window winding. On today's modern vehicles you will find that manufacturers will use a number of different recyclable materials throughout the interior to improve looks and style, and ensure that materials are used in a sustainable way.

Driving position

In the UK, vehicles are driven on the left, which means cars have right-hand drive, where the driver sits on the right. Driving on the left-hand side of the road evolved from the days when horses were the

Figure 1.18 Seat belt pre-tensioner fitted to a vehicle to improve safety of the passengers

main form of transport. Horse riders, who normally carried their swords on the left-hand side of their body, mounted their steeds on the animal's left side to avoid getting tangled with their swords. Also, jousting knights, carrying their lances under their right arm, naturally passed on each other's right. If you passed a stranger on the road, you walked on the left to ensure that your protective sword arm was between yourself and them.

In the case of motor vehicles, where the traffic is keeping to the left side of the road, the driver must sit on the right side in order to see that the road ahead is clear before overtaking. The UK, Ireland, Japan, Australia, New Zealand, India and many African countries drive on the left.

In most European countries and the USA, vehicles are driven on the right-hand side of the road and are consequently left-hand drive. Foot pedals in both right- and left-hand drive systems are normally arranged in the same order with the accelerator pedal on the right, brake pedal in the middle and, where a manual gearbox is fitted, a clutch pedal on the left.

Controls and instrumentation

The instrument panel fascia or dashboard is normally a one-piece assembly located within the cabin area facing the driver and mounted to the bulkhead by a supportive frame. On early vehicles, the controls and instrumentation were limited to basic switches or control knobs to operate simple features.

Included in the instrument panel was a speedometer, mechanically operated via a cable connected to the gearbox, together with other visual instruments or warning signals. Like today, all controls were within easy reach of the driver so that they never had to remove both hands from the steering wheel. Many controls, such as the indicators and windscreen washer and wiper controls, are mounted on the steering column so they can be operated without the hands leaving the wheel. This enables the driver to keep control of the vehicle at all times and stay focused on the road ahead.

Besides the main controls and instrumentation, the driver and front passenger have access to the heating and/or air conditioning controls as well as audio system, hands-free phone and satellite navigation controls. Also on the dashboard are instruments showing data such as speed, rpm, mileage, petrol level and temperature.

Figure 1.19 Modern vehicle instrument panel

On modern vehicles, due to the advancement of electronic technology, instrument panels and instrument clusters are digitally controlled. The driver is given instant and accurate information throughout each drive cycle undertaken. Information is communicated to the driver by means of warning lights or a digital messaging system. Some driving controls operate automatically or are voice-controlled; this can be seen in phone and audio features on many new vehicles.

1.2.3 Light and medium commercial vehicles

These small commercial vehicles are used for the conveyance of relatively light goods, usually over short distances, for example the type of vehicle used by tradespeople to carry their equipment or by shopkeepers to make local deliveries to their customers.

At the light end of this range the vehicle is classed as a van (Figure 1.20). Vans often utilise many of the components used by a similar-sized car in the manufacturer's range. In these cases, the term 'car derivative' is used. When fitting new parts, however, it should be taken into account that components such as clutches, braking systems and suspension units are uprated when they are used on commercial vehicles; this ensures that the parts can withstand the extra stresses. Car and van parts are similar in appearance, so it is not always obvious to the technician that the van components have been strengthened to take account of hard commercial use.

Figure 1.20 Car-derived light commercial vehicle (van)

Manufacturers normally offer a number of different body shapes and sizes to suit the customer's needs. When a vehicle is required for the transportation of bulky equipment, for example, materials carried by builders and decorators, an open body is often preferred. A light vehicle having this partly enclosed body is called a pick-up (Figure 1.21).

Small vans and pick-ups have two seats for the driver and one passenger and a standard of comfort comparable to the base model of the car from which the vehicles were derived.

Figure 1.21 Example of pick-up type vehicle

Most vans have a load-carrying capacity of about 0.5 tonnes. Since low-cost operation is an essential factor, these vehicles are often fitted with a diesel- (compression-ignition) type engine, although many are now fitted with electrical or hybrid power.

Medium-sized commercial vehicles

Larger vehicles, such as light trucks and minibuses, need to carry heavier loads, so they require a stronger construction and have to be specially designed to suit the application. Larger vans or medium-sized commercial vehicles often share platforms across manufacturers. This improves the cost in production and, therefore, the sale cost to the customer. While transmission and engine design may be sourced from passenger vehicles, they usually have bespoke body and chassis arrangements, with heavier duty steering and suspension to cater for the need to carry heavier loads. While engines are also often derived from passenger vehicles, manufacturers often change the power delivery as the vehicles are carrying heavier loads. This involves increasing the engine torque in many cases (see page 38). To improve operating efficiency, engines are generally diesel (compression-ignition), which provide good fuel economy over an equivalent petrol engine.

Medium-sized vans can come with either a separate chassis or a **monocoque** arrangement. Manufacturers generally provide a base chassis, but offer many alternative body types, including variations in length and height and the option for open or closed carrying areas to fit with specific needs (Figure 1.22).

Monocoque: vehicle design where the chassis arrangement and body are integrated into one structural unit.

Figure 1.22 Medium-sized light commercial vehicle

Figure 1.23 Light commercial vehicle with twin wheels for carrying extra weight

Four-wheel drive recreational and executive vehicles

These vehicles have their origins in the 1970s with the production of the Range Rover as a luxury version of the Land Rover. This was one of the first four-wheel drive (4×4) passenger vehicles with real off-road ability, along with high levels of passenger comfort.

The original Land Rover was built in 1948 to provide a vehicle that was designed to be extremely versatile in many conditions (Figure 1.24). With four-wheel drive, the Land Rover was able to take on some of the most extreme terrain, while also providing a vehicle that could carry passengers for day-to-day routine journeys.

Figure 1.24 Early four-wheel drive vehicle

Recreational vehicles (RVs) are increasingly popular and usually have four-wheel drive to enable operation in extreme or off-road conditions. Like light commercial vehicles, they may have either a separate chassis or monocoque designs. Engines are usually from the passenger vehicle range but in most cases have modifications to enable them to operate in extreme conditions, such as wading through water or operating on steep inclines. These vehicles often have sophisticated mechanical and electrical systems to improve traction. This is discussed in more detail on page 496.

Figure 1.25 Latest type of four-wheel drive vehicle from Land Rover – Range Rover Evoque

1.2.4 Heavy vehicles

Although this book concentrates mainly on light vehicles, a review of some heavier vehicles is included for comparison purposes.

All heavy vehicles or trucks are generally referred to as **HGVs** or articulated vehicles. A medium-sized vehicle has a maximum authorised mass of between 3.5 and 7.5 tonnes, while a large goods vehicle is constructed to carry or haul goods where the maximum authorised mass exceeds 7.5 tonnes. There is a maximum gross vehicle weight for large HGVs of 44 tonnes. These have at least six axles.

HGV: heavy goods vehicle.

Trucks

For long-distance transportation of goods a truck is usually used and these come in various shapes and sizes. A large flat platform is needed to carry the load. In many earlier designs this chassis was only provided above wheel height; no special effort was made to lower the frame, which usually consisted of two straight and deep side-members joined by several cross-members. This frame then supported the main components of the vehicle as well as the platform, which formed the basis of the body, and the driver sat in a cab at the front of the vehicle. Today's trucks often have lower frames to bring the centre of gravity down and make the truck more stable and aerodynamic.

The engine is usually a compression-ignition, diesel engine. It is fitted at the front and the driver sits high up at one side of it, with a seat for a passenger at the other side. Thus, the whole of the space from the engine rearwards is available for carrying the load.

To carry heavy loads the rear wheels either have twin tyres, fitted side-by-side, or special wide-section single tyres. Vehicles exceeding a certain total loaded weight are required to have six wheels carried on three axles, while even heavier vehicles are required to have eight wheels, two on each of four axles. These legal requirements are laid down in the Construction and Use Regulations drawn up by parliament. Since these are constantly liable to revision, those seeking further details of maximum permitted weights and dimensions of vehicles are advised to consult the regulations currently in force.

When six wheels are used, the two extra wheels may be carried on an additional axle at the rear of the vehicle (Figure 1.26). These extra wheels are usually, but not always, driven, but no provision is made for steering them. Figure 1.27 shows an alternative arrangement in which the extra axle is placed at the front, in which case the wheels are steered but not

Figure 1.26 A three-axle six-wheel HGV

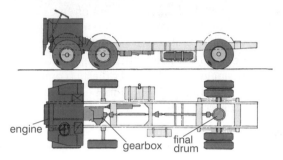

Figure 1.27 Alternative arrangement using twin front axles

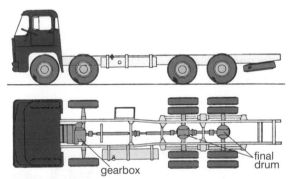

Figure 1.28 Eight wheeler using twin front axles and twin rear axles

driven. Eight-wheelers have two front axles (steered but not driven) and two rear axles (driven but not steered) as shown in Figure 1.28.

Trucks are allowed to tow a trailer on which an additional load can be carried. There is, in addition, a type of vehicle that consists of two parts: a four- or six-wheeled tractor (which does not itself carry any load) to which is attached, by a special turntable coupling, the front end of a semi-trailer, having two or four wheels at its rear end. In this way, some of the weight carried by the semi-trailer is supported by the tractor. The combination of tractor and semi-trailer is called an articulated vehicle. The trailer has retractable wheels on which its front end can be supported: this enables the tractor to be uncoupled and used with another trailer while its former trailer is being loaded or unloaded. An example of an articulated vehicle with a trailer is shown in Figure 1.30.

Figure 1.29 Articulated vehicle without trailer

Figure 1.30 Articulated vehicle with trailer

Figure 1.31 Single-decker bus with front entrance

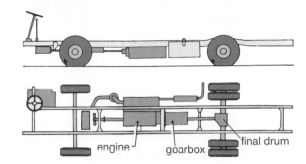

Figure 1.32 Single-decker bus chassis with engine laid on its side

Figure 1.33 Double-decker bus with rear entrance

Buses (omnibuses)

Buses are designed to transport large numbers of passengers. Up to about 40 passengers may be carried on a single floor or deck. Figure 1.31 shows a single-decker bus, which has its entrance to the front where the driver can see passengers boarding or alighting from the vehicle. On some earlier buses no doors were fitted to allow passengers quick access on or off the bus. Now, with improved safety requirements, all buses have doors to ensure the passengers get on and off the bus in a safe, controlled manner. The doors are operated by the driver or conductor to prevent passengers getting on or off while the bus is moving. In order to make room for the front entrance, the engine is often laid on its side below the frame, as shown in the illustration of the chassis (Figure 1.32).

A double-decker bus capable of seating about 60 passengers is shown in Figure 1.33. The Construction and Use Regulations stipulate a maximum height for the vehicle and a minimum ceiling height for both upper and lower decks. This means that the floor of the lower deck must be fairly close to the ground, at least along the central gangway between the seats. To permit this, the final-drive gears are not at the centre of the rear axle but are moved to one side, so that the gangway does not have to clear the highest point of the axle casing.

In early bus designs the engine was placed well forward directly over the front axle, and slightly to the nearside to allow the driver to sit beside it, leaving all the space behind the front wheels free for the accommodation of passengers. The gearbox was separately mounted on the nearside some way behind the engine, where it could be low enough to be completely below floor level, and the two propeller shafts – one between the engine and the gearbox and the other between the gearbox and the rear axle – were clear of the gangway.

In towns and cities there are usually short distances between stops and the speed of loading and unloading passengers is very important. At the rear of the bus shown in Figure 1.33 is a large platform about 300 mm above ground level and an easy step up from the edge of the pavement. From this platform another step up leads into the lower deck and a staircase leads to the upper deck. An issue with this arrangement is that the driver is unable to see passengers getting on and off except with the aid of mirrors, which do not give an adequate view of people on the platform or running to catch the bus. This is one reason why buses were usually manned by a conductor who indicated to the driver with a bell when it was safe to move.

A more modern design for a double-decker bus is shown in Figure 1.34. This has the engine positioned transversely at the rear and the entrance placed at the front in line with the driver.

Figure 1.34 Modern double-decker bus

By placing the platform at the front the driver can have a direct view of passengers boarding and alighting, as in the case of the single-decker bus shown in Figure 1.31.

Coaches

Vehicles of this type are designed to carry between 30 and 40 passengers over fairly long distances, in greater comfort than is provided in buses. Speed of loading and unloading is less important, but a larger amount of luggage accommodation is required due to the long-haul routes these types of vehicles travel. A chassis similar to that shown in Figure 1.32 is generally used, but more comfortable seats are provided. The entrance is either at the front or behind the front wheels.

Some buses and coaches are made with the body structure forming the main frame. Although this is not very common, it has the advantage of reducing total mass.

1.3 Vehicle structure

1.3.1 Frame/chassis

The component parts of a vehicle need a structure of some kind on to which they can be attached. Heavier vehicles, such as trucks, use a rectangular steel frame made up of two long side-members that are linked together by a number of cross-members, often called a ladder chassis arrangement. The other components of the vehicle, such as the engine and body, are then attached to this. The assembled vehicle without the body is called a chassis and the frame on its own is called the chassis frame. This construction is still used today across a number of vehicle variants because of its versatility and added strength for today's demands. Chassis construction was commonly used in the manufacturing of motor cars long into the 1950s and 1960s and allowed the body variant to be securely mounted. Today, you will still see some manufacturers using a version of this system, depending on the vehicle's design, functionality and demands.

Chassis frames consist of two channel-shaped side-members that run the full length of the vehicle's under-body layout. These two main members are held apart by a series of cross-members, located in key areas to enhance its overall frame strength. The cross-members are smaller in depth than the main members and are cold riveted or welded to the main members. Chassis frames are mainly made from steel with a low level of carbon content to reduce overall weight, especially on lighter-weighted vehicles. When the frames are constructed, additional steel bracing plates are added to strengthen those load-bearing areas. To reduce the overall frame weight, a series of machined holes positioned along the neutral axis of the frame are made that don't affect the overall strength. On some chassis systems, manufacturers add additional cross-type bracing to increase strength due to the added stress loads absorbed through the frame.

Early designs of chassis frames were found to have very poor resistance to **torsion**. This had a negative effect on the body frame, which at the stage of development wasn't designed to compensate for the weakness. Problems included movement between doors and the main pillars, causing creaking, broken windscreens and cracks appearing around body panel joints.

Torsion: the twisting of one end of an object relative to the other.

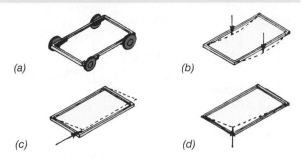

(a)

(b)

(c)

(d)

Figure 1.35 Distortion of a simple chassis frame

Distortion of a chassis frame consisting of two cross-members and two side-members is shown in Figure 1.35. These deflections are caused by the following forces:

1 Weight – the weight of the car and passengers causes the frame to sag, as in Figure 1.35b.
2 Road shocks – impacts and general vehicle motion produce deflection in the frame:
   - Lozenging – when the rectangular frame is pushed into a parallelogram shape (Figure 1.35c).
   - Twisting – a deflection at one corner of the frame (Figure 1.35d).

Manufacturers have to make the body and frame as light as possible, while offering maximum resistance to bending and twisting or torsional effects. Figure 1.36 illustrates the frames that are in general use:

- Channel
- Tubular
- Box

As design technology improved, manufacturers continued to use the chassis frame concept for the main support of the driveline and bodies. Different chassis frames, such as backbone (Figure 1.37) or box section (Figure 1.38) designs, were used to suit the ever-changing designs of the motor vehicle. Both were constructed using box section members running the length of the vehicle. The under body was supported by the frame using outrigger members – these were welded to the frame's spine to support the floor pan.

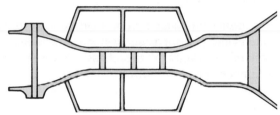

Figure 1.37 Backbone frame

Frame	Section	Behaviour
Flat ▬	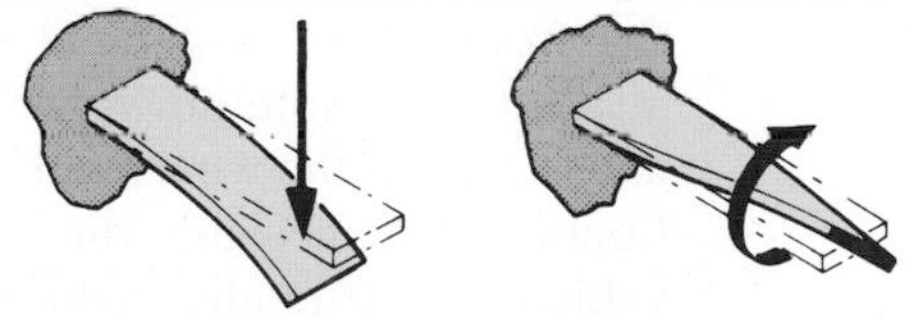	Offers little resistance to bending and twisting
Channel [	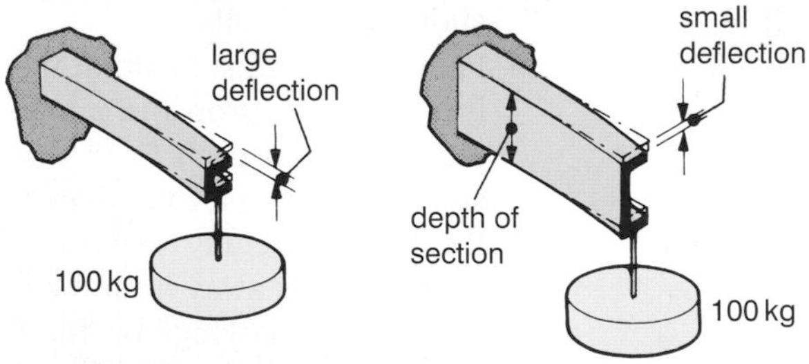 large deflection small deflection depth of section 100 kg 100 kg	Excellent resistance to bending Resistance increases as depth of section is increased
Tubular O		Excellent resistance to torsion Resistance increases as diameter is increased
Box ▯	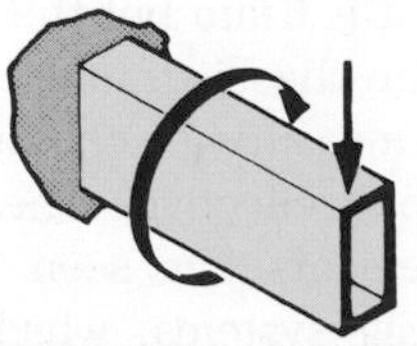	Good resistance to both bending and torsion

Figure 1.36 Frame sections

Figure 1.38 Box section

As car designs changed from rigid axle systems to independent suspension systems, the demand for different variants of the chassis became ever more important. The introduction of a chassis frame incorporating an energy-absorbing structure was to improve safety for the vehicle's occupants (Figure 1.39). Previous frames were designed as a rigid unit, but research showed that occupants were suffering a higher level of injuries in accidents with this design. Two key areas of the chassis frame at the front and rear of the frame structure were designed as crumple zones. If the vehicle was in a front or rear collision, the crumple zones would absorb the main impact by concertinaing the frame and reducing the impact forces. The outer body panels within the impact area would normally have to be replaced due to the extensive damage, but the central cabin area was protected. Producing an energy-absorbing structure designed to crumple in key areas was one of the first steps in vehicle crash safety to significantly reduce injuries to occupants in collisions.

Figure 1.39 An energy-absorbing frame with collapsible vehicle structure and airbags deployed

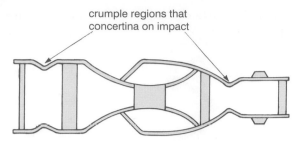

crumple regions that concertina on impact

Figure 1.40 An energy-absorbing chassis frame

Frame repairs

Frame repairs are required when a vehicle has been involved in a collision and has damage to the frame alignment. Depending on the severity of the impact, you can normally see if the frame alignment is out. To be sure that the alignment is within the manufacturing tolerances, it is important to identify the area of concern by completing the following frame alignment checks (Figure 1.41):

- Wheelbase check. Position the vehicle on a flat level surface with the front wheels in the straight-ahead position. Check the wheelbase position on both sides of the vehicle by measuring from the centre point of each wheel and comparing the results of each side to ensure the wheelbase is equal.
- Alignment check. Position the vehicle on a flat level surface and position a cord or straightedge against the rear wheel; rotate the steering until the front wheel is parallel with the cord or straightedge. Note down the clearance gap (if any) between the wheel and cord/straightedge. Continue to measure the other side of the vehicle. For true alignment both sides should show equal results.
- Plumb-line check. Position the vehicle on a flat level surface. Drop the plumb line down from the outside of each fixed shackle corner. This should give you a total of eight chalk marks on the floor. Carefully move the vehicle forward or backwards away from the measuring area to expose the markings on the floor. Connect up the marking points diagonally to the opposing fixed shackle points. Identify the centre line of the chassis frame and draw a line from the front to the rear. Now measure the diagonal lines across the centre line: they should all be equal. Generally, the tolerance allowed on this measurement is 6mm but this is dependent on the size of the chassis frame.

This form of measuring chassis alignment is fairly primitive but effective. The need for more accurate measurements has seen the development of sophisticated jig systems, which are now more commonly used by vehicle body repairers (Figure 1.42).

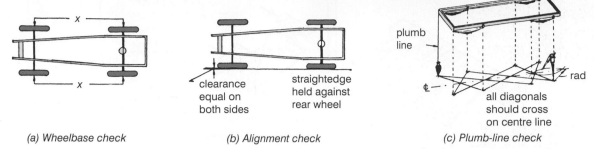

(a) Wheelbase check (b) Alignment check (c) Plumb-line check

Figure 1.41 Checking chassis alignment

The vehicle is mounted on the main jig support frame. Measuring is carried out by using specially designed braces that match the vehicle layout. If misalignment is identified, then the jig, along with jacks and chains, can realign the frame and the body repair can be completed.

Unless the frame has been heat treated, heating the chassis members sometimes improves the alignment process. Cracks can sometimes be welded or an additional reinforcement plate added to strengthen the repaired area. If incorrect jigging is carried out, then the vehicle alignment will be affected and the vehicle's handling will suffer. The latest jigs now use a laser-controlled, alignment measurement system, which greatly increases the accuracy of this process.

1.3.2 Unitary/integral construction

Modern cars are built with the body and the chassis integrated. This unitary/integral structure is much lighter in weight than the separate frame/chassis construction and is relatively cheap to mass-produce. The system uses a specially designed body to withstand the various load demands and stresses that occur when the car is in use. As early as the 1930s, the development of the all-steel body shell made it possible to withstand some of the various frame stresses and eliminated the need for a separate frame. With

further development, manufacturers found that they could mass-produce this design and respond quickly to the ever-increasing demands of their customers. Manufacturers also found that when constructing this type of body shell certain areas had to have additional strengthening to compensate for the added torsional stresses. Figure 1.43 shows key areas of the body shell, such as the scuttle, bulkhead, sills, pillars, floor and roof, all with added strengthening.

Along with this body construction, manufacturers have had to alter their body designs to include the structural requirements for suspension and driveline arrangements. The inclusion of sub-frames at the front and rear of the vehicle supported the driveline and suspension system accordingly. This arrangement allowed the suspension to become independent on each corner of the vehicle and advanced the evolution of different driveline layouts. Manufacturers had the option of using the conventional driveline layout, where the drive was transmitted to the rear wheels, or opt for the more commonly known transverse layout and have the front wheels as the driving axle. As manufacturers continued to develop this system, it became clear that the fixed-beam axle and chassis frame layout was becoming less popular to the average motor vehicle owner. Manufacturers have developed sub-frames made of steel, aluminium or

Figure 1.42 A vehicle mounted on a special vehicle jig for repair

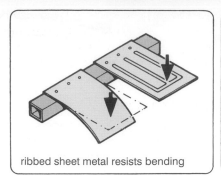

ribbed sheet metal resists bending

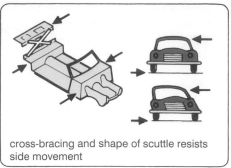

cross-bracing and shape of scuttle resists side movement

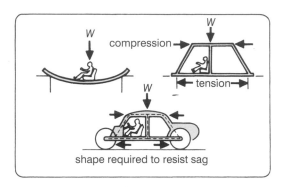

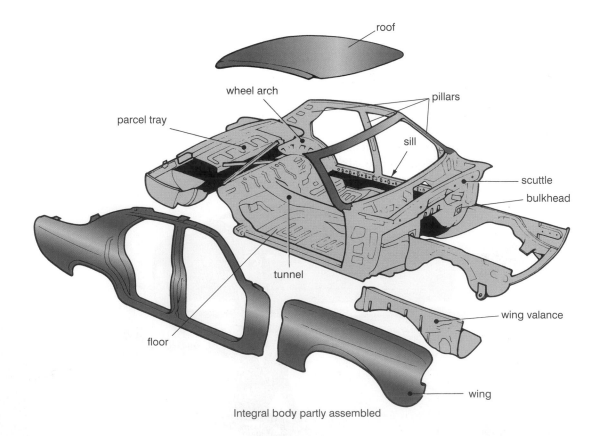

Figure 1.43 Integral body construction

other strong, lightweight metals to support or contain the required components. This technique, which uses the car's exterior to support the structural load rather than using an internal frame or chassis, is called a 'monocoque' arrangement and was first developed for aircraft construction (Figure 1.44).

The next key development stage of the body shell construction was the inclusion of crumple zones at the front and rear of the vehicle. Designing the body shell so that the structure absorbs a high level of the impact forces minimises the levels of injury to occupants in the central rigid cell of the vehicle.

Every motor vehicle designed and manufactured today has to undergo very stringent crash testing requirements (Figure 1.45). Manufacturers must obtain an 'N cap' test certificate prior to launching a new model range.

Early body shells were spot-welded together. However, as production technology has progressed with the increasing use of production lines and robotic machines, the space-frame structure has become more common (Figure 1.46). This gives a skeleton of high structural strength on to which all outer panels

are positioned. Manufacturers mainly use steel to construct the body skeleton, but aluminium or other strong, lightweight materials can be used for the outer panels to reduce the vehicle's weight and to meet today's environmental requirements.

Aerodynamics

Aerodynamic design was not something that concerned the early car manufacturers, but as vehicles became faster and manufacturing processes more sophisticated, the importance of aerodynamics to the efficient operation and performance of vehicles was recognised. Bolder designs started to be produced and vehicles became more eye-catching in their shape and style. Early panel construction, mainly done by skilled craftsmen using hand tools, gave way to mass production by robot-controlled machines (Figure 1.47). Manufacturers continually strive to improve their vehicles' aerodynamic design and environmental efficiency.

Figure 1.46 Steel body construction

Figure 1.44 Early car using sub-frame arrangement

Figure 1.45 Car in a rollover test

Figure 1.47 Robot-operated production

An aerodynamic body shape has a significant effect on overall performance. Manufacturers learnt that the greater the airflow resistance across the body structure, the higher the percentage rate of engine energy produced was lost. Therefore, designing the body shape to minimise this factor accurately would greatly increase the vehicle's overall performance and fuel efficiency.

Air resistance is given by the expression:

Air resistance = Drag coefficient × Area × Velocity^2

Vehicle manufacturers today simulate airflow dynamics by using a wind tunnel in much the same way as F1 racing teams. This enables manufacturers to produce designs and efficiencies that would have been unheard of only a few years ago. With the move to hybrid and electric-powered cars, these aerodynamic improvements have had a positive impact on mileage range, especially with purely electric-driven vehicles. With electric cars now able to drive over 300 km on one charge, they are providing a real alternative to many customers wishing to change from petrol- or diesel- powered vehicles.

For more on aerodynamics and other features that improve efficiency see section 1.4 and the feature on page 26.

Figure 1.48 Achieving excellent aerodynamic results with the Honda CRZ Hybrid

Interior and exterior design

Manufacturers found that it was very important to their customers to produce vehicles with the most up-to-date interior and exterior styling. For many years, chrome was a popular finish on external styling and embellishments. It both enhanced the external appearance and gave the vehicle some limited protection from minor impacts. Figure 1.49 shows the exterior of an older car using brightwork trim. With manufacturing skills and vehicle production demands ever increasing, so did the demand for using other types of materials in the interior and exterior finishing. Materials such as rubber, plastic and carbon were

used for the dashboard, centre consoles, bumpers, sill covers, wheel arch trims and valance fascia, to name just a few. The development of new materials for areas such as bumpers has also had the practical advantages of greatly reducing crash repair costs and injuries to pedestrians (Figure 1.50).

Another key area is the carpeting and insulation used in the vehicle's interior. At first, this wasn't considered to be an important factor in the early vehicle designs, but manufacturers began to realise that using good-quality insulation and carpets greatly reduced the unwanted engine and road noise entering the driving compartment. Just as important is the under-body protection and exterior paint finish. Some of the early manufactured vehicles had no under-body protection and the only colour available was black. Back in the early 20th century, Henry Ford is famously reputed to have told his customers that they could have any colour they liked as long as it was black. Customers today have such a wide choice of paint colour, finish and interior trim – it can be mind-boggling!

Figure 1.49 Exterior of an older vehicle with chrome trim

Figure 1.50 Exterior of modern car showing the emphasis on safety along with style

As the technology and variants of paint materials continue to advance, vehicle manufacturers now produce their vehicles using environmentally friendly water-based paints that have a long-lasting finish and protection against today's driving demands. With continuous advancements in body design, material technology and manufacturing skills, car owners today are driving vehicles with a high level of safety, luxury and comfort.

Jacking points

An important but little realised element of modern vehicle design is the need to incorporate key strengthened areas to provide suitable jacking points to allow the vehicle to be raised off the ground for inspection and routine maintenance. Common areas for strengthening are the floor pan or outer sill structures (Figure 1.51). All vehicles are generally supplied with a suitable jack, normally a small scissor or bottle jack. For more detailed inspection and professional maintenance, a trolley jack can be used with suitable axle stands for added support. For some jobs, this method may still have its limitations with regard to the amount of access a technician has, so they may choose to use a two- or four-poster ramp, which allows full access to all under-body areas and provides a safe working environment.

Whenever any jacking-up of a vehicle is carried out, great care must be taken to make sure that the jack, lifting pads or arms are located correctly prior to raising the vehicle. It is also important that personnel

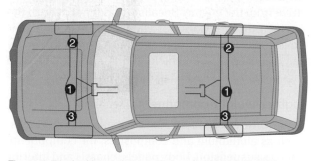

Figure 1.51 Jacking points on the underside of a vehicle

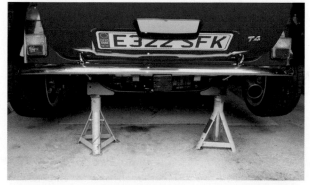

Figure 1.52 A car raised off the ground using axle stands

and any obstructions are clear from the vehicle being raised. Refer to the vehicle's handbook or workshop technical information for the correct jacking points and procedures, as jacking the vehicle in the wrong place could damage the vehicle structure.

Note: always read the operating instructions of the jack or ramp to make sure the equipment is suitable to lift the overall vehicle weight and that you understand the functionality. If you are planning to use a trolley jack to raise the vehicle, make sure that the vehicle is on a solid level surface and always use axle stands to give added support prior to working beneath the vehicle (Figure 1.52). Never use any other supporting device or object, such as house bricks, as an axle stand because this is extremely unsafe and you will put your life and that of others around you at risk. Applying the handbrake and using wheel chocks is good practice to add extra stability to the vehicle and prevent any additional movement taking place.

1.4 Vehicle efficiency and dynamics

Many manufacturers are now producing vehicles that are extremely efficient and produce very low emissions. This necessity has been brought about by many countries' governments signing up to an international agreement to lower the emissions of carbon dioxide (CO_2) each year. This agreement, called the Kyoto Protocol, was launched in December 1997 with the main goal of stabilising and reducing the greenhouse gases in the atmosphere to a level that will sustain the climate and prevent any dramatic changes.

The main gas that this agreement is concerned with in regard to the automobile industry is CO_2. This naturally occurring gas is thought to be contributing to climatic changes and, therefore, there is a need to limit its production where possible.

Manufacturers have tough targets to meet this agreement goal, so they have been developing innovative ways to lower the emission of CO_2 from their vehicles. Many manufacturers have used similar ways of achieving this and have called their vehicles special names to highlight them as lower-emission and high-fuel-economy vehicles. For instance:

- BlueMotion Technologies   – Volkswagen
- DRIVe   – Volvo
- BlueTEC   – Mercedes-Benz
- EfficientDynamics   – BMW
- ECOMOTIVE   – SEAT

Innovations in fuel economy and reduced emissions

Modern vehicles achieve excellent improvements in fuel economy and emission levels through very similar ways, including:

- stop-start systems
- lower-rolling-resistance tyres
- brake regeneration
- electronic power steering
- lighter-weight components
- lower-friction oils
- improved aerodynamics
- optimum gear change indicators.

Stop-start systems

Stop-start systems work by switching off the engine whenever the vehicle comes to a stationary position. As the vehicle approaches a stop point, the engine will cut out when the brake pedal is pressed, the vehicle comes to a standstill and the gearbox is put into neutral. When the driver is ready to move off and presses the clutch pedal to select first gear, the engine will start immediately and run as normal again until the next stop point. This system can save up to 20 per cent in fuel costs in an urban driving situation, along with big improvements to the emissions produced by the vehicle. The starting of the engine is carried out by very high-energy motors and generally takes about 400 milliseconds to start. This makes the system almost unnoticeable to the driver.

Lower-rolling-resistance tyres

These tyres roll along the road much more easily than conventional road tyres due to the compound (type of rubber) used and the tread pattern. These tyres have greater heat resistance and use anti-distortion materials to create less friction as the vehicle moves.

Figure 1.53 Lower-rolling-resistance tyre

With less friction and easier rolling the vehicle uses less fuel in propelling the vehicle along, thus also producing lower emissions.

Brake regeneration

When the vehicle brakes, the vehicle generates heat energy from the high amounts of friction. Normally this energy is lost to the atmosphere, but brake regeneration vehicles harness it. As the vehicle brakes or slows down by lifting off the accelerator pedal, the driven wheels rotate a generator to produce electrical energy. This electrical energy is then transferred to the vehicle's battery to charge it up. Because the battery is being charged by the vehicle slowing down or braking, there is less need for the engine-driven generator, called an alternator, to create the electrical energy to charge the battery. Because the alternator is not needed as much, it will not be drawing energy from the engine to drive it. This then saves on fuel, leading to better fuel economy and lower emissions.

Electronic power steering

Vehicles with normal hydraulic power steering usually have a hydraulic pump driven by the engine to pressurise the hydraulic fluid that is then used to assist the driver as they turn the steering wheel. This system uses energy from the engine and, therefore, uses fuel. The use of electronic, power-assisted steering is now becoming popular as it does not take drive from the engine. Because it does not absorb the engine power, it does not use fuel or lead to higher emissions. The electronic system is purely driven by the electrics of the vehicle and is often lighter and less complicated to install during production.

Lighter-weight components

Manufacturers have started to use lighter materials, such as aluminium and composites, for components such as suspension, body panels, chassis and interior trim. This means that the whole vehicle will weigh less, so the engine does not have to work as hard to move it along the road. This weight reduction greatly improves fuel efficiency and performance.

Lower-friction oils

By using oils with greatly improved lower-friction properties within the transmission, engine and final-drive units, the vehicle has much less wear and uses less energy to travel along the road. As the vehicle uses less energy, it uses less fuel and produces lower emissions.

Figure 1.54 *Aerodynamic wheels used to improve fuel economy and lower vehicle emissions*

Figure 1.55 *Rear spoiler used to improve aerodynamics at the rear of the vehicle*

Improved aerodynamics

Manufacturers have worked very hard to create vehicles that have less drag as they travel through the air. Some manufacturers use a number of systems to improve the aerodynamics:

- Active front grilles – these close off the airflow through the front of the car into the engine bay when the engine is cold to improve warm-up times, so the engine begins running at optimum temperature much more quickly. The closing of the grille also reduces air resistance around the front of the car, leading to improved fuel economy and lower emissions.
- Flat under body – this allows the air to flow underneath the car much more easily, providing much less air friction.
- Aerodynamic wheels – the air around the wheels does not create as much friction as the wheels rotate. By lowering this friction, the wheels are able to rotate more freely and the drag on the vehicle is less. This leads to improvements in fuel economy and lower emissions.

- Front and rear spoilers – these allow air to flow over the back window and down the rear of the car without creating air pressure build-up around the window area. At the front, the spoilers help direct the air around the front lower area of the vehicle and also around the tyres.

Optimum gear change indicators

The gear change indicators provide the driver with a visual signal when to change gear to maintain the optimum running efficiency of the vehicle. As the driver approaches the maximum torque point of the vehicle (usually around 2500–3000 rpm), the gear change light will signal to the driver to change up a gear, this ensures that the engine does not use unnecessarily high engine speeds that use a great deal more fuel and produce higher emissions.

By using all of these energy-saving technologies, the vehicles being produced today are getting more fuel-efficient and are producing fewer harmful emissions. It is hoped that these changes will continue to develop and ensure that the countries around the world meet their targets for emissions.

1.5   Vehicle maintenance

This book explains the fundamental operation of all mechanical, electrical and electronic systems used on motor vehicles both past and present. This section is about the importance of maintaining those systems, which will then increase the overall performance, efficiency and safety of the vehicle.

From the first ever motor vehicle produced, designers and engineers identified that the engine and all other vehicle systems would need regular maintenance or vehicles would quickly become unsafe or fail

completely. It wasn't uncommon for most vehicle owners to have their vehicle serviced two or even three times a year, depending on usage and driving conditions.

Early engines, such as steam or side-valve variants, needed continuous maintenance, for example, adjustments to valves or replacements of seals, to prolong their short running life. It wasn't until the spark ignition and the compression ignition engine emerged that maintaining the engine became more of a routine, depending on the driving requirements. Servicing intervals became a common factor in maintaining the engine and all other mechanical and serviceable areas. Changing the oil and filter every 3000 miles wasn't uncommon for many manufactured vehicles. This was due to the engine design and the quality of the oil and filtering used. As both the engine design and the quality of oil improved, vehicle manufacturers found that engine oil and filtering service could go to 6000 miles as long as the vehicle owner regularly carried out an oil level inspection. Today, engines still have to have oil and filter services, but they are now reaching 20,000 miles before renewal is required.

On early engines the valve system had to be adjusted at each service interval. This was due to the amount of wear and tear on each of the moving components and the quality of the oil used. Added to this, motor vehicle owners found that because of the poor quality of available fuels the engine cylinder head had to be removed and the valves de-coked to maintain the engine's performance.

As design and technology progressed, manufacturers started to produce engines with hydraulic followers, or lifters. These required better-quality oils and fuels. Other service items, such as ignition contact breaker points and condensers, have now been replaced by modern advanced electronic ignition systems. Again, ignition spark plugs had to be renewed every 6000 miles, but, in today's engines, some can be active for 100,000 miles before replacement. Oil filters and air filters are still serviceable items, but also have a greater life expectancy.

In early transmission and driveline systems, broken gears, shafts or bearings were a common problem. Manufacturers found that using different metals and better-quality oils greatly increased the service life of these components. It wasn't uncommon for most vehicles to have their gearbox and axle oils changed at each service interval and the propeller shaft joints greased to prolong their service life. As technology has progressed, we now find that such areas as the transmission or final-drive systems are now sealed for life unless any repairs are undertaken.

The chassis system on early vehicles also couldn't go without regular maintenance. Steering and suspension joints had to be regularly greased, otherwise excessive wear would result due to the poor road conditions and the materials used. Later steering and suspension systems used stronger and lighter metals and better rubber compound bushes. These components only need an annual inspection to confirm their condition. Early braking systems used a lever and/or push rod operation. This system was functional, but had limitations to its efficiency in stopping vehicles in an emergency. The introduction of the hydraulic braking system was a great advancement in engineering and safety.

The all-round drum brake system used on earlier vehicles was another area requiring regular maintenance. The introduction of disc brakes and ABS greatly improved vehicles' safety and requires less maintenance. The anti-lock hydraulic and electronically controlled systems, now fitted to modern vehicles, work in conjunction with the steering and suspension to provide an advanced safety system that continuously monitors the brake efficiency, notifying the driver of any issues concerning maintenance or stability. A modern engine management system now has the capability to measure, adjust and control the engine's performance to maximise its all-round performance.

Other areas, such as electrical systems, tyres, vehicle body and interior trim, all have forms of regular inspection, depending on the vehicle's usage. This again shows that as technology improves in these areas maintenance demands are reduced. Over the many decades of motor vehicle production we have seen a steady decline in the amount of maintenance that has to be carried out. To say that the motor vehicle will become maintenance-free is optimistic but, who knows, it might not be too far away.

2

Engines and engine technology

2.1 The internal-combustion engine

2.1.1 The solution for the automobile industry

The need to produce an engine that was able to meet the demands of industry and the public was met for a long period of time during the 1700s through the use of the rather large and awkward steam engine. This type of engine was able to produce a lot of power and, as time went on, became more and more efficient. The steam engine worked by producing steam in the large boiler and passing this under pressure to the cylinder that contained the piston. This steam then created pressure on the piston to force it down the cylinder to produce the rotary motion of the crankshaft linked directly to the wheels. One of the main problems with the steam engine was its size and weight. Along with this, the steam engine required a separate water tank and boiler to provide it with enough steam to operate in various conditions.

It wasn't long before the need to create a more compact power unit led to the development of an engine that was able to create the pressure inside the cylinder without the need to create steam pressure externally to the cylinders. The first fuel type used to create combustion within the cylinder to provide pressure to push the piston down the cylinder was coal gas. This was ignited within the cylinder to provide combustion pressure to move the piston down the cylinder bore, providing the rotary motion of the crankshaft. This was the first type of internal combustion engine. Unfortunately, this engine did not last very long as it still struggled to meet the ever-increasing demand for more powerful and efficient ways of creating engine power.

Designers worked on improving the engine and looked for a fuel that provided a much more controllable combustion process. The solution was to use fuels that were able to produce much more power during combustion. The best candidates were refined mineral oils derived from crude oil (a fossil fuel) as these could be introduced into the engine along with air and ignited on a timelier basis. This produced much greater combustion pressure and power. The need to increase this combustion pressure further led to the additional requirement to increase the heat within the cylinder to ensure that the fuel and air were burnt completely.

The initial solution was to ignite the air and fuel mixture with the use of a spark. This improved the combustion process creating higher pressures and heat generation, but it was still not enough. To improve this process further, engine designers found that pre-compressing the air and fuel in the cylinder before it was ignited created much higher combustion pressures. The principle of using pre-compressed air and fuel to create additional heat can be demonstrated by placing your finger over the end of a bicycle tyre pump and pushing the plunger down to create air pressure. You will notice that the heat generated at your finger increases as the air is compressed. This process is exactly what happens during the compression of the air and fuel in the cylinder. The additional heat increased the combustion pressure and ensured that most of the fuel was burnt during combustion due to the more tightly packed air and fuel mixture.

Soon designers found that there was an ideal ratio of air and fuel to achieve the best possible combustion. This ratio was approximately 14–15 parts of air to 1 part of fuel – 14–15 : 1. This air/fuel ratio provided much better combustion and, along with the increased compression created during the compression stroke and the addition of a spark to start the combustion process, the internal-combustion engine was soon becoming a very powerful and efficient unit. Designers worked on trying to control the ignition point of the air/fuel mixture through altering the timing of the spark. This started to make big improvements in creating a much more progressive combustion process, which led to improved power delivery.

On page 31 we examine alternative types of engines, including an internal-combustion engine that does not need the use of a spark to ignite the air and fuel but instead uses very high compression pressure to create enough heat to ignite the air/fuel mixture on its own. These engines are called compression-ignition engines or diesel engines.

In both the compression-ignition engine and spark-ignition engine, the combustion process creates very high pressures and generates high amounts of heat. This heat and rapid pressure rise is the basis of how the engine turns this combustion energy into reciprocation motion of the engine, through pushing the pistons down the cylinders to turn the crankshaft of the engine.

As you will start to understand, the whole combustion process is very rapid, especially when the engine speed starts to rise towards the higher revolutions per minute (rpm). At 6000 rpm, the engine is carrying

out the combustion cycle, including forcing the piston from the top to the bottom of the cylinder bore at approximately four thousandths of a second (4 milliseconds). The actual combustion of the air and fuel is much quicker.

Many people have debated whether the combustion process is actually an explosion or a very rapid burning process. You can make your own mind up after studying this section of the book.

Designers soon preferred the internal-combustion engine because it enabled high power outputs to be achieved in a fairly compact and integrated assembly compared with previous steam and gas powered units. The steam engine did, however, remain popular for a while due to its ability to generate exceptionally high power and where size was a less important factor. Steam locomotives and traction engines were still used to pull trains and run large industrial equipment through to the early 1960s.

As mentioned earlier, the internal-combustion engine runs on the use of fossil fuels created from refining crude oil. The difference between the compression-ignition and spark-ignition engines is in the way the fuel is ignited and burnt during combustion. For more detail on how these two engines differ, outlining the key differences in the engine cycles, see page 34.

2.1.2 Petrol engine history

The first commercially successful internal-combustion engine was made by a Frenchman, Etienne Lenoir, in 1860. It ran on coal gas, but worked on a cycle of operations that did not include compression of the gas before ignition: as a result, it was not very efficient. In spite of this it was, in some respects, superior to small steam engines at the time, and a great many were sold and did useful work driving machinery in factories. In 1862, Lenoir made a horseless carriage powered by his engine and possibly drove it on the roads, but he lost interest in this venture and nothing came of it.

A method of carrying out the cycle of operations required for the internal-combustion engine was described in a patent dated 16 January 1862, taken out by a French civil servant, M. Beau de Rochas. Since he did not have the means to develop the patent himself, the patentee offered it to Lenoir who, failing to realise its importance, turned it down.

In Germany, Dr N. A. Otto started the manufacture of gas engines in about 1866. His first engines were extremely noisy, though quite effective. However, in about 1875 Otto took out a patent describing a method of carrying out the cycle of operations that was identical with that of Beau de Rochas' 13 years earlier.

(It is, however, most unlikely that Otto had heard of the Frenchman or his patent.) Otto's new engine was an immediate success. It was much more efficient than Lenoir's and was very quiet – a characteristic that led to its being named 'Otto's silent gas engine'.

Lenoir, realising his mistake, began to manufacture engines working on the same principle. Otto, of course, sued him for infringing his patent rights, but Lenoir had no difficulty in proving that his engines were made under the earlier patent of Beau de Rochas, which had by now lapsed. The court proceedings finally brought poor Beau de Rochas the fame he deserved, and he was awarded a sum of money by the Academy of Sciences in Paris in recognition of his invention. Even so, the method of operation that he was the first to describe, and which is the one used in most modern engines, was for many years (and sometimes still is) known as the Otto cycle.

2.1.3 History of the compression-ignition (diesel) engine

The compression-ignition-type engine is often called a 'diesel engine' derived from the German engineer Dr Rudolf Diesel, who in 1892 took out a patent (No. 7241) on an engine that relied on the heat generated during compression to ignite a fuel of coal dust.

The fuel was forced into the cylinder by air pressure when the piston was at the end or near the top of its stroke. The intention of this design was to achieve a higher thermal efficiency or improved fuel consumption by using a compression ratio higher than that employed on petrol engines. In the early days of internal-combustion engines, pre-ignition (ignition before the spark) occurred in a petrol engine if the compression ratio exceeded a given value. In fact, this problem can still occur on modern engines if the compression is too high.

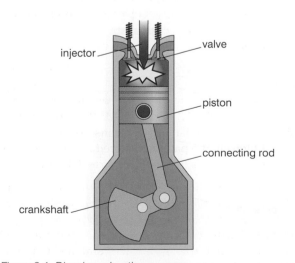

Figure 2.1 Diesel combustion process

Many authorities do not identify Dr Rudolf Diesel as the inventor of this engine, which was the predecessor of the modern compression-ignition engine today. They state that the patent (No. 7146), which was taken out in 1890 by a British engineer (Herbert Ackroyd-Stuart) and put into commercial production two years later, contained all the fundamental features of the modern unit. This patent, which was the result of practical development work on low-compression oil engines, included the induction and compression of air, as well as the timed injection of a liquid fuel by means of a pump (Figure 2.1).

To avoid taking sides in this controversy, the terms 'compression-ignition' or 'oil engine' are often used.

2.1.4 Petrol and diesel reciprocating engines: the main differences

There are two types of reciprocating engines, depending on the fuel used: these are petrol and diesel. Both of these types of engines share many similar operations and components, but the main fundamental differences are in the way the fuel is delivered, ignited and burnt to provide power.

Additionally, the petrol and diesel engine variants can also be split into two categories and this will depend on the operating cycle that is suited to meet its functional demands. So with the option of either a two-stroke or four-stroke engine being commonly available, this chapter covers the operating principles of both versions. Vehicle manufacturers over the years have found that the development of the four-stroke engine is more suited to everyday driving demands and is used widely across all light and commercial vehicles. For this reason, the four-stroke-type engine makes up the main content of this section to explain the differences between petrol and diesel engine operation.

The difference between the diesel and petrol engine is that the diesel engine requires fuel to be introduced into the combustion chamber under extremely high pressures, using a high-pressure fuel pump to provide the precise injection timing. These types of fuel pumps can provide accurate fuel metering and timing of fuel delivered, depending on drive cycle or driver demands. For a petrol engine to operate effectively, it does not need to rely on the same operating factors as a diesel engine. Early petrol engines used a device called a carburettor to control the metering and the fuel delivery. Up until 2000, carburettors where still being used on some variants of vehicles, however, due to emission requirements, we then saw the demise of this unit. Manufacturers now produce all cars fitted with highly complex fuel-injection systems to accurately control the amount of fuel entering the engine. This improves the efficiency of the petrol engine and allows it to produce excellent power along with lower emissions.

For diesel fuel to ignite within the diesel engine cylinders, it uses the very high heat generated through the use of high compression ratios. The pressure created through these high compression ratios is much higher than in a petrol engine. The petrol engine compression ratios are somewhat lower, so it will require alternative methods of igniting the air/fuel mixture. This process of igniting the fuel is completed by an electronically controlled spark or arc.

Over the years, the petrol engine has had to be refined considerably due to more stringent exhaust and other emissions legislation. Due to these changes in legislation, carburettors were gradually used less and the introduction of electronically controlled fuel-injection systems has become the normal route for vehicle manufacturers to take. Along with the fuel system changes, the ignition systems had to be upgraded to meet the demands of performance and emissions now required. Basic mechanical ignition systems have been changed to more advanced electronically controlled systems that are able to constantly monitor themselves and provide improved ignition timing control. These systems have developed to incorporate both the fuelling and ignition control and are often referred to as 'engine management systems' (EMS). When looking at current production vehicles, you will see that the process for controlling both petrol and diesel engines has become very similar.

Petrol engines now have much higher fuel pressures and inject fuel directly into the combustion chambers as seen with diesel engines.

This development has been driven by the need to ensure that each engine gains as much out of every litre of fuel burned as possible. It is also necessary that all new engines produce as little pollution as possible and provide as much power as possible.

In recent years, the management control of petrol and diesel fuel systems has been very similar. Although both have to meet stringent emission requirements, the legislation of diesel control has been more progressive. As previously mentioned, for a diesel engine to operate it requires high fuel-injection pressures compared to a current petrol engine, and sufficient compressed air to ignite the diesel fuel inside each cylinder. So, for today's diesel engines to operate efficiently, they run a complex EMS and do not rely on fuel pumps to deliver carefully metered fuel. They use a similar delivery method as petrol engines with a high-pressure fuel rail delivering fuel to individual electronically controlled injectors.

These injectors are opened and closed by the EMS at very precise rates to deliver the correct amount of fuel at any given engine speed.

The diesel and petrol engine share many major components and design features. Because of this, the description of the main parts of the reciprocating engine are generally the same for both types of engine, unless stated in the description. The issues specific to the petrol and diesel engines are covered on page 35.

2.1.5 The main components of the reciprocating engine

Figure 2.2 shows the main parts of an elementary engine:

1 The cylinder – in its simplest form, this is a tube of circular cross-section, closed at one end.
2 The gudgeon pin – this joins the connecting rod to the piston and allows rotational movement of the crankshaft and liner movement of the piston.
3 The piston – this fits closely inside the cylinder. Ideally, it would be perfectly gas-tight, yet perfectly free to move up and down inside the cylinder.
4 The connecting rod – this connects the piston to the crankshaft. At the piston end is a pin called the gudgeon pin, which is fitted into holes in the piston and the connecting rod to couple them together.
5 The crankshaft – this is the main shaft of the engine and is carried in bearings in the crankcase. Offset from the main part of the shaft is the crank pin, on which the connecting rod is fitted and is free to turn.

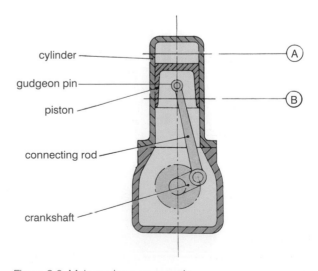

Figure 2.2 Main engine components

The arrangement is such that rotation of the crankshaft causes the piston to move up and down inside the cylinder: the lines A and B (Figure 2.2) indicate the limits of travel of the top of the piston. As the piston moves upwards, the space between its top surface and the closed end of the cylinder is reduced (i.e. the gas trapped in this space is *compressed*). As the piston moves downwards, the space above it is increased (i.e. the gas in this space *expands*).

The crankshaft can be rotated by pushing the piston up and down in the cylinder. Starting with the position shown in Figure 2.2, the crankshaft rotates clockwise as the piston is pushed downwards until the piston reaches the lowest point of its travel. At this point, the crank pin will be directly under the centre of the crankshaft, and the centre of the gudgeon pin, crank pin and crankshaft will all lie in a straight line. In this position, pressure on the piston will have no turning effect on the crankshaft, and this position is therefore called a **dead centre**. Another dead centre occurs when the piston is at the extreme top of its travel. These two dead centres, which are known as *bottom dead centre* (BDC) and *top dead centre* (TDC), mark the extreme limits of the piston's travel (Figure 2.3). Movement of the piston from one dead centre to another is called a *stroke*, and there are two strokes of the piston to every revolution of the crankshaft.

> **Dead centre**: the point at which the piston is at its upper or lowest point in the cylinder bore.

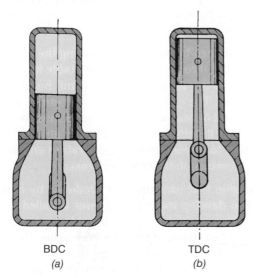

BDC   TDC
(a)   (b)

Figure 2.3 Top and bottom dead centres

Engine size

The usual method of indicating the size of an engine is to state the volume of air and fuel taken into the engine for each cycle of operations. This is clearly the volume contained in that part of the cylinder between the TDC and BDC positions of the piston.

The volume of a cylinder is given by the formula:

$$V = \pi r^2 h$$

Or:

$$V = \frac{\pi d^2 h}{4}$$

Where:

V = the volume of the cylinder

r = the radius

d = the diameter

h = the height or length

The internal diameter of the engine cylinder is called the bore, while the distance the piston moves between TDC and BDC is called the stroke. Representing these by d and l, respectively, the following formula can be written:

$$V = \frac{\pi d^2 l}{4}$$

Since this is the volume displaced or swept by the piston, it is called the displacement volume or **swept volume** of the cylinder. If the engine has several cylinders, as most have, the total swept volume of the engine is swept volume per cylinder multiplied by the number of cylinders.

If the bore d and stroke l are measured in millimetres and if n represents the number of cylinders, then the total volume (V_t) is:

$$V_t = \frac{\pi d^2 ln}{4\,\text{mm}^3}$$

$$= \frac{\pi d^2 ln}{4000\,\text{cm}^3}$$

$$= \frac{\pi d^2 ln}{4,000,000\,l}$$

(**Note**: $1000\,\text{cm}^3$ = 1 litre)

When the bore is equal to the stroke, the engine is called a 'square engine'. In a similar way, when the bore is larger than the stroke, the engine is called 'oversquare'.

> **Swept volume**: the volume of the cylinder from BDC to TDC including the combustion chamber.

Compression ratio

An important feature of the dimensions of an engine cylinder is the number of times the volume enclosed above the piston before compression is greater than that after compression. When the piston is at TDC, a space is left between the top of the piston and the end of the cylinder: the volume contained in this space is called the clearance volume. The volume enclosed above the piston at BDC consists of the clearance volume plus the swept volume and is called the total volume.

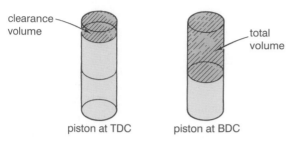

Figure 2.4 *Cylinder volume and compression ratio*

$$\text{Compression ratio} = \frac{\text{Total volume}}{\text{Clearance volume}}$$

$$= \frac{\text{Swept volume} + \text{Clearance volume}}{\text{Clearance volume}}$$

$$= \frac{\text{Swept volume}}{\text{Clearance volume}} + 1$$

2.2 The working principles of the four-stroke and two-stroke engine

2.2.1 Basic operating process

The piston is pushed down the cylinder by applying pressure to its upper surface. The method by which the pressure is produced is based upon the fact that if a gas is heated in a confined space, its pressure will increase. Figure 2.5 illustrates a simple demonstration of this fact: the apparatus is very simple and you can try it for yourself. Bore a hole in the cork of a bottle and into this hole push one end of a glass tube bent into a U-shape. Partly fill this tube with water and then push the cork into the bottle, holding the bottle upside down as shown. The difference in pressure between the air in the bottle and the air outside is shown by the difference (h) in the levels of the water at A and B. Warming the air in the bottle – even by holding it in the hand – will increase the pressure of the air in the bottle which, in turn, will push down the level at A and raise the level at B.

In an engine, the air can be heated to a very high temperature and a correspondingly high pressure is created inside the cylinder, thus exerting a considerable force on the piston.

Pressure above the piston can only push it downwards, and at the end of a downward stroke

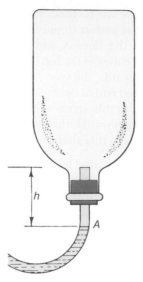

Figure 2.5 *Demonstration of increase in air pressure*

the pressure must be released and the piston moved back to the top of the cylinder before it can be pushed downwards again. The pressure is released by opening a hole in the cylinder called the exhaust port, and the piston is returned up the cylinder by the rotation of a wheel with a heavy rim – called a flywheel – fitted to the crankshaft. Once this flywheel has been made to turn, it will continue to rotate for several revolutions.

The air inside the cylinder could be heated by playing a flame on the outside of the cylinder. To reach the air inside, however, the heat would have to pass through the wall of the cylinder, so the air could be made no hotter than the cylinder. Much of the heat used would be lost by heating the cylinder and the air outside it.

This waste can be lessened by heating the air inside the cylinder directly: to do this a suitable fuel can be mixed with the air in the cylinder and burnt inside the engine. The cylinder will still, of course, absorb a good deal of heat, and arrangements must be made to prevent it getting too hot, but the air inside can be raised to a much higher temperature and so will reach a correspondingly higher pressure.

Any engine that uses the heat produced by burning a fuel to develop mechanical power is called a heat engine. One in which the fuel is burnt inside the engine is called an internal-combustion engine. Internal-combustion engines can use any one of a variety of fuels. Petrol is a liquid refined from crude petroleum, and is particularly suitable as a fuel for vehicles. It is liquid at normal temperatures and a vehicle can carry, in quite a small tank, enough to take it over 480 km (300 miles). Petrol gives off a flammable vapour even at quite low temperatures, enabling the engine to be started from cold with little difficulty.

2.2.2 Cycle of operations

Before either petrol or diesel can be burnt they must be vaporised and mixed with a suitable quantity of air. This mixture must then be introduced into the cylinder. This is done in two ways: through a hole called the inlet port or injected directly into the combustion chamber. Once inside the cylinder, the mixture is compressed before burning, since this greatly increases the pressure after burning. After compression, the vaporised fuel is either ignited by an electric spark, which, at the appropriate moment, jumps across a small gap on a sparking plug, screwed into the top of the cylinder, or through high compression ratios in the case of the diesel engine

After the fuel has burned and the resulting pressure has pushed the piston down the cylinder, the burned gases are released, as already mentioned, through the exhaust port. The inlet and exhaust ports are normally closed, but are opened at the correct times to allow the gases to pass through them.

The running of the engine involves the continuous repetition of four operations, which make up what is called the cycle of operations. These operations are continuously repeated, as long as the engine is running, in the following order:

1 The piston will move down to the bottom part of the cylinder and the inlet valve(s) will simultaneously open during this period. The charge is a mixture of fuel vapour and air for the petrol engine or just air for the diesel engine and some selective petrol variants will be drawn into the top area of the cylinder (above the piston). This is known as the induction stroke.

2 As the piston starts to move back up the cylinder, the inlet valve(s) will be closed. The force generated from the piston moving up the cylinder will compress the charge into the top area of the cylinder; this is known as the combustion chamber. Completing this part of the cycle will compress the charge and raise its temperature to a high level. This is known as the compression stroke.

3 As the piston reaches its highest point, the compressed charge will now be ignited. On a petrol engine, the charge will be ignited by the use of an electric spark, which then would burn the charge mass. In diesel engines, the injection of the diesel fuel into the charged heated air causes it to ignite and burn. In both cases, the ignited charge will force the piston back down its cylinder. This is known as the power or ignition stroke.

4 As the piston reaches its lower point within the cylinder it will then start to return back up. In doing so, it will start to force out the burnt gases from its cylinder through an opened exhaust valve. Once it reaches the top area of its cylinder, all of the gases will now be removed and the exhaust valve will be closed. This is known as the exhaust stroke.

The above operating procedure is better known as the four-stroke cycle. This is because the four operations coincide with the piston's movements (strokes) of travel from its highest positional point within its cylinder, moving down to its lowest point. A two-stroke cycle, which also uses the main principles of the induction, compression, ignition and exhaust strokes, has automotive application too, particularly in motorcycles, although there are significant differences in the details of operation between the two types. There is more on two-stroke engines on page 37.

If we refer to the engine cycle, you will identify that the explosion of the gases will force the piston on its way during only one of these operations. The remaining operations give no direct help, but actually impede the piston's movement, particularly the compressing of the gas. Thus, the work of the flywheel is not merely to push the piston back up the cylinder, but also to keep the crankshaft turning as steadily as possible between one impulse on the piston and the next.

2.2.3 Four-stroke cycle petrol spark-ignition engine

Petrol and diesel engine four-stroke cycles are very similar. The major differences between the two are at the point of fuel delivery during the compression stroke. Additional information on the diesel engine combustion process is on page 236.

In this method, one complete stroke of the piston is used to carry out each of the four operations forming the cycle of operations. Figure 2.6 shows the complete cycle. To complete the cycle, therefore, four strokes of the piston, occupying two revolutions of the crankshaft, are needed: consequently, the method is generally known as the four-stroke cycle.

The inlet and exhaust ports are closed by valves, which are mechanically opened at the correct times usually by a camshaft. If the engine runs on petrol, the petrol and air are mixed in the correct proportions by a carburettor, fitted to the outer end of the inlet port, or by fuel being injected into the inlet manifold or directly into the combustion chamber to mix with the air.

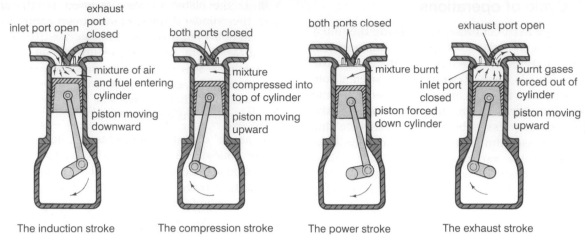

Figure 2.6 The operation of an engine on the four-stroke cycle

Starting with the piston at the top of its stroke, or TDC, as the crankshaft rotates the method of operation is as follows:

First stroke – the piston moves down the cylinder with the inlet port open and exhaust port closed, filling the cylinder with a mixture of petrol vapour and air. This is the induction stroke.

Second stroke – the piston moves up the cylinder with both ports closed, compressing the mixture into the combustion chamber at the top end of the cylinder. This is the compression stroke.

Third stroke – towards the end of the compression stroke an electric spark is made to jump across a small gap on a sparking plug screwed into the end of the cylinder within the cylinder head. This spark ignites the petrol vapour, which burns very rapidly, heating the gas in the cylinder to a high temperature and considerably increasing its pressure. The pressure forces the piston down the cylinder with both ports remaining closed. This is the power stroke.

Fourth stroke – the piston returns up the cylinder with the inlet port still closed but the exhaust port open, expelling the burnt gases from the cylinder. This is the exhaust stroke.

At the end of this stroke, the exhaust port closes and the inlet port reopens for the next induction stroke, which follows immediately.

Figure 2.6 illustrates these four operations. Observe the movements of the piston and operation of the valves as the crankshaft of an actual engine is rotated.

Flywheel effect

One of the issues associated with the four-stroke cycle engine is that the power strokes occur every four strokes of the piston. At low engine speed, there is a need to carry the engine over between the individual

power strokes due to the increased time taken between these strokes. This issue is overcome by the **flywheel** carrying the engine over between these non-power strokes. So the flywheel is designed to assist the engine crankshaft in completing its power stroke and then maintain its rotational activity to complete the other three strokes. The flywheel is attached to the end of the crankshaft and usually has the clutch or torque converter attached prior to the transmission assembly.

Flywheel: a large balanced weight that provides **inertia** to the crankshaft due to its large mass, helping to keep the crankshaft rotating between power strokes.

Inertia: the production of a uniform constant motion in one direction.

The flywheel's motion can be described by looking at a spinning car wheel when it is lifted from the ground; if a large amount of energy is input into the wheel to make it spin, the wheel will continue to rotate for longer due to its mass. So, in simple terms, if you want the wheel to maintain its rotational action, then the heavier the wheel the more energy it will store. The weight of the flywheel aids in this function due to its mass, assisting in rotating the crankshaft between power strokes.

The flywheel provides vital energy to maintain the crankshaft rotational action and provide the support to force each piston back up its combustion cylinder. During the compression, induction and exhaust strokes, opposing forces can be created on the crankshaft, so the energy from the flywheel assists in keeping the engine rotating at a constant speed.

Engines with a larger number of cylinders are not so dependent on the action of the flywheel due to the increased number of power strokes per crankshaft revolution. For example, an engine with eight cylinders has less dependency than an engine with four.

2.2.4 The two-stroke cycle

It has always been considered a disadvantage of the four-stroke cycle that there are three 'idle strokes' to every 'working stroke'. Between 1878 and 1881, a Scotsman, Dugald Clerk, developed an engine in which the cycle of operations was completed in only two strokes of the piston, thus providing a power stroke for every revolution of the crankshaft. This engine used a second cylinder and piston to force the fresh mixture into the working cylinder.

In 1891, Joseph Day invented a modified form of Clerk's engine, in which he dispensed with the second cylinder by using the space in the crankcase underneath the piston. He also avoided the use of valves by using the piston itself to cover or uncover the ports.

The two-stroke petrol engine

The operation of this engine (Figure 2.7) is as follows:

Beginning with the piston about halfway on its upward stroke (a), all three ports are covered. The upward movement of the piston compresses a fresh charge of mixture in the top of the cylinder, and at the same time decreases the pressure under the piston below the pressure of the atmosphere (the crankcase being seated).

Near the top of the stroke (b) the lower edge of the piston overruns the inlet port, allowing the pressure of the atmosphere to fill the lower part of the engine with fresh mixture from the carburettor.

At about the top of the stroke, the mixture above the piston is ignited in the same way as in the four-stroke engine, and with the same result: the high pressure of the burnt gases drives the piston down the cylinder.

A little below TDC (c), the piston covers the inlet port, and further downward movement compresses the mixture in the crankcase. Near the bottom of the stroke the top edge of the piston overruns the exhaust port, allowing the burnt gases to rush out of the cylinder under their own pressure.

Slightly further down the stroke (d) the transfer port is uncovered, and the mixture compressed below the piston flows into the cylinder above the piston, where it is deflected upwards by the specially shaped piston. This prevents the mixture shooting straight across the cylinder and out of the exhaust port.

As the piston rises on its next stroke, the transfer and exhaust ports are covered and the cycle of operations begins again.

In modern engines of this type, the deflector on the crown of the piston has been dispensed with, and the transfer port or ports (there are usually two) are shaped and aimed so as to direct the fresh mixture towards the top end of the cylinder away from the exhaust port.

It might be expected that the two-stroke engine would develop twice the power of a four-stroke engine of the same size, but experience does not confirm this. The operations are less effectively carried out and, despite the deflector on the piston, mixing the fresh charge with burnt gas cannot be avoided: there is usually some loss of fresh mixture through the exhaust port and incomplete scavenging of burnt gas from the cylinder. The main advantages of the two-stroke engine, therefore, are its greater simplicity and smoothness. It is commonly used for smaller-sized vehicles, such as motorcycles, and is seldom used for cars.

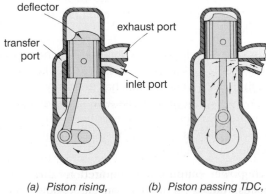
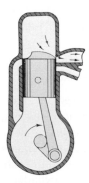
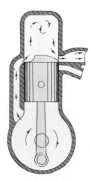

(a) Piston rising, compressing mixture above, decreasing pressure below. All ports closed

(b) Piston passing TDC, mixture above piston ignited, fresh mixture entering crankcase

(c) Piston moving downward. The fresh mixture in the crankcase has been compressed. The piston has just uncovered the exhaust port, and is about to uncover the transfer port

(d) Piston passing BDC exhaust and transfer ports open. Fresh mixture entering cylinder via transfer port, directed to top of cylinder by deflection on piston, driving out burnt gas through exhaust port

Figure 2.7 Operation of an engine on a two-stroke cycle

Two-stroke diesel compression-ignition engine

Although the two-stroke compression-ignition engine is not so popular as the four-stroke unit, some manufacturers regard the two-stroke engine's smoother torque, simpler construction and smaller unit as supreme advantages. Originally, this type was restricted to low-speed industrial and marine applications, but nowadays high-speed units arc fitted to commercial vehicles. The great disadvantage of the two-stroke petrol engine – the loss of fuel to the exhaust when both ports are open – does not apply to the compression-ignition engine, since the cylinder only contains air: therefore, it may be argued that the two-stroke cycle is most suitable for compression-ignition operation.

Figure 2.8 shows the sequence of operations for a simple two-port valveless form of engine.

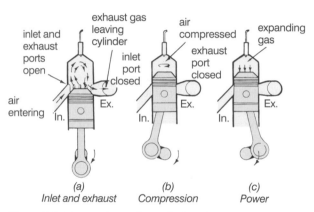

Figure 2.8 Two-stroke cycle – valveless form

Figure 2.8a shows the air entering the cylinder through the inlet port, and 'burnt' gas flowing to the exhaust system. As the piston ascends (Figure 2.8b) the inlet and exhaust ports are closed to provide the compression stroke. After the air has been compressed to a compression ratio of 12–16:1, the high temperature will ignite the fuel injected into the cylinder and produce the power stroke (Figure 2.8c).

To ensure that the engine receives adequate air charge, most vehicle applications normally employ a blower to pressure-charge the cylinder with air. However, it is possible to operate the engine by utilising the pressure waves or pulses in the exhaust system to induce the 'new' air into the cylinder.

Figure 2.9 shows a uniflow-type two-stroke engine, which is fitted with an exhaust valve and pressure-charged with a Roots-type blower. This improved arrangement provides better power output from the engine through improved engine breathing, as the engine is able to introduce more air and fuel into the combustion chamber and evacuate the exhaust gases more efficiently. This arrangement is claimed to give double the power of a four-stroke engine of the same capacity.

Opening the exhaust valve before uncovering the circumferential air ports allows the remaining gas pressure to start pumping out the exhaust gas. This is followed by an air charge approximately 30 per cent greater in volume than the cylinder capacity, to cool and scavenge the cylinder effectively.

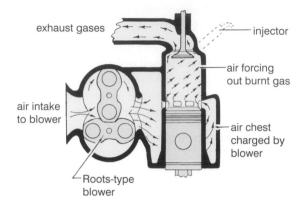

Figure 2.9 Uniflow-type two-stroke engine

2.3   Torque and power

2.3.1 Producing torque and power

Any discussion involving engines normally turns towards the 'power' output and how much 'torque' it produces. Torque and power are important terms when looking at engine performance and care must be taken that they are not expressed as the same thing. Torque and power are different measurements of the engine performance, with torque referring to the engine's ability to create turning power and power being the ability of the engine to do work over a period of time.

Thus, torque refers to the ability of an engine to pull or provide pulling power. This would be typically required in a vehicle that has to carry out heavy work for long periods, such as commercial vehicles carrying heavy cargo. Light cars having to pull loads, such as trailers or caravans, also require higher torque value engines.

High power outputs are required for high vehicle speeds. Racing cars and sports cars would generally have higher power engines than normal road cars.

You will see many cases of engines producing high torque and high power outputs. The normal method for an engine designer to produce an engine with high torque and power output is to increase the engine capacity and the number of cylinders. This combination of large engine capacity and higher number of cylinders was the normal route to higher performance engines. Now with the need to deliver good fuel economy and low emissions, this combination is changing more towards smaller capacity engines with forced induction and higher engine speeds. These engines produce similar power and torque, but much lower emissions and improved fuel economy.

An example of this can be seen with the Volkswagen TFSi engine. This engine is small capacity at 1400 cc but utilises turbo and supercharging to produce up to 180 horsepower and over 200 Nm of torque. Until recently, this sort of power and torque was only seen in much larger engines.

Figure 2.10 High power output, small-capacity engine incorporating turbocharging and supercharging

Diesel engines tend to produce more torque but less power than equivalent-sized petrol engines. This greater 'pulling power' makes diesel engines a popular choice for commercial vehicles. Petrol engines normally operate at higher engine speeds, enabling higher power outputs to be produced (see page 43).

2.3.2 Torque

Torque is a twisting or rotating force, for example the force that is applied to a shaft that needs to rotate, such as when you apply upward or downward pressure on a wrench or spanner to undo or tighten a bolt or nut. Torque is often referred to as the force that acts against a lever on a given length and also is expressed as a given weight, for example kilograms or pounds force. The length of the lever can be expressed in metres or feet. An example of a torque specification is 300 kg/m, which means that 300 kg of force are acting on a lever that is 1 m long.

Tightening a wheel nut (Figure 2.11) is a good example to demonstrate torque. If a short lever is used to turn the wheel nut, such as a 500 mm bar, then the amount of force required to act on the lever to tighten the wheel nut is quite high due to the lack of leverage available. If, however, a long lever is used, such as a 1000 mm breaker bar, then the force required is lower as the longer lever provides a big increase in leverage.

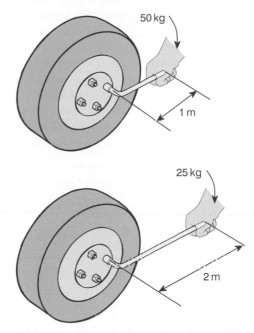

Figure 2.11 Tightening a wheel nut with a short and long lever

In order to tighten a wheel nut to a particular torque setting, a greater force must be applied to a shorter lever than a longer one. However, the actual amount of work done to tighten the nut is the same, no matter what the length of the lever. The difference is in the amount of *force* required. If, for example, the short lever is 500 mm long and the long lever is 1000 mm long (i.e. twice its length), the force required to tighten the wheel nut using the short lever is 50 kg force and the force required using the long lever would be half that, i.e. 25 kg force.

Note: the final torque result is the same with both levers, as they both apply the same twisting force to the wheel nut. It is the force *applied* that is different.

For instance:

Work done = Force × Distance

Therefore, if we have a lever of 500 mm and a force of 50 kg:

Work done = 50 kg × 0.5 m = 25 kg/m

If we increase the length of the lever to 1000 mm, we will have:

Work done = 25 kg × 1.0 m = 25 kg/m

This clearly shows that the length of lever is directly proportional to the input force required to obtain the same amount of work.

In summary, torque produced is directly related to the length of a lever and the force that can be applied to it.

Also note that the distance of movement when tightening a given bolt to a specified torque when using a longer lever is greater than when using a shorter lever. The amount of work done is the same, but the input of force is directly proportional to the length of lever – a longer lever requires less input force. You should always try to use a lever of suitable length for tightening or loosening fixings to avoid over stressing yourself. It should be noted though, that when tightening a fixing with a long lever it is very easy to over-tighten due to the lower effort you have to apply.

Figure 2.12 Work done tightening the wheel nut

Torque in an engine

When we use the term 'torque' applied to an engine, it refers to the twisting force available at the crankshaft. The combustion process creates the force that pushes the piston down the cylinder bore. This acts directly on the connecting rod and crankshaft forcing the crankshaft to rotate. The higher the expansion of the gases through combustion above the piston, the higher the force acting on the piston. Figure 2.13 shows the piston and connecting rod assembly, which is forcing the crankshaft to rotate.

When the piston starts its downward action within its cylinder, it is applying direct force on to the crankshaft's crank pin. We can regard the distance from the centre of the crank pin and the centre of the crankshaft as the lever length of the engine. This distance or measurement is often referred to as the 'crankshaft throw'.

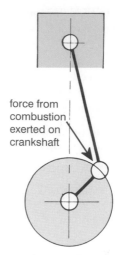

Figure 2.13 Piston and connecting rod applying force to the crankshaft

Torque is the force that is created when pressure is applied to the end of a lever, so applying the combustion forces created by the piston will then also generate increased torque. Generally, longer stroke engines have larger crankshaft throws, which then leads to larger torque produced.

Torque is not produced during the strokes of induction, compression or exhaust; it is only produced at the power stroke of a piston. Thus, a single-cylinder four-stroke engine, for instance one fitted to a motorcycle, will only produce torque once in every two revolutions of the crankshaft. This is why, when idling, the revs of these engines sound very low and lumpy.

Torque variation during the power stroke

When we look at torque and how it is produced, we see it is not constant through the piston and crankshaft motion. Pressure on the top of the piston increases when combustion occurs in the cylinders and the burning gases start to rapidly expand. The gases continue to expand while the flame spreads through the combustible mixture. As the piston is pushed down the cylinder due to the rapid pressure rise through combustion, the volume above the piston increases, leading to a pressure drop. This in turn reduces the force acting on the piston and crankshaft. This pressure rise-and-fall results in the torque varying during the power stroke.

The angle at which the connecting rod meets the crankshaft also has an effect, changing constantly as the crankshaft rotates. This angle change affects the torque produced. In Figure 2.14a, the piston is just past TDC and the angle between the connecting rod and the crankshaft makes it more difficult to transfer engine torque through to the crankshaft. In

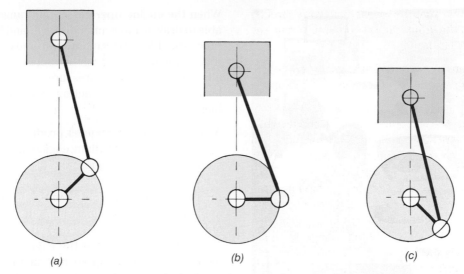

Figure 2.14 Torque variation due to different angles between the connecting rod and the crankshaft

Figure 2.14b, the connecting rod and the crankshaft are at right angles providing the optimum angle to transmit the turning force into the crankshaft. Figure 2.14c has the piston approaching BDC, producing a more acute angle between the connecting rod and the crankshaft. As in Figure 2.14a, this makes it more difficult to rotate the crankshaft.

As we have seen, force on the piston is only produced during the power stroke; the induction, compression and exhaust strokes do not produce torque at the crankshaft. Although the flywheel keeps the crankshaft rotating in between power strokes and also adds energy due to its mass, in effect torque at the crankshaft varies during the four-stroke cycle. So whether it is a two- or four-stroke engine, the 'effective torque' created at the crankshaft will be an average value of the generated torque produced throughout the operating cycle.

Measuring torque

Complex mathematical equations can be used to measure torque at the crankshaft, but engine torque is more usually measured rather than calculated using a *dynamometer*. Engine power is also measured using a dynamometer.

This is a device that applies a measured load to the engine while it is running in order to be able to create real-world driving simulation of the vehicle on the road. By applying known loads to an engine, it allows the torque produced at the crankshaft to be measured at different engine speeds. To gain the maximum torque that the engine can produce, the engine is operated at full throttle and load applied by the dynamometer. Once it gets to the point where the load applied prevents the engine speed from

increasing above a given speed (e.g. 3000 rpm), this gives the maximum effort the engine can provide at that speed. Increasing the load further will reduce engine speed, decreasing the load will increase engine speed. The torque can be measured or calculated because the load applied by the dynamometer is a known value.

To create the loading, the dynamometer actually applies a brake to the engine, hence the term 'brake dynamometer'.

Dynamometers come in various designs to cater for different needs. When checking the power and torque outputs of new engines, manufacturers use a version that mounts the engine on a frame or chassis. The crankshaft and flywheel are connected directly to the dynamometer device that applies the load. Some dynamometers use water to generate the resistance required to brake the engine and assess the power and torque. The dynamometer wheel is driven by the engine within the flow of water. Load is increased by increasing or decreasing the water flow. Modern dynamometers create the load using magnetic energy – adjusting the strength of the magnetic field to increase or decrease load.

So-called 'rolling road dynamometers' operate on the same principle as engine dynamometers, but the vehicle is driven on to the dynamometer so that the driving wheels rotate on a set of rollers (Figure 2.15). Rolling road dynamometers use either an electrical system or, more rarely, a water-based system to create the load. When using these rolling road dynamometers to measure torque and power the results are usually expressed in 'power at the wheels' due to the losses of power and torque through the transmission systems and road wheels.

Figure 2.15 Sports car on a rolling road dynamometer measuring power and torque outputs

Maximum torque

In an internal-combustion engine, the torque produced is directly proportional to the force acting on the piston during the power stroke. This force is produced by the sudden pressure rise created by combustion. Consequently, the more efficient the combustion, the greater the force acting on the piston and the greater the torque produced. Combustion efficiency can be increased by increasing the volume of air and fuel in the cylinder. Maximum torque can therefore be achieved by pressure-charging through the use of a supercharger or turbocharger to force more air and fuel into the combustion chambers. (Pressure-charging is covered in detail on page 133.)

Efficiency and engine speed

The way in which air and fuel is draw into the cylinders can be affected by a great number of variables. At the point when the inlet valve opens during the induction stroke, the piston is passing down the cylinder. This creates low pressure in the cylinder, causing air to be 'sucked' or 'drawn' into the cylinder.

In an engine running at high speed, there is very little time for air to enter the cylinder before the compression and power stroke. This can mean that the cylinder is not completely filled with a fresh charge (air or air/fuel mixture), although the high speed of the air coming through manifold and inlet ports (intake system) is also high, which helps to maintain the flow of air into the cylinders.

By contrast, when the engine is operating at low speeds, the movement of air through the intake system is slow, and this can also result in the cylinder not completely filling with charge.

When the engine operates at mid-range speeds, it is able to draw in large amounts of air and fuel due to the time available between power strokes. Consequently, this improved air/fuel mixture produces more efficient and higher-pressure combustion, which leads to a higher force acting on the piston, creating higher engine torque.

A great number of engines produce their maximum torque value at a medium engine speed. Figure 2.16 shows a typical torque curve for a petrol engine; from this, you will notice that the torque increases as the engine speed increases until the engine reaches approximately 3500 rpm when it starts to reduce, although the engine speed continues to increase. These results show that the engine is receiving the largest charge of air (or air/fuel mixture) at 3500 rpm, producing the greatest force on the piston and, therefore, greatest torque from the power stroke.

Engine designers have to take in many factors when working out how the engine is going to produce its power and torque, such as the use of the engine and the conditions it is going to operate in. These key factors inform the engine designers to work out how much air and fuel the engine is going to use and need at every given point within its operating limits. The timing of the opening and closing of the inlet and exhaust valves is a critical factor. Ideally, the timing of the opening and closing of the inlet and exhaust valves should vary according to different engine speeds, to ensure the right charge of air and fuel is placed in the combustion chambers. Traditionally in petrol engines, maximum torque was usually achieved at 50–60 per cent of maximum engine speed, for example at 3500 rpm for an engine with a 6000 rpm maximum speed (see Figure 2.16).

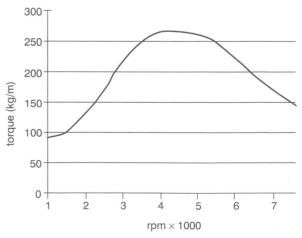

Figure 2.16 Torque curve for a traditional petrol engine

However, modern engines now have devices to achieve variable valve timing throughout the operating engine speed range. Engines with variable valve timing, along with other relevant engine design improvements, show that it is not unusual to have a consistently high torque value, from low through to high engine speeds, due to the ability to constantly alter the opening duration of the inlet and exhaust valves – although maximum torque is still often but not always produced at just over 50 per cent of the maximum engine speed. Figure 2.17 shows a torque curve for an engine fitted with variable valve timing; assess the improvement in torque produced at low engine speeds compared with the curve in Figure 2.16.

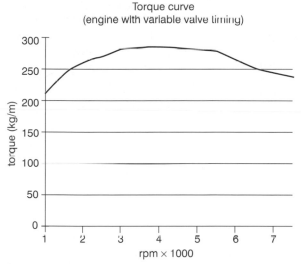

Torque curve
(engine with variable valve timing)

Figure 2.17 Torque curve of a petrol engine with variable valve timing

Torque units of value

There has not been universal consistency in the units used to express torque. In the USA and the UK, imperial measurements have traditionally been used – that is the 'pound foot' (lb ft), for instance 100 lb ft. In the metric system, you might see kilograms force (kgf) and metres, but any other weight or measurement of length could be used. There is now a general agreement in countries that use the metric system, including the UK, to use the Newton (N) as the unit of force and the metre (m) as the measurement of length. Torque is, therefore, normally quoted in Newton metres (Nm).

2.3.3 Power

Whether we are discussing electricity or engines, power is usually defined as the work done (energy converted) over a period of time. Work, power, force and torque are all different measurable aspects of an engine's performance and functions as it operates in various conditions.

The relationship between work and force can be illustrated in the example of a vehicle attached to a heavy trailer by a rope. If the vehicle provides enough force to tighten the rope, but not enough to move the trailer, then no work is done as the load of the trailer has not moved. If, however, the vehicle is able to apply a greater force, the trailer will move, meaning that work is being done. The further the trailer moves, the greater the amount of work done.

When talking about power in the automotive industry, we often use the term 'horsepower'. This term comes from the times when heavy loads were transferred using the power of horses and carts. Engine power is still often quoted in horsepower and 1 horsepower = 33,000 lb ft per minute or 74 W (0.746 kW).

Engine power

As it has been mentioned previously, torque is produced during the power stroke, and the highest point of torque is produced when the piston connecting rod is at or approaching right angles to the crankshaft. Power is generally related to the amount of work done by the engine and directly linked to the power stroke during the combustion process.

For example, a single-cylinder four-stroke engine that is operating at 1000 rpm will produce a certain amount of torque at the crankshaft during each of the individual power strokes, but each power stroke will only move the vehicle a short distance. If we take this theory further, the engine operating at 1000 rpm will have produced 500 power strokes due to the power stroke occurring every two crankshaft revolutions, this will have moved the vehicle over a relatively long distance. If we take this distance travelled over one minute, we have an indication of the power. For this reason, in theory, the faster the engine, the faster the rotation of the crankshaft, the greater the number of power strokes and the greater the total power. Therefore, using this theory, we can say that each power stroke produced by the engine produces the torque at the crankshaft, which leads to a higher number of power strokes providing an increase in engine power.

Remember that the force acting on the piston during the power stroke is directly proportional to the torque output of the engine. This can be seen in the use of pressure-charging (such as turbocharging), which produces higher combustion pressures leading to higher torque outputs. Obtaining the most power and torque from an engine will always depend on the amount of air and fuel in the correct ratio that can be added into the engine cylinders during combustion strokes. High amounts of air and fuel at the correct ratio will produce higher power and torque outputs.

Due to the amount of air and fuel entering the engine varying with engine speed, the typical results are that the engine produces the best torque value at a mid-range engine speed when the charge of air and fuel is highest. As the engine speed rises, the inlet and exhaust valves do not have as much time to force air and fuel into the engine and remove the exhaust gases; this results in the torque output reducing. The power will not necessarily fall at the same rate as there are a greater number of power strokes taking place at higher engine speeds.

If we take this theory to the extreme and presume the volume of fresh charge drawn into the cylinder remained constant irrespective of the speed of the engine, and we then doubled the speed of the engine providing twice the number of power strokes, the resulting power produced would also double. Remember that the torque produced at each power stroke would remain the same.

If, however, we look at the normal operating conditions of an engine and presume that the fresh charge of air and fuel mixture entering the engine reduces as the engine speed increases, then we would see that the engine power would not increase in direct proportion to the engine speed.

If we take this further with an example of an engine's power and torque delivery characteristics, an engine producing a power output of 100 **PS** at 2500 rpm may be delivering its peak torque at the same rpm when the maximum fresh charge is available. When the engine is running twice as fast, at 5000 rpm, the capability of the engine to intake air and fuel will be lower, at 75 per cent for example, therefore the torque output will be 25 per cent lower. At this point, each power stroke will deliver 75 per cent of its torque availability.

PS: pferdestärke = horse strength, a German unit similar to the traditional horsepower rating where 1 PS = 0.986 horsepower. An additional European specification for engine power used today is the kilowatt (kW), which equals 1.34 brake horsepower and 1.36 PS. For example, an engine with 100 kW of power is equivalent to 134 bhp and 136 PS.

At this point, we can see that the engine speed has doubled from the peak torque output at 2500 rpm, which in theory would mean a 100 per cent improvement in the power output at 200 PS. However, as the force produced at each power stroke is actually 75 per cent, the power output will be related. The peak power will theoretically be three-quarters of 200 PS, which is 150 PS.

Figure 2.18 shows a typical torque and power curve for a petrol engine. You will see that the torque produced by the engine is relatively low at low engine speeds until the speed of the engine starts to reach about 3000 rpm. At this point, the torque rises to its peak at 4500 rpm and then starts to drop. This torque reduction at higher engine speed is due to a reduction in the amount of the fresh charge of air and fuel entering the engine. When we then look at the amount of power produced, the engine is providing a relatively low amount of power at lower engine speeds until the engine reaches about 3000 rpm again, and then the power rises almost in a linear form to its peak at 6000 rpm. The power then starts to drop after 6000 rpm to the engine's maximum engine speed.

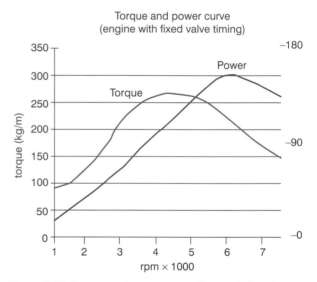

Figure 2.18 *Torque and power curves for a petrol engine*

As the engine speed rises, the fresh charge of air and fuel becomes much smaller as the engine has less time to draw the air and fuel into the engine, and so the engine power will start to reduce as the engine speed reaches towards its maximum. This is why many manufacturers now produce engines with variable valve control, as the engine is able to 'breathe' better at higher engine speeds due to the inlet valves being left open for longer to allow more air and fuel into the engine. Then, at low engine speeds, the valves are opened for shorter periods as the engine does not require the same levels of air and fuel.

To conclude, we can say that the power and torque produced by an engine is totally dependent on the amount of air and fuel in the correct ratio being able to enter the engine, and the timing of when this occurs along with the timing of the combustion process. The rated power output of an engine will be greater if the engine can draw in larger amounts of air and fuel in the correct ratio over a given period, for example one minute.

2.3.4 Power and torque characteristics of an engine

The need to be able to alter the power and torque characteristics of an engine has become more and more important in today's vehicles as manufacturers are now using the same basic engines across a wide range of vehicles. Each vehicle type has different requirements in power and torque. For example, a 2-litre engine used in a people carrier would need good torque characteristics for carrying more load and generally operating at lower engine and road speeds. If the same 2-litre engine from the same manufacturer was used in a performance hatchback, the engine would need better power characteristics due to the requirement that it operates at higher engine speeds and higher gear ratios.

The engine design has direct effect on the torque and power produced. By improving the breathing ability of an engine through changes to intake manifold, valves, camshaft opening period and cylinder head refinements, dramatic improvements can be made to the torque produced at specific engine speeds.

Manufacturers will always work towards a compromise when designing a particular engine. They will assess the main operating conditions in which the engine will perform, and then design it to be able to do this reliably for extensive periods of time. For example, an engine fitted to a sports car will be expected to operate at high engine speeds producing its power towards the peak rpm. This engine will be able to perform very well in such an environment, but if it was then asked to pull a heavy load, such as a trailer, it would not be able to produce the torque required to operate at lower engine speeds.

Most mainstream vehicles have to operate across many conditions, from pulling large loads (such as caravans) to travelling at high cruising speeds on the motorways. To enable these engines to have such wide operating characteristics, designers have introduced additional features, such as variable valve timing and variable valve lift technologies, along with variable intake systems and pressure-charging. These design features improve the ability of the engine to produce higher torque and power outputs without the requirement of operating the engine at such high engine speeds. Along with improvements to torque and power, engines today normally produce fewer emissions and provide improved fuel economy. Engine manufacturers will always have to compromise between performance and reliability, normally edging towards reliability for improved vehicle life.

2.4 Single- and multi-cylinder engines

2.4.1 Limitations of single-cylinder engines

The shape of a single-cylinder engine cannot be altered very much, and its size will depend upon its swept volume. This does not leave the designer much scope for making the engine compact so as to fit it into a smaller space in the vehicle. When several cylinders are used, the designer has a choice of different cylinder arrangements, allowing the engine shape to be varied to suit the space into which it must fit.

Virtually all engines used in vehicles (apart from motorcycles) are multi-cylinder, using from 2 to 16 cylinders. The reason for not using single-cylinder engines in cars or light commercial vehicles is due to the way the single-cylinder engine produces its power and torque. During the engine operating cycle, the torque produced by the power strokes continually alters due to the input of turning force to the crankshaft. In Figure 2.19, we can see that the torque input to the crankshaft is at its maximum during the engine's power stroke. During the compression, exhaust and induction strokes, the crankshaft requires an input of energy to keep it rotating. This effort is generated by the flywheel's stored energy, which is produced within the power stroke.

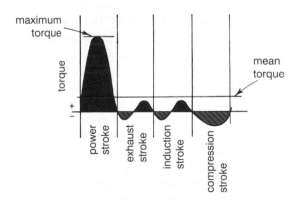

Figure 2.19 Torque fluctuations in a single-cylinder engine

With a large-capacity single-cylinder engine, such as that seen fitted to a motorcycle, the maximum torque developed may be high. However, because the torque developed by the power strokes is very irregular, creating a fluctuating torque curve, its average or mean value is very much lower.

The torque developed by the engine (especially a single-cylinder engine) is, therefore, rather erratic, especially at low speeds. A heavy flywheel is necessary to maintain crankshaft rotation in between power strokes, especially at lower engine speeds. Figure 2.20 shows that if a four-cylinder engine is used and the cylinders are working in succession, the mean torque is only a little less than the maximum torque. If we replace a single-cylinder engine with a four-cylinder engine where the total capacity is the same as the single-cylinder engine, we will find that each of the four cylinders individually generates a maximum torque value that is much lower than a larger single cylinder, due to the lower combustion pressures acting upon each of the four cylinders' pistons. However, the mean torque value of the four cylinders is likely to be greater than that of the equivalent single-cylinder engine. Additionally, torque delivery will be smoother due to the engine producing more power strokes per crankshaft revolution. The same transmission system can be used to transmit this increased mean torque as for the high-maximum-torque single-cylinder engine.

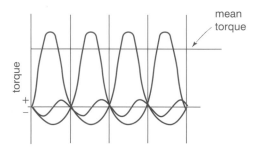

Figure 2.20 Torque fluctuations in a four-cylinder engine

Power output and the relation to engine speed

The volume of air inducted into an engine has a direct relationship on the power it can generate over a given period of time. Additionally, the capacity of the engine and the stroke of the crankshaft will have an influence on the power capabilities and the characteristics of the engine. Generally, the mass of the engine components along with the stroke of the engine will determine the maximum safe engine speed. For example, an engine with a short stroke and light engine parts will be able to operate at higher engine speeds and be able to accelerate and decelerate quickly, whereas an engine with a long stroke and heavier engine parts, such as a diesel engine, will react more slowly. This can be seen when comparing a large diesel engine with heavy internal components and a light aluminium petrol engine. Due to the forces created by the reciprocating parts of the engine, the lighter petrol engine will be able to have a higher engine speed than the large, heavy diesel engine.

For example, a single-cylinder engine with the same capacity as a four-cylinder engine will therefore have smaller parts, such as pistons and connecting rods,

and also a shorter stroke. The forces on these parts at a given engine speed will be considerably less on the four-cylinder engine than the single-cylinder engine as these parts have more mass. Multi-cylinder engines can safely run at higher speed, develop greater power and have longer life.

2.4.2 Number and arrangement of cylinders

Limitations on cylinder numbers

By increasing the number of cylinders it can be said that the engine will produce a smoother power and torque delivery due to the number of power strokes increasing per crankshaft revolution. However, this improvement to the power and torque delivery is gained with some sacrifices. Dealing with multi-cylinders is obviously more complicated than with a single-cylinder engine. The additional development requirements and the greater number of associated parts lead to an overall higher cost to produce a multi-cylinder engine. Additionally, today's engines require a highly complex EMS to be able to operate efficiently; this creates another development cost for the manufacturer. Multi-cylinder engines are essential for the running of a majority of the vehicles on the road; most light vehicles use engines with three, four, five, six or eight cylinders. Manufacturers are now moving towards smaller engines with three and four cylinders, as these produce lower emissions and have better fuel economy. Some of the more prestigious vehicles use larger engines, such as the Bugatti Veyron (Figure 2.21), a W16 engine based on the development of two eight-cylinder engines, but these are exceptional cases.

Figure 2.21 Bugatti Veyron W16 engine

Cylinder arrangements

There are four arrangements that may be used for multi-cylinders engines:

1 In-line – the cylinders are arranged in a single row, side-by-side and parallel to one another. They may be vertical, horizontal or inclined at any convenient angle.

2 Vee – the cylinders are arranged in two rows at an angle to one another. For two-, four- and eight-cylinder engines, the V-angle is usually 90°, and for six- and 12-cylinder engines it is usually 60° or occasionally 90° and 120°. There are, however, exceptions to this: for instance, most V4 engines use a V-angle of 60°. In each case, the crank pins are suitably offset in order to equalise the firing interval impulses.

3 Opposed – this could be regarded as a V-type engine in which the V-angle is 180°. The cylinders are usually placed horizontally.

4 W – this configuration is basically formed by creating very tight, almost overlapping banks of cylinders. If we take a W12 engine produced by Volkswagen, this has four banks of three-cylinder in-line arrangements. The engine could be termed a 'veevee' engine as it actually has two vee engines running within itself, but it has been termed the W engine. This arrangement creates very compact large-capacity engines.

Figure 2.22 W12 engine

Cylinder numbering

The cylinders of an engine are identified by numbers. When there is only one row of cylinders, they are usually numbered from one end to the other. However, in the case of other arrangements there is considerable variation in practice. A method put forward by the British Standards Institution (BS 1599:1949) may be summarised as follows:

The cylinders of in-line engines should be numbered 1, 2, 3, etc., commencing from the 'free' or non-driving end. In the case of vee or opposed engines, each group of cylinders should be numbered in the same manner, but groups of cylinders should be identified by letters

A, B, etc. The order of the lettering should be clockwise, looking at the 'free' or non-driving end of the engine, beginning at '9 o'clock' or the first after. This method is seldom used by motor-vehicle manufacturers: in V-type and opposed-type engines, the two groups of cylinders are sometimes identified as left (L) or right (R): sometimes one group of cylinders contains even numbers and the other odd; sometimes one group of cylinders is numbered consecutively, followed by the cylinders in the other group.

2.4.3 Firing order

The cylinders of a multi-cylinder engine are arranged to have their power strokes in succession, and the order in which the cylinders work is called the *firing order* of the engine. For smoothest running, the power strokes should be spaced at equal intervals, each interval being equal to the number of degrees per cycle of operations (720° for a four-stroke engine) divided by the number of cylinders. For a four-cylinder engine, the interval will be 720°/4 = 180° and for a six-cylinder: 720°/6 = 120°.

The firing order of an engine is determined by two things:

1 The arrangement of the cylinders and the cranks on the crankshaft. (This determines the possible firing orders.)

2 The arrangement of the cams on the camshaft. (This must be in accordance with one of the possible orders.)

Firing orders for some of the common types of engine are discussed in a little more detail on the following pages.

Four-cylinder in-line engines

Figure 2.23, in the form of a line diagram, shows the arrangement of cylinders and cranks in an engine of this type. Power strokes occur at intervals of 180° and the pistons move in pairs; 1 and 4 forming one pair and 2 and 3 the other. Suppose piston 1 is commencing its power stroke, then piston 4 will move down its cylinder on its induction stroke.

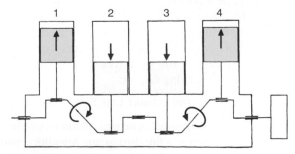

Figure 2.23 Arrangement of cylinders and crankshaft for a four-cylinder in-line engine

Piston 2 will move upwards on either its exhaust or compression stroke, and piston 3 will move up on either its compression or exhaust stroke. We can now make up a table showing the four strokes made by each piston during one cycle of operations.

From this table, we see that there are two possible firing orders for a four-cylinder engine. These are 1243 and 1342. Both are in common use.

In addition to taking the firing impulses, the crankshaft also has to resist the forces created when the pistons change their direction of movement. The arrows in Figure 2.23 indicate these inertia forces and the circular arrows show the effect on the crankshaft. By arranging the crank throws so that the two circular arrows oppose each other, it is possible to achieve reasonable balance of the engine as a whole.

The high speed and power produced by a modern engine makes the load on the crankshaft and centre bearing very high. Extra main bearings are provided between each crank throw to stiffen the construction. Figure 2.24 shows a typical crankshaft for a four-cylinder engine using five main bearings.

Figure 2.24 Crankshaft from a four-cylinder five-bearing engine

Six-cylinder in-line engines

Figure 2.25 is a line diagram of the cylinder and crank arrangement: (a) and (b) show alternative crankshaft arrangements as viewed from the front. In arrangement (a), commencing with pistons 1 and 6 at TDC, the next pair to come to TDC will be 3 and 4, followed by 2 and 5, and then 1 and 6 again. If piston 1 is commencing its power stroke, the next power stroke will occur in either of the cylinders 3 or 4, and the next in either of the cylinders 2 or 5. There are thus four possible firing orders:

132645, 135642, 145632 and 142635.

In the first three of these firing orders, all three cylinders in one half of the engine fire during one revolution and the three in the other half of the engine fire during the next revolution. In the fourth firing order, cylinders

in opposite halves of the engine fire alternately. This arrangement is generally preferable as it helps to obtain good 'distribution' of the air/fuel charge (see page 93). It is the only firing order in common use, though others have been used in rare cases.

If the cranks are arranged as shown in (ii), the pistons come to TDC in the order 1 and 6, 2 and 5, 3 and 4, followed by 1 and 6 again. In this case, the four possible firing orders are:

123654, 124653, 154623 and 153624.

Once again, it is only in the fourth firing order that cylinders in opposite halves of the engine fire alternately, and this is the one in common use.

Both alternative crank arrangements are used, and there are thus two alternative firing orders for a six-cylinder engine in common use – 142635 and 153624.

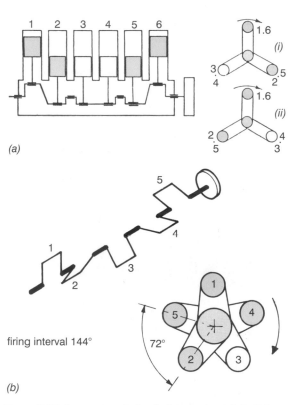

firing interval 144°

(b)

Figure 2.25 Arrangement of cylinders and crankshaft for a five- and six-cylinder in-line engine

Five-cylinder in-line engines

There are obvious manufacturing advantages of using similar-sized parts in the various engines offered by a vehicle producer. When this policy is adopted, there are occasions when a given vehicle requires an engine that has a power output and smoothness factor midway between that given by four- and six-cylinder units; this is achieved by using a five-cylinder layout. Similarly, there are cases when a six-cylinder in-line unit is too long and a V6 is too heavy.

Figure 2.25 (bottom) shows the throw layout of a five-cylinder crankshaft. The angle between the throws is 72°, the firing interval is 144° and a typical firing order is 12453.

Torsional oscillation

A six-cylinder crankshaft is long and slender. One end is attached to a flywheel, which rotates at a near-constant speed, whereas at the front end, the firing impulses cause the shaft to wind up and then unwind. If the shaft is made in the form shown in Figure 2.25, the rate at which the shaft would vibrate would be very high. As the firing impulses occur at a slower rate, no problem would arise from this vibration, but the shaft would whip due to the bending action caused by the centrifugal forces on each crank throw. Adding counterbalance masses (Figure 2.26) will reduce the whip, but these heavy masses will now cause the shaft to vibrate in a rotational direction (i.e. to speed up and slow down at a rate similar to that produced by the firing impulses).

Torsional oscillation: when a rotating mass generates a harmonic frequency through its mass, creating slight changes in rotational speed.

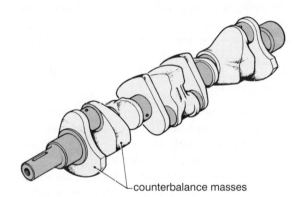

Figure 2.26 Six-cylinder crankshaft

At speeds where this occurs, the oscillation becomes severe and the irregular movement of the front end of the shaft can cause problems with valve timing gears, general vibration of the engine and, in severe cases, breakage of the shaft due to fatigue.

A torsional oscillation damper is fitted to prevent build-up of vibration at the speeds at which vibration is severe. The damper shown in Figure 2.27 consists of a small flywheel member bonded by rubber to a hub attached to the front end of the crankshaft.

At times when oscillation occurs, the constant speed of the flywheel member opposes the winding up and unwinding of the shaft. The extent of the vibration movement is reduced by means of the energy-absorbing rubber.

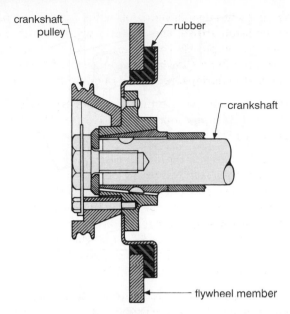

Figure 2.27 Torsional oscillation damper

Torsional oscillation dampers are not required on engines having short, stiff shafts, such as those used on four-cylinder engines.

V6 engines

Figure 2.28 (top) shows two banks of three cylinders set at an angle of 60° with a six-throw crankshaft also set at 60° between throws. Numbering of the cylinders is that used by a large manufacturer who produces V6 engines instead of the longer in-line units.

The firing interval is 120° and the banks are fired in the order: right, left, right, left, right, left. The 240° angle moved by the crank between adjacent cylinders in any one bank being fired gives good distribution. It will be seen that the cylinders in each bank fire in the order: front, centre, rear.

V8 engines

Figure 2.28 (bottom) shows the arrangement of cylinders in this type of engine: the cylinders are shown numbered in accordance with BS 1599. The earliest engines of this type used a crankshaft similar to that used in the four-cylinder in-line engine, as shown in (a). Later, the crank arrangement shown in (b) was adopted because it gives better balance. Power strokes occur at intervals of 90° in both cases, and the 'pairs' in which the pistons move are, for arrangement (a): 1A and 4R, 1B and 4B, 2A and 3A, 2B and 3B, giving eight possible firing orders. In the case of arrangement (b) the 'pairs' are: 1A and 2B, 1B and 3A, 3B and 4A, 4B and 2A, also giving eight possible firing orders. It could be an interesting exercise to work out these 16 possible firing orders for yourself.

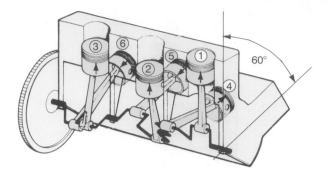

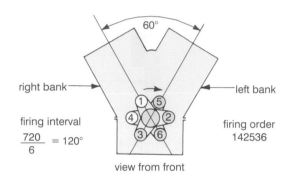

Figure 2.29 V10 engine used in a Dodge Viper

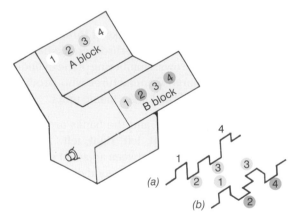

Figure 2.28 Cylinder and crank arrangements for V6 and V8 engines

V12 and V10 engines

The use of engines with more than eight cylinders is now fairly common, especially in larger more luxurious and high-performance vehicles. These engines tend to have capacities of 4 litres upwards. BMW use a V10 engine fitted to their M Power 5 Series car, this engine is highly complex and is based on the V10 engine used in Formula 1 cars.

Determination of firing order

It is necessary to know the firing order of an engine in order to be able to connect up the spark-plug leads correctly. There are several methods of discovering the firing order. It is sometimes marked on the engine, or on a plate on or near the engine. Failing this, the firing engine is invariably given in the workshop manual. If the engine is not marked and the workshop manual is not available, the following method can be used:

1 Remove the valve gear covers and note which the inlet valves are and which the exhaust is.
2 Rotate the engine in the direction in which it runs and watch the order in which one set of valves, inlet or exhaust, operate. This will give the order in which the inlet strokes or exhaust strokes occur, and the power strokes occur in the same order.

An alternative method is for the technician to use a cylinder pressure gauge inserted into the spark-plug holes and rotate the engine until the pressure rise is noted showing the compression stroke. In the absence of this equipment, the technician could position their thumbs and fingers over the plugholes (or fit corks in the plugholes suitably secured to each other), rotate the engine and note the order of 'compressions'. This should be done by rotating the engine by hand and not by the key and starter motor.

2.4.4 Engine balance

Severe vibration occurs if the engine is in a poor state of balance. This vibration can be caused by design factors or may result from poor maintenance of the engine. If vibration is to be minimised, attention must be given to the following:

- Primary balance
- Component balance
- Firing interval
- Secondary balance

Primary balance

When a piston passes through TDC and BDC, the change of direction produces an inertia force that attempts to keep the piston moving in the direction in which it was travelling before the change. This force, called the primary force, increases as the engine speed is raised. Unless counteracted, it will produce a severe oscillation in the vertical plane (i.e. in line with the cylinder axis).

Single cylinder

Figure 2.30 shows the primary inertia forces produced in a single-cylinder engine; the graph indicates the direction and magnitude of the force for one revolution of the crankshaft, taking the upward direction as positive. This shows that at TDC, the deceleration of the reciprocating masses (piston assembly and one-third of the connecting rod) generates an upward force on the engine.

At BDC a similar force is produced, but in this position the direction of the force is downwards. Consideration of the effect of these two forces will show that when the engine is running it will oscillate up and down at a frequency equal to the engine speed.

This vibration can be reduced by adding at A and B counterbalance masses that exert an outward force as the crank is rotated. By varying the size of the two masses, the outward force can be made to equalise the inertia forces F_1 and F_2. However, in positions other than the dead centres, the counterbalance masses would themselves produce an out-of-balance force. This would be unsatisfactory because it would only shift the plane of vibration from the vertical to the horizontal. Because of this, the counterbalance mass used on a single-cylinder engine is set to balance only half the reciprocating mass. As a result, vibration in the vertical and horizontal planes is expected; this means that all nuts and bolts used on vehicles propelled by single-cylinder engines should be securely locked.

Four cylinder

Figure 2.31 shows the crank throw layout on a four-cylinder in-line engine and the direction of the primary forces. Primary balance is achieved because the forces on the two pistons at TDC equal the forces on the pistons at BDC.

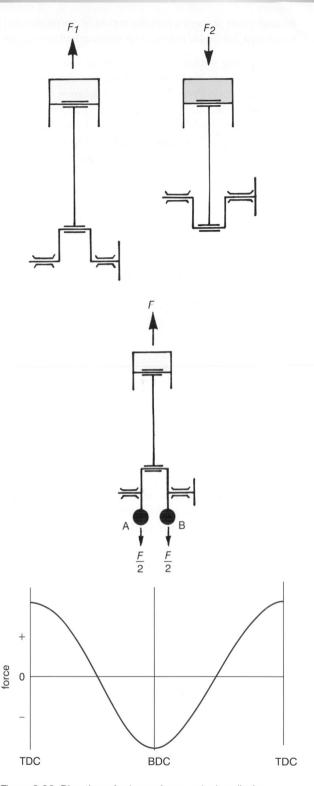

Figure 2.30 Direction of primary force – single cylinder

Figure 2.31 shows that the crankshaft throws are arranged so that forces acting on pistons 1 and 2 produce the opposite turning moment (called a couple) on the shaft axis to that given by the forces on pistons 3 and 4. The opposing couples introduced by this crank arrangement prevent a rocking action of the engine and, as a result, minimise fore-and-aft vibration of the engine.

The bending action on the shaft produced by the couples, and the high load on the centre main bearing, can be reduced by adding counterbalance masses to the crankshaft. Also, by using five main bearings to support the shaft (instead of the three commonly used in the past) a stiffer construction is achieved, which is essential on modern engines because of the high operating speeds.

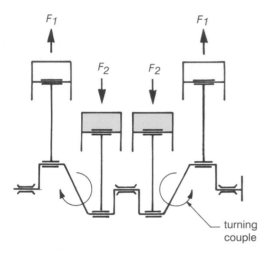

Figure 2.31 *Primary forces – four cylinders*

Three cylinder

Study of a three-cylinder in-line unit is useful because not only is it used as a 'straight' in-line engine, it also forms the basic unit for both the in-line six and V6 engines.

Figure 2.32 shows the crank layout and the primary forces when piston 1 is at TDC. Since the crank throws are set at 120°, the large force at each of the dead centres is balanced by the two smaller forces on the other two pistons. These smaller forces are the result of piston acceleration or deceleration as it approaches or leaves the end of the stroke.

Component balance

To minimise vibration, all components that have to rotate at high speed must be balanced. This is particularly important with large heavy components, such as a flywheel and clutch assembly. Although these two parts are balanced separately to within given limits, the mating of each part so that they 'run true' with the crankshaft axis is very important. This is achieved by using various location devices, such as **spigots**, **registers and dowels**.

Spigots, registers and dowels: devices used to ensure that two mating components are located centrally to avoid out-of-balance vibration occurring.

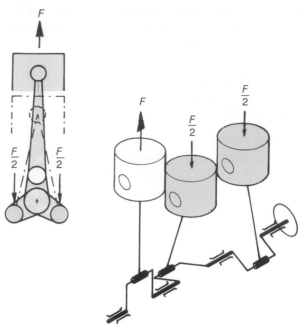

Figure 2.32 *Primary forces – three cylinders*

Ideally, the balancing of the crankshaft and flywheel assembly as one unit is desirable since it overcomes the **build-up of tolerances**. (Vibration due to this occurs when 'heavy spots' of each part are positioned so that they all act in the same direction.) Cost, both at the manufacture and repair stages, generally rules out the use of this one-piece balancing method on mass-produced vehicles.

Build-up of tolerances: a gradual build-up of the excess tolerances involved across the engine components. Individually, each tolerance is minimal, but when adding all of these together this can create an overall large tolerance causing an issue with vibration.

Reciprocating masses should also be balanced to achieve good primary balance. All parts that move in this manner should be selected so that they are all nearly equal in weight.

Balance of components generally covers two conditions: static balance and dynamic balance. The former can be carried out by placing the shaft and/or component on two horizontal 'knife-edges'; when released, the heaviest part moves to the bottom. Dynamic balance requires expensive apparatus, which rotates the part at high speed and indicates the extent and location of the heavy spots.

Imbalance is normally corrected by removing metal by drilling one or more holes in the component at the heavy point.

Firing interval

The angle turned by the crankshaft between power strokes of a multi-cylinder engine should be regular if maximum smoothness is to be achieved. Also, the more cylinders that are fired during the 720° period of the four-stroke cycle the lower the variation in the output torque, and the smoother the flow of power to the road wheels.

Secondary balance

The inertia forces considered during the study of primary balance are based on a piston movement, which is called simple harmonic motion (SHM). This type of reciprocating movement is shown in Figure 2.33a. Consider point P to be travelling at a constant speed around a circle of diameter AB, and another point N moving in a straight path from A to B.

Point N is said to move in SHM if it always keeps at the foot of the perpendicular NP.

Point N varies its velocity as it travels across AB and this is shown by the graph (Figure 2.33b).

Comparing the movement of an engine piston with SHM shows that during the first 90° rotation of the crank from TDC, the piston covers a greater distance; whereas within the range 90–180° a smaller distance is covered in the given time (Figure 2.33c). This produces the following effects:

1 The piston travels more than half the stroke when the crank is rotated from TDC to the 90° position.
2 Starting at TDC, the relative piston velocity for each 90° of crank movement is: fast, slow, slow, fast.
3 The piston *dwell* (the angular period where piston movement is small in relation to crankshaft motion) at BDC is far greater than at TDC.
4 The inertia force at TDC is far greater than at BDC.

This last point shows the reason why an engine designer needs to make a deeper study of engine balance if vibration is to be reduced. This study involves the analysis of secondary balance, which takes into account the difference between actual piston movement and the ideal SHM.

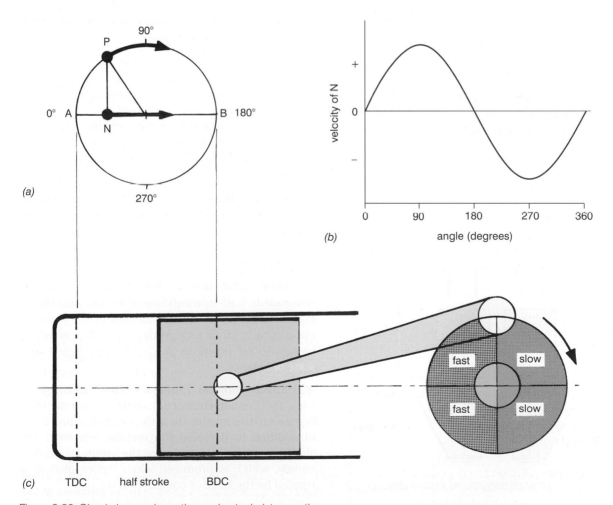

Figure 2.33 Simple harmonic motion and actual piston motion

Figure 2.34 shows the primary force produced by SHM, and the secondary force that must be added or subtracted to correspond to the actual motion. It will be seen that the frequency of the secondary force is twice the speed of the crank. By applying the information given by this graph, the direction of the secondary force can be determined; this has been added to the diagram of the engine shown in Figure 2.35. The result shows that a four-cylinder in-line engine has very good primary balance but has poor secondary balance.

The effect of this imbalance is to produce a vibration in the vertical plane at a frequency twice the speed of the crank. In the past, this vibration has been tolerated and, by using soft rubber engine mountings, the engine vibration is prevented from being transmitted to the remainder of the vehicle.

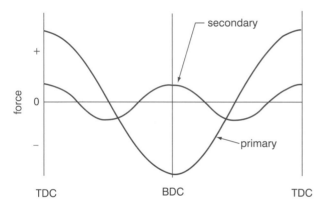

Figure 2.34 Graph of secondary force

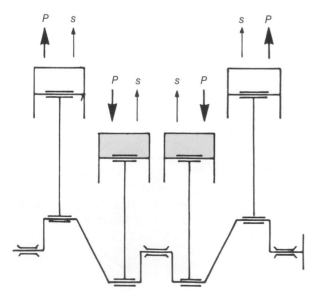

Figure 2.35 Direction of primary and secondary forces

In the three and six-cylinder in-line units and V6 the secondary forces balance out, so this is one reason why the six-cylinder in-line engine was used extensively in the past. Nowadays, the preference is for four-cylinder in-line units for engines up to about 2-litre capacity. This type has a high potential in respect of economy resulting from lower frictional losses. When it is combined with the use of a simpler EMS, a higher power/weight ratio can be obtained. In addition, the short, stubby crankshaft used on a four-cylinder unit does not suffer the severe torsional oscillation problems associated with longer shafts (see page 47).

Secondary harmonic balancer

An effective way of eliminating secondary forces is to use a secondary harmonic balancer. This was first used in 1911 by Frederick Lanchester to balance four-cylinder engines. Although this device was very effective, for many years soft rubber mountings have been used instead of a damper for cost reasons. In 1975, Mitsubishi of Japan produced a secondary balancer; in many ways this is similar in principle to the Lanchester type. This is now being made, under licence, by a number of companies and engines using this arrangement are much smoother in operation.

Figure 2.36 shows the principle of a secondary balancer. Two counterbalance shafts having offset masses are driven by the crankshaft at twice crankshaft speed. One counterbalance shaft is rotated clockwise and the other anticlockwise. Both shafts are 'timed' to the crankshaft so that when the piston is at TDC, both masses are set to exert a downward force.

To counteract the secondary force on the engine, the balancer must exert an opposing force only at the time when the force is needed. For four-cylinder in-line engines this is at a maximum when the crank is at 0°, 90°, 180° and 270°.

In Figure 2.36a and c, this balancing force is downwards and upwards respectively, whereas in Figure 2.36b and d, the two masses of the balancer oppose each other and produce a neutral effect; in these neutral positions the engine is already in a state of balance.

Mitsubishi Motors' Silent Shafts arrangement uses twin counterbalancing shafts with one shaft higher up the engine than the other (Figure 2.37). In addition to damping the vertical vibration, this shaft arrangement also damps the secondary rolling couple, which is produced when the crankshaft is rotated by the force of combustion.

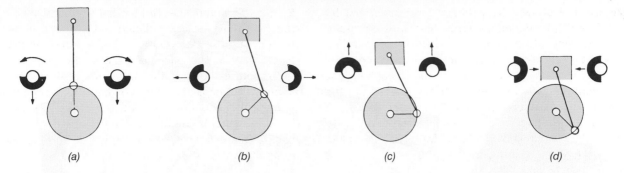

Figure 2.36 Principles of secondary balancer

The upper shaft turns in the same direction as the crankshaft and the vertical spacing of the shafts is 0.7 times the length of the connecting rod. Arranged in this way, the counterbalance masses set up a couple that opposes the rolling couple. Balance of the rolling couple cannot be achieved throughout the complete engine load range, so a shaft position is selected that will minimise the unbalanced couple during the most frequently encountered road load conditions. With this arrangement, the rolling couple of a balanced four-cylinder engine is better than that of a six-cylinder unit.

The Porsche 944 engine (Figure 2.38) uses a double-sided toothed belt to drive the counterbalance shafts. It is claimed that the balancer system on this engine reduces the noise level by 20 dB. Minimising the secondary vibration, especially at high engine speed, gives a reduction of the 'boom', which is felt and heard in the passenger compartment. In addition, a decrease in secondary vibration lengthens the life of engine auxiliaries, such as emission control equipment, electrical and fuel supply components and management systems that incorporate electronic devices.

The Land Rover Freelander i6 engine uses another type of balancer to eliminate the torsional vibration and crankshaft oscillation created through the rotational motion of the crankshaft at speeds. As the crankshaft speed increases and decreases through the action of going through the four-stroke cycle, the internal viscous damper (IVD) fitted to the opposite end of the crankshaft removes the vibration created, providing a smooth running six-cylinder in-line engine.

The IVD is constructed from a steel ring placed and enclosed within a housing filled with viscous fluid. (See page 128 for more information on viscous fluid fans.) The steel ring is radially journaled through a plastic bearing (Figure 2.39). As the crankshaft speed increases and decreases through its operation, the speed of the steel ring within the IVD

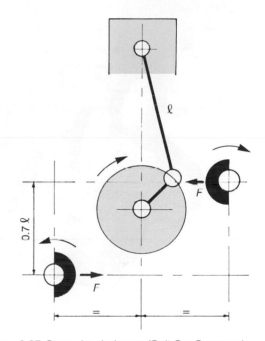

Figure 2.37 Secondary balancer (Colt Car Company)

is delayed in its rotational movement due to the viscous fluid. This delay counteracts the vibration created and therefore removes the unwanted vibration.

The function of the IVD is based on the braking effect of the silicone fluid and the steel ring's own inertia.

As the IVD operates, it creates a large amount of heat due to the friction created by the steel ring rotating in the viscous fluid. To ensure that the unit does not overheat, the unit has its own oil cooling delivered by three oil injectors. This keeps the temperature to about 140 °C.

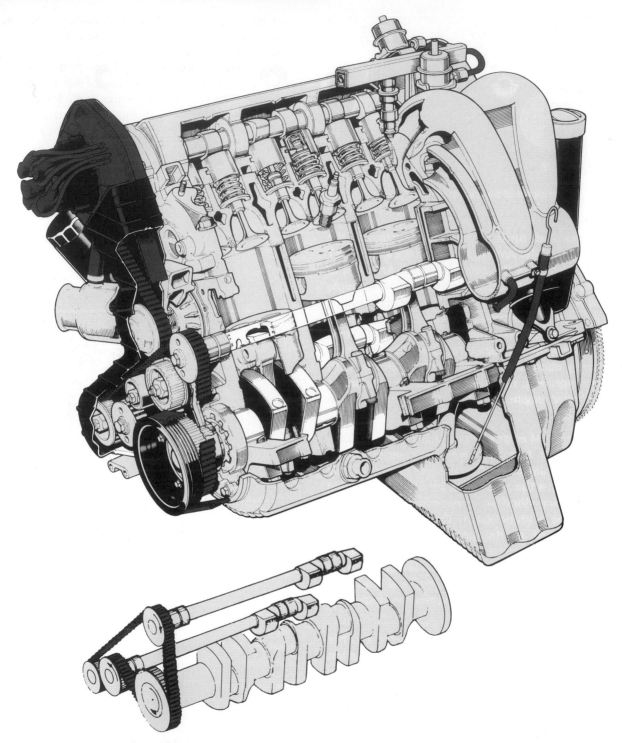

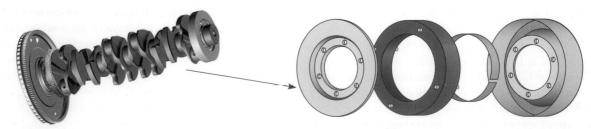

Figure 2.38 Secondary balancer fitted to Porsche engine

Figure 2.39 IVD and components

2.5 Crankshafts

2.5.1 Main features

The crankshaft is the part of a reciprocating engine that converts the power created from the power strokes of the pistons in the cylinders (linear power delivery) into rotational movement and passes it on to the transmission system, drive train and road wheels. The crankshaft of an engine is formed of a number of 'sections' (Figure 2.40). The main **journals** rotate in the main bearings and the crank pin, or crank journal, to which the connecting rod is fitted, is offset from the main journals by a distance called the crank radius. The webs connect the main journals to the crank pin, and where the journals join the webs a fillet or radius is formed to avoid a sharp corner, which would be a source of weakness. This is of vital importance in crankshafts that are subjected to particularly heavy loads.

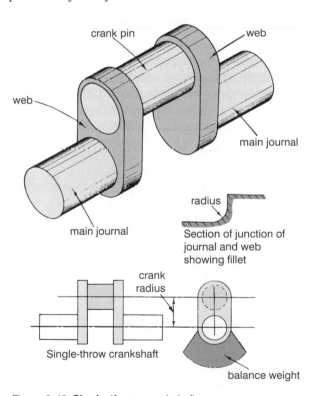

Figure 2.40 **Single-throw** crankshaft

Journal: the part of a shaft that rotates in a bearing.

Single-throw: where the piston or pistons are moved up and down the cylinder bore at the same time through TDC to BDC.

Balance masses

In some cases, the webs are extended to form balance masses, which are used in certain types of engine to ensure that the rotating parts are balanced as effectively as possible and will cause little or no vibration when the engine is running. It is not possible to completely balance the rotating parts of all engine types – this being one of the objections to the use of a single-cylinder engine, which is impossible to balance perfectly, though it can be made satisfactory for certain purposes. Figure 2.41 shows a crankshaft fitted to a multi-cylinder engine with extended webs to counteract the weight and create equal balance.

Figure 2.41 Crankshaft fitted to a multi-cylinder engine

In some engines in which the rotating parts are perfectly balanced, masses similar to balance masses may still be used: **centrifugal force** acting on the crank pins causes heavy loading of the adjacent main bearings at high speeds, and by extending the webs to form balance masses a counter-centrifugal force is applied in opposition to that on the crank pin, thus reducing the bearing loading. Masses used in this way are more properly known as counterbalance masses.

Centrifugal force: the tendency of an object to be thrown away from the centre as it travels along a curved path. Objects subjected to centrifugal force generally want to continue to move in a straight line from the central point of rotation.

Throw

There is sometimes some confusion as to the meaning of this term. It is often used as an alternative to crank radius, but early books on steam engines define the throw as the diameter of the crank pin circle (i.e. the throw is equal to the stroke of the piston). It might, therefore, be better to avoid the use of the term 'throw' in this sense and clarify what is intended by using the terms 'crank radius' or 'crank circle diameter' as appropriate.

The same word 'throw' is also used in a slightly different sense as the name given to a crank pin together with its adjacent webs and main journals. Thus, Figure 2.40 illustrates a single-throw crankshaft.

Crank pins do not always have a main journal on both sides. Figure 2.42 illustrates a two-throw crankshaft having only two main journals, the crank pins being connected together by a flying web.

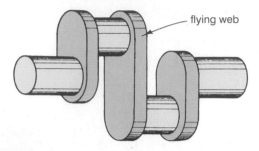

Figure 2.42 A two-throw crankshaft

Flywheel attachment

The flywheel is usually attached to the rear end of the crankshaft. The attachment must be perfectly secure and it should only be possible to assemble the flywheel in one position, partly because the flywheel is often marked to indicate the position of the number 1 crank pin, but more particularly because the crankshaft and flywheel, besides being balanced separately, are also balanced as an assembly. If the flywheel is not fitted in the same position as that in which the assembly was balanced, some imperfection of balance may arise that may cause vibration. (It is possible that the crankshaft itself may be balanced within the limits permitted, but not perfectly; the flywheel may also have a small but 'tolerable' imbalance. Should the crankshaft and flywheel be assembled so that the imbalance of the crankshaft and of the flywheel are 'additive', the resulting vibration might be eliminated by turning the flywheel through 180° on the crankshaft, and this latter position would be the 'correct' one.)

Figure 2.43 shows a more common method. A flange is formed on the end of the crankshaft, which is a close fit into a counter-bored hole in the centre of the flywheel. The flywheel is then secured by a number of screws, which pass through holes drilled axially through the flywheel face and screwed into threaded holes in the crankshaft flange. One or more dowels are fitted to relieve the screws of sharing loads, and the dowels, or screws, are often unevenly spaced to permit assembly in one position only. Bolts are sometimes used instead of screws; a suitable locking arrangement is provided for the nuts or screws.

Figure 2.43 Crankshaft – four-cylinder, five-bearing and flywheel mounting

2.5.2 Oilways

Engine-lubrication systems are discussed in detail on page 109, however, it is necessary to mention here the method by which oil is supplied to the crank pins. Oil is delivered under pressure to the main bearings, where it is fed into a groove running around the bearing at about the middle of its length. A hole is drilled through the crankshaft (Figure 2.44) running from the main journal, through the web to the surface of the crank pin. The main journal end of the hole moves around the groove in the main bearing as the shaft rotates, allowing a continuous supply of oil to pass to the crank pin.

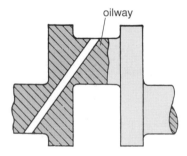

Figure 2.44 Oilway drilled through the crankshaft

Some large crankshafts have their crank pins and journal bored out to reduce the weight and, therefore, the reciprocating forces. The ends of these hollow pins and journals are usually closed by caps or plugs held in place by bolts (Figure 2.45) to prevent the escape of oil.

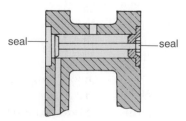

Figure 2.45 Method of sealing hollow journals

Oil retainers

The crankshaft projects from the rear end of the crankcase. Therefore, some of the oil that is pumped into the rear bearing to lubricate it will escape from the rear end of the bearing to the outside of the crankcase and be wasted. In addition, this will make a mess of the engine and possibly get into the clutch where it would be very undesirable.

Figure 2.46 shows two methods of preventing this escape of oil. Immediately behind the rear journal a thin ring or fin of metal is formed around the circumference of the shaft. Oil reaching this ring from the rear bearing is flung off by centrifugal force as the shaft rotates. This oil is then caught in a cavity from which a drain hole leads the oil back inside the crankcase.

Behind this flinger ring is a square-section helical groove or scroll, rather like a coarse screw thread, machined in the surface of the shaft. The outer surface of the shaft has a small clearance inside an extension of the rear bearing housing, and any oil that reaches this part of the shaft will tend to be dragged round with the shaft but at the same time be held back by the stationary housing: as a result, the oil will be drawn along the groove, the hand of which is such as to return it to the inside of the crankcase. In most cases, both the methods illustrated and described are used on the crankshaft: sometimes only one may be considered sufficient.

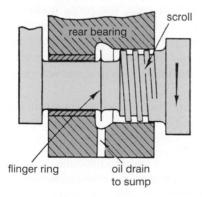

Figure 2.46 Scroll-type oil retainer

Figure 2.47 shows a section of a lip-type seal. Seals of this type have been used for many years in axles and gearboxes and are finding increasing use at both ends of the crankshaft. The seal consists of a specially shaped synthetic rubber ring supported by a steel shell and fitted into a recess in the crankcase or timing case. The ring has a shaped lip, which is held in light contact with the shaft by a garter spring. This type of seal usually replaces both the scroll and the flinger ring.

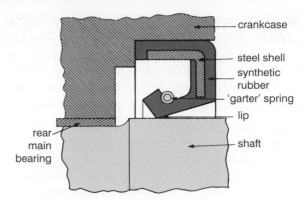

Figure 2.47 Section of lip-type seal

2.5.3 Clutch shaft spigot bearing

The power developed by the engine is transmitted through the clutch to the gearbox, and the shaft on which the driven part of the clutch is fitted is usually supported at its forward end in a bearing in the rear end of the crankshaft. This bearing, called a spigot bearing, usually consists simply of a bronze bush pressed into an axial hole in the rear end of the crankshaft (Figure 2.48), but sometimes a ball or roller bearing may be used.

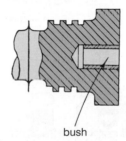

Figure 2.48 Clutch shaft spigot bearing

2.5.4 Front end or nose of the crankshaft

In most engines, the front of the crankshaft is used to drive the valve operating gear, along with auxiliary drive belts for components including air conditioning, alternators and power-steering pumps. The mechanism that operates the valves is usually driven by gears, chains or belts and the drive is usually taken from the front end of the shaft, although in a few cases it is taken from the flywheel end. The front end of the shaft is extended beyond the front main journal, the extension being parallel or sometimes stepped (i.e. the forward part is of slightly smaller diameter than the rearward part). On to this extension is pressed the timing gear, which drives the valve mechanism, and the pulley, which drives the auxiliary components: both are usually located on the shaft by **Woodruff keys** or are a **taper seat** arrangement. They are secured by a nut or screw threaded into the end of the shaft, which is tightened to a specific torque.

Woodruff key: a mechanical securing device to prevent a component rotating on a shaft. The key is a half-moon-shaped metal device that fits into a slot on the shaft. As it protrudes slightly, this forms a location for the slotted keyway of the fitted component and provides a means to locate and prevent rotation.

Taper seat: term used to describe the location of one component on to another through the use of a conical seating arrangement. The taper seat arrangement provides excellent centralising of two components and can also provide good sealing properties.

The timing gear is enclosed inside a cover called the timing case, but the pulley is outside this case. Oil-retaining arrangements, similar to those at the rear, are provided at this point, though the oil flinger is usually a separate part gripped between the timing gear and pulley bosses, and the scroll is formed on a rearward extension of the pulley boss.

Figure 2.49 shows a lip-type oil seal retained in the timing cover. The lip should be smeared with oil before fitting the pulley on to the crankshaft.

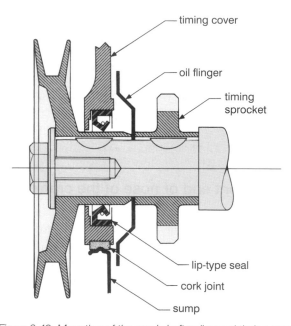

Figure 2.49 Mounting of the crankshaft pulley and timing gear

Some new engines fit the auxiliary drive at the gearbox end of the crankshaft to improve on the space required at the front of the engine. This arrangement takes its drive from the crankshaft via gears up to a power take-off where the accessories are driven at the relevant speeds. This system is called rear-end accessory drive (READ). Figure 2.50 shows an engine fitted with READ and illustrates the gear driven power take-off.

Figure 2.50 Rear-end accessory drive

2.5.5 Crankshaft materials

Crankshafts are made of high-quality steel or iron. These materials are processed by either **forging** or **casting**. Forging gives greater strength, but stiffness is of more importance than mere strength. Most modern shafts have large journals and a relatively short throw that allows the crank pins to overlap the journals when viewed from the end of the shaft. This feature allows the shaft to be cast; this gives a lighter shaft, which is cheaper to manufacture because it requires less machining. In addition, modern nodular irons are exceptionally strong and when ground to a fine finish and surface-hardened provide an excellent bearing surface. In this case, the term 'nodular' applies to the inclusion of minute rounded lumps of graphite (i.e. carbon); these particles are not combined with the base material so their existence in a free state classifies the material as iron and not steel.

Forging: the production of metal shapes through beating or compression of the heated metal using pre-formed shaped presses.

Casting: process used to produce metal components from liquid metal by pouring the heated liquid metal into a mould.

Following the initial forming, the shaft is ground to give a very smooth and accurately dimensioned surface of the journals and crank pins. Often the webs are not machined but, in the case of a high-performance engine, the shaft would be machined all over to reduce oil drag.

Unless special precautions are taken, the repeated load applied to the shaft and the continual torsional flexing of the shaft, especially in the region of the rear journal fillet, causes the shaft to fracture. This fatigue can be minimised by fillet rolling (Figure 2.51).

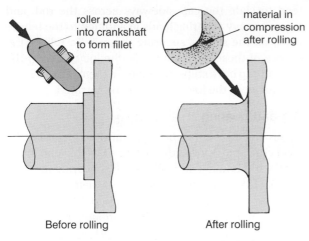

Before rolling   After rolling

Figure 2.51 Fillet rolling

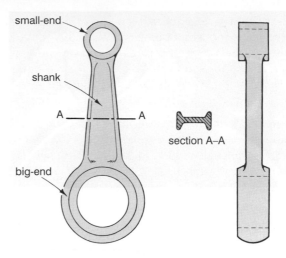

Figure 2.52 A simple connecting rod

For long life, there must be a large difference in hardness between the shaft and the bearing. Many modern engines use a comparatively hard bearing, so the journals and crank pins must be hardened. This is achieved by either **nitriding** or **induction hardening**. The former process involves heating the complete shaft to a temperature of about 500 °C in an atmosphere of ammonia gas for several hours. During this period, the steel absorbs nitrogen from the ammonia and forms a hard surface of iron nitride. The induction hardening method uses an electrical process.

Nitriding: heating steel together with ammonia or other nitrogenous material to increase the metal's hardness and resistance to corrosion.

Induction hardening: a process to harden the surface of steel where the surface is heated by exposure to an electromagnetic field and then quenched (cooled rapidly – usually by a water spray).

2.6   Connecting rods

2.6.1 General design

The connecting rod is a component that connects the piston to the crankshaft. It transfers the energy created in the cylinders through combustion from the piston to the crankshaft and allows rotational movement of the crankshaft between the connecting rod, crankshaft and piston.

Figure 2.52 shows a simple connecting rod. Owing to limitations of space inside the piston, the end that fits on the gudgeon pin is smaller than that which fits on the crankshaft, and these ends are called the small-end and big-end respectively.

The load due to gas pressure on the piston has a buckling effect on the shank of the rod. In the direction of the crankshaft axis, this tendency to buckle is resisted by the support provided by the gudgeon pin and the crankshaft, but no such support is provided to counteract buckling sideways. The shank of the rod is therefore generally made in an H section, which gives the greatest possible resistance to sideways buckling without excessive weight.

2.6.2 The big-end

The connecting rod shown in Figure 2.52 has a one-piece or solid-eye big-end. This can only be used if the crankshaft is of built-up construction (i.e. if the shaft is made in sections assembled and suitably fixed together, allowing the big-end to be slipped over the end of the crank pin before the shaft is assembled). While this practice was once common in single-cylinder motorcycle engines and has even been used in a few multi-cylinder car engines, it is much heavier and more expensive than the usual one-piece crankshaft construction described on page 57, and is seldom or never used in modern vehicle engines.

It is, therefore, necessary to split the big-end across the centre of the crank pin and bolt the two halves together after assembly on to the crank pin. The detachable portion is called the big-end cap. The bolts used are of high-tensile steel: their heads are specially formed to prevent them rotating while the nuts are being tightened, and the nuts are usually locked by split pins, tab-washers, or some other arrangement.

Wherever possible, the split is made at right angles to the length of the connecting rod (Figure 2.53), as this gives the best combination of tightness and strength. The piston and connecting rod are usually assembled together and the assembly then placed in position in the engine, either by passing the connecting rod through

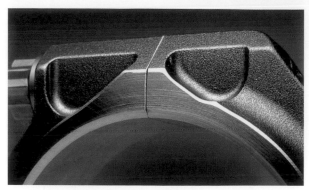

Figure 2.53 Split big-end

the cylinder from the top end, or entering the piston into the cylinder from the lower end. The removal of the piston and connecting rod assembly is made in the reverse way. If the crankshaft is in position, it is often impossible to get the piston past the crankshaft, especially if the shaft has balance weights. Though it would be quite practicable for the engine manufacturer to insert the pistons and connecting rods before fitting the crankshaft into its bearings, it is often necessary during repair work to remove one or more pistons. If the crankshaft also had to be removed just for this, a great deal of extra work would be needed.

On many modern high-speed engines, the size of the crank pins required to give the crankshaft the necessary stiffness makes the big-end so large that it is impossible for the connecting rod to be assembled or withdrawn through the cylinder if the big-end is split at right angles to its length. In such cases, the difficulty is overcome by splitting the connecting rod at an oblique angle and fixing the two parts together with screws (Figure 2.54).

At high engine speeds, large inertia forces act on the piston and impose loads on the connecting rod. This causes tensile stress around TDC and compressive stress around BDC. When the big-end is split perpendicularly, the inertia forces around TDC impose high tensile loads on the big-end bolts. On the other hand, when the rod is split obliquely, the forces also

tend to slide the cap sideways across the rod, and impose heavy shearing loads in addition to the tensile loads on the screws securing the cap. To relieve the screws of these shearing loads, the joint faces of the rod and cap have steps machined in them (Figure 2.54). Alternatively, the joint faces may be serrated.

Big-end bearing

To provide a suitable bearing surface to run on the steel crank pin, the inside surface of the big-end eye is lined with a thin coating of a special bearing metal. A popular alloy used for vehicle crankshaft and big-end bearings is 20 per cent tin-aluminium. This material, formed in a thin-wall bearing, combines high-fatigue strength with good surface properties and can be used without an overlay. When bonded together, the tin and aluminium form a network structure, so this material is sometimes called reticular tin-aluminium.

Where higher loadings prevail, either 6 per cent tin-aluminium or aluminium-silicon alloys may be used. The former has a high-fatigue strength and the latter a very high strength, but both materials require an overlay to improve compatibility and conformability. Bearings are described in more detail in Chapter 6.

2.6.3 The small-end

The construction of the small-end of the connecting rod varies according to the method of securing the gudgeon pin, which may either be fixed in the small-end or free to move. In the latter case, a solid-eye small-end is used, and this is generally lined by a bronze bush which is pressed in. One or more oil holes are drilled from the top of the rod to allow oil to reach the bearing surface: in some cases, a hole is drilled, through a thickening of the web of the shank, to carry oil from the big-end to the small-end under pressure from the big-end. A bushed solid-eye small-end is shown in Figure 2.55.

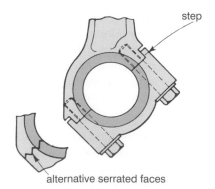

Figure 2.54 Big-end split obliquely

Figure 2.55 Connecting rod small-end for fully floating gudgeon pin

If the gudgeon pin is fixed in the small-end, it is usually done in one of the two ways illustrated in Figure 2.56 – (a) being the more common. The screw is arranged so that a small groove must be made in the surface of the gudgeon pin to allow the screw to be fitted; this provides positive endwise location of the pin independently of the clamping action of the screw, besides ensuring correct assembly. The screw is locked after tightening by some method such as the tab-washer illustrated in Figure 2.56.

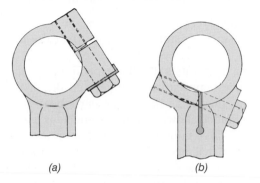

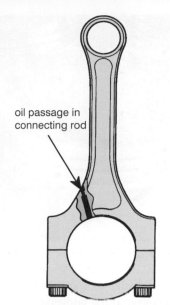

oil passage in connecting rod

Figure 2.57 Additional oil drilling in connecting rod for lubrication of the cylinder bores

(a)   (b)

Figure 2.56 Method of clamping gudgeon pin in the small-end

In many engines, a third method of securing the semi-floating gudgeon pin is adopted. This consists of making the pin interference fit in the un-bushed solid-eye of the connecting rod small-end. Assembly is usually carried out by heating the small-end of the rod causing it to expand and allowing the gudgeon pin to be fitted easily. On cooling, the rod contracts and grips the gudgeon pin securely. Special techniques are necessary for removing the pin.

2.6.4 Big- and small-end bearing lubrication

The lubrication of these components is extremely important, as lack of good lubrication will lead to very rapid deterioration and failure. Lubrication is achieved by oil passing through very accurate drillings through the crankshaft to the main bearing journals, then on to the big-end journals. From here, the oil flows through the big-end bearing and then through a drilling to the small-end bearing. Sometimes an additional drilling is placed part way up the connecting rod to supply a jet of oil to the cylinder bores as the crankshaft rotates to add additional lubrication for the pistons (Figure 2.57).

Note: when adding new crankshaft bearings, it is vitally important to make sure that the drillings in the connecting rod and crankshaft journals align with the bearings. Misalignment will cause immediate failure of engine components.

2.6.5 Connecting rod materials

Connecting rods are nearly always made from steel forgings, accurately machined where necessary. In high-performance engines, they are often machined all over to reduce weight to the minimum, and polished to remove surface scratches, which might lead to fatigue failure.

In a many cases, especially in more exotic engines, the connecting rods are an aluminium alloy. The main advantage of this is reduced weight, but a further advantage of aluminium is that it is a good material for bearings and aluminium rods can be used without any bush in the small-end.

2.7   Pistons, piston rings and gudgeon pins

2.7.1 The piston: main features

The purpose of the piston fitted to the reciprocating engine is to effectively provide a gas-tight seal inside the cylinder bore and allow the moving piston to be able to travel up and down the cylinder bore with minimal friction. The piston and the seal it creates within the cylinder allows the transfer of high pressure created during the combustion process to be transferred to the connecting rods and then on to the crankshaft.

Figure 2.58 shows the main features of a piston. The crown forms the upper surface on which the gas pressure acts, and the force due to this pressure is equal to the cross-sectional area of the cylinder multiplied by the gas pressure. This force, which acts along the

Figure 2.58 A piston assembly

centreline of the cylinder, is transmitted through the structure of the piston to the gudgeon pin bosses and then through the gudgeon pin to the connecting rod.

During the greater part of the stroke, the connecting rod operates at an angle to the centreline of the cylinder. This causes a side force to be applied by the piston to the cylinder wall (Figure 2.59), and it is necessary to provide bearing surfaces on the piston to carry this side force: these bearing surfaces are formed on the skirt.

To allow the piston to move freely in the cylinder it must have some clearance. In turn, this allows gas to leak from the combustion chamber past the piston. Since the greatest leakage occurs when pressures are highest and the gas is hottest, much of the oil film lubricating the piston will be burnt away or carbonised. After combustion the gases contain water vapour, carbon dioxide and, probably, small amounts of sulphur dioxide, which may contaminate the lubricating oil and lead to corrosion of the engine parts. To reduce the leakage as much as possible, piston rings are fitted into grooves formed on the piston just below the crown.

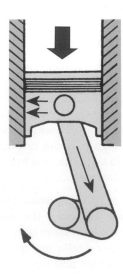

Figure 2.59 Side thrust of the piston caused by the angle of the connecting rod

The crown of the piston is directly exposed to the full heat of the burning gases during combustion. These gases are still extremely hot during the power and exhaust strokes: the piston absorbs a great deal of heat from these hot gases and will reach a very high temperature unless heat is removed from the piston quickly enough to keep its temperature within reasonable limits. The piston can pass this heat on to the cylinder walls through the piston rings and skirt, and it can do this better if the piston is made out of a type of metal that is a good conductor of heat.

Most metals expand with a rise in temperature, and since the piston gets hotter than the cylinder (which can be cooled more effectively), under running conditions it will expand more and the clearance between the cylinder and the piston will become smaller as the engine parts heat up. Thus, the clearance allowed when the engine is assembled must be large enough to allow for the decrease in clearance that occurs at running temperature, and the material used for the piston should preferably have a low coefficient of thermal expansion. Large clearances allow excessive side-to-side movement of the piston as the crank passes the dead centres and the connecting-rod angle changes, and this causes a noise called piston slap, which is objectionable.

Materials

Cast iron

Early engines had pistons made of cast iron. This metal has good strength and hardness at operating temperatures and forms a good bearing surface against the cylinder wall. However, it is relatively heavy, rather brittle and liable to develop cracks and not a particularly good conductor of heat. It has a coefficient of thermal expansion comparable with that of the cylinder, allowing quite small clearances to be used when cold, thus avoiding piston slap.

Aluminium

In its pure state, aluminium has a high coefficient of thermal expansion, is relatively soft and low in strength. The addition of about 12 per cent silicon and small quantities of other elements makes a strong alloy, which has a low coefficient of thermal expansion.

These are the main advantages of aluminium alloys for pistons:

1 Improved thermal conductivity, which makes for lower piston-crown temperatures. In turn, this causes less heating of the fresh mixture during the induction stroke, so that the mixture filling the cylinder is cooler and denser, leading to improved engine power output.

2 Reduced mass of the piston due to the lower density of aluminium, permitting the engine to run at a higher speed and so develop more power.

3 Because of its lower melting point, it can be cast in steel moulds or dies. This gives greater accuracy of casting and reduced costs if the pistons are made in large numbers.

4 Aluminium alloys are usually softer than cast iron and are easier to machine.

These are the chief disadvantages:

1 Greater coefficient of thermal expansion. This necessitates the use of larger clearances when cold, resulting in piston slap. This can be minimised by special construction of the piston skirt and by the use of alloys, which have a relatively low coefficient of expansion.

2 Aluminium is not as strong as cast iron, particularly at high temperatures. Therefore, it is necessary to use a greater thickness of metal to avoid distortion under load. While this reduces the saving of mass resulting from its lower density, it does increase the ability of the piston to conduct heat.

3 Aluminium is softer than cast iron, especially at high temperatures; this may lead to excessive wear of the ring grooves. Improved alloys have been developed and in some cases other methods have been adopted to overcome this difficulty.

4 Aluminium is more expensive than cast iron, though this is to some extent offset by its greater ease of casting and machining.

Composite construction

Attempts to combine the low weight and good heat conductivity of aluminium with the small clearances when cold permissible with cast iron or steel, resulted in a two-piece construction in which the crown and gudgeon pin bosses are made of aluminium and the skirt made of cast iron or steel.

Piston details

The crown

In its simplest form, the crown is flat and at right angles to the cylinder axis, and this involves only the simplest of machining operations. In some cases, the crown is slightly dished (Figure 2.60a). One reason for this is to make possible the use of higher compression ratios, should this become desirable, simply by reducing or eliminating the 'dish'. It is sometimes done to provide a particular form of combustion chamber.

Certain designs of combustion chamber require the piston crown to be made a particular shape, such as the domed crown (Figure 2.60b).

Note: whatever the shape of the crown, the effective force on the piston due to gas pressure is always given by multiplying the pressure by the cross-sectional area of the cylinder bore.

Figure 2.60 (a) Concave piston crown; (b) Domed piston crown

The ring belt

It is most important that this part of the piston is accurately made. In particular, each ring groove should lie in a plane at right angles to the cylinder axis. This part of the piston is generally given more clearance in the cylinder than the skirt, and does not normally bear against the cylinder. The ridges that separate the grooves are called *lands*.

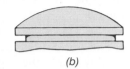

Figure 2.61 Piston ring belt

There are usually three or four of these grooves above the skirt, and sometimes one in the skirt below the gudgeon pin. These are discussed in greater detail later in this chapter on page 67 in connection with piston rings.

Pistons that are prone to ring groove wear can be fitted with an iron ring carrier, which is metallically bonded into the piston. This process provides good heat flow and ensures that the ring life is extended.

Gudgeon pin bosses

These must be connected to the piston crown in such a way that the loads that result from gas pressure are transmitted from the crown to the gudgeon pin without any possibility of distortion of the piston. The bosses are usually connected directly to the crown by substantial struts or thick webs.

It is important that the gudgeon-pin holes are bored accurately and with an extremely fine surface finish.

The skirt

The simplest form of this is illustrated in Figure 2.58, in which the skirt forms a downward tubular extension below the ring belt: this arrangement is called a solid skirt. It is the strongest form of skirt and is always used for engines where the loads on the piston are particularly great.

Many engines today use shorter skirt pistons as these provide very light piston assemblies. This can be seen in higher rpm engines such as variable valve timing-type engines. The lightness of the piston assembly allows the engine to be operated at higher rpm due to the lower weight having to be transferred up and down the cylinder bores. Figure 2.62 shows a piston with the shorter skirt compared with a conventional piston.

Figure 2.62 Short skirt pistons

To permit the use of small clearances with aluminium alloy pistons when cold, special types of skirt construction are used that involve some degree of flexibility of the skirt. For example, the skirt may be almost completely separated from the ring belt except at the gudgeon-pin bosses, and split down one side. This allows it to fit in the cylinder with very little clearance when cold; expansion due to a rise in temperature is taken up by reducing the width of the split. The split usually extends the full length of the skirt and is at a slight angle, to avoid leaving a ridge on the cylinder as wear occurs.

When assembling split-skirt pistons on to the connecting rod, it is important that the split side of the skirt is on the side that bears against the cylinder during the compression stroke, so that the unsplit, and therefore stronger, side takes the greater side thrust during the power strokes.

The high piston load of a modern engine has meant that the split skirt has been superseded by low expansion, solid-skirt pistons, such as the thermal slot or link strut types:

1 Thermal slot – a lateral thermal slot cut at the bottom of the ring groove on the thrust and non-thrust sides of the piston directs the heat from the hot (250 °C) piston crown to the gudgeon-pin boss regions. In some designs, these slots are extended axially downwards into the skirt

and terminate with a circular hole (Figure 2.63). Thermal expansion of the crown and bosses, combined with the effect of the gas load, pulls in the thrust faces and allows the piston to be fitted with a small clearance. To compensate for this action, the piston is oval when cold. These types of pistons are also sometimes called 'W' slot pistons due to the shaping of the lateral slots meeting the gudgeon-pin boss.

2 Link strut – pistons have special alloy steel (Invar) plates cast into the skirt. This material has an extremely low coefficient of thermal expansion, so the resistance given by these plates limits the expansion of the skirt.

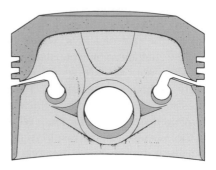
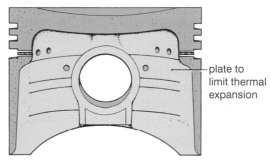

plate to limit thermal expansion

Figure 2.63 'W' slot piston and link strut piston

Piston clearance

The clearance left between the cylinder and piston when the engine is assembled will depend on the piston material, piston design and the operating temperature of the engine. Too small a clearance is likely to cause seizure, whereas excessive clearance results in gas blow-by, noise and high oil consumption.

For a particular engine, the manufacturer's manual should be consulted to obtain the actual clearances. In the past, a rough guide for piston skirt to cylinder clearance was taken as:

Cast iron	0.001 × bore diameter (mm)
Aluminium alloy, solid skirt	0.002 × bore diameter (mm)
Aluminium alloy, split skirt	0.001 × bore diameter (mm)

Design improvements and better materials have allowed the skirt clearance to be reduced. Many modern solid skirt, aluminium alloy pistons have a clearance as small as $0.0005 \times$ bore diameter. For example, a certain piston with a diameter 82 mm has a clearance of 0.041 mm; this is the distance between the cylinder and the thrust face of the piston.

The crown runs much hotter than the skirt, so the piston is slightly tapered to allow for this, the maximum clearance being given to the top. The taper is critical since too small a clearance at the top land causes the land to contact the cylinder and give scuffing and noise, whereas excessive clearance results in gas blow-by.

2.7.2 Piston rings

Piston rings prevent gas leakage through the clearance that must be left between the piston and the cylinder to allow the piston to move freely.

Figure 2.64 shows the main features of a piston ring: it is rectangular in section, and the nominal diameter is the diameter of the cylinder into which it is to fit. (This is measured on the ring with the gap closed, using a steel tape, which is passed around the ring and pulled tight.) A radial cut is made in the ring so that it can be placed in position in the groove on the piston. When in position in the cylinder, the gap between the ends of the ring, called the working gap, needs to be large enough to ensure that the ends of the ring do not actually touch, however hot the ring may get. When out of the cylinder, the actual diameter of the ring is larger than its nominal diameter. The gap, now called the free gap, is also larger than the working gap: this ensures that when in position in the cylinder the ring will exert an outward pressure against the wall of the cylinder along its whole circumference.

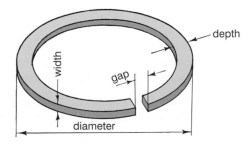

Figure 2.64 Piston ring dimensions

Figure 2.65 shows a section of the ring in position in its groove and filling the clearance between the cylinder wall and piston. The depth of the ring should be slightly less than the depth of the groove, to ensure that side forces acting on the piston are transferred to the cylinder via the bearing surfaces on the skirt and not through the piston rings, and also to ensure

that the clearance between the inner surface of the ring and the bottom of the ring groove is not less than the correct piston clearance.

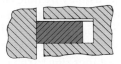

Figure 2.65 Plain rectangular-section piston ring

The width of the ring must also be slightly less than the width of the groove, to ensure that the ring will be perfectly free to move about in its groove. If the ring is too close a fit in its groove, it is liable to become securely stuck by carbonised oil after a period of use.

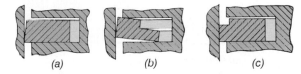

Figure 2.66 Special types of compression ring

Figure 2.66 shows that the ring has a rectangular cross-section. In some cases, this is slightly modified in one of three ways:

1 The outer surface of the ring is given a slight taper towards the top (about 1°). The purpose of this is to speed up the 'bedding in' process when the ring is new (Figure 2.66a).
2 The top inner corner of the ring is cut away, leaving the cross-section of the ring like a thick letter L. This serves the same purpose as the taper-faced ring above (Figure 2.66b).
3 The top outer corner of the ring is cut away (Figure 2.66c). This ring should be used when new top rings are fitted to worn cylinders. The cut-away portion avoids contact with the ridge that develops at the upper limit of ring travel in a worn cylinder. Some manufacturers call this ring a 'ridge dodger'.

Oil-control or scraper rings

The piston rings so far described are fitted for the purpose of preventing the escape of gas through the clearance between the cylinder and the piston and are called compression rings, pressure rings or gas rings. Piston rings also control the oil film on the cylinder wall in order to permit adequate lubrication without excessive quantities of oil getting past the piston and into the combustion chamber. In the combustion chamber, the oil would be decomposed and partly burnt, forming deposits of carbon on the combustion chamber walls and causing smoke in the exhaust gas. Special types of ring have been developed for this purpose, which are intended to glide over the oil film as the piston moves upward, but to scrape off all but a very thin film of oil on the downward stroke. Provision is made, usually by holes at the back of the ring groove or by chamfering the land immediately below the groove and drilling oil drain holes from this chamfer to the inside of the piston, to return oil collected by the scraper ring to the underneath of the piston. Figure 2.67 shows sections of several types of oil-control rings and their grooves. The bevelled scraper is the least severe in its action; the grooved type the most severe.

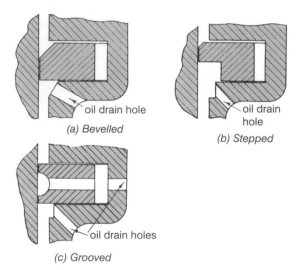

(a) Bevelled

(b) Stepped

(c) Grooved

Figure 2.67 Types of oil-control ring

Pistons are usually fitted with two or three compression rings and one scraper ring located in the bottom groove. In the past, an additional scraper ring was fitted around the skirt, but the desire for low bonnet lines has resulted in a reduction in the engine stroke and piston length: this means that there is insufficient space available for the skirt scraper ring.

Furthermore, the proximity of the piston to the oil being discharged from the bearings, combined with cylinder distortion, has demanded a scraper ring that exerts an outward pressure of about 3150 kPa (450 lbf in^{-2}): this is about 20 times as great as the standard iron types.

Figure 2.68 shows a steel oil-control ring. It consists of two narrow steel rails separated from each other by a specially shaped spacer. Large outward pressure is obtained by fitting an expander spring behind the ring. To avoid incorrect assembly, some designs combine the various ring elements into one unit.

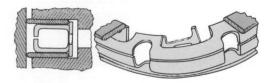

Figure 2.68 Steel oil-control ring

Fit of piston rings

When new piston rings are fitted to an engine, there are two important points to check (apart from ensuring that the ring is of the correct size and type) – the gap and the side clearance in the groove.

The correct figures for these are given in the engine manufacturer's service manual, but approximate values are given below for guidance.

Working gap

Water-cooled engines	0.003 × bore diameter
Air-cooled engines	0.004 × bore diameter
Side clearance in groove	0.04 mm (0.0015 in)

For example, a ring fitted to a water-cooled engine of bore 82 mm should have a gap clearance of 0.246 mm.

Measurement of working gap

This gap is measured by putting the ring, removed from the piston, into its cylinder and squaring it up by pushing it up against the end of the piston also placed inside the cylinder. The gap between the ends of the ring is then measured by feeler gauges. If the cylinder is worn, the ring should be in the least worn part of the bore when this measurement is made. Too small a gap can be rectified by carefully filing or grinding one end of the ring, preferably in a special jig that ensures squareness of the ends.

Piston ring materials

The most important properties of the material used for piston rings are as follows:

1 Wear resistance – especially (in the case of the compression rings) under conditions of somewhat scanty lubrication.
2 Elasticity – to ensure that the ring will maintain sufficient outward pressure against the cylinder wall to maintain contact with the surface of the cylinder.
3 Temperature tolerance – these properties must not be adversely affected by the temperatures to which the ring is subjected in use.

The material that most nearly fulfils these requirements is cast iron. In some cases, the wear resistance is improved by chromium-plating the outer face of the ring by a special process, but rings of this type are normally only used for the top compression ring.

In some oil-control rings the material used is steel, which is generally chromium-plated on the edges that bear upon the cylinder wall.

2.7.3 Gudgeon pins

Gudgeon pins need to be strong enough to carry the high loads imposed upon them by gas pressure on the piston and require a wear-resistant surface. They are therefore made of steel, usually alloyed with 3–4 per cent of nickel to increase toughness, and case-hardened to obtain a wear-resistant surface. Clearly, the ends of the hardened pin must be prevented from rubbing against the cylinder wall; otherwise it would soon score deep grooves in the cylinder surface.

There are two types of gudgeon pin, depending upon how they are fixed in position:

1 Semi-floating – securely fixed in either the piston or the connecting rod, usually the latter, as described on page 63. Although it was at one time common practice to fix the gudgeon pin in the piston by means of a screw threaded into one of the gudgeon-pin bosses, this practice has been discarded in favour of fixing the pin in the connecting rod. Movement is therefore confined to oscillation of the pin in the piston.

2 Fully floating – free to turn in both piston and connecting rod, and is generally used in engines in which the loads are particularly high. The pin is shorter than the cylinder diameter and is prevented from contacting the cylinder by one of the methods illustrated in Figure 2.69.

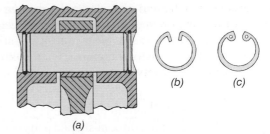

Figure 2.69 Location of gudgeon pin by circlips

The method shown at (a) consists of a spring steel ring called a circlip, which is sprung into a groove inside the gudgeon-pin hole after the gudgeon pin has been fitted – one at each end of the pin. The circlip is sometimes made of round-section steel wire and may have its ends bent inwards as shown at (b) to make it easier to fit and remove with pointed-nose pliers. Some circlips do not have the bent-in ends: in this case, the ends of the gudgeon pin are slightly chamfered as shown at (a) (this helps to prevent the circlip being forced out of its groove by endwise forces), and small notches are cut in the piston so that a pointed instrument can

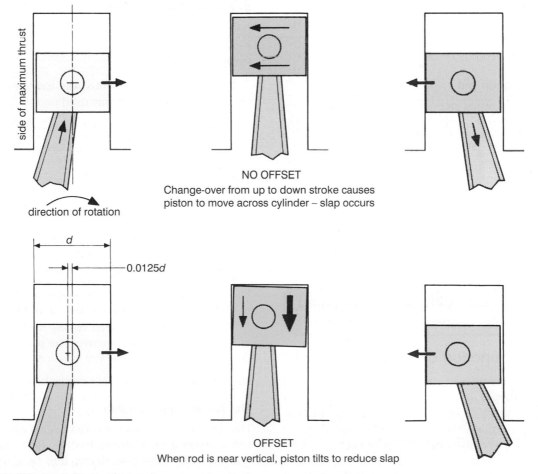

Figure 2.70 Effects of offset gudgeon pin

be inserted behind the circlip to remove it. Another type of circlip often used is the Seeger circlip (c), which is stamped from spring steel sheet. Special circlip pliers are used for fitting and removing this type.

Gudgeon pins are usually made tubular to reduce weight. An alternative method of preventing scoring of the cylinder is to fit mushroom-shaped pads of soft metal, such as aluminium or brass. The stem of the mushroom is a press fit in the bore of the gudgeon pin. This method is seldom used in modern engines.

Gudgeon-pin fit

The gudgeon pin is usually made a tight push-fit in the piston when cold: this eases off slightly when the piston reaches normal running temperature. You must not use force to remove a tightly fitting pin unless you do so very carefully, and great care must be taken to ensure that no force whatever is applied to the connecting rod, to avoid the risk of bending it. If possible, heat the piston in hot water or oil: if the piston cannot be immersed in oil or water, you can wrap rags soaked in hot water round the piston, after which the gudgeon pin can be pushed out easily without risk of damage.

A recent development is the use of an interference fit of the gudgeon pin in the small-end of the connecting rod. In effect, this is a semi-floating pin in which the interference fit is relied upon to hold the gudgeon pin in place.

Offset gudgeon pin

The skirt clearance needed for a solid skirt alloy piston has increased the occurrence of piston slap when the engine is cold. This noise can be reduced by offsetting the gudgeon-pin axis towards the side of maximum piston thrust (Figure 2.70).

At TDC, the slight tilting action eases the transfer of piston thrust from one side of the cylinder to the other. Since the offset is only about $0.0125d$, where d is the piston diameter, then care must be taken to observe the marking 'front' when the piston is fitted.

2.8 Intake, exhaust valves and valve-operating gear

2.8.1 The function of valves

It has been mentioned previously that the air/fuel mixture (charge) enters and exits the engine via a series of ports known as inlet and exhaust ports. These ports are fed via the valve assembly or valve train, as they are often called. These ports must be open only during that part of the cycle of operations when gas is required to pass through them. At all other times they must close sufficiently tightly to prevent the passage of gas at considerable pressure. It is the function of the **valves** to close the ports securely during these times. (**Note**: in the case of two-stroke engines, the ports can be closed by covering them with the piston, but a little thought will show that this method cannot be successfully used on an engine working on the four-stroke cycle.)

Valve: a component fitted to the engine, which opens and closes to let exhaust gases out of the combustion chamber and air and fuel into the combustion chamber at exactly the right moment in the engine cycle. Valves create a gas-tight seal when closed to allow the engine to build up compression and pressure during the four-stroke cycle.

In performing this function, the valves must:

- make a completely gas-tight seal in the ports when closed
- offer no opposition to the flow of gases when open
- require the simplest possible mechanism to operate them
- operate with the minimum of friction.

2.8.2 Types of valve

During the development of internal-combustion engines, several types of valve have been used. These are the main types:

1. The poppet valve – this was already in use on steam engines and was used on the early types of internal-combustion engines. It has proved so successful that its use has continued and is almost the only type to be used in modern engines.
2. The slide valve – also commonly used on early internal-combustion engines, but less satisfactory than the poppet valve. Now obsolete.
3. The sleeve valve – several versions of this type of valve have been used, the most successful being the Knight and the Burt-McCullum.
4. The rotary valve – several types of rotary valve have been developed and some have given very good results. They consist of rotating 'plugs' fitted across the ports, having holes, which, at the correct times, uncover the ports and allow gas to pass.

We can look at some of these valves in more detail.

The Knight sleeve valve

The Knight sleeve valve was developed around 1905 and consisted of a sleeve free to slide inside the cylinder with a second sleeve free to slide inside it, the piston moving within the inner sleeve. The sleeves were moved up and down inside the cylinder, and holes cut in the sleeves were arranged to uncover the cylinder ports at the correct times.

This valve was used by the Daimler Company from about 1909 until about 1933. It was also used by a number of continental manufacturers, such as Panhard, Minerva, Voisin, Peugeot and on a few Mercedes models.

The Burt-McCullum sleeve valve

The Burt-McCullum sleeve valve consisted of a single sleeve, which was given a combination of up-and-down motion and part-rotary motion inside the cylinder, holes in the sleeve uncovering the cylinder ports at the appropriate times. This was developed in about 1909 and was first used in the Argyll car in 1911. It has also been used in a few other cars, but its greatest success has been in aircraft engines, chiefly the large engines made by the Bristol Aeroplane Co. beginning about 1935. It was also used in the famous Napier 'Sabre' engine, a 24-cylinder engine developing about 3500 bhp, and in the last of the Rolls-Royce piston-type aero-engines, the 'Eagle', also a 24-cylinder engine developing over 3000 bhp.

Although these types of valve seemed to have many advantages over the cruder poppet valve, they have not survived in vehicle engines. Their main drawback was relatively high oil consumption and a smoky exhaust.

The poppet valve

A poppet valve is the only valve presently in use in vehicles. It is installed within the cylinder head (Figure 2.71), with its immediate attachments (Figure 2.72). The valve itself consists of a disc-shaped head having a stem extending from its centre at one side. The edge of the head on the side nearest the stem is accurately ground at an angle – usually 45° but sometimes 30° – to form the face. When the valve is closed, the face is

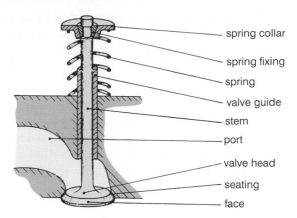

Figure 2.72 A poppet valve

pressed into contact with a similarly ground seating at the inner end of the port. Beyond the seating, the port curves smoothly away clear of the valve.

The condition and seating of the face is of vital importance in ensuring the gas-tightness of the valve. They are ground on special machines and the valve face is sometimes lapped into its seating with a very fine abrasive. Whether this is necessary, or even advisable if the grinding is sufficiently accurate, is often in dispute.

After a considerable period of use, the condition of face and seating deteriorates and allows leakage. This creates an issue with the engine through lowering the compression ratio as the gas escapes past the valve seat. If this occurs, the valves and the seats must be reground or lapped together. Special grinding machines have been developed for this purpose. In addition, the technician should be able to lap the valves together if they are not too badly worn using grinding paste and a valve lapping tool.

Figure 2.73 shows the face and seating in more detail. The seating is narrower than the face, to reduce the risk of trapping particles of carbon between the face and the seating, and to ensure a surface pressure great enough to provide a gas-tight seal. The thickness of the head indicated by the arrows is most important: a sharp edge, particularly in the case of the exhaust valve, is liable to become excessively hot and may cause 'pre-ignition' (ignition of the mixture inside the cylinder before the spark occurs).

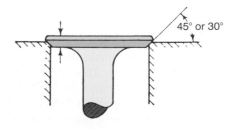

Figure 2.73 Valve face angles

Figure 2.71 Poppet valves fitted into a cylinder head

In a few cases, the exhaust valve face is ground to an angle about 0.5° less than the seat angle, as shown in Figure 2.74. There are three reasons for this:

1 The hottest part of the valve, under running conditions, is the stem side of the head, and the additional expansion of this side makes the face and seat angles equal at running temperatures.
2 The exhaust valve gets very hot (often red hot when the engine is running at full throttle) and is then less strong. Under these conditions, the spring load tends to cause the head to dish slightly, which can lift the inner edge of the face (nearest the combustion chamber) clear of the seating if the angles are the same when cold.
3 It reduces the risk of trapping carbon between the face and the seating. In this case, the face and seating cannot be lapped in.

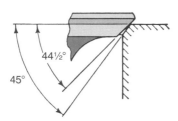

Figure 2.74 Valve face angle different from seat angle

2.8.3 The valve guide

The valve slides in a hole in the cylinder or cylinder head called the valve guide. There are generally three types of valve guide: shoulder, plain and integral (Figure 2.75). The valve guide must be perfectly true with the seating, and a small clearance is allowed between stem and guide to prevent any possibility of the valve sticking. Excessive clearance may lead to the seating being worn oval, and in the case of the inlet valve will allow air to leak into the mixture entering the cylinder. Valve stems are fitted with oil seals (Figure 2.75d) that prevent any oil entering into the combustion chamber during engine operation, especially during the induction stroke.

The guide is usually made in the form of a detachable sleeve to permit easy renewal when worn, but in some cases it is integral with the cylinder or head, since this assists the transfer of heat from the hot exhaust valve to the cooling system. In this case, wear is rectified by boring or reaming out the guide slightly and fitting a valve with an 'oversized' stem.

When the guides are detachable, they sometimes have a shoulder formed on them. They are an interference fit in the cylinder or head and are pressed into the shoulder. Guides without shoulders are easier and cheaper to make: when fitting, press these in to leave a definite length projecting from the head (Figure 2.75b).

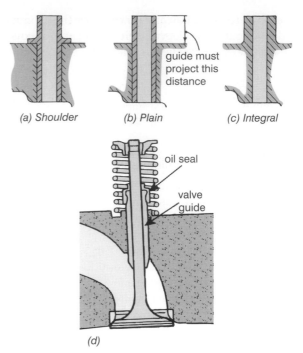

(a) Shoulder   *(b) Plain*   *(c) Integral*

(d)

Figure 2.75 Types of valve guides and valve fitted with valve stem oil seal

2.8.4 The valve spring

The spring returns the valve to its seat after it has been opened, and holds it there (assisted by gas pressure during the compression and power strokes) until it is next opened.

The spring must be strong enough to close the valve quickly at maximum engine speeds. The spring strength needed depends upon the weight of the valve and any other part of its operating gear that it has to move, and upon the maximum speed at which the engine is required to run. If the force exerted by the spring is insufficient, the valve will be late in closing at high rpm and so limit maximum engine speeds.

Valve springs are usually of the helical coil type (Figures 2.76a and b). Such springs are liable to surging at certain engine speeds, when the centre coils vibrate in a direction parallel to the valve stem. In extreme cases, this can lead to breakage of the springs, and can also allow the valves to bounce off their seatings after closing. This may be overcome in several ways:

■ The springs are so designed that when the valve is fully open they are compressed until adjacent coils almost touch, so preventing the build-up of excessive surging.
■ The coils are spaced closer together at one end than the other (Figure 2.76b). Springs of this kind must be fitted with the 'close' coils nearest the cylinder head.

Two (or occasionally three) springs are used, one inside the other. This does not prevent surging, but the two springs will not both surge at the same engine speed, and 'valve bounce' will be prevented. Also, if one spring breaks the second one will maintain pressure on the spring attachment and prevent the valve dropping into the cylinder.

Another type of spring occasionally used is the hairpin spring (Figures 2.76c and d). This is not liable to surge, but is more difficult to fit into the space available.

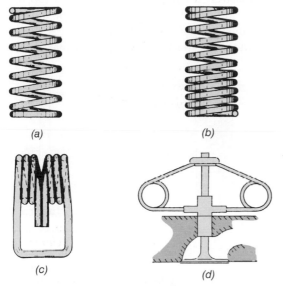

(a)   *(b)*

(c)   *(d)*

Figure 2.76 Types of valve spring

Valve spring fixing

Several different methods have been used to attach the spring to the end of the valve stem. Some commonly used methods are shown in Figure 2.77.

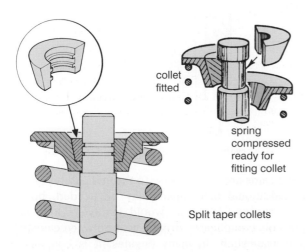

collet fitted

spring compressed ready for fitting collet

Split taper collets

Figure 2.77 Methods of fixing valve spring to valve stem

2.8.5 Materials

Exhaust valve

The exhaust valve is the hottest part of the engine. It is exposed to the full heat of the burning gas during combustion, and when the hot gases are released from the cylinder they sweep past the exhaust valve head. It is estimated that under full power conditions the exhaust valve reaches a temperature of around 700 °C. Consequently, a rather special steel is required to operate satisfactorily for long periods under these extreme conditions, so alloys containing varying amounts of manganese, silicon, nickel and chromium have been developed specifically for this purpose.

The exhaust valve is cooled by passing on its heat in two directions:

1 along the stem and through the guide into the cylinder head
2 directly into the cylinder head from the face to the seating when it is closed.

For extreme operating conditions, the valve stem is sometimes made hollow and partly filled with **sodium**, a very soft metal having a melting point of 98 °C. Under running conditions, the sodium is molten, and in splashing from end to end of the valve stem it assists the transfer of heat from the hot head. The heat travels up the valve stem and is transferred to the cylinder head where coolant channels in the cylinder head carry the heat away. This is an expensive form of construction and is only used when absolutely necessary. Sodium-filled valves are used when extra cooling is required due to the more extreme heat being generated by high-performance or forced induction engines.

Sodium: a very reactive metal that is completely sealed within the valve stem so that it does not come into contact with air or water.

Some valves are coated with aluminium to improve the heat transfer from the valve to the engine block. 'Aluminised valves' cannot be reground in the normal way because the surface coating is comparatively thin and manual grinding will damage the surface.

Inlet valves

Inlet vales are also made from high-tensile alloy steel usually containing nickel, chromium and molybdenum.

Intake valves

Titanium valves

In some more expensive engines, especially high-performance motorcycle engines, the use of titanium is sometimes seen in the manufacture of inlet and exhaust valves. Titanium is a very light, strong metal that is able to withstand wear extremely well but is much more expensive than the conventional materials used to manufacture valves. The reason for using titanium is to improve the efficiency and performance of the engine by lowering the weight that the camshaft and followers have to overcome to open and close the valve. By having lower-weight valves the energy required to open and close the valve is lowered, which leads to improved engine response.

Valve guides

Detachable valve guides are usually made of cast iron, although bronze is sometimes used, particularly for exhaust valves, because of its better heat-conducting properties.

Valve springs

The valve springs are usually made from spring steel, which contains about 0.6 to 0.7 per cent carbon and also small amounts of silicon, manganese and vanadium.

2.8.6 Valve position

The position of the valve in the cylinder head depends upon the design of the combustion chamber (see page 154). At this stage, it is sufficient to list the possible positions of the valves as follows:

1 Side valve or L-head – both valves are at one side of the cylinder, heads uppermost with the stems approximately parallel to the cylinder axis. To accommodate the valves in this position, the combustion chamber is extended sideways from the top of the cylinder forming a shape similar to an inverted letter L (Figure 2.78a). This arrangement is not used on modern engines.
2 Side valve or T-head – this is like the above except that inlet and exhaust valves are fitted at opposite sides of the cylinder. This arrangement, though common on early engines, has been obsolete for many years.
3 Vertical overhead valves (OHVs) – both valves are fitted over the top of the cylinder with their stems approximately vertical and parallel (Figure 2.78b), usually in a single row.
4 Overhead inlet and side exhaust or F-head – the inlet valve is arranged as in point 3 above and the exhaust as in point 1 (Figure 2.78c).
5 Inclined OHVs – both valves are fitted over the top of the cylinder head, but in two rows inclined at an angle to one another (Figure 2.78d).

2.8.7 Basic valve operation

The valves are moved to, and held in, their closed position by their springs. They are opened by cams carried upon one or more camshafts, which are driven by suitable gearing from the crankshaft. The cams do not usually act directly upon the valves since their rotary motion would impose a side force upon the end of the valve stem: to combat this side force **cam followers** are interposed between the cam and the valve. These followers may take one of two forms:

1 Tappets or cam followers, which rest upon the cams and are guided so they move in a straight line.
2 Rockers or levers, which rock upon fixed pivots.

Cam follower: a component that sits on top of the camshaft lobe. As the camshaft rotates, the movement of the camshaft lobe is transferred to the cam follower, which then operates the valve opening gear.

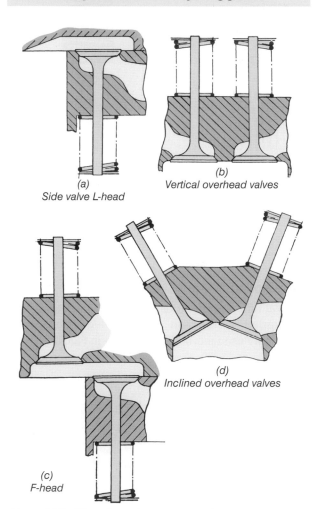

(a)
Side valve L-head

(b)
Vertical overhead valves

(c)
F-head

(d)
Inclined overhead valves

Figure 2.78 Alternative valve arrangements

If the cams are placed close to the ends of the valves, no additional mechanism may be needed, but in the case of OHVs this would involve a long and possibly complicated driving gear between camshaft and crankshaft. In many engines, it is considered preferable to place the camshaft reasonably near the crankshaft, so that a short and simple driving gear can be used. In such cases, the motion of the tappets is conveyed to the valves through push rods and overhead rockers.

In modern engines, overhead camshafts (OHCs) are used to improve on the distance between the valve opening mechanism and the valve assembly. Using OHCs involves more complicated drive mechanisms to drive the camshaft from the crankshaft. Due to the complexity of the camshaft arrangements, valve gear locations on modern, highly efficient engines are not easily operated with push-rod systems. Additionally, the drive systems for operating the valve gear using belts and chains are cheaper and more reliable and, combined with the operating performance of the OHCs arrangements, these are now the preferred option to push-rod systems.

Figures 2.79 and 2.80 show two arrangements for driving the valve gear. Figure 2.79 shows a direct-acting valve gear with the camshaft acting directly on to the follower and then the valve stem. Figure 2.80 shows a push-rod arrangement.

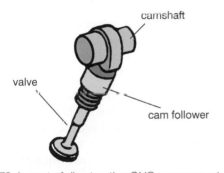

Figure 2.79 Layout of direct-acting OHC arrangement with the cam lobe acting directly on to the follower and then the valve stem

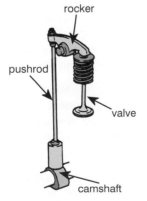

Figure 2.80 Push-rod layout with OHV with rocker shaft arrangement

Valve clearance

A valve is closed when its face is pressed into contact with the seating by the full force of the spring.

Figure 2.81 shows a simplified arrangement of valve, cam follower and camshaft. At (a) the valve is shown in the fully open position. As the cam rotates, the valve moves under the action of its spring (not shown) towards its closed position. At (b) a condition is shown in which the cam follower has reached the base of the cam before the face of the valve has come into contact with the seating. Since the cam follower cannot move downwards any further, the valve cannot completely close.

At (c) the cam follower is shown in the same position on the cam, but the valve face has reached the seating before the tappet has reached the base of the cam, leaving a gap or clearance between the end of the valve and the cam follower. This is called valve clearance or tappet clearance, and it is clear that in this case the cam follower cannot prevent the valve from closing properly.

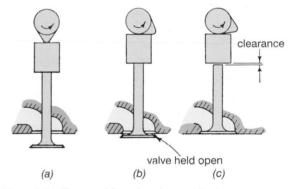

Figure 2.81 The need for valve clearance

There must always be a small clearance in the valve-operating gear when the valve is in its closed position to ensure that the valve will close completely. When the clearance is checked, allowance must be made for the fact that under different running conditions the amount of clearance will be altered by different temperatures due to different amounts of expansion of the valves, cylinder block and valve-operating gear. The valve clearance and the engine conditions under which it should be measured (i.e. engine hot or cold) are specified by the engine manufacturer, and it is most important that the clearance should be correct under the specified conditions. Excessive clearance will result in noisy operation and excessive wear. It will also cause problems with the engine running because having too much clearance will alter the opening and closing times of the valve timing. Too little clearance may result in the valve not fully closing under certain conditions. This causes loss of pressure in the cylinder and burnt exhaust valves (since one of the paths for the escape of heat is cut off if the valve does not close properly, and gas at a very high temperature will be forced at high speed through the gap between valve face and seating). The excessive heat will also damage the valve seat and valve face.

There is always provision for adjusting the valve clearance during assembly, usually (but not always) by means of an adjusting screw. In most cases, the clearance should be checked at intervals to ensure that it has not been altered by wear.

It is often assumed that the valve clearance is decreased as the engine becomes hotter, but this is by no means always the case. It is suggested that students check the valve clearances of a number of engines both hot and cold, and note the results.

Incorrect clearance will affect the angle of the cam at the instant the valve leaves or returns to its seat. Excessive clearance will cause the valve to leave its seat later and return it earlier in the cam rotation (i.e. the angle through which the cam – and therefore also the crankshaft – rotates while the valve is open will be reduced). Insufficient clearance will have the reverse effect.

Modern engines are fitted with hydraulic cam followers that alter the clearance between the cam follower and the valve stem automatically through hydraulic oil pressure. This system creates far greater control of the valve opening and closing times and also requires much less maintenance. When carrying out maintenance on an engine, the technician should always refer to the workshop manual to check what system is used as some modern engines still incorporate adjustable cam followers.

Valve rotation

During the opening and closing of the valve, small deposits can build up on the two faces causing wear and damage to the gas-tight seal between the valve seat and valve face. To overcome this problem, manufacturers build in a mechanism that rotates the valve during opening and closing operation. Two methods of valve rotation are used:

1 A method of rotating the valve through the camshaft lobe acting directly on to the follower. By having a slightly offset cam lobe and cam follower, the cam follower rotates slightly as the cam lobe strikes the follower. Because the follower is acting on top of the valve stem, this in turn rotates the valve slightly as it opens.
2 As the valve is opened by the camshaft lobe acting on the cam follower, the **collets** retaining the valve and valve spring become loose. In turn, this allows the action of the rotator to create rotational movement of the valve as it becomes unloaded. This is due to the rotator position between the top of the valve stem and

the valve spring. When the pressure is applied by the camshaft lobe striking the cam follower to open the valve, the pressure also acts upon the rotator and the valve rotates slightly as it opens. As the engine speed rises, the rotation speed becomes greater.

Collet: a locking device to secure the valve spring assembly to the valve stem.

2.9   Valve-operating mechanisms

2.9.1 Cams and camshafts

A cam is a component shaped in such a way that by its rotation it causes another part in contact with it to move in a different manner. There are many types of cams in use in different sorts of machines. In relatively simple engines, camshafts are rods made of forged or cast steel with lobes (cams) placed along their length that rotate and control the opening and closing of valves. In most modern multi-valve engines, separate shafts may be used for the inlet and exhaust valves. These can be termed 'twin cam' engines when looking at a straight engine such as a four-cylinder engine.

Valves within an internal-combustion engine are required to open and close to allow the fuel, air and exhaust gases to enter and escape the engine during the combustion process. It is important that the valves are opened and closed at critical times and for a critical length of time. The camshaft's purpose is to carry out this job in an extremely reliable fashion to ensure the engine operates at peak efficiency. The method for opening and closing the valve gear has not really changed since the conception of the reciprocating internal-combustion engine. The engineering accuracy and timing has altered over the years to obtain more efficient and powerful engines.

Camshafts are made of steel, either by forging or casting, with subsequent machining. Forged camshafts usually have the cams case-hardened, while the cams of cast shafts are generally hardened by chilling during casting.

The type of cam used to operate the valves of an internal-combustion engine is a relatively simple one, such as is illustrated in Figure 2.82. The cam follower remains stationary during that part of the cam's rotation when it rests upon the **base circle**, and its 'lift' begins at the point where the opening **flank** joins the base circle. At the peak of the cam lobe, the lift is at its maximum, and the follower falls as the closing flank passes beneath the cam follower. By the time it is again in contact with the base circle at the end of the closing flank, it will have returned to its original position.

> **Base circle**: the circle the cam follower describes when no valve lift is being applied.
>
> **Flank**: the part of the camshaft lobe that increases the speed of the opening and closing characteristics of the camshaft. The design of the flank can alter the speed at which the camshaft opens and closes the valves of the engine.

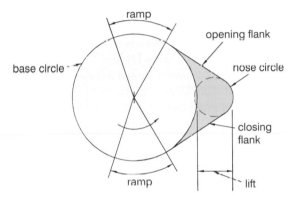

Figure 2.82 Details of a cam

In some engines, there may be comparatively large variations of clearance under different running temperatures, and to ensure quiet operation even when the clearances are large the flanks are joined to the base circle by ramps that extend over about 30° of cam rotation. When checking valve clearances, it is most important that the cam follower should be resting on the base circle of the cam. One way of ensuring this is to turn the engine to the position where the valve whose clearance is to be adjusted is at full lift, and then turn the engine one complete revolution. A simpler method is to note that in most multi-cylinder engines the pistons are arranged to move up and down together in pairs, so that if one of a pair is moving, say, upwards on its exhaust stroke, the other will also be moving upwards but on its compression stroke. Thus, to get any valve in the correct position for adjusting its clearance, the engine should be turned to the position where the corresponding valve in the other cylinder of the pair is at maximum lift.

Camshaft bearings

The camshafts are usually carried in plain bearings, but in some cases ball or roller bearings may be used. Many engines incorporate the bearings within the castings, especially when looking at aluminium cylinder head engines. In some engines, the shaft is moved into position from the front end of the engine, and to enable this to be done the bearings are larger than the cams. Most engines using multi-valve arrangements will have the camshafts fitted by splitting the cam carrier and laying camshafts in the bearings. It should be noted that in these cases it is very important to tighten the cam carrier down correctly using the manufacturer's sequence and torque settings. An example of this can be seen in Figure 2.83.

The camshaft is located endwise by some such arrangement as that shown in Figure 2.84, which also shows one of the methods used to secure the camshaft driving gear.

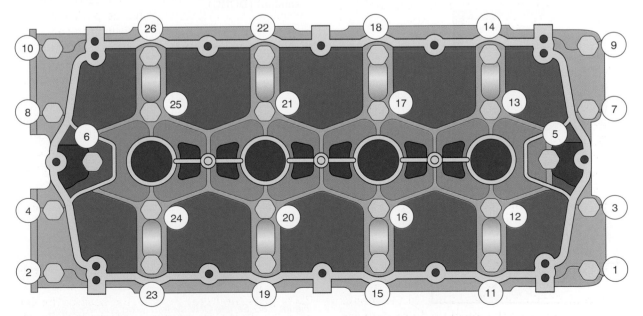

Figure 2.83 Camshaft carrier tightening sequence

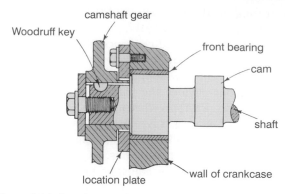

Figure 2.84 *Attachment of camshaft timing gear*

2.9.2 Camshaft location

Side-valve engines

Side-valve engines were a common early engine design. They had the camshaft located within the cylinder block close to the crankshaft. The valve operation was straightforward in this design as the valves were situated directly above the camshaft so they were opened and closed by means of a simple camshaft follower acting directly on to the valve stem (Figure 2.85). Due to the camshaft being situated close to the crankshaft, the drive arrangement was a simple chain and sprocket set-up. Some alternative arrangements used a gear drive, but this was often noisy in operation.

This type of engine is no longer used in modern vehicles as it does not allow a sufficiently efficient combustion process required by today's emission standards.

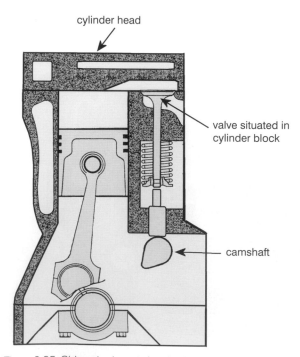

Figure 2.85 *Side-valve layout showing location of the camshaft*

OHV engines with push rods

The original OHV piston engine was developed by the Scottish-American David Dunbar Buick. It employs push-rod-actuated valves parallel to the pistons, and this is still in use today. This contrasts with previous designs that made use of side valves and sleeve valves.

Also known as a push-rod engine, the OHV engine variant normally will have the camshaft located inside the cylinder block. In a straight engine, the camshaft will normally be positioned just above or slightly to the side of the crankshaft, but immediately above the crankshaft when used in the V engine version. To operate the inlet and exhaust valves, you will identify that the engine is designed by utilising the operation of push rods or rods between the camshaft lobe and the valve rocker arms (Figure 2.86). Later OHV engine variants sometimes used followers or tappets to carry out the same functionality between the camshaft and push-rod layout. Later engine designs such as an OHC layout started to be used instead of the conventional OHV concept. This version of engine was similar in its design to its predecessor, but located the camshaft directly into the cylinder head and above the valve train, which in turn removed the need of the push rod.

As engine technology has progressed, the demise of the side valve and the push-rod engine is all but finished. The advancement of the OHC has progressed to now be the one version that can meet today's engine mechanical demands. Most vehicle manufacturers now produce their OHC engines with the option of a single overhead camshaft (SOHC) or a more complex layout of a double overhead camshaft (DOHC).

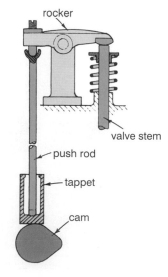

Figure 2.86 *Simple OHV system using push rods and rockers. The camshaft is located in the cylinder block.*

OHCs

If we refer to Figure 2.87, we can identify that the location of the camshaft is directly located above the valve train and combustion chamber. The camshaft then utilises the direct positioning of cam followers to operate between the valves and camshaft lobe. Comparing this arrangement to the earlier push-rod version shows that the OHC layout has fewer moving parts to complete the same operation of opening and closing the valves at a precise point of the engine cycle. A key difference is how the camshaft or camshafts are driven from the crankshaft. Whether it is belt, gear, or chain driven it is a more complex layout, but more manufacturers have found that the advantages of a better all-round performance and great design gives them the flexibility to meet today's driving demands. The removal of the push-rod activity has also allowed the cylinder head design to use longer and straighter ports. This design has then advanced the overall performance of the engine by optimising the port configuration, multi-valve layouts and improved breathing of the engine. Figure 2.88 shows a typical OHC arrangement.

As previously mentioned, the OHC layout needs to be driven by either a drive belt, chain or gear configuration. With this design, we also now see many engines with a multi-valve formation for each cylinder. This could comprise of a three-, four- or

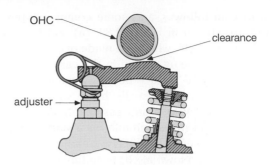

Figure 2.87 Simple OHC and rocker layout

even a five-valve per cylinder concept controlled by a variable valve timing system to maximise the engine's overall efficiency and power. This then allows the engine to have a greater engine speed and lower valve gear mass compared to the earlier cam in block layout.

2.9.3 Cam followers or tappets

Until fairly recently, cam followers have always been termed 'tappets'. This was due to the component that immediately contacts the cam lobe acting on the valve being tapped as the cam lobe rotated. Engine designers now usually refer to tappets as followers because these normally operate directly off the camshaft lobe rather than through push rods as seen in OHV arrangements. Tappets are one

Figure 2.88 OHC arrangement showing the valves acting directly on to the followers and camshaft

form of cam follower, and some common types of tappet are shown in Figure 2.89; (a) and (b) show barrel-type tappets, which are made of cast iron, the bottom surface being chilled in the casting process to provide a hard surface bearing against the cam. They are hollow and usually have 'windows' that help to reduce weight and assist lubrication. The tappet shown at (a) is suitable for a side valve and has a hardened adjusting screw to adjust the valve clearance. That shown at (b) is suitable for an OHV engine and operates a push rod, the lower end of which is located in the small hollow formed inside the base of the tappet. Both of these types of tappet operate directly in the cylinder block.

Figure 2.89c shows an earlier type of tappet for a side-valve engine. This type is usually made of steel and is carried in a detachable tappet block attached to the cylinder block by screws.

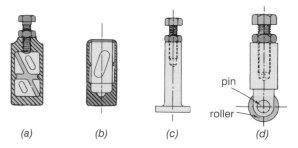

Figure 2.89 Types of tappet

These three types of tappet, and all tappets having a flat base, are used with cams that have convex curved flanks. Some cams have straight flanks, and these operate on followers having curved ends. In some cases, the tappet has a roller rotating on a pin (Figure 2.89d). This type is now seldom used, since for high-speed engines the roller must revolve much more rapidly round the flanks and nose than it does around the base circle, and at high engine speeds the angular accelerations of the roller involved are greater than can be achieved, and a considerable amount of skidding occurs. This being so, the more expensive roller construction might just as well be dispensed with and a plain rounded tappet base substituted. An additional weakness of this roller type is the pin, which is subjected to high shearing loads. Increasing the pin diameter to make it stronger raises the rubbing speed between pin and roller, and little is gained compared with a plain tappet. For low-speed engines, however, a roller tappet may have advantages.

Flat-based tappets are usually allowed to rotate in their guides; indeed, they are encouraged to do so since this reduces the rubbing speed between cam and tappet and spreads the wear over the whole of

the tappet base. Rotation of the tappet is encouraged by offsetting the tappet from the centre line of the cam or by grinding the cams with a very slight taper (about 1°), in which case the foot of the tappet is ground very slightly convex, forming part of a sphere of large radius. Roller tappets and curved-ended tappets must not, of course, rotate on their axes, and some means of positively preventing rotation must be provided.

OHC cam followers

Camshaft followers need to be strong so are usually made of steel. In OHC engines, where the cam is in line with (or above) the valve stem, the followers are arranged so that they sit directly over the valve and valve spring assembly. They are positioned between the cam and the valve stem in a machined bore in the cylinder head (Figure 2.90).

A pre-sized spacer or shim between the top of the valve stem and the internal face of the follower adjusts the clearance between the camshaft lobe and the camshaft follower. The shim thickness is carefully selected during the manufacturing stage of the engine to ensure the correct clearance is achieved. During service, this clearance will change, becoming too large or too small, due to the wear of engine components. To adjust this clearance, the technician takes measurements of the current clearance using a tool called feeler blades (Figure 2.91). When the measurement is taken, the most suitable shim will be chosen and replaced to bring the working clearance back to the manufacturer's standard. Some other camshaft followers fitted to OHC engines include a tapered adjusting screw that screws into the follower from the side and effectively replaces the shim. This type is far easier to alter and adjust the working clearance as no components

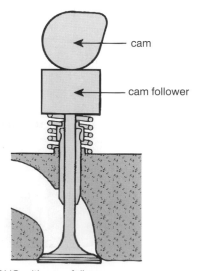

Figure 2.90 OHC with cam follower

need to be removed. Other types of OHC systems use hydraulic camshaft followers and rockers that act as cam followers. Figure 2.87 shows a typical example of a system using rockers acting as the camshaft followers.

Figure 2.91 Feeler blades

2.9.4 Hydraulic followers

Engine temperature depends on the operating conditions; as a result, the change in valve clearance is considerable. Setting of a clearance to suit an engine during its warm-up period will alter drastically when the engine is subjected to a period of high-speed or high-load use. This clearance variation will result in excessive noise and the change in valve timing will alter the power output.

Figure 2.92 shows the layout and operating principle of one type of hydraulic follower. The follower body (1) contains a plunger (2), which is formed into two chambers: a feed chamber (3) and a pressure chamber (4). Oil from the main lubrication system is passed to the feed chamber and then to the pressure chamber via a one-way ball valve (5). The oil flow from the pressure chamber is controlled by the amount of clearance between the follower body and the plunger. By accurately setting this clearance, a given amount of oil is allowed to escape up the side of the plunger each time the follower is operated. A follower spring (6) tends to force the plunger out of the follower body but, although this spring reduces the valve clearance to zero, it does have the strength to operate the engine valve.

When the valve is being opened (Figure 2.93a) oil in the pressure chamber is trapped, since the ball valve will not allow it to return back to the feed chamber. As a result, the upward movement of the tappet body pressurises the oil and causes the plunger to be moved a similar amount. During this stage, the follower behaves like a solid cam follower.

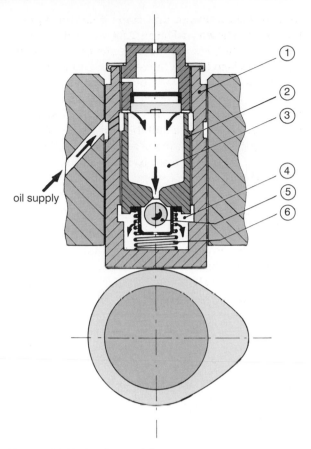

oil supply

Figure 2.92 Hydraulic cam follower

After the engine valve has closed (Figure 2.93b), the small leakage up the side of the plunger during the time that the oil was pressurised will mean that the pressure chamber requires more oil to make up for the oil loss. This is provided by allowing fresh oil from the feed chamber to pass the ball valve until the chamber is filled. During engine warm-up, the engine valve expands and this decreases the volume of oil in the pressure chamber needed to take up the play between the cam and the engine valve. This occurs over a period of time and is compensated for by the slight oil loss from the pressure chamber that occurs every time the tappet is operated. Consequently, zero valve clearance and correct seating of the valve is achieved irrespective of the temperature of the engine.

Slight oil loss from the follower occurs when the engine is unused for a period and this causes the followers to sometimes rattle for a short time after the engine is started. If this noise persists for more than about 10 seconds, the faulty cam followers should be replaced.

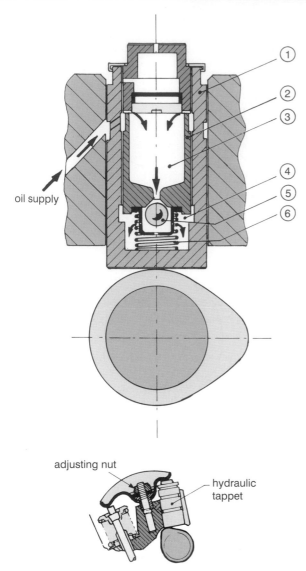

Figure 2.93 Hydraulic follower operation

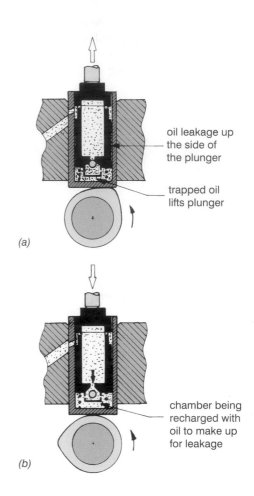

2.9.5 Push rods, rockers and OHC systems

Rocker assemblies are sometimes used instead of tappets and followers between the camshaft and valve; this arrangement can amplify the movement given by the cam by using different length rockers as levers. Valve clearance is adjusted by the screw at the pivot, or by mounting the rocker pivot (or the bush) eccentrically. Figure 2.94 illustrates two types. In Figure 2.94a an adjusting screw is shown as the means of adjusting the valve clearance. In the arrangement shown in Figure 2.94b the eccentric bush is a close fit in the rocker, but can be rotated in the rocker by a hexagonal flange at one end. The other end of the bush is threaded, and the bush is locked in the rocker by tightening a nut on this threaded end. To adjust the clearance, slacken the nut, rotate the bush to give the correct clearance and re-tighten the nut.

Figure 2.93 shows a layout that incorporates a hydraulic follower to operate a lightweight pressed steel rocker arm. No provision is made for manual adjustment because the hydraulic follower automatically takes up any clearance in the valve train. Each layout must contain some system of lubrication to reduce wear of the rubbing surfaces. Seals fitted to the valve stems ensure that oil used to lubricate the rocker assembly does not pass down the valve guides.

Many engines used to have OHVs operated by a camshaft in the crankcase, close to the crankshaft. This arrangement necessitates the use of push rods and overhead rockers to transmit the motion from the tappets to the valves, the usual arrangement being as illustrated in Figure 2.95a. The rockers pivot on a common rocker spindle supported in pillars attached to the cylinder head, and the rockers are spaced apart on the spindle by distance pieces, springs, or both. Valve clearance is adjusted by a hardened ball-ended screw in the end of the rocker, the screw fitting into a small cup formed in the top

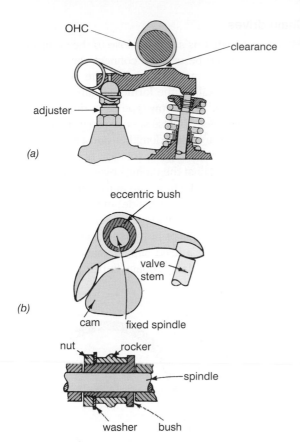

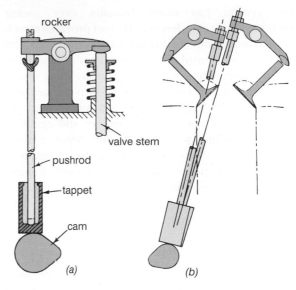

Figure 2.95 Push-rod operation on OHVs

Figure 2.94 Valve rocker with OHC

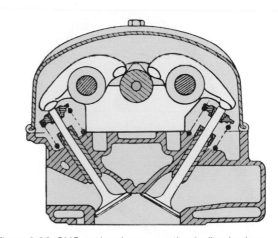

Figure 2.96 OHC and rockers operating inclined valves

end of the push rod; the cup retains oil to ensure lubrication at this point. The lower end of the push rod is ball-ended and is located in a cup formed in the tappet. Other more complex arrangements involved the rockers acting at right angles to the follower and push rod. This arrangement allowed for the valves to enter into the cylinder at greater angles (Figure 2.95b).

Rocker and push-rod construction

The rocker is usually made from a steel forging, but is sometimes formed from a steel pressing, and some are made in a special type of cast steel. The push rod may be made of a solid steel rod, the two ends being suitably 'formed' from the rod itself. Alternatively, the push rod may be tubular, of either steel or aluminium alloy, with separate hardened steel ends pressed on.

OHCs using direct-acting valve operation

Figure 2.96 shows an OHC where the valve arrangement is inclined. Here, rockers are operating the inclined valves. However, it is often preferred in engines with inclined valve arrangements to operate them by a camshaft positioned directly over each row of valves. This is called a double overhead camshaft (DOHC) system, as illustrated in Figure 2.97.

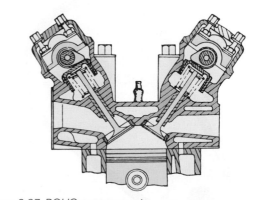

Figure 2.97 DOHC arrangement

This system has many benefits over rocker assemblies, as it uses fewer parts and provides direct-acting opening and closing actuation of the inlet and exhaust vales. The lobes of the cam act directly on the cam followers, which act directly on the valve stems. The system is now common on modern engines as it allows for higher engine speeds and lower emissions. The valve operation is both positive and accurate and the system is lighter, having fewer moving parts, allowing high engine speeds to be reached. To improve the power and emissions further, many manufacturers also incorporate variable valve timing technology (see page 145), as well as replace standard followers with hydraulic cam followers.

2.9.6 Camshaft drives

In an engine working on the four-stroke cycle, each valve must open once every two revolutions of the crankshaft, which makes it necessary for the camshaft to rotate at half-crankshaft speed (i.e. the speed ratio of crankshaft to camshaft is 2:1).

Chain drives

When the camshaft is situated close to the crankshaft, a short chain can be used to connect the crankshaft sprocket to the camshaft sprocket, the latter having twice as many teeth as the former (Figure 2.98a). The chain is either a single row-type or a duplex with a double row of rollers. Unless special provision is made, wear will cause the chain to lengthen and a rattling noise will be heard as the irregular rotation of the camshaft slaps the chain against the timing cover. Compensation for wear is achieved by fitting an automatic adjuster to rub on the non-driving (slack side) of the chain. Figure 2.98b shows a spring blade adjuster and in Figure 2.98c a hydraulic-type of automatic adjuster is used in conjunction with a fixed slipper made of a plastic material; the slipper damps chain 'flutter'.

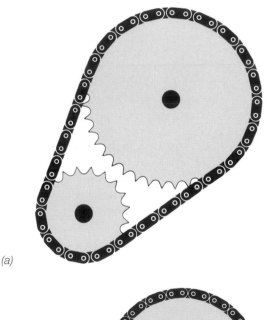

(a)

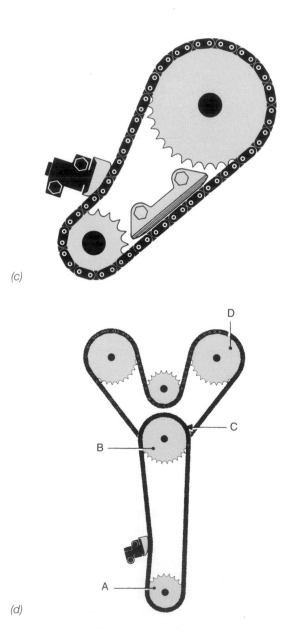

(c)

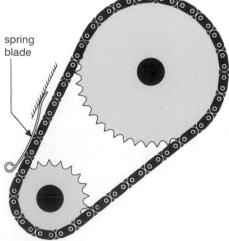

(b)

(d)

Figure 2.98 Camshaft chain drives

The camshaft is sometimes carried on the cylinder head and this means that a longer and more complex driving arrangement is necessary. The system used should operate with minimum noise and also must allow for thermal expansion of the block and head. Figure 2.88d shows a two-stage chain layout suitable for driving twin camshafts. In this case, the sprockets A, B, C and D give a speed ratio of $B/A \times D/C = 2:1$.

Automatic adjuster

The construction of the Renold short centre distance (SCD) auto adjuster is shown in Figure 2.99. The plunger in this compact-type of adjuster is forced against the chain by hydraulic oil pressure to compensate for chain wear, but return travel of the plunger is resisted by a ratchet. This non-return feature overcomes the need for undue pressure on the chain, which would cause power loss and extra wear.

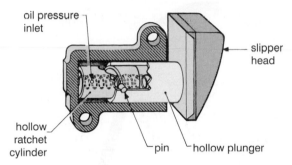

Figure 2.99 Renold SDC hydraulic adjuster

The rubber slipper head is bonded to a hollow plunger, which has a peg that engages in a helical slot in the ratchet cylinder. Oil pressure, supplied from the lubrication system, acts on the plunger to assist the spring in tensioning the chain. When chain wear occurs, the movement of the plunger causes the peg to push on the smooth face of the helical slot in the hollow ratchet and rotate the ratchet a small amount. Oil trapped in the adjuster acts as a damper and seepage past the plunger lubricates the chain. Return of the plunger in excess of that required to allow for thermal expansion is resisted by the peg engaging in one of the notches in the groove of the hollow ratchet.

Provision is usually made for the technician to lock the plunger to the ratchet for engine assembly purposes.

Figure 2.100 shows a characteristic layout of chain drive for an OHC engine. The camshaft is driven by a chain and this drives a second camshaft via gears. In a SOHC engine, the drive chain for the camshaft would be similar to Figure 2.100, but there would be no gear drive to the second camshaft. The second camshaft drive gear is one method of providing a drive to an engine with DOHC. On this arrangement, the chain is long. A guide is provided for it on the drive side

(which is the right-hand side in this example) to prevent the chain from moving out of alignment. A hydraulic tensioner acts on a tensioner blade on the slack side of the chain to ensure that the chain stays tight and to prevent any lashing during operation.

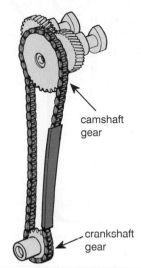

Figure 2.100 Chain drive to an OHC incorporating a gear drive to a second camshaft

A chain drive arrangement can still be used on DOHC engines where the camshafts are located further apart, but they will need a longer chain that will pass from the crankshaft and across two camshaft sprockets, one on each camshaft (Figure 2.101). This type of chain drive is used on many engines today, as it provides much longer service life than the belt arrangement described on page 86. To ensure that the chain tension is maintained, a tensioner is needed along with a chain guide to make sure that the chain does not move from the required path. Some early DOHC engines incorporated more intricate drive arrangements using two chains. One of the chains drove a camshaft drive sprocket from the crankshaft at a 2:1 ratio and the other chain took the drive from the camshaft drive sprocket to the twin camshafts at a 1:1 ratio. This design was seen on the Jaguar XK engine, which had a service life of over 40 years. This layout is shown in Figure 2.102.

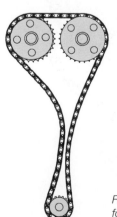

Figure 2.101 Chain drive arrangement for a DOHC engine

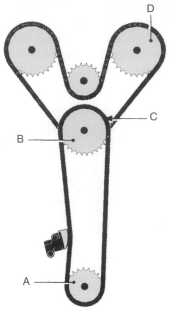

Figure 2.102 Complex chain drive for a DOHC engine

Gear drives

When the camshaft is fitted close to the crankshaft, a gear layout similar to that of Figure 2.103 gear drive can be used. Spur gears are noisy, so helical teeth are generally used. Sometimes the large camshaft gearwheel is made of a plastic material and, in cases where the distance is large, an idler gear is fitted. This type of arrangement is also seen on more modern engines using the READ arrangement mentioned in on page 60.

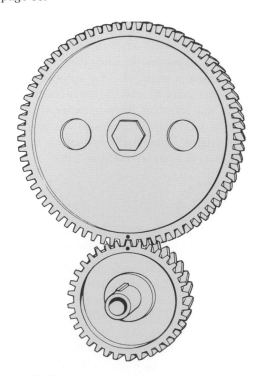

Figure 2.103 Camshaft gear drive

Belt drives

OHC engines are often driven by a rubber belt. The belt is notched to form teeth to maintain the correct valve timing (Figure 2.104). This type of drive is a cheap, quiet and efficient way of driving a camshaft that is mounted far away from the crankshaft. Also, this method enables the drive to be easily disconnected when the cylinder head has to be removed. Breakage of the belt can cause a problem especially if the piston strikes an open valve, but reinforced belt materials make belt breakage a rare occurrence. If the timing belt is removed for any engine repairs and is to be reused, the direction of the rotation should be noted to ensure that the belt is refitted in exactly the same way. Generally, if the engine repair requires the belt to be removed, it is good practice to change the belt for economical and engine safety reasons. The timing belt will often also

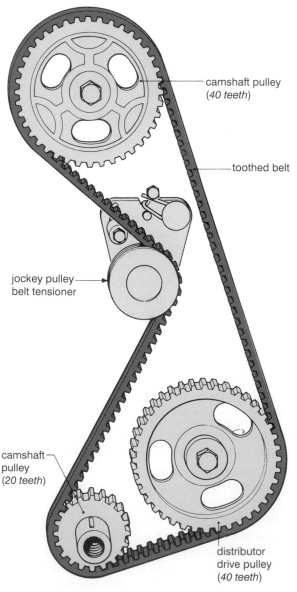

camshaft pulley
(*40 teeth*)

toothed belt

jockey pulley
belt tensioner

camshaft
pulley
(*20 teeth*)

distributor
drive pulley
(*40 teeth*)

Figure 2.104 Camshaft belt drive

drive other engine components, such as water pumps. Timing belts should always be replaced at the intervals recommended by the manufacturer, as failure of this important component is often very expensive.

Figure 2.105 shows two arrangements using a DOHC engine. This is similar to the chain drive arrangement shown previously. The first camshaft is driven by a belt; with gears taking the drive from the first to the second camshaft (Figure 2.105a). The second example is more conventional and uses the belt to drive both camshafts.

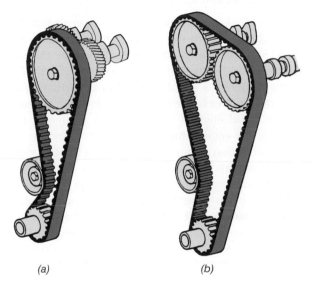

(a)   (b)

Figure 2.105 Two types of belt drive arrangement for a DOHC engine

Setting the valve timing

Whenever the camshaft drive is disconnected, the valves must be retimed to ensure that they open and close at the correct time in relation to the piston position. Timing gears and sprockets are normally marked, but where not, as in the case of a belt drive, the method is to set the camshaft and the crankshaft to the recommended positions before the drive is connected. Some manufacturers incorporate the facility to add locking pins to the drive gear to ensure that each gear is set in the correct position before removing the belt.

The new belt is then fitted and the locking pins are removed. It is very important to follow the manufacturer's instructions when fitting a new belt, as incorrect fitting may cause the engine to run incorrectly or even damage the engine.

Camshaft sprocket and gear attachment

The camshaft sprocket needs to be located securely on to the camshaft to avoid any movement while the engine is in operation. The usual method is to use the Woodruff key in a similar arrangement to the crankshaft pulley. Some camshaft sprockets are

located by the use of a taper seat arrangement. As the sprocket is tightened using the correct torque settings, the taper seat between the camshaft and the sprocket creates a secure locking of the two components. Other arrangements include the use of splines on the camshaft and sprocket to create and secure fitment.

2.10 Intake manifolds

2.10.1 Function of the intake manifold

Put as simply as possible, the function of the intake manifold in a petrol engine vehicle is to distribute the fresh charge of air and fuel to the individual cylinders of a multi-cylinder engine, and in a diesel engine to distribute the air supply to the individual cylinders where this meets with the injected fuel. There are, however, several difficulties to be overcome in designing a satisfactory intake manifold – difficulties so complex that one engine designer remarked that 'a certain amount of what can only be termed witchcraft is apparent' in the development of the intake manifold. These difficulties will be considered in two stages.

Airflow

If a single, straight, open-ended pipe is connected to the intake port of a single-cylinder engine, and the engine is driven by an electric motor, the engine will draw air through the pipe during its induction stroke. Towards the end of the induction stroke, the momentum of the gas in the intake pipe causes the gas to continue to flow towards the cylinder even after the piston has passed BDC. This inward flow of gas, combined with the upward movement of the piston at the beginning of the next stroke, causes a rise in pressure of the gas in the cylinder, which stops the inward flow of gas. This is the point at which the intake valve should close. If the valve timing is 'correct', the pressure at the port end of the intake pipe will be higher than the pressure at the open end, and this will cause the air to rebound away from the port, setting up an airflow along the pipe away from the closed valve. If the valve closes too late, this reverse flow will already have started before the valve closes. If the valve closes too early, the momentum of the gas will cause it to build up pressure at the valve end of the port still further, producing the same result – a reverse flow.

During this reverse flow, the gas will acquire momentum, which will cause the flow to continue until the pressure at the port end of the pipe falls below atmospheric pressure, and this will in turn cause a second rebound of gas into the port. These reversals of airflow in the pipe will continue for some time if there is little or no opposition to flow (the time for one complete oscillation depending upon the length of the pipe).

By selecting a suitable length of pipe, it is possible to arrange that, at the moment the intake valve opens, the gas in the pipe is moving towards the cylinder. The result is that more gas will get into the cylinder than would be the case if the gas was moving away from the port at the moment the valve opened, and a useful gain in power will be obtained. This, however, will only occur at one engine speed, and at other speeds the reverse effect will be produced. While this can be very usefully applied to engines required to deliver high power outputs over a very narrow speed range, such as racing engines, it is impractical for engines, such as those used in ordinary vehicles, which are expected to give good results over a wide range of speeds. To achieve this objective, the intake manifold should not be too long, and the length of pipe between the throttle body and each cylinder should be the same as near as possible.

Finally, to obtain the best flow of gas into the cylinder, the pipe should be of a large diameter and all bends should be gentle.

Petrol engine and diesel engine design differences

When looking at intake manifolds, it is useful to separate the design between petrol engines and diesel engines. In most petrol engines, the intake manifolds use a throttle valve or **butterfly valve** to control the volume of air passing to the engine. The throttle valve gives the driver control of the engine power by allowing the air to enter the manifold at a rate dependent on the need of the driver, which leads to the power required. This is usually controlled via a cable from the throttle pedal to the throttle valve, but new vehicles often now have the throttle valves controlled electronically (see page 227).

Butterfly valve: a disc that spins on its axis across the diameter of a pipe to regulate flow through the pipe.

Earlier engines used carburettors to add fuel to the engine at a suitable metered rate. These usually had the butterfly valve located within the carburettor body. Petrol engines today are fitted with fuel-injection systems; these still require a throttle mechanism and therefore a butterfly valve. The valve is usually fitted at the entrance to the intake manifold and is often called a 'throttle body assembly'. The fuel is added to the engine through the use of individual fuel injectors. The fuel injectors are normally fitted into the intake manifold where it locates against the cylinder head and intake ports.

Diesel engines only require air, rather than air and fuel, to be channelled to the engine. This is because the diesel fuel is delivered direct to each cylinder through injectors located directly in the cylinder head. The intake manifold is simply a means of distributing air from the air filter to the intake ports for each cylinder. Earlier diesel engines controlled the volume of fuel entering the engine through the injectors by the use of a distribution pump, so the use of a throttle valve was not required. Modern diesel engines do, however, tend to make use of throttle systems as they utilise injectors in a similar way to petrol injection, often called **common rail**. This refers to the injectors working from a common injection rail (Figure 2.107). So, there is a similarity with the petrol engine in that a throttle body may form part of the manifold to meter the amount of air entering the engine.

Common rail: arrangement in a diesel engine that uses a single pressurised fuel rail to supply fuel to the diesel injectors.

The use of variable length manifolds is now common to ensure that the correct gas flow is obtained at a range of engine speeds, further improving the performance and efficiency of the engine. This is described in more detail on page 94.

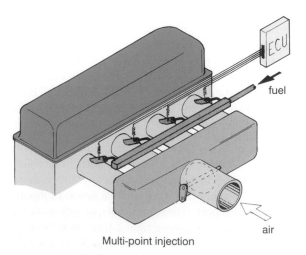

Multi-point injection

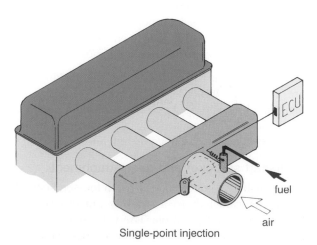

Single-point injection

Figure 2.106 Typical arrangement for a manifold with petrol fuel injection

Figure 2.107 Common rail diesel arrangement

Behaviour of fuel spray

It is the presence of the fuel spray in the air passing along the manifold that is responsible for most difficulties in the system. Since liquid fuel is much denser than air, it has a much greater disinclination to change either its speed or direction. Therefore, where changes of speed or direction occur in the manifold, the air responds to these changes much more quickly than the fuel.

Unless the speed of the flow of mixture along the manifold is kept at a fairly high level, the fuel spray tends to settle out on the floor and walls of the manifold and fuel will then not reach the cylinders in a form in which it can easily be vaporised.

It is thus clear that the cross-sectional area of the manifold must be small enough to ensure that the flow of mixture through it is sufficiently rapid to maintain the fuel spray in suspension in the air, even at low engine speeds: this is contrary to what is required to obtain the best filling of the cylinders.

There are three other factors that influence the extent to which the fuel remains in suspension in the airstream:

1 The fineness of atomisation of the fuel.
2 The pressure (or depression) in the manifold.
3 The temperature of the mixture in the manifold.

The finer the atomisation, the less likely are the fuel particles to separate out from the air, but a greater amount of evaporation will take place in the manifold. Evaporation within the manifold is undesirable because it reduces the weight of air and fuel that can be entered into the cylinder and the internal cooling due to vaporisation of the fuel inside the cylinder is lost. Since the fineness of the spray depends upon

the speed of airflow through the choke tube, the spray is coarsest when the speed of the mixture through the manifold is lowest (i.e. both conditions are at their worst at low speeds), and any attempt to improve either or both at low speeds merely reduces the possible power output at high speeds.

The lower the pressure or, put another way, the higher the depression in the manifold, the more rapidly the fuel evaporates in the manifold. Here, again, conditions are worst at low speeds and wide throttle openings.

Heating of the mixture encourages evaporation in the manifold and so helps to keep the fuel in suspension in the air, but it also reduces the possible power output for the reason stated above and because it reduces the density of the air. In this case, however, conditions are rather better, provided the heating is applied via the walls of the manifold, because the faster the mixture travels through the manifold the less time it has to absorb heat, and the mixture will pick up more heat under those conditions when it will be most helpful (i.e. at low speeds).

2.10.2 Features of manifold design

Enough has been said to indicate that manifold design is so complex that it is not possible to design one standard length and cross-sectional area of pipe that gives satisfaction under all conditions, and it is to be expected that a great deal of variation in manifold design will be found on vehicle engines.

For what may be called the normal types of vehicle engines, smoothness and economy are of more importance than sheer power. Thus, the manifold will be designed to provide the best possible distribution of mixture, both as to quantity and equality of air/fuel ratio, among the individual cylinders. Features that contribute to this are as follows:

1 Suitably sized pipe to maintain reasonably high mixture speeds at low engine speeds.
2 Introduce corners rather than gentle bends where changes in direction occur. The turbulence created at these corners assists in keeping the fuel in suspension in the air.
3 A fairly short manifold to avoid marked gain in power at one speed at the expense of a marked loss at some other speed.
4 Some means of applying heat to the manifold walls.

Manifold heating

Applying heat to the manifold and using this heat to vaporise the fuel is essential if the fuel mixture is to be evenly distributed to all cylinders, easily ignited and completely burnt. Moderate heating is required because excessive heat, as used in the past when the exhaust gases were made to come into contact with the intake manifold at a hot spot, lowers the volumetric efficiency (VE) (i.e. it reduces the ratio of the volume of air induced per cylinder per cycle to the swept volume of the cylinder.)

Heat is transferred to the manifold in three ways:

1 Conduction from the cylinder block through the manifold gasket.
2 Conduction from the coolant circulated through a jacket that surrounds the intake manifold.
3 Electronic heater located in the intake manifold.

In the first two options for heating the intake manifold, the conducted heat is absent until the engine warms up, so in addition to being provided with an extra-rich mixture (with its associated pollution problems) the engine will also be operating at lower power. The third option of fitting an electrically powered heating device assists in reducing the need for rich mixtures, so produces higher pollution for a minimum time during engine start-up from cold.

Figure 2.108 shows a water-heated manifold. Water from the coolant system is piped to a jacket adjacent to the carburettor and then returned by another pipe to the coolant system. An alternative design incorporates most of the intake manifold in the water jacket of the engine block.

Figure 2.108 Water-heated manifold

2.10.3 Typical manifolds

Various aspects of manifold design can be illustrated by studying some of the layouts used during recent years. These examples examine the use of carburettors and fuel injection, as the use of carburettors allows us to understand airflow in greater detail.

Four-cylinder in-line engines

The layouts shown in Figure 2.109 indicate various manifold arrangements that can be used for a four-cylinder engine.

Figure 2.109a is the cheapest arrangement and it was commonly used in the past for the more basic types of engine. Since the intake valves for cylinders 1 and 2 and cylinders 3 and 4 are adjacent to each other, the intake ports in the cylinder head can be joined together, or **siamesed**. This simplifies the head casting and allows a two-branch manifold to be used. For the majority of intake manifolds, aluminium alloy is used because the excellent thermal conductivity of this material allows the manifold to warm up quickly; also it is a lightweight metal. However, the siamesed arrangement has two serious limitations:

1 Poor VE due to the restriction of the gas flow caused by the large number of bends.
2 Severe induction robbery due to the overlap of induction strokes that occur in adjacent cylinders.

Siamesed: term used to describe the design of the exhaust and inlet ports as they are joined together to provide a simpler exhaust or inlet manifold and cylinder head design. The design allows one exhaust port, for example, to link two cylinders' exhaust ports together. This means that the manifold to this exhaust port carries both cylinders' exhaust gases away, leading to a simpler design and reduced production costs.

Power produced by an engine depends on the quantity of gas that can be charged into the cylinder during the induction stroke. For this reason, a high VE is a prime objective when designing an intake manifold. Since sharp bends in the tract reduce gas flow, an ideal manifold from a VE aspect should have gas paths as straight as possible.

Induction robbery, as the name suggests, means that some cylinders do not get their full share of new gas. Consequently, the total power output from the engine is low and the variation in power from the cylinders reduces the smooth running of the engine.

One of the two robbery periods can be seen by considering an engine with siamesed ports and a firing order of 1342. Bearing in mind that each intake valve opens early and closes very late, there is a large crank angle when the intake valves of cylinders 3 and 4 are open simultaneously. Towards the end of the induction stroke of cylinder 3, at high engine speeds the gas will be flowing freely into the cylinder at a very fast rate. Opening the valve in cylinder 4 will not encourage the gas to change its direction, so cylinder 4 will be starved of fuel until the valve in cylinder 3 has closed. This action is repeated for cylinders 2 and 1, so robbery occurs in two crank positions of the cycle. Both firing orders used on this design of manifold give similar robbery effects.

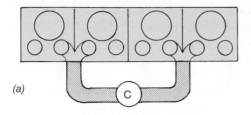

(a)

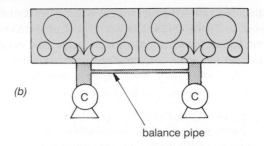

(b)

balance pipe

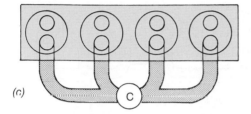

(c)

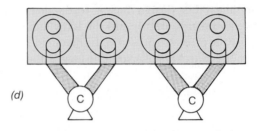

(d)

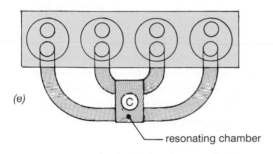

(e)

resonating chamber

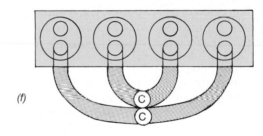

(f)

C = carburettor

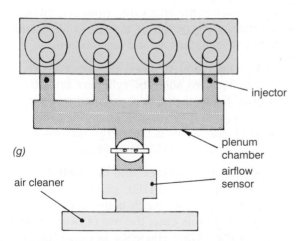

(g)

injector

plenum chamber

airflow sensor

air cleaner

Figure 2.109 Intake manifold layouts – four cylinders

On engines with carburettors and multi-branch manifolds, it is important that they have the throttle spindle parallel with the engine axis to avoid one branch being starved of mixture during part-throttle operation.

Figure 2.109b uses twin carburettors and, owing to the straighter air passages, the VE is raised, especially at high engine speeds. Robbery is still a problem here, and the irregular airflow through each carburettor requires a slightly richer mixture than before. The two separate manifolds are normally interconnected by a balance pipe, which gives smoother idling by equalising the depression in each manifold.

The cylinder head layout used in Figure 2.109c can be fitted with many different manifold arrangements. These options are often used by manufacturers to provide a range of engines, each with different power characteristics, to suit cars from the base model to the top-of-the-range carburettor version. The elimination of the siamesed ports overcomes the problem of robbery provided the individual tracts of the manifold are of adequate length.

Ideally, each cylinder should receive the same amount of air. The ratio of petrol and air should be identical and the additives contained in the fuel should not vary in quantity between the cylinders. The term 'distribution' is used to describe the ability of a manifold to meet these requirements, so the layout shown in Figure 2.109c gives a better distribution than the first layout. Although the layout is an improvement, the unequal length tracts mean that the distribution is still far from ideal. This is because the cylinders closest to the carburettor receive both a slightly richer and a larger quantity of mixture.

High power output at high speeds is the aim of the layout shown in Figure 2.109d. As with most applications of twin carburettors on four-cylinder engines, the irregular induction impulses through the carburettor generally result in higher fuel consumption than the single-carburettor version, but distribution is very good.

Figure 2.109e is a layout that uses only one carburettor to achieve good VE and distribution. As a result, a lively engine with good fuel consumption is obtained.

Sometimes this design has a resonating chamber between the carburettor and the individual tracts to amplify the pressure pulses in the manifold. Assuming the manifold tract is of a suitable length, these pulses build up a positive pressure in the region of the manifold side of the intake valve at the instant the intake valve opens.

The layout shown in Figure 2.109f has a twin-choke carburettor, with each choke supplying two cylinders in order to obtain a high power. The regular induction impulses through each choke improve the mixture quality, and any interference to flow due to robbery is eliminated.

In the past, the way to achieve good VE and ensure that each cylinder received its full share of mixture was to fit one carburettor to each cylinder. This was a very expensive and temperamental system that required constant balancing in order to keep the output of each carburettor equal to the others. The objectives and results of this layout can be equalled and improved by using a multi-point fuel-injection system (Figure 2.109g).

This layout passes air from a cleaner to a plenum chamber, which acts as an air reservoir and dampens the pressure pulsations. A chamber size of 0.8–1.2 of the engine capacity ensures a smooth flow of air through the airflow sensor so that it can accurately regulate the quantity of petrol to be injected. Fuel can be altered to many ratios across the engine speed and load requirements. This altering of fuel ratio is achieved by opening the injector longer or for shorter periods depending on the engine's needs. This provides greater control of fuel used and improves engine performance and lowers emission levels.

Six-cylinder in-line engines

The problems associated with four-cylinder manifolds are accentuated with long manifolds fitted to six-cylinder engines, so the power output and economy of this type of engine can be changed dramatically by altering the manifold layout. This point is illustrated by the two manifolds shown in Figure 2.110.

The siamesed port arrangement shown in Figure 2.110a uses a single intake and a three-branch manifold. This layout gives poor distribution as can

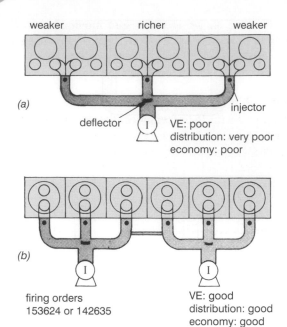

Figure 2.110 Intake manifold layouts – six cylinders

be verified by examining the sparking plugs after the engine has been in use: the two centre plugs normally have a sooty black deposit that indicates a rich mixture; the end plugs have a white deposit, which shows a weak mixture. With the addition of petrol fuel injection this issue is not as common, due to the intake manifold acting purely as a delivery tube of air to the cylinders and the fuel being injected directly onto the back of the inlet valve. However, this design can act as a restriction to airflow to all cylinders, creating an inefficient air and fuel mixture.

To avoid induction robbery, the firing order used must not fire two adjacent cylinders one after the other (i.e. if the engine is considered to be divided into two halves, the cylinders fire in the order: front, rear, front, rear). This is one of the reasons why the firing orders used are 153624 or 142635.

The use of twin intakes and a manifold layout, as shown in Figure 2.110b, gives a more costly arrangement but with much better distribution and a higher VE. In this case, the use of twin air intakes improves the engine efficiency because the airflow through the intake is regular and the fuel delivery is metered independently by each fuel injector.

Today, all vehicle engines utilise fuel injection to improve fuel distribution and VE. With each cylinder receiving fuel from an individual injector, there is much more control by the EMS in providing exactly the right amount of fuel for any given engine need. Now the intake manifold is simply providing a good clear route for the air to travel to the engine across all engine speeds. With fuel injection, we do not need the manifold to introduce as much swirl to mix the fuel and air as we are now just moving air to the cylinders. For this reason, the intake manifolds on fuel-injected engines are required to have smooth free-flowing tracts to transport the air.

Vee engines

Compared with in-line engines, the vee arrangement often gives a much shorter manifold design, due to the intake sitting above the engine feeding all cylinders. Some more modern engines can utilise very ornate shapes of manifolds to improve the length of the intake tracts, which improves engine performance and efficiency. They also introduce variable length manifolds to cater for different engine speeds. These are described later in this chapter.

Figure 2.111a shows a V6 layout with two tracts. Applying the firing order to the cylinder numbering system used shows that the banks fire: right, left, right, left, right, left. The interval between firing strokes in a given bank means that there is a similar interval between induction strokes.

A V8 manifold is shown in Figure 2.111b and, once again, the firing order and manifold shape are arranged to use each tract in alternate order so as to minimise the robbery caused by overlapping induction strokes.

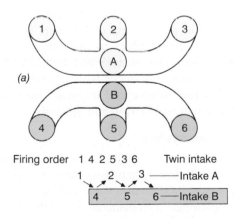

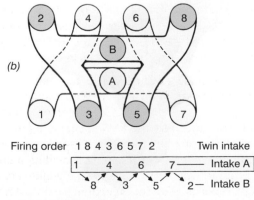

Figure 2.111 Vee engine intake manifolds

All engines utilising an electronic EMS will have one injector to feed fuel into the combustion chamber and usually incorporate twin intakes to feed fuel into each combustion chamber.

2.10.4 Manifold heaters

Fuel vaporisation is very poor during both the cold start and the warm-up period; this fact results in low power output, poor economy and high exhaust emissions.

To overcome the problem, many engines today are fitted with some form of electric heater to preheat the air and fuel as it passes through the intake manifold. Figure 2.112 shows two forms of heater that come into operation when the engine is below a set temperature and remain in use until the engine has warmed up. The heating element is switched on by the EMS when the ignition is switched on by the driver. The amount of time the heating element is switched on for is dependent on the outside air temperature. This is monitored by a temperature sensor, which sends a voltage signal to the EMS relative to the air temperature. When the temperature reaches a pre-determined limit, the EMS system will turn off the heater.

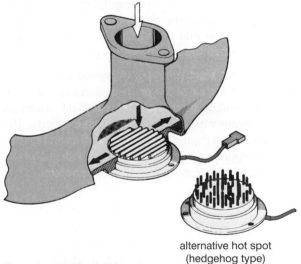

alternative hot spot (hedgehog type)

Figure 2.112 Manifold heaters

2.10.5 Induction systems for fuel injected engines

All engines now use multi-point fuel injection to meet the needs of the stringent emission regulations and provide the necessary power and efficiencies required from today's engines. By positioning the injectors very near to the intake ports on each cylinder head, precise control of the amount of fuel delivered is achieved. This provides excellent control of the whole engine's fuelling requirements. As with engines fuelled by carburettors, the intake manifold's aim is to provide filtered air to each cylinder where this can be then mixed with the fuel as it enters the intake port of the engine.

At the inlet port of the manifold, there is a throttle housing with a throttle butterfly. This opens and closes with the movement of the driver's right foot on the accelerator through a cable or sometimes a motor. Air enters the intake manifold into a large chamber often referred to as a plenum chamber. This plenum chamber creates a large reservoir of air and also acts to dampen down the air shockwaves developed by the opening and closing intake and exhaust valves. Air is then fed down each inlet tract to the intake port on the cylinder head.

Variable induction manifolds

Intake manifolds play a very important part in the ability of an engine to operate at peak VE. The air moving down the manifold is disrupted by the oscillating action of the opening and closing intake valves. The intake valves create shockwaves, which can alter the ability of the engine to draw in the air at certain engine speeds. Fixed length manifolds create a balance between performance and efficiency, but with the ability to alter the length of the manifold intake tracts the engine is able to operate in a much greater band of power and efficiency. By designing the manifold to be able to change length through the inclusion of valves, the oscillations in the manifold can be tuned so that the airflow is moving towards the engine when the intake valve is opened.

A longer inlet tract provides improved ability to fill the engine with air at lower to medium speeds, and a shorter length tract provides excellent ability to fill the engine with air at higher engine speeds. The cxample seen in Figure 2.113 shows a V6 engine system that incorporates a throttle housing with a throttle butterfly, a balance valve and six power valves.

Utilising the benefits of the variable intake allows the system to maximise its functionality in the three driving conditions: low speed, mid-range and high speed.

Low speed

When the engine is driven at low engine speed, the power valve and balance valve will be in their closed position. Having the facility of separate plenum chambers and longer primary tract gives the engine the benefit of improving breathing as you would achieve on a two- or three-cylinder engine. Also, to maximise the peak torque at the lower end speed, the primary and secondary plenum volume is designed to resonate at 2700 rpm.

Mid-range

While in the mid-torque-range, the plenum chambers are joined by activating the use of the balance valve and keeping the power valves closed, which then provides the use of longer primary tracts. In turn, this will provide a greater amount of torque (up to 3750 rpm) and increase the mid-range performance.

High speed

When the engine speed then increases to the upper controlled limits, the six power valves and the balance valve are fully open. This then provides the engine the benefit of breathing through the short tract plenum via the short primary tract chamber. Allowing this to proceed gives the benefit of a better-controlled balance within the torque range of 4000 rpm to its maximum range of 6250 rpm. This also allows the induction system to improve part-load fuel consumption. This is achieved by controlling the pumping losses that occur within these cycles, providing a better balance and improved fuelling at part load, through to 4000 rpm and upwards.

Variable intake system

The variable intake system (VIS) features an electronic throttle, two electronic actuators and a manifold absolute pressure (MAP) sensor that are all incorporated within the lightweight inlet manifold assembly.

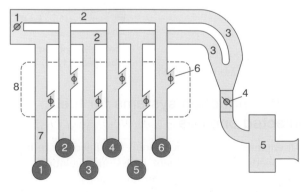

1   balance valve
2   main plenums
3   secondary tracts
4   throttle housing
5   air cleaner
6   power valves (6 off)
7   primary tracts
8   short tract plenum

Figure 2.113 Variable intake system fitted to a V6 engine

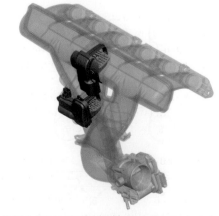

Figure 2.114 Inlet manifold with two electronic actuators

Naturally aspirated engines often have a smaller rpm range where the torque is high. On a turbocharged engine, where the incoming air to the cylinders is pressurised by the turbocharger unit and the over pressure enters the inlet manifold, a flat torque curve will be produced. This means that high torque is available over a large engine speed range.

For a naturally aspirated engine where the inlet manifolds correspond to prevailing atmospheric pressure, it is much harder to achieve high torque over a large engine speed range. Some of the functions that are used to achieve optimum filling of the cylinders are the variable camshaft timing (VCT) and adaptive inlet systems.

The VIS is usually used in conjunction with the VCT (see page 153) and camshaft profile switching (CPS) (see page 151) systems to control the airflow in the multi path inlet manifold to achieve optimum cylinder filling (volumetric efficiency).

Combining the VCT system allows the management system to maximise the opportunities of adjusting the inlet valves opening and closing periods. Common air pulsations are created within the inlet manifolds multipath system when the inlet valves are in their closed position. This is caused by the incoming air bouncing off the back of the inlet valves. The air pulsations can, if directed to the correct cylinder and the correct time, improve the engine's volumetric efficiency, achieving a high torque curve over a large speed range.

The air pulsations have, regardless of engine speed (rpm), a speed that corresponds to their frequency. By adjusting the route of the air pulsations through the inlet manifold tracks, it will be possible to synchronise the speed of the engine, ensuring that they arrive at the next cylinder to begin its next induction stroke at the correct time, and maximising the opportunity to provide optimum cylinder filling.

The VIS varies the length of the multipath inlet manifold to adjust the course of the inlet airflow and synchronise the frequency of the air pulse to the speed of the engine. The two electronic actuators control the direction of the airflow within the multipath inlet manifold. When controlling and combining the actuators' positions, from their fully open to fully closed position in relation to the engine speed, the air pulsations are then positively used throughout the engine's drive cycle demands. This in turn then provides optimum filling of the cylinders, which produces high torque over a wide engine speed range and greatly improve the engine's fuel efficiency.

Controlling the VIS actuators' positions, in principle, will produce three different torque curves. When the torque curves are combined, this produces a flat torque for a naturally aspirated engine, as shown in Figure 2.115.

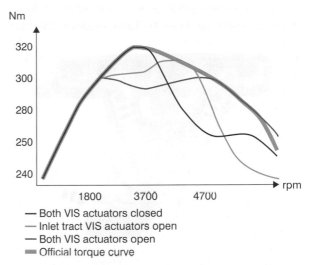

Figure 2.115 *Torque curve comparisons*

VIS principle of operation

Mounted within the inlet manifold main track assembly are the two electronic actuators, which are controlled by the electronic control unit (ECU).

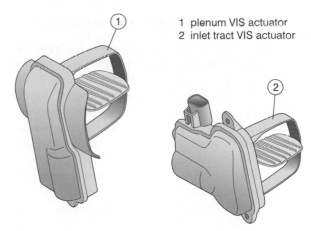

1 plenum VIS actuator
2 inlet tract VIS actuator

Figure 2.116 *VIS electronic actuators*

As previously mentioned, the VIS adjusts the length of the inlet track and plenum chamber using the two electronic actuators. The ECU can activate each of the actuators singularly or together to control the route of the airflow and so to maximise the inlet manifold's overall efficiency. The actuator will switch from an open position to a closed position on receiving an input signal from the ECU. The transmitted signal is switched, from a very low-level signal of about 1 V to a higher signal of around battery voltage, to open and close each of the actuators depending on the driving demands.

At engine speeds up to 2100 rpm, both of the actuators will be in their closed position. Cylinder filling is achieved by the exhaust gases leaving the combustion chamber, creating a low-pressure vacuum and enabling atmospheric pressure to force intake air into the cylinder at its correct period (Figure 2.117).

Figure 2.117 VIS operation up to 2100 rpm

At engine speeds from 2100 rpm up to 3800 rpm, both actuators are still set in the closed position. The air pulsations caused by closing of the inlet valves increases in frequency due to the high engine speed. The pulsations are forced around the multipath inlet system because the engine speed is still relatively low, so the pulsations have a long time to travel and reach the inlet valves on the next cylinder to begin its inlet stroke.

At engine speeds from 3800 rpm up to 4800 rpm, the inlet track actuator is cycled to the open position while the plenum chamber actuator remains in the closed position. The air pulsations caused by the closing of the inlet valves increase the frequency due to the higher engine speed. The pulsations are then forced through the short way, round the inlet manifolds multipath track. This is because the engine speed is higher, so the pulsations have a short time to reach the inlet valves on the next cylinder to begin its inlet stroke. This is shown in Figure 2.118.

Figure 2.118 VIS operation between 3800 rpm and 4800 rpm

At engine speeds above 4800 rpm, the inlet track actuator continues to stay open and the plenum actuator now also cycles to the open position. The air pulsations are determined by the short primary inlet pipes geometry, resulting in the total plenum volume being available to the entire cylinder (Figure 2.119). At this stage, the induction system is providing maximum airflow and supports the engine performance, depending on the driver's demands.

Figure 2.119 VIS operation above 4800 rpm

With the three systems working to providing optimum efficiency throughout the torque curve, the overall engine performance is maintained throughout its full rpm range and greatly improves the fuel consumption and emission control requirements.

2.11 Air cleaners and filters

2.11.1 Air cleaning and filtering systems

While an engine is running it will consume a very large volume of air, proportional to the engine capacity. This air may contain a large proportion of particles including dust, dirt, insects and moisture. These particles will find their way into the engine cylinders and mix with the lubricating oil to form an abrasive compound that will cause wear of pistons, cylinders and bearings. In an attempt to reduce such wear, air filters are generally fitted to the air intake system to remove these damaging particles.

These filters are often combined with intake silencers designed to eliminate or reduce the noise created by the airflow through the intake system. This noise varies from an intense hiss at small throttle openings to a roar at full throttle – often referred to as induction roar. Although generally this noise is limited in most vehicles, some sports cars are designed by

Figure 2.120 Air filter used on performance engine

Most filtering elements used in vehicles are now paper based. This filtering element is composed of a special grade of paper through which the air passing to the engine is drawn. A considerable area of paper surface is necessary to avoid restriction of the airflow. The necessary area is provided within a filter of reasonable size by making the paper into a large number of fine pleats as shown at (2) in Figure 2.121b.

This paper filtering element is surrounded by a pressed-steel frame and fitted into the lower part of the filter casing (4), and is enclosed by the cover (3) which is held in place by clips or screws. Air enters through the tube (6), passes through the paper element (2) and then to the carburettor through the connection (5). A silencing action is produced partly by the form of the tube (6) and also by the absorption of sound waves from the engine and carburettor by the paper element itself. An additional advantage of this type of filter is its small overall height.

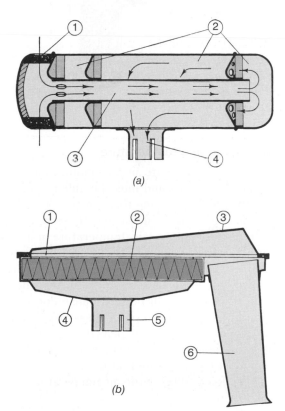

(a)

(b)

Figure 2.121 Typical simple air filter arrangement

the manufacturer to have a more tuned intake noise to provide the driver with a more 'sporty' sound enhancing the driving sensation. Intake noise levels are limited by legislation, so it is generally kept to a minimum. Manufacturers can get around this limitation by having intake systems that open separate valves at higher engine speeds and load, which then gives the more pronounced induction roar. At normal engine speeds the noise is kept to a minimum.

Figure 2.121a illustrates the construction of one type of air cleaner and silencer. Air first passes through the filtering element (1), which collects as much of the dust as possible, and then passes down the central tube (3) and into the throttle body or carburettor through the connection (4). The sound waves produced in the intake manifold are absorbed in the resonance chambers (2).

The filtering element shown in Figure 2.121 consists of a somewhat tangled mass of fine wire which is wetted with oil. As air threads its way through the wire mesh, dust sticks to the oil and the cleaned air passes on. Periodically (more often in very dusty conditions), the element should be thoroughly swilled in a can of paraffin (kerosene) to remove the trapped dirt. After drying, it should be dipped in clean oil and drained: this will leave a thin film of oil adhering to the wire mesh to collect more dirt.

Other materials used for filtering elements are cloth, felt and sponge. Most of these, like paper, cannot normally be cleaned and should be replaced at intervals as specified by the engine manufacturer. Some after-market filter elements, including the sponge type, can be cleaned using special soap. They are then dried and treated with a fine oil spray to provide finer filtering properties.

Some larger diesel engine vehicles utilise filter systems fitted with a vane arrangement within the filter cylindrical housing. As air enters the filter housing, a vortex is created which leads to the heavy dust particles being thrown outwards, creating a separation between the intake air. The cleaner air is drawn through the filter element into the intake manifold. This additional filtering action creates a much longer service life of the air filter element. Additional cleaning of the air filter housing is required during service. This extended service period is especially important with larger heavy goods vehicles that cover considerable miles.

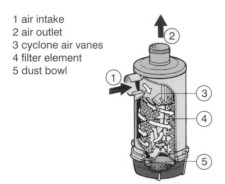

1 air intake
2 air outlet
3 cyclone air vanes
4 filter element
5 dust bowl

Figure 2.122 Typical simple air filter arrangement

Air cleaner intake temperature

Engines have to operate in an infinite number of operating conditions and must be able to perform efficiently whether driving through the hot Sahara Desert or frozen Iceland. During these operating conditions, the intake air temperature must be monitored and managed in the best possible way to ensure that the engine continues to deliver the power required. In very hot climates, the air entering the engine will be less dense due to the heat and will therefore contain less oxygen. The engine will not operate at its peak due to the lack of oxygen for combustion. In this instance, the intake system must try to ensure that the air entering the engine is cooled to bring the air temperature close to the optimum.

Some very basic systems using carburettors have an adjustable setting to change the intake from summer to winter by the means of a manually moved intake tube (6) (Figure 2.121b). This moves between picking air up from near the exhaust for winter to improve vaporisation and prevent icing in the intake and carburettor. The intake can then be moved towards the front of the vehicle for cooler air in the summer. In summer, the air is already hot, so further heating would result in low power, due to poor VE and overheating of the carburettor.

Automatic hot air intake system

Good vaporisation of the fuel is necessary if the vehicle is to conform to emission control regulations, so an automatic control is often fitted to ensure that the air intake temperature is correct.

The air cleaner has two intake tubes: one sited to induce cold air and the other tube set to receive hot air preheated by the exhaust manifold (Figure 2.123). Selection of the proportion of hot and cold air is by an air control flap valve, which is moved by a vacuum-operated diaphragm connected to the induction manifold. A thermo-valve mounted in the airstream in the air cleaner senses the temperature of the air entering the engine. When a given temperature is reached, say 25 °C, the thermo-valve opens and bleeds in air into the vacuum pipe. This destroys the depression in the diaphragm chamber and moves the valve towards the 'cool' position.

During slow-running and cruising conditions, the high manifold depression, for example above 50 **kPa**, will lift the diaphragm against the spring and move the air control vent to select hot air.

kPa: kilopascal – a measure of air pressure.

100 kPa = 1 atm = 1 bar = 14.7 psi

= atmospheric pressure at sea level

Air cleaner construction

The air cleaner is extremely important in ensuring the engine operates at its best and also has a long life. It is usually of a simple design. The filter is normally located in a housing, which is part of the whole intake system. This housing will be designed to improve airflow into the engine and also damp down any sound waves generated to lower the induction noise. The intake housing will affect the action of the airflow and reverse airflow (see page 89). The intake housing and associated components are all designed to work together to generate low noise, provide the engine with clean air, provide good engine performance and ensure that vehicle emissions are maintained at satisfactory levels during engine operation.

If the air filter is blocked or removed, this will have an adverse effect on engine performance. When looking at engines that are operating without any modifications, it is especially advisable to ensure that the manufacturer's standard air intake system is retained to ensure the engine performance is not affected.

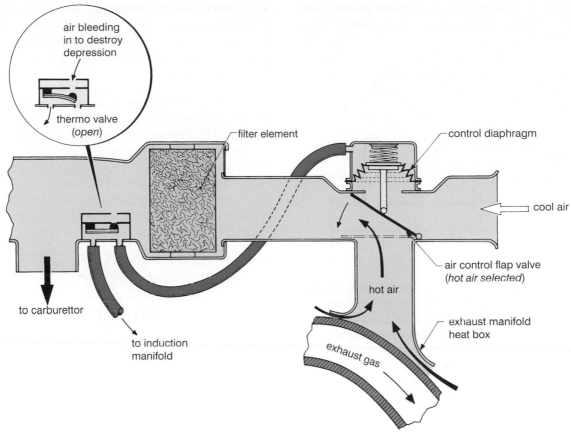

Figure 2.123 Automatic hot air intake system

2.12 Exhaust systems, silencers and catalytic converters

The exhaust system consists of four main parts and, in some newer diesel engines, a fifth part, which is designed to cut down on the particulates produced by burning diesel fuel.

1 The exhaust manifold – collects the exhaust gases from a number of cylinders and leads them to a single pipe.
2 The exhaust pipe – conducts the exhaust gases to a suitable point before discharging them into the air. This point is usually at the rear of the vehicle, but certain special types of vehicle (such as petrol tankers) may be required by law to discharge their exhaust gases at some other point.
3 The silencer – reduces the noise generated by the operating engine.
4 Catalytic converter – introduces a chemical and thermal reaction in the exhaust to reduce the level of unwanted gases produced through combustion.
5 Diesel particulate filter (DPF) – fits into the exhaust just after the exhaust manifold and before the catalytic converter. Its purpose is

to filter the diesel particulates produced by burning diesel fuel and prevent these from entering the atmosphere as they can cause breathing problems.

2.12.1 Exhaust manifolds

The exhaust manifold is designed to collect the gases produced by combustion from each cylinder and distribute them to the exhaust system. The manifold must do this in the most efficient way possible to prevent excessive back pressure in the exhaust system. When an engine is running at full throttle, the temperature of the exhaust gases may exceed 800 °C. To withstand such temperatures, exhaust manifolds are generally made of iron castings or fabricated from steel pipes and plate by welding.

Exhaust manifold design

The chief problem in the layout of an exhaust manifold is possible interference between cylinders. Consider the manifold shown in Figure 2.124, which is fitted to a four-cylinder engine having the firing order 1243. At the moment when piston 1 is approaching TDC at the end of its exhaust stroke, the momentum of the gas moving along the exhaust pipe should be helping to scavenge the burnt gas from the cylinder.

However, the exhaust valve of cylinder 2 would now be open and also discharging a cylinder full of burnt gas at high pressure into the manifold. The shape of the manifold will clearly result in some of this gas discharged from cylinder 2 entering cylinder 1, which will thus retain an unduly large proportion of burnt gas when its exhaust valve closes.

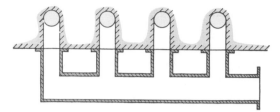

Figure 2.124 A simple exhaust manifold

The manifold shown in Figure 2.125 is an improvement on Figure 2.124, since the entry of each port into the manifold is curved so as to maintain an outward flow from each port rather than permit one port to blow back into another.

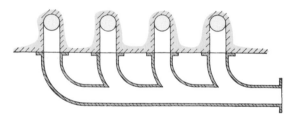

Figure 2.125 Improved exhaust manifold

Exhaust ports are sometimes siamesed to simplify and cheapen the cylinder head casting; a common arrangement is shown in Figure 2.126. Note the shaping of the end branches of the manifold to avoid interference between cylinders, and note also that this cannot occur between the cylinders served by the siamesed ports since, on a four-cylinder engine, exhaust strokes occur in these cylinders one revolution apart.

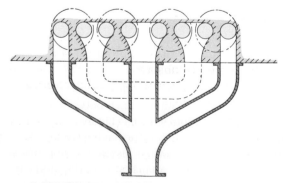

Figure 2.126 Exhaust manifold for a four-cylinder engine, one pair of exhaust ports siamesed

Interference can be completely avoided by having a separate pipe for each cylinder, but for ordinary cars and commercial vehicles this arrangement is too bulky and expensive. Furthermore, it is possible to use the gas pulsations from one cylinder to assist the flow of gas from another at certain engine speeds. This is done by joining separate pipes from each cylinder, first in pairs, making two pipes that are then joined into one. The lengths of the various sections of pipes are important, depending upon the engine speed at which the greatest benefit is desired; in a four-cylinder engine, the pairs of pipes to be joined are 1 and 4, and 2 and 3. Thus, when performance is an important consideration, a pipe layout similar to that shown in Figure 2.127 is used for a four-cylinder engine.

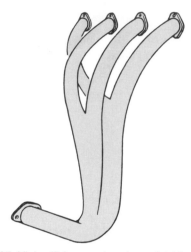

Figure 2.127 High-efficiency exhaust manifold for a four-cylinder engine

For six-cylinder engines, the cylinders that should be paired in this manner are 1 and 6, 2 and 5, and 3 and 4, but this is much more difficult to arrange compactly and neatly than in the case of a four-cylinder engine. It is, however, easy and convenient to use two manifolds: one for cylinders 1, 2 and 3; and the other for cylinders 4, 5 and 6, each of which groups have equally spaced firing intervals. The pipes from these two manifolds usually join at some distance from the manifolds, but in a few cases two completely independent exhaust systems are used, one for each group of three cylinders.

2.12.2 Exhaust pipes

Exhaust pipes are usually made of steel tubing, often protected against corrosion and oxidation by being coated with aluminium using a metal-spraying process.

Since engines are usually carried on flexible mountings, provision must be made for their movement relative to the frame. In some cases, there is a length of flexible exhaust piping between the pipes or manifolds bolted to the ports and the rear part of the pipe, which is attached to the frame by rigid brackets. Alternatively, the whole exhaust system is made up of rigid pipes and connections but is supported from the frame by flexible attachments, usually incorporating bonded rubber blocks.

Some high-performance vehicles have titanium exhaust pipes due to their excellent weight characteristics compared with steel. These are not widely fitted as they are very expensive.

Silencers (mufflers)

The exhaust noise of an 'un-silenced' engine is caused by the release of hot gas into the atmosphere in a series of high-pressure pulsations. This noise must be reduced to a level below the legal limit specified in the regulations.

Analysis of exhaust noise shows that, although it is made up of a number of different sounds or notes, it is possible to group the majority of the sounds into two main frequency bands:

1 Low frequency – caused by the air pumping action of the engine. This sound is also produced when the engine is motored over without combustion taking place.
2 High frequency – caused by the release and rapid expansion of very hot gas at a temperature of 800–1000 °C.

To damp these frequencies two silencers are needed: a capacity type for the low frequencies and an absorption type for the high frequencies.

Capacity-type silencers

Figure 2.128 shows this type. It consists of a large chamber in which the regular gas pulsations can be damped (smoothed out) by the bulk of gas contained in the chamber. Ideally, this expansion chamber should be large. However, because the available space often restricts the size, more than one capacity-type silencer is sometimes fitted. The damping of the low-frequency waves is achieved by fitting baffles to create a turbulent zone to break up the flow of gas in the silencer.

Baffles reduce the free flow of gas, so a bad design could cause a build-up of pressure in the exhaust system. This back pressure reduces engine power because any exhaust gas that is allowed to remain in the cylinder

(exhaust gas residual) will occupy space that would otherwise be filled with the fresh charge (i.e. a poor exhaust system can cause a reduction in the VE). The engine power suffers both from the loss of cylinder volume occupied by the exhaust gas residual, and from the heat of the burnt gas; the presence of this gas with its very high temperature heats the new charge as it enters, lowering its density and reducing its mass.

A well-designed, or finely tuned, exhaust system can improve engine power by using the negative and positive pressure pulses, which travel back and forth along the front exhaust pipe, to start the new charge flowing into the cylinder during the valve overlap period. An ideal pipe length gives a negative pressure pulse in the cylinder at the instant the inlet valve opens. The assistance given by the exhaust is only achieved at certain engine speeds, so the design should be tuned to give its support at the time when extra engine power is required.

Absorption-type silencers

The construction of this type, also called a Burgess silencer, is shown in Figure 2.129. It consists of a straight-through perforated tube, which is surrounded by a sound-absorbing material, such as glass fibre. Damping of the high-frequency sound waves is achieved by the material, which causes a slight retardation in the wave. When the wave returns from the outer chamber, it is out-of-phase with the vibration of the gas passing through the perforated tube, so the opposing action of the two waves smoothes out the high-frequency peaks.

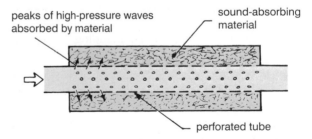

Figure 2.129 Absorption-type silencer

Composite-type silencers

The composite-type silencer (Figure 2.130) is a combination of the absorption- and capacity-type silencers. This combination is useful and cost effective, assuming space or ground clearance is sufficient for its installation.

Some silencers of this type have a number of tubes and/or chambers to produce out-of-phase sound waves that vibrate in sympathy with the main frequencies of the gas passing into the silencer; hence the term 'resonator' that is sometimes used to describe this type of silencer.

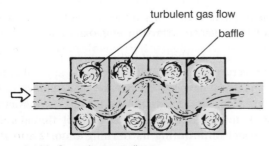

Figure 2.128 Capacity-type silencer

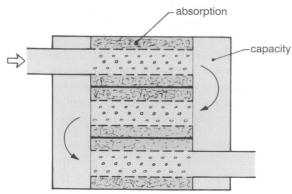

Figure 2.130 Composite-type silencer

Silencer material

Steam is one of the products of combustion. When the exhaust system is cold, the steam condenses to form water that either drips from the tailpipe or collects in the silencer until the system heats up. The combined effects of water and acids from combustion, high-temperature gas and water from the road produces a highly corrosive action that rapidly attacks the normal low-carbon steel exhaust system. This corrosion can be resisted by coating the steel with aluminium or by using a more expensive material such as stainless steel or titanium. Some after-market exhausts are manufactured from these expensive materials and are added as upgrades to the existing exhaust system.

2.12.3 Exhaust system design

Manufacturers spend a great deal of time and money in designing and engineering the exhaust system for their vehicles. The manufacturer has to take into consideration many key points including:

- engine performance
- noise
- emissions
- service life
- materials and cost
- installation design and space available.

All of these points have to compromise when the final components are manufactured. An exhaust made from stainless steel or titanium, for instance, is likely to perform better than one made from steel but cost is a limiting factor.

Engine performance can be improved by fitting a well-designed, finely tuned exhaust system using the negative and positive pressure pulses that travel back and forth along the front exhaust pipe to start the new charge flowing into the cylinder during the valve overlap period. The ideal length of an exhaust system is one that gives a negative pressure pulse in the cylinder at the instant the inlet valve opens.

Generally, the exhaust will perform best at a narrow engine speed range due to the length. The end design should be able to give its support at the time when extra engine power is required, normally at medium to high engine speed.

'Variable length' exhaust systems are used in some higher-performance vehicles. Here, valves alter the length of the exhaust system using a similar principle to that in variable induction manifolds. The Aston Martin Vantage is an example of a high-performance car that uses this system. The valves also allow exhaust gases to bypass the silencer to produce a free-flowing shorter exhaust at higher engine speeds. This creates more power through the use of positive and negative pressures to draw the exhaust gas from the engine and down the exhaust system. The valve closes during lower engine speeds when a quieter operation and lower power is required. Figure 2.131 shows an exhaust system fitted to a performance vehicle. Notice the smooth bends and larger diameter pipe. This is to prevent unwanted back pressure in the exhaust system.

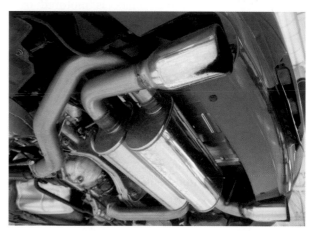

Figure 2.131 An example of performance exhaust system

2.12.4 Exhaust catalytic converter

For many years, vehicle manufacturers have been developing their engines to meet the market's demands. However, in recent times, the concerns over air pollution meant that a new device had to be developed to overcome these issues. Engineers and designers came up with a device called a 'catalytic converter' to monitor and treat the exhaust gases and remove those unwanted harmful pollutants before they entered the atmosphere.

On designing the catalytic converter, vehicle manufacturers had to also design a sophisticated management system to work alongside it. The management system was to be designed to monitor and adapt its parameters to control the amount of air/fuel ratio during its burning stage. This ratio is sometimes known as the **stoichiometric ratio**, and an ideal ratio of air/fuel will need to be 14.7 to 1. This then means that for each particle of fuel supplied, 14.7 parts of air will be burned to achieve this optimum ratio. To achieve this is somewhat of a challenge as the mixture will run lean or rich, depending on the driving demands or drive cycle conditions. Therefore, the management system has to continuously adapt its parameters to stay very close to the stoichiometric ratio. Figure 2.132 shows the construction of a catalytic converter.

Stoichiometric ratio: the theoretical optimum mix of air and fuel to create complete combustion.

A number of emission gases are produced during the combustion process:

- Nitrogen gas – a combination of monoxide and dioxide mixed with 78 per cent volume of air that is mostly drawn through the engine.
- Carbon dioxide – a product of the combustion process and the carbon deposits bond with the oxygen that is also drawn through the engine.
- Water vapour – another product of the combustion process and, like the carbon deposits, the hydrogen in the fuel will bond with the oxygen that is drawn through the engine.

The previous gases mentioned are mostly harmless, but on testing carbon dioxide it has been identified as a contributor to today's global warming problem. Although the EMS has been designed to provide an efficient control strategy, it is never perfect and other harmful emissions are produced in small amounts during the combustion process.

- Carbon monoxide (CO) – a colourless, odourless, poisonous gas, formed when there is a limited amount of oxygen.
- Hydrocarbons (HC) – the unburnt or partly burnt fuel particle. These particles can be broken down by being exposed to sunlight so they transform into oxidants. These oxides of nitrogen then break down the ozone layer when entering the atmosphere.
- Oxides of nitrogen – a contributor to unwanted smog and acid rain. This harmful pollutant can also cause human irritation to the nose and throat area.
- Fuel particulates – very small particles of the unburnt fuel that have escaped the combustion cycle. On entering the atmosphere, they can cause breathing problems. These particulates are generally found to be more harmful than the exhaust fumes produced by diesel engines.

The first three listed above are the three main emission pollutants that are regulated and managed by the intervention of a catalytic converter to greatly reduce the unwanted fumes entering our world.

How a catalytic converter is designed to reduce pollution

On designing the catalytic converter the vehicle manufacturers had to produce a unit that was to effectively reduce the unwanted toxic gases. It was known as the 'three-way catalytic converter' because of the three emission gases (unburnt hydrocarbons, carbon monoxide and nitrogen oxide molecules) that it had to monitor and reduce. The converter utilises two different catalysts to overcome the exhaust system demands: a reduction catalyst and an oxidisation catalyst. Each version is constructed using a ceramic structure coated in a metal catalyst, commonly using platinum or even rhodium and or palladium. The design of the assembly is to create an internal structure that is fully exposed to the hot exhaust stream gases. Using materials such as ceramic honeycomb, metal plate and ceramic beads (now almost an obsolete material) makes the construction of a catalyst very expensive to manufacture and purchase.

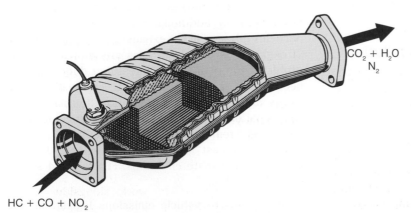

$CO_2 + H_2O$
N_2

$HC + CO + NO_2$

Figure 2.132 Structure of a catalytic converter

Figure 2.133 Exhaust emissions

The reduction catalyst

Within the construction of the catalyst you will see that it is divided into three sections. The first area is known as the reduction catalyst and it is where the assembly uses platinum and rhodium to minimise the amount of nitrogen oxides that are produced within the combustion process. As these molecules are drawn into the assembly, they will attach themselves to the catalyst membrane. This activity will then create a chemical reaction to break down these molecules and attempt to hold on to the nitrogen atom to collectively form nitrogen (N_2).

The oxidisation catalyst

The second stage of the catalytic converter is the oxidation catalyst area. In this area of the assembly, you will find that the unburnt hydrocarbons and carbon monoxide will be drawn over a platinum and palladium membrane, which then will cause a chemical reaction to reduce their mass within the exhaust gas flow.

The control system

Within the third stage of the catalyst you find a sensor that monitors the flow of the exhaust gases and is a functional part of the management control system to make sure the fuel injection and catalyst performs efficiently. The sensor is sometimes identified as an oxygen sensor, or as a lambda sensor, and it is normally mounted upstream of the catalyst. This means that the sensor is monitoring the exhaust gases before they enter the catalyst. This monitored information is then transmitted back to the engine control unit (ECU), identifying how much oxygen has been detected within the system. In turn, it allows the module to adjust its air/fuel ratio to increase or decrease the oxygen levels, and ensures that the system stays within the stiochiometric point and still continues to make sure that enough oxygen is being supplied to burn off those unburnt hydrocarbons and carbon monoxides within the oxidisation section of the catalyst.

2.12.5 Other ways to reduce pollution

Although the construction and performance of a catalyst does greatly reduce unwanted pollution, there is still a need to improve its overall efficiency. Manufacturers have identified from their research and testing that when the catalyst is in a cold state, the effectiveness of the assembly is reduced. So when a vehicle is started from a cold start condition, you will find that the catalyst will have a minimal effect on the pollutants produced until it reaches a suitable running temperature. This is always a key fact to remember if and when a vehicle needs to pass an emissions test for its MOT certification.

To improve this operating problem, firstly some manufacturers found that moving the catalyst nearer to the engine allowed hotter exhaust gases to arrive at the catalyst, which in turn assisted in heating up the catalyst faster during the engine's warm-up period. Unfortunately, this had a negative effect on some vehicles as the extreme high temperatures then reduced the life of the assembly. So, to overcome this, manufacturers devised a method of using heat shields to deflect some of the heat away so as to increase their life cycle.

In addition, manufacturers found that if the catalyst was preheated, then this would also improve its efficiency. This was achieved by using electric resistance heaters but, again, some manufacturers identified that using the conventional 12V electrical system didn't supply enough power to heat up the catalyst sufficiently, and most drivers didn't want to have to wait for the warm-up period to be complete before starting their vehicle.

Although the preheated functionality didn't work effectively on conventional vehicles, manufacturers of electric, hybrid and fuel-cell vehicles identified that the higher output battery packs supported the heat-up process and contributed to the lower emissions that they achieve.

Within the layout of the exhaust system the catalytic converter is the most expensive part. Therefore, it is necessary to ensure that they are well maintained and that the engine is kept in good running order. Any small misfires on the engine will cause the heat of the catalyst to rise very quickly, as the unburnt fuel leaving the engine's cylinders then ignites when it hits the catalyst causing very rapid heat build-up. Generally, a catalytic converter will last about 80,000–100,000 miles if it is well maintained.

Diesel particulate filters

Vehicles fitted with diesel engines are now generally fitted with an additional method to remove the particles released in the exhaust gases from this type of engine. The diesel particles are known to cause problems for people with breathing difficulties, so need to be kept to a minimum, especially within towns and cities and during short journeys. This additional device is called a diesel particulate filter (DPF) and it removes the diesel particulates (or soot) from the exhaust gas of a diesel vehicle, thereby reducing particulate emissions. Figure 2.134 shows the DPF in detail.

With changes to vehicle emissions legislation, the current **Euro 5** standards make DPFs as common in diesel car exhausts as catalytic converters are in petrol cars.

Figuro 2.134 Diesel particulate filter

Euro 5: the standards laid down by the European Commission with the aim of reducing emissions from vehicles. This standard deals with emissions from light passenger and commercial vehicles and came into force in 2009.

If you were to compare a DPF to a catalytic converter, you would identify that the DPF is not designed to allow free flow of exhaust gases but, instead, the DPF operates by forcing the flow of exhaust gases through the filter assembly. The internal structure of the filter is a series of channels that are blocked at alternate ends, which in turn then force the exhaust gases to flow through the cell wall, allowing them to exit the filtering process. Due to the cell walls being porous, they allow the continuous exhaust gas flow to take place, but the particulate matter that is flowing along within these gases is restricted and deposits itself on to the cell wall. By breaking down the gases and removing the deposits, it allows clean exhaust gases to exit the DPF out into the atmosphere. Meanwhile, the trapped deposits that are building up on to the cell wall will eventually be burnt off through one of two processes – passive and active regeneration. These processes are designed to create large amounts of heat within the exhaust and DPF systems to burn off the soot particles and then clear the filter. The temperatures created can be up to 600 °C. At this temperature, the particles trapped within the DPF are ignited, burnt away and expelled through the exhaust and catalytic converter.

Passive regeneration

The EMS will automatically activate the passive regeneration process as long as the vehicle is being driven on a suitably long drive cycle, allowing the DPF system to operate to its full functionality to burn off the particulates. Unfortunately, not all drivers complete a regular drive cycle to allow this process to be completed. Therefore, the vehicle manufacturers have built in to the EMS software an 'active' regenerative programme that then controls this process.

Active regeneration

During the active regeneration process, the ECU monitors the internal pressure of the DPF and, in turn, identifies how much soot is being stored within the cell chambers. Once the filter reaches about 45 per cent of its volume, the ECU will adapt its fuel parameters to increase the fuel timing which, in turn, will then increase the exhaust gas temperature. This programmed increase will activate the regenerative process and burn off any soot that is trapped within the DPF cell chambers.

If regeneration does not take place, perhaps due to a large amount of short journeys where the engine and exhaust system do not reach the required temperature, the DPF can become blocked. When this occurs, the pressure sensor fitted to either side of the DPF senses that the exit pressure is far lower than the inlet pressure. In turn, this will turn on the DPF warning light on the driver's display to advise that the vehicle should be taken to a dealer workshop for immediate repair. Continued driving of the vehicle in this state will cause damage and loss of performance as the exhaust gases are prevented from leaving the exhaust

Oxygen sensors

On a modern engine, oxygen sensors assume responsibility for the monitoring of the mixture strength. Oxygen sensors are commonly called lambda sensors. ('Lambda' refers to the Greek symbol λ, where lambda is a unit of measurement. Where the air/fuel ratio is said to be stoichiometric (14.7 : 1) this is known as $\lambda = 1$.)

Lambda is calculated by dividing the actual air/fuel ratio by the ideal (14.7 : 1). If an engine is running at the ideal air/fuel ratio, it can therefore be described as running at lambda 1 (14.7 : 1 divided by 14.7 : 1 equals 1). From this simple equation, it can be seen that if an engine is running rich, the lambda value will be less than 1 and if it is running lean, it will be greater than 1. Lambda is also sometimes described as excess air factor.

The lambda sensor is located in the exhaust pipe between the exhaust ports and the catalyst, normally in the exhaust downpipe. The lambda sensor signal is used by the EMS to maintain the air/fuel mixture at the correct ratio.

The oxygen or lambda sensor is designed to measure the amount of oxygen content that is being produced. This information is then electrically transmitted to the ECU, which then adapts its programmed parameters and makes sure the correct air/fuel mixture and other systems operate efficiently throughout its drive cycle. The lambda sensor signal operates between 0.1 V and 0.9 V. When the oxygen content in the exhaust is high, the lambda sensor voltage is low (0.1 V), when the oxygen content is low (rich mixture), the signal voltage is high (0.9 V). If the engine is running rich, there will be an excess of fuel and this will result in the majority of oxygen being burnt.

The lambda sensor is coated with a special ceramic material called zirconia (zirconium dioxide). Zirconia has a special property in that when it is exposed to two areas of differing oxygen content, a small voltage is produced. The sensor is then configured so that one side is in direct contact with the exhaust gas and the other in contact with atmospheric air. The greater the difference in oxygen across the sensor, the higher the voltage. The smaller the difference, the lower the voltage. Figure 2.135 shows the construction of a lambda sensor.

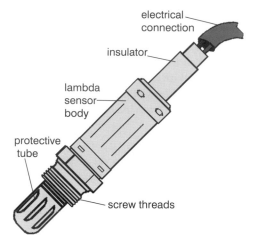

Figure 2.135 *Construction of a lambda sensor*

A lambda sensor will only start to produce a decent signal when hot. As the majority of emissions are produced by a vehicle when cold, it is important to heat the sensor up quickly so that the EMS can assume control based on a lambda sensor signal as soon as possible. To help the sensor to heat up quickly, two things are done:

1 It is positioned very close to the exhaust ports.
2 Sometimes an electrical heater element is also provided. The EMS controls the flow of current through this.

The lambda sensor is always used in conjunction with a catalytic converter as the converter only works effectively at stoichiometric ratio (or lambda 1). When the EMS is monitoring mixture strength through the use of the oxygen sensor, this is known as closed-loop control. The term is derived from the fact that the EMS decides what to put into the engine based on what it knows is coming out (like a loop). Engines rarely run on closed loop as a stoichiometric ratio is seldom suitable. (The driver only has to touch the accelerator to indicate a requirement to accelerate and that a rich mixture is required and the EMS will assume open-loop control, effectively ignoring the oxygen/lambda sensor.)

This version of lambda sensor is located on the output side of the catalysts. Sometimes it is known as a post-lambda sensor or downstream sensor. This sensor only monitors the performance of the catalytic converter and is not used to adjust any engine mixture. So its only functional activity is to identify that the catalysis is operating within its parameters and this is indicated by the sensor sending a constant output signal to the ECU. If the sensor then transmits a similar signal to the pre-catalysis sensor, then the ECU can adapt is parameters accordingly. If the imbalance continues, then a fault code it transmitted and stored in the memory of the unit. For this system to operate effectively, the air/fuel ratio must adjust every few seconds between rich and lean mixture.

2.13 Engine lubricants

2.13.1 The functions and properties of lubricants

A great deal of heat and friction build up inside an internal-combustion engine because of the many moving parts that act upon each other through sliding or rotating motion. Without means to protect each component, by creating a barrier between them, engine components would soon seize up and break. The lubrication system provides this protective barrier between each moving part preventing friction build-up and ensuring that heat generation is kept under control.

Friction and heat

When two surfaces come into contact, there is an opposition to relative movement between them – this is called friction. If the surfaces are clean and dry, the force needed to overcome friction depends on:

- the materials of which the surfaces are made
- the surface finish (i.e. whether rough, smooth or polished)
- the load pressing the surfaces together.

For any one pair of clean dry surfaces, it can be shown by simple experiments that the friction ratio is a constant number: it is called the coefficient of friction for those surfaces.

$$\frac{\text{Resistance to movement}}{\text{Load pressing surfaces together}}$$

When friction is overcome and movement between two surfaces occurs, work is done against friction and an equivalent amount of heat is generated at the surfaces. In a continuously running bearing, this heat must be dissipated into the surrounding air to keep the bearing temperature within reasonable limits.

Another result of movement between dry surfaces is wear of the surfaces. The rate of wear depends on the materials and also varies with the load and speed, but in a high-speed machine it is likely to be so rapid as to render the mechanism useless within a very short time.

If the surfaces can be kept apart, neither friction nor wear can occur, and that is the primary function of a lubricant – to separate the moving surfaces. Lubricants may be solid, liquid or gaseous, but liquids are by far the commonest and are almost universally used in vehicles.

An additional important purpose of the lubrication system is to reduce heat within the engine and carry this heat away to be dissipated to the surrounding air. This dissipation can be enhanced through the fitment of an oil cooler in line with constant airflow.

The liquid lubricant is pumped around the engine by the oil pump driven by the engine. This constant flow of oil through the engine components eases movement and absorbs heat away from the components, preventing excessive friction and heat building up. The oil is then passed to the oil reservoir (usually called the oil sump) at the base of the engine. The sump is in contact with the air and releases the heat into the atmosphere. As mentioned, an additional cooling method seen on many higher performance engines is an oil cooler. This is effectively a small radiator mounted directly in the airflow, which has the oil flowing through from the engine before being returned to the reservoir. Air flows through the fins of the oil cooler, constantly removing heat from the oil to the atmosphere, thus cooling the oil before it returns to the engine (Figure 2.136).

Figure 2.136 Example of an oil cooler

2.13.2 Properties of lubricants

Viscosity

When moving surfaces are completely separated by a film of liquid lubricant, the only resistance to motion is due to the **viscosity** of the lubricant. Thus, friction in a lubricated bearing depends upon the viscosity of the lubricant. However, the viscosity also influences the rate at which the lubricant is squeezed out from between two surfaces when load is applied (i.e. the greater the viscosity, the greater the lubricant's ability to withstand load). Hence, the lubricant should have a high enough viscosity to withstand the maximum load to be carried without causing excessive resistance to movement.

> **Viscosity**: a property of fluids by which they resist flow – the greater the viscosity the greater the resistance and vice versa.

The rating introduced by the Society of Automotive Engineers (SAE) is universally adopted to classify oils according to their viscosities. This method uses a number to represent the viscosity, for example SAE 20. The higher the SAE number, the higher the viscosity or, to use a more common expression, 'the thicker the oil'.

Engines in the past generally used a comparatively thick oil, such as SAE 50. However, the need to reduce both fuel consumption and cold-cranking loads has brought about the common use of much thinner oils, for example SAE 10. An even better economy can be achieved with the very thin oil SAE 5, but this can only be used on engines having extra-close-fitting bearings; this suitability can only be determined by seeking the manufacturer's advice.

Viscosity index

The viscosity of lubricants decreases with a rise in temperature; the extent of this change is measured by the viscosity index. A high index indicates a relatively small change in viscosity, while a low index indicates a large change. The lubricant used should have a suitable viscosity at its normal operating temperature in the engine. This means that when the engine is cold, the viscosity will be unnecessarily high, leading to poor circulation of the lubricant and excessive friction (oil drag), possibly even to the extent of making the engine difficult to start.

Multi-grade oils

In the past, the high-viscosity oil used in an engine during the summer made engine cranking difficult in the winter, so different grades were specified for the two seasons. Today, special additives that reduce the change in an oil's viscosity with temperature are often used, and this has meant that the same grade can be used throughout the year. These oils are called multi-grade or cross-grade, or given trade names that suggest the viscosity remains constant.

These oils can be recognised by the special SAE rating; this has two numbers separated by the letter 'W'. A typical oil is SAE 10 W 40: in this case, the oil is equivalent to SAE 10 when tested at a sub-zero temperature (hence the 'W' to indicate winter conditions), and has a viscosity of SAE 40 at the normal rated temperature.

Oiliness

This property is the ability of an oil to 'cling' or be attracted to a metal surface. The effect of this property is seen when a spot of oil is applied to a clean piece of metal; the oil film spreads out over the surface and resists being removed when wiped with a cloth.

The degree of oiliness varies with the type of oil; vegetable-based oils are excellent in this respect.

2.13.3 Oil types

The lubricant used for vehicle engines – and most other components – is oil. Oils are obtained from three main sources:

- Animal – purified and suitably treated animal fats, such as tallow and whale oil, are used for certain purposes, but decompose too readily to be suitable lubricants in modern vehicle engines.
- Vegetable – derived from plants, such as rape and corn. These also decompose too readily to be satisfactory, though one example, castor oil, was used quite extensively at one time. Its chief merit is its ability to lubricate under arduous conditions, but after a fairly short time treacle-like deposits are formed and it is now very seldom used.
- Mineral – derived from naturally occurring hydrocarbons. Oils of this type are refined from crude petroleum and are far more stable than other types. They form the basis of practically all modern lubricants and, though by no means perfect, they can be improved by the addition of certain chemicals known by the general name of additives.

Synthetic oils

Synthetic oils have increasingly been specified by manufacturers since the 1990s as the preferred engine and transmission oils to be used. Although synthetic oil is now more commonly used, more often in today's vehicles it is actually derived from the mineral formula. That is to say, synthetic oil is mostly polyalphaolefins (PAO) and comes from the purest part of the mineral oil refraction process. This process is the gas element that is achieved in production. A benefit of this PAO oil is that it can be mixed with the conventional mineral oil and not cause any internal engine failure. **Note**: it is generally best practice though to use the same type of engine oil in the engine to avoid any incompatibility issues.

Synthetic and mineral oil are compatible with each other and so they are unlikely to react negatively when coming into contact with other compounds. In the development stage of these oils, they have found that not adding the reactive carbon has minimised the possibilities of a chemical reaction that could create an acid solution and then cause possible internal failure within the engine or drive train.

Synthetic oil provides a high viscosity and stability at high operating temperatures. In the development of synthetic oil, manufacturers found that the use of additives allows the prevention of oil seal swelling and acts as a detergent, breaking down any carbon residuals. So, overall, it can be said that synthetic oil provides a more efficient lubrication application for today's engines.

Additives

Oil additives are more commonly used now to improve the oil's performance even further. Each additive can create different performance characteristics. Among the most important of these for use in engines are:

- oxygen inhibitors
- detergents
- viscosity index improvers
- anti-foam agents.

Oxidation inhibitors

At high temperatures, mineral oils tend to oxidise, forming hard deposits on the hottest surfaces with which they come into contact, such as the underside of the piston crown, and varnish-like deposits on parts not quite so hot, such as the piston skirt. Other products of oxidation may be carried in the oil and deposited in other parts of the engine. If these settle in oil passages, they may eventually reduce the oil flow to a dangerous extent. Today, oxidation inhibitors (or anti-oxidants) are added to the oil to reduce oxidation.

Detergents

As it circulates around the engine, the oil becomes contaminated with oxidation products and with burnt or partly burnt products of combustion that escape past the pistons. These usually consist of extremely small and relatively soft particles, which will not harm the bearings but tend to settle out and block up oil passages. These particles become baked hard around piston rings and restrict the free movement of the rings, eventually sticking them completely in their grooves.

The function of detergent additives is to keep these oxidation products in suspension in the oil so that they are not deposited inside the engine. The oxidation products are removed from the engine with the dirty oil when the oil is changed.

Viscosity index improvers

These are chemicals that reduce the change in the viscosity of mineral oil caused by change in temperature.

Anti-foam agents

Some engines suffer from the formation of foam or froth in the oil, and these additives are used to reduce this tendency.

2.13.4 Types of oil-based lubrication

Boundary lubrication

This form of lubrication relies on the 'oiliness' of an oil; that is, its ability to coat the surfaces and fill the cavities of low-speed rubbing components to ensure that metal-to-metal contact and subsequent wear is avoided.

In an engine, boundary lubrication is used for all sliding engine components other than the highly loaded bearings that require a pressure feed. The supply of oil for the boundary lubrication film is provided by splash; this comes from the oil thrown out from the crankshaft bearings.

Hydrodynamic lubrication

The bearings of a modern engine must withstand great loads and high rubbing speeds. If the surfaces are to be adequately held apart when subjected to these arduous conditions, the quantity of oil supplied must be sufficient both to fill the space between the shaft and bearing and to make up for the oil squeezed out from the bearing as it rotates. To ensure these requirements are met, the bearing is force-fed with oil at a pressure sufficient to maintain the supply while the engine is in use.

Highly loaded bearings rely on hydrodynamic lubrication to separate the surfaces. This is achieved by using the natural movement of the oil (hence the term 'hydrodynamic') to create an 'oil wedge' to lift and centre the shaft in the bearing.

Figure 2.137 shows the principle of this method of lubrication. The bearing is made larger than the shaft to the extent governed by the type of oil to be used and the expected thermal expansion.

When the engine is stationary, the shaft rests on the bottom of the bearing and is supported only by a thin oil film (Figure 2.137a). This boundary film provides lubrication when the engine is started.

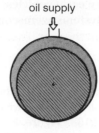

(a) Shaft stationary

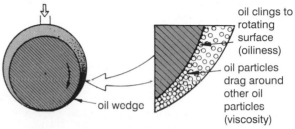

(b) Shaft starting to rotate

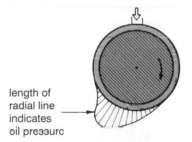

(c) Shaft rotating at high speed

Figure 2.137 Bearing lubrication and oil wedge principle

Initial rotation causes the boundary layer of oil on the shaft to move around with the shaft owing to its oiliness property. This movement, together with the inherent resistance of the oil particles to shear (viscosity), forces the oil between the surfaces to create a 'wedge' (Figure 2.137b). This wedge lifts and centres the shaft in the bearing (Figure 2.137c). This diagram also shows an indication of the pressure variation and its relationship to the oil wedge that is generated by the hydrodynamic oil film.

To achieve effective lubrication in the bearing, an adequate supply of good-quality oil at a suitable pressure must be provided to maintain the oil wedge.

2.14 The engine-lubrication system

2.14.1 Main features

The function of the lubrication system of an engine is to distribute the lubricant to all the surfaces needing lubrication. In the very early vehicles, simple – even crude – lubrication systems were considered quite satisfactory.

As early as 1905, the Lanchester Motor Company used a system in which a pump forced oil under pressure into the crankshaft bearings, and this has developed into the typical modern system, of which an example is shown in Figure 2.138. Figure 2.139 shows the same system in the form of a diagram, omitting all components not included in the lubrication system.

1 rocker spindle
2 oilway to rocker spindle
3 pipe to rocker spindle
4 oilway to gudgeon pin
5 camshaft bearing
6 dipstick
7 main oil gallery
8 outlet from pressure filter
9 oil jet to cylinder wall
10 oilway to big-end
11 oilway to main bearing
12 groove round main bearing
13 passage from pump to filter
14 pressure relief valve
15 pump
16 sump
17 inlet strainer
18 main filter

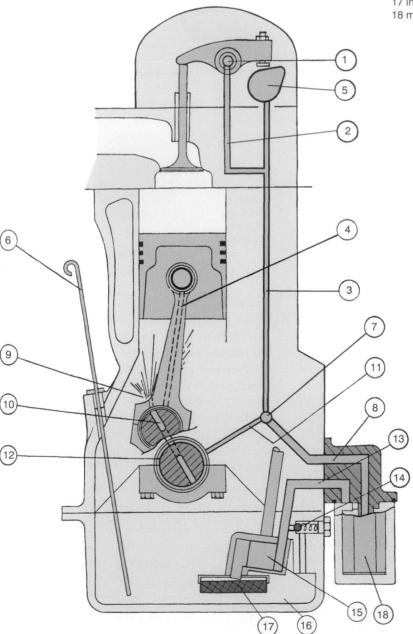

Figure 2.138 Typical base lubrication

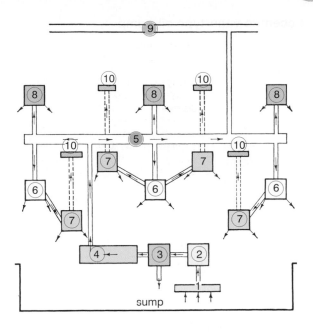

1 suction strainer
2 pump
3 pressure relief valve
4 main filter
5 main oil gallery
6 main bearing
7 big-end bearings
8 camshaft bearing
9 rocker shaft
10 gudgeon pins

Figure 2.139 Block diagram of lubrication system

In Figure 2.138, the oil is carried in the sump (16), in which the level must be high enough to cover the pump inlet but not so high that the crankshaft dips into the oil. A dipstick (6) is a simple means of checking the level of oil in the sump, though other means, such as a float indicator or an electric gauge, may be used. A mechanically driven pump (15) draws oil from the sump and delivers it via the main filter (18) to the main oil gallery (7). A rather coarse strainer (17) is fitted over the pump inlet to protect the pump from small hard objects, which would damage it.

Oil is supplied from the main oil gallery to the main crankshaft bearings and the camshaft bearings through passages drilled through the crankcase walls. A feed is also taken through an external pipe (3) and a drilled oil way (2) to the hollow rocker shaft on the cylinder head. Radial holes in the rocker shaft convey oil to the rocker bearings, and oil seeping through the bearings is splashed about the valve chamber to lubricate valve stems, push rods, etc. This oil eventually drains back to the sump via the push-rod enclosure, lubricating the tappets on its way. It is usual to have a restrictor in the supply to the valve gear, and oil seals are generally fitted to inlet-valve systems to prevent oil being drawn into the combustion chambers through the inlet ports.

Holes (10) drilled through the crankshaft convey oil from a groove (12) round the main bearing to the big-end: the groove is supplied from the main gallery (7) via the oilway (11), so that there is an uninterrupted supply to each big-end.

A small hole (9) drilled in a suitable position in the big-end bearing allows an intermittent jet of oil to spray on to the cylinder, and in some engines a hole (shown in dotted lines) is drilled through the shank of the connecting rod to take an intermittent supply to the small-end bearing.

Oil splashed off the crankshaft lubricates the remaining parts, and eventually drains back to the sump.

The quantity of oil delivered into the system by the pump depends upon the pump capacity and the speed at which it is driven. Exactly the same quantity must escape from the system, and this can normally happen only through the bearing clearances. As engine speed increases, the pressure in the system increases in order to force a greater quantity of oil through the constant bearing clearances. The pressure must be sufficient to ensure an adequate flow through the bearings at relatively low speeds, so that at higher speeds the pressure will be unnecessarily high, with risk of burst pipes or joints and excessive power loss in driving the pump. The pressure in the system is therefore limited by using a pressure relief valve (14).

2.14.2 Oil pumps

Several types of pump are used, including the following.

Gear-type oil pump

For many years this type was almost universal and it is still in common use. As shown in Figure 2.140, it consists of a pair of gear wheels meshing together in a casing (1), which fits closely around the tips of the teeth and the ends of the gears. One gear (2) is fixed to the driving spindle (3) and drives the other gear (7), which rotates idly on a fixed spindle (6). Inlet (4) and outlet (5) ports are cut in the casing on either side of the meshing point of the gears. When the gears rotate, they carry oil from inlet to outlet in the spaces between the teeth. As a tooth of one gear moves out of mesh with a space between two teeth of the other gear, oil flows in through the inlet to fill the void left. On the outlet side, oil is displaced through the outlet as a tooth of one gear moves into the space between two teeth of the other. Note particularly the direction of the oil flow and the direction of rotation (DOR) of the gears, shown by arrows.

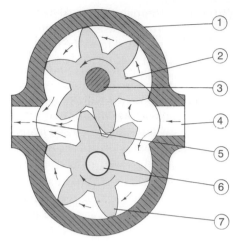

Figure 2.140 A gear-type oil pump

Eccentric rotor-type oil pump

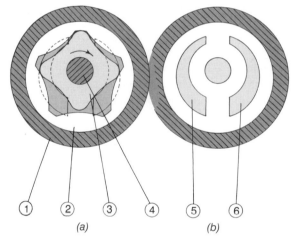

Figure 2.141 Eccentric rotor-type oil pump

In Figure 2.141, the casing (1) has a cylindrical bore in which is felted the outer rotor (2). The outer surface of this is cylindrical, but a number of lobes are formed on its inner surface. The inner rotor (3) has lobes formed on its outer surface, one fewer than the number on the outer rotor. It is fixed on the driving spindle (4) and mounted eccentrically in the casing so that each of its lobes makes contact with the inner surface of the outer rotor, dividing the space between the rotors into a number of separate compartments of varying size (i.e. the size of each compartment varies as the rotors turn). Inlet and outlet ports are cut in the end plate of the pump, and positioned so that the pumping compartments sweep over the inlet port (6) as they increase in size and over the outlet ports (5) as they decrease. The pump is shown assembled at (a): sketch illustration (b) shows the rotors removed to reveal the ports more clearly.

Eccentric vane-type oil pump

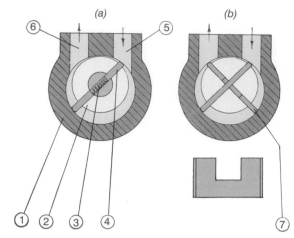

Figure 2.142 Eccentric vane-type oil pump

The earlier form of this pump is shown in Figure 2.142a. The casing (1) has a cylindrical bore in which is fitted the rotor (2) mounted on a shaft eccentric to the casing bore and touching it at one place. Spring-loaded vanes (4) are a close-sliding fit in a slot cut diametrically through the rotor, their outer edges being kept in contact with the casing bore by the spring (3). Oil is carried from the inlet (5) to the outlet (6) as the rotor turns.

A later version of this pump used on some modern engines is shown in Figure 2.142b. This has two one-piece vanes, each fitting in a diametral slot at right angles to one another. Each vane is cut away as shown at (7), and the bore of the casing is not truly cylindrical but shaped so that each vane touches the bore at both ends in all positions.

Internal/external-type oil pump

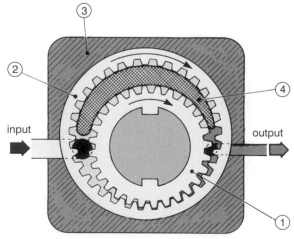

Figure 2.143 An internal/external-type oil pump

This type was introduced on automatic transmission units. Its compact size and ease in which it can be driven without the need for a separate drive shaft has made the pump popular for use in engines (Figure 2.143).

Normally, two flats on the 'front' end of the crankshaft are used to drive the inner gear (1); this meshes with and drives the outer gear (2), which is positioned off-centre. The outer gear is supported in a casing (3) and the wide region between the gears is filled with a crescent-shaped spacer (4); this projects from the casing.

At one end of the pump, two ports are formed in the casing to allow oil to flow to and from the pump. On the front face of the pump, a flat plate is fitted to blank off the gears and ensure that the only path for the oil is via the gear teeth.

Rotation of the crankshaft causes both gears to revolve in the same direction. This motion carries oil from the inlet to outlet side in the tooth spaces on both sides of the spacer. Since the teeth mesh together to give a drive, the oil cannot return back to the inlet side. As a result, there is a build-up of oil pressure.

As with most pumps, any wear that takes place will allow oil to escape back to the inlet and, as a result, will lower the pumping capacity and prevent the pump from building up its full pressure. Since the location of an internal/external pump makes it more difficult to remove, often it is recommended that the pump be inspected for wear when other work makes the pump accessible.

Internal/external pumps are more troublesome than eccentric rotor pumps if a car owner uses cheap oil that has no anti-foam agents. The air trapped in the system can pass to the hydraulic tappets and make them noisy.

Important note about pump priming

Pumps submerged in the sump oil are self-priming. This means that the level causes the oil to flow into the pump so as to wet the gears and bridge the clearances.

When a pump is mounted above the sump level, the pump must be primed by filling it with oil from a convenient external point. This operation is essential if, for any reason, the pump becomes dry, a condition sometimes created when the engine is assembled or when the engine has been allowed to stand unused for a considerable time.

To avoid drain-back of oil from the pump, some systems incorporate a valve between the intake filter screen and the pump.

2.14.3 Oil pressure relief valves

Figure 2.144 illustrates a simple type of relief valve, which consists of a ball held by spring pressure over a hole drilled into the main oil channel leading from the pump to the bearings. The pressure of oil in this channel exerts a force on the ball (5), tending to lift it off its seat against the load of the spring (3). The spring load is adjustable by screwing the cap (1) in or out, and locking it in the correct position by the locknut (2). When oil pressure is great enough to lift the ball off its seat, oil is allowed to escape from the main oil channel, thus relieving the pressure and preventing further rise. Oil escaping past the valve returns either to the sump or the pump inlet valve via the passage (4).

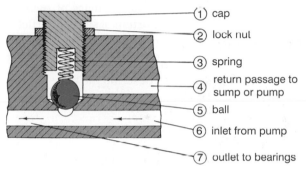

1. cap
2. lock nut
3. spring
4. return passage to sump or pump
5. ball
6. inlet from pump
7. outlet to bearings

Figure 2.144 Ball-type oil pressure relief valve

Figure 2.145 shows an alternative type of valve in which a plunger (4) replaces the ball, and an alternative method of adjustment is shown. In this case, the spring load is adjusted by adding or removing shims (2) above the spring.

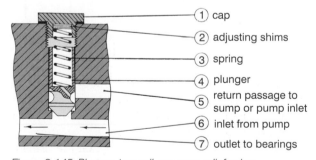

1. cap
2. adjusting shims
3. spring
4. plunger
5. return passage to sump or pump inlet
6. inlet from pump
7. outlet to bearings

Figure 2.145 Plunger-type oil pressure relief valve

2.14.4 Oil filters

The purpose of the filters in a lubrication system is to remove from the oil abrasive particles such as metals and carbon from the engine that would cause rapid wear of the bearings. If a fluid containing solid particles is passed through a porous material, the solid particles will be too large to enter the pores, or will become lodged in the tortuous passages of the pores, or pass completely through, depending upon the relative sizes of the pores and the particles.

Clearly, the finer the pores the smaller the particles the filter will remove from the fluid, but its resistance to the flow of fluid will be correspondingly greater. Thus, a very fine filter will need to have a very large surface area if the flow of oil to the engine bearings is not to be restricted.

A rather coarse wire mesh strainer is usually fitted at the pump intake to protect the pump against odd nuts, etc., lying about in the engine, or hard objects large enough to damage the pump. On the pressure side of the system a much finer filter is used. Today, the replaceable filter consists of about 4 m of resin-impregnated paper; this is pleated to expose a large external surface area to the oil and is retained in a cylindrical metal canister. The porosity of the paper is designed to trap nearly all particles of over 25 microns (0.025 mm), a proportion of smaller particles and any sludge.

The position of the filter in the lubrication 'circuit' governs the name used to describe the type; the two common types are:

- bypass
- full-flow.

Figure 2.146 shows the two arrangements. The full-flow type filters all the oil delivered to the bearings provided the filter is clean and the oil is not excessively viscous.

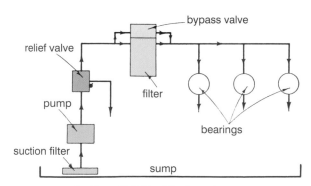

Position of full-flow filter in system

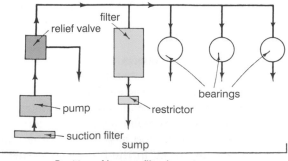

Position of bypass filter in system

Figure 2.146 Position of the filter in the system

Bypass filter

With this type only a proportion of the oil delivered by the pump is cleaned, so although this type filters out finer particles than the full-flow type as the oil returns to the sump, all the oil passing to the bearings is unfiltered. For this reason, most engines today use full-flow filters.

Full-flow filter

In addition to the filter material, this type incorporates a bypass valve that opens when the pressure drop across the filter exceeds about 1 bar (15 lbf in^{-2}). This valve opens when the filter is clogged, or when the oil is cold, to avoid oil starvation of the bearings.

Although this arrangement gives limited protection to the engine, the continued use of a filter that is not changed at the recommended time interval will, after a time, cause damage to the bearings because of the supply of unfiltered oil.

The replaceable full-flow filter is made in two forms:

- element type
- cartridge type.

Element-type full-flow filter

Figure 2.147 shows the construction of this type of filter. The assembly is mounted directly on the side of the crankcase by a pad, which overcomes the need for troublesome external piping. Today, most filters use a paper element. However, in some cases, a felt element, carried on a wire mesh frame and convoluted to give a large surface area, is occasionally fitted to suit world conditions.

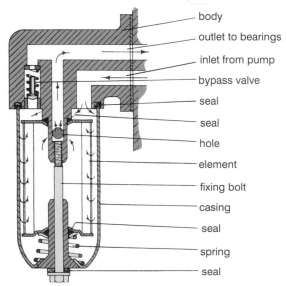

Figure 2.147 Element-type full-flow filter

The filter should be changed at the recommended intervals and this is carried out by removing the bolt at the base of the filter casing. This type has a number of seals and these should be renewed when the filter is changed. After renewing the element, it takes a few seconds for the engine to fill the filter, so the engine should not be accelerated during this time.

Cartridge-type full-flow filter

This type (Figure 2.148) is also called a spin-on filter. It is a 'throw-away' filter designed to simplify the task of removing and refitting.

The canister unit, often screwed directly on to the side of the engine crankcase and sealed with a synthetic rubber ring, houses a paper filter element and bypass valve. When changing this type of filter, it is important to make sure that both the 'O' ring and the oil filter housing surfaces are totally clean and that you smear a small amount of oil on the 'O' ring before fitting. By doing so, it will be easier to remove the filter again when it needs replacing.

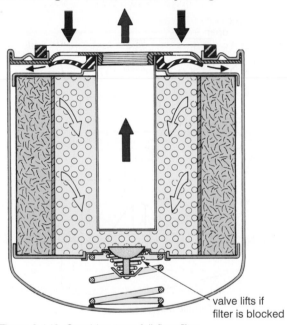

Figure 2.148 Cartridge-type full-flow filter

2.14.5 Valve stem sealing

An OHV mechanism, using either rockers or an OHC, needs a good supply of oil. This requires the valve stems to be fitted with effective seals to stop the oil trickling down the valve guides by gravity and, in the case of the inlet valve, being 'drawn in' by the manifold depression. Although this oil leakage is beneficial as regards stem wear, the oil consumption and exhaust smoke make sealing necessary.

Ineffective valve seals and worn guides can normally be diagnosed by allowing a warm engine to stand for about 10 minutes: on restarting, a puff of blue smoke is emitted from the exhaust.

Figure 2.149 shows arrangements for sealing a valve system. In some cases, special care is necessary when removing or refitting the valve to avoid seal damage.

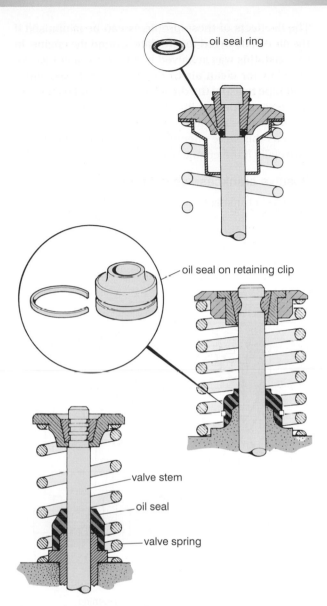

Figure 2.149 Valve oil sealing arrangements

2.14.6 Crankcase ventilation

If ideal conditions prevail within the engine, the air spaces in the crankcase, rocker cover and timing cover would be filled with a fine oil mist that coats all working parts. Unfortunately, this is not so, especially when the vehicle is used for short journeys. There are two main problems:

1 Blow-by of the pistons carries unburnt fuel, corrosive gases and steam into the crankcase.
2 Steam coming into contact with cold surfaces, such as the covers exposed to the cold airstream through the radiator, causes condensation. Water produced in this way mixes with the oil to form an emulsion called cold sludge – a dirty, black, smelly mess, which causes corrosion and obstructs oil flow.

The ill-effects of these problems can be minimised if the air can be urged to circulate around the engine. In the past, this was achieved by providing a crankcase breather for clean air to enter the crankcase and a vent pipe to expel the dirty fumes. Sometimes the end of the vent pipe was fitted with an airflow detector to lower the pressure and 'draw out' the fumes. Systems such as this were effective, but caused air pollution, especially if the engine was worn.

Positive crankcase ventilation

Positive crankcase ventilation (PCV) is necessary to conform to emission control regulations. This system uses a closed crankcase ventilation arrangement to prevent partially burnt fuel being discharged to the atmosphere. Instead, the fumes are returned to the induction system for burning in the combustion chamber.

Figure 2.150 shows the layout of a typical closed system. In this arrangement, the oil filler cap contains a calibrated passage and regulator valve that allows air to enter the crankcase only when the throttle is less than half open. At full throttle, the two hoses connected to the air cleaner and manifold convey the fumes to the induction system for burning in the engine.

To allow the engine to function correctly, especially during slow running, air must not be allowed to enter the system at points other than those designed for entry. This means that the oil dipstick must make an effective seal.

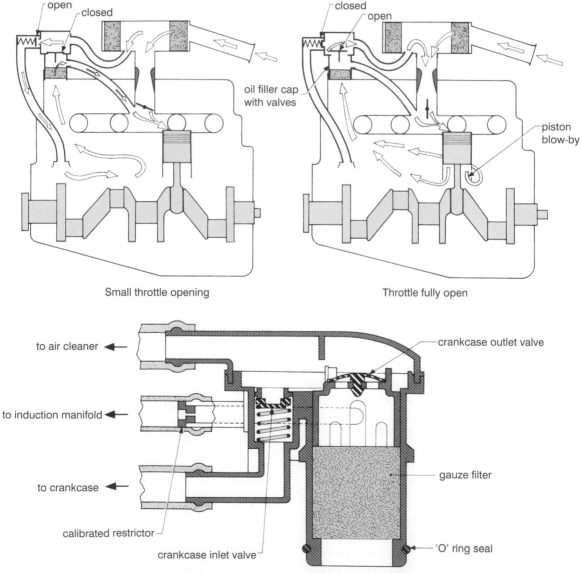

Small throttle opening

Throttle fully open

Section through oil filler cap that incorporates ventilaton valves

Figure 2.150 Closed engine ventilation system

2.14.7 Pressure indication

Mechanical-type pressure gauge

An indication of the oil pressure can be signalled to the driver by either a pressure gauge or a low-pressure warning light.

In the past, a pressure gauge system based on the Bourdon tube principle was used. The gauge of this system contains a Bourdon tube, which is a curved tube as shown in Figure 2.151. When pressure is applied to the tube via a small-bore copper or plastic tube from the engine, the tube tends to straighten out and this moves a needle across the scale on a gauge.

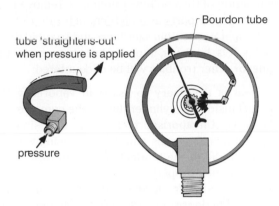

Figure 2.151 Pressure gauge – Bourdon type

This principle is still used today to operate a vacuum gauge, an instrument used for tuning an engine and for fault diagnosis.

Electrical-type pressure gauge

Modern vehicles use electrical/electronic systems to indicate to the driver when the pressure drops to a 'danger' point, or use an illuminated display to show the actual pressure.

Figure 2.152 shows a low oil pressure warning-light system. The pressure switch is fitted on the side of the engine and connected to the main oil gallery. When the engine oil pressure is low or the engine is not running, the oil pressure switch contacts are closed and the oil pressure warning light is illuminated due to the earth path through the oil pressure switch. When the oil pressure rises through the engine running, the pressure will act on the oil pressure switch and overcome the spring diaphragm pressure. This will cause the electrical circuit to break and extinguish the oil pressure warning light on the driver's display panel.

Many vehicles are now also fitted with an electronic oil pressure gauge system, which allows the driver to be able to monitor the oil pressure in the engine. The oil pressure sensor is located on the engine and

linked to the main oil gallery. This then picks up the engine oil pressure and converts this signal into an electronic signal back to the oil pressure gauge, indicating the engine oil pressure.

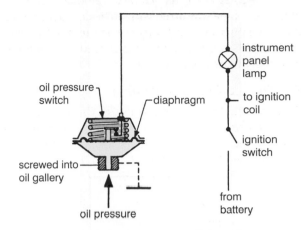

Figure 2.152 Low oil pressure warning-light system

In addition to pressure sensing, some vehicles use a 'hot wire' dipstick to indicate the level of oil in the sump; this electrical arrangement signals to the driver when the oil level is low.

2.15 The engine-cooling system

Most vehicles on the roads today are cooled by use of liquid-cooling systems. In most cases, the liquid is a mixture of water and a coolant additive designed to prevent freezing and corrosion within the engine and cooling system components. Although air-cooling is still seen on some vehicles, these are normally earlier types, apart from motorcycles, which still commonly use air-cooling on their smaller engines. Due to a majority of vehicles using liquid-cooling, we will concentrate on this area. Air-cooling will be mentioned only briefly.

2.15.1 The function of the cooling system

Today, nearly all engines are liquid-cooled as this provides the best method for controlling the heat generated by the engine through the combustion process. It is very important to maintain excellent cooling control of the engine to ensure that it is operating within conditions that provide peak performance and lowest possible emissions.

During combustion, and when the engine is operating at full throttle, the maximum temperature reached by the burning gases may be as high as 1500–2000 °C in a petrol engine. The expansion of the gases during the

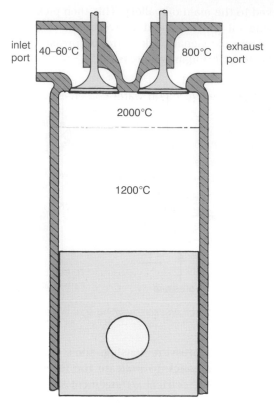

inlet port   40–60°C   800°C   exhaust port

2000°C

1200°C

Figure 2.153 Approximate gas temperatures in an engine

power stroke lowers their temperature considerably, but during the exhaust stroke the gas temperature may still not be far short of 800°C (Figure 2.153). All the engine parts that these hot gases come into contact with will absorb heat from them in proportion to the gas temperature, the area of surface exposed and the duration of the exposure; this heat will raise the temperature of the engine components. The temperature of even the exhaust gases is above red heat and far above the melting point of such metals as aluminium. Unless steps are taken to limit the temperature of the engine parts, a number of more or less serious troubles will arise:

1 The combustion chamber walls, piston crown, the upper end of the cylinder and the region of the exhaust port are exposed to the hottest gases and will reach the highest temperatures. The resulting thermal expansion of these parts will distort them from their correct shape, causing gas leakage, loss of power, valve burning and possibly even cracking of cylinder or head.
2 The oil film that should lubricate the piston and cylinder walls will be burnt or carbonised, causing excessive wear and even seizure of the piston.
3 Engine power output will be reduced by the heating of the fresh gas entering the cylinder, so reducing its density. The increased temperature of the fresh gas will also increase the possibility

of **detonation**, thus making a reduction in compression ratio necessary.
4 Some parts of the surface of the combustion chamber may become hot enough to ignite the fresh gas before the spark occurs: this is called pre-ignition, and will result in serious damage to the engine if it persists.

Detonation: when the fuel/air mixture ignites in the combustion chamber through excessive heat *before* the spark has occurred at the spark plug.

The function of the cooling system is to remove heat from the engine parts at a high enough rate to keep their temperature within safe limits and so avoid these troubles. It is, however, important not to overcool the engine, or other troubles will be encountered:

1 Heat is necessary to assist in vaporising the fuel inside the cylinder during the compression stroke. Unvaporised fuel will be deposited on cold cylinder walls and, besides being wasted, it will dilute the lubricating oil and destroy its lubricating properties.
2 Water vapour formed during combustion will condense on the cold cylinder walls, forming a sludge with the lubricating oil and corroding engine parts. Thus, the rate of wear is considerably greater when the engine is cold than when hot.

Experience suggests that the temperature of the cylinder head must be kept below about 200–250°C if overheating is to be avoided.

The cooling system needs to be designed in such a way that it is able to absorb different levels of heat from various areas around the engine. For example, where the heat generated is very high, such as the cylinder head, the coolant will need to have a large surface area to absorb the heat away from the combustion process; otherwise overheating will take place causing some of the issues mentioned earlier. At the base of the cylinder block the heat generated is lower, so the cooling system will not have such a large surface area contact with the engine. In this way, the general overall temperature will be maintained to an acceptable level to provide the peak running performance of the engine. The coolant is circulated around the engine to ensure that there are no localised hot spots; this is done through the use of a water pump, usually driven by the engine although sometimes electronically. The coolant galleries and tubes throughout the engine are different sizes to ensure the flow is maintained at a suitable rate.

There are two main systems in use, both of which dissipate heat removed from the cylinder into the surrounding air. The most common is liquid-cooling, although some smaller engines and earlier vehicles use air-cooling.

Direct air-cooling

In this system, more simply called air-cooling, heat is radiated from the cylinder and head directly into the surrounding air. The rate at which heat is radiated from an object depends upon:

1 the difference in temperature between the object and the surrounding air
2 the surface area from which heat is radiated.

Since (1) must be limited, the surface area of the cylinder and head exposed to the air must be increased, and this is done by forming fins on their external surfaces (Figure 2.154). It is also necessary to remove the heated air from around the cylinder and deliver a constant supply of cool air around and between the fins. This means that the cylinders must be sufficiently widely spaced to permit a suitable depth of finning all around them and the engine must be placed in an exposed position where the motion of the vehicle can provide the necessary supply of cool air. If it is necessary or desirable to enclose the engine, for the sake of protection or appearance, a fan must be used to supply the air, with suitable cowls to direct the air where it is needed.

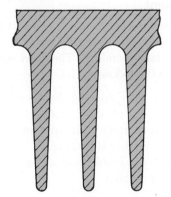

Figure 2.154 Section of fins on an air-cooled engine

Liquid-cooling

In this system, the outer surfaces of the cylinder and head are enclosed in a casing or jacket, leaving a space between the cylinder and the jacket through which a suitable liquid is circulated. The liquid generally used is water, which is in many ways the most suitable for this purpose, though it has certain drawbacks. During its passage through the jacket, the water absorbs heat from the cylinder and head, and it is cooled by being passed through a radiator before being returned to the jacket.

2.15.2 Comparison of air- and liquid-cooled systems

Air-cooling has several points in its favour:

1 An air-cooled engine should generally be lighter than the equivalent water-cooled engine.
2 The engine warms up to its normal running temperature very quickly.
3 The engine can operate at a higher temperature than a water-cooled engine.
4 The system is free from leakage problems and requires no maintenance.
5 There is no risk of damage due to freezing of the coolant in cold weather.

It has, however, a number of disadvantages:

1 A fan and suitable cowls are necessary to provide and direct the airflow. The fan is noisy and absorbs a fairly large amount of power. The cowling makes it difficult to get at certain parts of the engine.
2 The engine is more liable to overheating under arduous conditions than a water-cooled engine.
3 Mechanical engine noises tend to be amplified by the fins.
4 The cylinders usually have to be made separately to ensure proper formation of the fins. This makes the engine more costly to manufacture.
5 Cylinders must be well spaced apart to allow sufficient depth of fins.
6 It is more difficult to arrange a satisfactory car-heating system.

The main advantages of liquid-cooling include the following:

1 Temperatures throughout the engine are more uniform, thus distortion is minimised.
2 Cylinders can be placed close together and the engine made more compact.
3 Although a fan is usually fitted to force air through the radiator, it is smaller than that required in an air-cooled system and is thus quieter and absorbs less power.
4 There is no cowling to obstruct access to the engine.
5 The water and jackets deaden mechanical noise.
6 The engine is better able to operate under arduous conditions without overheating.
7 The engine is able to operate within its peak performance and lowest emissions band.

Its main disadvantages are as follows:

1 Weight – not only of the radiator and connections but also of the water: the whole engine installation is likely to be heavier than an equivalent air-cooled engine.

2 Because the water has to be heated, the engine takes longer to warm up after starting from cold.
3 If water is used, the maximum temperature is limited to about 85–90 °C to avoid the risk of boiling away the water.
4 If the engine is left standing in very cold weather, precautions must be taken to prevent the water freezing in the cylinder jackets and cracking them.
5 There is a constant risk of leakage developing.
6 A certain amount of maintenance is needed, for example, checking water level, anti-frost precautions, cleaning out deposits, etc.

2.15.3 Main features of an air-cooled system

The volume of air required to conduct a given amount of heat away from the cylinders of an air-cooled engine is about 2000 times the volume of water necessary to remove the same amount of heat and, in order to provide the necessary airflow around the cylinders of an enclosed engine, a powerful fan is essential. Figure 2.155a shows a fan of the simple curved blade type, known as an axial-flow fan because the direction of airflow is parallel to the axis of the fan spindle. This type of fan is sometimes used, but the radial-flow or centrifugal type (Figure 2.155b) is more often used, since it is more effective and a fan of smaller diameter can be used for a given airflow. This type of fan consists of a number of curved radial vanes mounted between two discs, one or both having a large central hole. When the fan is rotated, air between the vanes rotates with it and is thrown outwards by centrifugal force.

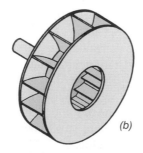

(a) *(b)*

Figure 2.155 Types of fan assembly

Figure 2.156 shows a simple air-cooled system for a four-cylinder in-line engine. A centrifugal fan (4), driven at approximately twice crankshaft speed, is mounted at the front of the engine and takes in air through a central opening (5) in the fan casing (6). From the fan the air is delivered into a cowl (3), from which it passes over the fins on the engine cylinders (1). Baffles (2) direct the airflow between the fins, from which the air picks up heat, so cooling the cylinders.

The in-line type of engine shown is not the most suitable for air-cooling, since the cylinders have to be placed further apart than would otherwise be necessary in order to allow enough air to flow between the cylinders. Vee-type engines, or horizontally opposed types, are better in this respect since the cylinders have to be spaced far enough apart to leave room for the crankshaft bearings: this allows a good airflow between the cylinders while keeping the total engine length short.

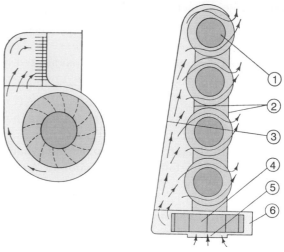

Figure 2.156 Air-cooled system for four-cylinder in-line engine

2.15.4 Main features of a liquid-cooled system

Liquid coolant

The liquid used to carry heat away from the cylinders and heads is almost invariably water, to which may be added certain chemicals. The chief advantages of water include the following:

1 It has a high specific heat capacity (i.e. a given amount of water, heated through a given temperature range, absorbs more heat than almost any other substance).
2 It is readily available in most parts of the world at little or no cost.

Water, however, has certain disadvantages:

1 It boils at a temperature somewhat lower than is desirable for best possible engine performance, especially at heights far above sea level where water will boil at lower temperatures due to the air pressure being lower.
2 It freezes at temperatures often encountered in winter in many parts of the world. Since ice expands with a fall in temperature, there is a considerable risk of cracking the cylinder blocks if freezing is allowed to occur.
3 There may be some trouble with corrosion of the metals with which it comes in contact.

These objections can be wholly or partly overcome in the following ways:

1 The temperature at which the coolant boils can be raised by operating the system under pressure. The way this is done is described on page 131, but the boiling temperature is raised by about 1 °C for every $4\,kN/m^2$ ($0.6\,lbf\,in^{-2}$) that the pressure is increased.

2 The freezing temperature of the coolant can be lowered by adding an antifreeze chemical. The one most commonly used is ethylene glycol, and a solution containing about 20 per cent of this in water is sufficient to give complete protection in the UK. The strength of the solution can be checked by means of a suitable hydrometer.

3 The risk of corrosion can be reduced or eliminated by the addition of suitable chemicals. These are usually included in the antifreeze solution.

Thermo-syphon system

The coolant must be made to circulate around the cooling system so that heat absorbed by the coolant around the cylinders can be dissipated in the radiator. The simplest method of producing this circulation relies upon the convection currents in the coolant. These result from the reduction in density caused by expansion of the coolant with increase in temperature. A system using this method of circulation is known as a natural circulation system, or a thermo-syphon system (Figure 2.157).

The basic system consists of a water jacket, which is connected by a synthetic rubber hose to a header tank. This tank forms part of the radiator, a heat exchanger made by connecting two tanks, header and lower, with a number of finned tubes to provide a large surface area for the disposal of unwanted heat. Airflow over the tubes and fins carries away the heat radiated

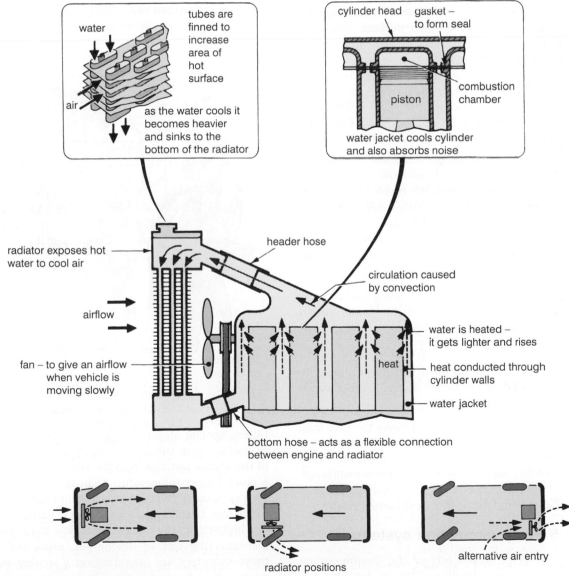

Figure 2.157 Liquid-cooling system

from the hot coolant, and so lowers the temperature of the coolant as it passes down the tubes. A bottom hose connects the lower tank to the jacket to provide a return path to the engine for the coolant.

When the engine is running and the vehicle is either stationary or travelling slowly, the airflow through the radiator is insufficient to give adequate cooling. At these times, overheating is avoided by using a fan to act as an air pump. Energy to drive the fan is often supplied by a belt driven from the crankshaft or, alternatively and more common today, the fan can be driven direct by an electric motor.

The principle of operation is based on three methods of heat transfer: conduction, convection and radiation – cooling of the engine takes place in this sequence.

Conduction

Heat flows from a hot substance to a cold substance. The hot internal parts of the cylinder pass the heat from one metal particle to the next through the walls to the comparatively cool outer surface. Coolant in contact with the metal surface receives the heat and carries it away.

Convection

This is based on the principle that at a temperature higher than 4 °C water gets lighter as it is heated (i.e. the density decreases as the temperature increases).

Coolant in the water jacket becomes heated and, since it becomes 'lighter', it will rise to the top of the jacket and flow through the header hose to the radiator. The hot water in the jacket will be replaced by colder water fed in from the lower tank of the radiator. When the flow is combined with the upward flow in the jacket, a natural circulation of the coolant is achieved, which is called convection.

Circulation due to the thermo-syphon action can only take place if the coolant level in the header tank is above the level of the header hose.

Radiation

Heat travels through air in a waveform similar to light. Radiated heat can be felt if your hand is placed close to a hot surface.

The purpose of a radiator is to transfer the heat from the coolant to the air. The air must move because, if it is stationary, the air temperature will soon become equal to the coolant temperature and heat transfer will cease. To avoid this problem, cold air is continuously supplied to the radiator and the heated air is carried away.

2.15.5 Pump circulation systems

Modern vehicles do not rely on the thermo-syphon system for engine cooling. This is because the bodyline of the vehicle prevents the use of a tall radiator and the large quantity of coolant required is too heavy to be carried around. When these disadvantages are combined with the slow cooling action and long delay before the engine reaches its optimum running temperature after cold starting, it is seen why a more positive and compact cooling system, as given by a pump, is now used universally.

Figure 2.158 shows the main features of a pump-assisted cooling system. The layout is based on the thermo-syphon system and uses a pump, generally belt driven, to promote circulation of the coolant. The increased rate of flow of coolant given by a pump system allows a smaller radiator and, where necessary, this can be mounted lower relative to the engine. Mounting the pump directly on to the cylinder block is common practice; this overcomes the need for an outlet hose between the pump and engine. The alternative is to make the pump a separate unit, which is convenient when the pumping capacity has to be increased to suit hot climates.

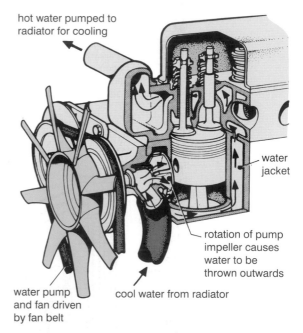

hot water pumped to radiator for cooling

water jacket

rotation of pump impeller causes water to be thrown outwards

water pump and fan driven by fan belt

cool water from radiator

Figure 2.158 Pump-assisted circulation of coolant

Unless special attention is given to the outlet flow of coolant from the pump, the cylinders at the end of the engine farthest from the pump will operate at a much higher temperature than those at the front. This is because the coolant will gain heat as it flows to the rear. Besides causing the rear cylinders to wear at a higher rate, the reduced heat flow to the coolant increases the risk of detonation, especially when these cylinders are operating on a weaker air/fuel mixture than the remaining cylinders.

One method of minimising this problem is to incorporate in the cylinder head a tube that runs from front to rear of the engine (Figure 2.159). Holes (2) formed in the tube (1) direct jets of 'cold' coolant around the outside of the exhaust valve seats and any other parts of the combustion chamber that need extra cooling. Holes in the **cylinder head gasket** allow convection currents to carry away the heat from the regions where the heat is less intense.

Cylinder head gasket: a component fitted between the cylinder head and cylinder block that creates a seal between the two components to allow pressure to build up in the combustion chambers and also prevents water and oil escaping from the engine or into the cylinders.

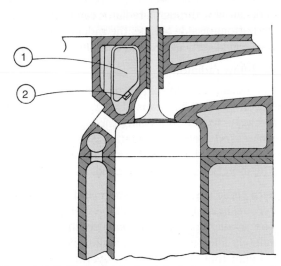

Figure 2.159 *Water distribution tube in the cylinder head*

The cooling pump (water pump)

Figure 2.160 shows a typical water pump. The body of the pump is generally a cast iron or light alloy casting, which carries a double-row ball bearing pre-packed with grease and sealed for life. The bearing must be robust because it has to withstand the radial load caused by the driving belt. Mounted on the spindle, and retained in position by an interference fit, is the impeller. This has either radial or curved vanes (Figure 2.161), which act as the means either to pressurise the coolant or to agitate the fluid sufficiently to produce a given flow. Various materials can be used for an impeller; it can be cast in iron, stamped in steel or moulded in plastic. The stamped impeller is very cheap but has a low pumping efficiency; as a result, the energy consumed lowers the fuel economy of the engine. A moulded impeller is more efficient but since this type suffers from bearing rotation and creep at the fixings, the cast impeller, shrouded in a manner to give a flow about three times greater than the stamped type, is favoured.

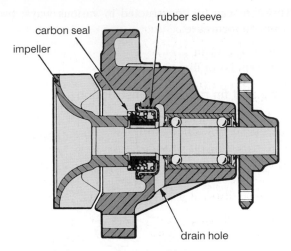

Figure 2.160 *A water pump assembly*

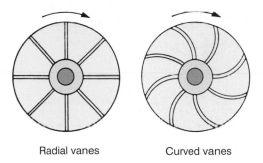

Radial vanes   Curved vanes

Figure 2.161 *The face of water pump impellers*

One of the most important parts of the pump is the seal between the impeller and casing. This is intended to prevent coolant entering the bearing, which would cause noise and rapid wear. The seal shown is retained in the casing and is a spring-loaded carbon type; this is bonded to a synthetic rubber sleeve fitted to allow for the difference in expansion between the carbon and the casing. An annular groove in the casing, on the bearing side of the seal, collects any coolant that might pass the seal; a drain hole at the bottom allows the coolant to drip from the pump – a sign that the pump seal is defective and the pump needs replacing.

Normally, the pump is situated at the front (crankshaft pulley end) of the engine and is driven at about crankshaft speed by a vee, flat or notched belt.

2.15.6 Radiators

The radiator is a liquid-to-air heat exchanger that consists of two tanks and a core or matrix from which heat is radiated from the coolant to the air. To be effective the hot coolant contact area exposed to air moving through the core should be as large as possible. Also, it should offer minimum resistance to the flow of air to ensure that the hot core is exposed to the coldest air.

The core can be constructed in various ways; two common forms are:

- tube and fin
- cellular or film type.

Tube and fin radiator construction

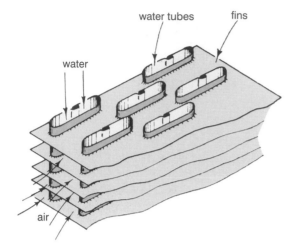

Figure 2.162 Tube and fin radiator construction

The tubes through which the coolant flows have a flattened oval section and are made of brass, about 0.125 mm thick. They are arranged in three or four rows and pass through a series of thin copper fins. The whole assembly is dipped in solder to bond the tubes and fins together.

A brass tank, fitted at each end of the core, connects with the tubes and provides a connection point for the synthetic rubber hoses that supply and receive the engine coolant.

Cellular or film-type radiator construction

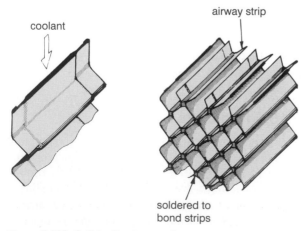

Figure 2.163 Cellular film-type radiator construction

Two forms of strip are used in this construction:

1 The waterway strip is a shallow trough with corrugated flanges. Two of these strips are placed together to form a water space similar in shape to a well-flattened tube.
2 The airway strip is deeply corrugated and is placed between the water tubes to increase the hot surface area.

After arranging the strips to form a matrix and fitting a tank to each end, the assembly is dipped in a solder bath to bond the strips and seal the waterways.

Radiators are now generally made from plastic and aluminium for lightness. The header tanks are usually plastic and connected together by an aluminium matrix.

Flow direction through a radiator

The coolant flow through a radiator can be from either top to bottom or side to side; the radiators giving this flow are called vertical-flow and cross-flow respectively.

Vertical-flow radiator

This is the earliest type of radiator and is designed to use the downward flow caused by natural convection as the water cools on passing through the radiator. The increased speed of circulation given by the pump overcomes the dependence on natural circulation, but the direction flow is unchanged.

Modern radiators are much wider and shorter than earlier designs, the actual shape being governed by the available space. To ensure the system is completely filled with coolant, a filler cap, combined with a vent that also acts as an overflow, is fitted at the highest point of the radiator.

On some cars with automatic transmission or high-performance engines, an oil cooler is used. This can be incorporated in the main radiator by mounting the oil cooler under the engine-cooling radiator.

Cross-flow radiator

Lower bonnet lines used in the last few years have meant that a wide, short radiator, often placed lower than the engine, is needed; this requirement is achieved with a cross-flow type. Used in conjunction with a pump, the system cools the water as it flows across the radiator. The two main engine hoses are connected to the end tanks; normally the 'hot' inlet to the radiator is situated higher than the outlet.

Figure 2.164 shows the layout of a typical cross-flow arrangement. This uses a separate reservoir that is often made of a transparent material to allow the coolant level to be checked. This reservoir also performs two other duties: it acts as an expansion chamber to allow for the change of coolant volume

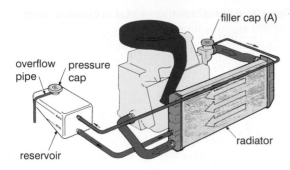

Figure 2.164 *Cross-flow cooling system layout*

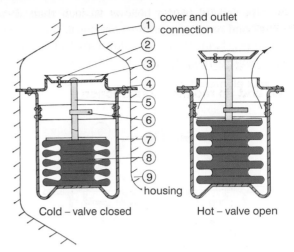

Figure 2.165 *A bellows type thermostat*

with change of temperature; and as a de-gas tank to condense the steam that collects at the highest point of the engine, the region under the filler cap (A).

Normal topping up of the system is made at the reservoir, but whenever the engine is drained, the system must be refilled at point A to avoid an air lock.

2.15.7 Temperature control of the cooling system

The cooling system must be capable of keeping the engine temperature within safe limits under the most arduous conditions, such as when climbing long, steep hills or at full throttle in hot climates. Since these conditions represent a very small proportion of the running time of most vehicles, it is clear that the cooling system will overcool the engine most of the time unless some method of reducing the effectiveness of the system when necessary is adopted. There are two ways in which this may be done:

1 By controlling the circulation of the water. This is the most common method and is done by a temperature-sensitive valve called a thermostat.
2 By controlling the airflow through the radiator by shutters or blinds.

Thermostats

There are two types: bellows type and wax element type.

Bellows type

This thermostat is seen in very early vehicles. The operating element is a sealed, flexible metal bellows (8) partly filled with a liquid that has a boiling point somewhat lower than the boiling point of water (such as alcohol, ether or acetone). Air is excluded from the bellows, which consequently contains the liquid and its vapour only, so that the pressure inside the bellows is due to the vapour pressure of the liquid. This varies with temperature, being equal to atmospheric pressure at the boiling temperature of the liquid: it is less at lower temperatures and greater at higher temperatures.

The lower end of the bellows is fixed to a frame (7), which is attached at its upper end to a circular flange (4), by which the thermostat is supported in its housing (9) that is usually formed in the outlet from the cylinder head to the radiator. A poppet-type valve (3) attached by a stem (5) to the top of the bellows controls a circular opening in the flange to regulate the flow of water. A flat spring blade (6) holds the stem in light contact with a V-shaped groove in a cross-member of the frame that supports the stem, and provides sufficient friction to prevent flutter of the valve.

At low temperatures, the pressure inside the bellows is lower than the atmospheric pressure outside and the bellows is contracted, holding the valve closed and preventing water circulating through the radiator.

As the water temperature increases, the hot water will collect around the thermostat, which is usually in the engine outlet connection, heating the liquid in the bellows and so increasing the pressure inside the bellows. At about the boiling temperature of the liquid in the bellows, the internal and external pressures will be equal, and the bellows will begin to extend and open the valve. This occurs at a temperature of about 70–80 °C. By the time the temperature has reached about 85–90 °C, the internal pressure in the bellows will have extended sufficiently to open the valve fully.

The thermostat will, therefore, perform two important functions:

1 It will shorten the time required to get the engine warmed up after a cold start.
2 It will prevent the temperature falling below about 70 °C when the engine is running at light loads.

A small hole (2) drilled in the valve acts as a vent to prevent air being trapped underneath the valve when the system is being filled, and a loosely fitting jiggle-pin prevents this hole becoming clogged.

The 'free length' of the bellows is such that when internal and external pressures are equal, the valve is open: thus, should the bellows develop a leak, the valve will remain open (i.e. the thermostat will be fail-safe).

The wax element type

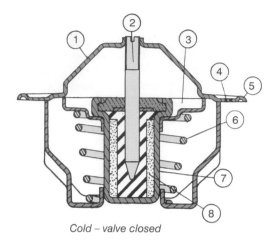

Cold – valve closed

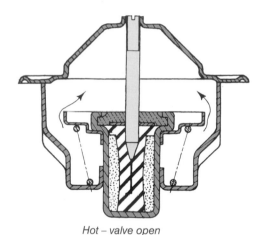

Hot – valve open

Figure 2.166 A wax-element-type thermostat

The operation of this type of thermostat (Figure 2.166) depends upon the considerable change in volume that occurs in certain types of wax at around melting point. The operating element is a substantial metal cylinder or capsule (7) filled with wax into which is inserted a thrust pin (2). A flexible rubber sleeve (8) surrounds the pin and is seated into the top of the capsule to prevent the escape of wax.

The thermostat is supported in its housing by the flange (5) in a similar manner to the bellows type, and the thrust pin (2) is attached to a bridge (1) spanning the flange. The valve (3) is attached to the capsule (7) and closes against an opening in the flange, being held in the closed position by the spring (6) when cold. The expansion of the wax during melting, forces the thrust pin out of the capsule, so opening the valve.

The useful life of this thermostat is claimed to be over 100,000 km; it is limited by a tendency for its opening temperature to increase because of deterioration of the rubber sleeve. It is much more robust than the bellows type, so that sudden and complete failure is extremely unlikely. This is just as well since failure would generally cause the valve to remain closed, resulting in overheating of the engine. However, if a leak develops in the rubber sleeve (8) below the thrust pin, the valve will stick open.

The hole (4) serves the same purpose as the hole in the bellows type (2) (Figure 2.165), and usually has a jiggle-pin also.

The opening temperature of wax-element-type thermostats is unaffected by coolant pressure, so this feature makes it suitable for use in most modern cooling systems.

Today, thermostats are often accompanied by bypass valves, which are operated electronically by the EMS. The bypass valves are usually located between the coolant outlets on the cylinder head and the supply line to the coolant pump. The purpose of the valve is to limit coolant flow to the coolant pump when the engine is warming up. The main part of the coolant flow is led to the heater matrix and back to the coolant pump.

The bypass valve helps the engine reach operating temperature more quickly. It regulates coolant flow in the thermostat housing to warm up the coolant more quickly. It remains open until the engine has reached operating temperature. Once reached, the thermostat and shut-off valve are completely open and the bypass valve is completely closed. At this stage, the large coolant circuit is open.

Use of the shut-off and bypass valves reduces warm-up time and allows the passenger compartment temperature to increase more quickly. The bypass and shut-off valves are regulated by the EMS through the information received from the coolant temperature sensor. Upon receipt of a signal from the EMS, the bypass valve completely or partially blocks coolant flow between the cylinder head coolant outlet and the coolant pump. Due to the engine being able to warm up quicker than normal, it will produce fewer emissions and use less fuel and also provide a warm driving compartment for the driver and passengers more quickly.

Radiator blinds

A very simple arrangement for controlling the airflow through the radiator is illustrated in Figure 2.167. A spring-loaded roller blind (4) is carried at the lower end of a rectangular channel-section frame secured to the front of the radiator. A cable control enables the blind to be raised to blank off as much of the radiator as may be necessary to maintain the required temperature. The end of the cable is taken into the driving compartment of the vehicle and incorporates some means of fixing the blind at a suitable height. It is desirable that a temperature gauge should be fitted to indicate to the driver the temperature of the cooling water.

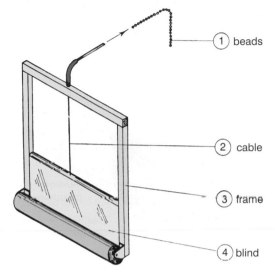

Figure 2.167 A simple radiator blind

Radiator shutters

This rather more complex arrangement for regulating the airflow through the radiator is illustrated in Figure 2.168. A rectangular frame fixed to the front of the radiator supports about 12 horizontal rods, each of which carries a metal strip about 40 mm (1½ in) wide. When these strips are all vertical, they blank off the airflow through the radiator, but by turning them 90° a free passage for air is provided.

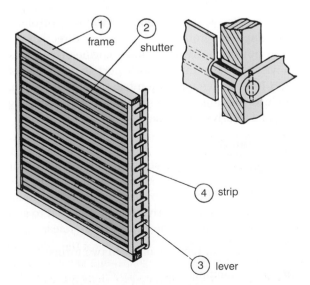

Figure 2.168 Radiator shutter assembly

Small levers fitted to one end of each spindle are connected to a vertical strip, which may be raised or lowered to open or close the shutters. This may be operated manually, as in the case of the blind, but the short movement necessary makes possible the use of a thermostat device.

Shutters such as these were once fitted to some of the more expensive types of vehicle and operated by a thermostat immersed in the radiator header tank. The arrangement used is normally fail-safe – any defect in the operating system results in the shutters being set in the fully open position.

In the past, shutters were rarely used on cars, but with the need to lower the air resistance of vehicles to improve on the efficiency and lower the emissions produced, the use of blinds or grille covers is now becoming more common.

Active grille roller cover

Wind resistance affects the vehicle's fuel consumption and hence environmental impact. The higher the speed, the greater the fuel consumption and environmental impact. The active grille's main function is to close the airflow through the cooling system and engine compartment and thereby reduce wind resistance.

The system consists of a roller cover with five plates that can regulate the opening to the radiator in a number of steps from fully open to fully closed. Although the purpose of the grille roller cover is to improve the wind resistance at higher speeds, the opening is also regulated in certain other driving situations, but then for faster warming of the engine.

With the adjustable grille cover the **Cd** value can be reduced, if necessary, by reducing the flow through the grille. It is at speeds above 70 kph that the grille cover is of most benefit.

> **Cd**: the coefficient of drag. The lower the Cd of a vehicle, the lower friction and air resistance it creates as it moves through the air and travels along the road. A lower Cd will improve the fuel economy and emissions produced by the vehicle.

The position of the disc plates is determined by taking into consideration engine temperature, air-conditioning compressor pressure, ambient temperature and vehicle speed.

The main reasons for regulating the roller cover are as follows:

- The air-conditioning system – at low speeds, the roller cover is open. At 70 kph, the roller cover starts to close.

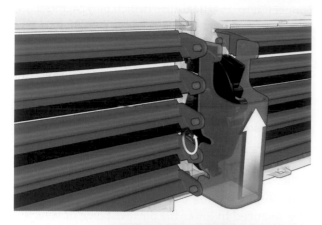

Figure 2.169 Active grille system

- Coolant temperature – normally the roller cover does not open because of high engine temperature. But if the car is driven under 40 kph for a long time and the engine temperature increases, then the roller cover is opened.
- High speed – if the car is driven at high speed (over 150 kph), the roller cover is opened.

High load – if the car has a trailer or is driven on a steep slope so that engine temperature increases, then the roller cover opens.

2.15.8 Cooling fans

In the simplest type of water-cooled system, the forward motion of the vehicle alone is relied upon to force sufficient air through the radiator. However, a positively driven fan gives a bigger airflow so that a smaller radiator can dissipate the required amount of heat. The simplest method of driving the fan is by a belt, usually the same belt that drives the alternator and the water pump: the engine-driven fan is often mounted on an extension of the water-pump spindle.

The fan is only needed when the air speed through the radiator is insufficient to control the temperature of the coolant. Other than at times when the vehicle speed is low, as in heavy traffic or hill climbing, the energy required to drive the fan continuously robs the engine of power and increases fuel consumption.

Although energy saving is achieved by aerodynamic shaping of the fan blades compared with pressed steel blades as used in the past, the modern vehicle achieves a better economy by using a drive system that 'cuts out' when fan operation is not needed. Two common systems are:

- electric
- viscous.

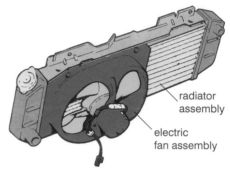

Figure 2.170 An electric fan cooling system

Electric fan drive

The fan is driven by a separate electric motor, which is only switched on when the cooling water reaches a predetermined temperature, for example 90 °C. The energy for the motor is controlled by either a thermostatic switch, sometimes a bimetallic type, fitted in the region of the header hose, or by a relay energised by a signal from the EMS via a temperature sensor located on the engine. This sensor will provide a voltage signal to the EMS that is proportional to a range of temperatures stored in the memory. The fan will be cycled in and out to maintain the appropriate temperature of the engine.

This type of fan is the most efficient way of controlling the engine temperature as it does not directly take engine power to drive it, unlike engine-driven fans and viscous fans that absorb certain amounts of power from the engine which takes fuel to generate, therefore providing more emissions and requiring more fuel to drive the vehicle.

Viscous fan drive

This type of drive has a disc-shaped clutch plate that is placed in a container of silicone fluid. The viscous drag of the fluid, caused by its resistance to shear, provides a non-positive drive that is designed to slip at an increasing rate as the engine speed rises.

Viscous drives for fans are made in two forms:

- torque-limiting
- air-sensing.

Torque-limiting fan drive

As the name suggests, this type is capable of transmitting to the fan a maximum torque that depends on the viscosity of the fluid. Figure 2.171 shows a typical construction. A clutch disc is sandwiched between the two halves of the casing, which is fitted with fluid seals to prevent leakage of the silicone fluid. Aluminium alloy is normally used as a material for the disc and casing.

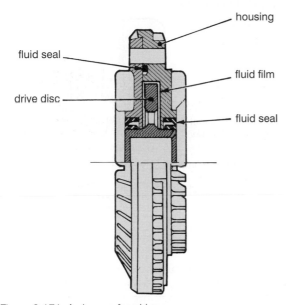

Figure 2.171 A viscous fan drive

This lightweight material is chosen because it has good thermal conductivity for dissipating the heat generated by the shearing action of the fluid: fins on the outside of the casing also aid the heat transfer from the coupling to the air.

The two graphs shown in Figure 2.172 show the performance characteristics of this type of drive.

Air-sensing fan drive

As well as torque-limiting, this type varies the fan speed to suit the temperature of the air that has passed through the radiator by controlling the amount of fluid in contact with the drive plate. When the temperature sensor detects that the coolant is below a temperature of about 75 °C, the fluid is evacuated from the drive chamber and the fan drive is disengaged. This saves more power than the torque-limiting type and also reduces fan noise.

Figure 2.173 shows an air-sensing fan drive. A spiral-shaped bimetal sensor is fitted at the front of the unit, and situated so that it is fully exposed to the air coming from the radiator. This sensor controls a valve arm, which is made to rotate through a small angle as the temperature changes and either cover or uncover an inlet port in the pump plate.

The fan is not needed at low radiator temperatures, so the sensor causes the valve plate to close the inlet port; this action stops the flow of fluid from the reservoir to the drive chamber. Since the existing fluid in this chamber is being pumped back to the reservoir continuously by the combination of centrifugal action and scoop movement, and no fluid is entering the chamber to take its place, the chamber soon empties and the drive disengages.

At high radiator temperatures, the thermostatic coil moves the valve arm and uncovers the inlet port; as a result, fluid flows from the reservoir to restore circulation between the reservoir and drive chamber and the drive to the fan occurs.

Figure 2.174 shows the performance characteristics of an air-sensing fan of the type fitted to light vehicles.

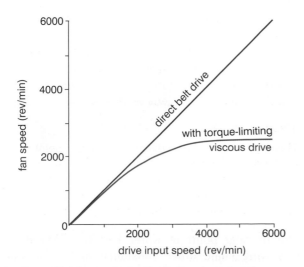

Figure 2.172 Viscous fan performance characteristics

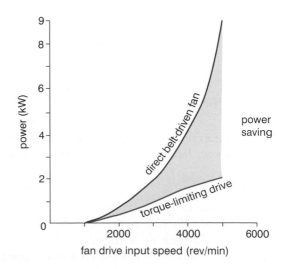

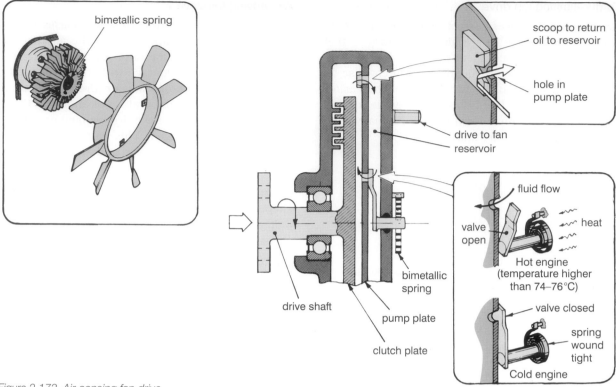

Figure 2.173 Air-sensing fan drive

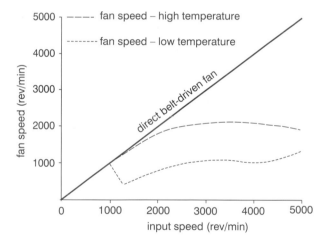

Figure 2.174 Characteristics of air-sensing fan

2.15.9 Use of antifreeze mixtures

One of the disadvantages of water as a coolant is the fact that in many parts of the world temperatures may drop below freezing during the winter months.

Water is peculiar in that its maximum density occurs at a temperature of 4 °C and from this point it expands with either a rise or fall in temperature. So long as it remains a liquid, this has no serious consequences, but solid ice expands as it freezes and will exert pressure on its container if it is sealed. If this happens to be the brittle cast-iron cylinder block, it is likely to

crack and this will result in a very expensive repair. A less drastic effect occurs when the expansion of the ice forces out the cylinder block core plugs.

These plugs, often made of brass and about 2 mm thick, blank off the core holes in the cylinder block. The holes are the result of the manufacturing process and are the places where the sand core, used to form the water jacket, is supported in the casting mould.

Prior to fitting, the plugs are shaped so that they are slightly convex. This allows the plug to be placed in the block recess and expanded by tapping the centre with a hammer, so as to allow the increase in its diameter to form a tight fit (Figure 2.175).

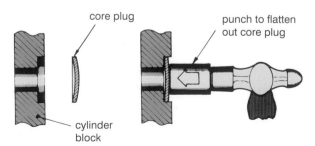

Figure 2.175 Core plug fitting

The freezing point of water can be lowered by dissolving some other substance in it. The one most commonly used is ethylene glycol. The effect of this liquid in lowering the freezing point of the coolant is shown in Figure 2.176. This graph shows that the coolant passes through a 'mushy ice' stage before it reaches the solid state that causes the structural damage. When partial freezing occurs while the vehicle is in use, the mushy ice that forms in the coldest part of the radiator tank interrupts the circulation and causes the engine to overheat.

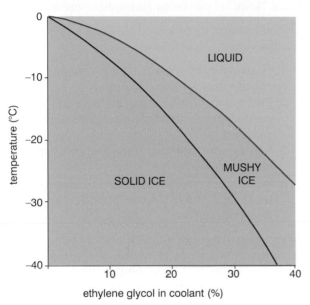

Figure 2.176 Effect of ethylene glycol on the freezing point of coolant

Ethylene glycol has the disadvantage of decomposing during use and forming acids that cause corrosion of parts, especially those made of aluminium alloy. To give protection to the many metals that come into contact with the coolant, suitable chemicals called corrosion inhibitors are added to the antifreeze solutions. In recent years, it has become common practice to leave the antifreeze in the cooling system for the whole year, rather than drain it at the end of the winter. In view of this, a reputable make of antifreeze should be used in order to give the engine all-year protection from corrosion.

In the UK, a coolant mixture containing 25 per cent antifreeze (i.e. one part antifreeze to three parts water) is often recommended to suit the conditions experienced during a normal winter. This proportion gives protection against ice damage down to -25 °C and gives coolant circulation down to about -12 °C.

Incidentally, the use of ethylene glycol in the coolant raises the boiling point; a 25 per cent solution raises it to about 103 °C.

Since the specific gravity of ethylene glycol differs from that of water, it is possible to check the proportion of antifreeze in the engine coolant by using a special hydrometer.

Use and disposal of antifreeze

Always ensure that you read the specification of the antifreeze to make sure that it is compatible with the engine being worked on. In many cases, antifreeze mixtures will mix but if you are not sure, the complete system should be drained and refilled with the new mixture.

As mentioned, antifreeze mixture can include ethylene glycol, an extremely toxic chemical to both humans and animals, which must be handled very carefully. Antifreeze should always be disposed of according to manufacturers' guidelines to avoid polluting waterways. Normally, automotive repairers will dispose of antifreeze in large containers that are then dispatched by specialist recyclers. Today, some antifreeze solutions are made from propylene glycol or other organic components, such as phosphate, and are silicate free. These are less toxic to humans and animals.

2.15.10 Pressurised cooling systems

Another disadvantage of water as a coolant is the fact that its boiling point is lower than the most efficient engine-operating temperature, and to prevent boiling and the formation of steam pockets around exhaust ports and sparking-plug bosses, it is necessary to keep the temperature of the water leaving the cylinder head below 85–90 °C.

The temperature at which a liquid boils rises as the pressure on it increases. In the case of water, the variation of boiling point with pressure is shown in Figure 2.177.

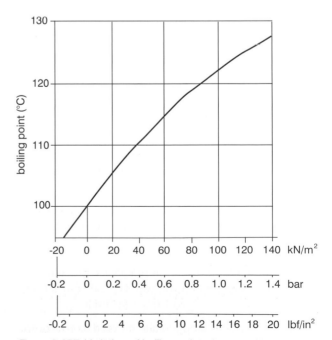

Figure 2.177 Variation of boiling point of water with pressure

Pressure can easily be imposed on the water in a cooling system by sealing it off from the atmosphere, so that any steam formed by the boiling water will raise the pressure and suppress further boiling until the temperature has risen still further. There is obviously a limit to the pressure that a radiator and rubber hoses can stand, and a pressure relief valve, such as that illustrated in Figure 2.178, is necessary. The one illustrated is incorporated in the header-tank filler cap.

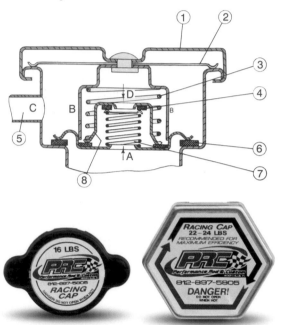

Figure 2.178 Pressure cap for coolant system

Starting from cold, the header tank will contain some air above the water at a pressure approximately that of the atmosphere. As the water is heated it expands, compressing the air. If the temperature rises sufficiently for boiling to begin, the steam formed will raise the pressure still further. This suppresses the boiling until the pressure in the header tank rises sufficiently to lift the pressure valve (8) against the loading of the spring (3), whereupon air and steam will be able to escape through the vent pipe (5). By this means, the system may be operated without boiling at a temperature slightly below that corresponding to the pressure needed to lift the valve.

The operating pressure that may be used with a cooling system is governed by the strength of the radiator and hoses. When this has been decided by the manufacturer, the appropriate radiator pressure cap is fitted. For information purposes, the 'blow off' pressure is stamped on the cap; typical values range from 0.5 bar (7 lbf in^{-2}) to 1.0 bar (15 lbf in^{-2}).

When the engine is stopped and allowed to cool down, condensation of vapour and contraction of the water

will reduce the pressure in the header tank. Should this pressure fall appreciably below atmospheric, there is a risk of the hoses and even the header tank collapsing. To prevent this, a vacuum valve (4) is fitted in the centre of the pressure valve and acts in the opposite direction (i.e. it is closed by a spring (7) assisted by positive pressure inside the header tank, but opens against the spring loading if header-tank pressure falls about 7 kN m^{-2} (1 psi) below atmospheric pressure).

The advantages to be gained by using a pressurised cooling system are as follows:

1 Elimination of coolant loss by surging of the coolant during heavy braking.
2 Prevention of boiling during long hill climbs, particularly, for example, in regions high above sea level.
3 Raising the working temperature improves engine efficiency.
4 It allows a smaller radiator to dissipate as much heat as a larger one, operating at a lower temperature.

Never remove the cap when the coolant temperature is above 100 °C, since the release of pressure will allow the water to boil violently: the resulting jet of steam and water from the open filler can cause serious scalds. At temperatures below this, the cap should be released slowly: it is designed so that the spring disc (2) (which is riveted between the cover (1) and the frame that contains the valves) remains seated on the top of the filler neck until after the seal (6) has lifted, so allowing pressure to escape through the vent pipe (5) before it can escape from the main opening.

Since bellows-type thermostats are sensitive to pressure changes, they are unsuitable for use in pressurised cooling systems. The wax element type does not have this disadvantage.

2.15.11 Sealed cooling systems

A further refinement of the cooling system consists of an arrangement whereby the system is kept completely full of coolant, expansion of the coolant being accommodated by providing an expansion tank into which the displaced coolant can pass and from which it can return to the system as the coolant in the system contracts on cooling. There are several variations of the arrangement, of which two are briefly described.

Figure 2.179 shows an addition to the pressurised system already described, the modification consisting of leading the vent pipe from the filler neck to the bottom of an expansion tank. A vent pipe is fitted to the top of the expansion tank, which may – though not necessarily – have a drain tap and a filler cap.

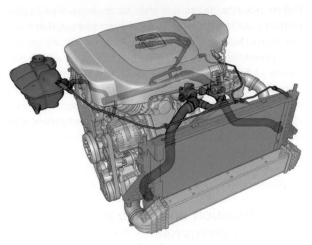

Figure 2.179 *Cooling system showing radiator expansion tank*

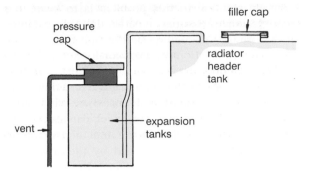

Figure 2.180 *Alternative radiator expansion tank*

The pressure cap differs from that shown in Figure 2.178 only in having a sealing gasket fitted between the filler neck and the spring disc (2). Some systems use a plastic, screw-type cap arrangement. This works in the same principle in pressurising the coolant system. A pressure release valve is incorporated into the cap to relieve any excess pressure.

The system is completely filled with coolant up to the top of the filler neck and the cap fitted. As the engine warms up the coolant expands, lifting the pressure valve off its seating, and some coolant passes into the expansion tank. Air displaced from the expansion tank escapes through the vent pipe. The expansion tank is seldom more than about half full under normal conditions.

As the engine cools down after stopping, the coolant in the system contracts, withdrawing coolant from the expansion tank back into the system through the filter cap vacuum valve – hence, the necessity for the gasket under the spring disc.

A variation of this system uses a plain, airtight filler cap on the header tank, the pressure and vacuum valves being contained in a small housing permanently attached to the header tank.

Figure 2.180 shows an alternative system in which the pressure cap is fitted on the expansion tank, which is connected to the top of the header tank by a small pipe. The filler neck on the header tank is sealed by a plain cap. The header tank is completely filled with coolant and a small amount of coolant is also put into the expansion tank. As the system warms up, coolant expands into expansion tank, which in this case is under pressure. As the system cools down, coolant from the expansion tank is drawn back into the header tank.

The advantages claimed for a sealed system are:

- it eliminates coolant loss by expansion
- it eliminates the need for periodic topping up, and prevents possible damage by neglecting to top up
- by excluding air from the main system, it considerably reduces corrosion of the components in the cooling system and deterioration of the antifreeze additives.

2.16 Supercharging and turbocharging (forced induction)

2.16.1 Principles of forced induction

The power that any internal-combustion engine can develop depends fundamentally upon the mass of air it can consume per minute. The normal method of filling or charging the cylinders of a four-stroke engine consists of allowing the pressure of the atmosphere to force air into the engine cylinders to relieve the partial vacuum formed when the pistons move downwards on their induction strokes. If the air is forced into the cylinders under a pressure higher than atmospheric pressure, a greater mass of air will enter the cylinder and the engine will be supercharged. This can be done by using some kind of air pump to deliver air to the engine: such a device is called a supercharger or turbocharger.

The supercharger's purpose is to provide the fresh charge for the engine at higher pressure than atmospheric pressure, which is delivered to conventional normally aspirated engines (unsupercharged). The increase in pressure of this fresh charge will then also create a much higher pressure during the compression stroke of the engine. When this occurs, the pressure build-up in the combustion chamber will be too high, leading to increased combustion chamber temperatures. This can create a premature ignition of the air/fuel mixture sometimes called pre-ignition.

A simple solution to this problem is to lower the compression pressures created in the cylinder by lowering the compression ratio. Due to this essential modification required for forced induction engines, compression ratios are normally lower than conventional normally aspirated engines. A downside of lower compression ratios is that these can lead to lower combustion efficiencies, which can also create higher emissions and increase fuel consumption. However, this is far outweighed by the advantage of higher engine power produced by introducing additional air into the cylinders.

Supercharging is extremely effective in enabling high power outputs to be obtained from smaller engines, improving the engine package size in vehicles to allow for improved design, aerodynamics and weight benefits. An initial disadvantage of this process is that fuel consumption can be higher unless additional arrangements are incorporated to offset the lower compression ratio, and to allow for the energy needed to drive the unit. This issue was especially noticed on earlier engines.

Today, manufacturers are able to make use of highly sophisticated EMSs to control fuelling and ignition very precisely. This means that supercharged engines can be both powerful and efficient. Also, the use of additional forced induction is now common with manufacturers for smaller engines to improve on fuel efficiency and lower the emissions produced. Volkswagen now use supercharging and turbocharging (twin chargers) on engines with capacity of 1400 cc that produce up to 180 bhp, something that used to require an engine capacity of at least 2000 cc. These engines provide excellent power to weight and fuel efficiencies.

2.16.2 Position and drive arrangements of the supercharger

The position of the supercharger in the induction system depends on the fuel system used. On early spark-ignition engines, the supercharger, or blower as it is often called, delivered air to the carburettor, but this system was later abandoned in favour of a position where it delivered the mixture from the carburettor to the engine. With the advent of petrol injection, the

Figure 2.181 Volkswagen twin-charger arrangement

arrangement has reverted to the original configuration: most modern superchargers only pump air.

The supercharger may be positively driven by a belt, chain or gears from the engine crankshaft. The drive arrangements found on today's superchargers include a facility to engage and disengage the drive to the supercharger to modulate the pressure produced. This is mainly done through the use of a magnetic clutch operated by the EMS. When the engine requires boost from the supercharger, the EMS will engage the clutch, which will in turn drive the supercharger forcing air into the engine.

Superchargers may also be driven by exhaust gases from the engine. This gas-driven type, the turbocharger, is favoured today because it uses the energy in the exhaust gas instead of using the power from the engine.

Turbocharging

The turbocharger is driven by the exhaust gases flowing from the engine through the exhaust manifold. The use of this fast-moving gas provides a means to generate movement of the turbine blades within the turbocharger, which in turn draws air into the turbocharger and forces it out at higher pressure. This is gained through 'free' energy and so is often the preferred route by manufacturers. Figure 2.182 shows a turbocharger *in situ* running at high temperatures.

Figure 2.182 Turbocharger running at high temperatures

It is sometimes claimed that the turbocharger is the answer to emission problems as well as present-day demands for a better fuel consumption, but the latter is difficult to obtain from a spark-ignition engine unless the unit is very carefully matched with the engine. This proviso is based on the fact that thermal efficiency (or fuel economy) depends on the compression ratio of the engine, and to make sure detonation is avoided, the ratio must be lowered when a supercharger or turbocharger is fitted. Yet, when dealing with the more modern engines seen in today's vehicles, manufacturers are able to use the powerful EMSs to allow higher compression ratios, therefore providing improved combustion efficiencies without the issue of pre-ignition and detonation.

Supercharged compression-ignition engines (diesel)

Supercharging is not limited to spark-ignition engines; compression-ignition engines may also be supercharged and may even be more suitable subjects for supercharging. A typical example of the introduction of a supercharger into a compression-ignition engine is where there is a need to raise maximum engine power to meet a legally permitted increase in the load carried by a vehicle. Instead of fitting a larger engine, many manufacturers have up-rated the power of the existing engine by using a turbocharger or supercharger.

In general, the problem of the compression ratio does not apply to compression-ignition engines, so the following gives a rough guide to the advantages gained by turbocharging a compression-ignition engine:

1 A four-cylinder turbocharged engine gives the power output of a six-cylinder unblown engine (normally aspirated).
2 A six-cylinder turbocharged engine gives the fuel consumption of a four-cylinder unblown engine (normally aspirated).

Two-stroke engines

A two-stroke engine, of course, does not have an induction stroke and relies upon air being forced into its cylinders by some kind of pump, but the engine is not supercharged unless the pressure of the air filling the cylinder is above atmospheric pressure. A two-stroke engine is normally pressure-charged by using a separate cylinder as a charging cylinder (as in the Clerk engine), by using the underneath of the working piston (as in the Day engine, see page 37) or by using some other kind of air pump such as a Roots blower (see page 136). Strictly, a two-stroke engine cannot be supercharged unless the exhaust ports are arranged to close before the inlet ports close.

2.16.3 Types of direct drive superchargers

The Roots blower

This device was patented about 1865 by F.M. and P.H. Roots in America and was used for a number of purposes including (in very large sizes) ventilating mines. Figure 2.183 illustrates the construction generally used for engine supercharging: depending on engine size, the width of the casing would be about 150–300 mm (6–12 in).

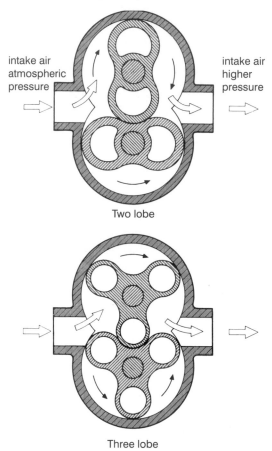

Figure 2.183 Roots blowers

It can be regarded as a form of gear pump in which each gear (called a rotor in the Roots blower) has only two teeth or lobes. (Some Roots blowers have rotors with three or even four lobes.) The rotors have a small clearance inside the casing and are carried on shafts, which are geared together outside the casing: one shaft is driven at approximately engine speed which then drives the other at the same speed.

The Roots blower is an air displacer and not a compressor: the air is not compressed within the blower but simply carried around from inlet side to outlet side in the spaces between the lobes and the casing. The pressure at the output side depends upon the relative swept volumes of the blower and the engine, and the speed at which the blower is driven.

The rotors operate continuously against the full delivery pressure and, thus, more power is absorbed in driving this device than would be required if compression took place within the blower: at low pressures this disadvantage is small, but it increases rapidly as pressure rises.

Owing to the rotor clearance there will be some 'back leakage' of air. This increases as delivery pressure rises and decreases as speed increases. Hence this type of supercharger is mostly used for high-speed engines and relatively low supercharge pressures.

The operation of this type of supercharger in a modern vehicle application would be similar to that described in the 'drive arrangements' section (page 86). The EMS will engage the blower through the use of a magnetic clutch to modulate the pressure produced. The Roots blower also requires oil to prevent the gear drive from seizing. During routine maintenance, it is good practice to check the supercharger oil level.

Vane compressor

In its simplest form, this compressor consists of a cylindrical casing in which is mounted eccentrically a cylindrical rotor carrying protruding vanes that divide the space between the rotor and the casing into a number of compartments, which vary in volume as the rotor turns.

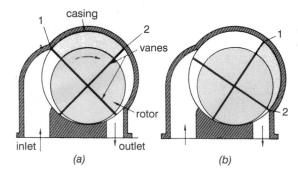

Figure 2.184 The principle of the vane compressor

In Figure 2.184a, the compartment shown shaded is in the position of maximum volume and the vane (1) has just cut off communication between this compartment and the inlet port. In Figure 2.184b, the rotor has turned to the position where the vane (2) is just about to open the compartment to the outlet port, and it can be seen that the volume of the compartment is now smaller than it was in Figure 2.184a. By altering the position of the leading edge of the outlet port, the amount of compression within the compressor can be altered, and this would normally be arranged to correspond with the required delivery pressure.

Figure 2.185 shows one practical form of this compressor which has, at various times, been marketed under the names of Centric, Arnett and Shorrocks.

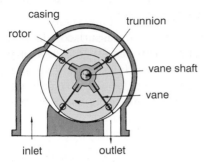

Figure 2.185 *The trunnion-type radial vane compressor*

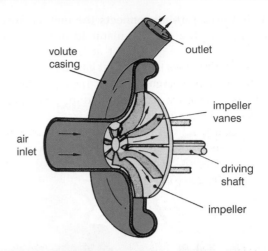

Figure 2.186 *Centrifugal blower*

The vanes are mounted on a shaft, which is placed centrally in the casing, each vane being carried on two ball bearings so that the vanes are always radial to the casing. The vanes pass through slotted rods or trunnions carried in the rotor and there is a very small clearance between the tips of the vanes and the casing. The rotor is driven at approximately engine speed by a belt, chain or gear drive.

One minor disadvantage of the vane compressor is the necessity for lubrication due to the sliding of the vanes in the rotor. While this is fairly easy to arrange, it is undesirable because oil mist carried into the engine may cause combustion difficulties, particularly in compression-ignition engines.

The centrifugal blower

If the Roots blower can be likened to a gear pump, the centrifugal blower can be simply described as a glorified water pump (as used in an engine-cooling system). The impeller is more carefully designed and made than the corresponding part of the water pump and is driven at considerably higher speed.

Figure 2.186 illustrates the construction. The shaft is driven at some five to six times engine speed: air is drawn in through the intake, carried around between the vanes of the impeller and thrown outwards by centrifugal force into the volute casing from which it passes to the inlet manifold.

The main benefit of the centrifugal blower is that a small size of blower can deliver a considerable quantity of air. However, it has two main disadvantages for automobile use:

1 It must be driven at very high speed (which introduces problems in the drive arrangements during rapid acceleration and deceleration).
2 It is only efficient over a very narrow range.

Turbo-type supercharger (turbocharger)

The difficulty in driving a centrifugal blower at very high speeds, and the loss of up to 35 per cent of the engine power to provide this drive, can be neatly overcome by using the energy contained in the exhaust gas to supercharge the engine. The combination of centrifugal compressor and exhaust-driven turbine is called a turbo-supercharger or turbocharger.

Attempts to apply this principle to engines have been made from time to time since the 1900s, but only within recent years has the method been applied to vehicles. The blades of a turbine have to operate at a high temperature of about 1000 °C, so only when a reasonably priced metal became available for the blades was it possible to make an economical unit. Today, nickel or nickel-chromium alloy iron is used.

Normally, a turbine of the radial flow type is used to drive the compressor. It has a similar construction to a centrifugal blower, but the gas flow through the unit is reversed (Figure 2.187). A cast-iron casing, formed like a snail's shell to feed the exhaust gas on to the periphery of the turbine blades, encloses the turbine. A flange on the part of the casing that forms the gas passage to the turbine connects the unit as closely as possible to the exhaust manifold of the engine. A connection at the gas outlet at the centre of the turbine casing allows the exhaust gas to be passed to a normal exhaust system.

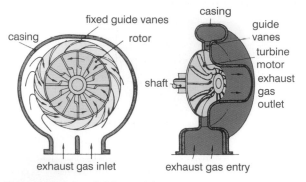

Figure 2.187 A radial flow turbine

When the unit is in operation, the exhaust gas, expelled from the engine cylinders at high temperature and velocity, is delivered into the casing that feeds the turbine rotor. Before the gas flows from the casing to the turbine, it first has to pass through either specially shaped passages or a ring of guide vanes; these ensure that the gas strikes the outer tips of the turbine blades tangentially so that the turbine can be driven in the required direction. As the gas flows towards the centre of the turbine, the blades slow it down. This action extracts energy from the gas and causes the turbine to spin at a high speed, in excess of 100,000 rpm under engine conditions in which the temperature and/or velocity of the exhaust gas is high.

The exhaust-driven turbine is supported by a shaft that transmits the drive to the centrifugal compressor. The casings of aluminium alloy and cast iron for compressor

and turbine respectively are bolted together to form a single unit; it is this assembly that is called a turbocharger or 'turbo' for short (Figure 2.188).

In view of the high speed of operation, two plain floating bearings (often made of cast iron) are needed to support the shaft (Figure 2.189). This type of bearing requires a pressurised supply of clean oil to resist wear and an adequate flow of oil to keep the bearings cool. The bearings are supplied with oil by a pipe connected to the engine's lubrication system. After passing through the bearings the oil is collected in a cavity, formed in the casing between the compressor and turbine, from where it is allowed to drain naturally back into the engine sump.

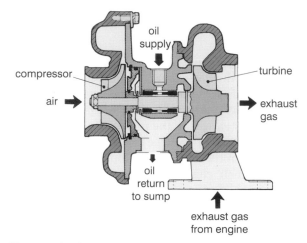

Figure 2.189 Section through a turbocharger

Gas and oil sealing is very important. Oil must not enter the compressor and exhaust gas must not pass to the bearings. The onset of either condition

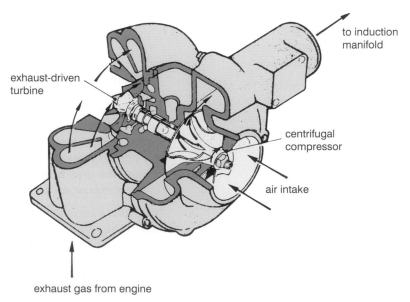

Figure 2.188 A turbocharger assembly

soon becomes apparent to the driver. Oil passing the compressor seal, especially when it is being pumped through by exhaust gas that is escaping from the turbine, produces a vast quantity of blue smoke. Any defect in the turbocharger that disturbs the action of the seals, such as shaft movement caused by worn bearings, soon shows up. Poor lubrication, caused by a lack of pressure or dirty oil, is a common cause of rapid bearing wear; this is accelerated when the shaft movement allows hot exhaust gas to escape into the bearings. When this occurs, the future life of the unit is limited to a few seconds.

Figure 2.189 also shows the bearing and seal arrangement. This design uses cast-iron sealing rings with a construction similar to a piston ring.

Special care of the turbocharger is needed to ensure that the bearings are not starved of oil when the engine is either started or stopped. The engine should not be accelerated either immediately after it has been started or just prior to switching off. (Bear in mind that it takes a long time for the turbine to come to rest.) In some cases, a turbo timer is fitted to the vehicle; this device prevents the engine from shutting down immediately when the ignition is turned off. When the driver switches off the ignition, the turbo timer will carry on running the engine for a predetermined time (one minute in many cases). After this time, the engine will stop. This can happen automatically so the driver does not need to be still with the vehicle. By using these devices the engine continues to supply oil through the turbo until it has stopped and cooled down.

2.16.4 Turbocharging for diesel and petrol engines

Fitting a turbocharger to an engine that was originally designed as a normally aspirated engine can produce some advantages as long as suitable modifications have taken place, including lowering the compression ratio. The advantages can include the following:

1 Improved torque and power produced, in many cases this can be 60 per cent and above. Due to the engine being smaller than a similarly powered normally aspirated engine, the power to weight benefit is high.
2 Fuel consumption can be improved through the use of forced induction.
3 The exhaust noise is reduced due to the turbocharger interrupting and smoothing out the exhaust pulses.

Diesel engine applications

Compression-ignition engines

Turbocharging has been commonly used on large compression-ignition engines for many years, since this type of engine is particularly suited to pressure-charging. Unlike the spark-ignition type, the compression-ignition engine does not suffer from compression limitations and, in addition, the air-only induction system of a compression-ignition unit combined with more under-bonnet space makes the fitting of a turbocharger much easier.

Today, diesel engine vehicles are often more powerful than their equivalent petrol-powered vehicles. With diesel producing more torque and benefiting from excellent fuel economy, the diesel engine has become very popular across European markets. With advances in EMSs, turbocharging and increases in fuel-delivery pressures, diesel engines have proved themselves to be extremely efficient and powerful. Manufacturers are now fitting diesel engines into many of their sports models due to this big improvement. An example of this can be seen with Peugeot fitting the 2-litre turbocharged diesel engine into the RCZ sports car.

Figure 2.190 Peugeot RCZ diesel sports car

Petrol engine applications

A car fitted with turbocharging was normally associated with top-of-the-range models designed to give a performance, especially acceleration in mid range, far above the norm. This is no longer the case as more manufacturers look to turbocharging to provide excellent performance with low running costs by using smaller engines with forced induction. Engines that are suitable for turbocharging conversion must be structurally strong enough to withstand the extra load and higher speed. Also, before the engine is turbocharged it must have its compression ratio lowered to avoid mechanical damage caused by combustion problems, such as detonation.

All current turbocharged engines use fuel-injection systems because these arrangements overcome the pressure problems that arise when carburettors are used and also ensure that the vehicle produces the lowest emissions possible. Careful matching of the turbocharger to a given engine ensures that the maximum boost (pressure above atmospheric) is limited to about 1.5 bar (22 psi) (i.e. the maximum pressure in the inlet manifold is atmospheric pressure plus 1.5 times atmospheric pressure).

Boost limitation and boost control

The exhaust gas of a petrol engine power unit is much hotter than that exhausted by a diesel engine, so this places extra stress on the turbocharger. Furthermore, current emission regulations relating to the discharge of NO_x mean that the boost must be reduced at times when this pollutant would normally be produced. This occurs at high engine speed and/or maximum load. Therefore, to meet this requirement, and also minimise the risk of engine damage, a boost-limiting valve is fitted (Figure 2.191). Under high load conditions, this poppet-type valve, which is often called a wastegate, is opened mechanically by a wastegate actuator to allow some of the exhaust gas to bypass the turbine and reduce its pumping action. In conjunction with the turbocharger, many modern power units also use an electronic EMS to set the ignition timing to suit the boost pressure. They also incorporate an electronic boost-control valve, which modulates the pressure produced by the turbocharger by altering the pressure acting upon the wastegate actuator.

NO_x: oxides of nitrogen. These gases are produced by the engine under very hot combustion temperatures, such as when fitted with a pressure-charging device like the turbocharger. They are pollutants.

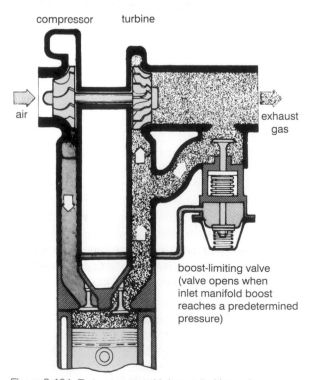

compressor   turbine

air

exhaust gas

boost-limiting valve (valve opens when inlet manifold boost reaches a predetermined pressure)

Figure 2.191 Turbocharger with boost-limiting valve

Electronic wastegate actuation is now common on many engines. This system uses the signals obtained from the sensors located on the engine to determine the precise level of boost required by the engine to meet the performance and emission requirements across the whole engine speed range. The operation of opening the wastegate is controlled by the EMS moving a solenoid or motor to open and close the wastegate through electronic signals. When the EMS notes a high boost pressure from the intake pressure sensor, it will operate the wastegate actuator solenoid or motor and modulate the pressure to avoid it rising too high. Along with this, the EMS will alter the fuelling and ignition settings to maintain the best performance and lowest emissions possible. In this way, the boost pressure is monitored in a much more accurate way than depending on the vacuum signal from the intake manifold alone.

An alternative method of limiting boost pressure is to use a pressure relief valve in the induction manifold; this opens when the boost reaches a predetermined maximum and allows air in the manifold to bleed to the atmosphere. These are sometimes called 'blow-off valves'.

Re-circulation and dump valves

Some turbocharged engines incorporate a valve either within the turbocharger or within the intake system to limit the pressure built up on the intake turbine of the turbocharger during a closed throttle position. When the engine is running at higher engine speeds, the turbocharger will be producing boost pressure pushing air into the engine through the open throttle. When the throttle is released, this built-up pressure has nowhere to go so acts upon the turbine impellor within the turbo slowing the turbine down. When the throttle is then opened and exhaust gases are pushed down the exhaust manifold, in order to spin up the turbocharger again the turbine has to build speed back up causing some lag. Fitting a recirculation valve or 'dump valve' as they are sometimes called (Figure 2.192) will release the pressure built up in the intake system when the throttle is closed, removing the pressure from the turbine blades allowing them to continue to spin at higher speeds until the throttle is then opened again and the turbo is able to build up boost pressure once more. This action improves the turbo response and limits the lag between gear changes when the throttle is opened and closed. Some after-market recirculation valves release this pressure to the atmosphere with a distinctive 'whoosh' noise. Manufacture-fitted valves release the pressure back into the intake system before the turbocharger and are much quieter.

Figure 2.192 Example of a recirculation or dump valve

Charge-air coolers (intercoolers)

Compression of the charge and its passage through a hot turbocharger raises the temperature of the air; this results in a reduction of the density of the charge. To overcome this problem, some diesel and petrol engines have a heat exchanger fitted between the turbocharger and engine (Figure 2.193). This unit, often called an intercooler, is generally an air-to-air exchanger and, by lowering the air temperature to around 50–60 °C, the VE is improved and the detonation tolerance is increased.

Figure 2.193 Example of an intercooler unit

An alternative to the intercooler is the air-to-liquid charge cooler. This component works in a similar way to an intercooler but also uses liquid coolant to cool the intake air even more. The air-to-liquid charge cooler is generally used where the engine is producing high-boost pressures and the need to limit the intake air temperature is vital. The charge cooler requires more plumbing and components than the intercooler and will generally require its own coolant and pump to circulate the coolant around the system.

Advantages and disadvantages of turbocharging petrol engines

The advantages of turbocharging a petrol engine are:

- higher torque for acceleration from low speed
- lower exhaust noise and emission
- better fuel economy due to a reduction in the pumping energy expended during the induction stroke. (Generally, this advantage is seldom achieved in practice because many drivers alter their driving technique to take full advantage of the extra power of a turbocharged engine.)

The main disadvantages of a turbocharged petrol engine, apart from the extra hazards created when incompetent drivers attempt to demonstrate the extra performance, are:

- higher initial cost of turbocharger and allied equipment
- higher repair and servicing costs, especially when other engine components are damaged by a defective unit
- delayed engine response after depressing the accelerator. Since the turbine takes a time to reach its effective speed, an acceleration delay occurs with older-type units. This is usually referred to as 'turbo lag'.

Variable-geometry turbochargers

Turbochargers are often related to noise, high NO_x emissions and 'laggy' performance. In the early years of development, this was the case and many high-performance vehicles suffered with large amounts of lag before huge amounts of power were introduced. This made driving these vehicles smoothly fairly difficult due to the all-or-nothing delivery. Today, manufacturers are able to produce engines that have excellent power and low emissions, along with vastly improved driving refinement.

This improvement is because of extensive design developments and improvements in fuel and ignition control with the use of highly complex and powerful EMSs. The turbo design has changed over recent years to enable big improvements in boost delivery without the large amounts of lag previously experienced. One of the main improvements is the introduction of variable-geometry turbochargers (VGTs), sometimes called variable-vane turbochargers.

The VGT is commonly used on diesel engines due to its ability to vastly improve the low-down engine power and torque values. Now the VGT is also used on petrol turbo vehicles as it produces the benefits of improved response and lower emissions. The VGT works by altering the flow of exhaust gases at the turbo inlet to optimise the exhaust gas flow over all engine speeds.

On normal turbochargers, the exhaust gas will flow over the turbine hitting the blades at the same pitch no matter what the engine speed. This works well over a narrow engine speed so can produce a delay in the performance produced (lag).

With the VGT, the exhaust gases are directed on to the turbine blades at different angles through the use of the movable vanes. The angle of the vanes (Figure 2.194) varies throughout the whole engine speed range through actuation of a device, which looks similar to the wastegate actuator. This action optimises the turbine behaviour throughout the engine speed range.

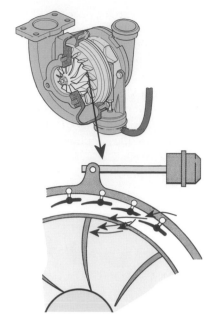

Figure 2.195 Vane position at lower engine speeds

Figure 2.194 VGT turbine blade arrangement

At low engine speeds the vanes are almost closed, as this narrow passage that the exhaust gas has to flow through increases the speed flowing over the turbine blades and ensures that the gas hits the blades at the optimum angle to produce the highest rotational torque on the blades. This action improves low-down engine speed response. Figure 2.195 shows the angle of the vanes at lower engine speeds producing high rotational torque on the blades.

As the engine speed increases, the exhaust gas speed will also increase. As this happens, the vanes are moved towards an open position directing the exhaust gases directly on to the turbine blades at a lower angle since the speed of the exhaust gas is able to spin the turbine at a suitable rate to generate the boost required (Figure 2.196).

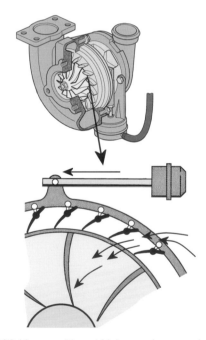

Figure 2.196 Vane position at higher engine speeds

The need for a wastegate is removed in this type of turbocharger as the action of the vanes continually alters the level of boost generated. The vanes are moved through the use of vacuum or electric stepper motors. Both are controlled by the EMS.

The benefits of using a VGT over a conventional turbocharger are that it can produce a much better response during lower engine speeds and improves the torque output of the engine. Fuel economy can also be improved due to the change to the power and torque produced by the engine at lower engine speeds.

Manufacturers have commonly used the VGT on turbo diesel engines, but only recently have they used a version on their petrol variants. It was the Porsche 997 (Porsche 911) that first used this type of turbo in its petrol-driven engine. Up until then, vehicle manufactures found it difficult to produce a VTG turbo that could withstand the higher temperatures that a petrol engine produces. The level of heat generated with a VTG turbo compared to a conventional assembly could reach around 200 °C higher. Porsche worked closely with BorgWarner and used a material developed from aerospace technology to construct a turbo assembly that could resolve these temperature issues.

2.17 Petrol four-stroke cycle in detail

2.17.1 Valve operation and the four-stroke engine

Earlier in this chapter the overall operation of an engine on the four-stroke cycle was described. We must now consider this more closely, particularly in connection with the opening and closing of the valves.

The first point to be appreciated is the fact that it is not possible for a valve to move from closed to fully open or vice versa instantaneously. In fact, the opening and the closing movements will each be spread over a considerable angle of crankshaft rotation. Thus, if a valve is required to be effectively open at the beginning of a stroke, it must begin to open before the dead centre: similarly, if it is required to be effectively open at the end of a stroke, it must not close completely until after the dead centre.

Even if the valves could be opened and closed instantaneously, the dead centres would not be the best points at which they should open and close except at very low engine speeds. The engine will give its best performance when the greatest mass of air and fuel is passed through the combustion chamber and burnt effectively. Consider an engine running reasonably fast. The most suitable point at which to open the inlet port depends upon conditions at the end of the exhaust stroke, and we will begin our study with the piston moving down the cylinder on the induction stroke and the inlet port already wide open (Figure 2.197). The downward movement of the piston reduces the pressure inside the cylinder so that the pressure of the atmosphere forces air through the carburettor and along the inlet pipe (i.e. the flow of air along the pipe is accelerated). The inertia of this air (its resistance to change of speed) causes it to lag behind the piston movement, so that by the time the piston has reached its maximum speed (about halfway down the stroke) the

pressure inside the cylinder is well below atmospheric pressure, but during the second half of the stroke, when the piston speed is decreasing, the airflow is able to catch up with the piston and the pressure inside the cylinder rises towards atmospheric pressure.

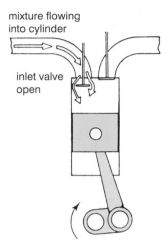

Air/fuel mixture entering cylinder during induction stroke

Figure 2.197 Induction stroke

At BDC the direction of piston movement reverses, but the momentum of the airflow along the inlet pipe towards the cylinder causes it to continue entering the cylinder until the piston has moved some way up the next stroke – provided the valve remains open (Figure 2.198). At some point during this stroke the upward movement of the piston increases the pressure inside the cylinder sufficiently to stop the inward flow of air and to begin to force air out of the cylinder (Figure 2.199), and the greatest possible amount of air will be trapped inside the cylinder if the inlet valve closes at this point. This will always be after BDC. How much after will depend upon engine speed, and the length and diameter of the inlet pipe and throttle opening.

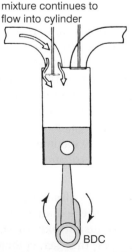

Momentum of mixture maintains flow into cylinder at BDC

Figure 2.198 End of induction stroke

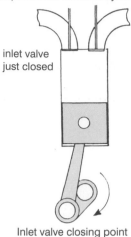

rising piston increases pressure inside cylinder
and stops mixture flow into cylinder

inlet valve
just closed

Inlet valve closing point

Figure 2.199 Compression stroke

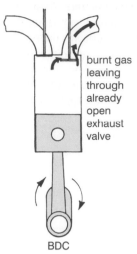

burnt gas
leaving
through
already
open
exhaust
valve

BDC

Burnt gas already escaping from cylinder at BDC

Figure 2.200 Start of exhaust stroke

At the end of the compression stroke the fuel is ignited and burnt, the gas pressure increases and the piston is forced down the cylinder on its power stroke. During the downward movement of the piston, the increasing volume lowers the pressure of the gas, but if the exhaust valve remains closed, the pressure will still be well above atmospheric pressure when the piston arrives at BDC. This pressure will offer a good deal of opposition to the upward movement of the piston during the exhaust stroke, even though the exhaust valve may now be open. Moreover, as the piston approaches BDC, the leverage exerted by the connecting rod on the crankshaft decreases rapidly and the pressure on the piston thus has a rapidly decreasing turning effect on the crankshaft. By opening the exhaust valve early, (i.e. before the piston reaches BDC) a good deal of the burnt gas is allowed to escape before the piston begins its upward exhaust stroke, and the pressure during this stroke – and consequently the opposition to the pistons upward movement – is very much reduced (Figure 2.200). The point at which the exhaust valve opens must be carefully chosen, so as to sacrifice as little as possible of the effect of the pressure in driving the piston downwards during the power stroke, while ensuring that as much gas as possible will escape before BDC to reduce to a minimum the opposition to the piston's upward movement during the exhaust stroke.

Thus, the exhaust gas is already moving out of the cylinder and along the exhaust pipe before the piston starts its exhaust stroke. During the stroke, the piston increases the gas velocity along the exhaust pipe. Thus, as the piston approaches TDC and its upward velocity decreases, the momentum

of the gas rushing along the exhaust pipe creates a partial vacuum inside the cylinder. As soon as the pressure inside the cylinder falls below the pressure in the inlet manifold, fresh mixture will begin moving into the cylinder if the inlet valve is opened. This can usually occur before the piston has reached TDC (i.e. by opening the inlet port before the exhaust port has closed, the momentum of the exhaust gas can be used to start the flow of fresh gas into the cylinder without any help from the piston) (Figure 2.201).

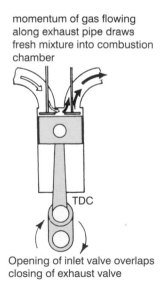

momentum of gas flowing
along exhaust pipe draws
fresh mixture into combustion
chamber

TDC

Opening of inlet valve overlaps
closing of exhaust valve

Figure 2.201 End of exhaust stroke

The fresh gas entering the cylinder will, of course, be drawn towards the exhaust port, displacing burnt gas. Placing the valves on opposite sides of the combustion chamber makes the fresh gas sweep right across the chamber on its way from the inlet port to the exhaust port. This ensures that the combustion chamber is thoroughly scavenged, or cleared of exhaust gas and filled with fresh gas. If the ports are very close together, it is possible for fresh gas to reach the exhaust port without displacing all of the burnt gas from the cylinder. The correct moment to close the exhaust port is the moment the fresh gas reaches it.

Thus, the opening point of the inlet valve and the closing point of the exhaust valve depend upon the following:

1 The velocity of the flow of exhaust gases along the exhaust pipe. In turn, this depends upon engine speed, throttle opening, the length and diameter of the exhaust pipe and the restricting effect of the silencer.
2 The pressure in the inlet manifold, which is dependent upon engine speed and throttle opening.
3 The position of the ports in relation to the combustion chamber and to each other.

The inlet valve usually opens a little before TDC and the exhaust valve remains open a little after TDC. Thus, for some angle of crankshaft rotation around TDC, both valves are open at the same time. The opening of the inlet valve overlaps the closing of the exhaust valve: this is the period of valve overlap.

While a large valve overlap may be beneficial at high engine speeds if the ports are arranged on opposite sides of the combustion chamber, it will make it impossible for the engine to idle or run slowly at light load. At low engine speeds and with small throttle openings the pressure in the inlet manifold is well below atmospheric pressure (as a vacuum gauge connected to the manifold will show). The quantity of gas exhausted from the cylinder is small and moves slowly, having very little momentum, so that it does not reduce the pressure in the cylinder appreciably below atmospheric pressure. Under these conditions, opening the inlet valve before the exhaust valve has closed will result in a rush of exhaust gas into the inlet manifold. Hence, on the following induction stroke the cylinder will be filled with a lot of exhaust gas and very little fresh mixture, which will almost certainly fail to be ignited when the spark occurs. If the engine will never be required to run slowly, for example a racing engine, this may not matter, but all engines used in normal vehicles are frequently called upon to idle smoothly and reliably, and for such engines the amount of valve overlap must be strictly limited.

To sum up, in a standard engine:

1 the inlet valve remains open after the piston has passed BDC at the end of the induction stroke. This is called the inlet valve closing lag
2 the exhaust valve opens before the piston reaches BDC at the end of the power stroke (exhaust valve opening lead)
3 the exhaust valve usually remains open after TDC at the end of the exhaust stroke (exhaust valve closing lag)
4 the inlet valve usually opens before the exhaust valve has closed (valve overlap) and usually before TDC (inlet valve opening lead)
5 the amount of lead or lag of valve opening or closing points and the amount of overlap will depend upon the design of the engine – particularly the port arrangement and inlet and exhaust systems – and upon the performance characteristics the engine is required to have.

The opening and closing points of the valves in relation to piston and crankshaft position are called the valve timing, and the correct timing for an engine – that selected by the engine manufacturers – is given either in the form of a table or by means of a valve timing diagram. Some examples of valve timing tables and diagrams are given in Figure 2.202, together with brief details of the engine to which they refer. A good exercise for students would be to make other valve timing diagrams of other engines to compare, especially when looking at lower-powered engines producing good fuel economy against higher-power engines with forced induction.

2.17.2 Variable valve timing and valve lift

The dynamics of airflow through an engine combustion chamber change dramatically over an engine speed range of 2000–6000 rpm. Using a standard valve drive arrangement is a compromise that allows the engine to start, run and provide strong acceleration with good cruising speeds, but engines are rarely ever in the **sweet zone**, which results in wasted fuel, reduced performance and excess exhaust emissions.

Sweet zone: the point in the engine operations where the intake charge is perfectly matched to the engine speed and performance requirements. The engine will be operating at peak efficiency.

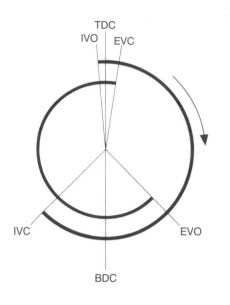

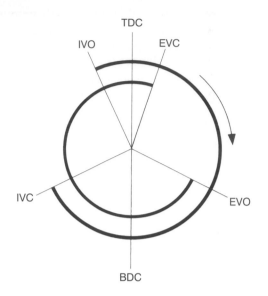

4 Cyl. OVH engine
swept volume 848 cm³
compression ratio 8.3 : 1
max. torque – 62 Nm AT
               2900 rev/min
max. power   – 31.3 kW AT
               4500 rev/min

4 Cyl. OHC engine
swept volume 1955 cm³
compression ratio 9.2 : 1
max. torque – 151 Nm AT
               3500 rev/min
max. power   – 72 kW AT
               5200 rev/min

IVO – inlet valve opens
IVC – inlet valve closes
EVO – exhaust valve opens
EVC – exhaust valve closes

Figure 2.202 Valve timing diagrams

Inertia forces apply when trying to get air to move – it is hard to get it moving and once moving is hard to stop. It has been mentioned previously that the intake valve will generally open before the piston reaches its TDC and will close when the piston reaches a point after BDC. The exhaust valve, however, will start to open when the piston reaches BDC and will close when the piston has just gone past TDC.

The air entering the engine will gain speed as the engine speed increases through the action of the pistons pulling air in through the inlet valves; this will still be the case even when the piston reaches the bottom of the stroke at BDC. Therefore, if the engine is not to lose any efficiency during this cycle and maintain the flow of air at a suitable rate, the valve timing will need to be altered as the engine speed changes.

Variable valve timing has been developed to increase engine performance, improve fuel economy and reduce exhaust emissions throughout the engine's operating range. The effect on fuel economy, power output and exhaust gas emissions is considerable.

Slow engine speeds

When an engine is running at slow speeds or idling, it is important to ensure that the air/fuel mixture is stable and of the correct ratio. This will ensure that the engine idles smoothly, produces the lowest emissions and picks up speed quickly as the engine is moved to medium and high speeds. In order to be able to do this, the variable valve timing system will retard the inlet valve timing. By retarding the valve timing so that the inlet valve(s) open later towards the point where the piston is at the start of the induction stroke at TDC, the exhaust valves will still be open to let out the gases and the cylinder will be able to be filled with a fresh charge of air and fuel without the contamination of exhaust gas. In this way, the engine is able to operate smoothly and produce low emissions.

If the inlet valve timing was left retarded to this level as the engine speed was increased, the cylinders would not be able to be charged adequately enough as the time allowed to fill the cylinders has been decreased by opening the inlet valve later. This would cause a loss of engine power at higher crankshaft speeds. In conclusion, retarding the inlet valve timing is good for low engine speeds but poor for high speeds and performance.

High engine speeds

When the engine is running at high speeds, there is a need to give more time for the cylinder to be charged with fresh air/fuel mixture due to the speed of operations. At this point, with an engine fitted with variable valve timing, it would be beneficial to advance the valve timing (open sooner) to allow the intake charge of air and fuel to enter into the cylinder by the depression created by the flow of exhaust gasses through the exhaust valve(s).

This flow of exhaust gases through the engine at higher engine speeds will improve the overall gas flow through the combustion chamber. By advancing the valve timing at higher engine speeds, the cylinders will have a longer period of time to be charged as the inlet valve(s) will be open for longer. This improves the VE of the engine, which leads to improved engine performance with higher power and torque being produced at higher engine speeds. When we look at an engine without variable valve timing, there is a compromise between advancing and retarding the valve timing due to it being set in one position. As most engines run across a mixture of low to mid engine speeds, manufacturers will design a camshaft that has a balanced power delivery across a wide band of engine speeds to provide a compromise between stable low emissions and performance.

If we look at an engine that operates at high engine speed for most of the time, such as an engine fitted to a sports car, the valve timing will be more biased towards the advanced side with lower necessity for smooth idling characteristics. These engines will idle at higher engine speeds than normal engines due to this larger valve advance and produce higher power outputs at higher engine speeds.

Variable valve timing systems today are not only able to alter the timing of the valve opening and closing period, but also alter the valve lift so that the valves can open wider and for longer during high engine speeds to give increases in power. The use of advanced EMSs allows this constant alteration between low and high engine speeds. The system will retard the valve timing and limit the opening of the valves during low engine speeds to provide good idle and low emissions, and then advance the valve timing and open the valves wider during high engine speeds for improved engine breathing. This all happens hundreds of times a second by the EMS constantly modulating the valve timing and lift.

By introducing a variable valve timing system to an engine, its running characteristics can be changed across the whole engine speed range providing an engine that produces both good power delivery and smooth low emission delivery.

There are many various types of variable valve timing systems in use today. Some incorporate just variable timing and others incorporate variable lift. Some systems now incorporate both systems together. The variable valve lift technology works by using low valve lift at lower engine speeds and then switching, literally in some cases, to higher camshaft lift at higher engine speeds.

Variable valve lift technology is also about allowing operation as a smooth low emission and high performance engine, which is not possible through fixed valve timing and lift.

Valve opening period

The period in which the valve(s) are open on a conventional valve train is governed by the profile of the camshaft lobe. When the engine runs at low speeds, the period the valve is open for allows adequate air and fuel to enter the cylinders to provide good performance and smooth running characteristics.

When the engine operates at higher speeds, the requirements for more air and fuel become greater. To ensure that the VE of the engine increases with engine speed, the period of the valve opening will also have to be increased along with the amount of lift. This increase in valve lift and/or longer valve opening period improves the efficiency of the engine through improved ability to breathe as enough air and fuel are allowed to enter the engine irrespective of the engine speed. This improves performance and fuel efficiency.

Variable valve control

Optimising the engine's fuel and air distribution is crucial in today's modern combustion engines. Manufacturers are always looking to develop their management systems to achieve the regulated environmental standards. In recent years, we have seen forms of mechanical device systems now being electronically controlled. Systems such as variable valve control, variable induction manifolds, and camshaft profile switch controlling greatly improve the modern engine's overall performance. In this section we will look at variable valve control and show the benefits of this system working collectively to improve emission control standards. The first system is the Valvetronic.

Valvetronic variable valve lift

As an example, we will look at the system fitted to the BMW, Peugeot and Citroën smaller engines called Valvetronic. It was introduced by BMW on the all-alloy, four-cylinder engine for the 3 series and has subsequently now been used by PSA Peugeot and Citroën across the smaller engine range.

The Valvetronic system incorporated with the engine unit and advanced electronic EMS avoids the need to use a normal throttle butterfly mechanism.

The Valvetronic system is able to not only alter the opening duration of the valves, but is also able to alter the lift of the valves continuously. The Valvetronic system utilises a conventional intake camshaft arrangement, but combines this with a secondary device that incorporates an eccentric shaft with levers and roller bearing followers. The eccentric shaft is continually adjusted through a very precise stepper motor arrangement. The movement of the stepper motor is dependent on the input signal from the throttle potentiometer. This movement of the stepper motor acting upon the eccentric shaft alters the opening duration and lift of the valve.

Figure 2.203 Valvetronic components

The Valvetronic system fitted to these engines removes the need and function of a conventional throttle butterfly by providing an infinitely variable intake valve lift. Valvetronic has its own management module separately housed in a unit away from the EMS. This is linked with the EMS incorporating a powerful computer processor.

The Valvetronic system provides many benefits:

- Reduced maintenance costs, through reduction of servicing and adjustment requirements and improved engine efficiency.
- Improved cold start behaviour due to the ability to alter the valve opening period and lift.

- Lower exhaust emissions as the engine is able to operate within its peak efficiency zone for a majority of the running period.
- A smoother running engine through constant alteration to valve opening time and lift across the whole engine speed and load range.

Valvetronic is able to operate on all petrol grades as it is able to compensate for lower octane fuel grades through alteration to valve opening period and lift specifications to avoid combustion knock normally associated with poor octane fuel. Also, the very high atomisation of the fuel as it is injected under higher fuel pressure assists in the ability of the system to provide a smoother operation with variation to fuel grades.

The whole Valvetronic system is built as one module and fitted to the cylinder head during engine manufacture.

One of the benefits of the Valvetronic system is its ability to gain at least a 10 per cent saving in fuel due to the engine being able to breathe more efficiently. These fuel savings are at their highest during slower engine speeds. Generally, manufacturers using this system will install a taller top gear to ensure that motorway cruising is done at slower engine speed to improve the fuel efficiency further. The Valvetronic system is another big step forward in manufacturers producing engines that are more fuel efficient and that produce lower CO_2 outputs. This is assisting in the global target for each country to produce lower greenhouse gases thought to contribute to global warming.

Operation

The EMS continually assesses the mass of air flowing through the throttle to the engine to calculate the exact amount of fuel required for each given point in the engine speed and load condition. The more the throttle is opened, the higher the mass of air entering the engine combustion chamber.

When the engine is running with small throttle angles, the throttle is only open a very small amount or is even totally closed. The pistons are still running, pulling in air through the virtually closed intake manifold. There is a partial vacuum or depression created in between the throttle and the combustion chamber. This situation creates some resistance to the sucking and pumping action of the pistons as they rise and fall in the cylinders, particularly during the non-power strokes, and this wastes engine energy. This phenomenon is known as 'pumping loss' and is especially noticeable during slower engine speeds when the throttle is in a closed or nearly closed position.

The Valvetronic system can reduce pumping loss by constantly altering the amount of air entering the combustion chambers during lower engine speeds through reduced valve lift; in some cases, the valves will remain closed if there is no need to introduce air into the engine. In this way, the Valvetronic system does not open the inlet and exhaust valves 100 per cent of the time like the conventional engine.

When you compare the Valvetronic engine with a conventional DOHC with multi-valve arrangement using regular mechanical or hydraulic followers, the Valvetronic system has other additional components including an eccentric shaft, stepper motor and an intermediate rocker arm (Figure 2.204) for each intake valve, which directs the desired opening lift on to the intake valve through the movement of the stepper motor. To make the intake valves open with greater lift, the rocker arms will push down deeper providing a greater pivot to open the valves. The opposite effect will be achieved by moving the rockers further up, hence providing less pivot and a smaller opening. In this way, the Valvetronic system is able to continually alter the opening lift of the intake valves to provide changes to the engine's breathing. This leads to the engine being able to take longer deeper breaths (higher valve lift) during higher engine speeds and shorter breaths (smaller valve lift) during lower engine speeds.

Operating parameters:

- Valve lift with the Valvetronic system is variable between 0 and 9.7 mm.
- Adjustment of the worm gear from one extreme to the other takes 300 milliseconds.

- Combined with conventional variable valve timing technology, the camshaft angle of rotation can be adjusted up to 60° relative to the crankshaft rotation.
- The intermediate arm is finished to a very high tolerance to ensure a totally accurate operation.
- The cams controlling the eccentric shaft are also finished to a very high tolerance to provide accurate control of the valve opening.

Additional benefits of the Valvetronic system:

- In Valvetronic engines the coolant is able to flow throughout the cylinder head to provide benefits in engine cooling.
- Due to the improvement in engine cooling, the water pump can be made smaller providing a benefit in reducing power consumption required from the engine to operate the water pump.
- As the engine is able to get up to operating temperatures quickly, the power-steering fluid is also warmed quickly reducing the power consumption on the engine through rotating the pump.
- The engine oil temperature is kept lower through the fitment of a heat exchanger between the engine coolant and the engine oil. This allows the engine to operate within its peak engine temperature for most of the operating time.

As the Valvetronic system utilises lower spring rate valve springs to limit the frictional loss during the opening and closing of the valves, the peak engine speed and efficiency will drop at over 6000 rpm. To improve this, higher rate valve springs could be used but this would cancel out some of the efficiencies saved through the Valvetronic operation.

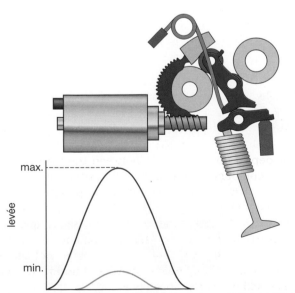 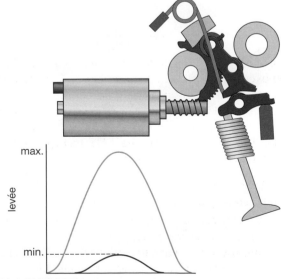

Figure 2.204 Valvetronic in high-lift breathing status and low-lift short breathing status

Camshaft profile switching (CPS)

Camshaft development has significantly changed in recent years. The timing of the camshafts and valve opening periods is crucial if all of the energy produced is to be used efficiently. Early camshafts were produced as solid shafts with a selected number of cam lobes, depending on the number of valves per cylinder. Manufacturers now use hollow camshafts to reduce their overall weight, and have increased the number of cam lobes, as most engines have a multi-valve system as their preferred operating option. With this system in mind, it is crucial that each valve is open and closed at the correct time, and energy loss is kept to a minimum.

Looking at Figure 2.205, showing the camshaft layout with CPS, you can firstly see that there is a key difference between the inlet camshaft compared to the exhaust camshaft. For each of the inlet valves located inside the cylinder head, the inlet camshaft features three lobes with two different profiles. The centrally located lobe is designed to open the inlet valve for its low valve lifting height and the outer two lobes are to open the same inlet valve when its high valve lifting height is demanded during its engine cycle. The key difference in valve opening heights is that on the low valve lifting height, the valve will open to a maximum of 3.6 mm, and when the CPS demands an increase in output, then the high valve lifting height will increase to 10 mm. The exhaust camshaft is also hollow to reduce weight, but uses the conventional cam lobes to open each individual exhaust valve per cylinder. The CPS is managed by the ECU and continuously adapts the system to maximise engine performance according to driver demands.

For the inlet and exhaust camshafts to carry out the CPS functionality, the followers used in this operation are also significantly different in design and functionality. The exhaust followers are mechanical, with an adjustable valve clearance that is set by using graded tappets. The inlet camshaft followers are hydraulic, which compensates for any wear, and the valve clearance is zero. The inlet followers are also two-piece devices to allow switching between the two inlet opening heights using an internal tappet locking mechanism.

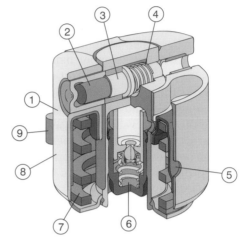

1   outer follower
2   outer locking pin
3   inner follower
4   inner locking pin with return spring
5   hydraulic valve adjustment oil inlet
6   hydraulic valve adjustment unit
7   outer follower return spring
8   anti-rotation lug
9   CPS function oil inlet

Figure 2.206 CPS hydraulic inlet follower

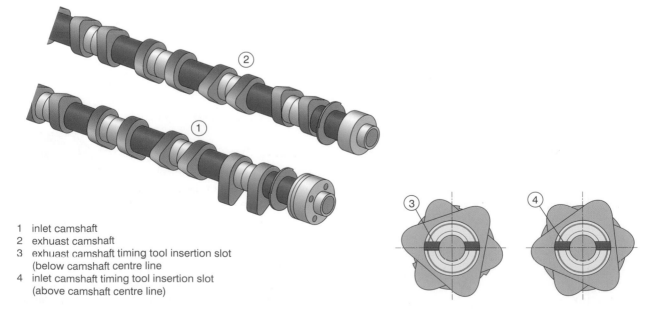

1   inlet camshaft
2   exhuast camshaft
3   exhuast camshaft timing tool insertion slot
     (below camshaft centre line
4   inlet camshaft timing tool insertion slot
     (above camshaft centre line)

Figure 2.205 Camshaft layout of CPS, also showing inlet camshaft arrangement

CPS inlet valve hydraulic follower

As you can see in Figure 2.206, there are a number of key elements in its construction for this device to operate the two different valve-opening heights. Clearly, at this stage, the mechanical devices can only be fully operational by the provision of an oil supply that is pressurised and controlled by the ECU and two control solenoids.

Inlet valve operation and control

Varying the point at which the inlet valve opens to the point at which the exhaust valve closes can yield a number of benefits. A high level of valve overlap, during which both the inlet and exhaust valves will be open at the same time, can encourage good cylinder charging at high engine loads as the incoming rush of inductive air purges the cylinder of any residual exhaust gases. While this is a benefit at high engine loads, it can be a disadvantage at low engine loads unless it is managed effectively. At low engine loads with minimal cylinder charge and high inlet, vacuum can lead to unpredictable charging as the exhaust backpressure will cause combustion instability, which will present itself as uneven idling and hesitation under light load conditions.

At moderate load conditions, the valve overlap is beneficial to the overall performance of the management system. At this stage the lower gas velocity eliminates any tendency for the incoming rush of charged air to purge the cylinder. The modest charged levels and reduced manifold depression means that a small quantity of exhaust gases will be drawn back into the cylinder. However, the higher intake gas speeds will ensure that good mixing of the exhaust gases with the high quantities of fresh, charged air maintains the stability of the combustion.

This process, working with the exhaust gas recirculation system, actually improves the volumetric efficiency of the engine by reducing the work that the engine has to perform when pumping fresh air charge into the cylinders, and improves the part load emission performance due to the exhaust gases being efficiently controlled.

As mentioned earlier in this chapter, the conflict between low load stability and high power output means engines with fixed valve timing systems have to compromise their overall timing process. This compromise attempts to balance the need for smooth and refined idle performance with very little or no valve overlap, with good high-speed power and torque output, where significant valve overlap is needed.

To overcome this operating issue, the use of variable valve timing along with the CPS is now popular. Mounted to the end of the inlet camshaft is a continuous VCT mechanism, which can adjust the point at which the inlet valve begins to open (relative to the fixed exhaust valve) over 60° of the crankshaft rotation.

Utilising the CPS, along with VCT, provides the management system with the option of two totally different profiles that opens the inlets valve at 3.6 mm and 10 mm heights, but also the valve opening period can be greatly increased to achieve a range from 175° to 310°. In Table 2.1, we can see the available valve lift and the valve opening and closing readings. This provides an increased range of control over the intake valve system to improve overall fuel efficiency and emission control.

Table 2.1 Valve timing data

Lifting height	Valve opens	Valve closes
Intake 3.6 mm	32° BTDC to 28° ATDC (after top dead centre)	120° ATDC to 180° ATDC or 60° BBDC (before bottom dead centre) to 0° BBDC
Intake 10.0 mm	37° BTDC to 23° ATDC	203° ATDC to 263° ATDC or 23° ABDC (after bottom dead centre) or 83° ABDC
Exhaust 10.0 mm	228° BTDC or 48° BBDC	12° ATDC

A full description and operation of the VCT mechanism is mentioned further on in this section.

CPS

The CPS system controls the lifting height of the inlet valves. At engine speeds up to approximately 3000 rpm the inlet valve will have a lifting height of 3.6 mm, and when the engine speed increases above 3000 rpm the valve lifting height increases of 10 mm.

The hydraulic tappet is located within the cylinder head above each of the inlet vales. A conventional hydraulic follower is allowed to move freely and rotate within its housing. A CPS hydraulic follower is not allowed to rotate due to a location lug installed into its housing. Each follower has a direct oil feed supply, which is controlled by two electronic solenoids. The controlled oil pressure acts on the locking pins within the followers' housing and, depending on its position, determines its operating height of opening.

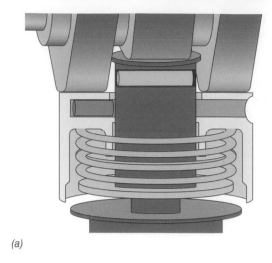

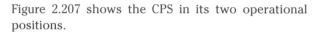

(a)

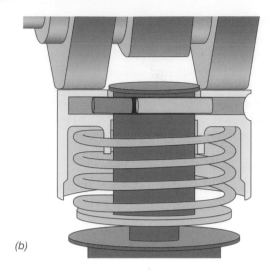

(b)

Figure 2.207 CPS in two operational positions

Figure 2.207 shows the CPS in its two operational positions.

In (a) the hydraulic follower is unlocked and the inner camshaft lobe transmits its force onto the inner section of the hydraulic follower. This then opens the inlet valve to a height of 3.6 mm and will continue this function up to engine speeds of 3000 rpm. The two outer cam lobes act onto the outer section of the hydraulic follower. The outer section of the tappet then compresses the valve return spring to compress and maintains that the follower is always in contact with the camshaft.

In (b) the hydraulic follower is locked as a one-piece assembly. This will occur when the engine increases above 3000 rpm and the two solenoids controlling the oil supply to each follower force the locking pins into place. This changes the camshaft profile to the out sections of the hydraulic follower. The outer camshaft lobes will act as the driving force and transmit its energy onto the outer section of the follower, increasing the valve opening height to 10 mm. The inner section is then locked in place with the outer section so the lower camshaft lobe becomes redundant until the engine drops below 3000 rpm.

Switching of all inlet valves occurs within one complete camshaft rotation and only when each tappet is in contact with the base section of the camshaft lobe and the valves are closed.

CPS solenoids

The position of the hydraulic follower locking pins is controlled by the ECU using two electro-hydraulic valves. The solenoids are located in the upper section of the cylinder head casing.

The CPS solenoid valves are electro-hydraulic seat-type valves with three operating positions:

- Inlet oil supply
- Oil supply return from the follower
- Oil return to engine sump

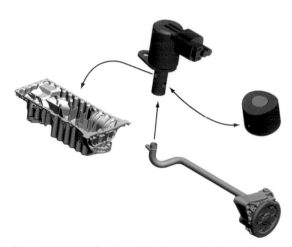

Figure 2.208 CPS solenoid system control layout

Positioning the solenoids at each end of the cylinder head provides improved control of the oil flow to the CPS followers.

When the solenoid valves are not activated they are held closed by the oil pressure on the inlet side. The solenoid valves are open between the hydraulic followers and return supply to the sump. This will then cause the oil pressure to be low on the followers' outer locking pin, and the valve lifting height will only be at 3.6 mm (Figure 2.209).

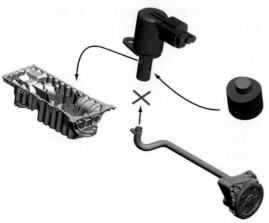

Figure 2.209 *System operating the hydraulic follower in the low-lift stage*

The ECU will monitor this activity and calculate when the solenoid must become active. The solenoid valves will close between the follower and the return to the engine sump, and open between the tappet and the oil pressure inlet side. This will result in high oil pressure on the followers' outer locking pin and forcing in on to the inner locking pin. When this activity is complete, the hydraulic follower will lock as a one-piece assembly and increase the valve opening height to 10 mm (Figure 2.210).

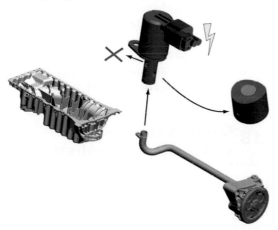

Figure 2.210 *System operating the hydraulic tappet in the high-lift stage*

For cold starting, the system is inactive and will only use the inner section of the hydraulic tappet to open up each inlet valve at 3.6 mm.

VCT mechanism

The inlet camshaft valve overlap is adjusted by the VCT mechanism, which allows the ECU to adjust the inlet camshaft position in relation to the crankshaft. This adaption allows the timing of opening and closing the inlet valve to be maximised, depending on engine load and driver demands. The VCT mechanism can adjust the point at which the inlet valve begins to open (relative to the fixed exhaust valve) over 60° of the crankshaft rotation.

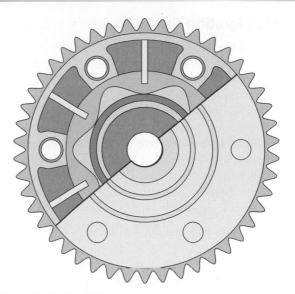

Figure 2.211 *The VCT*

The VCT is located on the end of the inlet camshaft and is a hydraulically controlled vane-type featuring a return spring, which returns the VCT mechanism to the retarded position when the engine is switched off or the hydraulic pressure has reduced below the operating level. The VCT rotor mechanism is secured to the end of the inlet camshaft, therefore, the oil pressure that is supplied to either side of the VCT vanes in turn moves the rotor in the required direction.

The ECM monitors the engine speed and torque demands and will adjust the valve overlap to achieve the optimum power, fuel efficiency and improved emission control. The hydraulic oil pressure is controlled by the ECU and activates an electronic solenoid valve to regulate the flow of oil pressure to the VCT mechanism.

The position of the inlet camshaft is determined by the ECM using a signal from the crankshaft position (CKP) sensor and the camshaft position (CMP) sensors. The ECM can then use the VCT solenoid valve to control the angle of the camshaft by controlling the flow of oil to the VCT mechanism. The VCT solenoid is controlled by the ECM using **pulse width modulation (PWM)** high frequency switching, which provides a rapid and precise control of the inlet camshaft position.

Pulse width modulation (PWM): a form of controlling the operation of electrical devices very accurately. Instead of just switching the device, such as a solenoid, on or off, PWM is able to modulate the opening and closing of the solenoid for very fine control by pulsing electrical signals to the device to keep it in a state between on and off. The rate at which the pulse is sent to the device is known as the frequency and is usually measured in hertz (Hz) or kilohertz (kHz).

2.17.3 Ignition timing

In the earlier part of this section (page 34), it was stated that the mixture was ignited towards the end of the compression stroke, and that after ignition has taken place the air/fuel mixture burns very rapidly and causes a very rapid pressure rise within the cylinder. When looking at the mixture burning process and pressure rise during the combustion process, it is obvious that this must be very quick in both cases as the piston will have moved halfway down the cylinder bore by the time this pressure is developed. This would create very low power.

To ensure that the maximum pressure is developed at the most optimum time, the combustion process should occur approximately 10° after TDC. Due to the mixture requiring some time to burn and create this very high pressure, the ignition point of the air/fuel mixture should be timed to occur before the piston reaches TDC. This means that the spark of the spark plugs must occur in advance of when the maximum pressure should occur. This is called ignition timing advance.

In order to ensure that the engine operates efficiently across the whole engine speed, the amount of advance and retard needs to be varied automatically. Most petrol combustion engines have the facility to continually alter the amount of ignition advance through mechanical or full electronic control. (These devices are looked at in more detail on page 207.) On earlier systems using basic contact breakers and vacuum advance and also simple electronic ignition systems, the need to set a base timing from which the automatic advance systems could then work from was necessary. The benefit of these automatic advance systems was that the ignition timing could be adapted to the varying operating conditions that the engine was subjected to.

As an example, the base timing could be set at 12° before TDC. The initial timing on earlier engines was usually set at idle speed and without the vacuum hose fitted to the vacuum advance. The timing is set with a strobe light that emits a flash of light each time the number 1 spark plug is fired. This then allows the technician to read off the crankshaft pulley the timing currently set on the engine.

As the engine speed rises, the ignition advance alters by increasing the amount of time before TDC that the spark plugs will fire. The time is increased or advanced due to the length of time the air/fuel mixture requires to enter the cylinders and ignite at higher engine speeds. To allow sufficient time for the combustion and pressure rise to happen, the ignition timing must be advanced ahead of the base timing.

However, when the engine is running under a load condition with wider throttle opening, the pressure in the cylinders will increase towards atmospheric pressure due to the higher volumes of air being able to enter the cylinders. In addition the air/fuel mixture entering the engine will become richer with more fuel entering the engine. Higher cylinder pressures and richer air/fuel mixtures will speed up the combustion process. If the ignition timing is set too far advanced in these conditions, the combustion process could happen too early – creating high pressure through combustion on top of the piston as it is still rising up the cylinder bores. This would cause early detonation and could lead to engine damage.

To prevent this occurring, the ignition timing is retarded through action of the mechanical advance mechanism or through electronic control. The mechanical advance mechanism uses vacuum created at the inlet manifold as an indicator of engine load. As the throttle is opened wider for acceleration, the depression within the manifold will drop. In turn, this will allow the advance mechanism to move back towards a more retarded ignition. As the engine then starts to cruise under a light throttle, the depression will be built back up so the advance mechanism will then move towards a more advanced ignition point.

To summarise, most engines have an engine speed-related advance mechanism and a load-related retarding mechanism. In the past, these advance and retard mechanisms were mechanical but modern electronic systems are now used to ensure consistently accurate and precise timing. There is more on ignition systems on page 201.

2.18 Combustion and combustion chambers

2.18.1 Combustion

The process of combustion in an engine is considered on page 34. For the purpose of this section of this chapter, it is sufficient to understand the following:

1 The rate of burning must be rapid, but not excessively so.
2 The rate of burning is influenced by several factors, of which temperature, pressure and turbulence are the only ones that concern us here.
3 The higher the compression ratio of the engine, the higher the thermal efficiency.
4 Combustion knock, commonly called detonation, is a form of extremely rapid combustion that is liable to occur under certain conditions. It is harmful and must be avoided. It occurs if the mixture is heated and compressed excessively during combustion. It is also influenced by the quality of the fuel.

The start of combustion in a spark-ignition engine starts when the arc of the spark plug ignites the air/fuel mixture entering the cylinders. This burning process continues until the flame has spread across the whole mixture charge. The burning process stops when the complete mixture is burnt, which is ideal combustion, and the piston is forced down the cylinder on its power stroke.

This process obviously only covers a small amount of the time taken during the complete four-stroke cycle, but it is critical on a number of important factors across the complete cycle. Excellent combustion will only take place if the initial compression of the air/fuel mixture is to an adequate level that is on the limit of being too high. If the compression of the air and fuel is too high, this may lead to pre-ignition as the air and fuel ignite too early. The temperature of the air and fuel as it is compressed during the compression stroke is also important; good temperature conditions will lead to good, even combustion. If the temperature is too low, this could lead to poor atomisation of the fuel, causing some of the fuel to leave the engine unburnt, raising emissions and also lowering efficiency of the combustion process.

Figure 2.212 illustrates the rise and fall of the pressure within the cylinder during the compression and power stroke.

The pressure within the cylinder during the compression stroke is dependent on the engine's compression ratio. If the compression ratio is low, for example 8:1, the overall compression pressure will be low.

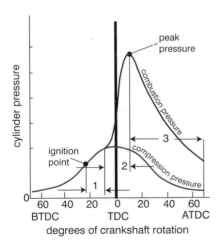

Figure 2.212 Cylinder pressures during compression, combustion and power stroke

First phase of combustion

This first phase of combustion in a spark-ignition engine takes place when the spark plug ignites the air/fuel mixture at the end of the compression stroke. As the burning process takes place, pressure rises along with the heat generated and this, in turn, forces the piston down in the cylinder due to the rapid pressure rise. This pressure rise takes place in the confined area between the upper part of the cylinder (combustion chamber) and the top of the piston. The pressure reached through this rapid burning process is far higher than the initial pressure reached through the compression stroke (Figure 2.212).

This first phase of combustion, commonly called the 'ignition delay period', refers to the time taken between the pressure rise through compression and the initial spark occurring from the spark plug. The ignition delay period has several key requirements:

1 The spark quality and timing of spark delivery.
2 The ratio of the air/fuel mixture.
3 The atomisation of the air/fuel mixture.
4 The temperature of the air/fuel mixture inside the cylinder that has been reached through the compression process.
5 The pressure created in the cylinder that has been reached through the compression process.

Due to the ignition delay period being a constant in time, the ignition point itself must be altered depending on the speed of the engine to ensure that the peak ignition time and compression pressure is reached before combustion.

Second phase of combustion

The second phase of combustion occurs during this rapid rise in pressure from the compression pressure to the combustion pressure period. This rise in pressure is created by the burning of the air/fuel mixture within the confines of the combustion chamber. The rate at which this pressure rises depends on a number of key factors that exist within the combustion chamber at this time. If we assume that all of the factors are correct during the first phase of combustion, the pressure rise during the second phase is dependent on the following:

1 Having the correct air/fuel ratio for the engine at the given point in time.
2 Good atomisation and mixing of the air/fuel mixture. Inadequate mixing of the mixture will lead to poor combustion and lower pressure created.
3 The shape of the combustion chamber. Good shaping of the combustion chamber will enable good flame spread and good pressure rise during combustion.
4 Spark plug position within the combustion chamber is important, as a well-placed spark will lead to improved combustion of the air/fuel mixture as it moves across the combustion chamber.

5 The amount of turbulence created as the air/fuel mixture enters the combustion chamber is important, as this will improve the ability of the flame to spread across the combustion chamber providing an even pressure rise as the mixture ignites.

Third phase of combustion

During the third phase of combustion, the pressure drops from phase two as the piston moves down the cylinder towards BDC and then towards TDC during the exhaust stroke. This pressure drop will alter depending on whether the first two phases have taken place successfully. As the piston moves towards the exhaust stroke, the exhaust valves will open to allow the gases to escape, leading to the first phase of combustion once more after the induction stroke.

Detonation and pre-ignition

Detonation, or as it is called sometimes 'pinking', is caused by high velocity shockwaves rebounding around the combustion chamber. This is often heard as a metallic-type tapping noise, hence the term 'pinking'. The noise sounds this way due to the sound waves created during the detonation being insulated through the cylinder block.

As combustion starts in the combustion chamber, the flame moves through the chamber at high speed progressively igniting the air/fuel mixture ahead of it. As the mixture burns, there is a pressure increase in the combustion chamber due to the increase in heat and combustion taking place. The rise in combustion pressure increases the temperature of the unburnt mixture. This increase in temperature places the unburnt mixture very close to ignition point and, therefore, is able to be ignited more easily when contacted by the flame front.

In well-designed combustion chambers the flame is able to spread evenly from the start of ignition through the spark plug to complete combustion of the mixture. This flame spread should be as even as possible in all directions of the combustion chamber for smooth progressive combustion to take place. This is often why manufacturers locate the spark plug in the centre of the combustion chamber to ensure that the combustion process is as even and as progressive as possible.

To bring this into context, if combustion took place in a tube, once the fuel is ignited by the spark plug the flame would spread along the tube's length and progressively burn the air/fuel mixture. As this flame spreads, the pressure and the heat of the combustion process will increase. This heat and pressure generated will travel through the unburnt fuel more quickly than the flame alone.

If a combustion chamber were designed in a similar way to the tube example, any unburnt mixture left in the chamber could suddenly ignite due to the heat travelling across the length of the chamber. This combustion of the unburnt mixture would occur before the flame spread reached it. This additional combustion process would create dangerous shockwaves that would disperse throughout the combustion chamber. When there is more than one area of unburnt mixture, the shockwaves can be duplicated, creating high shockwaves where these two combustion processes meet, causing engine damage and loss of performance.

Thus, we can see that the general design of combustion chambers plays a critical part in ensuring the combustion process is carried out efficiently, avoiding the possibility of pockets of unburnt mixture creating the chance of detonation or pre-ignition.

These small pockets of air/fuel mixture causing irregular shockwaves also create large amounts of additional heat due to the sudden combustion. Additional heat generated during combustion is undesirable, as this will cause areas within the combustion chamber to overheat leading to localised hot spots. These hot spots can cause additional pre-ignition issues as the air/fuel mixture can be ignited during compression before the spark plug is energised. The additional heat can lead to damage to the combustion chamber and associated components including cylinder walls, pistons, spark plugs, electrodes and the head gasket. Excess heat will also cause additional stress on the engine's cooling system.

Pre-ignition and detonation are similar in that they both lead to the air/fuel mixture igniting before the intended time triggered by the spark plug and the ignition system. However, pre-ignition is associated with the complete combustion process being started early. This condition causes the ignition of the air/fuel mixture to take place before the arcing of the spark plug has taken place. Detonation is different in that it usually occurs after or during the normal combustion process by igniting unburned pockets of air and fuel trapped within the combustion chamber.

Pre-ignition is usually caused by localised hot spots within the combustion chamber. These hot spots usually consist of parts of the cylinder head glowing red hot or carbon deposits being super heated causing them to become red hot. As the air/fuel mixture is compressed during the compression stroke in the engine cycle, the air/fuel mixture comes into contact with the localised hot spots and ignites before the spark plug has arced. This can cause damage to the engine as the piston tries to rise up the cylinder towards TDC. The pre-ignition of the air/fuel mixture creates a combustion situation that then tries to push the piston back down the cylinder. Due to the combustion process taking place at the wrong time during the compression stroke, this can lead to additional pressure rises and added stress on the engine components. This additional pressure wave is sometimes heard as a 'knocking'. This unwanted condition will lead to premature engine failure if left for a prolonged period. Lower engine power will also be experienced due to the lack of complete combustion occurring at the correct time in the compression stroke of the engine cycle.

Additional causes of pre-ignition can include excessive intake air temperatures or overheating of the engine because the mixture in the cylinder will be at a higher temperature and so closer to the ignition point. Any hot spots then act as the final means of igniting the mixture ahead of the sparking plug arc.

2.18.2 General principles of combustion chamber design

The power that can be obtained from an engine depends upon several key factors:

1 The VE – the amount of air that can be passed through the engine per minute.
2 The thermal efficiency – the efficiency with which the air can be mixed with fuel and burnt to release heat.
3 The mechanical efficiency – the efficiency with which the energy released by the burning fuel can be converted into mechanical work at the driving end of the crankshaft.

While the design of the combustion chamber can have little direct influence on the mechanical efficiency, it has a great deal to do with both the volumetric and thermal efficiencies. It has, however, an indirect influence on the mechanical efficiency.

Requirements for high VE

Chief requirements for high VE:

1 Large and unobstructed ports offering the minimum obstruction to the flow of gases.
2 The most suitable valve timing for the engine speeds and throttle openings at which the engine will most be required to operate.
3 A mixture temperature as low as possible at the moment the inlet valve closes. (Because of thermal expansion, the cylinder will hold a smaller mass of mixture if it is hot.)

Requirements for high thermal efficiency

In order to ensure that the engine is running at its very best, producing the optimum power for the amount of given fuel, we must look at the thermal efficiency of the engine is some detail. Some key factors affect the ability of an engine to operate within its peak thermal efficiency:

1 The highest possible compression ratio that can be used without knocking (detonation) occurring – detonation is created through the compression ratio being too high for the given quality of fuel. When the compression ratio is too high, the pressure created during compression ignites the fuel in pockets during the combustion process and creates unstable flame spread across the combustion chamber. This detonation process will create a poor pressure rise in the combustion chamber as the air/fuel mixture is not burnt in a smooth manner. Therefore, the pressure created will be uneven which, in turn, affects the power stroke delivery.
2 The minimum loss of heat to the combustion chamber walls – this depends upon the temperature difference between the hot gases and the walls, and upon the surface area of the walls. Since a high temperature is necessary to produce high pressure, it is important to reduce the surface area (i.e. to make the combustion chamber as compact as possible). This compactness has a further benefit – it reduces the time taken by the gas to burn, by reducing the distance the flame has to travel. It can be assisted by placing the sparking plug as near to the centre of the combustion chamber as possible.

Possibly the most important consideration in the use of a high compression ratio is the anti-knock rating (**octane number**) of the fuel used.

A fuel with a higher octane rating will have greater ability to withstand higher compression pressures due to its anti-knock qualities. Most fuel suppliers today offer petrol in two octane ratings. These are often around 95 **RON** for low octane rating and 99 RON for high octane rating. Higher performance engines often running forced induction require higher-octane fuel to prevent detonation.

Octane number: a scientific measurement of a fuel's ability to burn without detonation occurring through high compression ratios.

RON: research octane number.

Since high-octane fuels are more expensive due to the additional additives and refinery costs, a compression ratio must be chosen that balances thermal efficiency against fuel cost, bearing in mind the purpose for which the engine is to be used. (While a high compression ratio will result in lower fuel consumption for a given amount of work done, any gain may be entirely offset by the extra cost of the high-octane fuel necessitated by so high a ratio.

Figure 2.213 Examples of fuel available at a filling station

If running cost is of no importance, the fuel with the highest octane rating available may be used with a correspondingly high compression ratio.)

Anti-knock additives

In previous years, the use of anti-knock additives was common in petrol fuel. The additives were lead-based substances called tetraethyl lead and tetramethyl lead. These were used in small quantities to assist in raising the fuel's octane rating and therefore its anti-knock qualities. In these fuels, the lead acted as a retardant to the speed of the combustion process. This helped in preventing the fuel causing detonation during the combustion process. The use of these additives helped in the running of higher compression ratio engines, which create higher compression pressures.

However, lead is a serious pollutant so it was phased out in 1972. In addition, leaded petrol could not be used with catalytic converters because of the damage that lead causes to them. Unleaded or lead-free fuel is now the norm. Modern petrol fuels now use alternative additives to ensure that the fuel has adequate anti-knock qualities and to maintain the 95–99 RON figures required by today's vehicles.

Engine timing control to reduce detonation

Modern engines incorporate advanced ignition control systems within the engine management system (EMS). The ignition timing can be monitored and controlled at extremely fast speeds while the engine is running to make sure that it is running at peak of performance. The EMS can adjust the ignition timing by very small amounts while the engine is running. The timing will be balanced between the points of knock occurring, as this is where the highest point of combustion pressure is created.

The EMS uses devices called 'knock sensors' that detect when the engine is approaching the point of knock or detonation through shockwaves in the cylinder block. These shockwaves are picked up by the knock sensor, which then informs the EMS to retard the ignition timing in gradual steps until the knocking stops. The EMS will then build the ignition timing back up in small amounts until the engine is running at peak performance again. This process happens many times a second, so the driver will never notice any noise or disruption to the engine performance.

Combustion chamber design

The design of the combustion chamber can also contribute to the suppression of knocking. The risk of detonation is greatest in the last gas to burn – the end gas – and this risk can be reduced in two ways:

1 By getting the gas burnt as quickly as possible.
2 By arranging that the end gas is burnt in the coolest part of the combustion chamber: it is easier to do this by placing the sparking plug nearer to the exhaust valve (which gets very hot) rather than the inlet valve (which keeps relatively cool).

Turbulence

The rate at which the flame travels through stagnant gas is much too low to be of use in a high-speed engine, and it was realised many years ago that a violent agitation or turbulence of the gas is necessary to help spread the flame rapidly throughout the air/fuel mixture. There are two ways of creating turbulence:

1 By arranging the inlet port so that the mixture enters the cylinder obliquely and at high velocity, setting up a swirling motion that persists during the compression stroke. This is known as induction turbulence, and, though helpful, it is not by itself sufficient.
2 By designing the combustion chamber so that at TDC the piston approaches part of the cylinder head very closely, displacing mixture from this region with some violence. This action has been given the very descriptive name of 'squish', and turbulence created during the compression stroke is known as compression turbulence.

Mechanical efficiency

The positioning of the valves is one consideration in the design of the combustion chamber and, depending upon this, the valve-operating gear will be more or less complicated. The greater the complication of the valve gear, the more friction will be absorbed in operating the valves. This will also influence the cost of manufacturing the engine and, the maintenance it is likely to need.

Exhaust emission

Many countries have regulations that specify the maximum amount of undesirable exhaust products that may be discharged. When considering combustion chamber shape, the exhaust pollutants that influence the design are taken into account:

1 Carbon monoxide (CO) and hydrogen (H) – these gases are produced if the fuel mixture is not completely burnt.
2 Oxides of nitrogen (NO_x) – gases that are formed when the combustion temperature exceeds a given value.
3 The anti-knock quality of a fuel can be improved by adding additives to increase the octane rating.

In order to achieve a 'clean' engine, the engine designer must either produce a combustion chamber that does not generate pollutants or incorporate in the exhaust system a special catalytic converter to remove the problem gases. It takes time for the manufacturer to achieve the former, so in the changeover period, some vehicles have exhaust devices in order for them to operate in countries where emission limits are very strict.

Unfortunately, the engine modifications necessary to meet the regulations normally reduce the overall road performance and often increase the fuel consumption. When fuel conservation is necessary owing to restricted supplies, the emission requirements need careful attention by both the designer and the technician.

In general, the effects of the shape of the combustion chamber on the pollutants are outlined below.

Unburnt or partially burnt fuel

The chamber shape should be as compact as possible. Long narrow chambers, such as those used in the past on some OHV, over-square engines, gave a 'dirty' exhaust due to the difficulty of completely burning all of the charge in the short time available. This effect was very pronounced when the idling speed was low or under conditions of over-run when the ignition timing was unsuitable.

NO_x (combinations of nitrogen and oxygen)

Many early high-performance engines used a high compression ratio in conjunction with a very compact chamber. This gave a very high flame speed that produced an excessively high temperature. Although the power output was exceptional, the percentage of NO_x was far above the safe limit. Flame speed is the controlling factor, so the chamber shape must achieve a compromise in flame speed – too fast causes NO_x, too slow results in some of the charge being unburnt.

A further difficulty arises when the effect of engine load is considered. An engine set to give a 'clean' exhaust when idling or cruising often exceeds the NO_x limit when full throttle is applied. To overcome this problem, many engines have an arrangement that recycles some of the exhaust gas back into the induction manifold: the system is called exhaust gas re-circulation (EGR). The burnt gas mixing with the new charge slows down the rate of burning and so reduces the NO_x to an acceptable level. Valves controlling the flow of exhaust gas should only allow recirculation under full load conditions (i.e. at times when NO_x would be formed).

Unleaded fuel

As we have seen, the use of relatively cheap lead in petrol is not allowed due to pollution issues. In addition, lead damages catalytic converters so can't be used in vehicles fitted with these devices. Manufacturers have therefore had to find alternative additives to give the anti-knock and lubrication qualities once provided by lead. These are more expensive. As well as fuel additives, some manufacturers have moved towards using a lower compression ratio of the engine to prevent combustion knock. The combustion chamber shape selected for an engine must enable the engine to use a low-octane fuel and produce a high power output, together with good fuel economy – this is a difficult task for an engine designer.

2.18.3 Types of combustion chamber

With the above in mind, some of the more common types of combustion chamber can be considered.

The L-head combustion chamber

VE is not particularly high in this design (Figure 2.214). The arrangement of the valves at one side of the cylinder restricts valve size to about half cylinder diameter or less, and there are sharp bends through the ports and into the cylinder.

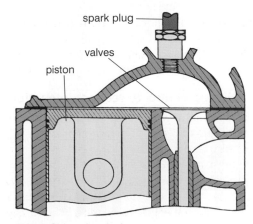

Figure 2.214 Side valve design

The chamber is not very compact, but there is a good deal of freedom in the choice of plug position to obtain the best results. The compression ratio is limited to about 7:1, as it is necessary to leave sufficient space above the valves to allow them a reasonable lift.

By bringing the surface of the head down close over the piston at TDC, leaving a suitable passage between the offset combustion chamber and the cylinder, both induction and compression turbulence are improved: it is, in fact, easy to get too much turbulence causing rough running through excessively rapid combustion.

The position of the valves makes possible the use of the very simplest valve-operating gear, and mechanical losses are the least possible.

Though popular at one time, this combustion chamber is now obsolete in vehicle engines on account of its low VE and restriction on compression ratio.

The 'bathtub' combustion chamber

The valves are placed vertically over the top of the cylinder (Figure 2.215), giving a better port shape leading directly into the cylinder. Thus, the gas flow – and VE – are much better than in the L-head design. The valves are arranged in-line, slightly offset from the cylinder centre, and the sides of the combustion chamber form a shape like an inverted bath (hence the name). Almost the only position for the sparking plug is the one shown, but this happens to fit in well with requirements, and the plug can be slightly nearer the exhaust valve than the inlet.

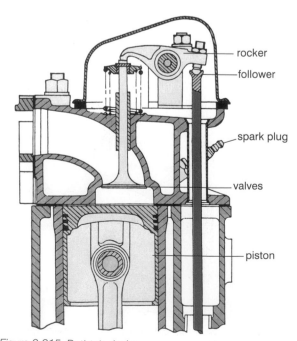

Figure 2.215 Bathtub design

The chamber is reasonably compact and, in some cases, the bathtub shape is angled to make it appear roughly heart-shaped when viewed from below.

There is little induction turbulence, but this is made up for by the very good compression turbulence produced by the squish effect. The squish area, as it is called, is placed on the side of the combustion chamber opposite to the sparking plug, to ensure a thorough sweep of fresh gas over the sparking plug as the piston approaches TDC.

The valves are often inclined to the port side of the cylinder head, to give a slightly reduced bend to the ports. This also gives a wedge-shaped combustion chamber, which makes for more effective control of flame speed. The sparking plug is fitted at the thick end on the wedge, thus giving a large area of flame front during the early stages of combustion and speeding up the first part of this process. As combustion progresses, the flame area is reduced, thus reducing somewhat the speed of the final stages of combustion and minimising the risk of detonation.

The hemispherical combustion chamber

It is commonly believed that the ideal shape for a combustion chamber is a perfect sphere. This belief is based upon the fact that the sphere has the smallest surface area per unit volume, and thus the heat loss to the combustion chamber walls is reduced to the minimum. In most other ways, however, this shape is most unsuitable. For instance, if the bore and stroke of the engine are equal, and the spherical combustion chamber is formed half in the piston and half in the cylinder head, the compression ratio is only 2.5:1, which is absurdly low. For a compression ratio of 8:1 and a similar form of combustion chamber, the stroke would need to be 4.66 times the cylinder bore. This would severely limit engine rev/min and place an unacceptable restriction on valve size.

However, a combustion chamber, the upper surface of which consists of a hemisphere formed in the cylinder head, has several important benefits. By inclining the valves at about 45° on opposite sides of the centreline (Figure 2.216), the valve diameter is much increased

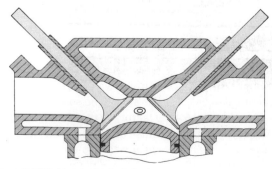

Figure 2.216 Hemispherical design

and a highly efficient port shape is obtained, giving excellent VE. This advantage is so important that where high power output is the main consideration, this type of combustion chamber works very well, but high NO_x emissions are a great disadvantage.

To obtain a high compression ratio the piston crown must be domed, giving the combustion chamber a shape like the peel of half an orange, having a high surface area per unit of volume, quite the opposite of the 'ideal' spherical shape. However undesirable this may be, it is of little importance compared with the advantages gained.

Induction turbulence can be arranged by having the inlet port at a slight angle to a cylinder diameter, and compression turbulence can be obtained by a suitable shape of piston crown.

The chamber is of a shape easy to machine all over, giving accurate control of compression ratio. Although the sparking plug cannot be fitted in the ideal position, it can be placed near the centre of the cylinder head, where good results are obtained.

The greatest drawback to this type of combustion chamber is undoubtedly the complication necessary in the valve-operating gear. The best method is DOHC (Figure 2.217), one directly over each row of valves, but this is also the most complicated and expensive. Alternative arrangements are:

- SOHC with rockers
- double side camshaft, push rods and rockers
- single side camshaft, push rods and rockers.

With improved designs, materials and lubrication the objections to the use of the hemispherical head are becoming less important, and the increasing emphasis on engine power output, even for 'production' cars, is resulting in the use of the DOHC layout (which has been used for practically all racing-car engines since about 1912).

The four-valve combustion chamber

A large-diameter valve is needed if good VE is to be achieved, but it is difficult to blend a large valve into a compact combustion chamber. This problem is minimised by using four valves: two inlet and two exhaust.

Figure 2.218 shows a typical four-valve chamber. Since the total port area of two inlet valves is greater than that given by one valve, it is possible to combine good breathing and economy with low

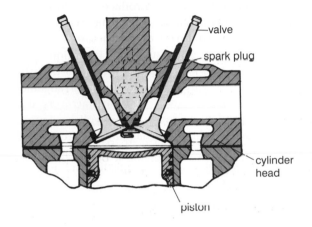

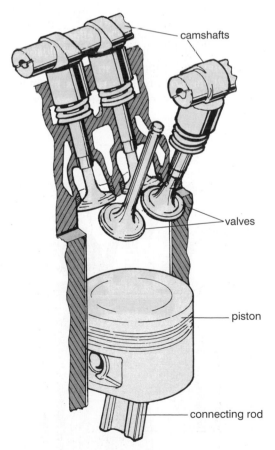

Figure 2.218 A pent roof combustion chamber with four valves per cylinder

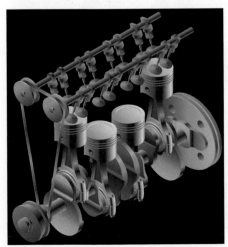

Figure 2.217 DOHC

exhaust emission. Inclining the valves to form a **pent roof**-type combustion chamber allows the sparking plug to be situated in the centre of the roof of the chamber. Four-valve engines can achieve more stable combustion over a wide fuel mixture range, so are suited for lean-burn designs (see page 231).

Pent roof: roof of a combustion chamber with a single plane sloping to one side.

The five-valve combustion chamber

Manufacturers have been able to develop the multi-valve engine further by introducing another valve within the cylinder head. This additional fifth valve is an inlet vale to improve the amount of air being drawn into the engine during the induction stroke. Additional valves increase the area of ports further than the four valves per cylinder arrangement, which leads to improved VE. Manufacturers using this arrangement today include Volkswagen and Audi. However, the first manufacturer to use this arrangement was Mitsubishi in their micro City car in 1989, this engine was under 600 cc and also used turbocharging.

Cross-flow, bowl-in-piston

In this design (Figure 2.220) the underside of the cylinder head is flat and a bowl in the piston forms the combustion chamber. The effect of having a machined chamber in the piston gives close control of the shape and capacity, so variation between cylinders of the compression ratio is minimised. A high ratio could be used if emission restrictions did not apply.

Figure 2.219 Five valves per cylinder combustion chamber

The flat head allows the large valves to open directly into the cylinder, so good breathing and scavenging is possible: this can be improved still further by increasing the bore/stroke to over-square.

Squish action around the chamber is obtained by the small piston-to-head clearance around the piston crown. In some engines, recesses are cut in the piston to prevent contact between the piston and the valve.

The term 'cross-flow' applies to the port arrangement: the inlet and exhaust manifolds are fitted on opposite sides of the engine. This feature gives space to use better manifold shapes, which further improves VE and exhaust scavenging (see page 143).

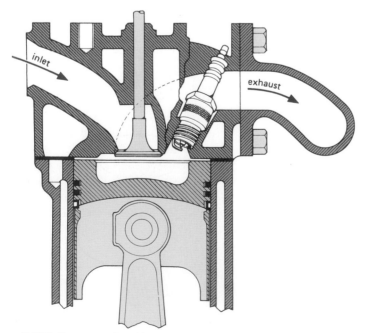
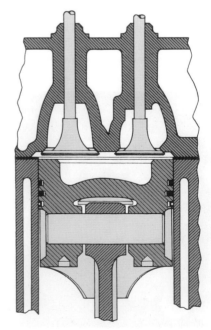

Figure 2.220 Cross-flow, bowl-in-piston design

2.19 Requirements of the fuel-delivery system

2.19.1 Introduction

As has been seen earlier, the power produced from an internal-combustion engine is the result of the heating of a gas in the form of air/fuel mixture and by burning this to cause rapid pressure build-up inside the engine cylinder. During one cycle of operations, the pressure acting on the piston varies widely, but it has an 'average' value, which is called the 'mean effective pressure' (MEP). The effort exerted by the engine is clearly proportional to the MEP, which depends upon engine design, compression ratio and the temperature to which the gas is heated by combustion.

2.19.2 Combustion of petrol

Petrol is a fuel that is particularly suitable for use in vehicles. It is a clean liquid that is easily stored (although reasonable precautions against fire are necessary) and which flows freely. It gives off a flammable vapour at quite low temperatures and when burnt liberates quite a large amount of heat.

Before petrol can be burnt it must be vaporised and mixed with a suitable quantity of air, since combustion is a process involving the chemical combination of a fuel with oxygen.

Crude petroleum, from which petrol is obtained, is a mixture of various compounds of hydrogen and carbon (called hydrocarbons), and petrol consists of those constituents of crude petroleum that have boiling points between the temperatures of, roughly, 30 and 200 °C.

Calorific value

The amount of heat liberated by complete combustion of unit mass of a fuel is called the **calorific value** of the fuel. For an average sample of petrol, the calorific value is about 44 MJ/kg.

Calorific value: the amount of heat liberated by complete combustion. This is measured in MJ/kg (megajoules per kilogram). You may also see it measured in calories – 1 calorie = 4.18400×10^6 megajoules.

Mixture strength

The mass of air per kilogram of fuel in a mixture of air and fuel gives the air/fuel ratio of the mixture and, as already noted on page 103, the air/fuel ratio for complete combustion – called the chemically correct mixture or stoichiometric mixture – is about 14.7:1 in the case of petrol.

A mixture having a greater proportion of fuel (i.e. a lower air/fuel ratio than 14.7:1) is called a rich mixture, while one having a greater proportion of air (i.e. a higher air/fuel ratio than 14.7:1) is a weak mixture. Within limits, both rich and weak mixtures will burn, but will produce different results.

Influence of air/fuel ratio

Mixtures having air/fuel ratios of less than about 8:1 or more than about 22:1 cannot normally be ignited in petrol engine cylinders. Within this range, variation of air/fuel ratio has a considerable influence on the engine's performance. (**Note**: it should be emphasised that the mixtures referred to are those in which the fuel is completely vaporised and thoroughly mixed with the air so that the proportions of air and fuel are the same throughout the whole bulk of the mixture. This is rarely the case in an engine cylinder under running conditions.)

It might be expected that the chemically correct mixture ought to give the best results, but this is not necessarily true. As already indicated, for instance, it is impossible, under normal running conditions, to ensure that the fuel is evenly distributed throughout the air, and under some conditions the fuel is not all completely vaporised when combustion occurs.

Main effects of variation of air/fuel ratio:

1 The MEP – this is found to reach maximum values with a slightly rich mixture. The upper curve of Figure 2.221 gives some idea of the way in which MEP varies with air/fuel ratio.

2 The rate of combustion – the speed of travel of the flame through the mixture varies in a manner roughly similar to the variation of MEP, being fastest with slightly rich mixtures and slowing down markedly as the mixture is weakened and to a lesser extent as it is enriched. One result of this is a tendency for the engine to run hotter if the mixture is weak.

3 The rate of fuel consumption – this is called the specific fuel consumption (SFC) and it is found to be lowest with mixtures that are slightly weaker than the chemically correct mixture, as shown by the lower curve in Figure 2.221.

4 Composition of exhaust gas – if an engine is supplied with the chemically correct mixture, the exhaust gas should consist of a mixture of carbon dioxide, water vapour and nitrogen. Owing to imperfect mixing of the air and fuel, however, it is found that there are in fact small amounts of both oxygen and carbon monoxide in addition to the other gases. If the mixture is made richer, the proportion of carbon dioxide in the exhaust gas decreases while the amount of carbon monoxide increases, and a small

amount of unburnt hydrogen is also found. As the limit of combustibility is approached, some unburnt carbon appears as sooty black smoke in the exhaust gas, and this is always a sign of excessive richness.

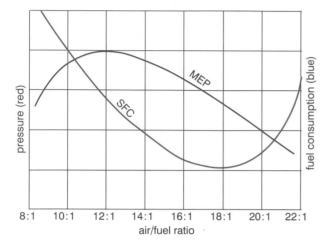

Figure 2.221 Effect on the MEP with changes in the air/fuel ratio

If the mixture is weakened from the chemically correct ratio, the proportion of carbon dioxide in the exhaust gas again decreases. Carbon monoxide is absent once the mixture has been weakened slightly, but the proportion of oxygen increases.

These changes in the composition of the exhaust gases can be used to estimate the air/fuel ratio on which the engine is running. A sample of exhaust gas can be analysed chemically: though this is impractical in a repair shop. An alternative is available in the form of an instrument called an exhaust gas analyser: this detects changes in the proportions of the gases by electrical means and indicates the air/fuel ratio on a scale.

Vaporisation

Since it is petrol vapour, and not the liquid, that burns, it is important that all the petrol supplied to the engine should be vaporised before ignition of the combustion mixture occurs. As liquids change into vapours they absorb heat (called latent heat), which they obtain from their surroundings. If petrol were to be vaporised in the carburettor, the latter would be chilled by the heat taken from it to vaporise the petrol, and moisture in the air passing through the carburettor would be condensed, deposited on the throttle and choke tube, and frozen. In this way, the passage through the carburettor would become blocked by ice and the engine would stop.

This could, of course, be prevented by arranging for the carburettor to be supplied with hot air drawn from

the region around the exhaust manifold. Overheating the air should be avoided for two reasons:

- It reduces power output. Since petrol vapour occupies a considerably greater volume than the equivalent quantity of liquid, a much smaller mass of petrol and air can be got into the cylinder if the petrol is in vapour form rather than liquid. If the air is heated any more than is absolutely necessary to prevent the formation of ice, there is a further loss of power due to the density of the air (and hence the mass of air in the cylinder) being reduced by the rise in temperature. It is not easy to regulate the extent to which the air is heated.
- If the petrol can be vaporised inside the cylinder, the heat absorbed during vaporisation will have a beneficial cooling effect on the inside of the combustion chamber, particularly when the engine is developing full power.

Thus, best results will be obtained if the fuel can be introduced into the cylinder in liquid form, provided it can all be vaporised before combustion. Since vapour is given off from the surface of a liquid, the rate of evaporation can be increased by breaking up the liquid into a fine spray of minute droplets. (To illustrate the principle, consider a millimetre cube – it has a volume of $1\,mm^3$ and a surface area of $6\,mm^2$. The cube can be cut up into eight smaller cubes each having sides 0.5 mm long and a surface area of $1.5\,mm^2$, giving a total area of $12\,mm^2$ for the same total volume. Hence, the smaller the size of the droplets forming a spray of fuel, the greater the surface area for a given volume.

Atomisation

Generally, the time is too short to vaporise the fuel completely before combustion, so additional means must be provided to break up the fuel mechanically into small particles by a process called **atomisation**. This breaks up the fuel either by subjecting it to a turbulent airflow or by pumping the fuel into the airstream through small holes in an injector. This action not only aids the production of a fast-burning mixture, but also helps to mix the air and fuel equally (i.e. it aims to produce a homogeneous mixture).

Atomisation: converting a substance into very small droplets.

Carburation systems

In the past, the bringing together of the petrol and air was performed by a carburettor. This device mixes the air and petrol in suitable proportions to obtain the desired performance from the engine; it also atomises the petrol to give good combustion.

Figure 2.222 shows in a simple format a carburation system to mix the fuel with the air drawn into the engine.

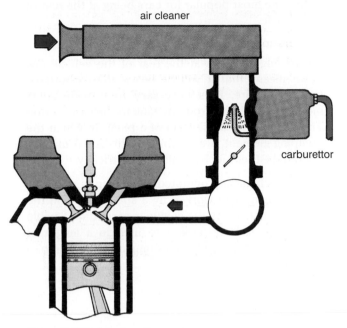

Figure 2.222 A carburation system

All engines today use a fuel-injection system instead of a carburettor. In addition to providing a selling feature, an electronic fuel-injection system should return a higher performance and improved emissions from the engine; so the engine will:

- develop more power to give a higher speed and to accelerate at a greater rate
- be more economical in its use of fuel
- produce lower emissions.

Fuel-injection systems

'Fuel injection' is the term used for any system that pumps fuel into the air supply in an atomised state. Current fuel-injection systems are electronically controlled and inject a quantity of fuel into the airflow of each individual cylinder. This has not always been

the case. Mechanical fuel-metering systems have been used in the past and fuel has not always been metered individually for the individual cylinders, it has been injected into the airflow at a single point with just one injector, very similar to a carburettor.

A modern multi-point fuel-injection system is fully integrated into the ignition system. It has fully electronically controlled, pulsed injection with the ability for full on-board diagnosis. Most full electronically controlled, fuel-injection systems have closed-loop emission control. Fuel is injected into the inlet air using multiple injectors. This ensures more accurate fuel metering and additionally ensures equal quantities of fuel are delivered to the individual cylinders.

Currently, this is the most common type of fuel injection fitted to modern petrol engines. In some systems, the fuel is injected continuously and on other systems the fuel is injected in pulses.

Continuous injection tended to occur on the earlier fuel-injection systems, whereas now the injection is pulsed. With pulsed fuel injection the injectors are opened by an earth signal sent from the EMS once per engine revolution.

This causes an atomised fuel cloud to hover around the inlet valve ready to be drawn into the combustion chamber. Figure 2.223 shows a multi-point fuel-injection system used today.

2.20 The fuel-supply system

The general fuel-supply system for a light vehicle consists of a fuel tank, fuel lines, filters, a pump, fuel-supply rail, fuel-return line and delivery devices, such as injectors or, on earlier vehicles, carburettors.

2.20.1 The fuel tank

Most tanks are constructed by soldering or welding steel, or by moulding plastic.

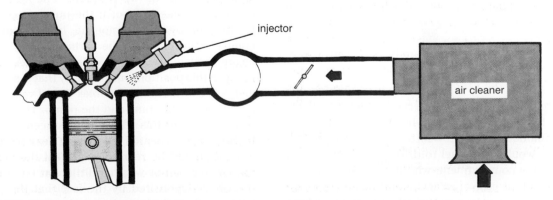

Figure 2.223 Multi-point fuel-injection system

Soldered tanks

The walls of the tank are made from tinned-steel sheets cut and bent to shape. The seams are either rolled or riveted before soldering, and the tank walls are internally supported at intervals by stiffeners. These consist of sheets that divide the tank into compartments, but are pierced with large holes so that, although they allow fuel to pass from one compartment to another, they prevent the fuel 'surging' from side to side of the tank.

Welded tanks

This construction uses steel pressings for walls and stiffeners, with welded joints and seams. The tank is often coated inside, and sometimes outside also, with tin or lead.

Plastic tanks

Materials such as high-density polyethylene can be easily moulded into irregular shaped tanks to fit into spaces situated away from accident impact zones. Extra protection against impact and exhaust heat can be given by using steel plates. Today, most fuel tanks are made from plastic as they are lightweight and recyclable.

Location of tank

It was at one time common practice on small and medium-sized cars to fit the tank as high as possible in the scuttle (between the engine bulkhead and the base of the windscreen). With the carburettor mounted fairly low at the side of the engine, the fuel could be allowed to flow to the carburettor by gravity, providing a simple and reliable system (Figure 2.224).

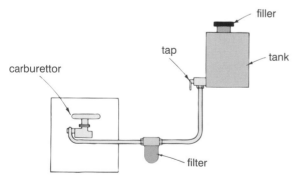

Figure 2.224 Gravity fuel system

In large cars and commercial vehicles, a tank of sufficient size could not be conveniently accommodated in the scuttle. Furthermore, any leakage would allow fuel to drip into the interior of the driving compartment, with a consequent risk of fire and, in the case of an accident, a split tank would allow petrol to leak on to the exhaust pipe at a point

where the pipe might be hot enough to ignite the fuel. Various alternative positions for the tank were tried – the most popular for cars being at the rear of the vehicle.

Carburettor fuel systems

Positioning the tank at the rear of the vehicle low down means that it will be below the carburettor level, therefore, it is necessary to provide some means of lifting fuel from the tank to the carburettor. This usually takes the form of a pump in which the pumping element is a flexible diaphragm: it may be operated either mechanically or electrically.

When mechanically operated, the pump is mounted on the engine and worked by a special cam on the engine camshaft. As the engine is carried on flexible mountings, it is necessary to include a length of flexible piping in the pipeline connecting the pump to the tank (Figure 2.225a).

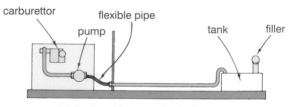

(a) Engine-driven mechanical pump

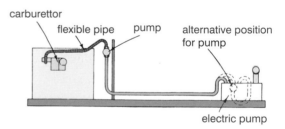

(b) Pump-feed fuel system

Figure 2.225 Layout of a simple fuel system

When electrically operated, the pump may be mounted in one of two positions. The first of these is on the engine bulkhead: the pump is connected to the tank by a rigid pipeline, but a flexible pipe connects the pump to the carburettor to allow for engine movement on its flexible mountings. With the pump in this position, one difficulty that is sometimes met is the formation of bubbles of fuel vapour in the pipe between the tank and the pump. There are two main causes for this – heat and reduced pressure. If the fuel pipe is heated by passing near the exhaust pipe, it should be rearranged, but if the heating is merely due to hot weather, little can be done. The trouble is aggravated by the fact that the pipeline between the tank and the pump, being on the suction side of the pump, is operating under a pressure less than atmospheric, a condition that encourages the formation of vapour. Thus, the alternative position for an electric fuel pump is close to the tank so that the main length of the pipeline is under pressure and the formation of vapour is discouraged. Both these positions are shown in Figure 2.225.

Fuel-injection systems

Engines that use a fuel-injection system instead of a carburettor have an electric pump fitted in, or close to, the fuel tank. When the pump is fitted in the tank, it is submerged within the fuel. The pump not only 'lifts' the fuel from the tank to the engine but also generates the pressure to inject the fuel into the engine manifold.

2.20.2 Fuel pumps

Mechanical fuel pumps

The constructional features of a pump of this type are shown in Figure 2.226. The upper part of the body (16) contains the inlet connection (1), the inlet valve (2), the outlet valve (3) and the outlet connection (4). The circular diaphragm (5) (made of fabric impregnated with synthetic rubber) is clamped around its edge between the upper (16) and lower (15) parts of the body. It is also clamped at its centre between two dished circular plates attached to the upper end of the diaphragm pull rod (6). A spring (7) is fitted between the lower diaphragm and the lower body pushes the diaphragm upwards. The pump is bolted to the wall of the crankcase. The lever (8) passes through an aperture to bear against an eccentric (9) on the engine camshaft, the end of the lever being pressed lightly against the eccentric by the spring (12). The lever pivots on a pin (10) on which is also pivoted a section link (13), the other end of which engages the lower end of the diaphragm pull rod.

When the engine is running, the lever (8) is rocked on its pivot. Movement of the lever towards the pump causes the step (11) on the lever to engage the link (13), which it moves about the pivot (10), so pulling the diaphragm and compressing the diaphragm spring (7). Movement of the lever (8) away from the pump allows the diaphragm to be moved upwards by the spring (7).

Downward movement of the diaphragm increases the volume of the pumping chamber above the diaphragm, holding the outlet valve (3) on its seat, but opening the inlet valve (2) and drawing fuel from the tank through the inlet connection into the pumping chamber. On the upward stroke of the diaphragm, pressure is applied to the fuel in the pumping chamber by the spring (7), closing the inlet

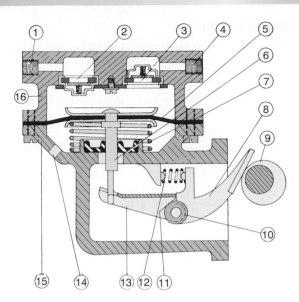

Figure 2.226 A mechanically operated diaphragm fuel pump

valve but forcing the outlet valve off its seat and delivering fuel through the outlet connection (4) and a pipe to the carburettor.

When the carburettor is full of fuel, a valve in the carburettor closes (see page 186), preventing the entry of any more fuel, and consequently fuel will now be unable to leave the pump. The diaphragm will thus be held in its lowest position by the fuel in the pumping chamber under the loading of the spring (7), although the lever (8) will maintain contact with the eccentric (9) through the influence of the spring (12). The pressure at which fuel is delivered to the carburettor is determined by the force exerted by the spring (7). This force in turn depends upon the dimensions of the spring and the extent to which it is compressed when the diaphragm is in its lowest position. Within limits, this may be varied by selecting a suitable thickness of packing to place between the pump mounting-flange and the engine crankcase, a greater thickness reducing the pressure slightly and a lesser thickness increasing it.

Should the diaphragm develop a leak, fuel can escape through a number of drain holes (14) drilled through the wall of the pump body.

Maximum fuel pressure at inlet and outlet points depends on the pump model. Typical values are:

- Inlet: vacuum of about 150 mm (6 in)
- Outlet: 21–35 KPa (3–5 psi).

Prior to about 1975, pumps were provided with a drain hole (14). Unless a seal is fitted around the rod (6), the hole would allow crankcase fumes to escape and so contravene emission regulations.

Electric fuel pumps

Note: fuel pumps fitted to petrol fuel-injection engines are discussed in detail on page 176.

Although electric fuel pumps have been extensively used in the past, the mechanical pump was preferred because it was cheaper. Also, the mechanical pump operates only when the engine is running, so the fire risk is reduced when the vehicle is involved in a crash.

The electric pump (Figure 2.227) consists of two parts: the pumping section, which is similar to the corresponding section of a mechanical pump; and the electrical unit, which operates the diaphragm.

Movement of the diaphragm (9) is effected by energising an electromagnet and attracting an iron armature (8). At the end of the stroke during which the fuel is entering the pump, the push rod (7) moves the toggle-spring assembly and clicks open the tungsten contacts (1): this interrupts the electrical supply to the magnet coil (2), allows the spring (3) to return the diaphragm and forces the fuel through the outlet valve to the carburettor. When the diaphragm reaches the end of its travel, the contacts close and the cycle is repeated.

This action will continue until the carburettor is full of fuel, when the diaphragm will be unable to make its return stroke, holding the contacts open until the carburettor requires more fuel. The pressure at which the fuel is delivered to the carburettor is governed by the strength of the spring (3).

Reference was made to the fire risk following a crash. To minimise this hazard, some vehicles have an inertia-actuated cut-off switch connected in the electrical supply to the fuel pump. A deceleration greater than 5 g (49 m/s^2) causes the switch to open.

2.20.3 Filters

All vehicles fitted with fuel injection and carburettors have a number of passages and small holes through which petrol must flow. Tiny pieces of dirt or droplets of water can obstruct the flow and prevent the correct functioning of the fuel system.

The petrol companies take a great deal of trouble to ensure that the petrol delivered by their pumps at filling stations is clean, but it is possible for dust to enter the tank of the car any time the filler cap is open, even for short periods. As fuel is taken out of the tank and delivered to the fuel system, air must be allowed

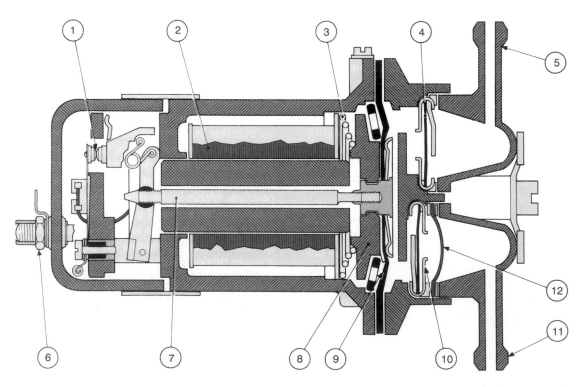

1 contact breaker points	7 pushrod
2 magnet coil	8 magnet armature
3 return spring	9 diaphragm assembly
4 outlet valve	10 inlet valve
5 outlet connection	11 inlet connection
6 electrical supply connection	12 filter

Figure 2.227 An electronically operated low-pressure fuel pump used on early carburettor systems

1 paper filter 2 strainer 3 support plate

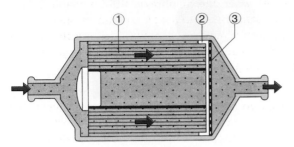

Figure 2.228 Section through a fuel filter

to enter the tank. It does this through a vent hole or pipe, and it may take in dust or moisture with it, the moisture subsequently condensing inside the tank. A small sump is usually formed at the lowest point of the fuel tank, with a drain plug to enable any water collected in the sump to be drained. The fuel supply to the engine is taken from the above sump level to minimise the possibility of dirt and water getting into the pipelines and eventually into the fuel system.

It is, however, a sensible precaution to fit one or more filters in the fuel system to trap dirt and water, preventing them from entering the fuel pump – where they might prevent a valve from closing properly or the fuel system from being able to deliver fuel correctly. Filters may be fitted in one or more of the following positions:

1 Around the outlet from the fuel tank.
2 At the fuel pump inlet.
3 At the carburettor inlet.
4 At any convenient point in the pipeline connecting the tank to the carburettor or fuel-injection system.

Filters used in conjunction carburettors generally consist of brass wire gauze of a mesh sufficiently fine to trap those particles of dirt that are large enough to cause trouble in fuel pumps and carburettors, and of an area large enough to pass more than the maximum fuel flow. If previously damped with petrol, these filters will also trap water.

Filters fitted to fuel-injection systems have much finer filtering properties and are usually made from fine nylon meshing or pleated paper. The pleats allow the largest filtration area possible within the given space. These types of filters are usually sealed and are replaced as an assembly during specific service intervals.

Replacement of filters

To ensure that the fuel system delivers fuel at the right pressure and without dirt or moisture, the fuel filter should be replaced at regular service intervals.

The intervals will be different for carburettor engines and fuel-injected engines. When dismantling the fuel system to remove the filter, care should be taken to ensure that the fuel pressure within the fuel lines is released safely – fuel under pressure can be sprayed in the technician's face or over hot engine parts, which could cause injury or damage. Care should also be taken when refitting the filter to ensure that it is fixed correctly, as some filters have flow direction arrows that must be adhered to.

2.20.4 Pipelines

For many years, the pipes used to convey the fuel from the tank to the carburettor were made of copper, a metal of great ductility, which enables it to be easily bent to shape, and possessing good resistance to corrosion. Copper, however, is relatively expensive and has been almost entirely replaced on modern vehicles by tinned steel or plastic.

Modern vehicles have their engines supported on flexible mountings, which permit fairly extensive movement of the engine relative to the frame, to prevent the transmission of vibration to the bodywork and passengers. It is therefore necessary to include a length of flexible piping in the pipeline. When a mechanical pump is used, this is fitted on the engine, and a length of flexible pipe connects the pump with the rigid part of the pipe, which is secured to the frame.

Plastic petrol piping, even when reinforced with braiding to improve strength, becomes soft and melts when exposed to excessive heat. In view of this, the pipe should be kept clear of the exhaust system.

Fuel-pipe connections

Where pipes are connected to tanks, pumps, filters, carburettors and fuel-injection rails, a secure but easily detachable connection is required. This usually takes the form of screwed connectors (Figure 2.229).

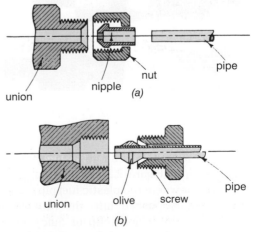

Figure 2.229 Types of pipe connection

That shown at (a) involves soldering the nipple on to the end of the pipe, but the type shown at (b) requires no soldering, the olive being compressed between the coned surfaces of the union and the screw as the latter is tightened. Since the olive is made of a relatively soft brass, it contracts on to the pipe making a fuel-tight connection. In a third type, not shown, the end of the pipe is flared out to mate with a suitable conical seating on the union.

With fuel-injected engines the fuel pressure can be very high, so the fuel connections need to be able to withstand this pressure. Connections like the one seen in Figure 2.230 shows the type of union often seen with high-pressure systems. This is called a banjo bolt type, which is sealed with the use of two copper washers.

Figure 2.230 Fuel filter connection on high-pressure system (banjo bolt type)

More modern fuel systems involve 'quick release' connections to allow fuel systems and components to be disconnected very easily and quickly. Many have cut-off valves incorporated within the release mechanism to prevent fuel leaking when disconnected.

Figure 2.231 Quick-release fuel connector with fuel isolation

A very simple connection used on low-fuel pressure lines can be seen in Figure 2.232. This is a simple push-on connector where the plastic fuel pipe, which is slightly flared, is pushed into the rubber fuel line and secured with a hose clip or quick-release retaining clip.

Figure 2.232 A push-fit-type fuel pipe connection

2.21 Electronic petrol injection – multi-point

2.21.1 Introduction

The term 'petrol injection' is used to describe any system in which the fuel is pumped or injected out in an atomised state to mix with the air supply.

All modern systems today are controlled electronically because this ensures the fuel quantity and quality is accurately set to suit the engine operating conditions. Multi-point fuel injection was previously only seen on higher-powered performance vehicles, but today strict emission control regulations demand precision in the metering of the fuel. Although petrol injection systems are more expensive, these systems are now used across all current production vehicles due to the economy and emission levels able to be obtained.

A petrol-injection system that delivers the correct quantity of highly atomised fuel at each inlet valve of the engine gives the following advantages, when compared with a normal carburettor and manifold layout:

- Lower exhaust pollution
- Lower fuel consumption
- Higher power output
- Smoother engine operation due to an even power output from each cylinder
- Even supply of anti-knock additives to each cylinder
- Automatic adjustment of the air/fuel ratio to suit operating conditions

2.21.2 Injector positions

Injection systems can be divided into two main groups: multi-point and single point. This classification is based on the number and positions of injectors:

1 Multi-point injection – separate injectors for each cylinder, each injector positioned close to the inlet valve of the engine.
2 Single-point injection – one injector only that discharges fuel into the airstream at the point used by a carburettor.

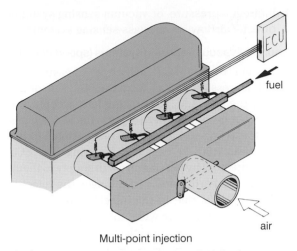

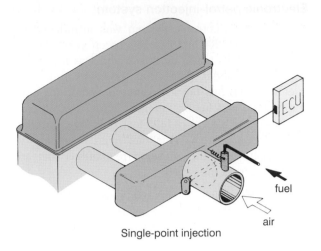

Figure 2.233 *Multi-point and single-point injection*

Figure 2.233 shows the general layout of both arrangements.

Multi-point injection

During the development period of petrol injection, which saw many uses on two-stroke engines and aircraft, the well-tried system used on compression-ignition (diesel) engines was applied to spark-ignition engines. On most of these applications, the injector sprayed fuel into the combustion chamber, but this direct-injection system required high fuel pressures and, unless the injection commenced in the early part of the compression stroke, vaporisation was poor.

Today, indirect injection is generally preferred (Figure 2.234), although many manufacturers are now moving towards direct-injection systems using very high injection pressures. In the indirect injection arrangement, an injector, operating at a low pressure, for example 2–3 bar (30–45 psi), is fitted to spray the fuel downstream into the air as it passes the inlet valve of the engine.

As the fuel spray needs only a comparatively low pressure, a simple injector construction can be used. It consists of a body screwed into the manifold, which encloses a spring-loaded conical valve that chatters to break up the spray. Fuel supply to the injector is carried by a plastic pipe.

Injection of petrol can be timed or continuous. In the former, fuel is sprayed into the airstream only when induction is taking place. The action of the injector opening with the fuel pressure behind it causes the fuel to atomise as it leaves the injector. This atomised fuel is then drawn into the cylinder through the opening intake valve.

The air-induction system comprising the air filter assembly, throttle body and intake manifold provides

a smooth flowing tract for the air to flow to the cylinder head. As mentioned on page 89, these items also act as a reservoir for the volume of air entering into the engine. This reservoir part of the manifold is often called the plenum chamber.

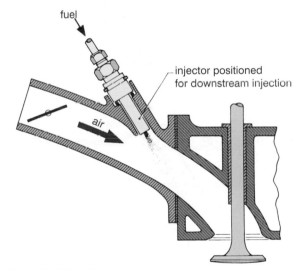

Figure 2.234 *Indirect petrol injection*

2.21.3 Metering methods

An ideal injection system must supply to the engine the correct quantity of atomised fuel to suit the engine speed and load. Also, the system must vary this quantity to allow for alteration in engine temperature and changes in air density caused by ambient temperature and altitude variations. The initial cost of the equipment generally indicates the number of special refinements used to cater for these variables.

Systems can be separated into two main types: mechanical or electronic.

Electronic petrol-injection system

The first full electronic system was introduced by Bendix in the USA in 1950. Seventeen years later, a similar unit was made by Bosch and was fitted to a Volkswagen model. Since that time, electronic fuel injection (EFI) has been a common system for both sports type and luxury category cars. Now all cars produced use a form of full electronically controlled fuel-injection system. This has been necessary to continually meet the emission regulations that are enforced across the world.

The full electronic systems use a solenoid-operated fuel injector. This opens at set times in the engine cycle, hence the term 'intermittent', and is held open for a period of time proportional to the quantity of fuel that is required.

A number of variations exist for fully electronic systems. The main difference between them is the way in which the airflow is measured; the two main systems are:

1 indirect – pressure- or vacuum-sensing systems
2 direct – airflow- or air-mass-sensing systems.

Pressure- or vacuum-sensing systems (speed density)

This system uses a MAP sensor to measure the manifold depression. Signals from the MAP sensor are passed to the ECU and, after taking into account the data received from the other sensors, the ECU signals the injector to open for a set time, proportional to the quantity of air that the engine is receiving. The ECU opens the injectors by passing an earth supply to them. The longer the earth supply, the longer the injector stays open; this is due to the injectors all having a permanent supply voltage when the ignition is switch on. The opening period of an injector is usually called the opening duration, as this is measured in time.

A good example of an early petrol EFI system – a straightforward pressure-sensed system – is the Bosch D-Jetronic. The D stands for *Druck*, which is German for pressure. Figure 2.235 shows the basic layout of this type of system.

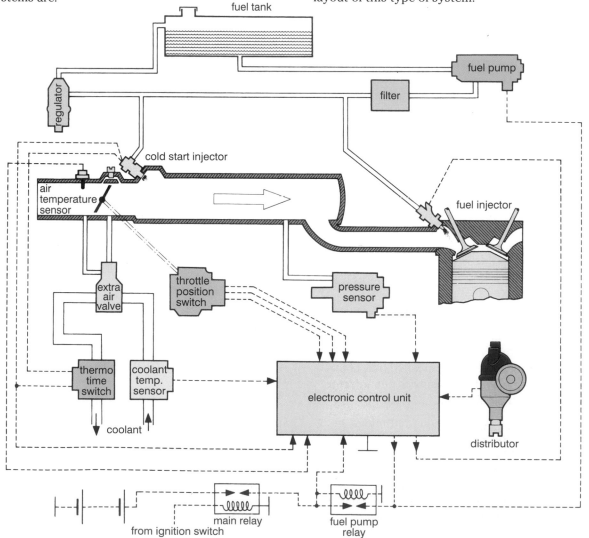

Figure 2.235 Petrol EFI system – pressure-sensed airflow – Bosch D-Jetronic

In this layout, the quantity of air induced into the engine for a given throttle opening depends on the manifold pressure. This is measured by a MAP sensor, which sends an electrical signal to the ECU to indicate the pressure inside the intake manifold. The quantity of air entering the engine is then calculated by checking the manifold pressure against the throttle potentiometer signal. This signal is processed by the ECU and is used to determine the period of time that the injectors should remain open.

This information is plotted on a graphical format called a map. The EMS uses these maps to determine the amount of fuel to inject at any given engine speed and throttle opening. An example of a map can be seen in Figure 2.236. From this map, you can see that at any given engine speed a relating value for fuel and engine load can also be referenced. This is exactly what the ECU will do when the engine is running to provide the best possible value for fuel and ignition.

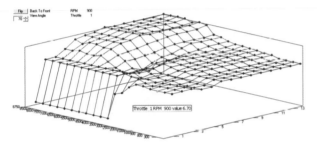

Figure 2.236 Engine management map showing fuel and engine load against engine rpm

Commencement of injection is triggered by either a switch in the ignition distributor or a sensor situated adjacent to the flywheel or crankshaft pulley. On early forms of the electronic injection system, such as the D-Jetronic system, all of the injectors were opened and closed at the same time on engines with four cylinders (banked injection), and for six-cylinder engines the injectors are operated in sets of three (i.e. three injectors spray at the same time).

In both cases, the injectors are triggered at each crankshaft revolution, which equates to twice during the complete engine cycle.

Later systems operate on the basis of injecting the fuel individually at the point of induction. This process is called sequential fuel injection and has the benefits of providing lower emissions and improved economy.

Also on earlier petrol fuel-injection systems, similar to the mechanical system explained on page 180 in this chapter, an extra cold start provision was required. This provided an additional injector in the intake manifold to inject fuel when the engine was cold. The additional fuel improved the cold starting of the engine.

The brain of the electronic system is the ECU; this receives messages from a number of sources (Figure 2.237) and, after comparing the data with the instructions programmed into its built-in memory or map, the ECU signals the injectors to operate accordingly. The amount of fuel injected is governed by how long the solenoid in the injector remains energised for, leading to the injector opening duration.

Figure 2.237 shows some of the other items that are used to control the system. The throttle position switch works in conjunction with the MAP sensor for measurement of airflow. The throttle switch in this case passes a voltage signal to the ECU to confirm that it is either in the opened or closed state. When the ECU notes that the throttle is closed and the engine is at idle speed, it will enable a slightly richer mixture through increased injector opening duration to give a smooth idle condition. At wide-open throttle, the ECU will note the MAP sensor readings also to determine the amount of fuel the engine requires. When the vehicle is travelling at speed and the throttle is closed by the driver taking their foot off the accelerator, the ECU will shut off the injectors to stop fuel being injected as the car is slowing down. When the driver then opens the throttle again to accelerate, the injectors will commence injecting fuel. This condition is known as engine overrun – fuel cut-off. This also improves the economy and emission levels of the engine.

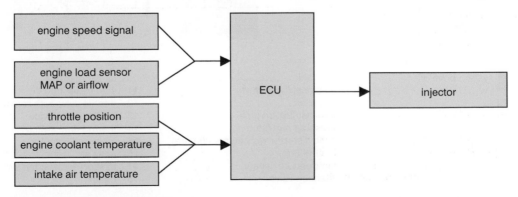

Figure 2.237 Input and output signals of an EFI system

The fuel pressure is created by an electronic fuel pump often situated in the petrol tank. The pressure of the fuel needs to be maintained at approximately 3 bar or 45 psi. The fuel pressure regulator is the component that controls the pressure. This is discussed later in this chapter on page 178.

Direct airflow- and air-mass-sensing systems

The petrol EFI system usually incorporates a device called an airflow/air-mass meter for measuring the quantity or volume of air entering the engine. Generally, there are two types of device:

- Airflow meter (vane or flap)
- Mass air meter (hot wire)

Both of these sensors produce a voltage output, which increases as the rate of airflow increases. This voltage signal is passed to the ECU to determine the fuel requirement of the engine; this is controlled by the duration of the opening period of the injector.

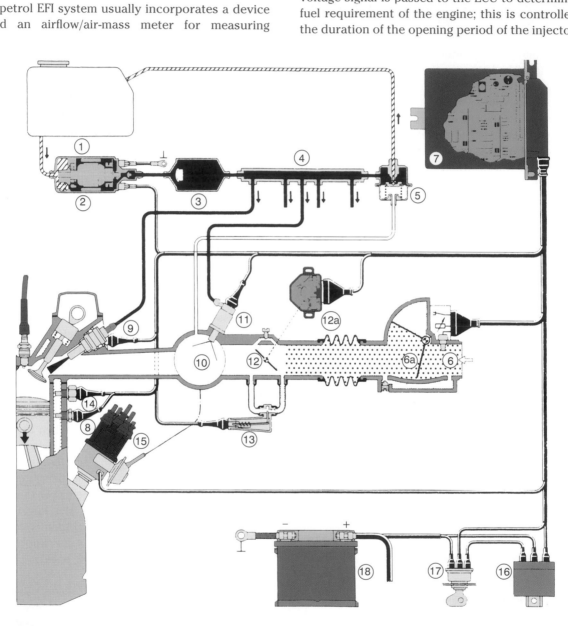

system pressure	1 fuel tank	10 intake manifold
'suction' line/return	2 electrical fuel pump	11 start valve
	3 fine filter	12 throttle valve with switch (12a)
atmospheric pressure	4 fuel-distribution pipe	13 auxiliary air device
	5 pressure regulator	14 thermo-time switch
intake manifold pressure	6 airflow sensor with sensor flap (6a)	15 ignition distributor
	7 control unit	16 relay set
	8 temperature sensor	17 ignition and starting switch
	9 injection valve	18 battery

Figure 2.238 Petrol EFI system – direct sensed airflow

Both types of sensors take account of the actual density of the air entering the engine, so it is possible to maintain the required air/fuel ratio to compensate for variations in atmospheric temperature and pressure. This feature is especially significant when the vehicle has to operate at different altitudes.

Vane or flap metering – Figure 2.238 shows the layout of a system similar to a Bosch L-Jetronic. The 'L' stands for *Luft*, the German word for 'air'.

The action of the flap sensor is similar to a spring-loaded door exposed to a movement of air. As the air speed (or density) is increased, the force on the door will also increase and will move it through an angle to a point where the force of the air equals the reaction of the spring. In the case of the vane, the position it occupies for a given airflow is registered by a potentiometer. The potentiometer voltage signal is then passed to the ECU to calculate the volume of air entering the engine. The purpose of the dampening chamber is to prevent the vane oscillating due to the airwaves moving forwards and backwards in the intake manifold.

Other than the arrangement for sensing the airflow, the basic system is similar to those previously described. The ECU uses the airflow meter, along with the throttle signal and MAP sensor voltage signals, to determine the amount of fuel to inject into the engine and when the spark at the spark plugs should occur. Fuel pressure, produced by the fuel pump, is maintained constant at 2–3 bar (30–45 psi) by a pressure regulator. Injector valves are actuated once per crankshaft revolution and fuel quantity is governed by the period that the injector is held open by the solenoid.

Hot-wire metering – the use of hot-wire air-mass sensors is now a popular choice with EMS designers due to its more compact design and accurate measurement of airflow.

The principle of the system (Figure 2.239) is based on the cooling action of air blown over a hot surface. Rate of heat transfer depends on the rate of airflow – a scientific fact easily demonstrated when you blow on a hot substance to cool it, for example a cup of hot tea.

The sensor has a hot wire element, which is heated by an electric current sufficient to maintain it at a constant temperature. When the airflow is increased, the cooling action is greater, so a larger current has to be passed through the wire filament to prevent a drop in its temperature. The voltage required to provide this current gives an indication of the

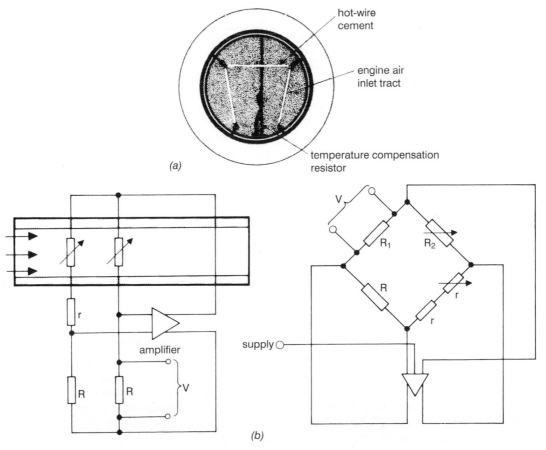

Figure 2.239 Hot-wire-sensing air-mass meter

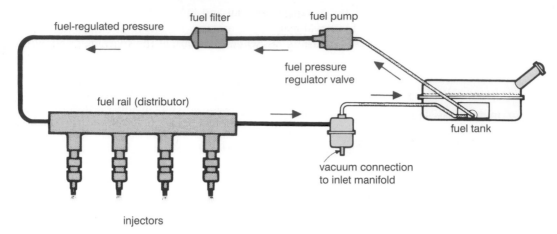

Figure 2.240 Fuel system

inducted air mass. This voltage is signalled to the ECU to enable the ECU to determine initially the basic quantity of fuel. The quantity is then slightly altered to take account of the signals it receives from other engine sensors.

Air temperature affects the accuracy of the system as described, therefore, to prevent temperature errors a compensating resistor is placed in the airstream. A change in air temperature causes this to alter its resistance and this compensates for the effect of a change of air temperature.

Today, many vehicles use air-flow/air-mass sensing because these systems allow the air/fuel ratio to be controlled within the limits required to meet emission regulations in force in various countries.

Although there are many different electronic systems of control in use throughout the world, the basic fuel-supply system and the supporting electrical circuitry are often similar. The following description of a typical system is intended to show the basic principle of the main hydraulic components.

2.21.4 Fuel-supply system

The fuel-supply system provides the injectors with adequate fuel at a pressure sufficient to allow the injectors to give good atomisation. The quantity of fuel injected depends on the fuel pressure, so this must not vary.

Figure 2.240 shows the main components of the fuel system, including the pump and fuel pressure regulator.

Pump

This is normally a roller-type rotary pump driven by a permanent-magnet electric motor (Figure 2.241). Rotation of the pump moves the rollers outwards and seals the spaces between the rotor and casing. As the fuel is carried around with the rotor, the combination of the rotor movement and the decrease in volume of the pumping chamber causes an increase in pressure.

Fuel from the pump passes through the motor; this aids cooling. More fuel is supplied than is needed; excess fuel is re-circulated back to the tank and this reduces the risk of vapour-lock problems.

Two ball valves are fitted in the pump: a non-return valve at the outlet and a pressure-relief valve limit the maximum pressure.

The pump is controlled by an ECU via a fuel pump relay, and the current supplied to the pump is sometimes passed through a ballast resistor to reduce the supply voltage. Note that this is not always the case on every system, so when checking for supply voltages check the workshop manual to make sure you are looking for the correct reading. The resistor is shorted-out when the engine is cranked to compensate for the lower battery voltage.

On switching on the ignition, the pump motor runs for a short time to pressurise the system fully. After this initial period the pump is stopped until the engine is cranked.

For safety reasons, an inertia switch is fitted in the electrical supply line to the pump relay. This switch opens if it is jolted, so, in the event of a collision, the pump ceases to operate. The switch can be reset by pushing down a protruding plunger.

Fuel pressure regulator

This controls the operating pressure of the system and is set to maintain a constant pressure difference (e.g. 2.5 bar or 36 psi) between the fuel line and the inlet manifold irrespective of throttle opening. It consists of a spring-loaded diaphragm and ball valve (Figure 2.242).

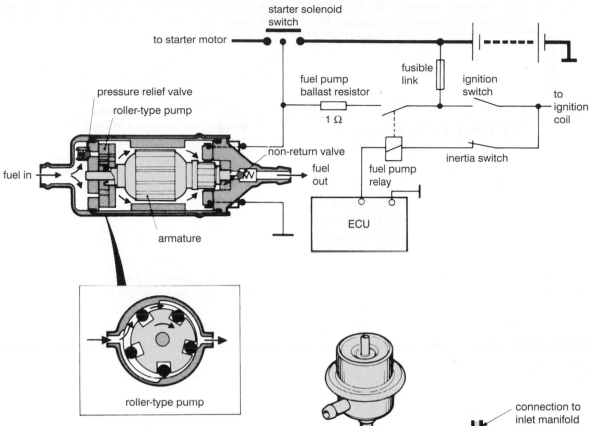

Figure 2.241 *Fuel pump and electrical supply circuit*

Manifold depression depends on throttle opening, for example engine load. Therefore, when the opening is small, the high depression encourages more fuel to leave the injector. To compensate for this, the fuel system operating pressure is lowered when the manifold depression is high. This is achieved by connecting one side of the regulator to the induction manifold. At times when the engine is operating under a light load, the regulator valve is slightly opened and the pressure is reduced.

Table 2.2 *Regulator control pressure*

Engine condition	Manifold depression	Typical operating pressures
Idling	Very high	1.8 bar (26 lbf in^{-2})
Full throttle	Very low	2.5 bar (36 lbf in^{-2})

Returnless fuel system

As we have seen with the mechanical fuel pressure regulator mentioned earlier, this component has an important job in maintaining the correct fuel delivery pressure to the fuel injectors. Many vehicles today incorporate a returnless fuel system, which is able to maintain the fuel delivery pressure without the need to re-route excess fuel back to the fuel tank. The reason for this system is to lower the emissions

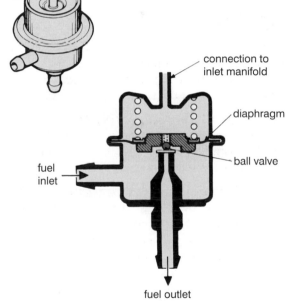

Figure 2.242 *Fuel pressure regulator*

of the vehicle by cutting out the need for warm fuel to be delivered back to the fuel tank, which creates higher hydrocarbon (HC) emissions from the fuel vapour. This system also lowers the production costs involved in the fuel-delivery system by having only one fuel pipe to the engine.

The returnless fuel system works by using a fuel pressure regulator within the fuel pump assembly within the fuel tank. The fuel pressure regulator is able to monitor the fuel pressure requirements of the engine by delivering fuel into the delivery system until the required pressure is obtained. At this point the excess fuel is bled back into the fuel tank past the regulator.

This system will normally operate at a higher pressure and the engine management will adjust the injector opening pulse width to maintain the correct fuel delivery at any given engine speed. Where a fuel pressure regulator was normally fitted into the fuel rail, a similar-looking component is fitted called a pulse damper. This device acts as a damper to the fuel-pressure delivery to maintain a constant pressure across the fuel injectors.

2.21.5 Injectors

The function of an injector is to deliver a finely atomised spray downstream into the throat of the inlet port. In addition, the injector must vary the quantity of fuel to suit the engine operating conditions; this is achieved by varying the time that the injector is open.

The required conical spray pattern (Figure 2.243) is obtained by pumping the fuel through a **pintle**-type nozzle. Fuel flow takes place when the nozzle valve is opened by a solenoid (Figure 2.244).

Pintle: pin or bolt.

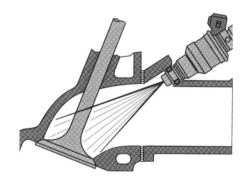

Figure 2.243 Fuel injector located in the intake manifold; spraying fuel on to the back of the inlet valve

Movement of the valve is limited to about 0.15 mm (0.006 in) and the period of time that the valve is open varies from about 1.5 to 10 milliseconds (0.0015 to 0.0100 seconds).

This variation in opening time alters the amount of fuel that is supplied to each cylinder per cycle. Open time depends mainly on the rate of airflow and engine speed, but engine temperature and fuel temperature also have a bearing on the amount of fuel that needs to be delivered.

In early systems, all injectors are electrically connected in parallel, so they all open and close at the same time. When the engine is warm, this opening normally occurs once every other revolution. Later systems open and close the injectors independently or sequentially in the same order and the firing order of the engine.

Changes in battery voltage can affect the opening duration of the injectors. Low battery voltage can lead to the injectors reacting more slowly or not opening completely due to the lower current passing to the injector circuit. Slower opening or limited opening duration will lead to weaker air/fuel mixtures as reduced quantities of fuel are injected into the combustion chamber than the ECU has originally calculated for. Many modern ECUs are able to monitor the battery voltage and recalculate the opening duration of the injectors to maintain an adequate engine running state until the battery condition improves. The ECU will also monitor the content of the exhaust gases to cross-check this calculation to ensure that the engine is running as efficiently as possible.

When the engine is cold started, extra fuel must be injected; this is provided by increasing the frequency of injections.

Injector opening and closing are by a solenoid and spring respectively.

2.22 Electronic petrol injection – single point

The single-point injection system is also often called throttle body injection because the single injector sprays fuel at a point on the air intake side of the

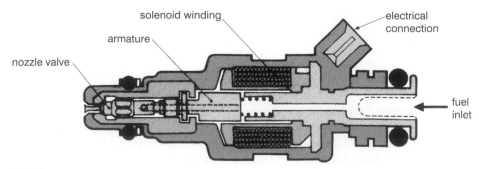

Figure 2.244 Fuel injector

throttle (i.e. the injection is made at the point where the carburettor would normally be situated). The single-point fuel-injection system was designed to provide more accurate control of fuelling as technology moved from the use of carburettors. However, manufacturers do not use single-point injection today as it is not able to meet stricter emission regulations imposed on the industry.

Although this system doesn't always compare well with full multi-point fuel injection, especially the advantages associated with good fuel distribution, its value should be assessed against a carburettor layout.

The call for better atomisation of the fuel, especially at low engine speeds, more precise control of the air/fuel ratio to meet current emission regulations, and additional demands to meet modern requirements for cold starting and warm-up, has forced many manufacturers to abandon the low-cost carburettor. Whereas the high cost of multi-point injection often does not warrant its use on some models of car, the use of a single-point system is a compromise. Also, this system is easier to control electronically than a carburettor, and because electronic systems are more sensitive in operation, the single-point system becomes an attractive proposition.

Figure 2.245 shows a typical throttle body injection layout that is similar to a Bosch Mono-Jetronic system. This shows a single solenoid-operated injector situated centrally in the air intake. It is supplied by a pressurised fuel system similar to that used in a multi-point layout.

Injected fuel is directed into a venturi-shaped region around the throttle, so the increased air speed at this point is used to break up the fuel further.

Airflow can be measured by a flap or hot-wire sensor. The ECU is mounted on this housing, so a compact layout is obtained. Other systems utilise a MAP sensor working in conjunction with a throttle potentiometer to determine the volume of air entering the engine. Since the ECU contains a microcomputer, it can easily process data from many other sensors also seen on the multi-point injection system. This includes engine temperature, intake air temperature, engine speed, etc.

Working in conjunction with these sensors, the ECU varies the amount of fuel injected to give deceleration cut-off and enrichment during cold start, warm-up, acceleration and full-load operation.

1 fuel tank
2 electric fuel pump
3 fuel filter
4 fuel-pressure regulator
5 solenoid-operated fuel injector
6 air-temperature sensor
7 ECU
8 throttle-valve actuator
9 throttle-valve potentiometer
10 canister-purge valve
11 carbon canister
12 lambda oxygen sensor
13 engine-temperature sensor
14 ignition distributor
15 battery
16 ignition-start switch
17 relay
18 diagnosis connection
19 central injection unit.

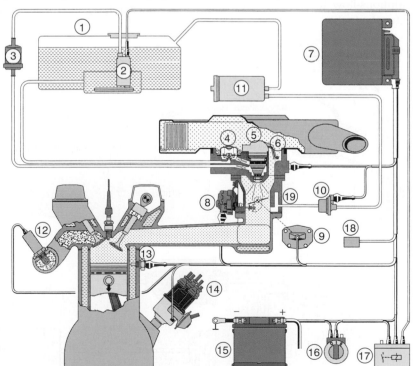

Figure 2.245 Bosch Mono-Jetronic throttle body injection system

When the engine is cold, fast idle of the engine is provided by an auxiliary air valve to pass excess air into the engine bypassing the throttle.

To improve the emission levels of the engines at this time, the single-point injection system was designed to work in conjunction with a three-way catalytic converter. In order for the catalyst to work at its optimum performance it has to be able to monitor itself hundreds of times a second to make sure that the air/fuel ratio stays as close as possible to the ideal ratio of 14.7:1. To enable the system to do this it is fitted with a sensor, called an oxygen or lambda sensor, in the exhaust system just before the catalytic converter. This provides a signal to the ECU in relation to the content of oxygen in the exhaust gases. The ECU then uses this information to lessen the fuel (weaken the mixture) or increase the fuel (enrich the mixture) to ensure that the fuel ratio stays within the ideal ratio.

The disadvantage of the single-point fuel-injection system is that, like the earlier carburettors, it is still not able to distribute the atomised fuel to the cylinders effectively. It should be noted, however, that this system did provide a step forward in economy and emission levels.

2.23 Mechanical petrol-injection system

The Bosch K-Jetronic is a mechanical system using the principle of continuous-flow fuel injection with airflow sensing to meter the fuel.

The operating principle is considered here by building up the system step by step. Figure 2.246 shows the basic system. A permanent magnet electric motor drives a roller-type pump, which pressurises the fuel sufficiently to give the required supply to operate the injectors. Maximum pressure in the primary fuel circuit is limited to 4.7 bar (about 70 lbf in^{-2}) by a pressure-regulator valve, and excess fuel from this valve is returned to the tank. The spring-loaded diaphragm forming an accumulator:

- holds the pressure in the line to aid hot starting
- slows down the build-up of pressure on starting
- smooths out the pulsations and reduces pump noise.

2.23.1 Fuel distributor and airflow sensor

This controls the quantity of fuel delivered to the injectors. The air sensor (Figure 2.247) consists of a venturi (1) in the induction pipe into which is fitted a movable disc (2). Attached to the disc is a counterbalanced lever (3), which acts on a control plunger (4). Mounted around the plunger are a number of diaphragm valves (5), one for each injector. The purpose of these valves is to provide a fuel supply to the injectors proportional to the movement of the control plunger.

When the engine is stationary, the disc (2) is resting in a closed position in the venturi. The lever (3) and control plunger will be in the lowered position and no fuel will pass from the waist of the plunger to the chamber above the diaphragm, so no injection will take place.

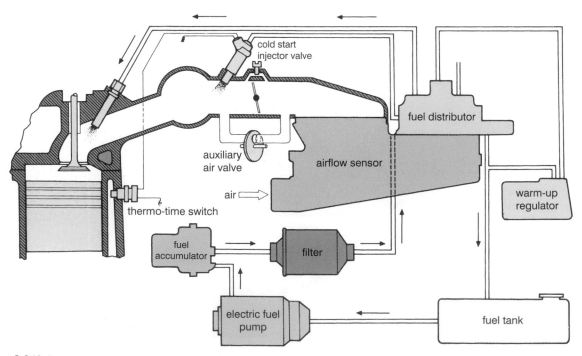

Figure 2.246 Basic layout of mechanical petrol-injection system

On starting the engine, the air movement through the venturi will lift the disc – the extent of the movement will be governed by the quantity of air flowing through the venturi. When the disc has lifted a set amount, the lever will raise the control plunger (4) and open a slit to allow fuel to the chamber. Although fuel pressure now acts on both sides of the diaphragm, the force of the spring moves the diaphragm downwards and opens the valve at the centre of the diaphragm to release the fuel to the injector. The flow of fuel from the chamber slightly lowers the downward force on the diaphragm, so a valve-open position is reached that corresponds to the amount that the control plunger is moved.

Opening the throttle will give a greater airflow, so the disc (2) will rise further, which, in turn, will raise the control plunger (4) and allow more fuel to pass to the chamber. This extra fuel flow will more than make up for the fuel that is 'escaping' past the valve to the injector, so the extra downward force produced by the fuel pressure lowers the diaphragm, opens the valve further and increases the quantity of fuel going to the injector.

From the description of the operation of the diaphragm unit it will be seen that it acts as a differential pressure valve. It regulates the pressure drop on each side of the diaphragm to a constant value of 0.15 bar (about 2 psi) irrespective of supply pump pressure, nozzle opening pressure or fuel flow.

The air/fuel ratio given by this system can be altered by varying the control pressure, which acts on the end of the control plunger. Reducing this pressure allows the sensor plate to move a greater amount for a given airflow and results in a richer mixture.

Cold starting

The layout of the system (Figure 2.248) includes a cold-start injector positioned downstream of the throttle. This electrically operated valve, together with the auxiliary air device, comes into operation when the thermo-time switch senses that the engine is cold.

Warm-up regulator

This controls the mixture enrichment during the cold-start and warm-up periods (Figure 2.249). It consists of a valve, operated by a bimetallic strip, which lowers the control pressure acting on the end of the control plunger when the engine is cold.

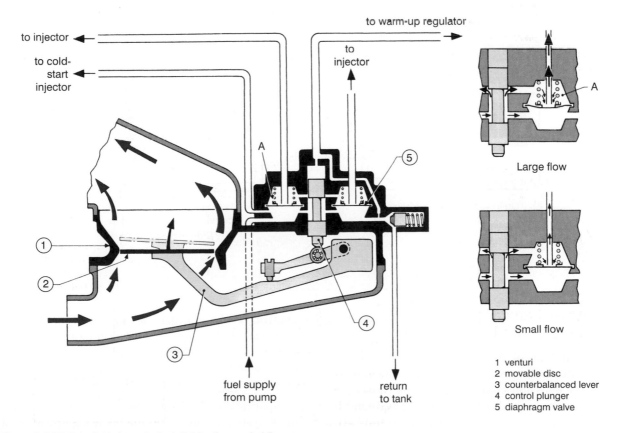

Figure 2.247 Bosch K-Jetronic fuel distribution and airflow sensor

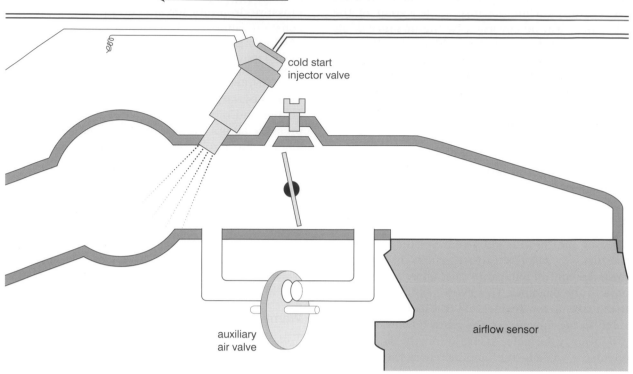

Figure 2.248 *Cold-start injector and auxiliary air device situated in throttle housing*

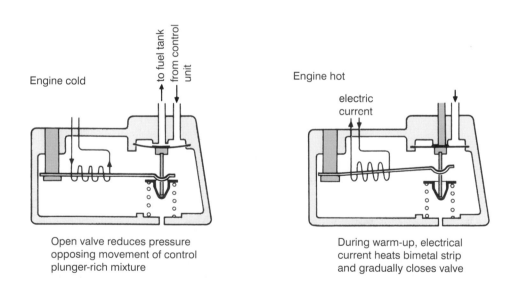

Figure 2.249 *Warm-up regulator*

2.23.2 Mechanical system with electronic control

Closer matching of the mixture to meet changing loads and operating conditions and the introduction of stricter emission control regulations caused the manufacturers to modify the K-Jetronic system. The modified system was called Bosch KE Jetronic; the letter E in the title signifies 'electronic'.

Control of the mechanical system by electronic means allowed the mixture to be set more accurately and, by virtue of the inherent 'intelligence' of the ECU, the modified system is able to vary the mixture to suit a wider range of operating conditions.

Comparing the KE system shown in Figure 2.250 with the K system Figure 2.247, the following are some of the differences:

- System-pressure regulator – more precise control of the system pressure is obtained by using a modified regulator valve, which takes into account manifold depression.
- Electro-hydraulic pressure actuator – functions as a fine mixture adjustment control to vary the air/fuel ratio slightly to suit all engine conditions, especially during warm-up, acceleration and full-load operation.
- ECU – acts as the brain of the system. It analyses the signals it receives from the throttle calve switch, airflow potentiometer and engine speed and temperature sensors, and then sends output signals to the actuators, which control the fuel mixture.

In addition, other features are included to allow fuel cut-off during over-run and, in countries where special emission laws were in force, the system controlled the mixture by utilising the variation in the oxygen content in the exhaust gas (lambda closed-loop system).

2.24 The simple carburettor

The term 'simple carburettor' refers to the basic type of carburettor. While it might be suitable for modern types of engine, it is important to understand these basic systems to appreciate the move to modern fuelling systems.

A carburettor consists essentially of two parts:

1 The means for regulating the entry of fuel to the carburettor according to the rate at which the fuel is used. This usually takes the form of a float chamber.
2 The means for atomising the fuel and mixing it with the necessary amount of air. This part is known as the mixing chamber.

These two parts are not necessarily separate from one another, but are usually situated within the carburettor body.

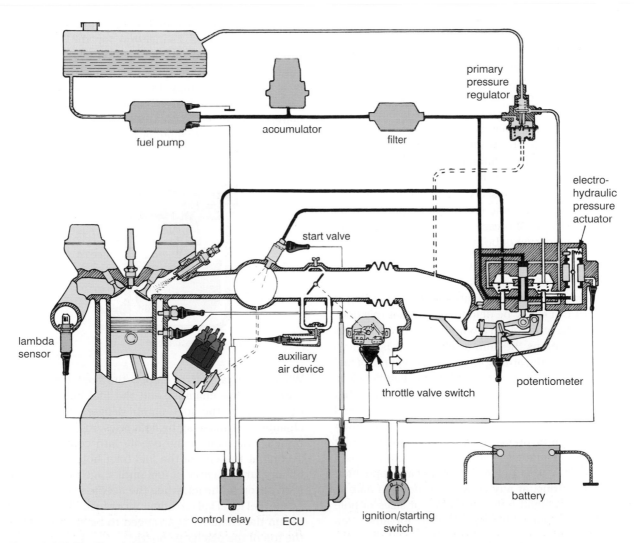

Figure 2.250 The Bosch KE-Jetronic fuel-injection system

2.24.1 The float chamber

The action of this is based upon the principle of the simple U-tube, which is illustrated in Figure 2.251.

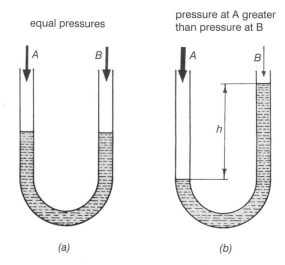

Figure 2.251 A simple U-tube

Figure 2.251a shows a U-tube partly filled with liquid: so long as the pressure acting at A and B are equal, the levels of liquid in the two limbs of the tube will be at the same height. However, if the pressure at A exceeds that at B, the level of liquid in limb A will be forced down and that in B raised. Thus, there will be a difference in the height (*h*) of the two levels, proportional to the difference between the two pressures, as illustrated in Figure 2.251b. Note that it is not the actual pressures that matter, but their *difference*, and the same effect will be produced by either an increase of pressure at A or a decrease at B, or by a combination of both.

Figure 2.252 shows the U-tube modified for use in the carburettor, the modifications consisting of an enlargement of the size of limb A and a shortening of limb B. (It can easily be demonstrated that this does not affect the principle in anyway whatsoever.) Under normal conditions the limb or chamber A is open to the pressure of the atmosphere, and is kept full of fuel to the level of the top of the limb B, or slightly below. If this level can be kept constant and limb B subjected to a pressure lower than that of the atmosphere, fuel will be drawn out from B at a rate that depends upon the difference in pressures and the opposition that the liquid encounters in flowing from A to B. It is a simple matter to provide the necessary opposition to flow by fitting, at any convenient point in limb B, a plug with a small hole, and different sizes of hole will clearly regulate the rate of flow for any given pressure difference.

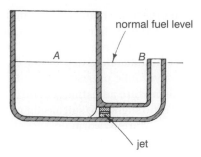

Figure 2.252 Modified U-tube as used in a carburettor

These drilled plugs are known as jets, and they are carefully calibrated and numbered by carburettor manufacturers to indicate the rate at which fuel flows through them under standardised conditions. The jets are externally threaded to screw into position and are easily interchangeable.

Figure 2.253 illustrates the manner in which the level in chamber A is kept constant. The top of the chamber is closed by a lid in which there is a small hole or air vent, by means of which atmospheric pressure is maintained on the liquid in the chamber. The lid also has a connection for the pipe from the fuel pump, and this connection leads to a hole entering the top of the chamber. Inside the chamber is a float, which may be made of hollow brass pressings, soldered together, or a suitable plastic material. Attached to the top of the float is a needle, the pointed end of which enters the hole by which the fuel comes into the chamber.

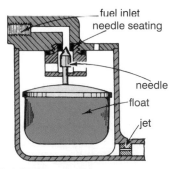

Figure 2.253 A float mechanism

When the chamber is empty, the float ties on the bottom of the chamber and the fuel inlet is open. Operation of the fuel pump delivers fuel to the chamber; as this fills, the float rises on the fuel level, bringing the end of the needle into contact with a seating at the end of the fuel inlet hole and cutting off any further entry of fuel until some fuel is drawn away through the jet, when the needle valve reopens as the fuel level falls to admit more fuel. The height of fuel in the chamber is arranged to be slightly below the top of the discharge nozzle.

2.24.2 The venturi

This device consists simply of a tube of which the bore diminishes smoothly to a throat and then smoothly enlarges to its original size (Figure 2.254).

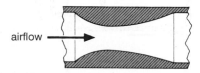

Figure 2.254 Venturi

Gas flowing along this venturi tube will increase in speed as it passes through the throat. The result of this is that the pressure of the gas will be reduced as its velocity increases, and will rise again as the velocity falls. This effect can be demonstrated by the apparatus shown in Figure 2.255. This consists of a series of glass tubes, which dip into a trough of coloured water. A blower (like a vacuum cleaner) is used to pass air through the venturi and the level of water in the tubes is noted when the blower is switched on. When there is no air flowing through the venturi, the level in all tubes is equal, but when air is moving through the venturi, the level in tube B will be higher than that shown in the other tubes. This indicates that the air pressure in the throat of the venturi is less than that which exists on each side of the restriction. Increasing the air speed through the venturi causes a greater drop in air pressure; in a similar way, if the throat of the venturi is made smaller, the drop in pressure for a given air speed will be greater. Whenever the air pressure is lowered below atmospheric pressure, the term 'depression' can be used, so in this case a venturi increases the air speed and forms a depression.

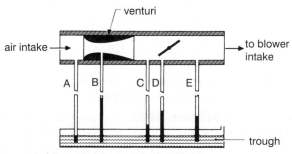

Figure 2.255 Demonstration of air pressure variation in a carburettor

The mixing chamber of a carburettor is the region around the venturi; it is situated in the induction pipe that supplies the engine with air. Fitted at the throat of the venturi, which is also known as the choke tube, is an outlet from a pipe or drilling that conveys petrol from the float chamber.

The combination of the depression created by the venturi and the petrol supply from the float chamber allows the petrol to mix with the air. Since the depression intensifies as the quantity of air passing through the induction pipe increases, the amount of petrol supplied to mix with this air will also increase.

2.24.3 The complete carburettor

Figure 2.256 shows a simple carburettor. The only component not so far mentioned is the throttle valve, the purpose of which is to regulate the engine power by controlling the airflow to the engine. The action of the carburettor is as follows.

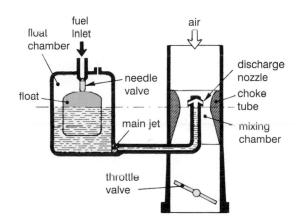

Figure 2.256 A simple single-choke carburettor

When the fuel supply is turned on, fuel enters the float chamber through the inlet connection, and rises in both the float chamber and also the fuel discharge nozzle. As the level rises, the float also rises and lifts the needle into the needle seating. This cuts off the entry of fuel when the level is just below the top of the discharge nozzle. If the engine is rotated, air is drawn in through the air intake and choke tube, producing a pressure drop or depression inside the choke tube. This depression draws fuel from the float chamber via the passage and jet into the mixing chamber. The rush of air through the choke tube will, if its velocity is great enough, atomise the fuel as it issues from the discharge nozzle. The mixture of air and atomised fuel will be drawn into the engine at a rate that depends upon engine speed and the extent of opening of the throttle valve. The driver controls the throttle by the accelerator pedal.

As the rate of airflow increases, because of either an increase in engine speed or a wider throttle opening or both, the depression in the choke tube also increases, thus drawing more fuel from the jet.

The size of the choke tube is selected so that the air velocity through it is sufficient to atomise the fuel at the lowest speed at which the engine is required to

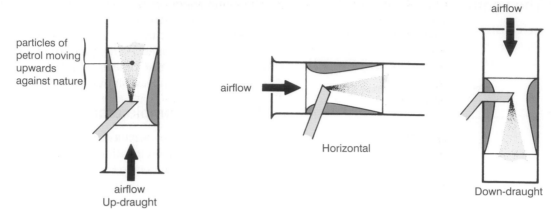

Figure 2.257 Attitude of choke tube

run. The desired mixture can be obtained by using a size of jet that allows the correct amount of fuel to flow and join the airstream.

Attitude of choke tube

In Figure 2.256 the axis of the choke tube is vertical. It does not matter whether the choke tube is horizontal, vertical, or at some intermediate angle (so long as the float chamber remains vertical) and carburettors are made with the choke tube in any of these attitudes, as shown in Figure 2.257.

The downdraught arrangement shown in Figure 2.257 was the most common arrangement. This was for two main reasons:

1 The flow of mixture into the manifold is assisted by gravity.
2 It enables the carburettor to be fitted in a very accessible position on top of the engine.

Variation of air/fuel ratio

The simple carburettor shown in Figure 2.256 would be suitable for a fixed-speed engine that operated against a constant load. But these conditions are quite different from those experienced by an engine fitted to a vehicle. When the load and/or speed of an engine fitted with a simple carburettor is increased, the mixture strength supplied by the carburettor becomes richer (i.e. the air/fuel ratio decreases as the speed or load is increased) (Figure 2.258).

This problem is overcome either by incorporating a compensation system or by using a carburettor design that uses the constant depression principle. The difference in construction that is used to overcome the mixture variation problem enables carburettors to be classified as:

■ constant-choke carburettors
■ constant-depression carburettors.

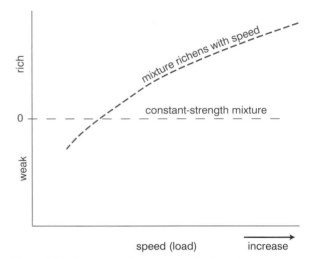

Figure 2.258 Mixture variation with a simple carburettor

As these names suggest, the former has a fixed size of venturi and incorporates a compensation system to maintain a near-constant air/fuel ratio. A constant-depression type has a variable choke, which enlarges as the engine speed and load increases. Externally the shape is quite different, so identification is simple.

2.25 Constant-choke carburettors

This type of carburettor is known as a fixed-choke, or variable-depression type because the depression in the fixed-sized venturi varies when the engine speed changes. This variation must be balanced by the fuel flow if weakness or richness of the mixture is to be avoided.

2.25.1 Need for mixture compensation

The change of mixture strength supplied by a simple carburettor is due to the fact that the carburettor

Figure 2.259 Constant-choke variable depression carburettor

is attempting to meter two different fluids: air and petrol. Air is a gas, which flows very easily, whereas petrol is a liquid, which is harder to get moving than a gas due to friction and density. In addition, petrol has a tendency for its particles to stick together and to the walls of the passage through which it flows.

By selecting suitable sizes for the choke tube and jet, it is possible to obtain a chemically correct mixture strength to suit a set engine speed. However, when this speed is increased, the subsequent increase in the depression would promote an excessive petrol flow. This enrichment with increase in speed and/or load is prevented by incorporating a compensation system in a carburettor.

2.25.2 Compensation systems

A compensation or correction system is necessary to maintain a near-constant air/fuel ratio. Careful matching of the jets to the system is necessary to avoid under-correction or over-correction; the former implies that the carburettor becomes richer, and the latter weaker as the speed or load increases.

Air-bleed compensation

This method of correction is the most common system in use today. The constructional details of the system vary between different makes, but the principle remains the same.

The arrangement shown in Figure 2.260 consists of an air jet that bleeds air into an emulsion, or diffuser tube, in the side of which are drilled a number of small holes. Petrol is supplied to the well via a main jet and the outlet from the well is situated in the venturi.

When the main jet is not in use, the petrol levels in the well and float chamber are similar, but when the venturi depression is sufficient to cause fuel to discharge from the outlet, the level in the well falls. This drop in level increases as the throttle is opened and when full throttle is reached the fuel level in the well is very low.

This opening of the throttle would cause a simple carburettor to supply a mixture that becomes richer

and richer as the speed increases. A correction system overcomes this problem by using the drop in fuel level in the well to expose air holes in the emulsion tube. When the mixture strength shows a sign of becoming rich, a hole is uncovered and air is bled into the system. This reduces the depression that is felt on the main jet and, as a result, restores the correct mixture strength.

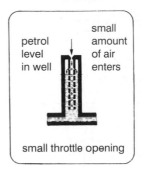
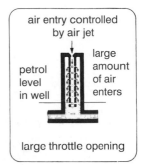

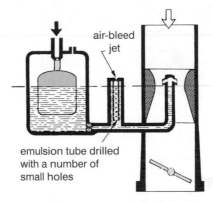

Figure 2.260 An air-bleed system

The action of this type of compensation system is similar to the glass and straw experiment shown in Figure 2.261.

With all bleed holes covered, the creation of a slight suction (depression) in the mouth causes fluid to move up the straw. Intensifying the depression increases the fluid flow. At this point, if one hole is uncovered the flow will decrease; the flow will decrease even further if more holes are uncovered. It is possible to adjust the flow of fluid by varying the number of holes that are uncovered.

Tuning the correction system to give a near-constant air/fuel ratio is achieved by altering the hole size and spacing in the emulsion tube to suit a given size of main jet. Some systems have an air-bleed jet (sometimes named the air-correction jet), which is detachable to enable its size to be changed. This air jet controls the maximum entry of air and is only effective at large throttle openings, because at smaller throttle openings the exposed holes in the emulsion tube control the entry of bleed air.

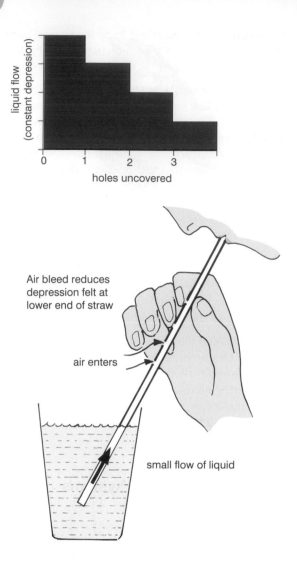

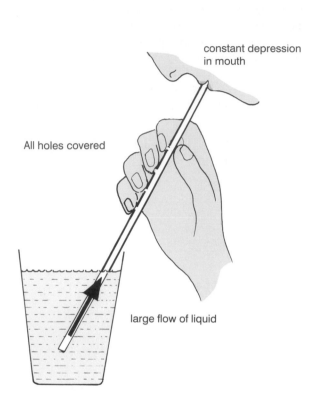

Figure 2.261 Effect of the air-bleed system

2.25.3 Slow-running and idle systems

A decreased airflow into the engine results in a reduction in the air velocity at the choke tube, and consequently the pressure at this point rises nearer to atmospheric pressure. If the carburettor is properly corrected, this will not alter the mixture strength, but it will result in a progressive coarsening of the spray owing to the reduced velocity of the airflow. Also, as the airflow is reduced, the velocity will eventually become insufficient to maintain the fuel droplets in suspension, owing both to their increased size and the low air velocity in the manifold. There will, therefore, be a speed below which the engine will not run, and this will depend primarily upon the size of the choke tube and, to a lesser extent, upon the diameter and length of the inlet manifold. The conditions necessary for good low-speed operation are quite unsuitable for developing reasonably high power at high speeds, and there is obviously a limit to the extent to which power at high rpm can be sacrificed to obtain a good low-speed operation.

The extreme condition of low air velocity through the choke tube occurs when the engine is running but not driving the car, and therefore has merely to develop sufficient power to overcome its own internal friction losses. This is the case whenever the vehicle is stationary but may be required to move at any moment, as, for instance, when halted in traffic or at traffic lights. For economy and comfort, the engine should run slowly and quietly, but respond instantly to the opening of the throttle when the time comes for it to drive the vehicle.

This condition of engine operation is known as slow running, ticking over or idling. The airflow through the choke tube is then not only too slow to atomise the fuel, but there is insufficient depression in the choke tube to draw fuel from the jets.

To pass the amount of mixture needed to keep the engine running at idling speed, the throttle is barely open, and the air velocity is greatest where it passes through the very small gap around the edge of the throttle. A vacuum gauge will show that the depression in the manifold is at its highest (about 380–450 mm or 15–18 in of mercury or 58 kPa below atmospheric pressure).

An arrangement similar to that shown in Figure 2.262 is used to provide a suitable mixture for slow running. A passage connects the float chamber, via the main jet, to an outlet positioned in the region of the throttle valve. Fuel flow is regulated by a slow-running jet or idling jet, and to ensure that fuel does not flow continually the top of the passage is taken above the fuel level in the float chamber. Siphoning is prevented by having an air bleed at the top of the inverted U of the passage and an adjusting screw adjacent to the throttle enables the volume of emulsified fuel entering the engine to be regulated to suit the condition of the engine. The speed at which the engine runs is determined primarily by the extent of the throttle opening; normally this is set by a throttle stop adjusting screw.

When the engine is idling, a strong depression exists on the engine side of the throttle, causing fuel to be drawn from the idling system. This fuel mixes with the air spilling past the edge of the throttle.

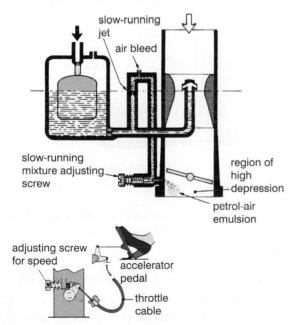

Figure 2.262 A slow-running (idle) system

Mixture strength for slow running

At idling speed only a whiff of mixture is needed to turn the engine over, and under these conditions the cylinder contains a comparatively large quantity of exhaust gas. This dilutes the new charge, so in order to provide an ignitable mixture, a charge that is richer than normal is provided during slow running. Today, this enrichment of the mixture is strictly limited because any unburnt or partially burnt fuel causes the exhaust to pollute the atmosphere. In view of this,

most later engines fitted with carburettors would not slow-run at a speed less than about 900 rpm.

Acceleration from idle

Opening the throttle from the idling position causes more air to pass the throttle. This lowers the depression (raises the pressure) and reduces the fuel discharge from the slow-running outlet. At the same time, the airflow through the choke tube causes the main jet system to come gradually into operation. This changeover does not always occur smoothly, with the result that any deficiency in fuel supply is accompanied by a sudden drop in engine power.

To avoid this transfer flat-spot, the arrangement shown in Figure 2.263 is used.

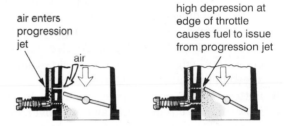

Figure 2.263 Two-hole idling system

At a throttle position where the 'flat-spot' would otherwise occur, one or more holes are drilled adjacent to the edge of the throttle valve to provide additional fuel discharge outlets. Fuel discharge from the upper hole is controlled by an interchangeable jet called a progression jet.

When the engine is idling, a high depression on the engine side of the choke causes petrol to discharge from the lower drilling. During this phase the progression hole will be above the throttle, so air will enter this hole, pass through the progression jet and bleed into the slow-running mixture to assist in the emulsifying process. As the throttle is opened, the rush of air past the edge of the throttle will create a depression in this region and will cause fuel to discharge from the progression outlet.

Idle speed adjustment

To meet emission regulations on carburettor engines, final adjustment of the idling system required a tachometer to set the engine speed accurately and an exhaust gas analyser to measure the quantity of carbon monoxide (CO) and hydrocarbons (HC) present in the exhaust gas.

Emission control

To meet the regulations, the slow-running system of a modern carburettor was designed to take into account the following:

1 Tamper-proof adjusting screws – screws provided for mixture alteration are arranged so that unqualified persons are deterred from altering the mixture. Adjusting screws are normally hidden in a recessed hole, which is sealed by a metal or plastic plug.

2 Carbon monoxide (CO) content in the exhaust – the mixture for slow running is set weaker than that used in the past. An exhaust gas CO test, taken after the slow running has been set, should show that the CO content is less than the value specified by the manufacturer – a typical maximum value is 1 per cent.

The weaker mixture needed to obtain this low value necessitates other carburettor alterations:

- Higher slow-running speed – the dilution effect of the residual exhaust gas on a weak slow-running mixture causes the engine to stall at a speed of 500–600 rpm. To give smooth, consistent engine operation, a slow-running speed in the range 800–900 rpm is used.
- Better mixing of the petrol and air in the slow-running circuit – the aim is to overcome a 'patchy' mixture. Fuel-rich regions in the combustion chamber give high CO emissions, whereas weak mixtures in the vicinity of the spark plug cause misfiring; this means that the complete charge for that stroke is exhausted and high hydrocarbon (HC) pollution results.
- Slow-running throttle bypass – a reduction in the richness of the slow-running mixture makes the engine very sensitive to slight alterations in the throttle position. A small amount of wear in the throttle spindle causes the butterfly valve to vary its closed position. Consequently, the engine may either race or stall when the throttle is released.

This problem can be overcome by making the valve close fully at slow running and providing a separate throttle bypass duct (Figure 2.264). Slow-running speed is controlled by a screw, which governs the quantity of mixture being supplied to the engine.

Unless carefully designed, this system is prone to throttle seizure when the carburettor cools after strenuous use of the engine.

Running on

When the ignition is switched off, the driver expects the engine to stop, but often the engine continues to run very erratically for a considerable time or until it is stalled by the dryer. During this running-on period, combustion is initiated by some part of the combustion chamber, such as a valve or spark plug electrode, that is hotter than normal. This extraordinary high temperature is often produced

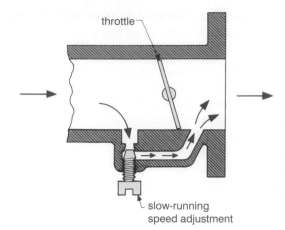

Figure 2.264 Throttle bypass

when the engine is operated on a weak mixture as needed to meet the emission regulations.

Various arrangements are used to overcome this problem; the method shown in Figure 2.265 is an electric solenoid, which cuts off the slow-running mixture when the ignition is switched off. This system is called an anti-run-on valve or anti-dieselling valve.

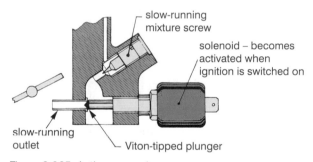

Figure 2.265 Anti-run-on valve

An alternative system uses a solenoid valve to open and allow air to enter the inlet manifold when the ignition is switched off.

2.25.4 Economisers and power systems

Under ideal conditions, a carburettor that supplied a chemically correct mixture (15:1) would cause the engine to produce maximum power and economy at all speeds and loads. In practice, the physical problems associated with distributing the correct amount of fully vaporised fuel to each cylinder makes it impossible to achieve this ideal. Even if it could be achieved, the difficulty of bringing each particle of fuel into intimate contact with the correct amount of oxygen needed to burn it completely into carbon dioxide (CO_2) and water (H_2O) makes the ideal remote from reality.

Varying the mixture strength supplied to an engine that is operating under load at a fixed speed causes the engine performance to change (Figure 2.266).

This graph plots the fuel used per unit of power against the torque output.

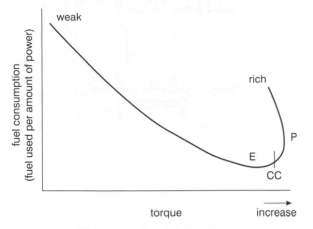

Figure 2.266 *Effect on varying air/fuel ratio*

When the air/fuel mixture is weak, the fuel economy is very poor and the torque output is low. As the mixture is enriched both the economy and torque improve, but after the lowest point of the curve (maximum economy) has been reached, further enrichment produces a slight increase in torque at the expense of economy. Continuing to enrich the mixture past the maximum torque point produces a drop in torque and a considerable rise in fuel consumption. Three points on this graph should be noted:

1 The chemically correct (CC) mixture strength gives neither maximum economy nor maximum power.
2 Maximum power (P) requires a mixture that is slightly rich.
3 Maximum economy (E) requires a mixture that is slightly weak.

In order to achieve both maximum power and greatest economy, the mixture strength supplied by the carburettor must be varied to suit the operating conditions (i.e. it must provide a slightly rich mixture for power and slightly weak mixture for economy). Emission regulations normally prevent the use of mixtures richer than 15:1, because they do not fully burn during combustion, so the engine power output at 15:1 is the maximum and the operating mixture range is on the weak side of this value.

The choke cannot distinguish between the high-load (power) and cruising (economy) conditions, so an alternative sensing source must be used. This is either the movement of the throttle or the pressure in the inlet manifold. Since the cruising and high-load conditions give a manifold depression that is high and low respectively, the variation in the manifold pressure is used by many systems to sense the load acting against the engine.

The devices used in a carburettor to vary the mixture strength to suit either the power or cruising conditions are called economisers or power systems.

In all cases, the weak cruising mixture is obtained by reducing the petrol flow through the main jet system. This can be achieved either by using a smaller jet or by reducing the pressure difference across the jet.

Restoration of the air/fuel ratio to 15:1 for power is achieved either by providing an additional path from the float chamber to the choke, or by exposing the main jet to the normal pressure difference.

Figure 2.267 shows a mechanically operated power valve. The smaller-than-normal main jet provides the cruising mixture. The throttle-controlled power valve, which comes into operation when the throttle is opened in excess of about 75 per cent, supplies extra fuel for power. In the high-load throttle range, the petrol flow through both the power and main jets gives a suitable mixture to enable the engine to develop its maximum power.

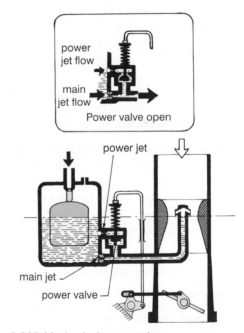

Figure 2.267 *Mechanical power valve*

Vacuum control of the power valve can be achieved by using a vacuum chamber diaphragm to act on a rod, which in turn controls the valve. Alternatively, the system can be arranged as shown in Figure 2.268. The diaphragm in this arrangement acts directly on the power valve, which can be made to control either the air bled into the system or the petrol flow.

Failure of a power valve is generally due to the diaphragm tearing. This prevents the mixture from becoming weak during cruising, so high fuel consumption results. Also, the torn diaphragm allows air to enter the manifold via the sensing passage; this causes unstable slow running.

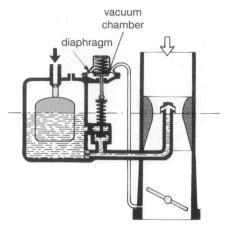

Figure 2.268 A vacuum-operated power valve

2.25.5 Acceleration pumps

Whenever the throttle is plunged open, there is a weakening of the mixture. One of the reasons for this is the delay caused by the reluctance of the fuel to respond compared with the fast action of the air. If the carburettor is already delivering a slightly weakened mixture to give maximum economy, the further weakening that occurs when the throttle is opened causes a delay before the engine responds; in some cases, it will cause the engine to misfire.

Whereas a carburettor without an economy system has small reserves of fuel on the outlet side of the main jet to allow for sudden increases in speed or load, an economy-type carburettor generally needs an acceleration pump. This delivers fuel into the mixing chamber when the throttle is plunged open.

There are two main types of acceleration pump: mechanical and vacuum-operated.

Mechanical type

The mechanical pump shown in Figure 2.269 is controlled by a linkage connected to the throttle. This linkage acts on a diaphragm, which draws fuel via a one-way valve from the float chamber and pumps it past a delivery valve fitted in the outlet passage. A separate jet, or restriction in the passageway, regulates the flow of fuel delivered by the pump.

When the fuel outlet pipe terminates in a region where the pressure is lower than atmospheric, there is a risk that fuel will discharge continuously, so a device such as a weighted valve, or air bleed into the outlet passage, is used to prevent this flow.

The pump must not discharge when the throttle is moved slowly. In Figure 2.269, this is achieved by

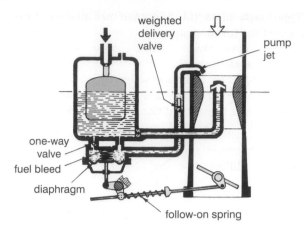

Figure 2.269 Mechanical accelerator pump

having a bleed to allow fuel to bypass the inlet valve of the acceleration pump when the throttle is opened slowly.

Most pump designs use a spring in the pump-operating linkage to increase the time that the fuel in the pump chamber is being discharged. This follow-on action also improves exhaust emission and economy.

Vacuum type

The pump shown in Figure 2.270 operates by using the sudden change in manifold pressure that occurs when the engine is accelerated. The pumping action is produced by the diaphragm spring; this is compressed when a high depression acts in the vacuum chamber. A sudden collapse of this depression allows the spring to discharge fuel into the mixing chamber.

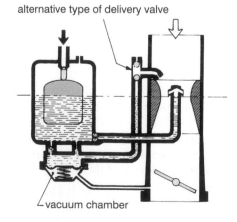

Figure 2.270 Vacuum-operated acceleration pump

2.25.6 Cold starting

Special provisions are necessary to start a cold engine. This is because the cranking speed of the engine is insufficient to allow the venturi to create an adequate depression. In addition, the slow-moving air entering the engine causes a large amount of fuel to be deposited on the walls of the inlet manifold. Since the manifold and cylinders are cold, very little vaporisation of the fuel takes place, so ignition of the charge under these conditions is very difficult.

Petrol consists of many different hydrocarbons (HC) and the fractions (groups of HC) that make up the fuel have different boiling points in the range 85–220 °C. A light-fraction fuel boils (vaporises) at a low temperature, whereas a heavy-fraction fuel does not boil until the temperature approaches 220 °C.

The provision of extra fuel during cold starting ensures there is an adequate supply of light-fraction fuels that are able to vaporise in the cold engine. If the quantity of gas formed by this vaporisation is sufficient, it is possible to ignite the gas and produce enough heat to drive the engine over, even though the cold oil is causing a large drag.

In the past, petrol suppliers helped to overcome the cold starting problem by providing a fuel for the winter period that incorporated a higher proportion of light fractions. This was then changed in the summer because highly volatile fuels cause vapour locks in the fuel lines when exposed to summer heat. Today, the fuel supplied at the pumps is more highly refined and this, along with the use of advanced EMSs, has prevented the need for this process.

Cold-starting systems used today can be divided into two main types:

1 Strangler
2 Separate starting carburettor

Strangler-type cold-starting system

Figure 2.271 shows the principle of a strangler. It consists of a flap valve, which is positioned at the air entry point of the carburettor. When the valve is closed, the strangulation of the air supply intensifies the depression felt at the venturi. As a result, extra fuel is supplied to provide a very rich mixture in the region of 8:1.

Once the engine has started, the richness of the mixture must be reduced to a point where the engine runs smoothly. This reduces the risk of rapid cylinder wear caused by neat fuel washing the oil film from the top part of the cylinders: also excessive fuel 'wets' or 'fouls' the spark plug and stops it functioning in the normal manner.

For historical reasons, the strangler is sometimes called the 'choke'. That is the reason why the name is occasionally marked on the driver's control knob. This control connects with a cable that acts on the

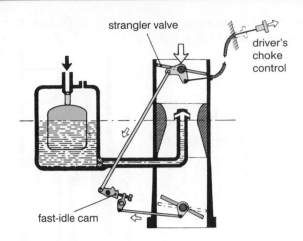

Figure 2.271 A simple strangler system

strangler valve; the first movement of the 'choke' control opens the throttle a small amount to give a fast idle to allow for the extra drag on the engine when it is cold.

The driver must not 'over-choke' the engine, because this action 'floods' the engine with fuel vapour and starves it of air.

To minimise the problems associated with 'over-choking', the strangler normally incorporates some arrangement to weaken the mixture as soon as the engine starts. Figure 2.272 shows an offset strangler valve that allows the moving air to act on the valve and partially open it after the engine has started.

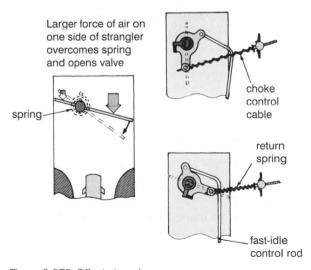

Figure 2.272 Offset strangler

Automatic strangler

Incorrect use of the 'choke' by the driver, especially the delay in returning it to the 'off' position, causes emission problems as well as those drawbacks previously outlined. To overcome these problems, the automatic choke was introduced.

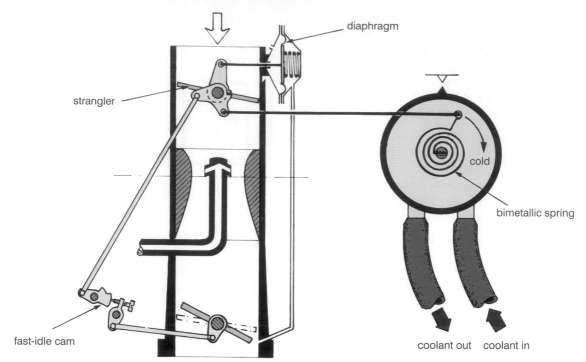

Figure 2.273 A simple automatic choke using a bimetallic strip

Figure 2.273 shows the principle of one system; this uses a bimetallic strip to sense the temperature of the coolant. When the engine temperature is less than about 15 °C, the bimetallic strip pulls the strangler to the closed position.

In the type shown, the driver should depress and then release the throttle prior to starting the engine. This allows the strangler and fast-idle cam to take up a position appropriate to the engine temperature.

After the engine has started, the strangler is partly opened by the diaphragm in the vacuum chamber; this is activated by the high depression created in the inlet manifold.

As the engine warms up, the rise in coolant temperature causes the bimetallic strip to gradually reduce its pull on the strangler. This takes place over a period of time, so both the richness and the fast-idle action are slowly changed to suit the engine temperature.

Normally two adjustments are provided:

1 The wind-up of the bimetallic strip governs the temperature at which the system comes into operation. Often marks are provided on the housing to suit the engine and climatic conditions under which it operates.
2 A fast-idle adjusting screw controls the engine speed during 'choke' operation. This screw should be clear of the cam when the engine is warm.

Separate starting carburettor

This system may be regarded as a separate carburettor attached to the main carburettor, therefore it incorporates its own jets and mixing chamber. This enables the cold-starting air/fuel ratio to be accurately controlled and the fuel and air to be well mixed to suit the conditions. The system may be operated by manual or automatic means.

Figure 2.274 shows the layout of a starting carburettor that is brought into action by means of a 'choke' cable, which rotates a disc (1). When the cable is pulled, the disc rotates and aligns a small orifice in the disc with a fuel passage connected to the float chamber. This movement also allows a large elongated hole at the bottom of the disc to uncover an outlet passage that leads to the main air intake on the manifold side of the throttle.

Providing the throttle is kept closed when the 'choke' is operated, the rotation of the engine by the starter motor causes the high depression in the manifold to be felt in the chamber (2). This depression causes air to enter the chamber by the bleed (3) and fuel to be drawn from the passage (6) after the fuel has been metered by the starter jet (4). When the system is not in use, a small quantity of fuel is held in the reserve well (5), so this fuel gives extra richness when the system is initially brought into use.

After the engine has started, an opening of the throttle by the driver reduces the depression in the chamber

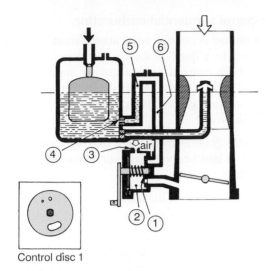

Control disc 1

Figure 2.274 Starting carburettor

(2); this decreases the quantity of rich mixture supplied by the starting carburettor. As the engine warms up, the mixture has to be weakened. This is achieved by rotating the disc a small amount to align a smaller orifice in the disc with the fuel-supply passage.

When a rich mixture is no longer required, the system is put out of use by pushing in the 'choke' to the 'off' position. This action rotates the disc and blanks off the fuel and outlet ports.

There are many variations of this system. Some designs use a cylindrical valve instead of a disc valve; in this configuration it is often operated automatically.

2.25.7 Constructional features for later types of carburettor

The rise of the importance of emission controls meant that modern carburettors, to supply air and finely atomised fuel evenly distributed in the proportion, needed to suit the engine operating conditions. These requirements could be met fairly easily if the engine operates at one constant speed, but wide speed ranges coupled with other variable factors, such as engine load, engine temperature, changes in atmospheric temperature, pressure and humidity, etc., make the carburettor's task very difficult.

Single fixed-choke carburettor

This type has been described in detail in the previous sections. Alterations over the years to this type of carburettor include the following:

- Inside air – an air vent to atmosphere (Figure 2.275) allows dirt to enter and vapour to escape from the float chamber, so a transfer passage (1) between the 'engine side of the filter' to the float chamber is provided. Any

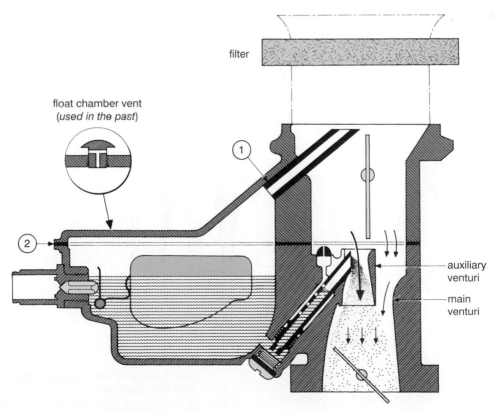

Figure 2.275 Inside air feature and auxiliary venturi

slight restriction of airflow through the filter does not affect the air/fuel ratio provided that the joint (2) makes a good seal.

■ Auxiliary venturi – placing a small venturi in a position such that its outlet is in the waist of the main venturi causes the fuel to mix with the air in two stages. Petrol joining the air flowing through the auxiliary venturi gives a petrol-rich initial mix, but on meeting the main airflow at the auxiliary venturi outlet the fuel is distributed evenly throughout the air mass and a constant air/fuel ratio is obtained.

Twin-choke carburettor

Engines such as the V6 and V8 normally required two carburettors. Cost and space was saved when the two carburettors were joined together to share a common float chamber.

Figure 2.276 shows a diagram of a dual-venturi downdraught unit. Normal practice is to arrange the manifold so that one venturi system supplies one set of cylinders and the other venturi the remaining cylinders. This layout shows why each venturi needs to be provided with its own system for cold starting, slow running, cruising and power.

The two throttle valves are interconnected and should be synchronised to give the same opening at all engine speeds.

Twin-barrel sequential carburettor

To obtain fuel economy, good atomisation of the fuel is needed. In a fixed-choke carburettor, this can be achieved by using a comparatively small-diameter venturi. Unfortunately, the restriction to airflow of a small venturi gives a poor VE and results in low maximum power.

When both economy and high maximum power are required, a multi-barrel sequential type carburettor is often fitted.

Figure 2.277 shows a diagram of this type. The two throttle valves are coupled together in such a way that the secondary throttle remains closed until the primary throttle has opened about two-thirds. When the throttle opens past this point, the linkage moves the secondary throttle so that both throttles reach the fully open position together. This sequential movement allows the primary barrel to supply all cylinders with a slightly weak, well-atomised mixture for cruising conditions. When power is required, the secondary barrel provides extra fuel and a good supply of air to meet power demands.

On some carburettors an auxiliary butterfly valve is fitted in the secondary barrel. Operated automatically, this valve closes when both throttles are open and the air speed through the venturi is low.

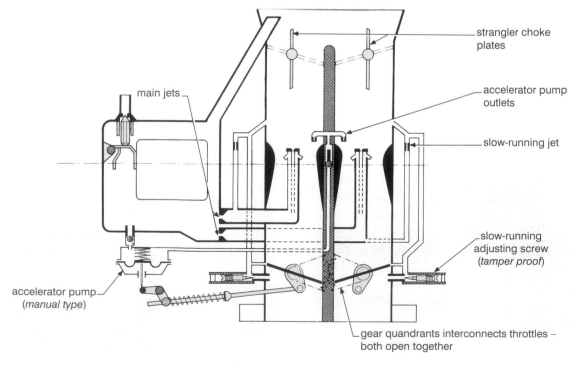

Figure 2.276 Twin-choke carburettor

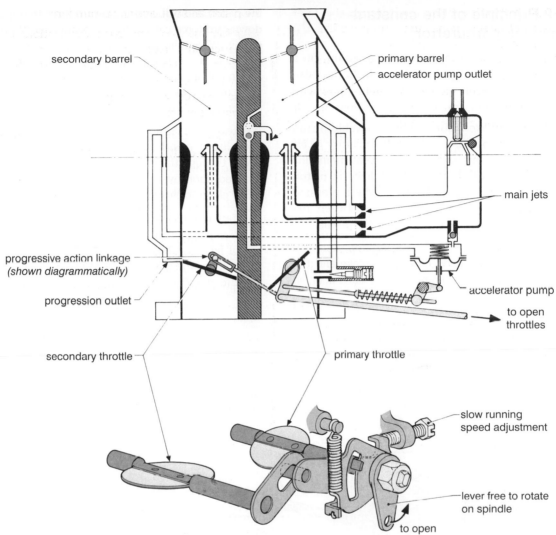

secondary barrel

primary barrel
accelerator pump outlet

main jets

progressive action linkage
(shown diagrammatically)

progression outlet

secondary throttle

primary throttle

accelerator pump

to open
throttles

slow running
speed adjustment

lever free to rotate
on spindle

to open

Figure 2.277 Twin-barrel sequential carburettor

Some higher performance vehicles use a four-barrel carburettor arrangement similar to the unit shown in Figure 2.278. This carburettor runs sequential choke in a similar way to the twin-barrel unit. The four-barrel unit delivers more air and fuel required for the larger capacity engines.

Figure 2.278 Four-barrel sequential carburettor

2.26 Variable choke – constant-depression carburettors

2.26.1 Constant-choke limitations

The varying depression that acts on the jet of a constant-choke carburettor makes it necessary to fit some form of compensating device to prevent mixture enrichment with increase in engine speed. Also, the size of the venturi is a compromise that gives neither maximum economy nor maximum power.

Carburettors working on a constant-depression principle do not suffer these drawbacks because they have a variable choke area, which alters to keep the choke air speed constant. This allows the air speed to be set to that required for good atomisation over the full engine speed range. Also, the constant depression over the jet overcomes the need for a compensating system.

2.26.2 Principle of the constant-depression carburettor

Figure 2.279 shows the basic construction of a constant-depression carburettor, which is also known as a constant vacuum, variable choke and variable venturi.

The venturi or choke is formed by a movable piston that alters the choke area to suit the quantity of air being supplied to the engine. An air vent maintains atmospheric pressure in the space below the piston and a communicating passage transfers the depression from the mixing chamber (the space between the choke and throttle) to the space above the piston.

When air is flowing through the carburettor, there is a difference in pressure between the air intake and the mixing chamber. This difference in pressure acts on the piston and will give an upward force to oppose the downward force caused by the piston weight and light spring. When the upward force due to air pressure difference is increased by opening the throttle, the piston will rise and the choke area will enlarge. Similarly, when the throttle closes, the mixing chamber depression reduces, the piston falls and the choke area decreases.

Whatever the airflow, the piston assembly always takes up a position that maintains a constant air speed through the choke to ensure that the petrol jet is acted upon by a constant depression – hence the name given to this type of carburettor.

As a tapered needle is attached to the piston, the rise or fall of the piston will vary the effective area of the petrol jet. By altering the taper of the needle, it is possible for the manufacturer to vary the fuel flow to suit the quantity of air being supplied at any speed.

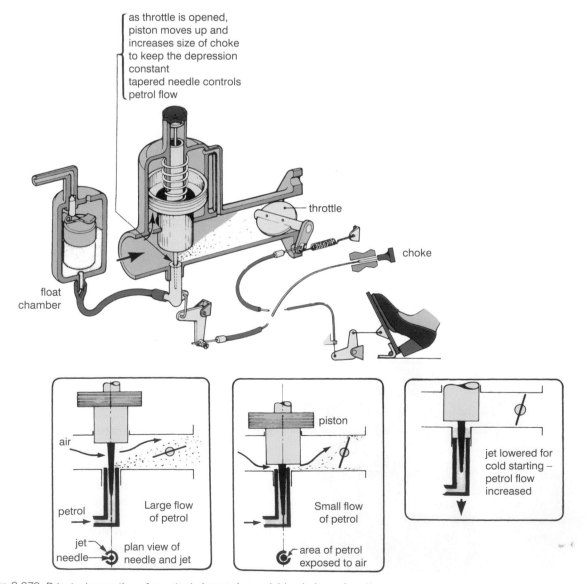

Figure 2.279 Principal operation of constant-depression variable-choke carburettor

SU type

Figure 2.280 shows a section through an **SU** constant vacuum type set in the cruising position. The main features include the following:

- Slow running – the piston will be lifted very slightly from the lowered position and the depression caused by the air rushing over the petrol jet will give a small fuel supply to suit the conditions. A separate slow-running jet system is unnecessary unless emission restrictions are strict.
- Throttle opening – as the throttle is opened, the mixing chamber depression is increased; this causes the piston to rise to a point where the mixing chamber depression is just sufficient to support the piston. The higher the piston moves, the larger the area of the jet and the greater will be the flow of petrol.
- Cold starting – a lever, operated by a cable control, lowers the fuel jet in relation to the needle. This enlarges the jet opening and increases the amount of fuel that is mixed with the air. The initial movement of the control cable slightly opens the throttle to give 'fast idle' action.
- Mixture adjustment – an adjusting nut acts as a stop to limit the upward movement of the jet. Unscrewing the nut lowers the jet and enriches the mixture throughout the entire speed and load range of the engine.
- Hydraulic damper – this restricts the rate of upward movement of the piston during acceleration and so gives a slight enrichment

of the mixture. The damper also reduces piston flutter caused by the irregular flow of air through the induction systems.

- Over-run limiting valve – this is a spring-loaded valve mounted in the throttle butterfly. When the engine over-runs (i.e. road wheels drive the engine) with the throttle closed, the valve opens to supply a fuel mixture, which reduces the exhaust pollution.

> **SU:** the name of the manufacturer of this type of carburettor. SU stands for Skinners' Union, with the Skinner brothers, George Herbert and Thomas Carlyle, being the founders of the company.

Zenith-Stromberg constant-depression type

Figure 2.281 shows the construction of this type. Whereas the SU type uses a piston, this carburettor has a synthetic rubber diaphragm. All of the other functions operate on the same principle as the SU carburettor.

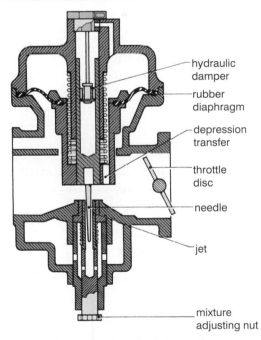

Figure 2.281 *The Zenith-Stromberg carburettor*

Electronic-controlled carburettors

As the emission regulations became more strict, manufacturers had to develop improvements on the fuel-delivery systems. These improvements meant that economy and emissions improved to provide more efficient running engines. Strict anti-pollution systems also forced the modification of the basic carburettor.

These requirements could only be met by a fuel system that was able to sense the engine's operating

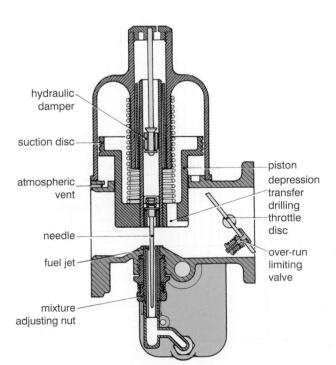

Figure 2.280 The SU carburettor

conditions accurately, and then use the information gained to provide a near-ideal mixture. Such an arrangement must be very sensitive and quick in operation, so electronic control systems were introduced to meet these requirements.

The features covered at this stage apply to a constant-depression carburettor, but many aspects considered also apply to other types of carburettor.

Figure 2.282 shows the layout of a typical electronic control system fitted to a constant-depression carburettor. This system was called electronic regulated ignition and carburetion (ERIC). In this system, four sensing devices are used to measure engine conditions and ambient (surrounding) changes that affect the operation of the carburettor. Electrical signals from these sensors are passed to a computer called an ECU, the brain of the system. During its manufacture, the ECU is programmed to show the action it should take in response to a given set of conditions, so this feature enables the carburettor to operate efficiently over a wide speed and load range.

The electronic system can be used to control:

- the mixture for cold starting
- slow-running and idle speed
- fuel cut-off when the vehicle is on over-run or the ignition is switched off.

Cold starting

Accurate measurement of ambient and engine conditions by electronic sensing ensures that the mixture supplied during cold starting is set to suit the engine temperature.

Figure 2.283 shows an auxiliary starting carburettor that is brought into operation when the cylindrical 'choke' is rotated by an electrical stepper motor. This type of rotary motor has a range of about three revolutions and is capable of moving in either direction through small angles such as 7.5°. The motor responds to an electrical pulse, so when a series of pulses is applied, it moves through a larger angle.

The diagram shows the 'choke' in operation, supplying an extra-rich mixture to augment that delivered by the main system. Air that enters the starting carburettor flows around the rotary choke and mixes with fuel coming from the float chamber. The quantity of air/fuel mixture is determined by the position of the rotary choke, which in turn is controlled by the stepper motor. As the engine warms up, the associated movement of the rotary 'choke' gradually reduces the mixture supplied by the system until eventually the fuel and air ports are cut off and the system goes out of action.

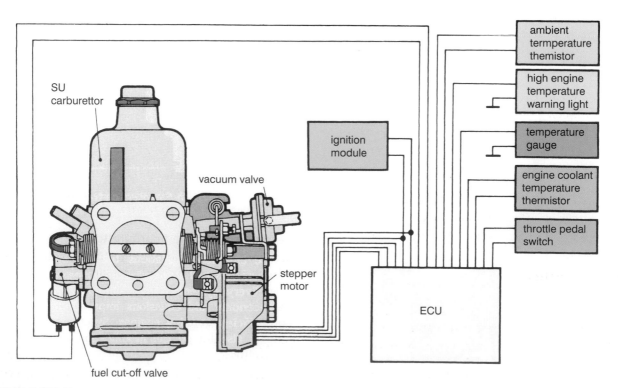

Figure 2.282 SU carburettor with ERIC control system

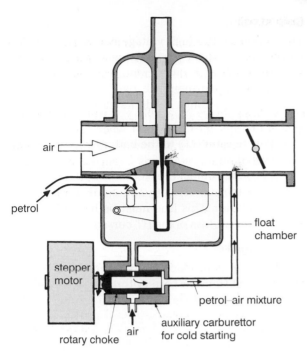

Figure 2.283 Carburettor with auxiliary starting system

Slow-running and idle-speed control

Many modern carburettors used a stepper motor to control the slow-running speed. This motor acts on a throttle stop and 'jacks' opens the throttle when the ECU detects that the engine speed is too low. Engines using this system can be set to slow run at a speed lower than normal without stalling.

In the SU type shown, the first movement of the stepper motor is arranged to control the throttle in a manner similar to that used on non-electronic carburettors.

Fuel cut-off

Economy can be improved by cutting off the fuel supply when power is not required. This can be achieved by using a solenoid valve to reduce the air pressure in the float chamber.

Fluid flow through any orifice is governed by the pressure difference that exists between the inlet and outlet sides of the orifice. In this case, petrol flow through the jet will cease when the air pressure in the float chamber equals the pressure on the output side of the jet.

Mixture control

Elaborate compensation systems as required on constant-choke carburettors can be eliminated by using an electronic system to control the mixture strength. This type of system sets the air/fuel ratio to suit operating conditions such as speed, load, temperature and throttle position of the engine, as well as the ambient temperature.

2.27 Ignition systems

2.27.1 The ignition system

Early engine designs used a hot-tube type of ignition system. This was an externally heated tube attached to the combustion chamber, which was designed to glow red and ignite the air/fuel mixture about TDC at the end of the compression stroke.

As engine speeds increased, the time (relative to crank position) at which the charge was ignited had to be set more accurately, so designers turned to an electric spark system invented by Lenoir.

Requirements of an ignition system

Towards the end of the compression stroke of an engine, an electric spark is required to ignite the air/fuel mixture. The spark has to have sufficient energy to start the charge burning and it must be timed to occur at the correct instant.

A system that produces a 'fixed' spark at TDC does not suit modern engines that are designed to operate at various load settings over a wide speed range. Instead, the spark must occur well before TDC to suit these conditions and, in addition, the spark timing must be precise and be made to vary when the conditions change. In early systems, the spark timing was adjusted by the driver, but modern units perform this duty automatically either by mechanical or electronic means.

Altering the timing to make the spark occur earlier in the operating cycle is described as 'advancing the ignition'. Conversely, the term 'retarding the ignition' is used when the timing is changed to make it occur later.

To obtain a high power output from an engine, the maximum cylinder pressure should occur at 10° after TDC, irrespective of engine speed and mixture/load conditions. Since it takes a comparatively long time for the burning fuel to build up to its maximum pressure, the spark must be set to allow for this time period. The angle of advance is enlarged when the load is decreased or if either the air/fuel mixture ratio or engine speed is increased. This timing change is necessary because the crankshaft moves through a larger angle during the extra time taken by the gases to build up to the maximum pressure.

Production of high voltage

Although early designs used a comparatively low-voltage trembler arrangement, the introduction of the high-voltage, timed spark system considerably improved engine performance. The voltage needed on a high-voltage system to produce a spark depends on the size of the **spark plug gap** and on the gas pressure in the cylinder. A normal gap is about 0.6–1 mm and, although only a small charge of about 600 V is required to produce a spark across this gap in the open air, it will take 10–50 times this voltage to fire a plug that is under pressure in an engine. Indeed, many electronic ignition systems produce over 50,000 V to deliver adequate energy to produce sparks at the spark plugs. This should be borne in mind when an ignition system is being tested – a spark produced at a plug outside the cylinder does not guarantee that it will spark when it is subjected to cylinder pressure.

Spark plug gap: the gap between the electrode of the spark plug and the earth point of the spark plug. This is set accurately to ensure that the ignition system can produce the correct spark delivery for the engine.

A high-voltage spark can be generated by a magneto or coil-ignition system.

Magneto

This is a small self-contained ignition unit, which generates pulses of high-tension current and distributes them to the appropriate cylinders at the correct time. Motorcycles and small single-cylinder engines use this system, but it is not used on modern cars.

Coil-ignition

This system uses electrical energy produced by a battery or alternator to supply the low-tension ignition current. The ignition coil transforms the voltage to that required to produce a high-voltage spark. Compared with a magneto, the coil-ignition system makes engine starting much easier. Also, it is simpler to control the maximum voltage to suit the conditions.

2.27.2 Coil-ignition systems

The conventional battery-inductive ignition system was introduced by Kettering in 1908, but it was not until the mid-1920s that the system was accepted as a successor to the magneto for use on cars.

Until recently, the main layout of a coil-ignition system, as it is commonly known, did not alter, but the current need to design 'cleaner' engines has demanded ignition systems that produce a higher energy spark that is timed far more accurately than before. Electronically controlled coil-ignition systems of the 'breakerless' type meet these requirements. To avoid confusion, the conventional system will be called the Kettering type.

Kettering type

Figure 2.284 shows the layout of a basic system that has been in use for many years. The main components are outlined below.

Ignition coil

This produces the high voltage necessary to cause a spark at the spark plug. It transforms the battery voltage of 12 V to a low-current, high-voltage charge that is needed to jump the plug gap. The ignition coil has two windings inside its case and these are connected to three external terminals:

1. Low tension (LT) to the battery via the ignition switch.
2. LT to the contact breaker.
3. High tension (HT) to the spark plug via the distributor. This lead must be highly insulated to prevent loss of the HT current.

Contact breaker

A HT current is produced by the ignition coil when the LT circuit from the battery through the coil to the vehicle frame (earth) is interrupted.

It consists of two contact points: a fixed contact, screwed down to a base plate, and a movable contact that is insulated from the metal parts that surround it. A cam, normally driven by the engine camshaft, operates the movable contact against the reaction of a strip-type spring. The number of lobes on the cam matches the number of cylinders, for example a four-cylinder engine has four lobes, so one revolution of the cam will give four sparks. On a two-stroke engine, one spark per revolution per cylinder is required, so the cam is driven at the same speed as the engine instead of half engine speed as required by a four-stroke unit.

A spark at the plug occurs at the instant the contacts separate, so the assembly is set (timed) in relation to the crankshaft to give a spark at the correct time.

Capacitor (condenser)

The capacitor, often referred to as a condenser, is connected in the circuit across the contact breakers (i.e. in parallel). This reduces arcing of the contacts and consequently gives a more rapid interruption of the LT circuit. Without the capacitor in the system, the contact breakers would burn out very quickly and the spark produced would be very weak.

Distributor

On a single-cylinder engine the HT lead from the coil is taken direct to the spark plug. A multi-cylinder engine has a number of spark plugs and each one of these has to be connected to the coil when the high-voltage charge is fed to the plug. The HT switch used to select the appropriate plug is called a distributor.

It consists of a hard plastic distributor cap, inside which is a rotor arm; this is turned at half crankshaft speed by a shaft that drives the contact breaker

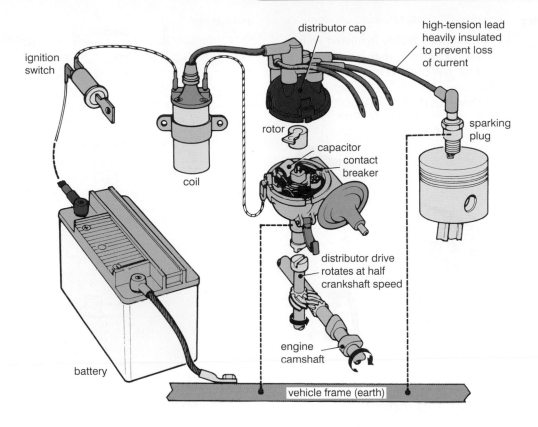

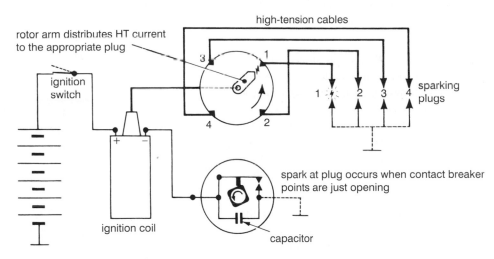

Figure 2.284 A coil-ignition system of the Kettering type

cam. The HT lead, or king lead, from the coil fits in the centre of the cap and a carbon brush rubs on the rotor to transmit the electrical charge.

At the instant the spark occurs, the rotor arm is set to 'point' to the 'segment' in the cap that is connected to the plug that requires the charge.

The distributor cap, rotor arm, contact breaker assembly and automatic advance systems are all incorporated in one unit; this is often called the distributor unit.

HT leads

Highly insulated with PVC plastics or thick rubber, the HT leads link the distributor to the spark plugs and ignition coil.

Radio, TV and electrical interference is reduced by using suppression leads having a high electrical resistance. The conductor used for the lead is either carbon impregnated cotton or glass fibre. These leads are generally made up in a set to suit the suppression requirements of the particular vehicle.

Spark plug

The spark plug consists of a highly insulated centre electrode and an earth electrode that is welded to a metal body. A typical gap of 0.6–1 mm between the electrodes enables a spark to be produced when a high voltage is delivered to the plug (Figure 2.285).

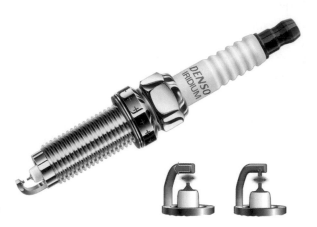

Figure 2.285 Example of a spark plug

2.27.3 Magnetism and induction

To help you understand the operation of ignition and other systems utilising magnetism, consider the following experiments.

Figure 2.286a shows a conductor passing through a piece of paper on to which are scattered some iron filings. When current flows through the conductor, the iron filings arrange themselves in a series of concentric circles. This indicates the presence of a magnetic field. If the process could be slowed down, you would see that on making the circuit, the field moves outwards from the conductor. When the flow of current is interrupted, a reverse action occurs – the field collapses.

Figure 2.286b shows a length of wire wound in the form of a coil. On closing the switch, the magnetic field surrounding each turn of the coil combines with other fields to produce a larger field. A soft iron core, mounted in the centre of the coil, concentrates and intensifies the field. This core becomes a magnet when current is flowing through the coil (Figure 2.286c); the magnetic strength is governed by the amount of current flowing, and the number of turns on the coil.

Figure 2.286d shows another coil, termed a 'secondary winding', which is wound over or placed near the original coil or primary winding. A **galvanometer** is inserted in the secondary circuit and the switch is operated. On closing and opening the switch, you will find that the galvanometer needle momentarily flicks one way on switching on, and then the other way on switching off. This was first discovered by Michael

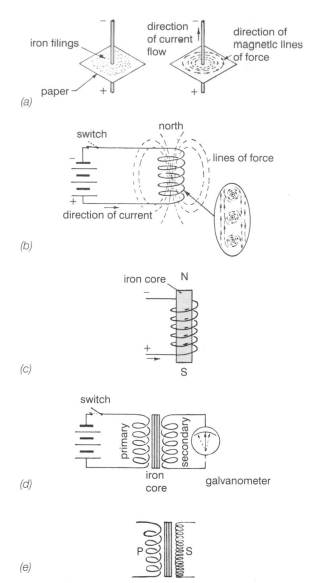

Figure 2.286 Magnetism and induction

Faraday in the 19th century, and from his experiments it was concluded that when a magnetic line of force cuts a conductor (or vice versa), an electromotive force (EMF) is induced in that conductor. The magnitude of the EMF depends on:

- the rate of change of magnetic field
- the number of turns on the coil.

In the apparatus shown in Figure 2.286d, the build-up of the field around the primary causes the lines of force to cut the secondary, and therefore an EMF is induced in the secondary.

Since the build-up is slower than the collapse, a much higher EMF is induced when the circuit is broken.

Galvanometer: an instrument used for detecting a small electrical current.

If the secondary winding contains more turns than the primary (Figure 2.286e), it is possible to obtain a higher voltage in the secondary circuit: for example if the secondary contains 100 times the number of turns wound on the primary, the EMF will be 100 times greater than the EMF in the primary, assuming the efficiency is 100 per cent. This increase in voltage is balanced by a proportional decrease in the current.

2.27.4 Principle of operation of a coil-ignition system

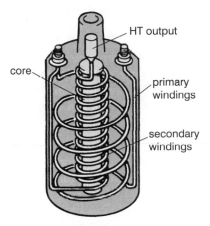

Figure 2.287 Internal construction of an ignition coil showing the primary and secondary windings

The layout of an earth-return (ER) coil-ignition system is shown in Figure 2.288. The system consists of two circuits: primary and secondary.

Primary circuit

Wound around a soft iron core in the coil are several turns of comparatively heavy enamelled wire. This is arranged in series with a battery, ammeter, switch and contact breaker. A capacitor is connected in parallel with the contact breaker.

Secondary circuit

A secondary coil winding, consisting of several thousand turns of fine enamelled wire, is wound under the primary. One end of this winding is joined to the contact breaker terminal, and the other end is connected in series with the distributor and spark plugs. R 'return path' from the plug, via earth, passes through the battery and primary winding, and so EMF induced in the primary winding is added to the large EMF produced in the secondary winding. This gives the coil a higher efficiency.

When the ignition is switched on and the contacts are closed, the current flowing in the primary winding sets up a magnetic field around the iron core of the coil. Opening the contacts, at a time when the spark is required, interrupts the current flowing in the primary circuit, and causes the magnetic field to collapse. During this collapse, the lines of force cut the secondary winding and induce an EMF in the secondary: a higher EMF than that acting in the primary is obtained, since the secondary contains more turns. The HT current is conveyed from the coil to the rotor arm, which, at this time, should be pointing to the correct distributor segment. This is the segment connected to the plug of the cylinder that requires ignition of the charge.

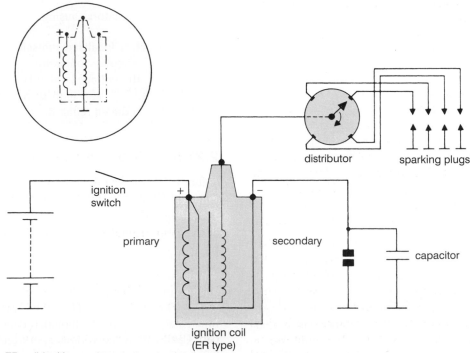

Figure 2.288 An ER coil-ignition system

Capacitor

A capacitor is fitted for two reasons:

1. It reduces arcing of the contacts.
2. It ensures a quicker collapse of the magnetic field.

A capacitor consists of two sheets of foil or metallic paper, which are separated from each other by at least two sheets of insulating material, such as waxed paper. These are wound into a cylindrical shape and inserted in a metal container. One sheet is joined to the earthed container, and the other sheet is connected by a wire or metal strip to the insulated side of the contact breaker.

When a voltage is applied to the terminals, a current can be made to flow into, but not through, the capacitor. This voltage charges the capacitor to a value equal to the supply voltage, and when this point is reached the flow of current ceases. If the supply is now disconnected, the charge will be retained for a time, but will gradually 'leak away'. When a charged capacitor is connected to a circuit bridging the terminals, the charge produces a current flow in a direction opposite to the original supply current.

In order to understand the function of a capacitor, consider the operation of an ignition system, which has the capacitor disconnected. As the contacts break, the lines of force cut the primary winding as well as the secondary, and therefore an EMF is also induced in the primary winding. This builds up to a pressure sufficient to cause a spark to jump the small contact gap. Arcing maintains current flow in the primary circuit, and thereby prevents the rapid collapse of the magnetic field, as well as causing serious burning of the contacts.

The action is in many ways similar to the hydraulic analogy shown in Figure 2.289. Water flowing along a pipe at great speed will produce a sudden pressure rise if the tap is shut off quickly. This pressure surge could lead to the discharge of a small amount of water through the 'closed' tap by lifting the tap washer off its seat.

Fitting an air dome to the system allows the water to flow into the dome as the tap is suddenly shut off, but after a short time the air forces the water back into the pipe.

The capacitor must perform a duty similar to the buffer action of the air dome. When the contacts part, the capacitor absorbs the self-induced current, and by the time the capacitor is fully charged the contacts have opened sufficiently to prevent a spark occurring at the contact breaker points.

Ignition coil output

The voltage required to produce a spark at the spark plugs with a gap of 1 mm and during the compression stroke of the engine is very high. In many cases, this is in excess of 50,000 V. This can be even higher on many newer electronic control systems and also if the mixture is weaker.

To meet the needs of the more modern engines, some enhancements had to be made to the basic ignition coil.

Oil-filled coil

Immersing the coil windings in oil gives three benefits:

1. The primary windings operate at a lower temperature. Therefore, the resistance is lower, which improves current flow.
2. It provides better insulation and greater resistance to moisture.
3. It reduces the **corona effect** (the corona effect can degrade insulators causing lower coil outputs).

Corona effect: a localised emission resulting from momentary gaseous ionisation in an insulation system when the voltage is high between two points or electrodes. This can lead to a degrading of the insulator and reduced reliability of the component.

2.27.5 Distributor construction

Figure 2.290 shows the construction of the complete contact breaker distributor assembly. This comprises the distributor, contact breaker assembly and automatic advance mechanism.

Distributor

A rotor arm, mounted above the cam and driven at half engine speed, is contacted by a spring-loaded carbon brush. This is fed by a HT cable from the coil, and housed at the centre of a moulded Bakelite distributor cap. Cables from the various spark plugs connect, in firing order, with brass or aluminium segments held in

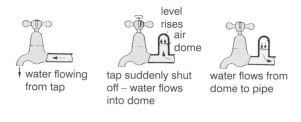

water flowing from tap

tap suddenly shut off – water flows into dome

level rises air dome

water flows from dome to pipe

current through closed contacts

contacts open current flows into condenser

current flows from condenser: contacts open sufficiently to prevent arcing

Figure 2.289 Action of a capacitor

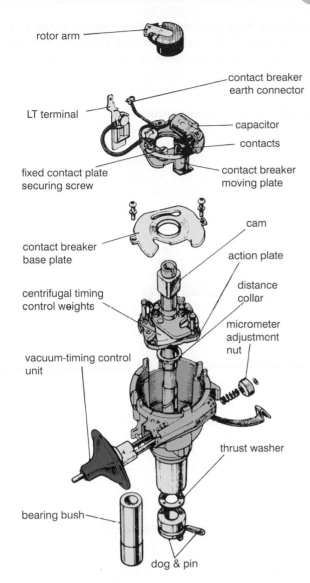

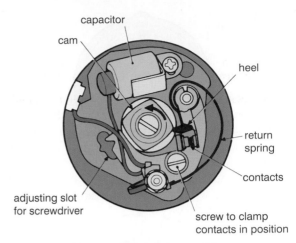

Figure 2.291 The contact breaker assembly

Figure 2.290 A conventional contact breaker distributor assembly

2.27.6 Ignition timing advance

Maximum cylinder pressure should be developed just after TDC. This generally means that the spark must be produced before TDC, since time is taken for the gas to build up to its maximum pressure. The time factor is fairly constant, but the angle moved by the crankshaft during this time varies in proportion to the engine speed. This means that, as the engine speed is increased, the spark must be advanced.

Alteration of the ignition timing to suit speed and load conditions is performed by two automatic advance–retard mechanisms:

- Centrifugal – advances the spark as the speed increases (i.e. speed-sensitive).
- Vacuum – uses induction manifold depression to advance the spark during light load (cruising) conditions (i.e. load-sensitive).

To advance the spark, either the cam is turned in the DOR or the base plate is moved against the DOR.

Centrifugal advance

The advancement of the distributor cam in the arrangement shown in Figure 2.292 is produced by two flyweights. These are pivoted on a base plate, which is driven around by the distributor shaft. A contoured face on the driving side of each flyweight acts against a cam plate; this is integral with the cam so that when the flyweights move outwards, the cam is rotated in the DOR.

The flyweight movement produced by a given increase in speed is determined by the strength of the two tension springs fitted between the base plate and cam plate. By carefully matching the spring strength and flyweight contour to the ignition timing requirement, a good engine performance can be obtained. A typical advance curve for a 'mechanical system' is shown in Figure 2.293.

the cap. These are positioned so that there is a small gap between the rotor and the segment. Ventilation slots, formed at the spigot joint between cap and main body, permit the escape of gases generated by the sparking.

Contact breaker

This consists of two tungsten contacts: a fixed earth contact and a movable insulated contact. This is linked by its return spring to a terminal on the side of the main body (Figure 2.291). A cam having four lobes (four-cylinder) or six lobes (six-cylinder) operates the contact. Elongated holes, through which the clamping screws pass, allow for adjustment. The contact is set to provide a cam lift or contact gap of the order of 0.36–0.40 mm.

A capacitor, earthed by a fixing screw to the contact base plate, connects with the insulated screw on the side of the main body.

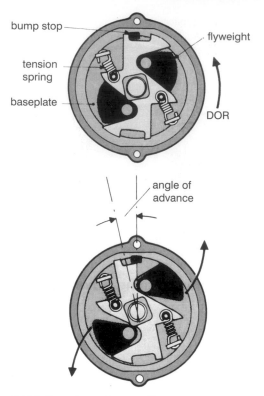

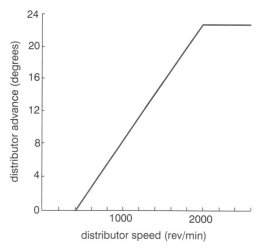

Figure 2.292 Speed-sensitive centrifugal advance mechanism

Figure 2.293 Typical advance curve of a centrifugal advance system

On some engines the rate of advance in the low-speed range has to be greater than at speeds over about 1000 rpm. This can be achieved by using springs of unequal strength with the stronger spring fitted slack on its post.

Vacuum-timing control

The normal centrifugal advance mechanism is sensitive to speed but cannot sense the degree of load on the engine. This means that maximum advance is restricted to avoid engine 'pinking'. The condition is particularly severe when an economy-type carburettor

is fitted. Weak mixture and slow burning of the fuel during part-load conditions demand a greater ignition advance than that used for maximum engine load. To overcome this problem, a vacuum control unit is often incorporated in the distributor unit.

The main construction is illustrated in Figure 2.294. The intake manifold pressure is felt at a drilling, generally in the vicinity of the throttle, which is communicated to a 'vacuum' chamber via a small bore pipe. This is fitted with a spring-loaded diaphragm and is linked to the distributor body.

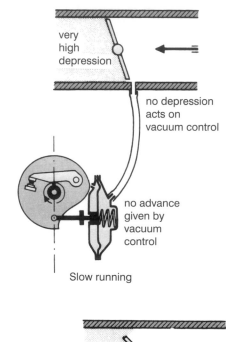

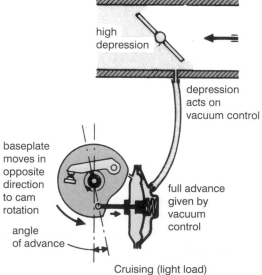

Figure 2.294 A vacuum advance system

During cruising conditions, a high depression acts on the diaphragm to give maximum ignition advance. When engine load is increased, the pressure alteration in the 'vacuum' chamber rotates the distributor to a position giving less advance.

Most modern units were built into the distributor, so only the contact breaker base plate needed to be rotated by the vacuum control.

Vacuum advance-control valves

To ensure that the engine meets strict emission regulations and obtain peak performance, precise ignition timing is essential. Control of the vacuum advance is often used to meet these requirements and this has meant that additional control valves, such as a spark delay valve, have been fitted in the vacuum pipe to control the advance given by the vacuum advance unit. A further development has been the introduction of dual diaphragm chambers; these are more sensitive to the variation in load on an engine.

Note: when checking ignition timing on an engine fitted with this conventional system, it is important to consult the workshop manual to confirm if the ignition timing is based on the vacuum pipe fitted or disconnected.

2.27.7 Spark plugs

The spark plug consists of a steel body, which retains a ceramic insulated centre. This electrode connects with the HT lead, and is generally made of a nickel alloy. One or more earth electrodes are welded to the body, and adjusted to produce a spark gap suitable for the engine. Most plugs today have a 14 mm diameter thread, but 10 mm and 18 mm are occasionally used. The length of thread, termed 'the reach', is governed by the distance through the cylinder head.

To function successfully, the plug must operate at the correct temperature. A low temperature allows oil and carbon to form on the insulator. This fouling causes the electrical charge to short to earth and leads to misfiring. When the plug temperature is too high, the plug electrodes get too hot and pre-ignition occurs.

The heat range of the plug is governed mainly by the distance between the electrode tip and the heat transfer washer. Figure 2.295a shows a plug that can disperse its heat quickly. This is known as a cold or hard plug, and is suitable for an engine that has hot cylinder conditions, for example high-performance engines. Moving the copper transfer washer away from the electrode (Figure 2.295b) raises the plug temperature to give a hot plug.

Interference

Whenever an electric spark occurs, waves of electrical energy are radiated. These cause interference with domestic television receivers and car radios. To limit this interference, the law stipulates that some

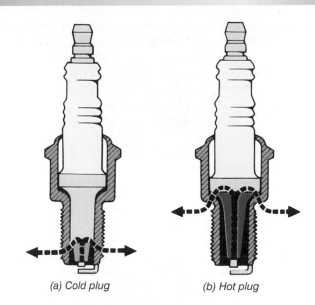

(a) Cold plug   *(b) Hot plug*

Figure 2.295 Spark plug heat range

effective form of suppression must be used. The ignition is the main offender, so special devices are fitted to the HT circuit. These generally take the form of resistors of value between 5000 and 25,000 ohms, which can be incorporated in:

- a special HT lead
- a special carbon brush fitted between rotor and centre distributor terminal
- a fixed resistance, which is inserted in the HT lead.

Spark plug electrodes

The electrodes of a spark plug are subjected to a great deal of abuse when fitted to an internal-combustion engine. High levels of heat, gas pressure and corrosion constantly bombard the spark plug electrodes, along with the very high voltages occurring every time the arcing occurs when the spark plug is fired.

Spark plug electrodes were mainly manufactured from a nickel alloy as this was relatively cheap and produced adequate performance. However, with the improvement in engine performance and increase in combustion chamber pressures, there was a need to supply spark plugs that could operate under these conditions in a reliable manner. These newer spark plugs had their cores made from copper, which allowed them to handle the greater voltages needed in higher combustion chamber pressures. The use of copper improves the conductivity of the spark plug, providing greater energy at the electrode tip. The improvement to conductivity also improves the thermal efficiency of the plug, reducing the heat at the electrode tip.

Today, manufacturers use much more expensive materials when producing spark plugs, such as platinum and iridium. Iridium is a much harder-wearing metal than platinum and has a greater resistance to heat with a melting point of approximately 2450 °C. The use of these precious metals improves the efficiency of the spark plug by improving the conductivity and resistance to wear. The improvement in conductivity lessens the load on the ignition system to provide enough energy to create the arcing at the electrode. By using metals such as iridium, the voltage required can be up to 5000 V less.

The voltage required to discharge the spark at the electrode tip is dependent on the shape and size of the electrode itself. Using a thinner tip made from very high conductivity material improves the spark discharge and requires less energy to do so. By using a more rounded, fatter tip, the energy required to discharge the spark plug is higher, making it more difficult for the ignition system. Although there are obviously benefits with using a thinner electrode tip to improve the spark discharge, there is a downside due to its shorter service life.

As the spark plug wears, a larger spark plug gap can be created. This gap can cause misfiring and associated problems. Vehicle manufacturers are always looking for opportunities to extend the service life of components to increase the time and mileage between main services. The use of copper-cored spark plugs causes problems in that the electrode will wear before the extended service period is met. To improve this, as mentioned earlier, the spark plugs generally used today are made using more precious metals, such as platinum or iridium. These plugs dramatically extend the serviceable life of the spark plug. It is common for many new vehicles to have a spark plug service life of 60,000 miles, as opposed to 12,000 miles with standard copper-core spark plugs.

Many of the latest spark plugs also use dual electrode tips ranging from 2–4 in number (Figure 2.296). The additional electrodes do not necessarily produce additional sparks but will vastly improve the service life of the plug as more that one electrode wears.

Figure 2.296 Dual electrode spark plug

Centre electrode polarity

When a metal is heated it emits electrons, which are negative charges of electricity. The hottest part of a spark plug is the centre electrode, so if this is arranged to be of negative polarity, then the electron flow due to the heat will be in the same direction as the charge given by the ignition coil. A centre electrode having negative polarity gives a more effective spark for a given coil output.

The centre electrode polarity is controlled by the direction of the coil windings in relation to the battery polarity. In order to obtain a 'negative spark', the LT connections on the coil are now marked '+' and '−'.

2.27.8 Contact breaker setting

Dwell angle

Setting the contact breaker gap used to be done by rotating the cam until it was in the full lift position, and then measuring the gap between the points with a feeler gauge. The method was often inaccurate because it was impossible to take into account the position the cam occupied when the engine was running. Any wear in the driving shaft bearings gave an incorrect gap, which led to incorrect timing of the spark and often caused poor ignition performance at high engine speeds because of the comparatively short time that current was flowing in the primary circuit. Furthermore, operation of most contact sets causes a transfer of metal from one contact to the other and this results in a 'pip' building up on one contact and a 'hole' forming in the other. This would defeat the feeler gauge method unless the 'pip' was ground away.

Modern electrical testing equipment generally incorporates a meter, which measures the dwell angle and this is used as an alternative to the feeler gauge method. As applied to ignition units, dwell is the period that the contacts are closed during a cam movement equal to the angle between the cam lobes. (This statement gives the common definition but readers may find cases where the term 'dwell' is used to indicate the 'open period'.)

Figure 2.297 shows a diagram of a cam suitable for a four-cylinder engine. In this case, the closed period or 'dwell angle' is 60°. This is typical for a four-lobe cam, whereas a cam used with a six-cylinder engine generally has a dwell angle of 35°; both cases give a tolerance of about ±2°.

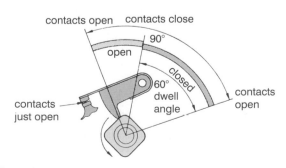

Figure 2.297 Dwell angle

Some manufacturers stated the setting as percentage dwell. This indicates as a percentage the period that the contacts are closed or:

$$\text{Dwell (\%)} = \frac{\text{Dwell angle (closed)}}{\text{Angle between camlobes}} \times 100$$

The dwell angle for the cam shown in Figure 2.297 is:

$$\frac{60}{90} \times 100 = 67\%$$

Double contact breakers

Consideration of the dwell angles of units fitted to four- and six-cylinder engines show that dwell angle is reduced as the number of cylinders increases. If a single contact breaker were used on an eight-cylinder engine, then the short dwell period would seriously affect the coil's performance at high speeds. To overcome this problem, a double contact breaker is often used (Figure 2.298).

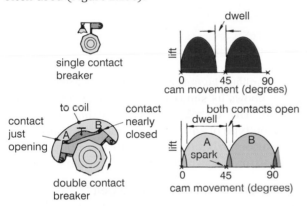

Figure 2.298 A double contact breaker

Contact set A is connected in parallel with set B so the circuit is only interrupted when both contacts are open simultaneously. As soon as contact A opens to give a spark at the plug, the other contact closes to re-establish the primary circuit.

2.27.9 Ballast resistor

The maximum output from a normal coil decreases as the engine speed is increased, so in order to give a more constant output a ballast resistor is sometimes fitted in the primary circuit. This should not be confused with the resistor fitted to improve cold starting.

At low engine speeds, the relatively large current flow in the LT circuit causes the resistor to get hot, increase its resistance and so limit the current flow. When engine speed is high, the resistor runs cooler.

2.27.10 Starting problems

Starting difficulties with modern engines are rare and when they arise the trouble can often be blamed on inadequate servicing or faulty circuits within the ECU.

Whenever certain models are prone to a particular fault, then attention is focused on possible causes and this generally leads to either a modification or a recommendation of a suitable repair or treatment. Two examples of problems associated with ignition system failure are dampness and low battery voltage.

Dampness

Dampness may be caused by under-bonnet condensation, climatic conditions or any means that allows water to come into contact with HT ignition leads. Moisture on these leads causes the HT current to short to earth; consequently, this external 'leakage' of electric current prevents a spark occurring at the plug. In the past, the manner in which this trouble was avoided was to protect the equipment by preventing moisture from coming into contact with the HT system. If this precaution was not followed, then it meant that in cases where a distributor cap was fitted, the unit along with leads attached, had to be removed and taken to a warm place to dry out.

To help prevent this situation the use of a conductive water repellent spray can be applied from an aerosol can to the ignition equipment. This spray acts as a barrier to the moisture and prevents future trouble, and in cases where the leads are already damp, a spray from the aerosol normally overcomes the problem and allows the engine to start. In most cases, the best option is to make sure the ignition system is kept out of direct moisture and also kept free from dirt, as this attracts moisture.

Low battery voltage

This is often the cause of an engine failing to start on a cold morning. If the life of the battery is nearing its end, the high starter motor load is sufficient to lower the voltage at the ignition coil to a value less than 9 V. Under these conditions the coil is unable to provide the voltage necessary to produce a spark at the plug, even though the starter motor is still operating successfully. This problem is not helped if the driver operates the starter motor for periods longer than about three seconds at a time, since the longer the motor is operated the lower the battery voltage will become. Ideally, between each starter operation a period is given for the battery to 'recover'.

Some manufacturers recognised this problem and altered the ignition system to a form similar to that shown in Figure 2.299. This diagram shows that the normal 12 V coil has been replaced by a 7.5 V coil and a ballast resistance inserted in series in the primary circuit. When the engine is running, the resistor drops the voltage from 12 V to 7.5 V. During the starting phase, the starter switch shorts out the resistor and applies full battery voltage to the ignition coil.

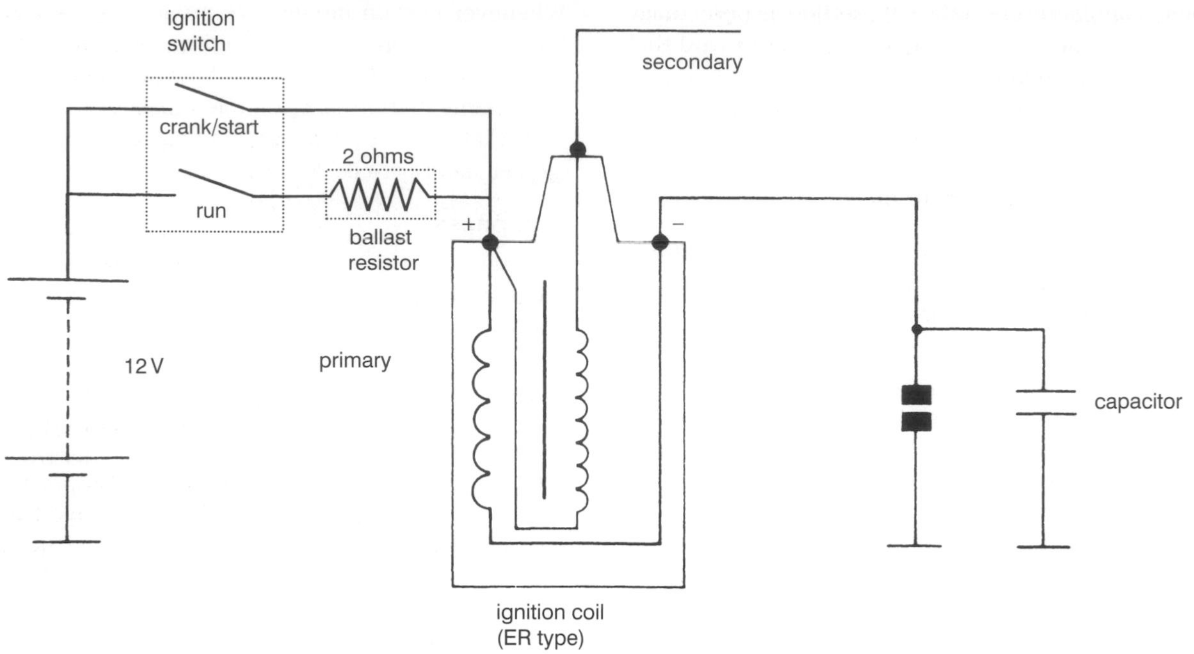

Figure 2.299 A ballast resistor ignition system

2.27.11 Electronic ignition

Although the conventional ignition system gave good service, the two problems of pollution and fuel economy demanded that improvements were made. Modification or elimination of the contact breaker was the main alteration because the traditional contact breaker has the following drawbacks:

1 Ignition timing varies from specification. The timing alters owing to:
   ■ wear at heel, cam and spindle and erosion of contact faces
   ■ contact bounce and inability of the heel to follow the cam at high speed.
2 Dwell angle variation due to change in engine speed or wear at contacts.
3 Servicing requirements are frequent.
4 Cannot effectively control a current greater than about 3 A.

Electronic ignition systems

The main functions of a conventional contact breaker arrangement is to:

1 trigger the system when the spark is required
2 interrupt the primary current flow to induce a high voltage in the secondary circuit.

Breakerless ignition systems, sometimes called transistorised ignition systems, use solid-state electronic devices to perform the two contact breaker duties. Normally they work in conjunction with a low-inductance ignition coil (see pages 212–213).

The simplified layout of an electronic system (Figure 2.300) shows its similarity to a conventional ignition system. The distributor assembly incorporates a common type of automatic advance mechanism and HT distributor, but the contact breaker is replaced by a transistorised switch to 'trigger the spark'.

Limitations of a conventional coil

The conventional ignition coil primary winding has a large number of turns. During operation of this coil, interruption of the primary circuit mutually induces an EMF into the secondary and self-induces into the primary winding an EMF of polarity similar to that which existed before the circuit was broken.

Self-inductance slows down the rate of build-up and collapse of the magnetic field and this is one reason why the performance of the standard ignition coil falls as engine speed is increased. The problem becomes acute on engines that demand a large number of sparks per second, for example a multi-cylinder two-stroke engine or an eight-cylinder unit.

Low-inductance coil

A low-inductance (low-resistance) ignition coil has a smaller number of turns on the primary winding so as to reduce self-inductance. This gives a sharp interruption when the circuit is broken, but the lower primary resistance means that the current flow is much greater; normally it is about three times as great, so contact breaker life is much shorter.

In addition to good high-speed performance, the low-inductance coil also gives a good energy release during the spark period, so these advantages make this type of coil popular. Increased use of this coil type is accompanied by the need for a circuit breaker, which does not have the drawbacks associated with the conventional contact breaker arrangement.

2.27.12 Trigger systems

Figure 2.300 shows the main layout of an electronic ignition system. The distributor unit is similar to a conventional unit, with the exception that the contact breaker is replaced by an electronic switch called a pulse generator. This device generates an electrical pulse to signal to the control module when a spark at the plug is required. The action is similar to the trigger of a gun – when the trigger is operated the control module breaks the primary circuit; this causes the ignition coil to produce the HT charge.

The three main types of pulse generator are:

- inductive
- Hall
- optical.

Inductive pulse generator

Figure 2.301 shows one type of inductive pulse generator suitable for a four-cylinder engine. It consists of a permanent magnet, coil winding and iron rotor, which acts as a reluctor to vary the flux flow. Two leads connect this unit with the control module.

When the tooth of the reluctor passes the permanent magnet, the change in magnetic flux induces an EMF in the coil. Since this EMF varies between 0.5 and 100 V (the actual output depending on the speed of movement), the voltage variation, together with the change in frequency, provides a sensing signal that can also be used for purposes other than spark triggering.

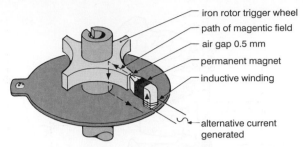

Figure 2.301 Inductive pulse generator

The size of the air gap is critical and should not need to be altered during normal servicing of the vehicle.

Some manufacturers do not use the distributor unit, if fitted, as a pulse generator. Instead, they use either the flywheel teeth or a toothed ring fitted at the end of the crankshaft. Naturally, any damage to the 'teeth' on this ring affects the ignition performance.

Hall pulse generator

Figure 2.302 shows a distributor unit fitted with a Hall generator; it gets this name because the system is based on the **Hall effect**.

Hall effect: this occurs when an electric current passing through a conductor is subjected to a magnetic force at right angles to its flow. This creates a potential difference in current flow at right angles to the direction of current flow and the magnetic field. This phenomenon is a result of forces called Lorentz forces, named after an American physicist called Edwin Herbert Hall.

The unit consists of a permanent magnet, vane and semiconductor chip called a Hall integrated circuit (IC), which is supplied with a voltage from the battery.

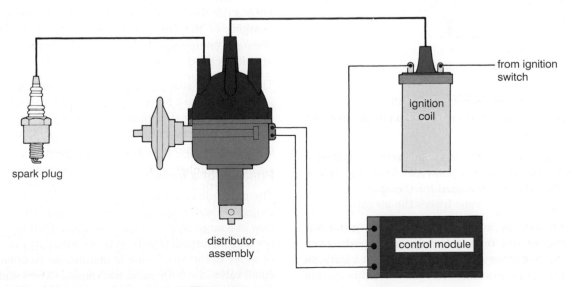

Figure 2.300 The layout of an electronic ignition system

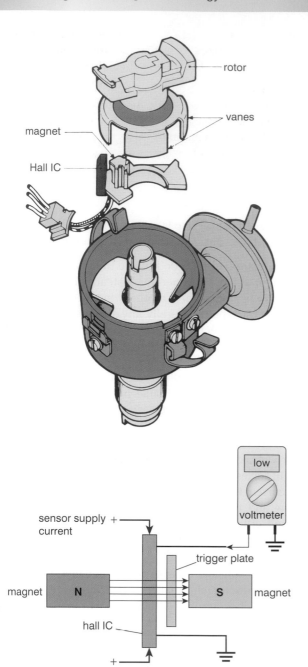

Figure 2.302 Hall pulse generator

A three-core cable connects the Hall generator with the control module; the leads are Hall IC signal-input, Hall IC-output and earth.

As the vane passes between the magnet and Hall IC, a change in magnetic flux causes the chip to switch the sensor off and on; the signal for the spark occurs at the instant when the vane leaves the air gap.

With the ignition switched on, the Hall generator produces its full output to trigger a spark (even when the engine is being turned over by hand), so care should be exercised when handling this system owing to the risk of receiving an electric shock.

Optical pulse generator

This system senses the spark point by using a shutter to interrupt an infrared light beam projected by a light-emitting diode (LED) on to a **phototransistor**. Figure 2.303 shows a conventional distributor unit modified to take an optical trigger.

Phototransistor: a semiconductor switch that is sensitive to light intensity.

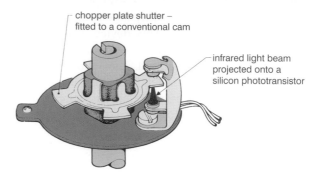

Figure 2.303 Distributor modified to take an optical trigger

2.27.13 Control modules

The purpose of the control module (also referred to as an ignition module or amplifier) is to switch the primary circuit current on and off in accordance with the signal it receives from the pulse generator. Most vehicles fitted with electronic ignition layouts use an inductive storage system.

In basic electronic ignition systems the control module is often located within or on the distributor; this simplifies the wiring and improves reliability. In addition to its switching duty, the module also varies the dwell so as to control the maximum output voltage applied to the spark plugs. At low engine speeds the dwell period is small and at higher engine speeds the dwell period is longer. This improves the charging of the coil and therefore ensures a more constant energy spark. Systems having this feature are often called constant energy systems.

The inductive storage system uses a primary circuit layout similar to a Kettering-type, except that a robust power transistor (Darlington transistor) in the control module is used to make and break the primary circuit (i.e. to do the same job as a contact breaker).

Principle of a transistor

The principle of a transistor is shown in Figure 2.304. Using the water analogy, it will be seen that water flow in a large pipe C to E can be controlled by water pressure in a small pipe B. At times when the pressure of water in the small pipe is insufficient to open the small valve, the large valve will remain closed and the main flow will be interrupted.

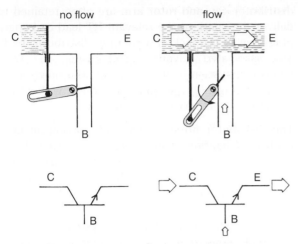

Figure 2.304 Principle of operation of a transistor using a water valve as comparison

A transistor functions in a similar way; it will not allow current flow between E and C unless a small voltage is applied to B. This switching feature of a transistor is of great value, because it enables a large current to be controlled by a very small current. In this application it is used as an alternative to a relay, but whereas a relay is comparatively large and uses moving parts, a transistor is very small and is a solid-state device.

Primary current switching

A simplified layout of the circuit is shown in Figure 2.305. The power transistor is connected, by terminals C and E, in the primary circuit between the ignition coil and earth, and terminal B is connected to the trigger section of the electronic circuit.

The transistor is switched 'on' when its base B receives a small current which is signalled by the trigger. When this takes place, the primary circuit is closed and the ignition coil is able to build up its magnetic flux. At the time when the trigger pulse signals that a spark is required, the current to the transistor base is interrupted and the primary circuit is broken.

The action of the module can be demonstrated by connecting a test lamp between 'earth' and the 'module side of the ignition coil'. Assuming the module and trigger are functioning correctly, a slow rotation of the engine causes the light to go on and off.

2.27.14 Computer-controlled ignition systems

Manufacturers have had to develop ignition systems to cope with the continued demand to produce engines that are more fuel efficient, produce lower emissions and also provide more power. The ignition system plays a large part in meeting these demands through providing more accurate spark delivery and improved reliability with longer service intervals. The use of computer-controlled systems has been the natural move from basic electronic ignition systems. These ignition management systems eliminate the mechanical automatic advance arrangements; instead, the timing of the spark, in relation to the trigger signal, is set in accordance with the data held in the pre-programmed memory unit of the computer.

A number of sensors are positioned around the engine to measure operating conditions, such as coolant temperature, engine load, engine knock, engine speed and intake air temperature. Signal data is fed from these sensors to the computer or ECU and, after comparing this data with its memory, the ECU is able to determine the correct ignition setting to maintain the optimum engine running performance.

The ECU-controlled ignition system is able to finely tune the ignition timing characteristics of the engine by monitoring the output signals from the sensors

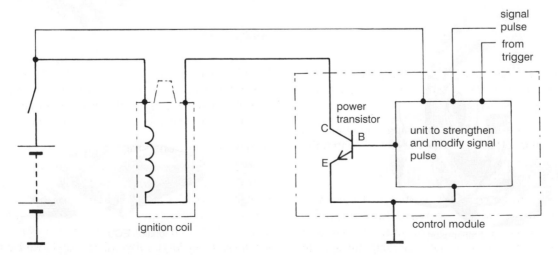

Figure 2.305 An electronic trigger ignition system (breakerless)

located around the engine. During the engine warm-up cycle, the ignition system will monitor the engine coolant and intake temperature. To improve on the emissions produced when the engine is colder, the ignition timing can be advanced. This alteration allows the air/fuel mixture a little longer to burn, leading to fewer emissions produced by the combustion process.

Engines fitted with ECU-controlled ignition systems are usually fitted with a sensor to monitor the knock generated by the combustion process. The knock sensor can detect the onset of detonation occurring during combustion (Figure 2.306). When this sensor signals to the ECU that combustion knock is taking place within the cylinder, the computer slightly retards the ignition setting. By continually monitoring the engine, the use of a knock-limiting system allows a greater control of the ignition advance and provides an ignition system that can operate at optimum levels.

Engine speed and position is monitored through the use of an inductive crank position sensor. This is usually fitted on the flywheel side of the engine, although some engines pick up the engine speed signal from the front crankshaft pulley. The engine speed sensor removes the need for the distributor and associated drive mechanisms, as the ECU will be able to work out the exact position of the engine as it rotates passed the crank position sensor. The

distributor cap and rotor arm are often retained to deliver the spark to the relevant HT lead and spark plug. Due to the lack of a rotating distributor body and associated advance mechanisms, the ECU-controlled system is able to maintain a much more accurate control of the ignition advance without the need for regular service adjustments.

The distributor fitted to a vehicle having an ECU-controlled ignition system only needs to fulfil its main duty, namely to distribute the 'spark' to the respective cylinders. The advance and retard of the ignition timing is carried out by the ECU, which is receiving the important data from the various sensors. A development of this system has led to the total elimination of the distributor as a means to deliver the required HT spark to the plugs. This incorporates individual ignition coils to deliver the HT spark directly to the spark plugs. This system is often called a distributorless ignition system.

Distributorless system

The distributorless ignition system (DIS) is also called wasted spark ignition.

This system completely eliminated the need to have a distributor by connecting the pairs of spark plugs of 'complementary' cylinders in the manner shown in Figure 2.307. From this image, you will notice that

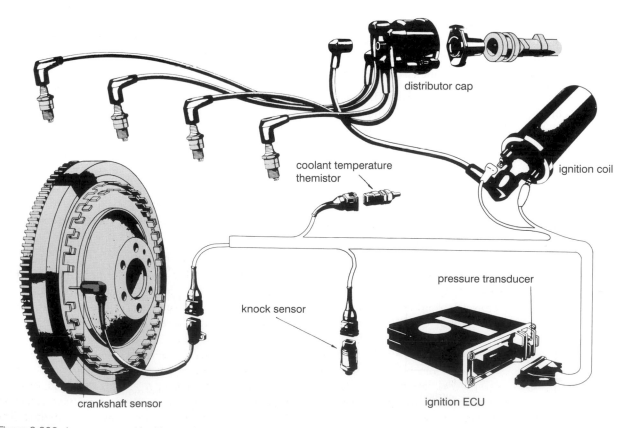

Figure 2.306 A programmed ignition system

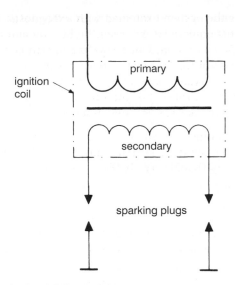

Figure 2.307 A DIS principle

secondary windings are connected directly to the spark plugs and the primary windings are connected internally in the ECU and have no internal connection within the ignition coil. These coils are connected to pairs of spark plugs. For example, in a four-cylinder engine this will mean that coil one will be connected to spark plugs 1 and 4 and coil two is connected to spark plugs 3 and 4. This is important if checking the resistance values during diagnosis.

When the primary is interrupted in the normal way, the HT voltage produces a spark at both spark plugs (1 and 4 in the case of a four-cylinder engine). Since only one cylinder is primed for ignition, the spark in the other cylinder, which is ending its exhaust stroke, will not perform any useful function other than complete the secondary circuit.

2.28 Engine management

2.28.1 The requirement for EMSs

Vehicles produced today are highly advanced with an enormous amount of technology built into even standard vehicles. The need to add technology has been forced by the customer requiring more equipment, enhanced vehicle performance, improved fuel economy, lower emissions and improved safety. Manufacturers have continually developed vehicles to provide these requirements along with meeting increasingly strict regulations around vehicle emissions and safety. The engine fitted to today's vehicles still operates on the general four-stroke cycle of induction, compression, power (ignition) and exhaust. The main difference now is that all engines are fully controlled by advanced EMSs.

Earlier engine-control systems managed the ignition and fuel systems separately. Now the systems are fully integrated and manage the fuelling, ignition and emission control systems in one unit. This unit is usually called the engine control module or ECU.

History

Towards the end of the 1980s, governments proposed changes in current emission regulations; this led to an agreement for manufacturers to produce engines with cleaner emissions. This decision led to the need to improve the fuel-delivery system from a carburettor to a fully electronically controlled management system. Some vehicles modified the carburettors to be electronically controlled, but the increasing demands for lower emissions and improved fuel economy caused these systems to be changed for a more suitable alternative.

Electronic petrol injection was then introduced and this provided a more accurately metered fuel delivery leading to improvements in vehicle emissions. These systems also have the benefit of providing substantial improvements in engine performance and fuel economy. These ignition and fuel-management systems use an array of sensors and actuators to provide data and to operate the components. These sensors are often used across both systems as they provide essential information about the running of the engine required by both parts of the management system. Both the ignition and fuel-delivery management systems use a stored map in their memory, which outlines the exact point at which to fire a spark plug or open an injector across the complete engine operating range.

The programmed ignition system, discussed earlier in this chapter on page 215, was a leap forward in controlling the precise point at which the spark plugs had to be fired. It utilised many common sensors located on the engine to adapt itself with changes in engine performance (i.e. with the use of knock sensors). The petrol fuel-injection system was then left to maintain a fixed fuel delivery based on its own sensor information.

The next inevitable step was to integrate these two electronic control systems to produce one EMS, which led to the development of one ECU. This new ECU, or ECM (engine control module), shares the information from all of the sensors fitted to the engine to provide very precise control of the fuel and ignition systems. This integration also allows both systems to work together in providing improved fuel economy, performance, emissions and reliability. The increasingly strict requirements for lower emissions have forced the need to fit an exhaust catalyst. This unit provides a further reduction in emissions through chemical reactions. The catalyst can only operate correctly if it is able to monitor the exhaust gases leaving the engine along with the engine operating systems to maintain the emission levels required. This continual loop of gathering sensor information and making adjustments carried out by the ECU is known as 'closed loop', due to the ECU making all of the judgements without outside intervention. The idle speed is also accurately controlled by the system.

Figure 2.308 shows input and output signals of a typical ECU.

As mentioned previously, the modern engine has to be able to provide a balance between good performance, excellent fuel economy and low emissions. These demands are met through the development of the EMS alongside the engine development itself. An added benefit of the EMS is that it is able to monitor the changes in engine performance through wear and deterioration of service items and make necessary changes to the fuel, air and ignition supply to maintain a suitable level of emissions and performance. The ECU has an integrated self-diagnostic facility that constantly monitors the sensor and actuator signals. If the ECU detects a fault, the system registers it in the ECU memory and usually signals to the driver. The driver can then take the vehicle to a repair centre

to have the system examined with a diagnostic scan tool. This equipment will read the ECU memory and highlight any stored faults. The technician can then use this information to carry out a repair.

Note: the EMS is a combination of the fuel and emission control systems. For ease, these are described separately in the next section to aid understanding.

2.28.2 Ignition system

Within the ignition side of the EMS, the main control of the primary ignition circuit is still maintained by using a process similar to that seen in the contact breaker ignition system. This involves a continuous making and breaking of the primary ignition circuit. The ECU can monitor the idle condition of the engine and increase or decrease the ignition advance to ensure that the ideal remains stable and provides the least possible emission levels.

The DIS is now used in most vehicles today. This system provides improvements in the spark generation to meet the needs of the higher combustion pressures and weaker air/fuel mixtures. In some cases this system can also be called the wasted spark system; it is termed in this way due to the spark plugs connected in pairs firing at the same

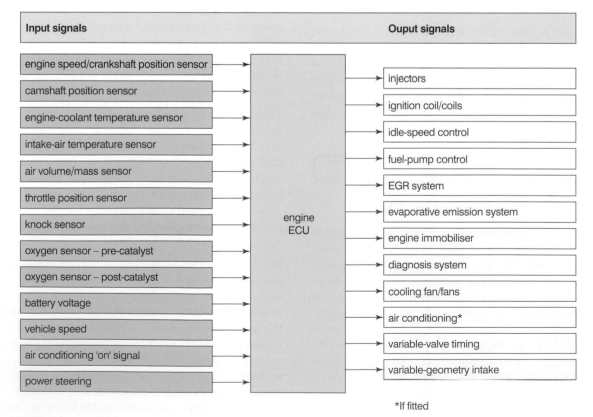

Input signals		Ouput signals
engine speed/crankshaft position sensor		injectors
camshaft position sensor		ignition coil/coils
engine-coolant temperature sensor		idle-speed control
intake-air temperature sensor		fuel-pump control
air volume/mass sensor		EGR system
throttle position sensor	engine ECU	evaporative emission system
knock sensor		engine immobiliser
oxygen sensor – pre-catalyst		diagnosis system
oxygen sensor – post-catalyst		cooling fan/fans
battery voltage		air conditioning*
vehicle speed		variable-valve timing
air conditioning 'on' signal		variable-geometry intake
power steering		

*If fitted

Figure 2.308 A typical EMS (used to control the functions of the various components, such as the injectors, coils and idle speed actuator), input signals and output signals

time irrespective of whether the other engine cylinder is on its compression stroke. The DIS is discussed in more detail in on pages 216–217. An alternative system that is able to produce similar performance is the compact coil type, providing one coil per spark plug (Figure 2.309). These coils are fitted directly to the top of the spark plug and so there is no need to have secondary HT leads. The individual coils have their own primary circuit and are controlled by the ECU. This control involves the switching of the primary circuit by an ignition amplifier that is normally integral with the ECU.

coil acting directly on spark plug

spark plug

Figure 2.309 An example of a compact coil unit fitted to each spark plug

The coils are fired in the same order as the engine firing order. The ECU provides a primary trigger for the coils through inputs from the engine position sensor and also the camshaft-position (CMP) sensor. For example, if an engine with a four-cylinder engine has a firing order of 1342, then the spark for each cylinder ignition coil will occur in that order.

As the engine needs to rotate twice for each cycle of operations, there is a need to be able to determine when cylinder 1 piston is at TDC near completion of the compression stroke. This is due to the fact that cylinder 1 piston could be at either compression or exhaust stroke. Thus, the ECU needs to know

when cylinder 1 is nearing TDC completing the compression stroke.

As the camshaft rotates once per cycle of operation, it is also critical that the ECU can determine the position of the camshaft lobes. This function is carried out by the CMP sensor, also known as the cylinder identification sensor. The sensor is positioned adjacent to a toothed section of the camshaft. The sensor provides the ECU with the position of the camshaft as it is closing the valves on cylinder 1 on the compression stroke. This gives the ECU the information required in order to start the fuelling and ignition strategy at cylinder 1, thereafter the ECU can determine the remaining cylinders.

2.28.3 Fuel systems

The fuel-injection system used in modern engine management is very similar in its basic functions to the ones described earlier on page 170. The main aim of the fuel-delivery system within an EMS is to provide fuel to the engine at exactly the right time in the right amount and adjust itself to maintain low emissions. EMSs use information from various sensors and actuators around the engine and engine compartment to carry out this task. The following sensors are part of this system.

Air sensing

The volume of air entering the engine is a very important factor to monitor and measure. EMSs either monitor the intake manifold pressure using a MAP sensor or sense mass airflow entering the intake manifold generally by using a hot wire or hot film mass airflow sensor (Figure 2.310).

The hot wire air mass meter has a platinum wire suspended in the flow of air and a voltage applied to it by the ECU. The resulting current flow heats the wire. A **thermistor** is used to sense the temperature of the wire and when the target temperature is reached the voltage is maintained. The flow of air across the wire cools it, and the ECU has to apply a higher voltage to achieve its target wire temperature. The degree of cooling created by the airflow is in direct proportion to the amount of airflow, and the voltage required to achieve the target temperature is therefore also in direct proportion to this. The ECU interprets the voltage as airflow volume. Figure 2.310 shows the basic connections to the hot wire air-mass meter.

Thermistor: a resistor whose resistance varies significantly with temperature.

On a cold day, the cooling effect will be greater for a given amount of airflow; therefore, the required

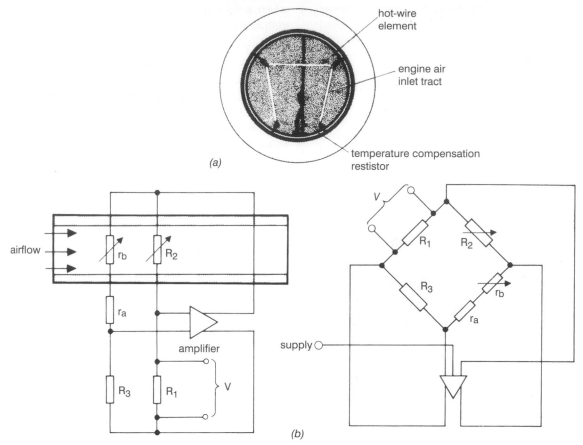

(a)

(b)

Figure 2.310 Diagram showing the operation and connections to a hot wire air-mass meter

voltage will be higher. The ECU interprets this as an increase in airflow and will increase fuel-injection volume correspondingly. This is just what is required as cooler air is denser and, therefore, each cylinder will receive a greater amount of oxygen per intake stroke. This sensor is therefore a true air-mass sensor.

The hot film-type air-mass sensor operates using very similar principles to the hot wire type. In the hot film-type sensor, the wire is replaced by a thin film resistor made from platinum.

Figure 2.311 Hot film-type air-mass meter

Throttle position

The ECU needs to know the position of the throttle for many reasons, including acceleration, enrichment, fuel cut-off on over-run, cruising and traction control. When the driver presses hard on the accelerator pedal, the throttle opens fully. The air will increase in volume with very little delay, but the fuel being heavier is slower to react. This creates a momentary lean period, which often manifests as a flat-spot or hesitation. You have seen that a carburettor overcomes this problem through the use of an accelerator pump. EMSs have no such pump, only the injectors. The ECU senses that the driver has moved the throttle to the fully open position by monitoring the throttle position sensor. This enables the ECU to increase the quantity of fuel injected to prevent the generation of a flat-spot and provide progressive power delivery.

Figure 2.312 shows the principle behind the throttle position sensor. The ECU applies 5 V to the resistor track. The moving contact effectively divides the resistor track into two resistors wired in series with one another.

As the moving contact moves (it is connected to the throttle linkage), it will adopt a position that dictates

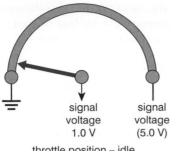

signal
voltage
1.0 V

signal
voltage
(5.0 V)

throttle position – idle

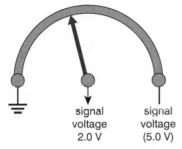

signal
voltage
2.0 V

signal
voltage
(5.0 V)

throttle position – part throttle

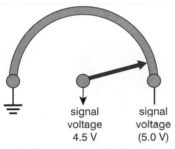

signal
voltage
4.5 V

signal
voltage
(5.0 V)

throttle position – full throttle

Figure 2.312 Throttle potentiometer operation

the comparative length of the two resistors. If they are the same length, then the voltage will be half supply (2.5 V) in the middle where the moving contact is. The moving contact is connected to the ECU via the harness and the ECU senses 2.5 V. This it interprets as 50 per cent throttle opening. All voltages sensed in between fully closed and fully open represent a known throttle angle to the ECU. This type of sensor is often referred to as a potentiometer.

Crankshaft position sensor

The crankshaft position (CKP) sensor is usually fitted so it lines up with the engine flywheel, but in some cases they are fitted to point at the crankshaft pulley. The CKP sensor picks up a signal from a component called a reluctor ring, which is a steel ring with square teeth. The square teeth are arranged to allow the sensor to pick up engine speed and position information. The CKP sensors normally have a wiring harness and connector attached with three wires; these wires are two signal wires to feed the

alternating current (AC) signal created back to the ECU and an earth screening connected to the vehicle body through the ECU.

The CKP sensor is usually an inductive-type sensor but can also be a Hall-effect type, which operates much like the Hall-effect distributor mentioned on page 213. The inductive-type sensor produces a sine wave output voltage signal much like the one seen in Figure 2.313. The AC voltage is started through the reluctor ring moving past the CKP sensor by creating a magnetic flux.

Figure 2.313 CKP sensor

As the engine speed increases, the speed at which the reluctor passes the CKP sensor will also increase. In turn, this raises the frequency and magnitude of the sensor output voltage. The signal generated by an inductive CKP sensor will be about 6.5 V AC. This constant change in magnitude and frequency is passed to the ECU to calculate the engine speed and, therefore, the relevant fuelling and ignition required. The engine speed is calculated by the number of teeth passing the CKP sensor and the speed at which they pass. The teeth are positioned at equal intervals apart from TDC, where generally there are two teeth missing to provide a reference point for the ECU to synchronise engine position.

The CKP sensor signal is very important for the running of the engine as there is no back-up signal generated if this fails. Failure of this sensor would stop the engine immediately. If the sensor failed during an engine start condition, the engine would not be able to start due to no crank position signal being generated for the ECU to start ignition and fuel delivery.

Generally, if this sensor or any other sensor fails, a fault code will be stored in the ECU along with battery voltage, coolant and intake temperatures recorded at the time the sensor failed. This information can be used by the technician to try and diagnose the sensor failure. When this or another sensor fails, the ECU will switch on the malfunction indicator lamp (MIL). Also, if the CKP sensor fails, the tachometer will also fail due to the loss of engine speed signal.

CMP sensor

The CMP sensor is located in the area of the camshaft usually in the upper area of the engine. The purpose of the CMP sensor is to assess the position of the camshaft in relation to the crankshaft. The CMP signal is generated in the same way as the CKP signal and is used to inform the ECU of the correct ignition timing order and fuel injection point. Additionally, with an engine fitted with variable-valve timing control, the CMP will signal accurate operation of the camshaft position adjustment. Generally, the CMP sensor generates its signal from four teeth on the camshaft that are of different shapes. This ensures that the CMP signal can determine the exact position of the camshaft during engine running conditions.

When a Hall effect-type sensor is fitted, it will not generate the same AC wave (sine wave) form like the inductive-type sensor. The Hall-effect sensor will generate a square waveform, which enables the ECU to interpret the signal more clearly due to the very sharp edges of each signal generated. If the CMP sensor fails while the engine is running, it will illuminate the MIL in the same way and alter the engine performance by moving the engine settings map into a default setting, often losing sequential fuel injection and implementing basic ignition timing settings. The ECU will store a fault code to allow the technician to interrogate the system and trace back the fault.

Ambient barometric pressure sensor

The ECU incorporates an integral ambient barometric pressure sensor. This internal sensor is supplied with a 5 V feed and returns a linear voltage of between 2–4.5 V, dependent on the air pressure around the vehicle. The air pressure and density is important to know as the ECU can alter the fuelling and ignition requirements for the engine depending on the air density. For example, if the vehicle is travelling along a high mountain road, the air pressure and density will be lower than normal.

Therefore, the fuel and ignition values will have to be altered to compensate for less oxygen content in the air, otherwise it would run too rich.

Temperature

Sensors are used to monitor various areas of temperature around the engine compartment. This includes intake air temperature, coolant temperature, ambient air temperature and, in some cases, exhaust temperature. Figure 2.314 shows two sensors used to measure intake air and coolant. The sensors work by the ECU passing a 5V supply to the sensor and receiving a signal voltage back to the ECU. The return signal voltage is dependent on the resistance value of the sensor at the given temperature. The temperature sensors work on a negative temperature coefficient (NTC) basis; as the temperature rises the resistance falls, so as the engine temperature rises the return voltage will also rise due to the resistance falling within the sensor.

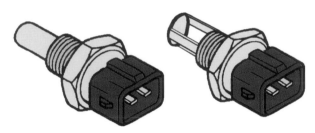

Figure 2.314 Engine-coolant and intake-air temperature sensors

When an engine is cold it will require a richer mixture, this is achieved by the ECU receiving a low-voltage supply back from the sensor due to the higher resistance value. As the engine warms up, this resistance value will start to drop causing the voltage to rise. The relating voltage values are stored in the ECU map, which will relate to fuel and ignition values.

The engine temperature sensor is also able to control the operation of the cooling fans through the ECU. As

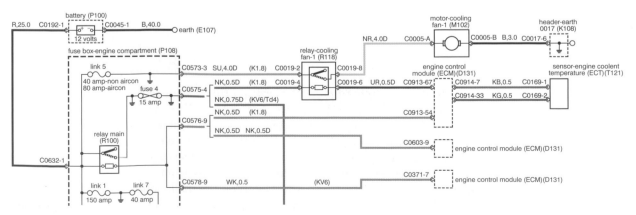

Figure 2.315 Engine management-controlled fan circuit

the engine temperature rises to 85–90°C, the ECU will provide an earth path to the fan relay to energise the relay windings. This will then allow power to the fans to commence cooling of the radiator. Figure 2.315 shows the fan relay circuit of an engine management-controlled fan system.

The additional temperature sensors operate in a similar way and are placed in suitable locations to sense the relevant temperature.

Combustion knock

Combustion knock is monitored by the knock sensor, generally an engine is fitted with one knock sensor per bank of cylinders. For example, if an engine has four cylinders it will have one knock sensor; if an engine has eight cylinders in a 'V' formation, it will have two sensors. Figure 2.316 shows a knock sensor.

Figure 2.316 Knock sensor

A knock sensor consists of a piezoceramic crystal. This is another example of a piezoelectric element being put to use on a modern EMS, with the other being a type of MAP sensor used to calculate the pressure within the intake manifold. Piezoelectric elements come in two main types: those that experience a change in resistance and those that physically generate a voltage when deformed. The knock sensor is a good example of a piezoelectric element that generates voltage when deformed through vibration.

When an engine runs, it will generate vibrations within the cylinder walls. When the vibrations turn to knocking through pre-ignition, for example, the sensor vibrates and a voltage is generated. This can vary between as much as 10 V and as little as 1 V, depending upon the manufacturer. This voltage indicates to the ECU that the engine is knocking and it will start to progressively retard the ignition timing to a point where the knocking stops. When the engine stops knocking, the knock-sensor voltage will reduce to zero and the ECU will start to progressively re-advance the ignition timing until knocking is detected again. This is known as a closed-loop control and it enables the ECU to keep the timing right on the threshold of knock, therefore generating maximum power for minimum fuel consumption with low emissions.

Catalytic converters and oxygen sensors

The continual need to meet strict emission regulations has meant that all cars produced are now fitted with a catalytic converter. The catalytic converter is able to reduce harmful gases produced during the combustion process. These gases are carbon monoxide (CO), hydrocarbons (HC) and nitrogen oxide (NO_x), and are converted to water (H_2O), oxygen (O_2), carbon dioxide (CO_2) and nitrogen (N_2), which are generally harmless, apart from CO_2 which is a **greenhouse gas**. See Figure 2.317 showing the gases entering the catalyst and exiting after going through the catalyst element.

Greenhouse gas: gas whose increased presence in the atmosphere is believed to contribute to global warming, for example carbon dioxide (CO_2).

The oxygen sensor provides feedback signals to the ECU to enable closed-loop control of the air/fuel ratio. On modern vehicles, generally two sensors are installed, one pre-catalyst and one post-catalyst. Each oxygen sensor produces an output voltage, which is inversely proportional to the oxygen content of the exhaust gases. In some cases, the oxygen sensor can also be

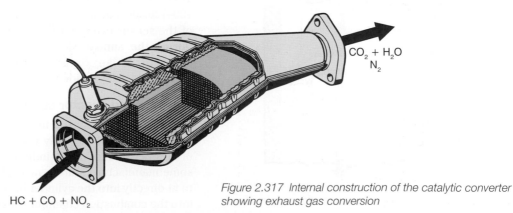

$HC + CO + NO_2$

$CO_2 + H_2O$
N_2

Figure 2.317 Internal construction of the catalytic converter showing exhaust gas conversion

called the lambda sensor due to its measurement of the air/fuel ratio where perfect combustion happens at 14.7:1 ratio, which equals lambda 1.

The oxygen sensor or lambda sensor consists of a sensing element made from zirconium; this has a ceramic coating that is able to absorb exhaust gas. The outer surface of the sensor is subjected to direct contact with the exhaust gases and the inner surface is exposed to the air surrounding the sensor.

Zirconium has a special property – when exposed to two areas of differing oxygen content, a small voltage is produced. If the engine is running rich, there will be an excess of fuel. This will result in the majority of oxygen being burnt. Higher voltage will be produced by the sensor where there is a greater difference between the oxygen content in the ambient air and the exhaust gas. Where the difference between the oxygen content is smaller, the voltage will also be lower. The working range of the sensor is about 0.1 V to 0.9 V.

As mentioned earlier, the value 'lambda' is often used to describe how rich or lean an engine is running. It is calculated by dividing the actual air/fuel ratio by the ideal (14.7:1). If an engine is running at the ideal air/fuel ratio, it can therefore be described as running at lambda 1 (14.7:1 divided by 14.7:1 equals 1). Taking this equation, it can be seen that if an engine is running in the rich region (i.e. below 14.7:1), the lambda value will be less than 1, and if the engine is running lean (i.e. higher than 14.7:1), the lambda value will be greater than 1. Lambda is also sometimes described as excess air factor.

Figure 2.318 shows the construction and operation of an oxygen sensor. (1) shows the protective layer placed on the tip of the oxygen sensor; this is made from hard-wearing and heat-resistant ceramic. (2) shows the electrodes subjected to the exhaust gas flow and ambient air. (3) shows the zirconium-sensing element. A represents the ambient air and B represents the exhaust gas.

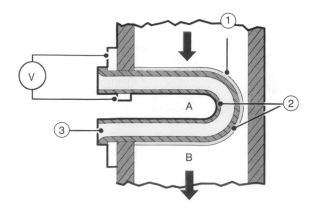

Figure 2.318 Construction and operation of an oxygen sensor

Figure 2.319 shows a simple graph outlining the general voltages produced in relation to the air/fuel ratio

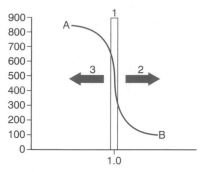

1 lambda window
2 lean AFR
3 rich AFR

Figure 2.319 Effect of air/fuel ratios (AFR) on the oxygen sensor voltage

Oxygen sensors require heat to be able to operate effectively. The sensor will start to operate at about 350 °C, but to react quickly enough during changes to the exhaust gas content the sensors need to be at approximately 600 °C. To make sure the sensors are running as quickly as possible, they are often heated by passing current through a heating element from a relay operated by the ECU.

The ECU will constantly assess the signals received back from the oxygen sensors. If at any point the engine management detects a signal that is unlikely, it will log a fault code in the memory. This fault code will be logged against engine speed, engine temperature and engine load to ensure that the technician is able to understand some background behind the fault. The ECU uses the signals from the oxygen sensors to set a majority of the engine adaptations, so it is very important to gain an accurate signal.

If an oxygen sensor is failing, the engine may have symptoms of poor running and give off a strong smell of rotten eggs from the exhaust (caused by an increase in hydrogen sulphide).

The life span of the oxygen sensor is usually about 100–120,000 miles. During this time, the efficiency of the sensor can deteriorate – this may be noticed during the annual MOT where the emissions are checked, as an oxygen sensor that is working incorrectly will provide unacceptable emissions.

Injectors and injector control

The injectors supply the fuel to the engine. A multi-point system will normally inject fuel on to the back of the open intake valves (indirect injection), although some manufacturers are now designing the injectors to fit directly into the cylinder head and inject directly into the combustion chamber (direct injection).

The injector is a solenoid-operated valve. The injector requires a power supply and an earth connection in order to operate. Most systems will supply a constant power supply to the injector and switch the injector on/off by switching the injector earth circuit, although there are a few systems that switch the power supply circuit. The injector is opened electro-mechanically and closed by spring pressure acting on the injector pintle.

Problems can arise when the valve becomes coated in deposits, absorbing the atomised fuel, leading to lean mixtures. The injector has a very fine spray pattern. Not all injector spray patterns are the same; the spray pattern will depend on the system/engine type. Top-feed injectors normally have a fine mesh filter in the top of the injector. Side-feed injectors are now becoming more common; the fuel can flow through the injector in the fuel rail, overcoming fuel rail temperature problems.

Single-point systems use an injector very similar to the side-feed injector, although the injector pintle is normally replaced by a ball valve. The ball valve provides the correct spray pattern for the fuel to be sprayed on to the throttle butterfly. The single-point systems use a much lower fuel pressure (approximately 1 bar). The fuel is injected above the throttle butterfly and therefore is not subjected to intake manifold pressure changes.

The length of time the injector remains open will depend on the ECU input signals. With a cold engine, the fuelling requirements will be higher than normal, therefore, the opening duration will be longer (approximately 6–14 milliseconds). As the engine warms up and therefore requires less fuel, the injection duration shortens. When the engine is at idle and at the correct operating temperature, the injection duration is typically 2–3 milliseconds.

During high load (wide-open throttle, acceleration), more fuel is required and the injection duration lengthens, dependent on the ECU input signals. During vehicle deceleration (over-run situations), fuel is not required and therefore under certain conditions (engine speed above 1500 rpm and the throttle closed) the injection duration will be very short or, in most cases, disappear completely (only the supply voltage is available with no earth path). Figure 2.320 shows an example of the waveforms generated by the injectors.

These waveforms and duration figures are only guidelines; they will differ from system to system. Therefore, always refer to vehicle specific information before checking any signals, etc.

The injectors are operated by the ECU in various strategies. In most cases, the ECU will run the injectors in a sequential strategy, which follows the firing order of the engine. On occasions where the

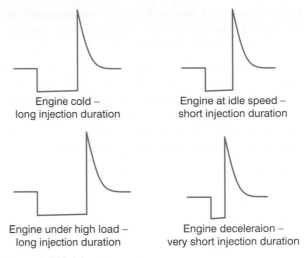

Engine cold – long injection duration

Engine at idle speed – short injection duration

Engine under high load – long injection duration

Engine deceleraion – very short injection duration

Figure 2.320 Injector waveforms

engine is required to provide more power, some EMSs can run the injectors in a 'banked' strategy, which opens and closes all of the injectors at the same time giving maximum fuel delivery. Other strategies include 'grouped', which operates the injectors in pairs. For example, with a four-cylinder engine this would operate 1 and 4 together and 2 and 3 together. This strategy can sometimes be used on cold starting to make sure adequate fuel enters the engine.

Idle speed and maximum engine speed

Engine idle speed is regulated by the idle air-control valve (IACV) and the ECU. The IACV is also known as a stepper motor. In some cases, the construction is slightly different but the operation is the same. Figure 2.321 shows a selection of IACVs and stepper motors. The ECU uses two methods of idle-speed control:

■ Ignition timing adjustment
■ IACV stepper motor

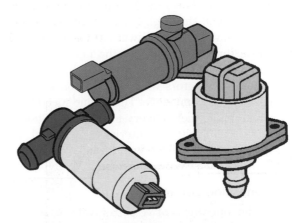

Figure 2.321 Types of IACVs and stepper motors

At a point where the engine idle speed starts to waver and the engine does not have any other loads (e.g. air conditioning), the ECU will utilise the ignition timing along with the IACV to try and regulate the idle speed. The use of both ignition timing and the IACV provides very quick correction to the engine idle speed, ensuring that it falls within the ECU's tolerance. When the engine is subjected to additional loads, such as the air-conditioning compressor or the power steering being operated, the ECU will raise the idle speed accordingly through the use of the IACV.

The engine idle speed signal is acquired from the CKP sensor, but the ECU will also reference input signals from the following components:

- Alternator
- Air-conditioning system cooling fan status
- Air-conditioning compressor on/off status

When the ECU receives signal data from the inputs above, it will calculate the required change to idle speed to compensate for this additional load to prevent a stall condition or 'hunting' of the idle speed above and below the required setting. The IACV is mounted directly on to the intake manifold adjacent to the throttle valve. The IACV works by opening and closing a bypass port to allow air to flow around the throttle valve and enter the engine. Where a higher engine speed is required, the IACV will open the bypass port further to allow a larger volume of air to flow around the closed throttle and create a higher idle speed. Inversely, if the engine idle speed is too low, the port will be closed to limit the amount of air bypassing the throttle. Another purpose of the IACV is during deceleration – when the throttle is closed, the IACV will open slightly to reduce the depression in the intake manifold, which improves the emissions produced by the engine.

Maximum engine speed is controlled by the ECU taking a reference signal from the CKP sensor. This is checked against the stored maximum speed in the ECU's memory. If the engine speed approaches the maximum allowed, the ECU will cut fuel delivery to the engine through turning off the injectors. When the engine speed has then dropped below the maximum, the injectors will be turned back on and fuel delivery will commence. The engine speed is cut through stopping fuel delivery instead of ignition to prevent any unburnt fuel entering the exhaust and catalytic converters, which would cause overheating and damage to the catalyst element.

Other emission controls

During the operation of a petrol vehicle, a large amount of fuel vapour is generated from the fuel stored in the fuel tank. On earlier vehicles, this vapour was left to vent into the atmosphere, which added to the emissions created by the vehicle's engine. On modern vehicles, the fuel vapours are not allowed to

enter the atmosphere so a system had to be designed to prevent this. This system is called the evaporative (EVAP) emission system (Figure 2.322).

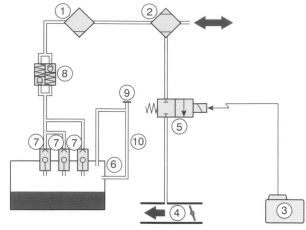

1 vapour separator
2 EVAP canister
3 ECU
4 throttle
5 purge valve
6 fuel tank
7 rollover valve
8 two-way valve
9 fuel filler cap
10 filler tube

Figure 2.322 The charcoal canister EVAP emission system

The system comprises a two-way valve, a vapour separator, an EVAP canister, a purge valve and interconnecting vent pipes. The vent pipes are connected to the system components and the fuel tank by quick-release connectors. On the fuel tank, the vent lines are connected to three rollover valves. These are float valves that prevent fuel from entering the vent pipes due to fuel slosh or if the vehicle overturns.

Fuel vapour, generated in the tank as the fuel heats up, is stored in the tank until the pressure is sufficient to open the outward venting side of the two-way valve. When the two-way valve opens, excess pressure is released through the vapour separator and the EVAP canister to the atmosphere. The vapour separator and the EVAP canister remove fuel from the vapour and relatively fuel-free air vents to the atmosphere. When the fuel tank cools and vapour pressure decreases below ambient pressure, the two-way valve opens and outside air is drawn through the EVAP canister and vapour separator into the tank.

Some of the fuel removed from the vapour vented from the fuel tank is stored in the EVAP canister. Since there is a limit to the volume of fuel that can be stored in the EVAP canister, when the engine is running fuel is purged from the EVAP canister through the purge valve and burned in the engine.

When an engine is running under hot conditions, oxides of nitrogen (NO_x) can be produced in large quantities. NO_x is generated when oxygen and nitrogen are combined in hot combustion temperatures. To lower the production of NO_x, the temperatures of the combustion chamber must be lowered during engine operation situations.

To do this, many engines are fitted with EGR systems. This system re-circulates some of the exhaust gases leaving the engine back into the intake manifold and back through the engine. The action of passing exhaust gases back through the combustion process lowers the overall temperatures to prevent the production of NO_x. This operation is only carried out under certain engine operating conditions, such as cruising, where the driver will not notice the process taking place.

EGR does not take place during engine idling as this would affect the engine idle speed. With the addition of variable-valve timing to some engines over the past few years, this has also improved in lowering the amount of NO_x produced by increasing the overlap of the exhaust valves to allow a small amount of exhaust gas into the combustion chamber during the induction stroke.

Other controls and sensors

The EMS will control various operations on the vehicle that interact with the engine. These can include:

- variable-valve timing
- variable-valve lift
- traction control (TCS)
- dynamic skid control (DSC)
- variable-induction systems
- air-conditioning compressor.

Further enhancement of EMSs in today's vehicles involves the use of an electronic throttle control. This is sometimes called 'drive by wire' by some manufacturers. Most earlier types of EMSs used a linkage directly to the throttle body from the accelerator pedal. The throttle position is then calculated by the feedback from the throttle potentiometer to the ECU. Using an electronic throttle system (Figure 2.323) eliminates the need for a throttle cable. Extremely accurate throttle positions can be managed by the ECU via input from various sensors and a throttle pedal potentiometer mounted directly on the accelerator pedal.

This system comprises three main components:

- Electronic throttle control valve
- Accelerator pedal position (APP) sensor
- ECU

When the accelerator pedal is depressed, the APP sensor provides a change in the monitored signals.

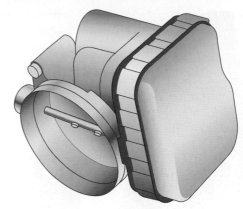

Figure 2.323 Electronic throttle body

The ECU compares this against an electronic 'map' and moves the electronic throttle valve via a pulse width modulated control signal, which is in proportion to the APP angle signal.

The system is required to:

- regulate the calculated intake air based on the APP sensor input signals and programmed mapping of the ECU
- monitor the driver's input request for cruise control operation
- automatically position the electronic throttle for accurate cruise control
- perform all dynamic stability control throttle control interventions
- monitor and carry out maximum engine and road speed cut out.

The APP sensor shown in Figure 2.324 sends pedal position information input by the driver back to the ECU. The sensor has two potentiometer tracks to provide the pedal movement signals. The signals from the two tracks are used by the ECU to determine fuelling for engine operation, and also by the ECU and the automatic transmission ECU to initiate a kick-down request for the automatic transmission.

The ECU monitors the outputs from each of the potentiometer tracks and can determine the position, rate of change and direction of movement of the throttle pedal. The 'closed throttle' position signal is used by the ECU to initiate idle-speed control and also override fuel cut-off.

Alarm and immobilisation systems

Manufacturers have now had to ensure that all vehicles produced are able to sustain any tampering from criminals. This has been enforced by the insurance companies to reduce car theft. Many manufacturers fit alarm systems combined with advanced immobilisation systems to prevent the vehicle being broken into and driven away without

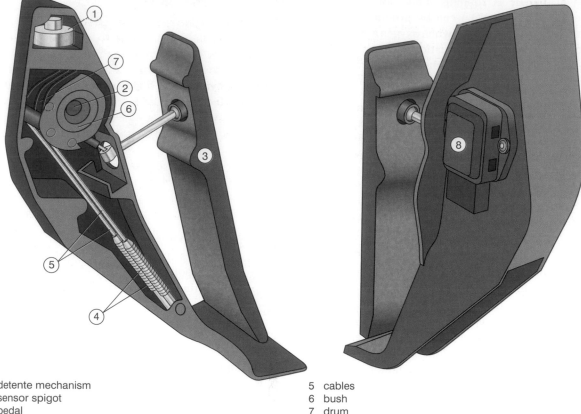

1   detente mechanism
2   sensor spigot
3   pedal
4   springs

5   cables
6   bush
7   drum
8   APP sensor

Figure 2.324 APP sensor

the keys. The immobilisation systems are integrated into the EMS to provide a robust method to prevent the vehicle being started without the correct key. The immobilisation systems usually work by having a coded key matched to the vehicle. The key is often programmed to the vehicle's security and EMS by the manufacturer and, where spare keys are required by the manufacturer's main dealers, using special diagnostic equipment. When the key is inserted into the ignition barrel, it transmits a coded signal to the immobilisation system. If the immobilisation system recognises this coded message, the EMS will start the engine as normal. If, however, the key is not recognised, the EMS will prevent the engine from running by cutting the starter motor operation, along with the fuelling and ignition systems. This then prevents the vehicle being driven away by anyone except the correct key holder.

Fault monitoring

As mentioned throughout this section, the EMS includes a facility to monitor the system operation and store any faults that may occur during the time when the engine is running. These faults are stored in the erasable programmable read-only memory (EPROM) area of the ECU. The driver will notice a fault when it occurs as a malfunction light will

appear on the instrument display. The technician can then read the memory for the faults stored and also read 'live' data coming from the ECU using diagnostic equipment similar to that seen in Figure 2.325 to understand the fault and carry out a repair. If an EMS has a fault with a sensor, the ECU is often able to provide a default figure for the sensor to allow the driver to get the vehicle home or back to the vehicle repairer. This condition is known as 'limp home' condition.

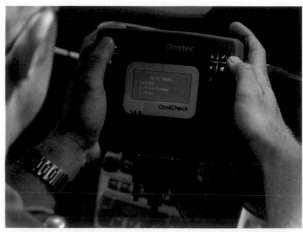

Figure 2.325 Diagnostic equipment being used to read the ECU memory

2.28.4 Direct injection

In this section, the main type of petrol fuel injection described has been the indirect type. This system sprays fuel from the injector on to the back of the inlet valve and then into the engine. Many manufacturers are now moving towards the production of direct injection systems very similar to the diesel-injection system. Direct injection systems are being used to improve on the emissions produced by the combustion engine. Direct injection systems can reduce fuel consumption and emission levels by approximately 25 per cent. The direct injection systems allow greatly reduced air/fuel ratios up to 40:1 during some engine running conditions. These ratios are due to improvements in intake and combustion chamber design. These new engines are designed to generate much more turbulence within the cylinders when the fuel is injected.

The injectors are located directly in the cylinder head and spray fuel into the combustion chamber near to the inlet valve and spark plug. The injection timing and spray patterns can be altered during the engine's operation to maximise the power generated from the fuel injected. The fuel is delivered to the engine from the tank via an electronically driven pre-supply pump located inside the fuel tank. The pressure generated by this pump is in the region of 3.5 bar (50 psi). The pressure regulator fitted as an integral part of the pump assembly maintains this pressure and returns any excess fuel back to the fuel tank.

The fuel is then passed to a high-pressure engine-driven pump, which boosts the pressure between 80–130 bar (1160–1900 psi). This high fuel pressure is monitored by a fuel pressure sensor located in the fuel rail. If the fuel pressure exceeds the maximum, the ECU will return some fuel from the high-pressure pump back to the fuel tank via a solenoid valve.

The high-pressure fuel is then passed to the injector fuel rail; the fuel rail acts as an accumulator for the fuel waiting to be injected into the engine through the injectors. The fuel rail has a pulse damper fitted, which absorbs some of the pulses generated by the high-pressure fuel pump.

The injector opening point (timing) and the duration are controlled by the ECU interpreting information from all of the sensors and actuators located around the engine. The injectors fitted to direct injection engines require much higher electrical current to initially open. This is due to having to overcome the much higher fuel pressures. These higher current requirements can often need additional electronic control external to the ECU.

The direct injection system has many strategies for injecting fuel into the engine, all depending on different engine conditions.

Idle speed and low engine loads

During low engine speeds, the direct injection system retards the injection timing to a point where the fuel is being injected towards the TDC point of the piston on the compression stroke. At this point, the air in the cylinders is highly compressed. Therefore, when the fuel is injected in the combustion chamber, the fuel swirls around the spark plug region. As the air is already highly compressed, the injected fuel is resisted from penetrating the whole of the compressed air but finely atomises in the area around the spark plug. At this point, the air/fuel ratio is about 14–15:1 ratio around the spark plug. The air/fuel mixture is protected from condensing by touching the cold cylinder walls by a layer of air and exhaust gas; this improves the thermal efficiency of the engine. This mixture of air and fuel along with the air and exhaust gas is called the 'stratified charge'. The air/fuel ratio at this point across the combustion chamber is about 30–40:1. Improved fuel economy through very lean mixtures is achieved by using the stratified charge process.

The torque produced by the engine at this point is directly proportional to the volume of fuel injected into the combustion chamber. The volume of air entering the engine through the throttle has little effect on the torque output. The direct injection systems use the electronic throttle systems described earlier on page 227. This allows very accurate setting of the throttle to maintain the engine power and ensure the emissions are low. As the engine operates in very lean conditions, the temperature of the combustion chambers can become very hot. As mentioned previously, hot combustion temperatures can create high NO_x emissions. The direct injection system incorporates EGR to bring these temperatures down to satisfactory levels. CO_2 levels are also improved through the use of very lean mixtures.

Medium to high engine loads

As the engine load increases, there is a need to advance the injection timing to inject fuel into the engine earlier when the inlet valve is open. At this point, the cylinder is filled with an evenly displaced mixture of air and fuel at a ratio of about 14.7:1. This richer mixture improves engine response and power output. The volume of air inducted into the engine has a direct relationship to the power and torque the engine can produce and this is controlled through the throttle opening.

Transition between low and high load conditions

As the engine moves from low load and idle conditions to high power output and higher load conditions, the ECU has to make some changes to ensure this is done smoothly. At low engine speeds and when idle, the throttle is wide open, controlled by the ECU through the electronic throttle system. As the engine moves between this condition and high load condition, the throttle is closed momentarily by the ECU. By closing the throttle, the pressure in the intake manifold drops below atmospheric pressure, which produces a richer mixture. At the same time, engine torque output is dropped through retarding the ignition timing. This process provides a seamless changeover between the two operating states. The opposite occurs when the engine moves from high load to low load.

2.29 Vehicle emissions

Figure 2.326 Chrome car exhaust

2.29.1 Emission legislation

Environmental considerations have forced many countries to introduce regulations to limit the pollution caused by vehicles. It is claimed that emissions from vehicles damage human health, plant life and the environment. This problem is particularly severe in areas where the geographic and climatic conditions create an atmospheric envelope that traps the pollutants. The main pollutants and their sources are shown in Table 2.3.

The countries around the world that first introduced stringent controls were Australia, Japan, Sweden and the USA, in particular the state of California. In recent years, as these countries lowered the maximum allowable emission limits, other countries, including those of the EEC, introduced their own standards. Each year sees a tightening of the standards, so manufacturers have to update or modify their vehicles continually to meet the particular requirements laid down for the country in which the vehicle is to be sold. Since 1998, the average CO_2 emissions for new cars have fallen by over 17 per cent. This is a good improvement but there is still more work to be done to meet the 2012 target of 130 g/km.

Exhaust gas

The exhaust gas contains unburnt fuel called hydrocarbons (HC), partially burnt fuel called carbon monoxide and oxides of nitrogen (NO_x) caused by hot combustion temperatures.

Table 2.3 The main pollutants and their sources and effects

Pollutant	Origin	Effects
CO (carbon monoxide)	Incomplete combustion or partially burnt fuel	Poisonous to human beings when inhaled. CO adheres to haemoglobin in the blood and prevents oxygen being carried to body cells.
HC (hydrocarbons)	Unburnt fuel, vaporised fuel escaping from fuel system	Irritates eyes and nose. Cancer risk. Odour.
C (carbon)	Partially burnt fuel	Smoke – restricts visibility. Can be carcinogenic (cancer-causing constituents). Odour.
NO_x (oxides of nitrogen, mainly NO and NO_2)	Very high combustion temperatures cause nitrogen to combine with oxygen	Toxic to humans. NO_x combines with water to form nitrous acid, which causes lung disorders. It combines with other exhaust products to give eye and nose irritants; also affects nervous system. Smog.
Pb (lead)	Added to petrol to raise octane rating	Toxic to humans. A cumulative poison causing a wide range of physical and mental disorders. Causes irreversible damage to children.

Crankcase

During engine operation emissions are created in the crankcase by fuel and oil vapour, along with emissions passed into the crankcase through combustion passing the piston rings. These emissions need to be controlled through various systems.

Fuel system, including fuel tank

Hydrocarbon (HC) vapour emissions are produced by fuel stored in a vehicle's petrol tank.

One of the consequences of producing cleaner engines with lower emissions is that the devices used also have the effect of increasing fuel consumption and lowering power output. Manufacturers have to continually push the boundaries of engineering to prevent this happening as lower fuel efficiency and power outputs are less attractive to customers. Many manufacturers will only fit the required emission control systems relevant to the market that they are being sold in.

2.29.2 European Union regulations for petrol engines

Before any new vehicle is sold in a European Union (EU) country, a number of vehicles must be submitted to the regulating body of a Member State to enable tests to be carried out to confirm that the vehicle type meets current EU standards. This EU-type approval procedure includes engine test cycles on a minimum of five vehicles to ensure that emission levels are within current limits.

To ensure that new vehicles comply with EU regulations, they have to pass real-world drive cycle tests that reflect the normal operation in an urban rural environment. The engine has to be started from a normal cold condition and then driven on real driving cycles, which include operating at various engine speeds including motorway cruising. During the test situation, the vehicles are attached to a mobile dynamometer.

Current emission regulations for passenger vehicles can be seen in Table 2.4. This outlines the emission regulations from 1992 to future Euro 6 regulations in 2014.

Earlier emission regulation limits were determined on the cubic capacity of the engine; during 1993 this was changed to the Euro 1 emission regulations, which all new vehicles had to meet from this point forward. Gradually, new regulations have been introduced that bring the emission levels down further to the current Euro 5 emission regulations.

Engines submitted for test must be designed to run on unleaded petrol, as this is the only type of petrol now available. In addition, the petrol filler pipe must be designed to prevent the tank from being filled from a petrol pump delivery nozzle having an external diameter of 23.6 mm or greater. This regulation means that nozzles of pumps supplying lead-free petrol have to be smaller than those used on pumps that dispense leaded fuel.

The method adopted by an engine designer to meet the emission limits depends on the technology available to a manufacturer. The cost of fitting a catalyst, and its accompanying fuel mixture control system, on small and medium-sized cars, forced many manufacturers to develop lean-burn engines. Tests show that this type of engine gives a good fuel economy and a much lower emission level than other conventional engines. It was expected that the lean-burn type would meet future emission requirements, but the introduction in 1989 of a more stringent standard based on a new European extra-urban driving cycle (EUDC) has meant that to attain the new limits the lean-burn engine needs an exhaust catalyst.

The emission regulations discussed so far relate to the petrol engine. Diesel and dual-fuel engines have to comply with separate EU emission regulations.

Diesel engines must also meet emission standards and, as in the case of petrol engines, the limits laid down by the EU are gradually being reduced to give a cleaner environment. The Euro emission regulations for a diesel engine can be seen in Table 2.5.

Table 2.4 *Euro emission regulations for petrol passenger vehicles*

Emission tier	Date	CO (g/kg)	HC (g/kg)	NO_x (g/km)	NO_x + HC (g/kg)
Euro 1	July 1992	2.72	–	–	0.097
Euro 2	January 1996	2.2	–	–	0.5
Euro 3	January 2000	2.3	0.2	0.15	–
Euro 4	January 2005	1.0	0.10	0.08	–
Euro 5	September 2009	1.00	0.100	0.060	–
Euro 6	September 2014	1.00	0.100	0.060	–

Table 2.5 Euro emission regulations for diesel passenger vehicle

Emission tier	Date	CO (g/kg)	HC (g/kg)	NO_x (g/km)	NO_x + HC (g/kg)
Euro 1	July 1992	2.72	–	–	0.097
Euro 2	January 1996	1.0	–	–	0.7
Euro 3	January 2000	0.64	–	0.5	0.56
Euro 4	January 2005	0.5	–	0.25	0.30
Euro 5	September 2009	0.500	–	0.180	0.230
Euro 6	September 2014	0.500	–	0.180	0.170

2.29.3 Control of engine emissions

Various design modifications and extra fitments are necessary to control engine emissions. The following is a summary of the main features.

Carbon monoxide

This is produced when a cylinder receives either a rich mixture or a poor quality (patchy) mixture. Methods of improvement are listed below.

Closer control of mixture strength

The fuel supplied to the engine by the fuel system undergoes very accurate measurement, especially under slow-running and cold-starting conditions.

Improved distribution of the fuel

Sequential fuel injection is one way of overcoming this problem. Good distribution was difficult with carburettors and single-point injection.

More precise engine tuning

Advanced EMSs have removed the need for technicians to tune the engine, as the ECU checks and retunes itself during engine operation.

More compact combustion chamber

Modern engine designs promote very compact high compression ratio combustion chambers.

Throttle position systems

Opening the throttle slightly when slow running or when decelerating reduces HC emissions.

Precise ignition timing

Ensuring very accurate timing of the ignition can dramatically improve the emissions of an engine. The EMS is able to do this hundreds of times a second.

Hydrocarbons

These are produced when fuel vaporises and escapes to the atmosphere from the fuel system, or when the fuel is unburnt in the cylinder. Methods of improvement are listed below.

Closed crankcase ventilation system

Unburnt fuel passing the pistons and entering the crankcase is prevented from escaping to the atmosphere by a positive crankcase ventilation (PCV) system. The unburnt fuel is returned to the induction system.

Sealed fuel system

A fuel (EVAP) emission control system seals the fuel tank and float chamber, collects the vaporised fuel, passes it through a charcoal-filled canister and delivers it to the induction manifold for combustion in the engine cylinders.

Altering the advance of the ignition

By retarding the ignition timing during slow running or when decelerating dramatically improves the HC emissions. The ECU is able to carry out this task.

Mixture adjustment during deceleration

The EMS is able to carry out very precise control of the fuel injected into the engine under many different running conditions. The ECU can cut fuel altogether when the vehicle is decelerating if the engine speed is over 1500 rpm.

Exhaust gas oxidation

Many engines cannot be 'cleaned up' internally to meet the emission limits, so a catalytic converter has to be fitted in the exhaust system. This looks similar to a large conventional silencer, but is much heavier and more costly.

Carbon dioxide

The production of carbon dioxide (CO_2) occurs as a direct product of complete combustion along with water (H_2O) and nitrogen (N_2). Although perfect combustion does not take place in real-life situations, the more efficient the combustion process, the greater the levels of CO_2. To ensure engines produce the lowest possible harmful emissions, the air/fuel ratio is kept as close to the perfect 14.7 : 1 ratio as possible. Any fault in the ignition process causing the emission levels to rise will create a lower CO_2 value. As we know, CO_2 is not harmful to humans as a gas but it is now being blamed for the change in climate and global warming. To ensure that vehicles produce the lowest CO_2 possible, they must be highly efficient and use the lowest possible amounts of fuel. Changes to aerodynamics can greatly help to reduce CO_2, along with lower resistance tyres and more efficient engines.

Oxygen

Oxygen is essential for combustion to take place. When this is combined with fuel (HC) the complete combustion will create CO_2 and H_2O with no HC in the exhaust gas. If the air/fuel mixture is rich, then no O_2 will be produced as it will be completely used during the burning of the fuel. If the mixture is lean, the exhaust will emit higher levels of O_2 as insufficient fuel will cause poor combustion. Weak mixtures can be down to air leaks in the intake system as well as low fuel content. Misfire conditions due to poor ignition can create high O_2 content in the exhaust gas, as the complete cylinder of air is expelled through the exhaust without combustion taking place.

Oxides of nitrogen

The atmosphere in which we live and breathe consists of 78 per cent nitrogen and 21 per cent oxygen by volume. Although nitrogen contributes over three-quarters of the make-up of the air that is drawn into the combustion chamber, it is not used in the combustion process. During the combustion process under high load, the temperature within the combustion chamber can reach in excess of 1370 °C. When nitrogen and oxygen are subjected to temperatures above 1093 °C, the oxygen and nitrogen begin to combine. This combination of nitrogen and oxygen form harmful oxides, called oxides of nitrogen. These oxides of nitrogen include nitrogen dioxide and nitrogen monoxide.

Due to the high temperatures needed to mix the nitrogen and oxygen, it is the only one of the pollutants produced by the engine that increases as the stoichiometric fuel mixture is reached. If the high temperature within the combustion chamber is not reached, then the chemical reaction does not take place and only nitrogen and oxygen will be exhausted. For this reason, the best way to reduce the concentration of oxides of nitrogen is either to reduce the combustion chamber temperature or restrict the time that the combustion chamber is at the high temperature.

The production of oxides of nitrogen is at its highest level when the air/fuel ratio is approximately 16:1. Above or below this ratio the concentration of oxides of nitrogen is reduced. When the engine is running lean, oxides of nitrogen are reduced as the temperature within the combustion chamber is reduced. When the engine is running rich, the concentration is reduced due to the reduction in oxygen entering the combustion chamber.

It is now known that combustion chamber temperature affects the amount of oxides of nitrogen that are produced. Ignition timing affects the temperatures generated within the combustion chamber. When ignition timing is advanced or retarded, the temperature within the combustion chamber will change. Advancing the ignition timing when the engine is running, either at or near the stoichiometric fuel mixture, will cause the combustion chamber temperature to rise.

Engine designers have carried out many improvements over the years to reduce the levels of NO_x. These have included the following.

Decrease the flame speed during combustion

Using EGR, the combustion process can be slowed down when the engine is under higher load conditions.

Combustion chamber design

The shape of the combustion chamber can alter the flame speed to improve the levels of NO_x production. When combined with lower compression ratios, the NO_x production is lowered further.

Increase in air/fuel ratio

The highest NO_x production comes from a high combustion flame speed combined with an air/fuel ratio approximately 16:1. An engine running weak mixtures with excess air will have lower combustion temperatures and lower NO_x production. Lean-burn engines run in this configuration, which greatly reduces NO_x emissions. The EMS in this type of engine has to have very accurate ignition timing settings to ensure that the performance is not affected too greatly. Direct injection engines running with very high fuel-injection pressures and excess air are also able to produce lower NO_x emissions as described earlier.

Ignition timing alteration

Ignition timing control can assist in lowering the production of NO_x by preventing the ignition timing advancing too much during the time when the throttle is open; this prevents sudden rises in combustion chamber temperature.

Valve timing

Variable valve timing can help reduce NO_x production by altering the valve overlap period during induction. By introducing a small amount of exhaust gas during induction, the combustion chamber temperatures can be kept lower.

Intake-air temperature

By having lower intake-air temperatures the production of NO_x can be reduced by lowering the combustion temperatures. Engines fitted with a pressure-charger utilise an intercooler to lower the temperature of the air entering the engine.

Three-way catalyst

NO_x production from an engine can be greatly reduced by running an EMS with closed-loop control alongside the fitment of a three-way **catalyst** in the exhaust system.

Catalyst: a material that produces a chemical action without undergoing any change itself.

In two-way converters the catalyst material changes the gas by oxidising the HC and CO emissions to form H_2O and CO_2. Later designs of converter necessary to meet tighter emission limits also have to remove O_2 from the nitrogen oxide compounds; these converters are called three-way.

2.29.4 Converter construction

There are two basic types of converter: monolith and pellet (bead). In the monolith type, the large catalyst surface area needed for exposure to the gas is achieved by using a honeycomb construction, whereas the pellet type has a number of aluminium coated wire baskets to support the catalyst covering.

At present, the precious metals platinum, palladium and rhodium are the most suitable catalyst agents; the actual metal used, or mixed combination, governs the type of converter.

A two-way oxidising type uses platinum and palladium, whereas the three-way oxidising/reducing converter uses platinum and rhodium. Since each converter has a weight of about 4 g of precious metal, cheaper converters using base metals such as copper and chromium are being developed. At present, these metals are more prone to being 'poisoned' by small quantities of sulphur present in the fuel.

All converters become ineffective if the catalyst comes into contact with lead. Failure to use a lead-free fuel results in lead being deposited on the catalyst surface; this causes the catalyst to be isolated from the gas.

Monolith type

The construction of this 'single block' type converter is shown in Figure 2.327. In this type the aluminised ceramic or steel honeycomb forms a stable and secure base for the catalytic deposit of precious metals besides providing a gas exposure area equivalent to several football pitches.

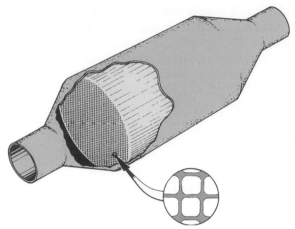

Figure 2.327 A monolith-type catalytic converter

When used with a lean-burn engine, a two-way catalyst uses the excess oxygen exhausted from the engine to react with the hydrocarbons. In the case of a three-way catalyst fitted to a normal engine, the nitrogen oxide content in exhaust gas acts as the oxidising agent to promote combustion of CO and HC to CO_2 and H_2O, while the nitrogen oxides, being stripped of their oxygen, are reduced to nitrogen.

The three-way catalyst only operates effectively when used with a fuel control system, such as a 'closed-loop' electronic EMS; this ensures that the air/fuel ratio is maintained at the precise stoichiometric point (chemically correct ratio).

Pellet type

Figure 2.328 shows a diagram of a dual-bed, three-way converter.

In the layout shown, the first bed contains a three-way catalyst and the second bed an oxidising catalyst. The first bed reduces the NO_x to basic nitrogen and then uses the released O_2 to oxidise some of the HC and CO. Secondary air, introduced by a pump to a chamber between the beds, mixes with the remaining HC and CO and allows the gas to be fully oxidised after it passes through the second bed. During this process a considerable amount of heat is generated.

For a converter to operate efficiently, and to avoid a fire hazard in the area of the converter, the engine must NOT:

- use leaded fuel
- be slow-run for long periods
- be tested by shorting-out the spark plugs to earth
- be compression-tested for long periods
- operate in a condition that delivers neat fuel to the exhaust system.

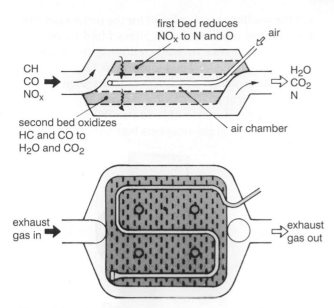

Figure 2.328 *Action of a dual-bed three-way catalytic converter*

2.29.5 Lean-burn engine

During recent years, some engines have been designed to operate efficiently on lean mixtures up to about 22:1. When compared with conventional engines, the lean-burn arrangement gains in fuel economy and has a lower level of emission. For engines of a capacity less than 2 litres, the lower emissions levels, the retention of a high compression ratio and the ability of the engine to use low-octane unleaded fuels make the lean-burn design attractive.

Two major sources of unburnt HC in a conventional engine are:

1 Crevices in the combustion chamber that trap the unburnt mixture, especially those crevices in the regions of the piston ring and head gasket.

2 Absorption and desorption of HC by the oil film and combustion chamber deposits.

Attention to these factors, together with features that give high turbulence at low loads without sacrificing VE for full-load operation, enables the engine to operate satisfactorily on lean mixtures. At steady cruising speeds this gives a reduction in the HC emission, and because the combustion temperature is lower, the NO_x emission is also reduced. Lean-burn engines have lower power tosses from pumping, heat transfer and dissociation (fuel breakdown at high temperature into its separate chemical 'elements' without being burnt), so these factors contribute to the higher fuel economy.

Most designs of lean-burn engine use a four- or five-valve combustion chamber and have specially shaped inlet ports that speed up and direct the incoming mixture to give barrel swirl – a gas movement shown in Figure 2.329a.

The tumbling motion of the gas continues until the latter part of the compression stroke; at this stage the main swirl motion is broken up into small swirl patterns (Figure 2.329b). It is this 'micro-turbulence' action, generated just prior to the point of ignition, that allows the engine to operate on lean-burn mixtures.

Lead

To comply with EU and UK regulations, the lead (Pb) additive in fuels has gradually been reduced from 0.84 g/l in 1972 to zero in 1998.

By the early 1990s, the EU, in company with many other countries, only allowed the manufacture of engines that are suitable for operation on lead-free fuel. Since January 2000, many countries have now banned the use of leaded fuel. Oil companies have

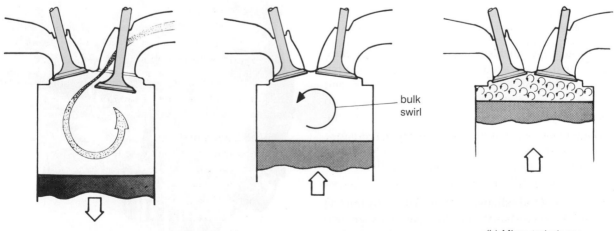

(a) Barrel swirl

(b) Micro-turbulence

Figure 2.329 *Turbulence in a lean-burn engine*

developed lead replacement fuels (LRP) for engines unable to run on lead-free fuel. This fuel uses potassium additives. In the future, this fuel will not be available as fuel manufacturers find the additional expense in refining this fuel uneconomical. Separate additives are now available for earlier engines.

2.29.6 Emission testing

Each new vehicle sold has to comply with local market emission regulations. For example, a vehicle sold into the UK market today must comply with current EU regulations, Euro 5, which lays down the maximum levels of vehicle emissions allowed. These limits can be seen in Tables 2.4 and 2.5 on pages 231 and 232. Many countries have mandatory emission testing and, in some cases, the random exhaust gas checks are carried out at the roadside by the enforcement service. In the UK, each vehicle has to undergo an MOT test after the first three years of a vehicle's registration, and then annually after that. This test assesses the general condition of the vehicle and also tests the exhaust emissions.

The equipment used to test the emissions from an engine is called an exhaust gas analyser. Although this equipment is used to carry out the emissions test during an MOT, it is also an effective diagnostic tool that should be used when fault-finding on a poorly running vehicle. Generally, most exhaust gas analysers will check the following gases:

- Oxygen (O_2)
- Carbon dioxide (CO_2)
- Carbon monoxide (CO)
- Hydrocarbons (HC)
- Oxides of nitrogen (NO_x)

Some exhaust gas analysers are now capable of providing the technician with more detail on the air/fuel ratio of the vehicle and display this as a lambda reading. The chemically correct air/fuel ratio of 14.7:1 is expressed as lambda = 1 on the display. A reading of less than 1 would indicate the air/fuel ratio of being on the richer side and a reading of more than 1 would indicate a leaner mixture.

The exhaust gas analyser must be calibrated before use to ensure an accurate reading. This is often carried out by an engineer on a regular basis, and the machine must also be warmed up before use to make sure that it is correctly operational. After warm-up has taken place, the machine will carry out a self-test, which includes a leak check to ensure that no air is entering the system during the test as this would dramatically alter the results.

The content of the exhaust gas is measured by putting a probe into the exhaust pipe. The gas analyser then draws a sample of the exhaust gas down the tube into the machine. The exhaust gas content is then analysed

and the readings are displayed for the technician. The gas analyser has a series of filters fitted to prevent any unwanted soot or water entering the analyser. These should be checked on a regular basis to avoid inaccurate readings and analyser faults. Figure 2.330 shows a typical example of a modern gas analyser. Diesel engines are also able to use the gas analyser and are subjected to emissions test during the MOT.

Figure 2.330 Exhaust gas analyser

2.30 The diesel four-stroke cycle in detail

2.30.1 Four-stroke operation

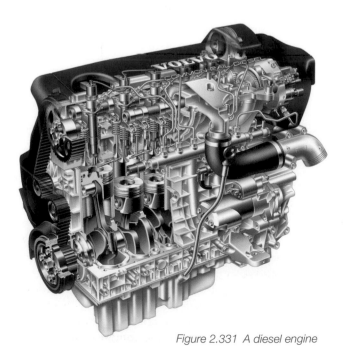

Figure 2.331 A diesel engine

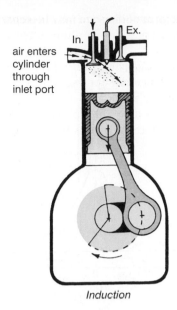

Induction

air enters
cylinder
through
inlet port

In.　Ex.

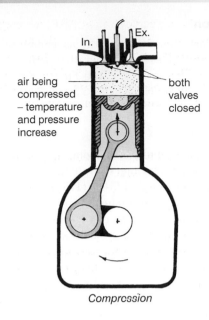

Compression

air being
compressed
– temperature
and pressure
increase

In.　Ex.

both
valves
closed

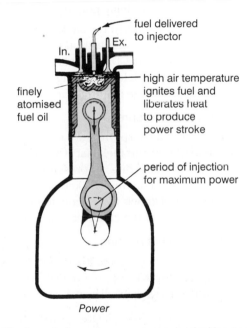

Power

fuel delivered
to injector

In.　Ex.

finely
atomised
fuel oil

high air temperature
ignites fuel and
liberates heat
to produce
power stroke

period of injection
for maximum power

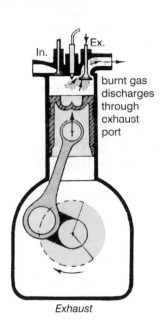

Exhaust

In.　Ex.

burnt gas
discharges
through
exhaust
port

Figure 2.332 The four-stroke cycle – a compression-ignition engine

In many ways, this operation is similar to the four-stroke petrol cycle; both occupy 720°, or two revolutions of the crank, to complete the four strokes – induction, compression, power and exhaust.

Figure 2.332 shows the sequence of operations, and also the main constructional differences between petrol and compression-ignition engines (i.e. the elimination of the carburettor and the substitution of a fuel injector in place of the spark plug). A difference that is not apparent is the compression ratio, which is much higher in the case of the compression-ignition engine. Some engines have ratios as low as 11:1 or as high as 26:1, whereas petrol engines seldom use a ratio greater than 11:1.

The sequence that follows is for a conventional diesel engine using a standard-type diesel fuel pump.

Induction

The descending piston increases the cylinder volume and decreases the pressure. Atmospheric pressure forces air through the open inlet port into the cylinder.

Compression

Both valves are closed and so the ascending piston compresses and raises the temperature of the air. For a compression ratio of 14:1, the final temperature and pressure will be 650°C and 3.5 bar (500 lbf in⁻²) respectively.

Power

Just before TDC, fuel oil, having a self-ignition temperature of 400 °C, is injected into the cylinder at a high pressure, for example 175 bar (175 atmospheres), by means of a high-pressure fuel pump. After a short delay, the fuel begins to burn and liberates heat, which raises the pressure to 6.2 bar (900 lbf in⁻²), providing the thrust necessary for the power stroke. The amount of power is controlled by the period of injection (i.e. the quantity of fuel injected).

Exhaust

As the piston nears the end of the power stroke, the exhaust port is opened. The ascending piston pumps out the burnt gas in readiness for the new cycle.

The temperatures and pressures quoted are approximate and are only intended as a guide, since engine design and other factors can alter conditions considerably.

2.30.2 Diesel combustion

Combustion process

Combustion in the chamber of a petrol engine originates at the spark plug and then progresses throughout the cylinder. In the case of the compression-ignition engine, combustion of the fuel is started by the heat of the air in the chamber. As the fuel 'droplet' passes through the air, it absorbs heat, and, if the temperature is high enough, the fuel will vaporise and ignite. Wide distribution of the fuel occurs during the heating phase and so combustion will begin at many points in the chamber. In the case of one type of direct injection engine, once ignition has taken place, most of the burning will tend to concentrate in zones fairly close to the injector. These zones must be fed with air in order to sweep away the burnt gases and supply the oxygen necessary for complete combustion. Lack of oxygen in the combustion region leads to black smoke in the exhaust. Since power is governed by the quantity of fuel injected, and this, in turn, is limited by the point at which smoke is emitted, some system must be used to introduce an orderly supply of air to the fuel. The airflow is called swirl, a term used in preference to turbulence, since this expression implies a disorderly movement.

Phases of combustion

Figure 2.333 shows a time-base indicator taken from a compression-ignition engine that is operating at full load. Ricardo indicated that the combustion process

that gave this form of diagram may be separated into three phases.

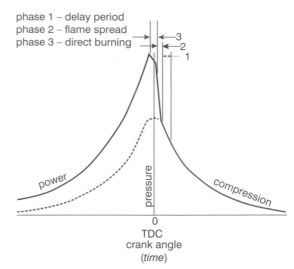

Figure 2.333 The phases of diesel combustion

Phase 1: Ignition delay period

This is the time taken (or angle turned by the crank) between the start of injection to the commencement of the pressure rise. During this important period, the injected fuel particles are being heated by the hot air to the temperature required for the fuel to self-ignite.

Phase 2: Flame spread

This causes a sharp pressure rise due to the sudden combustion of the fuel that was injected during the first phase. The rate of pressure rise governs the extent of the combustion knock. This is commonly called 'diesel knock' and is considered to be the main disadvantage of the compression-ignition engine.

Phase 3: Direct burning

The direct burning of the fuel as it enters the chamber gives a more gradual pressure rise. When the engine is operating at less than full load, this phase does not exist.

Consideration of the diagram shows that if the delay period is shortened the quantity of fuel in the chamber is less so the engine is quieter and smoother. Design factors that increase swirl, atomisation and temperature give a shorter delay period, but perhaps one of the most important factors is the ignition quality of the fuel.

Unlike petrol, compression-ignition fuels must be capable of igniting in a heated air mass without the aid of an electrical spark. The ability of a fuel to ignite, or its 'ignition quality', is expressed as a cetane rating. Classification is obtained by comparing the fuel with a good fuel (cetane) rated as 100, and a poor fuel (alpha-methylnaphthalene) rated as zero. Most commercially available fuels have a cetane rating of about 50.

2.31 Diesel engine combustion chambers

2.31.1 Types of combustion chamber

There are many good designs of compression-ignition combustion chambers, each arranged so as to provide an effective swirl pattern. These designs can be divided broadly into two main classes:

- Direct injection
- Indirect injection

In the former, fuel is injected directly into the closed end of the cylinder, whereas in the latter type, fuel is sprayed into a separate small chamber, which is connected to the cylinder by a small passage or throat.

2.31.2 Direct injection

Figure 2.334 shows the essentials of an open-type combustion chamber. For many years, the direct injection (DI) type shown has been used on heavy vehicles and, in a slightly modified form, is currently the most popular for car engines.

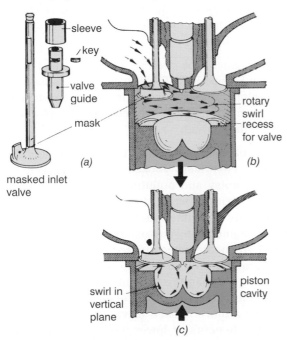

Figure 2.334 Compression-ignition combustion chamber – DI type

A deep cavity, machined in the piston, contains most of the air, since at TDC the piston is very close to the flat cylinder head. To obtain the necessary compression ratio, OHVs are essential. Shallow recesses in the piston crown provide clearance for the valve heads. (Inaccurate setting of the valve timing allows the valves to strike the piston.) A multi-hole injector allows finely atomised fuel under high pressure, of approximately 175 bar for a regular diesel pump, to penetrate the fast-moving air and just enter the cavity of the piston.

Swirl is produced in two planes: vertical and horizontal. The ascending piston causes the air to be directed into the cavity and move in the manner shown in the diagram. As the piston approaches TDC, this motion will be speeded up because of the squish action of the air between piston and head. Horizontal or rotary swirl can be obtained by inclining the inlet port tangentially to the cylinder, or masking the inlet valve. Figure 2.334 shows the latter arrangement, which is the most popular. Combining both swirl movements gives a vortex airflow in the cavity, and ensures a good supply of oxygen to the combustion region.

2.31.3 Indirect injection

Up until the mid-1980s, the indirect injection (IDI) type was commonly used on small compression-ignition engines as fitted to light vehicles. Compared with the traditional heavy vehicle DI engine, the IDI ran more smoothly and, since the IDI type used tower injection pressures, the engine was more able to operate over a large speed range.

Many IDI combustion chambers have been based on the Ricardo Comet design shown in Figure 2.335. In this arrangement, a swirl chamber is connected to the main chamber by a throat, which is allowed to operate at a higher temperature than the surrounding metal.

Air is pumped through the hot throat into the chamber during compression, so by the end of this stroke the antechamber contains very hot air in a high state of swirl. Fuel injected into this fast-moving air mass is quickly atomised into a very fine state. This atomisation is very effective even though the fuel is injected in the form of a 'soft' spray by a pintle or single-hole nozzle set at a comparatively low pressure (e.g. 100 bar).

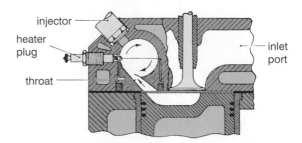

Figure 2.335 Compression-ignition combustion chamber – IDI type

After combustion has been initiated in the swirl chamber, burning fuel, together with the unburnt and partially burnt fuel, is carried into the piston cavity in the main chamber. When the injection period is increased to produce a higher engine power, most of the fuel that is injected towards the end of the spraying period does not ignite until it mixes with the air in the main chamber. This ensures that during the combustion period the burning can continue for a relatively long time until it finally reaches a stage at which the fuel cannot find sufficient oxygen. Beyond this point, black smoke starts to be emitted from the exhaust; this smoke point dictates the maximum amount of fuel that can be injected without sacrificing economy and also represents the maximum power that can be legally obtained from the engine.

In an IDI engine, the combination of hot air and excellent atomisation gives a short ignition delay. Compared with the DI type, the intensity of diesel knock is lower, the engine runs more smoothly and the cetane rating of the fuel that is required can be lower with IDI engines.

2.31.4 Preheating system

All compression-ignition engines require some special provision for cold starting. The injection of a larger quantity of fuel, and the greater amount of easily ignitable fractions contained in the injected charge, are generally sufficient to start a cold DI engine, but the greater heat losses of IDI units require these engines to have extra cold-start provisions. Compared with ratios of about 16:1 that are used with DI, the IDI engines use higher ratios in the order of 22:1; in some cases a ratio as high as 30:1 is used.

In addition to the cold-starting requirement, a high compression ratio is also used to raise the thermal efficiency (i.e. economy, to that of the DI engine). This feature tends to counteract the greater heat loss due to the larger surface area of an IDI combustion chamber.

When cold starting an IDI engine, one or more of the following are used:

Heater plug

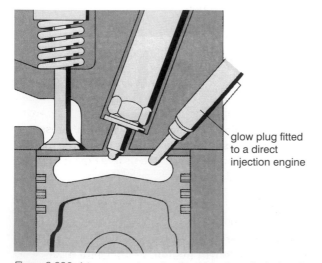

Figure 2.336 A heater or glow plug fitted into the cylinder head

glow plug fitted to a direct injection engine

The heater plug is a hot bulb, often called a glow plug (Figure 2.336) that is fitted in the swirl chamber. The air in the chamber is heated by electrical means for a few seconds prior to starting a cold engine. Today, these plugs are often controlled automatically.

Manifold heaters

The manifold heater is an electrical unit fitted to preheat the air as it passes through the inlet manifold to the cylinder.

Pintaux injector

The pintaux injector is a pintle-type injector that has an auxiliary hole to direct fuel down the throat of the chamber during the cranking period. This improves the heating of the fuel during compression to improve initial start combustion.

2.31.5 Modern power units used in light vehicles

Light vehicles fitted with the diesel engine are a very popular choice by customers. Most small-capacity diesel engines fitted in today's vehicles have excellent fuel economy and very low emissions. Power outputs from small-capacity diesel engines have risen due to more advanced fuelling systems and turbochargers.

Diesel engines took over 53 per cent of the new car sales in Europe in 2007, so manufacturers have had to develop this power unit to produce more and more refinement to ensure that the customer keeps coming back to their brand.

In the earlier years of the diesel engine light vehicle, customers looked at this power unit as slow, noisy and polluting but now, due to the manufacturing specifications, the diesel engine is virtually as refined as the equivalent capacity petrol engine. Many customers now prefer to drive diesel engine vehicles due to the power delivery. The torque produced by a diesel engine is usually much higher than the equivalent petrol engine, so there is less need to run the engine at high speeds, creating a more relaxed driving experience along with the benefits of lower fuel consumption and emissions.

2.31.6 Perkins Prima

An example of the advancements in development of the diesel engine could be seen with the introduction of the Perkins Prima engine. This engine was produced for light vehicles and had a 2-litre capacity.

Traditionally, IDI was the system normally associated with small compression-ignition units. Perkins

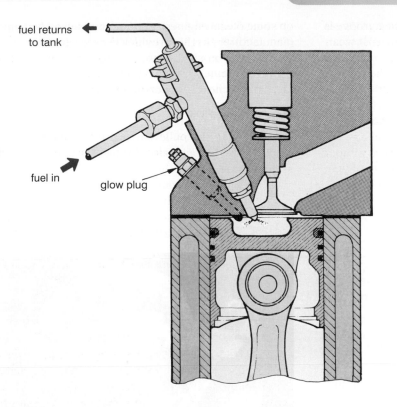

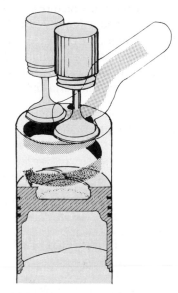

high-speed rotary swirl
produced by inclined inlet port

Figure 2.337 The Perkins Prima combustion chamber

departed from the norm because they found that the IDI was less efficient because of its high energy consumption; this was caused by the high compression ratio and large pumping losses that resulted from the rapid movement of air between the main chamber and the swirl chamber.

Figure 2.337 shows the layout of the combustion chamber. The bowl-in-piston combustion cavity, together with an inclined (helically shaped) inlet port to achieve high-speed rotary swirl, gave high power and excellent economy up to a rated engine speed of about 4500 rpm; a speed range higher than the majority of other units in use at the time.

Automatic glow plugs were used for cold starting; these came into operation when the driver turned the ignition key. It is claimed that these aids allowed the engine to be started in temperatures well below freezing. During the cranking period the injection timing was advanced to give easier combustion, but when the engine fired the injection timing was quickly returned to normal; this reduced noise and gave smoother operation during warm-up.

The engine weighed little more than a spark-ignition engine, even though it was built to withstand the stresses of turbocharging.

2.32 Main components of the diesel engine

The higher cylinder pressures of compression-ignition engines demand stronger components, although for production economy reasons, manufacturers of light compression-ignition units often use some engine components, such as cylinder blocks and crankshafts, which are interchangeable with the spark-ignition versions.

2.32.1 Components

Cylinder block

Due to the higher combustion pressures within a diesel engine the cylinder block is normally produced from cast iron. This material provides the extra strength required to handle the additional pressures of the combustion process and the force of the heavier components during their movement through the engine cycle.

Pistons

Pistons are usually made of aluminium alloy, often with steel inserts in the skirts to control expansion, and are made longer than the spark-ignition piston so as to accommodate the combustion cavity. Three or more piston rings are used and the top ring groove is generally armoured by using an insert to resist wear.

Crankshaft

Crankshafts have to be more robust to withstand the higher pressures and shock loads, and the fillets are normally rolled to improve fatigue life. Generally the main bearings, situated between each crank throw, are copper-lead and the big-end bearings are either fully copper-lead or copper-lead/tin-aluminium, with the heavier-duty material fitted to the connecting rod side of the bearing.

Cylinder head

As with spark-ignition engines the purpose of the cylinder head is to seal the top of the engine cylinder and create a combustion chamber. The cylinder head also houses the inlet, exhaust valves, injectors, glow plugs and camshaft(s).

The cylinder head in compression-ignition and spark-ignition engines has to withstand the very high compression pressures. In the compression-ignition engine, these pressures are higher than in a spark-ignition engine due to the higher compression ratios. Most cylinder heads today are made from aluminium, as this is lighter than the cast cylinder heads previously used.

Intake manifold

Intake manifolds serve a different purpose because they do not have to convey a combustible charge. Air cleaning and induction silencing are still necessary, so these functions, together with other functions such as manifold heating for starting, speed governing and turbocharging, require the use of a suitable manifold.

2.32.2 Valve timing

The valve timing periods for light vehicle compression-ignition engines are similar to those used on the spark-ignition engine because the breathing requirements are basically the same. Heavy compression-ignition engines have a much lower maximum operating speed (e.g. 2000 rpm) because of the mass of the components, so in these the valve periods are smaller; inlet valve angles of 10° before to 40° after, and exhaust angles of 40° before to 20° after are typical on heavy engines.

2.32.3 Valve-operating gear

The diesel engine uses similar valve-operating gear to that found on the petrol engine. There are various options available to manufacturers. The most common type of drive arrangement is the toothed rubber timing belt, as this provides relatively quiet operation and fairly long service life (100,000 miles

on some diesel engines). Chain drive is used by some manufacturers as this provides very low maintenance and service costs. Figures 2.338 and 2.339 show both arrangements fitted to a modern diesel engine. When replacing the timing belt during service, it is essential that the engine timing is set accurately before removal of the old belt. This is often carried out by pinning the pulleys to avoid any movement of the crankshaft, camshafts and fuel pump during belt removal. After fitting the new belt, the engine timing should be checked again along with the belt tension. If a valve gear drive belt fails during operation, severe engine damage will usually occur as the pistons hit the open inlet or exhaust valves.

Figure 2.338 Diesel engine fitted with toothed belt-driven valve gear

Diesel engines can have various valve arrangements, from two valves per cylinder (one inlet and one exhaust valve) to four valves per cylinder (two inlet valves and two exhaust valves). Most modern diesel engines have moved towards four valves per cylinder, due to the benefits of improved breathing by increasing the amount of air entering the engine and improving the exhaust gas flow when it leaves the engine. Recent technological developments have forced engine designers to rethink the combustion chamber designs to improve on the CO_2 and NO_x emissions. Some designers are now moving back to two valves per cylinder to lower the amount of swirl in the combustion chamber to improve on the CO_2 output.

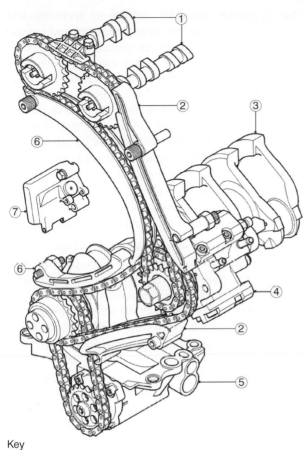

Key

1 camshaft	4 fuel pump	7 mounting bracket
2 RH chain guides	5 oil pump	
3 crankshaft	6 LH chain guides	

Figure 2.339 Diesel engine fitted with chain-driven valve gear

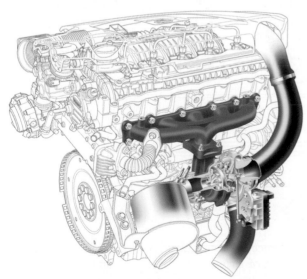

Figure 2.340 DPF system fitted to a modern diesel engine with turbocharger

2.32.4 Engine lubrication

High combustion temperatures and elements such as sulphur in the fuel make the diesel engine more prone to deposits of carbon, formation of gums around the piston rings and lacquer deposits on the side of the pistons.

These conditions are minimised by using a heavy-duty detergent oil. Detergent additives in these special oils maintain engine cleanliness, and dispersant additives hold the carbon and soot in suspension in the oil so that the foreign particles harmlessly pass around the system until the oil is next drained. It is essential that diesel engines have the correct oil, especially on the later engines fitted with DPF systems. The DPF system is fitted to the exhaust manifold on the latest diesel engines. This system collects the diesel particulates exhausted by the engine during the drive cycle. The particulates are then burned off when the engine reaches correct running condition. Figure 2.340 shows a DPF system fitted to a diesel engine.

2.32.5 Advantages and disadvantages of diesel engines

Compared with a petrol engine of the same size, a diesel engine has the following advantages:

- Fuel economy – the high compression ratio gives a good thermal efficiency (35–40 per cent indicated) and provides the driver with approximately 30 per cent more miles to the gallon.
- Reduced risk of fire – at room temperature, the low volatility of diesel-engined road vehicle (Derv) fuel makes ignition difficult.
- Lower CO_2 emissions – the diesel engine produces lower CO_2 emissions compared with the same capacity petrol engine.
- Higher torque output – the diesel engine produces higher torque outputs at low engine speeds, providing improved towing and cruising ability.

The disadvantages are:

- High initial cost – due to expensive fuel-injection equipment and more substantial engine construction.
- Lower maximum power output – earlier diesel engines generally produced lower power outputs than the equivalent petrol engine. Today, the difference is minimal due to the more advanced fuelling systems and the use of turbocharging.
- Lower power/weight ratio – generally, the diesel engine is heavier than the equivalent petrol engine, which leads to a heavier vehicle. Due to the improved torque outputs of the diesel engine, this is not a big disadvantage.
- Greater noise in operation – the diesel engine produces higher levels of noise during combustion (combustion knock) than a petrol engine.

2.33 Mechanical aspects of the diesel fuel system

2.33.1 Mechanical systems

Early diesel engines used air pressure to deliver the fuel into the cylinder, but today the fuel is delivered by high-pressure pumps driven by the engine's crankshaft. The fuel is passed to the injectors through small-bore steel pipes or lines. The basic fuel pump system or jerk pump, which is shown in simplified form in Figure 2.341 is often termed mechanical or solid injection, since the ejection of the fuel is brought about by the action of the plunger on a 'solid' column of oil.

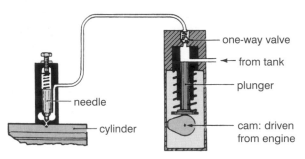

Figure 2.341 *Principle of the mechanical system of fuel delivery*

The equipment must be capable of metering and delivering the fuel at the correct pressure and precise time. When it is said that the volume of fuel injected into the cylinder per cycle is often less than the volume of a small pin head, and the variation between cylinders must not exceed 2 per cent, you must appreciate that the injector system is a high-precision unit. Very close limits and small clearances for example; the clearance between plunger and barrel is less than $3\,\mu m$ (0.0001 in). The diesel fuel system demands special precautions to prevent dirt from entering the system. Clean fuel, regular replacement of filters, and close attention to cleanliness during overhaul of equipment are all essential if the apparatus is to perform its exacting task.

A layout of a typical system is shown in Figure 2.342. A low-pressure feed pump or gravity supply ensures that the injection pump receives a continuous flow of clean filtered fuel. The system incorporates many filters: a fine gauze unit is fitted on the inlet side of the pump, and a felt, cloth or paper filter is inserted between feed pump and injection pump. Injection, in the case of a four-stroke, occurs every other revolution and, therefore, the injection pump must be driven from the timing gears or camshaft at half engine speed. At the appropriate time, fuel under high pressure is conveyed to the injector by fuel

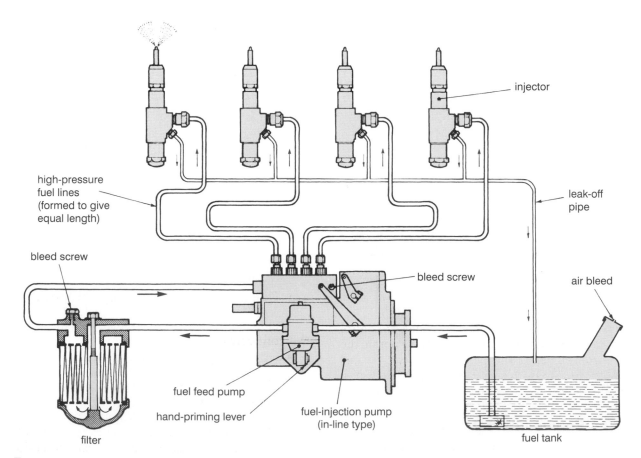

Figure 2.342 *Layout of a compression-ignition fuel-injection system*

lines, which should be of equal length to maintain an equal injection delay (period between the time when a high pressure builds up in the pump and the time when fuel begins to spray from the injector).

Lubrication of the main working parts of the system is usually done by the fuel oil itself: a predetermined leakage past the injector needle is directed to waste or returned to the fuel tank.

The pump will not function correctly if air is present in the system, and therefore venting screws or valves are provided at various points to allow air to be bled out. This is necessary after disturbance of supply lines or 'running-out' of fuel. A priming lever, generally fitted to the feed pump, allows the feed pump to be operated manually. With the air vent (bleed screw) open, operation of the feed pump forces a column of fuel through the line and allows the air to be driven from the system.

2.33.2 The injection pump

Until recently, modern diesel engines were fitted with either an in-line pump or a distributor pump: the former is similar in basic construction to the pump produced by Robert Bosch over 50 years ago, whereas the distributor pump has been in production for as many years. The comparatively low initial cost of the latter made this type attractive to many manufacturers.

Since both pumps have been produced in large numbers, this chapter describes each type.

Diesel engines today are fitted with more advanced fuel systems called common rail fuel-delivery systems. These systems deliver fuel in a similar process to the petrol fuel-injection systems described on page 162. A more detailed explanation of common rail is discussed on page 263.

2.33.3 In-line pump

Figure 2.342 shows an in-line, four-element enclosed camshaft type of pump, and Figure 2.343 illustrates the construction of one pumping element. This unit comprises the following.

Pumping element

A steel plunger moving through a constant stroke reciprocates inside a close-fitting steel barrel. The plunger is partly machined away to produce a control helix and vertical groove. An inlet and spill port in the barrel communicates with a gallery fed from the fuel tank. Location of the barrel is provided by allowing a screw in the casing to register in a recess adjacent to the spill port in the barrel.

Partial rotation of the plunger varies the output from zero for stopping the engine to maximum for starting. Between these limits a variable supply of fuel is necessary to meet the engine power and speed requirements.

The operation of the pumping element is shown in Figure 2.343. The positions of the element are as follows:

A When the plunger is at BDC, the depression in the pump chamber causes fuel to enter both ports.

B This position, known as the point of port closure (or spill cut-off with this type of pump), is generally regarded as the theoretical point of injection. Both ports have been covered, and so the ascending plunger raises the pressure of the fuel to produce injection.

C Injection stops when the edge of the helix uncovers the spill port. Pressure is relieved by fuel passing down the vertical groove, around the waist of the plunger and out of the spill port.

D Rotation of the plunger causes the helix to uncover the spill port either earlier or later, to give less or more fuel respectively.

E Moving the plunger to make the vertical groove coincide with the spill port means that the port will remain open; therefore no fuel will be delivered and the engine will come to rest.

Plunger control

Two lugs on the plunger fit into slots in a control sleeve on to which is clamped a toothed quadrant. This quadrant engages a rack cut in the control rod, which runs the length of the pump. By moving the quadrant relative to the sleeve, the output from each element can be calibrated or equalised.

Drive

Symmetrical cams, set to give the appropriate firing order, act on a roller follower and tappet block. A screw or shim adjustment between tappet and plunger allows the time of the start of injection of one element to be varied in respect to the other elements. A four-cylinder engine has a phase angle (the interval between injections) of:

$$\frac{360°}{\text{No. of cylinders}} = \frac{360°}{4} = 90°$$

The operation for setting this angle is known as phasing.

Delivery valve

The delivery valve (Figure 2.344) performs two duties:

1 The conical seat acts as a non-return valve preventing the return of fuel from the high-pressure pipeline when the spill port opens. This allows the pump chamber to recharge and also enables air or gas to be purged from the pipeline via the injector.

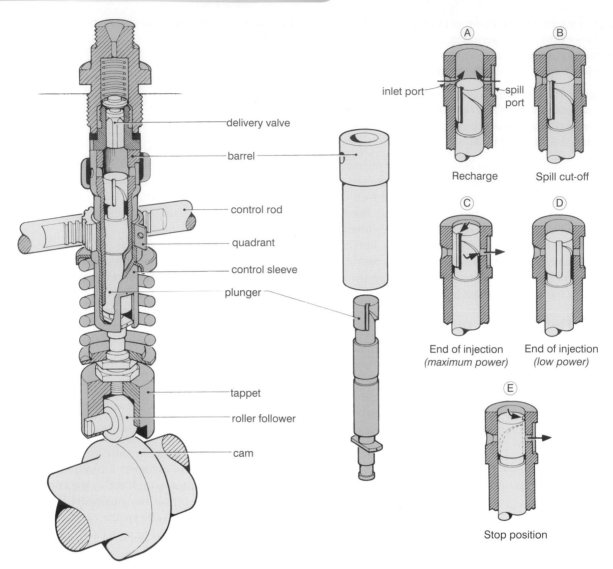

Figure 2.343 *The injection unit inside an in-line fuel-injection pump*

2 If air can be eliminated from the high-pressure pipeline, the pump will often operate satisfactorily without a delivery valve: on the opening of the spill port the pressure at the injector will fall rapidly to pump inlet pressure giving a sharp closing of the injector. The fitting of a non-return valve, however, traps pressure in the pipeline while the injector is still open. This pressure can only be relieved by fuel continuing to pass the injector at a diminishing pressure, resulting in the last few droplets of fuel merely 'dribbling' out, causing incomplete combustion, carbon formation, smoky exhaust and high fuel consumption.

The collar below the conical seat acts as a piston and withdraws a small amount of fuel from the high-pressure pipeline as the valve closes, causing the necessary rapid pressure drop to ensure a sharp cut-off to injection.

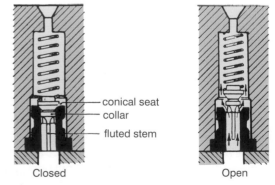

Figure 2.344 *Delivery valve*

Governor

Higher gas pressures in the cylinder of a compression-ignition engine usually demand stronger components than those used in a petrol engine. Strength is normally improved by increasing the component dimensions, but this also increases weight and leads to engine damage if the speed exceeds a given value, which is governed by the components' strength/weight ratio.

A pump with a rising output characteristic (i.e. for a given control rod setting the output increases with speed, and compression pressures, which are substantially the same at idling as at maximum speed) makes it difficult to obtain a steady idling speed – this causes the engine either to race or to stall.

Limitation of maximum speed and control of the engine at idling speed are the two main duties performed by the governor. If the unit attends to these two duties only, it is known as an idling and maximum speed governor, whereas a unit that regulates throughout the speed range is termed an all-speed governor.

There are three main types of governor:

■ Mechanical
■ Pneumatic
■ Hydraulic

Mechanical governors

The type shown diagrammatically in Figure 2.345 is an idling and maximum speed governor, which is often used on heavy-vehicle engines. Mounted at the end of the injector pump, it consists of two weights, which are rotated by the pump camshaft. Springs exert a force in an inward direction on the weights, and bell cranks link each weight to the bottom end of

a floating lever: the top end of the lever is connected to the control rod and the centre is mounted on an eccentric, which is rotated by the accelerator pedal.

The diagram shows the governor in the engine-stationary position, and in this condition the weights are fully retractable to hold the control rod in the maximum fuel position in readiness for starting the engine. When the engine fires, rotation of the weights causes the centrifugal effect to overcome the spring and move the weight out to the position shown by Figure 2.345b, which causes the control rod to be withdrawn to the 'idling' setting. In this position the weights are being controlled by the outer (weaker) springs only, so sensitive control is possible.

Assuming the pedal is not depressed, any increase in speed produces a slight outward movement of the weights and this moves the control rod in the direction that reduces the fuel delivery. In a similar way, stalling is prevented by the weights moving inwards, which causes the control rod to increase the fuel delivery.

Between idling and maximum speeds, the weights maintain the same position, and appear to be locked together. During this phase, downward movement of the accelerator pedal rotates the eccentric and moves the control rod in a direction that increases the fuel delivery.

As maximum speed, for example 1800–2000 rpm, is reached, the high centrifugal force acting on the weights will overcome the strong outer springs and move the weights outwards (Figure 2.345c). This motion, when

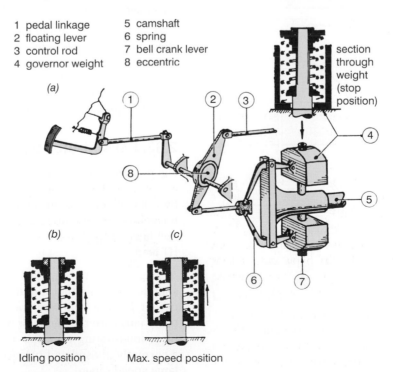

1 pedal linkage
2 floating lever
3 control rod
4 governor weight
5 camshaft
6 spring
7 bell crank lever
8 eccentric

section through weight (stop position)

(a)

(b)　　*(c)*

Idling position　　Max. speed position

Figure 2.345 Idling and maximum speed mechanical governor

transmitted to the control rod, decreases the quantity of fuel delivered, and reduces the engine power, irrespective of the position of the accelerator pedal.

A small quantity of engine oil, contained in the separate governor housing, lubricates the moving parts. Check the level at regular intervals, for example every 3000 km (2000 miles).

A number of adjusting nuts, screw and stops are employed with this type of governor. Do not disturb the settings unless you have special tools and the necessary knowledge.

Pneumatic governors

In-line pumps fitted to light compression-ignition engines often use this all-speed type of governor. Holding the accelerator pedal in a set position, the governor will maintain a constant speed up to a point where the load on the engine is too great.

Figure 2.346 shows the main construction of this type. A spring-loaded diaphragm, connected to the control rod, is mounted to seal a chamber, which is linked by a pipe to a venturi control unit in the inlet manifold. A butterfly valve, fitted in the waist of the venturi, is connected directly to the accelerator pedal.

When the engine is at rest, the diaphragm spring forces the control rod to the maximum fuel or excess fuel position. (Many pumps are fitted with an excess fuel device. This is a manually operated control fitted

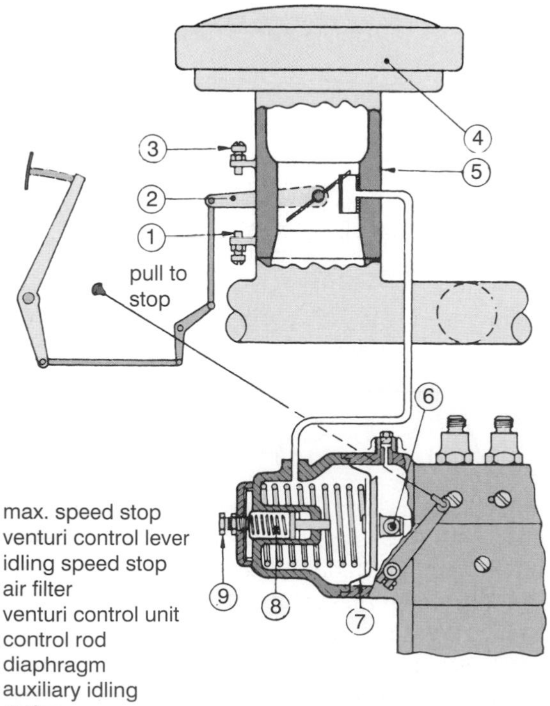

1 max. speed stop
2 venturi control lever
3 idling speed stop
4 air filter
5 venturi control unit
6 control rod
7 diaphragm
8 auxiliary idling spring
9 auxiliary idling set-screw

Figure 2.346 A pneumatic governor system

at the end of the pump, which enables extra fuel to be delivered for cold starting. It cannot be operated from the driving position.)

Closing the accelerator pedal after starting produces a depression in the venturi and diaphragm chamber. This causes atmospheric pressure to force the diaphragm and control rod to the idling setting. With the pedal in any set position, an increase in speed intensifies the venturi depression, which reduces the control rod opening: a decrease in speed will produce the opposite condition.

As the accelerator pedal is depressed, the butterfly valve is opened and the venturi depression is decreased. This causes the spring to open the control rod and increase the engine speed until a balance is reached between the spring thrust and venturi depression.

A stop screw, acting on the lever controlling the butterfly valve, limits the maximum speed. When the valve reaches its stop, any tendency for the engine to increase speed will intensify the venturi depression and reduce the control rod opening.

A 'stop' control on the dash enables the driver to override the governor and move the control to the 'no-fuel' position.

Note: do not start the engine with any part of the governor system disconnected as the engine could enter a condition where the engine speed will not be able to be controlled.

Hydraulic governors

This type is used with in-line pumps where smooth, slow idling speeds are demanded, for example coaches, but high cost tends to limit its use. A gear-type oil pump, driven from the end of the pump camshaft, supplies oil through various valves to operate a piston linked to the control rod.

2.33.4 Distributor-type pumps – Lucas

Figure 2.347a shows a DPA-type pump suitable for a four-cylinder engine. Connected to the engine by a flange and driven by a splined shaft, this unit resembles the distributor used on a petrol engine; fuel lines to the injectors occupy the position of the HT leads.

A single-element, opposed plunger pumping unit supplies fuel to either a four- or six-cylinder engine; except for the cam and the number of ports, the other parts are the same for both engines. Operated by a non-rotating cam, the single element provides a correctly phased and balanced output over a very large speed range.

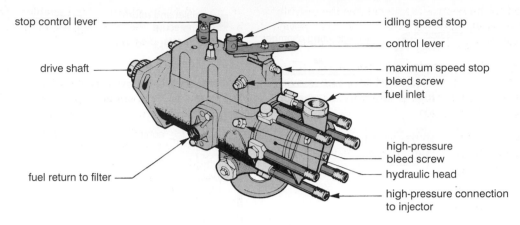

(a) Distributor pump fitted with mechanical governor

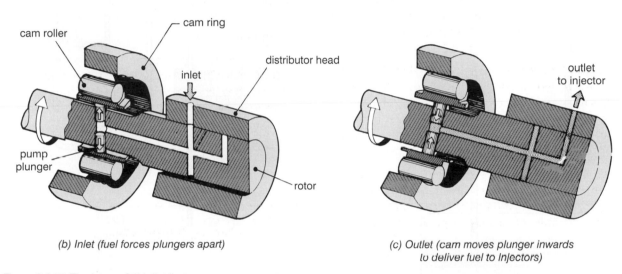

(b) Inlet (fuel forces plungers apart)   *(c) Outlet (cam moves plunger inwards to deliver fuel to injectors)*

Figure 2.347 The Lucas CAV distributor pump

The pumping unit, shown diagrammatically in Figure 2.347b, consists of two plungers mounted in a rotor, which turns in a fixed hydraulic head. Ports in the head and rotor line up in certain positions to allow either inward or outward flow of oil. Figure 2.347b shows the inlet port open. Pressure from a transfer pump fitted at the end of the main pump, directs fuel oil along the centre of the rotor to force out the plungers. Figure 2.347c shows that the uncovered outlet port will allow the cam to force the plungers together and discharge the fuel to the injector.

Cam ring shape

Dribble is eliminated by using a special cam design to stop fuel delivery sharply (Figure 2.348). At the end of each pumping stroke the roller, which operates the pumping plunger, suddenly moves outwards and drops the pumping pressure.

This retraction arrangement overcomes the need for a delivery valve.

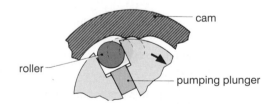

Figure 2.348 Cam ring shape to retract roller

Fuel system

Figure 2.349 shows a typical fuel system. A feed pump supplies fuel, via a filter, to a sliding vane transfer pump, which directs the oil through a driver-controlled metering valve to the rotor. Transfer pump pressure is limited by a regulating valve, and oil, which escapes from the pumping element, returns to the filter after lubricating the working parts.

The quantity of fuel delivered to the injector is governed by the position of the metering valve. The diagram shows a partly opened valve restricting

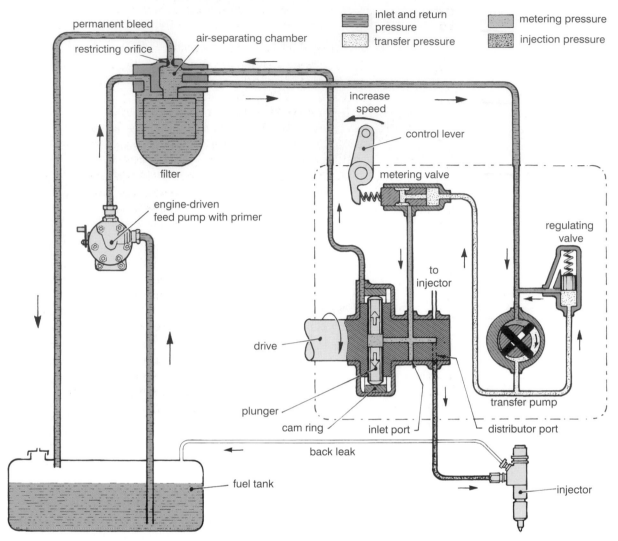

Figure 2.349 Fuel systems for Lucas CAV distributor pump

the flow of oil to the rotor. This reduction in oil flow prevents the full outward travel of the plungers; hence the shortened stroke gives reduced fuel and lower engine power.

On fitting a 'new' pump, it is essential to fill the pump completely with clean fuel oil before attempting to start the engine. Various venting screws are provided to bleed the air from the system.

The absence of delivery valves in the high-pressure lines makes it necessary to bleed these lines; bleeding is carried out by slackening the union nuts at the injectors and cranking the engine. Before operating the starting motor to purge the air, the appropriate personal safety precautions should be taken to avoid contact with the high-pressure spray.

Automatic advance mechanism

An automatic advance mechanism is provided for engines that have a wide speed range. This consists

of a spring-loaded piston, which rotates the cam ring against the DOR when the transfer pump output pressure increases (Figure 2.350).

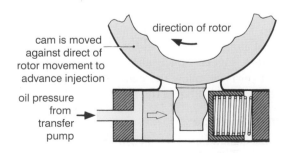

Figure 2.350 An automatic advance mechanism

Governor

The governor used is either a hydraulic or mechanical type.

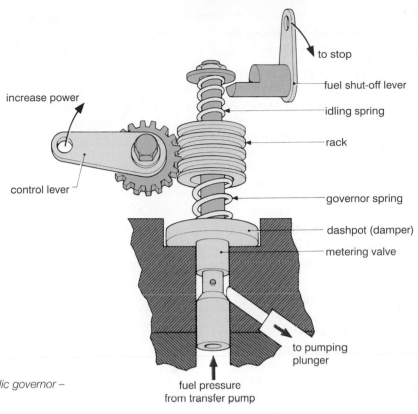

increase power

to stop

fuel shut-off lever

idling spring

control lever

rack

governor spring

dashpot (damper)

metering valve

to pumping plunger

fuel pressure from transfer pump

Figure 2.351 Hydraulic governor – distributor pump

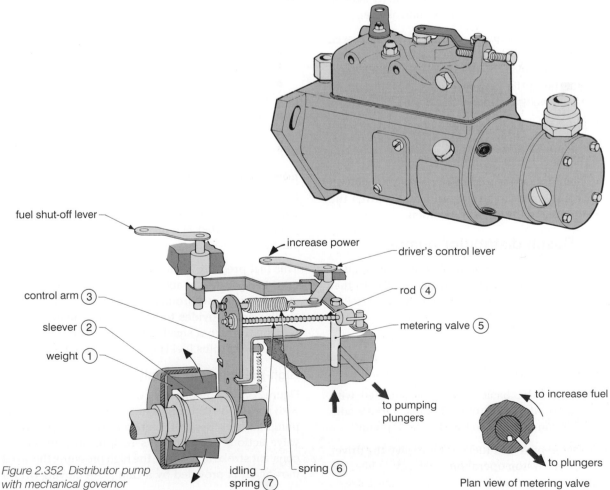

fuel shut-off lever

increase power

driver's control lever

control arm ③

rod ④

sleever ②

metering valve ⑤

weight ①

to pumping plungers

spring ⑥

idling spring ⑦

Figure 2.352 Distributor pump with mechanical governor

to increase fuel

to plungers

Plan view of metering valve

Hydraulic governor

Control of engine speed is achieved by utilising the transfer pump and the fuel metering valve (Figure 2.351).

The driver controls the valve through a spring, so if the driver depresses the pedal a given amount, the valve will open wide and allow the speed to increase. The build-up in engine speed increases the transfer pump pressure; this gradually moves the metering valve towards the closed position until a point is reached at which the speed will not increase any more. These events recur throughout the range.

Mechanical governor

This type is recommended when more precise control of the engine speed is required. It can be recognised by the longer pump housing, which is needed to accommodate the flyweights.

Figure 2.352 shows the constructional details of a simplified layout. Rotation of the input shaft causes the weight (1) to be thrown outwards and move a sleeve (2) against a control arm (3). The pivot on this arm causes the upper part of the arm to move in the opposite direction, which pulls on the rod (4) and closes the metering valve (5). All of these movements are resisted by the control spring (6): the tension on this spring is given by the driver's control lever.

When the driver requires an increase in power, movement of the control lever extends the spring. The larger force given by the spring resists flyweight movement until the engine speed is sufficient to enable the flyweight to move.

Under idling conditions, tension is removed from the main governor spring and a light idling spring (7) is used to resist movement of the flyweights.

At any time the engine can be stopped by a shut-off lever. This overrides the governor and moves the metering valve to the 'no fuel' position.

2.33.5 Bosch distributor pumps

Figure 2.353 shows a Bosch VE-type pump fitted in a self-bleeding fuel system layout similar to that used on many light vehicles. VE stands for 'Verteiler' which is German for distributor or divider.

As with other rotary pumps, this type has one pumping element and a number of high-pressure outlets, one for each engine cylinder.

In addition to the basic features associated with modern distributor-type rotary pumps, various add-on modules can be fitted to the Bosch VE pump:

- Solenoid-operated fuel cut-off to give the driver a key start/stop operation.

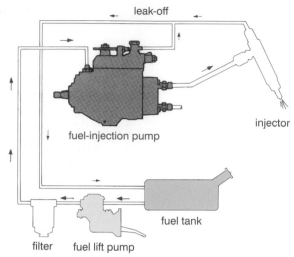

Figure 2.353 A Bosch distributor pump fuel system

- Automatic cold-starting module to advance the injection.
- Fast-idle facility to give even running during warm-up.
- Torque control for matching the fuel output with the fuel requirement.

The simplified section through the pump (Figure 2.354) shows the layout of the basic sub-systems; these include:

- low-pressure fuel supply
- high-pressure fuel supply and distributor
- fuel shut-off solenoid
- distributor plunger drive
- automatic injection advance unit
- pressure valve
- mechanical governor.

Low-pressure fuel supply

Driven at half crankshaft speed by a drive shaft, a transfer pump having four vanes delivers fuel to the pumping chamber at a pressure set by the regulating valve.

This fuel pressure, which rises with engine speed, is used to operate the automatic advance unit. Also, it gives an overflow through the pump body, which aids cooling and provides the self-bleeding feature. After passing through a small restriction at the top of the pump, the surplus fuel is returned to the fuel tank.

High-pressure fuel supply

Figure 2.355 is a simplified view of the pumping chamber with part of the distributor head cut away to show the pump plunger. Besides rotating in the head to give a valve action, the plunger is reciprocated through a constant stroke to produce the high pressure; this axial movement is provided by a cam plate moving over a

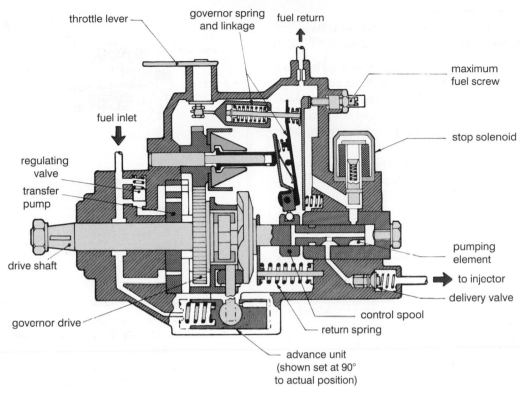

Figure 2.354 The Bosch VE distributor pump (simplified)

roller ring. The quantity of high-pressure fuel delivered to the injector via the outlet bore is controlled by the position of the control spool. This feature varies the effective pumping stroke; it increases as the spool is moved towards the distributor head.

In the position shown in Figure 2.355a, the rotation of the plunger has caused one of the metering slits to open the inlet passage; at this point all outlet ports are closed. Prior to this, the plunger had moved down the chamber to create a condition for the fuel to enter and fill the high-pressure chamber.

Slight rotation of the plunger closes the inlet port and causes the single distributor slit in the plunger to open one of the outlet ports. While in this position the plunger is moved up the chamber to pressurise the fuel and deliver it through the outlet bore to the injector.

The position of the plunger at the end of the injection period is shown in Figure 2.355b. At this point, the control spool has already allowed a considerable movement of the plunger before the cut-off bore in the plunger has been uncovered; this port exposure instantly drops the pressure and terminates the injection.

Further pumping movement of the plunger causes the fuel in the pumping chamber to be returned to the pump cavity. With the spool set in this maximum fuel position, which corresponds to the fuel requirement for starting, a movement of the control spool to an extreme position away from the distributor head reduces the output to a minimum; this is the spool setting for slow running.

Fuel shut-off

The 'no fuel' or 'stop' position is provided by a solenoid-operated valve; this cuts off the fuel supply to the inlet passage when the 'ignition' key is switched off.

Distributor plunger drive

The plunger must be rotated and reciprocated and Figure 2.356 shows how this is achieved.

Rotation of the drive shaft, at half crankshaft speed (for a four-stroke engine), is transmitted via a yoke and cam plate to provide rotary motion to the pump plunger.

Reciprocating motion is provided by the rotation of a cam plate as it moves over four roller followers fixed to a roller ring. In a pump suitable for a four-cylinder engine, four lobes are formed on the cam plate and contact between the plate and rollers is maintained by two strong plunger return springs. A yoke positioned between the drive shaft and the cam plate allows the plate to move axially while still maintaining a drive.

Pressure valve

A delivery valve having a similar construction to that used on in-line pumps is fitted in the distributor head

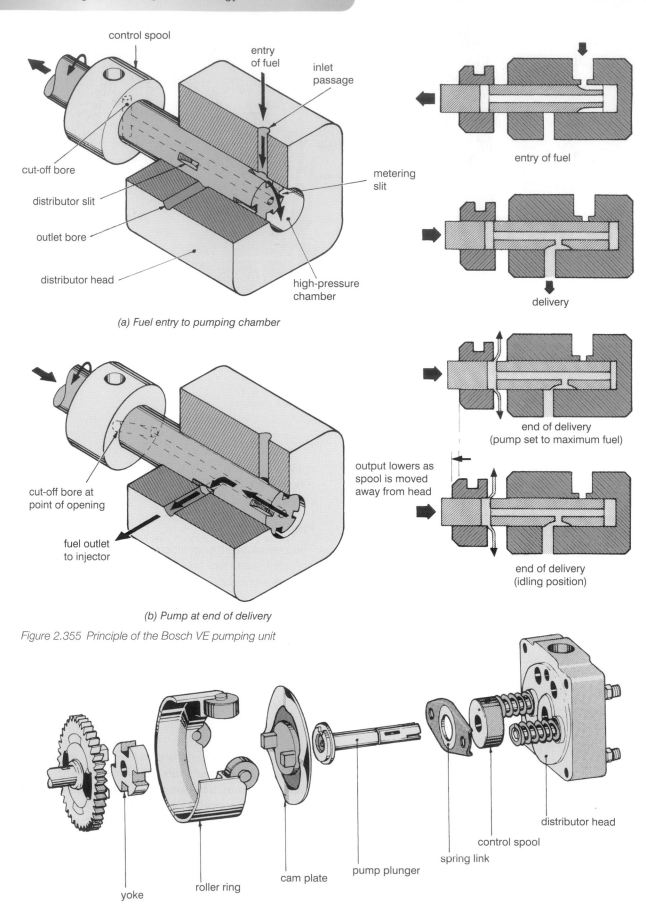

control spool

entry of fuel

inlet passage

cut-off bore

distributor slit

outlet bore

distributor head

metering slit

high-pressure chamber

entry of fuel

delivery

(a) Fuel entry to pumping chamber

cut-off bore at point of opening

fuel outlet to injector

output lowers as spool is moved away from head

end of delivery (pump set to maximum fuel)

end of delivery (idling position)

(b) Pump at end of delivery

Figure 2.355 Principle of the Bosch VE pumping unit

distributor head

control spool

spring link

yoke

roller ring

cam plate

pump plunger

Figure 2.356 Plunger drive

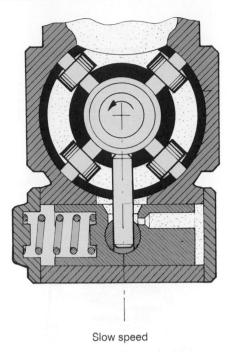

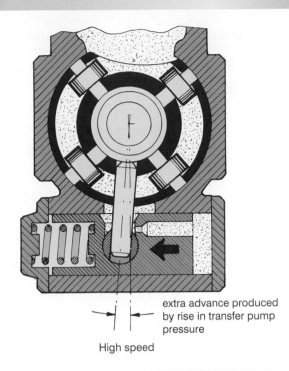

extra advance produced
by rise in transfer pump
pressure

Slow speed   High speed

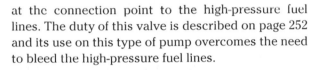

Figure 2.357 Principle of the automatic advance

at the connection point to the high-pressure fuel lines. The duty of this valve is described on page 252 and its use on this type of pump overcomes the need to bleed the high-pressure fuel lines.

Automatic injection advance unit

The roller ring assembly is not fixed rigidly to the casing; instead, it can be partially rotated through an angle of up to 12° to allow the automatic advance mechanism shown in Figure 2.357 to vary the injection timing.

When the pump is rotated, fuel under pressure from the transfer pump is delivered to the timing advance chamber via the pump cavity. A rise in the pump speed causes the transfer pump pressure and flow to increase; this moves the timing-advance piston against its spring, which in turn, causes the actuating pin to rotate the roller ring in a direction opposite to the DOR of the drive shaft.

Governor

The Bosch VE pump is fitted with either a two-speed or an all-speed governor. The layouts of these types of governor are similar, but differ in the arrangement of the control springs.

Figure 2.358 shows the main construction of a two-speed governor. This type controls the engine during the phases of idling and maximum-speed operation. At other times, the driver has near-direct control of the quantity of fuel delivered and hence the power output of the engine.

The centrifugal governor, which consists of a series of flyweights, is driven from the drive shaft through gears having a ratio that steps up the speed. The high-speed flyweight rotation given by this ratio ensures good sensitivity of the governor, especially during the idling phase.

An increase in engine speed, and the associated centrifugal action on the flyweights, produces an outward force that pushes a sliding sleeve against a control lever system. Movement of this lever, which is connected at its lower end to the control spool on the pumping plunger, can only take place when the sliding sleeve is able to overcome the reaction of the spring that is in use at that time.

Starting

With the accelerator pedal half-depressed and the governor stationary, the starting spring pushes the sliding sleeve towards the flyweights and moves the control spool to the maximum fuel position.

Idling

When the engine starts, the release of the accelerator combined with the outward movement of the flyweights, causes the lever to move the control spool to the minimum fuel position. When the engine is operating in this phase, smooth idling is obtained by the interaction of the flyweights and idling spring.

With the accelerator pedal lever against the adjustable idling stop, any small speed increase causes the flyweights to exert a larger force on the

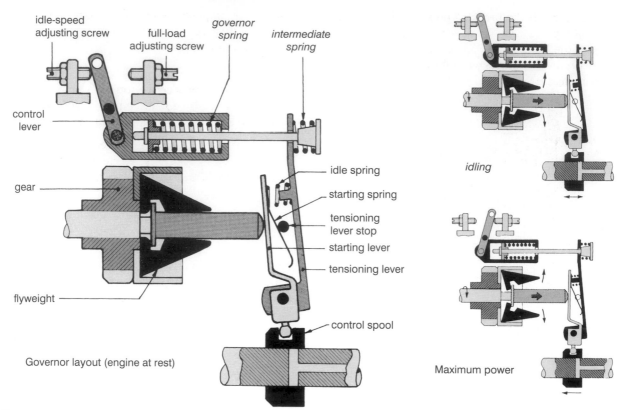

Figure 2.358 Governor – Bosch VE mechanical type

sliding sleeve. This slightly compresses the idling spring and, as a result, the spool control lever moves the spool and reduces the fuel delivery.

Any slight drop in engine speed produces the opposite action, so smooth idling under governor control is obtained.

Mid-range operation

Once the idling range has been exceeded the larger governor force puts the idling and starting springs out of action. At this stage the intermediate spring comes into use to extend the idle control range and so smooth the transition from idle to mid-range operation. The intermediate spring is stronger and provides a flexible link between the driver's pedal and the control spool lever, so that when the accelerator pedal is depressed a slight delay in engine response is introduced.

Beyond this phase any movement of the accelerator produces a direct action on the control spool.

Maximum speed

During mid-range operation, the preload of the main governor spring causes the spring assembly to act as a solid block. But when the engine reaches its predetermined maximum speed, the force given by the flyweights equals the spring preload.

Any further speed increase allows the flyweights to move the spool control lever. This reduces the quantity of fuel being delivered and so keeps the engine speed within safe limits.

2.33.6 Injectors

The purpose of the injector or sprayer is to break up the fuel to the required degree and deliver it to the combustion region in the chamber. This atomisation and penetration is done by using a high pressure to force the fuel through a small orifice.

Vehicles in the UK use a type of injector that incorporates a valve. This closed system is responsive to pump pressure – raising the pressure above a predetermined point allows the valve to open, and stay open until the pressure has dropped to a lower value. The 'snap' opening and closing of the valve give advantages that make this system popular.

The complete injector (Figure 2.359a) consists of a nozzle and holder, which is clamped to form a gas-tight seal in the cylinder head. A spring, compressed by an adjusting screw to give the correct breaking (opening) pressure, thrusts the needle on to its conical seat. Fuel flows from the inlet nipple through a drilling to an annular groove about the seat of the needle. A thrust, caused by fuel acting on the conical face X, will overcome the spring and lift the needle when the pressure exceeds the breaking pressure. The opening of the valve permits discharge of fuel until the pressure drops to the lower limit. Any fuel that flows between the needle and body acts as a lubricant for the needle before being carried away by a leak-off pipe.

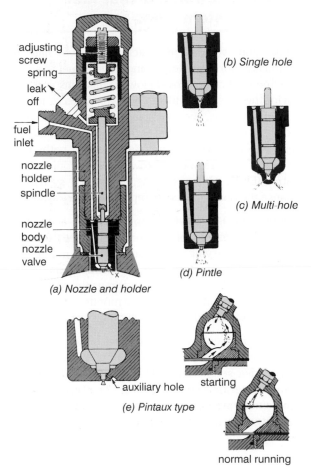

Figure 2.359 The injector

Nozzle types

There are three main types of nozzle:

- Single-hole
- Multi-hole
- Pintle

Single-hole (Figure 2.359b)

A single orifice, which may be as small as 0.2 mm (0.008 in), is drifted in the nozzle to give a single jet form of spray. When this nozzle is used with indirect injection systems, a comparatively low injection pressure of 80–100 bar is used.

Multi-hole (Figure 2.359c)

Two or more small orifices, drilled at various angles to suit the combustion chamber, produce a highly atomised spray form. Many engines with direct injection systems use a four-hole nozzle with a

high operating pressure of 150–250 bar. A long-stem version of this type simplifies the accommodation of the injector in the head.

Pintle (Figure 2.359d)

Swirl chambers can accept a soft form of spray, which is the form given by a pintle type of nozzle when set to operate at a low injection pressure of 110–135 bar.

A small cone extension on the end of the needle produces a conical spray pattern and increases the velocity of the fuel as it leaves the injector. This type tends to be self-cleaning.

The elimination of heater plugs on some light IDI engines has been made possible by the invention of a special pintle nozzle known as the pintaux (pronounced 'pintawks') type (Figure 2.359e). Starting conditions produce a small needle lift, and so fuel passes through the small auxiliary hole and is directed to the hottest part of the chamber. Under normal running pressures, the full lift of the needle discharges the fuel through the main orifice.

2.33.7 Injector servicing

With the engine at its operating temperature, the colour of the exhaust smoke, if any, acts as a guide to injector operation and is also used to assess the condition of an engine. The general rules relating to smoke colour are as outlined below.

Black smoke

This colour results when all the injected fuel is not being burnt. It means that either the engine is receiving too much fuel or is receiving insufficient air (rich mixture).

The fuel will not be completely burnt if the injector fails to atomise the fuel correctly or if any engine condition, such as poor compressions or incorrect valve timing, delays the start of combustion.

The fuel-injection timing can also create a black smoke situation. If the timing is too far advanced, the compression pressures and temperature will be lower causing a delay in igniting the fuel resulting in retarded ignition point. If the injection timing is too far retarded, the injected fuel will burn rapidly due to the higher compression temperatures. The ignition point of the fuel will burn some but not all of the fuel resulting in the remainder of the fuel exiting through the exhaust as fuel particulates (black smoke).

Blue smoke

Blue smoke coming from any engine is a sign that lubricating oil is being burnt. Any mechanical condition that allows lubricating oil to enter the combustion chamber will result in blue smoke.

The engine operating condition at which smoke is emitted often acts as a guide to the cause, for example a puff of smoke emitted when the engine is started, after it has been allowed to stand idle for a few minutes, suggests that valve guides or valve stem seals are worn.

White smoke

Incorrect fuel pump timing of the engine produces this colour smoke, but it should not be confused with the natural white colour of water vapour (steam); this occurs when a cold engine is started and the steam partially condenses as it passes through the cold exhaust system.

In addition to the emission of black smoke, faulty injectors cause low-power output and intense engine knocking (diesel knock).

A faulty injector can often be traced by listening to the change in engine note, which occurs when one injector at a time is cut out by slackening the pipeline union. Before this is attempted, special personal safety precautions must be taken:

1 Diesel fuel should not be handled if it can be avoided. Where fuel is likely to come into contact with hands, gloves or a barrier cream should be used. This prophylactic cream reduces the risk of a skin inflammation disease (dermatitis).
2 Fuel oil under injection pressures can penetrate the skin, so no part of the human body should be exposed to fuel spray from an injector.
3 Eye protection in the form of safety glasses should be used to prevent fuel under pressure (low or high) from entering the eyes.
4 A well-ventilated work area, with special extraction equipment, is needed to prevent atomised fuel from being inhaled into the lungs.

Injectors should be regularly cleaned, adjusted and tested. This servicing requires special cleaning tools and equipment in order to carry out the following tests:

1 Seat tightness (front leak) – this ensures that the nozzle valve seat is sound when the pressure is below the opening pressure.
2 Needle wear (back leak) – this indicates the amount of fuel that is passing from the needle or pressure faces to the leak-off pipe.
3 Pressure setting – the opening pressure, sometimes called the breaking pressure, must be checked and, if incorrect, reset to the recommended pressure.
4 Spray pattern – the spray pattern of the injector when it is operating under its working pressure should be observed. A poorly atomised spray of streaky appearance indicates that the nozzle orifice is partially blocked.

When refitting an injector to the engine, a new seat washer should be used and the damping arrangement should be tightened to the correct torque.

2.34 Electronic diesel fuel system

Engine and vehicle manufacturers have had to continually work on developing engine fuel systems to be more efficient, provide lower emissions and also provide the consumer with more power. When we looked at petrol systems, the manufacturers moved towards electronic control systems to improve the efficiency. Diesel engines have the same development paths with the manufacturers moving towards electronic diesel control (EDC). This system is a 'bolt on' system to enhance the Bosch VE fuel pump and delivery system.

Although the Bosch VE pump is able to accurately control the amount of fuel being injected into the engine under varying load conditions, it is not able to monitor external factors, such as engine temperature, air density and emissions. With the use of EDC these additional external factors can be monitored to ensure that the diesel fuel delivery is much more precise.

Fuel delivery is controlled by the use of two actuators located within the distributor pump. These devices are called a solenoid-operated timing device and a solenoid-operated control spool. The EDC pump has many similarities in its construction with the Bosch VE-type pump, including the fuel shut-off and the fuel-delivery plunger.

Figure 2.360 shows the layout of an EDC system – inputs and outputs

Input devices of the EDC system comprise the following:

- CKP sensor
- Start of injection sensor
- Fuel temperature sensor
- Coolant temperature sensor
- Intake-air temperature sensor
- MAP sensor
- Vehicle speed signal
- Throttle position sensor
- Servo unit potentiometer (drive potentiometer) on quantity servo control unit
- Clutch switch
- Brake switches
- Cruise control selector (if fitted)

CKP sensor

The engine flywheel has a reluctor disc attached to it to provide a reference for the CKP sensor. The reluctor ring consists of equally positioned pins around the circumference of the flywheel. These allow

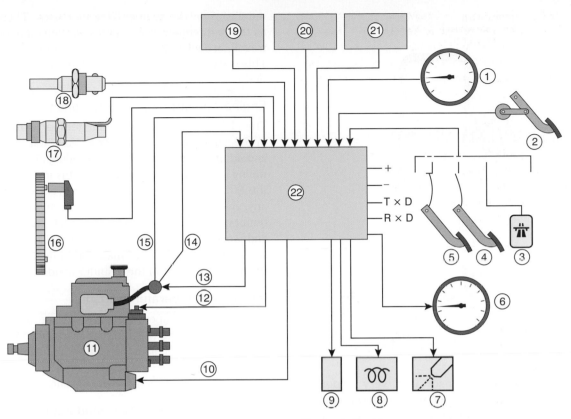

Figure 2.360 Layout of an EDC system showing inputs and outputs with EGR

1   vehicle speed signal
2   throttle position sensor – linked to accelerator pedal
3   cruise control selector (optional)
4   brake switch
5   clutch switch
6   engine speed signal
7   diagnostic lamp
8   glow plug lamp
9   heater time relay
10 injection timing device
11 fuel-injection pump

12 stop solenoid
13 quantity servo control unit
14 quantity servo control unit potentiometer
15 fuel temperature sensor
16 CKP sensor
17 start of injection sensor
18 coolant temperature sensor
19 MAP sensor
20 mass airflow sensor
21 EGR modulator valve
22 ECU

the CKP sensor to generate a signal to establish the engine speed and position. The CKP sensor can be the inductive type or Hall effect type, depending on the manufacturer and age of the engine. The CKP sensor is usually mounted in the gearbox bell housing and sits pointing adjacent to the flywheel and reluctor ring. The inductive-type CKP sensor has a hardened plastic body with a permanent magnet situated in the centre. The CKP sensor has a critical air gap between the tip of the sensor and the reluctor ring, where a magnetic flux is created as the flywheel rotates and the reluctor ring pins pass the tip of the CKP sensor.

This magnetic flux is continually disturbed as the pins move past the sensor and creates a voltage pulse within the field windings around the magnet in the sensor. This voltage pulse is an AC voltage and is sent to the ECU so it can calculate the engine speed and position.

As the flywheel rotates through a complete revolution, the voltage pulses created are transmitted to the ECU through the signal wire from the sensor. The ECU is able to determine the engine speed by calculating the number of pulses generated over a given time and it is also able to calculate the engine position through a missing series of pins around TDC; as the sensor passes the missing pins, the voltage pulse stops creating a vital TDC reference point for the ECU. The CKP sensor output voltage is used along with the start of injection sensor to calculate the injection timing more accurately.

Start of injection sensor

Figure 2.361 shows an example of an injector with an integrated start-of-injection sensor. The start-of-injection sensor, or needle-lift sensor as it is sometimes called, is fitted to one of the diesel engine's fuel injectors.

1 setting pin   4 cable
2 sensor winding   5 plug
3 pressure pin

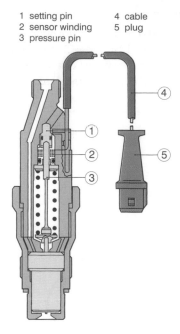

Figure 2.361 Injector with integrated start-of-injection sensor

The start-of-injection sensor is a very important component in ensuring the diesel injection timing is adjusted to be as accurate as possible during engine running. The sensor is essentially a field winding arrangement surrounding the shaft of the injection needle. The field windings receive a direct current (DC) voltage supply from the ECU, which then creates a magnetic field.

As the fuel pressure rises within the fuel injector, the needle will lift off its seat. As this takes place, the shaft of the needle will move within the field windings, interrupting the magnetic flux created. This process creates an AC voltage in the coil windings, which is then passed back to the ECU as a start-of-injection reference point.

The start of injection signal, together with the CKP sensor, is used by the ECU to calculate the exact point of injection. This is then adjusted by the ECU through the injection timing solenoid (described on page 262) to provide a continual alteration of the diesel injection timing during engine running. By altering the injection timing so accurately, the EDC system is able to provide excellent engine performance, low emissions and good fuel economy.

Fuel temperature sensor

The diesel fuel temperature sensor is used by the ECU to monitor the fuel temperature to assess its density. Cold diesel fuel is denser than hot diesel fuel. This information is important in calculating the exact amount of fuel to inject into the engine. The sensor is a NTC-type resistor. This means that the resistance will

reduce when the temperature increases. Therefore, as the fuel temperature increases, the voltage signal travelling back to the ECU via the sensor will increase. This is used by the ECU to calculate the temperature of the fuel.

Engine-coolant temperature sensor

The EDC system uses an engine temperature sensor in the same way as any other EMS. When an engine is cold, it will require different fuelling and injection timing settings to a hot engine, so it is important that the ECU is able to calculate the correct settings for any given engine temperature. The engine coolant temperature (ECT) sensor is also an NTC-type resistor and works in the same way as the fuel temperature sensor. The sensor is normally fitted near the top of the engine, usually in the cylinder head.

Intake-air temperature sensor

The intake-air temperature (IAT) sensor is used by the ECU, along with the information received from the MAP sensor, to calculate the volume and density of air entering the engine. Hot air is less dense, so the ECU will have to make adjustments to the fuelling of the engine.

Exhaust gas recirculation modulator valve

The exhaust gas recirculation (EGR) modulator valve is used to control the level of EGR taking place during specific engine running conditions. This valve is controlled by the ECU and is usually located in the engine compartment. EGR is used to introduce exhaust gases into the combustion chamber at certain engine running conditions to lower the combustion chamber temperatures. By lowering the combustion chamber temperatures, the production of NO_x is lowered.

Manifold absolute pressure sensor

The pressure inside the intake manifold is measured by the manifold absolute pressure (MAP) sensor. This is usually mounted directly on to the intake manifold or attached via a flexible pipe. The sensor is a silicon diaphragm-type sensor, which is able to react to changes in air pressure and send an electrical signal back to the ECU to calculate the fuelling and injection timing required. When the air pressure in the intake manifold changes, the pressure is detected by the sensor and this causes the silicon diaphragm to deflect. As the diaphragm deflects it changes its length and, in turn, alters the length of the resistors in the diaphragm. By changing the length of the resistors, the resistance value also changes, which then alters the electrical signal returning back to the ECU. This constantly changing voltage value returning back to the ECU is converted to a pressure reading and combined with other readings, including intake-air temperature for the ECU, to calculate the correct fuelling and injection timing for the engine.

Mass airflow sensor

The mass airflow (MAF) sensor is found within the intake pipe to ensure that it is able to monitor the volume of air entering the engine. The MAF sensor fitted to EDC systems is normally a hot film-type sensor, which has the surface of the sensor heated by the ECU through an electrical current. The temperature of the film is maintained at a constant temperature. As the air flows over the MAF sensor, it has a cooling effect on the hot film and the ECU can calculate the volume of air entering the engine by how much more current is needed to maintain the temperature of the hot film. If a larger amount of air is drawn into the engine through higher engine speeds, this will create more cooling of the film, which in turn leads to a greater current required to maintain the temperature. The ECU uses the MAF sensor information to control the levels of EGR during engine running conditions.

Vehicle speed signal

The ECU is able to calculate the vehicle speed through inputs from the ABS ECU. The vehicle speed data is used to ensure that functions such as cruise control and idle stabilisation are able to operate correctly.

Throttle position sensor

The throttle position (TP) sensor is linked directly to the throttle pedal and sends a signal to the ECU of the exact angle of movement. When the ignition is switched on by the driver, the position of the throttle is given to the ECU through the TP sensor. As the throttle pedal is moved, the TP sensor causes the voltage through the sensor to vary, which is then sent back to the ECU to calculate the throttle position. The ECU uses this information to calculate:

- required engine speed
- rate of acceleration
- rate of deceleration.

The signal from the TP sensor is set to show a positive voltage for accelerate and negative for decelerate. This information allows the ECU to provide acceleration enrichment or deceleration fuel cut-off during over-run conditions.

Servo unit potentiometer (drive potentiometer) on quantity servo control unit

The ECU uses the signal from the potentiometer to work out the position of the control spool situated within the injection pump quantity servo control unit.

Clutch switch

The clutch pedal switch is fitted to the clutch pedal to inform the ECU when the clutch pedal is depressed and released. The ECU uses this information for driver aids, such as cruise control and idle stabilisation or anti-stalling.

Brake switch

The brake pedal switch is normally a twin contact device and is used by the ECU to operate the brake lights and also to disengage cruise control along with instigating fuel limiting during braking.

2.34.1 Output devices

The output devices of the EDC system include the following:

- Quantity servo control unit
- Stop solenoid
- Injection timing device
- Heater time relay
- Diagnosis and pre-heater lamps
- Fuel consumption indicator in instrument pack

Quantity servo control unit

The quantity servo control unit is located within the fuel-injection pump. It is used to accurately control the volume of fuel delivered to the fuel injectors.

The quantity servo control unit (Figure 2.362) is a rotary magnet mounted on an eccentric shaft. The eccentric shaft is, in turn, attached to the control spool of the fuel pump. The rotary magnet has a return spring fitted and its movement is controlled by the control coil windings. Maximum fuel delivery is achieved through the magnet rotating about 60°. At one end of the eccentric shaft is the control spool and the other end is linked to the rotary potentiometer.

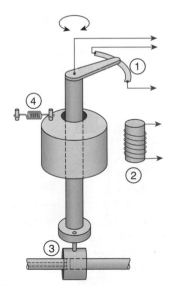

1 rotary potentiometer
2 control coil
3 control spool
4 return spring

Figure 2.362 Quantity servo control unit

As the ECU energises the control coil through input signals for the throttle pedal, the rotary magnet will move with the eccentric shaft, which then creates linear movement of the control spool. The movement of the control spool allows more or less fuel to be delivered to the injectors, depending on its position. When the control coil is de-energised, the rotary magnet and eccentric shaft will return to the start position through the action of the return spring. The control spool provides very accurate fuel delivery to achieve the required engine performance.

Stop solenoid

The stop solenoid fitted to the EDC system works in a similar way to the conventional stop device fitted to distributor-type diesel pumps. It is fitted to the high pressure part of the fuel-injection pump and receives a battery voltage supply when the ignition is switched on to open the solenoid, allowing fuel to flow. When the ignition is switched off, the supply is cut and the solenoid is closed which shuts off the fuel flow to the injectors.

Injection timing device

The diesel injection timing is controlled by the injection timing device (Figure 2.363). This component consists of a spring-loaded plunger and solenoid and is fitted in the fuel-injection pump assembly. The injection timing device moves through the influence of fuel pressure within the pump. The operation of the solenoid is controlled by the ECU sending a pulse frequency signal to switch the solenoid on and off at various rates, depending on engine speed and load.

To retard the injection timing, the solenoid is energised, which results in a fuel pressure drop inside the pump. To advance the timing, the solenoid is de-energised, which results in a fuel pressure increase inside the pump.

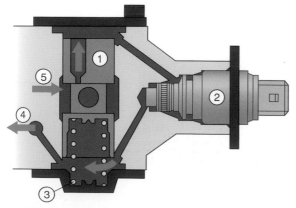

1 plunger
2 solenoid
3 spring
4 pump feed pressure
5 pump internal pressure

Figure 2.363 Injection timing device

Heater time relay

As with normal conventional diesel engines, the EDC system utilises glow plugs to improve cold-engine starting. The time that the glow plugs are switched on with the EDC system is controlled by the heater time relay through the ECU; the length of time will depend on variables such as engine temperature and ambient temperature.

Fuel-injection pump

The fuel-injection pump (FIP) in Figure 2.364 is driven from the crankshaft in the same way as a conventional distributor diesel pump. This can be through chain, belt or gear drive. The pump is a vane-type arrangement and it delivers fuel under high pressure to the fuel injectors. The fuel quantity and pressure is regulated by the movement of the control spool (described on page 261). As the control spool is moved through the signals received from the TP sensor, the fuel-delivery rate will be increased or decreased depending on the engine requirements. The fuel pump assembly contains the following components, which either send or receive signals from the ECU.

Fuel quantity servo unit

This component regulates the amount of fuel delivered to the injectors by moving the control spool.

Servo unit potentiometer

The servo unit potentiometer is used by the ECU to calculate the exact position of the control spool for accurate fuelling of the engine.

Injection timing device

The injection timing device continually regulates the injection timing of the engine through the internal pump pressure.

Fuel temperature sensor

The fuel temperature sensor references the fuel temperature and sends the signal back to the ECU to finely adjust the fuelling requirements of the engine.

Stop solenoid

The stop solenoid cuts off the fuel supply to the pump when the ignition is switched off and allows fuel delivery when the ignition is switched on.

Due to the increase in vehicle crime, manufacturers have to fit immobilisers to vehicles to prevent the vehicle from being driven away without the owner's permission. Earlier immobiliser systems used simple devices that isolated the fuel-delivery plunger or cut off the power supply to the fuel-delivery pump. More modern systems now incorporate coded signals from

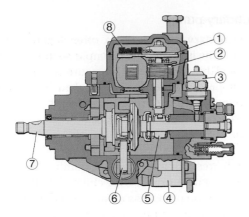

1 rotary potentiometer
2 quantity control servo unit
3 stop solenoid
4 injection timing device solenoid valve
5 control spool
6 timing device plunger
7 drive shaft
8 fuel temperature sensor

Figure 2.364 EDC fuel-injection pump

transponders located within the ignition key which send coded messages to the ECU. If the ECU does not recognise the coded message, the ECU will not permit the engine to start.

Transponder: a transmitter that sends a signal to a receiver device. This can be a coded, encrypted signal or straightforward radio signal.

2.34.2 Electronically controlled common rail diesel fuel system

The following information is based on a three-litre six-cylinder engine. The principles of operation will be the same as other types of common rail diesel fuel-injection systems.

The common rail engine is equipped with a high-pressure common rail fuel-injection system. With this fuel-injection process, a high-pressure pump delivers a uniform level of pressure to the shared fuel line (the common rail), which serves all the fuel-injection valves. Pressure develops to the optimum level for smooth operation. This means that each injector nozzle is capable of delivering fuel at spray pressures of up to 1350 bar (20,250 psi).

The common rail system disconnects fuel-injection and pressure generation functions. Fuel-injection pressure is generated independently of engine speed and fuel-injection volume and is available in the fuel rail for injection to the cylinders.

The fuel-injection timing and volume are calculated in the ECU and delivered to each engine cylinder by the injectors, each of which is actuated by energising the appropriate solenoid valve.

The fuel system is divided into two sub-systems:

- Low-pressure system
- High-pressure system

1 air-mass meter	4 high-pressure accumulator(rail)	7 coolant temperature sensor
2 ECU	5 injectors	8 fuel filter
3 high-pressure pump	6 crankshaft speed sensor	9 accelerator-pedal sensor

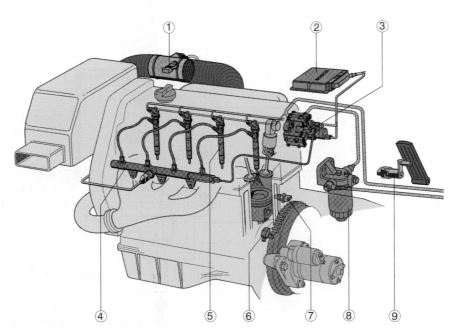

Figure 2.365 A common rail fuel system

The low-pressure system features the following components:

- Fuel tank
- Advance delivery pump
- Outlet protection valves
- Auxiliary delivery pump
- Fuel filter with inlet pressure sensor
- Pressure relief valve (LP system)
- Fuel cooler

The high-pressure system features the following components:

- High-pressure pump
- High-pressure common rail
- Pressure control valve
- Rail pressure sensor
- Injectors

The low-pressure system pressure is approximately 1.5–5 bar (22.5–75 psi) and returns pressure of less than 0.6 bar (9 psi). The pressure in the high-pressure end is 200–1350 bar (3000–20,250 psi).

Fuel tank

The fuel tank is usually constructed from moulded plastic. It incorporates a low-pressure advance delivery pump, fuel sender unit and a rollover valve to prevent fuel leakage through the vent in the event of an accident.

Fuel advance delivery pump

The electrical fuel pump is located inside the fuel tank. The pump transports fuel from the fuel swirl pot towards the engine. The pump is controlled by the ECU via the fuel pump relay.

Secondary pump

The secondary fuel pump is often located on the outside of the fuel tank. The pump is an in-line electric pump and boosts the fuel pressure for delivery to the high-pressure pump. The pump is activated at the same time as the electric fuel pump by the ECU controlling the fuel pump relay.

High-pressure fuel-injection pump

The high-pressure fuel-injection pump is located on the engine and is driven by a chain or belt from the crankshaft. The pump has an approximate maximum delivery pressure of 1350 bar.

The high-pressure fuel pump fitted to a common rail diesel fuel system is the vital link between the low-pressure and the high-pressure fuel systems. The high-pressure pump has to make sure that there is the right quantity of fuel delivered at the right pressure over all of the operating conditions of the engine. This will also include the delivery of additional fuel, which can be required to assist in rapid starting of the engine where an increase in fuel rail pressure is required. Figure 2.366 shows the high-pressure pump in detail.

Diesel fuel is delivered via a fine tolerance filter to the high-pressure fuel pump inlet port and also the safety valve which is located behind the inlet part of the pump. Diesel fuel is then directed through the throttle bore into the low-pressure duct. The low-pressure duct is directly connected to the cooling and lubrication circuit of the high-pressure pump; it does not have an engine oil feed for lubrication.

1. cut-out valve
2. exhaust valve
3. sealing unit
4. high-pressure connection to fuel rail
5. pressure control valve
6. ball valve
7. fuel return
8. fuel supply
9. safety valve
10. low-pressure duct
11. pump drive shaft
12. eccentric cam
13. pump element
14. element chamber
15. suction valve

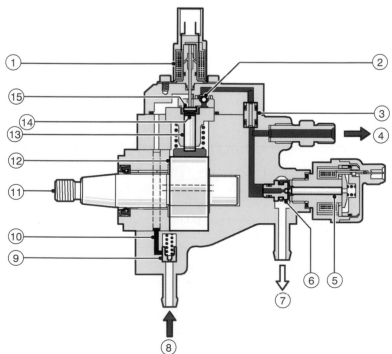

Figure 2.366 Common rail high-pressure fuel

The pump drive shaft is driven via a chain or belt drive from the crankshaft at more than half of the engine speed (usual max. 3300 rpm). The high-pressure pump is often a three-piston type with an eccentric cam acting upon the three pistons. The pump pistons move up and down depending on the cam shape.

If fuel pressure within the low-pressure duct rises higher than the pressure required to open the suction valve (0.5–1.5 bar, 7.5–22.5 psi), the advance delivery pump will be able to force fuel under pressure into the cylinder chamber when the piston moves down its bore on the suction stroke. During the time that the fuel is forced into the cylinder chamber, the intake valve will close if the piston reaches a point where the dead centre is exceeded. At this point, the fuel will be sealed in the cylinder chamber. The fuel is then compressed by the piston in the intake line. The exhaust valve will open when the desired pressure is achieved in the fuel rail. The highly compressed fuel then enters the high-pressure fuel system.

The pistons within the pump will continue to deliver fuel under pressure until they reach the TDC point known as the delivery stroke. As the pistons go beyond this point, the pressure will then fall, which in turn closes the outlet valve. The fuel will no longer be under pressure and the pistons will move downwards towards the suction stroke.

During this operation, if the pressure within the cylinder chamber falls below the pressure in the low-pressure chamber, the intake valve will open to allow the start of the process again.

The high-pressure fuel pump continually operates to ensure that there is sufficient high-pressure fuel in the fuel rail. The rail pressure is regulated by the pressure control valve.

As mentioned previously, the high-pressure fuel pump generates the pressure required in the fuel system through the use of a three-piston radial pump arrangement. This allows three delivery strokes per revolution of the high-pressure pump, giving a uniform load on the engine during its operation.

The power required to drive the high-pressure fuel pump will increase with engine speed and the set pressure in the fuel rail, known as delivery pressure. Due to the high-pressure pumps fitted to common rail diesel engines needing to provide large quantities of fuel, there is normally an excess amount of compressed fuel available during engine idling or low-load conditions. As this excess fuel is no longer subjected to pressure once it has left the pump and flowed away in the return line to the fuel tank, the initial energy created during compression is also lost and heats the fuel.

The excess fuel returned to the fuel tank down the return line is also passed through a fuel cooler to prevent the fuel from heating too much.

Pressure control valve

On the common rail diesel engine, the fuel pressure control valve is located at the high-pressure pump.

The function of the fuel pressure control valve is to maintain the fuel pressure in the fuel rail according to the requirements of the engine; this is based on engine load and speed. If at any point the pressure in the fuel rail becomes too high, the fuel pressure control valve will open allowing some of the volume of fuel to pass back to the fuel tank via a collector line. When fuel pressure is too low, the control valve will close to allow pressure to build.

The pressure control valve is activated by the ECU through an armature via a coil field winding. A ball is pressed into a seal by the armature, which acts to create a tight seal between the high and low-pressure side of the fuel rail. At times when the armature is not activated, the ball is able to return to its seat by the action of a return spring.

The pressure control valve has two control circuits:

- Electrical control circuit for setting a variable pressure value in the rail
- Mechanical control circuit for equalising high-frequency pressure fluctuations

The function of the electrical control circuit is to act as a compensator for any slow pressure fluctuations in the fuel rail and the mechanical system compensates for the faster pressure fluctuations. At times when the pressure control valve is not activated, the high pump pressure is exerted on the intake side of the control valve. Due to the control valve not being energised, the pressure will build up to a point where the pump pressure is greater than the spring force holding the ball on its seat. At this point, the valve will be forced open by pump pressure. This pressure will be set to about 100 bar (1500 psi).

At a point when the fuel rail pressure is required to increase, the control valve will be activated providing a magnetic force along with the spring. The pressure control valve is modulated between mechanical spring force and electromagnetic force until there is a balance of pressure between each force. The force of the armature through magnetic force is directly controlled by the current sent from the ECU. The current is pulsed at a relatively low frequency to create a modulation of the pressure control valve.

Fuel rail

The common rail diesel engine is equipped with a fuel rail in a similar fashion to petrol fuel injection. The common fuel rail is fitted along the cylinder head in parallel with the fuel injectors.

The function of the fuel rail is to supply the fuel injectors with the right amount of fuel at the right pressure. This allows the injectors to have a constant fuel pressure, even when the injectors are opened and closed, providing the engine with very accurately metered amounts of fuel. The fuel rail is subjected to very high fuel pressures and care should be taken if working in this area. Fuel pressure should always be relieved before removing any components.

In most cases, the fuel rail will have a fuel pressure sensor fitted either at the end of the rail or in the middle. This monitors the fuel pressure and informs the ECU if it requires more pressure from the pump or less.

Fuel rail pressure sensor

On the common rail engine, the fuel rail pressure sensor is usually fitted into the rail at one end or in the middle. The function of the sensor is to monitor the fuel pressure in the rail and inform the ECU through a voltage signal. Figure 2.367 shows the fuel pressure sensor.

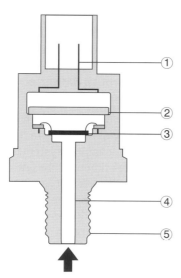

1 electrical connections
2 evaluation switch
3 diaphragm with sensor elements
4 high-pressure connection
5 retaining thread

Figure 2.367 Fuel rail pressure sensor

The fuel pressure sensor works in a similar way to the MAP sensor. The sensor has a diaphragm that consists of a semiconductor material. As the fuel pressure fluctuates, it will act on the diaphragm and alter the shape. As the shape is stretched through pressure the resistance value of the sensor will change. This continual alteration of resistance changes the voltage signal coming out of the sensor back to the ECU. The ECU will be able to recognise and continually change voltage values to work out the pressure in the rail.

The pressure sensor has a supply voltage of 5V, which is the same for most sensors on the EMS. As the resistance changes in the sensor, due to the pressure acting on the diaphragm, the returning voltage will increase and decrease around 5V. The deflection of the diaphragm is related to approximately 1 mm per 500 bar (7500 psi) pressure. It is vital that the system is able to monitor the fuel rail pressure very accurately to maintain the correct fuelling of the engine. If the fuel rail pressure sensor fails, the ECU will utilise an emergency function by working with the pump pressure control valve until the vehicle can be repaired.

2.34.3 Injectors

The injectors are arranged in the central area above the combustion chambers in the cylinder head. Figure 2.368 shows the injectors in detail.

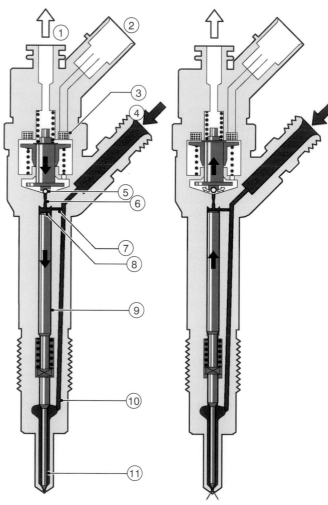

1 fuel return (outlet)
2 electrical connection
3 activation unit 2/2 solenoid valve
4 fuel supply (inlet), high pressure from rail
5 valve control chamber
6 ball valve
7 inlet throttle
8 outlet throttle
9 valve control piston
10 supply channel to nozzle
11 nozzle needle

Figure 2.368 Common rail fuel injectors

The injector can be divided into four main sections:

- Hole nozzle with injector needle
- Hydraulic servo system
- Solenoid valve
- Connections and fuel channels

The high-pressure connection (4) guides the fuel through the channel (10) to the nozzle and also through the supply throttle (7) in the control chamber (5). The control chamber is connected to the fuel return line (1) by the outlet throttle (8), which is opened by a solenoid valve. When the outlet throttle is closed, hydraulic force on the valve piston (9) exceeds that on the pressure stage of the injector needle (11). Subsequently, the injector needle is pressed into the seat and seals the high-pressure channel off from the engine compartment. Fuel cannot enter the combustion chamber, although it is constantly pressurised at the high-pressure connection.

When the injector activation unit is actuated, the outlet throttle is opened. This reduces the pressure in the control chamber, and therefore the hydraulic force on the valve piston.

As soon as the hydraulic force drops below that on the pressure stage of the injector needle, the injector needle opens, which allows the fuel to enter the combustion chamber through the spray apertures. This indirect activation of the injector needle via a hydraulic force increasing system is used because the force required to open the injector needle using the solenoid valve cannot be produced directly. The control quantity required in addition to the fuel quantity injected enters the fuel return line via the control chamber throttle.

In addition to the pilot control volume, fuel is also lost (leakage quantity) at the nozzle needle and valve piston guides. The control and leakage quantities can be up to 50 mm^3 per stroke. They are guided back to the fuel tank via the fuel return line with a manifold, to which the overflow valve, high-pressure pump and pressure control valve are connected.

The function of the injector can be subdivided into four operating statuses when the engine is running and the high-pressure pump is delivering fuel:

- Injector closed (under high pressure)
- Injector opens (start of injection)
- Injector fully open
- Injector closes (end of injection)

At a point when the engine has stopped and the fuel pressure in the fuel rail has fallen, the nozzle spring will close the injector. When the injector is at rest the solenoid valve, called a 2/2 solenoid valve, will not be activated so will be closed. Because the 2/2 solenoid is not activated the throttle will be closed, so the ball valve will be pressed into the lodgement by the valve spring force. The fuel pressure in the fuel rail will now accumulate in the valve control chamber and the same pressure will be felt at the chamber volume of the nozzle. The fuel pressure forces applied to the control piston and the spring pressure to the nozzle ensures that the injector needle is closed at this stage.

At a point when the injector is activated by the ECU, the 2/2 solenoid valve is activated by a sharp current input. This ensures that the valve is opened very quickly. The force of the valve spring and armature is overcome by the force of the electromagnet, which causes the final throttle to open.

The current applied to the electromagnet is lowered after approximately 450 milliseconds to create a holding current. This is possible due to the reduced air gap between the valve and the magnet.

At the point when the control valve is opened, the drain throttle will allow fuel to leave the valve control chamber and flow to the cavity above and then to the fuel return line back to the fuel tank. As the pressure in the valve control chamber drops, the pressure in the chamber volume of the nozzle will be higher as this is subjected to the fuel rail pressure from the high-pressure pump. The result is that the lower pressure now acting upon the control piston is overcome by the pressure at the nozzle and the injector needle will start to open to provide injection of fuel.

The injector opening speed is dependent on the difference in fuel throughput between the inlet and outlet throttle. The control piston will reach its maximum stroke after about 2.0 mm; at this point it will be held there supported by a cushion of fuel. The cushion of fuel is provided due to the flow of fuel from the inlet and outlet throttle. At the maximum stroke of the control piston, the injector nozzle is completely open and fuel is injected under fuel rail pressure into the combustion chamber.

At the point when the ECU has determined that the injection is finished, the 2/2 solenoid valve is deactivated and the armature is forced down under the valve spring force. The armature will act up on the ball, which then closes the throttle outlet. Wear on the ball and the lodgement is limited by the reset spring, which prevents excessive downward force. By closing the outlet throttle, the fuel pressure will accumulate in the control compartment of the inlet throttle. This increase in pressure then acts upon the head of the control piston. The pressure on the control piston will now be greater than the pressure acting upon the nozzle chamber so the injector will close. The speed of closing the injector is dependent on the fuel throughput in the inlet throttle. The injection process stops when the injector needle hits the lower limit point and rests in its seat.

Fuel filter

The fuel filter is often located in the engine compartment or, in some cases, it is fitted underneath the vehicle near the fuel tank. The function of the fuel filter is to clean the fuel before it reaches the high-pressure fuel pump, preventing wear and damage to the very fine tolerance components. In some cases, a bimetallic valve is fitted in the fuel return line to prevent heated fuel residue from mixing with cool fuel from the tank, which can cause paraffin residue to block the filter.

A fuel pressure sensor is also fitted into the fuel filter housing. This measures the fuel pressure being delivered to the high-pressure fuel pump from the low-pressure fuel pump. This sensor allows the ECU to monitor the fuel pressure flowing to the high-pressure pump and make any adjustments required to maintain a constant pressure through the pump and on to the fuel rail.

Pressure relief valve

A pressure relief valve is fitted between the fuel filter and the high-pressure pump to limit the pressure to about 2–3 bar (30–45 psi) received at the inlet to the high-pressure pump. This relieves any excess pressure at the inlet to the high-pressure pump by diverting the fuel back into the fuel return line. The pressure relief valve therefore protects the high- and low-pressure pump from overload damage.

Fuel temperature control

The temperature of the fuel is important is ensuring the common rail system operates efficiently. It is controlled by a bimetallic valve, mentioned previously, in the fuel filter section. The fuel is returned straight to the fuel tank if it is less than 85 °C. If the fuel temperature is higher than 85 °C, it is sent back to the tank via a fuel cooler, which is usually mounted at the front of the vehicle in full flow of air. When the engine starts from cold, the warm fuel is partially redirected through the secondary pump to warm the fuel further to improve cold starting. In some hotter climates the fuel cooler may also have a small electric cooling fan fitted to ensure that the fuel temperature is maintained to the correct level.

Glow plugs

The operation of glow plugs has been mentioned in the previous diesel section (page 240). Their main purpose is to improve engine starting by warming the air inside the combustion chamber. The glow plugs will also assist in reducing the amount of fuel required for cold starts and, therefore, lower the levels of black smoke. By introducing warmer air during cold starts, the injection timing does not need to be so advanced, which can cause high levels of diesel knock.

The glow plug consists of a tubular heating element that sticks out into the combustion chamber. The heating element is a wire filament encapsulated within a hardened magnesium oxide powder. A heating coil is located at the tip of the heating element. Behind the coil a control coil is fitted in series. The function of the control coil is to check that the heater coil does not overheat.

2.34.4 Common rail EMS

The common rail EMS is very similar in operation to a petrol EMS in that it works from information stored on a chip called maps. The maps are pre-programmed pieces of data that allow the EMS to determine the exact fuelling, timing and EGR requirements of the engine over any given load or speed. Figure 2.369 shows the main components in the common rail EMS

The ECU is normally an adaptive module. This means that it can 'learn' the driver and vehicle characteristics. This improves the engine running performance by continually altering the parameters depending on driving styles and also engine wear. This ongoing adjustment to the fuelling and injection timing as the engine wears means the emissions are able to be maintained at the legislated levels during the service life of the engine.

The ECU is able to determine when specific functions are operated by using a programmed strategy. The EMS has many sensors placed around the engine to provide data to the ECU enabling decisions to be made on how the engine should be run. The ECU also has the ability to instigate a fail-safe mode if a sensor fails to provide data through malfunction. This means that if a sensor such as a coolant temperature sensor fails, the ECU will use a default value for that sensor until the problem is rectified. For example, it will use a value of 40 °C to ensure that the engine continues to operate until the repair can be carried out. In cases where a default value cannot be made, such as a CKP sensor, the ECU will stop the engine.

The ECU uses stored data to operate the engine management outputs such as fuel pump or fuel injectors. This data is known as 'calibration' data and is combined with the data received from the inputs such as air temperature, coolant temperature, throttle position, etc. to determine the output signals to the **actuators**.

Actuator: a device that receives signals from the ECU to produce an operation. Examples include a fuel injector, fuel pump and EGR valve.

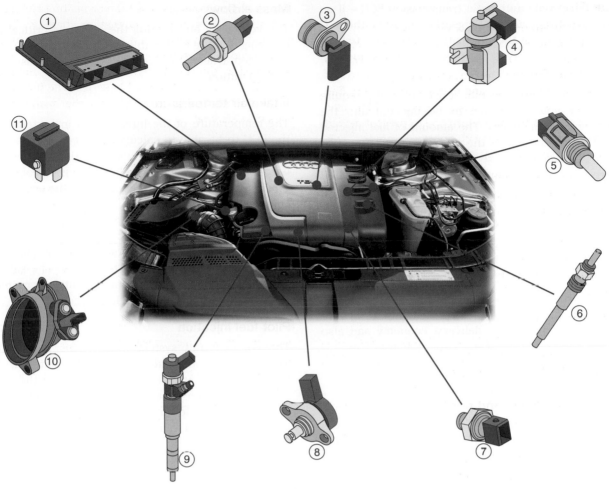

1 ECU
2 fuel rail pressure sensor
3 CKP sensor
4 EGR modulator
5 fuel temperature sensor
6 glow plugs

7 oil pressure switch
8 fuel rail pressure control valve
9 fuel injectors
10 mass airflow/inlet-air temperature sensor
11 main relay

Figure 2.369 Common rail engine management components

The ECU fitted to a common rail diesel fuel system uses strategies such as:

- smoke limitation
- active surge damping
- automatic gear change
- fuel reduction
- engine cooling
- combustion noise limitation.

At times when the engine is idling or has a full throttle position, the ECU will reference the data stored in the fuelling map to respond to the signals received from the APP sensor. To ensure that the most optimum fuelling is provided for these conditions, the ECU will utilise the data received from the following sensors:

- CKP sensor
- APP sensor

- Engine coolant sensor
- MAF/inlet air temperature sensor
- Fuel rail pressure sensor

Once the data has been received and checked against the data stored within the map, the ECU will then control the engine acceleration by using the following controllers and actuators:

- EGR modulator – this will be closed for a cleaner combustion.
- Fuel pressure control valve – this will allow an increase in fuel pressure supplied to fuel rail.
- Electronic fuel injectors – the ECU will alter the injector duration.
- Air-conditioning compressor clutch relay – this will be de-energised during wide open throttle to lower the load exerted on the engine and provide more power.

- Electronic automatic transmission ECU – if an electronic automatic gearbox is fitted, the ECU will request the automatic gearbox ECU to kick-down the gears to provide more torque and acceleration.

When the engine is cold, it will normally require a larger volume of fuel to be injected into the combustion chambers. The amount of fuel injected will be dependent on the signal received from the coolant temperature sensor. The ECU will also use this signal to determine if the glow plugs are required to be operated through the glow plug relay and, if so, for how long. When the engine is hot, the ECU will implement normal fuelling strategy as no excess fuel is required.

2.34.5 Injection control

When the engine is operating, it is essential to provide precisely the correct amount of fuel to ensure smooth power delivery, economy and also limit emissions produced at the exhaust. The ECU controls the opening duration and also the injection timing through assessing the following data.

Crankshaft speed and position

The information received from the CKP sensor is used to determine the exact engine speed and injection timing and also calculate the volume of air entering the engine.

CMP

The information received from the CMP sensor is used to calculate the positions of the camshaft against the crankshaft for injection timing control.

Injection timing map

The map stored in the ECU for injection timing is used to cross-reference the input data signals received to make sure the injection timing is accurately controlled.

Engine coolant temperature

The engine coolant temperature is used along with the data received from the CPK sensor and fuelling map to provide very precise control of the injection quantity.

Fuel rail pressure

The data received from the fuel rail pressure sensor is used by the ECU to finely tune the injector opening times, which is sometimes called the injector duty cycle, to adjust any fluctuations in fuel rail pressure. For example, if the fuel rail pressure is slightly low, the injection duration may be increased to compensate.

Mass airflow

The volume of air entering the engine is critical in ensuring that the ECU is able to calculate the volume of oxygen available for correct fuelling and also for EGR operation.

Intake air temperature

The temperature of the intake air is important for the ECU to be able to calculate and compensate as required. For example, if the air entering the engine is cold, it is denser and has a higher oxygen content. The ECU will then adjust the fuelling of the engine to compensate for this higher volume of oxygen.

Accelerator pedal position

The signals from the APP sensor are used by the ECU to monitor the demand from the driver. The signal will essentially determine the power output required from the engine for any given driving condition.

Pilot fuel injection

The common rail system utilises this facility to lower the engine noise normally associated with diesel-powered engines. The ECU will open the fuel injectors very briefly just before the main injection opening to provide an initial lower pressure flame in the combustion chamber. This helps reduce the shock of the main charge, which often causes diesel knock.

Smoke limitation

When the engine is operating at lower speeds, the turbulence in the combustion chamber is lower, which could cause issues with the fuel mixing with the air, leading to higher amounts of smoke being produced. The common rail system overcomes this by providing very high injection pressures at lower engine speeds to create excellent atomisation of the fuel as it enters the combustion chamber. Although the injection pressures are very high, the ECU will ensure that there is not too much fuel injected in relation to the amount of oxygen present.

Active surge damping

The active surge damping allows smooth gear changes to be made by the automatic gearbox, by the ECU reducing the fuelling at the point of gear change to lower the torque output momentarily. This ensures that the gear changes do not create a surge to the engine power delivery and that they are carried out almost without the driver and passengers noticing.

Variable nozzle turbocharger

The variable nozzle turbocharger (VNT) is able to continually alter the exhaust gas flow over the turbine to provide varying levels of boost. For example, when the guide vanes directing the exhaust gas are closed, the flow of exhaust gas to the turbine wheel is increased, leading to additional boost pressure.

The pressure within the intake manifold created through the boost pressure from the VNT is sent back to the ECU by a boost pressure sensor. The ECU uses this voltage signal to determine the amount of boost allowed for any given engine load condition. The boost is controlled by a boost-control solenoid valve, which is attached through a vacuum pipe to the boost-control vacuum actuator on the VNT (in a similar position to a conventional wastegate controller on a conventional turbocharger). The amount of vacuum acting upon the control actuator will depend on the ECU calculating the required level of boost for the engine at any one time. The amount of vacuum will operate between approximately 0 mbar and 640 mbar depression, depending on the engine manufacturer. When the vacuum is at its highest, the vanes in the VNT are fully closed, which provides maximum boost pressure.

Immobilisation

The ECU plays a major role in the immobilisation of the vehicle. The ECU prevents engine fuelling until it receives a valid coded signal from the immobilisation ECU. The coded signal from the immobilisation ECU is supplied in the form of a rolling code, preventing the code from being copied or bypassed. When new, the immobilisation ECU is blank and is programmed with a starting code. The code is then used as a base point for the rolling code when the immobilisation ECU is synchronised to the ECU during manufacture.

Once synchronised, the ECU and the immobilisation ECU are not interchangeable and operate as a matching pair. When a new ECU is fitted to a vehicle during service, the new immobilisation ECU must be supplied with a code that matches the vehicle. The rolling codes in the new immobilisation ECU and the existing ECU must be synchronised using diagnostic equipment.

Information for this section was based on Land Rover Technical Information on Range Rover TD6 engine 2005.

2.35 Engines – routine maintenance

2.35.1 Engine maintenance

The routine maintenance of the modern vehicle is critical to ensure that it provides reliable service throughout its life. Routine maintenance covers a wide variety of systems, with each system having different levels of service throughout their life. The technician will normally follow a manufacturer's service maintenance check schedule when carrying

out service operations to ensure that all areas are assessed, checked and serviced to the required standard. Modern vehicles have longer service intervals than earlier vehicles, this is due to the higher grade materials used in vehicle manufacturing and also the grades of lubrication now used across the engine and transmission systems. Generally, vehicles now require service maintenance at 12,000–20,000 miles. Due to the engine oils having to last up to 20,000 miles they must be of a very high grade. It is important when replacing the engine and transmission oils that the same or equivalent oil is used. The manufacturer's service data should be checked prior to using an oil to make sure it meets the required standard.

Incorrect specification oil can lead to premature wear and failure of engine and transmission components. In diesel engine vehicles the incorrect grade of engine oil can lead to blockages in the DPF system due to higher soot build-up from lower specification engine oils.

2.35.2 Engine oil and filter

Engine oil and oil filters should be changed within the recommended service periods issued by the manufacturers. This can be expressed in two ways to the driver:

- Time-based, for example every 12 months
- Mileage-based, for example every 12,000 miles

If the driver is not covering 12,000 miles in the year then obviously the engine oil will need to be changed every 12 months. Throughout its life, engine oil carries out several functions while it is circulating around the engine and its components. Engine oil lubricates, removes harmful substances, prevents corrosion, removes heat, and carries particles through to the oil filter to prevent them causing wear to the engine.

When changing the engine oil, care should be taken to wear appropriate protective clothing including:

- overalls
- safety footwear
- protective gloves.

Engine oil, especially used engine oil, is harmful to the skin and contact should be avoided or kept to a minimum. Protective gloves prevent the engine oil coming into contact with the skin and causing problems.

To change the engine oil, the engine should be run to normal operating temperature in a well-ventilated area or with exhaust extraction fitted. The vehicle should be raised using a suitable vehicle hoist or ramp. The oil filler cap should be removed to allow air to enter the engine when the sump plug is removed. A suitable oil container should be placed under the vehicle's sump and the sump plug should then be removed, taking care to avoid any scalding from the hot engine oil. The engine oil should then be left to drain for a few minutes to ensure that all of the old oil is removed. The sump plug should then be wiped and fitted with a new sealing washer and refitted to the sump and tightened to the correct torque.

The engine oil filter is then removed using a suitable filter wrench or strap. Again, care should be taken to avoid contact with the oil as it escapes from the filter and housing. Wipe the filter housing and sealing area and fit the new oil filter. It is good practice to smear a thin layer of oil on the oil filter sealing ring when refitting, as this will improve the seal and assist when removing the filter again during the next service. Tighten the new filter (cartridge type) by hand. Clean around the engine to avoid any engine oil dripping from the engine.

Lower the vehicle and fill the engine with the correct specification engine oil and check the level using the dip stick fitted to the engine. **Note**: do not overfill the engine as this will cause damage and can increase exhaust emissions due to the burning of the engine oil.

Ensure that the waste engine oil is disposed of correctly within the local authority guidelines.

Figure 2.370 Engine oil and filter change

2.35.3 Engine-cooling system

The coolant level, as with other fluids, is checked visually during each of the periodic services. The coolant level will naturally drop over a long period of time so it must be replenished when required. Low coolant level may also indicate a leak or fault within the engine; this should be investigated further to avoid damage to the engine caused by overheating.

Precautions

When removing the radiator cap when the engine is hot, great caution must be used. The following procedure must be used:

- Place a thick cloth over the radiator cap.
- Start to loosen the cap slowly until steam starts to come out.
- Leave the cap in that position until the steam stops.
- Loosen the cap further until steam starts to come out again.
- Leave the cap in that position until the steam stops.
- Continue this procedure until the cap is released and no steam is being emitted.

Refill the radiator with the correct coolant fluid, as some fluids are water-based and some fluids are oil-based. If the engine is using oil-based coolant, there is usually a sticker under the bonnet to warn the driver. When replenishing the coolant fluid, make sure the correct amount of antifreeze is added.

Antifreeze requires replacing approximately every three years or 36,000 miles. To check the antifreeze condition and mixture ratio a special tool called a hydrometer should be used. This tool assesses the specific gravity of the coolant mixture to determine the ratio of antifreeze and water.

Figure 2.371 Checking antifreeze strength

Condition of cooling system components

The engine-cooling system has to cope with a range of environmental conditions during its operation. During very harsh cold weather, the cooling system has to be able to protect the engine against freezing and allow the engine to warm up quickly for the passengers and also for the engine to be operating in its peak temperature. During hot weather, the cooling system has to be able to maintain the peak engine running temperature without overheating while in slow-moving traffic and also during cruising speeds. To ensure that the cooling system continues to meet these requirements, regular checks should be made to the cooling system components:

- Check all hoses for damage and cracking, especially where they connect the engine to the radiator as these hoses are subjected to continual flexing.
- Check the condition of the drive belts for the water pump and fan (if engine driven).
- Check the condition of the radiator cap or expansion tank cap to make sure the seal is in good working order. Faulty seals will cause the engine to overheat as the water is unable to be pressurised.
- Check for general leaks around the cooling system connections.
- Check the condition of the radiator and carefully clean any debris that may be caught in the fins as this can affects the cooling capability of the radiator.

2.35.4 Valve clearances

The intake and exhaust valves operate with a small clearance tolerance between the valve and the camshaft. This clearance is important as it allows for heat expansion during engine operation. If the clearance gap is too small when the engine is cold, the engine may suffer a misfire condition as the engine warms up due to the valve staying open slightly as the components expand. If the gap is too large, a great deal of noise will usually be heard as the valves are opened and closed by the camshaft, the valve lift will be less as the gap has to be taken up before the valve is opened.

In order to make sure the engine operates correctly, engines *not* fitted with hydraulic followers require inspection during service to check the valve clearances. Before the valve clearances are checked, it is best practice to check the manufacturer's data for the setting procedures as these differ between engines. Some engines require adjustment through a simple arrangement (Figure 2.372), with a lock nut and threaded adjuster. Other engines require the technician to measure the clearances and the replace shims located on the camshaft follower to gain the correct valve clearance. In all cases, the technician will use feeler blades to check the clearance between the camshaft and the valve follower.

2.35.5 Ancillary drive belts

The drive belts used to operate components (including power-steering pumps, fans, alternators, high-pressure pumps for suspension, air-conditioning, etc.) utilise strong rubber belts with reinforced fibres. During the service life of these belts, it is important to check the condition of the belts looking for cracks, oil contamination or stretch. A worn belt will cause slippage when the engine is rotating, especially when the alternator or power steering is put under load. This slippage will be heard by the driver as a loud

Figure 2.372 Checking valve clearances

screech. When replacing the ancillary drive belt, it is important to make sure the tension is correct to avoid damage to the new belt and also the components being driven by the belt. Also check the pulleys and bearings of the components driven by the belt, looking for general wear and play in bearings.

The belt must be changed at the intervals laid down by the manufacturer, which can be between 24,000 miles and 100,000 miles.

When the timing belt becomes worn it can become cracked or damaged or, in severe cases, the teeth may physically come away from the belt. Depending on the vehicle and manufacturer, the amount of damage that this may cause can vary from no damage to complete destruction of the engine. As the compression ratios on modern engines are now higher for both petrol and diesel, the clearance between the valves and the pistons has been reduced, so the amount of damage caused is generally very high.

Figure 2.373 Ancillary drive belt arrangement

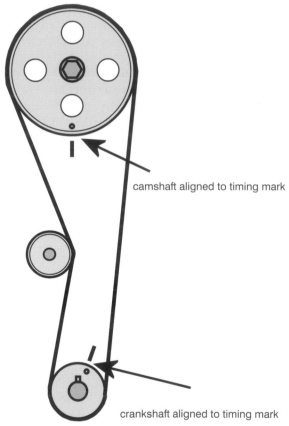

camshaft aligned to timing mark

crankshaft aligned to timing mark

Figure 2.374 Timing belt – aligning marks on cam and crank pulleys

2.35.6 Timing belt

The timing belt is used to drive the engine's camshafts, water pump and high-pressure fuel pump on common rail diesel engines and DI petrol engines.

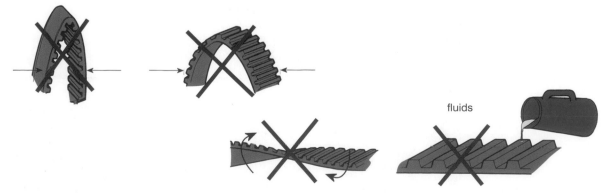

fluids

Figure 2.375 Timing belt premature failure through twisting, bending, and oil and water on belt

Precautions

- Follow manufacturer's procedures for the removal and refit of the cam belt.
- Do not bend or twist the belt.
- If refitting the same belt after a repair, ensure that it is fitted in the same DOR and not over-tensioned.
- Do not allow the belt to be contaminated with either oil or water.
- Remove any oil or water from the components on which the belt will run.
- Use a belt-tensioning tool to ensure that the belt is neither too tight nor too loose.

2.35.7 Engine – general

During the service interval the technician should check for general engine operation making sure that there are not any unusual noises or running problems. Checks for oil and coolant leaks should be carried out around the engine. If a leak is found, the area should be cleaned and rechecked to ensure the exact location is identified before work is carried out. Any engine misfires or abnormal running should be investigated to prevent longer-term damage. Initial checks on the engine's ignition system should be carried out to determine a running problem and then check compressions and mechanical components. Misfires can cause damage to other components, such as catalytic converters, so these should be rectified quickly.

2.35.8 Exhaust system

The exhaust system should be inspected as part of a routine service. Check for the security of the exhaust mountings and general condition of the exhaust system. Excessive corrosion of the exhaust system will lead to failure so it should be replaced. Any leaks from joints should be rectified, as leakage of hot exhaust gases can lead to heat damage of surrounding components. Condition of the catalytic converter should be checked visually and also through use of an exhaust gas analyser. A failure of the catalytic converter will show higher emission levels than required for the MOT. High emissions may not be the sole result of a faulty catalytic converter, so checks on the fuel and ignition system should also be made.

2.35.9 Road testing

Road testing should be use to check for faults reported by the customer and also to assess the repair that has been carried out. Only drivers with suitable insurance and driving licences should carry out this procedure. During road testing, the technician will use sight, feel and sound to check for problems with the vehicle. Over time, the technician will develop greater skills in assessing vehicles through road-testing procedures.

Figure 2.376 Exhaust system – checking mountings, joints and leaks

Figure 2.377 Carrying out a road test

2.36 Petrol fuel system – routine maintenance

2.36.1 Fuel system maintenance

The fuel system is required to store the fuel in a suitable container and supply the engine with clean fuel in the correct metered quantity across all engine operating conditions. The fuel system components that require inspection and maintenance are:

- fuel tank and fuel-supply lines
- fuel filters
- injection system.

2.36.2 Fuel tank and supply pipes

The fuel is stored in a fuel tank normally located at the rear of the vehicle. The fuel tank is normally made from plastic on more modern vehicles and is often protected by a guard to avoid any road debris damaging it. The fuel tank should be visually inspected for leaks, security and damage, the fuel lines should be checked for leaks and security and the fuel tank filler cap should be checked for correct sealing and security. The fuel filler cap has three functions:

1 Prevent fuel leakage
2 Prevent fuel vapour (HC) escaping
3 Prevent fuel from being removed from the vehicle illegally

2.36.3 Fuel filter

The fuel filter has an important role in ensuring that all fuel delivered to the engine is clean and free of any foreign particles or water. If any particles enter the fuel-injection system, they can cause damage to the injectors and pump. Therefore, it is very important to make sure the fuel filter is changed in line with the manufacturer's service requirements.

The fuel filter is normally located in a securing bracket and will have a direction of flow for the fuel when passing through it. Before removing a fuel filter, it is very important to make sure that the fuel pressure is removed from the fuel lines. The fuel system will normally hold some residual pressure when the engine is switched off, especially on fuel injected vehicles. To depressurise the fuel system it is recommended to read the workshop manual to ensure that this is done correctly. When the filter is removed, care should be taken to ensure that any fuel is collected safely to avoid any fire hazards. Replace the fuel filter and union washers if fitted, ensuring that the direction of flow is correct, and tighten the unions. For fuel-injected vehicles, turn on the ignition to run the fuel pump and check for any leaks. Run the engine and check again.

Diesel fuel filters are replaced in a similar way to this process but, in some cases, it is important to manually prime the fuel system to remove the air after replacing the fuel filter. If this is not carried out, the engine will not start. Follow the workshop manual process to ensure the operation is carried out correctly.

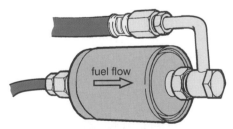

Figure 2.378 Fuel filter replacement

2.36.4 Petrol fuel injection

The modern fuel-injection system requires little maintenance during its service, especially the latest types as no physical adjustments can be made to alter the running of the engine. On systems fitted with throttle cables, these should be checked for wear and adequate free play. Any sticking cables should be replaced as they could cause a serious incident if the throttle is stuck open when the vehicle is running.

On earlier systems, the idle speed and idle mixtures could be adjusted by adjusting an air-bleed screw similar to the one shown Figure 2.379. The idle mixture was altered by adjusting a screw located in the airflow meter; this sent a signal to the ECU to alter the injection opening time during idle conditions. A shorter opening time produces less fuel and, therefore, a weaker mixture (Figure 2.379).

EMSs now do not have any physical adjustments as the parameters are controlled by the ECU through inputs from the sensors around the engine. Some systems allow adjustment only through the use of diagnostic equipment similar to that shown in Figure 2.380.

Faults on the EMS are logged in the ECU memory and the technician is able to read these faults and interrogate the ECU with the use of the diagnostic equipment. The technician can read live data from the sensors and actuators to determine the running condition of the system to diagnose engine running faults.

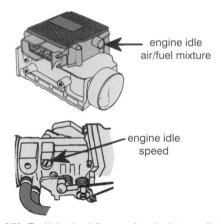

engine idle
air/fuel mixture

engine idle
speed

Figure 2.379 Fuel injection idle speed and mixture adjustments

Figure 2.380 Diagnostic test equipment connected to the vehicle to measure parameters and carry out checks on EMS

2.37 Ignition systems – routine maintenance

2.37.1 Ignition system maintenance

Lack of maintenance of ignition systems, especially Kettering-type systems, causes more breakdowns than any other engine fault. The following points outline some of the important tasks that should be periodically carried out.

Spark plugs

These should be removed at the recommended times (e.g. every 10,000 km), cleaned, re-gapped, tested (if equipment is available) and refitted. Carbon can be cleaned off with a wire brush but is best removed by sandblasting; if this method is used, then all traces of sand must be removed from the plug, especially from the thread.

The gap is measured with a feeler gauge and adjustment is carried out by bending the earth electrode.

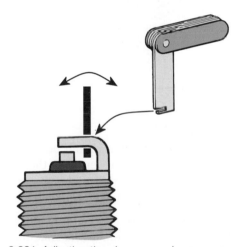

Figure 2.381 Adjusting the plug gaps using a gap gauge tool

On refitting, the plug should be tightened to the correct torque. If a torque wrench is unavailable, then the following technique can be used:

- Gasket seat – tighten 'finger-tight' and then rotate the plug one-quarter of a turn with a plug spanner.
- Taper seat – ensure that the seat is clean, tighten 'finger-tight' and then use a plug spanner to rotate the plug one-sixteenth of a turn.

Platinum- and palladium-tipped spark plugs

These types of spark plugs have a very long service life (100,000 km/60,000 miles). It is important to ensure that if the engine is fitted with these plugs as original equipment that they are replaced with the same specification, as engine running problems can be caused by using lower specification spark plugs. Gaps on these types of spark plugs are often over 1 mm so care should be taken in ensuring the correct gap is maintained.

2.37.2 Contact breaker

Contact breakers are no longer fitted to current production vehicles but an understanding of their service requirements is useful. About every 10,000 km (6000 miles) a new contact set should be fitted. After fitting the new contacts, they must be adjusted to the recommended gap. This can be measured with a feeler gauge after setting the cam in a position where the contacts are fully open.

Use of a dwell meter gives greater accuracy when setting the contact gap. An increase in the gap reduces the dwell and advances the spark; for example, if the dwell angle is reduced by 5°, then the timing will be advanced by 5°.

Ignition timing

Marks are normally provided on the crankshaft pulley to enable the ignition timing to be set. An outline procedure is as follows: first the engine is warmed up and then stopped to allow a stroboscope to be connected to plug lead 1. After restarting the engine, the slow running is set to the recommended speed and the flashing light is directed on to the moving pulley. The 'freezing' of the motion enables the position of the timing marks to be observed. (**Note**: it also gives the impression that other moving parts are stationary, so care must be taken to avoid injury.)

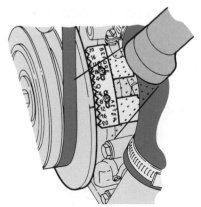

Figure 2.382 Checking of ignition timing using a strobe light

Correct timing of the spark is important. If the spark is over-advanced, pinking and perhaps engine damage will result. Retarded timing causes poor power, increased fuel consumption and overheating.

2.37.3 Maintenance of electronic systems

In addition to maintenance of common items such as spark plugs, the various electronic units are tested for serviceability by using special test sets. After making initial checks on external wiring and multi-pin connectors, individual units are then tested as recommended; if found defective, they are either exchanged or replaced.

Full EMSs require very little maintenance; any faults occurring while the engine is running are stored in the memory of the control unit. These faults can then be checked using diagnostic equipment to read the fault codes or view the system operation.

Care should be exercised when handling these extra-high-voltage units: in some cases, a shock can be fatal.

2.38 Diesel engine – routine maintenance

2.38.1 Diesel engine maintenance

The diesel engine is now very popular with customers due to its ability to provide improved fuel economy along with petrol engine performance. Modern diesel common rail fuel-delivery systems operate in a similar way to the petrol EMSs. Diesel engines and the fuel-delivery systems require extremely clean fuel to operate efficiently. Many of the components within the fuel-delivery system have very fine tolerances which, if contaminated with dirt or water, will lead to premature wear and failure.

2.38.2 Fuel system maintenance

The diesel fuel system has similar maintenance requirements to a petrol fuel system these include:

- fuel tank and supply lines
- fuel filters
- fuel-injection components.

The fuel tank and supply lines are the same as in petrol fuel systems.

Fuel filters

Diesel fuel filters are available in two different types depending on the vehicle and manufacturers' preference. These two types are:

- element-type
- cartridge-type.

Element-type fuel filter

To replace any fuel filter on a diesel engine, it is necessary to drain off the excess fuel pressure in the system and also in the fuel filter housing. This should be drained into a suitable container and disposed of correctly. To change the element-type fuel filter, it is necessary remove the lower filter housing and O rings. Clean the lower filter housing using a lint-free cloth and then remove the filter assembly. Replace the filter assembly and refit the lower housing (Figure 2.383) along with the new O rings. Tighten the housing screws and ensure the drain screw is also tightened. Loosen the bleed screw located in the top of the filter housing and bleed the fuel system using the required manufacturer's procedures. Tighten the bleed screw when all of the air is evacuated. Start the engine and check for leaks.

Figure 2.383 An element-type diesel fuel filter

Cartridge-type fuel filter

The cartridge-type fuel filter should be replaced by unscrewing the filter body and removing the complete cartridge assembly. Replace the filter and O rings and bleed the system referring to the workshop manual.

Note: always dispose of the filter assemblies in the correct manner to avoid contamination of the environment.

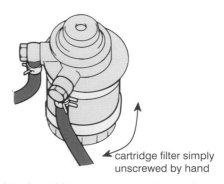

cartridge filter simply unscrewed by hand

Figure 2.384 A cartridge-type diesel fuel filter with sediment trap

Water sediment filter

Many diesel engines also have a water sediment filter fitted to the fuel system. This device traps any water held in suspension in the diesel fuel due to moisture build-up in the fuel tank assembly. It is important to ensure that all water is removed from the diesel fuel before it enters the fuel-delivery system to avoid corrosion and damage occurring to the very low tolerance components. The water sediment filter is often an integral part of the cartridge type-fuel filter assembly. It is good practice to drain the water during interim services to prevent water building up during vehicle operation. This is done by loosening the sediment filter and allowing the fuel and water to drain for a moment. Tighten the sediment filter and run the engine to check operation. Often diesel fuel systems incorporate a water-in-diesel sensor. This sensor illuminates a light on the driver's display if there is too much water present in the fuel system, warning the driver to have the water drained or filter replaced.

2.38.3 Diesel engine – general

The diesel engine requires similar checks to the petrol engine to ensure that it continues to operate efficiently. The diesel engine is required to pass a smoke test during an MOT test to ensure that it is not producing too many diesel particulates. High levels of black smoke emitted from a diesel engine indicate that too much fuel is being delivered to the engine. Checks should be made to ensure that filters are clean and injectors are not worn when diagnosing this problem. On modern common rail systems, high levels of black smoke can also be caused by a faulty high-pressure pump or faulty fuel pressure sensor causing the pump to produce too much fuel pressure. A diesel specialist should be consulted when diagnosing these types of faults.

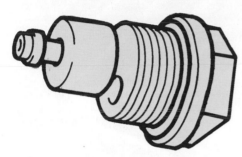

Figure 2.385 A diesel fuel water sediment filter

Figure 2.386 Diesel black smoke

3

Transmission systems

Figure 3.1 Transmission gears close up

3.1 The gearbox and gear ratios

3.1.1 Reason for a gearbox

The internal-combustion engine used in modern vehicles will operate over a limited effective speed range, for example 1500–7000 rpm, producing a comparatively low torque (turning effort). If the speed drops below the lower limit, or if the load is too great, the engine will stall and the vehicle will come to rest.

If a vehicle did not have a gearbox, the following disadvantages would soon become apparent.

Poor acceleration from rest

The clutch would have to be slipped for a considerable time to avoid stalling the engine. A road speed of about 24 kph (15 mph) would have to be reached before full engagement could take place, and during this time the driving force at the wheels (**tractive effort**) would only be slightly greater than the force opposing the motion of the vehicle (**tractive resistance**). The acceleration is governed by the difference between the tractive effort and resistance. If this difference is small, the acceleration will be poor.

Tractive effort: the force required to move an object or vehicle forward.

Tractive resistance: the opposing force that the tractive effort must overcome to create movement.

Poor hill-climbing ability

A gradient increases the resistance and this will mean that as soon as a hill is tackled, the engine will slow down and eventually stall. This could be overcome by employing a large engine with a high torque output, but it would be uneconomical.

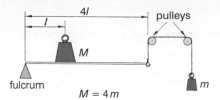

Vehicle cannot be driven at low speeds

As the vehicle speed is decreased, the engine speed will also be decreased. Slipping of the clutch would be necessary to avoid stalling if the vehicle had to be driven at low speeds.

No neutral or reverse

It would not be possible to keep the vehicle stationary without stalling, so the clutch would always have to be disengaged when the vehicle wasn't moving. This also makes the vehicle difficult to manoeuvre.

3.1.2 Gear leverage

Figure 3.2 shows a simple means of applying leverage with a person using a lever to assist the vehicle in moving forward. When the person applies effort without a lever, there is not sufficient force to provide forward motion. When using the lever and pivoting this at the bumper, the person is able to produce forward motion due to the duplication in force through the length of the lever. Indeed, the length of the lever provides a multiplication of force applied from the same amount of effort from the person.

Figure 3.2 Human effort is reduced by using a lever

Figure 3.2 highlights the importance of fitting a gearbox.

Other mechanical devices are able to produce similar results, although not necessarily using levers. Components such as gears can provide a multiplication of force from a given input. Figure 3.3a shows another simple form of lever using weights and pulleys. The force applied to the end of the lever utilising weight m and pulleys can lift a weight four times as great (weight M). This simple experiment shows that a small input force can be amplified using the lever system.

Figure 3.3b shows how two discs may be used to obtain leverage. In this example, a mass acting on shaft C will support a larger mass on shaft D. This arrangement may be considered as a simple gearbox, the engine connected to shaft C and the road wheels to shaft D. In this example, the output torque is double the engine torque, and if disc B is made three times the diameter of A, the output torque will be

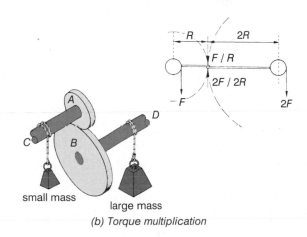

(a) Large mass lifted by a small mass

(b) Torque multiplication

Figure 3.3 Gear leverage

trebled. This appears to produce something for nothing, but speed must be taken into account. It will be seen that as the torque increases, the speed decreases proportionally and, therefore, the power remains the same, assuming the mechanism is 100 per cent efficient.

In Figure 3.3b the speed ratio (movement ratio) is also called the gear ratio, and in this case is $2:1$, which indicates that two revolutions of the input shaft are required to rotate the output shaft by one revolution.

Belts, pulleys and friction drives were used on early designs of the motor car, but the introduction of a sliding gearwheel arrangement saw these systems gradually disappear.

3.1.3 Determination of gear ratios

Obtaining a high maximum vehicle speed, combined with good acceleration and economy over the whole speed range, requires a system of gearing that allows the engine to operate at the speeds at which it develops its best performance. Maximum engine power, torque and economy all occur at different engine speeds, so this makes the task of matching the gear ratio difficult, especially when variable operating conditions and driver demands have to be taken into account.

Setting of the numerous gear ratios takes into account the engine requirement to suit a given operating condition (Table 3.1).

Table 3.1 Engine requirements

Operating condition	Requirement
Maximum vehicle speed	Maximum engine power
Maximum acceleration	Maximum engine torque
Maximum traction	Maximum engine torque
Maximum economy	Engine at mid-range speed and under light load with a small throttle opening

Today, the type of engine fitted to a light vehicle generally requires a gearbox that gives five forward speeds and a reverse (i.e. a set of five different forward gear ratios in addition to reverse gear). This gives a reasonable performance to suit most driving conditions, including economy.

There are, however, vehicles fitted with six-, seven- or even eight-speed gearboxes. It should be noted that a high gear is one that has a ratio with a low numerical value (i.e. a ratio of 1:1 is higher than the ratio of 2:1.)

The lower the gear, the greater the reduction between the engine and the road wheels; this means that, for a given engine speed, the road wheel speed is lower.

Maximum vehicle speed

Maximum vehicle speed is achieved when the vehicle is set in its highest gear and the throttle is held fully open.

To minimise friction losses in the gear that is used for most of the time, a ratio of 1:1 (direct drive) is chosen for 'top gear'. Consequently, the setting of 'top gear' is really the choosing of a final-drive ratio to suit the diameter of road wheel and engine characteristic.

Figure 3.4 shows the considerations that have to be made to ensure that a vehicle can attain a high maximum speed. It shows the balance between the power required and the power available. Data for the former is given by the brake power curve of the engine; for the latter, data is obtained by calculating the power needed to overcome the tractive resistance of the vehicle when it is moving along a level road.

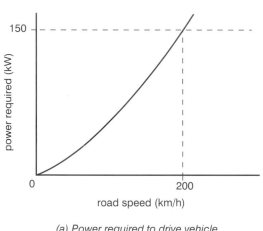

(a) Power required to drive vehicle

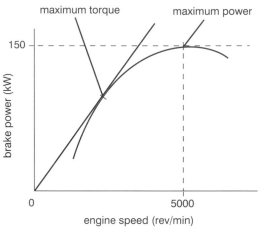

(b) Power available to drive vehicle

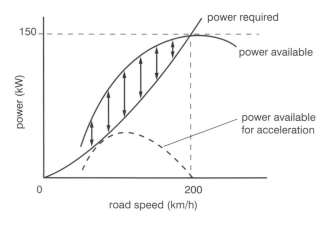

(c) Curve shows balance between power available and power required

Figure 3.4 Power graphs

Tractive resistance, sometimes called total resistance, includes:

1 air resistance – due to movement of the vehicle through the air
2 rolling resistance – due to friction between the tyre and road. Largely influenced by the type of road surface
3 gradient resistance – increases as the steepness of the incline (hill) acts against the vehicle motion.

Figure 3.4a indicates that the power needed to propel a given vehicle increases with the cube of the speed. This means that if the speed is doubled, the power required is eight times as great. In this example, a power of 150 kW is needed to drive the vehicle at 200 kph.

The power output of the engine fitted to this vehicle is shown in Figure 3.4b. This power curve shows that the engine produces a peak brake power of 150 kW at 5000 rpm.

If the maximum road speed is to be as high as possible, the gear ratio of this vehicle must be set so that the peak of the 'power available' curve occurs at a road speed of 200 kph. In this case, an engine speed of 5000 rpm drives the vehicle at 200 kph.

Overall gear ratio (gearbox ratio × final-drive ratio)

Once the relative positions of the two curves have been decided, it is then possible to examine the general performance with respect to acceleration. The vertical difference between the two curves is the surplus power available for acceleration, so this can be plotted as a separate curve to show the speed at which maximum acceleration is achieved.

Assuming friction is neglected, it must be appreciated that a gearing system neither increases nor decreases power (i.e. the power output from a transmission system is similar to the engine brake power irrespective of the gear ratio).

In view of this, a change in the gear ratio of the vehicle shown by the curves in Figure 3.5 will cause the peak P to move horizontally from the position it occupied in Figure 3.4c. Lowering the ratio (curve A) moves the 'power available' curve to the left and raising the ratio (curve C) moves it to the right. These two conditions are called under-gear and over-gear respectively.

In both conditions the maximum possible speed is reduced but this is not the prime consideration. Table 3.2 shows the advantages of the two gearing conditions.

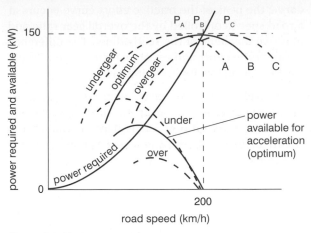

Figure 3.5 Under-gear and over-gear

Table 3.2 Advantages of under-gear and over-gear

Condition	Advantages
Under-gear	More power for acceleration, so vehicle responds quicker
	Flexible top gear performance, so less gear changing is necessary when the vehicle encounters higher tractive resistances
Over-gear	Lower engine speed for a given road speed, so: • better economy • lower engine noise level • less engine wear

The advantages of under-gearing can be used to overcome the disadvantages of over-gearing and vice versa. A comparison of these two conditions shows that under-gearing is more suitable for the average car, so under-gearing to the extent of about 10–20 per cent is common. This means that the engine power peak occurs in 10–20 per cent before the maximum possible vehicle speed is reached, although having more gears available allows for better matching of the gearing.

Maximum traction

Once the designer has set the overall top gear ratio, the bottom gear ratio (first gear) is then decided. This gear is used when moving off and is also needed when maximum tractive effort is required, so as to enable the vehicle to climb very steep hills.

Tractive effort is based on engine torque, so maximum tractive effort in a particular gear occurs when the engine is developing its maximum torque. In Figure 3.6a, the top gear performance, which was previously plotted as a difference in power, is shown as a balance of forces. It can be seen that the driving force curve is similar in shape to the engine torque curve; the peak of the tractive effort curve occurs at a road speed controlled by the overall gear ratio and effective diameter of the road wheel. The difference between the effort and resistance curves represents the force available for acceleration.

Figure 3.6b shows the effect on the tractive effort curve of lowering the gear ratio. In this case a bottom gearbox ratio of 4:1 is used to amplify the tractive effort sufficiently to meet the hill-climbing requirement.

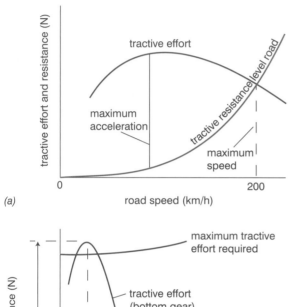

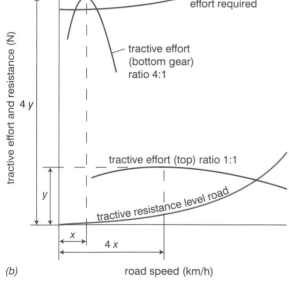

Figure 3.6 Tractive effort curves

The gradual engagement action of the clutch must be used to provide a tractive effort build-up sufficient to move the vehicle on the steep hill represented by the graph. Once the clutch is fully engaged, and the engine is operating in the region of maximum torque, a small acceleration is possible – this assumes the engine speed does not drop too low.

The bottom gearbox ratio is calculated by dividing the maximum effort required by the maximum effort available in top gear.

Intermediate gear(s)

Having set the top and bottom gearbox ratios, the intermediate ratios are then inserted so that they form a geometric progression (GP). This means that all the individual ratios advance by a common ratio. For example, assuming the top and bottom overall ratios are 4:1 and 16:1 respectively, then the sets of ratios for the three- and four-speed gearbox are:

- three-speed gearbox: 4, 8 and 16 (common ratio 2)
- four-speed gearbox: 4, 6.35, 10 and 16 (common ratio 1.59)

To obtain optimum speed and acceleration performance, the engine should be operated in the speed range between the limits of maximum torque and maximum power. The wider this operating range, the smaller the number of ratios required to bridge the gap between top and bottom. Most modern car engines have a narrow range, so gearboxes fitted in conjunction with these engines normally have at least five-speed boxes, even six or seven speeds in some cases.

In a gearbox fitted with six gears, fifth normally would have a 1:1 ratio with sixth being an overdrive because it has a ratio that steps up the speed; as a result, it drives the output shaft faster than the engine.

> ### 3.2 Different types of gears and gearboxes

3.2.1 Types of gearing

Various types of gearing are used on a motor vehicle, but gearboxes employ one or more of the following:

1 Spur gears – teeth parallel to axis, used on a sliding-mesh gearbox. Mainly in reverse gear system.
2 Helical gears – teeth inclined to axis to form a helix. Gives increased strength and quieter operation.
3 Double helical gears – two sets of opposing helical teeth.
4 Epicyclic or planetary gears – spur or helical gears rotating about centres that are not stationary.

Types 2 and 3 are used on constant-mesh and synchromesh gearboxes. Most automatic gearboxes use epicyclic gearing.

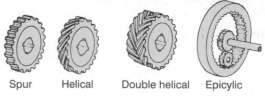

Spur   Helical   Double helical   Epicyclic

Figure 3.7 Types of gears

Gear material

The gear teeth have to resist severe shock loading and wear, so a case-hardened steel is used to provide a tough core and a hard surface.

3.2.2 Manual gearboxes

Gearboxes today may be divided into two main groups: manual and automatic. Manual gearboxes require the driver to have full control of the gearbox. Usually the driver will use a manual control lever to select the most appropriate gear ratio to suit the driving conditions. This has been developed further with the use of automated selecting manual gearboxes. This type of gearbox operates as a manual gearbox but has electronic or hydraulic gear shifting devices. This can speed up the gearshift and also allow the driver to have automatic gear shifting. These are explained in more detail on page 346.

In addition to reverse, the number of 'speeds' (gear ratios) provided in a modern gearbox is four, five, six or even seven in some cases. In the past a three-speed gearbox was commonly used for cost reasons.

The main types of manual-change gearbox are:

- sliding-mesh
- constant-mesh
- synchromesh.

Today, the synchromesh is the most common type in use. The layout of this type has been developed from the other two, and it is for this reason that the now obsolete sliding-mesh type is used for initial study.

3.2.3 Automatic

The term 'automatic gearbox' refers to a gearbox type that is able to change gears without the aid of the driver throughout the vehicle operating conditions. Once the driver has made the initial selection to determine the direction in which the vehicle is to move (Figure 3.8) and the gear range to be used, the other decisions are made by the transmission control module or 'brain' within the gearbox.

Figure 3.8 Automatic gearbox selector

In the USA, a gearbox is called a transmission. This explains why an automatic gearbox is sometimes called an automatic transmission unit.

Today, many automatic gearboxes use an epicyclic gear system. The required gear is obtained by holding or driving a part, or parts, of the gear train by means of a friction clutch or brake. The brakes and clutches are controlled by a hydraulic system; this either incorporates its own sensing system, or uses electronics to monitor the engine and vehicle operating conditions.

In addition to the four–eight speed epicyclic gearbox, most automatic systems require the fitment of a fluid clutch arrangement, called a torque converter, between the engine and gearbox. This replaces the normal friction clutch and fulfils two duties: it automatically disengages the engine from the transmission when the engine speed is below about 1000 rpm; and also provides an infinitely variable torque and speed ratio to bridge the steps between the gearbox epicyclic ratios.

In the UK, the combination of a torque converter and automatic gearbox forms an automatic transmission system.

3.2.4 Continuously variable transmission

The power output of a normal engine varies with the engine speed. At slow speeds the output is very low, so if good vehicle performance is required, the engine would have to rotate much faster; it would need to operate at a speed at which it develops its maximum power.

This story is repeated when the torque output and fuel economy are considered. Maximum torque occurs at a different speed from that for maximum economy, and neither of these speeds coincides with the point of maximum power.

This constant engine-speed requirement for the achievement of any one of the three performance factors is not possible with a conventional gearbox; this is because the engine speed has to be continually changed to suit the vehicle speed. As a result, the engine only gives its best at the vehicle speed appropriate to the point of maximum engine torque, power or economy.

A gearing system having an infinitely variable ratio would give a performance as shown in Figure 3.9 – this is called an ideal tractive effort curve. In this case, the engine is kept at the speed at which it gives its maximum power and the road speed is altered by varying the gear ratio.

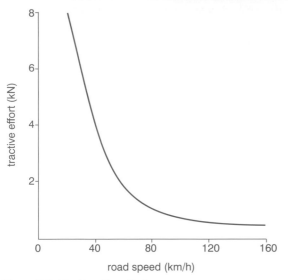

Figure 3.9 Ideal tractive effort

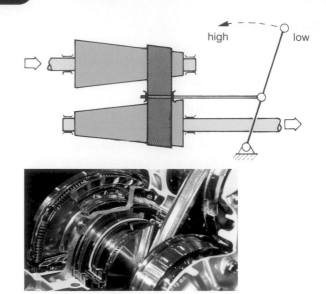

Figure 3.10 A simple CVT system and modern gearbox

An approximation to the ideal curve can be obtained from any system that operates according to the principle of the system shown in Figure 3.10. This particular arrangement is not very practical, but the layout shows the basic idea behind this method of gearing.

Continuously variable transmissions (CVT) have now become more popular due to the benefits of having no steps in between gear changes, which provides improved economy and lower emissions. Some vehicles,

such as hybrid vehicles, use the CVT arrangement for this purpose, which further improves the economy provided when using electric motor and petrol engine configurations. One of the first mass-produced vehicles with CVT was the DAF. This vehicle had a belt and pulley layout, which was called the variomatic CVT system (Figure 3.11). This was pioneered by the Dutch manufacturer and was fitted as standard to the small cars they produced in the late 1950s.

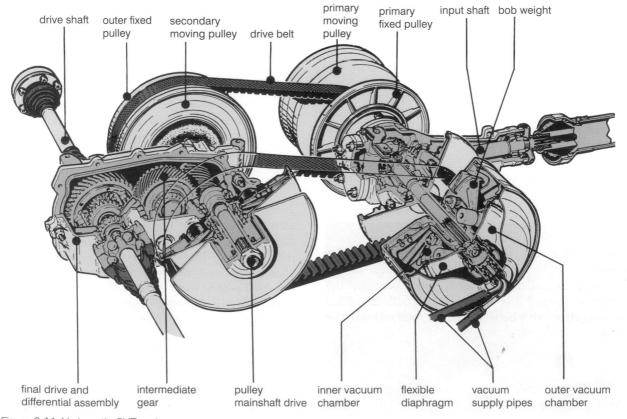

Figure 3.11 Variomatic CVT system

3.2.5 Stepped transmission

A comparison of the traditional gearbox curves with the ideal curve is shown in Figure 3.12. This graph indicates why the term 'stepped transmission' is used to describe any system that gives this kind of stepped output.

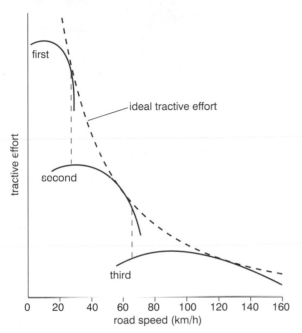

Figure 3.12 *Conventional stepped transmission*

Gearboxes originally having only three forward gears needed the engine to operate over a very wide speed range; this meant that the tractive effort at many road speeds was far less than the ideal. Increasing the number of ratios gives a considerable improvement and this is used on many heavy vehicles, as well as modern passenger vehicles, although passenger vehicles will incorporate fewer gear ratios than heavy vehicles. When the number of ratios is increased to about 10, the combination of the narrow engine range needed to 'bridge the gap' between the ratios, and the close approximation of the actual tractive curve to the ideal, allows the engine to be operated around its best speed.

An approach to the ideal tractive effort curve is achieved by using an automatic gearbox with a torque converter. Although the converter is very inefficient at low engine speeds, the effect of the converter's infinitely variable ratio between the limits of about 2:1 to 1:1 gives a smooth transition and positive drive between the stepped ratios of the main automatic gearbox (Figure 3.13).

3.2.6 Other types of gearbox and transmission

Many gearboxes fitted to vehicles today take examples of manual and automatic transmission systems and

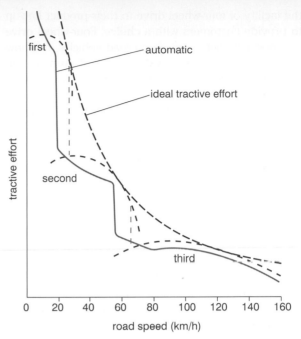

Figure 3.13 *Tractive effort with a three-speed automatic gearbox*

link them together to provide gearboxes that are able to operate like a manual transmission, but with the gear changes by an automated mechanism using either electronic motors or hydraulic assistance. The use of this automated gear change set up allows the driver to choose between driving the vehicle in a fully manual gearbox mode, with the gear changes being carried out by the use of paddles or using the stick to shift forwards or back to move up and down the ratios, or in automatic mode with the gearbox electronic control unit (ECU) deciding when to change gear. In both cases, the systems are electronically controlled and often provide very rapid gear changes leading to improved performance and economy. These new transmissions are covered in more detail on page 346.

3.3 Drive configuration

3.3.1 Drive arrangements

The general drive configuration of a vehicle usually depends on its expected function and purpose. The engine produces power to move the vehicle along the road surface. This power is transmitted via a transmission system incorporating a gearbox and final-drive assembly. The majority of light vehicles have four wheels, although there are a few three-wheeled vehicles still seen on the roads today. The drive configuration layouts therefore either two- or four-wheel drive.

A majority of four-wheeled vehicles utilise a two-wheel drive layout. These will be front- or rear-wheel drive. It is now more common for some manufacturers to add the facility of four-wheel drive to their product line-up to provide customers with a choice. Four-wheel drive was normally only seen on off-road vehicles, but now it is available across a wide choice of normal road vehicles from family saloons and hatchbacks to estate and sports cars. A four-wheel-drive system produces benefits from increased traction due to all four wheels propelling the vehicle, especially in lower friction situations.

Three-wheeled vehicles usually transmit the power from the engine to the rear wheels via a final drive in the rear axle. There are, however, some smaller engined three-wheel vehicles that situate the engine over the front steered wheel and pass the drive directly to this wheel. Some independent manufacturers producing higher-powered three-wheeled vehicles utilise a drive arrangement with the single wheel at the rear and two wheels at the front. The rear wheel is often driven by a powerful motorcycle engine via a chain or propeller shaft.

Manufacturers' choice of drive arrangement is normally dependent on the market and purpose of the vehicle. Each type of drive arrangement from front-wheel drive to four-wheel drive has advantages and disadvantages, which are taken into consideration by the vehicle designers when producing new vehicle types.

3.3.2 Rear-wheel drive

Traditionally, cars were of the rear-wheel drive layout (Figure 3.14). This was where the rear wheels acted as the driving wheels and the front wheels swivelled to allow the car to be steered. Locating the main vehicle drive components and engine units in this way provided the technician with improved accessibility, but also impacted on the passenger space through the installation of a transmission tunnel to locate the propeller shaft down the length of the passenger compartment. Rear-wheel drive provides good traction in dry and firm-grip conditions. However, on loose surfaces and under acceleration in wet conditions, rear-wheel drive vehicles tend to snake and lose grip, causing the rear of the car to move sideways requiring continual correction of the front (steering) wheels if a straight path is to be maintained.

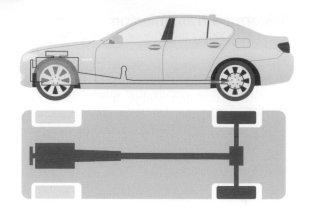

Figure 3.14 Rear-wheel drive layout

3.3.3 Front-wheel drive

The benefits of having a more compact arrangement have made the front-wheel drive layout a popular choice for manufacturers (Figure 3.15). The demand for smaller cars has increased as quickly as the demand for more economical vehicles; this has pushed manufacturers into producing more compact designs, which usually incorporate front-wheel drive. Accommodating all the major components under the bonnet has allowed more space in the vehicle for the occupants and removed the need for a transmission tunnel. The drive axle is now combined in a transaxle arrangement, and this allows the output shafts from the engine and gearbox to move in the same direction and use shorter drive shafts to the road wheels. The drive shafts are fitted with an inner and outer joint, known as a constant velocity joint (CV joint), which ensures an even speed is obtained as it rotates, reducing vibration even when drive is being transmitted through large angles. One disadvantage to front-wheel drive is a lack of grip under heavy acceleration and hill climbing, as the weight of the vehicle moves towards the rear, un-weighting the front wheels. The steering can also be heavy without the use of power steering; however, handling is improved, especially in wet conditions.

Figure 3.15 Front-wheel drive

Mounting the main units (engine, transmission, clutch, etc.) as one assembly sometimes makes it more difficult to gain access to components for repair or service. In some cases, access to the clutch can require the engine to be removed from the vehicle due to space around the engine, transmission and vehicle body being limited. With the benefits of improved component materials, the cost of major repairs is kept to a minimum.

3.3.4 Four-wheel drive

Four-wheel drive has long been associated with all-terrain and off-road vehicles, but is increasingly being fitted to normal road-going vehicles. Four-wheel drive is safer because it transmits drive to all four wheels and, therefore, reduces wheel spin or loss of traction, especially in wet, muddy or icy conditions. Additionally, the positive drive to all four wheels assists in the braking of the vehicle, especially when using the transmission to slow the vehicle down as all four wheels will create traction when the vehicle decelerates.

When four-wheel drive vehicles are fitted with conventional differential systems, the same issues will be apparent when one wheel loses traction, as all of the torque will be lost through the spinning wheel. For these reasons, many manufacturers fit an additional differential between the front and rear axles and also fit limited slip differentials that prevent excessive wheel spin, making sure the engine's power and torque are transmitted to as many wheels as possible.

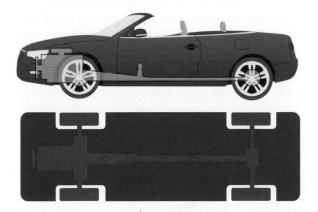

Figure 3.16 Four-wheel drive

Four-wheel drive systems are relatively expensive to produce and can cause the vehicle to be less fuel economical due to the extra weight and drag associated with these systems. Some manufacturers now produce vehicles that are four-wheel drive on a part-time basis. These systems operate as a front-wheel drive system until the front wheels lose traction,

then the system will engage the rear wheels to provide additional traction. When all four wheels have gained traction of the road surface, the rear wheels will be disengaged. This system provides the benefits of four-wheel drive but without the penalty of additional fuel costs associated with full-time four-wheel drive. Figure 3.16 shows a four-wheel drive layout.

3.4   Rear-wheel drive layout

3.4.1 Advantages

Rear-wheel drive layouts can provide a wide variety of advantages to the vehicle manufacturer. The design of the rear-wheel drive layout is simplified by placing the main components in a line down the centre of the vehicle; this gives good vehicle balance and provides a simpler construction process. The advantages produced with this layout are:

- simple manufacturing process and construction layout
- vehicle weight can be evenly distributed to provide excellent vehicle balance front to rear of the vehicle, leading to improved vehicle handling and stability
- vehicle components are relatively accessible and maintenance procedures are improved, leading to lower costs for the customer
- lower effort required to steer the vehicle
- various-sized engines can be fitted relatively easily
- linkage to the main components is made simpler as they are generally situated closer to the driver, such as gear change cables
- the manufacturer has more options in designing the suspension system to provide different arrangements for different types of vehicles using the same vehicle platform.

Larger vehicles tend to use rear-wheel drive layout in preference to front-wheel drive, as this allows larger engines to be fitted relatively easily.

3.4.2 Torque reaction

'To every action there is an equal and opposite reaction.' (Newton's third law of motion)

When referring this statement to the transmission system, it implies that every component that produces torque, such as the engine, will also suffer an equal reaction. In the transmission system's case, this is the differential and drive shafts rotating the wheels.

In the rear-wheel drive layout, to prevent the rear axle casing turning in the opposite direction to the driving wheels, a support system must be utilised in the form of the suspension system and vehicle body.

An additional example can be seen in Figure 3.17, showing a tractor with its rear driving wheels stuck in a ditch. As the driver tries to accelerate out of this situation, they must be careful to avoid the torque reaction causing the tractor to rotate around the centre point of the wheels causing the front wheels to lift off the ground.

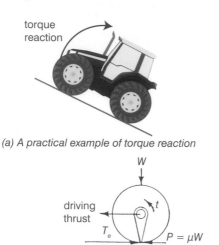

(a) A practical example of torque reaction

(b) Lever action of a wheel

Figure 3.17 *Torque reaction and torque acting on a lever*

3.4.3 Driving thrust

If torque (t) is applied to the wheel, which in this case can be considered as a lever (Figure 3.17b), this produces a tractive effort (T) at the road surface, and an equal and opposite force at the axle shaft. To propel the vehicle forwards, the driving thrust must be transferred from the axle casing to the vehicle body or frame.

The maximum tractive effort is limited by the frictional force (P) of the tyre on the road surface. The tractive force depends on the coefficient of friction (μ) between the tyre and the road and the load (W) exerted on the wheel.

3.4.4 Transmitting driving thrust to the vehicle body and controlling axle torque reaction

When the vehicle is powered forwards by the engine and transmission system, a force is applied to the rear wheels. This force must be harnessed to provide forward movement. The vehicle body or chassis provides this by taking the force generated by the transmission system and engine.

A drive system is an arrangement for transmitting the driving thrust from the road wheels to the vehicle body. The system used must also incorporate a means

for resisting the movement of the main components due to torque reaction.

In the past, leaf springs were normally used for the rear suspension of a vehicle. These springs were often utilised to provide the thrust and torque reaction functions of the drive system.

The axle casing has to be able to resist the torque reaction, as this will try to rotate the axle around itself as the torque is transmitted to the road wheels through the final-drive assembly.

On pre-1950 motor cars, there were four notable drive systems in use. Since that time, these basic systems have been modified to suit modern requirements. The drive systems were:

- Hotchkiss open-type
- Four-link (semi-Hotchkiss)
- Torque-tube
- de-Dion.

Although these systems are rarely used today in their original form, they are included here to show the arrangements used to resist the various forces associated with the propulsion of a vehicle. This knowledge should help in the diagnosis of many of the 'knock, clonk and vibration' faults associated with drive systems.

Hotchkiss open-type drive system

This once popular arrangement is shown in Figure 3.18. Two rear leaf springs, longitudinally mounted, are connected to the frame by a 'fixed' pivot at the front, and swinging shackles at the rear. A universal joint is fitted at each end of the exposed or 'open' type propeller shaft, with provision made for alteration in shaft length, which occurs when the springs are deflected.

Torque reaction is resisted by damping the axle to the springs by means of 'U' bolts. Under heavy driving conditions the springs will deflect up at the front and down at the rear, and vice versa during braking. This movement will help to damp driving shocks and improve transmission flexibility. Since the axle continually moves up and down, the need for a rear universal joint is clear.

Driving thrust is transferred from the casing to the spring by the friction between the two surfaces, and then transmitted through the front section of the springs to the vehicle frame. If the 'U' bolts become loose, the spring centre bolt (axle location bolt) will have to take the full driving thrust, and the high shearing force will quickly fracture it.

Four-link (semi-Hotchkiss) drive system

Some car manufacturers use helical springs in conjunction with a live rear axle. Helical springs

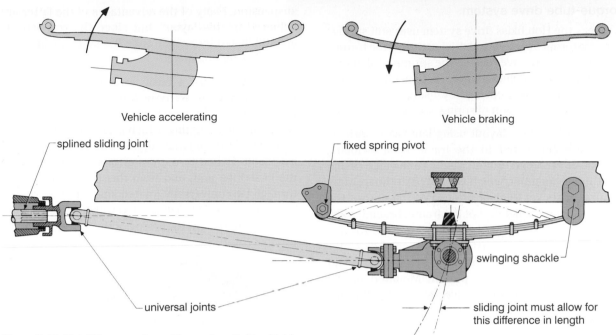

Vehicle accelerating

Vehicle braking

splined sliding joint

fixed spring pivot

swinging shackle

universal joints

sliding joint must allow for this difference in length

Figure 3.18 Hotchkiss open-type drive system (light vehicle)

cannot take driving and braking thrust, torque reaction or give lateral support to the rear axle, so extra parts must be fitted to fulfil these functions.

In the layout shown in Figure 3.19, the rear axle is positioned by upper and lower trailing suspension arms; these arms transmit driving thrust and prevent rotation of the axle casing. Sideways movement of the axle is controlled by a transverse stabiliser called a **Panhard rod**; this rod connects the rear axle to the vehicle body. Rubber mountings at each connection point reduce noise transmission, eliminate the need for lubrication and also provide slight flexibility to allow for drive movement and geometric variations during spring deflection.

Panhard rod: (also called a Panhard bar or track bar) part of a vehicle's suspension designed to prevent sideways movement. It is a rigid bar that connects the rear axle on one side to the car body on the other. It allows up and down movement, but not lateral movement.

At first, it would appear that the helical spring gives a reduction in the unsprung weight, but when the weight of the additional locating arms and rods needed for this arrangement is added, the unsprung weight difference is very small. However, the accurate positioning of the axle in this system is an advantage.

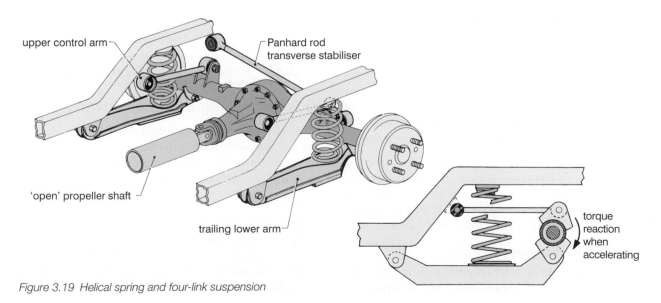

upper control arm

Panhard rod transverse stabiliser

'open' propeller shaft

trailing lower arm

torque reaction when accelerating

Figure 3.19 Helical spring and four-link suspension

Torque-tube drive system

Whereas the Hotchkiss drive system uses stiff springs to resist torque reaction and driving thrust, the torque-tube or enclosed drive relieves the springs of all duties other than their intended purpose. This means that a 'softer' ride can be achieved by using either 'softer' springs or another form of spring, for example helical.

Figure 3.20 shows a layout using laminated springs, which are connected to the frame by a swinging shackle at each end. Bolted rigidly to the axle casing is a tubular member, which is located at the front by a ball and socket joint positioned at the rear of the gearbox or cross-member of the frame. Bracing rods, connected between the axle casing and the torque-tube, strengthen the construction. A small diameter propeller shaft is fitted inside the torque-tube and splined to the final-drive **pinion**. Mounted in the centre of the ball joint is a universal joint to allow for angular deflections of the drive.

> **Pinion**: small gear wheel that is engaged or engages with a larger gear wheel to provide a gear ratio.

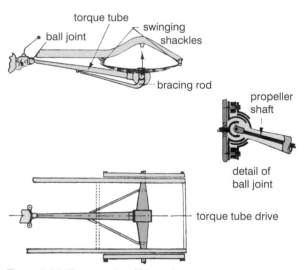

Figure 3.20 Torque-tube drive system

In this arrangement, the torque reaction and driving thrust are taken by the torque-tube. When the forward thrust from the ball is taken on the rear housing of the gearbox, means must be provided to transfer this force through the gearbox mountings to the frame.

Helical or torsion bar springs may be used as alternatives to laminated springs, and in these cases side movement of the axle must be controlled by fitting some form of transverse stabiliser, for example a Panhard rod, between the frame and the axle.

de-Dion drive system

The de-Dion axle is often regarded as the halfway stage between the normal axle and independent suspension. Many of the advantages of the latter are achieved in this layout, but since the rear wheels are still linked by an axle tube the system cannot be classed as independent.

Figure 3.21 shows a basic arrangement: laminated springs are connected to the frame by a 'fixed' pivot at the front and a swinging shackle at the rear. Each spring carries a hub mounting, which is rigidly connected to a tubular axle beam that supports the wheel on a stub axle shaft. Bolted to a cross-member of the frame is the final-drive unit, and from this the drive is taken through two universally jointed shafts to the wheels. The main propeller shaft is fitted with a universal joint at each end to allow for flexing of the frame.

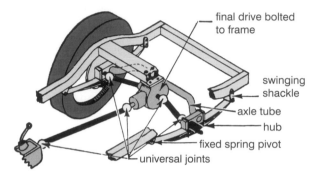

Figure 3.21 de-Dion drive system

Torque reaction of the final-drive casing is taken by the frame, and the driving thrust is resisted by the springs.

The major advantage of this layout is the reduction in unsprung weight. This ensures that wheel spin is reduced by allowing the light driving wheels to follow the contour of the road surface closely. Wheel spin is caused, too, by the tendency of the normal axle to rotate around the pinion when a high propeller shaft torque is exerted. This lifting effort of the wheel is eliminated with the de-Dion system and weight is equally distributed.

3.5 Front-wheel drive layout

3.5.1 Advantages and disadvantages

Concentrating the engine and transmission system in one unit and placing the assembly at the front of the vehicle to give front-wheel drive, produces the following advantages and disadvantages.

Advantages:

- Compact construction
- Flat floor of passenger compartment – no propeller shaft tunnel or gearbox bulge
- Good traction because majority of weight is taken by the driving wheels

- Engine can be mounted transversely, which either reduces bonnet length or increases the size of the passenger compartment
- Good steering stability – driving thrust of the wheels is aimed in the direction that the vehicle is intended to follow. Also the layout rarely suffers from the over-steer characteristics described in the steering section

Disadvantages:

- Heavier steering
- More tyre wear on the front tyres due to steering and powering the vehicle
- More complicated driveline arrangements to transmit power to the driven wheels while allowing them to steer the vehicle

Although front-wheel drive vehicles need more complicated drive shaft arrangements, the many advantages make the layout very suitable for a small car.

3.5.2 Transverse engine layout

Figure 3.22 shows a typical front-wheel drive layout. The transversely mounted engine is bolted to a unit called a transaxle. This unit gets its name from the two words 'transmission' (a term used in the USA for gearbox) and 'axle'. In the past, the general term 'rear axle' often applied to the gearing as well as the axle casing, but nowadays the various drive arrangements make it necessary to restrict the use of the name 'rear axle' to the member that performs the axle duty. The two main components inside the axle of a rear-wheel drive vehicle are the final drive, for example **crown wheel** and pinion, and the differential.

> **Crown wheel**: gear wheel set at right angles to its driver gear; usually the crown wheel is larger than the driving gear (normally a pinion).

The early four-speed gearbox shown in Figure 3.22 has two shafts: an input shaft splined to the clutch; and a mainshaft connected to the final-drive pinion. A bevel gear final drive is necessary when the engine is mounted longitudinally, but in the layout shown the engine position allows the use of normal helical gears. Drive from the final drive is transmitted through the differential to the two drive shafts. Speed variation due to drive shaft angularity is prevented by using constant velocity universal joints at each end; the inboard joint at each side being of the plunge type.

During acceleration, or at times when the engine is used as a brake, torque reaction tends to make the engine rotate about the crankshaft, so suitably spaced engine mountings are fitted to resist this movement. The wheel hub assembly to which the drive shaft is fitted on a front-wheel drive vehicle is connected to the lower end of the suspension strut assembly. To prevent the strut moving laterally, a component called a track control arm is fitted between the strut and the vehicle body or sub-frame. Driving thrust and braking torque are taken by the suspension components, in particular the tie bar fitted from the track control arm to the body (Figure 3.23).

Generally with this configuration the drive shafts are of unequal length due to the transmission being situated at one side of the engine bay. When torque is transmitted to the drive shafts from the transmission system, there tends to be different torque reactions in each drive shaft. The shorter drive shaft will tend

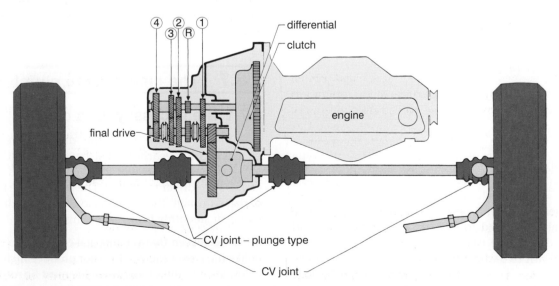

Figure 3.22 Front-wheel drive layout

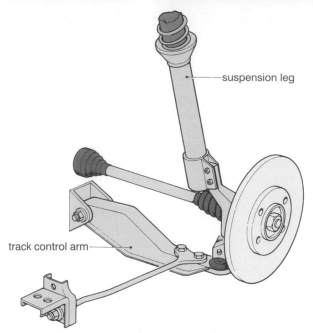

Figure 3.23 Front-wheel drive suspension layout

to transmit more of the torque, as this is less likely to twist or be affected by the torque input. In these cases, the vehicle may pull to one side when accelerating. This occurrence is called 'torque steer' and mainly affects higher powered front-wheel drive vehicles. To counter this problem, manufacturers tend to fit split drive shafts and a centre bearing to the longer drive shaft or alter the suspension geometry.

3.6   Four-wheel drive layout

3.6.1 Advantages

A four-wheel drive, sometimes called a 4WD or 4×4 (four by four), vehicle transmits a drive to all of its four wheels instead of two wheels, as is common with the majority of light vehicles.

There are two main traction problems with a two-wheel drive (4×2) vehicle:

- Loss of traction during cross-country operation
- Loss of adhesion during acceleration

Four-wheel drive addresses both of these problems.

The intended use of the vehicle governs the type of four-wheel drive system that is offered by the manufacturer.

Vehicles in the four-wheel drive category are generally designed to work efficiently both on and off-road. In some cases, these vehicles provide the driver with two-wheel drive during normal road use and then four-wheel drive when the front wheels lose traction, or if the driver engages the rear axle through

electronics or a simple lever. This system is called part-time four-wheel drive. Many larger vehicles, such as the Range Rover and Discovery, use a full-time four-wheel drive system that constantly drives all four wheels.

High-performance cars with four-wheel drive that are built for fast road operation generally also use four-wheel drive at all times; this gives improved handling and additional safety. In this case, the full weight of the car is spread over all of the driving wheels. This full utilisation of the vehicle weight considerably increases the tractive effort that can be applied to the car; as a result, a high rate of acceleration can be achieved.

Four-wheel drive vehicles offer the following advantages over front and rear-wheel-drive vehicles:

- The vehicle weight is distributed over all four driving wheels and, therefore, provides improved traction and stability.
- Wheel spin is limited and traction improved on acceleration as all four wheels receive torque from the engine and transmission system.

Torque reactions in four-wheel-drive vehicles are similar to both front- and rear-wheel-drive vehicles, so similar components are used to resist the movements created.

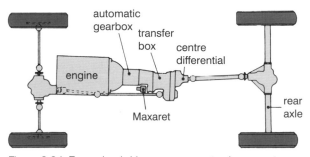

Figure 3.24 Four-wheel drive arrangement using a centre differential

3.7   The single-plate clutch

3.7.1 The necessity for a clutch

In order to change gear, the drive between the engine and the gearbox must have the ability to be temporarily disconnected. The vehicle clutch system enables the driver to do this. The progressive take-up of drive through the clutch also allows the driver to move off smoothly from a standing start.

It has been seen that the internal-combustion engine, unlike the steam engine, does not produce high power at low speeds; therefore the engine must be rotating at a speed at which sufficient power is developed before the drive to the wheels is established. This condition rules out the use of a dog clutch (Figure 3.25a), since the connection of a rotating engine to a stationary transmission shaft would damage the transmission and jolt the vehicle. The clutch used must allow the drive to be taken up smoothly so that the vehicle can be gradually moved away from the stationary position.

Once moving, it will be necessary to change gear, and so a disengagement of the engine or transmission is required. This is also part of the clutch's function.

The clutch takes up the drive smoothly; it also disengages the drive. These two duties can be performed by various mechanisms; the friction system is considered to be one of the most effective and efficient. Hydraulic and electric systems are also employed on motor vehicles.

3.7.2 The friction clutch

The operation of a friction clutch is demonstrated by the two discs shown in Figure 3.26b. If discs A and B are connected to the engine and transmission respectively, then when the discs are held apart no drive will be made. When A is moved to contact B, the friction between the surfaces will allow a drive to be transmitted. The extent of this drive will be governed by the force that pushes the discs together. Therefore, if the force is gradually increased, the drive transmitted will increase proportionally. This will allow the vehicle to move smoothly from rest.

When the drive is engaged, both discs must rotate at the same speed, and so the clutch designer must ensure that there is enough pressure and friction to produce this condition. During the life of the clutch, faults may develop that restrict pressure or friction; therefore the clutch will slip and the performance of the vehicle will be affected.

The clutch shown in Figure 3.26 is a construction developed from Figure 3.25. Both sides of the friction plate are utilised, and this means that double the torque (turning moment) can be transmitted before slip takes place. The friction plate, or driven plate, is sandwiched between the engine flywheel and the pressure plate, and the design is known as a single-plate clutch.

A multi-plate clutch is a unit that employs a number of driven plates and is described on page 301.

3.7.3 Single-plate clutch

This is the most common type of clutch in use, and has the advantage of producing a quick disengagement.

Figure 3.26 shows a simple clutch with a driven plate (1) splined to the primary shaft (2) of the gearbox. Riveted to the plate is a pair of linings or facings (3), which used to be made of asbestos but are now made of alternative heat-resistant materials that have a satisfactory coefficient of friction and other useful properties. The pressure plate (4) is located by a number of studs (5), and is forced towards the flywheel (6) by means of springs (7). A withdrawal sleeve (8) allows the clutch pedal (9) to act on the clutch forks (10) and push the pressure plate away

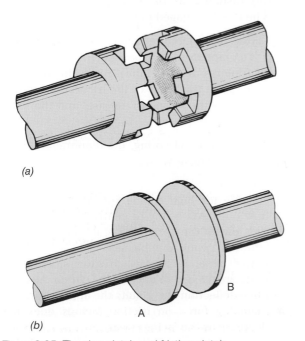

(a)

(b)

Figure 3.25 The dog clutch and friction clutch

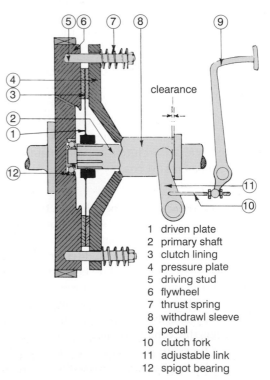

1 driven plate
2 primary shaft
3 clutch lining
4 pressure plate
5 driving stud
6 flywheel
7 thrust spring
8 withdrawl sleeve
9 pedal
10 clutch fork
11 adjustable link
12 spigot bearing

Figure 3.26 Construction of simple single-plate clutch

from the flywheel. An adjustable link (11) is set to give a small clearance between the clutch fork and the withdrawal sleeve to ensure that the full force of the springs is felt on the driven plate.

This clearance allows the pedal a small amount of free movement, which, measured at the pad of the pedal, is normally about 25 mm (1 in). At the centre of the flywheel is fitted a spigot bearing (12), which locates the front end of the gearbox primary shaft and allows for the difference in speed between the two members. This bearing can take the form of a ball race or plain bush; the former is normally sealed with a metal cover to prevent the lubricant being thrown out on to the linings. The plain bearing type is generally manufactured from phosphor-bronze, and made porous so that the bush can be impregnated with graphite to make it self-lubricating.

Single-plate clutch operation

When the driver depresses the pedal, the clutch forks push the pressure plate away from the flywheel to remove the spring pressure from the driven plate. This allows the plate to run free, and therefore disengages the engine from the transmission.

On releasing the pedal, the spring thrust forces the pressure plate towards the flywheel and sandwiches the driven plate between the two surfaces. This movement of the pedal must be gradual, or the full force of the springs will be suddenly applied to the driven plate and cause a jolt. When the pedal is fully released, the drive can take two paths – it can be transferred directly from the flywheel face to the driven plate, or it can be taken via the studs and pressure plate to the rear face of the driven plate.

Close attention should be given to this second drive path because the existence of an excessive clearance between any two parts in this drive path leads to noise and a jerky operation of the clutch. The path, via the pressure plate, is designed to take half the transmitted torque of the clutch, so modern units use efficient arrangements to convey the drive from the flywheel to the pressure plate.

During the engagement of the clutch, the force transmitted to the driven plate must be applied gradually. Since any jerky movement of the pressure plate gives a more pronounced judder at the road wheels, the flywheel/pressure plate connection must avoid, or limit, the slip-grip action caused by friction at this point. Most probably the clutch in Figure 3.26 will suffer from this drawback, which will be evident at a time when the vehicle is moving off from rest (i.e. when the pressure plate is moving towards the flywheel and driving torque is attempting to resist this axial movement).

The majority of motor manufacturers use single-plate clutches, which are produced by a variety of manufacturers, including Unipart, Motoquip, Borg and Beck. More specialist clutch systems are produced by manufacturers such as AP Racing. The types of spring used to provide the clamping force are as follows:

1 Diaphragm spring – universally used for cars and light commercial vehicles.
2 Coil spring – although multi-coil spring clutches were used for all vehicles in the past, nowadays this type is only used on heavy vehicles.

Diaphragm spring clutch

This type of clutch is very compact; it has few working parts and a spring that is particularly suited to light vehicles.

The force needed on the pressure plate is provided by a diaphragm spring. This is a circular, slightly conical, tempered steel disc with radial slits cut from its centre to give flexibility.

Whereas a coil spring gives a force that progressively increases with deflection, a diaphragm spring exerts a force that varies as its shape is altered. At first, the force gradually increases like the coil spring, but after the diaphragm spring has reached its 'flat' position, the force decreases and then increases once again (Figure 3.27). In many ways, the spring action is similar to that which occurs when pressure is applied to the convex end of a 'tin' can – when sufficient force is applied to move the can end past its flat position the end 'clicks' rapidly to its full inwardly dished state or, in the clutch's case, this would be the disengaged position.

When fitted to a clutch mounted on a flywheel, the spring is compressed just beyond the point where it is flat (point A on the graph). Set in this position, the reduction in thickness of the friction facing due to wear causes the spring to 'release' and the force to increase.

Compared with a coil spring, the diaphragm spring offers the following advantages:

- Compact
- Suitable for high engine speeds. Coil springs bow outwards owing to centrifugal action and this lowers the spring force; it can also cause vibration owing to imbalance
- Lower pedal force. Less friction since fewer parts are needed to operate the clutch. Also the force-deflection curve suits the application
- Clamping force on friction facings does not decrease as the facings wear

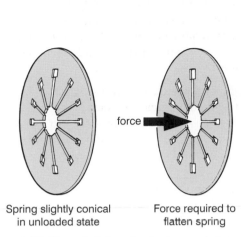

Spring slightly conical   Force required to
in unloaded state   flatten spring

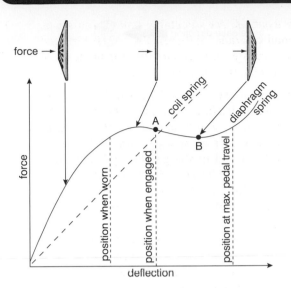

Figure 3.27 Characteristics of a diaphragm spring

Pressure plate construction

Figure 3.28 shows the construction of a diaphragm spring clutch. This particular design uses only five main working parts: cover; diaphragm spring; fulcrum rings; pressure plate; and driving straps. Turnover tabs on the cover hold the fulcrum rings, which act as a pivot for the diaphragm spring. As the cover bolts are tightened, the pressure plate pushes the diaphragm spring away from the flywheel and deflects the spring to a near-flat shape. In this position the reaction of the spring on the pressure plate provides the clamping force on the driven plate.

A single-plate clutch has two driving surfaces; the flywheel and the pressure plate. In the clutch shown in Figure 3.28, a strap drive is used to transfer the drive from the cover to the pressure plate. Three flexible steel straps working in tension allow the pressure plate to move smoothly towards and away from the flywheel, but prevent rotational movement relative to the cover.

Disengagement of the clutch compresses the spring and, as the graph shows, the force required by the driver is less in the disengaged position (B) than that needed at the commencement of the pedal travel. This is opposite to that given by a coil spring clutch.

A release bearing, attached to either the diaphragm spring fingers or to the clutch fork, moves the inner ends of the fingers of the diaphragm spring towards the flywheel to disengage the clutch. This forward movement of the inner part of the spring causes it to pivot on the fulcrum rings and move its outer part away from the pressure plate. With the spring damping force removed, the spring straps pull the pressure plate away from the driven plate and disengage the drive to the driven plate.

Release bearing

The purpose of the release bearing is to transmit the force applied by the driver from the clutch fork, which is pivoted to the bell housing, to the rotating diaphragm spring. In the past, a graphite block held to the clutch fork contacted a flat plate secured to the diaphragm spring fingers, but today most clutches use a ball race. This race is sealed with metal end covers to retain the lubricant. In some cases, the ball release bearing is connected to the clutch fork by a flexible plastic compound, which allows the bearing to align itself with the centre of the clutch and give smooth clutch operation.

When the clutch is engaged (i.e., drive is taking place), a small clearance should exist between the release bearing and the diaphragm. This clearance, which is normally measured at the pedal pad and called free-pedal movement, is necessary for two reasons: it keeps the release bearing clear of the rotating spring; and also ensures that the full spring thrust acts on the pressure plate. As the clutch facing wears, the clearance decreases, so unless periodic adjustment is made, the clearance will disappear and the clutch will start to slip.

The driven plate

The important features incorporated in the design of a driven plate can best be seen by considering the disadvantages of using a plain steel plate with a lining riveted to each side. Disadvantages are as follows:

- Buckling of the plate due to heat
- Drag, due to the plate rubbing against the flywheel when the clutch should be disengaged
- Very small movement of the clutch pedal between the engaged and disengaged positions – the clutch is said to be in the *in* or *out* class – with very little control between these points

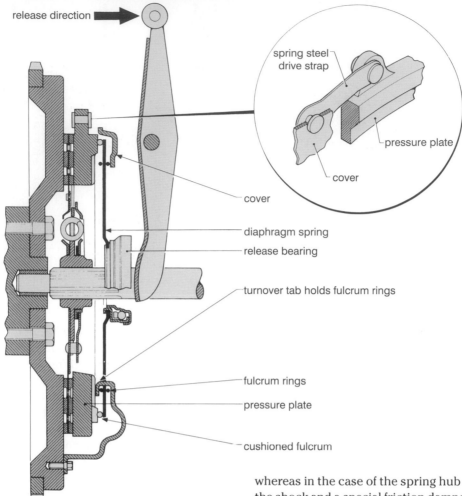

Figure 3.28 Diaphragm spring clutch

To overcome these problems, the plate is normally slotted or set in such a manner as to produce a 'flexing' action. This is generally known as crimping and Figure 3.29 shows one form. Each segment is dished a small amount so that the linings tend to spring apart when the clutch is engaged.

If the clutch is in the driving position and the pedal is depressed, the driven plate will tend to jump away from the flywheel to give a 'clean' disengagement. While in this position the linings will be held apart, and air will be pumped between the linings to take away the heat. During engagement, axial compression of the driven plate spreads the engagement over a greater range of pedal travel and, therefore, makes it easier to make a smooth engagement.

Figure 3.29 shows a driven plate that is riveted to a splined hub. This arrangement is used occasionally, but in most cases the hub is mounted independently of the main plate, and the drive between the two components made possible by either fitting a series of springs or bonding the hub to the plate by means of rubber. Rubber takes shocks and also absorbs shocks, whereas in the case of the spring hub the spring takes the shock and a special friction damper fitted between the plate and the hub absorbs the energy of the shock. By using one or other of these hub centres it is possible to absorb the torsional shocks due to clutch take-up or the more troublesome engine vibrations, which cause transmission noise and rattle.

Multi-coil spring clutch

This type of clutch has been the standard clutch for a number of years, but the popularity of the diaphragm spring type for cars has meant that the multi-coil spring clutch is now only used on heavy vehicles.

Pressure plate construction

A series of coil springs is positioned between the pressed steel cover and the cast iron pressure plate. Spring steel straps are used to transmit the drive from the cover to the pressure plate. Four release levers, pivoting on fulcrum pins supported in adjustable eyebolts, connect the release lever plate to the small struts placed between the lever and the pressure plate. These struts improve the efficiency of the release mechanism and, in conjunction with the steel driving straps, allow the pressure plate to move smoothly when taking up the drive: a jerky action will cause clutch judder. The release bearing can be either graphite block or ball race type.

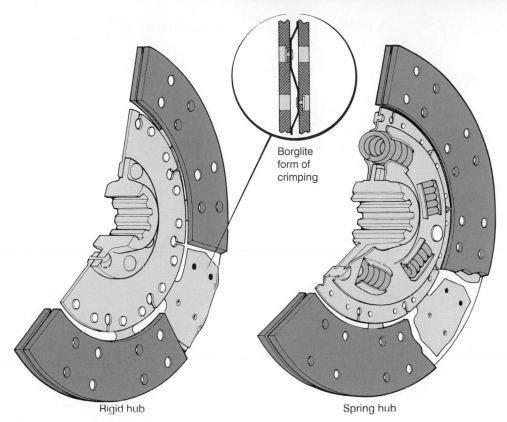

Borglite form of crimping

Rigid hub   Spring hub

Figure 3.29 Driven friction plate construction

The cover plate assembly is bolted to the flywheel; this is flat-faced for clutches having a driven plate diameter of less than 330 mm (13 in) and pot-type (recessed) for larger clutches. Balance is most important for all clutches and, since hole clearance is necessary for the cover retaining bolts, means must be provided to keep the clutch concentric with the flywheel: dowels perform this duty.

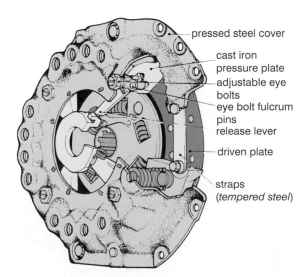

pressed steel cover

cast iron pressure plate
adjustable eye bolts
eye bolt fulcrum pins
release lever

driven plate

straps (*tempered steel*)

Figure 3.30 Multi-coil spring clutch

Large driven plates have a tendency to spin (i.e. to continue rotating after the clutch pedal is depressed). To limit this trouble, the plate should be made as light as possible. Some manufacturers use a small disc brake (also known as a clutch stop) to bring the driven plate to rest. This brake is mounted on the non-rotating part of the release bearing and when the pedal is depressed approximately two-thirds of its travel, the brake contacts a disc on the primary shaft.

3.7.4 Pedal linkage

The external linkage between the pedal and clutch may be either mechanical or hydraulic.

Figure 3.31 shows two systems that are used. The mechanical system has an adjuster to enable the correct free-pedal movement to be maintained. If the clearance is non-existent, wear on the release bearing will occur and clutch slip will result. (This effect can also be produced if the driver rests their foot on the pedal.) When the clearance is too great, the pedal will reach the end of its travel before the clutch is disengaged and this 'drag' will make it difficult to engage gear. The hydraulic system does not have this adjustment as the free play is taken up by the hydraulic fluid. In some cases, there is a small adjustment available at the slave cylinder on to the release fork to finely adjust the clutch action.

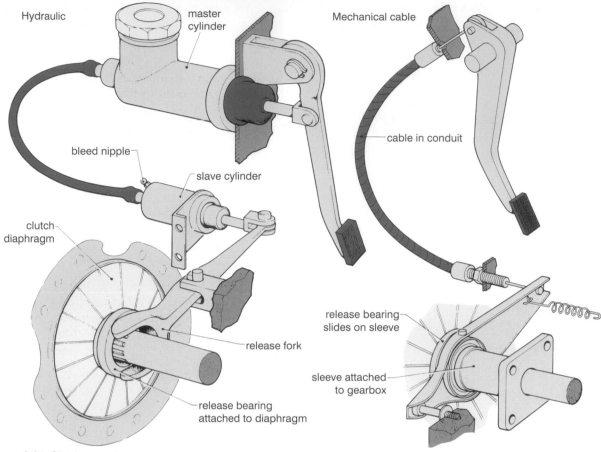

Figure 3.31 Clutch operating systems

The mechanical systems shown in Figure 3.31 have a pedal mounted on the frame of the vehicle and a clutch cross-shaft on the engine. Rubber-mounted engine bearers allow the engine to move a considerable amount in all directions. If the clutch pedal is partly depressed, any fore and aft movement of the engine will adversely affect the smooth operation of the clutch and 'judder' will result. To prevent this, some manufacturers employ a tie-rod to limit the engine movement, but this arrangement defeats the object of using flexible engine mountings.

You will see that engine movement has no effect on hydraulic and cable systems.

Automatic clutch adjustment

During vehicle operation, the type of mechanical linkage shown in Figure 3.31 causes the free-pedal movement to increase when the cable stretches; this extension is quite common when a cable is used to operate a mechanism. Periodic adjustment must be made to allow for this to avoid clutch drag; this results when the free-pedal movement is excessive. Some manufacturers consider this task undesirable, so in these cases an automatic adjuster similar to that shown in Figure 3.32 is provided.

The type shown in Figure 3.32 uses a conventional cable arrangement from the clutch to the point where the cable normally connects to the clutch pedal. At this point the cable is attached to a ratchet; this is moved to operate the clutch by a pawl connected to the end of the pedal.

After the automatic take-up of the adjuster that follows the replacement of a cable, a downward movement of the pedal causes the pawl to lock into the ratchet and pull the cable.

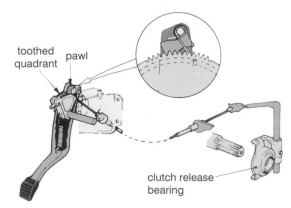

Figure 3.32 Automatic clutch adjustment

When wear causes the slack movement to increase to more than the pitch of one ratchet tooth, the spring partially rotates the ratchet and causes the pawl to jump a tooth; this takes up the cable slack and resets the free-pedal movement to the required amount.

3.8 The multi-plate clutch

3.8.1 Transmitting high torque outputs

The torque transmitted by a plate-type clutch depends on four factors; these are shown in the following formula, which is used to calculate the torque capacity:

$$t = sp\mu r$$

Where:

t = torque transmitted (Nm)

s = number of friction contact

p = total spring thrust (N)

μ = coefficient of friction

r = mean radius (m)

Or, alternatively, a formula to calculate the torque transmitted by a clutch can be expressed as:

$$T = 0.5\mu W(r_1 + r_2)n$$

Where:

T = torque (Nm or Nmm)

W = total spring force (N)

The W is sometimes replaced by the letters Fa.

r_1 = external radius of the friction disc (mm)

r_2 = internal radius of the friction disc (mm)

r_1 and r_2 are used to calculate the mean radius of the friction plate i.e. $\dfrac{r_1 + r_2}{2}$

μ (*mu*) = coefficient of friction

n = number of pairs of frictional faces (two for a single-plate clutch)

There are cases where the spring thrust, friction or clutch radius must be restricted, so in these cases the number of plates has to be increased to ensure that the maximum torque can be transmitted without slip. A clutch having more than one driven plate is called a multi-plate clutch.

Although this type of clutch was widely used on cars up to about 1930, the numerous advantages of the single-plate clutch, especially its ability to disengage the drive completely (its resistance to drag), has meant

that a multi-plate unit is now rarely used as a main transmission clutch between the engine and gearbox.

A modern use of a multi-plate type is in automatic gearboxes. This type of gearbox needs a number of clutches to hold the various gear elements and, since the clutch diameter in this application is limited, a multi-plate clutch is commonly used.

Figure 3.33 shows the main constructional details and represents a main clutch of the type used on early motor vehicles. Bolted to the flywheel is a cover that engages, by means of slots, with a series of lugs on the outer plates. These plates, which may be plain steel or fitted with cork or friction material inserts, act on inner plates, which are splined to a hub. Thrust springs push the plates together to form a drive.

To disengage the clutch, the end plate is withdrawn to compress the springs and release the other plates. It is difficult to ensure that all plates disengage, and to remedy this defect the plates are either dished or fitted with small springs to push the plates apart.

The clutch may be either wet or dry; the advantage of using the former is that it reduces the fierce engagement by allowing the engine oil to flow into the clutch housing. The clutch employed in automatic gearboxes is generally of the wet type, and is operated by a piston controlled by hydraulic pressure. **Sintered** bronze plates are used in many designs. The porous surface traps the oil to give long life and smooth operation.

Sinter: manufacturing process in which powdered bronze or compressed paper is partially fused to make it solid but porous.

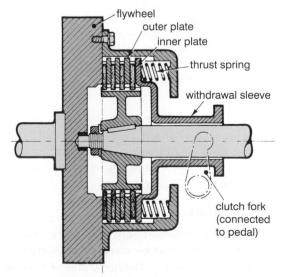

Figure 3.33 Simple multi-plate clutch arrangement

3.9   The sliding-mesh gearbox

3.9.1 Basis of the modern manual gearbox

The sliding-mesh gearbox was popular on cars up to about 1930, but today it is rarely used. Nevertheless, many modern gearboxes have been developed from its configuration. The basic layout of a four-speed and reverse gearbox is shown in Figure 3.34. The various spur-type gears are mounted on three shafts:

- Primary shaft (alternative names: input, clutch or first motion shaft)
- Layshaft (countershaft)
- Mainshaft (output or third motion shaft)

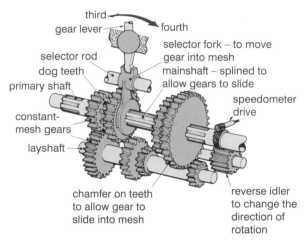

Figure 3.34 Four-speed and reverse sliding-mesh gearbox

3.9.2 Primary shaft

The primary shaft transmits the drive from the clutch to the gearbox at the engine side of the transmission system. The shaft is supported by a spigot bearing positioned close to the splines on to which the clutch driven plate is connected. The main load on this shaft is taken by a bearing; normally a seated radial ball type, positioned close to an input gear called a constant-mesh pinion.

The gear is so named because it is always in mesh with a larger gear, a constant-mesh wheel that is part of the layshaft gear cluster. **Note**: a small driving gear is called a pinion and a large gear a wheel. The term 'cog' is not used.

3.9.3 Layshaft

The layshaft, which is normally fixed to the gearbox casing, supports the various-sized driving pinions of the layshaft gear cluster. Bearings placed between the shaft rand gear cluster resist the radial load set up when the gears are forced apart. The type of bearing depends on the load it has to withstand; for a comparatively light load, a phosphor-bronze plain bush is suitable, but heavy-duty applications call for a more efficient bearing, such as a caged needle roller. Gear noise occurs when a high driving torque causes the gears to move apart. To keep the shaft distance constant, a more rigid bearing is used, for example an uncaged needle roller bearing. In most cases, the end-float of the layshaft gear assembly, and in consequence the alignment of the gears, is controlled by flat thrust washers situated between the gear cluster and the casing.

3.9.4 Mainshaft

This splined output shaft carries spur gearwheels that slide along the shaft to engage with the appropriate layshaft gears. At the 'front' end, the mainshaft is supported by a spigot bearing situated in the centre of the constant-mesh pinion. A heavy-duty radial ball bearing is fitted at the other end to take the force of the gears as they attempt to move apart. The load on this bearing is at a maximum at the time when first gear is engaged and high torque is being produced.

3.9.5 Gear selector

The gear lever transfers the input from the driver to the gear selector mechanism. The selector is a fork mounted on a rod, which fits into a groove in the gear. The function of the fork is to slide the gear wheel along the mainshaft so that the gear can engage and disengage with the matching gear pinion mounted on the layshaft. A striking mechanism is an alternative name for this arrangement; in a similar way, the rod is sometimes called a rail.

A four-speed gearbox needs three selector forks; these slide on, or move with, three separate rods. Normally one fork controls the first and second gears, and the second fork controls the third and top gears. Reverse has a separate fork, longer than the other two, because it has to fit around the lower-positioned reverse gear.

3.9.6 Gear wheel positions when different gears are selected

Refer to Figure 3.35 while reading through this section. It shows a four-speed gearbox with reverse type for simplicity.

Neutral

All mainshaft gear wheels are positioned so that they do not touch the layshaft gears, this enables them to rotate freely. A drive is taken to the layshaft, but the mainshaft will not be turned while in the neutral position.

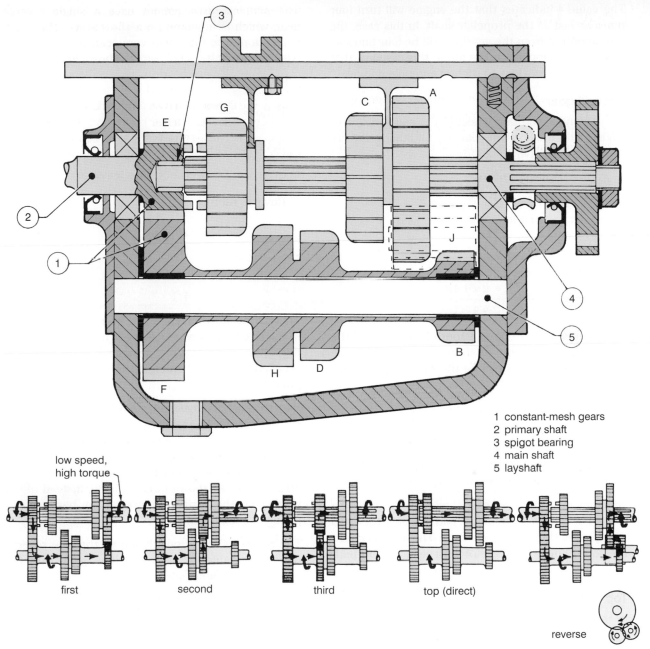

1 constant-mesh gears
2 primary shaft
3 spigot bearing
4 main shaft
5 layshaft

low speed,
high torque

first   second   third   top (direct)

reverse

Figure 3.35 Gear positions (sliding-mesh). Four-speed and reverse sliding-mesh gearbox.

First gear

The first-speed gear wheel (A) on the mainshaft is slid backwards to engage with pinion B on the layshaft; all other gears are positioned in neutral. In this gear, the reduction in speed that occurs as the drive passes through the constant-mesh gears (E and F) is reduced further by the first-speed gears (A and B).

The gear ratio (also called the movement ratio or velocity ratio) is given by:

$$\text{Ratio} = \frac{\text{Number of teeth on driven wheel}}{\text{Number of teeth on driving wheel}} = \frac{\text{Driven}}{\text{Driver}}$$

Since two sets of gears are used in a gearbox, then:

$$\text{Ratio} = \frac{\text{Driven}}{\text{Driver}} \times \frac{\text{Driven}}{\text{Driver}}$$

Note: the ratios are multiplied together to determine the overall gear ratio.

$$\begin{aligned}
\text{First gear ratio} &= \frac{F}{E} \times \frac{A}{B} \\[4pt]
&= \frac{40}{20} \times \frac{40}{20} \\[4pt]
&= 2 \times 2 \\[4pt]
&= 4:1
\end{aligned}$$

The value 4 indicates that the engine will turn four times as fast as the propeller shaft. In this case, the torque output from the gearbox will be four times as great as that applied at the input; this assumes that there is no energy loss to friction and oil pumping.

Second gear

The second-speed gearwheel (C) is slid forward to engage with the layshaft gear (D); all other gears are set in the non-driving position.

$$\text{Ratio} = \frac{\text{Driven}}{\text{Driver}} \times \frac{\text{Driven}}{\text{Driver}}$$

$$\text{Second gear ratio} = \frac{F}{E} \times \frac{C}{D}$$

$$= \frac{40}{20} \times \frac{35}{25}$$

$$= 2 \times 1.4$$

$$= 2.8 : 1$$

When the same size of gear tooth is used for all the gears in a gearbox, the total number of teeth on the various sets of gears will be the same. In this case, the total number is 60.

Third gear

In this gear position, gear wheel G is slid in to mesh with gear H. Since the size of the layshaft gear (H) is larger than the gear (D) that was used to give second gear, a slightly higher ratio than second is obtained.

Sometimes it is necessary when diagnosing a particular fault to consider the path taken by the drive as it passes through the gearbox. This path is called the power flow. In the case of third gear, the flow path is: Primary shaft to gears E, F, H and G to mainshaft.

Top gear

In this layout, fourth gear is a direct drive; namely a gear that gives a ratio of 1:1. It is obtained by sliding gear G to engage its dog teeth with the corresponding teeth formed on the end of the constant-mesh pinion E. Engagement of the dog clutch locks the primary to the mainshaft and this gives a 'straight-through' drive. In this gear, the power flow is not transmitted through any gear teeth so the energy loss is small (i.e. the efficiency is high). Losses would be even smaller if it were possible to reduce the churning effect of oil by the layshaft, but this oil movement is necessary to provide lubrication of the gearbox.

Reverse gear

Sliding a reverse gear between any two gears on the layshaft and mainshaft is the method used to change the direction of rotation (DOR) of the output shaft.

The simplest arrangement uses a single reverse gear, which is mounted on a short shaft. This shaft is positioned so that the reverse can slide and mesh with the two first-speed gears as shown in Figure 3.35.

The gear ratio is:

$$\text{Ratio} = \frac{\text{Driven}}{\text{Driver}} \times \frac{\text{Driven}}{\text{Driver}} \times \frac{\text{Driven}}{\text{Driver}}$$

$$\text{Reverse ratio} = \frac{F}{E} \times \frac{J}{B} \times \frac{A}{J}$$

In this case, J cancels out, thus leaving:

$$\text{Reverse ratio} = \frac{F}{E} \times \frac{A}{B}$$

$$= \frac{40}{20} \times \frac{40}{20}$$

$$= 2 \times 2$$

$$= 4 : 1$$

This is the same ratio as for first gear and, irrespective of the size of the reverse gear (J), it will be seen that the ratio always remains the same. For this reason, it is called an idler – it changes the direction, but does not alter the ratio.

With the idler arrangement, some drivers persistently slip the clutch to maintain a low reversing speed. Excessive clutch wear resulting from this practice is minimised when the reverse ratio is set lower than first gear. This is achieved by using a reverse gear arrangement as shown in Figure 3.36. Instead of the single idler, the compound reverse gear has two gear pinions joined together.

The reverse shaft is positioned so that the reverse pinions are able to mesh simultaneously with the appropriate layshaft and mainshaft gears.

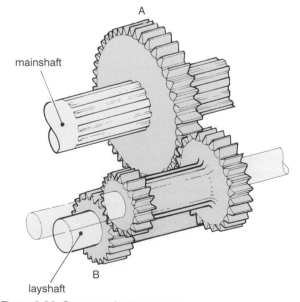

Figure 3.36 Compound reverse gear

3.9.7 Gear changing

When one gear is moved to engage with another gear, noise will result if the peripheral (outside) speeds are not the same. To avoid this, the driver of a vehicle having a sliding-mesh gearbox performs an operation called double-declutching.

On changing up, for example from first to second, the clutch driven plate, primary shaft and layshaft gear cluster must be slowed down by re-engaging the clutch while the lever is positioned in neutral. The engine slows down more quickly than the layshaft assembly, so a braking action on the layshaft assembly is obtained.

The opposite is required when changing down; the layshaft must be sped up. To achieve this, the engine is reconnected to the gearbox while the lever is in neutral, and the accelerator pedal is depressed. When the layshaft assembly has sped up by the required amount, the accelerator is released, the clutch pedal depressed and the gear lever moved to the lower gear. Finally, as the clutch is being released, the engine must be accelerated sufficiently to match the engine speed to the road speed.

A chamfer on the engagement side of each gear tooth is provided to allow for an easier entry of the sliding gear. However, if the driver makes a bad change, in addition to the loud noise created by the gear teeth rubbing against each other, burring of the teeth will occur and in some cases the teeth will chip or break off.

3.9.8 Selector mechanism

A fork of the type shown in Figure 3.37 is used to slide a gear wheel along the mainshaft in order to select the appropriate gear. It is mounted on its own rod and links the driver's gear stick to the sliding gear wheel. Two selector forks are required for a three-speed and reverse gearbox, and three forks are needed for a four-speed unit. The gear stick can be a direct-acting lever or it can be mounted remote from the gearbox.

Every gearbox must be fitted with the following:

- Selector detent – holds the gears and selectors in position and so prevents gear engagement or disengagement due to vibration.
- Interlock mechanism – prevents two gears engaging simultaneously; if this occurs, the gearbox will lock up and shaft rotation will be impossible. (Severe damage will occur if the interlock device is omitted during a gearbox overhaul.)

Selector detent

Figure 3.37a shows a typical arrangement suitable for a layout having the selector fork locked to the rod. The device consists of a steel ball that is pressed into a groove in the rod by a spring.

Into the rod are ground three grooves; these correspond to the rod positions for neutral and for the two gears served by the selector. Retention of the rod is governed by the strength of the spring. In cases where the spring strength is adjustable, it must be set sufficiently strong to prevent the gear from jumping out of mesh, but not so strong that it makes gear changing difficult. Each selector rod has a separate spring-loaded detent.

Interlock mechanism

Every gearbox must have some form of safety device fitted to prevent two gears, for example second and top, engaging at the same time. This mechanism is fitted in addition to the selector detent. Although the interlock device takes a number of different forms, the arrangement shown in Figure. 3.37b is one of the most common.

This system uses a plunger and two balls; the diameter of each ball is greater than the spaces between the rods. When one of the outside rods is moved, the full diameter of the rod presses its adjacent ball into the groove ground in the centre rod. This action retains the centre rod in the neutral position and also pushes the plunger against the second ball to lock the other rod.

From the neutral position, movement of the centre selector rod carries the plunger with it and allows the full shaft diameter of the rod to push both steel balls into the grooves machined in the outer rods.

Figure 3.37b shows the technician who has to dismantle the selector mechanism that the rods cannot be driven out unless they are set in the neutral position.

When dismantling a gearbox for repair, it is advisable to ascertain the type of interlock used on the particular gearbox; this is because during cleaning it is easy for either a ball or the plunger to drop out. If this is not noticed when the box is reassembled, the high risk of gearbox seizure, and the effect of this on a moving vehicle, will cause many problems.

3.9.9 Lubrication

In the past heavy gear oil was used as a lubricant for a sliding-mesh gearbox. If the box were in use today, then oil similar to that used in a rear axle, such as extreme pressure (EP80–90) would be suitable; this assumes that precautions had been taken by the

Neutral postion

In gear

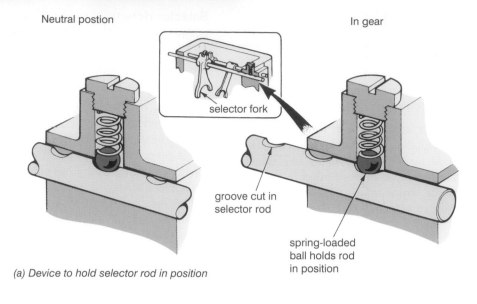

selector fork

groove cut in
selector rod

spring-loaded
ball holds rod
in position

(a) Device to hold selector rod in position

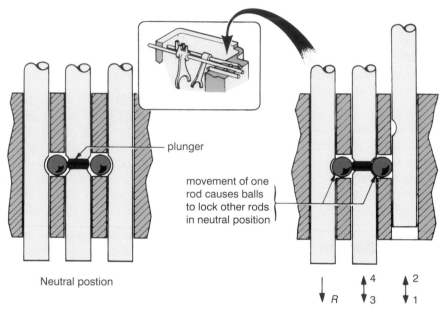

plunger

movement of one
rod causes balls
to lock other rods
in neutral position

Neutral postion

R   4   2
     3   1

(b) Ball and plunger type of interlocking mechanism prevents two gears engaging at the same time

Figure 3.37 Selector mechanism

manufacturer to avoid corrosive attack by this oil on non-ferrous materials such as phosphor-bronze.

The gearbox oil level is set at layshaft height. Rotation of the gears on this shaft carries the lubricant around with the gears in a pump-like manner; this simple method ensures that all meshing teeth have an adequate supply of oil. Splash lubrication, set up by the churning action of the oil by the layshaft gears, is the method used to lubricate the other gearbox parts.

Some form of oil sealing arrangement at the front and back ends of the gearbox is necessary. This prevents loss of oil and possible contamination of the clutch friction facings.

3.9.10 Power take-off arrangement

In addition to the mechanism used for driving a vehicle along a road, a power supply is often required for operating various external items of auxiliary equipment.

A light truck having a tipping mechanism is one example, but the most varied application of power take-off units is associated with specialised off-road vehicles. Many agricultural operators regard this type of light vehicle as a transportable power source for driving saws, drifts, pumps, etc.

Figure 3.38 shows a typical power take-off arrangement that is driven from the gearbox layshaft. The extra take-off gear, which is mounted on a flange provided on the side of the gearbox, is slid in to mesh with one of the sliding-mesh gears of the layshaft by a separate selector lever.

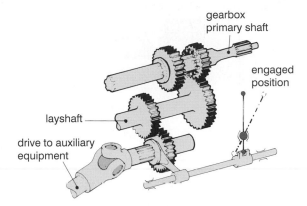

Figure 3.38 Power take-off arrangement

3.10 Constant-mesh and synchromesh gearboxes

3.10.1 Evolution from sliding-mesh system

The sliding-mesh-type gearbox discussed on page 302 is no longer used by manufacturers. Many of the design features in the constant-mesh-type gearbox, however, have evolved from the sliding-mesh-type of gearbox arrangement. To ensure that a full understanding is obtained of the constant-mesh-type gearbox it is useful to ensure that the more basic sliding-mesh is understood.

3.10.2 Disadvantages of the sliding-mesh

Although the mechanical efficiency of the sliding-mesh gearbox was high, it suffered from two great disadvantages:

- Gear noise due to the type of gear
- The difficulty of obtaining a smooth, quiet and quick change of gear without the application of great skill and judgement

Gearbox designs introduced over the past decades have been developed to overcome these disadvantages. The first step in the development came when the constant-mesh gearbox was introduced.

3.10.3 Constant-mesh gearbox

This was first used on cars in the early 1930s, but gave way after only a short time to other designs, although it is still used on commercial vehicles and tractors.

The main feature is the use of the stronger helical or double helical gears, which lead to quieter operation. Each pair of gears is in constant-mesh, and gear operation is obtained by locking the respective gear to the mainshaft by means of a **dog clutch**.

Dog clutch: device that joins together two shafts, by means of teeth in one part that engage in slots in the other, in order to transmit motion.

The layout of the box follows the sliding-mesh arrangement previously described, and Figure 3.39 shows the main details of the third and top-gear section. The mainshaft gear wheels are mounted on bushes or needle rollers, and are located by thrust washers. When the gear is required, a dog clutch, which is splined to the mainshaft, is slid along by the selector to engage with the dog teeth formed on the gear. This has the effect of locking the gear wheel to the shaft. There will still be noise if the dog teeth are not rotating at the same speed when the engagement is made, and so double declutching is necessary, but damage caused by a 'bad' change will be limited to the dog clutch.

3.10.4 Synchromesh (constant-load type)

The constant-mesh gearbox provided a number of improvements over the sliding-mesh gearbox, with the reduction in gear noise being one of the major benefits. However, a certain amount of skill was still required to produce a quick, quiet change. The difficulty was in double-declutching, and the purpose of carrying out this operation was to equalise the speeds of the two sets of dog teeth before engaging the gear. It soon became apparent that some device was required to synchronise the speeds mechanically, and when the system was invented it was known as the synchromesh gearbox.

The first type of synchromesh gearbox used in Figure 3.40 shows the main details of the unit controlling third and top gear. Fundamentally, the gearbox is laid out in the same manner as a constant-mesh, with the exception that a cone clutch is fitted between the dog and gear members.

The female cone of this clutch is formed in a hub, which has internal and external splines. A series of spring-loaded balls are carried in radial holes in the hub, and these push outwards into a groove machined in a sleeve. The selector fork controls the position of the sleeve, which has splines of the same pitch as the dog teeth on the gear.

The initial movement of the selector and sleeve carries the hub towards the gear and allows the cones to contact. At this point, the friction between

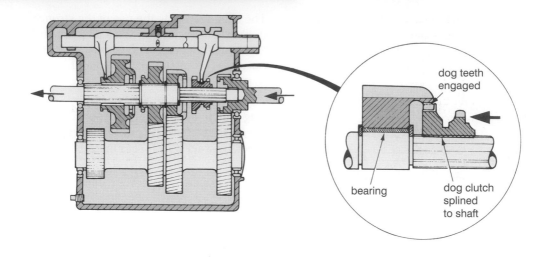

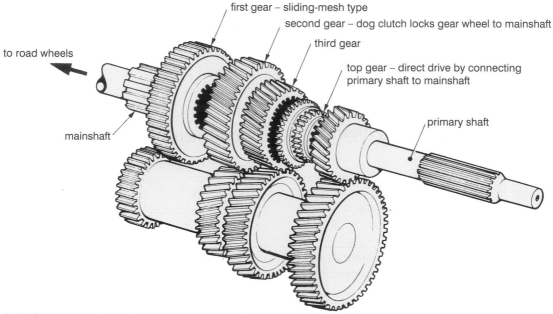

Figure 3.39 Constant-mesh gearbox

the cones adjusts the speed of the gear wheel to suit the hub and mainshaft. Extra pressure on the lever will allow the sleeve to override the spring-loaded balls and positively engage with the dogs on the gear.

If the gear change is rushed, there will not be enough time for synchronisation, and the change will be noisy. The time taken for the speed to be equalised is governed by the frictional force that exists at the cone faces. This force is controlled by:

- total spring strength
- depth of groove in sleeve
- angle of cone
- coefficient of friction between cones.

Therefore, if, because of mechanical defects, any of these factors is reduced, synchronisation will take a longer time and noise will probably be heard. This time factor has presented problems for the lubrication specialist, since the high-viscosity oil required by the gears takes a considerable time to disperse from the cones. The solution to this problem was to use a lower viscosity oil (similar to medium engine oil SAE 30) and provide a series of grooves on the cone face to cut through the oil film and disperse the lubricant. Until recently, it was considered essential to drain and refill the gearbox every 8000 km (5000 miles) in order to remove the particles worn from the cones and gear teeth. With extended service schedules now in operation this mileage has been increased considerably, and some manufacturers have recommended that after the first change no further changes are necessary.

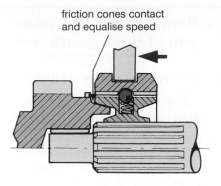

friction cones contact and equalise speed

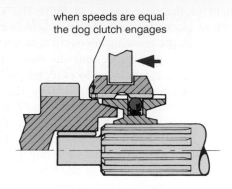

when speeds are equal the dog clutch engages

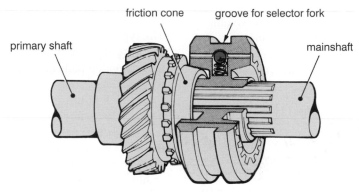

friction cone   groove for selector fork

primary shaft   mainshaft

Figure 3.40 Principle of the synchromesh gearbox

3.10.5 Baulk ring synchromesh

The baulk ring system, which is sometimes called blocker ring or inertia lock, is a later development of the constant load system, used in the manufacture of modern gearboxes, and is designed to overcome the main disadvantage of the earlier design – noise or crashing of the gears due to a quick change.

Two main features are incorporated in the baulk ring system:

1 The cone pressure or load is proportional to the speed of change.
2 An interception device prevents positive gear engagement until the speed of the two members is equal.

Various constructions are used to produce these features. Figure 3.41 shows one system in common use.

Operation

Three spring-loaded shifting plates, which push out from the hub into a groove in the sleeve, fit into slots in the baulking cone. Each slot is wider than the plate; the clearance on each side is equal to half the pitch of the splines on the sleeve. The baulking cone, which is made of phosphor-bronze, has specially chamfered teeth on the outside, of a pitch similar to that of the dog teeth on the gear sleeve.

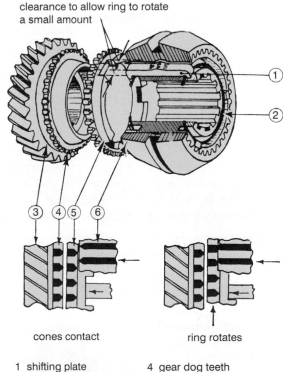

clearance to allow ring to rotate a small amount

cones contact   ring rotates

1 shifting plate
2 circlip spring
3 gear
4 gear dog teeth
5 baulking cone and ring
6 sleeve

Figure 3.41 Baulk ring synchromesh unit

Movement of the gear lever will move the sleeve and shifting plates towards the gear selected. The plates will push the baulking cone into light frictional contact with the gear cone, and the difference in speed will allow the gear cone to carry the baulking cone around to the limit controlled by the plate (half spline movement). Extra pressure on the lever will tend to move the sleeve towards the dog teeth of the gear, but if the two members have different speeds, the dog teeth on the baulking ring will block the passage of the sleeve. In this position the splines on the sleeve are touching the teeth on the baulking ring, and therefore if a greater force is applied to the lever, a greater force will act between the cones and synchronisation will be achieved in a shorter time. As the speeds become equal, the plates assume a central position in the slots of the baulking ring, and all teeth line up; therefore the sleeve can now pass the baulking cone to engage positively with the dog teeth on the gear. The torque is now able to be transmitted to the mainshaft through the whole assembly, which includes the gear wheel, sleeve and synchro hub.

With the baulk ring synchromesh system, gear changes can be made quickly without any engagement noise. If the gear is unable to engage on the first movement of the gear lever, extra pressure can be applied to the baulk ring ensuring the relative speeds are matched to allow synchronisation. Quicker and quieter gear changes are made using this type of synchromesh gearbox, resulting in less wear on the transmission system and reduced driver fatigue.

3.11 Rear-, front- and four-wheel drive gearboxes

3.11.1 Rear-wheel drive gearboxes

Figure 3.42 shows, by means of an exploded view, the gear layout of a simple four-speed and reverse gearbox suitable for a rear-wheel drive car. This gearbox uses a baulking-ring-type synchromesh on all forward speeds. To simplify the construction, a sliding-mesh arrangement is used for reverse.

The type of baulking ring shown in Figure 3.42 is different in construction from that shown in Figure 3.41, but the basic principle is the same.

The type of unit shown in Figure 3.42 utilises the hub to press the synchro cones together. It uses three spring-loaded balls in the hub to lock the hub initially to the striker ring, and three tangs on the baulking ring, which fit into slots in the hub, give the baulking action. Circumferential movement of the ring, relative to the hub, is arranged by having a clearance between the sides of the tangs and hub. This ensures that the ring can move each way, to the extent of half a spline, to block the passage of the striker ring as it attempts to engage with the dog teeth on the gear.

Reverse gear is arranged with the teeth of the reverse idler gear meshed on to the teeth of the sleeve used to select first and second gear. When the driver selects the reverse gear, the reverse idler gear engages and

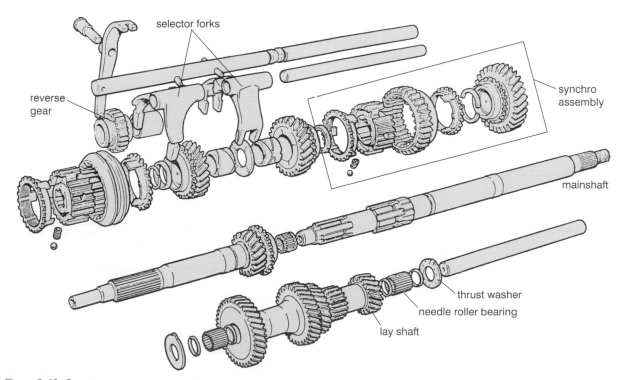

Figure 3.42 Gear layout four-speed and reverse gearbox

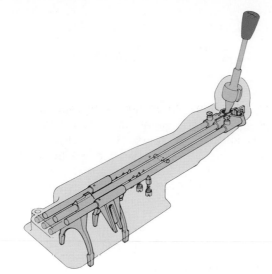

Figure 3.43 Remote control lever

meshes with the gear on the layshaft cluster, which then transfers the torque through the first and second gear sleeve through to the mainshaft, but in reverse direction.

Uncaged needle rollers are used in this layout to support the layshaft gears. This bearing arrangement is now common because, in addition to having low friction, the extra rigidity of a needle roller compared with a plain bush gives a more precise gear mesh. As a consequence, the noise is reduced when the gearbox is loaded. This construction makes it more difficult to reassemble the box, but with the aid of a dummy layshaft of equal length to the gear cluster the task is made easier.

Every gearbox must have some provision to prevent the escape of oil. For flange joining, either the fitment of a paper-based sealing joint or, on metal-to-metal faces, the application of a sealing compound is used.

Leakage along the shafts and through the bearings is normally prevented by fitting lip-type seals. These are positioned on the clutch side of the primary shaft bearing and at the universal joint end of the gearbox extension housing.

Speedometer drive

The speedometer is driven by means of a skew gear from the main shaft. A steel worm, mounted on the mainshaft and located in the gearbox extension housing, generally drives a plastic moulded pinion; this is connected to either a flexible cable or an electrical transducer.

Gear change mechanism

The seating position often means that the gearbox selectors are situated well forward of the driver's body. In the past, a long 'floppy' lever was used, but nowadays the rigidity of a short lever and a remote control mechanism enables the driver to select the gears with greater precision.

Five-speed and reverse gearbox

Over the last decade, the fitment of five-speed transmission systems to vehicles has led to improved fuel consumption and lower emissions due to the overdrive facility of the fifth gear. Modern vehicles incorporate additional gears and often have six forward gears, which is sometimes extended to seven speeds in manual transmissions, and even eight in some automatic transmission systems. The term 'overdrive' means that the propeller shaft turns faster than the engine, so in a five-speed gearbox the fourth gear is the normal 'top' or direct-drive gear.

Figure 3.44 shows a heavy-duty five-speed gearbox in which all gears, including reverse, are synchromesh. Helical gears are used throughout and each gear on the mainshaft is supported on needle rollers; this reduces noise and improves efficiency. The gearbox casing, which is ribbed to avoid distortion under load, is a lightweight aluminium alloy die-casting.

In recent years, computer-controlled manufacturing processes have made it possible to produce gears with great accuracy. This allows running tolerances to be reduced, which in turn leads to a quieter operation. These developments allow for the use of oils of low viscosity, so by expending less energy to rotate the layshaft the gearbox efficiency is improved. In the gearbox shown in Figure 3.44, very thin oil, similar to that used in automatic transmissions, is recommended.

In common with many other five-speed gearboxes, the fifth-speed gear of the box shown is situated at the rear of the gearbox.

Reverse detent

Some form of 'blocker' arrangement is fitted to a gearbox to prevent the accidental engagement of reverse gear when the vehicle is moving forward. The simplest form is a spring-loaded detent; this must be overcome by the driver before the lever can be moved to the 'reverse' position. To overcome this spring, the driver either has to lift the gear lever or exert extra pressure on it.

Five-speed gearboxes sometimes use a gear lever pattern of movement (gate pattern), whereby fifth and reverse are in the same plane, for example fifth and reverse are obtained by forward and backward movement of the lever respectively. In these cases, a positive gate lock is often used.

In the gearbox shown in Figure 3.44, the driver has to lift a collar on the gear lever to engage reverse.

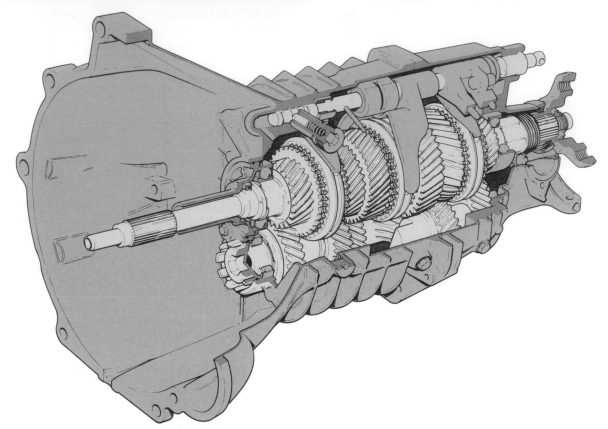

Figure 3.44 Five-speed and reverse gearbox (Ford type)

3.11.2 Front-wheel drive gearboxes

A transversely mounted engine and transmission assembly is the common arrangement for a front-wheel drive vehicle. This compact transaxle configuration normally requires the gearbox input and output shaft to be at the same end, so a two-shaft layout is used.

Since a simple (single-reduction) system of gearing is used instead of a compound (double-reduction) system, a layshaft is not needed.

Figure 3.45 shows the layout of a five-speed and reverse gearbox. In this design, each shaft is supported by a ball race at the non-driving end; at the other end the radial load is much heavier, so a roller race is fitted. Axial thrust on each shaft is taken by a radial-type ball bearing, so this locates the shaft and maintains alignment and takes the thrust of the helical gears. The **spigot bearing** needed with a layshaft-type gearbox is unnecessary with the two-shaft layout, so this gives a more rigid gear assembly and a quieter gearbox results. A further improvement can be made when needle rollers are used to support the gears on the shafts.

Spigot bearing: a small needle roller bearing that sits in the middle of the flywheel.

Gear change mechanism

Some form of remote control mechanism is essential because a long lever is far too flexible.

The linkage used must be capable of transmitting two distinct motions: longitudinal movement of the gear as it is moved from, say, first to second, and transverse movement as needed for the selection of another pair of gears.

Figure 3.46 shows the principle of two systems in common use: a single rod linkage; and a twin cable arrangement.

During operation, movement of the engine due to torque reaction is accommodated by either using a universal joint or relying on the inherent flexibility of the cable.

Speedometer drive

Front-wheel drive layouts normally have the skew gear mounted adjacent to the final-drive assembly. This drive point is more accessible than the output shaft of the gearbox. In earlier gearboxes, the speedometer was connected to the speedometer gear drive via a cable. However, modern gearboxes no longer use cables to transmit the vehicle speed to the speedometer, instead they use an electronic

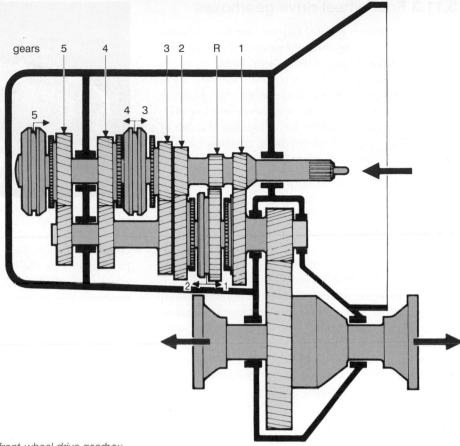

Figure 3.45 Layout of five-speed front-wheel drive gearbox

speedometer drive. The speed of the vehicle is transmitted via a **transducer** located inside the gearbox driven from the final drive. This transducer sends a signal via a cable to the speedometer fitted in the driver's display. Many vehicles fitted with an anti-lock braking system (ABS) now use the ABS ECU to send vehicle speed signals to the speedometer from the ABS wheel speed sensors.

Transducer: an electrical device that transforms one sort of energy into another, for instance converting variations in a physical quantity, such as speed, into an electrical signal.

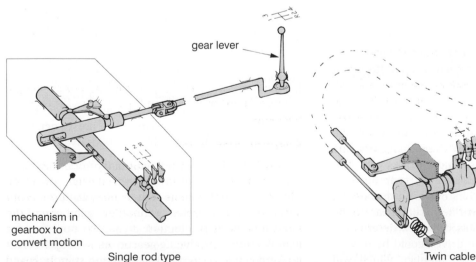

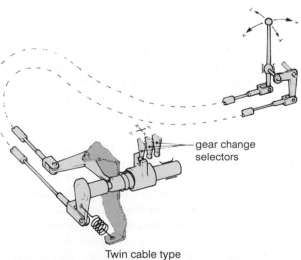

Figure 3.46 Gear change mechanism

3.11.3 Four-wheel drive gearboxes

Four-wheel drive vehicles require the transmission system to distribute torque between the front and rear axles. In many cases this is split 50/50, although some vehicles more biased to road use will have different torque split arrangements, for example 70/30 split front to rear. The gearboxes fitted to four-wheel drive vehicles usually have the same number of ratios as front- or rear-wheel drive vehicles, ranging from five to six forward gears.

Four-wheel drive vehicles normally have an additional component within the transmission system to pass the drive to the front and rear axles. This is called a transfer box and it is usually located on the end of the gearbox. Many smaller four-wheel drive vehicles, especially those biased to the road, have a gearbox that is adapted from the front-wheel drive unit. The drive to the rear wheels is normally taken from a transfer box attached to the output shaft of the gearbox. This can be seen in Figure 3.47, with the transfer box being attached to the differential output on the flywheel side of the gearbox. The right-hand wheel will then take its drive from the transfer gearbox along with the rear wheels.

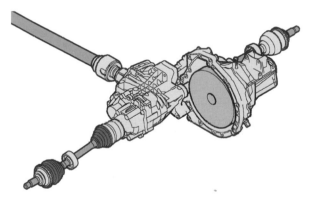

Figure 3.47 Transmission layout of a five-speed gearbox on a four-wheel drive vehicle

3.12 Automatic gearbox (gear system and fluid coupling)

3.12.1 Introduction

Once the driver has confirmed the direction the car is to move in, automatic gearbox systems change gear automatically during a drive cycle. The driver manually selects the desired gear and the automatic gearbox takes up its drive. From then on, the automatic gearbox identifies what gear to be in during its drive cycle. This could be determined by a number of factors. The driver could be driving in a controlled or aggressive manner, which will affect the automatic gear change routine. The road

Figure 3.48 View of the inside of an automatic gearbox

characteristics will also affect the automatic gearbox performance if the car is being driven up or down acute inclines. In each case, the automatic gearbox identifies the factors and selects the preferred gear to keep the car under control.

In the past, the automatic gearbox was often considered to be a luxury, but today many drivers regard this unit as a desirable essential. This popularity has led to the introduction of many different types of box. Two-pedal control (i.e. the elimination of the clutch pedal), together with automatic gear selection, reduces driver fatigue because it overcomes the need for tedious clutch and gear-change operations. Consequently, the simpler control of the vehicle enables the driver to concentrate on the other essentials of vehicle handling, especially the safety aspects.

Some early designs of automatic transmission were criticised because they robbed the driver of gearbox control. Modern units have overcome these drawbacks by allowing drivers to override the gearbox when they wish to take full command. More recently, the incorporation of electronic gearbox control has enabled the gearbox to be operated in a mode to match the driver's technique and performance requirement, for example sports mode and economy mode.

Up until the mid 1970s, the majority of automatic gearboxes used on light vehicles were made by Borg Warner. This company offered a range of units to suit engine sizes between 1.5 and 5 litres. Based on production numbers, one of the most successful gearboxes was the Model 35 and its derivatives.

Today, most vehicle manufacturers produce a gearbox either of their own design, or made under licence to some other manufacturer. With automatic transmission technology being one of the most advanced production areas, we now see car manufacturers producing gearboxes with up to eight forward gears to support the emission standards and improve fuel efficiency.

Automatic transmission units

To understand the fundamental operating principles of an automatic transmission, we need to break it down into key areas. Other than the continuously variable transmission (CVT) systems, most modern automatic transmissions consist of two main units: a main gearbox and a fluid clutch.

The function of these main parts is as follows:

Main gearbox – automatically provides a series of stepped ratios to enable the vehicle to overcome road conditions needing a large driving effort; also allows the vehicle to operate over a wide road-speed range. This is achieved by using a configuration of gears referred to as planetary or epicyclic gears. In addition to the provision of neutral and reverse, the modern gearbox also has a positive parking lock and a means for the selection, and 'hold', of a particular gear.

Fluid clutch – automatically disconnects the drive when the engine speed is low and gradually connects it as the vehicle is moved from a stationary position. It is either a fluid coupling or fluid converter; the latter is often called a torque converter because, in its simple form, it can double the output torque from the engine. In addition, the converter is able to reduce the torque amplification gradually as the output speed of the converter increases.

3.12.2 Planetary gearing

Planetary gearing, also called epicyclic gearing, is a system in which one or more of the gear elements rotates around another gear in a similar manner to the way that the planets revolve around the sun. Conventional gearing systems have the gears on shafts mounted in fixed positions, but planetary systems use the movement of some of its gears, together with their mounting shafts, to produce the required motion and gear ratio.

A planetary system can be arranged in many ways and, since this type of gearing offers many advantages, it is used in a number of different automotive components, the most common being the automatic gearbox.

'Epicycle' can be defined as a small circle rolling around the circumference of a larger circle. When using this principle in a gearing system, you will see a small pinion gear rolling around the outside of the larger gear. To simplify this understanding, imagine our solar system of planets rotating around the sun. The small pinion gear is known as a planet gear and the larger gear is the sun gear. This is then known as epicyclic gearing, as shown in Figure 3.49.

As in Figure 3.49, you will identify that the sun gear is fixed to its shaft and the planet gear is the gear that achieves the rotational movement. The number of rotations will be determined by the amount of teeth that both gears have. It should be noted that when a planet gear revolves around a fixed sun, the number of revolutions it makes, relative to the observer, is always one greater than the obvious. For example, if the planet gear has 20 teeth and the sun gear has 40 teeth, then the planet gear will rotate three times as it travels around one circumference of the sun gear.

Another type of planetary gearing uses an internally toothed ring gear. This is shown in Figure 3.50 and is known as an annulus. The annulus meshes its internal toothed gearing to the planet pinion gear. When the

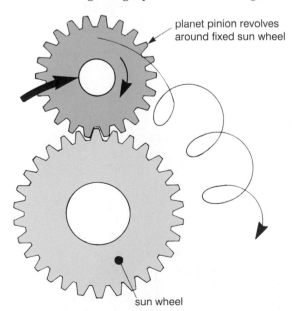

planet pinion revolves around fixed sun wheel

sun wheel

Figure 3.49 Epicyclic gear action – planet revolving around a fixed sun wheel

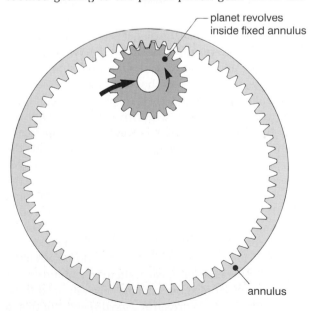

planet revolves inside fixed annulus

annulus

Figure 3.50 Epicyclic gear action – planet revolving inside a fixed annulus

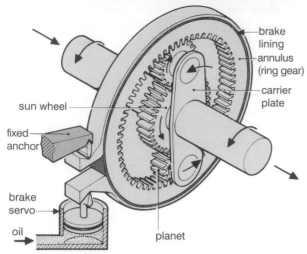

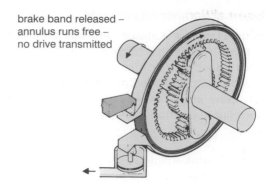

brake band released –
annulus runs free –
no drive transmitted

Figure 3.51 A simple epicyclic gear train

annulus is fixed, the planet rotational movement causes it to rotate around the inside the annulus. If you then compare this action with the previous sun and planet rotational activity, you will conclude that the planet gear will have to rotate many more times around the annulus to complete the same cycle.

Simple epicyclic gear trains

The most common epicyclic gear arrangement is known as the 'Simpson gear'. This uses a sun and annulus system with two or more planet gears positioned within its assembly (Figure 3.51). In this assembly, the input shaft is connected to the sun gear and output shaft is connected to the planet gears via a planet carrier plate. An external contracting friction brake band surrounds the circumference of the annulus to hold it stationary when necessary.

Whenever the annulus brake band is released, the natural resistance to movement of the planet carrier output shaft will cause the planet gears to become idler gears. This will result in the forward-moving sun gear driving the annulus gear in the opposite direction. At this stage, no drive would be transmitted through the gear train to the output shaft (Figure 3.51, right-hand illustration). To obtain a positive drive through the gear train, the brake band around the circumference of the annulus has to be applied. This then holds the annulus in a fixed position and the driven sun gear rotates and drives the planet gears to walk around the internal gearing of the annulus (Figure 3.51, left-hand illustration). The planet carrier and output shaft rotate in the same direction as the input shaft, but at a much slower rotational speed. The speed at which the output shaft is driven is determined by the ratio between the gears. For the epicyclic gear train to transmit drive, at least one of the members of this unit will need to be held stationary or is driven at a fixed speed. For this to be achieved, the system uses friction brake bands or a multi-plate clutch assembly to perform this function.

Figure 3.52 shows the action of a planet pinion gear as a lever. When the annulus is held stationary by the brake band and the sun gear is rotated through a small angle (A), the planet lever pivots about a tooth (fulcrum) on the annulus gear. This action causes the centre of the lever to prise forward the planet carrier and rotate it about its axis to the extent of angle B. The movement of the planet carrier now rotates the output shaft. A comparison of the movement of the input shaft with the output shaft is shown in the angle achieved between A and B. This indicates that a gear train of this size produces a reduction between the input and output shaft to achieve about a 3:1 ratio.

Gear ratios

To work out the gear ration of an epicyclic gear train, you need to determine the number of teeth on the sun gear and the annulus. To identify this, you need to calculate the following:

$$\text{Ratio} = \frac{A + S}{S}$$

Where:

A = number of teeth on the annulus

S = number of teeth on the sun gear

Example: if $A = 100$ and $S = 20$, the gear ratio is $6:1$

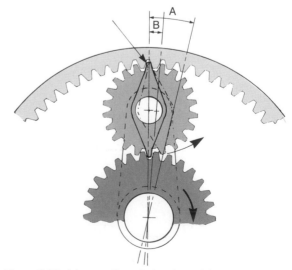

Figure 3.52 A lever action of planetary pinion

Brake action

When an epicyclic gear train is used in any form of gearbox, the friction brake action overcomes many of the drawbacks associated with gear engagement in a conventional gearbox. The brake is both quick and quiet in its operation and during engagement the slipping action prevents a sudden jolt. This feature could be used in a transmission system to perform the function of the main clutch, but rapid wear of the brake would occur. It is therefore necessary to retain the main clutch so that the brake can be applied at a more controllable rate, giving a smooth operation together with a good friction material life.

As gear engagement is provided by the brake mechanism, and since the need to disconnect the power is avoided, the main clutch only has to function as a device to take-up the drive when the vehicle is moved off from rest. A fluid clutch meets this need, so this type of clutch is normally fitted in conjunction with an automatic gearbox.

Figure 3.53 show the principle of using a system of both multi-plate disc clutch and brake band clutches when applied to the sun gear. Compared to a manual gearbox and clutch arrangement, this gives the automatic transmission a key advantage, enabling the delivery of power from the engine to the gearbox to be smooth. This ensures that there is progressive take-up of drive as the vehicle pulls away from a standing start. Additionally, the fluid coupling adds to the overall refinement of this gearbox when fitted with this type of clutch arrangement.

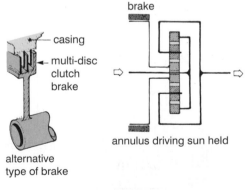

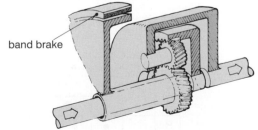

Figure 3.53 Brake applied to sun wheel

Gear ratio

The number of teeth on the sun wheel and the annulus of a simple epicyclic gear train govern the gear ratio. This is given by:

$$\text{Ratio} = \frac{A + S}{S}$$

Where:

A = number of teeth on annulus

S = number of teeth on sun wheel

Example: if A = 100 and S = 20, the ratio is 6:1.

Brake applied to sun gear

There are many occasions when an epicyclic gear train system is required to provide a comparatively high gear ratio. The ratio can be achieved by connecting the gear elements in the manner that is shown in Figure 3.53 (also Figure 3.54, 1.2:1 forward). To achieve this, the brake is applied to the sun gear; the input shaft is connected in such a way that it drives the annulus gear. Either the brake band or a multi-disc clutch can be used to hold the sun gear in a stationary position. This applies the same principle as mentioned previously in the gear leverage example. The point of contact between the planet gear and sun gear makes the planet the lever and sun gear the fulcrum.

The ratio achieved by this arrangement is:

$$\text{Ratio} = \frac{A + S}{A}$$

Using the same number of teeth as in the previous example: A = 100 and S = 20.

The ratio of this drive arrangement is 1.2:1.

This calculated ratio obtained is very close to direct drive (1:1), so this gear configuration has many uses.

Simple epicyclic drive arrangement

A simple epicyclic drive arrangement comprises a sun, planet set and an annulus. Another type of epicyclic gearing system is called the compound epicyclic drive arrangement, which uses one epicyclic drive assembly driving another.

Figure 3.54 shows how different gear ratios, together with forward and reverse, can be obtained from a simple epicyclic gear arrangement. These are achieved by altering either the brake band position or the input drive point. By using a number of clutches and brake bands with this simple assembly, various interconnections can be made to achieve a gearbox speed range such as first, second direct drive, reverse and neutral. A neutral position is not needed when a fixed ratio is required, so in this case the 'braked' element is often an integral part of the housing.

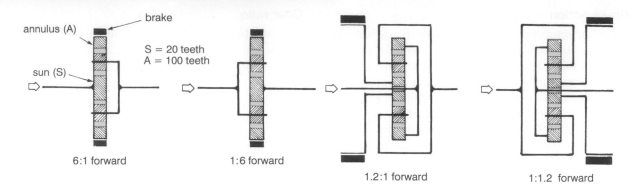

6:1 forward   1:6 forward

S = 20 teeth
A = 100 teeth

annulus (A)   brake

sun (S)

1.2:1 forward   1:1.2 forward

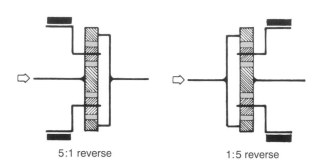

5:1 reverse   1:5 reverse

Figure 3.54 Various methods of connecting a simple epicyclic gear train

Construction

Note that Figure 3.54 shows a simplified epicyclic gear diagram with only one planet pinion gear being used. The arrangement of only one planet pinion gear is impracticable because a single pinion would give an unbalanced thrust on the sun and annulus members, as they are forced apart under load. Using three planet pinion gears that are equally spaced will overcome the imbalance of thrust. Figure 3.55 shows a version of a simple epicyclic gear unit, with each planet pinion being supported by a ball race that is fixed to a short shaft attached to the planet carrier assembly. This carrier assembly then acts as the arm of an epicyclic unit.

The illustrations of epicyclic gear assemblies show spur gear types. These are straight-cut gear teeth that were used in early versions of this gear construction. Now helical type gears are more commonly used (Figure 3.55). The helical type gear provides a quieter meshing of gears, but they need low-friction thrust washers in between them to resist the axial force set up by the tooth angle.

obtained by using both brake bands and multi-plate clutches together, which are used to hold selected epicyclic elements stationary allowing the drive to be transmitted through the transmission assembly.

Figure 3.56 shows a compound gear train arrangement that uses two clutches and two brake bands to provide the three forward gear ratios and a reverse gear. This configuration shows the basic principles of operation of a compound epicyclic gear train (Table 3.3).

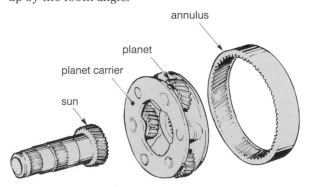

annulus

planet

planet carrier

sun

Figure 3.55 Simple epicyclic gear train

Compound gearing

Most automatic gearboxes use two or more epicyclic units to form a compound gear train assembly. Some of the internal elements in these units are permanently interconnected. The way this is achieved depends on the manufacturer's design and overall gearbox construction. The engagement of a particular gear is

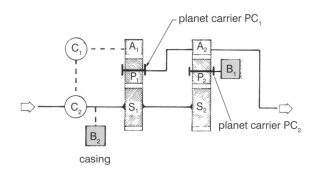

	C_1	C_2	B_1	B_2
N				
1	●		●	
2	●			●
3	●	●		
R		●	●	

Figure 3.56 Compound epicyclic gear train ZF planetary pinion

Table 3.3 Action of a compound gearing system

Gear	Clutch and brake engagement	Operation
First	C_1 and B_1	When vehicle is stationary, drive to A_1 causes the idler action of P_1 to drive S_1 in the opposite direction. This motion applied to S_2 allows the idler action of P_2 to drive A_1 forward at a slow speed. Even when the output shaft starts to move, the relative motion of the gear members remains the same.
Second	C_1 and B_2	Drive to A_1 causes the planet carrier PC_1 to be driven around the faced sun S_1 at a speed slightly faster than in first gear. Rear unit is inoperative.
Third	C_1 and C_2	Driving both S_1 and A_1 causes the complete unit to revolve as one; this gives a direct drive. Rear unit is inoperative.
Reverse	C_2 and B_1	Driving S_2 and holding PC_2 in the rear unit causes P_2 to act as a reverse idler. Front unit is inoperative.

Unidirectional clutches/free-wheel units

The unidirectional clutch is also referred to as a free-wheel or one-way clutch. Its action is similar to that used on a bicycle in that it transmits drive in one way and not the other. Used in manual transmissions, the free-wheel unit was often fitted as a separate assembly behind the gearbox. When used in this application, it enabled the vehicle to be free-wheeled or coasted when the road conditions were favourable for its use. This did slightly improve fuel efficiency, but a distinct disadvantage of the unit was the increased wear on the brake linings due to the increased use by the driver as there was no engine braking available. The device also enabled the driver to make a gear change on a manual gearbox without operating the main clutch. Once the vehicle is in motion and the driver releases the throttle pedal, this causes the one-way clutch to disconnect the road wheels from the gearbox. This then removes the driving loads from the gears and allows easy movement of the gear change lever. If the driver didn't want the free-wheel feature, then the unit was locked by a gear to give a fixed-wheel condition. This was necessary to obtain reverse gear, so provision was made to lock the unit automatically when reverse gear was selected.

Modern applications

In more recent times, manufacturers of automatic gearboxes have used unidirectional clutches. This type of clutch can also be found in torque converters and overdrive units. The unit limits the movement of a particular member within the assembly to rotate in one direction only. This then provides the simple means of holding or driving one part of an epicyclic gear train assembly so it can rotate only in one direction.

Types of unidirectional clutches

There are two main types of unidirectional clutch used in an automatic gearbox epicyclic gear train:

- Roller-type
- Sprag-type

Roller-type

The roller-type (Figure 3.57) uses a number of parallel rollers sandwiched between the inner member and the inclined cam face of the cylindrical outer member. This assembly uses a series of concertina-shaped strip springs to wedge the rollers between the two faces of the housing.

The unidirectional clutch application shown in Figure 3.57 is from a version used in a torque converter assembly to control the directional movement of the **stator** within the housing of the converter. The inner member is rigidly secured to the converter housing.

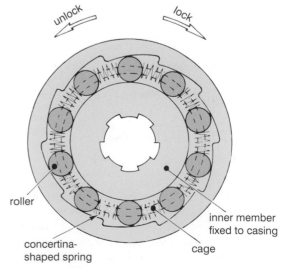

Figure 3.57 Roller-type unidirectional clutch

An anticlockwise movement of the outer housing releases the rollers from the inclined cam faces and of the outer housing assembly. This allows the outer member to rotate freely during this application. If the direction of the outer track is reversed, then the rollers are forced between the inner member and the outer inclined cam faces of the outer member. The rollers are then wedged between these members to prevent any slip taking place. In this case, the clutch will be fixed when the outer track is turned clockwise, and free when moved anticlockwise.

> **Stator**: a component that redirects fluid when it returns from the turbine in a torque converter. The stator increases the efficiency of the torque converter.

Sprag-type

The main difference between the sprag-type and roller-type design is that the sprag-type uses a number of inclined wedges called sprags (Figure 3.58). The wedges are held in a spring cage and positioned between the inner and outer cylindrical tracks of the assembly. The springs are designed to twist the sprags in the wedge direction and keep them in contact with both tracks. When the inner member is rigidly secured to a component casing, an anticlockwise movement of the outer track releases the wedge action of the sprags and, as a result, allows the outer track to move freely. Reversing the direction of motion of the outer track, the friction between the sprag and the track greatly increases the wedge action and prevents any slip taking place between the members. In this case, the clutch will be fixed when the outer track is turned clockwise, and free when moved anticlockwise.

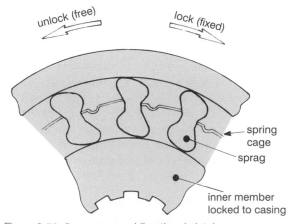

Figure 3.58 Sprag-type unidirectional clutch

Unidirectional clutch faults

The two operating states of a unidirectional clutch are free and fixed, so the two main faults are that the clutch is free when it should be fixed and fixed when it should be free, leading to slip and seizure respectively. A broken spring is a common cause of slip, and a fractured roller or sprag causes seizure because the unit wedges in both directions. To correct these faults, the complete free-wheel unit would need to be replaced.

3.12.3 Fluid clutch or fluid flywheel

This arrangement was originally intended for marine use, and was invented by Dr Hermann Föttinger in 1905. It was not until 20 years later that a British engineer (H. Sinclair) introduced the fluid drive on a motor vehicle. With this drive, the transmission is connected to the engine by hydraulic means, which provides an effective damper to the torsional vibrations set up by the engine, a smooth take-up to move the vehicle from rest and, in the case of the converter, a device to amplify the torque.

The hydraulic coupling

This unit is often known as a fluid flywheel, since it usually forms a component part of the main engine flywheel.

Principle of the fluid-coupling flywheel

You will understand the principle of operation if you consider the following steps. Figure 3.59a shows a 'grapefruit' member, which is filled with a fluid and rotated. The fluid is thrown tangentially outwards and upwards.

If a plate is held over the member (Figure 3.59b), the fluid will strike and tend to rotate the plate in the same direction. The force and torque acting on the plate will depend on the speed of rotation – the greater the speed, the greater the force, since more energy is given to the fluid.

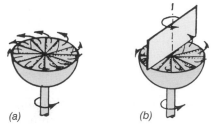

(a)   (b)

Figure 3.59 Principle of the fluid flywheel

In Figure 3.60a, the plate is replaced by another 'grapefruit' member, which receives the drive and re-diverts the fluid back to the driving member. The 'fluid' circuit can be traced by following the path taken by a particle of fluid. Rotation of A will cause the particle to move outwards from point 1 to 2. This is brought about by the resistance of the fluid to movement in a circular path. (A body will move in a straight line unless acted upon by a force. So, if you consider a plan view of A, you will see that the straight-line path will take the particle to the outside.) The farther from the centre the particle moves, the faster it will have to travel; consequently, energy will be extracted from the engine.

The shape and outward motion will force the particle upwards and cause the tangential flow to strike the vanes of member B, the force of impact being governed by the speed difference of the two members. At point 3, the energy possessed by the particle is less than at point 2, since the force of impact causes energy to be given up in the form of heat. This fact means that the energy remaining in the particle is less than that given to it by the engine, and therefore the output speed will be lower than the input.

The fluid following the particle will push it, against its natural tendency, to point 4. During this movement, the linear speed of the particle is decreased and energy is given up to drive the output shaft. If the speed of both members is the same, the outward force at point 4 will be equal to that at point 1, and no circulation will take place. Since the operation depends on fluid passing from one member to the other, it is fortunate that the driven member B rotates more slowly.

As the particle moves from point 4 to 1, the engine will have to supply extra energy to speed up the fluid. This is necessary because the fluid is rotating more slowly than the driving member and is acting as a brake on the engine. A fluid converter uses an extra member to overcome this braking effect.

Figure 3.60b shows the main constructional details of a fluid coupling. Oil of a type similar to light engine oil (SAE 30) is introduced to the level of the filler plug, which leaves an air space for expansion. To allow for the difference of speed, a bearing is fitted between the driven and driving members, and a guide ring is sometimes incorporated to provide a smooth flow path for the fluid.

When the engine is driving, the oil circulates in the direction shown: fast when the driven member is stationary, but slowing down as the two members approach the same speed. Under 'overrun' conditions, the direction of oil flow in the axial plane is reversed, and a drive from the output shaft to the crankshaft provides 'engine braking'.

Apart from a periodical check on the oil level, the coupling needs very little attention. If a fault arises, it is normally either:

- overheating, due to excessive slip, which may be caused by a low oil level, or
- noise, due to bearing wear, which allows the faces of the members to touch.

3.12.4 The hydraulic converter

This component fulfils one of the most important tasks in a modern automatic transmission system and, in its simplest form, provides an infinitely variable ratio up to approximately 2:1. It is also responsible for duties performed by the fluid coupling. More complicated types are capable of providing greater torque ratios.

Principle of operation

Before considering the operation of the converter, an appreciation of the following experiments may be of help. Anyone who has used a hosepipe will realise that the water leaves the nozzle at a considerable speed. A moving fluid possesses energy and this means that it is capable of doing work. Directing a flow of fluid on to a plate causes the fluid direction to change and the extent of this change governs the force that acts on the plate (Figure 3.61).

Varying the speed of the fluid by adjusting the tap also alters the force of impact; a low fluid speed contains very little energy and therefore only exerts a small force on the plate.

The force of impact can be varied by moving the plate so that it is tending to travel with the fluid. During

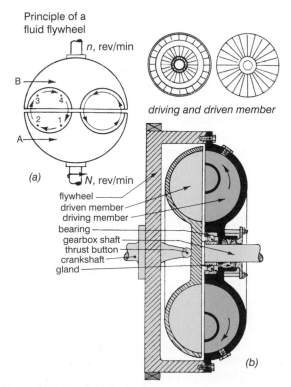

Principle of a fluid flywheel

n, rev/min

driving and driven member

N, rev/min

flywheel
driven member
driving member
bearing
gearbox shaft
thrust button
crankshaft
gland

(a)

(b)

Figure 3.60 The fluid flywheel

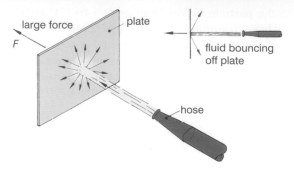

Figure 3.61 Fluid exerting a force on to a plate

this movement, the speed of the fluid relative to the plate is slower than in the previous case, so the impact force will be less. If it is possible to move the plate at the same speed as the fluid is moving, then no impact will take place, consequently no force will be produced on the plate.

Figure 3.62 shows a curved plate. In this case, the fluid strikes the plate with a velocity (v) and the curved surface redirects the fluid back at a velocity ($-v$) towards its source. Double the force is obtained with this arrangement, since the plate not only stops the fluid but also has to send it back at the same speed.

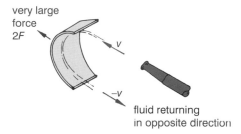

Figure 3.62 Effects of a curved plate

Mounting a series of these plates on to a shaft (Figure 3.63) forms a simple turbine. Each plate, which is now called a vane, will extract the energy from the moving fluid to produce a turning action on the shaft.

Consideration of the previous experiments will show that:

- low velocity of the fluid produces a small turning movement or torque
- high torque occurs when the fluid velocity is high and the shaft speed is low
- gradual decrease in torque occurs as the shaft speed increases.

The term 'fluid' is chosen since the previous experiments can be conducted with air or any liquid, and the arrangements considered could be applied to gas turbines, turbochargers or hydraulic converters since the basic principle is similar.

Having established the basic idea of the turbine, the means of fluid supply will now be examined. From the previous description it will be appreciated that the energy is contained in a particle of fluid by virtue of its velocity, so a compact device is needed to eject fluid at high velocity. In the case of the torque converter, this is provided by a centrifugal pump, which in principle is similar to the type used in a cooling system or supercharger.

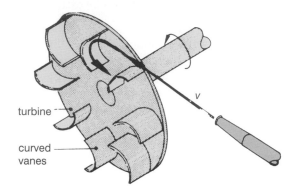

Figure 3.63 Energy extracted from fluid to give turning movement

Figure 3.64 shows the basic features of the pump. Rotation of the member will cause the particle of fluid (p) to move in the path shown. Initially, the movement is towards the outside of the member and the greater distance it has to travel in one revolution at this point shows that its velocity has been increased. Work has to be done by the engine to achieve this increase in the energy content of the particle. Shrouding the pump with a container causes the fluid to move away from the pump as shown in Figure 3.65. The diagram shows the fluid moving around the circumference and it is the velocity in this direction that governs the driving force that is being delivered by the pump. The resemblance between the flow given by the pump and the nozzle shown in Figure 3.63 should now be apparent and the effect of engine speed on the pump's performance will be easy to understand – low engine speed will give a small flow (low velocity) of fluid and, consequently, each particle will contain only a small amount of energy.

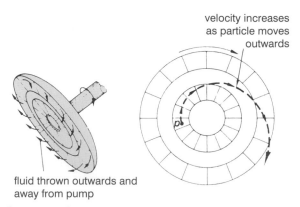

Figure 3.64 Pump action

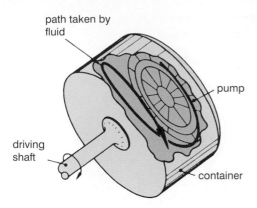

Figure 3.65 Container fitted to pump

Placing the pump adjacent to the turbine (Figure 3.66) and making the pump act as the container shows how the drive from the engine is achieved. The pump imparts energy to the particle as it moves towards the outside. This energy is extracted by the turbine by moving the fluid inwards towards the shaft, thus causing it to slow down.

To summarise this stage:

Pump: Speeds up particle   Imparts energy

Turbine: Slows down particle   Extracts energy

Figure 3.66 is similar to a fluid coupling and, in this form, the torque output is always less than the torque input.

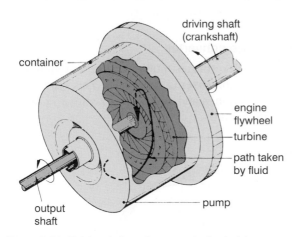

Figure 3.66 Fluid path from the pump to the turbine

Applying the earlier analogy of the hosepipe would indicate that when the turbine is turning slower than the pump, the force of impact of the fluid striking the turbine vanes should give a torque increase. This would be true if the fluid did not have to return to the pump, but since this fluid is to recirculate then the speed of the fluid compared to the speed of the pump vane must be considered. To give a high impact force on the output member, the pump must be turning at a higher speed than the turbine, so when the fluid is returned to the

pump it is travelling slower than the pump vane. In this condition, the vane will strike the slower moving fluid particle and this will give a force that is acting against the motion of the pump (i.e. the fluid will tend to act as a brake on the pump). The greater the speed difference between the pump and turbine, the greater the impact force on the turbine, but this will also result in a larger braking action on the pump. To obtain a torque multiplication, this braking action must be eliminated. This is achieved by fitting a separate member called a stator (stationary member) between the turbine and the pump. Mounted on an extension of the gearbox casing, the stator consists of a number of vanes, which are shaped in the manner shown in Figure 3.67. Fluid returning to the pump is redirected such that it now enters the pump at a suitable speed and direction. If the path of the oil returning to the pump is considered, the system could be shown diagrammatically as in Figure 3.68.

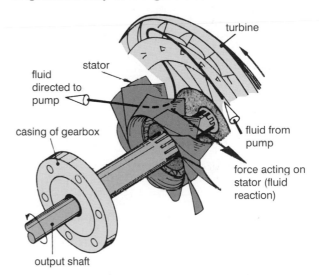

Figure 3.67 Action of the stator

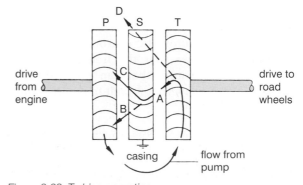

Figure 3.68 Turbine operation

Fluid from the pump acts on the turbine (T), but if the turbine is turning slower than the oil, then the oil will be deflected in the path marked A, the stator will act as a reaction member and will direct the fluid from path B to path C; a suitable direction for the pump to receive the fluid. As the turbine speed is increased, fluid path A will gradually change until it is taking path D. Fluid attempting to flow in path D will now be obstructed by the stator vanes and the disturbance caused by this obstruction would give a considerable drop in efficiency. To limit this drawback, a unidirectional clutch (free wheel) is fitted between the stator and the extension of the gearbox casing. As soon as the fluid strikes the back of the stator vanes the clutch will unlock and the fluid will then pass along path D to the pump. Once this occurs, the unit will act similarly to a fluid coupling.

Figure 3.69 shows the torque output in relation to turbine speed for a given speed of the pump. It will be seen that the output torque is approximately equal to input torque when the turbine speed is about 90 per cent of the pump speed.

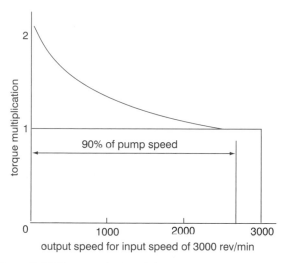

Figure 3.69 Torque output variation

Three-element torque converter

Figure 3.70 shows the arrangement of a three-element, single-stage converter. This type is quite common and is used in conjunction with many different types of automatic gearbox. Examination of Figure 3.70 shows that the free wheel is the only mechanical feature that can produce faulty operation of the converter. A fault in the free wheel can give:

- slipping stator – causes the fluid to enter the pump at the incorrect angle; therefore full torque multiplication cannot be obtained. This fault is detected by a stall test.
- seized stator – fluid striking the back of the stator vanes cannot make the stator free wheel at the appropriate time, so the fluid acts as a severe brake on the engine and produces overheating of the converter. Gearbox diagnosis is covered on page 384–6.

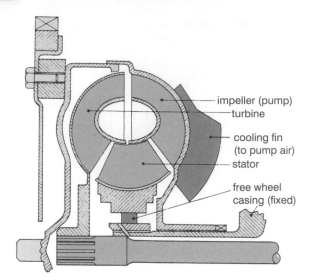

Figure 3.70 Three-element, single-stage torque converter

Torque converter fluid

The fluid for the converter is normally supplied by the automatic gearbox and it is generally a low viscosity mineral oil that contains additives to improve lubrication and resist frothing. **Cavitation** noise caused by air in the converter is minimised by pressurising the fluid to about $138 \, kN/m^2$ (20 psi).

Cavitation: bubbles in a liquid. These can cause noise if they occur in torque converter fluid.

Multi-stage converter

When greater torque multiplication is required, a multi-stage converter is often used. This type uses a series of turbines and stators and Figure 3.71 shows the main features.

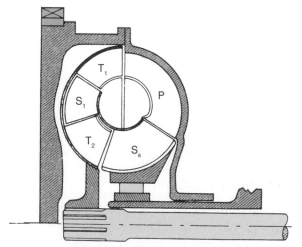

Figure 3.71 Layout of a multi-stage torque converter

Under conditions of low turbine/pump speeds, the fluid will follow the path shown in Figure 3.72 and the energy in the fluid is gradually extracted as it passes through each stage.

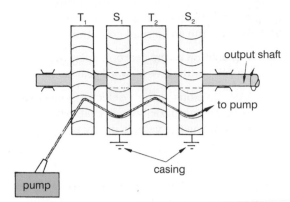

Figure 3.72 Principle of a multi-stage torque converter

3.12.5 Torque converter lock-up clutch

One of the inherent problems associated with using the torque converter to transmit engine power to the automatic gearbox is that, due to using fluid to transfer this drive, a certain amount of slippage will occur, which leads to wasted energy and increased fuel consumption. Generally, the slippage at the turbine wheel is about 4 per cent of the output. To prevent this from happening, during vehicle cruising conditions where it would be beneficial to have a complete 1:1 ratio between the impellor driven from the engine and the turbine driving the transmission, a lock-up clutch is used. When this is engaged, the impellor and the turbine are locked together and no slippage will occur.

When the lock-up clutch is disengaged, the fluid is under pressure within the torque converter and flows on either side of the clutch (Figure 3.73). Due to the pressures acting upon the clutch being equal, the plate will disengage and allow the normal operation of the torque converter to be maintained. To engage the clutch, the vehicle will need to be travelling at cruising speed with low load on the engine. At this point, the automatic gearbox hydraulic system will remove pressure from between the clutch plate and the impellor casing. The clutch lock-up will only operate when the gearbox is in top gear.

In early automatic gearboxes, the lock-up clutch was controlled by the automatic gearbox hydraulic circuit via a **governor**, but in later versions an ECU monitors and controls this function.

Governor: a device that automatically regulates the supply of fuel, steam or water to an engine.

The excess automatic gearbox fluid is transferred back to the gearbox sump pan by the hydraulic control valve system. As the fluid is evacuated from one side of the clutch, the pressure on the remaining

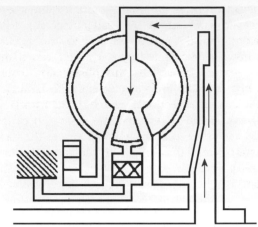

Figure 3.73 Lock-up clutch – disengaged

side increases, this forces the clutch into contact with the impellor casing. This action locks the impellor and turbine together allowing them to rotate as one unit without any slippage (Figure 3.74). As the vehicle speed reduces and the gearbox changes down a gear or the load on the engine increases, automatic gearbox fluid is diverted under pressure to act on the clutch plate between the impellor casing. This reaches a point where the hydraulic pressures on both sides of the clutch are equal, causing the clutch to disengage. As this occurs, the torque converter will revert to its normal operation.

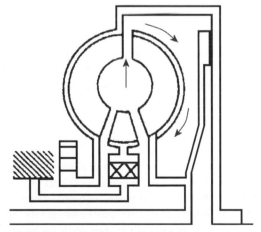

Figure 3.74 Lock-up clutch – engaged

3.13 Automatic gearbox (operation)

3.13.1 Automatic gear selection

In order to ensure that the engine makes good use of its power to move the vehicle along, the automatic gearbox has to have a balance of suitable gear ratios. The engine power is transmitted through to the automatic gearbox via the use of a fluid coupling or, in today's motor vehicles, a torque converter.

Figure 3.75 The gear selector

The selection of drive is firstly chosen by the driver, depending on the vehicle's parked position. Up to the late 1990s, when selecting forward gears the driver would have had a selection of up to five gear ratios. This maintained the performance throughout each drive cycle. Most automatic gearboxes were designed with a three-speed transmission to support engine demands. However, as manufacturers were always looking to produce high-performance engines with lower emission outputs, the automatic transmission had to adapt to meet those demands. Today, automatic gearboxes generally now have six gear ratios, but some higher power vehicles can have either seven or eight ratios to support and maximise the engine demands of achieving low emissions, fuel economy and performance.

In an early, basic automatic vehicle operation, when the driver selected their preferred forward-moving gear (normally drive, 'D') drive was taken up once the handbrake was released and the driver applied pressure to the accelerator pedal. The gearbox took up drive in first gear and then, depending on driver demands, changed up or down. This concept was reliant on driver inputs on the brake or accelerator, which controlled the mechanical and hydraulic systems within the automatic transmission. Again, in later automatic transmission systems, the driver inputs are just as important, but with an electronic control module monitoring and adapting the settings. The automatic gearbox is now more popular within the motor industry and customers.

3.13.2 Selector features

In early automatic transmissions, the driver had the options of park, reverse, neutral and drive, with the addition of first and second gears as additional forward gears. In later automatic transmissions, the addition of a third or even fourth gear was supplied to support the emission and fuel efficiency demands. Today, automatic gearboxes can have up to eight gears providing very close ratios for improved acceleration

and long top gears for low rpm cruising. Gearboxes today also incorporate advanced computer control systems that communicate with other vehicle systems to ensure that the gearbox is always in the correct gear for the given road conditions.

For this explanation of the gearbox operation, we will look at a gearbox with three forward gears and reverse.

For safety reasons, the selector mechanism incorporates an inhibitor switch that prevents the driver from starting the vehicle in any position other than park or neutral.

P – park. In most automatic transmissions, this function is operated by a mechanical parking **pawl** mechanism. The parking pawl is mounted inside the gearbox housing and locks a gear that is connected to the output shaft of the automatic transmission. With the pawl in its locked state, any take-up of drive is prevented and it acts as secondary brake to support the handbrake when the vehicle is parked on an incline. Also, when park is selected, the engine can still run in a stationary position. This allows the driver to select a sub-system, such as air conditioning or heating, to maintain a suitable cabin temperature.

Pawl: a curved bar or lever mounted on a pivot, the free end of which engages with the teeth of a cog or ratchet so that the cog or ratchet can only turn in one direction.

R – reverse. Rearward movement of the vehicle is achieved in this position. Reverse has only one gear ratio to operate from and aids manoeuvring activities when in confined areas or parking.

N – neutral. If neutral is selected, then this allows the engine to run without applying any power through to the automatic transmission. Also, neutral allows the vehicle to move without power from the engine and allows the vehicle to be towed for a short distance. If prolonged towing takes place, then the risk of internal damage is likely due to the lack of oil flow.

D – drive. Drive is identified as the normal automatic mode that enables the transmission to operate the whole range of forward gears automatically. The selected gear ratio adopted is determined by the driving conditions and driving style undertaken.

2 – second gear. If the driver selects second gear, then the transmission will only operate within the second gear parameters and not step up to a high gear to allow increased output of the transmission. The gearbox will always start off in first gear and step up into second depending on the driver demands. Once engaged, and depending on the drive cycle, it will drop down if the vehicle speed decreases to a crawling speed.

1 – first gear. First gear selection will provide the driver with the option of the automatic gearbox's lowest gear ratio only. When this gear is selected, there will be no free-wheeling action and the gearbox provides a suitable function for engine braking. If the driver selects this gear position option, then there is no up-shift functionality and drive is limited to the gear ratio that is permitted by the automatic transmission.

3 and 4 – third and fourth gear. Modern automatic transmissions are provided with these additional gears to allow the driver a wider selection depending on driving conditions. Sometimes these gears are used as an overdrive gear, or they can be manually selected by the driver. The overdrive functionality is sometimes controlled via a switch that is located within the gear selector lever. With the automatic transmission active in drive, the driver has the additional option of pressing the overdrive button and when the driving conditions are met the overdrive facility becomes active.

3.13.3 Mechanical gear train

Within the construction of an automatic transmission, most gear train layouts are fundamentally the same. The following two variants show the basic concepts that are representative of automatic transmissions using two interconnected epicyclic gear trains, which form the compound system layout.

Figure 3.76 shows how a braking action can be performed on various elements of the gear train by using the multi-plate clutch system. One advantage of this concept is that it provides a smoother gear change and eliminates the need for brake band adjustments. The automatic transmission layout provides three forward gear ratios and one reverse. This automatic transmission layout using an epicyclic gear train is very common with a number of manufacturers.

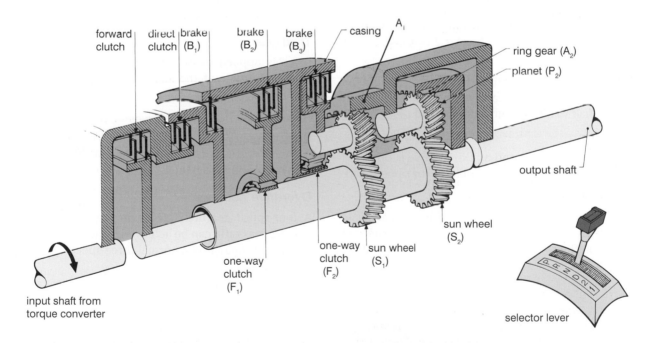

Gear	Fwd clutch	Direct clutch	F_1	F_2	B_1	B_2	B_3	Ratio
1	•						•	2.452 Lock-up
2	•					•		1.452 Lock-up
D1	•			•				2.452
D2	•		•					1.452
D3	•	•						1.000
R		•					•	2.212

Figure 3.76 Gear train layout and a table showing gear ratios and clutch/brake selection

Example 1: operation of a simple three-speed gearbox

When D3 is selected ('D' is selected on the gear lever and third gear is engaged) the forward clutch is applied, giving a gear ratio of $1:1$.

Note that gears listed as 1 and 2 on the table provide engine braking and are when the driver has selected either 1 or 2 on the gear lever.

D1, D2 and D3 on the table refer to when the driver has selected D and the gearbox is in full automatic mode. In this situation there is no engine braking available.

First gear

Drive is applied to A and the front planet carrier is held either by the free wheel F_2 (D1 position D, gear 1 engaged) or the brake B_3 (position 1, gear 1 engaged) (1).

Forward motion of A_2 drives both S_1 and S_2 in the opposite direction; this causes P_1 to act as an idler and drive A_1 in a forward direction.

Second gear

Drive is applied to A_2 and the sun S_2 is held by either the free wheel F_1 (position 2, gear 2 engaged, D2) or the brake B_1 (2).

Forward motion of A_2 'walks' the planet P_2 around the fixed sun S_2; this action causes the planet carrier and output shaft to move as given by the ratio $\frac{A+S}{A}$.

Third gear

Drive is applied to A_2 and S_2. Direct drive is obtained because both gear members rotate at the same speed.

Reverse gear

Drive is applied to S_1 and the front planet carrier is held by the brake B_3. The forward-moving sun will drive A_1 in the reverse direction; the planet P_1 will act as an idler.

Example 2: operation of an alternative three-speed layout

The gear train layout used in Figure 3.77 was used by Ford on their C3 Bordeaux generation gearboxes, and is similar to that used by other manufacturers.

The automatic transmission provided a five-position selector, marked P R N D 2 1, and controlled the action of two clutches, two brake bands and a free wheel.

First gear

Drive is applied to A and the rear planet carrier is held by either the free wheel (D1) (position D, gear 1 engaged) or the rear brake B_2 (1).

The resistance to movement of the output shaft, which is connected to the front planet carrier, causes the front planet to drive the two suns S_1 and S_2 in the opposite direction. With the rear planet acting as an idler, the annulus A_2 is driven around slowly in a forward direction.

Second gear

Drive is applied to A_1 and the front brake B_1 is applied to hold S_1. The speed reduction is given by the front gear set, the ratio being $\frac{A+S}{A}$.

Third gear

Drive is applied to A_1 and S_1. This causes both A_1 and S_1 to rotate at the same speed; direct drive is obtained.

Reverse gear

Drive is applied to S_2 and a brake holds the rear planet carrier. Reverse is obtained by the rear gear set, the planet P_2 acting as an idler.

Overdrive gear set

A four-speed gearbox having an overdrive as the highest gear ratio can be achieved by adding an extra gear set at the rear of a normal three-speed epicyclic train.

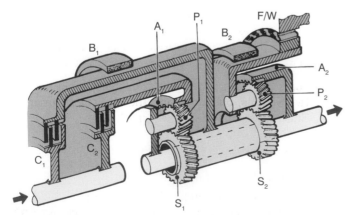

Gear	C_1	C_2	B_1	B_2	F/W
1		•		•	
2		•	•		
D1		•			•
D2		•	•		
D3	•	•			
R	•			•	

Figure 3.77 Layout of the compound gear train (Ford C3) and table showing clutch and brake bench operation to access each gear

In the overdrive layout shown in Figure 3.78, fourth gear is obtained by holding sun S_3 by a brake; the drive is applied to the planet carrier PC_3. Driving the planet carrier around the fixed sun causes A_3 to rotate at an overdrive speed as given by the ratio $\dfrac{A}{A+S}$.

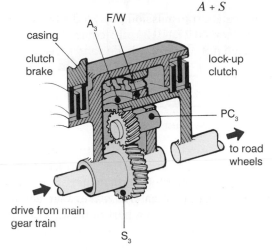

Figure 3.78 An overdrive gear set (ZF)

In other gear positions, the overdrive gear set is put out of action by either the lock-up clutch or the free wheel; the former is used for reverse and also for gear positions designed to give engine braking.

3.13.4 Multi-plate clutch actuation

A number of brake bands and multi-phase clutches are fitted in an automatic gearbox. Clutches are used to connect the gear train to the input shaft and band brakes are fitted to hold a part of the train stationary.

In a number of modern gearboxes, clutches are sometimes used instead of brake bands; this makes the gearbox more compact and lightweight; it also overcomes the need for adjustment that must be carried out periodically to compensate for friction lining wear.

Oil pressure, produced by a pump driven at engine speed from the fluid converter, is distributed by control valves to the appropriate clutch and brake when actuation of these parts is required.

Multi-plate clutches

Numerous wet-type, multi-disc clutches are fitted and most of these operate on the same principle. Figure 3.79 shows a typical construction.

Two sets of steel plates, inner and outer, are connected alternately by protruding tabs to the hub and drum respectively. Bonded to the faces of the inner plates is a friction material having either a hard or comparatively soft texture. A hard facing is made of a **cellulose** compound, or synthetic fibre, bonded together with a phenol resin to obtain a suitable friction value. A soft facing, which is based on a compound of paper, is more

porous and elastic. Paper-based facings normally give a smoother and quieter take-up when operated over a wide range of temperature and pressure.

> **Cellulose**: a natural, insoluble substance made by plants.

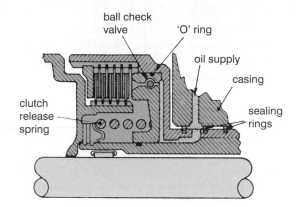

Figure 3.79 A multi-plate clutch

When the clutch is to be engaged, oil under pressure is supplied through a drilling, in either the casing or the shaft, to the clutch-operating cylinder. Leakage of oil between moving parts and loss of pressure needed to operate the clutch, is prevented by fitting a number of synthetic rubber 'O' rings and square-section, cast-iron seals.

Torque transmitted by a given multi-plate clutch depends on friction value and operating pressure, so one of these is the cause when clutch slip occurs. Drag between the plates when the clutch is disengaged is an energy drain, so provision is made to separate the plates. A large clutch release spring returns the operating piston and, in some cases, the steel outer plates are slightly dished. Immediately after the clutch has been disengaged, the centrifugal action of the residual oil in the operating chamber would apply the piston and cause slight drag. This is prevented by having a check valve to release the pressure.

When oil pressure operates the clutch, the check valve is held closed, but removal of this pressure allows the ball to move outwards – owing to the centrifugal effect – and open the release hole.

Some automatics have a clutch that is operated by two pistons, one small and the other large in area. This construction, shown in Figure 3.80, allows the thrust on the plates to be varied to suit the conditions; this achieves a smoother operation.

Clutch slip

The term 'clutch slip' clearly describes the fault accurately and gives the same symptoms as with a manual gearbox clutch. If the fault is allowed to

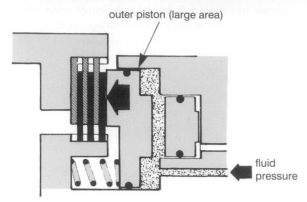

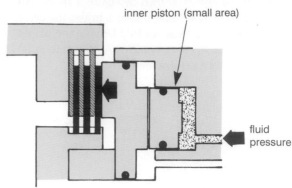

Figure 3.80 Clutch operation with two pistons

continue, then the accelerated wear of the friction faces, together with the effect of high temperature caused by the continuous slip action taking place, can only be rectified by renewing the clutch or brake band assembly.

To investigate for clutch slip, a stall test needs to be carried out. Carrying out the test procedure in each gear would confirm which clutch pack or brake band assembly is faulty. For stall test procedures, always refer to the vehicle manufacturer's technical information confirming their recommendation of testing.

3.13.5 Brake band actuation

Normally two or more brake bands are fitted in a gearbox to prevent rotation of the gear members. An external contracting, single-band type brake is used and Figure 3.81 shows the basic construction. The band is anchored at one end to the casing to resist the rotational force and is actuated by a hydraulic servo at the free end. Maximum braking torque is achieved by sitting the anchor in such a position that the rotational force of the drum produces a self-wrapping action.

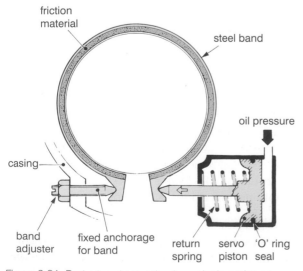

Figure 3.81 Brake band actuation by a single-acting servo

The spring steel brake band is internally lined by bonding to it a hard friction material. When the brake is applied, this material makes contact with a steel drum connected to a part of the gear train. An adjuster to compensate for wear is normally provided at the band anchor. The screw for this adjuster is often carried through the gearbox casing to simplify maintenance. Adjustment of the band normally involves releasing the lock nut and then tightening the screw to a given clearance or torque setting.

Various types of servo actuator are used to suit the gearbox; the common types are:

- single-acting
- delay
- double-acting.

Single-acting servo

The basic type shown in Figure 3.81 consists of a single hydraulic piston fitted in a cylinder that is fixed to the gearbox casing. Fluid leakage past the piston is prevented by a synthetic rubber 'O' ring and a spring is fitted in the chamber to return the piston. The force exerted by a servo must be sufficient to prevent slip of the drum, so bands controlling gears having a high torque output are fitted with a servo cylinder, which has either a large area or a high operating pressure.

Delay servo

When the vehicle is in motion, a sudden engagement of a brake causes a jolt. Harsh changes and jolts should not occur with well-designed automatics because they incorporate special devices to minimise this problem; one of these is the delay servo shown in Figure 3.82.

The delay feature is achieved by using a second (inner) spring and a piston rod that can slide through the piston, instead of being rigidly attached, as in the basic type. When fluid pressure is applied, the initial piston movement compresses the inner spring. Once this has taken place, positive contact between the piston and rod is made and the full force is applied to the brake in the normal way. The cushioning action of the inner spring gives a gradual application of the brake; also it damps the vibration produced by the band during the initial stage of engagement.

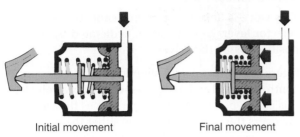

Initial movement   Final movement

Figure 3.82 A delay servo

Double-acting servo

On this type, fluid can be directed to one or both sides of the piston. In Figure 3.83a, fluid under pressure supplied at A will act on the small-area part of the piston and apply the servo in the normal way. When an equal fluid pressure is applied to A and B (Figure 3.83b), the piston will move in the 'release' direction. This is due to unequal thrust produced on the piston by the fluid pressure acting on the side of larger area.

A double servo is used to provide a smooth change between second and third gear; in this case, application of the brake gives second gear. When a certain speed is reached, a change to third is made by directing fluid from a single line to the appropriate clutch, and also to the 'release' side of the servo. Besides reducing the number of hydraulic lines, this arrangement gives a quick down-change because as soon as the fluid is released from one side of the servo, the second gear immediately comes into operation. The majority of automatic gear changes are made while the drive is being transmitted through the gearbox. If a brake, or clutch, were released before the next gear units were partly applied, then the engine would suddenly speed up. This condition is called flare-up; it is prevented by overlapping the engagement of the new gear with the disengagement of the old gear. If the period of overlap is too great, then a harsh gear change condition, sometimes called tie-up, results. This occurs because the two 'gears' oppose each other (i.e. each gear attempts to drive the output shaft at a speed dictated by its ratio, with the result that the gearbox partially locks up).

Brake slip

As with the clutch slip previously mentioned, the term 'brake slip' describes the fault accurately and gives the same symptoms as with a manual gearbox clutch. If the fault is allowed to continue, then the accelerated wear of the friction faces, together with the effect of high temperature caused by the continuous slip action taking place, can only be rectified by renewing the clutch or brake band assembly.

To investigate for clutch slip, a stall test needs to be carried out. Carrying out the test procedure in each gear would confirm which clutch pack or brake band assembly is faulty. For stall test procedures, always refer to the vehicle manufacturer's technical information confirming their recommendation of testing.

3.13.6 Hydraulic control of actuators

The clutches and brake bands of most automatic gearboxes are operated by hydraulic means. A pump, driven at engine speed from the torque converter, generates the fluid pressure; this pressure should be sufficiently high to lock the clutch plates or brake drum, but not so high as to waste energy. Distribution of fluid to the clutches and brakes is by means of a control valve, called a manual valve, linked to the driver's selector lever.

Valve operation

Although many valves are used in automatic gearboxes, the basic principle of operation of each valve is the same. At this stage, the construction and operation of some of the valves is considered.

Regulator valves (relief valves)

The main purpose of this type of valve is to limit the hydraulic line pressure to a given maximum. The three main types, shown in Figure 3.84, are ball, plunger (piston) and spool.

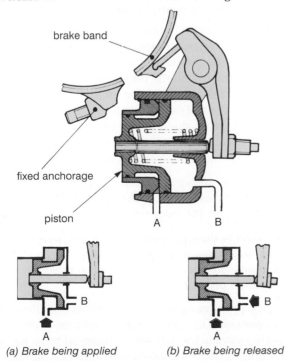

brake band

fixed anchorage

piston   A   B

B   B

A   A

(a) Brake being applied   *(b) Brake being released*

Figure 3.83 A double-acting servo

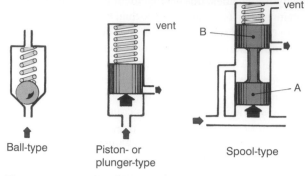

Ball-type Piston- or Spool-type
plunger-type

Figure 3.84 Types of regulator valves

Ball and plunger-type relief valves

Ball and plunger-type valves are similar to those used on engines. When the pressure acting on the valve produces a thrust greater than the force exerted by the spring, then the valve lifts and so prevents any further increase in the pressure. The operation is based on the relationship:

Thrust = Pressure × Area

Spool-type relief valves

Simple spool valves are similar to the plunger type except that they are waisted (reduced in area at the centre) to control the fluid flow. In Figure 3.84, the areas of A and B are the same, so the pressure in the waist region will exert an equal thrust upwards and downwards; as a result, the pressure in this region will not affect the movement of the valve.

When pressure is sufficient to lift the valve, a port is uncovered. Fluid will then flow to the waisted part of the valve from where it is either returned to the reservoir or passed to a line that acts on another part of the system.

Differential spool valves have two spool 'plungers' of different diameter similar to the type shown in Figure 3.85. As fluid pressure begins to build up, the spool will move to the right; this is because the effective area of B exposed to the fluid is larger than that of A. The actual movement of the spool is controlled by the spring strength. The spring is situated in a chamber that is vented to avoid a pressure build-up behind the valve. When the pressure reaches a set value dictated by the spring, the spool uncovers the port C; this spills out the fluid and prevents any further rise of pressure.

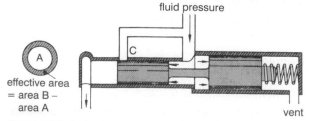

effective area
= area B –
area A

Figure 3.85 A simple pressure regulator valve

Control valves

The purpose of this type of valve is to direct the fluid to a hydraulic line that either activates or controls the appropriate clutch and/or brake.

Manual control valve

This valve is linked by a rod or cable to the driver's selector lever, so its position is dictated by the gear position set by the driver.

Figure 3.86 shows a very simple manual valve used to control forward and reverse movement of a vehicle. In this case, operation of the lever moves the valve and uncovers the port that supplies either the forward or reverse gear actuators. Positive location of the valve is obtained by a selector ball detent arrangement.

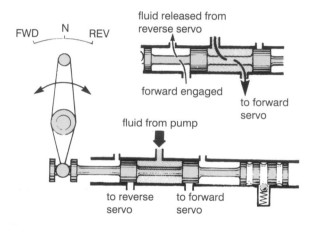

Figure 3.86 A simple, manual control valve to control forward or reverse gear

Pressure-sensitive control valves

The basic system for the automatic control of the gear changes must sense the speed of the road wheels. A hydraulic system of control uses a governor for this purpose. Mounted on the output shaft, the governor generates a fluid pressure that increases as the road speed rises. Control valves, connected to the governor fluid circuit, sense the pressure in this circuit. At the appropriate time, the valve operates and directs the fluid through the lines to engage the new gear.

Figure 3.87a shows a spool valve with a fluid connection at each end. If the areas of the faces A and B are equal, the valve will:

- move to the right when the fluid pressure at C is greater than at D, and vice versa
- remain in a central position when pressure at C equals pressure at D.

Any pressure given by the fluid at E will have no effect on the movement of the valve, because the thrust tending to move the valve to the right will be balanced by an equal and opposite thrust acting on the other face. In many ways, this is similar to the action of the two springs.

Making the area of one spool larger (Figure 3.87b) will cause the pressure acting on the larger area to give a greater thrust on the valve than that given by a similar pressure at C.

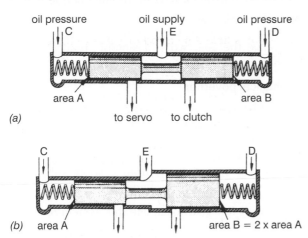

(a)

(b)   area A   area B = 2 x area A

Figure 3.87 A spool valve controlling flow to either the servo or the clutch

3.13.7 The hydraulic system

The hydraulic system described in this chapter does not represent an actual system used in any particular make of gearbox; instead, it illustrates the basic principles of automatic control by using a much simplified system. From this base system, you should be able to comprehend the construction and operation of a modern unit.

The system is considered in a series of stages.

Stage 1

Figure 3.88 shows the layout of a simple fluid supply system used to operate a clutch and torque converter.

Pump

Normally, an internal–external gear pump is used (refer to the engine section on page 111 for information on the oil pump operation). This pump is driven at engine speed by tangs formed on the torque converter casing. The fluid is drawn from the reservoir and passed to the pump through a fine screen-type filter, so as to remove any small dirt particles.

Since most modern automatic gearboxes have only one pump at the input, it is not possible to tow start the engine. This is because the engine and pump will be stationary, so pressure will not be generated in the system to activate any clutch and brake – neutral will result.

Primary regulator

This spool valve controls the line pressure that is applied to the manual valve. In the system shown, the line pressure always remains constant. (This is

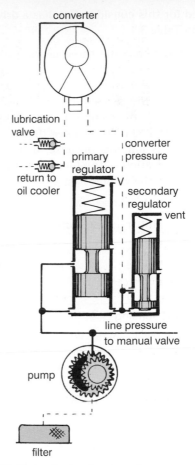

Figure 3.88 Hydraulic circuit   stage 1

unsuitable for a modern gearbox because the high pressure needed to prevent slip under conditions of high torque will give harsh changes when the engine is lightly loaded.)

Fluid released from the valve is passed back to the inlet side of the pump instead of being discharged into the reservoir. This action saves energy that would be used if the fluid had to be drawn through the fine-mesh filter screen.

Secondary regulator

Line pressure is too great for the converter, so the secondary regulator acts as a pressure reducer. A portion of the fluid returning from the converter passes either to an oil cooler or to a line that provides low-pressure lubrication of the gearbox.

Manual valve

Under the control of the driver, this valve distributes the fluid to the various valves, clutches and brakes. In the position shown in Figure 3.89, the fluid is delivered to the front clutch at line pressure.

Sequence of clutch and brake application

The order in which the clutch and brake actuators are applied depends on the type of gear train. The layout used for this consideration has a drive range as shown in Table 3.4.

The table shows that the three gears in the drive range all use the front clutch; the particular gear in this range is determined by the actuation, or non-actuation, of the rear clutch and brake. Use of the front clutch in this manner is common to many other gearboxes. It should be noted that wear on the forward clutch is minimal because, unlike the rear clutch, the application of the forward clutch is only carried out when the vehicle is stationary.

Table 3.4 Clutch and brake operation

Gear	Front clutch	Rear clutch	Brake band
D1	•		
D2	•		•
D3	•	•	•

Speed and load sensing

Gear changes must be made when a predetermined road speed is reached, so some form of sensor is necessary to 'tell' the gearbox when to change the gear. Automatic gearboxes use one of the following to determine the speed of the output shaft:

- Mechanical governor
- Hydraulic governor
- Electronic speed sensor

The speed sensor must work in conjunction with a shift valve (change valve); the duty of this valve is to direct the fluid to the clutches and servos so as to change the gear when a suitable road speed is reached.

Mechanical governor

This centrifugal system consists of two bob-weights, which throw out against the resistance of a spring as the speed of rotation increases. The governor is driven from the output shaft, and movement of the bob-weights operates a hydraulic spool valve that directly controls the gear changes.

Today, very few gearboxes use this system of speed sensing.

Hydraulic governor

This type was developed from the mechanical governor. It uses a spool valve, sensitive to a centrifugal effect given by its rotation, to generate a fluid pressure that increases with speed.

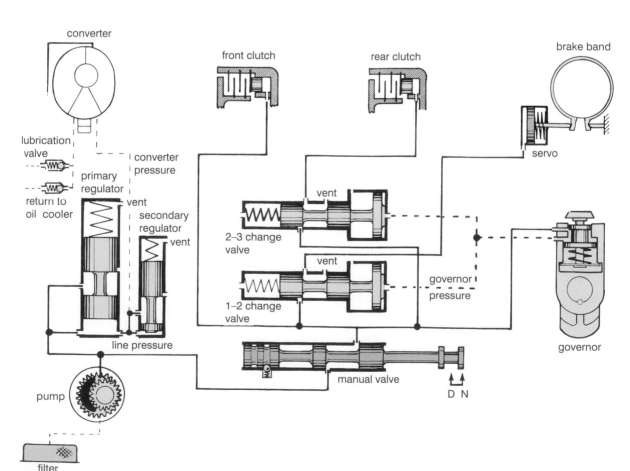

Figure 3.89 Hydraulic circuits – stage 2

Electronic speed sensor

An indication of the road speed is needed for many electronic systems used on modern vehicles. This data is provided by some form of magnetic sensor fitted close to the output shaft of the gearbox. Signals from the sensor are passed to an ECU for processing, so that the data can be used for a particular electronic system such as gearbox control.

Stage 2

When comparing Figure 3.89 with Figure 3.88, the former has the addition of two change valves or shift valves and a hydraulic governor.

Change valves or shift valves

Two valves are shown in Figure 3.89. One valve controls the up and down changes between first and second (1–2 shift valve) and the other the changes between second and third (2–3 shift valve).

A simplified shift valve is shown in Figure 3.90. Line pressure from the manual valve acts at A and the line supplying the appropriate clutch or servo is connected at port B. Movement of the valve against the spring is produced by pressure of the fluid from the governor at port C. When the governor pressure is sufficient to overcome the spring, the shift valve moves and connects port A with port B. This allows line pressure to act on the servo or clutch so as to produce the change of gear. By fitting a stronger spring to the 2–3 shift valve (or making the valve smaller in area), the 2–3 valve is made to open at a much higher governor pressure than the 1–2 valve.

The diameter of plunger D is larger than plunger E. This feature is effective after the valve has opened

and its use prevents a gear-hunting action. This action is a severe vibration of the vehicle caused by the shift valve oscillating between the open and closed positions. Once the valve starts to open, the extra thrust on piston D adds to the thrust given by governor pressure; as a result of this added thrust, the valve is opened fully. This arrangement makes the up changes occur at higher road speeds than the down changes.

Hydraulic governor

This valve is a form of regulator valve; its duty is to alter the fluid pressure in the governor line in keeping with the road speed: as speed increases, the pressure rises. When the governor pressure is high enough, it causes the shift valves to operate and allow the next gear to be selected.

It should be noted that the examples shown in Figure 3.91 have two shift valves (for gears 1–2 and for 2–3). If the spring pressure in shift valve 2–3 is stronger than the spring fitted to shift valve 1–2, then the governor fluid pressure will have to be higher to overcome the shift valve 2–3. In this way, the governor fluid pressure is required to be lower to change from first to second gear than to change from second to third.

The principle of operation of a governor is shown in Figure 3.91. The governor is fitted to the gearbox output shaft. The governor assembly contains a valve body and in the centre of this slides a bob-weight. A spring pushes the valve outwards towards the bob-weight. This construction gives a two-stage characteristic and, as shown by the graph, the high-pressure rise, in relation to a small speed increase during the first stage of its operation, gives good

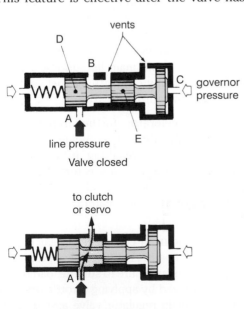

Figure 3.90 A gear change shift valve (change valve)

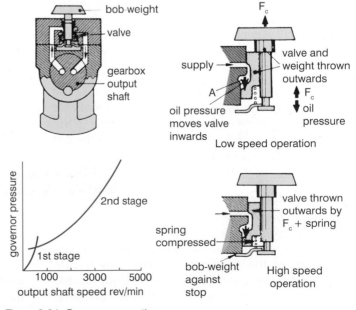

Figure 3.91 Governor operation

sensitivity; this ensures that the 1–2 gear change always occurs at the same speed.

At speeds less than about 500 rpm the first stage applies. During this stage, the bob-weight and valve act as a solid unit, so under bob-weight control the valve opens and closes the supply port as the weight moves outwards and inwards. The change in governor output pressure is achieved by the action of the fluid on face A.

Following an increase in speed, the valve moves outwards and the supply port is opened. This causes the fluid pressure acting on face A to rise until it produces a sufficient thrust to move the valve inwards and close the supply port. A further increase in speed causes this operation to be repeated but, in view of the greater centrifugal effect, the pressure in the valve chamber must reach a higher value before it can close the supply port. The second stage starts when the bob-weight stop contacts the governor body. From this point onwards, the balance between the opening and closing of the valve is achieved when: centrifugal force on valve = thrust of fluid on face A.

Stage 2 operation

The automatic selection of three gears can be achieved by the layout shown in Figure 3.89.

When 'D' is selected, the manual valve supplies line pressure to the front clutch and, with the aid of a free wheel, first gear (D1) is obtained. Line pressure is also applied to the other valves in the system, but all of these valves are inactive.

As soon as the vehicle moves, rotation of the output shaft produces a governor pressure and this acts on both shift valves. At a speed controlled by the strength of the spring in the 1–2 shift valve, the governor will generate sufficient pressure to open the valve. This action allows line pressure to act on the brake servo and give second gear (D2).

A further increase in road speed causes the governor pressure to rise further until it reaches a point where it overcomes the stronger spring in the 2–3 shift valve. At this speed, the opening of the 2–3 valve causes line pressure to act on the rear clutch and give third gear (D3).

Load sensing

The road speed at which the up and down gear changes occur varies with the load of the engine (i.e. the speed at which the changes occur increases with movement of the accelerator pedal). This feature mimics the technique used by a driver: light throttle pressure, early changes; heavy throttle pressure, delayed changes.

Various methods are used to sense the 'driver's mood' and most automatics use one of the following:

- Throttle valve, manually operated
- Throttle valve, vacuum-operated
- Electronic control

Manually operated throttle valve

The function of this valve is to produce, in a separate line, a fluid pressure that increases as the accelerator pedal is depressed. This throttle pressure, applied to the end of the shift valves, opposes the governor pressure that acts on the other end of the valves and, as a result, alters the point at which the shift valve operates.

The throttle valve is normally operated by a cable. This connects a lever on the side of the gearbox to some part of the carburettor throttle linkage. As the throttle is opened, the cable is pulled. This action rotates a cam in the gearbox and compresses a spring that acts on the valve.

Stage 3 operation

Figure 3.92 shows how a simple throttle valve is positioned in the fluid system to control flow and pressure to the throttle line (the dotted line leading from the throttle valve).

With the throttle closed, line pressure from the manual valve cannot pass the spool of the throttle valve, but if the throttle is opened a given amount, the spring on the cam side pushes the valve to the right. This partially uncovers the port that connects with the manual valve, and allows fluid to spill past the throttle valve so as to generate a pressure in the throttle line. A connection between this line and the chamber at the end of the throttle valve causes pressure to be felt 'behind' the valve. As pressure builds up, the valve moves slightly to the left; this reduces the flow from the main line until a balance is reached, as with many other valves, between the valve opening and the output pressure.

Depressing the accelerator further repeats this sequence; the only difference being that the increased spring thrust, resulting from the new position of the cam, requires a greater pressure in the throttle line to 'balance' the valve. So the more the throttle is depressed, the greater the pressure in the throttle line.

Besides acting as the main controller of gear change speeds, the throttle line pressure can also be used to vary the regulated line pressure to suit the load on the engine. This is achieved by applying throttle pressure to the end of the main regulator valve assembly. As the pressure increases or decreases, the gearbox will change gears up and down the gear ratios.

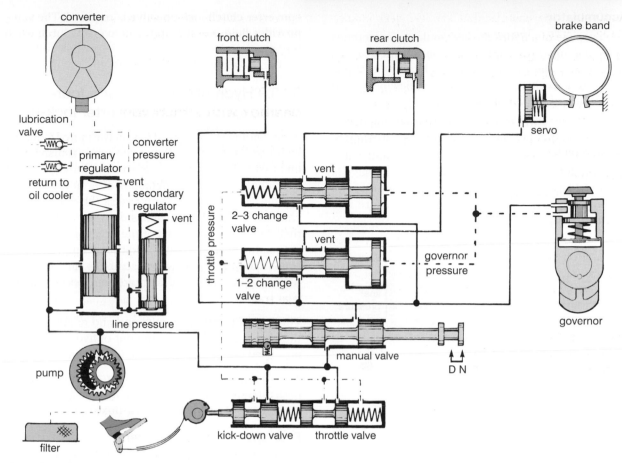

Figure 3.92 A hydraulic circuit – stage 3

Vacuum-operated throttle valve

The depression within the inlet manifold gives a good indication of the engine load, so some automatics have a throttle valve that is controlled from a vacuum chamber situated on the side of the gearbox. The overall action of this type of throttle valve is very similar to that of the manually operated valve.

Electronic control

A sensor, controlled by either manifold pressure or throttle position, signals the engine load to an ECU. After processing the signal, the ECU energises a solenoid to move the appropriate shift valve and change the gear. Some gearboxes that use this system also have a vacuum chamber connected to the manifold to vary the line pressure to suit the conditions.

Kick-down valves

There are occasions when a driver requires quicker acceleration, such as when overtaking. When this occurs, it is necessary to select a lower gear to place the engine within its higher power band and the gearbox in a ratio to take advantage of this higher power. On an automatic gearbox, this is achieved by full depression of the accelerator pedal to a position called 'kick-down'.

In a basic system, a movement of the pedal to this position opens a kick-down valve in the hydraulic system; this causes a sudden drop in pressure in the throttle line. Up to a certain speed in each gear position, this drop in pressure produces an immediate down change of gear.

In Figure 3.92, the kick-down valve is situated between the throttle valve and the cam. When the pedal is fully depressed, the cam moves the kick-down valve to the right, causing a pressure increase in the throttle line.

3.13.8 Additional features

The modern automatic gearbox has a number of features in addition to the basic system previously described. These are fitted to make the gear changes smoother, the vehicle more economical and to give the driver more control over the gearbox. The extra parts include the following.

Modulator valve

This type of valve is fitted to reduce the pressure in a part of a given line to suit some special operating condition, for example fitted in the throttle line supply to the regulator valve. In this case, it modulates (makes less violent) the rise in throttle pressure that acts on the regulator.

Accumulator

The purpose of a hydraulic accumulator (sometimes called a damper) as applied to an automatic gearbox is to reduce the rate at which a clutch or brake is actuated. It cushions the shock by delaying the full application of the fluid pressure.

Figure 3.93 shows an accumulator consisting of a spring-loaded piston in a chamber that is connected in the fluid line between the shift valve and clutch (or brake servo). When the shift valve is opened, the time taken for the fluid to compress the accumulator spring ensures that the pressure rise in the line is gradual.

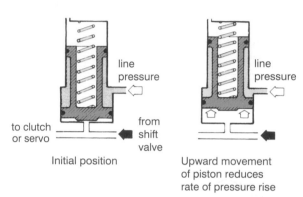

Figure 3.93 Accumulation action

Torque converter lock-up

Within the construction of most modern torque converters you will find a lock-up clutch assembly, which is designed to assist in the torque converter's efficiency throughout each drive cycle undertaken. Locking the torque converter at higher speeds prevents any slippage, which can generate heat and use engine power. Therefore, the vehicle will be more efficient. To operate the clutch assembly, a torque

converter clutch lock-up valve is required. The valve provides fluid pressure to the converter clutch when top gear is selected and the road speed is sufficient for the converter slip to be bypassed.

3.13.9 Hydraulic system for a four-speed gearbox with torque converter lock-up

As technology has evolved within the motor industry, manufacturers are now using automatic transmission units with four, five, six, seven or even eight gears to support the driving demands of a modern motor vehicle. However, when you assess the development changes within the transmission unit, you will find that they are adaptations of the original three-speed automatic gearbox, with additional epicyclic gear trains and/or overdrive assemblies incorporated within the housing to form a more complex compound gear train.

The addition of ECU monitoring and adaptations to the gear train reduce the amount of hydraulic valves now used to operate the internal functionality.

The following information provides a basic understanding of the hydraulic system now used in most four-speed automatic gearboxes.

Four-speed hydraulic system

Figure 3.94 shows a common hydraulic valve block arrangement that is seen in most modern automatic transmissions. This illustration is from a ZF transmission. This transmission system has three forward gears, along with an overdrive fourth speed with a torque converter lock-up clutch assembly. The gearbox also provides neutral, park and reverse gears. Figure 3.95 outlines the ZF hydraulic circuit and shows the various valves and associated components integral with the hydraulics.

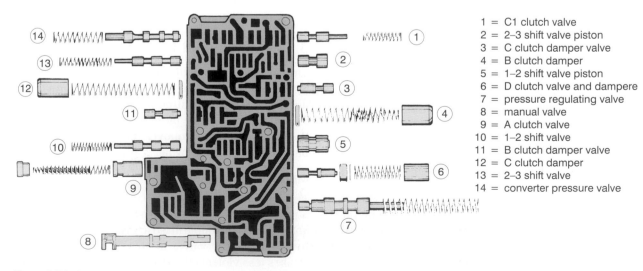

1 = C1 clutch valve
2 = 2–3 shift valve piston
3 = C clutch damper valve
4 = B clutch damper
5 = 1–2 shift valve piston
6 = D clutch valve and dampere
7 = pressure regulating valve
8 = manual valve
9 = A clutch valve
10 = 1–2 shift valve
11 = B clutch damper valve
12 = C clutch damper
13 = 2–3 shift valve
14 = converter pressure valve

Figure 3.94 A hydraulic valve block ZF four-speed gearbox

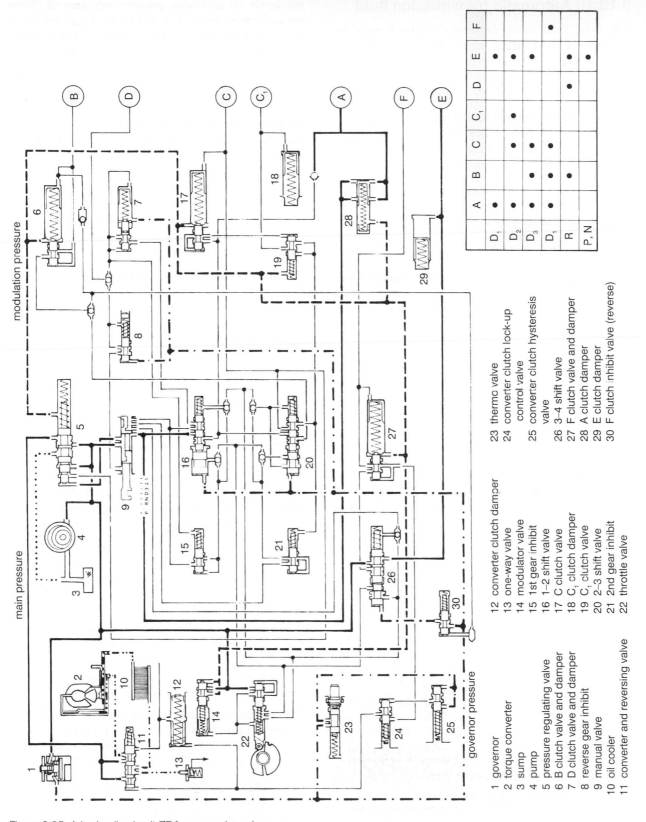

	A	B	C	C_1	D	E	F
D_1	•	•	•			•	
D_2	•	•	•	•		•	
D_3	•	•	•			•	
D_1	•	•	•		•		•
R	•	•				•	
P, N						•	

1 governor
2 torque converter
3 sump
4 pump
5 pressure regulating valve
6 B clutch valve and damper
7 D clutch valve and damper
8 reverse gear inhibit
9 manual valve
10 oil cooler
11 converter and reversing valve
12 converter clutch damper
13 one-way valve
14 modulator valve
15 1st gear inhibit
16 1–2 shift valve
17 C clutch valve
18 C_1 clutch damper
19 C_1 clutch valve
20 2–3 shift valve
21 2nd gear inhibit
22 throttle valve
23 thermo valve
24 converter clutch lock-up control valve
25 converter clutch hysteresis valve
26 3–4 shift valve
27 F clutch valve and damper
28 A clutch damper
29 E clutch damper
30 F clutch inhibit valve (reverse)

Figure 3.95 A hydraulic circuit ZF four-speed gearbox

3.13.10 Automatic transmission fluid

The fluid used in an automatic gearbox must be capable of performing many functions; it must operate the torque converter, actuate the clutches and brakes, and lubricate the various gears and bearing surfaces.

Each one of these duties demands special properties, so it is essential that the fluid actually used contains a wide range of additives that will more than satisfy the recommended specifications.

In traffic conditions, a torque converter gets very hot and, although an oil cooler is now common, the high temperature reached by the fluid must neither cause excessive oxidation nor vary the viscosity adversely to make the gear changes harsh or noisy.

Additives to resist wear of the rubbing surfaces and foaming of the fluid are also essential because a long period between fluid changes is demanded.

Another important consideration is the need to use a fluid that gives a stable friction value. A fluid of the incorrect type can cause the clutch and brake unit to engage either too quickly or too slowly, depending on the type of fluid used.

Most modern gearboxes use a fluid made to the General Motors specification DEXRON® II. Earlier gearboxes often used an ATF (automatic transmission fluid) to the Ford standard F.

It should be noted that the fluid used must be of a specification to suit the design of the box; clutch and brake problems occur if the wrong type of ATF is used.

Fluid level

A dipstick is normally used to indicate the correct volume of oil within the automatic gearbox. On most automatic gearboxes, you will find that the dipstick is located within the engine compartment. Usually, it is marked to show the level when the fluid is hot. Since the reservoir level varies with the position of the selector, it is essential to set the lever as recommended and run the engine at the suggested speed. A number of faults arise if the level is either higher or lower than that recommended.

3.14 Electronically controlled automatic gearbox

3.14.1 Improved efficiency and other operational benefits

Modern automatic gearboxes are usually fully electronically controlled and have the ability to adapt efficiently to maximise performance output. They are controlled by an ECU with a series of actuators and sensors that provide accurate functionality responding to the drive cycle and driver demands.

A fully electronically controlled automatic gearbox has many advantages over the earlier more simple mechanical/hydraulic gearboxes. By utilising ECUs to manage the operation of the gearbox, the correct gear selection can take place to optimise driving conditions. The automatic control module normally communicates with the ECU, but some manufacturers have integrated the two modules as one power train control module. Many of the sensors that the automatic gearbox uses to monitor or adapt are also used by the EMS, so integration of the two is logical to provide rapid interaction in some functions.

The communication between both of these modules is critical to provide good engine torque (or power) if and when the automatic transmission demands. On today's systems, engine torque is controlled normally by the use of an electronic throttle as this is the most efficient system. Known as 'drive by wire' and combined with adaptations to the fuelling and ignition timing, this enables rapid changes in engine torque and better efficiency to be achieved.

If the gearbox module notifies the ECU that a gear change is required, then instant adaptation of the throttle position, fuelling or timing can take place to achieve a brief change in the engine torque. This then ensures such a smooth gear change that the driver may not notice the change when acceleration or deceleration takes place.

It is also possible for the ECU to adapt and influence the gear change operation. For example, if the driver decides to overtake another vehicle by putting the engine under full load and on completion of this activity the driver releases the throttle quickly, then the engine management control module can indicate this reduced engine load to the automatic gearbox control module. This then would notify the automatic gearbox module to immediately change up into a higher gear to suit the demands.

The information that is continuously transmitted between both modules enables a rapid initiation of gear changes that would not be possible with a mechanical system.

Most common electronically controlled automatic transmissions now have a five-, six-, seven- or even eight-speed gearbox. The highest gear is normally an overdrive gear, which would work in conjunction with the lock-up clutch to achieve good economy.

As well as providing a smoother and more responsive gear change, the electronically controlled gearbox helps to improve the emissions produced by the engine. If there is an imbalance between the engine control system and the automatic gearbox, then emission levels will be affected. For example, incorrect gears will be selected if the throttle position control is not matching its set parameters, resulting in situations such as driving up a steep hill slowly in top gear with the throttle fully open, which will have a significant effect on emission levels.

Ensuring that the gear change and gear selection are matched to the driving conditions and driving style enables the management systems to achieve legislated emission levels.

3.14.2 Operation of the electronically controlled gearbox

Sensors and actuators

Electronic sensing of the operating conditions that affect the behaviour of an automatic gearbox has many merits over 'mechanical' sensing. For this reason, a number of modern units now use electronic devices, both to sense the conditions and to control the shift valves.

Figure 3.96 shows a layout of an electronically controlled automatic gearbox. Clutch chambers and brake servos are hydraulically operated, as in

a conventional system, so pressure regulators are needed as well as a manual valve to distribute the fluid. In this system, the number of hydraulic valves is considerably reduced; this is because the various tasks performed by these valves are now undertaken by the ECU. The interface between the electronic and hydraulic systems occurs at the shift valves. Each hydraulic shift valve is controlled by a solenoid; this is energised by the ECU when operation of the valve is required.

Speed, load and temperature sensing

Engine speed

The engine speed is normally monitored by a sensor located on the engine block. The crankshaft position sensor monitors the crankshaft speed and position during every engine cycle. This information is then transmitted to the ECU to identify these inputs and adapt its controlling to suit the vehicle's demands.

Vehicle speed

Within the design of the earlier mechanical automatic gearboxes, the governor was fitted to the output shaft and this then controlled the hydraulic pressure applied to the change valves. When the vehicle speed increased, the pressure applied to the change valve also increased in proportion to the vehicle speed required.

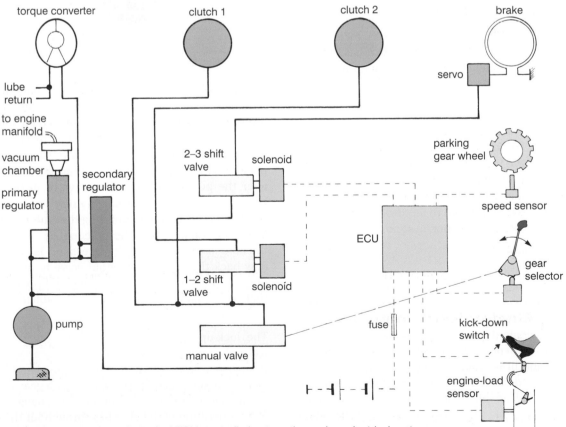

Figure 3.96 Schematic layout of a typical ECU-controlled automatic gearbox electrical system

An electronically controlled automatic gearbox monitors the vehicle speed by using a vehicle-speed sensor. Commonly, this sensor is fitted to the output shaft of the automatic gearbox, but manufacturers now integrate this function by using a wheel-speed sensor from the ABS system. The wheel-speed signal is transmitted to the ABS control module, which then notifies the automatic transmission control module of this input reading. The automatic transmission module then uses this information, along with the engine speed and load signals, to determine when gear changing should take place.

Additional speed signal

Some automatic transmission systems may also be fitted with additional speed sensors. These may be installed to monitor the input speed transmitted into the transmission. This speed signal information is used by the control module to adapt its parameters and to provide a smoother engagement of the different gear ratios, depending on variations of engine torque throughout every drive cycle. The type of speed sensor used within this system is an inductive or magnetic type, which passes an AC voltage signal on to the control module to confirm the rotational speed of the input shaft. To support this function, an inhibitor switch is usually fitted to the transmissions selector linkage to allow the starter motor to function only when the selector lever is in park or neutral.

Vehicle driving load

On earlier, mechanically controlled automatic gearboxes, the engine load was monitored and adapted using a throttle cable that was connected to the throttle linkage. When the throttle pedal was operated, the movement adjusted the position of the throttle valve in the valve body. With the electronically controlled automatic gearbox, the engine load is adapted by the means of a throttle position sensor in conjunction with the air mass sensor and the manifold absolute pressure sensor. Both sensors are standard on a modern EMS to monitor the air volume and load within the induction system.

Oil temperature sensor

The oil temperature within an automatic gearbox is a crucial element of its correct functionality. If the temperature is incorrect, then the viscosity of the oil and therefore the rate at which it will flow through the hydraulic elements of the gearbox will be affected. This will influence the operational speed of the clutches and brake bands engaging and disengaging during the drive cycle. The oil temperature is monitored by an oil temperature sensor normally located near to the valve body. This sensor transmits accurate temperature information back to the control

module. This, again, is vital information that the control module needs in order to produce smooth gear changes.

Basic operation

The automatic gearbox control module controls the operation of the gear selection using actuators, which are electrically operated solenoids. The solenoids operate and position the hydraulic change valves and, where fitted, the lock-up clutch. The solenoids are an integral part of the internal valve block that is located within the gearbox housing (Figure 3.97).

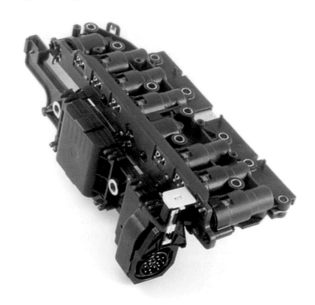

Figure 3.97 Solenoid valves fitted to the valve body

The control module will energise or de-energise the required solenoids to adapt their parameters when a gear change is required. Thus, energising a selected solenoid within the valve body will increase the line pressure and adapt the change valve to its selected position. The increase in the line pressure will then alter the position of the change valve in the valve body, which then increases pressure to be applied to the relevant piston controlling the clutch or brake band actuation. When the solenoid is disengaged, the fluid in the mainline (line pressure) is allowed to flow back through the solenoid valve to an exhaust or drain port in the valve. The fluid and pressure are therefore exhausted back through the solenoid valve and returned to the gearbox sump.

The lock-up solenoid within the torque converter will only operate depending on the gear selection (fourth gear in this example), road speed and engine load. To maintain and provide a smooth gear change, accumulators are used to support the change valves in the operation of the clutches throughout the drive cycle of the vehicle.

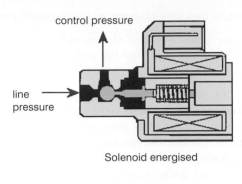

control pressure

line
pressure

Solenoid energised

exhaust

Solenoid de-energised

Figure 3.98 Solenoid valves in an energised and de-energised state

Line pressure

To control and maintain the desired line pressure, regulating valves are used in both mechanical and electronic automatic transmission units. If the line pressure is controlled electronically, a single primary regulating valve is used within the valve body. Its operating position is determined by the line pressure

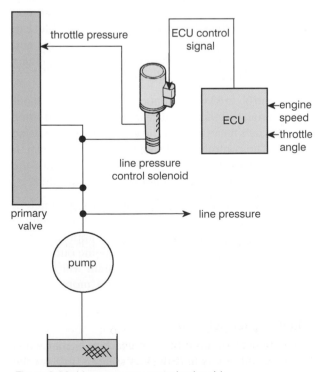

throttle pressure

ECU control signal

ECU

←engine speed
←throttle angle

line pressure control solenoid

primary valve

line pressure

pump

Figure 3.99 Line pressure control solenoid

control valve. Figure 3.99 shows how the position of the electronically controlled solenoid has to be continuously altered to provide the correct line pressure to suit the automatic gearbox operating conditions. The adaptations to the line pressure solenoid are controlled by the control module and are influenced by input signals and information received from various engine and gearbox sensors. The ECU adapts the line pressure by varying the electrical control signals applied to the solenoid, which in turn ensures that the gear changes are at the correct vehicle and engine speed and provide a smooth operation at all times.

Reduced number of hydraulic valves

Figure 3.100 shows a modern six-speed electronically controlled automatic gearbox. If you compare this version to an earlier conventional automatic gearbox, you will see that there are fewer hydraulic valves used in its operation. The reduction of a number of hydraulic valves and other components, such as governors, is due to the ECU now controlling solenoid functions.

Figure 3.100 An electronically controlled gearbox

Kick-down

On earlier automatic transmissions the kick-down facility was achieved by using a throttle cable or linkage system, which was connected on to the kick-down valve located within the gearbox. In the modern automatic gearbox, this is now electronically controlled by means of a throttle position sensor or a kick-down switch, which is connected to the linkage. When the driver demands full throttle, the control selects a lower gear to suit the driving demands. This will only be achieved if all driving parameters are met between the engine management and automatic gearbox control. If confirmed, then the driver will experience an increase in acceleration and be able to carry out the driving requirements. If driving demands are reached or throttle position has changed, then the control module will adapt and reselect a suitable gear depending on driver demands.

Gear selection

The driver selects the direction of drive by operating the gear selector lever. The lever is connected to the automatic gearbox via a cable, mechanical linkage or electronically.

Park

When park (P) is selected, the parking pawl engages and locks the internal drive of the transmission to prevent movement of the vehicle when it is left unattended.

Initial gear selection

When the driver selects their preferred gear, the position switch that is either located on the gear lever housing or on the side of the transmission will send a signal to the control module identifying the lever's position. On receiving this information, the automatic gearbox will activate its solenoids to select the preferred gear and allow the gearbox to operate.

Safety

To remove any accidental movement from its park position, many vehicle manufacturers are fitting a park lock solenoid. If the driver wishes to select a gear, then the ignition must be switched to the 'on' position and pressure will need to be applied to the brake pedal. If all parameters are met, then a solenoid located within the selector mechanism energises and allows the movement of the lever from its park position to the driver's selected position.

Smooth selection process

On selecting a forward gear, the control module will engage first gear and proceed to take-up drive in a forward motion. On a modern automatic gearbox, the control module may initially engage a higher gear, such as third, when drive is selected. This then limits the torque applied and reduces the possibility of the vehicle trying to take off by lurching forwards. Once the control module adapts its parameters and identifies that this risk is minimised, then the control module selects first gear to allow for a smooth take-up of drive from a stationary position.

Mode selection

On today's more modern, electronically controlled automatic gearboxes, drivers will have additional options to select from, for instance 'economy' or 'sports' mode, by pressing a switch or by a selective movement of the gear lever. For these modes to be available to the driver, the electronic interactions of the automatic gearbox control module and the ECU allow the reconfiguration of the engine performance in conjunction with changes to the gearshift pattern.

Note: on some vehicles the manufacturers have a similar function available but only adapt one of the two control systems to provide the addition function.

When the driver chooses economy mode, then the automatic control module will adapt its parameters to change into a higher gear and, at the same time, the ECU will also adapt its parameters to reduce its engine speed. In turn, this will provide a more efficient and lower emission operation. When the driver chooses sports mode, the automatic gearbox changes gear at a higher engine speed and the engine performance is increased by changes in the fuel and ignition parameters. The increase in performance also increases the fuel consumption. The driver, therefore, has the option to select a mode to suit personal preferences and driving conditions.

On some electronically controlled automatic transmissions the driver will have the additional option of a 'snow' mode setting. In this mode, the control modules will adapt to provide a higher gear selection to reduce torque to the driven wheels, which in turn will reduce the amount of wheel spin and loss of traction.

Adaptive operation and artificial intelligence

With the development of electronically controlled systems, some vehicle manufacturers now use automatic gearboxes that are 'artificially intelligent' and will adapt to different conditions depending on driving demands and vehicle stability. In reality, the electronic systems used on both adaptive and artificially intelligent systems are somewhat different, but both identify and learn their drivers' inputs and can also pre-judge driving conditions by receiving input information from other control systems.

The control module continues to monitor all input signals from the engine and gearbox sensors, and using these signals it can identify the way the vehicle is being driven. The control module adjusts its output signal to adapt its parameters and provide the driver with the desired performance or economy that is requested.

The control module may also adapt its parameters for driving on an incline. For example, if the vehicle is being driven uphill, then it may be appropriate to select a lower gear to improve the engine output and maintain its driven speed. The system will select a lower gear if the driver has applied more throttle movement.

Manual gear selection

A key benefit of an automatic gearbox is that when the transmission is in drive it is still possible for the driver to select another gear manually by using the gear lever. This facility gives the driver the option of selecting first, second or third on a four-speed gearbox to provide the addition of engine braking in very low gear ratios.

Sequential gearbox

On modern automatic gearboxes, there is the facility to allow the driver to select the gear manually in a sequential order. For example, the driver can select from first to second, second to third and third to fourth (Figure 3.101).

Figure 3.101 Gear selection options

Just as in the operation of a manual gearbox, but without the need to operate a clutch pedal, the driver selects first gear to move off and then changes up into the desired gear depending on driving demands. On changing down, the driver will operate the selector lever in the reverse direction to enable the selection of a lower gear in the same sequential manner.

If on down-shifting the driver tries to select a lower gear but the engine speed is too high, then the control module will not allow this down-shift to take place, thereby protecting the engine and gearbox from damage.

On operating the gear selector, the selection signal is transmitted and received by the automatic control module, which then will adjust its parameters to adapt the appropriate solenoid to select the preferred gear ratio. The driver is notified of the current position by a digital display on the instrument panel.

On some models, the driver is provided with the additional gear selection within the steering wheel assembly. The driver may choose to use these gear selection controls so their hands always remain on the steering wheel. Two buttons or selector control paddles are provided to control the up and down shift of the gearbox. **Note**: on some manual gearboxes, they may also have the adaptive functionality to allow sequential change control. In addition to the above variants, some manual gearbox systems also have a hydraulic system to move the selector. For this system to operate, the control module monitors the hydraulic system by receiving input signals from sensors. The control module operates the hydraulic system, which in turn operates the clutch in its conventional way. The driver can then have the option of changing gear with the gear selector lever or by using the steering wheel buttons or paddles.

With the control module monitoring and adapting the actuation of the gear change and clutch mechanism, it is also possible to select a fully automatic gear change process even though the gearbox and clutch are essentially a manual type. A number of vehicle manufacturers, such as Ferrari, use the same manual gearbox fitted with either manual selection and clutch operation or electro-hydraulic selection and actuation.

Fail safe

For most modern electronically controlled automatic gearboxes, the control module will have a limited operation strategy to revert to if an internal or electrical fault occurs during a drive cycle. The driver will experience a reduction in performance and a warning light or message on the instrument panel. In most cases, the vehicle will adapt to a default setting, better known as 'limp home' mode. This mode allows the vehicle still to be driven but at a greatly reduced output. The driver would normally have the option of reverse gear to aid manoeuvring and third gear as a forward gear. The control module would store a fault code within its memory and the distance travelled on that journey. The logged fault code gives a description of the concern and any reference data to support it. When the vehicle goes in for repair, the technician uses a scan tool to read the fault code and carry out an investigation to confirm the fault. The vehicle would only have to be picked up by the recovery services if there was a major electronic failure, internal mechanical failure or a total loss of transmission fluids.

3.15 Dual clutch transmission systems

3.15.1 Description

Figure 3.102 Dual clutch transmission gear lever

Dual clutch transmission (DCT) systems are a type of semi-automatic transmission and have become more popular with manufacturers looking for the option to use an automatic gearbox manually, but with increased shift speed.

3.15.2 Operation

DCT, also known as a twin-clutch gearbox, direct shift gearbox or double clutch transmission, uses two separate clutches for odd and even gear sets. The two separate manual transmissions and their clutches work as one unit and are contained within one housing. The driver can manually change gears if they don't want to operate in fully automatic mode, although the changes are still operated by the system's electro-hydraulics.

The secret to the system's ability to change gear very quickly lies in the fact that the two clutches operate different gears. Odd numbered gears (1, 3, 5 and 7) are operated by a larger outer clutch, while arranged concentrically within it a smaller clutch drives the even numbered gears (2, 4 and 6). While torque from the driven wheels is being applied to one clutch, the other clutch can be disconnected. This allows the pre-selection of one gear while the vehicle drives in another. The fact that this system allows very quick

and smooth gear changes makes it suitable for both ordinary road cars and high-performance cars.

Torque converters are not needed in a DCT system. Instead, they mainly use oil-bathed, wet multi-plate clutches, similar to the clutches used in most motorcycles, though dry clutch versions are also available.

The DCT originated in France in the 1930s. However, it was never fully developed by its inventor Adolphe Kégresse and the first working models weren't built until the 1980s when advances in electronics made it possible to have computer-controlled ECUs. Porsche racing cars were the first to use the system and the first production car to use it was the 2003 Volkswagen Golf Mk4 R32. Volkswagen named the gearbox direct-shift gearbox (DSG) (Figure 3.103).

Figure 3.103 Direct-shift gearbox

As performance and economy become more important in the production of modern vehicles, a number of manufacturers are now developing dual clutch and gearbox systems and there are several different versions on the market. The following companies are among those that offer these systems:

- BMW
- Bugatti
- Fiat
- Ford
- General Motors
- Volvo
- McLaren
- Mitsubishi
- Porsche
- Volkswagen
- Peugeot
- Citroën

Advantages

- The fuel economy of vehicles fitted with the DSG is usually better, seeing up to 15 per cent improvement over a standard automatic gearbox.
- Due to the seamless gear changes of the DSG there is no loss of torque from the engine.
- The speed at which the DSG gearbox changes gear is very quick, with up-shifts of 8 milliseconds due to the next gear being pre-selected prior to change.

- Gear changes are very smooth.
- The gear change is maintained, providing exactly the same gear change speed, irrespective of throttle position or gearbox mode.

Disadvantages

- The driver requires very sensitive use of the throttle to avoid unnecessary down-shifts through the kick-down facility of the gearbox. This is done by refraining from full throttle use or using the manual gear change facility through the gear stick or paddles.
- The overall efficiency of the gearbox is affected by the use of the wet clutches. This can cause some loss of power when compared with a conventional manual transmission system.
- The gearbox oil used in DSG gearboxes is very specific and requires changing at more regular service intervals than a conventional gearbox. This increases the cost of the vehicle using this type of gearbox.
- The cost to manufacture the DSG gearbox is greater than a conventional manual gearbox, which leads to overall greater vehicle costs for the customer.
- The gear-shift time taken when a gear selected is not the chosen ratio by the gearbox ECU can be higher at approximately 1100 milliseconds. However, this is still obviously quick in normal terms.
- Due to the multi-plate clutches, the torque handling ability of the DSG gearbox is limited.
- The DSG gearbox is heavier than a conventional manual gearbox, which can impact on the **power to weight ratio** of the vehicle.

Power to weight ratio: the ratio given between the power output of the vehicle and the overall vehicle weight, for example 200 bhp per tonne.

3.16 Electronic gear shift transmission systems

3.16.1 Description

Electronic gear shift (EGS) is essentially a manual gearbox with electronic motors to shift the gears and operate the clutch mechanism for the driver automatically. The main structure of the gearbox is similar to a manual gearbox apart from some additional features, such as a gearbox actuator, clutch actuator and a gearbox ECU. This type of gearbox can be driven in full automatic mode or manual sequential mode. The driver has a simple gear selector in the driving compartment similar to an automatic gear selector, but with fewer options – just neutral, automatic, reverse or manual.

3.16.2 Operation

When the driver selects automatic, the gearbox ECU will signal to the clutch actuator to depress the clutch, allowing the gearbox actuator to select first gear. The vehicle will remain stationary until the driver depresses the accelerator pedal. At this point, the gearbox ECU will signal to the clutch actuator to release the clutch gradually to take-up drive and allow the vehicle to move forward. As the engine approaches the pre-determined engine speed, the ECU will then signal to the clutch actuator to depress the clutch and then the gearbox actuator to select the next gear. During this time of changing the gear, the ECU will signal to the engine management to move the throttle and engine torque back to allow a smooth gear change. When the gear is selected, the EMS will then bring the throttle and engine power back to allow acceleration. This process happens in approximately 0.4 seconds.

When the vehicle is placed in manual mode, the gear changes are initiated by the driver flicking a steering wheel-mounted paddle. This informs the gearbox ECU of a gear change requirement. If the engine speed rises towards the maximum engine speed, the gearbox ECU will change gear automatically to avoid damage to the engine.

When the vehicle approaches a stationary position, the gearbox ECU will register the road speed from the road-speed sensor located in the transmission system and also from the ABS system. As the vehicle slows down, the gearbox ECU will change down the gears to provide some engine braking. When the vehicle is virtually stationary, the gearbox ECU will signal to the clutch actuator to depress the clutch and the gearbox actuator to select first gear.

The EGS system has many other individual functions to ensure that all eventualities are covered during the operation of the vehicle, but this explanation should give a brief overview of the system.

3.17 Continuously variable transmission systems

3.17.1 Introduction

The **continuously variable transmission (CVT)** was originally developed back in 1955 and was known as the Van Doorne system. The Dutch company DAF was one of the first manufacturers to use such a system,

Continuously variable transmission (CVT): able to provide an infinite number of seamless gear ratios. There are no step changes between the ratios due to the transmission consisting of two cone-shaped pulley wheels, which constantly change size, leading to changes in gear ratio and output drive speed.

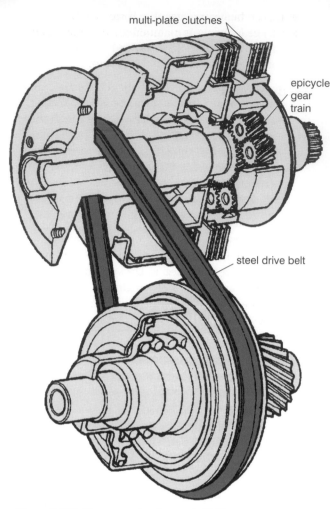

Figure 3.104 Components of an early CVT

and even when Volvo acquired DAF they continued to produce a Volvo variant of this system.

Other manufacturers, such as Fiat and Ford, then introduced a CVT-type gearbox system that was very similar in concept to the original Van Doorne system. The Ford CTX (continuously variable transaxle) uses the same belt-drive principle as the Van Doorne unit, but instead of using two rubber drive belts in tension, the Ford CTX employs a single steel belt that works in compression. The transmission unit is suitable for front-wheel drive cars up to 1.6 litres, and it is claimed that it is more economical than a conventional automatic gearbox. Since the development of these early versions of CVT, many other manufacturers are now producing their own versions to support the market demands.

In order to be able to support the demands of the power train (engine area), both types of gearbox (manual and automatic) require gradual changes in gear ratio to allow progressive build-up of speed of the vehicle. Within the automatic and manual gearboxes, the gear train consists of either conventional gear clusters or the use of epicyclic gear sets combined with clutch and brake-band packs. A CVT-type gearbox can provide the driver with a wide range of gear ratios throughout its operating range. A key benefit is that, depending on the driving conditions the vehicle is experiencing, the CVT can adapt its gear ratio to suit and maintain this throughout that period. It can select a specific engine speed and alter the gear ratio from a higher to a lower ratio and revert back to the higher ratio when the vehicle speed changes during that stage of its drive cycle. Another key benefit of a CVT transmission system is that it controls the engine speed to maintain specific engine rpm and, thus, optimises the reduction of exhaust emissions and fuel consumption.

Early CVT systems were designed to drive the rear wheels, but more recently manufactured designs are front-wheel drive versions. Most manufacturers use no more than a 1.6-litre engine to drive the transmission system, but as technology and development advance it is expected that many manufacturers will use engines with greater torque and power to drive CVTs.

Basic layout

Figure 3.104 shows that the CVT system is built around an enclosed vee belt, which runs between two adjustable cone-shaped pulleys. The primary pulley is connected to the engine via a single-stage epicyclic gear train having compound planets, and the secondary pulley is connected through a pair of reduction gears to the final drive.

One half of the primary pulley, which is connected directly to a hydraulic servo, is moved when a change in gear ratio is required. By altering the width of the pulley, the effective diameter can be gradually changed while drive is being transmitted. Belt tension is maintained by varying the diameter of the secondary pulley; this is achieved by using a strong spring to push the two halves of the secondary pulley together.

Two multi-plate clutches control the epicyclic gear train to give forward and reverse motion; one clutch connects the sun wheel and planet carrier together to give forward, the other locks the annulus to the transmission casing to provide reverse. These clutches are immersed in oil and are designed to slip at low speed; this feature allows the car to 'creep' when manoeuvring.

The thrust belt consists of a large number of vee-shaped steel elements retained on two steel bands. When the belt is driving, each steel element transmits thrust by pushing against its neighbour.

The hydraulic system and driver controls are similar to a conventional automatic transmission. When the driving mode is selected, hydraulic pressure from an engine-driven pump acts on the appropriate clutch actuator. With the vehicle in motion, ratio changes are brought about by the action of the hydraulic valve unit; this varies the pressure that is applied to the pulley servo in accordance with the signals it receives from the engine and road-speed sensors.

When the vehicle is accelerated or decelerated, the behaviour of the engine initially seems strange to drivers who normally use conventional systems. Since the CVT system selects the best ratio to suit the conditions, the engine does not have to be accelerated through each gear before the vehicle reaches its operating speed.

Later CVT designs used the same belt principle as the Van Doorne unit, but instead of the two rubber belts in tension they employed a single steel belt that worked using compression (the transmission of power is achieved by the steel belt pushing the output pulley rather than pulling).

3.17.2 Operation of the modern CVT

Within the transmission housing, there are two sets of multi-plate clutches controlling the epicyclic gear train and providing the forward and reverse motion. For the forward drive motion, one of the clutch assemblies is connected to the sun wheel and planet carrier. For the reverse gear motion, the second epicyclic gear train locks the annulus to the gearbox casing. Both epicyclic gear train assemblies are submerged in gear oil and are designed to allow some slip functionality at low engine speed. This gives the transmission the benefit of been able to operate without a clutch plate or a fluid coupling, and also allows the vehicle to creep when manoeuvring at lower speeds.

The internal construction of the CVT is built around the enclosed steel vee belt, which is located between the two adjustable cone-shaped pulley assemblies. The belt is made up of a large number of vee-shaped steel elements constrained within the main outer steel bands. When drive is taken up, the vee belt rotates within the cone-shaped pulleys and each steel element of the belt transmits thrust against the cone assemblies.

The primary cone pulley assembly is connected to the engine input drive and utilises a single-stage epicyclic

Figure 3.105 Steel vee drive belt

gear train consisting of a set of compound planets gears. The secondary cone pulley is connected to the final-drive assembly and uses a pair of reduction gears to maintain its output control. On the primary cone assembly, one half of the drive cone is fixed and the other section is connected directly to the main hydraulic servo assembly. This cone section will then move inwards or outwards to provide the change in gear ratio when required. Altering the width of the cone pulley assemblies effectively alters the diameter at which the steel vee belt sits within each section of the assembly, thus producing an increase or decrease in speed.

To maintain the tension of the steel vee belt, the secondary cone pulley works in conjunction with the operating changes of the primary cone assembly. For example, if the primary cone pulley gets narrower, then the secondary cone pulley will get wider. For this functionality to be achieved, the system uses a strong steel spring to maintain constant pressure on the two secondary cone pulleys, forcing them together. Both moving sections of the primary and secondary cone pulleys are positioned diagonally opposite each other preventing any misalignment of the steel vee belt throughout its drive cycle. If a low ratio is required, then the two halves of the primary cone pulley are positioned wide apart from each other providing a small diameter pulley. The position of the two halves of the secondary cone pulley are then set close together and provide a large diameter pulley. The actual position of the steel vee belt is centralised between the two drive pulleys, and variable changes occur when an increase or decrease in engine speed determines the gear ratio requirements. For example, if the engine speed increases, then the two primary cone pulley halves will slowly move closer together producing a larger diameter; simultaneously, the two secondary cone pulley halves will then separate and produce a smaller diameter. This operating principle will increase the gear ratio to a much higher level and provide an overdrive facility. For an overdrive function to be achieved, the secondary pulley assembly must be rotating 2.5 times faster than the primary pulley assembly.

If you compare the CVT hydraulic system and driver controls to the conventional automatic transmission, you will see that they are very similar in many ways. As the driver selects a preferred driving mode, the hydraulic system comes into operation and controlled oil pressure from the engine driven oil pump acts on the selected clutch actuator to provide the drive to be taken up. Throughout the vehicle's drive cycle, the variation of gear ratio is controlled and maintained by the hydraulic valve body. Oil pressure varies depending on the pressure applied on the pulley servo in accordance with the signal received from the EMS and input signals from road-speed sensors. To maintain a smooth take-up of drive, the two pulley assemblies are continuously jetted with oil. The oil jet is located within the transmission housing. To maintain its operating temperature and prevent overheating of the transmission oil, the system is also supported by an oil cooler.

Gear selection

The CVT gear selector is similar to a conventional automatic transmission in many ways. The driver will have the options of P, R, N, D and L (park, reverse, neutral, drive and low) as the selected positions available on the gear selector assembly. The selector lever will be connected to the transmission by a flexible steel cable, which connects on to the manual control valve within the valve body assembly of the transmission.

Park

If the driver selects park, the mechanism acts directly on the secondary cone pulley, internally locking the secondary cone pulley within the transmission casing and preventing any movement of the front wheels.

Reverse

With reverse selected, the reverse clutch is applied and the rotational function of the annulus is prevented. With this function selected, the planet carrier drives the planet gears, which in turn will operate the sun gear to be connected to the primary cone pulley. This then will provide the take-up of drive and move the vehicle in a reverse motion. Just as conventional automatics and even manual gearboxes allow, when the reverse gear is selected it will maintain a suitable gear ratio to suit the vehicle speed.

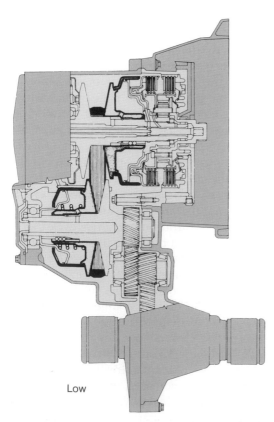

Low

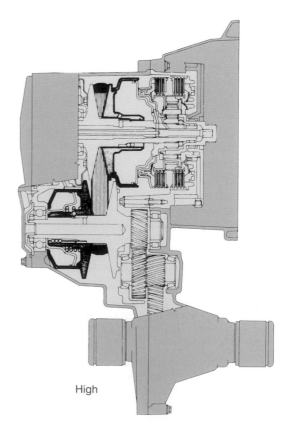

High

Figure 3.106 The modern CVT

Neutral

When neutral is selected, no activation of clutches takes place and, therefore, no drive is transmitted through the gearbox.

Drive

When the driver selects drive forward, the clutch is applied and the gear assembly rotates as one assembly. The drive is transmitted directly to the primary cone pulley. The gear ratio will be controlled by the driver applying pressure on the throttle pedal, which in turn will increase engine speed and gearbox output speed.

Low

If the driver decides to select low gear, then the gearbox will operate at a low speed output. This option is preferred and suited to mountainous driving conditions, if the vehicle is being used for towing conditions or it can be used for engine braking during deceleration. If required, a higher gear ratio can still be selected. The acceleration and deceleration behaviour between the engine and gearbox may seem strange compared to a normal transmission. Since the CVT can provide a progressive gear ratio throughout its driving range, the engine doesn't have to accelerate and reach its optimum speed level before changing up to the next gear.

Note: if a vehicle fitted with a CVT needs to be towed, then the front wheels must be raised clear of the ground to prevent internal damage occurring within the transmission assembly.

Other vehicle manufacturers have produced other variants of the CVT concept. Versions such as 'Toroidant' and 'Hydrostatic' for instance, are now offering effective challenges to the conventional automatic gearbox.

3.18 Overdrive systems

3.18.1 Introduction

To 'overdrive' means to drive faster. In the case of the transmission, the propeller shaft rotates faster than the engine when the overdrive system is in use. Used mainly when the vehicle is cruising, the overdrive gear gives improved petrol consumption, reduces engine wear and produces less engine noise. Today, most overdrive systems are built into the gearbox. This comparatively cheap arrangement gives an extra gear. Where a four-speed box is used, the fifth gear is an overdrive.

In the past, many three- and four-speed gearboxes had a separate overdrive unit fitted as an optional extra behind the gearbox. The common type used was made by Laycock and this was developed from the de Normanville unit. This is the type considered here.

Mounted either in place of the rear extension housing (or in front of the final drive), the overdrive transmitted the power in all gear positions. This meant that it had to be strong to withstand the torque developed in the low ratio gears.

Used in these locations, the overdrive gear set could also be engaged when the intermediate gears were selected in the main gearbox. This was a useful feature because its use converted a normal three-speed gearbox into a five-speed one. Road conditions for which top gear was too high and second gear was too low could be matched by using second gear and overdrive to give a ratio that fell between the main ratios. Operated by an electrical switch, the overdrive could be quickly engaged without having to use the clutch. Torque developed by the lower gears was too great for the overdrive unit, so an external inhibitor switch was fitted to disengage the overdrive during reverse and low gear operation.

Construction and operation

The simple epicyclic gear set used in this type of overdrive gives either direct or overdrive gear and is operated electro-hydraulically. The electrical system, controlled by the driver, activates a hydraulic system to move a cone-type clutch forwards and backwards to either hold or drive a sun gear.

The layout of the gear-train set is shown in Figure 3.107. Drive is applied to the planet carrier and the sun wheel, which is mounted on a bearing on the input shaft, and can be connected by a friction cone-type clutch to either the annulus or the casing.

Direct drive

Spring pressure pushes the cone clutch to the right to connect the sun wheel to the annulus and lockup the complete gear assembly. Drive from the engine is taken through the free-wheel unit: the cone and gear unit accommodate overrun and reverse conditions, since the free wheel will not transmit a drive in the reverse direction.

Overdrive

Oil is placed under pressure from a pump driven by the input shaft. This pressure acts on pistons, which force the cone clutch against the casing to prevent the sun wheel from rotating. The input shaft will move the planets forward and cause them to rotate around the fixed sun. This motion will drive the annulus slightly faster than the input shaft, to give overdrive. The overdrive may be engaged without using the main clutch, and thus the operation is quick.

If the transmission is in its low gears or in reverse, then the overdrive operation is not permitted. The torque developed by the transmission in its lower

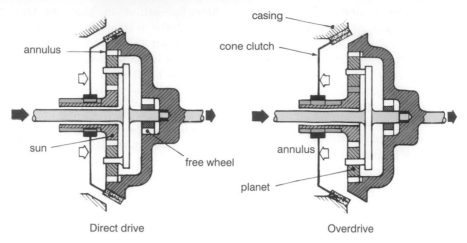

Direct drive

Overdrive

Figure 3.107 Overdrive gear train layout

gears is too great for the overdrive to operate, so an external inhibitor switch is fitted to the gear selector mechanism to disengage the overdrive during lower gear and reverse gear operation.

3.19 Propeller shafts and drive shafts

3.19.1 Introduction

Propeller shafts

The propeller shaft, or prop shaft, is historically known as a part on an aircraft or boat that transmits drive to the final-drive unit. Looking at an aircraft, the propeller shaft transmits the drive from the engine to the propeller, which then provides the forward thrust to move the aircraft. When referring to the propeller shaft fitted to a motor vehicle, this component transmits the torque from the transmission system to the final-drive unit or differential unit. The drive is then directed to the wheels through the drive shafts linking the wheels to the final-drive unit.

Generally, when we discuss the propeller shaft, it is in reference to rear- or four-wheel drive vehicles. The propeller shaft is a tubular component and is often a one- or two-piece construction, depending on the distance between the transmission and the final drive. By adding a two-piece construction, this can prevent an issue called **whip** (see page 353).

Whip: term used to describe the bowed deformation of a propeller shaft.

Drive shafts

Drive shafts are used in rear-wheel drive, front-wheel drive and four-wheel drive vehicles. The drive shafts transmit the torque from the transmission system

through the final-drive unit to the driven wheels. These shafts are smaller than the propeller shaft, usually being the width of the vehicle. The drive shafts can be tubular or solid in design, depending on the vehicle.

3.19.2 Propeller shafts

The propeller shaft must be strong to resist the twisting action of the driving torque and it should be resilient to absorb the torsional shocks. Also, it must resist the natural tendency to sag under its own weight because vibration occurs when the centre of gravity does not coincide with the axis of the shaft.

A tubular section propeller shaft is normally used because it has the following merits:

- Low weight
- High resistance to misalignment, especially sag
- Good torsional strength (a tubular shaft is only slightly weaker than a solid shaft of similar diameter)
- Low resistance (low inertia) to changes in angular speed that arise when a Hooke-type coupling is used to drive the shaft

Refer to section 3.20 on page 354 for more on Hooke-type couplings.

A propeller shaft often rotates at high speed, especially when the overdrive gear or top gear is in use. Therefore, the shaft must be made and repaired to meet good balance limits. In fact, when looking at a vehicle running at 7000 rpm in a gear of 1 : 1 ratio, the propeller shaft will be rotating at the same speed. It is important, therefore, that during manufacture steel shafts are balanced correctly. During this operation, small patches are spot welded on to the 'light parts' of the tube to correct any imbalance.

Even when the static alignment of a shaft is perfect, the weight of the shaft makes it bow at the centre. When this is excessive, rotation of the shaft causes the bow to increase owing to the centrifugal effect. This deformation, or whip of the shaft, sets up a vibration that becomes severe as it approaches the whirling speed. The critical speed at which this condition occurs depends on two vital dimensions: the mean diameter of the tube, and the length of the shaft. Whirling speed is raised when either the diameter is increased or the length is decreased.

Many rear- and four-wheel drive vehicles need a longitudinal propeller shaft that has to span a great distance between the gearbox and final drive. In these cases, the driveline is normally divided and a bearing is fitted to support the shafts in the region where they are split (Figure 3.108). This bearing is mounted in rubber to absorb any vibration that would otherwise be transmitted to the body.

Where a solid or 'live' axle is fitted there will be axle movement as the vehicle moves over the road surface and the suspension absorbs the undulations. To accommodate this movement, universal joints are fitted to both ends of the propeller shaft. The joint at the front connected to the transmission is required to accommodate body movement and transmission system movements. The rear joint allows the axle to move up and down during suspension movements. Since it is nearly impossible to maintain the correct drive angles of Hooke-type couplings fitted to a two-piece shaft layout, many modern arrangements use one or more constant velocity (CV) joints (refer to the next section on page 354 for CV explanation).

As the axle moves up and down or twists at an angle through torque reaction, the distance between the axle and the transmission system will alter. To ensure that the propeller shaft can take up this alteration in length, a sliding joint is fitted to the transmission end. This arrangement incorporates a splined joint that allows the propeller shaft to move in and out of the transmission output shaft during axle movements (Figure 3.108).

Composite propeller shafts

The composite propeller shaft shown in Figure 3.109 is a modern alternative to the divided arrangement. The tubular shaft is made of composite materials containing carbon fibre. This material is extremely strong when woven together with epoxy resin. This is then bonded to a steel spigot for connection to the universal joints. The use of carbon fibre propeller shafts is normally limited to motor sport vehicles, such as Formula 1 cars, where the weight of each component is critical. These propeller shafts can handle larger torque inputs

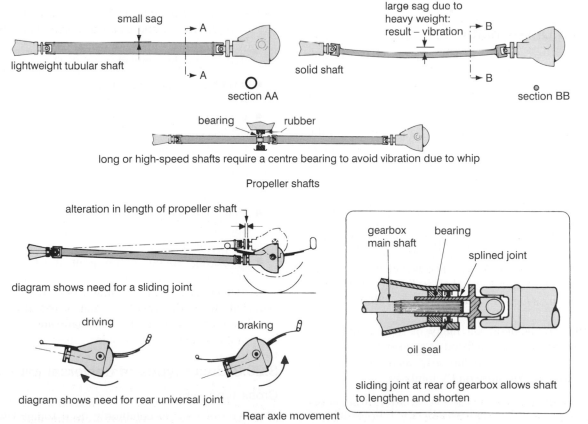

Figure 3.108 Propeller shaft features

than the steel versions but are very expensive. For this reason, manufacturers do not normally fit these types of propeller shafts as original equipment.

Compared with a conventional two-piece propeller shaft arrangement, the advantages of the composite carbon-fibre shaft are as follows:

- Weight reduction by about 50 per cent
- High internal shock absorption
- Good noise, vibration, harshness (NVH) performance
- Exceptional corrosion resistance

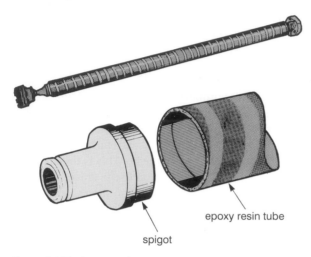

Figure 3.109 A composite carbon-fibre propeller shaft

3.19.3 Drive shafts

Since these shafts are comparatively short in length, they are often made solid to give clearance to allow for movement of the suspension. Where space is not restricted the lightweight tubular section can be used.

The short distance between the road wheel and the final-drive housing, combined with a large road wheel movement due to suspension deflection, means that both the maximum drive angle of the universal joints and the length variation of the shaft are great. A CV joint at each end of the drive shaft meets the angle requirement and a plunge CV joint accommodates the length change during suspension movement.

Rear-wheel drive vehicles having independent rear suspension need a drive shaft to link the road wheel to the fixed final-drive assembly, which is usually mounted directly to the vehicle's body or a **sub-frame** arrangement. On many of these vehicles, a plunge-type CV joint is fitted at each end of the drive shaft to accommodate the suspension movements. (See page 357 for more on CV joints.)

Sub-frame: supporting frame to which the engine or suspension of a car without a true chassis is attached.

3.20 Universal and CV joints

3.20.1 Introduction

A universal joint, sometimes called a Carden joint, allows the drive to be transmitted through a variable angle.

The need for a universal joint is shown in Figure 3.108. This is a rear-wheel drive layout having the gearbox mounted on the frame and the rear axle bolted to the road springs. Road shocks will deflect the springs to the position shown. This will alter the angle of the propeller shaft relative to the gearbox and final drive and, unless a universal joint is fitted to each end of the propeller shaft, the shaft will bend and fracture.

A similar problem occurs on front-wheel drive vehicles. In this case, one end of the drive shaft is connected to a fixed transaxle assembly and the other end is attached to a wheel hub that moves up and down with the suspension spring. In addition to giving flexibility in this direction (plane), the outer universal joint must allow the road wheels to be steered through a large angle of about 25°.

3.20.2 Requirements

A simple joint consisting of a flexible fabric disc secured to the shaft by metal forks meets the basic requirements, but this type is only suitable for driving a low-speed shaft through a very small variable angle. This type of joint is still used for some engineering applications, but it fails to meet the requirements expected of a modern universal joint. These are:

- **strength** – high torque must be transmitted with the minimum energy loss due to friction
- **compactness** – space is limited so the joint must be small and robust
- **large drive angle** – modern road springs allow large wheel deflections, so the joint must be able to accommodate the large drive angle given by this movement
- **shaft balance** – severe vibration occurs if the shaft runs out-of-true, so the joint must maintain good alignment
- **operating speed** – the joint must operate efficiently at high speed under conditions of high torque and variable drive angle. This requirement must be combined with the need for the joint to have a long life and minimum maintenance.

3.20.3 Basic types of universal joint

Cross-type joint

This type of joint is commonly used today. Often, it is called a Hooke-type coupling because it was developed from the joint claimed to have been invented by the scientist Robert Hooke in the 17th century.

The joints in Figures 3.110a and b, which show the basic and developed form respectively, have two yokes set at 90° to each other. These yokes are joined to each other by a cross-shaped **trunnion** block and, in modern joints such as those made by Hardy Spicer, contact between the two parts is made by needle roller bearings held in a hardened steel cup retained in each arm of the yoke. Alignment of the trunnion is achieved by making the bottom of the cup contact the end of the block.

Trunnion: a cross pin arrangement able to locate and support a drive shaft on either side and allow transfer of torque through a larger range of angles.

Lubrication of the bearings is provided by using a special viscous oil, similar to that used in a final drive, which is contained in a reservoir formed by drifting out the centre of the trunnion arms. The oil is introduced either by a lubrication nipple or by pre-filling a small reservoir that will last for the life of the joint. An oil seal retained on each arm of the block presses against the cup and prevents the escape of the lubricant.

The cups are retained in the yoke either by **circlips** or staking. Peening over the edge of the yokes to stake the cups makes replacement of worn parts in the

joint more difficult; in this case, it is recommended that the complete shaft assembly is replaced when the joint is worn. The merits of this type of joint are:

- compactness
- high mechanical efficiency
- ability to drive through a large occasional 'bump' angle (maximum about 25°)
- accurate centring of shaft, hence the joint is suitable for high speed operation.

Circlips: circular fasteners that clip into place and are used to join two components together allowing rotational but not lateral movement.

Lubrication failure, especially in cases where a 'grease' nipple in the trunnion block is missed when the vehicle is serviced, causes the needle rollers to indent and damage the bearing surfaces. This type of wear gives a slight angular movement, allowing the slackness in the joint to produce a noise often described as a 'clonk' during the changeover from drive to over-run and vice versa. Failure to rectify this fault, accelerates the rate of wear and this soon leads to misalignment and severe vibration.

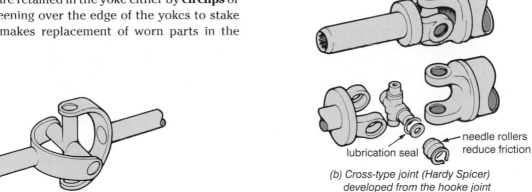

(b) Cross-type joint (Hardy Spicer) developed from the hooke joint

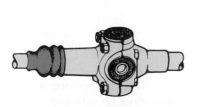

(a) Hooke-type joint

(c) Cross-type with rubber bushing to absorb vibrations

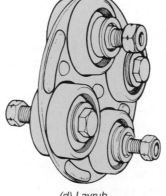

(d) Layrub

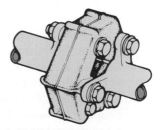

(e) 'Doughnut' rubber coupling

Figure 3.110 Types of universal joint

Rubber joints

One disadvantage of the cross-type joint is its lack of flexibility in relation to the absorption of torsional shocks and driveline vibrations, especially when a comparatively rigid transmission system is used. A smoother and less harsh drive can be obtained by using one or more rubber joints in the transmission driveline. Various types of rubber joint are in use; these include:

- Moulton-type
- Layrub-type
- doughnut-type.

Moulton-type

This rubber trunnion joint (Figure 3.110c) is based on a Hooke-type coupling, but uses moulded rubber bushings to transmit the drive between the trunnion and yokes. The synthetic rubber mouldings require no lubrication and their resilience damps the torsional shocks that are generated when the drive is transmitted through an angle.

Layrub-type

Originally made by the Laycock Company and constructed of a series of rubber bushings, the name 'Layrub-type' is used to describe this joint (Figure 3.110d). It consists of a number of moulded rubber blocks, with specially shaped cavities at the ends, which are sandwiched between two steel pressings. Each shaft is connected by means of a fork to alternate rubber blocks.

This construction allows the rubber blocks to deform and allow the drive to be transmitted through a small angle. In addition, the blocks accommodate small axial and angular movements for shaft length alteration and torsional damping.

Although the coupling is rather large in diameter, the Layrub-type offers the following advantages:

- No lubrication required
- Capable of driving through bump angles up to about 15°
- Allows for axial movement, hence no splining of the shaft is necessary
- Flexibility damps shocks and insulates vehicle from transmission noise

Doughnut-type

Although rather large, the great flexibility of this type provides a soft cushion to absorb the majority of torsional shocks produced by the action of other joints or by vibration from either the engine or road wheels. Figure 3.110e shows that the synthetic rubber coupling is near circular in shape, and is moulded around cylindrical steel inserts that are bolted alternately to the three-arm forks attached to the shafts.

The merits of this coupling are similar to the Layrub-type.

3.20.4 Speed variation of a Hooke-type coupling

When a Hooke-type coupling is transmitting a drive through an angle, the output shag does not rotate through 360° at a constant speed. Instead, the speed varies every 90° of rotation, and the rate of movement for one revolution is fast, slow, fast, slow (Figure 3.111).

This cyclic speed variation, and its associated vibration, is insignificant when the drive angle is less than about 5°, but becomes much more intense as the angle is increased.

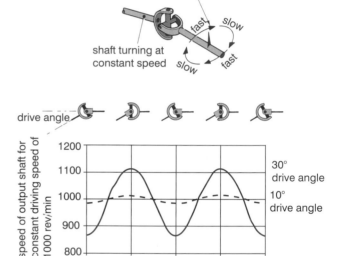

Figure 3.111 Speed variation with Hooke-type joints

One method of achieving a constant speed output from the propeller shaft is to mount two Hooke-type couplings, either back-to-back or positioned in a certain way at each end of the propeller shaft. In both configurations, the relative positions of each coupling must be arranged so that the speed change of one coupling is counteracted by the other. The 'phasing' of Hooke-type couplings, as applied to two separate driveline layouts, is shown in Figure 3.112.

This diagram shows that to restore a constant speed, two conditions must be satisfied:

1 Yokes at each end of the propeller shaft must be positioned in the same plane.
2 The drive angle of each coupling must be equal.

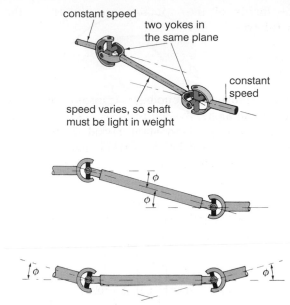

Figure 3.112 Phasing of Hooke-type couplings

3.20.5 CV universal joints

A CV universal joint is a type that provides an output shaft speed equal to that of the input in all shaft positions within the working range of the joint. Today, these joints are often used in drivelines because of their smooth operation. They were originally introduced for situations where the drive angle was large, for example at the wheel end of a front-wheel drive vehicle when the steering is set in the full-lock position.

Geometry of a typical CV joint can be appreciated if the action of a Hooke-type coupling is considered. The speed variation of a Hooke-type joint is caused by the alteration in leverage between the yokes and trunnion block. When the coupling is viewed from the side and the input shaft is rotated through 90°, the trunnion block is seen to oscillate back and forth from the vertical through an angle equal to the shaft drive angle.

A constant angular velocity condition occurs with this joint when the trunnion block is at the mid-point of its rocking movement. If this condition could be maintained, a CV universal joint would be obtained (i.e. constant-velocity conditions are achieved when the connecting device between the driving and driven 'yokes' is positioned in a plane that bisects the angle of drive).

The various CV joints in use have a construction that is based on either the twin Hooke-type coupling arrangement or the 'angle bisect' principle.

The following CV joints are in use:

- Tracta
- Rzeppa
- Bendix-Weiss
- Tripode

Tracta CV joints

The need for CV joints was discovered in 1926 when the first four-wheel drive vehicle was made in France by Fenaille and Grégoire – the Tracta (traction-avant) car. When the second car was made, the driveline incorporated CV joints and the type used on that car is now known as a Tracta joint. This type is now made by Girling and Figure 3.113 shows the main details.

Reference to the line sketch shows that the operating principle is similar to two Hooke-type joints: the angles are always kept constant and the yokes are set in the same place.

The joint is capable of transmitting a drive through a maximum angle of about 40° and its strong construction makes it suitable for agricultural and military vehicles, but the friction of the sliding surfaces makes it rather inefficient.

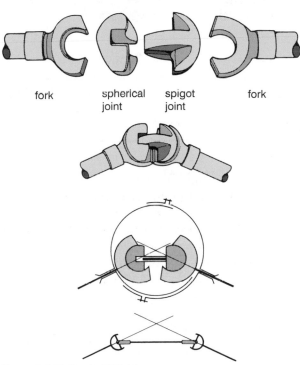

Figure 3.113 Tracta CV joint

Rzeppa-type CV joint

This joint was patented by A.H. Rzeppa (pronounced Zeppa) in America in 1935. The development of this type is in common use today; it is called a Birfield joint and is made by Hardy Spicer.

Figure 3.114 shows the construction of a Birfield joint and the line sketch shows the principle of operation.

Constant velocity is achieved if the device (steel balls in this case) connecting the drive shaft to the driven shaft rotates in a plane that bisects the angle of drive: the Birfield joint achieves this condition.

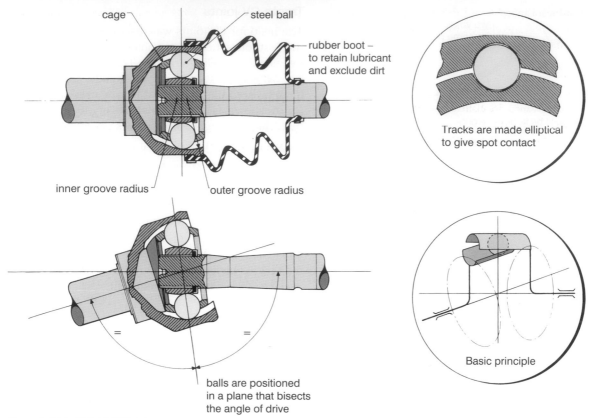

Figure 3.114 Birfield CV joint

Drive from the inner to outer race is by means of longitudinal, elliptical grooves, which hold a series of steel balls (normally six), that are held in the bisecting plane by a cage. In the original Rzeppa joint, the cage position was controlled by a small plunger fitted between the two shaft centres, but noise was a problem. In the Birfield design, the plunger is omitted. Instead, the balls are made to take up their correct positions by offsetting the centres of the radii for inner and outer grooves.

A Birfield joint has a maximum angle of about 45°, but this angle is far too large for continuous operation because of the heat generated. Lubrication is by grease – the appropriate quantity is packed in the joint 'for life' and a synthetic rubber boot seals the unit.

Bendix-Weiss-type CV joint

This type was patented in America in 1923 by Weiss and later developed by Bendix. It is now known as a Bendix-Weiss and produced in the UK by Dunlop. Figure 3.113 shows a simplified drawing of this type. The two forks have grooves cut in their sides to form tracks for the steel balls. There are four tracks, so four balls are used to transmit rotary motion and a fifth ball placed at the centre of the forks locates the two forks and resists the inward force. The driving balls

work in compression, so two balls take the forward drive and the other two operate when reverse drive is applied. The complete joint is contained in a housing filled with grease. Maximum angularity is about 35°.

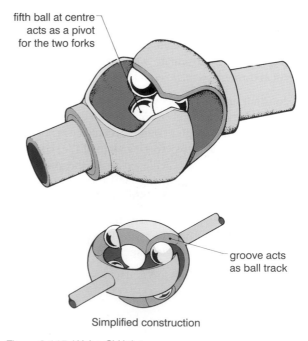

Figure 3.115 Weiss CV joint

Constant velocity is achieved in a manner similar to the Rzeppa – the balls always take up a position in a plane that bisects the angle of drive.

Tripode-type CV joint

This compact joint has been developed over the past 35 years and, in view of its ability to operate efficiently at high speed, it is now the most common type of joint used in drive arrangements where independent suspension is used.

Besides providing good resistance to high-speed centrifugal effects, the construction of this joint, combined with the reduced working clearances achieved by modern production techniques, produces a transmission driveline with good noise-vibration harshness (NVH) performance.

In the construction shown in Figure 3.116, the three-armed support (tripod) carrying the spherically shaped rollers is fixed to the outer housing. On both sides of each driving fork, which also has three arms, grooves are cut to form a bearing track for the rollers.

Drive through the joint is produced by the force exerted by the side of the driving fork on the rollers. This force is transmitted to the tripod and joint housing.

Alteration of the drive angle causes the roller to move backwards and forwards along the grooved track as the joint rotates through one revolution. A small clearance is given between the roller and track to permit this movement.

Homokinetic motion is achieved with a Tripode joint because of the path taken by the rollers with respect to the contact point on the track.

> **Homokinetic motion**: constant velocity. Homokinetic joints allow a rotating shaft to transmit power through a variable angle, at a constant rotational speed.

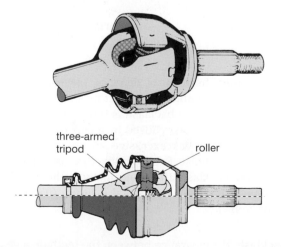

Figure 3.116 Tripode CV joint

three-armed tripod   roller

This type of fixed joint accepts an occasional drive angle up to about 45°.

3.20.6 Plunge joints

Suspension movement causes an alteration in length to many driveline shafts, so a special CV joint called a plunge joint must be used to allow for this. The alternative is to use splines to allow the joint to slide back and forth along the shaft, but lubrication often causes a problem.

Two plunge joints in common use have been developed from the fixed Birfield and Tripode types.

Birfield plunge joint

Development work on the original Rzeppa joint by Löbro in Germany in the late 1950s produced the type known in this country as the Birfield CV joint. In 1960, the Löbro company redesigned this fixed-type joint and produced it in a plunge form to satisfy the needs of front-wheel drive vehicles that were gaining favour at that time.

The constructional features of this joint are shown in Figure 3.117. In this type, the grooves that act as the tracks for the balls are straight instead of curved; this allows the shaft length to vary up to about 50 mm.

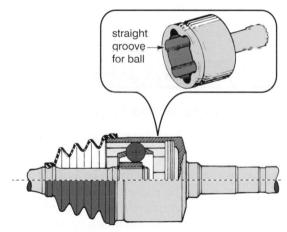

straight groove for ball

Figure 3.117 Birfield plunge joint

When the shaft angle is increased, the rolling action of the balls in the inner and outer grooves positions the cage in the bisecting plane to give a CV drive.

The maximum drive angle of 22° is considerably less than that in the fixed type, so in front-wheel drive vehicles the plunge joint is positioned at the engine end of the drive shaft.

Tripode plunge joint

Comparing the tripode plunge joint in Figure 3.118 with the fixed tripode joint (Figure 3.116) shows that the basic construction is similar. The main difference is that the plunge joint has roller tracks that are straight instead of curved.

The type shown permits a maximum plunge of 55 mm and a drive angle up to 25° but, as with all types of CV joint, the working angle should be less than 10°.

Later types of tripode-type plunge joints use either ball or needle roller bearings to reduce the friction between the contact surfaces. These improve the NVH performance and allow the joint to operate efficiently at high speed.

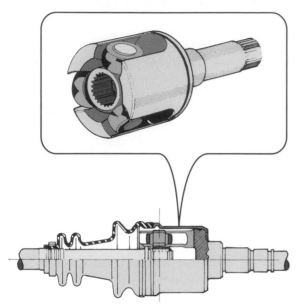

Figure 3.118 Tripode plunge joint

3.21 Final-drive gears

3.21.1 Purpose of the final drive

The purposes of a final drive, as applied to a rear axle, are:

- to transmit the drive through an angle of 90°
- to gear down the engine revolutions so that a 'direct top' gearbox ratio may be employed. In the case of cars, this requires a final-drive ratio of approximately 4:1.

These functions can be performed by bevel or worm gears.

3.21.2 Bevel gears

The geometry of a bevel gear layout may be considered by referring to Figure 3.119. This represents two friction cones: A – the crown wheel; and B – the pinion. To avoid slipping and wear, the apex of the pinion must coincide with the centre line of the crown wheel. If the pinion is incorrectly positioned, the peripheral speeds of the crown wheel and pinion will not be equal. Mounting the gear in the correct position will show that the angle of the bevel is governed by the gear ratio.

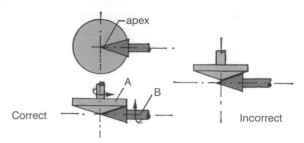

Figure 3.119 Friction cones representing bevel-gear drive

Types of bevel gear
Straight bevel

Figure 3.120 illustrates the main features of the bevel type of gear. Tapered teeth, generated from the centre, are machined on the case-hardened steel gears, and then ground together to form a 'mated pair'. The DOR of the axle shaft will be determined by the position of the crown wheel relative to the pinion. (It is possible on some vehicles to fit the crown wheel on the wrong side, and this gives one forward and several reverse ratios.)

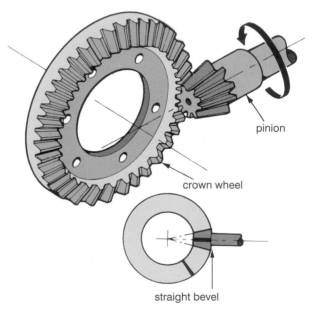

Figure 3.120 Straight bevel gear

Adjusters in the form of distance pieces, shims or screwed rings enable the correct mesh and **backlash** to be set. When the backlash is too small, expansion due to heat and wear caused by a lack of lubrication will result, whereas excessive clearance produces slackness and noise. Each manufacturer recommends a suitable backlash; this is normally in the region of 0.15 mm (0.006 in) for cars and 0.25 mm (0.01 in) for heavy vehicles.

Backlash: the clearance between the teeth on a gear.

Spiral bevel

Although the straight bevel was cheap to produce and mechanically efficient, the meshing of the gears caused an objectionable noise, which was reduced when a **helical** form of tooth was employed. Naturally, it is impossible to generate a helix on a tapered pinion, so the gear is known as a spiral bevel.

> **Helical**: shaped like a helix (a three-dimensional spiral).

The construction of the gear is shown in Figure 3.121. A number of teeth, generated from the centre of the crown wheel, form (in the case of the pinion) a left-handed spiral. This direction causes a large outward thrust on the drive and a smaller inward thrust on the over-run; therefore pinion-bearing wear will increase the backlash rather than cause seizure of the gear.

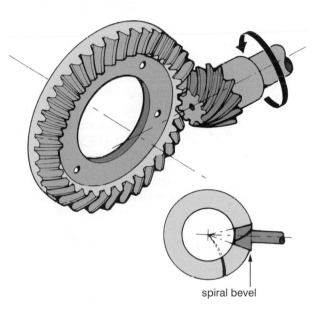

spiral bevel

Figure 3.121 Spiral bevel gear

Since the crown wheel teeth are inclined to the pinion, you will notice that the tooth pressures are much higher. The straight (i.e. no additives), high-viscosity gear oil, which was satisfactory for the straight bevel type, gave poor results when used in spiral bevel units. The oil film broke down under the high loads, and allowed rapid wear and scoring to take place. Special oils to lubricate the surface after rupture of the oil film were developed and these are known as EP (extreme pressure) lubricants. They contain various additives, such as sulphur, chlorine and phosphorus compounds, which react chemically at high temperatures with the metal surface to form a compound of low frictional resistance.

Hypoid

The hypoid type of gear shown in Figure 3.122 is the popular form in use today. The pinion axis is offset to the centre line of the crown wheel. It can be placed above or below the centre, but in the case of cars is always placed below to give a lower propeller shaft and a reduction in the tunnel height. Pinion offset varies with the application, but an offset equal to one-fifth of the wheel diameter is often used.

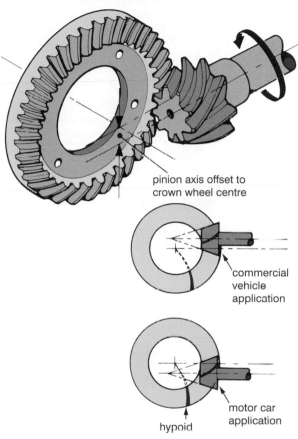

pinion axis offset to crown wheel centre

commercial vehicle application

motor car application

hypoid

Figure 3.122 Hypoid bevel gear

By lowering the axis, it will be seen that the tooth pitch of the pinion increases, and so, for a given ratio, the pinion diameter can be larger (30 per cent for normal offset). This gives a stronger gear and is the main reason for its adoption on commercial vehicles.

It is often said that a hypoid is halfway between a normal bevel and a worm drive. In the former case, a rolling action takes place, whereas in the latter the motion is all-sliding. By increasing the sliding motion in the hypoid gear, meshing noise is reduced, but the high temperature and pressure of the oil film is a strain on the lubricant. To deal with this, special EP oil is employed, which contains more active agents than those used with the normal spiral bevel. These oils contain expendable EP agents to resist scuffing and wear at high temperature, and a fatty acid to improve boundary lubrication at low temperature.

3.21.3 Worm and wheel

Today, this expensive form of drive is rarely used as a final drive on light vehicles, but it is still used on heavy vehicles. It is included in this chapter because this important type of gear has a number of other applications on motor vehicles.

Various arrangements (Figure 3.123) can be used to give a very quiet and long-lasting gear, but efficiency is not as good as with the bevel (94 per cent against 98 per cent).

The gear ratio of a worm and wheel is given by:

$$\text{Ratio} = \frac{\text{Number of teeth on wheel}}{\text{Number of starts on worm}}$$

You can see that this type of gear provides a large reduction in a small space. The worm may be mounted below (under-slung) or above (overhead) the wheel. An hourglass or Hindley worm embraces more teeth than the straight worm but adjustment is more critical.

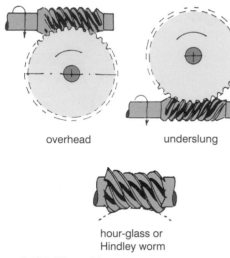

overhead   underslung

hour-glass or
Hindley worm

Figure 3.123 Worm drives

Friction caused by the sliding action of the worm is reduced by using a worm wheel of phosphor-bronze and a worm of case-hardened steel, but even with this material the unit gets rather hot. A large, well-cooled sump is used to reduce oxidation of the oil. This occurs at a high temperature and causes the oil to thicken. To improve the boundary lubrication, a vegetable-based oil is sometimes used as an alternative to straight gear oil.

3.21.4 Bevel-drive adjustment

Current types of bevel drive operate under severe conditions, but will give satisfactory service provided the gear is adjusted correctly. Every manufacturer gives detailed information of special tools, clearances, etc., and you should refer to this before attempting such an important overhaul.

The following general points should be a guide:

- Noise from the final drive is caused by bearing defects or incorrect meshing (the latter may be caused by bearing wear). Generally, noise or 'whine' on the drive occurs when the gear is too deep in mesh, and noise on the over-run is caused by insufficient depth of mesh.
- Whenever a final-drive noise develops, determine the cause as soon as possible. Misaligned gears will 'mate' to the new position wearing to each other.
- The mating of the gears may make it impossible to obtain a quiet operation even when the adjustment is corrected. If repair is delayed, you will probably require a new crown wheel and pinion, as well as a bearing.

Preloading of bearings

Adjustable taper roller bearings are commonly used in a final-drive assembly to support both the crown wheel and pinion.

If each bearing was set by adjustment to give a small clearance between the rollers and tracks, then end-float and misalignment of the gear would result. This would lead to gear noise and premature bearing failure, due to incorrect meshing and uneven loading respectively. Even when the clearance is eliminated, the elasticity of the bearing material will still give similar effects unless this is taken into account.

To overcome these problems, all adjustable bearings used for final drives are preloaded. This means that the bearings are forced together (using the adjustment facility provided) to the position occupied by the bearings when the unit is under full load.

In the case of pinion bearings, the extent of this pre-compression is indicated by the torque required to rotate the pinion in its housing; for example, a torque of $1.36\,\text{Nm}$ ($12\,\text{lbf in}^{-2}$) is required to rotate the pinion. The recommended preload normally states the conditions under which it should be measured, for example with the bearings dry and the oil seal removed.

Figure 3.124 shows two ways of checking the preload of a pinion.

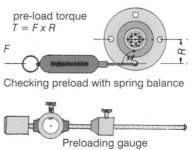

pre-load torque
$T = F \times R$

Checking preload with spring balance

Preloading gauge

Figure 3.124 Measurement of preload

Pinion adjustment

The method of adjustment of the pinion bearing preload depends on the type of spacer used to hold the bearings apart. Figure 3.125 shows the two main arrangements: a rigid spacer and a collapsible spacer.

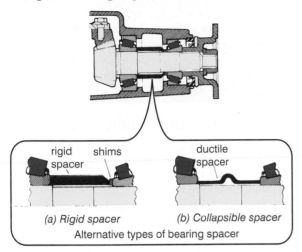

Figure 3.125 Pinion bearing adjustment

A bearing arrangement controlled by a rigid spacer has a series of shims to control the static load on the bearings (Figure 3.125a). On this type, the pinion nut has to be fully tightened before the preload is measured; if it is found to be incorrect, then shims have to be either added or removed.

This type of spacer simplifies the task of renewing the pinion oil seal because the bearing preload is not altered by seal replacement provided the pinion nut is fully tightened.

Time is saved on the preload operation when a collapsible spacer (Figure 3.215b) is used. In addition to holding the bearings in alignment, this **ductile** steel spacer collapses under pressure from the pinion nut, and so allows the preload to be set in one operation. With the pinion, bearings and seal in position, the nut is tightened only sufficiently to give the recommended preload. When the torque is correct, the nut is locked in position. A ductile material has very little elasticity, so if the bearing preload is too high, a new spacer is required.

Ductile: a property of a material meaning it can be drawn into a wire and is therefore pliable, not brittle. For instance, copper and steel are ductile, plastic is not.

Greater care must be taken with units having a collapsible spacer when a new pinion seal has to be refitted to cure an oil leak. Prior to unlocking the nut, the precise position of the nut relative to the pinion must be noted. Unless this action is taken, the crown wheel will have to be removed so that the pinion bearings can be preloaded.

The pinion position, relative to the crown wheel, must be set accurately in order to position the apex point of the pinion correctly. Noise, in the form of a 'whine', and possible breakage of the gear teeth is likely to occur if this is not done.

In the past, the initial position of the pinion was set by aligning it with the edge of the crown wheel teeth. Nowadays, a special 'dummy pinion' jig is used for this operation.

Crown wheel adjustment

After setting the pinion, the crown wheel is fitted to the assembly. When doing this, it is important to fit the correct bearing cap, because these are not interchangeable.

Backlash

Backlash is adjusted at this stage by moving the crown wheel towards or away from the pinion. Before taking the final measurement of backlash with a clock gauge, it is wise to check that the crown wheel **run-out** is within the recommended limits.

Run-out: the deviation from centre of a round object as it rotates, such as a wheel and tyre.

Meshing

Meshing of the gear is carried out by applying a smear of marking compound to the driving side of a few crown wheel teeth, and then turning the pinion in the DOR while applying a resistance to the crown wheel.

The marking obtained indicates the mesh of the gears with respect to pinion position and backlash. Figure 3.126 shows the change, in relation to the correct marking, when the pinion position is changed. It should be noted that the 'correct' marking shows only a limited contact between the teeth under light-load test conditions. When full load is applied to the gear, the contact area covers the complete tooth.

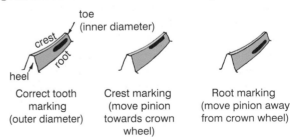

Figure 3.126 Crown wheel tooth marking

Crown wheel preload

Housing rigidity and accurate gear alignment are essential with a hypoid gear if the low noise level feature of this type is to be achieved. This means that slackness in the crown wheel bearings must be eliminated by preloading.

Various methods are used to measure the preload; the most common is to measure the spread (outward deflection) of the bearing caps when the adjusters are screwed together. For example, a preload cap-spread of 0.1 mm (0.004 in) means that after preloading the side bearings the distance between the bearing caps has increased by 0.1 mm.

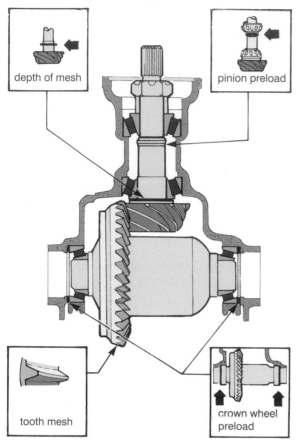

Figure 3.127 Final-drive adjustments

When shims are used to control the backlash, the preload is achieved by increasing the shim thickness on each side of the crown wheel; the shims are added after the backlash has been set. Axles having this construction need a special tool to 'spread the caps' before the crown wheel assembly is removed or refitted.

A visual summary of the main adjustments is shown in Figure 3.127.

3.22 The differential

3.22.1 Purpose of the differential

If both rear wheels were connected to a common driving shaft, two effects would soon show up:

- Rapid rear tyre wear
- Difficulty in steering from the straight-ahead position

Figure 3.128 shows that the outer wheel must travel a greater distance when the vehicle is cornering: therefore, if the wheels are interconnected, the tyres will have to 'scrub' over the road surface and tend to keep the vehicle moving straight ahead. These effects can be minimised by driving one wheel and allowing the other to run free, but the unbalanced driving thrust and unequal cornering speeds make the arrangement unpopular. The solution to the problem came in 1827 when Péqueur of France invented the differential. This mechanism allows the wheels to rotate at different speeds, but still maintains a drive to both wheels.

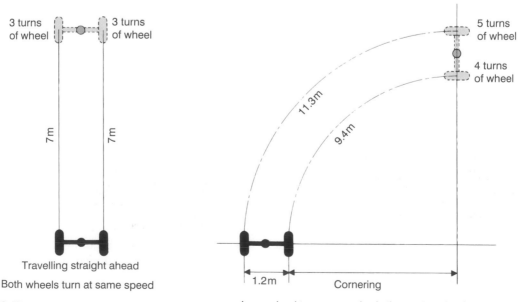

Figure 3.128 The need for a differential

3.22.2 Principle

Consider an axle like the one shown in Figure 3.129a. The two discs shown are linked by shafts to the wheels and interconnected with a lever. When a driving force is applied to the centre of the lever, each disc will receive an equal share of the inputted driving force (i.e. half the driving force).

The movement of the discs will depend on the resistances opposing the directional motion of the shafts (i.e. the resistances at each wheel). If the resistance is the same at each wheel, the driving force will be equal across the two wheels and the vehicle will travel in a straight-ahead direction.

If large amounts of resistance act on disc B, the lever will tilt and push disc A forward. This condition is shown in Figure 3.129b.

When a force (F) is applied to C at the centre of the lever, each disc will receive an equal share (i.e. half the force applied). The movement of the discs will depend on the resistances (R) opposing the motion of the shafts. If a larger resistance acts on disc B, the lever will tilt and push disc A forward a greater amount.

Increase in distance moved by A = Decrease in distance moved by B

Increase in speed of A = Decrease in speed moved by B

Therefore: $A + B = 2C$

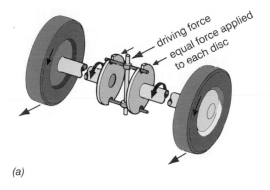

(a)

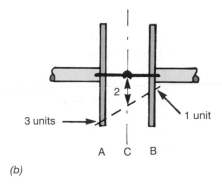

(b)

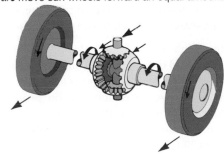

When vehicle is moving in a straight path, planet gears move sun wheels forward an equal amount

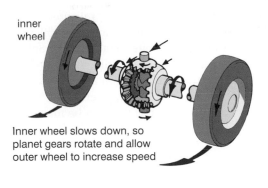

inner wheel

Inner wheel slows down, so planet gears rotate and allow outer wheel to increase speed

(c)

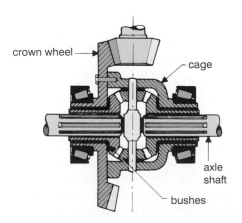

crown wheel

cage

axle shaft

bushes

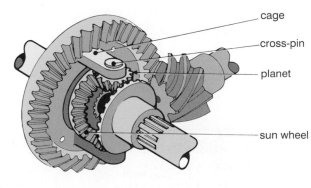

cage

cross-pin

planet

sun wheel

(d)

Figure 3.129 The action of a differential

In Figure 3.129c, the disc system is replaced by bevel gears, which are called sun wheels (discs) and planets (levers). The drive is applied to the cross pin and will push the planet gears forward to exert an equal torque on each sun wheel irrespective of the speed. When the vehicle turns a corner, the inner wheel will slow down and cause the planets to rotate on their own axis to speed up the outer wheel. Straight-ahead motion of the vehicle will allow the whole unit to rotate at the same speed.

The complete differential is shown in Figure 3.129d. This arrangement shows a crown wheel bolted on to a differential cage. This cage supports the sun wheels on plain bearings and transmits the drive to the cross pin.

Light cars only need two planet gears, but four gears are necessary on heavier vehicles to reduce tooth pressures. Lubrication is provided by the final-drive oil, which can splash through holes in the differential cage.

Differential lock

If one driving wheel of a two-wheel drive vehicle loses adhesion, the propelling force is considerably reduced and this results in the vehicle being immobilised. On these occasions the differential action is undesirable. Therefore, on vehicles designed to operate over poor surfaces, a differential locking arrangement is often fitted.

Differential action can be prevented by locking together any two individual units of a differential and Figure 3.130 shows one arrangement. Splined to a differential sun wheel is a sliding dog clutch member, which engages with dog teeth formed on the cage of the differential. The clutch is engaged by means of a fork and movement of this can be made by a lever fitted on the outside of the axle.

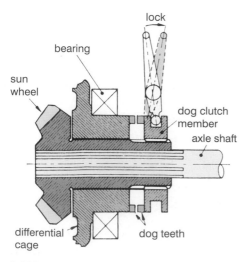

Figure 3.130 A differential lock assembly

In the engaged position, the sun wheel, and consequently the rear wheel connected to this sun gear, is made to turn at the same speed as the cage. Locking one sun gear to the cage in this way ensures that the other sun gear also turns at the same speed.

Limited-slip differential

Although a high mechanical efficiency is desirable for the majority of mechanical components, it is a disadvantage in the case of a differential. In addition to the reduced traction over slippery surfaces, a 'low friction' differential fitted to a high-powered vehicle limits acceleration and causes excessive tyre wear. Observation of such a vehicle during acceleration shows that torque reaction of the engine tends to lift the left-hand driving wheel off the ground. When this is accompanied by an uneven road surface, the presence of excessive wheel spin is apparent. In order to restrict these drawbacks, the differential action is opposed by artificially increasing the friction between the sun wheel and the differential cage. Arrangements having this feature are called limited-slip differentials.

There are three basic mechanical types of differential that give this, or a similar action; these are:

- mechanical limited-slip differential
- visco-differential
- torsen limited-slip differential.

Mechanical limited-slip differential

Figure 3.131 shows the layout of one type of differential, which is bolted to the crown wheel.

A multi-disc clutch pack fitted behind each sun wheel has the inner and outer plates splined to the sun and cage respectively. Since bevel gears are used, an axial thrust will be developed that will be proportional to the torque applied by the crown wheel to the differential. Under low torque conditions, the differential will function in the normal way, but if the torque is increased, the clutch pack will be loaded and this will resist rotation of the sun gear at a different speed from that of the cage (Figure 3.132).

To increase the load on the clutch pack further, many designs incorporate:

- a Belleville disc-spring washer between the cage and the clutch discs of each pack to provide an initial load on the discs
- angled cam faces between the cage and the cross pins. Driving thrust exerted by the cage on the pin causes the pin to force the planets against the side gear ring. When four planets are used two separate pins, flexibly linked at the centre and having opposite cam faces, cause two planets to act on one clutch pack and the other two to exert force in the opposite direction.

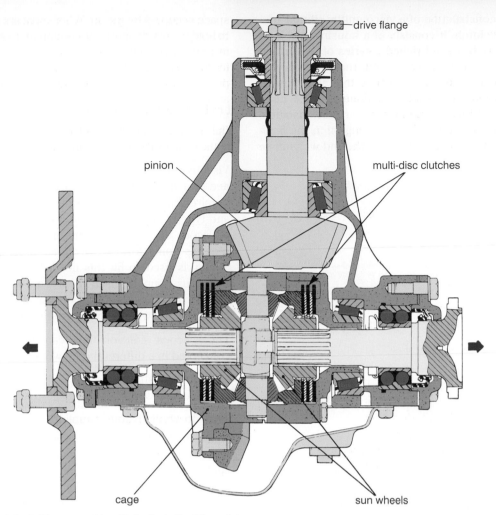

Figure 3.131 A final-drive assembly with limited-slip differential

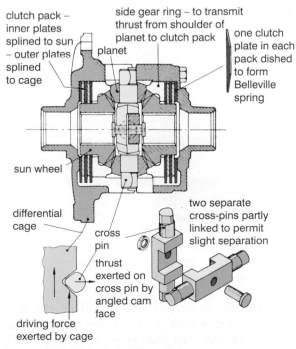

Figure 3.132 Limited-slip differential

The action of this type of differential should be remembered by the technician. With only one driving wheel lifted off the ground, a drive transmitted to this wheel from the engine can cause the vehicle to be driven forward.

Visco-differential

The visco-type differential has been used more and more by manufacturers over the years. It combines a standard differential with a viscous coupling. This transmission application uses the coupling as a viscous control device to regulate the speed difference between the two driving wheels.

Whereas the locking action on a mechanical limited-slip differential depends on input torque, the viscous type depends on the speed difference of the driving wheels. Very little resistance is offered when the speed difference is small, but the resistance progressively builds up as the difference increases. Compared with the mechanical limited-slip differential, it is claimed that this type gives lower tyre wear, easier steering and lower stresses in driveline components.

The basic construction of a visco unit is similar to a multi-plate clutch. It consists of a housing and hub, between which is sandwiched a series of perforated metal plates (Figure 3.133). Alternate plates are attached to the hub and housing; this also acts as a container for the viscous silicone fluid. A heat-resistant seal, made of fluorinated rubber, isolates the silicone fluid from the lubricating oil in the final-drive assembly and ensures that the fluid will suffice for the life of the coupling.

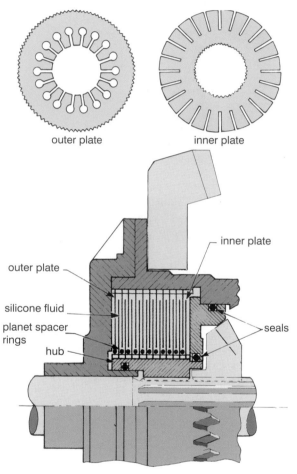

Figure 3.133 A visco-differential unit

The operating principle of the coupling is based on the fact that the shear force (drive) given by the fluid on a plate depends on the shear rate (speed difference). By using a high-viscosity fluid, the coupling can be designed to output a comparatively high torque, which progressively builds up as the shear rate is increased.

The relationship between torque and shear rate is affected by a number of factors such as fluid viscosity, the gap between plates and plate perforation. By varying these design factors, the coupling can be 'tuned' to suit the application.

Prolonged slipping of the coupling generates heat and this causes the fluid to expand and take up some of the space occupied by the air. Where spacers are not used to hold the plates apart, the combination of the increase in air pressure due to fluid expansion and the reduction in fluid pressure in the gaps causes the plates to be pushed together. This gives metal-to-metal contact and at this point (hump) the coupling temporarily departs from its viscous mode operation. As it passes through this phase, the torque output rises considerably; in some designs it can be six times as great.

Viscous couplings can be used to control front, centre and rear differentials. Each application has different requirements in view of its position, speed of operation and type of vehicle to which it is fitted. For example, a viscous control unit at the rear of a powerful car requires some form of overload protection, so the 'hump' is used to fill this need. On the other hand, a viscous coupling used for a front-wheel drive car should have no 'hump', because a unit with this characteristic would adversely affect the steering.

The viscous control unit can be installed and connected in a differential in two ways:

- Shaft-to-shaft
- Shaft-to-cage

Shaft-to-shaft viscous coupling

Figure 3.134 shows a bevel-type differential having a viscous control unit connected between the two axle shafts, the hub holding the inner plates joined to one shaft and the housing with its outer plates connected to the other shaft. Space is made available for the unit at the centre of the crown wheel by moving the differential to one side.

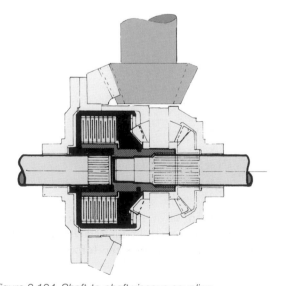

Figure 3.134 Shaft-to-shaft viscous coupling

When the car is moving with no wheel slip in a straight line, the control unit is not in operation. But at times when the shaft speed is different, such as when one driving wheel loses adhesion or when wheel spin occurs during acceleration, the resistance offered by the unit ensures that the driving torque to both wheels is maintained.

Shaft-to-cage viscous coupling

The cheaper arrangement shown in Figure 3.135 has the housing of the viscous control unit integral with the differential cage and the hub connected to one axle shaft.

The speed difference between the cage and axle shaft is half the difference of the road wheels, so compared with the shaft-to-shaft type, the shaft-to-cage unit must have a torque characteristic about three times greater to achieve the same locking effect.

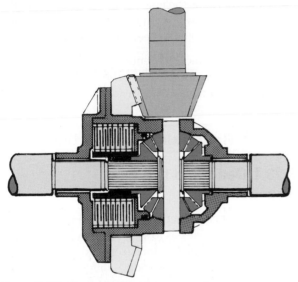

Figure 3.135 Shaft-to-cage viscous coupling

The viscous coupling is an extremely effective and compact device in limiting the slip between axles to provide improved traction. The viscous coupling is also used in many four-wheel drive vehicles between the front and rear drivelines. The viscous coupling allows a difference in front- and rear-wheel drive speeds, and also creates a type of differential lock between the front and rear wheels if the wheel speeds become high due to loss of traction. More information on four-wheel drive is provided in section 3.24 on page 374.

3.22.3 Torsen limited-slip differential

The word 'torsen' is derived from **tor**que **sen**sing, which describes how this limited-slip differential operates. Figure 3.136 shows the torsen limited-slip differential unit.

The assembly comprises a final-drive gear (bolted to the differential casing), two helical gears splined to the drive shafts and three pairs of element gear assemblies arranged at 120° within the differential casing. Each of the element gear assemblies comprises

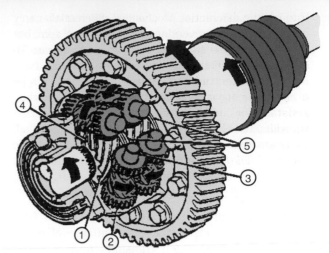

1 helical side gear
2 element gear assembly – worm and spur gear
3 journal pin
4 thrust washer and spacer washer
5 two thrust washers and needle roller bearing

Figure 3.136 Torsen limited-slip differential

a worm gear and two spur gears running on a journal pin. The worm gears are in constant mesh with the helical gears, and the spur gears mesh with those of the adjoining element gear assembly. Axial thrust of the helical gears is controlled by a combination of thrust washers and needle roller bearings located at each end of (and between) the two gears.

Operation

When a wheel connected to the torsen differential loses traction, a difference in torque across the axle causes the gears in the torsen differential to bind together. This binding together creates friction, which leads to a limiting of the speed difference between the two wheels, thus limiting slippage. The gear design in the differential assembly determines the **torque bias ratio**. For example, if a manufacturer is designing a vehicle, they may wish to alter the way the differential operates between models to alter the handling characteristics. One particular torsen differential may be designed with a 5:1 bias ratio. This means that it is capable of applying up to five times more torque to the wheel that has good traction.

Torque bias ratio: ratio of torque between wheels with good traction and poor traction. The ratio represents how much more torque can be sent to the wheels with the highest traction than is sent to the wheels that are spinning or have lost traction.

3.22.4 Electronic differential control

The need to improve vehicle dynamics through improved road holding, traction and stability has led manufacturers to re-think how traction can be improved through the differential. Mechanical differentials carry out a good job in preventing unwanted wheel spin, but they can react too slowly or harshly in some cases. To improve this requirement, some manufacturers have moved to an electronic controlled differential. This type of arrangement has been used by motor sport for a while and it is now finding its way on to today's production vehicles. The 'E' differential, as it sometimes called, is designed to give improved traction and dynamic stability. The electronically controlled differential continuously adapts to both the driver's demands and the amount of grip available at each individual wheel.

Operated by an internal electric motor and ball-and-ramp mechanism, the differential contains a multi-plate clutch, which transmits torque to the wheel with most grip and, therefore, maximises the car's traction. The multi-plate clutch assembly is designed to prevent excessive differential slip, but differs fundamentally from a conventional traction control system, which uses the brakes to counteract differential slip after it has occurred.

Active differential control for precise driving

Active differential control is fully automatic and can vary its locking torque and, therefore, the proportion of torque sent to each driven wheel depending on surface conditions and power applied. Its subtle control strategies optimise traction at each wheel, improving acceleration on low-grip surfaces but also potentially improving stability when required.

Active differential control is designed to work with other systems, such as traction control and the ABS function. The active differential control (ADC) system can significantly improve overall vehicle performance and provide more precise driving feel.

Design features

Incorporated within the differential assembly are two additional planet gears to enhance the higher driving torque loads transmitted through the differential. Also, using a multi-plate clutch and actuator assembly installed on the left-hand sun gear actively controls the torque flow through the differential. The clutch biases the torque from the differential to the wheel with the higher grip and prevents the wheel with the lower grip from spinning. A temperature sensor installed in the cover provides a differential oil temperature signal to the control module, to prevent excessive use damaging the multi-plate clutch. The control module monitors and receives input information from a number of other systems such as wheel speed, steering angle, automatic transmission speed, temperature information and axle ration. Using an electric motor and reduction gearbox adjusts frictional loading of the multi-plate

clutch. For accurate control of the differential, the module adapts its strategy to provide a balance for regular differential preloading function and a slip control to deliver a torque output of up to 2000 Nm.

If a fault occurs with the electronic differential, the control module records an error code and displays a warning in the driver's display. These messages can include the following:

- 'Differential has reached the overheat threshold. System deactivated until temperature returns within limits.'
- 'Fault has occurred with electronic differential. System deactivated until fault rectified.'

Any fault will cause the loss of the limited-slip facility, but the system will maintain normal differential action until the fault has been rectified.

With the electronic differential now being used on modern vehicles, drivers have the added support of all-round traction and stability for optimum grip.

3.23 Rear axle construction

3.23.1 Dead and live axle arrangements

Axles of solid construction are referred to as dead or live axles. A live axle has to support the vehicle weight, and also incorporate the final drive and drive shafts to move the vehicle and provide a differential allowing the vehicle to turn around corners in the road. The dead axle merely has to carry the weight of the vehicle and support the non-driven wheels. Live axles are now generally used with commercial vehicles where the need to carry heavy loads favours their rugged construction. Some four-wheel drive vehicles also use the live axle arrangements for strength and durability. Vehicles today rarely use dead axles, due to their inability to provide good control of the road wheels.

3.23.2 Axle casing construction

The type of axle casing dictates the method that must be used to remove the final-drive assembly. Today, the casing used will be either a banjo or carrier-type. In the past, a type known as a split (trumpet) casing was occasionally used. These three types are shown in Figure 3.137.

Banjo axle

The tubular axle section is built up of steel pressings welded together and suitably strengthened to resist the bending load. The centre of the casing, combined with the axle tube on one side, resembles a banjo – hence its name.

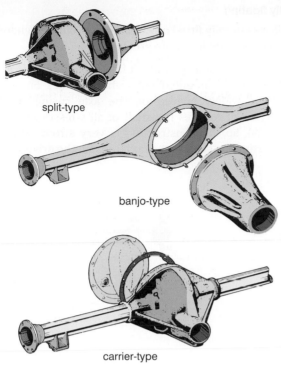

split-type

banjo-type

carrier-type

Figure 3.137 Types of rear axle casing

The final-drive assembly, which is mounted in a detachable malleable iron housing, is secured to the axle casing by a ring of bolts. When this assembly is in position, the axle shafts are slid in from the road wheel end of the casing.

On some banjo axles a domed plate is bolted to the rear face of the casing. Removal of this plate allows the final-drive gears to be inspected and, in cases where the axle shaft is secured to the differential, enables the axle shaft to be unlocked from the sun gear (side gear).

A lubricant-level plug, set at a height of about one-third up the crown wheel, is screwed into the domed cover or the final-drive housing. The level is normally just below the axle tubes, so lubrication of the hub bearings is by splash caused by rotation of the crown wheel.

Note: overfilling of the lubricant-level plug should be avoided because this swamps the oil seals and causes oil to enter the brakes.

When in operation, the final drive gets hot, so some form of air vent is provided to release the pressure in the axle casing; this prevents oil being forced past the seals.

Carrier axle

This type of axle casing is more rigid in its construction than the banjo type and is often used to support a hypoid gear. The final-drive assembly is mounted directly in a rigid malleable cast iron carrier into which the axle tubes are pressed and welded.

Extra rigidity is obtained by using reinforcing ribs that extend from the pinion nose to the main carrier casting. Access to the final-drive gear is by means of a domed plate at the rear of the casing. Specialist tooling is required to carry out maintenance procedures on this type of axle.

3.23.3 Axle shafts

The axle shaft transmits the drive from the differential sun wheel to the rear hub. The various types may be compared by considering the stresses the shaft has to resist. Figure 3.138 shows a line sketch of a simple shaft, which is subjected to:

- torsional stress due to driving and braking torque (Figure 3.138a)
- shear stress due to the weight of the vehicle (Figure 3.138b)
- bending stress due to the weight of the vehicle (Figure 3.138c)
- tensile and compressive stress due to cornering forces.

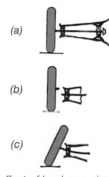

(a)

(b)

(c)

Figure 3.138 The effect of load on a simple axle shaft

Types

Axle shafts are divided into three main groups, depending on the stresses to which the shaft is subjected:

- Semi-floating
- Fully floating
- Three-quarter floating

Semi-floating

Figure 3.139a shows a typical mounting of an axle shaft suitable for light cars. A single bearing at the hub end is fitted between the shaft and the casing, so the shaft will have to resist all the stresses previously mentioned. To reduce the risk of fracture at the hub end (which would allow the wheel to fall off), the shaft diameter is increased. Any increase must be gradual, since a sudden change in cross-sectional area would produce a stress-raiser and increase the risk of failure due to fatigue. (Fatigue may be defined as breakage due to continual alteration of the stress in the material.)

Although the final-drive oil level is considerably lower than the axle shaft, the large amount of 'splash' would cause the lubricant to work along the shaft and enter the brake drum. Sealing arrangements normally consist of an oil retainer fitted at the hub end (the lip of the seal is positioned towards the final drive).

Fully floating

This is generally fitted on commercial vehicles where torque and axle loads are greater.

The construction (Figure 3.139c) consists of an independently mounted hub, which rotates on two bearings widely spaced on the axle casing. This arrangement relieves the shaft of all stresses except torsional, so the construction is very strong. Studs connecting the shaft to the hub transmit the drive, and

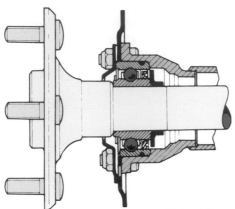

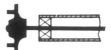

(a) Semi-floating (commonly used on cars)

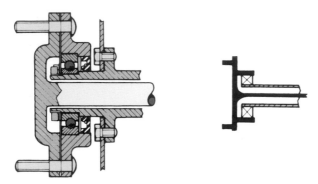

(b) Three-quarter floating (rarely used today)

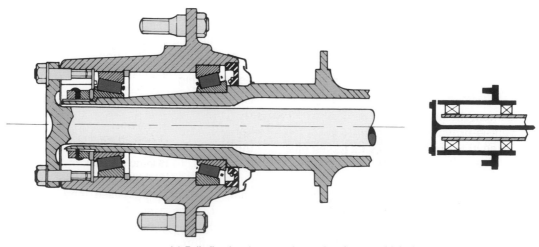

(c) Fully floating (commonly used on heavy vehicles)

Figure 3.139 Rear hub construction

when the nuts on these studs are removed the shaft may be withdrawn without jacking up the vehicle.

Three-quarter floating

Having defined the semi and the fully floating shaft, any option between the two may be regarded as a three-quarter floating shaft. Figure 3.139b shows a construction that has a single bearing mounted between the hub and the casing. The main shear stress on the shaft is relieved, but all other stresses still have to be resisted.

Axle shaft material

A tough, hard material must be used to withstand the various stresses, resist spline wear and provide good resistance to fatigue. A medium, carbon-alloy steel

containing such elements as nickel, chromium and molybdenum is the usual choice. There is a balance between durability and lightness of components on the modern motor vehicle; in this case, the use of strong material is the only option.

3.23.4 Font live axles

Front live axles are generally used on four-wheel drive vehicles, such as the Land Rover Defender. The use of live axles provides improved strength and durability, which is important in an off-road vehicle subjected to harsh terrain. The live front axle construction is very similar to the live rear axle, with a differential final-drive unit linked via drive shafts to the road wheels.

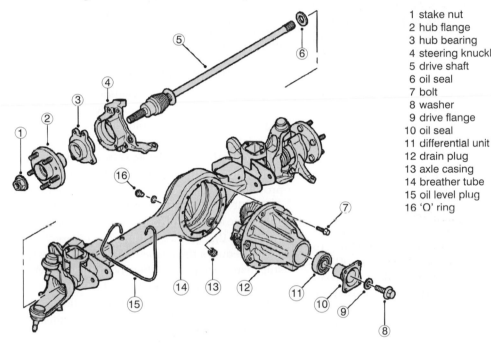

1 stake nut
2 hub flange
3 hub bearing
4 steering knuckle
5 drive shaft
6 oil seal
7 bolt
8 washer
9 drive flange
10 oil seal
11 differential unit
12 drain plug
13 axle casing
14 breather tube
15 oil level plug
16 'O' ring

Figure 3.140 Front live axle component layout

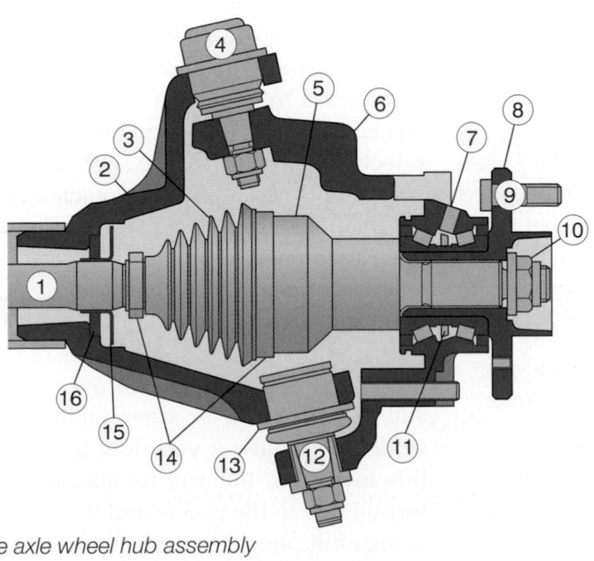

1 drive shaft
2 axle casing
3 gaiter
4 upper ball joint
5 CV joint
6 steering knuckle
7 hub bearing
8 hub flange
9 wheel stud
10 stake nut
11 ABS sensor ring
12 tension collet
13 lower ball joint
14 securing bands
15 shield
16 oil seal

Figure 3.141 Live axle wheel hub assembly

One of the major differences in the front live axle is the addition of swivel wheel hubs to allow the steered wheels to turn with the input from the driver. The swivel wheel hubs are a large arrangement pivoted at the top and bottom with ball joints to allow the wheels to turn. The wheel hubs house the CV joints required to pass torque from the drive shafts to the driven wheels through various steered angles. Figure 3.140 shows a live front axle arrangement and Figure 3.141 shows the wheel hub assembly housing the CV joint.

3.24 Four-wheel drive systems

3.24.1 Types of four-wheel drive

A four-wheel drive vehicle, sometimes called a 4WD or 4×4 (four by four), transmits a drive to all of its four wheels instead of two wheels, as is common with the majority of light vehicles with front- or rear-wheel drive only.

There are two main traction problems with a two-wheel drive (4×2) vehicle; these are:

1 loss of traction during cross-country operation
2 loss of adhesion during acceleration.

The intended use of the vehicle governs the type of four-wheel drive system that is offered by the manufacturer.

Vehicles in the Land Rover and Range Rover category pride themselves in offering the ability to provide excellent on-road driving dynamics without compromising the benefits of excellent off-road capabilities. Many four-wheel drive vehicles use two-wheel drive on 'hard' surfaces and restrict the use of four-wheel drive to cross-country work, where the vehicle is likely to encounter low-traction surfaces that could lead to a complete loss of traction from the two driving wheels. These types of vehicles are classed as part-time four-wheel drive. The drive to the other axle can be instigated in two ways:

- Manual operation by the driver
- Electronic control

The main benefit of operating in two-wheel drive on normal road conditions is that the vehicle will be more economical due to less drag of the transmission system driving the additional axle.

Most Land Rover vehicles are classed as full-time or permanent four-wheel drive, as all four wheels are constantly driven to provide added traction across all road conditions.

Many high-performance cars that are generally built for road operation also use four-wheel drive at all times; this gives improved handling and extra safety.

Figure 3.142 Land Rover vehicle operating off-road

In this case, the full weight of the car is spread over all of the driving wheels. This full utilisation of the vehicle weight considerably increases the tractive effort that can be applied to the car; as a result, a high rate of acceleration can be achieved.

Cross-country operation

The limitation of a conventional two-wheel drive vehicle is soon appreciated when it encounters the rough terrain and muddy conditions normally associated with cross-country operations. In these situations, the rear wheels soon lose their adhesion. Consequently, the traction available is insufficient to provide a drive. The normal differential adds to these difficulties because if the adhesion of one driving wheel is lost, the drive to the other wheel is generally too low to propel the vehicle. Although a differential locking device reduces the chance of this occurring, there are still many occasions when both driving wheels are rendered ineffective. The four-wheel drive is provided to overcome this situation – when either front or rear axles lose traction the other axle maintains a drive to move the vehicle out of the difficulty.

Figure 3.143 shows a typical, simple layout of a four-wheel drive vehicle's transfer box. Mounted behind the main gearbox, this transfer gearbox unit divides the drive between the axles and normally incorporates extra gears to provide a very low ratio. The transfer box is generally controlled by two gear levers; one for selecting four-wheel drive and the other to give 'high' or 'low' gear. Many new vehicles now incorporate an electrical system to switch between high and low ratios using a motor. The transfer box contains a series of gears to deliver the torque from front to rear, and also a set of epicyclic gears to alter the ratio between high and low. Low range is used when the vehicle has to navigate over very rough terrain and manoeuvre over steep inclines and drops. The vehicle will have a very low top speed when using this low ratio, but will be able to climb very steep terrain due to the power and the torque of the engine being multiplied through the transfer box ratio.

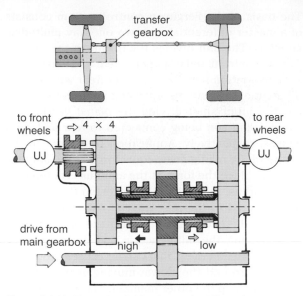

Figure 3.143 *Four-wheel drive layout for off-road use*

Drive to the front wheels is transmitted via the final drive, differential and drive shafts. Steering movement of the front wheels is accommodated by fitting extra universal joints at the wheel end of the drive shafts and, in order to overcome vibration, the CV-type of joint is generally used.

The four-wheel arrangement shown in Figure 3.143 should not be operated on a hard-surfaced road because of the risk of transmission 'wind-up'. When a vehicle using this arrangement turns a corner, the mean speed of the front wheels is higher than that of the rear wheels, so the speed difference causes the propeller shafts to deflect, winding up the transmission (a similar effect to that of winding up an elastic band). Drivers disregarding this instruction often cause serious injury to anyone changing a wheel due to the torsional stress being built up in the drive shafts.

To overcome the wind-up problem and make the vehicle suitable for four-wheel operation on hard surfaces, a third differential between the driving axles is needed. This differential is now more commonly fitted to four-wheel drive vehicles as it provides the driver with full-time four-wheel drive. However, one issue with this centre differential may occur when the vehicle is carrying out cross-country work. If any of the road wheels lose traction, the power and torque will be lost through this one wheel unless a differential lock is used or the slipping wheel is restricted through a limited-slip differential or traction control. Figure 3.144 shows a four-wheel drive system with a centre differential. The centre differential is usually located within the transfer gearbox and often incorporates a viscous or torsen limited-slip arrangement.

Hard surface operation

Tractive and braking efforts are limited by the adhesive force on the road wheels; this force is calculated from:

Adhesive force = Coefficient of friction × Load on wheel

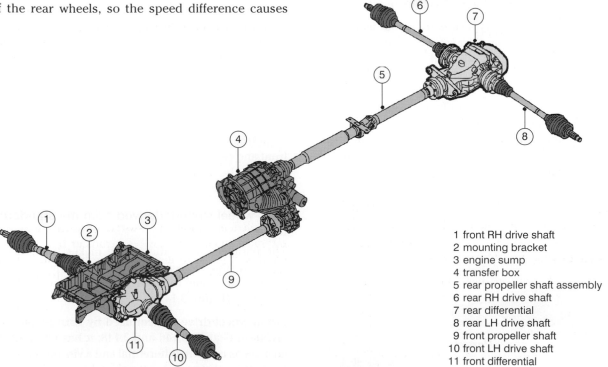

1 front RH drive shaft
2 mounting bracket
3 engine sump
4 transfer box
5 rear propeller shaft assembly
6 rear RH drive shaft
7 rear differential
8 rear LH drive shaft
9 front propeller shaft
10 front LH drive shaft
11 front differential

Figure 3.144 *Four-wheel drive system with centre differential fitted within the transfer gearbox*

By using this expression, it can be seen that the total weight of the vehicle must be fully utilised if the maximum adhesive force is to be obtained.

When only two driving wheels are provided, the loss of 'weight' on the non-driving wheels proportionally reduces the adhesive force; as a result, the maximum tractive effort that can be safely applied to the vehicle is limited.

Beyond the point where the tractive effort equals the adhesive force, the driving wheel spins; this spinning not only limits the rate of acceleration, but can also lead to loss of control of the vehicle with dangerous results. This effect also relates to braking, as skidding occurs beyond the point where the braking force equals the adhesive force.

By spreading the driving and braking forces over all of the wheels, greater safety is achieved. Backing-up this force distribution with a device for sensing the approach of wheel spin or slip, and then adjusting the effort accordingly, leads to even greater safety.

Cars of this type are not designed for serious off-road use, but they do give the all-weather driver an added sense of security for tackling icy or wet conditions.

3.24.2 Ferguson Formula

One of the first people to appreciate the importance of 'all-wheel drive' was Harry Ferguson, the inventor of the lightweight tractor. He took out a patent on the 'Ferguson Formula' (FF) in 1954, and this was used on a Jensen sports car in the early 1960s.

Figure 3.145 shows a typical early layout as applied to a Jensen sports car. A transfer box, containing the sensing mechanism, is adjacent to a centre (third) differential and propeller shafts transmit the drive to front and rear axles. A **Maxaret** unit prevents the possibility of the rear wheels locking during braking. Driven by the transmission, it senses the mean deceleration of front and rear road wheels and just before the wheel locks the hydraulic pressure to the brake is relieved.

Maxaret: one of the first anti-lock braking systems to be used on road vehicles introduced by Dunlop.

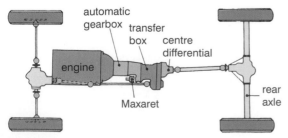

Figure 3.145 Ferguson Formula transmission layout

The basis of the Ferguson control system consists of a master differential and two one-way multi-disc clutches. The unit divides the torque in the ratio of 37 per cent front and 63 per cent rear and allows for a speed variation between front and rear wheels. The differential is a simple epicyclic gear train, which has the input shaft driving the planet carrier, the annulus and sun being connected to rear and front wheels, respectively. Application of a force to the centre of the planet gives equal force at the annulus and sun. Since the force at the annulus is acting at a larger radius, the torque is greater, so this member is connected to the rear wheels. As with a normal differential, speed variation can take place. In this arrangement, the difference in speed between the output shaft and the planet carrier causes the planet to rotate around the slower-moving gear, a motion that speeds up the other member. The extent of this speed variation is limited by the control unit and, in this particular design, the front wheels are only permitted to over-run the rear ones by 16.5 per cent, while the rear wheels can only over-run to the extent of 5.5 per cent. Once this limit is reached, a multi-disc clutch locks the planet carrier (input shaft) to the sun wheel (front output shaft) (i.e. the centre differential is put out of action). This action can occur during acceleration or when the vehicle is braking.

3.24.3 Four-wheel drive using viscous coupling

Unless some form of control is used to limit the action of a centre differential, the loss of adhesion at any one wheel will cause the vehicle to become immobile. On the other hand, if a centre differential is not fitted, then driveline components will be stressed because of transmission wind-up. A compromise is achieved by using a viscous coupling. This can be arranged in one of two ways: it can be used either as a control unit to limit the speed difference between front and rear wheels, or as a viscous transmission to connect the front drive system to the rear when the conditions demand it.

Four-wheel system derived from the standard drive

The parallel axis of the engine makes it necessary to use a transfer gearbox; on some vehicles this is positioned behind the main gearbox (Figure 3.146) or alongside (Figure 3.147).

A four-wheel drive system used by Ford utilises the layout in Figures 3.146 and 3.148; it has an epicyclic gear set as a centre differential and a viscous coupling to control the speed difference between the front and rear wheels. The input shaft of the differential

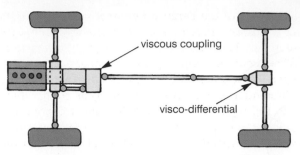

Figure 3.146 Four-wheel drive layout – a longitudinal engine when viewed from the underside

is connected to the planet carrier and the front and rear-wheel output shafts are linked to the sun wheel and annulus respectively. This gives a torque split between the front and rear axles of 34:66 – a typical proportion for this type of car.

At the front, a standard differential is fitted on the right-hand side of the engine and a drive shaft, fitted with CV joints, transmits the power to the right-hand front wheel. The drive train to the left-hand front wheel necessitates an intermediate shaft, which, owing to the location of the engine, has to pass through the engine sump before connecting with the left-hand drive shaft. The rear axle is driven in the normal manner; this includes a two-piece propeller shaft and a visco-differential.

Compared with a two rear-wheel drive vehicle, the front axle steering geometry must be modified to take into account the different driving conditions.

On this car the power take-off to the offset output shaft, which connects with the front axle shaft, is by means of a silent chain. The viscous coupling is a shaft-to-shaft design. Connected 'between the axles' in

this manner, the coupling senses the speed differences between the axles and gives a torque difference twice the value of the torque transmitted by the coupling.

Control of drive by the coupling to the front and rear wheels varies with the operating conditions. When the mean speed of front and rear wheels is nearly equal, the coupling is ineffective. However, as the speed difference increases, the coupling resistance and associated locking rise progressively.

Complete loss of adhesion at any wheel causes a large slip in the coupling; as a result, the coupling exerts a high-locking torque on the gears so as to maintain a drive to the wheels that are attempting to spin. Extended use of the coupling under maximum slip conditions would soon cause it to overheat. Therefore, to give it protection the coupling is designed to go into the 'hump mode'.

Four-wheel drive systems derived from the front-wheel drive

The basic front-wheel drive arrangement is comparatively easy to adapt to a four-wheel drive system because the complicated parts of the assembly, namely the front drive layout and steering geometry, is already in place.

Most front-wheel drive cars use a transaxle, so the drive is taken from this unit through a centre differential to the rear wheels (Figure 3.147).

The torque distribution proportion varies with the make of car. It depends on the weight distribution, in particular the location of the engine and the characteristics that are desired. The front/rear proportion varies from about 56:44 to 35:65.

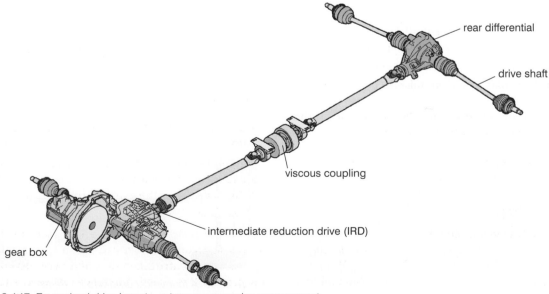

Figure 3.147 Four-wheel drive layout – a transverse engine arrangement

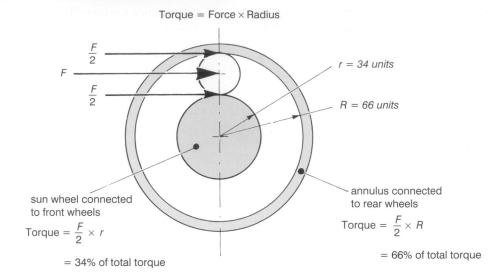

Torque = Force × Radius

$\frac{F}{2}$

F

$\frac{F}{2}$

$r = 34$ units

$R = 66$ units

sun wheel connected
to front wheels

annulus connected
to rear wheels

Torque = $\frac{F}{2} \times r$

= 34% of total torque

Torque = $\frac{F}{2} \times R$

= 66% of total torque

Epicyclic differential to divide front/rear torque in the proportion 34/66

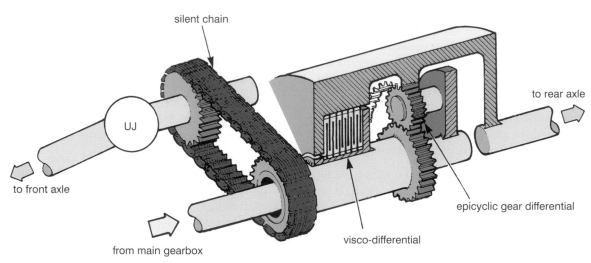

silent chain

UJ

to rear axle

to front axle

from main gearbox

visco-differential

epicyclic gear differential

Figure 3.148 Four-wheel drive transfer box (Ford)

Most centre differentials use an epicyclic gear set. This is controlled by a viscous coupling mounted in one of two ways:

■ Shaft-to-shaft between take-offs to front and rear axles
■ Between input drive and take-off to either the front axle or rear axle

Variable four-wheel drive

This system achieves the benefits of four-wheel drive, but without the drawbacks of a permanently connected arrangement.

The viscous transmission layout shown in Figure 3.147 uses a propeller shaft and viscous coupling to interconnect the two axles. A centre differential is unnecessary, but a free wheel is fitted in the rear axle final-drive gear.

During normal operation, when the axle speeds are nearly equal, the coupling ensures that the rear wheels are only driven to a very limited extent (i.e. the vehicle behaves like a normal front-wheel drive system). However, when the front wheels lose their

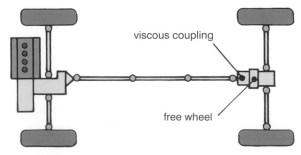

viscous coupling

free wheel

Figure 3.149 A four-wheel drive viscous transmission with free wheel

adhesion, the difference in speed causes the coupling to make use of the rear wheels for propulsion.

The free wheel ensures that no drive is transmitted from the rear axle to the engine during overrun, so this feature makes the arrangement suitable for use with ABS. A free-wheel-locking device, operated by an electro-pneumatic system when reverse gear is selected, makes four-wheel drive available for reversing.

Manufacturers have adapted this system using a viscous coupling unit as shown in Figure 3.150. This system is fitted within the propeller shaft, which connects the transaxle through the intermediate reduction drive (IRD) to the rear final-drive unit. The system can be used with manual or automatic vehicles with minimal alterations.

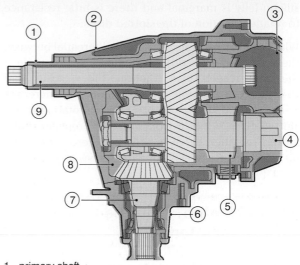

1 primary shaft
2 main casing
3 differential unit
4 RH housing
5 laygear
6 pinion housing
7 rear output pinion
8 hypoid gear set
9 intermediate shaft

Figure 3.151 Intermediate reduction drive

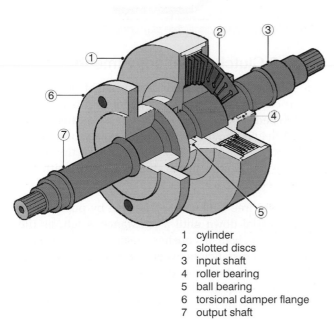

1 cylinder
2 slotted discs
3 input shaft
4 roller bearing
5 ball bearing
6 torsional damper flange
7 output shaft

Figure 3.150 Viscous coupling unit

The IRD is fitted in place of the conventional transfer box and is attached to the manual or automatic gearbox. The combination of the two units provides drive to the front and rear wheels. The IRD incorporates a differential unit to control the proportion of drive delivered to each front wheel and, in addition, operates in conjunction with the viscous coupling unit (VCU) to give the vehicle a self-sensing four-wheel drive system. The unit comprises a main casing, a right-hand housing, a primary shaft, an intermediate shaft, a differential unit, a laygear, a hypoid gear set, a rear output pinion and a pinion housing (Figure 3.151).

The VCU automatically controls the transfer of drive to the rear wheels by limiting the speed differential

between the front and rear propeller shafts. The unit is supported in two propeller shaft bearings attached to the floor cross-member. The VCU comprises a short cylinder, which contains an input shaft supported in a roller bearing race at the front and a ball bearing race at the rear. Within the cylinder, slotted discs are alternately attached to the outer surface of the input shaft and the inner surface of the cylinder. An output shaft is welded on to the rear of the cylinder. The input shaft is attached to the front propeller shaft and the output shaft is attached to the rear propeller shaft.

On some models, a torsional damper is bolted to a flange on the output shaft to cut down on vibration through the transmission.

The VCU cylinder is a sealed unit filled with a silicon jelly. The viscosity of the silicon jelly increases when subjected to shear stresses. When there is a speed differential between the front and rear propeller shafts, adjacent slotted discs in the VCU rotate in relation to each other. The shearing action of the rotating slotted discs increases the viscosity and resistance to rotation of the silicon jelly.

The rear wheels are usually under-driven with this system and, in effect, pulled along by the front axle. Therefore, in most conditions, the vehicle is effectively front-wheel drive, with the rear wheels turning the rear propeller shaft slightly faster than the IRD drives the front propeller shaft. Since the speed differential is low, the increase in viscosity of the silicon jelly is marginal and there is little resistance to relative rotation of the slotted discs.

When there is a significant speed differential between the front and rear propeller shafts, for example if the front wheels lose traction, the viscosity and resistance to rotation of the silicon jelly increases to a level that slows or stops relative rotation of the slotted discs. With the front and rear propeller shafts locked together, drive is thus transferred from the IRD to the rear wheels providing four-wheel drive.

3.25 Clutch – routine maintenance

3.25.1 General maintenance

Apart from minor adjustments on some systems, the clutch assembly and mechanism do not require any maintenance. Clutch life depends on the way in which the car is driven. High mileage and the frequency of clutch use can be a factor and slipping of the clutch can cause excessive wear. For example, a car that has been used mainly for motorway driving requires fewer gear changes than a car that is frequently used around town and is constantly stopping and starting. Therefore, the clutch wear will be greater on the car used around town.

The way the clutch is engaged will also cause the clutch to wear, and driving with your foot on the clutch or slipping the clutch when pulling away in the wrong gear will cause the clutch to wear out.

As the clutch wears, the free play in the clutch pedal decreases. This makes the clutch slip, causing further wear on the clutch lining. Too much free play at the pedal and the clutch will not disengage, making it difficult to change gear.

Many vehicles have self-adjusting clutch mechanisms, therefore no adjustment is necessary. This type adjusts the cable length as the clutch wears. Hydraulic clutches use the position of the **slave cylinder** to allow for clutch wear. Clutches without a self-adjusting mechanism should be checked and adjusted during routine maintenance or as per the manufacturer's recommendations.

> **Slave cylinder**: a component used to actuate another component through hydraulic pressure received from a main hydraulic cylinder called a master cylinder. For example, a clutch slave cylinder operates a clutch release bearing through hydraulic pressure created by the driver acting upon a master cylinder attached to the clutch pedal.

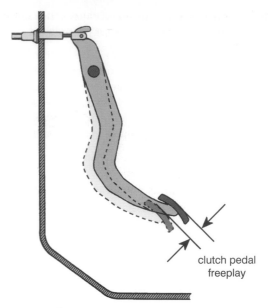

clutch pedal freeplay

Figure 3.152 Clutch pedal free play and adjustment

3.25.2 Clutch pedal adjustments

In some cases, the clutch pedal height and biting point can be adjusted by the pedal stop behind the clutch pedal. Before carrying out this adjustment, the pedal height should be checked by measuring from the floor of the vehicle to the surface of the pedal. Usually, the clutch pedal should be level with the brake pedal.

The pedal free play can be checked by pushing the clutch pedal down until a resistance is felt, as the release mechanism pushes against the pressure plate. This distance between the resting position of the pedal and the point where resistance is felt is the free play, which usually measures around 15–30 mm. Adjustments can be made on cable-operated clutches by altering the length of the cable, and on hydraulic clutches by adjusting the push rods in either the master or slave cylinders.

3.25.3 Clutch maintenance

Hydraulic clutches require the fluid level to be checked during service. A slightly reduced level could be caused by wear on the friction plate. If the fluid reduces greatly, then a more serious problem such as a leak in the system is likely. If the fluid drops too much, the system could introduce air to the fluid lines. This air would make the clutch travel decrease as the air rather than the fluid is compressed.

Early vehicles had separate reservoirs for the clutch and brake fluid but, as the same fluid is used, these days the reservoir is more commonly shared.

Lubrication of the clutch release mechanism components is not possible due to their location, so this is done during production or if the vehicle requires a repair in the system. The vehicle should be road-tested before and after any repairs to check for faults such as slipping, dragging, judder and the fierceness of operation.

Figure 3.153 Topping up the clutch reservoir

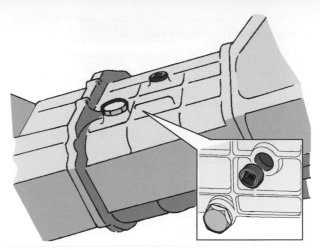

Figure 3.154 Manual gearbox oil level check and filler plug

3.26 Manual and automatic gearbox – routine maintenance

3.26.1 General checks

Gearboxes do not require maintenance during servicing unless the gearbox oil is changed on a service schedule. Due to such high-quality materials being used today, wear in the gearbox is kept to a minimum. Other than checking the oil level, carrying out a visual inspection for leaks and checking gear selection during a road test, the gearbox generally needs little attention.

Before checking the oil level the vehicle should be on a level surface, preferably a lift for ease of checking the underside of the vehicle for gearbox leaks.

3.26.2 Manual gearbox

Gearbox oil lubricates and cools the gears and bearings inside the gearbox. The gears rotate and force the oil out between them at high pressures.

Most manufacturers only recommend the checking and topping up of oil in the gearbox, but some specify the oil should be changed at certain mileages. Usually there are two plugs situated in a gearbox, one on the side for checking and topping up and one at the bottom for draining the gearbox oil if necessary. Only the specified oil from the manufacturer should be used to prevent premature failure of the gearbox.

3.26.3 Automatic gearboxes

The oil in an automatic gearbox does the same job as in a manual gearbox, but also includes lubrication of multi-plate, wet-type clutches that are immersed in the oil along with the brake bands to prevent premature wear. It also acts as a hydraulic fluid, providing hydraulic pressure for the valve body and torque converter. As an automatic gearbox produces a lot of heat, the oil also acts as a coolant, and automatics have an oil cooler fitted to the system that allows the oil to be cooled down as it passes through.

Unlike manual gearboxes, oil changes are usually required in automatic gearboxes as the oil gets broken down by the wear occurring to the brake bands and clutches and it loses its lubricating properties. Drain plugs are sometimes fitted to automatics, but usually the gearbox sump has to be removed to drain the oil. It is also recommended that the filter in the pickup system is changed at the same time.

The gearbox oil level on an automatic should only be checked using the dipstick when the engine is hot, with the engine running and the gear lever in the park position, as this is when the torque converter is full of oil and a correct reading will be available.

Transaxle gearboxes used on front-wheel drive layouts often incorporate a final-drive differential unit. These types of gearbox often have separate gear oil for the final-drive unit and the gearbox. The final-drive unit will usually use a hypoid differential gear oil and the automatic gearbox will use automatic transmission fluid.

Note: it is important to check that the correct grade of oil is used, otherwise the transmission may not operate correctly and damage may occur. The two are separated by the fitting of a seal to the output shaft of the automatic gearbox.

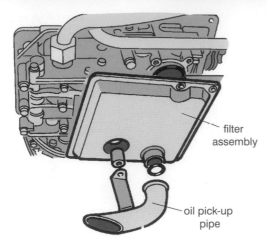

filter
assembly

oil pick-up
pipe

Figure 3.155 Automatic gearbox oil filter

3.26.4 Four-wheel drive gearboxes

If a transfer box is fitted as part of the four-wheel drive transmission system, it is normally filled with separate oil from the main gearbox. This should be checked separately from the main gearbox and may use different oil. This should always be checked before adding new oil. Some four-wheel drive systems using electronic clutch engagement to deliver torque to the rear wheels incorporate separate units within the rear differential unit. In many cases, these units require special specification oil that is normally obtained from the manufacturer's main dealer. It is very important to use the correct oil, as operation of this system will be affected by the incorrect oil type.

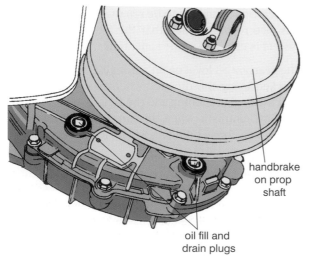

handbrake
on prop
shaft

oil fill and
drain plugs

Figure 3.156 Four-wheel drive gearbox and transfer box

3.27 Propeller shaft and drive shaft – routine maintenance

3.27.1 General maintenance requirement

Drive shafts and propeller shafts have universal joints that move through varying angles as they rotate. These joints need to be lubricated to prevent premature wear and seizure. Earlier vehicles were sometimes fitted with lubrication nipples and could easily be lubricated at maintenance intervals. Most modern vehicles have sealed-for-life joints and need no maintenance as long as they are always covered by the rubber **gaiters** protecting them.

Gaiter: a device used to seal a joint to prevent the ingress of dirt and water and also to prevent the lubricating grease escaping from the joint, which would cause premature wear.

3.27.2 Propeller shaft

Propeller shafts usually have cross joints fitted, such as Hooke-type joints. As the shafts rotate through varying angles, it is necessary for a suitable lubricant to be used to prevent vibration, noise and wear of these joints.

Some vehicles are fitted with grease nipples to allow grease to be injected via a grease gun during routine maintenance. Later types are sealed during manufacture and require no maintenance. It is essential that the correct type of grease is used for different applications and the manufacturer's specification should be referred to. Most propeller shafts have a sliding joint fitted and if these are not sealed, they will also require lubrication.

When carrying out routine maintenance of the propeller shaft area, a visual inspection of the joints and bearings should be carried out, along with inspection of the oil seals to make sure no gearbox oil is leaking. Bearings and joints should be checked for excessive free play, which could lead to failure of the joint. Propeller shaft faults can normally be diagnosed by vibration being felt through the vehicle as it is being driven, which alters in accordance to the vehicle speed. A knocking noise may also be heard on power take-up through worn joints or bearings.

3.27.3 Drive shaft

CV joints are fitted to drive shafts to allow for suspension movement and the steering of the front wheels. CV joints are usually sealed from the manufacturer with a molybdenum-based grease, which is prevented from leaking out of the joint by a rubber bellows-type gaiter, also known as a drive shaft boot. This also stops water and dirt ingress from road conditions causing premature wear. The gaiter can perish over a period of time causing it to crack and split, allowing the grease to escape and the joint to become worn. This will cause a knocking noise when driving, especially when turning or manoeuvring in tight spaces with the steering on full lock. This noise is caused by the metal components of the joint wearing on each other. During cornering more stress is placed on the joint. If any noise is heard from a CV joint, it will normally require replacing immediately before terminal failure occurs, causing the vehicle to become immobilised.

3.28 Clutch – fault diagnosis

3.28.1 Clutch-release mechanism

The clutch-release mechanism is usually made of metal as it handles a great deal of stress during operation. Nylon or plastic bushes are used within the set-up to help ensure that the clutch-operating mechanism is as smooth and quiet as possible when the clutch is depressed. As the clutch is constantly in use, the lubrication of the linkage reduces over time, resulting in increased friction requiring the driver to use more effort to depress the pedal and operate the clutch.

Cable-operated clutches use a nylon sleeve to separate the inner and outer cables that acts as a lubricant to lower the friction when the cables are moved during gear changes. When wear takes place, friction increases between the two cables and the effort required to operate the clutch increases. This is noticeable when the driver pushes the clutch and a more 'notchy' feel is felt within the clutch pedal.

3.28.2 Clutch assembly

Faults in the clutch assembly can become apparent due to the loads and forces from the engine and transmission during operation.

There are four main clutch faults:

1 Slip
2 Spin or drag
3 Judder
4 Fierceness

Slip symptoms

Under acceleration, the engine revs increase without an increase in vehicle speed. This can be accompanied by a smell from the burning friction faces as the friction material overheats. In a clutch slip condition, the vehicle will be difficult to accelerate, especially when under load or going up an incline.

There are various possible causes of clutch slip. The following is a list of the most common issues that can create a lack of pressure being applied to the clutch friction plate:

- Lack of free play at pedal
- Worn clutch friction plate linings
- Partial seizure of pedal linkage
- Defective pressure plate (seized or broken springs)
- Oil contamination of clutch plate

Spin or drag symptoms

Clutch spin and drag symptoms are often grouped together as they are similar and are both associated with design faults.

- Difficult to engage first and reverse gears from neutral – a grating noise can be heard when selecting reverse gear.
- The vehicle jolts when changing gear while driving due to the poor clearance of the clutch plate, friction plate and flywheel.
- The vehicle continues to transmit drive from the engine to the gearbox even when the clutch is fully depressed as the clutch is unable to disengage.

Possible causes of these problems, created by poor separation between the two driving surfaces and the flywheel and clutch cover are:

- an excessive amount of free pedal movement
- low fluid levels or ingress of air in the system
- fouling or wear on the linkage, preventing the pedal from being depressed
- oil-contaminated facings causing one face to stick to a driven surface
- defective driven plate or seizure on splines of the main shaft
- misalignment of friction faces
- partially seized or collapsed spigot bearing.

Judder symptoms

Clutch judder is noticeable mainly when letting out the clutch to take-up drive from the engine through the transmission system. It is a low frequency vibration, which can be transmitted through the engine and transmission and through the vehicle body.

Possible causes of clutch judder are from any defect that prevents the smooth engagement of the clutch:

- Jerky pedal operation: sticking cable or slip/grip movement of a pivot
- Excessive engine movement during take-up of drive

- Oil-contaminated facings
- Defective pressure plate
- Misalignment of friction faces
- Defective driven plate; broken springs in the hub
- Defective diaphragm spring, causing imbalance in the clamping force of the pressure plate

Fierceness symptoms

Clutch fierceness is felt when the clutch is gradually released, but the biting of the clutch is very sudden. This is felt as a jolt through the vehicle and the transmission system. Damage to the transmission and engine mountings can occur if this is not rectified.

Possible causes for clutch fierceness are any defects that allow the clutch take-up to be faster than the movement of the pedal. These include:

- partial seizure of the pedal linkage or contamination of the clutch fluid in the system
- oil-contaminated driven plate
- misalignment of the friction faces.

Clutch bearing noise symptoms

Clutch-release bearing noises are usually heard when the clutch is depressed as the release bearing makes contact with the clutch cover. A noisy clutch release bearing should be investigated and rectified fairly quickly, as this could link to a worn clutch assembly. Failure of the release bearing would result in an inoperative clutch system, as the driver would be unable to disengage the clutch to change gear. The noise usually disappears when the pedal is released as the bearing is no longer put under stress.

Possible causes of a noisy clutch release bearing are:

- incorrect clutch free play adjustment
- worn spigot bearing noise – usually a whining noise
- worn clutch cover.

3.29 Manual gearbox – fault diagnosis

3.29.1 General diagnosis

The gearbox is attached to the engine and transmits the power from the engine to the wheels through various gears and ratios under enormous forces. This can lead to components becoming worn or failing over time. Faults range from gear selection problems to noises coming from the gearbox caused by component failure. Selector linkages can sometimes require adjustment as the components wear or if the gearbox has been removed and refitted for any reason. Road testing the car is the most common way

of diagnosing a fault within the gearbox, as engine speeds and loads can be varied to reproduce a fault. If a gearbox has to be stripped down, it is advisable to carry out checks to the other gears and bearings while apart. Most manufacturers now replace a gearbox rather than repair it due to the costs involved in stripping and rebuilding it.

Example diagnosis

To diagnose gearbox faults, it is important to ensure that you understand the transmission system; this will assist in the diagnosis through a good understanding of the working principles. If it is possible to determine when a fault occurs, for example when only in one gear, it is possible that the fault exists within that gear or the corresponding gear it meshes with.

If it is difficult to engage second gear during acceleration, the selector or synchromesh unit should be suspected as the probable cause. If the gearbox has a constant whine through all gears and when travelling in neutral, the differential bearings may be worn. After any gearbox repair is carried out the vehicle should be thoroughly road-tested to ensure it has been repaired correctly.

Table 3.5 Manual gearbox faults

Fault	Cause
Gear whine	a Lack of oil b Gear-tooth wear c Bearing wear d Shaft misalignment
'Knocking' or 'ticking'	a Chipped gear tooth b Foreign matter wedged between gear teeth c Defective bearing
Jumping out of gear	a Defective selector detent (e.g. broken spring) b Shaft misalignment due to worn bearings c Worn gear teeth
Gear fails to select	a Incorrect adjustment between gear stick and selector b Defective selector

3.30 Automatic gearbox – fault diagnosis

3.30.1 General diagnosis

The automatic gearbox consists of more complex systems and components than the normal manual gearbox unit. For this reason, the diagnosis of any faults with an automatic gearbox should be researched using the manufacturer's technical manual initially, to ensure that the technician has a good understanding of the operational features. Table 3.6 shows some of the main areas to look at when diagnosing any of the symptoms listed; this should be a first assessment prior to any further deeper inspection.

Before carrying out any diagnosis with the automatic gearbox it is recommended that the oil level and condition should be visually assessed, as this can give some good clues to various faults. For example, if the gearbox oil is dirty and the car is not changing gear smoothly or is slipping when changing gear, it is more likely that the oil contains particles of the clutch or brake bands due to wear of these frictional surfaces.

3.30.2 Common faults and their causes

It should be noted that regular maintenance through servicing activities should prevent most problems with the automatic gearbox. Table 3.6 lists a series of symptoms accompanied with possible causes and faults.

Table 3.6 Automatic gearbox faults

Area	Cause	Fault
Fluid	Low level	Starvation of the pump prevents the hydraulic system from operating correctly; faults range from non-engagement of gears to erratic operation
	High level	Governor strikes oil surface, so change speeds are affected
	Poor quality	Rough gear changes. If oil is contaminated with grit particles, then a valve may stick; the resulting fault is related to the part of the system controlled by the valve
Selector lever	Incorrect adjustment	Some gears, particularly those at the end of the travel, will not select (Lever should be adjusted when it is at mid-point of selector range.)
Throttle cable	Incorrect adjustment	Road speed at which changes take place will be either too high or too low
Starter inhibitor	Incorrect adjustment	Starter will be active in positions other than P and N

After checking the gearbox oil for any contamination and ensuring it is at the correct level (check manufacturer's manual for the method of checking gearbox oil as this can differ), if a fault from the table is not apparent, the technician should carry out a series of tests to diagnose the problem.

Test sequence

1 Carry out a road test with the vehicle to assess the gearbox operation, taking note of how the gearbox changes gear and if there are any unusual noises.
2 Carry out a stall test. This tests the torque converter operation for stator slip and the brake bands and clutches for slip. The stall test should not be carried out for a prolonged period, as it creates a large amount of heat within the gearbox.
3 Carry out a pressure test on the gearbox hydraulic system. Pressure take-off points are normally provided on the gearbox to enable a pressure gauge to check the line pressures. This detail will normally be available from the gearbox manufacturer.

3.30.3 Stall test

The stall test is used to assess the condition of the torque converter and associated components. The main mechanical components that can create a faulty operation of the torque converter are the unidirectional clutch or free wheel. A fault with the unidirectional clutch can produce:

- a slipping stator – causing the fluid to enter the pump at the incorrect angle; therefore full torque multiplication cannot be obtained
- a seized stator – preventing the fluid striking the back of the stator vanes from making the stator free wheel at the appropriate time, so the fluid acts as a severe brake on the engine and produces overheating of the converter.

A stall test indicates whether slip is occurring at the converter free wheel or in the gearbox. A general outline of the method is as follows:

1 Check that the engine is warm and that it is in good condition. A low engine power will give a false result.
2 Connect a **tachometer** to the engine.
3 Chock the wheels and apply the handbrake and footbrake.
4 Run the engine, select 'D' (or position recommended by the manufacturer), fully depress the throttle and note the maximum engine speed, which should be about 1800 rpm.

Warning: during this test the engine power is absorbed by the converter fluid and this causes a rapid temperature rise. The duration of the test should be less than 10 seconds.

Table 3.7 Stall test results

Typical result	Probable cause
Below 1000 rpm	Converter free wheel slip
About 1200 rpm	Engine not giving full power
Above 2000 rpm	Gearbox clutch or band slip

Tachometer: instrument for measuring the speed of an engine, usually in revolutions per minute.

The automatic gearbox does not have many adjustments to alter the general running performance; these are normally limited to brake bands, starter inhibitor switch and the gear selection cable and mechanism. It may be necessary to carry out these types of adjustments after replacing any of the gearbox components.

3.30.4 Electric control diagnosis

Most gearboxes fitted to today's vehicles have either full or part electronic control. This electronic control involves the use of a gearbox ECU, linked to sensors and actuators within the gearbox, and also other systems such as the engine and engine management.

When diagnosing faults with ECU-controlled transmissions, the technician will interrogate the ECU with diagnostics equipment, this will read any faults stored in the ECU's memory. Faults stored in the ECU's memory are normally from failure of an electrical component, such as a pressure sensor, etc. To assess the operational condition of the gearbox, it may be necessary to read the data from the ECU as the vehicle is travelling to understand how the system is performing. From this data, the technician will be able to assess the condition of components to trace the cause of the fault.

Figure 3.157 Diagnosing transmission faults

4

Chassis systems

4.1 Introduction

The vehicle's chassis system consists of three main areas:

- Steering system
- Suspension system
- Braking system

The way the vehicle responds to the road and driver inputs is all down to the design features of the chassis system, which the vehicle manufacturer has built into the vehicle dynamics. Vehicle fundamentals across the chassis system areas have not changed dramatically since their conception. The main difference in all of the chassis system areas is the inclusion of lighter weight, higher grade and more accurately manufactured materials. Additionally, vehicles today now incorporate a great deal of electronic control systems to improve vehicle safety, handling and refinement.

On earlier vehicles, the driver had full control of all the systems through the inputs through the steering and braking system. Now the vehicle monitors the inputs from the driver to decide what is best for the vehicle and the driver. This can be seen with anti-lock braking systems (ABS), which monitor road wheel speed and vehicle dynamics and make alterations to individual brakes to bring a vehicle back in control of the driver. Earlier vehicles depended on the driver to alter the pressure on the brakes to avoid a skid condition, or the driver's skills in preventing a vehicle from sliding off the road. The following section gives a full understanding of the fundamentals of the vehicle's chassis systems and provides an insight into technology now found on today's vehicles.

4.2   Directional control and stability

The fact that vehicles today often travel at high speeds illustrates the need for good steering, but perhaps even more important is efficient maintenance and fault rectification. Steering fault diagnosis can often place great demands on the technician's basic knowledge, so it is essential in the interests of road safety that they have a thorough understanding of this subject. This is due to the modern vehicle being very dependent on the steering and suspension geometry and set up. Most modern vehicles have settings for front and rear suspension and steering, with many incorporating something called **passive steering** into the rear suspension. Passive steering is discussed later in this section on page 413 but, in general terms, this enables the rear wheels to take different lines depending on the cornering speeds through deflection in suspension components. For these reasons, it has become very important for the technician to be able to diagnose and repair steering and suspension systems effectively to maintain the vehicle's dynamics.

Passive steering: when the vehicle's rear wheels are able to take a different line through suspension deflection or suspension design. Alterations to suspension mounts can create a change to the road wheel alignment as weight is transferred to that wheel. This can improve the handling through adding toe-in to the rear wheels during cornering.

Basic principles

The steering mechanism must enable the driver to:

- maintain easily the straight-ahead motion of the vehicle, even on uneven surfaces and at high speeds
- change the path of the vehicle without undue effort.

Swinging-beam system

The geometry of steering may be understood by considering the layout of a vehicle (Figure 4.1). A swinging axle beam, mounted on a turntable (or pivot) on the frame, turns the wheels and allows the vehicle to move around an imaginary centre (Ic). You will see, in the position shown, that all wheels are at right angles to radial lines drawn from Ic, and each wheel forms a tangent to the curved path that the wheel is actually taking. The natural tendency of a wheel is to travel in a straight path, and it is obvious that a curved path will cause greater tyre wear. This wear can be kept to a minimum if misalignment is limited through accurate set-up of the steering system.

Swinging-beam system: a simple steering system consisting of a solid beam axle mounted centrally through a pivot to allow the steered wheels to move.

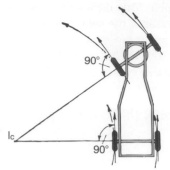

Figure 4.1 Swinging-beam system

Ackermann layout

Many of the disadvantages of the swinging-beam system were overcome in 1817 when a Munich carriage builder, named Lankensperger, first introduced the fixed-beam, double-pivot system. In 1818, his agent in England, Rudolph Ackermann, took out a patent on the system, which is known as the Ackermann layout and versions of this are widely used by vehicle manufacturers today.

The steering layout should position the wheels at angles shown in Figure 4.2. In 1878, Charles Jeantaud, a French coachbuilder, demonstrated that this condition must be fulfilled if tyre wear is to be minimised. The diagram shows that the difference in the front wheel angles depends on the ratio T/W (T = track width, W = wheelbase length). The Ackermann layout does not fully achieve the conditions shown by Jeantaud in all wheel positions; normally it is accurate only when the wheels are straight ahead and in one position in each left-turn and right-turn wheel setting.

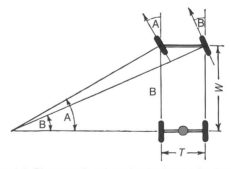

Figure 4.2 Diagram showing why the inner wheel must be moved through a larger angle

The main details of the layout are shown in Figure 4.3. Each wheel hub is mounted on a stub axle that swivels on either ball joints or a kingpin to give the steering action. Linkage connecting the two stub axes together comprises two track arms and a track rod. The Ackermann layout is obtained by positioning the kingpin (or swivel joints) and the **track rod** joint on an imaginary line, which is inclined to the centre line of the vehicle. This means that when a track rod is fitted to the rear of the swivel centres, it is shorter than the distance between swivel centres. Although this is satisfactory on heavy vehicles, it is not used on cars because of the engine position; instead, the track rod is set forward of the wheel centres.

Track rod: a joint that connects the steering arms to the steered wheels of the vehicle to input driver steering requests, these allow rotational and linear movement of the steering and suspension system.

Figure 4.4 shows the steering angles when the track rod length is equal to the swivel centre distance; both wheels will move through the same angle. Setting the track arms and shortening the track rod to give an Ackermann layout will cause the angles to vary when the wheels are turned. The action will be seen if the track rod is moved a given distance to the left: the left-hand track arm approaches its effective crank angle (rod and arm at 90°) and this gives the arm a small angular movement, whereas on the right-hand side the arm moves away from the effective crank angle and increases the arm and wheel angle. The difference in angle between the two wheels increases as the wheel is turned.

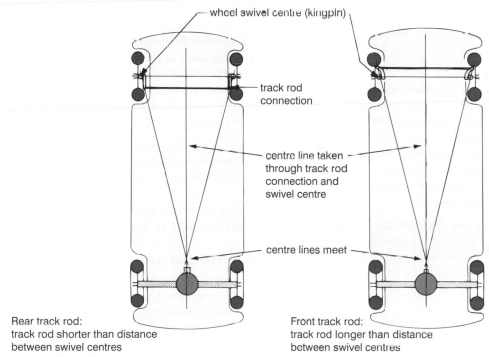

Figure 4.3 *Ackermann steering system*

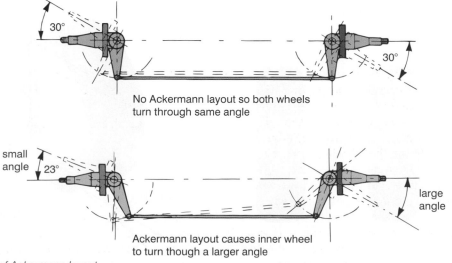

Figure 4.4 *Effect of Ackermann layout*

It should be noted that the essential feature of the system is the position of the track arm connection in relation to the steering swivel axis and not the shape of the track arms. However, any distortion of the arms due to vehicle impact will cause misalignment and incorrect wheel angles. The setting of the track arms can be checked either by placing the wheels on turntables and measuring the angles, or by checking the amount that the wheels move out-of-parallel when one wheel is steered through a given angle – this latter test is called 'toe-out on turns'.

4.2.1 Oversteer and understeer

Slip angle

Previous steering geometry has been based on a vehicle using 'hard' tyres. Low-pressure tyres used on modern vehicles take a different path when subjected to a side force. Figure 4.5 shows a plan view of a wheel travelling in the direction A.

If a side force acts on the wheel, tyre deflection will cause the wheel to take path B, although the wheel is still pointing in the original direction. The angle between the path that the wheel is actually taking and the plane of the wheel (AA) is termed the slip angle. (This term is misleading since no slip is actually taking place: 'creep angle' might be a better term, but 'slip angle' is in common use.)

The slip angle caused by the deflection of the sidewall of a given tyre is proportional to the side force acting on the tyre. This statement is true up to the point where adhesion is lost and the tyre starts to slide sideways. During the non-slip phase the following applies:

$$\text{Cornering power (N/degrees)} = \frac{\text{Side force (newtons)}}{\text{Slip angle (degrees)}}$$

The cornering power (CP) of a tyre is governed by:

1. inflation pressure – an increase raises the CP
2. tyre construction – a radial-ply tyre has a higher CP than a diagonal-ply tyre
3. tyre size – a low-profile tyre has a smaller wall so a higher CP is achieved
4. camber (tilt) of wheel – tilting the wheel away from the side force increases the CP
5. load on the wheel – if the load is varied from the normal, then CP will decrease.

(See page 449 for further details about tyre construction.)

Self-aligning torque

When a side force acts on a tyre, the wall deflects to give a slip angle. Observing a wheel that is rotating in this condition shows that the side deflection of the tyre is greater at the point where the tyre leaves the road as it revolves (Figure 4.5). This effect produces a self-aligning **torque** (*t*), which attempts to turn the wheel to align itself with the actual direction that the wheel is taking.

The effect of this torque is felt by a driver of a vehicle that is travelling along a highly cambered road – the steering will 'pull' to one side.

Torque: the turning or twisting force to produce rotation around an axis.

Oversteer and understeer

Tyre slip angles affect the steering characteristics of a vehicle by causing either oversteer or understeer. A side force, caused by wind, road camber or cornering forces, produces a slip angle at each tyre.

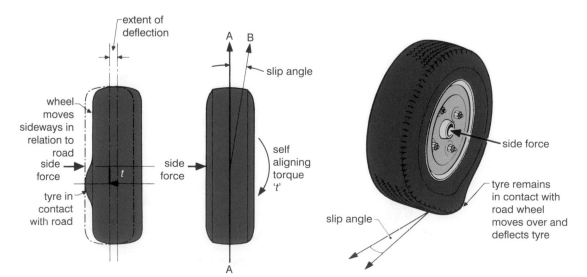

Figure 4.5 Slip angle and self-aligning torque of the tyre

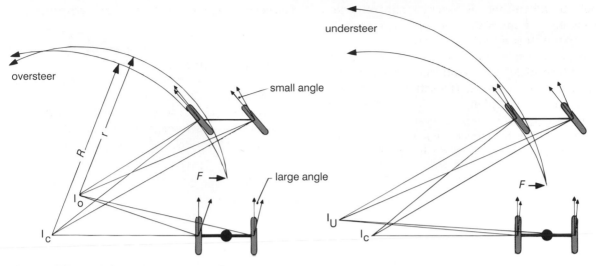

Figure 4.6 Effects of slip angles

When the rear slip angles are greater than the front (Figure 4.6), the vehicle will turn more sharply than normal – a condition called oversteer. To correct this, the driver has to straighten up the steering wheel – a difficult feat under cornering conditions. When this is linked to the fact that the sharper turn causes a further increase in the cornering force, then it will be apparent why oversteer is regarded as dangerous in most conditions. Some drivers, such as rally drivers, will use oversteer to their advantage in bringing the back of car around to improve corner exit speeds, but this should not be attempted by normal drivers. A mixed tyre arrangement, which uses radial-ply on the front and diagonal-ply on the rear, increases the oversteer effect, so for safety reasons it is made illegal to use this tyre arrangement.

Oversteer can also be caused by:

- moving the centre of gravity towards the rear by increasing the load on the rear of the vehicle
- lower tyre inflation pressure at the rear than that recommended
- large load transference from inner rear wheel to outer rear wheel when cornering.

Understeer is produced when the front slip angles are greater than the rear. This tends to cause the vehicle to move away from the side force and makes the vehicle take a path of larger radius than normal. A reasonable degree of understeer is desirable, but if it becomes excessive 'hard' steering results. Most automotive manufactures 'dial in' a certain amount of understeer into production vehicles, as this is a safer condition compared with oversteer and it is easier to correct by removing power to allow the front tyres to regain grip.

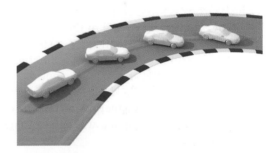

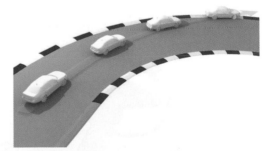

Figure 4.7 Oversteer and understeer situations

4.2.2 Steering mechanism

The mechanism used to link the driver's steering wheel to the road wheels depends on the type of suspension system. Modern layouts have been developed from the basic system shown in Figure 4.8. Today, the use of this system is confined to light commercial vehicles.

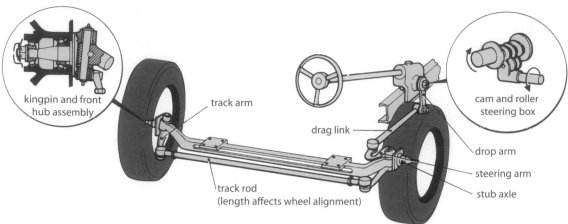

Figure 4.8 Steering layout – light commercial vehicle

Steering for light trucks and some off-road vehicles

The steering column, set at an angle to suit the driving position, contains a shaft (mast), which is connected to the spoked steering wheel either by a taper and key or by **splines**. At the lower end of the column, a steering gearbox is fitted and this moves a drop arm. A ball joint on the bottom end of the arm joins it to a drag link, which pushes and puffs a steering arm mounted on a stub axle. Construction of stub axles takes various forms; the arrangement shown is called a reversed-elliot type. Phosphor-bronze bushes in the stub axle provide for steering movement of the road wheels around a kingpin, which is retained in the axle beam.

In the UK, the steering box controls the right-hand (off-side) wheel and movement of the other wheel is by means of the track rod linkage.

Spline: a mechanical mounting that incorporates grooves or slots. This allows two items to be attached together to enable them to rotate as one unit. Some splines allow rotational movement and sliding movement if they are not locked.

Steering for cars

Figure 4.9 shows a typical steering layout for a car. Independent suspension is normal for this type of vehicle, so a split track rod, made up of two or three separate pieces, is necessary to avoid a change in the steering geometry when one or both wheels strike a bump in the road. A rack-and-pinion-type steering rack naturally takes the place of the centre link of a three-piece track rod and also eliminates the need for a drag link. These features, together with its comparatively direct action, make this type of steering set-up attractive for cars and light vehicles.

Steering movement of the wheels is normally provided by widely spaced ball swivel joints situated at the outer connection points of the suspension arms.

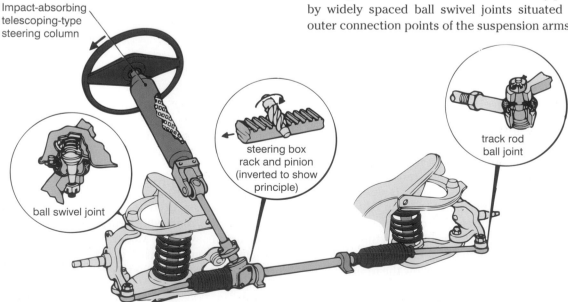

Figure 4.9 Steering layout for a car without power-assisted steering

All steering systems fitted to modern vehicles will have power-assisted steering (PAS) to lessen the driver's effort to steer the vehicle, especially heavier vehicles or vehicles fitted with wide profile wheels and tyres. Assistance will be in two forms:

- Hydraulic pressure delivered by an engine-driven or electric pump
- Electric delivered by a motor situated directly on to the column or rack assembly

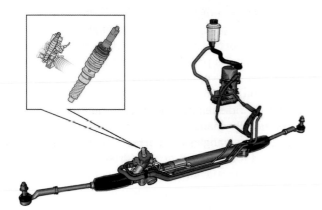

Figure 4.10 PAS layout showing hydraulic with electronic pump

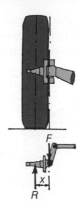

Figure 4.11 Layout showing the need for centre-point steering

Centre-point steering appears to be ideal, but the 'spread' effect of the pneumatic tyre causes the wheel to 'scrub' and give heavy steering and an increase in tyre wear.

4.3 Camber, caster and swivel-axis inclination

4.3.1 Centre-point steering

Figure 4.11 shows a vertical wheel and kingpin arrangement. This has the following disadvantages:

1 Large splaying-out effect of the wheel. The wheels are pushed along by the force (F), which is opposed by the resistance (R). These two forces produce a couple ($F \times x$), which becomes very large when the front brakes are applied.
2 Heavy steering owing to the distance between the kingpin and wheel centre. The wheel has to be moved in an arc around the pin, the radius being x.
3 Large bending stress on the stub axle and kingpin.

To overcome these problems, the wheel and kingpin are arranged so that the 'offset' distance (x) is reduced. When the offset is eliminated (i.e. when the centre line of the wheel meets the centre line of the kingpin at the road surface), the condition is termed 'centre-point steering'. This can be obtained by (a) camber, (b) swivel-axis inclination or (c) dished wheels.

4.3.2 Camber

Wheel camber is an important factor in the vehicle's handling and stability. There are two camber angles utilised: positive and negative camber. Positive camber is noticeable when viewing the front of the vehicle, as the front wheels will be leaning out at the top and in at the bottom. Negative camber is noticeable as the front wheels will lean in at the top. Incorrect camber setting will have an effect on the vehicle's tyre wear. Too much negative camber will create excessive wear on the inner edges of the tyres; too much positive camber will cause the tyres to wear on the outside edges.

The camber setting is critical in making sure that the vehicle travels in a straight line and is stable during cornering. If the camber angles are set differently on each side of the vehicle, this can create a problem with the vehicle pulling to one side – the vehicle will generally pull to the side of the wheel with the greater positive camber setting. Many vehicles do not have adjustable camber as this is set by the suspension components during the vehicle design. If these vehicles require adjustment, they will have to be adjusted by replacing a suspension component that is possibly bent or worn.

Positive camber

When the wheel has positive camber, the stresses on the stub axle and the tendency for the wheels to splay out is reduced considerably.

However, the wheel angle (leaning out) caused by having positive camber will result in different rolling radii where the tyre contacts the road. The result of this is a cone effect of the tyre, which causes the outer edge of the tyre to wear as more vehicle load is placed on this area. Positive camber also reduces offset, which results in lighter steering. You will see some heavier vehicles using positive camber for this reason.

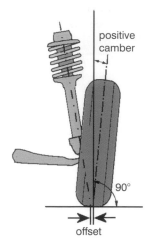

Figure 4.12 Positive wheel camber

As mentioned earlier, one implication of having positive camber is the cone effect of the tyre as it touches the road surface. This cone effect will cause the wheels to try and steer the car away from the wheel with the most positive camber. Because of this, when both wheels have the same amount of positive camber, they will both try and turn the steered wheels outwards in opposing directions. As both wheels will produce the same force, this is cancelled out causing the vehicle to travel in a straight line.

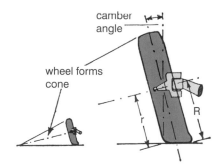

Figure 4.13 Positive wheel camber creating tyre deflection

As the wheels will have a tendency to try and turn outwards, this will cause the tyres to scrub and wear on the outside edges. To try and counter this problem, vehicles with this set-up normally have a small amount of toe-in. As both wheels will have the same amount of toe, this will cancel out the forces created.

Negative camber

Negative camber is found when the wheel is tilting in at the top when viewed from the front. Negative camber reduces the angle of the wheel when the

vehicle is cornering, providing a larger tyre footprint on the road surface. As the tyre is able to have more of its surface area on the road, this improves the vehicle's stability and handling during cornering. A problem associated with having a more pronounced negative camber setting is that the added wheel offset will normally create heavier steering and increase inner tyre wear.

When a vehicle is designed, the wheel alignment and settings are an important factor in making sure the vehicle handles correctly and does not wear out tyres too quickly. The design engineers have to create the correct settings for when the vehicle is travelling and is part loaded. This is due to the fact that when the vehicle travels along the road, the suspension and ride height of the vehicle constantly change. As ride height changes, the camber angle will also generally change. To ensure that the camber and other steering angles are correct, the vehicle should be loaded to represent normal driving conditions. In this condition, the camber can be set to ensure that it provides the best compromise in vehicle handling and tyre wear.

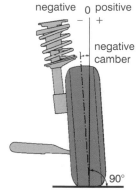

Figure 4.14 Negative wheel camber

Figure 4.15 Car using a large amount of negative camber

For many years, the trend has been to set the camber from zero to slightly positive, to offset vehicle loading. However, the current trend is to set slightly negative settings to increase vehicle stability and improve handling. Camber angles on road cars rarely exceed 2°, but as you can see on some competition cars this angle can be exceeded to give greater stability through corners as the tyre rolls on to the contact patch during high-speed cornering. An issue with this will be tyre wear while driving in a straight line.

Kingpin or swivel-axis inclination

Tilting the kingpin outwards at the bottom produces an angle between the kingpin centre line and the vertical, which is known as kingpin inclination (KPI) or swivel axis inclination (Figure 4.16). Most layouts require KPI of 5–10°, in order to obtain the required offset. The larger angles are used when the designer moves the wheel away from the kingpin to accommodate brakes, bearings, etc.

As the wheel is turned, it will move in the plane AA, and will lift the front of the vehicle: this produces a self-centring action. When vertical kingpins are used, a simple yoke-and-pin type of steering joint can be used at each end of the track rod. An inclined kingpin causes the joint to move from the plane BB, upwards at one end of the track rod and downwards at the other. A ball joint is necessary at each end of the rod to allow for this motion.

Dished wheels

By slightly dishing the wheel (Figure 4.17), the amount of camber and KPI may be reduced. The light pressed-steel or alloy wheel must not be excessively dished, or the strength will be diminished due to the excessive stresses created.

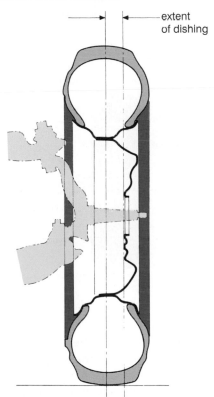

Figure 4.17 *A dished wheel*

Negative offset (negative scrub radius)

In the past, positive offset was used. This was obtained by making the centre line of the wheel meet the swivel axis at a point just below the road. The offset distance, measured at the road surface between the two centre lines, should be equal to ensure that the inward or outward 'pull' of one wheel balances the 'pull' of the other wheel.

When one front tyre deflates, the positive offset on that side will increase. This will cause the vehicle to pull violently to that side and will make it difficult for the driver to maintain control, especially if the brake is applied (Figure 4.18).

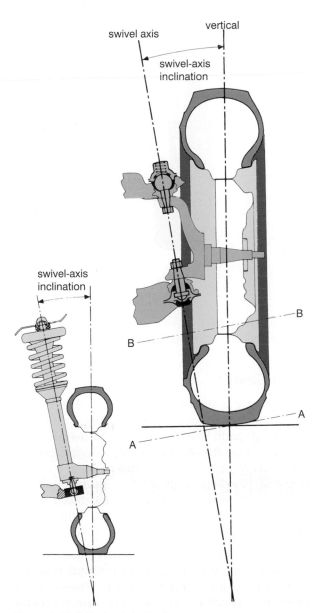

Figure 4.16 Swivel-axis inclination

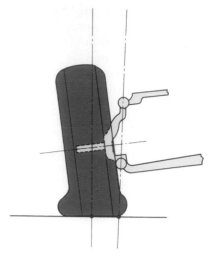

Tyre deflated – offset has increased

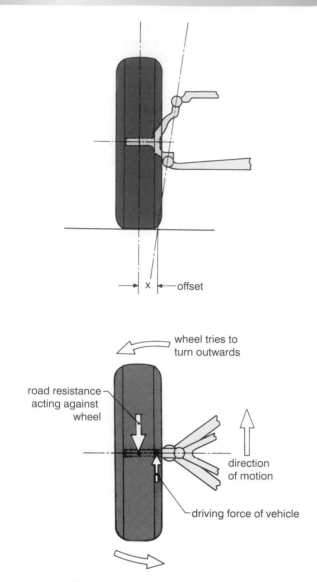

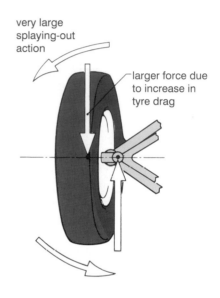

Figure 4.18 Positive offset

Road safety is improved when negative offset is provided by the manufacturer. It is obtained by inclining the swivel axis in order to give an intersection point well above the road surface. With this geometry, the effect of tyre deflation is to shorten the offset. Although the rolling resistance is increased, this shorter offset robs the deflated tyre of leverage to change the direction of the vehicle.

A further safety feature of negative offset is achieved when the front brakes are unbalanced owing to poor adhesion of one wheel or failure of one front brake. Even under these adverse conditions the vehicle can still be brought to rest in a straight line. For example, if the right-hand front brake failed (Figure 4.19), the geometry would cause the braking action of the left-hand wheel to steer the wheels to the right to counteract the loss of brake drag on the right-hand side of the vehicle. This inbuilt action relieves the driver of a difficult control problem. Also it makes the negative offset layout particularly suited to a diagonally connected split-line braking system.

4.3.3 Caster

Wheel caster is applied to enable the driver to 'feel' the straight-ahead position so that they may steer a straight path. When cornering, a torque must be exerted on the steering wheel to overcome the self-centring or castering action, which tends to keep the wheels pointing straight ahead. From this introduction, it will be seen that too much caster produces hard steering, whereas too little causes 'wander'.

The action of this steering feature may be understood by considering the operation of a simple furniture caster fitted to a trolley (Figure 4.20a). When a force is exerted on the trolley, it moves in the direction of the force. The effect of this force on the caster is shown

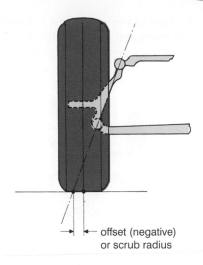

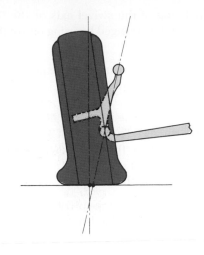

offset (negative)
or scrub radius

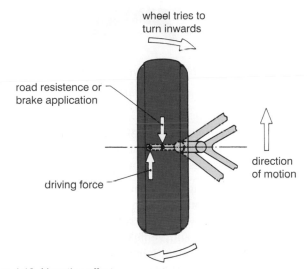

wheel tries to
turn inwards

road resistence or
brake application

driving force

direction
of motion

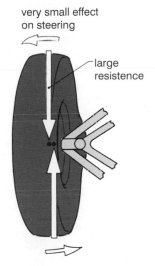

very small effect
on steering

large
resistence

Figure 4.19 Negative offset

in the diagram: the force *F* acting at the pivot and the resistance acting at the wheel produce a couple that rotates the caster to a position where the wheel is following the line of thrust.

On a vehicle, the pivot centre line is normally made to strike the road in front of the centre of contact of the wheel. In this case, the wheel will follow the path taken by the pivot centre line, which will always be in front of the vehicle.

Caster can be obtained by mounting a vertical kingpin in front of the wheel (Figure 4.20b) or by inclining the kingpin forward at the bottom (Figure 4.20c) to give caster angle. The latter is simpler, and most manufacturers use this arrangement. The angle is generally 2–5°; but, once again, reference must be made to the manufacturer's recommendation for caster angle and tolerance (normally +/–0.5° for all steering angles).

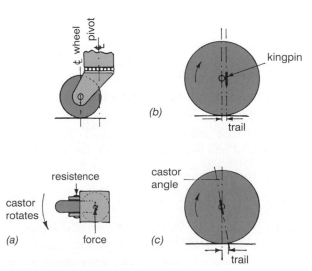

¢ wheel
¢ pivot

kingpin

trail

(b)

resistence

castor
rotates

force

(a)

castor
angle

trail

(c)

Figure 4.20 Wheel caster

The inclining of the swivel axis or the tilting of the kingpin can be arranged by using one of the following methods:

1 Upper independent suspension members mounted slightly to the rear of the lower members.
2 Tilting the axle beam of a light truck by:
   a fitting wedges between axle and spring
   b mounting the axle towards the front of a laminated spring
   c inclining the laminated spring.

Figure 4.20 shows the pivot centre line making contact with the road in front of the centre line of the wheel; this is called positive caster. This geometry is common for a rear-wheel drive arrangement, but is unsuitable for front and four-wheel drive vehicles. This is because the conditions shown in Figure 4.20 are then reversed. Most vehicles that use the front wheels as driving wheels have negative caster, but since this is only a general rule, reference to the manufacturer's data should be made when checking the steering geometry.

Figure 4.21 shows the caster angles applied to a vehicle suspension system. As you can see, this vehicle has negative caster as usually seen on front-wheel drive vehicles.

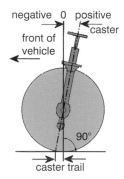

Figure 4.21 Wheel caster applied to front-suspension system

4.3.4 Wheel alignment

Both wheels should be parallel when the vehicle is travelling forward in a straight path. To achieve this basic condition, an allowance must be made for the change in alignment between the stationary and moving positions. The forces on a moving wheel take up the clearance in each ball joint and produce a slight deflection of the linkage. This action causes the road wheels to splay in or out, depending on the geometry of the steering and whether the drive is by the front or rear wheels.

Most rear-wheel drive vehicles have the wheels set so that the distance, measured at hub height, between the front of the wheel rims is 1.5–3.0 mm shorter than that measured between the rear of the same wheels. When the wheels are set in this way, they are said to toe-in. Figure 4.22a shows a toe-in setting of 3 mm.

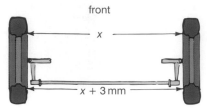

(a) Wheel alignment

(b) Section through tyre tread

Figure 4.22 Toe-in and toe-out conditions

In a similar way, if the distance at the front of the wheels is greater than that at the rear of these wheels, then the expression toe-out is used.

The toe setting is determined by the manufacturer by carrying out tests to find the value that gives minimum tyre wear and creates the best compromise between wear and vehicle handling and stability. If the wheel alignment is incorrectly set, the tyres will wear unevenly. If the vehicle has too much toe-in, this will create excessive scrubbing of the tyres' outside edges as the vehicle travels along the road, and the tyres will point inwards towards the centre line of the vehicle. If the wheel alignment is set with too much toe-out, the tyres will wear on the inside edges as they are pointing away from the centre line of the vehicle.

In the past, a trammel gauge was employed to measure the wheel alignment, but today either an optical or an electronic gauge using lasers is used. Figure 4.23 shows the latest type of alignment equipment. Prior to aligning the wheels, certain preliminaries should be undertaken; these include:

- checking the tyre pressures
- setting the correct load on the vehicle
- positioning the wheels in the straight-ahead position
- moving the vehicle forward to 'settle the steering'
- checking the run-out (buckle) of the wheel; the maximum run-out should be positioned so that it does not affect the alignment measurement.

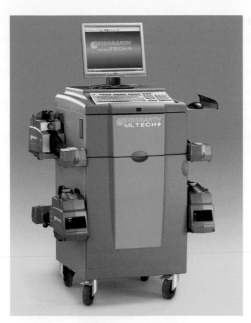

Figure 4.23 Four-wheel alignment equipment used to check and set up the vehicle's suspension and steering system

Left- and right-handed screw threads on the track rod are often provided to alter the length of the rod for correction of the alignment. Equal adjustment of the two outer rods is necessary if the layout has a rack-and-pinion steering box. Failure to do this will have two effects: firstly it will alter the position of the steering wheel with the result that the horizontal spokes will be misaligned; and secondly the steering locks will be unequal along with the incorrect toe-out during cornering.

Incorrect wheel alignment can be recognised by the wafer edge of rubber left on the side of the tread pattern after it has been scraped over the road surface (Figure 4.22b). An examination of the position of the feather gives an indication of the fault; a wafer of rubber on the inside of the tread suggests that the wheels are toed-in, and vice versa. This feathering of the tread is often more pronounced on one tyre than the other.

The combination of road camber and the action of the tyre's self-righting torque causes both front wheels to turn towards the nearside. This movement affects the steering geometry and shows why a manufacturer may recommend a toe setting that appears to contradict basic theory. Interaction between the various geometry aspects of a modern vehicle makes it difficult to pinpoint the cause of a fault from a given symptom. Therefore, after carrying out the preliminaries, a front-end check covering all aspects of geometry is advised.

Adjustment for rear wheel alignment is provided on some vehicles fitted with independent rear suspension, especially vehicles with four-wheel drive.

Rear-wheel toe is just as important as front-wheel toe, especially on vehicles with independent rear suspension and front- or four-wheel drive. On a solid rear axle, the rear toe will not change unless there is damage to the axle casing. With an independent suspension set-up, each wheel must be treated individually in relation to the vehicle centre line. Unlike front-wheel toe where the steering system centres any side-to-side variation, at the rear the toe of each wheel will cause instability if incorrectly adjusted, showing a tendency to pull the vehicle to one side.

The ideal situation would be to have zero wheel toe at the rear, although a small amount of toe-in at the rear can improve stability in a straight line. Excessive toe-in in either direction will cause rapid tyre wear, although in competition cars the rear wheels are often set to toe-in with front-wheel drive to 'dial out' understeer and induce a small amount of oversteer. This is not normally set up on everyday road cars as this type of vehicle characteristic would not be suitable for most drivers.

4.4 Steering components

4.4.1 Steering gear systems

The steering gearbox provides the driver with a lever system to enable them to exert a large force at the road wheel with the minimum effort, and to control the direction of vehicle motion accurately.

The overall ratio between the steering wheel and the road wheel varies from about 18:1 to 35:1, depending on the load on the road wheels and the type of steering.

As the ratio is raised, a large number of turns are required to move the wheel from lock to lock: this makes it difficult to make a rapid change in vehicle direction.

By varying the efficiency, the degree of reversibility (a reversible gear transmits motion from steering wheel to drop arm and vice versa) can be controlled, to enable the driver to 'feel' the wheels, yet not be subjected to major road shocks.

4.4.2 Types of steering gear

A number of different types of steering gear have been used over the years, including the steering box and rack-and-pinion.

The steering box is commonly used in larger vehicles, such as commercial-type vehicles, although some four-wheel drive vehicles use this system due to its strength. Various types of steering box have been used, which include:

- worm and sector
- screw and nut
- recirculating ball
- cam and peg
- worm and roller.

Today, most modern light vehicles utilise the rack-and-pinion steering system due to its flexibilities in size and mounting.

Worm and sector

This type has been developed from one of the earliest designs of steering box, a worm and wheel. A case-hardened steel worm and sector are located by bearings in a malleable iron or light alloy casing. Figure 4.24 shows the worm connected to the inner column and the sector forming a part of the rocker shaft.

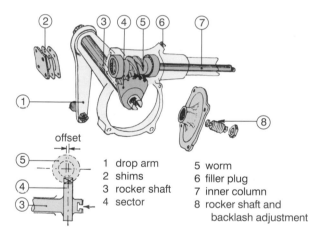

1	drop arm	5	worm
2	shims	6	filler plug
3	rocker shaft	7	inner column
4	sector	8	rocker shaft and backlash adjustment

Figure 4.24 Worm and sector steering box

Most steering boxes are provided with the following adjustments:

1 End-float of inner column – generally shim adjustment.
2 End-float of rocker shaft – shim or screw adjustment.
3 Backlash between gears – gears can be moved closer together.

The greatest wear takes place in the straight-ahead position of the box, so the gear is normally made with a larger backlash in the lock positions. This reduces the risk of seizure at full lock when the box is adjusted to compensate for wear. It is essential to reduce end-float and backlash to a minimum, but tight spots must be avoided.

Steering box lubrication is provided by filling the box to the level of the plug with normal gear oil.

Screw and nut

A phosphor-bronze or steel nut is screwed on to a multi-start Acme thread formed on the inner column. Rotation of the nut is prevented by a ball fitted in the rocker arm. Axial thrust of the column is taken by a single ball race fitted at the top end, and the nut sliding in the housing supports the lower end. The end-float of the inner column is adjusted by the nut at the top end.

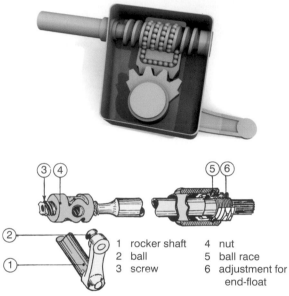

1	rocker shaft	4	nut
2	ball	5	ball race
3	screw	6	adjustment for end-float

Figure 4.25 Screw and nut steering box

Recirculating ball

A higher efficiency (90 per cent as opposed to 50 per cent) is achieved by using a nut with steel balls acting as 'threads'. The type shown in Figure 4.26 uses a half nut with a transfer tube, which feeds the balls back to the nut. A peg on the nut is located in the rocker arm.

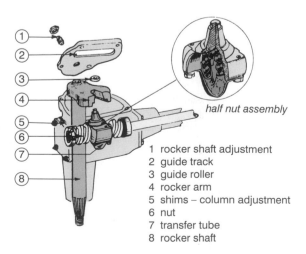

half nut assembly

1 rocker shaft adjustment
2 guide track
3 guide roller
4 rocker arm
5 shims – column adjustment
6 nut
7 transfer tube
8 rocker shaft

Figure 4.26 Recirculating ball steering box

Cam and peg

A tapered peg in the rocker arm engages with a special cam formed on the inner column. The end-float of the column is controlled by shims, and an adjusting screw on the side cover governs the backlash and end-float of the rocker shaft.

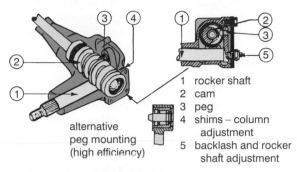

1 rocker shaft
2 cam
3 peg
4 shims – column adjustment
5 backlash and rocker shaft adjustment

alternative peg mounting (high efficiency)

Figure 4.27 Cam and peg steering box

A modified form, known as the high-efficiency cam and peg gear, uses a peg, which is allowed to rotate in bearings in the rocker arm.

Worm and roller

A roller follower fitted to the rocker shaft engages with an hourglass worm. The small offset of the roller to the worm enables an adjusting screw to control backlash and end-float of the rocker shaft.

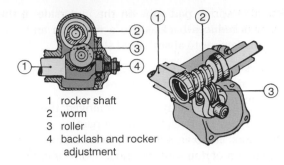

1 rocker shaft
2 worm
3 roller
4 backlash and rocker adjustment

Figure 4.28 Worm and roller steering box

4.4.3 Rack-and-pinion steering arrangement

Today, the rack-and-pinion-type steering arrangement is the most popular on cars and light trucks, especially vehicles fitted with independent suspension. The steering column connects to the rack-and-pinion through a universal joint, and this allows for angular changes between the column and rack-and-pinion. The rack-and-pinion is constantly meshed with the steering rack and, as the driver turns the steering wheel, this rotational force is transmitted to the steering rack. This rotational force enables the driver to move the steering rack to either the left or right, and as the steering rack is connected to the wheels through the steering rack ends, directional change is achieved. An

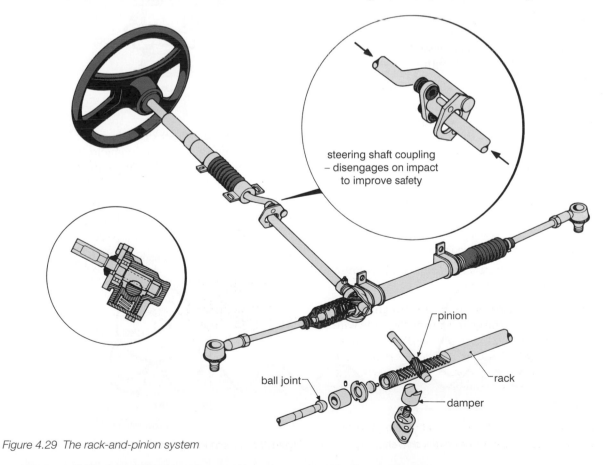

steering shaft coupling – disengages on impact to improve safety

pinion

rack

ball joint

damper

Figure 4.29 The rack-and-pinion system

adjustable spring pad rubs on the underside of the rack; this reduces backlash to a minimum and also acts as a damper to absorb road shocks.

The rack-and-pinion steering system is widely used as it has the following advantages:

- The need for relay rods is removed, this makes the rack lightweight and compact.
- There is no maintenance needed, just visual checks of items like the rack boots for cracks or wear.
- The rack-and-pinion is directly meshed to the rack itself, and this improves steering response.
- The amount of resistance generated by this system is very small, which reduces the amount of effort needed by the driver.

Variable ratio rack-and-pinion

To overcome the heavy steering and lack of progression when fitting a normal rack-and-pinion steering system and introducing large steering angles, the fitment of a variable ratio rack is sometimes used. These steering racks give the benefit of altering the ratio and, therefore, the effort required by the driver to turn the steered wheels.

The ratio of the steering rack is made variable by altering the pitch of the teeth on the rack to be gradually less towards the end of the rack assembly. The pitch of teeth on the pinion gear are more uniform. Decreasing the pitch (distance between the teeth) of the teeth on the rack means that there are more teeth for the given rack length.

As the driver inputs a turning force into the steering wheel from straight ahead, the wheels will move through a given angle, for example 25°. Due to the pitch of the teeth on the rack being larger, the distance the rack moves will be greater. As the driver continues to move the steering wheel towards full lock, the distance the rack moves will be less for the given input from the driver due to the pitch of the teeth becoming less.

As the driver approaches full lock, the effort will become less due to the increased leverage of the rack-and-pinion caused by the change in rack teeth pitch leading to a change in gear ratio. This increase in gear ratio reduces the effort required to turn the steering wheel. In this way, the driver obtains excellent responsive steering around the straight-ahead position and also gains easier steering towards full lock for manoeuvring the vehicle and parking.

4.4.4 Steering joints

The various steering rods and levers are connected by ball joints, which allow universal movement. Most modern vehicles use self-lubricating types similar to the one in Figure 4.31. Fitted on either side of the plated steel ball is a split moulded bearing, which is compounded with a specially developed metallic lubricant. These types of ball joints are sealed for life and require no maintenance. The boot covering the ball joint stops dirt and moisture getting in, preventing premature wear.

4.4.5 Front hubs

The general construction of the front hub will change between vehicles due to the different requirements

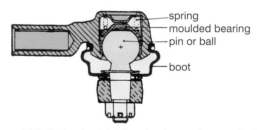

spring
moulded bearing
pin or ball

boot

Figure 4.31 A steering joint (service free and non-adjustable)

of front- and rear-wheel drive layouts. If looking at a front- or four-wheel drive vehicle, the front hub assembly will have to accommodate the fitment of the drive shaft, together with the hub bearings. In a rear-wheel drive vehicle, the front hub assembly will have to carry the wheel hub and bearings alone.

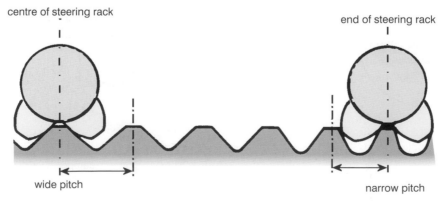

centre of steering rack

end of steering rack

wide pitch

narrow pitch

Figure 4.30 A variable ratio rack (note the difference in pitch for the teeth at the end and the centre of the rack)

Non-driving hub

Figure 4.32 shows a typical bearing arrangement for a non-driving hub. Two adjustable taper roller bearings, spaced as widely apart as possible, are fitted between the stub axle and the malleable iron or steel cast hub.

The hubs are lubricated by packing each bearing and half the cavity between the bearings with a grease suitable for the brake system. Whereas a limesoap grease of medium consistency is suitable for a shoe brake, a grease base having a high melting point, such as lithium or bentone, is essential for hubs used with disc brakes. A lip-type synthetic rubber seal prevents the escape of grease and the ingress of moisture and dirt.

Driving hub

A typical hub arrangement used for a front-wheel drive vehicle is shown in Figure 4.34. The stub axle housing contains two bearings that support both the wheel hub and driving shaft, which is typically part of the constant velocity joint (CV joint). The wheel bearings used will be dependent on the general vehicle requirements and the load needed to be carried. The normal types of bearings are either roller ball or taper roller bearings. **Note**: different types of bearings will have different tightening procedures that must be followed to avoid damage. For more information on these types of bearings see Chapter 6, page 582.

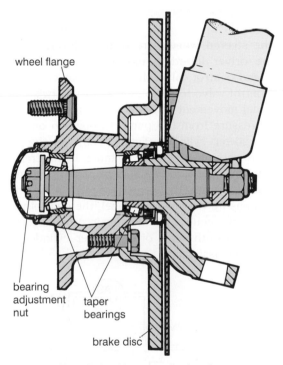

Figure 4.32 Front hub with taper roller bearings

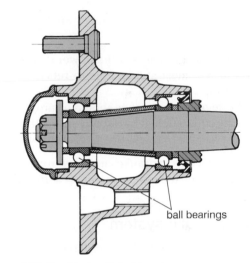

Figure 4.33 Front hub with ball bearings

This type of hub is adjusted by tightening the nut until all clearance is eliminated and then slackening it off one 'flat'. To achieve a more accurate setting, some manufacturers recommend that the adjusting nut is tightened to a specified torque before releasing the nut a given amount. This method should not be confused with preloading. A hub bearing has to withstand heat from the brakes, so it needs a running clearance; this grade of fit is quite different to that obtained after a bearing has been preloaded.

An alternative bearing arrangement is shown in Figure 4.33. This uses two angular contact type ball races, which are held apart by a rigid spacer. The nut on this non-adjustable hub must be tightened fully to the correct torque loading.

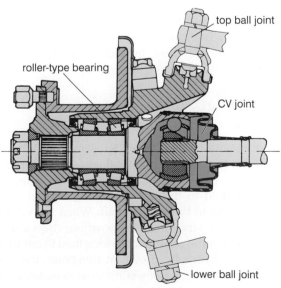

Figure 4.34 Front hub (front-wheel drive arrangement)

4.5   Power-assisted steering

With increased loads on steered wheels and wider section tyres, the large effort required at the steering wheel makes the driver's job very tiring and difficult, especially when steering the vehicle at low speeds such as parking. Improvements such as an increase in the mechanical efficiency of the steering system or lower steering box ratios help to reduce driver fatigue, but if the latter is not limited the increased number of turns made by the steering wheel to move it from lock to lock becomes troublesome. When steering effort exceeds a safe maximum, some method must be found and power assistance is the answer. Most vehicles now have power-assisted steering (PAS) fitted as standard.

The power assistance arrangement should achieve certain requirements:

1 It must be 'fail-safe' – if the power system fails, the driver must still be able to retain effective control.
2 The degree of assistance should be proportional to the effort applied by the driver, and the driver must be able to retain the 'feel' of the wheels.

On light vehicles, hydraulic and electronic power assistance is used to help the driver steer the vehicle.

4.5.1 Hydraulic system

Hydraulically operated power-assisted systems are based on either a constant pressure or constant flow layout – the former employs a hydraulic accumulator to store the pressure, whereas the latter has fluid flowing around the system continuously until assistance is needed.

Figure 4.35 shows the essential components required to operate a constant flow system with a rack-and-pinion steering system. In addition to the normal steering components, the system requires:

- a pump
- a control valve
- a ram cylinder.

The hydraulic pump shown in Figure 4.35 has a reservoir for the hydraulic fluid as an integral component to the design. This reservoir supplies hydraulic fluid to the power-steering control valve that connects to the pinion shaft. When the vehicle is driven in a straight-ahead position, the valve is placed in a neutral position, allowing fluid to circulate through the hydraulic circuit. At this point, the fluid pressure acting on the power cylinder is equal, so no assistance is given to the steered wheels.

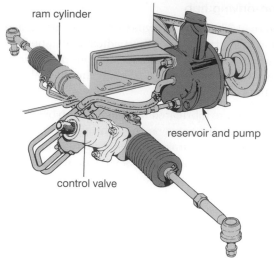

Figure 4.35 PAS system

As the steered wheels are turned, through action of the driver inputting movement to the pinion shaft and control valve, the torsion bar connecting the control valve to the pinion shaft will twist. This torsional movement of the control valve will direct fluid pressure from the pump through to one side of the power cylinder (Figure 4.36). As the fluid pressure acts on the power cylinder, it will create a force to that side of the cylinder providing assistance to driver in turning the steered wheels. As the driver straightens up the steering wheel, the control valve will sit in the neutral position again providing equal pressure to both sides of the power cylinder and therefore no assistance.

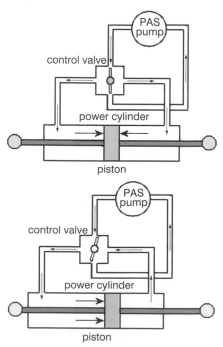

Figure 4.36 PAS layout; driving with wheel in straight-ahead position and during turns

Hydraulic pump

This is generally an eccentric rotor or eccentric vane-type driven by the vee belt from the engine crankshaft. Some pumps fitted on new cars are electronic to improve on the efficiency of the engine by not drawing power from the belt via the crankshaft.

The pump is supplied by hydraulic fluid from either an integral reservoir or a remote arrangement. The type of fluid used is normally an automatic transmission fluid (ATF) type, which has a low viscosity.

Pressure is created in the pump by the rotation of the vane or rotor, this fluid under pressure is sent to the spool control valve. The maximum pressure that the pump can produce (normally $7\,\text{MNm}^2$ or $1,000\,\text{lbf in}^{-2}$) is controlled by the pressure relief valve. Normal pressure increases are generally proportional to the engine speed due to the direct linkage with the power-steering pump. Any excess pressure released by the pressure relief valve is redirected back to the fluid reservoir.

In many modern production vehicles, the power-steering system will also incorporate a system to alter the power assistance depending on the road and engine speed. This is done by fitting a valve in the system, which allows full pressure during low-speed manoeuvring to increase the assistance for the driver (Figure 4.37). During higher road speeds and engine speeds, the valve will modulate the pressure through the hydraulic steering system to limit the amount of assistance and enable the driver to 'feel' the road and the steered wheels, which in turn improves the vehicle's handling and stability. This valve is usually activated via a control unit, which receives signals from around the vehicle such as road speed, steering angle, engine speed and vehicle roll. During low-pressure requirements the excess pressure is returned to the inlet side of the pump.

A power-steering pump is normally driven directly via a belt from the engine's crankshaft. As the steered wheels are turned, the power-steering pump will generate pressure to provide assistance. As this occurs, the power-steering pump will draw power from the engine, putting the engine under load. If the engine is idling, this would cause the engine speed to drop and possibly stall. To avoid this, most engines incorporate a facility to provide a slightly higher idle speed when the power steering is operated. This is called an 'idle-up' device.

The idle-up device fitted to earlier vehicles with carburettors and mechanical fuel-injection used a vacuum switch integrated into the high-pressure line from the hydraulic power-steering pump. The vacuum switch was connected to a vacuum pipe from the throttle valve. As the power-steering fluid pressure rose through the power steering being operated, the pressure was sensed at the vacuum switch. This opened the switch to allow a small amount of air to bypass through to the engine side of the throttle valve, and this provided a slightly higher engine idle speed. As the power steering returned to the straight-ahead position, the pressure dropped and the vacuum switch closed.

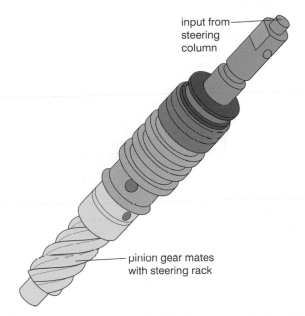

input from steering column

pinion gear mates with steering rack

Figure 4.37 Pressure valve fitted to alter pressure in steering rack according to need

More modern vehicles fitted with engine management systems (EMS) use a pressure switch fitted to the high-pressure power-steering pipe. This switch monitors the pressure in the power-steering system and provides a signal to the electronic control unit (ECU) when the hydraulic pressure is high. The ECU will then signal to the idle control device to increase the engine idle speed to compensate for the additional load on the engine. As the steering returns to a neutral position, the pressure drops and the ECU's signal from the pressure switch informs the ECU to bring the idle speed back to the normal setting.

Control valve

Figure 4.38 shows a rotary-type control valve, which is controlled by a torsion bar that is positioned between the steering shaft and the pinion of the steering box. The valve, commonly called a rotary control valve, is a shaft with a series of flutes encased by a sleeve, which has the same number of internal axial grooves. The ports situated around the outside of the sleeve and shaft pass the oil from the pump supply to the lines connected to the ram chambers.

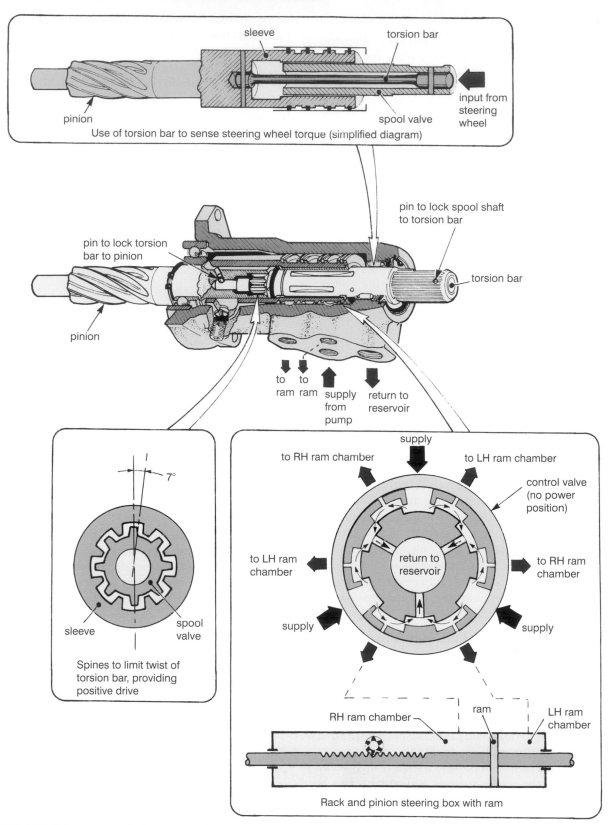

Figure 4.38 Rotary-type control valve operation

The torsion bar is limited to twisting about 7° in each direction by a series of splines between the shaft and sleeve. Any angle below this transmits torque applied by the driver to the steering box pinion via the torsion bar. This provides a fail-safe feature to provide a mechanical drive from the steering shaft to the pinion in the event of a failure of the power system.

The amount of twist of the torsion bar and the movement of the rotary valve are directly proportional to the effort applied by the driver through the steering wheel. As the torsion bar twists through about 0.5°, this will give the start of power assistance as the fluid is able to start to move through the spool valve and out to the hydraulic ram. As the amount of twist rises, so does the amount of fluid pressure and therefore assistance. At the point of about a 4° twist, the system will be at the point of maximum assistance.

With the valve positioned in the straight-ahead 'no-power' position shown in Figure 4.38, all the ports are open. At this stage, oil is allowed to pass directly through the valve and return to the reservoir providing no assistance.

As the driver manoeuvres the vehicle, the wheels will turn against the resistance of the road surface and cause the torsion bar to twist; this twisting action allows the valve to rotate relative to the sleeve, which cuts off the oil flow both to the reservoir and to one side of the ram. Also at this time, the ram is subjected to oil under pressure. This oil pressure builds up sufficiently to create movement of the road wheel and return the torsion bar to the no-torque position. Oil displaced during this stage from the unpressurised ram is returned to the power-steering fluid reservoir.

Whenever the steering is held on full lock, the hydraulic oil pressure builds up to its maximum. When the system reaches a predetermined pressure, a relief valve, fitted within the pump, opens and allows oil to return to the pump inlet.

Other types of control valve are available, including the spool valve and the flapper valve. The spool valve-type control valve carries out the same operation as the rotary valve-type. It redirects the pressurised oil from the power-steering pump to the correct side of the power piston. The main difference is that the spool valve moves up and down rather than rotating like the rotary valve. The control valve shaft and the pinion are again connected via a torsion bar, so if the power-steering pump fails, steering can still be achieved.

The spool valve is fitted inside the valve sleeve and the two are connected together via two steel balls. The whole unit is connected to the pinion gear via two sliding pins. As the pinion rotates, the spool valve rotates in the same direction but also moves up and down by approximately 1 mm. The sleeve valve is secured to the pinion gear via a slide plate and snap ring; this stops the sleeve valve from moving up or down.

As the driver turns the steering wheel, this turning force is transmitted through the control valve shaft to the pinion gear via the torsion bar. As force is applied to the torsion bar due to the friction between the tyres and the road, the torsion bar begins to twist. The control valve shaft moves in proportion to the amount of twist of the torsion bar, thus raising or lowering the spool valve by the screwing action of the balls.

Figure 4.39 Spool valve fitted to steering box

The amount that the torsion bar twists controls the amount of upward or downward movement of the spool valve. This is in relation to the sleeve valve. When the steering wheel is turned to the right, the spool valve moves upward, and when the steering wheel is turned to the left, it moves downward.

This movement sends pressurised fluid to either one side of the power piston or the other, creating assistance.

The flapper-type control valve (Figure 4.41) is used with the recirculating ball-type steering system found in steering boxes, and is integral with the torsion bar. The high-pressure oil generated by the power-steering pump is first directed through valves V_1 and V_2. These valves control the direction in which the fluid flows. Fluid is allowed to flow from the pump to one side of the power-steering piston and back to the reservoir, depending on which direction the driver turns the steering wheel. These first two valves form flapper no. 1.

The second two valves act as pressure-control valves, controlling the pressure at the power-steering piston, depending on the amount of force generated by the drive turning the steering wheel. These two valves form flapper no. 2. If the steering wheel is in the straight-ahead position so the control valve is in neutral, all four of these valves are open. Therefore, there is no pressure difference at the power-steering piston. If the driver now turns the steering wheel to the left, V_1 of flapper no. 1 is opened and V_2 is closed. Flapper no. 2 will also be operating at this point, partially opening valve V_3 and fully opening V_4. By opening and closing these valves, pressure will rise at point A forcing the piston to the right, thus giving assistance to the driver.

An example of this operation can be seen in Figure 4.41, which shows the valve operation in turning right.

As the driver turns the steering wheel to the right, pressurised fluid will travel through valve V_2 to the right-hand side of the power piston. If the driver continues to turn the steering wheel, then the pressure acting on valve V_4 caused by the increased force generated by the driver will close V_4 tightly. This will cause the fluid pressure to rise, giving maximum assistance to the driver. As the amount of turning force exerted by the driver is reduced, so is the amount of twisting of the torsion bar. This causes valve V_4 to open slightly, thus reducing the amount of assistance given.

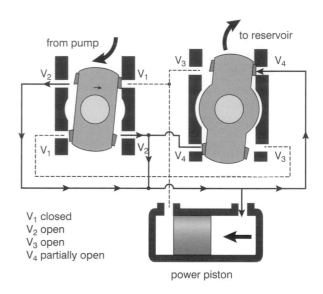

V_1 closed
V_2 open
V_3 open
V_4 partially open

Figure 4.41 Valve operation – turning right

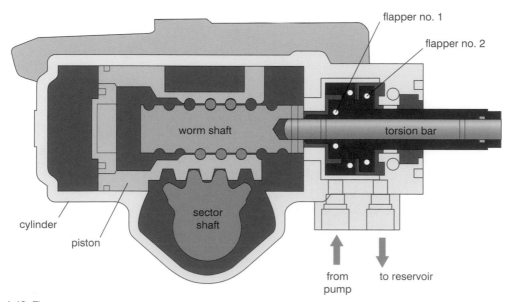

Figure 4.40 Flapper valve

Power assistance for steering boxes

The steering box PAS system operates in a similar manner to that of a rack-and-pinion PAS system. This system also has an engine-driven pump to produce the hydraulic pressure. The control valve and the ram cylinders are either located externally from the steering box (Figure 4.42) or located internally in the steering box.

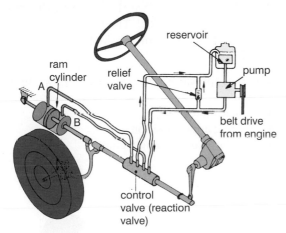

Figure 4.42 Steering box PAS layout

The control valve remains in the neutral position giving no power assistance when there is no torque applied to the steering wheel by the driver. As the steering wheel is turned by the driver, the turning force travels along the steering column to the power-steering control valve. This then opens the port to direct power-steering fluid pressure to the ram to provide assistance to the steering. As the steering wheel is then turned in the opposite direction, the pressure in the hydraulic system is diverted by the control valve to the opposite side of the ram, which provides assistance to the driver.

4.5.2 Electro-hydraulic PAS

In conventional PAS systems, an engine-driven power-steering pump generates the hydraulic pressure needed to assist the driver in steering the vehicle. With electro-hydraulic PAS (EHPAS), the engine-driven pump is replaced by an electric motor. There are two main advantages to this type of system:

1 The speed of the pump can be controlled via the engine's ECU, and by varying the speed of the pump progressive steering can be achieved easily.
2 There is no power loss due to the driving of the vane pump as with conventional PAS, producing improved economy and lower emissions.

The layout of the system makes it particularly suited to mid-engine front-wheel drive vehicles, as all the components can be grouped in the front of the vehicle.

Road speed signals picked up from the ABS system are sent to the power-steering ECU to inform the system of vehicle speed and, therefore, required assistance. A warning light is also fitted to the system to alert the driver if there is a malfunction within the system.

The vane pump assembly incorporates the vane pump, reservoir, pump motor and the power-steering ECU. The vane pump and reservoir supplies the steering gearbox with the appropriate amount of fluid, depending on vehicle speed and steering conditions. The pump motor drives the vane pump, and also transmits the steering conditions back to the ECU, as the amperage needed by the motor changes. A power-steering ECU then controls the speed of the electric motor based on signals received from the speed sensor and the pump motor. Idle-up functions are also controlled via the power-steering ECU.

When there is an increase in electrical load, rpm is increased to reduce poor engine performance. If there is an actuator malfunction, the power-steering

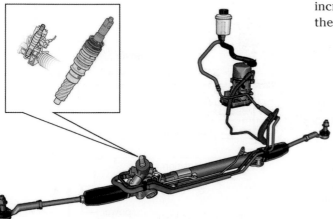

Figure 4.43 Electro-hydraulic power-steering system used on the Volvo S60

ECU is able to switch off the relay and stop motor operation. It is also able to output diagnostic codes to help find any malfunctions in the system.

The engine's ECU sends a signal to the power-steering ECU when the vehicle is started if the engine is cold or if the engine speed is low. This enables the power-steering ECU to make the appropriate adjustments. Finally, the power-steering relay supplies power to the pump motor.

Signals from the pump motor and the vehicle speed sensor are sent to the power-steering ECU. The ECU judges the condition of the vehicle and adjusts the fluid flow accordingly. The fluid flow is adjusted by either speeding up or slowing down the motor.

The pump motor control consists of three maps: normal; non-steering; and 0 mph vehicle speed. As the vehicle speed increases, the pump motor speed decreases as a reduction in voltage is applied.

Actions taking place during vehicle speed increase:

- Wheel speed increases
- Wheel speed sensors inform ABS ECU
- ABS ECU informs EHPAS ECU
- EHPAS ECU reduces motor pump speed
- Reduction in pressure/assistance level

Actions taking place during vehicle speed decrease:

- Wheel speed decreases
- Wheel speed sensors inform ABS ECU
- EHPAS ECU increases pump motor speed
- Increase in pressure/assistance level

4.5.3 Electronic PAS

Electronic PAS (EPAS) systems have become increasing popular with manufacturers. They are more compact and can be easily adapted to many different vehicles by adapting the control software to suit driving characteristics. These systems are also able to improve vehicle emissions and economy levels of the vehicle as they do not draw energy from the engine-driven pump. Hybrid and electric cars also use these types of systems due to not requiring an engine-driven pump.

The EPAS system uses an electric motor acting on the steering column using a worm gear and gear wheel. The steering column is in two halves linked with a torsion bar. The torque sensor measures the relative position of the two sections of the steering column. The example shown in Figure 4.44 uses optical-type sensors. An LED and phototransistor are arranged either side of a shadow plate fixed to the steering column. The outputs from the phototransistors are processed by the sensor circuit to produce a turning signal. The ECU calculates the required assistance

level using this signal and controls the motor accordingly. It also provides a diagnostic system.

Principle of operation

The EPAS system provides the following control functions:

- Road-speed-sensitive power assistance
- Assisted steering return

Both of these functions are the result of the motor voltage control by the ECU. The ECU determines the voltage supply to the motor based on the following data:

- Force applied to the steering wheel by the driver
- Vehicle speed
- Steering angle position
- Speed of steering angle change

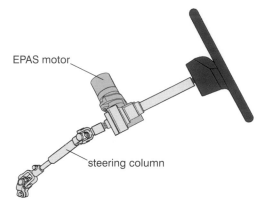

Figure 4.44 EPAS system showing motor attached to the steering column

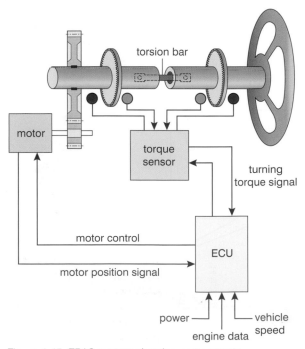

Figure 4.45 EPAS system showing components

The torque sensor measures the input force applied by the driver. When the driver turns the steering wheel, the torsion bar between the two halves of the steering column will twist. The amount of twist is proportional to the force applied. The output signal of the two phototransistors will move out of phase.

The size of the phase change will be proportional to the twist in the torsion bar and, therefore, to the force applied by the driver.

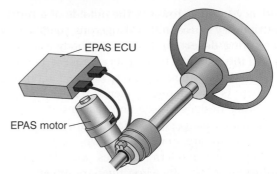

Figure 4.47 ECU and EPAS system

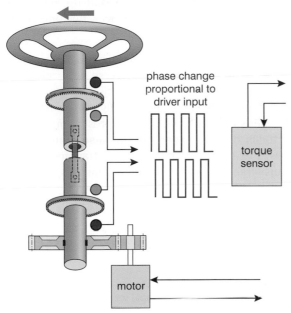

Figure 4.46 EPAS torque sensor operation

The torque sensor will also measure the steering angle position and the speed of angle change. The steering angle position is calculated by counting the number of pulses from the phototransistor. The speed of steering angle change is proportional to the frequency of the signal from the phototransistor. The torque sensor circuit measures these three parameters and then outputs a digital signal to the EPAS ECU.

The EPAS ECU combines this data with the road speed to calculate the direction and speed of the motor and, therefore, the assistance required for the driver.

Fault-finding with EPAS

Troubleshooting EPAS systems is actually much simpler than you may think. Invariably, the motor, gear housing and torque sensor will be integrated with the steering column as a single assembly. Diagnosis of a system defect becomes a simple matter of confirming that the input signals, power source and ground are correct at the ECU, then confirming that the ECU connections between the torque sensor and the motor are correct. The operation of the system will also be supported by diagnostic codes from the ECU,

Figure 4.48 Scan tool used to interrogate the EPAS system

allowing technicians to identify the problem area very easily through the use of a suitable scan tool.

One of the downsides of this type of arrangement is that many drivers will report less 'feel' for the road and feedback from the steered wheels compared with a hydraulic arrangement. Manufacturers are now overcoming this issue through more advanced control unit software, which is able to give the driver more communication with the steered wheels and how the vehicle is reacting to the inputs the driver is giving through the steering wheel.

4.6 Rear-wheel and four-wheel steering

4.6.1 Rear-wheel steering by altering suspension geometry (passive rear steer)

It has been known for many years that the front-to-rear wheel alignment plays a significant part with respect to directional stability of a vehicle. This is clearly shown when a car has worn suspension bushes; often the lack of stability makes it dangerous to drive due to the wheels taking incorrect directional movements, especially during cornering and braking.

Up to the mid-1950s, the majority of vehicles suffered from oversteer (i.e. the rear of the vehicle had a tendency to steer towards the outside of a turn). A contributory cause to this dangerous condition was rear spring deflection initiated by body roll, which caused the rear axle to alter its alignment. Improved axle location systems helped to reduce the problem, but there is an inherent tendency to oversteer with the earlier designs of axle and suspension systems. The obvious dangers associated with an oversteer characteristic are now well known, so to improve stability most modern vehicles are designed to understeer, especially when they are driven at high speed.

One step towards an understeer characteristic can be achieved by using the natural transfer of the vehicle's weight during cornering to 'steer' the rear wheels. This action is produced either by misaligning the rear axle or, in the case of a vehicle fitted with independent rear suspension, by utilising a change in geometry of the rear suspension system.

The suspension geometry can be tuned to react in different ways, especially during cornering, through the fitment of special flexible bushes. These react to the load exerted on them as the vehicle turns. The different loading causes the bushes to deform, causing the suspension geometry to change slightly. For example, when cornering, the outside loaded rear wheel may toe-in slightly to improve the vehicle turn into the corner. It is important to make sure that these types of suspension bushes are fitted correctly to avoid any vehicle handling issues. Suspension components should also be tightened under the weight of the vehicle to ensure that the bushes are preloaded correctly to avoid over twisting bushes during suspension movement.

Figure 4.49 shows an independent rear suspension layout. The adjustable transverse link allows for the toe-in of the wheel to be adjusted if necessary. The fixed transverse link is slightly shorter than the adjustable link, which promotes a small amount of toe-in during cornering. This also minimises the effects of bump steer. The bush attaching the fixed transverse link to the rear sub-frame has a very soft

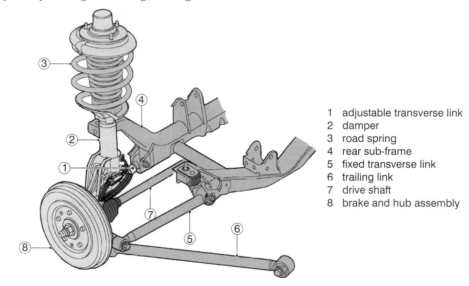

1 adjustable transverse link
2 damper
3 road spring
4 rear sub-frame
5 fixed transverse link
6 trailing link
7 drive shaft
8 brake and hub assembly

Figure 4.49 Rear suspension system on Land Rover Freelander using arrangement to introduce passive rear steer

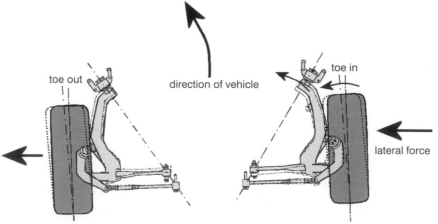

Figure 4.50 Rear suspension geometry changing during cornering

initial movement rate, which becomes progressively harder as the rate of deflection increases. The three remaining bushes in the fixed transverse and the adjustable transverse links are of hard construction, which give precise handling and minimises brief steer effects. The soft bush allows for small amounts of toe-in during cornering.

The added benefits of this type of suspension arrangement is that it can provide additional stability during braking through providing some toe-in and also changes to the camber during cornering.

Many vehicles today offer a form of rear steering often called 'passive rear steer' to counteract normal vehicle tendencies. For example, Subaru used a passive steering system on the Impreza to correct the rear wheels' tendency to toe-out, and Peugeot used passive rear steer on the 306 model to improve rear wheel turn during cornering.

4.6.2 Four-wheel steering systems

Difficulties in ensuring the rear wheels are taking the most accurate route when the vehicle is turning can be further enhanced by the use of a four-wheel steering system (4WS). In 1988, two car manufacturers, Honda and Mazda, offered 4WS on some of their models. Today, many other car manufacturers utilise the 4WS system, including Mitsubishi and Nissan.

Advantages of 4WS

Compared with a conventional two-wheel steer system, it is claimed that 4WS offers the following advantages:

1 Superior cornering stability
2 Improved steering responsiveness and precision
3 High-speed straight-line stability
4 Notable improvement in rapid lane-changing manoeuvres
5 Smaller turning radius and tight-space manoeuvrability at low speed

Relative wheel angles

The direction that the rear wheels steer in, relative to the front wheels, depends on the operating conditions.

During low-speed manoeuvring, wheel movement is pronounced, so the rear wheels are made to turn in the opposite direction; this simplifies the positioning of the car in situations such as when parking in a confined space (Figure 4.51). Since the rear wheels are made to follow the path on the road taken by the front wheels, the rear of a 4WS car does not cut in in the normal way, so the risk of hitting an obstacle is greatly reduced.

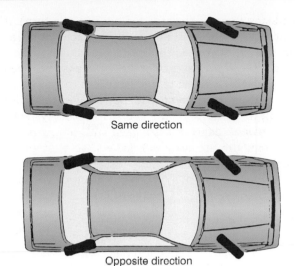

Same direction

Opposite direction

Figure 4.51 4WS wheel angles (angles exaggerated)

High vehicle speed

At high speed, when steering adjustments are subtle and generally small, the front wheels and rear wheels turn in the same direction. This action causes the car to move in a crab-like manner rather than move in a curved path; this arrangement is beneficial at times when the car has to change lanes on a high-speed road. The elimination of the centrifugal effect and, in consequence the reduction of body roll and cornering force on the tyre, improves the stability of the car and makes it easier and safer to control.

Wheel angle control

The two basic systems in use vary in the way that the wheel angles are controlled. Honda uses mechanical rear steering, whereas the Mazda arrangement has a rear 'gearbox' that is both power-assisted and electronically controlled.

Both systems use a power-assisted rack-and-pinion steering box for the front steering gearbox, with a take-off connection to control the rear steering gearbox via a centre, or transfer, shaft. Two or more universal joints on the shaft are provided to allow for small drive angle variations.

1988 Honda 4WS system

This early system is steer-angle dependent (i.e. the movement of the rear wheels is controlled by the angular movement of the front wheels).

For steering wheel angles up to about 130°, the rear wheels are arranged so that they turn through a small angle in the same direction as the front wheels. As the front wheels are steered beyond that angle, the rear wheels gradually straighten up and then turn through a comparatively large angle in the opposite direction (Figure 4.52).

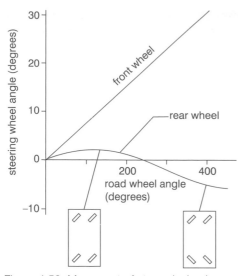

Figure 4.52 *Movement of steered wheels (Honda mechanical)*

Control of the rear wheel angles is obtained by an epicyclic gear mechanism in the rear steering gearbox (Figure 4.53). Meshing with a fixed annulus is a large planet gear that is driven by an eccentric on the input shaft. A short shaft, integral with the planet and offset from the centre of the planet, transmits a drive by a slider and guide to a stroke rod; this is connected to the rear wheel track rods (Figure 4.54a).

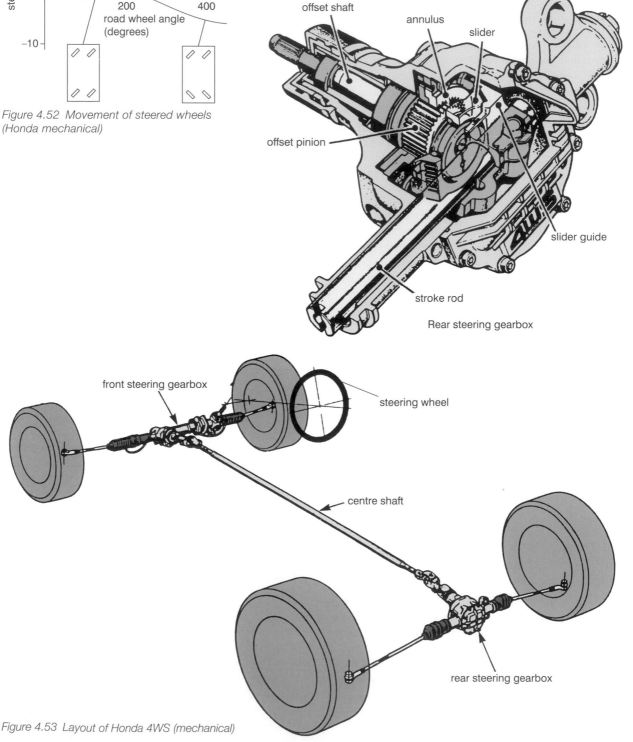

Figure 4.53 *Layout of Honda 4WS (mechanical)*

Slight rotation of the input shaft causes the planet to rotate and this slightly moves the offset output shaft in the same direction as the input (Figure 4.54b). As the input shaft carries the offset shaft towards the top dead centre (TDC) position (Figure 4.54c), the stroke rod moves back to the central position – at this point the rear wheels are set in a straight-ahead position.

Further rotation of the input shaft and planet to the full-lock position (Figure 4.54d), gives a maximum displacement of the stroke rod and a corresponding movement of the rear wheels.

The rear gearbox is maintenance free; it is packed for life with grease. The centre shaft couplings are splined to both steering gearboxes and a master spline at each connection point ensures that the units cannot be incorrectly phased on assembly.

Mazda 4WS system

In this system, the rear wheels are steered by a hydraulically operated power unit, which is electronically controlled according to steering wheel angle and vehicle speed (Figure 4.55).

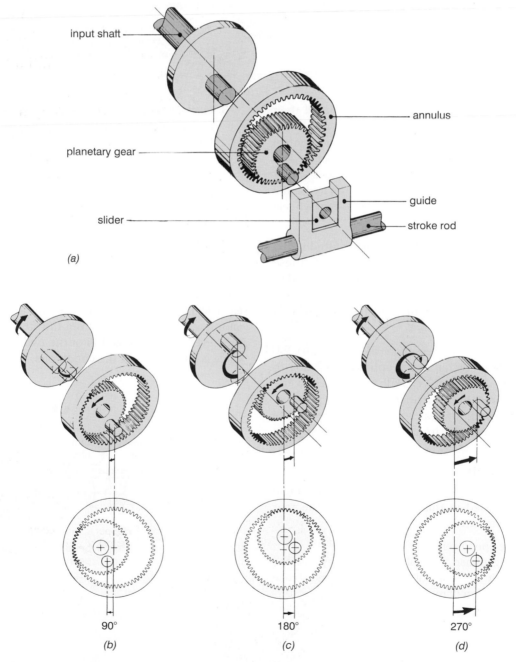

Figure 4.54 Epicyclic gear action (Honda)

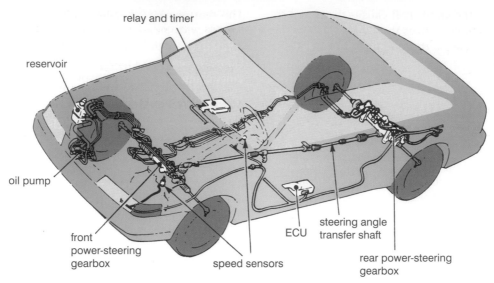

Figure 4.55 Mazda 4WS layout

The Mazda arrangement is more complicated than the Honda system, so has more things to go wrong. However, as is normal with other advanced control systems, special fail-safe devices are incorporated. In this system, it takes the form of a centring lock spring and special safety solenoid. In the event of hydraulic or electronic failure, these devices set the rear wheels to the straight-ahead position.

This system uses two electronic sensors fitted to the transmission output and speedometer drive; these measure the vehicle speed. The signals are passed to an ECU, which has a built-in memory that is used to 'tell' the hydraulic system the direction and angle to set for the rear wheels.

At speeds considerably less than 35 kph (22 mph), the rear wheels are steered in the opposite direction to that of the front wheels. As 35 kph is approached, the rear wheels are moved to the straight-ahead position. Above this speed, the rear wheels are steered in the same direction as the front wheels but the angle is limited to 5°.

Main components

The block diagram (Figure 4.56) shows the main components used in this system to steer the rear wheels. These include:

1 vehicle speed sensors
2 steering phase control unit – conveys to the hydraulic ram control valve the required stroke and direction of movement

3 electric stepper motor – alters the yoke angle and bevel gear phasing according to the signals it receives from the ECU
4 rear steering shaft – transmits the position of the front wheels to the bevel gear in the steering phase control unit
5 control valve – controls the hydraulic pressure supplied to the ram cylinder
6 hydraulic ram cylinder – steers the rear wheels according to the requirements.

The steering phase control unit (Figure 4.56) alters the direction and angle of the rear wheels. From the electrical pulses passed from the ECU to the stepper motor, and the movement from the steering shaft to the bevel gear, the position of the hydraulic control valve is altered to suit the conditions.

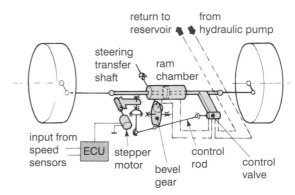

Figure 4.56 Schematic diagram showing layout of rear-wheel steer unit (Mazda)

4.7 Steering systems and wheel alignment – routine maintenance

4.7.1 Steering systems maintenance

Maintenance requirements for non-PAS systems

The maintenance checks on non-PAS systems are very small but some of the checks needed are described here.

Steering wheel installation

By moving the steering wheel in all directions, it is possible to check that the steering wheel has been correctly installed. This test will also check that the main shaft bearing is not loose and that the steering wheel is secured correctly to the main shaft.

Steering wheel free play

While sitting in the driver's position steering wheel free play can be checked. Place the steering wheel in the straight-ahead position and check that the front wheels correspond to the steering wheel. Now move the steering wheel slightly to the left or right without the wheels actually moving. Check the manufacturer's specifications for the amount of free play allowed. If there is excessive free play, then one of the following problems may have occurred:

- Worn steering linkage
- Steering wheel not secured properly
- Worn wheel bearings
- Worn steering rack, or incorrect adjustment of steering gear
- Loose main shaft joint

Wear in the steering linkage

Raising the front of the vehicle off the ground and moving the wheels back and forth is the recommended method for checking the wear in the steering linkage. If there is excessive movement, then either wheel bearings or worn steering linkage are possible causes. To raise the front of the vehicle, either use a two-poster ramp or a trolley jack; if a trolley jack is used, then axle ramps must be used to support the vehicle.

Wheel bearing play

As with the steering linkage, the wheel bearing play can be checked by first raising the front of the vehicle off the ground and then gripping the wheel at the top and bottom and checking if there is any play in the wheel. If there is play, then the same task must be carried out with the brakes applied. If the amount of play is reduced and not eliminated totally, then it is probably not a wheel-bearing fault.

Steering joints and gaiters

Check around all of the steering linkages from the steering column down through the steering rack and to the rack rods and track rod ends. There should be little or no play in these areas. Check the dust gaiters located on the steering rack and the track rod ends, as any damage to these will cause water and dirt ingress, which will accelerate the wear of these components and lead to possible seizure.

Maintenance requirements for power-steering systems

Power-steering leaks

Checks should be made on power-steering systems to ensure that there are no leaks throughout the system. Any leakage from pipes or unions should be rectified immediately, as excess fluid loss could lead to failure of the power-steering system.

Power-steering pressure check

With EHPAS, it is important to understand the pump pressure when diagnosing faults associated with lack of assistance. To check pressure you will need a special pressure gauge, which can be fitted into the power-steering pressure line to the steering rack. Figure 4.57 shows an example of this type of gauge. When the gauge is fitted, the system will have to be bled of any air to ensure that you gain an accurate reading. To bleed a hydraulic power-steering system the reservoir must be filled with the correct grade of fluid, the engine is then run up to approximately 1000 rpm. When the engine is at this speed, the steering is then turned from lock to lock to run the pump and circulate the fluid around the system. This should be done several times until all of the air is evacuated from the system.

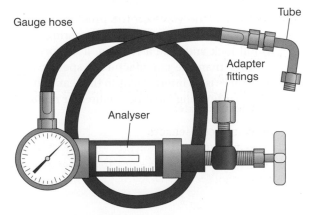

Figure 4.57 Power-steering pressure gauge

The pressure check sequence is as follows:

1 Close the valve on the pressure gauge and check the reading displayed. Compare the reading obtained against the manufacturer's specifications. If the pressure is low, replace the power-steering pump.

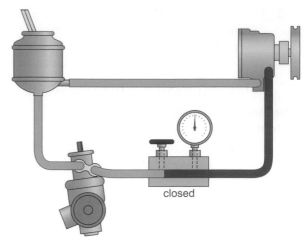

Figure 4.58 Pressure check – step 1

2 Re-open the valve on the pressure gauge and take a reading at 1000 rpm and at 3000 rpm. Check the manufacturer's specification and if the difference between the two readings is too great, then replace the flow control valve within the power-steering pump.

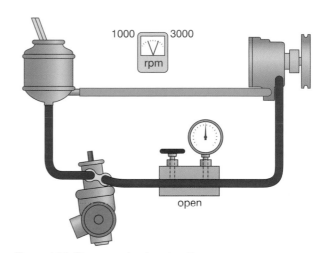

Figure 4.59 Pressure check – step 2

3 Check that the valve on the pressure gauge is still fully open. Then turn the steering wheel to full lock and take a reading. If the pressure is lower than the manufacturer's specification, then there is an internal leak in the gear housing. The gear housing must be repaired or replaced.

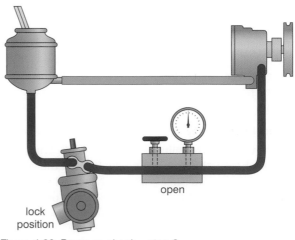

Figure 4.60 Pressure check – step 3

4.7.2 Diagnosis of steering faults

The following table summarises the various steering faults that can occur.

Table 4.1 *Steering faults*

Fault	Possible cause	Diagnosis
Car pulls to one side	Set back	Check the position of the front wheels. Are they in line?
	Incorrect camber	Car will pull towards the side with the most positive camber. Check for worn ball joints, control arm bushes, sagging or broken springs, bent strut assembly.
	Uneven tyre inflation	Check that both tyres carry the same pressures. The car will pull towards the side with the lowest pressure.
	Mismatched tyres	Both front tyres must be the same size, same design and approximately the same amount of tread. Mixing of radial-ply and cross ply tyres should not take place.
	Incorrect caster	Caster must be the same on both front wheels. Check for worn control arms or strut bushes.
	Dragging brake	Corroded brake calliper pistons and misaligned handbrake cables can cause brakes to drag. Car will pull towards side with dragging brake.
	Misaligned rear axle	Rear axle steer is caused when the rear axle is not perpendicular to the vehicle's centre line. Check rear suspension for worn control arm bushings, sagging springs.
	Power-steering problem	Check for even steering balance by raising the front wheels off the ground and running the engine. There should be no tendency for the steering to go to one side. If there is, check for leaky control valve. Steering should be equal in both directions.
	Problem tyre	Faulty tyre construction may cause steering pull.
Car wanders	Loose steering parts	Inspect tie rod end, idler arm and steering assembly mountings.
	Worn steering gear	Adjust the components if possible. If no adjustment is available, parts should be replaced and set up correctly.
	Incorrect caster	Incorrect caster adjustment can make the car unstable. Check also for worn strut or control arms and bushes.
	Wheel bearings	If loose, remove and inspect for damage.
Vibration	Bent or out-of-round wheel rims	Inspect wheels for damage and that they are true.
	Improper tyre balance	Correct tyre balance.
	Worn suspension parts	Check components and bushes for wear and damage. Inspect tie rod ends, idler arm and steering gear mountings.
	Worn wheel bearings	Check for play and adjust or replace.
	Damaged or worn brake components	Check discs, pads and callipers.

4.7.3 Wheel alignment

Under normal conditions, it is not necessary to check the wheel alignment at every service interval, although it must be checked during the pre-delivery inspection. Wheel alignment does need to be checked when a fault occurs, which will normally be evident due to abnormal tyre wear.

There are numerous components and systems that can affect wheel alignment. If a component is physically worn, then adjusting the wheel alignment will not solve the problem. The components that suffer from wear and can affect the wheel alignment are:

- tie-rod ends
- steering linkage
- wheel bearings
- suspension components.

Other factors that can affect wheel alignment are:

- tyre pressure
- vehicle ground clearance
- tyre run out
- difference between left and right wheelbase
- wheel alignment being carried out on uneven ground.

Most wheel alignment data supplied by the manufacturer is given with the chassis to ground clearance at a specified height. This height is usually with the vehicle unloaded, although some manufacturers prefer the vehicle to be weighted with the equivalent of four passengers to settle the suspension. The reason for this is that loading the vehicle will affect both the camber and caster angles. There are other checks that can be carried out during road tests to determine steering and wheel alignment faults. These include checking that the vehicle travels straight ahead without pulling to the left or right, and also that the same is true while braking. Any abnormal noise from the steering and suspension components, and unusual movement of the steering wheel, may also signify a fault. If any of the above problems occur, then wheel alignment must be checked, together with any suspected faulty components.

Wheel alignment is checked using special calibrated equipment (Figure 4.61). Before the vehicle wheel alignment is checked, it must be placed on a flat surface and turn plates should be positioned under the front wheels. The equipment is attached to the vehicle's wheels by the technician and the measuring heads are then centred. When the equipment is switched on, the laser projects a line on the opposite head and measuring scale. By reading off the measuring scale on each measuring head the technician is able to determine if the wheel alignment is correct. If adjustment to the wheel alignment is required, the technician will adjust the suspension or steering to set the wheel to the correct manufacturer's setting.

Figure 4.61 Wheel alignment equipment

The readings are then checked again when all settings have been adjusted. The steering and suspension settings that can be checked by the equipment are:

- wheel toe (toe-in or toe-out)
- wheel camber (negative and positive)
- wheel caster (positive and negative)
- wheel set back (alignment of wheel axle).

4.8 Elements of suspension systems

The purpose of the suspension system is to isolate the driver and passengers from most of the road shocks and wheel movements as the wheels pass over the road's surface. To carry out this role, the suspension system is located between the road wheels and the vehicle's chassis or frame. The suspension system should be able to:

- provide a balance between maximum passenger comfort and maximum safety, along with meeting certain aspects of cost and reliability
- meet all technical requirements that a modern vehicle has to cope with, along with being relatively easy to maintain and as low in cost as possible
- take the road shocks generated through the road wheels and isolate these from the occupants, allowing them to travel in comfort while also ensuring that the vehicle has good handling characteristics and stability. This is done by ensuring that the road wheels always remain in contact with the road surface and that the suspension geometry is maintained during acceleration, braking and cornering to improve the vehicle's handling dynamics
- transfer the braking and engine power to the vehicle body and road wheels without creating an unstable situation.

In order to achieve these requirements, the suspension system should have a low unsprung weight to maintain the best possible road holding and vehicle stability.

Suspension systems have become more complex over the years to provide vehicles with excellent ride and handling characteristics, along with high levels of safety and security. Suspension systems now incorporate advanced materials to reduce weight, and often include electronics to continually adjust the settings enabling the driver to obtain the maximum driving enjoyment from the vehicle. While suspension systems have become more complex and elaborate they are all built on the basic format described in this section. Interested readers might wish to explore the advancements made in suspension systems in more detail using other resources.

4.8.1 The suspension assembly

The suspension assembly is made up of the following components:

- Road spring
- Dampers
- Suspension linkage

Road spring

The road spring supports the vehicle's weight and determines the vehicle's ride height. The spring absorbs road shocks and allows the wheels to follow the undulations of the road surface. This last point is important to ensure that the driver has control of the vehicle. If the road wheels leave the ground, control of the vehicle is lost. Springs can be made from several different materials, each having different characteristics in the way they react.

Dampers

Dampers are used to absorb some of the energy stored in the spring. This reduces the likelihood of the vehicle body bouncing as it passes over bumps in the road surface. When the vehicle strikes a bump in the road, the wheel deflects and compresses the spring. If this compression was left to deflect, it would oscillate – causing the wheel to lose traction on the road and thus making the vehicle unstable.

Almost all dampers, or shock absorbers as they are sometimes incorrectly called, are hydraulic telescopic. We do not tend to call dampers shock absorbers because it is the complete suspension system that is involved in absorbing the shocks from the road surface and not just the damper.

Suspension linkage

The vehicle body is connected to the wheels by the suspension linkage, which allows for movement between the body and the road wheels. There are many components used in a vehicle's suspension layout.

4.8.2 Suspension systems

When looking at suspension systems as a whole, they are generally categorised into two main types:

- Rigid axle
- Independent

The rigid axle type connects the two wheels at the front or at the rear on the same axle, which is then subjected to movement when either wheel negotiates a bump in the road. The independent type, as its name suggests, allows the independent movement of each road wheel across each axle. There are, however, systems that combine elements of both types, with each wheel on an axle indirectly connected to each other through the use of connecting beams that prevent them from being totally independent.

Rigid axle suspension

In a non-independent arrangement, the wheels on the front or rear of the vehicle are connected usually by a tubular axle or beam axle. The layout of this type of system is very simple and very strong, which makes it suitable for larger or heavier vehicles, including HGVs and buses, as well as some off-road vehicles, such as Land Rovers, where strength is important. A disadvantage of this system is that the movement of one wheel affects the wheel on the other side and can have an adverse effect on the vehicle's handling.

Three advantages of rigid axle suspension are that it provides good wheel travel, axle articulation and ground clearance, which are essential attributes for off-road use.

Independent suspension

The independent type suspension system offers many advantages over the rigid arrangement, as each of the road wheels are able to move independently of each other across the axle. Because of this, the road wheels are able to keep good contact with the road surface and maintain excellent wheel geometry during cornering. These benefits provide additional comfort and improved vehicle handling, which in turn provide a safer vehicle.

The body of the vehicle and its mass are supported by the suspension road springs. This is referred to as the sprung weight (i.e. everything acting down on the springs). The other chassis areas, such as axles, wheels, tyres and brakes, are not supported by the suspension system and are called unsprung weight.

Unsprung and sprung weight

Large unsprung masses on a vehicle are undesirable as they have a negative effect on vehicle handling and behaviour. For this reason, vehicle designers try to keep the unsprung weight as low as possible.

Low unsprung weight helps to produce a suspension system that responds sensitively to road irregularities, giving maximum comfort and handling performance. Improvements to unsprung weight can be made through use of lighter suspension and wheel materials, such as aluminum. If the spring does not have to react to heavy loads on top of the weight of the vehicle, it can respond to suspension inputs much more quickly and therefore ensure that the handling behaviour of the vehicle is improved. Examples of vehicles using

1 radius arms
2 panhard rod
3 shock absorbers
4 bump stops
5 air springs
6 rear axle

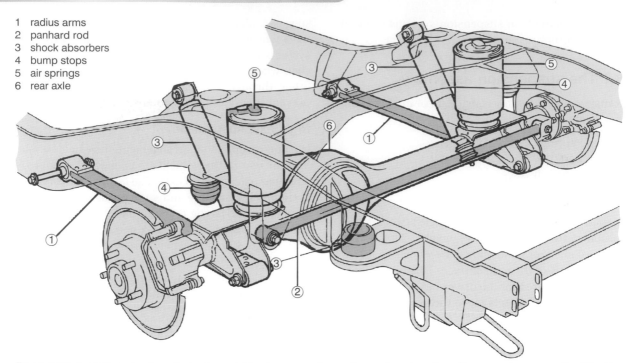

Figure 4.62 A relatively modern design for a rigid axle suspension system using air springs. These systems are often fitted to light commercial vehicles, but are now rarely used on passenger cars due to the weight.

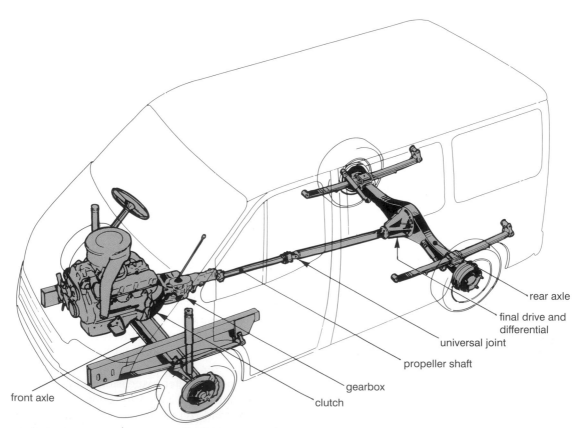

Figure 4.63 A medium-sized commercial vehicle with rigid front and rear axles, both fitted with leaf-type springs. This type of arrangement has gradually been replaced by independent front suspension with rigid rear axle, as this provides improved vehicle handling and comfort.

Figure 4.64 A more modern type of set-up with independent front and rear suspension

this benefit of having very low unsprung weight are Formula 1 cars where the suspension arms connecting the wheels to the vehicle's body are made from carbon fibre. Carbon fibre material is extremely light and allows the suspension to react very quickly to inputs from the driver and the race track, ensuring that the handling of the car is at its best.

The forces acting on the sprung weight of the vehicle are varied and all have to be kept in check. These are generally described as:

- pitch
- roll
- squat
- bounce
- yaw.

Pitch

Pitch occurs when the front of the vehicle dives and the rear rises, or vice versa. This occurs not only under acceleration and braking, but also over bumps in the road. The amount of pitch or, more precisely, the pitch accelerations, are a major determinant of ride quality.

Figure 4.65 Pitch

Roll

When cornering, the centrifugal forces acting at the centre of gravity produce a rolling action transverse to the direction of travel. For example, if a vehicle is driving round a right-hand bend, the vehicle will roll to the left, away from the corner.

The amount of this roll is dependent on the spring rate, centrifugal force and the distance between the centre of gravity and the roll axis (leverage).

The roll axis can be approximated by establishing the parts of the body (through the front and rear axles) that remain at rest when being rocked sideways. These are known as roll centres.

Figure 4.66 Roll

Squat

This occurs when the vehicle accelerates quickly, causing the rear of the car to push down as the turning motion of the wheels is taken up by the suspension system. This is especially seen on rear-wheel drive vehicles.

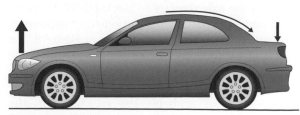

Figure 4.67 Squat

Bounce

This happens when the vehicle compresses its suspension across the front and rear axles at the same time, providing a linear movement of the whole vehicle. This could be created with an amalgamation of rolling and pitching. Bounce is often seen when the vehicle is driving along a road with evenly spaced dips and peaks.

Figure 4.68 Bounce

Yaw

Yaw is the rotational or oscillatory movement of a vehicle around a vertical axis passing through the centre of gravity. It can be affected by the location of the major components and side forces acting on the vehicle, for example crosswinds.

The heavier the components and the farther apart they are in the vehicle chassis, the higher the moment of inertia. Therefore, the vehicle will resist turnings or yaw motion to a greater extent than when the components are lighter and situated nearer the vehicle centre.

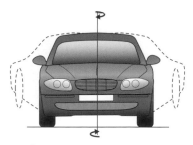

Figure 4.69 Yaw

4.9 Requirements of a spring

4.9.1 Purpose of a spring

Mounting the axle directly to the frame of a vehicle would subject the occupants and general components to severe shocks. This can be seen in Figure 4.70a, which shows the upward movement of the frame when the wheel strikes a bump. In this case, the vertical acceleration would cause considerable discomfort: most probably the reluctance of the vehicle frame to move upwards quickly (inertia)

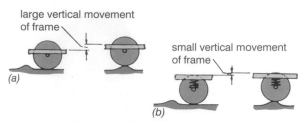

Figure 4.70 Effect of fitting a spring

would buckle the wheel. (You will have observed this effect when riding a bicycle over a bump.)

In addition, if the vehicle is moving along the road at a greater speed, the wheel may even get to a point where it actually loses contact with the road surface. This would be due to the wheel hitting the bump in the road wanting to continue to rise in a vertical motion through its own inertia even after the road surface has dropped away. If this is then repeated several times due to the road surface being rather bumpy, the road wheel can lose contact with the road a large amount of the time. This situation would lead to the instability of the vehicle due to the loss of traction.

A spring fitted between the wheel and the frame allows the wheel to move up and down without causing similar movement of the frame (Figure 4.70b). This spring absorbs road shocks, and allows the wheel to follow the irregular contour of the road surface: for this purpose, the wheel assembly should be as light as possible.

Road shocks can be further reduced by fitting a 'spring' to the wheel; this is achieved through the fitting of a pneumatic tyre.

The term 'suspension system' includes many components, such as springs, dampers, linkages, tyres, struts, etc. Therefore, the suspension system provides a means of isolating the road bumps and shocks from the vehicle and its occupants. The main benefits of the suspension system are improved grip between tyre and road surface, improved passenger comfort and limitation to driver fatigue and isolation of noise travelling between the road wheels and the vehicle chassis and body.

4.10 Types of spring

Various forms of springs can be used. These are:

- metal – laminated, helical and torsion bar
- rubber
- pneumatic (gas and air suspension).

Each type of spring has different characteristics and different uses. The following section explores these types of springs and outlines their properties in relation to each other.

4.10.1 Types and characteristics of metal springs

Laminated or leaf springs

The steel-laminated or leaf spring provides a very low-cost and simple connection to the axle and makes this type very popular for rear suspension systems on earlier cars and larger vehicles.

The main details of a semi-elliptic spring are shown in Figure 4.71. A main leaf, rolled at each end to form an eye, has a number of leaves clamped to it. To ensure a constant stress throughout the spring, the leaves are graduated in length. Rebound clips transmit the load to some of the lower leaves during the return motion of the spring and eliminate the need for fitting a large number of leaves above the main plate. Rubber bushes, fitted in each eye, allow for movement of the spring and act as noise insulators. Alteration in spring length is accommodated by a swinging **shackle**.

Shackle: pivoted link connecting a suspension spring to the body of the vehicle.

The stiffness or **rate** of a leaf spring is governed by the following:

1 Length of spring – shorter spring, higher rate
2 Width of leaf – wider spring, higher rate
3 Thickness of leaf – thicker leaf, higher rate
4 Number of leaves – greater number, higher rate

Rate: also called stiffness, is the force required to deflect the spring.

To obtain a 'soft' ride, a low-rate spring is required and this will deflect a larger amount under a given load. Normal springs have a constant rate and give a deflection that is proportional to the load (Hooke's law). However, if the lower leaves are set to a reverse camber, a stiffening up of the spring will occur as deflection increases: this is called a progressive or variable-rate spring.

As the laminated spring deflects, the plates or leaves slide over each other and cause inter-plate friction. Although this has a beneficial damping effect, the 'hard' ride, noise and wear it creates make it necessary to reduce this friction as much as possible. Earlier designs of spring had to be sprayed with penetrating oil, but today special features are incorporated to eliminate the need for periodic attention. These include:

- synthetic rubber buttons fitted at the ends of the leaves
- reducing the number of leaves (as the number is reduced, the width must be increased)
- inter-leaf plates of low friction material.

To gain the full advantage of the second point above, many springs in use today have only one leaf. Overstressing at the centre of the spring is avoided by using a tapered leaf; thin at the ends and wider and thicker in the centre.

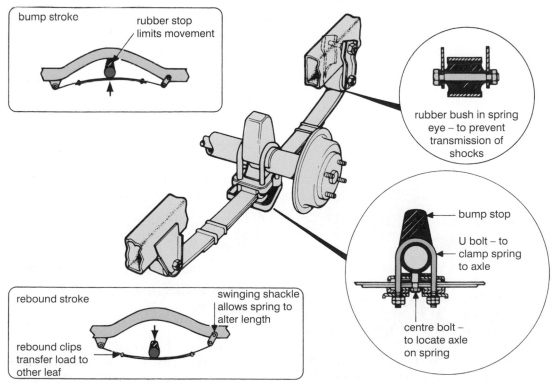

Figure 4.71 Laminated or leaf spring

Hooke's law of elasticity

Robert Hooke was a British scientist living in the 17th century. He first proposed what we now know as Hooke's law in 1660 and defined it clearly in 1678. He summarised it in a Latin phrase: *Ut tensio, sic vis*, meaning: 'As the extension, so the force'.

Hooke's law of elasticity is an important tool when looking at how the suspension systems react to bump and rebound when the vehicle is travelling along the road surface. Hooke's law states that when a spring is extended or compressed as the vehicle hits a bump or drops down a dip, the load applied by the vehicle's weight is in direct proportion to the deflection. When looking around the vehicle, we can see that there are many materials that work on this principle. As long as the directly proportional load does not exceed the limit of the material, Hooke's law is a useful one to consider when choosing the correct suspension system or spring pressure for a vehicle. For example, if a vehicle is expected to carry a load of 500 kg but the spring is only capable of holding 400 kg, the vehicle's suspension will not be able to take the load and the vehicle will 'bottom out' on its suspension. Materials that have this linear-elastic property and relate to Hooke's law of elasticity are known as 'Hookean' materials.

Mathematically Hooke's law is fairly simple and is stated as:

$$F = kx$$

Where:

x is the stretch or compression of the spring (in SI units: N or $kgms^{-2}$ or kgm/s^2)

F is the force exerted by the material (in SI units: N or $kgms^{-2}$ or kgm/s^2)

k is a constant called the rate or spring constant (in SI units: Nm^{-1} or kgs^{-2} or kg/s^2).

To determine whether there is a stretch or compression in the spring, we use a method of signs. If the spring is compressed, both x and F are negative (–) and when stretched both are positive (+).

Helical springs

The helical spring is made from high-grade steel wire formed into a coil. The rate of the spring is governed by the length and diameter of the wire. The wire is wound in the form of a coil, so the length will be controlled by the diameter of the coil and the number of active coils.

This spring is often used in conjunction with independent suspension and is, therefore, most commonly used on modern light vehicles including light commercial vehicles. Figure 4.72 shows a helical spring arrangement in a front suspension.

1 panhard rod
2 radius arm
3 coil spring
4 damper
5 anti-roll bar

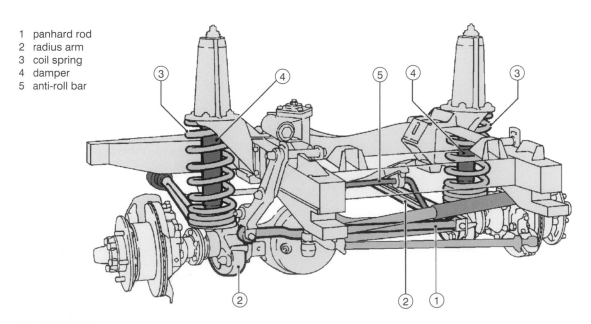

Figure 4.72 Helical coil spring suspension system

Helical or coil and torsion bar springs are superior to leaf springs in terms of energy storage (energy stored in a given weight of spring), but whereas the leaf spring fulfils many duties, the other types require extra members and these can add to the basic weight. Recent developments of suspension systems have seen many improvements in this area and many manufacturers now use lighter materials for suspension components, improving on the unsprung weight characteristics of the vehicles.

Many helical spring suspension set-ups today use variable rate springs. These offer a variation in the 'stiffness' of the spring dependent on the amount of compression. For example, when the vehicle is driving along a road that is straight and flat, the helical spring will act as a softer suspension giving good occupant comfort due to the diameter of the wire used at the top of the spring. However, when the vehicle is driven around a corner, the spring will compress and the rate of the spring will rise as the diameter of the wire increases further down the spring. Due to this rise in spring rate, the suspension will stiffen, which will limit body roll and improve vehicle handling. An example of this type of spring can be seen in Figure 4.73.

On some vehicles, helical springs are used to support the dead axle fitted at the rear of a front-wheel drive vehicle. Figure 4.74 shows a typical layout in which the spring acts directly on the axle. Axle location at the top and bottom is provided by the top-mounting of the damper and the trailing arm. Besides providing fore-and-aft stiffness, the lower arm in conjunction with the damper tube absorbs the braking torque.

Lateral movement of the axle is resisted by a steel Panhard rod. The rod has a rubber bush at each end where it is bolted to the axle and body.

On higher-performance vehicles, a rear stabiliser bar, or anti-roll bar as it is sometimes called, is often fitted; this reduces roll when the car is cornering. The stabiliser bar restricts the body movement of the vehicle as it corners; this improves the vehicle's

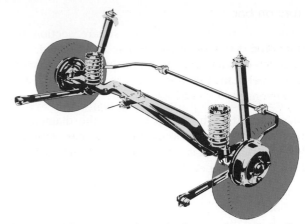

Figure 4.74 *Rear suspension using beam axle and helical/coil springs*

stability and handling by keeping the vehicle flatter when subjected to these cornering forces. The stabiliser bar is essentially a type of torsion spring that reacts to the movement of the vehicle body independently of the suspension travel. The stabiliser bar is covered in more detail on page 442.

An alternative suspension set-up using helical springs and a solid rear axle can be seen in Figure 4.75. This type of suspension uses the beam as a type of torsion bar or stabiliser bar. These types are often called 'H' frame set-ups due to their shape.

The vehicle weight during cornering is transferred towards the outside of the corner causing the inner side of the vehicle to become lighter. The increase in body weight due to the cornering forces trying to push the vehicle towards the outside of the corner, compresses the outer spring and the movement of the vehicle body extends the inner spring. The weight transfer causes the rear axle beam to twist. The vehicle's body height is retained through the opposing force created by the twisting action of the torsion bar axle, this works in a similar way to the stabiliser bar.

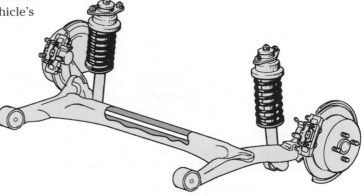

Figure 4.75 *Beam axle where beam functions as a torsion bar, sometimes called 'H' frame arrangement*

Figure 4.73 *Progressive rate helical/coil spring*

Torsion bar

This is a straight, circular or square section bar anchored to the chassis frame at one end, and connected by a lever or wishbone-shaped member to the wheel at the other end.

Figure 4.76 shows a torsion bar suspension system on a car. At each end of the bar, the diameter is increased and splines connect the bar with the levers. Adjustment is often provided at the frame end to 'level' the suspension.

Since the coil spring is a form of torsion bar, the rate of both springs is governed by the same factors – length and diameter. If the length is increased or the diameter is decreased, the rate will decrease (i.e. the spring will be softer).

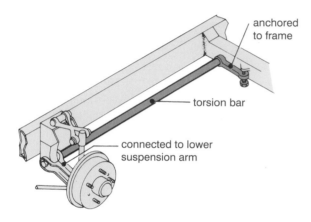

Figure 4.76 Torsion bar spring arrangement

Spring material

The material used for springs must be capable of withstanding high stresses and resisting fatigue. Early designs used high-carbon steel, but today low-percentage alloy steels, such as silico-manganese, are used.

4.10.2 Types and characteristics of rubber suspension

Rubber springs, loaded in compression or shear, can be used as the main suspension spring, or fitted in conjunction with metal springs to modify the suspension characteristics. Many suspension arrangements employ a large rubber 'bump' stop to stiffen the suspension spring at maximum deflection.

Much weight can be saved with this form of suspension because rubber can store more energy per unit mass than any other type of spring material.

Figure 4.77 is a simplified drawing of the rubber suspension system used on the original Mini. The spring is positioned between the frame and the top

link of the suspension system. By connecting the spring to a point near the link pivot, deflection of the spring can be reduced to a minimum without reducing the total wheel movement.

This design of spring gives a rising-rate characteristic (i.e. it is 'soft' for small wheel movements but becomes harder as the spring deflects).

The energy released from the spring after deflection is found to be considerably less than that imparted to it. This **hysteresis** is an advantage, since lower-duty dampers may be used.

Hysteresis: internal loss of energy that lags behind changes in the effect causing it.

Some rubber suspension systems have a tendency to 'settle down' or 'creep' during the initial stages of service and allowance must be made for this.

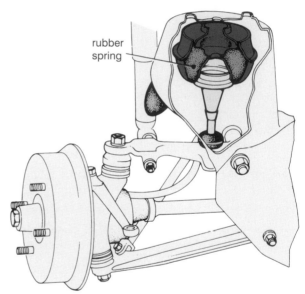

Figure 4.77 Rubber spring suspension

Hydrolastic suspension

This system is a development of the rubber-type suspension arrangement and is intended to improve the vehicle's resistance to pitch – the tendency of the body to oscillate in a fore-and-aft direction. This movement is produced if the front springs compress and the rear springs extend simultaneously. The continuous forward and backward pitching motion gives a most uncomfortable ride and this would be serious if the frequency of vibration of front and rear springs were the same.

The hydrolastic layout on a vehicle consists of rubber displacer units (Figure 4.78), which are interconnected and mounted between the frame and the independent suspension linkage controlling the wheel. The interconnection is made with two pipes;

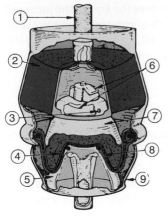

1 interconnecting pipe
2 rubber spring
3 damper bleed
4 butyl liner
5 dampered piston
6 damper valve
7 fluid separating member
8 rubber diaphragm
9 tapered cylinder

Figure 4.78 A hydrolastic displacer unit

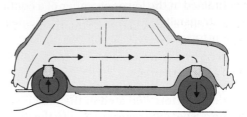
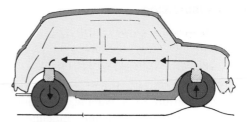

Figure 4.79 Action of hydrolastic units

one to link the left-hand side units together and the other to do a similar job on the right-hand side. The system is pressurised with a liquid (water + alcohol + anti-corrosive agent) after the air has been extracted.

Each displacer unit comprises a rubber spring, a metal separating member holding two rubber damper valves, a rubber diaphragm attached to the suspension linkage holding the wheel and a metal body, which is secured to the chassis of the vehicle.

Road irregularities normally tend to cause the vehicle to pitch, roll and bounce, so the operation of the system under these conditions will be considered.

Pitch

A sudden upward movement of the front wheel causes the diaphragm to displace the fluid through the damper. This action will, in turn, force fluid along the pipe to the rear unit where it will move the diaphragm and raise the rear of the vehicle to the level of the front (Figure 4.79). When the front wheel descends, the fluid is returned and the vehicle settles back in its normal riding position. During this sequence, the fluid has to pass the damper valve in each unit, so restriction to fluid flow at the valves and in the pipeline damps out the pitch oscillation tendency.

Roll

When a vehicle is cornering, centrifugal action causes the body of the vehicle to tilt or roll outwards and this action is apparent when 'soft' conventional springs are used. The hydrolastic system is 'soft' when a single wheel is moved, but if, as when cornering, the two outside suspension units are loaded, a stiffening of the system occurs. Under this type of loading fluid is not displaced from one unit to the other. Instead, the increased fluid pressure deflects the rubber springs and these provide a marked resistance to the roll of the body.

Bounce

This is a condition that causes the four wheels to deflect at the same time, so all the hydrolastic units will perform similarly to the outer units when they were reacting to roll.

4.10.3 Pneumatic suspension

Hydro-pneumatic suspension

This system differs from the normal metal/spring suspension in a number of ways. One main difference is that the suspension unit is supported by a mass of gas, which remains constant irrespective of the load carried by the wheel.

Gas pressure increases progressively as the volume is reduced and this desirable feature means that the suspension stiffens as the load on the wheel increases.

Furthermore, if the suspension is compressed even more, the gas will form a progressive rate spring as it will stiffen when a greater load is exerted upon it. This creates a spring stiffness in direct relation with the load input through the road wheels. Figure 4.80 shows the basic principle of a hydro-pneumatic system.

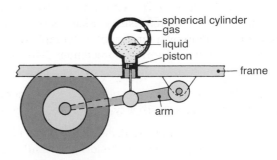

Figure 4.80 A hydro-pneumatic suspension system

Liquid contained in the lower chamber of a container is used to transmit the force from the suspension piston to nitrogen gas, which is stored in the upper chamber of the container. Between the upper and lower chambers is a strong rubber diaphragm, this ensures that the fluid and gas are kept separate and also transfers the force created in the fluid chamber through the suspension compression to the chamber filled with gas.

Hydragas suspension

This system has been developed from the hydrolastic type of suspension, the main difference being that the rubber spring is replaced by a pneumatic spring.

Figure 4.81 shows the layout of one of the four hydragas units fitted to a vehicle. The units are interconnected in pairs by a fluid pipeline, which links the front unit with the same-side rear unit. This line equalises the liquid fluid pressure in the two units to reduce the fore-and-aft pitching motion, which is most noticeable on short-wheelbase vehicles.

The unit consists of three main parts: a nitrogen gas spring; a fluid displacer; and a damper valve block. Bump movement of the wheel suspension arm deflects the diaphragm and pressurises the fluid. If the pressure in the other displacer unit and interconnecting pipe is similar, then the fluid will not flow through to the other displacer, but it will flow through the bump valve in the damper valve block into the chamber. The pressurised fluid acts on the diaphragm causing the gas to be compressed. Compressing the gas creates a resistance to the suspension arm movement, and this resistance progressively increases the more the gas is compressed. On rebound, the fluid flows in the opposite direction through the rebound valve in the damper valve block. Energy, which causes the spring to oscillate, is absorbed as the fluid is passed through the damper.

The action of the interconnecting fluid lines in relation to pitch, roll and bounce is similar to that of the hydrolastic system.

Citroën system

This pneumatic spring system has a hydraulic control, which not only allows the driver to adjust the ground clearance of the vehicle, but also maintains this set clearance irrespective of the load carried. Figure 4.82 shows the layout of a system similar to that used by

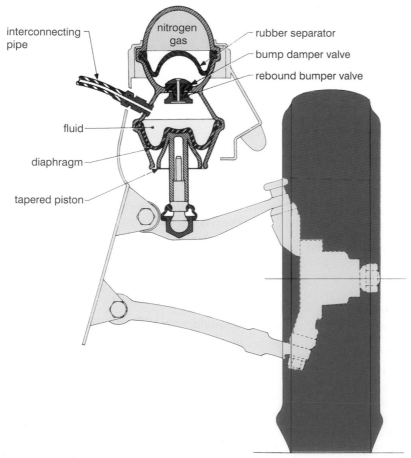

Figure 4.81 Hydragas suspension

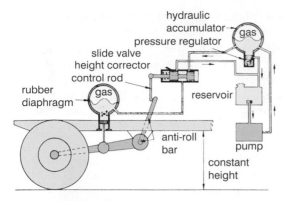

Figure 4.82 Layout of hydro-pneumatic suspension system

Citroën. Each wheel is mounted on a suspension arm, which is supported by a pneumatic spring. Connected transversely, between the suspension arms at the front and rear, are anti-roll bars, and these are linked to height correctors by means of control rods. An engine-driven pump supplies oil under pressure to a hydraulic accumulator and this is connected to the height control or levelling valves.

As the vehicle is loaded, the downward movement of the vehicle structure causes rotation of the anti-roll bar. This moves the slide valve and uncovers the supply port to allow oil to flow from the accumulator to the suspension cylinders. When the vehicle reaches a predetermined height, which can be varied by a selector inside the car, the anti-roll bar and control rod move the slide valve back to the 'neutral' position. A decrease in load gives a similar sequence except that valve movement causes the oil in the suspension cylinder to be discharged back to the reservoir.

A delay device or dashpot is incorporated in the height corrector valve to prevent rapid oil flow past the valve when the wheel contacts a bump or dip in the road. Without this dashpot, sudden movements of the wheel would mean that the valve is continually working and this would give an unsatisfactory operation.

Damping is provided by partially separating the oil in the spherical chamber from the cylinder in which the piston slides. Small holes, closed by disc-type valves, allow the oil to flow to and from the cylinder and sphere in a manner similar to other hydraulic dampers.

In the Citroën application, the hydraulic pressure is also used for power assistance in steering, braking and gear changing. One model employs a braking system with independent front and rear brake circuits, interconnected with the hydraulic suspension system. This arrangement proportions the effort applied at each brake to the load carried by the wheel.

Air suspension

The full air-suspension system is designed to ensure that the vehicle maintains the correct ride height at all times, regardless of road conditions or load. The system has an air spring fitted at each wheel to provide full independent control. In many cases, the air-suspension system will incorporate a facility for the driver to alter the ride height of the vehicle for different driving conditions, such as a raised ride height for off-road driving and a low ride height for easier access. While the vehicle is in motion, the system will automatically alter the ride height to maintain the appropriate level and also improve road-handling dynamics. During constant driving on a motorway at speeds over 60 mph, many systems will lower the ride height of the vehicle to improve aerodynamics and stability.

When the vehicle is in a cornering or heavy braking situation, the adjustment of the ride height will be disabled for safety reasons. This avoids any sudden disturbance of the vehicle that could cause the driver to lose control or the vehicle to be unresponsive. The ride height changes are also disabled if a vehicle door is opened to avoid possible damage, for example, by the door being caught on a stationary object, such as a wall, as the vehicle ride height is dropped.

The air-suspension system described in this section is based on a system used on a Range Rover. It is a fully electronically controlled system with many functions allowing excellent ability off-road and also providing comfort and good road holding for on-road driving. The system uses height sensors at each corner of the vehicle to monitor the ride height at all times. The air-suspension ECU also has the ability to self-monitor the system and provide 'health checks' to make sure all functions are operating correctly. If the system detects a fault with any component or sensor reading, the ECU will notify the driver through a warning lamp on the driver's display. This can then be investigated by a technician through the use of special diagnostic equipment.

This system described utilises fully independent front and rear suspension, which is able to offer better ride characteristics when compared with live axle arrangements seen on earlier vehicles.

Air-suspension system used on a Range Rover

Front and rear suspension

The independent front and rear suspension offers a reduction of unsprung mass over the conventional beam axle design. The suspension geometry features positive ground-level offset for improved control under braking. The suspension arms have been designed for maximum ground clearance. Suspension geometry on the front can be adjusted via the strut

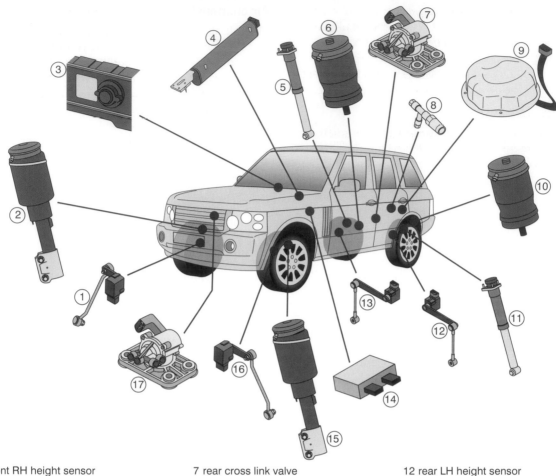

Figure 4.83 Air-suspension system used on a Range Rover

1 front RH height sensor	7 rear cross link valve	12 rear LH height sensor
2 front RH strut assembly	8 external pressure relief valve (where	13 rear RH height sensor
3 air-suspension control switch	fitted)	14 air-suspension ECU
4 reservoir and valve block	9 compressor	15 front LH strut assembly
5 rear RH damper	10 rear LH air spring	16 front LH height sensor
6 rear RH air spring	11 rear LH damper	17 front cross-link valve

top mount for camber and on the steering rack track rod ends for toe-in. At the back, the camber and toe can be adjusted via eccentric bolts.

The air suspension comprises:

- air springs
- two cross-link valves
- cross-link valve assembly
- air reservoir, pressure sensor and valve block and pump
- height sensors
- air-suspension ECU
- air supply pipes
- external pressure-relief valve
- air-suspension fascia control switch.

Air springs

Each air spring has a top plate assembly, an airbag and a base piston. The airbag is made from a flexible rubber material, which allows the bag to expand with air pressure and deform under load.

1 cover
2 seal plate
3 nut
4 front air spring
5 air hose connector
6 rear air spring

Figure 4.84 Air spring assembly

On the side of the top cap is a connector that allows for the attachment of the air hose from the cross-link valve. The piston is made from plastic and is shaped to allow the airbag to roll over its outer diameter. The base of the piston has a splined stud in the centre for correct positioning of the air spring into the lower wishbone.

Two cross-link valves

The cross-link valves comprise a single large solenoid valve with connections to the LH and RH air springs, and also connections for each air spring from the reservoir mounted valve block. The solenoid-operated valve is controlled by the air-suspension ECU. When the solenoid is energised, the cross-link valve connects the two air springs together, allowing air to flow between them if required. This provides additional articulation of the suspension improving the off-road capabilities of the vehicle and an improvement in low-speed ride comfort. The air-suspension ECU senses that the vehicle is off-road by comparing rapid changes in signals from the height sensors. The operation of the cross-link valves is fully automatic, requiring no driver intervention.

Air reservoir, pressure sensor and valve block and pump

The unit comprises a piston compressor, a 12V electric motor, a solenoid-operated exhaust valve, a pressure-relief valve and an air dryer unit to ensure that no moisture enters the system. The electric motor, compressor, air dryer and pressure-limiting and exhaust valve are mounted on flexible rubber mountings to reduce operating noise.

1 electrical connector
2 RH air spring supply/return
3 RH air spring supply/return from valve block
4 cross-link valve body
5 LH air spring supply/return
6 LH air spring supply/return from valve block

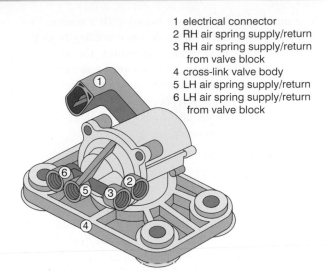

Figure 4.85 Cross-link valve assembly

The reservoir supplies pressurised air to the four air springs via the valve block to enable the air-suspension system to carry out ride height changes. The reservoir is a large aluminium tank, which holds the air required to adjust the volume of air in the system. This is monitored for pressure by a sensor located in the reservoir so that the pump does not add too much air, which would cause damage.

Height sensors

A height sensor is fitted in each corner of the vehicle to monitor the ride height of the vehicle. These are mounted on the front and rear sub-frames, with a mechanical link to the suspension lower arms.

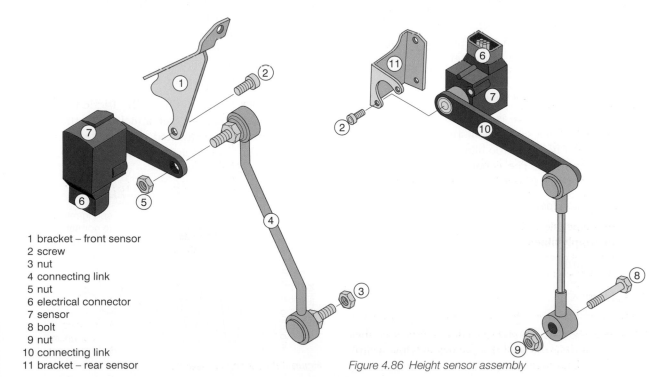

1 bracket – front sensor
2 screw
3 nut
4 connecting link
5 nut
6 electrical connector
7 sensor
8 bolt
9 nut
10 connecting link
11 bracket – rear sensor

Figure 4.86 Height sensor assembly

The units contain a circuit board with a sensor. The sensor is supplied with a reference voltage from the air-suspension ECU, which measures the returned voltage to determine the sensor arm position. Therefore, when the suspension changes height the return voltage changes proportionally, so the ECU then understands the current vehicle height and can make changes if required.

Air-suspension ECU

The air-suspension ECU monitors vehicle ride height via the four height sensors. Under normal operation, the ECU will monitor ride height of the vehicle through receiving information from the height sensors and driver demands. Under continued cruising conditions, the ECU will even lower the vehicle approximately 20 mm for improved aerodynamics and a lower centre of gravity for improved handling. During off-road conditions, the driver will request the ECU raises the vehicle for improved ground clearance by operating the air pump, opening the valve block and filling the air springs with air until the height sensors note the required vehicle height has been achieved. At this point the valve block will close to prevent any more air entering the air springs. When the vehicle then returns to normal road conditions and speeds, the system will exhaust air from the air springs to bring the vehicle back down to its normal height. The system can also lower the vehicle right down on to its bump stops if requested, to allow passengers to exit or enter the vehicle with greater ease.

This system is very flexible and provides excellent capability for off-road and normal road vehicles.

Air-supply pipes

The system uses interconnected nylon pipes to connect the components together. Routing of these pipes is very important to avoid failure of the system.

External pressure-relief valve

An external relief valve is fitted to the system as a safety device. This component relieves pressure in the system if it becomes too high, thus protecting the major components. The general pressures this unit operates at are 12–13 bar (176–191 psi).

Air-suspension fascia control switch

The air-suspension ECU is able to provide four different ride heights on the Range Rover:

- Standard
- Off-road
- Motorway
- Access

The ride heights are selected via the rotary control switch. Rotating the switch upwards or downwards selects a different ride height. The centre of the rotary

switch contains the 'hold' switch. This prevents the air-suspension ECU from automatically changing from the currently selected ride height, and prevents the user selecting a new ride height.

4.11 The damper

4.11.1 Purpose of a damper

When the wheel strikes a bump, energy is given to the spring via the suspension units and road wheel, this is then deflected. When the bump is passed, the road wheel tries to return back to its original position rebounding or releasing the stored energy. This will carry the spring past the normal position to set up an oscillating motion. This action is similar to the movement of a pendulum – a freely suspended pendulum will oscillate for a considerable time after being struck. Anything made from a springy type of material, such as rubber, will respond in the same way.

Think of a football being dropped from height. It will continue to bounce for some time and each time it hits the ground it absorbs energy and then releases it again as it bounces back into the air. This will continue until the football has released all of its energy. To stop these oscillations you could place a hand over it to prevent it gaining height and then falling to the ground. As the energy of the football is absorbed into the hand the bouncing ceases.

Similarly, in order to give a comfortable ride in today's vehicles, a device must be fitted to absorb the energy stored in the spring and so reduce the number of oscillations occurring between the initial bump and the return of the spring to the rest position. This is the function performed by the damper (often misleadingly called a shock absorber).

Early damper designs utilised the friction between two sets of plates, one set attached to the frame and the other set connected to the axle. This type converted the 'spring' energy to heat.

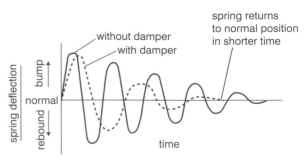

Figure 4.87 Spring oscillation curves

4.11.2 Hydraulic dampers

Today, the main type of damper used is the hydraulic tubular damper. This dissipates the energy by pumping oil through small orifices. Resistance of the hydraulic damper, due to the oil flowing through the orifices, increases as the speed of spring deflection increases, whereas the earlier friction damper gave a constant resistance. The resistance to spring movement can apply to the rebound stroke only (single-acting), or to both the bump and rebound strokes (double-acting). Alternatively, it can offer a differential action by resisting both strokes but exerting a greater action on the rebound.

There are two main types of hydraulic damper:

1 Lever – used in earlier vehicles
2 Direct acting (telescopic)

Lever type

Figure 4.88 shows a diagrammatic view of a lever-type damper, which is mounted to the vehicle frame and connected by a lever and link to the axle. The horizontal cylinder contains two pistons, which are fitted with recuperator and pressure valves. A thin, mineral-base damper oil is introduced to the level of the bottom of the filler plug.

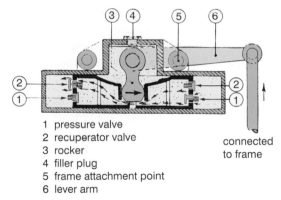

1 pressure valve
2 recuperator valve
3 rocker
4 filler plug
5 frame attachment point
6 lever arm

connected to frame

Figure 4.88 A lever-type damper

Bump movement of the axle operates the damper pistons and displaces oil from one chamber to the other. Oil exerts pressure to open the pressure valve, flows through an orifice to provide resistance, and passes through the open recuperator valve to break down the depression created in the other chamber. Rebound of the spring produces a similar action in the opposite direction.

The actual damper differs from Figure 4.88 in various ways – the valve construction and position are different, and in some designs the cylinders are mounted vertically.

Telescopic direct-acting type

As the name suggests, this type of damper is directly connected between the body and the suspension member that moves with the road wheel.

It is made either as a separate bolt-on unit or as an integral part of a suspension system. Direct-acting dampers are made in two basic forms: single-tube and twin-tube.

Single-tube damper

The operating cylinder is a single tube, closed at the bottom end by a cap, which is attached to an eye or stem for connection to the moving part of the suspension. A piston fitted with two-way reed valves slides in this tube, which covers a series of holes through which oil can pass. The piston is attached to a rod that passes through a guide retained in the top of the tube. The rod is attached to the vehicle body and rubber bushes at the attachment points isolate road shocks and allow for slight angular movement of the damper body. A rubber seal, held in place by fluid pressure, is positioned adjacent to the guide to prevent the escape of fluid. An abutment plate fitted to the piston to limit the stroke provides a flat surface for contact with the top seal when the damper is fully extended. A tubular shield, attached to the rod member, is fitted to protect the rod from dirt and stone damage.

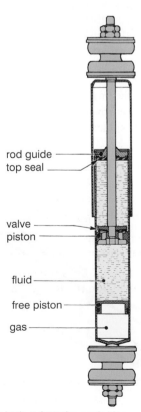

rod guide
top seal

valve
piston

fluid

free piston

gas

Figure 4.89 A single-tube telescopic damper

A chamber at the base of the damper, sealed by a free piston, contains a quantity of inert gas. When the damper is completely filled with thin-type mineral oil, this gas is in a compressed state.

On the bump stroke, the inner movement of the piston displaces oil from the bottom to the top chamber. The energy needed to pump the oil through the drillings and deflect the piston valves provides the damping action. By varying the size of the 'bump' and 'rebound' orifices, the resistance of each stroke can be altered to suit the requirement.

For a given downward movement of the piston, the volume available for the oil in the upper chamber is less than that required by the oil, so when this action occurs the free piston moves slightly downwards.

The single-tube construction has a number of merits: it can displace a large quantity of fluid without fluid aeration or noise and be consistent in service even when installed at a large angle to the main suspension movement. The potential energy stored in a deflected suspension spring is converted into heat by a damper, so with this design good heat dissipation from the damper to the airflow is achieved.

Denting of the single working tube by stones must be avoided, so this is a good reason for placing the damper at the centre of the helical suspension spring.

On MacPherson suspension systems (page 441), a single-tube, gas-pressurised damper is used as a main suspension 'leg'. In this application, a more robust rod guide is fitted to enable it to act as a top bearing to accommodate steering movement.

Twin-tube damper

An extra tube is used on this type to form both a reservoir for the fluid and an overflow region to accommodate fluid due to rod displacement and expansion.

The base valve at the bottom of the working chamber has three duties to perform: it controls the outward flow of fluid into the reservoir during the 'bump' movement, the fluid return on the 'rebound' stroke, and the bleed leakage for reducing the damper's resistance during slow-speed suspension movements.

The life of a direct-acting damper depends on its fluid-sealing ability, so great attention is paid to the design of bearing and seal. The hard chrome-surfaced piston rod works in a sintered iron guide bearing, which is lubricated by a small amount of fluid forced through the bearing on each stroke. A multi-lipped rubber seal placed on the outside of the bearing cuts the fluid off the rod and returns it to the reservoir.

Baffles in the reservoir prevent violent movement of the fluid, which would otherwise cause aeration. Any fluid in an aerated state that is allowed to enter the working chamber would render the damper ineffective, so for extra protection a fluid containing special anti-foam additives is used.

Baffle: something that restricts the movement of fluid in a system.

The long stroke of a direct-acting damper allows the working pressure to be much lower than the lever-type damper. In view of this, the direct-acting type is more reliable, and is also cheaper to manufacture.

Although the best performance is achieved when the dampers are mounted vertically, many suspension layouts in use today, especially those used to support a live rear axle, have the dampers set 'diagonally' to improve the stability of the suspension.

Dampers do not offer any resistance to slow-speed body roll, because the inherent bleed feature in the damper allows this movement to take place. High-speed roll is resisted, but manufacturers generally fit

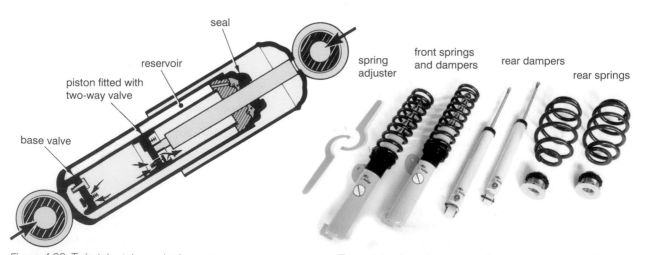

Figure 4.90 Twin-tube telescopic damper

seal
reservoir
piston fitted with two-way valve
base valve

spring adjuster
front springs and dampers
rear dampers
rear springs

Figure 4.91 A performance coil-over damper assembly

a transverse stabiliser, often called an anti-roll bar, to control the roll motion.

Some performance vehicles and track vehicles are fitted with a unit that incorporates the damper and helical spring. These are usually called 'coil-over' dampers and are often made from aluminium to lower the weight of the suspension system and improve the unsprung weight characteristics. These units are also fitted with an adjustment facility for the dampers and springs to fine-tune the behaviour of the suspension for different driving styles and road conditions. Many of these dampers have over 16 positions for the dampers, allowing for a very wide range of conditions. Spring rates and vehicle ride heights can be changed by raising or lowering the spring seat on the unit using a special shaped spanner.

Although sophisticated equipment for oscillating the dampers to test their operation is available, most manufacturers recommend the simple test carried out by pressing down with your hand on the corner of the car. By noting the number of oscillations made by the spring for the body to come to rest, the effectiveness of the dampers can be ascertained.

4.11.3 Magnetic ride dampers

Dampers have continually evolved to provide improved performance and vehicle control. Dampers designed to perform in high-speed conditions often give a hard ride due to the roll stiffness and the damper rates increasing. This would not normally be suitable for everyday driving so a compromise between vehicle handling and driver/passenger comfort has to reached.

Some manufacturers have started to use a new form of damping technology – magnetic ride dampers. This system has been developed to resolve the balance between comfort and performance driving dynamics. This new system continually adapts itself to the road and driver inputs. These inputs include steering, braking, gear-changing speeds, road speeds and vehicle roll and yaw. This alteration to the damper settings happens within an extremely short period of time (approximately 5–6 milliseconds). The regular oil-filled damper contains a specific grade of oil; however magnetic ride dampers contain special fluid called **magnetorheological fluid**.

Magnetorheological fluid: a synthetic hydrocarbon oil in which is suspended microscopic magnetic particles measuring between 3 and 10 microns.

When the driving conditions require damper stiffness to be altered, the control unit provides a voltage to a small coil in the damper. This creates a magnetic field in the magnetorheological fluid, aligning the magnetic particles. The particles lined up across the damper body provide a restrictive channel for the fluid to pass through the piston channels. This restriction will cause the damper stiffness rate to rise, altering the dynamics of the vehicle. This process takes place much quicker than in a normal mechanical adaptive damper.

Figure 4.92 shows the magnetic ride operation. When the tiny iron particles are subjected to the magnetic field, they are aligned in the direction of the magnetic flux. Due to the positioning of the electromagnetic coil in the damper, the damper fluid and iron particles are energised to provide a magnetic flux that runs exactly transversely to the inlet ports in the damper piston. When the damper piston moves, the aligned iron particles create flow resistance in the flowing suspension fluid providing an increase in damper rate.

By adding more current to the electromagnetic field, the rate of the damper will increase due to the resistance of the fluid increasing. The energy is controlled in relation to driving dynamics and impulses from the road. This means that for every road situation, optimal damping power is available. This damping power produces a more comfortable feel or sportier vehicle handling.

The magnetic ride dampers can provide many different levels of damping, leading to changes to the vehicle handling. The control unit for the dampers receives signals from many areas around the vehicle to constantly analyse the current vehicle situation. The driver is able to select at least two modes of operation: 'normal' for usual driving conditions and 'sport' via a switch mounted in the driving compartment.

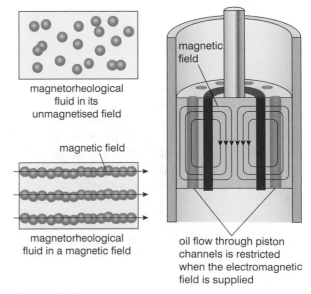

magnetorheological fluid in its unmagnetised field

magnetic field

magnetorheological fluid in a magnetic field

magnetic field

oil flow through piston channels is restricted when the electromagnetic field is supplied

Figure 4.92 Magnetic ride damper operation

When the vehicle's dampers are placed in the 'normal' setting, the fluid is more viscous and the degree of damping less pronounced. The vehicle will generally act in the usual way with adequately controlled body roll and pitch. It will feel like a well set-up, comfortable suspension system. This setting is ideal for day-to-day driving.

When the vehicle dampers are placed in the 'sport' mode, the fluid becomes less viscous. This change in viscosity provides a suspension system with very firm characteristics, leading to improved body control and grip. The body movements are restricted from the very moment the steering is turned into a corner, leading to a much more settled vehicle through the turn. This setting provides a very stable condition at each road wheel, which results in improved driver feel for the road surface.

Magnetic ride dampers do not have any moving parts, unlike regular mechanically activated dampers. This benefits the operational speed of the system to a near instantaneous response. The damping rate is directly proportional to the current applied to the electromagnet, so it can be adjusted extremely easily and quickly by the control system. This means the magnetorheological dampers respond almost in real time with great sensitivity to impulses from the road, allowing the greatest possible driving dynamics and maximum comfort.

4.12 Rigid axle suspension

4.12.1 Advantages and disadvantages of rigid axle arrangements

The rigid axle arrangement is one of the simplest forms of construction to connect left- and right-hand road wheels together and to allow them to move with the suspension system. Due to this arrangement being so simple, it has some key advantages still used by manufacturers today:

- Number of components is low due to the simplicity of the arrangement
- Requires little service maintenance
- The constructional strength of the axle can be made high by increasing the gauge of the materials, this leads to this type of arrangement being suitable for large heavy goods vehicles
- As the axle moves, the wheels alter their alignment accordingly providing low tyre wear

It can be seen, therefore, that the rigid axle has some key advantages, making it suitable for a large number of light and heavy commercial vehicles. However, the rigid axle does have some limitations:

- As the weight of the axle is high, the suspension system has to be able to cope with this weight resulting in a greater unsprung weight.
- When one wheel hits a bump in the road, the opposite wheel will react in the opposite direction leading to an unsettled ride.

4.12.2 General construction and applications of a rigid axle

Rigid axles were once common in a large number of passenger vehicles, but now with the improvements of independent suspension systems they are no longer used. Light and heavy commercial vehicles still utilise this arrangement as it provides a strong positive axle arrangement.

Where the rigid axle is used on the rear of a commercial vehicle it normally incorporates a final-drive unit and drive shafts to power the rear wheels. These are called live axles. If the rigid axle does not contain any drive units, it is called a dead axle.

Springs and axle location

Rigid axles were normally fitted with heavy leaf spring arrangements across light and heavy vehicles. Some commercial type vehicles still use this arrangement. The leaf spring also acts as a linkage for the suspension to the axle casing. Additional suspension control linkages are not normally fitted to axles with leaf springs as they provide good resistance to braking and acceleration forces.

Today, vehicles with rigid axles generally use coil spring or air-suspension systems as these provide greater vehicle control and handling dynamics. Some four-wheel drive vehicles still use rigid front and rear axles. When this is the case, there is a need to control wheel movement through the use of leading and trailing arms connecting the axle to the vehicle body. This arrangement offers benefits over leaf springs, such as improved ride quality due to the coil or air springs purely controlling the weight of the vehicle. The axle is prevented from moving from side to side during cornering and torque transfer by the addition of a Panhard rod.

Front-wheel drive vehicles often have an adaptation of the rigid rear axle but use coil springs or a torsion bar arrangement. Figure 4.93 shows a typical rigid rear axle, which has trailing arms locating the axle to the vehicle body.

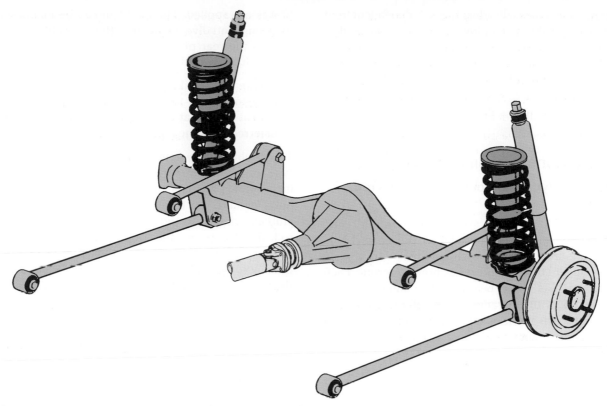

Figure 4.93 Rear axle using coil springs and with leading arm for axle location

4.13 Independent front suspension

4.13.1 Disadvantages of beam axles

In order to appreciate the advantages of independent suspension, you should consider the disadvantages of the beam axle:

1 Small maximum spring deflection, therefore 'hard' springing, vertical axle movement is limited by the clearance between the axle and the engine.

2 Steering geometry is not accurately controlled:
   a Figure 4.94a shows the alteration to camber angle that occurs when one wheel strikes a bump. Sudden changes in camber angle cause the wheels, which are acting as a form of gyroscope, to 'flap' around the kingpin. (This fault is known as wheel shimmy.)
   b Figure 4.94b shows the difference in caster angle when the spring is deflected.

3 High unsprung weight – maximum wheel adhesion is not obtained.

4 The engine normally has to be situated behind the axle to give clearance. If the engine can be moved forward, it may be possible to accommodate all the passengers within the wheelbase – this gives greater comfort.

5 Poor 'roll stiffness' at the front tends to produce oversteer – the front springs have to be mounted close together.

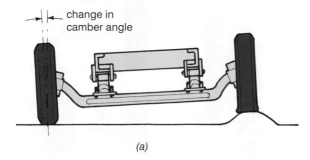

(a)

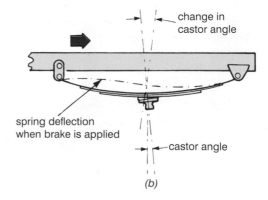

(b)

Figure 4.94 Steering geometry alterations

To overcome these disadvantages, independent front suspension (IFS) is employed. This term is used to describe any system for connecting the wheels to the frame in which the movement of one wheel has no effect on the other wheel.

Many types of IFS have been used in the past, but now most designs fall under the heading of transverse link system.

4.13.2 Transverse link system

Wishbone type and double-link/radius rod types

The main details of this system are shown in Figure 4.95. Two links, often parallel in the normal ride position, are made in a wishbone shape to provide fore-and-aft stiffness and resist braking torque. Each wishbone has three bearings: two inner bearings connecting with the frame and an outer one attaching to the stub wishbone, and the upper end to a point on the frame just above the upper wishbone.

Because the lower wishbone pivot points on the link-type system are normally set parallel to the road, the front of the car 'dives' towards the ground when the brakes are applied. This problem can be minimised by using anti-dive geometry; this is achieved by placing the rear pivot point of the lower wishbone higher than the front pivot.

When the front brakes are applied, the action of the braking torque on the inclined wishbone generates a vertical force that counterbalances the extra load transferred from the rear to the front wheels.

The double-link system (Figure 4.96) and wishbone type are similar in some ways, but the double link incorporates a simpler wishbone construction. Two links, mounted in the normal manner, connect the stub axle carrier to the frame. A semi-trailing radius rod, fitted between the lower link and the frame/chassis, resists longitudinal dynamic loads and braking torque. The spring can be positioned above the top axle carrier. Rubber or plastic (PTFE) bushes are fitted at the inner ends of the wishbone, and in many cases a ball joint at the outer end enables the stub axle to swivel. Springing can be provided by using coil springs in the position shown or above the upper wishbone, or a torsion bar at points A or B (Figure 4.95).

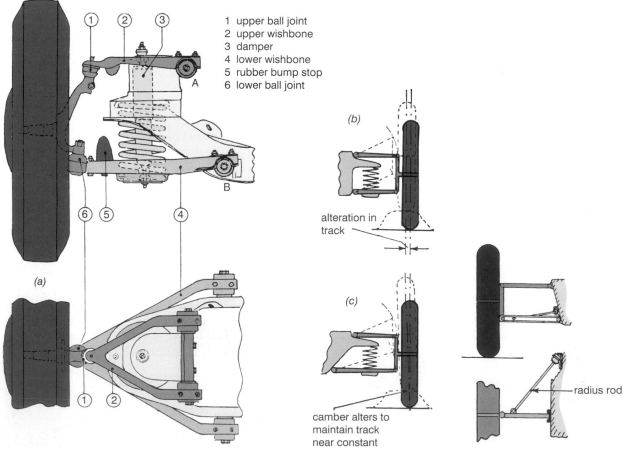

1 upper ball joint
2 upper wishbone
3 damper
4 lower wishbone
5 rubber bump stop
6 lower ball joint

(a)

(b)

alteration in track

(c)

camber alters to maintain track near constant

radius rod

Figure 4.95 Transverse link system – wishbone type

Figure 4.96 Double-link and radius rod

As with the full wishbone systems, early designs used wishbones of equal length, but the track variation (Figure 4.95b) caused considerable tyre wear although the camber remains unchanged. Track variation can be reduced by using wishbones of unequal length, the longer one at the bottom (Figure 4.95c). Now the camber angle changes to negative on bump and cornering, which can improve stability but will also increase tyre wear slightly.

A constant caster angle is achieved with this design by mounting the top wishbone slightly behind the lower one.

In order to obtain the maximum wishbone length without restricting engine space, the wishbone axis is sometimes inclined towards the rear.

Either a piston-type damper is mounted to incorporate the inner bearings for the top wishbone, or a telescopic damper is fitted in the centre of the coil spring. In cases where torsion bar springing is used, a large movement of the telescopic damper can be achieved by mounting the damper diagonally: the lower end is connected to the outer end of the lower link, or a torsion bar can be connected to the inner ends of the lower link.

MacPherson type

Figures 4.96 and 4.97 shows the main details of this type of suspension. A long telescopic tube incorporating the damper is pivoted at the top end and rigidly connected to the stub axle at the lower end. Track control is maintained by a single transverse link, attached to the chassis by rubber or nylon bushes and connected to the stub axle by a ball joint. The coil spring is located between the fixed and floating suspension members. Both front suspension lower links are interconnected by a stabiliser bar, which also provides the required fore-and-aft stiffness.

In early designs, the caster, camber and swivel-axis inclination was usually set in production and could not be altered. However, today, with modern suspension set-ups and the need for improved road holding and handling, suspension systems often incorporate many adjustments on front and rear wheels. Adjustment of these systems should be done with accurate calibrated equipment to ensure optimum results are achieved.

The swivel-axis inclination is the angle formed between the vertical and the line taken from the centre of the strut thrust bearing to the centre of the ball joint, which connects the strut to the track control arm. For tyre clearance purposes, the strut is set to a smaller angle than the swivel-axis inclination.

Setting the top of the strut towards the vehicle centre allows the manufacturer to obtain the advantages of a negative offset (negative scrub radius) for the steering.

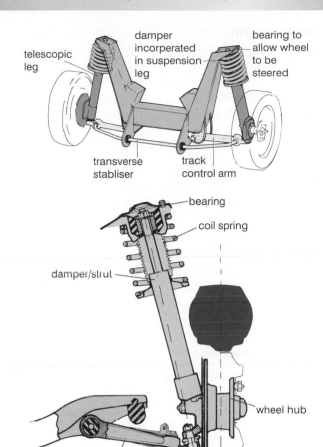

Figure 4.96

Figure 4.97 The MacPherson strut arrangement

Swinging arm

Two leading or trailing arms of equal length (i.e. longitudinally mounted links), are connected between the frame and the stub axle carrier. The spring can be mounted above the top arm or a torsion bar may be connected to the arm at the frame location point (Figure 4.98).

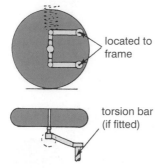

located to frame

torsion bar (if fitted)

Figure 4.98 Swinging arm arrangement

Track-rod linkages

The one-piece track rod used with beam axle layouts is unsuitable for the majority of IFS systems because wheel alignment would be altered if one wheel was deflected up or down. The stub axle carrier in many IFS systems moves in an arc, so in order to eliminate misalignment, the track rod connection must move in a similar arc. This condition can be met by using a three-piece track rod similar to the types shown in Figure 4.99.

Adjustment of the rack-and-pinion system is provided on both outer track rods. When resetting the wheel alignment, it is necessary to adjust each rod an equal amount and use accurate calibrated equipment.

Unequal adjustment of the track rods results in:

- incorrect steering wheel alignment
- one steering lock being greater than the other
- incorrect toe-out on turns.

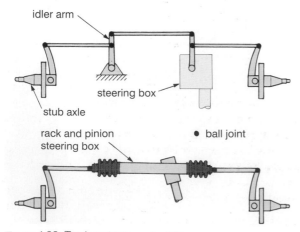

idler arm

steering box

stub axle

rack and pinion steering box

• ball joint

Figure 4.99 Track-rod linkage for IFS

Anti-roll bar or stabiliser bar

The anti-roll bar is fitted to the vehicle's suspension system to limit the amount of body roll the vehicle has during cornering. On independent suspension systems, the anti-roll bar normally connects the left and right-hand suspension units together. It is usually connected to the lower suspension arms and the vehicle body or sub-frame. The roll bar has bushes linking it to the vehicle body to allow it to twist freely. As the vehicle goes round a corner, the vehicle weight will transfer to the outside wheels causing the body to roll. The anti-roll bar counters this roll by the twisting action of the bar acting on the vehicle body and suspension on the opposite side and tries to pull the body down limiting the roll condition. Figures 4.100 and 4.101 show this action with the right- and left-hand side of the bar producing a counteraction when one side is deflected through body roll.

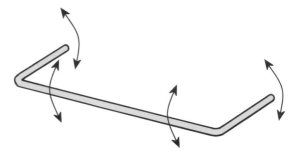

Figure 4.100 Anti-roll/stabiliser bar

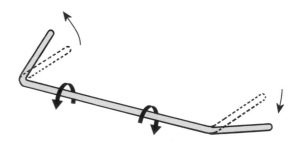

Figure 4.101 Anti-roll/stabiliser bar effect

The anti-roll bar will not alter the suspension stiffness as when the left and right suspension units go up and down the roll bar is free to rotate and is not subjected to torsional twisting. When the vehicle corners, the weight on the outer side of the vehicle will cause the spring to compress and the inner spring will expand as the vehicle body rises. This action will cause the anti-roll bar to twist in opposite directions. This twisting creates energy within the anti-roll bar, which is subjected to the opposite side suspension unit. As this opposite reaction is transferred to the suspension unit, it pulls the body back down on to the suspension spring leading to lower roll. Anti-roll bars are usually made from heat-treated solid steel. This material is very resistant to fatigue and maintains its shape when stressed. Many manufacturers are now making these roll bars from hollow steel, which is giving the same characteristics but the weight is greatly reduced. Stiffness of the bar is governed by the diameter of the bar and the length of the arms connected to the lower suspension points.

4.14 Independent rear suspension

4.14.1 Advantages of independent rear suspension

Many of the advantages of IFS apply to independent rear suspension (IRS), but the most important item is the reduction of unsprung weight. The final-drive unit and the brakes are the heaviest items so if 'inboard' brakes are fitted to a frame-mounted final drive, as much as 50 per cent reduction in unsprung weight can be achieved.

Many of today's vehicles are front-wheel drive. Although many of the suspension systems described in this section feature final drive, many of these systems also apply to front-wheel and four-wheel drive layouts.

The similarity between IRS and the de-Dion drive often makes it difficult to draw a dividing line, but if the definition of independent suspension is remembered, a division can be made. In general terms, any suspension system that connects the wheels to the chassis or body and has independent movement from all other wheels on the vehicle is said to be independent.

4.14.2 Types of IRS

Parallel link system

Two wishbone-shaped links, mounted transversely, connect the wheels to a backbone-type frame (Figure 4.102a). Springing is provided by longitudinally mounted torsion bars, which connect with the lower wishbone. Modern vehicles now tend to use coil springs in these arrangements. The coil springs are fitted between the wishbone and vehicle body. On rear-wheel drive arrangements, the drive is transmitted from the final-drive unit through CV joints, which form part of the drive shafts.

Swinging arm

An alternative method of mounting the wheels is provided by the trailing arm system shown in Figure 4.102b. A spring, mounted as shown, or a torsion bar, acting at the pivot, may be used. One popular light car used to use a rubber spring instead of the normal metal type shown.

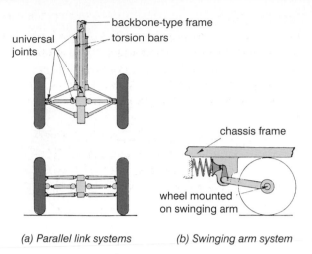

(a) Parallel link systems   *(b) Swinging arm system*

Figure 4.102 IRS

Swinging half-axles

This system consists of two axle tubes, which are jointed to the final-drive housing to allow the wheel to rise or fall (Figure 4.103). To allow for the change in drive angle, universal joints are fitted at the centre of each axle joint.

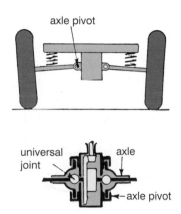

Figure 4.103 Swinging half-axles

Transverse link and coil springs

An arrangement similar to that shown in Figure 4.104 was used for many years on Jaguar cars. The road wheel is located in the transverse plane by a tubular suspension link at the bottom and a drive shaft at the top. Non-plunge universal joints are fitted at each end of the drive shaft to allow for shaft movement. The diagram shown shows how old wire wheels were fitted to the drive shafts using splines and centre knock-on wheel nuts. Later vehicles used conventional wheel stud arrangements seen today, so would have different hub arrangements.

Longitudinal stiffness and driving thrust duties are performed by a longitudinally mounted radius arm, which connects the wheel end of the link to the vehicle body.

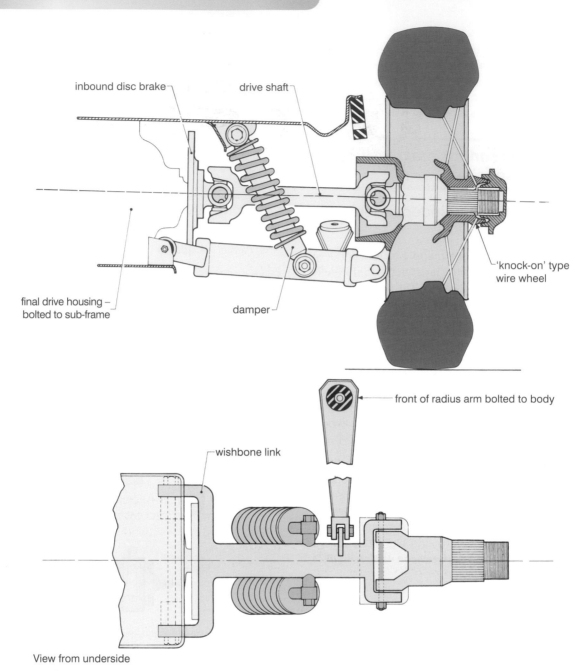

inbound disc brake

drive shaft

'knock-on' type wire wheel

final drive housing – bolted to sub-frame

damper

front of radius arm bolted to body

wishbone link

View from underside

Figure 4.104 Transverse links and coil springs

Torque reaction caused by driving the wheels and torque from the inboard disc brakes are both taken by the final-drive housing. This housing is bolted to a sub-frame on to which the complete rear suspension is assembled.

As the two 'links' are of different length, a variation occurs in the rear wheel camber angle when the springs are deflected. Camber angle is adjusted by shims fitted between the brake disc and the universal joint flange.

Semi-trailing arm and coil spring

This system supports the rear hub by a wishbone-shaped suspension arm mounted diagonally on to

a sub-frame, which could also carry the final-drive housing in rear- and four-wheel drive arrangements. By arranging the suspension arm in this way, the wheel is supported both laterally and longitudinally (Figure 4.105).

Driving torque reaction is transferred from the final-drive housing to the sub-frame and, as in similar arrangements, the construction prevents the tendency of the right-hand rear wheel to lift during hard acceleration. Braking torque and driving thrust are taken by the suspension arms.

Rubber is extensively used at the suspension arm pivots and for mounting the springs and

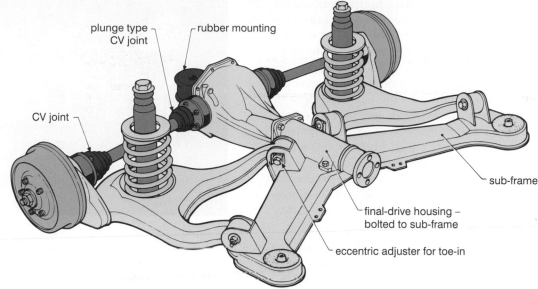

Figure 4.105 Semi-trailing arm and coil spring system

sub-frame to the body: this gives flexibility, reduces the transmission of vibration and noise, and overcomes the need for lubrication. To allow for alteration of wheel alignment (toe-in), one mounting of each suspension arm is fitted with either eccentric adjusters or shims.

The suspension may also incorporate changes in camber as the suspension moves during cornering and when passing over bumps.

Transverse link and strut

The layouts shown in Figure 4.106 for independently mounting each rear wheel are similar in basic construction to the MacPherson IFS system. This system is often used on front-wheel drive vehicles that have no rear drive shafts. Variations of this system have been produced over the years as this arrangement provides excellent suspension and wheel control.

The stub axle is rigidly attached to a long vertical strut that incorporates the suspension damper, and a transverse link, in the form of a wishbone or arm, controls the wheel track. Resistance to backward movement of the road wheel is provided by a longitudinal tie bar; this links the lower end of the strut with the vehicle body to give a stable three-point mounting for the suspension.

The helical spring can be fitted in one of two positions: it can be mounted either on the transverse wishbone or around the strut in true MacPherson style.

On some systems, a spring having coils of differing radii is fitted to improve comfort by providing a variable rate. As this progressive-type spring is being compressed, the larger diameter end-coils close up.

This action shortens the effective working length of the spring and stiffens the suspension.

As with many other IRS systems, the camber angle changes as the wheel is deflected. This feature is utilised to alter the tyre's cornering power so, by careful design, excellent handling characteristics of the vehicle can be achieved.

Since rubber is used at all mounting points, slight deflection of the suspension layout causes a change in wheel alignment. To allow for this, it is common to set the rear wheels so that they toe-in a small amount. On non-adjustable layouts, it is important to replace all washers and spacers in the place from which they were removed. Other layouts often incorporate an eccentric bolt on one of the track control arms.

Figure 4.106 Strut-type IRS

A variation on this system uses bottom suspension arms and a fixed top arm, along with a transverse link sometimes called a 'control blade'. The damper is mounted to the bottom arm by a pivot to allow movement and the top mounted to the body. As the suspension components are mounted on a separate sub-frame, which is bolted to the vehicle body with rubber isolators, the system provides excellent noise isolation and an improved centre of gravity. This system can be used with front- or rear-wheel drive arrangements and, due to the geometry of the suspension components and the action of the control blade, it possesses excellent resistance to dive, pitch and roll, which improves the handling characteristics.

Figure 4.108 Checking dampers for leaks

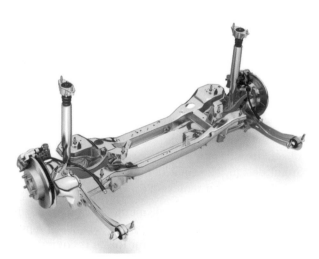

Figure 4.107 Control blade suspension arrangement (Ford)

4.15 Suspension – routine maintenance and diagnosis

4.15.1 Suspension checks

Suspension system checks are relatively simple and are as follows:

- Check security of suspension fittings and components.
- Check operation of dampers.
- Check ride heights.
- Check for wear and leaks.

Dampers

Figure 4.108 shows where to check for damper leaks. Damper operation can be checked by a simple 'bounce test' as shown on page 447. Uneven tyre wear and poor road holding often indicate weak damper operation.

Ride height

Checking the suspension ride height of a vehicle should be carried out on flat non-sloping workshop floor. Ride heights should be checked in accordance with manufacturer's instructions, for example, tyre pressure settings, no person on-board, and specified amount of fuel in the tank. The measurement is best taken with a solid rule or bar calibrated to the manufacturer's dimensions. Use of a tape rule is not recommended.

Figure 4.109 Points where ride height is measured

4.15.2 Common suspension system faults and common causes

1 Incorrect ride height (unequal or low):
   - Broken spring or fault with spring seating, for example corrosion at MacPherson strut top mounting
   - Damaged or bent suspension arms as a result of kerbing, etc.
2 Cracked, perished or worn mountings or bushes:
   - Usually due to high mileage or long vehicle life

3 Suspension noise:
- Excessive free play or wear in components or mountings
- Loose suspension components or fixings
- Worn damper
- Lack of lubricant

4 Excessive travel or movement in suspension components:
- Worn, loose or broken suspension components
- Worn dampers

5 Fluid leakage from dampers and hydraulic components:
- Worn dampers due to high mileage or arduous service conditions
- Loose hydraulic connections or cracked pipes or hoses

6 Worn dampers:
- Carry out bounce test and observe results

Damper bounce test

To carry out a vehicle bounce test, each corner of the vehicle should be pushed down vertically. An observation of the vehicle's reaction should then be carried out (Figure 4.110). The vehicle should react by rebounding two or three times if the damper is in good order.

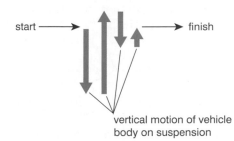

Figure 4.110 Damper bounce test

If the damper rebounds/oscillates more times, the damper should be inspected further. The technician should check for leaks and security to the suspension and vehicle body. Leaks may be visible around the dirt gaiter, as oil will leak past the damper piston seals if it is worn.

vertical motion of vehicle
body on suspension

Figure 4.111 A good damper reaction to the bounce test

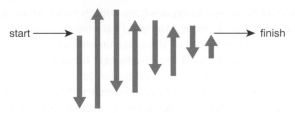

start →   finish

Figure 4.112 A damper that is worn and oscillates too many times during a bounce test

If a damper is suspected of being worn, it should be replaced with the opposite side damper at the same time. Single dampers should not be fitted, as this can unbalance the vehicle's handling.

4.16 Wheels

4.16.1 Requirements and types of wheels

A wheel must be light, to enable the tyre to follow the contour of the road, and strong, to resist the many forces acting on it. It must be cheap to produce, easy to clean and simple to remove. These conditions are met by the detachable-disc type of pressed steel or cast aluminium wheel: this is usually bolted directly to the hub assembly. In most cases, spherically seated nuts or bolts ensure a rigid mounting. To reduce the risk of the wheel accidentally coming off, some manufacturers use 'left-hand' threads on the nearside and 'right-hand' threads on the offside; the direction of thread is generally indicated by an L or R on the nut. All wheel nuts or bolts should be tightened to the correct torque to ensure that they are seated correctly.

Figure 4.113 Types of vehicle wheel, including wheel trims, that improve the aerodynamics

The wire or spoke-type wheel, which was common up to about 1935, is still used on some sports and racing cars. Modern designs use tangential spokes to transmit driving and braking forces; inner and outer sets of spokes are connected to the hub shell as wide apart as possible to provide lateral stiffness of the wheel. A centre-lock or knock-on mounting is used, whereby the drive is taken by serrations and the shell is located between two cones, one formed on the hub and the other on a single large nut screwed on to the hub to retain the wheel. Left-hand threads on the offside hubs and right-hand threads on the nearside hubs are generally used to prevent the nut working loose. This quick-change type of wheel is strong and light and ensures good circulation of air to the braking system, but is difficult to clean.

During recent years, the lightness of the wire wheel and the ease of cleaning of the pressed steel wheel have been combined in a wheel made of light alloy. Although much more costly, the appeal of attractive aluminium and magnesium alloy wheels has made this type popular for use on most common cars. A light alloy wheel is cast to shape and then machined to give the final finish.

The advantages of an alloy wheel over a pressed steel wheel are:

- lighter weight (able to provide a rigid and wider wheel without the disadvantage of extra weight)
- conducts heat away from the brakes and tyres more efficiently
- increased **wheel track** width, resulting in better cornering performance
- enhances the appearance of the vehicle
- can be cast and machined to more precise tolerances that ensure more accurate steering geometry.

Wheel track: the measured distance between two wheels on the same axle.

The main disadvantages of alloy wheels compared to pressed steel wheels are their lack of resistance to accidental damage, as well as their increased expense.

Some alloy wheels require the tyre to be removed from the inner side of the wheel to avoid damaging both the tyre and the wheel.

Note: under no circumstances must an inner tube be fitted to a tyre fitted to an alloy wheel.

The three main types of vehicle wheel are shown in Figure 4.114. These are alloy, steel and wire wheels. The last image shows a steel wheel with a wheel trim fitted, showing that even steel wheels can look rather attractive. This example is a specially designed wheel trim to improve airflow around the wheels.

4.16.2 Types of rim

Well-base rim

Figure 4.114 shows the main details of this construction, which is generally used for car tyres. The drop centre or well enables the tyre to be pressed into this recess, so that the opposite side (adjacent to the valve) may be levered over the rim flange. The air pressure in the tyre causes the bead to ride up the slight taper (5°) and 'lock' the tyre to the rim. Rim diameter and width is often found stamped into the centre of the wheel and is also stated on the tyre. For example, a tyre 145/70 × 13 is fitted to a 13 in diameter rim; the 145 refers to the nominal sectional width of the tyre in millimetres, and the 70 refers to the sectional height.

Flat-base three-piece rim

The stiff, heavy-bead tyres used on heavy vehicles require a detachable-flange type of rim. A split lock ring, like a large circlip, holds the flange in position. When the flange is pushed towards the tyre, the lock ring may be removed.

Light alloy

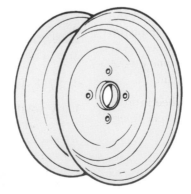

Pressed steel disc

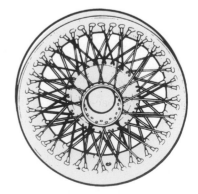

Wire

Figure 4.114 Types of vehicle wheel

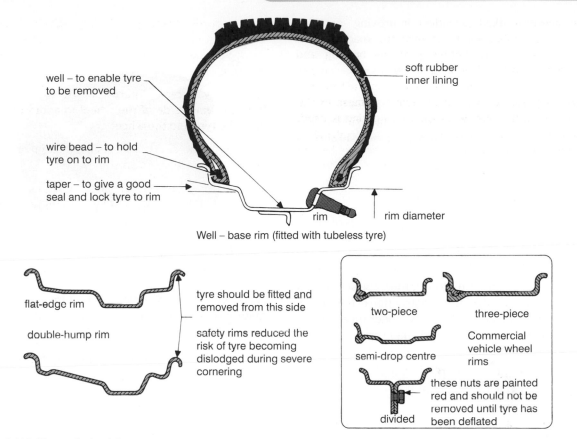

Figure 4.115 Types of wheel rim

Semi-drop centre rim

This two-piece rim is a compromise between the well-base and the flat-base rim, and is suitable for light trucks. A split, detachable flange simplifies removal and the slight taper enables the tyre to 'lock' to the rim. The small well must be used when the tyre is being removed.

Flat-based divided rim

Mainly used on military vehicles, this type of rim is made in two sections and bolted together by a ring of nuts adjacent to the rim. On no account must you remove these nuts when changing a wheel.

4.16.3 Space-saver wheels

A spare wheel has to be carried on a vehicle in case one of the tyres develops a puncture. Various locations are used to carry this wheel, the most common place being the luggage space at the rear of the car.

To reduce the space taken up by the spare wheel in order to improve the luggage capacity, some manufacturers fit a special small-diameter, thin spare wheel.

This space-saver-type wheel should only be used in an emergency to allow the car to be driven to a repair location. Sometimes this type is called a 40–40 wheel; the car should not be driven faster than 65 kph (40 mph) over a distance greater than 65 km (40 miles).

Alternatively, some manufacturers use sealing kits. A 12V compressor is used to pump in a mixture of air and sealant to temporarily seal a puncture. The recommended speed and distance when using this sealant to carry out an emergency repair is 80 kph (50 mph) and a 200 kilometre (125 mile) distance.

Self-supporting run flat tyres can also be fitted to the vehicle using reinforced sidewalls that support the vehicle weight if the tyre goes flat. These should be replaced within 50 miles.

4.17 Tyres

The dictionary definition of a tyre is a band of iron, steel, rubber, etc., placed round the rim of a wheel to strengthen it or reduce vibration.

4.17.1 The pneumatic tyre

Early solid rubber tyres certainly strengthened the wheel, but did little to improve the comfort. It was not until R.W. Thomson in 1845 invented the pneumatic tyre that high-frequency vibration could be reduced. This idea was developed by J.B. Dunlop in 1888 for cycle use and was quickly applied to motor vehicles. An airbag or inner tube was contained in a cover so that the vehicle was 'floated' on a cushion of air.

The modern tyre, besides improving comfort, increases the **adhesion** between the road and the wheel to give satisfactory grip for braking and steering in various driving conditions.

> **Adhesion**: the ability of two substances to bond together. In the case of a tyre and the road surface, this is the ability of the tyre to grip to the road surface without losing traction.

4.17.2 Tyre construction

Figure 4.116 shows the constructional details of a tyre. On this tyre, the casing must resist the expansion of the inner tube, especially when the tube is subjected to road shocks. Fracture of the casing causes the tube to blow out (i.e. burst the tyre); thus, the strength of the tyre is governed by the construction of the casing. Tyres fitted today do not have an inner tube and are called tubeless. These tyres are made up from 10 core components:

1 Bead core – made from rubber covered steel wire and is used to hold the tyre firmly on the wheel rim.
2 Apex – made from synthetic rubber and influences the steering precision, ride and comfort.
3 Inner liner – made from butyl rubber and seals the inside of the pressurised tyre.
4 Textile carcass – made from **rayon** or polyester cords embedded in rubber. This keeps the inflated tyre in shape and links the bead to the tread area.
5 Bead reinforcement – made from rayon, nylon or polyester cords embedded in rubber. This influences the directional stability of the tyre.
6 Flange cushion or rim strip – made from synthetic rubber and ensures that there is an air-tight seat on the rim and prevents chafing of the rim flange.
7 Steel cord belt – made from high-strength multi-cord steel. This stabilises the tread area and provides shape retention and increased mileage performance.
8 Cap-ply – made from nylon cords and improves the high-speed stability of the tyre.
9 Side wall – made from rubber and protects the carcass from damage and weathering.
10 Tread – made from synthetic and natural rubber. This influences the grip, rolling resistance and handling characteristics of the tyre.

> **Rayon**: a textile fibre made of cellulose. The fibres are woven together to form a strong material.

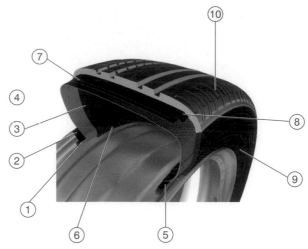

Figure 4.116 Tyre construction

Heavy vehicles and some cars require even stronger materials, so more steel cords are needed in these cases.

The *bead* consists of a number of hoops of steel wire that are responsible for retaining the tyre on the rim. The casing is wrapped around the bead wire and moulded into shape.

The *tread* is bonded to the soft rubber that encloses the casing. The material used is natural or synthetic rubber, which is compounded with chemicals such as carbon-black to produce a hard, abrasion-resisting substance. Various tread patterns are used to clear water and grease off the road, so that the tyre can 'bite' into the surface. An excellent grip, especially on soft surfaces, can be obtained by transversely slotting the tyre to form bold tread bars, but when used on hard roads this type is rather noisy and generally causes the 'heel and toe' form of tread wear.

The tread pattern should be selected to suit the operating conditions:

1 Normal touring – requires a tread that gives quiet operation and provides effective adhesion under wet, dry and greasy conditions.
2 High-speed operation – places emphasis on the heat generated, the noise level and the increased adhesion of the tyre to the road.
3 Cross-country tyres – have to bite into mud, snow and loose surfaces, so heavy tread bars are needed. Extensive use of this type of tyre on hard highways causes noise and component wear.
4 Winter tyres – have wide tread grooves providing additional traction and remain flexible at low temperatures due to an increased proportion of natural rubber in their construction. Winter tyres should be fitted in sets of four and speed ratings can be reduced. Chains can also be fitted to tyres to gain extra traction in snow and ice.

Figure 4.117 Winter tyre tread and tyre with snow chains fitted to gain extra traction in snow and ice conditions

Some dos and don'ts in fitting tyres:

- **Always** replace tyres in axle pairs.
- **Never** mix tread pattern designs across axles.
- Where possible, use same brand and pattern family of tyre across an axle.

Energy-saving tyres

Today, the need to ensure that vehicles provide the most miles per litre of fuel used has increased the range of tyres available, especially specific energy-saving tyres. These tyres have been designed to have lower rolling resistance, which then leads to the

vehicle having to do less work to propel it along the road. As less work has to be done by the engine, less fuel is used. The lower rolling resistance is created by using different materials in the rubber, along with the improved tread pattern to create less drag as the wheel rotates. Many manufacturers now fit these tyres to their vehicles as standard equipment to improve the fuel consumption and also the emissions produced by the vehicle.

Figure 4.118 Energy-saving tyre with low rolling resistance

Tread pattern design

There are many different types of tread pattern. The ones most commonly seen are:

- asymmetric – pattern design must be fitted the correct way round. They can be fitted in any position on the vehicle
- directional – pattern design for specific directional rotation only. They must be fitted in direction of rotation (DOR)
- multi-directional – pattern design may be fitted either way round on the rim.

4.17.3 Tubeless tyres

Tubeless tyres are now basic equipment for modern vehicles. The inside of the casing and outer surface of the bead is lined with a soft rubber, which forms an air-tight seal with the rim and eliminates the need for a separate tube. There are two main advantages:

1 Better air-sealing qualities are obtained providing the cover is correctly sealed to the rim.
2 The soft inner liner of the cover provides a puncture-sealing arrangement. On fitting or removing this type, be very careful to avoid damaging the bead.

Resistance to a side force

The extent of the side deflection produced when a side force acts on the tyre governs the actual path taken by the wheel. This side deflection (Figure 4.119) is increased when the inflation pressure is low, but is controlled to a very large extent by the construction of the tyre.

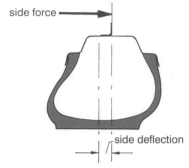

Figure 4.119 Effect of side force on a tyre during cornering

Diagonal-ply

Figure 4.120 shows a tyre with the carcass composed of several layers of casing plies. The cords forming one ply run at an angle of about 100° to the cords of the adjoining ply, and each cord of the ply forms an angle of approximately 40° to the bead. This type is also called cross-ply and has been in use for a long period. Cross-ply tyres are usually found on earlier vehicles and are not generally fitted to modern-day passenger vehicles, although some commercial and agricultural vehicles still use them.

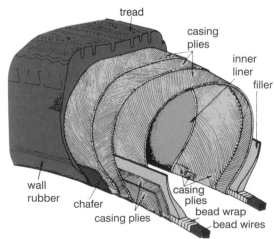

Figure 4.120 Tyre construction – diagonal-ply

Radial-ply

Figure 4.121 shows a tyre with the cords arranged in such a manner that they form an angle of 90° to the bead (i.e. the cords are radially disposed to the wheel). This type has the great advantage that it offers a large resistance to side deflection and its effect on the vehicle handling is very noticeable. A vehicle fitted with cross-ply tyres often suffers from side drift when

it corners and gives the impression to the driver that the tyres are sliding on the road, whereas radial-ply considerably reduce this effect. In a similar manner, if the vehicle **oversteers** badly, then this could be reduced by fitting radial-ply to the rear axle. These 'stiffer' tyres will reduce the slip angle of the rear wheels and will produce a safer and more stable condition. This mixing of radial-ply and cross-ply tyres on a vehicle must be used with great care and under no circumstances must radial-ply be fitted to the front axle when cross-ply are used on the rear wheels. Mixing in this configuration is illegal because of the oversteering problem, so care is needed to identify the tyres correctly. Today, radial-ply tyres can be identified by the word 'radial', which is moulded on the wall of the tyre and the 'R' in the tyre size description – for example 145×70×R13. Prior to the general introduction of this method the means of identification was to note the type letters and refer to the manufacturer's catalogue.

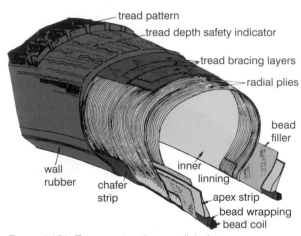

Figure 4.121 Tyre construction – radial-ply

Oversteer: a condition when the rear wheels lose traction and try to overtake the front of the vehicle causing a slide condition. This is usually countered by turning the steered wheels into the slide.

Table 4.2 Diagonal and radial-ply advantages

Diagonal-ply	Radial-ply
Lighter steering at low speed	About 80 per cent longer life
Not so critical with respect to steering geometry	Lower rolling resistance, so fuel consumption is improved
Smoother ride at low speed	Side deflection is reduced, so the vehicle corners without drift
Cheaper	Full width of tread is held on the road when the car is cornering, so grip is improved, especially on wet roads

Belted and braced tyres

Figure 4.121 shows that, in addition to the radial cords, a number of layers of breakers are used. These bracing layers act as a belt around the circumference to stabilise the tread and resist the enlargement of the tyre on inflation, since the radial cords do not offer the same resistance to tyre enlargement as the cross-ply cords. Textile materials used for these breakers give a tyre that is sometimes called a belted type, whereas steel cord breakers give a braced tread type.

Tyre profile

The 'section height' to 'section width' of early tyres was approximately equal and this aspect ratio was considered as 100 per cent. As increased demands were made for improved vehicle stability, the cornering power of tyres was raised by reducing the aspect ratio. Today, low-profile tyres having ratios of about 80 per cent and ultra-low-profile types of 35 per cent are in common use. These 'wide oval' tyres, and other similarly shaped tyres, can be identified by relating the dimensional markings on the tyre to the manufacturer's handbook.

4.17.4 Valves

Figure 4.122 shows the main details of the Schrader one-way valve used in conjunction with a tubeless tyre. In this case, the valve is inserted in the rim, whereas in separate-tube designs it is vulcanised, or bolted, to the tube.

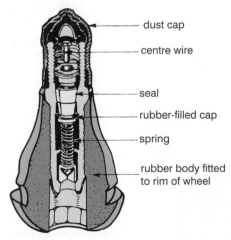

Figure 4.122 Schrader valve

- dust cap
- centre wire
- seal
- rubber-filled cap
- spring
- rubber body fitted to rim of wheel

The core is threaded into the stem until the tapered, hard rubber section forms a seal with the stem. Spring pressure forces the centre wire and rubber-filled cup on to its seat to prevent an outward flow of air. A dust cap acts as an extra air seal and prevents entry of dirt.

4.17.5 Inflation pressure

Inflation pressure is governed by the load carried by a given tyre, although manufacturers vary the pressure to modify the steering characteristics. Large-section tyres use a lower pressure for a given load, and so greater comfort is achieved, but the resistance to rolling is increased. The pressure recommended by the manufacturer is applicable to a cold tyre (i.e. it is the pressure before the tyre is used), and takes into account the average pressure rise ($28\,kN/m^2$ ($4\,lbf$ in^{-2})) that is caused by the temperature increase during use. Recommended pressure is normally suitable for sustained speeds up to 130 kph (80 mph), but a higher pressure is advised if speeds or loads are increased.

Under-inflation or overloading leads to rapid wear on each side of the tread and internal damage to the casing, whereas over-inflation wears the centre of tread.

Tyre pressure monitors

The tyre pressure monitoring systems (TPMS) signal if the pressure drops too low in one or all of the tyres. To measure the tyre pressures, there is a sensor integrated within the air valve in each wheel (Figure 4.123). In the event of low air pressure in any of the tyres, the driver is warned by a message in the driver display. This can usually be switched off if, for instance, winter tyres are fitted without TPMS.

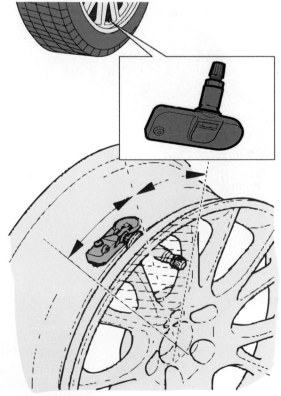

Figure 4.123 TPMS sensor located in the air valve of the wheel and tyre assembly

When removing a tyre from a wheel that has this system, it is important that a distance of 20° or 100 mm (whichever is greatest) either side of the valve is avoided by the tyre removal equipment. This is to prevent damage to the sensor when removing the tyre.

When replacing a worn tyre, the valve section must always be replaced. The typical sensor battery life is 10 years. A specialist tool can be used to read out the sensor's ID number and the current pressure of the tyre.

When replacing the tyres with this system, the driver will normally have to drive the vehicle for 1–2 miles for the system to recalibrate and the warning light to extinguish.

Tyre marking

Local statutory regulations based on EC recommendations specify the classification markings that must be shown on the sidewall of a modern tyre. If the tyre is to be sold in the USA, additional data must be included.

Figure 4.124 shows an example of the markings required on a tyre intended for sale in Europe and the USA.

Speed rating

Tyres are marked to show the maximum recommended speed. The speed markings are indicated by letters representing 'speed', 'high speed' and 'very high speed', T, H, V, Z and W being the most common.

Example: 165 SR 13 is a radial tyre of size 165 × 13 and reference to the manufacturer's manual shows that the speed marking 'S' represents a maximum speed of 180 kph (113 mph). The alternatives for this size of radial tyre are shown in Table 4.3.

Table 4.3 Alternatives for radial tyre 165 SR 13

Size	Speed limit
165 HR 13	210 kph (130 mph)
165 VR 13	over 210 kph

Table 4.4 shows speed symbols and the maximum speeds.

To use this information, if we look at 205/50 R15 91V as an example tyre:

205 – is the section **width** measured in millimetres.

50 – is the **aspect ratio** (or profile) expressed as a percentage.

1   type of tyre: tubeless or tubed type
2   size designation: 175 – width of tyre in mm
 ▪ S – speed rating
 ▪ 14 – rim diameter in inches
3   TWI stands for tread wear indicators
4   EC standards: 88 – maximum load per wheel
5   S – speed rating
6   casing material and number of plies
7   tread material and number of plies
8   maximum inflation pressure when cold, stated in psi or bar
9   US standard for giving maximum load per wheel
10   manufacturer's name
11   EC approval marks
12   EC approval marks
13   US approval marks
14   manufacturer's coding

Figure 4.124 Sidewall tyre markings

R – is the construction type (i.e. radial tyre).

15 – is the wheel rim diameter of the tyre expressed in inches.

91 – is the **load index**.

V – is the **speed rating** 205/50 R15 91V 240 kph (140 mph).

Table 4.4 Speed ratings for tyres

Speed symbol	Speed (kph)	Speed symbol	Speed (kph)
A1	5	J	100
A2	10	K	110
A3	15	L	120
A4	20	M	130
A5	25	N	140
A6	30	P	150
A7	35	Q	160
A8	40	R	170
B	50	S	180
C	60	T	190
D	65	U	200
E	70	H	210
F	80	V	240
G	90	Z	over 240

Width: the tread width measured in millimetres. This builds up the tyre footprint that contacts the road surface.

Aspect ratio: the 'height' of the tyre expressed as a percentage of the tyre width. Lower profile tyres have lower aspect ratios. Higher performance tyres usually have lower profile tyres. Lower profile tyres have less flex in the tyre wall, so can provide a more responsive steering feel but be at the cost of ride comfort.

Load index: measurement relating to the safe loading of the tyre. This is important as the manufacturer will recommend specific load ratings for a vehicle and these must be adhered to for vehicle safety and insurance purposes.

Speed rating: the safe maximum speed the tyre is able to sustain for prolonged periods while loaded. This is important to note when replacing tyres, as a tyre with too low speed rating may fail during vehicle operation. Insurance may also be void if incorrectly rated tyres are fitted to a vehicle.

The tyre manufacturer should be consulted if a tyre is required for a vehicle that is to be subjected to either a high maximum speed or a high consistent speed.

Ply rating

This is an indication of the strength of a tyre and currently does not represent the number of layers that form the casing of the tyre.

Ply rating combined with tyre size are two factors that determine the legal maximum load (plated load) that can be carried by each axle of a commercial vehicle.

Run-flat tyres

Manufacturers are always looking at improving vehicle safety and lowering the vehicle weight. The fitment of run-flat tyres is now standard equipment on some vehicles. The purpose of the run-flat tyre is to give added stability if the tyre suddenly loses pressure and to allow the vehicle to be driven at lower speeds (65–80 kph/40–50 mph) for approximately 80 km (50 miles) until the vehicle can be taken to a tyre specialist for a replacement. This removes the need for a heavy spare tyre and improves the amount of luggage area in the vehicle.

The run-flat tyre works by having stiffer side walls that are designed to be driven on at lower vehicle speeds if the tyre deflates. The tyre walls are made from rubber that is able to withstand the normal excessive heat build-up experienced from running a vehicle on flat tyres. This gives the driver the added security of knowing that the vehicle will remain stable during a sudden tyre blow out.

One issue with run-flat tyres is that due to the stiffer side walls the vehicle ride may be affected, causing a slightly stiffer less compliant suspension system as the tyre is not able to absorb the smaller shocks delivered by the road surface.

An additional design of run-flat tyres is a tyre that incorporates a inflation canister within the tyre and wheel design. The tyre inflation canister is strapped to the wheel within the well area. If the tyre deflates suddenly, the weight of the vehicle on the flat tyre will burst the canister causing the gas and tyre repair fluid to be expelled rapidly. This action re-inflates the tyre and the repair fluid plugs the puncture. This allows the vehicle to be safely driven to somewhere where the tyre can be replaced.

4.17.6 Tyre wear

As a vehicle drives along the road surface, the tyre tread is subjected to a great deal of stress through the acceleration, cornering and braking forces transmitted. The tyre tread gradually wears over time as the vehicle demands its grip and traction needs. The tyre surface is gradually put down on to the road surface so the tread depth becomes less and less. If the vehicle is driven more aggressively, the tyre's rubber will deteriorate more quickly, leading to the need to replace the tyres as they approach the legal tread depth limit. Tyres should be subjected to careful assessment during service periods and also on regular occasions by the driver to ensure that they deliver their optimum level of performance.

Worn tyres can dramatically alter the handling and braking performance of a vehicle so it is very important to ensure that they are in the best possible condition. Generally, the contact patch of a tyre on a regular vehicle is less than the size of a piece of A5 paper. For this reason, tyres are one of the most important areas of maintenance.

Tyre pressures are also very important in ensuring that the tyre delivers its maximum level of traction and grip. In many cases, the tyre pressures should be altered with different vehicle loads so it is important to check the manufacturer's recommended settings.

During routine inspection, tyres should be checked for the following defects:

- Inflation pressures
- Wear and tread depth
- Damage

Tread wear indication

The tread of a modern tyre has a pattern that changes when the tread has worn down to a given limit. This safety feature allows an observer to determine the danger limit quickly without having to use a tyre tread depth gauge.

Interchanging tyres

At present, there are various recommendations regarding the interchanging of tyres, so tyre manufacturers' guidance should be followed. Generally, cross-ply tyres should be interchanged at frequent intervals if uniform tyre wear is to be achieved. Longitudinal changes (L/H front to L/H rear, etc.) and diagonal changes (R/H front to L/H rear and spare to L/H front, etc.) are normally advised.

Some manufacturers of radial-ply tyres recommend that the front tyres are not moved to the rear because of the different wear pattern of front and rear tyres.

Legal requirements

Legislation exists to prevent the use of a vehicle that is fitted with defective tyres. The current regulations specify the following tyre faults:

- The use of unsuitable tyres
- Under-inflation
- Break in the fabric in excess of 2.5 cm (1 in) or 10 per cent of the section width
- Lumps or bulges
- Exposure of cords
- Tread depth less than minimum. The law requires a tread depth of at least 1.6 mm across the central three-quarters of the breadth of tread around the entire circumference of the tyre

A tyre with a puncture outside the central tread area must be replaced according to British Standard (BS) recommendations.

rapid wear at shoulders

rapid wear at centre

wear on one side

feathered edge

bald spot(s)

under-inflation

over-inflation

excessive camber

incorrect toe misalignment

steering slackness brake drum or disc wear or distortion worn dampers unbalanced wheels

Figure 4.125 Abnormal tyre wear

The preceding list of faults is intended to outline the requirements, and it is recommended that the current regulations be read in order to acquire an accurate understanding of the legal requirements.

Tread wear patterns

The type of irregular wear pattern of a tyre tread is often a good indication of a specific mechanical fault in the steering, braking or suspension system.

The life of the tread on a tyre depends on the service it receives and on the manner in which the car is driven. The life is shortened if the tyre is subjected to rapid acceleration and braking, high-speed cornering and excessive scrubbing by abuse of the power steering.

Figure 4.125 shows the main types of abnormal wear and the cause(s) of each.

Normal wear – tyre wear is unavoidable. As a tyre wears, it loses its level of grip and safety. It is recommended that tyres are replaced at 3 mm, although the legal limit is 1.6 mm. Correct inflation pressures, driving style and road types can all affect tyre wear.

Shoulder wear – tyre worn on both edges, but not in centre of tread. This is caused by under-inflation, causing uneven contact with the road and wear on edges of tyres.

Centre wear – tyre worn in centre but not on edges. This is usually caused by over-inflation.

Uneven wear – tyre worn on inner or outer edges. Usually caused by wheel alignment/geometry problems.

Tread distortion – cracks or deterioration of the tread. Usually caused by tyre ageing or under-inflation, causing excessive flexing of the tread.

Sidewall cracking – cracking of the sidewall of the tyre. Perishing of the rubber is usually caused by age, low mileage and poor storage conditions.

Impact damage lumps/cuts – lumps or cuts in the tyre sidewall. Caused by potholes, kerb damage or damage caused by objects in the road.

4.18 Wheel balancing

Independent suspension systems and modern, small-diameter, large-section wheels demand extra care and attention to wheel balancing.

Although tyre manufacturers balance the tyre and tube, it is often necessary to balance the complete wheel assembly to ensure that the wheel rotates free from vibration.

Wheels out of balance may be the result of (a) static unbalance, or (b) dynamic unbalance.

Before balancing the wheel, ensure that you:

- clean all mud and dirt off the wheel and the tyre
- inflate the tyre to the correct pressure
- inspect the wheel and the tyre for damage
- ensure that the wheel is installed correctly
- remove all weights.

4.18.1 Static unbalance

This is apparent when the wheel is mounted on a horizontal shaft having low-friction bearings (Figure 4.126a). The wheel always comes to rest in one position, which indicates the presence of a 'heavy spot' directly below the wheel axis. (A bicycle wheel shows this action clearly.) A wheel used in this condition will tend to cause the unbalanced centrifugal force to lift the wheel off the road periodically (Figure 4.126b), and produce conditions known as 'wheel hop', 'shimmy' and uneven tyre wear.

4.18.2 Dynamic unbalance

Figure 4.126c shows a wheel in good static balance, but when this wheel is rotated the centrifugal forces acting on each 'heavy spot' will not balance, since the forces are not acting through the same line. In this diagram, the wheel axis tends to rotate around the kingpin in a clockwise direction, whereas the opposite applies to Figure 4.126d. Serious dynamic unbalance causes the wheel to 'flap' around the kingpin, a condition known as wheel shimmy.

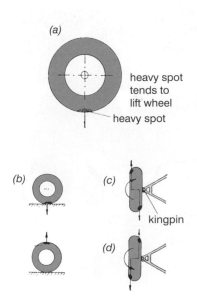

Figure 4.126 Unbalanced wheels

4.18.3 Wheel balancing

There are two methods of balancing wheels, either on or off the vehicle.

Balancing off the vehicle

The advantages of balancing off the vehicle are that:

- all wheels (driven or undriven) can be easily balanced
- wheels can be balanced while the vehicle is not available.

Balancing on the vehicle

The advantage of balancing on the vehicle is that out-of-balance forces of drum and hub are taken into consideration.

The disadvantage of balancing on the vehicle is that all the components must be replaced in the same place or the balance of the wheel will be adversely affected.

General precautions

Always use the correct adhesive weights for alloy wheels and never use steel wheel weights for alloy wheels.

4.18.4 Wheel-balancing machines

Wheel-balancing machines enable the technician to determine the position and extent of the correcting mass, which must be clipped on to the rim to create a balanced wheel assembly. Simple equipment can be used to detect static unbalance, but since the wheel

Figure 4.127 Wheel balancer (off vehicle type)

must be rotated to determine dynamic unbalance, more costly apparatus is necessary. Training should be carried out when using off and on car balancers as they can be very dangerous due to the wheels rotating at very high speed.

4.19 Wheel and tyre – routine maintenance and diagnosis

4.19.1 Tyre pressures

Having the correct inflation pressure in the vehicle's tyres not only optimises the performance but also increases the driver and passenger personal safety when driving.

As a guide, you should check the tyre pressures at least once a month and before long journeys. Ignoring this advice runs the risk of decreasing the grip and increasing the braking distances. There is also a risk that the tyres could be damaged and the lifespan will decrease. The fuel consumption will also be affected with the wrong pressures, especially if they are under-inflated as this creates extra drag when the car rolls.

The recommended tyre pressure levels for front and rear tyres are often different due to the weight and balance of the vehicle, along with the size often being different.

The correct pressures for your vehicle can normally be found in the owner's manual. The information may also be marked on the vehicle (e.g. on the driver's door pillar, or on the inside of the petrol flap). In most cases, two different sets of pressures are given:

- For 'normal' driving conditions.
- For a loaded vehicle (with extra people or heavy items on board).

To check the tyre inflation pressures, you will need a tyre pressure gauge or use the gauge on the inflation equipment found at most garages and petrol stations.

Cold weather

In severe cold weather, it is often better to fit winter specification tyres to ensure that the vehicle gains maximum available grip of the roads. Also, it is important to check the pressures of the tyres if the outside temperature is low due to the pressure of the tyres dropping during cold temperatures. In many cases, the pressure can drop 2–3 psi in cold temperatures.

Wheel alignment

The alignment of the front and rear wheels on a vehicle are extremely important for two reasons:

1 Stability and road-holding of the vehicle
2 To minimise tyre wear and prolong the life of the tyres

Wheel alignment should be checked using special equipment designed to assess the angles of each road wheel in relation to the vehicle's position. In many cases, wheel alignment can be altered through knocks to road wheels or hitting potholes. When a wheel is pushed out of alignment, it will cause the vehicle to take a path not chosen by the driver. It will cause a pulling of the vehicle to one side or create instability of the vehicle during cornering. There are many types of wheel alignment equipment that can check all four wheels at the same time or just two wheels. All equipment should be operated by a technician who is trained to ensure that the most accurate measurements and settings are obtained. Wheel alignment data is obtained in the vehicle's workshop manual.

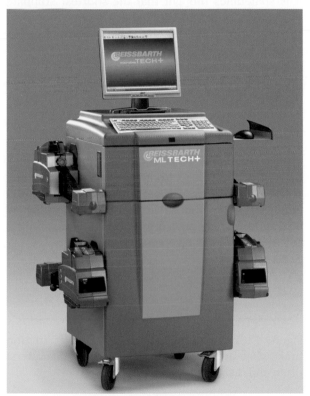

Figure 4.128 Wheel alignment equipment used to set up the vehicle's steering and suspension

Tread depth

Tread depth should be measured on regular occasions to ensure that tyres remain legal. Equipment used to measure tread depth is simple in design and can have digital or analogue readings (Figure 4.129). The simplest design consists of a sliding measuring scale with a depth pin used to drop into the grooves of the tyre. The flat base of the depth gauge is positioned on to the tyre across a tread groove of the tyre.

The depth pin is then pushed into the groove of the tyre. As the pin moves down into the groove, measurement will then become visible on the sliding scale of the depth gauge. The further the pin moves down into the groove, the greater the tread depth of the tyre. Digital gauges work in the same way but have a readout displayed on the gauge. Generally, this should be checked across the whole width of the tyre, so three to four measurements may be taken. As mentioned earlier, the current legal requirement is to have 1.6 mm of tread over three-quarters of the tyre, with the remainder being visible tread.

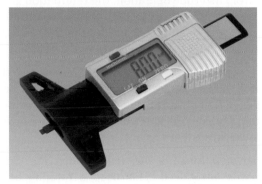

Figure 4.129 Tyre tread depth gauge – digital type

4.20 Braking principles

4.20.1 Purpose of a brake

When a vehicle is accelerated, energy supplied by the engine causes the vehicle speed to increase. Some of this energy is instantly used up in overcoming frictional and tractive resistances, but a large amount remains stored in the vehicle as kinetic energy.

The existence of kinetic energy is seen when a vehicle is moving and neutral is selected. The vehicle does not immediately come to rest; instead, it travels for a considerable distance before it becomes stationary. In this case, the stored energy is slowly being converted and used to drive the vehicle against the resistances that oppose the vehicle motion. Reliance on these resistances to slow down a vehicle would cause many problems, so an additional resistance, called a brake, is needed to convert the energy at a faster rate. The purpose of a brake is to 'convert kinetic energy to heat energy'.

The speed of the energy conversion controls the rate of retardation of a vehicle (i.e. its rate of deceleration).

Heat generation at the brake is obtained by rubbing a fixed pad or shoe against a rotating object driven by the motion of the vehicle. In the early days, this was achieved by pressing a wooden block against the steel tyre of a road wheel (Figure 4.130).

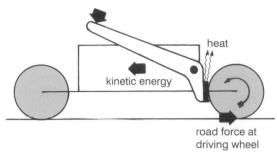

Figure 4.130 The principle of the brake

Apart from its crude operation, the retardation given by this single brake was limited both by the friction between the tyre and road and by the fact that the braking action was only applied to one wheel.

Fitting brakes to the other wheels increases the stopping power, so when a braking system was introduced that utilised the full 'weight' of the vehicle by fitting a brake to all four wheels, a far more efficient and powerful system was obtained.

A large step forward was made when the drum brake was introduced. This used a rotating drum (fixed to the wheel) on to which a brake shoe was pressed. Originally, an external contracting band was used, but this got very hot owing to the difficulty in radiating the heat to the surrounding air. The internal expanding type was a natural development and an early type is shown in Figure 4.131.

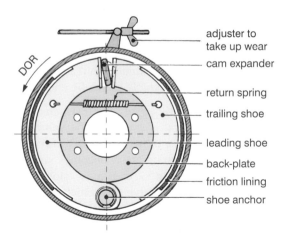

Figure 4.131 Cam-operated brake shoe arrangement

Stopping distance and tyre adhesion

The strength of the force pressing a shoe against a drum governs the resistance to rotation of a road wheel. During this operation the road surface has to drive the wheel around. The limit of this driving force is reached when the resistance of the brake equals the maximum frictional force that is produced between the tyre and road. The latter is called the adhesive force and can be calculated from the expression:

$$\text{Adhesive force} = \frac{\text{Load on}}{\text{wheel}} \times \frac{\text{Coefficient of}}{\text{friction}}$$

When the limit is reached, the wheel starts to skid, so extra force on the brake shoe will not produce any increase in the rate at which the vehicle slows down, no matter how good the braking system. This situation is apparent when a vehicle is braked on a slippery surface: slight pressure on the brake soon locks up the wheel and very poor braking results. This shows that the adhesion between the tyre and road is the main factor that controls the minimum stopping distance.

Road adhesion is affected by:

- type of road surface
- condition of surface, for example wet, dry, icy, greasy, etc.
- design of tyre tread, composition of tread material and depth of tread.

It is sometimes thought that the shortest stopping distance is achieved when the wheel is locked to produce a skid. This idea is false because experiments show that the force required to 'unlock' a tyre is greater than the force required to keep it locked over the surface. It should be noted that a wheel held on the verge of locking not only gives the shortest braking distance, it also allows the driver to maintain directional control of the vehicle as the wheels are allowed to continue to rotate. Although many drivers can modulate their braking in an emergency to prevent the wheels from locking and maintaining control of the vehicle, most vehicles now have ABS fitted, which prevents the wheels from locking by altering the brake pressure to the individual brakes automatically in an emergency situation.

4.21 Main types of brake system

Figure 4.132 shows the two main types of friction brake that are commonly used by manufacturers: drum and disc.

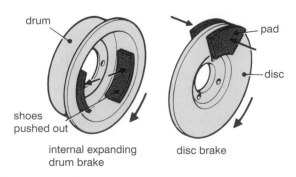

Figure 4.132 Types of brake – drum and disc

Both types use a fixed (non-rotating) shoe or pad that rubs against a moving drum or disc. The friction between the rubbing surfaces is increased by attaching a special friction material to the fixed component (i.e. brake pad or shoe). In the past, this friction material had a high asbestos content, but the health dangers associated with the dust from this substance has forced manufacturers to replace it with a safe asbestos-free material.

Note: although asbestos brake linings are no longer fitted, care should be taken when working on the braking system as the dust generated is still dangerous if inhaled. Masks should always be worn when working around the brake linings. The manufacturer's instructions should be understood before attempting to dismantle a brake assembly.

4.21.1 Introduction to drum brakes

This internal expanding type of brake uses two shoes that are attached to a back-plate, which is fixed to a stub axle or axle tube. Each shoe has a 'T' section and a friction lining is riveted or bonded to the outer face of the shoe. At one end of the shoe is a device for expanding the shoe when the brake pedal is depressed. In a simple brake (Figure 4.132), a cam is used as a shoe expander, but modern layouts fitted to cars use hydraulically operated pistons for this purpose.

All shoe-type brakes must have some arrangement to prevent the shoes rotating with the drum. The shoe anchor, which must be rigidly attached to the back-plate, takes the form of a large pin that passes through the shoes, or a housing against which the shoes are located.

Simple arrangements of springs pull the brake shoes on to the back-plate and also return the shoes to the 'off' position after the brake has been applied. In some cases, separate springs are used to perform the retention and return functions.

The inner cylindrical surface of the cast iron drum is ground to give a smooth surface on to which the brake linings can rub. The drum is generally attached to the hub flange by small countersunk screws and retained securely by the wheel nuts. If possible, the drums should be exposed so that a good flow of air over the drum is achieved to dissipate the heat and prevent loss of brake efficiency that occurs when the unit gets very hot. Some drum assemblies have fins arranged around the outer surface to increase the drum surface area and improve cooling.

Some form of adjuster is provided at each brake to take up excessive clearance due to wear of the friction facing. Since a large leverage is needed between the brake pedal and shoe, a large movement of the shoe would mean that the brake pedal would strike the floor before the brake is fully applied. This dangerous condition is avoided by either manually adjusting the brakes periodically, or having an automatic adjuster that continually sets the shoes so that they are always positioned very close to the drum. Drum brake components can be seen in Figure 4.133.

Advantages of drum brakes

For many years, vehicle manufacturers used drum brakes as the main braking system on both front and rear axles because of their simplicity and low manufacturing costs. As vehicle technology

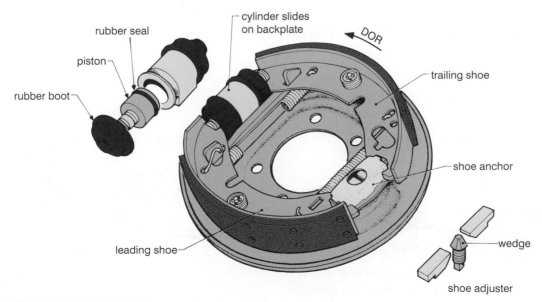

Figure 4.133 Drum brake components

progressed, manufacturers developed more advanced braking systems with disc brakes and it was thought that these would eventually entirely replace drum brake systems. However, although they are not as popular, vehicle manufacturers still use the drum brake principle on rear axles because it provides some key advantages over the disc brake layout.

One key advantage of the drum brake system over other systems is that it provides a 'self-servo action'. This action occurs when the rotating brake drum provides assistance to the brake shoes by trying to draw them out towards the drum lining face. When brake pedal pressure is applied, the brake shoes will move outwards towards the brake drum lining face and braking force will be applied when both are mated. This duel application of exerted pressure and rotational forces creates a greater force and produces better braking efficiency.

On the single leading shoe format of drum brakes the leading brake shoe is used to produce the self-servo action while the trailing shoe acts at a reduced rate. This application is reversed when the vehicle is driven in the opposite direction. The trailing brake shoe now becomes the leading shoe and provides the self-servo action. This then provides the driver with self-servo action and greater braking forces in both forward and reverse directions.

Disadvantages of drum brakes

A major disadvantage of the drum brake operation is 'brake fade'. This condition occurs when the temperature between the two friction linings increases so much during braking that it causes a reduction in the braking performance. The driver then has to apply greater pressure to the brake pedal to try to obtain the same braking efficiency. This condition normally arises when the vehicle is driven

for long periods and the brakes have been used regularly to slow the vehicle down from high speeds or downhill descents.

Another cause of brake fade is when regular braking raises the temperature to a level that boils the brake fluid. If this occurs, then air bubbles and moisture are created within the hydraulic system and braking efficiency is reduced.

The maximum braking torque that the drum brake system can produce is affected by the friction created between the brake shoe linings and the drum, and the effect this has on the shoe. The overall braking efficiency and torque produced is also affected by the service condition of the brake linings. Manufacturers have found that regular inspections and the use of more modern friction materials with anti-fade properties can reduce some of the brake fade experience.

Parking brake (drum type)

Manufacturers normally also use a drum brake system to provide the parking brake on models with drum brakes on the rear axle. For the normal braking system to become active, the driver applies footbrake pressure to operate the hydraulic circuit. This hydraulic pressure then forces the brake shoes on to the brake drum lining face and brake application takes place. For the parking brake system, the driver uses a separate handbrake lever. The mechanical lever is connected to a cable system that runs to the rear braking system. The cable is connected to the rear brake shoes within the brake drums using a mechanical linkage to operate. On applying the parking brake, the lever is pulled up and the movement of the cables operates the mechanical linkage to move the shoes outwards. The brake shoe lining grips on to the brake drum lining face to stop the rear wheels from rotating.

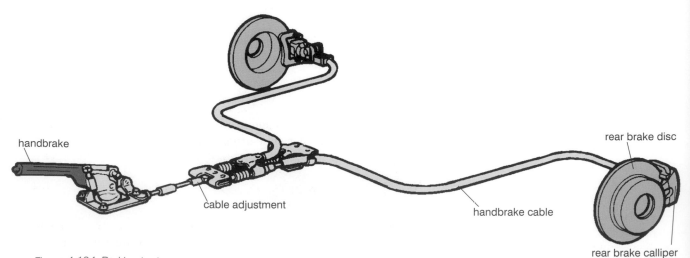

handbrake

cable adjustment

handbrake cable

rear brake disc

rear brake calliper

Figure 4.134 Parking brake arrangement

Most vehicle manufacturers have designed their parking brake systems to operate on the rear brakes, but some have produced systems connected to the front brakes. This is a good functional alternative, but the design set-up is more complex due to the steering application and wheel movement. Manufacturers of four-wheel drive vehicles also have parking brake systems with the brake drum fitted to the transmission system. It is normally fitted to the propeller shaft system and mechanically operated to lock the transmission when applied.

4.21.2 Introduction to disc brakes

The disc brake was developed to minimise the fade problem seen in drum brakes. When brake fade occurs, the driver has to apply a much larger effort to effect braking and, in extreme cases, it becomes impossible to bring the vehicle to rest. The problem arises when a drum brake is continually operated for long periods, for example when a vehicle descends a long mountain road. In such cases, excess heat is generated and cannot be dissipated quickly enough. This is because in drum brakes the heated regions are shrouded by metal.

To solve the problem, the way the heat is released from the brakes during their operation needs to be improved.

Disc brakes address this problem. They consist of an exposed disc, which is attached to the hub flange; the two friction pads are pressed on to this disc to give a braking action (Figure 4.135). The pads are moved by hydraulic pistons working in cylinders formed in a calliper that is secured to a fixed part of the axle.

Figure 4.135 Disc brake and calliper

When hydraulic pressure is applied to the two cylinders held in the calliper, the pistons move; this action forces the friction pads into contact with the rotating disc that is often made from cast iron or other materials, such as carbon or ceramic on high-performance vehicles. The sandwiching action of the pads on the disc gives a retarding action and heat generated from the energy of motion is conducted to the disc.

As a large part of the disc is exposed to the air, heat is easily radiated, with the result that the brake can be used continuously for long periods before serious fade occurs. Since the friction pads move at a right angle to the disc, any drop in the friction value does not affect the force applied to the pad, so this type of brake is not so sensitive to heat build-up.

No assistance is obtained from the rotating disc to aid the driver in the application of a disc brake, so to achieve a given retardation a disc brake requires a greater pedal pressure than that needed for a drum brake. Manufacturers recognised that the driver would need additional assistance to apply enough braking force to slow down or stop the vehicle. Consequently, power assistance and servo assistance were developed. Both systems are discussed on page 484.

Adjustment for pad wear is automatic on a disc brake, so minimum attention is required. However, the level of brake fluid should be inspected periodically as this will fall as the brake pads wear. The open nature of the system means that pads can easily be inspected for wear and, assuming there has been no corrosion, worn pads can be easily replaced.

4.22 Brake operating systems

Today, brake shoes and pads are generally operated hydraulically, apart from the handbrake as this needs a mechanical linkage for safety. Up to the mid-1930s, most systems were mechanically operated and this type is considered for the purpose of appreciating the features offered by modern systems.

4.22.1 Mechanically operated brake system

Figure 4.136a shows the layout of a simple mechanical system. Four adjustable rods or cables link the brake-shoe operating levers to a transversely mounted cross-shaft. The footbrake and handbrake controls are connected to the cross-shaft by links having elongated holes to allow independent operation of each control.

In this system, each brake will receive its share of the brake pedal force only when the mechanism is balanced (i.e. set up so that each shoe contacts the drum simultaneously). If one brake has a much smaller shoe-drum clearance than the others, all of the driver's force will be directed to that brake; as a result, the unbalanced braking action will cause the vehicle to 'pull' violently to the side on which this brake is situated.

Compensation devices were fitted in the layout to overcome this problem and Figure 4.136b shows a simple arrangement for balancing two brakes.

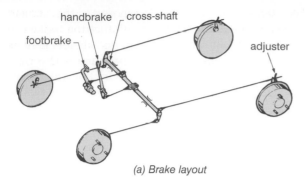

(a) Brake layout

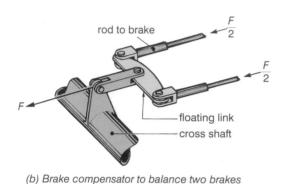

(b) Brake compensator to balance two brakes

Figure 4.136 Mechanical brake layout

A fully compensated brake system ensures that each brake is applied at the same time and that each one receives its share of the braking effort. To achieve this condition, the mechanical system shown would require three compensators: front (to balance the front brakes); rear (for the rear brakes); and centre (to equalise front and rear).

The large force on the brake shoe is achieved by using a compound lever system. The larger the leverage, the smaller the force needed on the brake pedal. However, if a very large leverage is provided, the brake will require frequent adjustment to counteract wear of the brake linings.

To comply with vehicle legislation, a vehicle must have a handbrake (parking brake) to hold the car stationary when the vehicle is left unattended. If for any reason the main braking system fails, then the handbrake can also function as an emergency brake.

Legal requirements insist that hydraulically operated brake systems must be fitted with a mechanical handbrake that acts on at least two wheels. Normally, a rod or cable is used to link the handbrake with a mechanical lever-type shoe expander fitted to the rear brakes. A strong, flexible cable between the mechanical lever and the rear brake system allows the cable to be routed logically throughout the under-body area and also allows for suspension and body movement.

To operate the handbrake mechanism, the driver would normally pull up the lever, which in turn operates a ratchet and pawl mechanism. Pulling up the lever to its 'on' position will apply the mechanical brake mechanism to a lock position. On disengaging the lever, the pawl will release from the ratchet and the applied pressure on the cable and mechanical system is released.

Figure 4.137 Mechanically operated handbrake

4.22.2 Hydraulically operated brake system

Vehicle manufacturers identified very early that the mechanical braking system had some limitations and that a hydraulic braking system could produce much higher efficiency levels than the mechanical designed system. Using a hydraulic system over a mechanical system is more suited for vehicles with independent suspension and where the brake pressure balance between all braking wheels is fully compensated. Hydraulic systems also allow the fluid pressure to be transmitted and applied more responsively, depending on driver demands and driving conditions.

The basic layout of a master cylinder is shown in Figure 4.138. This component is the main operator for the hydraulic system, supplying the brake callipers and wheel cylinders with the fluid required when the driver brakes. Small-bore pipes or tubing (Bundy tubing) are used to connect up the master cylinder to each of the brake callipers or wheel cylinders. Hydraulic brake fluid is contained within all of the components and pipework for instant application. The master cylinder also has a reserve of fluid stored in a reservoir mounted on to its housing for additional supply if required.

Brake operation

When the footbrake is depressed by the driver, the pedal acts on a piston in the master cylinder and pumps fluid through the lines into the wheel cylinders and callipers. As the pressurised fluid enters the wheel cylinders and callipers, the pistons move outwards to bring the shoe or pad into contact with the drum or disc. After movement has been taken up, the force on the master cylinder piston further pressurises the fluid in the system and applies a force to each brake. At this stage, the greater the force that is applied to the pedal, the higher the pressure produced in the system.

The pressure of the fluid in each wheel cylinder and calliper produces a force on the piston, which is applied to the brake. Since fluid may be regarded as being incompressible, and the pressure is the same

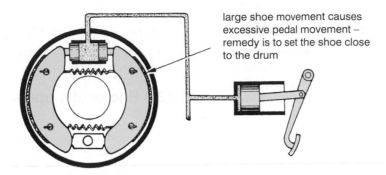

large shoe movement causes excessive pedal movement – remedy is to set the shoe close to the drum

Brake requiring adjustment

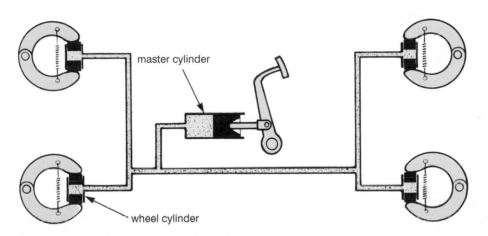

master cylinder

wheel cylinder

Hydraulic brake layout

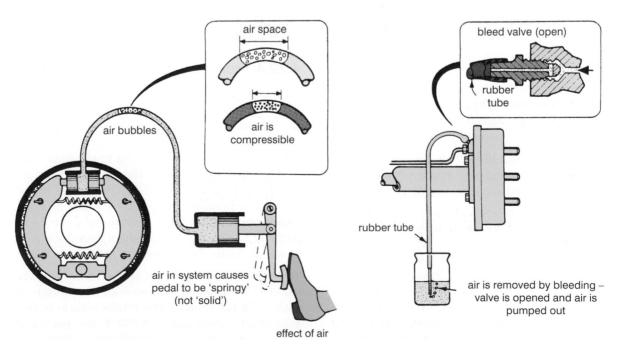

air space

air is compressible

bleed valve (open)

rubber tube

air bubbles

air in system causes pedal to be 'springy' (not 'solid')

effect of air

rubber tube

air is removed by bleeding – valve is opened and air is pumped out

Figure 4.138 Simple hydraulic brake operation

throughout the system, the thrust on any part of the system is proportional to the area of that part. In view of this fundamental law, the force applied to the pistons can be varied to suit the application.

Any air that is present in the system causes the brake pedal to lose its 'solid' feel (i.e. the pedal becomes *springy*). This is dangerous because the required fluid pressure cannot always be built up before the master cylinder piston reaches the end of its travel. Although the compressibility of the air does not prevent the build-up in fluid pressure, its elastic nature makes it necessary to remove the air after any part of the system has been disconnected. This operation is called *bleeding* and valves are fitted at each wheel cylinder and calliper to allow the air to be removed.

The single-line system shown has one major disadvantage: if a fluid leak occurs in any part of the system, then brake failure results. On these occasions, it is hoped that the driver realises that the handbrake is the emergency brake; although it acts on two wheels only, it enables the vehicle to be safely brought to rest.

For safety reasons, modern vehicles use a dual-line system. This layout ensures that at least two brakes can be operated by the footbrake in the event of a leak.

Brake fluid

For a hydraulic braking system to operate effectively at all times it needs to have properties to overcome adverse conditions, specifically it should have a low freezing point, a high boiling point and a low viscosity. The brake fluid must be non-corrosive and act as a lubricant for the main brake system components. Components such as the master cylinder, callipers and wheel cylinders have internal rubber seals and moving parts. The external pipework and flexible hoses used in the braking system need the same protection. Brake fluid is **hygroscopic**, but the rate at which it absorbs moisture is determined by its type and the usage of the braking system.

Most vehicle manufacturers recommend that the braking system is checked periodically and that a brake fluid service is carried out every two or three years.

Hygroscopic: the ability to absorb moisture.

Today, vehicle manufacturers have a greater choice of fluids depending on their vehicle system requirement and demands. Early systems used a vegetable-based or a mineral-based fluid to operate the hydraulics, and it was critical for the technician to identify which type was to be used. If by accident the technician was to top-up a vegetable-based system with mineral-based

fluid, it would cause the rubbers seals within the master cylinder, callipers and wheel cylinder to fail in a very short period of time. Therefore, it is important to note that the correct specification of fluid is used when topping up or when carrying out a brake fluid service.

Note: further information about brake fluid can be found in the hydraulic operating system section of this book on page 483.

4.22.3 Pneumatic operating systems

Pneumatic operating systems are commonly used across a wide range of vehicles. Low-pressure systems are used on light vehicles and this is normally operated by the driver applying additional boost when required. The high-pressure systems or full compressed air braking system is used on heavy goods vehicles. This would be too heavy, bulky and expensive for a light vehicle.

Manufacturers have identified that if they use a combination of part-compressed air and part-hydraulic air, this helps to reduce the pedal pressure to a more comfortable effort. This type of 'air over hydraulic' system is used on light trucks in the three-tonne category.

Manufacturers moving towards the use of disc-type braking systems use the assistance of a vacuum servo to support the application of the brakes when applied. The servo assembly uses the manifold depression or vacuum generated by an engine-driven pump to assist the driver in applying the brake.

Manufacturers of four-wheel drive variants use a pressurised fluid system to provide the driver with additional brake force assistance when required.

4.22.4 Front/rear brake apportionment

To obtain the correct apportionment between the front and rear brakes, the system has to be designed to accommodate the inertia acting on the centre of gravity when the vehicle is experiencing deceleration. This moves the load forward on to the front brakes while the rear brake load is reduced. If the system is not designed to compensate for this, then the rear brakes will prematurely lock up, causing a brake in balance from front to rear. Load transfer can be seen in Figure 4.139, where the weight of the vehicle moves forward over the front wheels as the vehicle brakes.

To have an understanding of the change in wheel loading, we need to consider and appreciate the set-up of a typical rear-wheel drive vehicle having a static load distribution of 50/50. If this system was under test conditions, it would show that 75 per cent of the total weight would be forced on to the front wheels under maximum braking application. To improve this balance, we need to adapt this system so the front brakes provide about 60 per cent of the retarding forces generated. Having a 60/40 apportionment provides a better balance, increases the safety aspects and reduces the possibility of the front wheels locking up before the rears. The 60/40 ratio can be achieved by using:

- discs at the front and low-capacity drum brakes at the rear
- larger area wheel cylinders at the front
- larger diameter drums at the front
- more effective brakes at the front.

Figure 4.139 Weight transfer under braking

4.23 Brake arrangements

As we have seen, brake arrangements can be divided into two main classes: drum and disc.

4.23.1 Drum brakes

Drum brakes are much less popular than they were in the past, with most modern light vehicles having no drum brakes at all. However, some will still use a drum arrangement for the parking brake system. Some light vehicles will have hydraulically operated drum brakes fitted to the rear, while having disc brakes fitted to the front.

The drum/disc arrangement allows more brake force to be applied to the front wheels. Also, the simple application of a mechanical handbrake to the rear drum brake make this type an obvious choice for a rear brake. Due to the performance and extended service intervals of modern vehicles, the rear brakes tend to be disc arrangements.

Various brake shoe arrangements are used; these include:

- leading and trailing shoe
- twin leading shoe (2LS)
- duo-servo.

Leading and trailing shoe brake

Figure 4.140 shows the layout of a leading and trailing shoe brake. The shoes are hydraulically expanded by two separate pistons fitted in a wheel cylinder fixed rigidly to the back-plate. Rotation of the shoes with the drum is prevented by an anchor pin that is securely mounted on the back-plate, so as to resist the full braking torque. A strong spring is fitted to return the fluid and shoes when the brake is released. By mounting this spring on the back-plate side of the shoes, the shoes are pulled against high spots of the back-plate, formed to provide a bearing surface for the brake shoe. A snail cam or eccentric, mounted behind each shoe, provides for manual adjustment of the shoes. These cams can be partially rotated with the aid of a wrench without removing the drum; they are positioned so that each shoe is set as close to the drum as possible without causing excessive binding (rubbing). Adjustment on more modern vehicles tends to be automatic. This is discussed on page 470.

When the vehicle is stationary, hydraulic pressure forces both shoes outwards. After the clearance has been taken up, an equal force is applied by each shoe to the drum.

This equal force does not apply when the vehicle is moving. Instead, the drag of a moving drum on the friction linings causes one shoe to be applied hard and the other to be pushed towards the off position. As a result, the braking torque produced by the shoes is in the ratio 4 : 1.

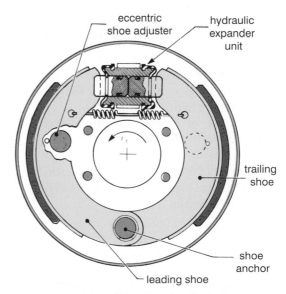

Figure 4.140 Leading and trailing shoe brake layout

The shoe that does the most work is called the *leading shoe*, and this can be identified by the fact that it is the first shoe in the DOR after the hydraulic expander.

Conversely, the other brake shoe is called the *trailing shoe*. Since the work done by the leading shoe is much greater, the rate of lining wear on this shoe is higher than the trailing shoe. This means that unless a thicker lining is used on the leading shoe, it reaches its wear limit well before the trailing shoe. On most new shoe linings you will notice this difference in lining thickness as you inspect or replace the brake shoes.

On the layout shown, the unequal wear pattern can be taken up by the floating pistons in the wheel cylinder. If this were not so, some provision would be needed to allow the brake shoes to be adjusted so that they can be centralised with the drum.

Self-servo action

Self-servo action is the effect of drum rotation on a brake shoe. This can be demonstrated by the arrangement shown in Figure 4.141. Applying an equal force to the free end of the two levers, and rotating the drum in the direction shown, causes the frictional force on lever A to increase the loading on the shoe. The opposite effect is produced on lever B; here the frictional force acts against the force *F*, so this lever, which represents the trailing shoe, is not pressed so hard against the drum.

Reversing the direction of the drum changes the action and this converts the leading shoe into a trailing shoe, this is beneficial when the vehicle is travelling backwards.

The term 'self-servo' is used to describe this self-apply condition and Figure 4.142 shows the three factors that vary the amount of self-servo that acts on a leading shoe:

1 Position of shoe tip – self-servo is increased as the leading edge of the friction lining is moved towards the hydraulic expander.
2 Coefficient of friction (μ) of the lining – an increase in the friction value gives a larger self-servo action.
3 Position of the shoe anchor – moving the anchor towards the centre of the drum increases the self-servo action.

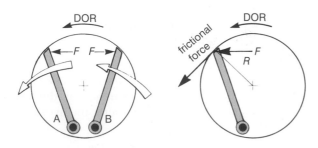

Figure 4.141 Self-servo

Effects of self-servo

To obtain a leading and trailing shoe brake that has a high braking power (large drum drag for a given application force), a large self-servo action is required. The idea is to use the energy from drum rotation to minimise the effort applied by the shoe expander through the hydraulic pistons.

The negative servo action on the trailing shoe must be minimised in order to obtain a powerful brake. Often, this is achieved by placing the friction lining of the trailing shoe nearer to the expander than is used in the case of the leading shoe. Attention to this feature must be given when reassembling a brake, because if the shoes are reversed a fierce braking action, and possible *grab* (lock-up), will result.

A number of problems arise when a large self-servo action is relied on to give a powerful leading and trailing brake. Since self-servo action relies on friction, any fall-off in the friction value seriously affects brake performance. Normally this occurs when the brake reaches a critical temperature; as a result, serious fade occurs.

Another drawback of a brake that uses a high self-servo is the variation in braking power that occurs when the force applied to the shoe is varied. Ideally, the ratio drum drag : applied force should be constant because this gives a progressive braking action. This was not the case with many leading and trailing shoe brakes used in the past; instead, the brake power increased with pedal pressure and often the brake locked up without warning.

Floating shoes

Figure 4.143 shows a leading and trailing shoe brake fitted with a wedge-type adjuster. In this design, the brake shoes butt against an adjuster unit that acts as a fixed anchor for the shoes. Both shoes are free to float up and down on the anchor; this arrangement allows for shoe centralisation and also reduces the tendency of the brake to grab.

When this type of brake is applied, the two shoes are pushed outwards to contact the drum. Rotation of the drum forces the leading shoe directly against the anchor; the reaction of the trailing shoe is taken through the expander to the leading shoe.

Note the position of the brake linings on the shoes on this design. This asymmetrical layout means that care is needed to ensure that the linings are refitted in their correct positions after overhaul. Also, it is important to check that the assembled back-plates have not been interchanged with their shoes from left to right, and vice versa.

Handbrake operation is by a lever and strut mechanism.

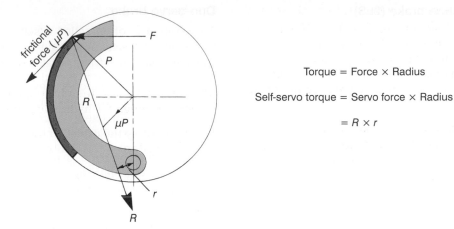

Torque = Force × Radius

Self-servo torque = Servo force × Radius

= R × r

Direction of self-servo force

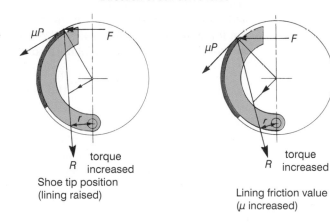

torque
increased
Shoe tip position
(lining raised)

torque
increased
Lining friction value
(μ increased)

torque
increased
Shoe anchor position
(pin moved towards
centre of drum)

Figure 4.142 Factors affecting self-servo torque

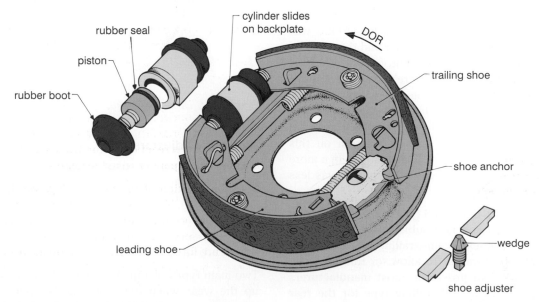

Figure 4.143 Leading and trailing shoe brake components

Twin leading shoe brake (2LS)

Before the universal adoption of the disc for front brakes, the 2LS was commonly used. Each shoe had its own expander, which was positioned so that both shoes were subject to a self-servo action (Figure 4.144).

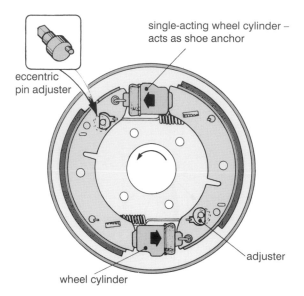

Figure 4.144 Twin leading shoe brake arrangement

An interlinking pipe behind the back-plate provided an equal hydraulic pressure to each single-acting cylinder. The cylinder housings acted as a shoe anchor for the floating shoes, so the cylinders were rigidly attached to the back-plate.

Compared with a leading and trailing shoe brake, the 2LS type had the following advantages:

1   Even lining wear – because both shoes did an equal amount of work, a longer life was achieved, the brake ran cooler and the need for adjustment was less frequent.
2   Equal self-servo – there were two effective shoes so a more powerful, stable brake was obtained.
3   Greater resistance to fade – less reliance was placed on one shoe to do the major share of the braking, so the self-servo action on this shoe could be reduced. This resulted in a more progressive brake and, as a result, it was less sensitive to heat.

One disadvantage of the 2LS type showed up during reversing. Unless special double-acting linkage was provided, both shoes became trailing shoes when the car travelled backwards. To allow for this problem, and the handbrake provision, most manufacturers retained the leading and trailing type for the rear brakes.

Duo-servo brake

This system is often called a self-energising brake. It is a very powerful brake, but its effectiveness falls tremendously if the friction value decreases.

Figure 4.145 shows a modern, hydraulically operated duo-servo brake. The operating principle is based on the use of drum energy to considerably boost the force applied by the driver.

When the leading shoe is pushed out into contact with the forward-moving drum, the frictional force causes it to rotate partially with the drum. The shoe movement produced by this self-wrapping action is transmitted through a floating adjuster to the trailing shoe, which brings the shoe into contact with the drum. With the trailing shoe against the anchor pin and the shoe-to-drum clearance having been taken up, the force applied by the expander is supplemented by the self-energising action of both shoes.

To minimise the delay before the self-energisation assistance comes into action, the trailing shoe is held on the anchor pin by a stronger return spring; this means that the expander only moves the leading shoe. In this case only, the leading shoe is called the 'primary shoe'; it gets this name because the shoe is made to contact the drum before the secondary shoe.

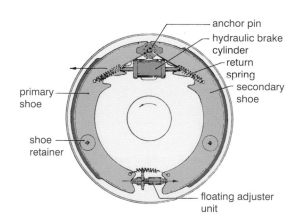

Figure 4.145 Duo-servo brakes

Automatic adjusters

Various methods are used to provide some form of automatic adjuster to set the shoes the correct distance from the drum.

Adjustment of front disc brakes is automatic, so to reduce servicing costs most modern rear drum brakes are fitted with separate automatic adjusters.

Two main types of adjuster are used: one type takes up the wear when the footbrake is operated; the other type is controlled by handbrake operation.

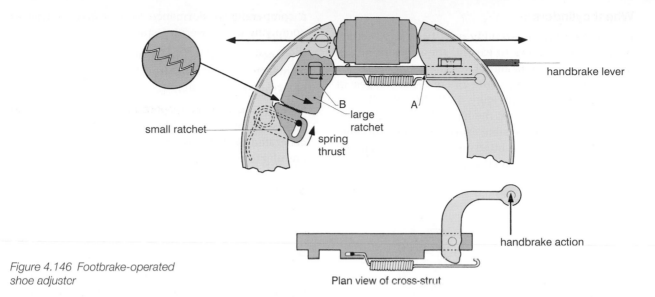

Figure 4.146 Footbrake-operated
shoe adjuster

Plan view of cross-strut

Footbrake-operated shoe adjuster

Figure 4.146 shows one of the many arrangements that uses the footbrake to take up wear. This type uses a cross-strut, retained to one shoe by a spring, and two ratchets mounted on the other shoe. A spring acting on the small ratchet pushes the fine saw-like teeth towards the large ratchet, which has a slot to receive the cross-strut. When the brake is set up correctly, a small clearance exists at B.

When the shoe-to-drum clearance is small, brake operation allows the ratchets to move with the shoe. However, when the outward movement of the shoes exceeds the clearance at B, the strut holds back the large ratchet and causes it to jump a tooth. Consequently, when the brake is released, the return movement of the shoe is less than before.

The handbrake operates in the normal way – a cranked lever acts directly on one shoe and the reaction on the pivot pushes the strut against the locked ratchets to expand the other shoe.

Handbrake-operated shoe adjuster

This system utilises the movement of the handbrake to take up lining wear; Figure 4.147 shows one arrangement. In this case, the shoes are held apart to give the correct shoe-to-drum clearance by a threaded strut, which is expanded by a ratchet-toothed wheel. This is moved by a pawl connected to the handbrake lever.

As lining wear takes place, the movement of the handbrake lever increases. When this movement exceeds a given limit, the pawl jumps a tooth on the ratchet. The handbrake action following this relative tooth-to-pawl movement lengthens the threaded strut and sets the shoes closer to the drum.

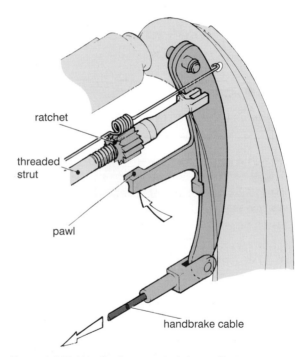

Figure 4.147 Handbrake-operated shoe adjuster

Duo-servo adjustment

Duo-servo-type brakes often utilise the self-wrapping movement to control the length of the floating adjuster. Some pawl and ratchet arrangements use the forward motion of the car to give the adjustment, whereas others only operate in reverse.

Shoe-release

Sometimes drum removal is difficult if the drums have become grooved. To allow for this, a hole is often provided in the back-plate in the region of the automatic adjuster to back off the shoes to allow the drum to be removed without damaging the shoes and drum.

Wheel cylinders

A shoe-type brake assembly uses two single-acting-type wheel cylinders to expand the shoes in a twin leading shoe brake and a double-acting type for a leading and trailing shoe brake. These types of cylinder are shown in Figure 4.148. Wheel cylinders are fitted with a valve at the highest part to allow air to be bled from the system. Normally, only one valve for the two cylinders is fitted on a 2LS brake assembly; this valve is provided on the upper cylinder.

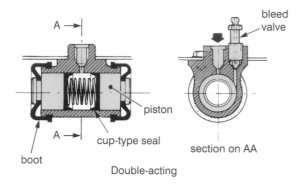

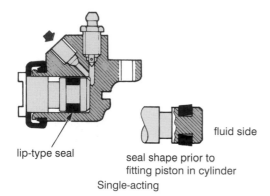

Figure 4.148 Types of hydraulic wheel cylinder

Brake shoe frictional material

We have seen that, in the past, asbestos fibres were commonly used as the brake lining friction material. These were either woven or moulded and then bonded with a resin to give a friction facing in the required form. Asbestos combined strength with good thermal and friction qualities, and was relatively cheap to produce.

Based on research carried out over many years, it has been identified that breathing in asbestos dust greatly increases the risk of lung cancer and other respiratory problems. Following this research, the use of asbestos in braking systems and many other applications has been banned. Manufacturers have been forced to developed brake and clutch linings using asbestos-free materials. Although this has increased the manufacturing costs, it has greatly reduced health risks and new materials now display

a comparable performance to asbestos, as well as complying with governing standards.

The new materials used vary between vehicle manufacturers, but range from **Kevlar** to a combination of steel and mineral fibres.

Note: it is very important to ensure that masks are used when working on the brake linings as the dust generated from the brake pads and shoes can still be harmful to your respiratory system.

Kevlar: the brand name of an extremely strong synthetic fibre used to reinforce rubber and other materials.

Bonded friction linings

Early versions of brake linings were secured to the brake shoe by the means of brass, copper or aluminium rivets. The modern arrangement is to use a specially cured adhesive to stick the facing on to the brake shoe. As well as giving greater strength and a more accurate profile, this method of attachment also improves heat flow and eliminates scoring of the drum rubbing surface by the grit-embedded rivets.

Although bonding allows more wear to take place, it is recommended that as a general rule the facing should be changed when it has worn down to one-third of its original thickness. Most vehicle manufacturers provide specification data to identify the minimum thickness permitted before replacement is required.

4.23.2 Disc brakes

Disc brakes are now favoured by all manufacturers of cars, as this type offers a number of advantages.

1 The disc surface on which heat is generated is directly exposed to the air, allowing easier dissipation of heat and giving a greater resistance to fade.
2 Independence of self-servo effect. The non-assisted brake may require more effort but its action is progressive (i.e. the brake gives a braking torque proportional to the applied force).
3 The brake is not so sensitive to friction changes.
4 Self-adjusting linings or pads are used, which are easily replaced.
5 Pedal travel does not increase as the disc heats up – heating a drum causes expansion that increases pedal travel.
6 Weight of disc brake arrangements is generally lighter than drum.

With modern vehicles now demanding higher levels or performance and refinement, car manufacturers generally fit disc brakes to both the front and rear wheels of light vehicles.

Figure 4.149 Brake disc arrangement running red hot

Two-piston calliper

The construction of a light-duty disc brake is shown in Figure 4.150. A split calliper assembly, rigidly attached to the stub axle carrier, houses the cylinders and two opposed pistons, which act directly on friction pads mounted on each side of the disc. Since the pads are visible, the degree of wear may be easily determined. They are replaced by removing the split pins and pad-retaining springs.

A rubber seal, mounted in a groove in the cylinder, prevents fluid leakage and also retracts the piston and pad after application of the brake (Figure 4.150b). This feature not only compensates for lining wear, but also keeps each pad close to the disc. A dust shield is fitted between the calliper and the piston to prevent ingress of water and dust, which could cause corrosion and seizure of the piston.

Internal drillings link the two fluid chambers, and a rubber hose supplies the calliper with fluid from the master cylinder. A bleed screw is fitted to each calliper to allow the brakes to be bled during servicing.

Four-piston calliper

When greater braking force is required, a four-piston calliper unit may be fitted. These are often fitted to high-performance vehicles where improved brake force is required to slow the vehicle down. The four-piston brake calliper is also used in conjunction with a tandem master cylinder to provide a safer application when operated with the servo assistance.

Figure 4.151 shows a high-performance four-piston calliper arrangement. These callipers are generally made of light aluminium alloy to improve the unsprung weight characteristics.

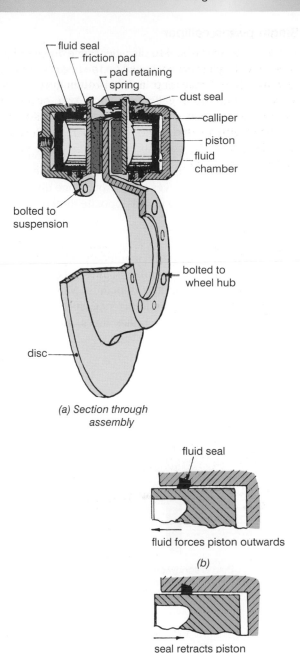

(a) Section through assembly

(b)

Figure 4.150 A two-piston calliper disc brake

Figure 4.151 High-performance four-piston brake calliper

Single-piston calliper

The limited road wheel-to-disc clearance on vehicles with a steering geometry based on the negative offset (negative scrub radius) principle is often insufficient to accommodate a calliper having two opposed pistons. In these cases, a single-piston calliper similar to Figure 4.152 is used.

The piston housing is keyed to the pad housing, which is bolted to the wheel suspension member. Hydraulic pressure moves the piston in one direction and the piston housing in the opposite direction.

4.23.3 Brake discs

Brake discs are generally manufactured from grey cast iron and come in a number of different diameters, depending on the vehicle demands. Vehicles that require increased braking efficiency, such as sports cars, can use cast iron brake discs. However, in recent years, some have progressed to use ceramic or carbon fibre-based discs.

The brake discs are secured to the wheel hub by bolt fixings. The discs rotate at the same speed as the road wheels and the exposed frictional surface of the disc is kept cool by the airflow drawn through the wheel when the vehicle is moving. In recent years, vehicle manufacturers have used either solid or ventilated discs, depending on the vehicle's driving requirements.

Solid discs

Solid discs have two frictional surfaces that the brake pads grip when brake pedal pressure is applied. The radiated heat produced is dissipated throughout the disc frictional surface and housing area. Prolonged heavy braking will lead to the brake discs overheating, causing brake fade and possible brake vibration through the steering or brake pedal.

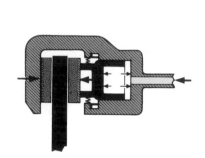

Disc is sandwiched by the action of the piston and the reaction of the cylinder

Diagram shows that negative offset layout needs a compact calliper

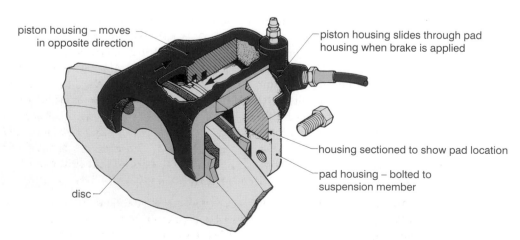

piston housing – moves in opposite direction

piston housing slides through pad housing when brake is applied

housing sectioned to show pad location

pad housing – bolted to suspension member

disc

Figure 4.152 A single-piston floating calliper

Figure 4.153 Solid disc

On later vehicles, manufacturers now use solid discs on the rear brakes where the braking force is less and the manufacturing costs are reduced by not using a drum brake set-up.

Ventilated discs

Like solid discs, ventilated discs also have two frictional surfaces, but these are separated by an air space. The frictional surfaces are joined by fins that are designed to draw cool air into the centre of the disc when it is rotating. This design feature supports the cooling of the disc when high temperatures are generated during braking, therefore preventing brake fade and increasing the life of the brake pads.

Ventilated discs are commonly used on the front braking system where the braking forces over the front wheels are much greater due to the weight transfer during the braking process. Other versions of ventilated discs also have additional drillings found in the brake frictional surface. This design allows a greater amount of air to flow over and through the disc assembly, and also allows gas build-up during heavy braking to escape, thereby improving braking efficiency. Another version of this type of brake disc has machined grooves milled into the frictional surface, arranged in a radial fashion from the disc centre to allow the gas build-up to escape more quickly and help deglaze the brake pads. This then helps to provide cleaner and quieter brake application when the pads mate with the frictional surface of the brake discs.

If the vehicle is fitted with a solid brake disc for its rear braking application, then the centre hub of the disc is sometimes used as a brake drum to support the function of a handbrake mechanism. Inside the hub of the disc will be a small set of brake shoes

Figure 4.154 Vented disc

connected to the cable mechanism and operated by the driver using the handbrake lever. On operating the lever, the connected cable will operate the brake shoe mechanism and the shoes will move outwards towards the internal face of the disc hub. Some vehicle manufacturers have used other versions of this system, where a complicated arrangement using the brake callipers provides the handbrake facility.

4.22.4 Brake pads

The brake pad has a great deal of work to deal with when it is pressed on to the brake disc during braking. The pad is usually made by bonding a frictional surface to a steel backing plate. The brake pads are held in place by a brake calliper and are arranged in pairs on each wheel. The steel backing plates are mounted into the calliper with the frictional surface facing the brake disc. As the driver presses the brake pedal, the brake pads are forced on to the brake disc through hydraulic pressure. The squeezing of the pads on to the brake disc slows the vehicle down. This process generates a great deal of heat through friction between the pad and the disc. The heat is then transferred to the brake pads and calliper and also to the brake disc. The frictional energy created also transfers some of the pad material on to the brake disc, causing wear of the pads. Brake pads will generally last up to 24,000 miles, depending on the driver's braking technique.

As mentioned previously, brake callipers fitted to normal road vehicles have two brake pads per calliper on each wheel. The brake calliper is fitted to the wheel hub, which is then attached to the suspension unit.

Some high-performance vehicles and racing cars can have additional brake pads and callipers fitted to each wheel to create greater braking forces. In some cases, the frictional material can be different across each pad set to create progressive braking performance.

The life of the brake pad is dependent on the braking technique and vehicle performance. The brake pads will be assessed for their condition during routine servicing and if they are not likely to last to the next service, they will be replaced. Some brake pads will incorporate a pad wear warning device to alert the driver when the pads are worn to a low limit. Some systems incorporate a piece of soft metal fixed into the brake pad metal backing, which is connected to a warning light on the driver display. As the pad wears to a point where the soft metal touches the brake disc, the light will illuminate due to the brake disc creating an earth path for the lamp.

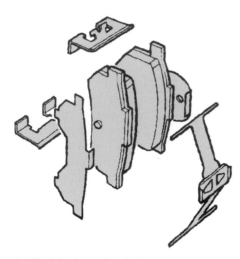

Figure 4.155 A brake pad and shim

Brake pads can come in many different types depending on their functional requirements. Some vehicles will have softer pads to create a more aggressive braking performance, and others will use harder frictional material for greater durability and a less aggressive braking feel. It is important to use the brake pad that is specified for the vehicle, as it will be manufactured to the vehicle's specifications and performance. Racing and high-performance cars will generally have softer brake pad material to give greater braking force, but these will wear more quickly.

Brake pad materials

In the past, brake pad material incorporated asbestos to help in preventing the pad material overheating. This has been replaced over the last decade with materials that are not prone to cause health problems. These alternative materials include cellulose, mineral fibres, **aramid**, chopped glass, steel, copper fibres and ceramics. The wear rate of discs and brake pads

is always a compromise between having extremely long-lasting brake frictional components, and ones that can create excellent braking performance. Additionally, the brake components will be manufactured to be quiet in operation and be more environmentally friendly in their construction and disposability.

A brake pad that offers excellent braking performance from cold operating temperatures and requires a low brake pedal pressure will be manufactured from a high coefficient material. Pads that are required to have a more sustainable progressive braking performance, with good heat efficiency, will be made from material with a lower, more constant coefficient of friction. These pads will also require higher brake pedal force.

> **Aramid**: a tough, heat-resistant synthetic fibre.

High-performance vehicles creating high braking temperatures can use a semi-metallic brake pad material. This provides high strength to the pad and conducts heat away from the brake discs efficiently. A disadvantage of this type of pad material is that the pads can create greater disc wear due to the high abrasive properties; the brakes can also be noisier.

Recently, some manufacturers have started to introduce ceramic braking materials to brake pads with copper fibres. These provide very high temperature sustainability for high-performance braking and over a longer period. This type of brake pad also provides less brake fade and brake dust during brake application. An additional benefit to ceramic material brake pads is the quieter braking when compared with conventional brake pad material.

4.24 Hydraulic operating systems

4.24.1 Benefits of hydraulic systems

Hydraulically operated braking systems are very popular and are generally used with light vehicles.

They offer the following advantages:

- Fully compensated – each brake receives its full share of the pedal effort from the master cylinder.
- High efficiency – the efficiency of the hydraulic system is greater than that of the mechanical layout.
- Good steering and suspension movement – suitable for vehicles having independent suspension. They allow the steered wheels to move without interference.

- Brake pressure can be changed by modifying the distribution of the master cylinder – the force exerted on a piston is governed by the piston area: the larger the area, the greater the thrust. For example, if the manufacturer requires a greater thrust on the trailing shoe, a larger piston can be used.

4.24.2 Layout of system

Figure 4.156 shows a simple, single-line hydraulic layout used to operate a drum and disc brake system. When the driver applies brake pedal pressure to the system, the master cylinder feeds hydraulic fluid to each of the wheel cylinders. Each cylinder then operates and moves the brake shoes outwards towards the brake drum. The master cylinder has an integral reservoir to store an additional amount of fluid to support the system's demands. Regulations

demand that a separate mechanical parking brake system must be provided on at least two road wheels. This then enables the driver to stop the vehicle in the event of the hydraulic system failing. In the system shown in Figure 4.156, the handbrake would operate the rear brakes to stop the vehicle from moving.

4.24.3 Master cylinder

Brake manufacturers offer two main types of master cylinder: single-cylinder and dual-cylinder (tandem) for use with single-line and dual-line system layouts respectively.

Single-cylinder type

Construction

Figure 4.156b shows the layout of a single-type master cylinder.

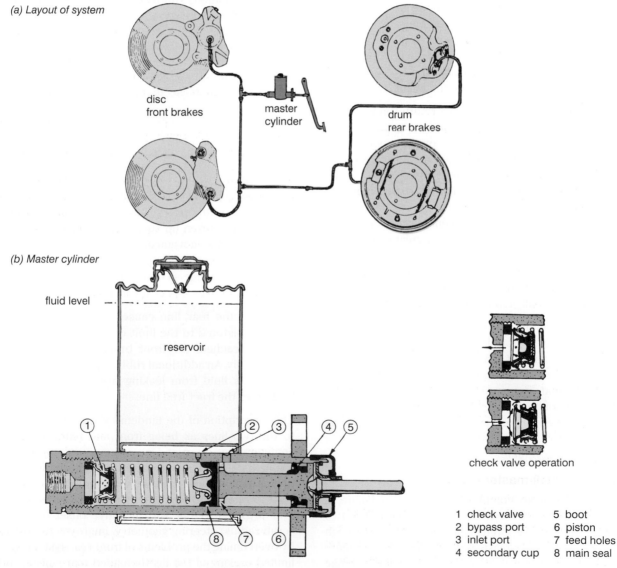

(a) Layout of system

disc
front brakes

master
cylinder

drum
rear brakes

(b) Master cylinder

fluid level

reservoir

check valve operation

1	check valve	5 boot
2	bypass port	6 piston
3	inlet port	7 feed holes
4	secondary cup	8 main seal

Figure 4.156 A hydraulic brake system using single-line master cylinder

Linked to the pedal by an adjustable push rod is a piston (6), which is sealed by a main rubber cup (8), held in position by a spring, and seated on a thin washer to prevent the rubber entering the feed holes (7). An inlet port (3) allows fluid around the waist of the piston; leakage of this fluid is prevented by a secondary rubber cup (4). Outward travel of the piston is limited by a circlip, and a rubber boot (5) excludes the dirt. A 0.7 mm bypass port (2), counter-bored half-way with a drill of 3 mm diameter, is positioned just in front of the main cup. A check valve (1), fitted at the outlet end of the cylinder, ensures the non-return of aerated fluid during the bleeding process.

Operation

When the brake pedal is depressed, the piston forces the fluid into the line until all shoe movement has been taken up. Thrust on the pedal will then pressurise the system and force each shoe against the drum. If shoe movement is too great (i.e. if the shoes require adjustment), the piston will reach the end of its travel before the brake applies. To overcome this problem, the driver should pump the pedal: a quick return of the piston creates a depression in the main chamber and causes fluid to flow through the feed holes and over the main cup to recharge the cylinder.

On release of the brake, the shoe return springs pump the fluid back to the master cylinder: any excess fluid in the line, caused by 'pumping' or expansion due to heat, is returned to the reservoir via the bypass port. Blockage of this small port prevents the return of the fluid and leads to the brakes 'binding', so to ensure that the main cup does not obstruct the port when the brake is off, a small free pedal movement is given. Continued binding of the brakes will create a great deal of heat in the friction surfaces, which will lead to overheating of components and possibly cause the brake fluid to boil. Boiling brake fluid can introduce air into the brake system, which will create poor braking performance.

A braking system depends on having good-quality brake fluid throughout the brake lines. If at any point there is a leakage of brake fluid from a brake line or braking component, the braking system will lose its ability to create pressure to force the brake linings on to the friction surfaces. This loss of brake pressure is often called brake system failure, and can cause the driver to have a serious accident through loss of control of the vehicle.

Tandem (dual) master cylinder

In order to avoid complete brake system failure, a tandem-type master cylinder is used. Due to the two independent brake circuits being controlled through the use of one brake master cylinder, a hydraulic failure in one brake line will result in the loss of one brake circuit only. This will still provide an effective but much reduced brake performance. When this occurs, it is hoped that the driver remembers that the handbrake is independent, because with this the driver is able to bring the vehicle to rest in reasonable time.

Construction

In general, the tandem cylinder may be considered as two single cylinders mounted end to end and Figure 4.157 shows the close similarity between this conception and the actual layout.

The cylinder contains two pistons, one directly connected to the pedal and the other operated by fluid pressure. Each piston, which is fitted with seals to prevent fluid leakage, controls a separate line to either the front or rear brakes. At each of the two outlet points, a check valve is fitted. One return spring is positioned between the pistons and a stronger return spring, acting on the independent piston, ensures that the pistons are forced back to their stops. Fluid is supplied through ports similar to the solo cylinder and the reservoir is divided into two parts to prevent a total fluid loss when one line fails.

Operation

Under normal conditions, the movement of piston 1 causes an increase in the fluid pressure in the chamber controlled by piston 1. Pressure from this chamber is transmitted to the front brake line and to piston 2, which, being free to move, will pressurise the rear brake line to the same extent as the front line.

Assuming a failure occurs in the front line, the movement of piston 1 will discharge fluid at the fracture and will allow the two pistons to contact. Although this stage has taken up some of the pedal travel, the remainder of the movement is available to operate the rear brakes. Repeated applications of the brake will eventually discharge all of the fluid from the portion of the reservoir that supplies the faulty section.

Failure in the rear line causes the initial pressure to move piston 2 to the limit of its travel. Once this point is reached, the front brake can be operated successfully. An additional rubber seal fitted to piston 2 prevents fluid from leaking from the serviceable section to the fractured line.

This description of the tandem cylinder has referred to the two lines as being front and rear, but other configurations do exist. One common arrangement is a split line diagonally linked system: this connects the brakes diagonally into two separate circuits – left-hand front to right-hand rear, and vice versa (Figure 4.158). This layout, together with negative offset (negative scrub radius) steering geometry, improves the safety by overcoming the problems of front-rear systems (i.e. limited braking of the lightly loaded rear wheels and spinning of the vehicle if the rear wheels lock).

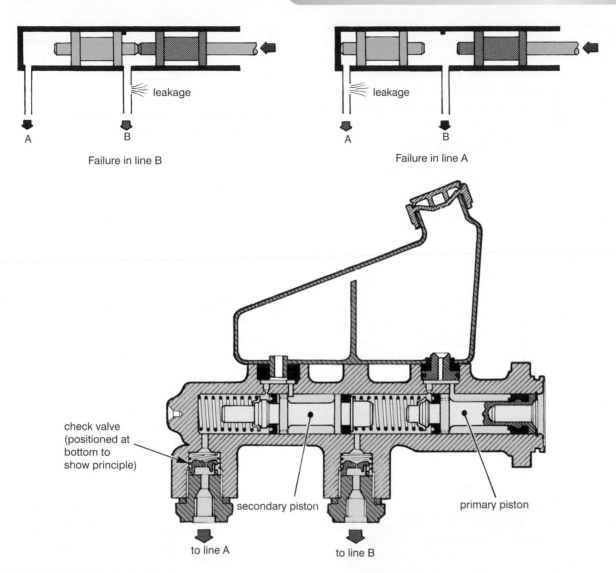

leakage

A   B

Failure in line B

leakage

A   B

Failure in line A

check valve
(positioned at
bottom to
show principle)

secondary piston

primary piston

to line A   to line B

Figure 4.157 Tandem master cylinder

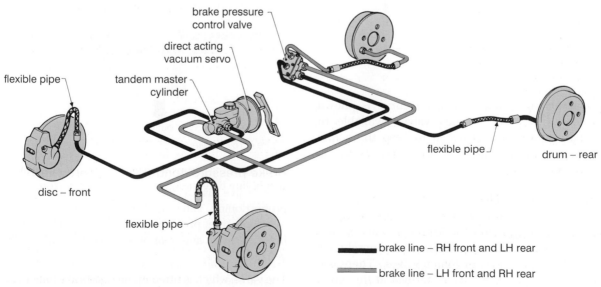

brake pressure
control valve

direct acting
vacuum servo

flexible pipe

tandem master
cylinder

flexible pipe

disc – front

flexible pipe

drum – rear

brake line – RH front and LH rear

brake line – LH front and RH rear

Figure 4.158 Split line diagonally linked system

A more expensive method uses four-piston callipers on each front disc, each pair supplied by independent lines from the tandem cylinder. Failure of one line ensures that the other line keeps both front brakes and one rear brake in operation.

4.24.4 Valves

Brake pressure proportioning valve

The amount of weight pushing down on a road wheel will affect the amount of braking force the brake can accept before wheel lock-up occurs. If a wheel is heavily loaded, it can brake harder than a wheel that is only lightly loaded. The more tyre to road friction, the less likely that it will lock up during heavy braking. When a vehicle is travelling forward and the brake is applied, the weight distribution moves towards the front. As the weight distribution moves towards the front of the vehicle, the rear wheels become increasingly likely to lock up. There is a variety of valves available to the manufacturer to combat this problem.

Figure 4.159 shows the shift of weight distribution under braking. To help prevent rear-wheel lock-up during heavy braking, brake line pressure acting on the rear brakes is reduced. The rate of this variation varies from vehicle to vehicle and is set by the manufacture.

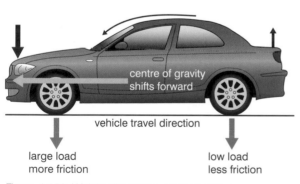

Figure 4.159 Weight distribution under braking

An example of an ideal pressure curve is shown in Figure 4.160. The various valves available to the manufacturer are designed to keep the actual pressure curve as close to the ideal curve as possible. (The dotted line shows what the rear wheel pressure would be without any valve fitted.) As soon as it goes above the ideal curve, the brakes would be susceptible to lock-up. With the valve activated, the actual curve stays below the ideal curve and shows safe rear-wheel braking pressures. The general term for these valves is 'proportioning valves'. There is a wide selection and the ones described in this book are the most common.

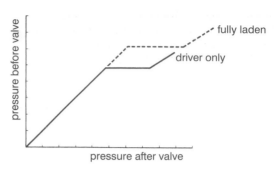

Figure 4.160 Control valve performance

Mechanical brake proportioning valve

The brake pressure proportioning valve in Figure 4.161 is fitted in the rear brake line. The valve is designed to reduce the risk of the rear wheels locking during heavy braking by limiting the brake pressure acting on the rear brakes. The valve consists of a spring-loaded plunger contained within a body. When the fluid pressure is relatively low, it will not overcome the spring, so the same pressure will act on all brakes.

When the brake is applied, fluid will initially pass to the rear brakes, but as the pressure is increased and a predetermined pressure is reached, the valve will close. Any further increase of fluid pressure is only applied to the front brakes.

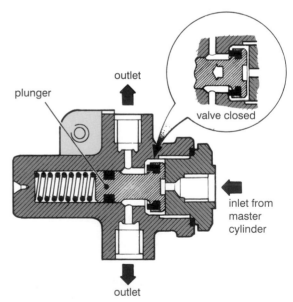

Figure 4.161 Brake pressure proportioning valve

Brake pressure control valve (inertia valve)

This valve is a development of the pressure proportioning valve and is particularly suited to overcome the problem of the large load variation between front and rear wheels of front-wheel drive vehicles.

The valve, which is fitted in the rear brake line(s), is an inertia-sensitive pressure-reducing valve that operates when the vehicle decelerates at a predetermined rate. When this occurs, the valve temporarily shuts off the rear line and allows the extra force on the pedal to increase the front brake pressure further. After a given pressure is reached, the valve restarts the pressure supply to the rear brakes but at a reduced rate (Figure 4.161). The unit takes into account vehicle weight transfer and attitude during braking, and is sensitive to vehicle loading and road conditions.

Figure 4.162 shows the construction of a valve suitable for a common rear brake circuit; a system having independent lines has two valves mounted side by side. The unit consists of a cylinder, mounted to the car body at a given angle, which contains a stepped piston and a steel ball.

At low vehicle deceleration rates, fluid enters the inlet port, passes around the ball and through the piston drilling to the rear brakes – pressure is equal in front and rear brake lines.

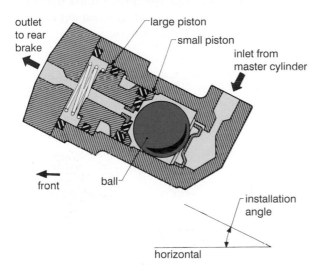

Figure 4.162 Brake pressure control valve (inertia type)

When the rate at which the vehicle slows down produces an inertia force sufficient to roll the ball up the sloping cylinder, then the ball shuts off the fluid supply to the rear brakes. When this occurs, the difference in piston area causes the outlet pressure to remain constant, even though the inlet pressure is being increased. At a given point, governed by the piston areas, an increase in inlet pressure starts to move the piston so as to give a proportional pressure to the rear brakes. Pressure in the two lines at this stage is given by:

$$\text{Inlet pressure} \times \text{Small area} = \text{Outlet pressure} \times \text{Large area}$$

Pressure differential warning actuator

This is a warning device to illuminate a 'brake failure warning lamp' if the pressure difference in the two brake lines differs by more than a given amount.

Failure of one brake line causes the pistons in Figure 4.163 to move and operate the electrical switch. The switch will remain closed until the pistons are reset.

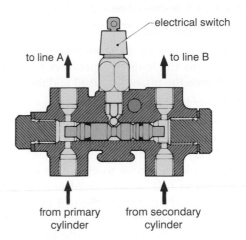

Figure 4.163 A brake pressure differential warning actuator

Load-apportioning valve

The purpose of the load-apportioning valve is to supply a quantity of pressurised hydraulic brake fluid to the rear brakes within its controlled limit in proportion to the load carried by the rear wheels. The load-apportioning valve helps to reduce the risk of a rear-wheel skid at times when the rear wheels are lightly loaded. The valve arrangement also ensures proportioning of the brake pressure when the rear wheels are heavily loaded.

The valve is designed to reduce the risk of a rear-wheel lock-up at times when the rear of the vehicle is lightly loaded, but also ensuring that the proportioning of the brake pressure to the rear wheels is correct when the rear wheels are heavily loaded. This type of valve is commonly fitted to vehicles such as estate cars and light commercial vehicles, as these types of vehicle are more likely to carry heavy loads in the rear. Where a single brake line is used, only one load valve is required. However, if the brake system incorporates a diagonal split line arrangement, there is a need to fit a valve to each line to provide stability under braking. The valve housing is bolted to a fixed part of the vehicle body and either a compression or tension spring is used to sense the load on the rear wheels. This spring connects the valve-operating lever to a part of the suspension system that moves in proportion to the vehicle load.

Figure 4.164 shows the construction of the valve. The operating lever acts directly on a piston that incorporates a ball valve. When the brake is 'off', the piston is at the bottom of the bore and the ball valve is held open by a push-rod fixed to the valve body. In this position the fluid can pass freely between the inlet and outlet ports. Upward piston movement takes place when hydraulic pressure is applied to the valve. This is achieved by making the area exposed to the fluid on the upper part of the piston larger than the area on the bottom part.

Operation – light load

The force exerted by the external spring on the piston governs the hydraulic pressure that must be applied before the piston is raised and the ball valve is closed.

When the load is light, only a small force is exerted by the spring on the piston. As a result, only a comparatively low pressure is needed to move the piston upwards so as to close the valve. When the pressure at this closure point is exceeded, full pressure cannot be applied to the rear brake; instead, any further increase in pedal force will cause the piston to control the valve so as to supply a pressure that is lower and proportional to the pressure applied to the front brake.

Operation – heavy load

As the load on the rear wheels is increased, a deflection of the suspension causes the external

spring force to increase. To overcome the extra force exerted by this spring on the piston, a higher fluid pressure must be built up before the piston is able to rise. Consequently, full pressure on the rear brakes is maintained until a much higher pedal force is applied.

Faults

Besides possible leakage of the seals, fracture of the external spring is likely. This breakage will cause the valve to reduce the pressure supplied to the rear brakes considerably. When the valve is defective, the complete unit is usually replaced.

The type shown in Figure 4.164 has an adjusting screw between the lever and piston. This controls the point at which the valve comes into operation (i.e. the front/rear braking ratio for a given rear-wheel load). Setting the adjusting screw up correctly requires the use of special tools, including a brake pressure gauge and a set of vehicle scales to set the load of the vehicle to gain the correct brake pressure. Always refer to the manufacturer's test procedures when working on the brake system.

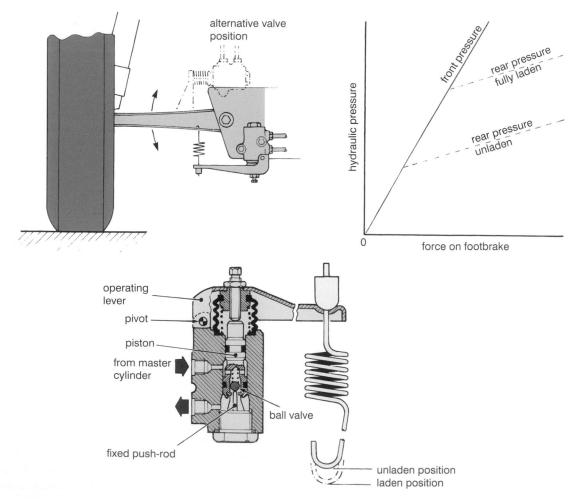

Figure 4.164 A load-apportioning valve

4.24.5 Electronically controlled brake proportioning or electronic brake force distribution

Weight transfer during braking places the majority of the vehicle's weight over the front wheels and axles as the inertia of the vehicle is thrown forwards. When the vehicle brakes, the suspension at the front will compress and the rear will extend. At this point, due to more weight acting upon the front wheels, greater grip will be available on the front wheels. As the rear suspension is extended and the weight transferred to the front, the rear wheels have lower levels of grip.

If the braking force applied to the front and rear wheels is the same at this point, the rear wheels will tend to lock due to the lower levels of grip available, which could create an unstable braking situation. Generally, most vehicles have a type of brake proportioning device that limits the brake pressure to the rear wheels and sends higher pressure to the front wheels. With the electronic brake force distribution (EBD), the brake pressure ratio is fixed between the front and rear.

The EBD system works in conjunction with the vehicle's ABS by monitoring the braking on the front and rear axles. If the ABS assesses that the rear wheels are about to lock, the ABS, through an electronic brake pressure control valve, will limit the brake pressure to the rear axle to prevent lock-up and skidding occurring. This system always ensures that the vehicle has the optimum braking performance across each axle in all conditions, including while towing and carrying heavy loads.

The ABS monitors the road wheel speeds and can sense when a wheel or axle is about to lock under braking. When this happens, the EBD system though the ABS limits the pressure to the axle, preventing a locking of the brakes and causing the vehicle to become unstable.

4.24.6 Brake fluid

Brake fluids must conform to the international standards introduced in the USA by the Society of Automotive Engineers (SAE) and Department of Transportation Federal Motor Vehicle Safety Standard (FMVSS).

The main requirements of a fluid:

- Low viscosity – the fluid must flow easily over a wide temperature range and be able to operate in very cold conditions.
- Compatibility with rubber components – besides resisting corrosion of metal parts, the fluid must not chemically react with the rubber seals, etc. (i.e. it must be non-injurious to the system).
- Lubricating properties – to reduce friction of moving parts, especially rubber seals.
- Resistance to chemical ageing – the fluid should have a long life when stored and must be stable when in use.
- Compatibility with other fluids – the fluid must mix with other fluids in its class.
- High boiling point – to avoid vaporisation when in use and heated by the brake action.

Most brake systems use a glycerine-alcohol (glycol) fluid with additives incorporated to allow it to meet the specifications. Since a number of different fluids are available, some vegetable and some mineral-based, the manufacturer's recommendation should be consulted before a system is serviced. This is essential because if a minute quantity of mineral oil is introduced into a system designed to operate on a vegetable-based fluid, the rubber seals will be severely damaged.

Boiling point of brake fluid

Glycol-based brake fluids are hygroscopic; this means that they absorb water from the atmosphere over a period of time. As a result, the boiling point lowers and in extreme circumstances causes complete failure of the brakes because of vapour locking. This condition is produced when the fluid in a part of the system is heated above its boiling point sufficiently to vaporise the water in the fluid. Once this occurs, the elastic nature of the steam allows the pedal movement to reach its limit of travel before it can build up sufficient pressure to apply the brakes effectively.

In view of the hygroscopic nature of most brake fluids, the SAE and FMVSS specifications require the fluid to have a wet boiling point and dry boiling point in excess of the stated value. The 'wet' boiling point is the temperature at which a fluid containing 3–3.5 per cent of water boils and produces steam bubbles.

In the case of a typical fluid such as SAE J 1703C, FMVSS 116 DOT 3, the 'wet' boiling point must be above 140 °C. Although this is higher than the 120 °C of fluids used in the 1950s, for safety reasons it is still necessary to change the fluid in a brake system every year. Bearing in mind that a brake fluid absorbs about 5 per cent water in this time, and that this contamination lowers the boiling point to about half its original value, then the need to change the fluid is evident.

To take account of the rising demands placed on brake fluids, especially in the field of disc brakes, the US Safety Regulations are continually being updated. Fluids that meet the DOT 4, DOT 5 and DOT 5.1 standards are now available, and some new fluids that have wet/dry boiling points of 190–270 °C permit the fluid renewal interval to be extended to 2–3 years.

Table 4.5 Boiling points for common brake fluids

	Dry boiling point	Wet boiling point
DOT 3	205 °C (401 °F)	140 °C (284 °F)
DOT 4	230 °C (446 °F)	155 °C (311 °F)
DOT 5	260 °C (500 °F)	180 °C (356 °F)
Dot 5.1	270 °C (518 °F)	190 °C (374 °F)

To prevent the brake fluids absorbing water during storage, they should be stored in sealed containers.

Brake fluid testers are available for use in the vehicle workshop. The tester is used to check the general condition of the brake fluid, including the water content and boiling point. A sample from the fluid reservoir is taken and analysed. This process aids the technician during service procedures in determining the age of the fluid and whether or not it needs changing.

The chemical properties used to produce brake fluid have some similarities with paint remover, so under no circumstances should brake fluid be allowed to come into contact with the paintwork of the vehicle. If any fluid accidently drips on to the paintwork, then it should be washed off with water immediately as it will react with the vehicle paint and cause damage. Always take extreme care when topping up the fluid

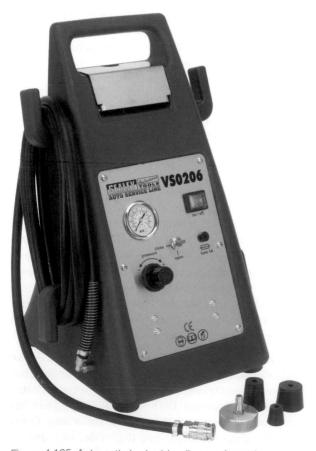

Figure 4.165 Automatic brake-bleeding equipment

reservoir by protecting nearby body panels. Never just wipe off any spillage; always use water because fluid residue can eat into the paintwork and discolour the area over a period of time.

Bleeding the brakes

This is necessary whenever air has entered the system or if the brake fluid has absorbed water over time. When bleeding all of the brakes at once, it is usual to start at the wheel farthest away from the master cylinder. The main steps in the operation are:

1 Ensure that the reservoir is full.
2 Attach one end of a rubber tube to bleeder valve and immerse other end in fluid contained in jar.
3 Open bleeder valve and slowly pump pedal until air bubbles cease to appear. Close bleeder valve as pedal is being depressed.
4 Repeat at all wheels.
5 Top up reservoir.

Automatic brake-bleeding equipment is available that connects to the fluid reservoir and fills the system as well as pressurising it to push the fluid through the master cylinder, pipes, ABS pump/modulator, valves and callipers. These are best used on vehicles with ABS systems.

4.24.7 Faults

The main faults and their causes are shown in Table 4.6.

Table 4.6 Main brake faults and causes

Fault	Cause
Pedal requires pumping	Shoes require adjustment
Springy pedal	Air in system
Spongy pedal (pedal creeps downwards)	Leakage in system, e.g. fluid passing main rubber cup

4.25 Servo operation

When the force that a driver can comfortably apply to the footbrake is insufficient to slow the vehicle down at the required rate, some form of assistance must be given. The boosting force used to reinforce the driver's effort is called servo assistance.

In the past, the assistance given by brake drum rotation (self-servo) kept the pedal force low, but when powerful disc brakes were introduced and vehicles became faster and more powerful, some other form of assistance was needed. Today, servo assistance for light vehicle brakes is provided by either pneumatic or hydraulic means: vacuum assistance for medium cars; hydraulic assistance for heavy cars and vehicles fitted with ABS; and compressed-air assistance for some light trucks and minibuses.

4.25.1 Vacuum assistance

The vacuum-operated servo is the most popular form of servo assistance. The term 'vacuum' is misleading because most systems use the depression formed in the induction manifold of the spark-ignition type of engine as a source of servo energy. In the case of a diesel engine, this energy is not available at the manifold due to the lack of a throttle valve and depression, so an engine-driven 'vacuum' pump (exhauster) is used to provide the required assistance.

All servo systems must be fail-safe, so if, for example, a fault develops in the vacuum unit, the main braking system must still be able to operate, albeit with a pedal force considerably greater than normal.

Progressive operation of the servo is a further requirement; this means that for light pedal pressure, the assistance given by the servo is proportional to the pedal effort. Figure 4.166 shows the relationship between the hydraulic pressure that acts on the brake cylinders (both with and without servo assistance) and the pedal effort. The servo valves provide a gradual increase in the assistance up to the knee point; at this point maximum vacuum assistance is given. Any rise in output pressure beyond the knee point is a direct result of the increased pedal effort.

Vacuum servos in use today are called suspended vacuum types, because when the vehicle is in use and the brakes are off, 'vacuum conditions' exist on both sides of the servo piston. When the brake is applied,

air from the atmosphere is bled to the chamber on one side of the piston to give the pressure difference. This arrangement allows the servo to respond quickly and is a considerable improvement on the earlier type that was atmospheric suspended; this air was present on both sides of the piston and this had to be 'drawn out' before assistance could be provided.

There are two main types of suspended-vacuum servo: indirect and direct.

Indirect-acting servo

This type is sometimes called a remote type because it is mounted remote from the pedal in the hydraulic line between the single master cylinder and the wheel cylinders. Generally, this type is not used today in production vehicles, although you may see it as an after-market fitment to earlier vehicles that were not originally fitted with servo assistance or where the performance of the braking system has been improved due to performance upgrades.

Figure 4.167 shows a servo suitable for a medium-sized car; it consists of three main items:

1 Vacuum cylinder containing a spring-loaded diaphragm
2 Slave hydraulic cylinder
3 Control valve actuated by hydraulic pressure

With the engine running and the brake off, the unit will be as shown in Figure 4.167a. The vacuum valve will be open and equal 'vacuum' pressure will be felt on both sides of the diaphragm.

Application of the pedal produces a hydraulic pressure on the brakes and also raises the valve piston in the servo. This movement closes the vacuum control valve and opens the air valve to allow a breakdown of the 'vacuum' in the outer chamber of the vacuum cylinder.

Air pressure difference causes the booster diaphragm to apply a thrust on the slave-cylinder piston, which boosts the thrust given by the driver's foot on the brake pedal (Figure 4.167b). 'Proportional' braking is obtained by allowing the difference in air pressure, felt by the booster diaphragm, to act on the control valve diaphragm: as the difference increases, the diaphragm will overcome the hydraulic pressure acting on the valve piston and close the air valve (Figure 4.167c).

Release of the pedal drops the hydraulic pressure to allow the valve piston to return and open the vacuum control valve. Air is quickly evacuated from the outer chamber of the vacuum cylinder and a spring returns the diaphragm. A hole in the centre of the slave-cylinder piston ensures that the brake can still be operated if the servo fails.

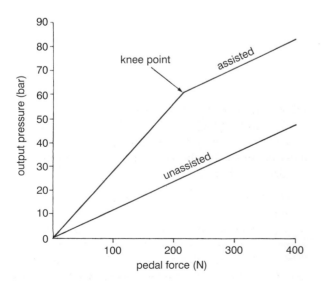

Figure 4.166 Servo assistance

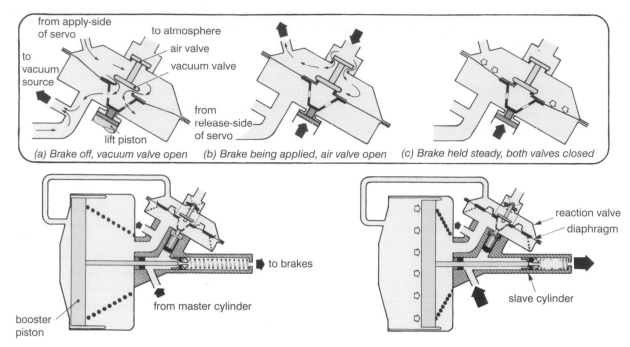

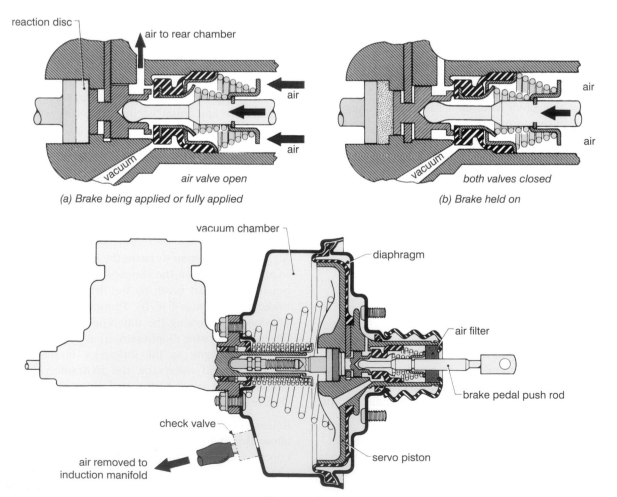

Figure 4.167 Suspended-vacuum servo – indirect type

Figure 4.168 Suspended-vacuum servo – direct type

Apart from general inspection of hoses etc., the only attention the unit requires is the periodic cleaning of the air filter.

The popularity of a tandem-operated hydraulic system has made the indirect type obsolete in modern vehicles.

Direct-acting servo

Today, the direct-acting, suspended-vacuum servo is designed as original equipment for cars and light commercial vehicles and has the advantage that it can be used with either single or tandem master cylinders. It gets its name from the fact that the pedal linkage is directly connected to the servo.

Figure 4.168 shows the position of the unit when the engine is running, the brakes are 'off' and the servo piston is 'suspended in vacuum'. Atmospheric pressure has been removed from both servo compartments and passed to the engine manifold through the pipe and non-return valve in the front of the vacuum chamber. Evacuation of air from behind the rubber-diaphragm-seated piston is through a control valve linked to the footbrake pedal.

Movement of the brake pedal initially closes the vacuum valve and then opens the air valve (Figure 4.168a). This allows air to flow through the filter and valve to the rear chamber. Atmospheric pressure is now acting on the rear chamber and a vacuum acting on the front chamber. The difference in air pressure between the two chambers produces a force on the piston that boosts the effort applied by the driver, as the atmospheric pressure is greater than the vacuum or depression.

As the servo piston starts to move, it will exert a force on the master cylinder push-rod through a rubber reaction disc. Pressure on this spongy disc will cause it to squeeze back and close the air valve (Figure 4.168b). In this position, the driver's efforts will be supplemented by a servo boost that is proportional to the effort applied: this feature enables the driver to 'feel' the load applied to the brake and also gives a progressive operation.

Further movement of the pedal will reopen the air valve and the previous events will be repeated up to the 'knee point'. Beyond this stage, the driver will be able to keep the air valve open; this indicates the limit of servo assistance.

Release of the brake pedal causes the air valve to close and the vacuum valve to open. This will restore the vacuum suspension of the piston and allow the spring to return the piston to the 'off' position. In the event of vacuum failure, the brakes can still be applied without servo assistance.

The assistance given by a vacuum chamber is proportional to the area of the piston (i.e. the larger the area, the greater the assistance). Accommodating a very large cylinder adjacent to the footbrake on a modern car is difficult and various systems are used to overcome the problem. One arrangement is to fit a servo cylinder with two pistons mounted in tandem. This arrangement effectively increases the surface area of the servo assistance, providing higher levels of braking pressure.

Vacuum supply

Although many servo units operate directly from the induction manifold, an improvement in performance and extra safety is achieved by using a vacuum reservoir to 'store vacuum' (Figure 4.169). This type of system is normally seen on larger light or light commercial vehicles.

The manifold depression, if any, of a diesel engine cannot be used to operate a brake servo, so a separate engine-driven pump is fitted. This pump, or exhauster, produces a 'vacuum' of about 500–600 mm of mercury.

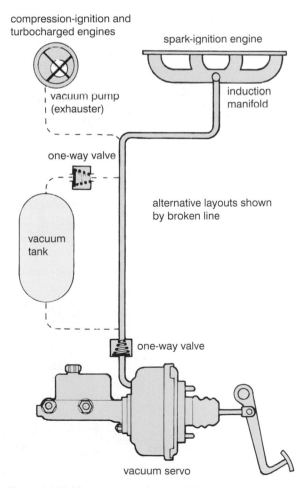

Figure 4.169 Vacuum servo layout with vacuum store

On electric vehicles, there is also a need to generate this assistance due to the lack of an engine. This is done through an electric vacuum motor driven from the vehicle battery supply.

4.25.2 Hydraulic assistance

Unless an effective servo is fitted, a considerable effort is required to stop a heavy motor car or light truck. Since the pressure difference of a vacuum arrangement is limited, a system is needed that provides a much greater source of energy; this can be achieved with a hydraulic servo because this type of system operates on a pressure of 55–82 bar (800–1200 lbf in^{-2}).

The hydraulic power produced by the engine-driven pump of this system can also be used to provide for other servo needs, for example power-assisted steering, lifts, etc.

Figure 4.170a shows a diagrammatic sketch of a continuous-flow hydraulic servo system.

Mounted behind the conventional master cylinder, the servo valve is supplied with fluid from a multi-cylinder radial pump, which is driven from the engine or transmission. The diagram shows the brakes in the 'off' position, and in this state the fluid can easily pass between the master-cylinder piston and servo valve to a drilling that leads back to the reservoir.

Depression of the pedal initially closes the conical servo valve and causes the pump to build up a pressure in the region A, which will tend to force the piston and valve apart. The piston has a larger area than the valve, and so the thrust exerted on the piston will be greater than that acting on the valve and brake pedal. This area ratio governs the assistance given to the driver. As soon as a given pressure, which will depend on the force applied to the pedal, has built up, the servo valve will partially open to maintain the pressure and give assistance. If the pedal force is exceptionally high, a pressure relief valve will open and allow fluid to escape to the reservoir.

Release of the pedal returns and opens the servo valve, releases the brakes and restores uninterrupted flow of fluid from the pump to the reservoir.

Continuous-flow system with accumulator

The assistance given by the continuous-flow system depends on the pump speed, so a 'hard' pedal is felt when the pump is stationary or rotating slowly. To overcome this disadvantage, a hydraulic accumulator is normally incorporated into the system.

Figure 4.170b shows the layout of the system, which uses the same pump and master cylinder as the previous example.

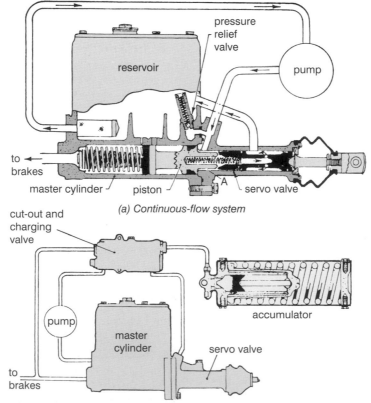

(a) Continuous-flow system

(b) Continuous-flow system with accumulator

Figure 4.170 Hydraulic servo system

The accumulator or pressure storage cylinder contains a spring-loaded piston or airbag, which is acted upon by the fluid: the higher the fluid pressure, the more the bag or spring is compressed. A cut-out valve maintains the accumulator pressure in the range 55–82 bar (800–1200 lbf in^{-2}), and a charging valve, activated by fluid pressure from the output or brake line side of the master cylinder, releases fluid from the accumulator to act on the servo valve, should the pump be incapable of supplying the necessary fluid.

Whenever you have to disconnect any part of this system, it is essential that you discharge and drain the accumulator. This can be done by pumping the brake pedal many times with the engine or electrically driven pump switched off.

4.25.3 Compressed-air assistance

On light trucks and minibuses, an alternative to a hydraulic servo is a compressed-air servo; this is generally called an air/hydraulic (air over hydraulic) or Airpac system because compressed air is used to boost the force applied by the driver to a hydraulically operated brake.

The system is based on the layout shown in Figure 4.171. Air pressure, generated by an engine-driven compressor, is stored in a reservoir adjacent to the servo chamber; this houses a piston that operates another piston that controls the main hydraulic brake line. When the brake is applied, a valve directs compressed air into the servo cylinder to boost the pedal effort.

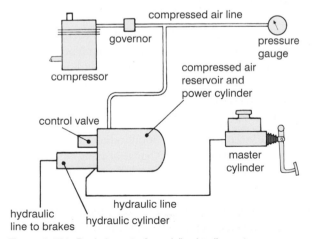

Figure 4.171 Basic layout of an air/hydraulic system

4.26 Anti-lock braking systems

4.26.1 History

The anti-lock braking system (ABS) has been fitted to vehicles since the 1960s. Its function is to improve the safety of the driver and passengers by preventing the wheels from locking during heavy braking situations. When a road wheel locks, the driver is unable to control the direction of the vehicle due to the loss of traction.

ABS was first introduced on aircraft to help pilots during landing. With ABS, the aircraft was able to land on the runway in a much safer manner without the pilot having to worry about the wheels locking, which could cause the aircraft to become unstable. The first production ABS fitted to aircraft was in 1929 and designed by an aircraft and automobile engineer called Gabriel Voisin. A well-known ABS called the Dunlop Maxaret system was first seen on production aircraft in the 1950s and is still in use today.

Soon automobile manufacturers started to take notice of this ABS and decided that it would be a great benefit for the drivers of vehicles on the road. One of the first systems in use was a mechanical ABS, which had some limited use on a few types of road cars including the Jenson FF and also on a racecar called the Ferguson P99. This mechanical system worked out to be fairly unreliable and also too expensive for wider commercial use, so was only used for a short period of time. A form of brake control was fitted to the Austin 1800 in 1964, which used a valve to alter the brake force between the front and rear axles when any wheel locked. This system provided some additional stability of the vehicle but was not particularly refined.

The first electronic system used on production vehicles was produced by Bosch and Mercedes Benz for use on the larger Mercedes Benz vehicles. This system was launched in 1936 and was really the first sophisticated system in operation. By today's standards this system was comparatively slow, but it did provide real progress in the technology of providing the type of ABS seen on vehicles today.

In 1971, the first real four-wheel sensed ABS came into production; this was manufactured by Bendix in a commercial partnership with car manufacturer Chrysler. It provided true electronic control and used far fewer moving parts when compared with the Bosch/Mercedes Benz system. The system was called the 'Sure Track' system and provided a real leap forward in braking performance and safety.

Manufacturers such as Bosch have continued to develop the ABS, which is now fitted to almost all new production cars and, in some cases, motorcycles. The ABS now integrates with other systems on many cars to provide additional stability control systems, producing even safer vehicles.

4.26.2 Need for an anti-lock system

The ABS is designed to ensure that the driver is able to maintain control of the vehicle during heavy or emergency braking situations. The ABS will provide shorter braking distances due to the lack of wheel lock, which allows the tyres to maintain greater friction with the road surface. ABS can be relied on too much by some drivers, which can in fact cause accidents through braking too late. Also, with road conditions such as snow or ice, the ABS can actually increase braking distances due to the lack of ability to create a wedge of snow between the tyre and road surface. The wedge acts as an additional frictional advantage in these conditions. A vehicle should never be driven beyond its or the driver's ability.

Since ABS came into widespread use in production cars in 1978, it has made considerable progress. Recent versions not only handle the ABS function itself (i.e. preventing wheel locking) but also traction control, brake assist and electronic stability control.

While we know that ABS has a function to ensure that the vehicle can stop in the shortest possible distance in a straight line, the additional advantage is that the vehicle adhesion through the tyres with the road surface is maintained while the vehicle is taking sudden manoeuvres to avoid an accident. When a driver manoeuvres their vehicle in a different direction to avoid an obstacle, they have to rely on the tyres to obtain suitable grip depending on the vehicle speed or road conditions, otherwise trying to steer or even change direction is almost impossible. Normally, the vehicle would take an undesirable direction because of the driver's delayed reaction (no one can react instantaneously) and then because of the speed and grip obtained. ABS consequently assists in preventing the tyres losing traction during heavy braking. This improved stability of the vehicle gives the driver the opportunity to maintain control of the vehicle during critical emergency conditions.

Although it is true to say that braking distances in wet conditions or on slippery surfaces will be greatly reduced, the action of the ABS (i.e. any direct reduction in braking distance when driving in a straight line), should be regarded as a bonus rather than the objective.

Drivers find it difficult to assess the force that should be applied to the brake pedal to make an emergency stop and bring the vehicle to rest in the shortest possible distance. This is because it is impossible to take into account the many varying factors, such as the frictional properties of the road and tyres, and the condition of the surface, for example wet, dry, greasy or icy, and the speed at which a judgement has to be made. This generally means that the driver applies either too much or too little pressure on the pedal. The effects of these actions:

1 Pedal pressure is too high – one or more of the wheels skid over the surface with the result that:
   a stopping distance is increased because the adhesion between a skidding wheel and the road is less than that given by a wheel that is held on the verge of locking
   b directional control is jeopardised. In the case of a rear-wheel skid, the vehicle turns from front to rear.
2 Pedal pressure is too low – stopping distance is increased, which can result in impact with an obstacle.

The adhesion between the road wheel and road surface is governed by the coefficient of friction. This varies considerably when the condition of the road surface is changed, for example the friction value of a dry asphalt road falls from about 0.8 to 0.15 when it is covered with black ice.

To understand the mathematics of slip ratio, we need to understand that the speed a vehicle is travelling in prior to braking is the same as the speed of the road wheels. When the vehicle has to brake quickly, the road wheels will slow down quicker than the vehicle, at this point wheel slippage will occur. This wheel slippage can be calculated using a simple formula:

$$\text{Slip ratio} = \frac{\text{Vehicle speed} - \text{Wheel speed}}{\text{Vehicle speed}} \times 100$$

On a dry surface, the adhesion varies as the percentage of wheel slip changes from 0 per cent (no slip) to 100 per cent (locked wheel sliding over the surface). Figure 4.172 shows how the longitudinal and transverse adhesion of a tyre on a typical surface changes as the amount of slip is increased.

The curve representing longitudinal adhesion for a given condition shows that a braking force set to hold a wheel at about 15 per cent slip provides the maximum retarding force.

Vehicle stability, with respect to its tendency to slide sideways, is indicated on the graph by the transverse adhesion curve. The adhesion in this direction falls as soon as the wheel starts to skid, so if any serious skidding occurs, this can quickly lead to loss of control, especially when the driver is making a steering correction or when the vehicle is cornering.

Vehicle stability and control is maintained by limiting the amount of wheel slip while the vehicle is braking. The ABS provides the driver with additional stability during heavy braking by generally achieving a slip

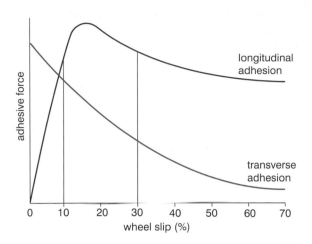

Figure 4.172 Adhesive force and wheel slip

ratio of about 10–30 per cent. This level of slip allows the driver to be able to maintain control even when driving around a corner or making an avoidance manoeuvre.

Although the ABS is able to operate across a wide variety of road conditions, it is still very important to ensure that the driver takes appropriate additional care when driving the vehicle on surfaces such as snow or ice, as the stopping distances will be increased tremendously in these situations.

If the vehicle is driven in adverse conditions, such as snow or loose surfaces including gravel, the operation of the ABS will generally provide very little if any improvement to the stopping of the vehicle. A vehicle with no ABS builds up gravel or snow in front of the tyre creating some additional resistance that helps to stop the vehicle. When ABS is fitted, this additional frictional build-up will not occur. For this reason, it is quite normal in some situations, such as in a car rally where there are often loose surfaces and snow, to not make use of ABS. Experienced rally drivers have the ability to sense the braking action of the road wheels very quickly, and they are able to use the locking action of the brakes to promote additional control of the vehicle during cornering by unbalancing it to give extra slippage and rotate the car through a slide. This enables the driver to set up the vehicle for a corner before they have actually arrived at the corner apex. The rally driver may, therefore, be able to switch off ABS operation for given road sections.

Note: some drivers may be concerned about the noise of the ABS operation as this can create a fairly loud buzzing noise accompanied by a vibration of the brake pedal. This is quite normal as the ABS operates due to the actuation of the solenoids and pump within the system.

4.26.3 Types of ABS

Various types of ABS can generally be classed into two groups: electronic and mechanical. The difference between them is the manner in which wheel slip is sensed, monitored and controlled. Various types of ABS brakes are fitted to vehicles, but mechanical types of ABS are no longer used by today's manufacturers. All systems fitted to current vehicles are based on a fully electronically controlled format, and it is this type we shall cover here.

4.26.4 Electronically sensed ABS

Whereas early designs of electronic systems were intended as 'add-on' units, the latest generation of ABS units is incorporated into the hydraulic brake circuit to form an integrated brake system. The master cylinder and vacuum servo used in original designs are assisted or sometimes replaced by a hydraulic pump-assisted braking unit; this provides both normal braking and anti-lock functions.

Skid sensing of each wheel is provided by sensors, some of these sensors are electromagnetic or Hall effect. These measure and communicate to an ABS ECU any rapid change in speed of rotation of the wheel (i.e. the sensors indicate the percentage slip that is taking place at each wheel).

All electronic ABS units are designed in such a way that if failure occurs, normal braking can be maintained. This is called 'fail safe'.

Although ABS units look like they are integral with the vehicle braking system, operation is achieved by intruding into the brake pressure lines. Therefore, these systems are often referred to as intrusive systems. Indeed, many of the latest ABS units incorporate advanced assistance programmes, such as emergency brake assist, pedestrian avoidance and vehicle stability control systems.

Layout of system

Figure 4.173 shows the layout of the main components of a four-wheel, four-channel regulated ABS. The system may be divided into two sub-systems: hydraulic and electronic.

Hydraulic components

The hydraulic components fitted to an ABS usually consist of:

- master cylinder
- brake lines
- high-pressure pump
- brake callipers/wheel cylinders
- accumulator
- expansion chambers.

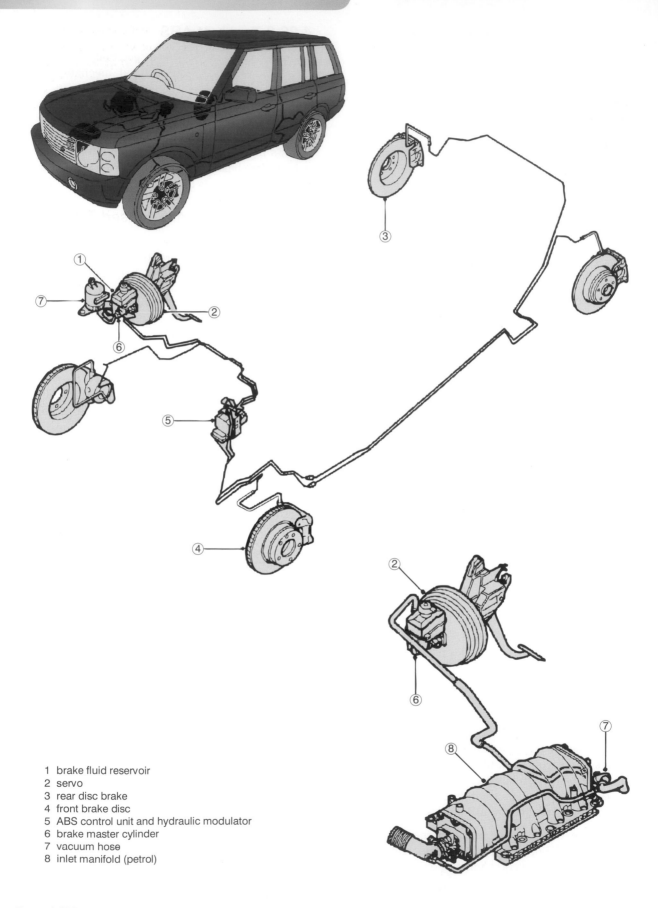

1 brake fluid reservoir
2 servo
3 rear disc brake
4 front brake disc
5 ABS control unit and hydraulic modulator
6 brake master cylinder
7 vacuum hose
8 inlet manifold (petrol)

Figure 4.173 Layout of four-wheel, four-channel ABS

Generally ABS units today have four lines and are four-wheel sensed. This system will incorporate eight solenoid valves in the modulator. Each line has an inlet and an outlet valve.

Electronic components fitted to the ABS generally fall under the following headings:

- ABS ECU
- ABS modulator
- Solenoid valves
- Brake switch
- Wheel speed sensors

Using Figure 4.174 as an example of an ABS hydraulic system, the following is an explanation of the processes involved in an ABS operation during normal braking. More detail of this operation is on page 494.

1 When the pedal is pressed (1), the shuttle valve (2) is moved by hydraulic pressure and opens line A.
2 As the shuttle valve moves, it also triggers valve switch (3).
3 This informs the ECU that the pedal has been pressed.
4 Pressure will be fed down line A to the front brakes.

During normal braking, the inlet valves (4) are in the open position and the outlet valves (5) are in the closed position. This allows the front and rear brakes to be applied in the normal way. If the ECU detects via a wheel sensor that a wheel is about to lock, the system will go into ABS mode. The inlet valve of that wheel will be closed and the outlet will remain closed – this is called 'pressure maintenance'.

If, however, the wheel is still locking, then the outlet valve will be opened and the pump (7) will be activated drawing fluid pressure away from the calliper or drum – this is called 'pressure decrease'.

When the ABS ECU then recognises that all wheels are rotating at the same speed, the process will start again with full brake pressure being applied through the open inlet valves (4) to the brake callipers or wheel cylinders – 'pressure increase'. This process can happen many times a second until the vehicle has come to a halt or the brakes are released and normal driving is resumed.

Due to the pump running and the inlet and outlet vales modulating the pressure to the brakes, the driver will feel and hear the operation. This is normal, although some drivers may recall this after ABS operation has taken place.

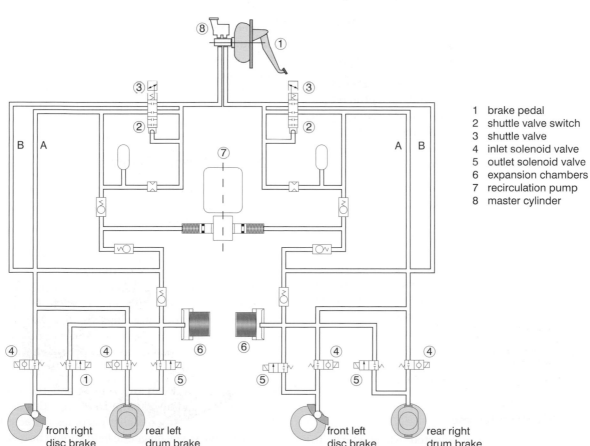

1 brake pedal
2 shuttle valve switch
3 shuttle valve
4 inlet solenoid valve
5 outlet solenoid valve
6 expansion chambers
7 recirculation pump
8 master cylinder

Figure 4.174 Hydraulic layout of ABS

Operating principle

To recap on the operation in more detail, the three phases of ABS operation are:

A Pressure maintain phase
B Pressure decrease phase
C Pressure increase phase

Normal brake operation – during the normal braking operation, the brake fluid pressure will not be influenced by the ABS at all. This is due to the ABS usually only operating during a wheel-lock situation, so it has no influence on the general braking operation.

Phase A: pressure maintain

At this point, the braking of the vehicle is causing the road wheels to slow down, the ABS then detects that one or more of the road wheels is slowing down at a quicker rate than the other road wheels – this is done through the signal from the wheel speed sensor. The ABS will note that this could lead to the wheels locking up. At this point, the ABS will prevent brake pressure being applied to the wheels slowing at a quicker rate to prevent them from locking, this is done by closing off the inlet solenoid to those wheels. The brake pressure will then increase on the wheels with greater traction, creating a balanced braking action. This process will happen many times a second and can move from different wheels very quickly.

Phase B: pressure decrease

When a sensor signals the starting of a wheel skidding, the ECU closes the input valve and opens the return valve in the valve block. This causes reduction in fluid pressure in the appropriate line so that the risk of wheel locking is reduced. The surplus fluid coming from the return valve passes to the reservoir.

To commence operation of the ABS, the ECU opens the main valve, so that pressurised fluid in the booster chamber flows over the cup seal of the master cylinder into the pressure chamber in the forward part. This replenishes the fluid returned to the reservoir by the return valve, as well as provides both front brake circuits with a pressure proportional to the pedal force. During normal brake operation, the fluid from the booster circuit passes to the rear brakes at a pressure proportional to the pedal force. For ABS regulation of the rear wheels, the single return valve in the line reduces the pressure equally for both rear wheels based on select-low operating principle.

Phase C: pressure increase

When the speed of the affected wheel starts to increase, the sensor signals free running of the wheel. An ABS input valve in the regulated fluid line is opened to increase the pressure up to a point where the percentage slip is greater than required. This regulated cycle is repeated about 12 times per second. At this frequency, the vibration of the wheel and suspension assembly is avoided. ABS will execute the pressure hold and pressure reduction phases in direct response to the data received via the wheel speed sensors, which is processed by the ABS ECU. If a wheel lock is still detected, the process will start over again with the pressure maintain phase.

The three phases of the ABS operation are applied as necessary to help maintain wheel speed deceleration consistent on all four wheels. This functionality will then help to ensure that vehicle control is maintained and the braking distances are reduced.

Signals from the sensors are transmitted to an ECU, which contains two microprocessors; these compare the input signals received from each wheel with those obtained previously. If they find that a wheel is starting to skid, an output signal is transmitted to actuate a return valve, which slightly releases the pressure in that particular hydraulic line. By monitoring about 8000 sensor signals per second and taking action within a few milliseconds, the ECU is capable of providing a lock-free state of all wheels to ensure safe deceleration and good vehicle stability.

Warning lamps are fitted to signal to the driver any fault in the pressure and electrical sections of the ABS. Self-checking electrical pulses continually pass around the circuit and valves to monitor the system and set the anti-lock mechanism in the fail-safe mode if a defect is detected. A dashboard lamp signals this information to the driver.

4.26.5 ABS components

Wheel-speed sensors

A wheel-speed sensor is located at each wheel, sensing the rotation of an exciter ring with 40 to 60 teeth. The sensors are often an electromagnetic type. When the vehicle is in motion, the inductive sensors (AC output) send signals to the ECU (Figure 4.175). The front exciter ring is often fitted to the outside diameter of the CV joint inside each front hub assembly. The rear exciter rings are often part of the rear hub assembly. (Hall-type sensors are now being used on the latest systems as they provide a stronger and cleaner signal.)

Note: the gap between the sensor and the exciter ring is pre-set and no attempt to change this setting should be made. Any metallic particles attracted to the casing due to the magnetic field should be cleaned off. This is to prevent any incorrect calculations occurring during operation.

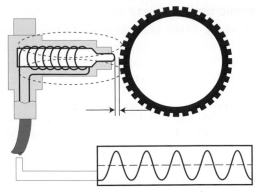

Figure 4.175 ABS wheel-speed sensor arrangement

Modulator and ECU

The modulator usually has the ECU integrated as one compact unit. This reduces the size and wiring required. The modulator chooses the solenoid valves, pump required and brake pressure switch required for ABS operation.

Figure 4.176 ABS modulator and ECU

All signals from the wheel speed sensors and brake pedal are fed to the ABS ECU to process and act upon if ABS operation is required. The ECU will operate the solenoid valves during ABS operation to instigate the three phases of ABS mentioned previously on page 494. This operation will take place at least 10–15 times a second to avoid locking wheels during braking. The ECU and hydraulic modulator are often available as separate service components. The ABS ECU can be investigated by diagnostic equipment to check for faults or system information for diagnosis.

Pump

The pump is fitted to increase and decrease pressure in the brake lines during ABS operation. During the pressure decrease phase, the pump will run and draw pressure away from the locking wheel's brake calliper and divert it back to an accumulator and brake fluid reservoir. During the pressure increase phase, the pump can generate higher brake pressure to apply the brakes again to slow the vehicle down.

Brake-by-wire

Brake-by-wire is a further development of the vehicle braking system. Like with other systems, such as engine management, the physical link between driver inputs and the actuators is becoming less evident. The brake-by-wire system is a development of the braking system used by some higher levels of racing cars. The system itself is based on a dual circuit hydraulic system (described in this chapter on page 478), but instead of the brake command being controlled by the driver's foot through hydraulics, it is controlled by electronics. Like the drive-by-wire throttle pedal (described in Chapter 2, page 227), the brake pedal is connected to a variable resistor or **rheostat**. As the driver pushes the pedal, the rheostat sends a higher voltage signal to the ECU.

The control unit will then signal an actuator to operate the hydraulics in the same way as a hydraulic dual circuit system. The brake-by-wire system allows the brake pedal to be placed anywhere in the driving compartment and it is not subjected to complicated plumbing of the brake master cylinder.

One issue with the brake-by-wire system is that drivers do not gain the normal 'feel' from the brake pedal during a braking situation. The feel through the brake pedal is important to allow the driver to have an understanding of the pressure being input into the brake system. The brake-by-wire system overcomes this by the system placing a resistance in the brake pedal proportional to the input pressure. The brake-by-wire system will not allow the brakes to be applied too harshly, as it will monitor the road wheel speed, steering angle and front and rear axle speed difference to avoid any locking of the brakes through the ABS and by lowering the actuation pressure.

A future advancement of this system, which could be available in the near future, utilises individual electric motors placed at each road wheel that are connected to the brake calliper. As the driver inputs a pressure through the brake pedal, the control unit will register this input pressure in the same way as previously explained. The control unit will then decide, after taking into account the variables around vehicle road speed, steering angle and pedal pressure, the brake pressure to implement on each road wheel through the actuation of the individual motors. This process takes milliseconds and does not require any mechanical parts, apart from the motors, and does not use hydraulics.

Rheostat: device that measures electrical resistance.

4.26.6 Vehicle stability control systems

Dynamic stability control

The dynamic stability control (DSC) system is designed to improve the lateral stability of the vehicle in all driving situations. DSC optimises vehicle stability even in critical driving situations. The system controls dynamic stability when accelerating and when starting from a standstill. Additionally, it identifies unstable driving behaviour, such as understeering and oversteering, and helps to keep the vehicle under control by manipulating the engine output and applying the brakes at individual wheels. Some noise may be generated when the brakes are applied. The system is ready to operate each time the engine is started. The indicator lamp in the instrument pack extinguishes shortly after the engine has been started. If the indicator lamp flashes, the system is active, regulating engine output and brake forces. Without DSC engaged, the vehicle may be driven as normal, but at the limit of adhesion its behaviour will be less predictable. Therefore, it is recommended not to switch off the DSC under normal driving conditions.

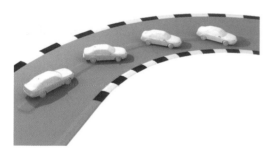

Figure 4.177 Vehicle in counter-steer using DSC during cornering

Traction control system

The traction control system (TCS) incorporated in ABS for the detection of slip can also be used to control and limit the maximum traction force utilised for the vehicle propulsion. This arrangement was first introduced by Harry Ferguson in 1954. The control is achieved by blocking the compensating function of the differential in certain driving situations by using a computer. This partial differential locking action is obtained by using ABS components to provide a braking action on a skidding wheel. When both driving wheels undergo excessive slip, the ECU, in addition to acting upon the brakes, alters the engine throttle setting to reduce the driving torque. Some of the new generation ABS layouts are designed to easily accommodate a TCS module.

Electronic brake assist

The electronic brake assist system (EBA) is designed to enhance the braking control of the ABS system for the driver. The EBA includes two functions that are programmed into the control electronics of the ABS ECU.

The first EBA function is designed to provide the maximum braking force available during rapid (panic) braking situations. The ABS control module senses inputs from the brake pedal switch and the signal from the brake pressure sensor on the master cylinder. The criterion for activation of EBA is the speed at which brake pressure builds up with the brake pedal depressed. The criteria required for EBA activation are:

- brake switch ON
- brake pressure build-up threshold value met
- vehicle road speed higher than 8 kph (5 mph)
- vehicle not in reverse
- not all wheels in ABS operation.

If the threshold for EBA activation is achieved, the ABS control module will activate a pressure build-up phase through the hydraulic pump unit. The pressure at all wheels is increased up to the ABS operation point. This occurs even if the driver does not achieve the ABS operation point with the pedal.

The front and rear axle brakes are controlled individually. ABS operation will continue until the driver releases the pedal and the pressure in the master cylinder drops below the threshold value stored in the ABS ECU.

The second EBA function is also designed to enhance a driver-initiated braking procedure. The EBA will build up the pressure in the rear brake circuit when the front brakes are already in an ABS regulation cycle. The additional braking pressure at the rear wheels will shorten the stopping distance. The following criteria must be met before the ABS control module will activate EBA:

- Both front wheel brakes in ABS operation
- Vehicle speed higher than 8 kph (5 mph)
- Vehicle not in reverse
- EBA and pressure sensor test OK
- Rear wheels not in ABS operation

The sensitivity of this system can often be adjusted via diagnostics equipment. Usually this is left in the higher-sensitivity setting for safety.

Hill descent control

Hill descent control (HDC) is designed for off-road use to automatically slow the vehicle and maintain a steady speed on steep gradients. This function allows the driver to focus on steering and controlling the vehicle without having to use the brakes to slow the vehicle.

HDC is activated manually through the switch located on the fascia area. HDC can be selected under conditions where the vehicle is in a low speed condition of less than 32 kph (20 mph). The HDC lamp in the instrument pack indicates HDC selection status. When activated, the vehicle's speed is held to approximately 8 kph (5 mph) by the ABS ECU pulsing the brakes to maintain the speed.

The following conditions must be met before the HDC will activate:

- HDC switch operated.
- Vehicle speed less than 32 kph (20 mph).
- Accelerator pedal pressed less than 15 per cent.
- Downhill driving recognised through angle sensor.

Figure 4.178 A vehicle using HDC is slowed automatically and maintains a steady speed

Corner braking control

Corner braking control (CBC) improves stability control while braking through corners. As the vehicle enters a corner the weight of the vehicle shifts to the outside wheels through centrifugal force. With non-CBC equipped vehicles, if the driver brakes while driving through a corner, an equal hydraulic force is applied to each wheel. Though the pressure is equal, the grip available for braking is unequal at the tyre footprint due to the increased weight on the outside wheels.

With a CBC-equipped vehicle, the feature regulates the applied pressure to the wheels based on the rate of cornering. When the driver brakes an unequal hydraulic pressure is applied to each side of the vehicle. Though the brake application pressure to each wheel is unequal, the dynamic of the vehicle's weight transfer compensates for the unequal pressure. As a result, braking effort is distributed in proportion to the grip available ensuring that lateral grip is maintained.

4.27 Electronic handbrake system

Today, vehicles are increasingly fitted with electronic handbrake systems that are operated by a switch in the vehicle. These systems work by using a motor, which pulls the cable acting on the rear brakes to apply the handbrake and hold the vehicle stationary. An example of this arrangement is seen in Figure 4.179. These systems require additional inspection during service to ensure that they are adjusted correctly. Normally, the electronic handbrake will apply automatically when the vehicle is switched off and will release automatically when the vehicle pulls away. This avoids the need for the driver to remember to apply and release the handbrake avoiding accidents and also overheating the parking brake components if the handbrake is not released correctly.

Some vehicle manufacturers that now use the electronic handbrake do provide a manual override device to overcome any possible electronic failure. These types of devices are normally accessible through a compartment in the vehicle and are connected to the cable system to allow disengagement. Other manufacturers have designed their system so that the only way to override the electronic handbrake is through using a diagnostic tool to talk to the ECU.

4.28 Brake – routine maintenance

Just like any other system on a vehicle, the braking system will need to be maintained. The braking system has critical operating factors that cannot afford to be ignored and needs to be inspected and adjusted to maintain efficiency. The driver must take some responsibly to make sure that their vehicle is in the best condition at all times. To ignore this responsibility could put the vehicle's occupants and other road users or pedestrians at risk if an incident occurs. Accidents always happen when you least expect them and the outcome of applying the brakes to slow down a vehicle does have some unknowns until the vehicle comes to a stop.

Visual inspection, looking for damage or leaks can sometimes identify issues within the braking system. Seeing any damage or leakage should always be investigated and rectified as it could cause other issues. Hearing unusual noises while driving and when applying the brakes could indicate a possibility of worn components or a build-up of contamination on the brake linings. If any of these issues occur, they should be investigated and rectified at the earliest opportunity.

Most modern braking systems do now have some built-in safety measures, which also provide the driver with identified information. This is normally indicated by warning lights or warning messages transmitted to the instrument panel.

4.28.1 Foot pedal

Vehicle owners can carry out some basic checks regularly to make sure that the braking system is functioning correctly. Most experienced drivers know how their vehicle's brake pedal should feel and quickly identify when it doesn't feel right. The brake pedal should feel solid when the engine is not operating and have an element of sponginess when the engine is running. This is because the engine is supplying vacuum to the brake servo to support the brake application. If the pedal pressure doesn't change when the engine is running, then there is a possibility of a servo problem. If, when applying pressure to the brake pedal, the movement travels a long way down, this could indicate that the brake linings are worn to an undesired limit or the system might be experiencing a component failure or fluid leakage. Further investigation should be made.

4.28.2 Handbrake

With the handbrake, the driver should again be familiar with the amount of travel it completes until it locks and holds the brakes on. There are regulations to the amount of travel allowed and most conventional handbrake systems allow between four to six clicks of the lever. Later electronic handbrakes don't have this function and just have an on/off facility. If the handbrake does have excessive movement or is not holding the brakes when applied, then an inspection of the system is needed.

4.28.3 Brake linings and brake fluid

For most drivers, it is very difficult to know what condition the brake linings are in, so they are reliant on other aspects. Some manufacturers provide wear-level sensors located within the lining assembly. This wear indication is then transmitted to the driver by a warning light being illuminated on the instrument panel.

Regular inspection of the brake fluid level would give some indication of a problem, but this is not always accurate. The reservoir normally has a level indicator on it and it is very important that it stays above the minimum. Having a brake fluid service at the manufacturer's recommended time scale is important, as the fluid absorbs moisture and over a period of time will become ineffective. It is *not* recommended to top up the fluid unless you are instructed, because carrying out this activity could cause other issues to arise.

Only a regular inspection to carry out adjustments or replacements can guarantee the braking system is working to the manufacturer's and the government's standards.

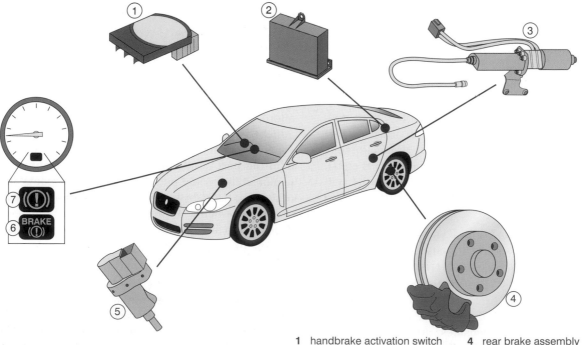

Figure 4.179 Electronic handbrake system

1	handbrake activation switch	**4**	rear brake assembly
2	handbrake control unit	**5**	footbrake switch
3	handbrake cable motor assembly	**6**	handbrake warning symbol
		7	brake warning symbol

CHAPTER 5

Vehicle electric, safety and comfort systems

5.1 Introduction

In today's world electricity is one of our major energy sources that one takes for granted in powering everyday appliances from a house light bulb to a mobile phone. What we should remember, and also understand, is that electricity was used in a basic form on the motor car back in the 1900s. Motor cars were mainly mechanical in their design and functionality for many years, however, they did have some primitive electrical functions and control. Early motor cars had electrical systems for lighting, starting, battery charging, ignition systems and other ancillary systems. Many of the electrical systems used on early motor cars are mandatory system requirements for today's motor car.

As technology has continued to progress at a rapid pace, the motor car electrical architecture is now one of the main advancement areas. We now see our motor cars produced with advanced engine management control, electronic gearbox and final-drive systems, electronic stability programmes, comfort and safety restraint systems as standard features. Additional ancillary systems such as electric windows, central locking, memory seats, security and in-car entertainment (ICE) systems are also just a few to mention. Many of these are now also mandatory systems that car owners take for granted as standard equipment. With these customer expectations, we now find that the complexity of the motor car electrical systems has greatly increased.

For many years within the motor industry, workshops had a designated electrical specialist that only focused on resolving electrical issues. Most workshop technicians had good mechanical knowledge but were always reliant on the electrical specialist to come to their aid on identifying and rectifying electrical problems. As motor car technology progressed, it became clear that today's technicians must also have a good level of electrical knowledge to become an 'all-rounder' and to be able to use advanced diagnostic equipment to support their diagnostic routines.

With this in mind, we must not forget that any advanced electronic system that is now used on the modern motor car needs the basic electrical functionalities to operate. To minimise the possible incorrect diagnoses, or even damaging an expensive control module, this electrical section provides an overview of the basic operating principle of electrical fundamentals, and helps support the underpinning knowledge required when having to carry out diagnostic routines.

5.1.1 Main electrical circuits within today's vehicles

The main source of electrical power comes from the battery. This important component is the electrical energy source when the engine is not running. The battery is connected to the individual circuits throughout the vehicle. To identify the individual circuit used on a motor vehicle, it is better to categorise them into sub-systems for their functionality control.

Charging circuit

The charging circuit supplies the electrical energy when the engine is running and also maintains the battery output to achieve its fully charged state.

Starting circuit

This circuit provides the high amperage electrical energy to enable the engine to be cranked at a high enough speed for it to start and run.

Ignition circuit (earlier vehicles)

The ignition circuit provides the electrical energy to run the engine's ignition system. It produces high voltage at the spark plugs at many different conditions to ignite the air/fuel mixture. This system is integrated within the engine management system (EMS). The voltage produced by today's ignition

systems is very high (40,000–100,000V), so care should be taken when working around this area.

Fuel-injection circuit (earlier vehicles)

On earlier vehicles, this circuit provided the engine control system with the electronic functionality to supply the correct volume of fuel and air needed to achieve its optimum injection strategy.

Engine management circuit

Today, vehicles generally have an integrated EMS, which includes the ignition system and fuel-injection system. The EMS also controls the emission systems to ensure that the engine does not produce too many harmful gases.

Lighting circuit

Ever since the motor car was designed, the exterior lighting system has evolved from a basic single filament bulb in each lamp assembly to today's more advanced Xenon and light-emitting diode (LED) lighting. Now controlled by an electronic control unit (ECU), the lights can activate far quicker and are much brighter, which provides a higher level of all-round safety. In addition to this, motor vehicles now have headlamps that automatically switch back and forth from dip beam to main, and can also adjust their setting to follow the road ahead depending on steering wheel movement. With clear, visible instrument panel warning indications given to the driver, and interior lighting design to provide its occupants with suitable comfort and convenience, the conventional lighting system has moved on a long way.

Auxiliary circuit

The auxiliary circuit combines all of the other various systems now required for today's modern motor vehicle. Systems such as windscreen wipers, washers, horn, interior heating and ventilation are now standard. In addition to these, we now have electronic controlled systems including anti-lock braking systems (ABS), climate control, stability programmes, safety restraints, ICE and satellite navigation.

5.2 Basic principles of electricity

Despite all of the technology now seen in motor cars, we must not forget that without the fundamentals the electrical system would have no function. For many years, technicians used basic test lights or analogy meters to test electrical circuits – the level of their knowledge and experience with electric diagnostics determined the outcome of the repair to the vehicle.

Today's technicians now have a greater selection of electrical equipment available to support them in diagnostic routines but, again, they must not forget the basic principles of the electrical systems.

The modern motor car now uses complex ECUs and communication systems to control vehicle systems. While this does make the car's electronic systems more reliable, it does give the technician the added pressure of not only knowing how to use the diagnostic equipment but also needing a greater understanding of the complex system functionalities.

What we must understand is that the diagnostic equipment only gives *guidance* to the technician on information it receives. Sometimes the technician should revert to using wiring diagrams and a multi-meter to confirm a reading before condemning an expensive control module. Remember, even a loss of a power or ground within a circuit can affect an electronic module's functionality.

5.2.1 Electrical key terms

Before we go into detail explaining different terms used in electricity, Table 5.1 lists the most common

terms used within the motor industry and a brief description of their meaning. For a more detailed description, it is advised that you refer to the relevant areas in this chapter.

5.2.2 Comparing an electrical circuit to a water circuit

To break down some of the misconceptions of an electrical circuit, it is best to start at a point where we can compare it with another more familiar system. A water circuit works on the same principles as an electrical circuit because both systems are pressurised during their operation. To compare both systems, we would use a pressure gauge on a water circuit and a voltmeter on an electrical circuit. Before connecting a gauge to a water circuit, the gauge would indicate a reading of zero – this is known as atmospheric pressure. Connecting a pressure gauge to an active water circuit will show the running pressure of the system. For example, if the pressure reading is 12 bar, then this means that there is 12 bar of pressure above zero (atmospheric pressure) within the water circuit.

Table 5.1 Common electrical terms

Ampere	(amps or A) unit of measurement for flow of electric current, equal to one coulomb per second
Conductor	a substance or object that allows electrical current to flow easily
Electrical charge	a fundamental property of particles that causes them to be repelled or attracted to other electrically charged matter
Electric circuit	the pathway along which electrical current flows
Electric current	the flow of electrical charges through a conductor, measured in amperes
Electric field	the area surrounding a charged particle or object; it exerts force on other charged bodies in the same space
Electrode	a conductor by which electrical current leaves or enters an object or electrical device
Electromagnetism	the fundamental interaction of magnetic forces and electric currents in nature
Electron	an elementary particle that has negative electrical charge; found in all atoms, it is the main carrier of electricity in solid objects
Insulator	a material that prevents the flow of electricity
Ion	a molecule or atom that has electric charge as a result of losing or gaining electrons
Kilowatt-hour	a unit of energy consumption equal to 1000 watts per hour
Neutron	an elementary particle that has no electric charge; it forms part of the nucleus of most atoms
Ohm	(Ω) a unit of measurement, it expresses the electrical resistance in a circuit
Proton	an elementary particle that has a positive electrical charge; found in all atoms, its charge is equal to the negative charge of an electron
Resistance	the degree to which a material opposes the flow of electric current
Static electricity	electrical charge that is not moving (i.e. static); it often builds up due to friction
Voltage	the driving force behind the flow of electricity
Watt	(W) the unit of measurement for electrical power, equal to one joule per second

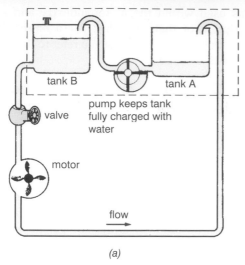
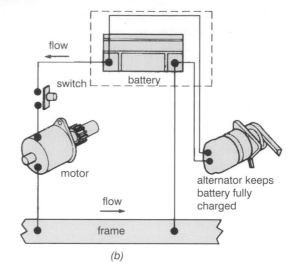

(a) (b)

Figure 5.1 Comparison of water and electrical circuits

Pressurised water circuit

Figure 5.1 shows water contained within two tanks (A and B). Tank A is vented to the atmosphere, so the pressure in this tank is the same as atmospheric pressure (zero). Tank B is pressurised.

Tanks A and B are connected by an electrical pump. When the system is active the pump draws water from tank A and feeds it to tank B. Water is forced by the pump into tank A, which is then pressurised, so the water would attempt to flow down the tap and out of tank A. With the tap closed, water will not be able to flow and tank A's pressure will keep rising. A safety switch could be installed that would switch off the pump if pressure rose to a certain limit, for example 12 bar above atmospheric pressure. However, water will flow through the tap and pass through the motor if the tap is open. The motor is then operated by the flow of water (forced under a pressure of 12 bar), which in turn could drive a machine.

The water will use almost all of its energy to drive the motor. However, as the water is continually pushed around the system, it will return from the motor to tank A. Once this occurs, it will stay there without pressure. This demonstrates that it is the pressure itself that drives the motor. If there is any amount of pressure left over from the return journey to tank A, it would vanish as soon as the water reached the open space of the tank (which would now be at atmospheric pressure – zero in this case).

It is important to note that it's the *higher pressure* in tank B that makes the water flow through the motor and back to tank A. To enable flow, there must be a pressure difference (i.e. if tanks A and B had the same pressure, then the flow of the water would not occur). In this example the pressure difference is 12 bar.

The following calculation shows:

(12 bar in tank B) − (0 bar in tank A) = 12 bar

Electric circuit

To compare the results from the water circuit and transforming it to an electrical circuit we now need to use a voltmeter to measure the electrical pressure produced. Before you connect the voltmeter to the electrical circuit, the meter reading would indicate zero. Instead of the water tanks, we now have a battery as the source provider. The battery provides the circuit with 12 V when active and 0 V when no circulation is taking place. So if we connected the voltmeter to the active circuit, the meter reading will indicate 12 V and 0 V when disconnected. This, again, gives us a 12 V pressure difference.

Table 5.2 Comparison of water circuit with electrical circuit

Figure 5.1a	Figure 5.1b
Water circuit	Electrical circuit
Water tanks	Battery (stores energy)
Outlet pipe tank B	Positive terminal (high pressure outlet)
Return pipe on tank A	Negative terminal (zero pressure connection)

As per the water tanks, when the circuit is switched on the electricity passes through the motor and the energy rotates the motor assembly, which then powers a machine or device. The motor uses all of the electricity in this process (i.e. there is no energy or 'pressure' left in what flows back to the negative terminal).

The higher pressure of water in tank B can be compared with the higher pressure at the positive terminal of the battery circuit. Once again, the difference in pressure is what causes the water or electricity to flow in both examples:

- High pressure from tank B forces water flow to tank A.
- High pressure at positive terminal forces electricity flow to negative terminal.

'Voltage' is the term used to indicate electrical pressure and **volts** (V) is the unit of measurement.

The following calculation shows a pressure difference is 12 V:

$$\text{12 V at the positive terminal} - \text{0 V at the negative terminal} = 12\,V$$

Volt: unit of electrical pressure (potential difference), which creates the flow of electricity.

When describing the pressure difference between two points in a circuit we use the term 'potential difference'. Once again, the water tank analogy is not perfectly accurate but it is still a useful, though basic, explanation of electrical flow.

Electromotive force

The difference in pressure level between positive and negative terminals generates energy known as **electromotive force (EMF)**. The EMF is what drives the electrical current between the battery terminals.

Electromotive force (EMF): in automotive terms, this is the voltage or charge produced by a generator or battery in an electrical circuit. This charge can often be stored in devices such as coil windings: this is often called 'potential energy'.

5.2.3 Pressure/voltage measurements

Water pressure measurement

From understanding the basic principles previously detailed, we are now going to add a pressure gauge to the water circuit. Attaching a pressure gauge to the outlet terminal at tank B (Figure 5.2a) would show 12 bar of pressure, but the gauge would actually be comparing tank B's pressure with atmospheric pressure. If you used a gauge with an attachment to be connected to tank A, then a more accurate comparison of the tank pressures would be obtained.

Electrical pressure measurement

Similarly, adding a voltmeter to the electrical circuit would provide an actual comparison of the electrical 'pressure' between the two circuit points. In Figure 5.2b, if the positive terminal has one test probe voltmeter attached and another probe is attached to the negative terminal, then the electrical 'pressure' would show as 12 V on the voltmeter. What is being

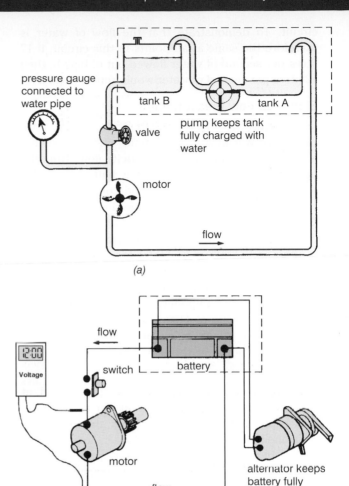

Figure 5.2 Measuring pressure in a water circuit and an electrical circuit

measured between the voltages at both terminals is the potential difference or 'pressure'.

5.2.4 Water and electrical flow measurement

Water flow measurement

For the water to flow around the circuit, a complete circuit must be in place from tank B through to tank A (Figure 5.1a). With the tap in the open position, water can return to tank A by flowing through the circuit. The rate of water flowing through the circuit is dependent on the water pressure at tank B, combined with any restrictions in the pipework. **Note**: the motor itself restricts the flow of water; it reduces the rate of flow through the circuit, similar to the restriction caused by a pipe blockage.

The measurement of water flow could be quoted in litres per second, and measured at any point in the circuit. To demonstrate that the flow of water is therefore the same at all points in this circuit, if 12 litres per second of water flowed out of tank B, then 12 litres per second of water would return to tank A.

Electrical flow measurement

Looking at the electrical circuit in Figure 5.1b, electricity will flow in the circuit when the switch is in the 'on' position. The electricity flows from the battery positive terminal to the battery negative terminal, via the cable (wire) and components. The voltage or 'pressure' applied to the circuit determines the amount of electricity that flows in a circuit (i.e. the pressure or potential difference between the positive and negative terminals). In addition, the level of electricity flow will depend on any 'resistances' (or restrictions) in the circuit. These resistances are usually electrical components attached to the circuit. Therefore, looking at Figure 5.1b, it is the electric motor that restricts the flow of electricity – compare this to the motor in the water circuit, which also restricts the flow of water.

'Current flow' is the rate, or amount per second, at which electricity flows through an electrical circuit. It is expressed in amperes (A) but this is usually shortened to **amps**. Using the water flow example again, amperes can be compared with litres per second of water flow. So, to simplify this, if there is 12 amps of electrical flow from the positive terminal, then 12 amps has to pass back to the negative terminal. Therefore, the flow of electricity, or current, is the same throughout this circuit.

> **Amp**: rate of flow (current). The rate at which the electricity will flow through the circuit.

5.2.5 Measuring resistance to flow

Looking at the water circuit we know that the water flows through the pipe. The pipe's diameter (bore size) would affect the resistance to flow: a large bore pipe would provide less resistance to flow; a very small bore pipe would further reduce the flow of water. To take this further, if a length of the pipe is flattened so that it stops the flow almost completely, this will be a very serious restriction to the water flow.

Figure 5.3a shows a motor being driven by the flow of water. The flow here will be restricted if the motor is connected to a mechanical device (for example, a pulley wheel joined to a rope and bucket). The rotation of the motor will resist the weight and therefore restrict the flow of water.

Figure 5.3b is an electrical circuit, and therefore the flow of electricity will be affected by resistances. Electrical components such as motors or lightbulbs can be the cause of such electrical resistances. Sometimes resistances are deliberately included in circuits to control or restrict the electrical flow, for example using a dimmer switch on a lighting circuit. A simple dimmer switch acts as a resistance that can be changed to control the flow of electricity; the light is dimmed when the flow is reduced.

In Figure 5.3b, we can compare the dimmer switch in an electrical circuit with a tap in a water circuit. If we gradually close the tap, the flow of water will gradually reduce. Similarly, as a dimmer switch is turned down, the flow of current is reduced as the resistance across the switch increases. Resistance is measured in 'ohms'. (The omega symbol (Ω) is often used to represent ohms.) A higher number of ohms mean a higher amount of resistance.

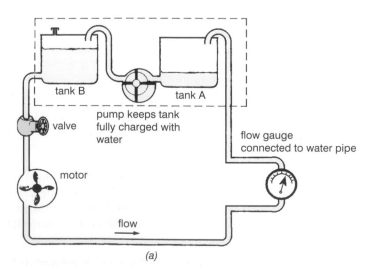

(a)

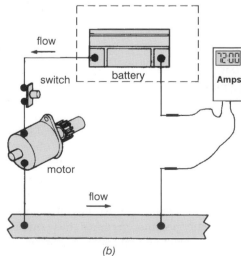

(b)

Figure 5.3 Measuring flow in a water circuit and an electrical circuit

5.2.6 Relationships between volts, ohms and amps

So far we have looked at the three main elements of electricity: pressure, rate of flow, and resistance. When trying to identify electrical problems, it is useful to remember the purpose or function of these three elements.

Before covering such terms in more detail, there is a little background work to recap on. Firstly, an important point to remember is that although we often term current as flowing, it is in fact the charge that flows, but for simplicity we will continue to use the term 'current flow', as it is commonly referred to in this way and highlights that the charge of electricity passes along a conductor, such as a wire or circuit board, towards the consumer component. It may well be viewed that all conductors, including wires and consumers, contain stationary charges irrespective of whether or not they are connected within a circuit. It may be viewed that all conductors, including wires and consumers, contain stationary charges irrespective of whether or not they are connected within a circuit. It is only when these charges flow through a conductor/consumer that the circuit may begin to operate or 'do work'. At this point a current is created. So what makes the charges flow? Well, referring to the previous information in the water tank analogy, you can view the battery as being a sort of 'charge pump', and it is this component that causes the charges within an electrical circuit to flow.

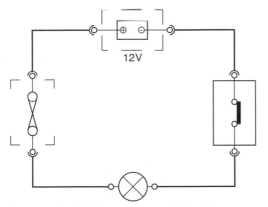

Figure 5.4 Basic circuit

Consider the basic circuit shown in Figure 5.4. When the switch is open and the bulb is not lit, the entire circuit is 'full' of stationary but moveable charges. Close the switch and the battery creates an electrical pressure that forces the charges to move. You can liken the circuit to the analogy of the water circuit, and now the battery is the component that drives it. These charges move towards the battery from the bulb, pass through its cell and continue to exit into the other side of the circuit towards the

bulb. It is the bulb that offers the circuit resistance and gives off light and heat as charges pass through it. It is the flow of these charges that can be referred to as an electrical current. However, it is the charge itself that flows.

Remember:

- a current is created by the movement of charge
- all conductors are 'full' of stationary charge
- charge is moveable when connected within an electrical circuit
- the battery provides the electrical pressure required to force the charges around the circuit
- the consumer component provides resistance to the flow of charge.

Voltage

Essentially, this is the electrical energy (V) stored in the battery that creates an electrical current by forcing electrons from positive (high potential) to negative (low potential) within a circuit.

Voltage is known as conventional flow and, strictly speaking, this is defined as 'energy per unit charge'.

For example, 1 volt is equal to 1 joule of energy per coulomb of charge.

Put simply, voltage can be considered as the electrical 'pressure' that creates a current, therefore delivering the unit charge to the consumer. The higher the voltage, the higher the 'pressure' and, therefore, greater amount of energy per unit charge.

Remember: a voltmeter always displays *potential difference*.

Current

Current can be viewed as being the volume or rate of charge flow within a fixed time period. Measured in amperes, 1 amp is equal to 1 coulomb of charge flowing each second.

For example, the larger the measured current within a circuit, the greater the amount of charge and, therefore, energy each second that may be perceived to be flowing in it.

When measuring current it is important that you select the correct tool, depending upon the amount of current likely to be tested in the circuit.

For circuits up to approximately 10 A, a standard digital multimeter equipped with an ammeter may be used. Most ammeters contain a fuse to protect it during measurement. The fuse rating should always be confirmed before making any tests.

The ammeter should be connected into series with the rest of the circuit (Figure 5.5). In this example, the circuit protection fuse has been removed and the ammeter connected across the two pins of the fuse holder. Ensure you have selected the correct lead position on the face of the digital multimeter. Failure to adhere to this will result in damage to the equipment. For an accurate reading, the circuit must be switched on and operational.

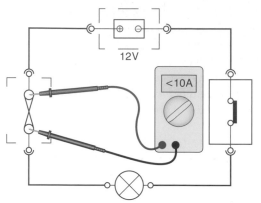

Figure 5.5 Use of a digital multimeter checking amps in a circuit (notice this is connected in series)

For circuits with a current of more than 10 A, an inductive current clamp should be added to the circuit as demonstrated in Figure 5.6.

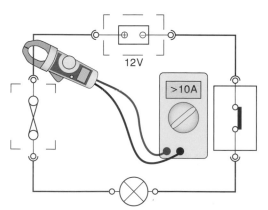

Figure 5.6 Current clamp being used to test for amps higher than 10 A

First make sure that the current clamp is fitted in the direction of electron flow; this is usually embossed on to the device. The clamp measures the current by monitoring the magnetic flux that builds around the wire, as an electrical current exists within it. In most cases, inductive current clamps are only suitable for measuring current and for testing circuits that are above 1 A (i.e. they are not suitable for measuring small levels of current).

Resistance

Resistance can be defined as being 'the opposition to an electrical current. It is like having an area of 'friction' within the circuit. This measurement is taken in **ohms**.

In a basic series circuit, the higher the resistance employed, the lower the current will be.

This relationship was discovered by the German physicist Georg Simon Ohm, hence Ohm's law.

Remember, a number of factors can affect the resistance of a component, such as:

- length of the cable
- the cross sectional area of the cable
- temperature
- resistance of the actual component itself.

Ohm: resistance to flow.

Often a resistance is an electrical component such as a switch or a motor. These components are called 'electrical consumers'.

To again draw comparison with the water circuit:

- Circuit voltage (pressure) increase = increased rate of flow
- Circuit voltage decrease = decreased rate of flow
- Ohms (resistance) increase = decreased rate of flow
- Ohms decrease = increased rate of flow.

Therefore, flow rate is dependent on the voltage (pressure) and the ohms (resistance) of a circuit.

5.2.7 Electrical power

The more energy there is flowing around a circuit (be it water or electricity), the more energy there is available to be harnessed. By increasing the rate of flow, you can increase the amount of power generated. Fitting an electrical component to a circuit, such as a lightbulb, will create a resistance that cannot be altered. A variable resistance (such as a dimmer switch) could be fitted, and then by increasing the resistance of the dimmer switch the flow would be reduced.

However, if we wanted to *increase* the brightness of the lightbulb instead, the current flow would have to be increased in turn by increasing the pressure (voltage) in the circuit. When we turn up the dimmer switch (increase the voltage) we can observe a change in the brightness of the bulb, however there is also a unit of measurement to represent power output of the bulb itself.

Power is measured by the watt (W), where 1 watt is equal to 1 joule of energy per second.

In context, most circuits on vehicles operate at a battery voltage of approximately 12 V (energy per unit charge), but the amount of current (rate at which energy is flowing) in individual circuits varies.

Comparing the amount of power required to operate a starter motor against a side lamp bulb is a good example (Figure 5.7). Both will operate at 12 V. The rate at which that energy is delivered to the starter motor (current) must be dually increased, perhaps at a rate of 150 amps. Compare this to the side lamp bulb, which also requires 12 V, however only at a rate of 0.5 amps.

- Power is, therefore, the relationship between voltage and current.
- Power = Voltage × Current.

Figure 5.7 Comparing current draw between a bulb and a starter motor

Ohm's law

Ohm's law explains the relationship between volts, amperes and ohms; this may be written as:

1 volt is required to force a current of 1 ampere through a resistance of 1 ohm.

The law can also be expressed in the equation:

Voltage = Current × Resistance

or

$V = I \times R$

Where:

V = voltage

I = current in amperes (A)

R = resistance in ohms (Ω)

Electrical properties	Unit of measurement	Symbol
'Pressure' or potential difference	Volt	V
Current (flow)	Ampere	A
Resistance	Ohm	Ω
Power	Watt	W

Table 5.3 Summary of electrical units and symbols

By knowing two out of the three values, the third value can then be calculated. Below are three examples that show this calculation using Ohm's law:

Example 1

In the circuit in Figure 5.8, the resistance is 4 Ω and the current flowing is 3 A.

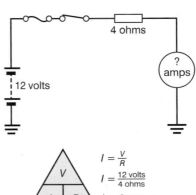

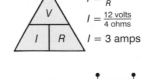

$I = \frac{V}{R}$

$I = \frac{12\ volts}{4\ ohms}$

$I = 3\ amps$

Figure 5.8 Using two of the three electrical values to calculate the third value

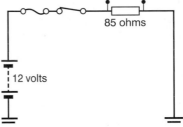

Figure 5.9 Formula for calculating ohms

Example 1 using Ohm's law shows:

$V = I \times R$

$= 3A \times 4Ω$

$= 12V$

Calculation formula is: Volts = Amperes × Ohms

Example 2

In Figure 5.8, the voltage applied to the circuit is 12 V and the current flowing is 3 A. Using Ohm's law, the resistance of the circuit can be calculated:

$$R = \frac{V}{I}$$
$$= \frac{12\,V}{3\,A}$$
$$= 4\,\Omega$$

Calculation formula is: Ohms $= \dfrac{\textbf{Volts}}{\textbf{Amperes}}$

Example 3

In Figure 5.8, the voltage applied to the circuit is 12 V and the resistance in the circuit is 4 Ω.

Using Ohm's law, the current flow in the circuit can be calculated:

$$I = \frac{V}{R}$$
$$= \frac{12\,V}{4\,\Omega}$$
$$= 3\,A$$

Calculation formula is: Amperes $= \dfrac{\textbf{Volts}}{\textbf{Ohms}}$

5.2.8 The effects of electrical energy

When current passes through a conductor, for example a cable or wire, it can cause three different effects:

1 Heat
2 Light
3 Magnetism

Heat

Heat is generated when electricity flows through a wire. Certain types of wire are constructed to allow large amounts of heat to be produced. A heated rear window element or a cigarette lighter are two good examples of this electrical energy effect.

Light

The glow of light is generated when electricity flows through particular types of wire. A lightbulb is a good example of electricity flowing through a wire causing it to produce a bright light. **Note**: light will also generate heat.

Magnetism

A magnetic field is generated when electricity passes through a wire. The magnetic field is essentially the same as that of a normal magnet but it is created by the flow of electricity, thereby producing an 'electromagnet'.

Generating magnetism in this manner produces only a weak field and the longer the wire, the stronger the magnetism. However, it is impractical to use long pieces of wire. By winding a long wire into a tight coil, it can be fitted into a smaller space, resulting in a stronger magnetic field.

Producing a magnetic field in this way can make it more versatile. If an electromagnet is placed beside another magnet (either a normal magnet or electromagnet), the two magnets will repel or attract each other. This method can be used to produce movement of components. For example, if one magnet is fitted to a rotating shaft, when it is then repelled by the another magnet it will make the shaft rotate, and a simple electric motor will be created.

Good examples of electromagnets used within vehicle electrical circuits include the ignition coil, alternator, starter motor and solenoids including relays and injectors.

5.2.9 Conductors and insulators

Conductors

A material that freely allows the flow of electrical current (i.e. has a very low resistance to current flow) is called a conductor. Copper is used in the construction of electrical cables because it has a low level of resistance. Other materials such as platinum, gold, silver and certain forms of carbon are also suitable for conducting electrical current.

Resistance within the circuit will be affected by the:

- type of cable
- cross-sectional area of cable
- length of cable
- thickness of cable (remember how the size of the water pipe affects resistance to water flow)
- temperature of cable (resistance usually increases with temperature in most types of cable).

Insulators

An insulator is a material, such as rubber or PVC, which resists or opposes the flow of electricity. An electrical cable is usually covered with insulation material to protect it against other cables or the body structure. If the insulated wire touches another piece of bare wire or the body of the car, then the insulator stops the energy passing across. In the event of the insulation failing, the energy would pass across to the other metal and create a **short circuit**.

Glass, plastics and porcelain are also suitable for insulating electrical currents. Some are more suitable for specific uses, depending on their properties.

Short circuit: a short path back to a battery's negative terminal, which can result in circuit damage, fire or even explosion.

Semiconductors

Semiconductive material, such as silicon and germanium, has less resistance than insulators, but more resistance than conductors. It can be useful for electronic components such as control modules. Their atomic structure is different to that of conductor materials and, therefore, behaves differently. They will not conduct current in their pure state; however when they are combined with very small amounts of foreign matter their atomic structure changes. This then enables current to pass through the material.

Properties of semiconductors

- When the temperature of the semiconductor increases, so will its resistance, sometimes significantly.
- Mixing additional substances with a semiconductor increases its ability to conduct electricity.
- When a semiconductor is exposed to a light source its resistance will change and light can be generated as current is passed through it.
- Semiconductors are commonly used to control the flow of current in an electrical circuit.
- Semiconductors are widely used in electronics.

Diodes, transistors and microchips are good examples of electronic devices that use semiconductors.

A temperature sensor used within the EMS is a good example of a component that uses this semiconductive function. This is because a semiconductor resistance changes with temperature, and temperature change is indicated by change in a circuit's current and voltage.

Semiconductors are used as electronic switches. When the driver switches on a primary circuit that uses a semiconductor within its operation of control, the semiconductor will act as a switch to control one or more secondary circuits if required. Although a mechanical switch such as a relay can be used for this purpose, a semiconductor switch will operate many times faster and is a lot smaller in its design.

5.3 Electrical circuits and calculations

5.3.1 Understanding the difference between conventional flow and electron flow

In the 1700s, Benjamin Franklin began experimenting with electricity and set a number of precedents for which he developed terms, concepts and definitions.

It was discovered that a flow of charge is created by having a high potential (electron surplus) and a low potential (electron deficiency) connected in a conductive circuit. Franklin labelled the high potential (electron surplus) 'positive' and low potential (electron deficiency) 'negative', and so conventional flow moved from the positive to the negative (Figure 5.10).

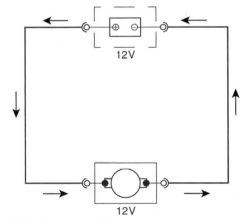

Figure 5.10 Conventional flow

However, research later identified that flow of charge actually moves from the negative (electron surplus) to the positive (electron deficiency). This is known as electron flow and is shown in Figure 5.11.

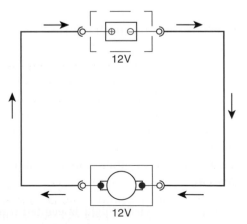

Figure 5.11 Electron flow

So assessing the above information and Figure 5.11, does it really matter which way we refer to charge flow? The answer is, not really; just as long as we are consistent with definitions and the use of graphics and symbols.

The terms 'positive' and 'negative' are well-established and even mathematical concepts, such as Ohm's law, in most cases remain valid no matter which way you consider charge flow. As such, most wiring diagrams show the conventional flow from positive to negative.

5.3.2 A simple circuit

Figure 5.12 shows a simple circuit. The circuit layout is constructed by using a lamp and switch, which is then connected to a battery. In Figure 5.13 the same circuit is shown, along with standard electrical symbols.

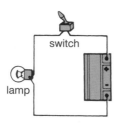

Figure 5.12 A simple circuit with a lamp and switch connected to a battery

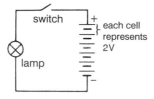

Figure 5.13 A simple circuit illustrated with electrical symbols

Figures 5.12 and 5.13 show the layout of a simple circuit. A simple on/off switch with a set of electrical contacts controls the flow of electricity.

If the switch is turned 'off', then the contacts of the switch will be in the open position. This is commonly known as 'open circuit' (i.e. the circuit is broken and current cannot flow within the circuit, therefore preventing the bulb from lighting up).

If the switch is turned 'on', then the contacts will be closed. The circuit will then become live and the current will flow, passing through the switch and on to the bulb filament. This will cause the fine wire of the filament to glow. In other words, it will become **incandescent**.

Incandescent: when visible light is emitted through the heating of a filament until it is white hot.

5.3.3 Earth return

When an electrical component is connected to a battery source by two cables, one of the cables is called the supply and the other is the earth or return. Using the metal body and frame of the vehicle as a part of the circuit reduces the length of cable and simplifies the layout. The frame is referred to as earth (or ground) and joined to one of the battery terminals. In normal cases, the negative terminal is 'earthed' and the polarity of the vehicle is called 'negative earth'.

The term 'return' is linked with the current flow in a circuit. By substituting the vehicle body for the return cable, an earth return system is formed (Figure 5.14). The alternative two-wire arrangement, known as 'insulated return', is seldom used other than for special-purpose vehicles, for example petrol tankers.

Note: battery terminals must be connected to give the correct earth polarity. Serious damage to components, especially those containing electronic devices, will occur unless the equipment is connected to give the correct polarity.

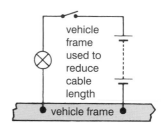

Figure 5.14 An earth return circuit

5.3.4 Types of circuit

There are two types of electrical circuits used within the modern motor vehicle, although occasionally a combination of both can be used. The two circuits are known as 'series' and 'parallel'.

Series circuit

In Figure 5.15, the circuit is fitted with two bulbs, one directly after the other. They are therefore known as being 'in series'. When the circuit is switched to 'active' the current will flow from the battery positive terminal, and will have to pass through both bulbs before it returns to the negative battery terminal.

A disadvantage to using a series circuit is that if one of the bulb filaments is faulty, then the current will not be able to flow to both bulbs and neither will be active.

Note: when testing a series circuit, the current flow through the circuit is the same at any point.

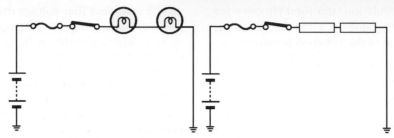

Figure 5.15 A series circuit (shown with bulbs and with resistor symbols)

The total resistance (R_T) of the circuit is equal to the sum (addition) of the two resistance values in the circuit. That is:

$$R_T = R_1 + R_2$$

For example, if:

R_1 and R_2 are $2\,\Omega$ and $4\,\Omega$

Then:

$$R_T = 2\,\Omega + 4\,\Omega$$

$$= 6\,\Omega$$

To calculate and identify the amount of current flow, you need to use the formula of Ohm's law. **Note**: the calculation must include the circuit's total resistance.

As most light vehicle electrical circuits use 12V systems, the current flow in the circuit is:

$$I\,(\text{current}) = \frac{V}{R_T}$$

$$= \frac{V}{R_1 + R_2}$$

$$= \frac{12\,V}{2\,\Omega + 4\,\Omega}$$

$$= \frac{12\,V}{6\,\Omega} = 2\,A$$

Parallel circuits

Figure 5.16 shows a parallel circuit, which has been created by fitting two bulbs together side by side. Both bulbs are connected to the battery positive terminal as well as the battery negative terminal. With this layout, each bulb will receive equal battery voltage.

A key advantage of using parallel circuits in motor vehicles is to improve safety and awareness for other vehicle users. For example, if one bulb fails to light up within a side light circuit, then the other bulbs within the circuit will continue to remain lit and visible.

To calculate the total current flowing through the switch in Figure 5.16, we will need to identify the total value of each resistance in the circuit. However, it's important to remember that there are effectively two circuits (i.e. bulb current 1 + bulb current 2 = total current).

For this calculation, we must use Ohm's law to identify its values:

$$I\,(\text{current}) = \frac{V}{R_T}$$

With R_1 value being $2\,\Omega$ and R_2 being $6\,\Omega$, then the current flow through each resistance is as follows:

For R_1 $\qquad = \dfrac{12\,V}{2\,\Omega}$

$I\,(\text{current}) = 6\,A$

For R_2 $\qquad = \dfrac{12\,V}{6\,\Omega}$

$I\,(\text{current}) = 2\,A$

The total current flowing through the circuit

$$= \frac{\text{Current}}{\text{through } R_1} + \frac{\text{Current}}{\text{through } R_2}$$

$$= 6\,A + 2\,A = 8\,A$$

If the total current flow and the supply voltage are known, then we can calculate the total resistance of the circuit using Ohm's law:

$$R_T = \frac{V}{I} = \frac{12\,V}{8\,A} = 1.5\,\Omega$$

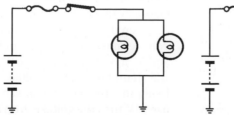
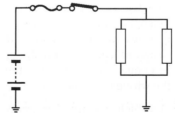

Figure 5.16 A parallel circuit (shown with bulbs and symbols)

So assessing this calculation, the total effective (or combined) resistance value of a parallel circuit is always lower than that of the smallest resistor.

The total resistance of a parallel circuit can be calculated in another way by using this formula:

$$\frac{1}{R_T} = \frac{1}{R_1} + \frac{1}{R_2}$$

In this instance:
$$\frac{1}{R_T} = \frac{1}{2} + \frac{1}{6}$$

Or in another way:
$$\frac{1}{R_T} = \frac{3}{6} + \frac{1}{6}$$

Or:
$$\frac{1}{R_T} = \frac{4}{6}$$

Therefore:
$$\frac{R_T}{1} = \frac{6}{4} = 1.5\,\Omega$$

These calculations have demonstrated that the total resistance is lower than the value of the smallest resistor.

For day-to-day general vehicle work or electrical testing, a technician is unlikely to use this formula. However, there may be times when certain diagnostic problems arise where this underpinning knowledge of parallel resistance calculations will be useful.

5.3.5 Voltage drop

Voltage drop is an excellent diagnostic assessment of any given circuit when looking for faults. We've already established that for an electrical circuit to be active, current will need to flow. If a circuit has a resistance, then the voltage (potential difference) will fall as the current passes through the resistance. If we were to test each side of the resistance, we would identify that the voltage on both sides is different. This difference in the voltage is called 'voltage drop'.

Note: the current must be flowing in the circuit in order to create voltage drop.

Due to the extremely high internal resistance of a voltmeter, it is recommended that the majority of circuit testing is performed using the following method.

When checking a circuit for voltage, the voltmeter should be connected in parallel across the circuit to avoid damage to the meter. When checking for amps, the meter should be connected in series so that the circuit current passes through the meter. In some cases, when checking for amps an inductive amps clamp is best, as this allows the circuit to be assessed without disconnecting any of the connectors by placing the inductive clamp around the wiring to be checked.

The majority of modern vehicle electrical systems are now controlled using electronic modules. You can be confident that voltage drop testing will not in any way damage sensitive components within these units. In addition to this, voltage drop testing will give you a far clearer result than, for instance, resistance or continuity testing, thus building your confidence during fault diagnosis.

The most important rules to remember when voltage drop testing are:

- a reference voltage is first obtained from a known good supply for comparison with your measurements
- the circuit is active (switched on) even if the consumer is not working.

Note: resistance is only active in a closed circuit. If a circuit is not closed (switched on) then the voltage drop method will not measure a resistance.

Voltage drop across a single resistance

Figure 5.17 shows a single resistance within the circuit. The 85 ohm resistor effectively uses up all of the energy (or voltage) in the circuit, so we can identify that the voltage drop across a single resistor in a 12V circuit will equal 12V.

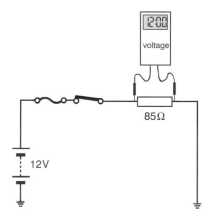

Figure 5.17 Voltage drop across a single resistance

At the start of the resistance the voltage applied is 12V, but as the resistance uses all of the existing voltage, the voltage at the end of the resistance will be 0V. Therefore, the voltage drop will be expressed as 12V across this single resistance.

Voltage drop across resistances in series

Figure 5.18 shows a circuit with two resistances connected in a series. In this case, the total available voltage must drop across both the resistances – R_1 and R_2. If both R_1 and R_2 are the same value, then they will share the existing voltage equally between them. Using this theory we can see that if each resistance uses 6V, then the voltage drop across both resistances would be expressed as 12V.

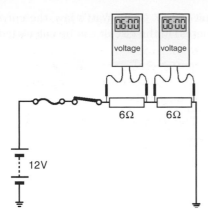

Figure 5.18 Voltage drop across two equal resistances in series

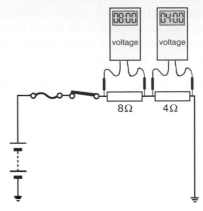

Figure 5.19 Voltage drop across two series resistances (with different values)

If two resistances are connected in series but have two different values, then the voltage drop will likewise be different across each resistance. However, the total voltage drop across the two resistances will still equal the total available voltage. This means that in a 12V circuit the values of the two series resistances would be of no concern; it would still be a 12V total voltage drop. Both resistances share the entire voltage available.

Ohm's law can be used to calculate the voltage drop across the resistances (see page 501). If two of the three values are known, then Ohm's law calculation can be applied.

$$V_{drop1} = R_1 \times I \text{ (current)}$$

$$V_{drop2} = R_2 \times I \text{ (current)}$$

Note: the supply voltage equals the sum of the voltage drops across the resistances in the circuit.

To calculate the voltage drop across each resistance, refer to Figure 5.19. The calculations show that current flow in the circuit must be calculated first:

$$I = \frac{V}{R_T}$$

$$= \frac{V}{R_1 + R_2}$$

$$= \frac{12V}{4\Omega + 2\Omega} \text{ (lowest common denominator)}$$

$$= \frac{12V}{6\Omega}$$

Once again, looking at Figure 5.19, the voltage drop across each resistance can be calculated.

$$V_1 = R_1 \times I \text{ (current)}$$

$$= 2\Omega \times 2A = 4V$$

$$V_2 = R_2 \times I \text{ (current)}$$

$$= 4\Omega \times 2A = 8V$$

If we add the total voltage drop across the two resistors, this will be equal to the supply voltage (V_T) (i.e. the battery voltage).

$$V_T = V_1 + V_2$$

$$= 4V + 8V$$

$$= 12V$$

When resistance values in the circuit are the same, the supply voltage is evenly split between the resistances. For example, with circuit supply voltage at 12V and three resistances connected in series each with a value of 2Ω, then the voltage drop will be 4V at each resistance.

The three resistance values in themselves are irrelevant; if they are all equal, then the voltages will be equally distributed across the three resistances, still creating a 4V voltage drop across each resistance.

Voltage drop across resistances in parallel

If we look at resistors connected in parallel in a circuit, we must remember that each of the resistors are in fact independent of each other and act as a single resistance. This is due to parallel circuits supplying full voltage to each resistor or load device, because each resistance has the full available voltage applied from the battery positive terminal to one end and the battery negative terminal to its other end. Therefore, when we look at the calculation required to work out the voltage drop in a parallel circuit we must calculate each resistance independently as a single resistance.

5.3.6 Calculating power (watts)

As covered earlier in this chapter on page 507, energy or power is generated when electricity flows in a circuit. This energy or power comes in the form of heat, light or creating movement (electric motors or solenoids).

We have seen how Ohm's law defines the ohm; similarly, we can use Watt's law to define the watt. The term 'watt' comes from a Scottish engineer called James Watt (1736–1819) and is the unit used to measure the amount of electricity used by a device in which the potential difference is one volt and the current is one ampere.

Power is expressed in watts (W) and the definition of power is work done in a given time.

Power can be calculated from Watt's law using this formula:

Power = Current × Voltage

or   Watts = Amperes × Volts

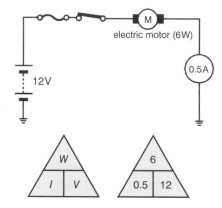

Figure 5.20 Power or watts in a circuit

Similar to Ohm's law, if two of the values are known, the third value can be calculated. The following examples demonstrate how.

Example 1

In the circuit in Figure 5.20, the voltage applied to the circuit is 12V and the current flowing is 0.5A. Using Watt's law, the power (watts) applied to the circuit can be calculated:

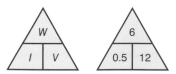

Figure 5.21 Calculation using Watt's law

The above calculation in Figure 5.21 shows:

$W = I \times V$

$= 0.5\,\text{A} \times 12\,\text{V}$

$= 6\,\text{W}$

Calculation formula is: Watts = Amperes × Volts

Example 2

In the circuit in Figure 5.22, the power produced within the circuit is 6W and the voltage applied to

the circuit is 12V. Using Watt's law, the current flow (*I* in amperes) in the circuit can be calculated:

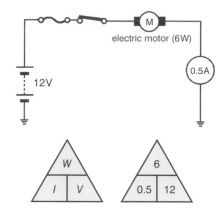

Figure 5.22 Calculation using Watt's law

The above calculation shows:

$I = \dfrac{W}{V}$

$= \dfrac{6\,\text{W}}{12\,\text{V}}$

$= 0.5\,\text{A}$

Calculation formula is: Amperes = $\dfrac{\text{Watts}}{\text{Volts}}$

Example 3

In the circuit in Figure 5.20, the power produced within the circuit is 6W and the current flow (*I* in amperes) is 0.5A. Using Watt's law, the voltage applied in the circuit can be calculated:

Figure 5.23 Calculation to find voltage using Watt's law

The above calculation shows:

$V = \dfrac{W}{A}$

$= \dfrac{6\,\text{W}}{0.5\,\text{A}}$

$= 12\,\text{V}$

Calculation formula is: Volts = $\dfrac{\text{Watts}}{\text{Amperes}}$

5.3.7 Open and short circuits

There are two types of common faults that can occur in a circuit:

- Open circuit
- Short circuit

Open circuit

When electrical current is unable to flow due to a break in the circuit, this is termed an 'open circuit'. A switch is the most common component used to provide an intentionally open circuit. The 'on and off' flow of current within the circuit is controlled by the switch.

Another form of open circuit occurs when there has been a fault within the electrical circuit (see Figure 5.24).

Due to the break in the cable, the flow of current is prevented and the circuit cannot work. In Figure 5.24, an ammeter is used to measure the amount of current or amperes, also forming part of the circuit itself. In effect, the meter measures the flow rate and indicates the amount of current in the circuit. In the case of this circuit, the reading on the ammeter will be zero due to the break in the wire, which is causing an open circuit.

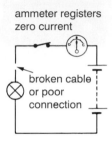

Figure 5.24 An open circuit

Short circuit

If a flow of current can choose to either pass through a resistance or through a piece of wire, most of the current will pass through the latter. Electricity will always take the path of least resistance between the battery terminals. For example, if the cable supplying power to a headlight accidentally chafes through and touches the vehicle body and connects to the earth connection (Figure 5.25), the current will take the route of least resistance and divert straight to earth rather than carrying on to the headlight, which creates some resistance.

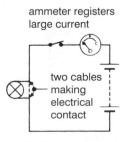

Figure 5.25 A short circuit

The unwanted outcome is that the full amperage or current flow from the battery going directly to earth will cause large heat build-up due to the circuit no longer containing any load device to absorb the power. This can result in the current flow becoming so high that the wiring could melt. In this event, some extra form of protection would be needed.

To protect the circuit, a fuse is normally fitted in the supply circuit. This will act to protect the wiring and other components as it will break or blow and cause an open circuit situation. As mentioned, an open circuit does not have current flow. This then protects the rest of the circuit and prevents a possible fire. Insulation fitted to cables varies in thickness and is directly proportional to the size of cable and the current flowing through the cable. A higher core thickness cable carrying high current, such as a starter motor cable, will have thicker insulation.

5.3.8 Fuses and other circuit protectors

A fuse is a short length of thin wire or metal that is designed to melt and break the circuit if the current exceeds the rated value marked on the fuse. Provided it is of the correct rating, a fuse reduces the risk of fire in the event of a short circuit.

A number of fuses, or other forms of thermal circuit breaker, are fitted to protect the various circuits of a vehicle (Figures 5.26 and 5.27). Some electrical components require a comparatively large current, so in these cases a fuse having a high 'amperage' is specified. Fuses are generally fitted to the supply side of the circuit, usually as near as possible to the positive battery or supply terminal such as a switch or relay.

Figure 5.26 Early types of fuses – glass tube and ceramic

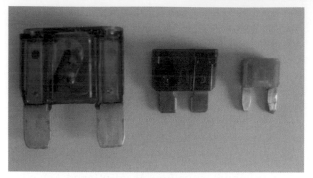

Figure 5.27 Blade type fuses in three different sizes

If a fuse blows, it must be replaced with the same size and type and the cause of the blow should be investigated. If the fuse blows immediately when the new fuse is placed in the fuse box, a short circuit situation should be followed up. This process involves isolating each of the components on the circuit until the fuse no longer blows.

Many fuses fitted today are of the blade type because they are slim and compact. These come in three different sizes and are colour coded with the ampere capacity written on the fuse body.

The fusible rating ranges from 5 A up to a maximum protection of 30 A.

J Case fuses

The J Case fuse is a common type of fuse used in today's vehicle electrical systems. They are used in electrical circuits that have a need for protection, rating from 30 A up to a maximum of 60 A.

Figure 5.28 J Case fuses

Bolt-down fuses (fusible links)

Within the automotive electrical system some components will demand or generate high levels of power. In these instances, fuses need to be able to protect these circuits. These fuses are high amperage and often called 'fusible links'; they are normally available in 40–500 A. The fusible link has thicker wire acting as the fuse to allow for the higher amperage

running through the circuit. Fusible links will react in the same way as normal fuses when subjected to a dead short or higher amperage current by melting the wire to create an open circuit and provide protection. Sometimes they are known as mega fuses because of their protection rating (Figure 5.29). If at any time a fusible link blows, it should be replaced and the circuit should be assessed for any faults, such as short circuits, prior to the vehicle running on the road.

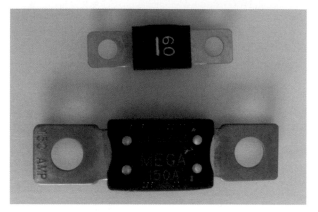

Figure 5.29 Bolt-down fusible links

Circuit breakers

Some circuits with a heavy draw on current, such as sunroofs or electric windows, are protected by circuit breakers. Once a certain level of current is reached, the circuit breaker will stop the current from flowing (this is called 'tripping') and the circuit will no longer work. These are similar in operation to the circuit breakers found in household electric systems.

Circuit breakers can either reset themselves automatically once the current has returned to a safe level, or they can be reset manually.

5.3.9 Switches

In most conventional circuits the flow of electricity is controlled via a switch. The internal structure of the switch comprises a set of contacts; these can be either open or closed. An open contact breaks the circuit so current is unable to flow. When the switch is turned on, the contacts close, allowing the electrical current to flow through the circuit. Vehicles have many types of switches fitted that control different circuits. These include push-on/off switches, lever-operated switches, rotary switches and temperature/pressure switches.

Push-on/off switches

Push-on/off switches are simple in design and are frequently used to control many electrical circuits in a motor vehicle. Figure 5.30 shows a selection of different options but all are of the push-on/off type.

Figure 5.30 Push-on/off type switches fitted in a car interior

Figure 5.32 Rotary headlight switch

Lever-operated switches

These types of switches are conventionally used to operate items such as the indicators and wipers. This type of multi-contact switch controls a number of functions needed by the driver, depending on driver demands and external conditions. For convenience and accessibility, they are normally fitted to the top of the steering column. The switch is fitted at the bottom of the lever and by pushing the end of the lever up or down different circuits will function (Figure 5.31). Lever-operated switches often also house a multi-function unit that handles a large number of components and data across the auxiliary and lighting circuits.

Figure 5.31 Lever-operated switch assembly

Rotary switches

This type of switch is operated by turning the knob, which in turn moves a set of contacts at the bottom of the shaft. A good example of a rotary switch is a headlight dial (Figure 5.32). Also in Figure 5.32 you can see a different version of a rotary switch designed for adjusting the brightness of the instrumentation lighting. Rotary switches can also be used for adjusting heater fan speeds, or even as an ignition switch on the steering column.

Temperature/pressure switches

In modern vehicles many components are operated automatically through the use of temperature and pressure switches. These switches perform their operation without the need of input from the driver because the contacts are activated by temperature or pressure.

Temperature-operated switches

A switch used to control the cooling fans uses a set of contacts contained within the body of the switch (or sensor). This is placed within the flow of coolant around the top hose region. The contacts remain open when the coolant is below the threshold temperature (e.g. 85°), and when a predetermined higher temperature is reached, the contacts then close and pass an earth supply to a relay, which will then supply current to the cooling fans (Figure 5.33).

Figure 5.33 Temperature-operated switch

Pressure-operated switches

This type of switch would normally be located within a circuit that needs to monitor the pressure of its operating fluid. The switch contacts will be closed when the pressure of the fluid is at its lowest, but when the pressure increases to its predetermined level, the contacts will open.

A pressure switch can be used to detect low refrigerant pressure in an air-conditioning system. This would then prevent the compressor being run, which would cause a great deal of damage. Many pressure-operated switches also provide a warning light, situated in the instrument cluster to warn the driver of any failure, such as low oil pressure (Figure 5.34).

Figure 5.34 Pressure-operated switch

5.3.10 Relays

Incorporated within most electrical circuits you will find a relay as part of the system's control functionality. Relays come in a number of different sizes and a wide variety of current ratings and types, depending upon the circuit application (Figure 5.35a). All relays function as an electrically operated remote switch, where they use a relatively low current flow to control the operation of a circuit that has a much higher demand on current flow.

Figure 5.35a Selection of relays fitted to a fuse box

In Figure 5.35b the relay is used to switch on the headlight circuit. The headlights have a relatively high current requirement operating at around 15–20 A. Most relays are located within a junction box for containment to reduce the amount of wiring but, if needed, the relay could be located nearer to the headlights to, again, reduce the length of wiring required.

The relay itself can be activated by a very low current; this means that only a very thin wire is needed between the headlight switch and the relay, which in turn allows the switch to be designed for low current values. However, a thicker wire would be needed from the relay to the headlights because it's carrying a higher current. The use of thinner wire to act as the switch circuit and thicker wire to carry the higher current to the headlights keeps the amount of wire to a minimum, which lowers the weight of cable required for a given circuit.

When the driver switches on the headlights a low current is passed through the relay. This low current closes the relay switch allowing the main supply (battery positive) to flow via the fusible link to the headlight circuit and on to the headlamp units. Using a relay enables the manufacturer to use less high-amperage cable to power the circuits, as the relays can be mounted close to the headlamp units. This reduces the chance of resistance build-up and also provides lighter **wiring harnesses**.

> **Wiring harness**: the cabling routed throughout the vehicle to provide electrical power to each component. It is designed to be as light and strong as possible to ensure that no faults associated with open, short or high-resistance circuits occur.

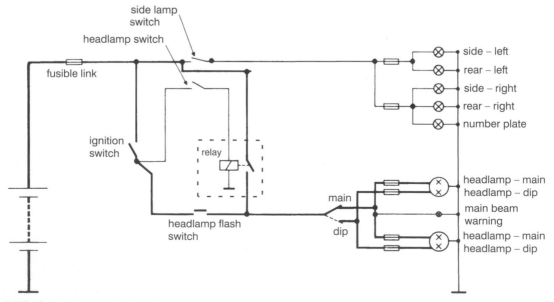

Figure 5.35b A relay in a simple headlight circuit

Using long wire to carry a high current can result in an unacceptable voltage drop and a subsequent reduction in current flow. This would affect the operation of the light bulbs or other electrical items. In addition, there are safety concerns when high currents pass through long pieces of wire. The current flow can generate heat in the wire and switch contacts, which could cause them to fail and even result in fire. To avoid each of these scenarios, the costs associated with using a relay have to be low to be attractive to the manufacturer and beneficial in the production of the vehicle itself. The added benefit of a less heavy wiring harness makes the use of relays cost effective.

Relay construction and operation

To understand the principle function of a relay, we need to establish how they are constructed and how the relay functions when energised. As mentioned previously, a relay is a type of switch with a very important purpose. It switches high current circuits on and off that would quickly damage a normal switch due to the current flow through the switch assembly. If a relay was not used, the switch itself would be too big as it would require 'heavy' contacts. A relay has 'heavy' switch contacts and it can be installed anywhere on the vehicle near the component it will operate.

Figure 5.36 shows the internal structure of a relay and included is a relay image from a wiring diagram.

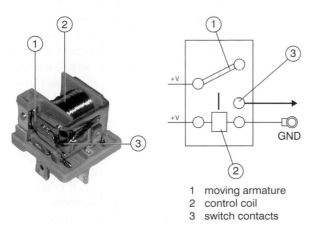

1   moving armature
2   control coil
3   switch contacts

Figure 5.36 Internal structure of a relay and simple wiring diagram

Two relay standards exist:

- DIN (Deutsches Institut für Normung)
- ISO (International Organization for Standardization)

Note: the translation for the German '*Deutsches Institut für Normung*' (DIN) is the 'German Institute for Standardization'.

To identify the difference between the two relay standards, both manufacturers use different terminal numbering. This is normally visible on the base or outer housing of the relay.

Table 5.4 Relay standards and terminal numbering

ISO	DIN	Designation
1	86	Switched feed
2	85	Ground
3	30	Ignition or constant feed
4	87a	Switched feed change over
5	87	Switched feed from relay to consumer

Figure 5.37 shows the two versions.

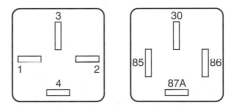

Figure 5.37 Two versions of relay pin arrangements

Although we have identified two manufacturing versions, you will find that there are a number of functional versions available depending on the system that the relay is operating within. These types are known as:

- 4-pin normally open
- 4-pin normally closed
- 5-pin change over.

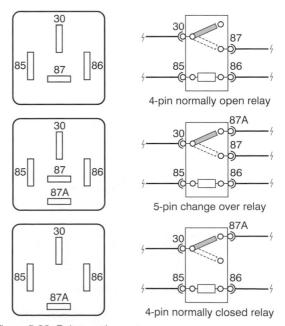

4-pin normally open relay

5-pin change over relay

4-pin normally closed relay

Figure 5.38 Relay versions

The internal structure of the relay contains two contacts that form a switch. When the relay is inactive, they are usually open and become closed when a small magnetic field is created alongside the contacts.

Also within the relay housing is a coil winding assembly. The coil winding assembly acts as an electromagnet when energised to provide the means of switching the contacts in order to open and close the main high amperage circuit. The coil windings are energised by a low current switch circuit utilising thin low amperage cabling and a simple switch device usually operated by the driver. When the switch is operated the low amperage current will flow through the relay coil windings creating an electromagnetic field. This will cause the relay contact to close, creating a circuit.

The main circuit terminals within the relay are connected to the main power feed from the battery, or another fused circuit, and to the consumer component (e.g. the heated rear window or cooling fans). As the low amperage circuit energises the coil windings, the contacts close in the relay allowing the main current to flow through the relay to the electrical consumer.

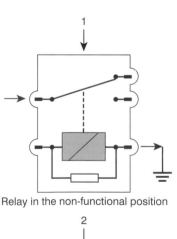

Relay in the non-functional position

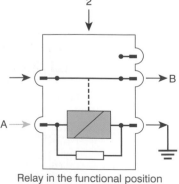

Relay in the functional position

Figure 5.39 A relay in a non-functional position (1) and then active (2)

This process can also be reversed (i.e. the circuit is opened or switched off by using a relay that is normally closed when not energised and open when energised). Additionally, some relays are able to operate two circuits by using two sets of contacts and two output terminals; this can be useful on circuits such as main beam lamps where two lamps need to be switched on simultaneously. When the headlamps are in the dipped, low beam position the relay contacts are in their normal closed position; when the driver selects main high beam the relay coil windings are energised through a low amperage feed from the main beam switch. This leads to the relay contacts being opened to disconnect the dipped low beam but also connect the main beam circuit. These types of relays are called 'change-over relays', where two circuits are controlled using one relay.

5.3.11 Cables

Throughout the vehicle's electrical system, each component is connected to the supply by low-resistance cables (wires). Generally, copper cables that are usually stranded to give good flexibility are used to connect components. As many electrical systems are fitted to today's vehicles, it has become common practice to run several cables along a single path; these cables are bound together to form a 'loom' or wiring harness. Wiring harnesses allow neat routing of cabling around the vehicle and prevent the possibility of chafing against the metal frame and breakage of the cable due to vibration. Wiring harnesses are secured to the vehicle body using various securing clips to prevent further movement and chafing. Many harness outer protection sleeves are also heat retardant, especially when routing through the engine bay area, to prevent damage from the heat of the engine and exhaust.

The quoted-size of a cable refers to the diameter of the wire and the number of strands. If the cable is too small for its length or for the current it has to carry, it will overheat and produce a voltage drop, which affects the performance of the component to which it connects, for example a light will not give its full brightness or a starter motor will not rotate at the correct speed.

Many different-sized cables are used throughout the vehicle depending on the size of current required for the given components. Most of the circuits on the vehicle have a wire diameter of approximately 0.30 mm, apart from heavy current draw components such as starter motors or alternators. When a defective cable is renewed it should be replaced with a cable of similar size. If a new circuit is to be installed, the maximum current load should be estimated in order to ascertain the cable size needed. See Table 5.5 for cable ratings.

Table 5.5 Cable ratings

Number and diameter of strands (mm)	Nominal CSA of core (mm²)	Resistance per meter 20°C (Ω)	Approximately continuous current rating (A)	Equivalent American gauge (size)	Typical application
9 / 0.30	0.85	0.0294	5.75	19	LT ignition side/tail lamps
14 / 0.25	0.70	0.0271	8.00	19	
14 / 0.30	1.0	0.0189	8.75	17	General purpose
28 / 0.30	2.0	0.0094	17.50	14	Headlamps
44 / 0.30	3.0	0.0064	25.50	12	Battery supply and actuator circuits
65 / 0.30	6.0	0.0031	42.00	9	Dynamo alternator circuits
84 / 0.30					
97 / 0.30	7.0	0.0027	50.00	8	Alternator and ammeter circuits
120 / 0.30	8.5	0.0022	60.00	8	Alternator and ammeter circuits
37 / 0.71	15	0.0011	105.00	-	Starter cables
37 / 0.90	25	0.008	170.00	-	
61 / 0.90	40	0.0005	300.00	-	
61 / 1.31	60	0.0003	415.00	-	
266 / 0.30	20	0.0010	135.00	-	

Cable covering and coding

Generally, PVC or plastics are used to insulate most cables around the vehicle, apart from where there is high heat. PVC and plastics are relatively inexpensive to use and also provide good electrical insulation and resistance to fuel, petrol and oil. However, it should be noted that PVC gives off dangerous fumes when heated.

To help identify each cable, the cable coverings are colour coded. The colour codes used on a vehicle depends on the manufacturer. Table 5.6 shows an example of some colours that have been used for the principal circuits. In addition to the main colour, on some cables you will see a tracer colour running along the length of the wire or, in the case of some European cables, a coloured band. The colour of the tracer identifies the part of the circuit formed by this cable.

For example, a cable shown as WG has a white base colour and a green tracer.

In recent years, a number of car manufacturers have modified their colour coding. The main change is that you now see two letters to identify the colour of the cable. For example, a brown cable is identified as BN. If the brown cable has a trace colour of white, the code BN-WH will be visible. See Table 5.7 for additional colour-coding references.

Table 5.6 Colour coding and abbreviations for principal circuits

Circuit cable	Colour	Abbreviation
Earth connections	Black	B
Ignition circuits	White	W
Main battery feed	Brown	N
Side lamps	Red	R
Auxiliaries controlled by ignition switch	Green	G
Auxiliaries not controlled by ignition switch	Purple	P
Headlamps	Blue	U

Table 5.7 Additional colour coding for automotive wiring

Previous code 1	Previous code 2	Colour	New code
BK	B	Black	BK
BU	U	Blue	BU
GN	G	Green	GN
GY	S	Grey	GY
O	O	Orange	OG
R	R	Red	RD
P	P	Violet	VT
Y	Y	Yellow	YE
W	W	White	WH
T	N	Brown	BN

5.3.12 Connectors

Cable connections are very important in ensuring electrical circuits maintain excellent continuity at all times. The need to prevent damage through vibration and ingress of moisture or dirt means that these connections have to be watertight and very secure. With more electrical equipment found on today's vehicles and the use of advanced computer systems to control engine management and transmissions, it is very important to make sure that these connections are not damaged or subjected to abuse.

Figure 5.40 shows a typical plug-and-socket harness connector, which is used to join a number of cables. At the ends of the connector, the terminals are exposed; this provides a test point for meter checks.

On circuits where there is very low current such as the inputs into an EMS, these could be significantly affected by a poor connection that offers a high resistance. As the EMS is highly dependent on the information received from the sensors to operate efficiently, any chances of poor connectivity or high resistance will cause the EMS to operate incorrectly. This could lead to the EMS misinterpreting devices such as the coolant temperature sensor, which could lead to incorrect fuelling of the engine. On many newer vehicles the use of gold plating is used on the connector pins. This can be seen on supplemental restraint systems where the control unit must fire the airbags at very high speeds. The use of gold ensures that the resistance is kept to a minimum, as gold is an excellent conductor of electricity.

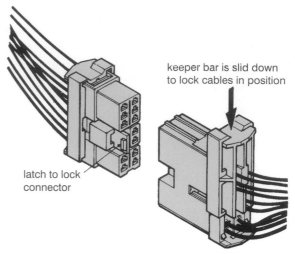

Figure 5.40 Typical plug-and-socket harness connector

5.3.13 Wiring diagrams

Wiring diagrams are very important in diagnosing faults within a circuit. The wiring diagram gives a pictorial view of the circuit and allows the technician to trace the circuit operation without the initial need to interfere with the vehicle's wiring harness. Each manufacturer has their own preferred method

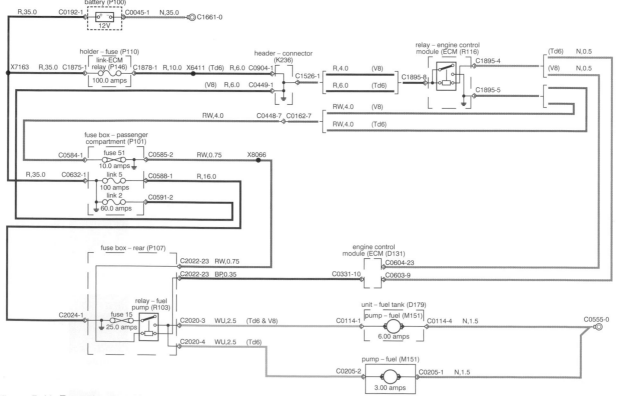

Figure 5.41 Example of a wiring diagram showing a fuel pump circuit

of producing wiring diagrams, so it is important to understand the basic concepts before following a given diagram. An example of a wiring diagram can be seen in Figure 5.41; this shows the fuel pump circuit. You will notice a great deal of detail on the diagram, which helps the technician to locate connectors, earth points and components and identify colour of wires and power distribution. Generally, it takes some time to understand these diagrams in detail. In this example diagram, we need to locate the ECU as we would like to check the 'N' (brown) wire going to the connector C0604-23.

The C0604 equates to the connector number 604 and the 23 equates to pin number 23. The technician would then look up the location of C0604 to find specifically where this is on the vehicle. Figure 5.42 shows where this is located. Using the electrical library, we can see that the ECU and the connector are inside the E-box, which is inside the engine bay. Connector C0604 is also the second connector along. The pin details to the right show that pin 23 is the 'N' (brown) wire.

Electrical symbols

As shown in Figure 5.41, the use of symbols is very important to ensure that the technician is able to follow the circuit in detail and identify components. In Figure 5.41, you can see that symbols for the relay, fuses, pumps and battery have been used. Due to a large number of different components being used in today's vehicles, there is a need to have a standard format for manufacturers to follow to ensure that the technician is able to follow the wiring diagrams. The symbols used in wiring diagrams will vary slightly between manufacturers.

For many years, vehicle manufacturers have used the British Standards Institution (BSI) electrical symbols shown in BS 3939-1:1986 throughout their wiring diagrams. Figure 5.43 shows some of the main symbols used. Standardised symbols help when having to work on different vehicle ranges, but note that the European equivalent may be slightly different.

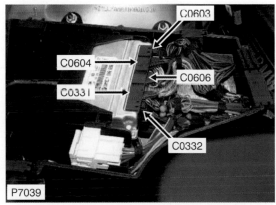

Cav	Col	Cct
1	NW	3
3	YN	3
4	YB	3
7	NU	31
8	YW	3
9	Y	3
10	YR	3
11	YR	3
13	NR	3
14	BW	3
15	B	3
16	BR	3
17	BU	3
19	N	3
23	N	3

Description: Engine control module (ECM) – V8
Location: Inside E-box

no connector face

Colour:
Gender:

Figure 5.42 Connector location using electrical library

Description	Symbol
Direct current Alternating current	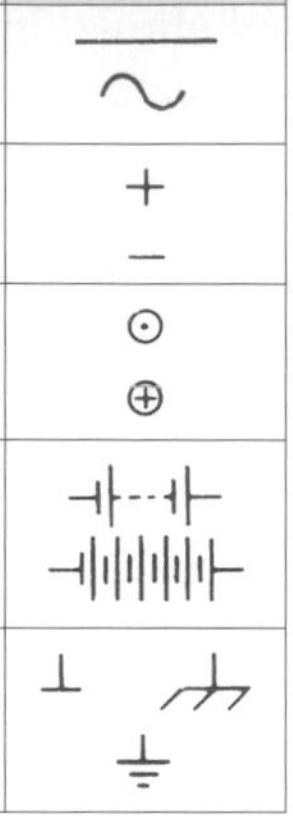
Positive polarity Negative polarity	+ −
Current approaching Current receding	⊙ ⊕
Battery 12 V (Long line is positive)	
Earth, chassis frame Earth, general	

Description	Symbol
Conductor (permanent) Thickness denotes importance Conductor (temporary)	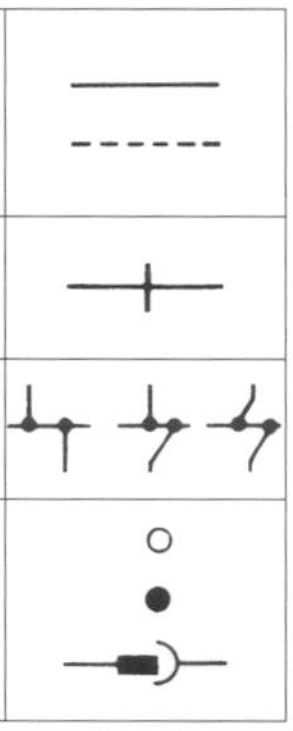
Conductors crossing without connecting	
Conductors joining	
Junction, separable Junction, inseparable Plug and socket	o ●

Description	Symbol
Variability: applied to other symbols	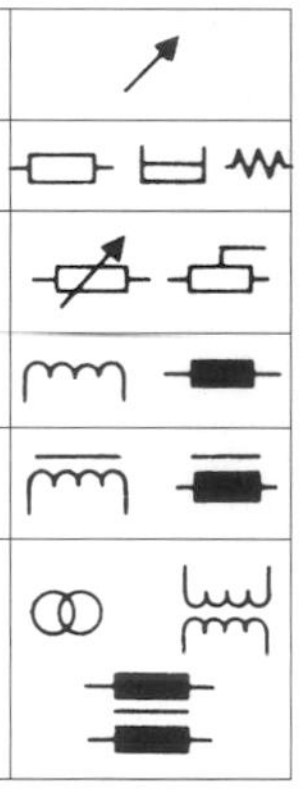
Resistor (fixed value)	
Resistor (variable)	
General winding (inductor, coil)	
Winding with core	
Transformer	

Description	Symbol
Diode, rectifying junction	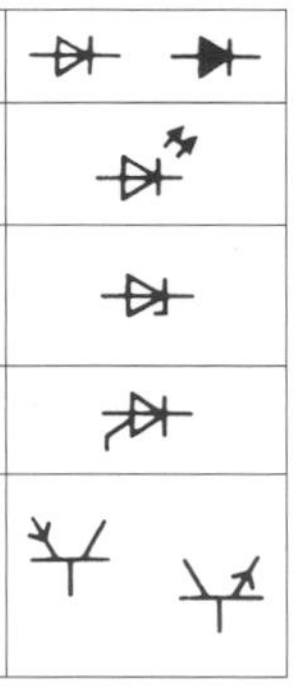
Light-emitting diode	
Diode, breakdown: Zener and avalanche	
Reverse blocking triode thyristor	
PNP Transistors NPN	

Description	Symbol
Lamp	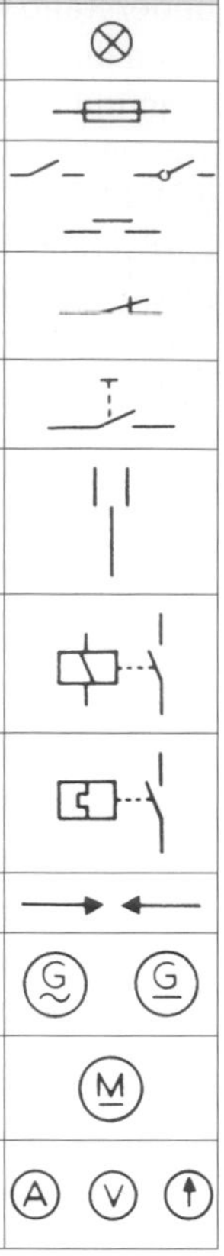 ⊗
Fuse	
Switch ('make' contact, normally open)	
Switch ('break' contact, normally closed)	
Switch (manually operated)	
Switch (two-way)	
Relay (single winding)	
Relay (thermal)	
Spark gap	
Generator AC and DC	
Motor DC	Ⓜ
Meters: ammeter, voltmeter, galvanometer	

Description	Symbol
Capacitor, general symbol	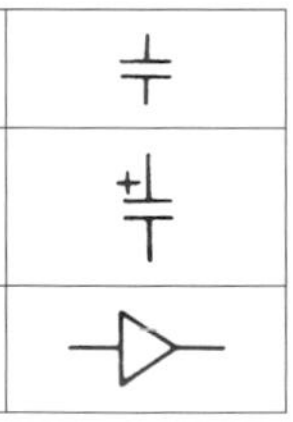
Capacitor, polarised	
Amplifier	

Description	Symbol
N-type channel Junction field effect transistor (FET) P-type channel	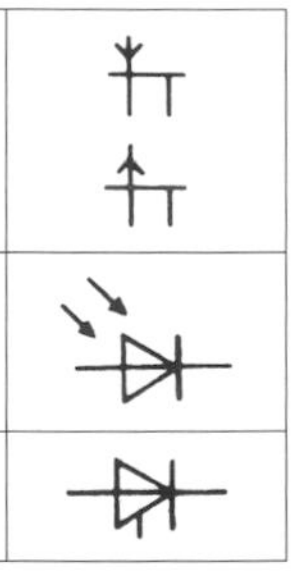
Photodiode	
Thyristor	

Figure 5.43 Examples of electrical symbols

5.4 The battery

5.4.1 Introduction to lead–acid battery

The purpose of a battery is to 'store' the electrical energy needed to operate the vast electrical components when the engine is stationary or when the output from the alternator is low. The battery does this by converting the electrical energy supplied to it into chemical energy, so that when an electrical current is required the energy flow can be reversed (i.e. the chemical energy is converted back into electrical energy).

As the battery supplies energy to the electrical components on the vehicle this energy needs to be replaced to ensure that the battery remains in a fully charged state. Generally, the alternator, driven by the engine, carries out this task by producing electrical energy through the use of an electromagnet rotating within a series of windings. On more recent vehicles, electrical energy is also created through the action of the vehicle slowing down or braking. This is called regenerative braking. This process takes some of the load from the alternator, and thus the engine, so provides improvements to emissions and economy. This is discussed in more detail in Chapter 7 on page 593.

Lead–acid battery

Most vehicles use a lead–acid battery. This type of secondary (reversible in charge/discharge) battery has lead plates immersed in an electrolyte (liquid solution) of sulphuric acid (H_2SO_4) and distilled water.

There are various types of lead–acid battery:

- Conventional
- Low-maintenance
- Maintenance-free

5.4.2 Conventional battery

This type of battery has been used for many years and has been refined during this time. Most batteries are now maintenance-free, so require no checking or servicing. By understanding the concepts of the basic lead–acid battery, the technician is able to understand the progression to maintenance-free batteries used today.

The battery shown in Figure 5.44 consists of a polypropylene or hard rubber container; this houses a number of separate cells of 2V nominal voltage. A 12V battery has six cells connected in series by lead strips; a series arrangement means that the cells are interconnected with the positive terminal of each cell joined to the negative of the adjacent cell.

An alternative method of connection is to link all positive terminals together and all negative terminals together; an arrangement called parallel. This cell layout is not used on vehicles because it gives a total voltage of only 2V instead of 12V. On occasions when a parallel arrangement is used, the capacity is increased; this is the period of time when

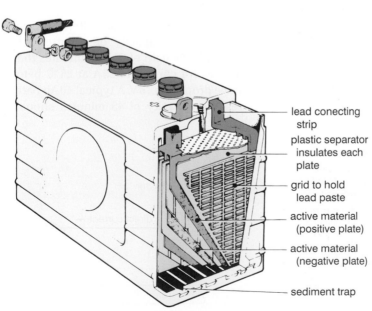

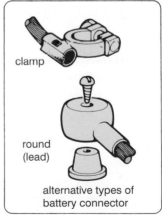

clamp

round (lead)

alternative types of battery connector

lead conecting strip

plastic separator insulates each plate

grid to hold lead paste

active material (positive plate)

active material (negative plate)

sediment trap

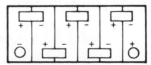

lead strips connect the cells in series – the positive plates in one cell are connected to the negative plates in the adjoining cell

Figure 5.44 Battery – conventional type

a battery supplies a given voltage before it becomes discharged. When six 2V cells are connected in parallel the capacity is about six times as great as that given by the series arrangement.

Note: the use of higher voltage batteries is also common especially in heavy goods vehicles where a 24V battery is used.

Each cell is made up of two sets of lead plates (positive and negative), which are placed alternately and separated by an insulating porous material. The plates on the conventional battery consist of a lattice-type grid of lead-antimony, which retains the active lead oxide paste material.

A moulded cover seals the cells and either individually screwed caps or a one-piece detachable cover allows the cells to be periodically topped up with distilled water. Vents in the cover permit the gas to escape; this is evident during the charging process and when the battery is used in a discharged state.

Various types of terminal posts are used. Some batteries have a post with a hole to enable the connector to be clamped; others use a cylindrical post around which the connector is fitted.

It is essential that the battery is connected to the vehicle in a way that gives the correct earth polarity. Extensive damage to electrical components will occur if the polarity is incorrect. Terminals are marked '+' (positive) and '–' (negative); when cylindrical posts are used, the larger diameter is positive. Also the colours red (or brown) and black (or blue) are used to indicate positive and negative respectively.

Cell action

As the battery discharges (gives out its energy) the lead in the plates undergoes a chemical change and the acid becomes 'weaker' (i.e. the 'specific gravity' decreases).

To reverse the action, an electrical charge is supplied from an alternator. This changes the lead plates back to their original chemical form and 'strengthens' the electrolyte. A charge current has to pass through the battery in one direction, so a direct current (DC) must be used. To produce the chemical reversal of the plates, the charge current flows in the opposite direction to the current given out by the battery, so the connection between the battery and the alternator (or bench charger) must be positive to positive (Figure 5.45).

Voltage variation

When the battery is 'taken off charge' the terminal voltage or potential difference (PD) is about 2.1V, but this quickly drops to 2.0V, where it remains for the major part of the discharge period. Towards the end of the discharge period the PD falls rapidly until a fully discharged value of 1.8V is reached. These values represent PD, so current must be flowing at the normal discharge rate when the voltage reading is taken.

Terminal voltage towards the end of the charging period rises to 2.5–2.7V, but this quickly falls to about 2.1V when the charge current ceases.

Capacity

The total area of the plates governs the length of time that a battery will supply a discharge current; this represents the capacity of a battery and is often expressed in ampere-hours (Ah). A battery rated at 38Ah, based on a 10-hour rate, should supply a steady current of 3.8A for 10 hours.

'Reserve capacity' is an alternative method of expressing the capacity of a battery. This rating indicates the length of time in minutes that a battery will deliver a current of 25A at 25°C before the cell voltage drops to 1.75V. A typical 40Ah battery having a reserve capacity of 45 minutes should keep the

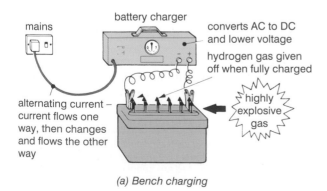

(a) Bench charging

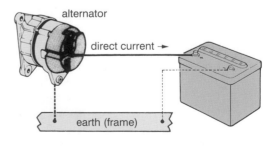

(b) Battery charging by the vehicle alternator

Figure 5.45 Battery charging methods: a) Bench charger; b) Vehicle charging system

vehicle in operation for this time after the charging system has failed, provided the electrical load is normal.

Maintenance of conventional-type batteries

Regular maintenance is needed to keep this type of battery in good condition. This work includes the following tasks.

Battery fitting

Extensive damage to electrical components results if the earth polarity is accidentally reversed.

Mounting bolts and brackets should hold the battery firmly in place, but the bolts should not be over-tightened.

Note: when removing or refitting a battery, the earth lead should be removed first and fitted last. This reduces the risk of the spanner arcing to earth.

For safety reasons, the earth battery terminal should be disconnected before work is carried out on engine parts that are liable to rotate. When working on a modern vehicle, extra care should be taken when disconnecting the battery before work commences. In-car entertainment and security systems often need re-coding when the battery is disconnected; it is good practice to ensure that you have these details before disconnecting the battery. Also, on some vehicles the EMS will need to be re-initialised once the battery is reconnected, so the technician should consult the workshop manual beforehand.

Electrolyte level

The electrolyte should be maintained at the correct level (for example 6 mm above the plates) by topping up with distilled water. Frequent topping up indicates that the battery is being over-charged.

Terminal corrosion

Corrosion is reduced by coating the terminal with petroleum jelly or silicone grease. A corroded terminal is cleaned by immersing the terminal in ammoniated warm water or soda dissolved in water. This solution can also be used to neutralise acid spillage on vehicle body parts.

Use of jump leads

In the event of a discharged battery, an engine can sometimes be started by temporarily connecting another battery to the car battery using jump leads. To do this, the two batteries are connected in parallel (positive to positive and negative to negative). After the engine has started and run for a few minutes, the engine must be allowed to slow-run before the jump leads are disconnected; making sure that the earth lead is removed first. It is good practice to connect the earth jump lead directly to the engine, rather than the negative post of the battery, as this improves current flow. Usually, you will be able to utilise an engine-lifting eye or the main earth connection.

Battery hazards

An acid burn should be treated immediately with sodium bicarbonate solution or, failing this, clean water. Acid splashed into the eye should be bathed immediately in clean water and medical attention should be sought as soon as possible.

Sometimes the acid supplied to a garage needs to be 'broken down' to weaken it before it is used to fill a new battery. For safety reasons, the dilution must be carried out in a glass or earthenware container by adding acid to water and *not* water to acid.

Acid splashes on clothes can be neutralised with an alkali, such as ammonia, if holes are to be avoided. Gloves and goggles should be worn when handling or pouring acid; it is also advisable to wear an acid-proof apron.

A large quantity of hydrogen is released from the cells when charging continues beyond the fully charged state. There is a great risk of explosion from this highly flammable gas when connecting the terminals, so care must be taken to avoid a spark. After bench charging, it is wise to let the battery stand for a time before fitting it to the vehicle, especially when the car incorporates a central-locking door system.

Battery tests

These tests should be performed in accordance with the battery manufacturer's recommendations. The following tests relate to a conventional battery and are intended as a guide.

Hydrometer

The specific gravity (or relative density) of an electrolyte is measured by a hydrometer; the readings indicate the state of charge (Figure 5.46). Values quoted represent the weight of the electrolyte in relation to the weight of an equal volume of water. Typical values are:

- Fully charged   1.280 (specific gravity)
- Half-charged   1.200 (specific gravity)
- Fully discharged   1.150 (specific gravity)

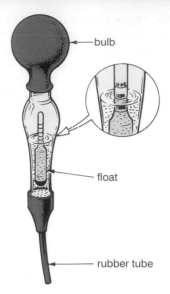

Figure 5.46 Use of a hydrometer

bulb

float

rubber tube

Electrical load test

Also called a high-rate discharge test and drop test, this equipment indicates the ability of a battery to supply a large current similar to that required to operate the starting motor. The test shows the battery voltage during the time that a large current is being 'drawn' from the battery.

This is a severe test and must not be prolonged beyond the recommended time. It should only be performed on a fully charged battery.

A 30 Ah battery in good condition, tested against a load of about 100 A, should show a reading of 8–10 V for a period of 15 seconds.

5.4.3 Low-maintenance battery

Improved materials and new construction techniques have reduced the need for a battery to be periodically topped up with distilled water to replace losses due to gassing. These new style batteries are fitted to modem vehicles because the reduction in maintenance is an attractive selling feature.

Use of these batteries has been made possible by the improved control of charging rate and voltage obtained from an alternator system compared with dynamo charging equipment.

Gassing has been reduced by changing the grid material from lead–antimony to an alloy of lead–calcium.

When the low-maintenance battery operates with a good charging system and at normal temperature, the electrolyte only has to be checked once a year or at 80,000 km intervals.

Other than in its grid material, the construction of a low-maintenance battery is similar to the conventional type. Since the performance characteristics are based on proven designs, it is normally possible to fit a low-maintenance battery in place of a conventional battery.

5.4.4 Maintenance-free battery

The maintenance-free battery shown in Figure 5.47 differs in several respects from the conventional battery. The most significant features are that the battery is sealed, except for a very small vent hole, and that it requires no service attention other than to be kept clean.

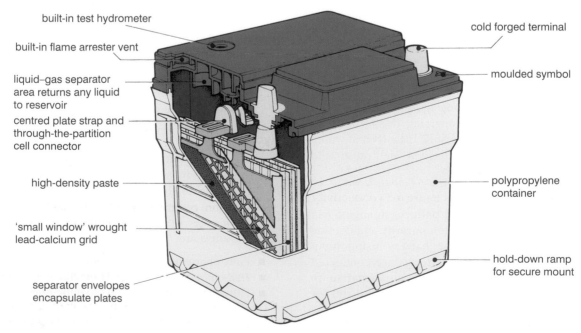

built-in test hydrometer

built-in flame arrester vent

liquid–gas separator area returns any liquid to reservoir

centred plate strap and through-the-partition cell connector

high-density paste

'small window' wrought lead-calcium grid

separator envelopes encapsulate plates

cold forged terminal

moulded symbol

polypropylene container

hold-down ramp for secure mount

Figure 5.47 Battery – maintenance-free type

A test indicator is fitted in the top cover to register the state of charge. The indicator is a form of hydrometer that signals the battery's condition by changing colour. The type illustrated shows green when the battery is charged and serviceable, and green/black or black when recharging is required. A yellow light indicates that an internal fault is present; in this condition the battery must not be charged or tested. Furthermore, jump leads must not be used when this fault is indicated; instead, the battery should be replaced and the alternator output checked.

If the battery is discharged to a point where it cannot crank the engine and as a consequence the engine has to be started either by jump leads or by pushing the car, then it will be impossible for the alternator to recharge the battery. When a battery is in this condition it must be removed and bench charged; this is necessary because the voltage needed to recharge it is higher than that given by the charging system of the vehicle.

5.4.5 Gel battery

The gel battery or, as it is sometimes called, the gel cell battery, is very similar in its operation as the normal lead acid battery, except the watery acid is set as a gel.

The normal electrolyte is replaced by a sulphuric acid mixed with silica, which creates the gel electrolyte. This has benefits as the battery does not have to be kept in an upright position and is also able to sustain greater heat and vibration compared to a normal wet cell battery.

Unlike the wet lead acid battery, the gel battery does not lose electrolyte through evaporation so is maintenance free and will not require checking over the life of the battery.

During a vehicle collision, if the battery is damaged it will not spill neat acid as the solid mass of gel will stay intact. This is a real benefit in preventing injury to vehicle occupants or the recovery operator.

The gel battery is very similar in its chemical construction to a normal non-sealed battery apart from utilising a different component in the lead plates. The normal antimony found in wet lead acid batteries is replaced by calcium for its improved conductivity and because it's less toxic.

The gel battery requires a different method for charging as it will be damaged by using a regular battery charger. It requires a slower lower amperage charge cycle to avoid damage so care should be taken when charging these types of batteries.

The gel battery is being used more extensively in automotive applications due to its improved durability and lighter construction. Motorcycles and race cars have been using gel batteries for some time as they resist the forces of cornering and high vibration much better than wet lead acid batteries.

5.4.6 Battery monitoring system (BMS)

The battery monitoring system (BMS) has become necessary on modern vehicles, which incorporate a great deal of electrical equipment that can drain the battery, and require a steady electrical feed to avoid malfunction. The BMS is designed to measure battery voltage, current and temperature to calculate the capacity, state of charge, and current performance expected from the battery unit. The BMS module is located on the negative terminal of the battery and it supplies the battery state of health (SOH) to the vehicle's power management system (PMS). The PMS utilises this information to optimise the battery state of charge (SOC).

If, over a period of time, the electrical charge used by the vehicle is more than the alternator can develop, the PMS will compensate for this by lowering the power consumption of comfort equipment, such as heated front and rear screens and seats. When the SOC returns to normal the PMS will alter the electrical feed to normal consumption.

The BMS can also forecast when extra power is required from the alternator, such as at idle speed, and will increase the idle speed to increase power delivery of the alternator. The BMS continually assesses the power consumption of the vehicle and is able to provide very precise control of the power generation, which leads to reduced fuel consumption and emissions as the alternator is loaded at precise times.

5.5   The charging system

When the engine is running, the charging system provides electrical energy for the operation of the vehicle components; also, it must maintain the battery in a fully charged state. To fulfil these duties, the generator of the charging system must convert mechanical energy to electrical energy.

There are two types of generator:

- Dynamo, commonly used in the past
- Alternator, which is now standard fitment

5.5.1 Principle of the alternator

The origin of the generator goes back many years. In 1831, Michael Faraday performed an experiment to show that an electric current was generated when a magnet was moved in a coil of wire (Figure 5.48). He demonstrated that during the inward movement of the magnet, the needle on the meter moved; this showed that an electric current was flowing in the coil circuit. Withdrawal of the magnet caused the (centre zero) needle to move in the other direction; this indicated that the current was flowing in the opposite direction. At times, when there was no relative movement of the magnet and coil, electrical energy was not generated in the coil circuit.

Faraday went on to demonstrate that the electrical energy generated depended on three things:

1 The strength of the magnetic field
2 The length of the conductor exposed to the magnetic field
3 The speed at which the magnetic field is cut

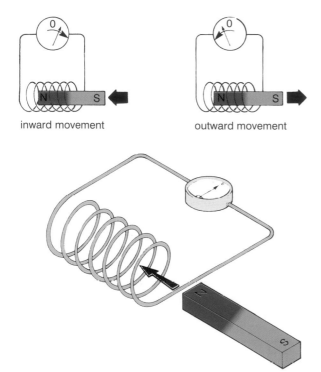

Figure 5.48 Generation of electric current

A modern alternator-type generator uses the principle of electromagnetic induction established in Faraday's experiment: a magnet is rotated inside a coil of wire. In this coil, an EMF (electromotive force) is generated, which causes an electric current to be forced around the circuit.

Using the following steps, the function of each part of an alternator can be appreciated.

Generation of an alternating current

Figure 5.49a shows a shaft-driven permanent magnet positioned in a soft iron C-shaped stationary member (stator). This stator provides an easy path for the magnetic flux between the N and S poles of the magnet. Figures 5.49b–d show how the magnetic

lines of force (flux) vary in density and direction as the magnet is rotated.

In Figure 5.50, a voltmeter is placed across a coil of wire wound around the stator. Rotation of the magnet generates an EMF, which varies, as shown by the graph, with the magnet position. The polarity of the magnetic flux in the stator changes as the magnet is rotated, so an **alternating current (AC)** is produced. The amount of current depends on the three factors given by Faraday; since the only variable is the speed, then the faster the magnet is rotated, the higher the output.

> **Alternating current (AC):** an electrical current that is constantly being changed from + to − by an AC generator. This produces an AC waveform.

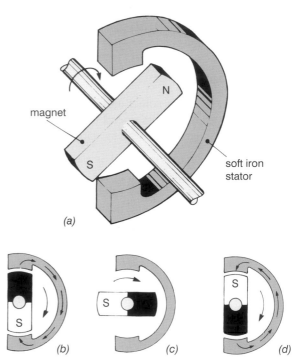

Figure 5.49 Path of magnetic flux

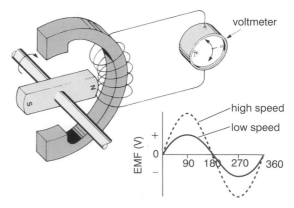

Figure 5.50 Generation of AC output

Space and weight are very important, so the alternator must be designed to give the highest possible output. One step towards improved efficiency is to use a multi-pole magnet arranged as shown in Figure 5.51. In this case, the magnet is placed coaxially with the shaft and, by means of soft iron 'fingers', two extra poles are formed on the rotating member (rotor). This arrangement doubles the output and makes the unit more efficient.

As before, the output increases as the speed rises up to a point where the rapid changes in current flow prevent any further increase in output. This feature is advantageous because the machine protects itself from being overloaded.

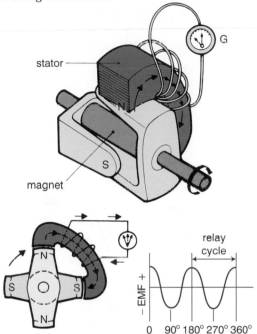

Figure 5.51 Output from a multi-pole magnet

Multi-phase output

To utilise more of the rotor poles, another stator winding is added in the position shown in Figure 5.52. This gives two independent outputs as shown by the graph. The stator winding B gives an output that peaks at a rotor position 45° after the EMF peak of winding A (i.e. the output from the two windings is 45° out of phase and is called two-phase output).

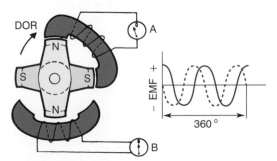

Figure 5.52 Multi-phase output

Similarly, if another stator winding is added and all three are spaced out around a multi-pole rotor, then a three-phase output is obtained (Figure 5.53). As the number of magnetic poles is increased, each individual cycle will be shorter; therefore, the larger number of AC cycles produced in one revolution of the rotor will produce a comparatively smooth peak output of current.

Control of magnet strength

When the engine is turning over very fast, the very high EMF output from a permanent magnet type alternator causes both damage to the machine and overcharging of the battery. To overcome these problems, the permanent magnet on the rotor is replaced by an electromagnet. This arrangement allows the strength of the magnetic field to be easily controlled by varying the current supplied to the winding; the greater the current passed to the 'field', the stronger the magnet.

Figure 5.53 shows the parts of a modern alternator that generate the electrical energy; the type shown is a three-phase, 12-pole machine. Current to the rotor field is delivered via slip rings; these are two rings of copper on to which rub two carbon brushes.

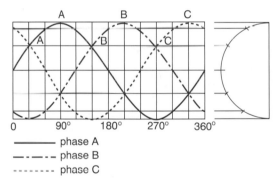

Figure 5.53 Three-phase output

The three sets of stator windings, which are interconnected together in a star or delta arrangement, have three output leads – one for each phase.

5.5.2 Rectification of alternating current to direct current

The AC produced by the alternator is unsuitable for battery charging due to the current reaching the battery terminals rapidly alternating from positive to negative, so no complete charge can be passed to the battery. For this reason, the output must be rectified (changed) to direct current. Today, this is achieved by using a semiconductor device called a diode, which forms part of a component called a rectifier or diode pack found in today's alternators.

Semiconductors

Certain materials, such as silicon and germanium, are neither good electrical conductors nor insulators; instead, they come in a borderline category. If semiconductor crystals are doped in a special way by adding traces of certain impurities and then arranged with other semiconductors, a range of solid-state electronic devices can be obtained. The most common devices are called diodes and transistors.

The diode is an electronic 'valve' that allows current to flow in one direction but not the other. It is represented by the symbol shown in Figure 5.54a. The arrowhead indicates the direction in which the diode freely conducts a **conventional flow** current.

> **Conventional flow**: when current is assumed to flow from positive to negative.

Diode rectifier

Figure 5.54b shows how a diode can be used in a simple circuit to rectify AC to DC. The one-way action of a single diode blocks the 'reverse' current flow and gives an output, called half-wave rectification, as shown by the graph.

Four blocking diodes, set to form a bridge circuit (Figure 5.54c), are needed to ensure that half the output is not lost (i.e. to achieve full-wave rectification) (Figure 5.54d). With the diodes arranged

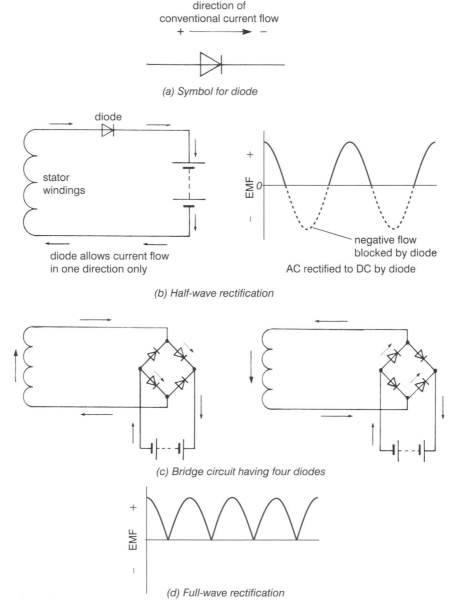

(a) Symbol for diode

(b) Half-wave rectification

(c) Bridge circuit having four diodes

(d) Full-wave rectification

Figure 5.54 Current rectification

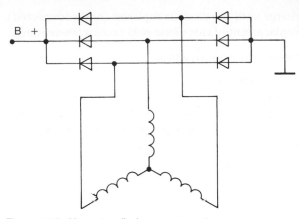

Figure 5.55 Alternator diode arrangement

in this manner, the battery is always supplied with a DC charge, irrespective of the current polarity generated in the stator windings.

A three-phase output from an alternator with three stator windings requires a rectifier having six output diodes arranged in the manner shown in Figure 5.55. This diode network ensures that the current output is always in one direction. Irrespective of the position and direction of the current-flow arrow on the stator windings, the terminal B+ will always be positive.

Battery reverse flow

When the engine is stationary, and at other times when the alternator output voltage is lower than the battery voltage, current would tend to flow from the battery to the alternator and discharge it. Whereas the

old dynamo charging system needed a cut-out switch in the main line to prevent this current drain, the one-way characteristic of the diodes in an alternator rectifier automatically prevents this happening.

This inherent feature means that the main output terminal on the alternator is subject to full battery voltage. Therefore, when the alternator is either disconnected or removed it must be remembered that this connection is 'live'.

5.5.3 Voltage output control

The output from an alternator must be limited to a voltage of about 14.2V; this value equals the potential difference of a battery that is nearing its fully charged state. Setting the alternator to this maximum will allow it to charge at a high rate when the battery is discharged, but as the battery approaches its fully charged state the charging rate will gradually reduce to zero.

Alternator output is controlled by varying the current supplied to the rotor field. The regulator performs this current control function by using electronic devices in the form of diodes and transistors. These are retained in a 'micro' metal container, which is mounted under the alternator cover.

Solid-state devices, such as diodes and transistors, are highly sensitive to heat and voltage surges. Therefore, during operation and repair, precautions need to be taken to ensure that a regulator (and rectifier pack) is protected from exposure to these conditions.

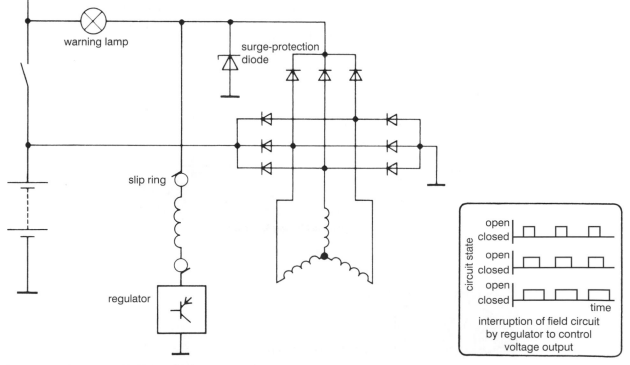

Figure 5.56 Regulator of field current surge protection

5.5.4 Alternator operation and construction

The alternator circuit (Figure 5.56) includes a charge warning lamp to signal to the driver when the system is not operating. In addition to this duty, the warning lamp circuit is used initially to excite the field. On switching on the ignition, the small current needed to operate the lamp also passes through the rotor winding and regulator to earth. This creates a weak magnetic field sufficient to commence the charging operation when the alternator starts to rotate. Naturally, this operation will not occur if the bulb has 'blown'. Unless 12V is obtained from the lead, which has been disconnected from the 'IND' terminal, the alternator will not charge.

When the unit is operating, three field diodes supply the field with a current as dictated by the regulator. As the engine speed rises from stationary or slow running, the output voltage at the field diodes also rises. This reduces the current through the warning lamp and causes the lamp to become dim and finally 'go out'.

Surge protection diode

Breakdown of the main transistor in a regulator occurs if the alternator is charging and a poor connection, or similar fault, causes the voltage to increase suddenly. To avoid this damage, a **surge**-protection diode is sometimes fitted between the 'IND' lead and earth. This special diode only conducts when the surge voltage exceeds a given value.

Surge: a sudden rise in electrical current; without a form of surge protection this sudden rise could damage the electrical components.

Failure of this diode, following a fault, often causes it to conduct the field supply continuously to earth, so with the field shorted out, the alternator will not charge until the diode is replaced (or disconnected). Replacement of this diode only takes a few minutes.

Alternator construction

The construction of a modern alternator is shown in Figure 5.57. The unit is usually driven by a belt at a speed higher than the crankshaft, so it produces a good output even when the engine speed is comparatively low.

Alternators can operate at speeds up to 15,000 rev/min and require a high belt tension to prevent slip when a large current is being produced. In view of these operating conditions, ball bearings are used to support the rotor.

Cooling air is pumped through the machine by a cooling fan driven by the rotor shaft.

Smart alternators

Some alternators used on the latest motor vehicles (since around 2010) are termed as 'smart alternators'. These systems are able to connect and disconnect themselves depending on the amount of charge required by the vehicle. By doing this, the drag from being rotated by the engine is lowered and improvements to the fuel economy and emissions are gained. These alternators also have the ability to change from being an alternator to a starter motor. This is used on stop–start systems where the engine is cut when the vehicle becomes stationary in traffic and then starts immediately when the clutch is depressed or the foot is taken off the brake pedal. The engine starts in a fraction of a second due to the high-energy starter/alternator being able to spin the engine over very quickly. Stop–start systems are now fairly common on newer vehicles and are producing excellent savings in CO_2 production.

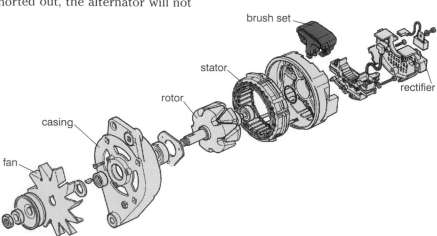

Figure 5.57 Exploded view of an alternator

5.6 The starter system

An electrical starter motor is required to crank the engine over at a speed of about 100 rev/min to enable the fuel to be atomised and the mixture to be compressed sufficiently to start the engine. This cranking used to be achieved by the driver turning a starting handle, but today all cars use an electric starting system.

To obtain sufficient cranking torque from the robust electric motor, a large current is needed. On a cold morning this may be up to about 500 A, so thick, short supply cables and a good battery capable of delivering this high current are needed.

The complete system may be considered in three sections:

- Electric starter motor
- Starting circuit
- Mechanical engagement systems

5.6.1 Operating principles of the starter motor

The motor converts electrical energy supplied from the battery into mechanical power; this is achieved by using an electromagnetic principle similar to that employed for the generation of electrical energy seen in an alternator. In a starter motor, this is reversed to provide turning motion through the use of an electromagnet and field windings.

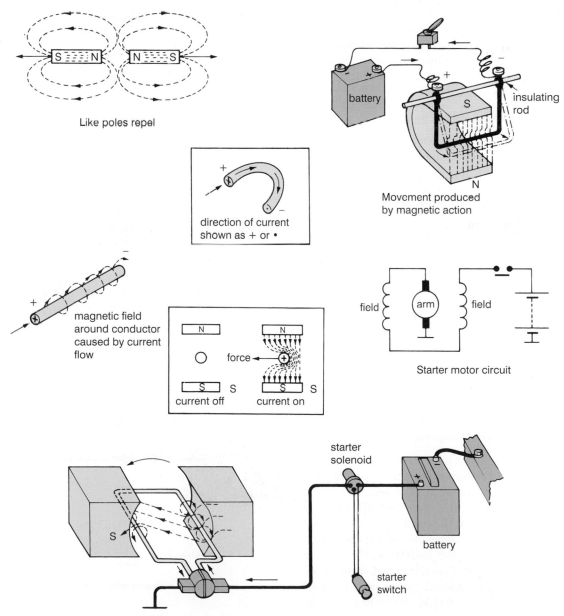

Figure 5.58 Principle of the starter motor

When two 'like' poles of two magnets are brought together, the magnets push each other apart. From this experiment, the expressions 'like poles repel' and 'unlike poles attract' are obtained.

A motor uses the 'repel action' to produce a force (Figure 5.58). This force produces motion when a current-carrying conductor is placed in a strong magnetic field; the force is caused by the bending of the flux lines. Flux lines may be regarded as elastic bands: when the bands between the poles are stretched, a force is created.

By bending the conductor in the form of a loop, and using carbon–copper brushes to conduct the current to copper commutator segments joined to a conductor situated in a magnetic field, a partial rotation of the loop is achieved. Full rotation can be obtained by using more loops (windings) placed in different angular positions. These loops are wound around a soft iron armature (to concentrate the field) and are joined to commutator segments, so as to allow a current to flow to each individual loop as it passes through the densest part of the field.

Formation of the magnetic field

Most starter motors have a wound electromagnetic field, which is normally connected in series in the main circuit. This arrangement produces a strong field because all of the current that is supplied to the motor must pass through the field windings. There is, however, an alternative to this series arrangement called series-parallel arrangement.

These different field winding and armature arrangements can be seen in Figure 5.59. These arrangements are all about ensuring that the most is made of the current available to ensure that maximum torque can be obtained from the starter motor. To obtain a high torque from a motor that is required to operate at a low cranking speed demands a large supply of electrical power from the battery. To ensure that the torque of the motor is maintained, there is a need to use low-resistance conductors in the motor since the power (watts) is the product of the voltage and current (amperes).

Generally, the voltage in a light motor vehicle is fixed to approximately 12 V. Due to this fact, the only way to increase the power developed by the motor is to keep the current flow (amperage) high. High amperage is achieved by ensuring that the conductor and winding resistance are as low as possible. As we have seen in Watt's law, the lower the resistance, the greater the current flow. This then results in higher power or watts. For this reason, manufacturers produce field windings and armature coils from strips of copper or aluminium, and use high conductivity copper–carbon

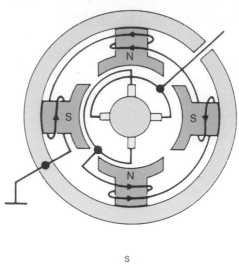

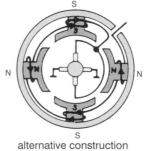

alternative construction

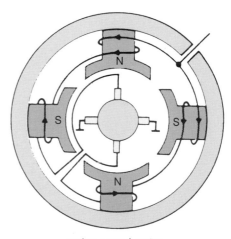

series-wound motor

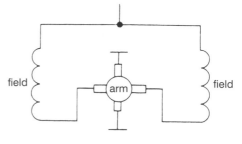

series-parallel motor

Figure 5.59 Field winding arrangements

brushes to transfer the electrical energy to the slip rings. Additionally to this, the other components included within the motor such as supply cables, connectors and terminals must also be made from materials that can handle the large currents to avoid any unnecessary voltage drop, which could cause slow or low-powered starter motors and increase the risk of over-heating.

Many of today's vehicles use smaller, more compact starter motors that use a permanent magnet field. These motors are lightweight and achieve their high torque output by using an epicyclic gear between the motor and the driving gear.

Four-brush motors

A reduced resistance and greater current flow can be achieved by using four brushes instead of two. The four-brush machines are made in either a series-wound or series-parallel field arrangement (Figure 5.59).

Figure 5.60 shows another type of four-brush, four-pole motor complete with drive. This type of motor has a field winding bent in a waveform, which provides four poles in the order N-S-N-S and a face-type commutator; this uses brushes situated on the side of the armature instead of the more common radial position associated with a cylindrically shaped commutator.

5.6.2 Starter motor and solenoid circuit

Figure 5.61a shows a pictorial view of a typical cable layout for a starter motor. The diagram shows two earthing straps; these are used to complete the circuit. Partial failure of either one of the straps will seriously reduce current flow and, as a consequence, will affect motor operation. In addition, the alternative 'earth paths' from the battery to the motor through such parts as engine controls will cause local heating.

The inclusion in the circuit of a solenoid allows the length of heavy-duty cable to be kept to a minimum. The voltage drop increases with the length, so when a long cable is used the potential difference applied to the motor is considerably less than that obtained across the battery.

Switching is achieved by a pair of heavy-duty copper contacts in the solenoid. These contacts are closed by a low-current winding in the solenoid. It is energised when a remote switch, normally actuated by the ignition key, is operated (Figure 5.61b).

The solenoid has two windings: a closing coil and a hold-on coil (Figure 5.61c). These are connected in parallel with each other so they both operate when the driver's switch is closed. When the motor is in operation, only the hold-on coil is in use; this feature reduces the solenoid operating current.

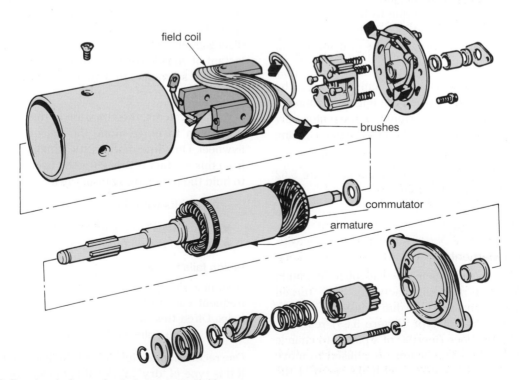

Figure 5.60 Four-brush, four-pole starter motor and drive

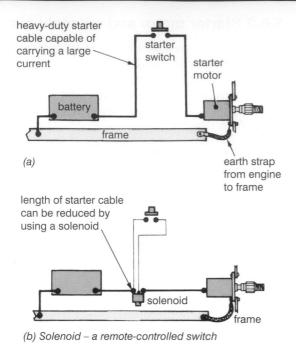

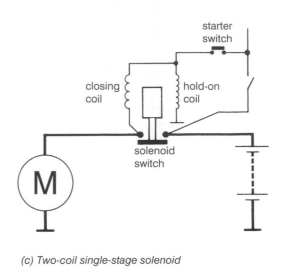

(c) Two-coil single-stage solenoid

(b) Solenoid – a remote-controlled switch

Figure 5.61 Starter motor circuits

The audible click given from the solenoid when it operates is a useful aid for diagnosis; for example, a repeated clicking sound from the solenoid suggests that the hold-on coil is defective.

5.6.3 Starter motor engagement with the engine

A low gear ratio between the starter motor and the engine enables sufficient torque to be developed to turn the crankshaft. This ratio is obtained by using a pinion on the motor to drive a large gear formed on the flywheel.

Permanent engagement of the pinion causes the armature to over-speed when the engine is running, so a mechanism is used to ensure that the pinion only connects with the flywheel when the engine is being started.

The two engagement systems shown in Figure 5.62 are used on light vehicles; they are:

- inertia engagement
- pre-engagement.

Inertia engagement

The inertia-type arrangement was once common on vehicles, but now manufacturers have turned towards the pre-engaged type due to its more reliable operation. The inertia type (Figure 5.63) relies on the natural reluctance (inertia) of a pinion to change its state of motion. This feature is utilised to move the pinion so that it engages with the teeth of the flywheel when the armature starts to rotate.

The pinion is mounted on a helix, which is splined to the starter motor armature. Sudden rotational movement of the armature rotates the helix, but owing to its inertia, the pinion remains stationary; this causes the pinion to slide along the helix and engage with the flywheel teeth. A 'lead-in' (chamfer) is present on both the pinion and flywheel teeth to aid this initial engagement.

When the engine fires the increase in engine speed spins the pinion along the helix and causes it to disengage from the flywheel teeth. The shock at the instant of engagement and disengagement is severe, so a large spring is fitted adjacent to the helix to act as a cushion.

On some systems, the vibration of the engine causes the pinion to move along the helix and touch the flywheel. On some models, the 'tinkling noise' given from this contact is prevented by using a light spring to hold the pinion away from the flywheel.

Possible faults with this type are:

- pinion fails to engage
- jammed pinion (seized engine).

Pinion fails to engage

Assuming the speed of rotation is sufficient, the most frequent cause of a 'sticking pinion' is dirt on the helix. Often this is due to the presence of oil on the splines, which collects dust from the clutch.

One recommended lubricant is Molykiron (SAE 5) but if this type of 'dry' lubricant is unavailable, then the helix should be left in a dry state after cleaning.

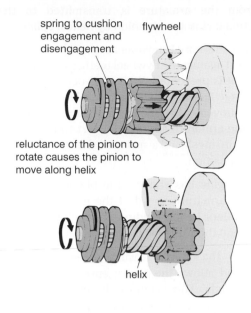

spring to cushion engagement and disengagement

flywheel

reluctance of the pinion to rotate causes the pinion to move along helix

helix

Figure 5.62a Inertia engagement system

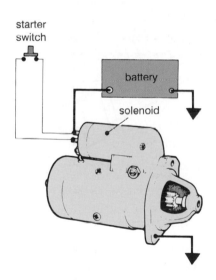

starter switch

battery

solenoid

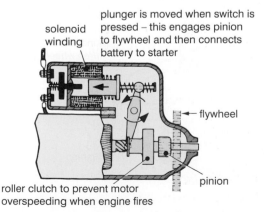

solenoid winding

plunger is moved when switch is pressed – this engages pinion to flywheel and then connects battery to starter

flywheel

pinion

roller clutch to prevent motor overspeeding when engine fires

Figure 5.62b Pre-engagement system

Figure 5.63 Pre-engaged starter motor

Jammed pinion

This occurs after the driver has attempted to start the engine. It is caused by local wear on the flywheel ring gear. On a four-cylinder engine, this wear takes place in two regions (and on a six-cylinder, three regions) because the engine normally comes to rest in one of these positions.

When the flywheel tooth wear becomes excessive, the force of pinion impact, combined with shaft flexibility, jams the teeth together and locks the engine.

An emergency method that can be used on a car with a manual gearbox is to engage top gear and 'rock the car' by pushing it backwards and forwards. The normal method is to remove the motor and examine the flywheel teeth for wear and the starter spindle for alignment. The appropriate repair is then carried out.

A ring gear is normally a 'shrink fit' on the flywheel, so after removing the worn gear the new gear is heated to the limit recommended to expand the ring; then it is pushed into place, making sure that the chamfer is on the correct side.

Pre-engagement starter motors

This type was originally confined to diesel engines, but now the pre-engaged type is the most common starter motor used by manufacturers across petrol and diesel cars. The change from the inertia type to a pre-engaged drive on petrol engines was due to the difficulty of maintaining pinion engagement with an inertia drive when an engine 'part-fires' during the cranking period.

The use of this type of starter motor drive takes into account the special starting requirements of a compression-ignition (CI) engine. These include:

- component inertia – considerable torque is needed to rotate the crankshaft initially and accelerate it to the cranking speed
- cranking speed – the cranking speed of a diesel engine should be higher than that of a petrol engine to initiate combustion
- high compression pressure – during the cranking period the CI engine draws in a full charge of air and compresses it to a much higher pressure than a petrol engine. As a result, the cranking torque is high and the speed is too irregular to maintain engagement of the starter pinion.

Figure 5.64 shows the constructional details of a pre-engaged type of starter motor. A solenoid plunger is connected to an operating lever; this is pivoted to the casing at its centre and forked at its lower end to engage with a guide ring. This ring acts against a unidirectional roller clutch and pinion. Helical splines, formed on the armature shaft, engage with the driving part of the unidirectional clutch. These splines cause the pinion to rotate slightly when the clutch and pinion are moved axially. A strong return spring in the solenoid holds the lever and pinion in the disengaged position.

When the starter switch is operated, the two-coil solenoid windings become energised and the plunger is drawn into the core. This initial action causes the lower end of the operating lever to move the guide ring and pinion assembly towards the flywheel teeth. This movement, aided by the slight rotation of the pinion, normally gives full engagement of the gears. After this initial action, extra travel of the solenoid plunger causes the main contacts to close: this connects the battery to the motor.

Drive from the armature is transmitted to the unidirectional clutch and pinion by helical splines.

Sometimes the initial movement causes the pinion teeth to butt against the flywheel teeth; as a result, full engagement is prevented. When this occurs a spring in the linkage flexes and allows the solenoid plunger sufficient movement to close the main contacts. As soon as the armature and pinion start to rotate, the teeth slip into mesh and a spring pushes the pinion to its driving position.

After the engine has started, the pinion speed will exceed the armature speed. If the motor is still in use, the rollers in the unidirectional clutch will be unlocked and the clutch will slip to protect the motor.

Release of the starter switch de-energises the solenoid and allows the return spring to open the switch contacts. This occurs well before the pinion disengages and so avoids over-speeding of the

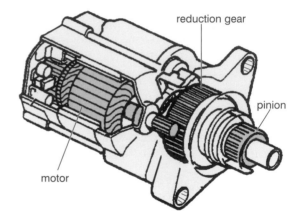

Figure 5.65 Reduction-type starter motor

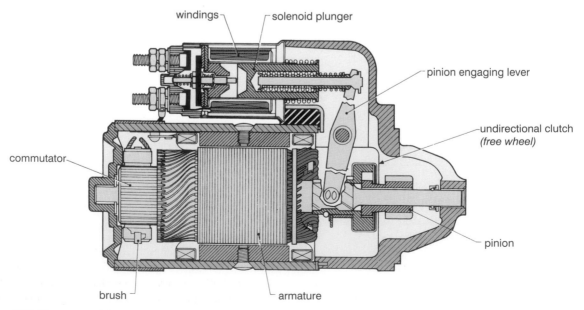

Figure 5.64 Pre-engaged-type starter motor

motor. Further movement of the plunger causes the operating lever to withdraw the pinion fully from the flywheel.

Reduction-type starter motors

Many manufacturers today now fit reduction-type starter motors (Figure 5.65). These are very compact and lightweight and incorporate a reduction gear system to increase the torque output.

The idea of the compact reduction-type starter is to create a very powerful starter motor in a small design. The reduction gear system increases the torque output, along with a small high-torque motor. The reduction-type starter motor is pre-engaged and incorporates a unidirectional clutch and pinion to prevent damage to the motor when the engine starts.

The motor is able to spin at a much higher speed than a conventional-type starter motor due to the arrangement of the motor windings and brushes. The use of the reduction gears enables the starter motor to use the high torque output with the gear ratio of about 3:1 to provide a rotation speed suitable for the engine application. This arrangement provides excellent initial turning of the engine when cold and – due to the torque of the motor and the reduction gears – is able to maintain this rotation speed for a greater length of time. This combination provides improved starting characteristics, especially for the modern higher compression ratio engines.

Note: the solenoid acts directly on the pinion, and pushes the pinion into the flywheel ring gear.

5.7 Lighting systems

Figure 5.66 Xenon headlight assembly

The modern vehicle incorporates many different lights to meet the requirements of the law and the needs of the driver. These lights are grouped in separate circuits:

Stop–start technology

With the need to continually improve on the average fuel consumption and emissions produced in modern cars, manufacturers have now started to fit a system that can improve the amount of fuel used by up to 20 per cent. This system is called 'stop–start'. As its name suggests, this system is designed to stop and start the vehicle's engine at pre-determined times, thus saving fuel, especially when idling in slow-moving traffic.

The system works by incorporating a new type of alternator that can also act as a starter motor. The 'stop and start' principle is to put the engine into standby mode when the vehicle is stationary (e.g. at a stop sign, a red light or in a traffic jam), and to restart it immediately and totally transparently for the user. With a manual gearbox vehicle, the system works when the vehicle is put into neutral at speeds under 20 kph and the clutch is pressed and released. The car will then stay in this standby mode or 'eco mode' until the clutch pedal is depressed to select first gear.

Stop–start systems start the engine much faster than standard starter motors due to the very high output from the reversible alternator. Additional voltage is acquired from a very high power capacitor. This capacitor is charged when the engine is running by the high output alternator and then is able to boost the voltage during start conditions to ensure the engine spins over very quickly, providing an almost seamless start condition. The capacitors provide an additional 5 V and 4 KW of power during the start condition.

Batteries fitted to stop–start vehicles are also improved and are generally gel filled rather than the normal acid type. These batteries are able to charge and discharge very quickly without generating any gases.

1 Side and rear lamps, including lamps for the number plate, glove compartment and instrument panel.
2 Main driving lamps (headlamps), including a dip to avoid dazzle of other drivers.
3 Daytime running lights, used to improve road safety through increased visibility. These are usually front lamps incorporated in the main headlamp assembly or separate LED lights.
4 Rear fog lamp(s) for 'guarding' the rear of the vehicle in conditions of poor visibility.
5 Auxiliary driving lamps (front fog lamps).
6 Reversing lamps to assist the reversing of the vehicle and warn other drivers and pedestrians.
7 Brake lights to warn a following driver that the vehicle is slowing down.

8 Directional indicators and hazard warning lights, which are required to flash at a given rate. Hazard warning lights are designed to warn other road users in situations where the vehicle has stopped or broken down.

9 Instrument panel lights for signalling either the operation of a particular light unit, or the presence of a fault in a section of a lighting circuit.

5.7.1 Circuit arrangement

A very simple circuit consists of a battery, switch and lamp. When more than one lamp is controlled by a single switch, the lamps are arranged in parallel; this ensures that full battery voltage is applied to each lamp so as to obtain maximum brilliance.

To save weight, most lighting circuits use an earth return layout, so good clean connections are needed at the numerous earthing points. A 'dirty' connection (i.e. poor earth) causes a high resistance; this reduces the voltage applied to the lamp and results in a poor light.

Circuit diagrams

These are shown in either a location or compact theoretical form; the former layout shows each component in its relative position, whereas the latter makes the diagram simpler to follow. Figure 5.67 shows a simplified lighting circuit represented in both forms.

This parallel circuit has the lamps controlled by three switches:

- Switch 1 operates the side and rear lamps. It also supplies switch 2.
- Switch 2 operates the headlamps and supplies switch 3.
- Switch 3 distributes the current to either the main beam or the dip-beam headlamp bulbs.

Circuit protection

A single fuse, mounted in the main supply cable, protects a circuit in the event of a severe short. This simple protection system cannot be used in the external lighting supply cable because all lights will

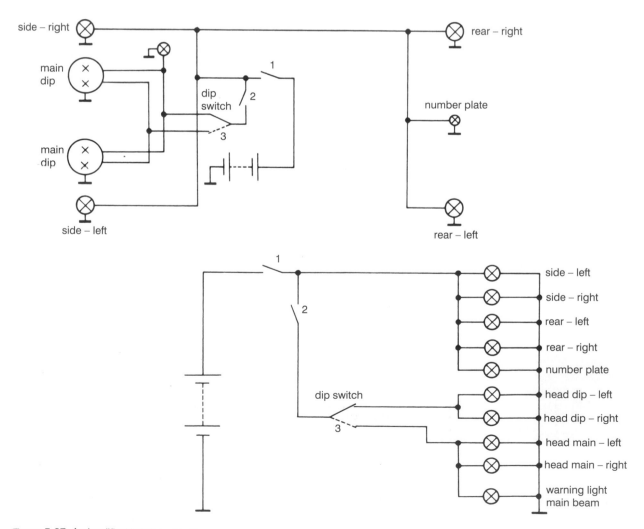

Figure 5.67 A simplified lighting circuit

go out when the fuse fails; a dangerous situation when the vehicle is travelling at speed along a dark road.

To avoid this danger, manufacturers either fit separate fuses for each light system, or refrain from fusing the headlamp circuit altogether. Figure 5.68 shows a lighting system that incorporates a series of fuses. **Note**: the circuits are arranged in parallel to ensure that if a fuse blows, this will only affect one light for safety reasons.

Relay control

The use of high-powered lighting requires the use of a relay to act as a heavy-duty switch. Without a relay the circuit would require heavy cabling to connect the switch and headlight, which is not favourable in circuit design due to the weight and size of switches. For this reason, the relay is used to switch the current to the lighting on and off; this is switched by a low current from the switch assembly. Using a relay improves the wiring harness design, as the manufacturer can locate the relays together and limit the harness weight and size to the switches around the instrument area (see page 518 for more detail on relays).

5.7.2 Filament lamps

The main details of a single centre contact (SCC) side lamp bulb are shown in Figure 5.69a. Enclosed in a glass container is a helically wound tungsten filament; this is held by two support wires, one attached to an insulated contact in a brass cup and the other soldered to the cap to form an earth. A low-wattage vacuum bulb of the type shown has the air removed to reduce heat loss and prevent oxidation of the filament. The type of bulb shown is secured in its holder by a brass bayonet cap (BC); alternative fixing methods are the miniature screw cap (miniature Edison screw – MES) and the capless type.

To produce a brighter light, filaments of driving lamps are made to operate at a higher temperature. The lamp is filled with an inert gas, such as argon, and its pressure increased slightly. Heat loss from the filament due to gas movement is reduced by winding the filament in a tight helix.

Some driving lamps have two filaments to give a main and dip beam (Figures 5.69b and c). One end of each filament is connected to the cap and the other ends are soldered to the two lamp contacts. These bulbs usually have bulb holders that prevent the bulb from being fitted incorrectly; they can only be fitted in one way.

Tungsten–halogen bulb

Because of its high light output, many modern driving lamps are fitted with a tungsten–halogen bulb, which is also called a quartz–halogen bulb (Figure 5.69d). Quartz is used instead of glass and by filling the lamp with halogen gas, vaporisation of the filament, which leads to blackening of the glass and filament erosion, is reduced. Another advantage of this type is that its more compact form allows more precise focusing. The tungsten is used in the manufacturing of the bulb element as this is much harder wearing and is therefore able to last longer.

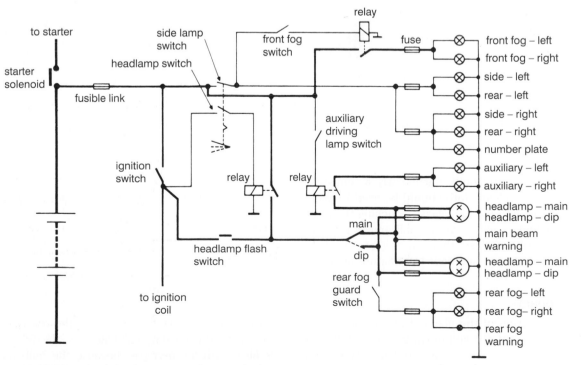

Figure 5.68 Lighting circuit that incorporates fuses and relays

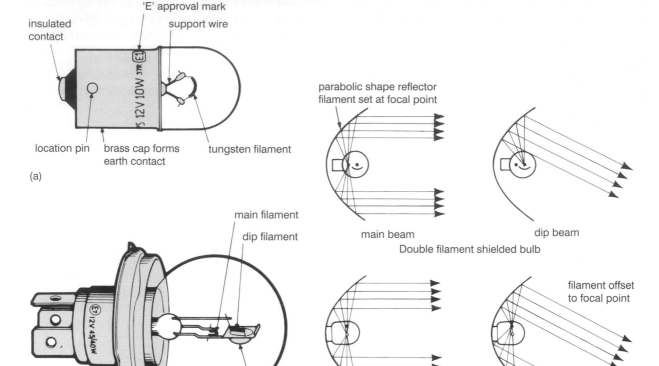

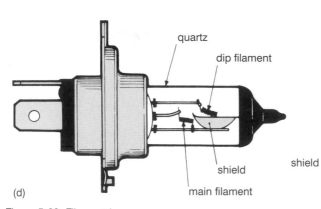

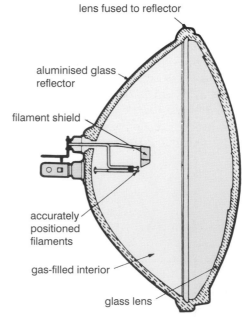

Figure 5.69 Filament lamps

When replacing any bulb, particularly a tungsten–halogen type, a clean cloth should be used to avoid touching and staining the 'glass'. Touching the glass with your fingers will leave a small grease print on the surface of the glass; this can increase the heat density on that spot and cause premature failure of the bulb.

Sealed beam

Accurate location of the filament at the focal point and elimination of dirt and moisture on the reflector are both achieved with a sealed beam lamp unit (Figure 5.70).

Figure 5.70 Sealed beam lamp unit

An aluminised glass reflector, fused to the lens, supports the main and dip tungsten filaments; the whole unit is filled with an inert gas. Because the bulb has no independent glass envelope, tungsten deposits are spread over a very large area, so the light efficiency of a sealed beam unit remains high for a long period of time.

The sealed beam unit has two disadvantages: it is costly to replace when a filament fails; and sudden light failure occurs when the lens becomes cracked.

Lamp marking

Regulations state that all bulbs, and other lamp parts, used on a vehicle must be marked with the letter 'E' and a number that identifies the country where approval was given. This mark indicates that the part conforms to the EEC standard specified for a given application.

Reflector

A highly polished aluminised reflector of parabolic shape concentrates and directs the light rays in the required direction (i.e. dipped and main beam situations). Positioning the main beam filament at the focal point of the reflector gives parallel rays and maximum illumination (Figure 5.71). This is achieved by a pre-focus bulb to site the filament accurately.

Some vehicles use a multi-segment reflector with several different focal lengths moulded together to form the light unit. These 'homofocular' plastic reflectors are very narrow, which allows them to blend in with the body contour.

Lens

A glass lens, consisting of several prismatic block sections, distributes the light to obtain the required illumination. The design of the lens pattern attempts to achieve good illumination for both main and dip positions: a concentrated long-range illumination for the main beam; and a wide spread of light distributed just in front of the vehicle for the dip beam. Regulations insist that to avoid dazzling oncoming drivers, the lens must deflect the dip beam downwards and also offset it towards the nearside.

Four-headlamp system

Optically, it is difficult to produce a single lens and reflector unit that gives an illumination that satisfies both main and dip conditions.

To overcome this drawback some vehicles have four headlamps: two for long-distance illumination; and two for lighting the area immediately in front of the car. Each one of the outer lamps has two filaments: a dip filament situated at the focal point to give good light distribution; and a second filament positioned slightly away from the focal point to provide near-illumination for main-beam lighting. When the lamps are dipped the inner lamps that give long-distance illumination are switched off.

For accommodation reasons, the lamps used in a four-headlamp arrangement are often smaller than those used on a two headlamp system. Many current vehicles incorporate two headlamps within one unit on each side of the vehicle to provide a four-headlamp arrangement. These often also incorporate the direction indicators and daytime running lights. See Figure 5.72 for an example of this type of arrangement.

Figure 5.72 Four-headlamp arrangement incorporating direction indicators and daytime running lights

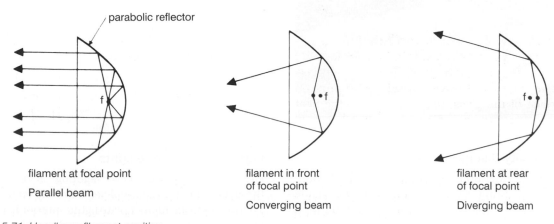

filament at focal point
Parallel beam

filament in front of focal point
Converging beam

filament at rear of focal point
Diverging beam

Figure 5.71 Headlamp filament position

5.7.3 New headlamp technologies

Headlamps found on many of today's vehicles are very complex and provide extraordinary levels of lighting compared with the standard halogen types mentioned earlier. These headlamp systems utilise advance technologies with their own control modules and, in some cases, include directional lighting, which automatically follows the direction of the road through inputs from the steering.

Modern headlamps incorporate much more complex designs than conventional older headlamp units. They use many different reflective segments that when placed together produce a geometric reflector design. Each of these segments helps to make up the headlamp's intensity. By transferring the lighting control solely to the reflector, it means headlamp designers have more leeway to mould a clear cover lens to the body shape of the vehicle. This aesthetic consideration cannot be easily achieved with cylindrical lenses.

Projection headlamp systems (as they are sometimes called due to the beam being more intense) use optical lenses that project an image or desired illumination pattern, dependent on the market the vehicle is in, on to the road surface.

As well as creating a more aesthetically pleasing headlamp unit with increased lighting power, the segmented headlamp and projection system designs must also comply with the strict lighting standards established for all headlamps. The lighting standard for the UK is the Ground Vehicle Lighting Standards, developed by the Society for Automotive Engineering (SAE).

Usually, the headlamp covers are made from high impact-resistant clear plastic, which can be designed to follow the contours of the vehicle's body to provide excellent aerodynamics and attractive body shapes.

Figure 5.73 Headlight unit using geometric-type reflector

High-intensity discharge headlamps

As we have mentioned earlier in this chapter, traditional lighting systems utilise bulbs made of tungsten or halogen – these both require a superheated filament for illumination.

The latest headlamp technology, high-intensity discharge (HID) headlamps, doesn't use any filament at all. You will notice that vehicles fitted with HIDs have a distinct bluish tint to the light that they give out. HID bulbs create light in the same way as a mercury vapour lamp, whereby a high-pressure gas is excited between high-voltage electrodes. The bulbs contain xenon gas, hence the reason why HID headlights are often called xenon headlights.

When the driver switches on the headlamp the xenon gas turns into a white-hot plasma light almost immediately. The brightness of a single HID bulb is as bright as two incandescent filaments. Once turned on, light output of a HID headlight is three times that of halogen. In addition, it has the benefit of using very low current draw from the gas once the electric arc is started.

To start the arcing of the two capsule electrodes requires very high voltage at approximately 25,000 V and a current flow of 20 A. When the lamp is lit, this falls dramatically to an operating voltage of approximately 80 V and a current flow of 3.5 A. To ensure that the headlamp assembly lights up correctly and reliably, the HID headlamp systems incorporate an ECU as seen in Figure 5.74. This ECU also links with the suspension system to constantly alter the levelling of the headlamps during operation to avoid dazzling other drivers. The lower running current of these HID lights also reduces the load on the alternator and battery system.

The light from these units will seem almost white because its colour temperature is hotter than halogen. One of the advantages is that HIDs offer much greater illumination, and therefore visibility, of road signs and street reflectors. The intensity of the light means that the bulbs are usually set behind projector beam headlight assemblies, which enables tight focusing of the beam. A distinct cut-off area for the light should minimise glare for oncoming traffic; the self-levelling function is very important when using these HID headlamps due to the light being so much brighter than normal filament lights – the oncoming drivers could be severely dazzled and may lose control of their vehicle.

To prevent injury from the high voltages when working on these systems, the technician should always ensure that they follow the workshop manual and manufacturer's precautions.

Light-emitting diode lights

Light-emitting diode (LED) lighting is now used throughout many of the vehicles currently on the road. This ranges from number plate lights, interior lights, tail lights, side lights, daytime running lights and now even

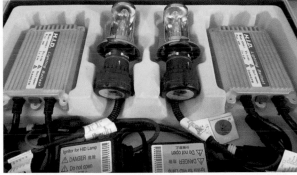

Figure 5.74 HID xenon headlamp assembly and control unit

includes main headlamps. The use of LEDs has become more popular due to the benefits of the LED lights requiring much less voltage and current to deliver their light. The LED lighting systems include a large number of LEDs to provide extremely bright lighting, which utilises very low power. The low power consumption is very important, especially when looking at hybrid and full electric vehicles, to ensure that the vehicle's battery has a longer range. Figure 5.75 shows LED lights integrated within the headlamp assembly; they surround the headlight in a radial manner to provide daytime running lights and side lights.

Figure 5.75 LED lighting within a headlamp assembly

5.7.4 Additional vehicle lighting

As mentioned earlier in this chapter, motor vehicles have a wide variety of lighting providing many different functions. Generally, the additional auxiliary lighting found on vehicles today utilises less powerful bulbs due to the functional requirements. Lighting such as directional indicators, side lights, tail lights and number plate lights will use filament-type bulbs with many different wattage requirements. It is very important to check the wattage of the replacement bulb before you fit it to avoid incorrect operation. This is especially important where the fitment is of the same design. Auxiliary lighting on current production vehicles is now moving towards the use of LED lights, so there should be no problems associated with selecting the correct type and wattage bulb as LED systems are generally fitted as a complete unit.

5.8 Auxiliary lighting and equipment

Vehicles today incorporate a great deal of additional electrical equipment, over and above the statutory requirements, that is designed to enhance the driver's and passengers' journey, as well as making the journey safer. This increased level of equipment in vehicles is driven by the manufacturer's constant striving to provide more added benefits, thus encouraging customers to purchase their vehicles over others. Therefore, the levels of equipment are constantly rising right across the price ranges. Equipment now found on fairly basic specification vehicles is at the sort of level you would have only found on very expensive executive vehicles 5 to 10 years ago.

Motor vehicle evolution has shown a trend of previously non-essential items becoming a statutory requirement, for example warning horns, windscreen wipers and washers, directional indicators and brake lamps. Today, all new vehicles produced must be fitted with these basic systems, and statutory regulations, framed by the European Union, govern their construction and method of operation. Increasingly, other non-essential features and systems are being fitted to meet customer demand.

Auxiliary equipment fitted on a modern vehicle includes the following:

- Horn – the law requires an audible warning device, which emits a continuous note that is neither too loud nor harsh in sound.
- Windscreen wipers – the law requires windscreen wipers that operate effectively.

- Windscreen washers – the law requires a screen washer to be fitted to clean the driver's side of the windscreen.
- Directional indicators – the law requires that three coloured signal lamps are fitted in approved positions on *each* side of the vehicle, together with a telltale indicator on the instrument panel. The rating of each lamp is specified, together with the flashing rate (60–120 flashes per minute).
- Brake lamp – the law requires the fitting of a lamp that automatically lights up when the brake is applied.
- Reversing lamp – the law states that no more than two white lamps may be used, the wattage of each lamp not being greater than 24 W. Regulations also cover the switching requirements of such lamps.
- Instrumentation systems – the driver instrumentation fitted to vehicles is very important and ranges from very comprehensive to basic, depending on the manufacturer and price level of the vehicle. The basic instrumentation fitted includes: fuel level; coolant temperature; and vehicle condition monitoring arrangements for detecting system faults, such as failure warning lights.

Other auxiliary electrical equipment fitted to a vehicle may include:

- clock
- interior and courtesy lights
- fan and heater motor, air conditioning and climate control
- rear and front window heaters/demisters
- electric window winding motors
- central door locking and alarm/immobiliser systems
- ICE systems
- door mirror adjustment and mirror heating systems
- sunroof control motors
- satellite navigation systems
- telephone systems
- seat position motors
- refrigeration
- reversing camera
- parking sensors
- television and DVD
- emergency response system.

Note: lighting regulations are revised periodically and vary from one country to another. When replacing a lamp or a single bulb it is necessary to make sure that the replacement is of the correct standard to comply with your local regulations. UK standard units will have the 'E' mark stamped upon the unit. This shows that the lamp is certificated under the European commission for safe use.

Electrical systems fitted to vehicles are usually fused, either in groups or individually. Vehicles both large and small use a large number of fused circuits to protect the wiring, components or system operation.

Fuses, along with additional types of circuit breaker, are normally located together in one or two places on the vehicle. Normally, the vehicle will have a fuse box located in the engine bay and also inside the vehicle. The fuse box located in the engine bay area will house all of the fuses and relays required for the operation of the major units, such as engine management, fuel pump, lighting, air-conditioning compressor, fans, automatic gearbox and ABS. The fuse box located inside the vehicle will handle the auxiliary equipment inside the driving compartment, such as electric windows, electric sunroof, ICE, cigarette lighter, satellite navigation and interior illumination. A circuit layout showing some of the main items of auxiliary equipment is shown in simplified form in Figure 5.76, together with typical fuse ratings.

Figure 5.76 shows that each item of equipment is supplied by its own individual circuit. Due to the vast amount of equipment and many functions of today's vehicles, it is impossible for manufacturers to supply one wiring diagram to show all circuits, as this would be far too big and complicated to follow.

Instead, each circuit is published individually so that technicians are able to follow a single circuit. For example, one wiring layout for the EMS, another for the charging system and another for the starting system. This makes diagnosing faults more straightforward.

Most manufacturers now publish this material electronically, rather than in paper form, either using CD-ROMs or the internet. This has the added benefits of less clutter (i.e. fewer paper manuals), less printing, information being easier to update and the ability to use search engines to locate information much more quickly than looking through a large paper manual.

The wiring diagrams also show the location of units and connectors to further improve diagnostics. This information is necessary to reduce the time taken in locating electrical problems. Due to the large subject area and limited space available in this book, the study of auxiliary systems will only provide information on simple instrumentation. For additional information on other systems, refer to the companion book published in this series, *Fundamentals of Automotive Electronics*.

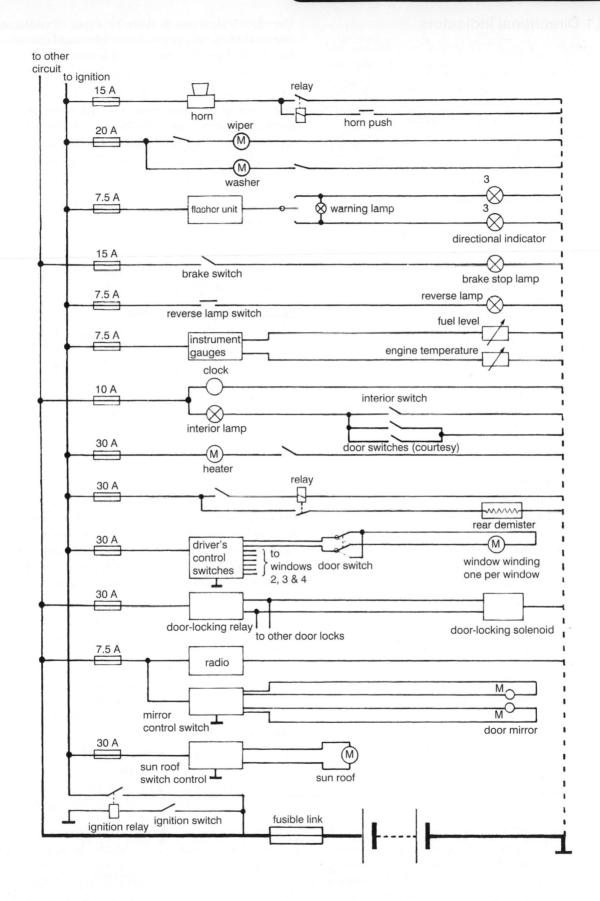

Figure 5.76 Auxiliary circuits

5.8.1 Directional indicators

The circuit in Figure 5.77 shows an indicator and hazard warning system. This circuit works when the indicator switch is moved to the left or right. As the switch is moved, the current from the ignition switch through the fuse flows through the flasher unit to the relevant indicator light. The current is interrupted by the flasher unit to provide a regular pulse, which produces the flashing of the indicator lamps.

If the vehicle breaks down or is unexpectedly stationary, the driver is able to warn other drivers by switching on the hazard warning lights. The driver activates an additional switch (hazard lights) to pass current to the whole circuit to enable all of the direction indicators to flash at the same time.

There are various types of flasher units available to control the repetitive flashing action of the indicators: thermal, capacitor, and electronic. The units have three electrical connections: 12 V supply, output to the lamps, and earth. Each type of flasher unit has to meet road legislation, which includes an audible and visual warning to signal the failure of a lamp. The thermal flasher unit causes the lamps to stay on if a lamp has failed, whereas the electronic type causes the remaining lamps to flash at a quicker rate.

Thermal-type flasher unit

The heating effect of an electric current to bend or extend a metal strip is used in this type of flasher. One design incorporates two bimetallic strips, where each strip is wound with a heating coil and fitted with a contact. When current passes through the coil the strips bend, which opens and closes the contacts.

The electrical circuit is made by a pair of contacts, one located on the centre of the ribbon and the other fixed to the base. The flasher unit is installed in series with the lamps, so that current to these lamps passes though the metal ribbon, vane and contacts.

Operation of the switch is instantly indicated by the signal lamps. The heating effect of this current increases the length of the metal ribbon, which allows the vane to click upwards to its natural position. Consequently, the contacts are opened, which breaks the circuit and extinguishes the signal lights. After a short time, the ribbon cools down and contracts as heating is discontinued. This clicks the vane downwards and once again closes the contacts to repeat the cycle of events. Since the time taken to heat the vane depends on the current, the flash frequency is governed by the lamp load.

Electronic-type flasher unit

Electronic flasher units are more efficient than the thermal flasher units. The electronic-type flasher can provide a direction indicator signal load of up to 98 W without altering the flash frequency. This is also the same for the hazard warning lights, where they can operate for many hours of continuous use.

The system normally incorporates an electromagnetic relay to control the current to the signal lamps. The relay method of switching also provides an audible signal, as it is not affected by the high-voltage spikes produced during the switching operation. In addition, the relay contacts have very little voltage drop. The drop across the relay contacts is about one-tenth of that of a transistor. Even though **transistor switching** is ideal for high-speed applications, the relay is still preferred for slow-speed, heavy-current switching action.

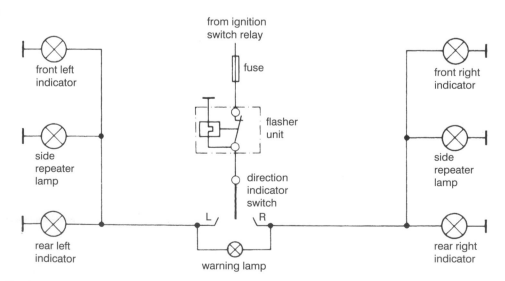

Figure 5.77 The indicator/hazard lamp circuit

Transistor switching: transistors are very small semiconductors capable of switching on and off very quickly through the input of tiny voltage signals. They have no moving parts, so make very reliable switching devices in electrical control circuits.

The basic system of a typical flasher unit uses a printed circuit board, which contains an integrated circuit, capacitor, relay and three resistors. The integrated circuit chip has three main sections: an oscillator to pulse the supply voltage; a relay driver; and a lamp failure detector. The integrated circuit controls the operating voltage of the chip and ensures constant flash frequency over a supply voltage range of 10–15 V.

5.8.2 Thermal-type instrument gauges

These types of instruments have given way to more accurate and advanced electronic systems. However, it is important to understand a basic-type gauge before you are able to follow more advanced systems. The operation principles of thermal fuel and temperature gauges are very similar. The gauge circuits are supplied with a constant stabilised voltage and the gauge indicator needles use the bending action of a bimetallic strip when it is heated. The bimetallic strip is made from two different strips of metal with different heating properties. For example, the use of brass and steel is common. When the strip is heated by the current passing through it, or around it in a coil of wire, the brass and steel expand at different rates, causing the strip to bend with the metal that expands at the greatest rate on the outside.

Fuel gauge

If we take the fuel gauge as an example (Figure 5.78), the bimetallic strip is heated by current passing through the coil of wire that is wrapped around it. This strip then bends with the heat generated, which leads to movement of the gauge.

The bending of the strip is directly proportional to the amount of current flowing through the heating coil. The greater the current, the higher the temperature and, as a result, the more bending action will take place.

The voltage stabiliser's job is to provide a constant voltage to the gauge. The earth path from the gauge then passes through a variable resistor in the tank sender unit (potentiometer) through to the earth point.

Due to the constant change in resistance as the moving contact passes over the resistive track, the connection to earth alters. This alteration in the earth changes the current flow through the gauge. When the moving contact is connected to a float assembly and positioned in the fuel tank, the float will move as the fuel level alters. This causes the resistance to earth to alter, leading to a change in the current flow through the fuel gauge. This change in current then moves the needle indicating the fuel level.

When the fuel tank is full the potentiometer will provide little resistance, as it will give a straight path to earth (Figure 5.78). This will lead to higher current flow and therefore heat generated in the coil windings, which leads to more bending of the bimetallic strip. This moves the needle to the 'full' position on the gauge. As the fuel is used, the float will fall and the resistance will increase as the arm moves around the potentiometer.

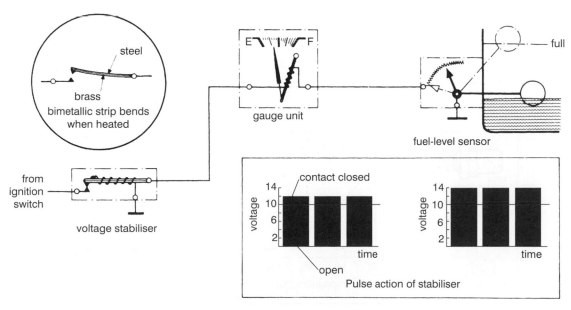

Figure 5.78 A thermal-type fuel gauge

This higher resistance provides lower current flow and lower heat generated at the coil windings. This leads to the needle on the gauge bending less and moving towards the 'empty' point on the gauge.

To ensure that the reading on the gauge remains stable and does not display a false reading, it is important to make sure the voltage applied is also stable. This is achieved through the use of a voltage stabiliser. Vehicles today have a more accurate electronic-type voltage stabiliser compared to the bimetallic-type stabilisers fitted to earlier vehicles.

Note: care should be taken to avoid an explosion when testing the operation of this system with the sensor. The sensor must be removed from the fuel tank. Any sparks generated near to the tank where petrol vapour is present will be dangerous and could cause the fuel to ignite.

Engine temperature sensor and gauge

The principles of the conventional-type thermal temperature gauge are very similar to that of the operation of the fuel tank sender unit. The temperature gauge is directly related to the resistance of the earth return through the temperature sensor, instead of the fuel tank sender unit potentiometer. As a result, the voltage supplied must also be stabilised in the same way to ensure that an accurate reading is obtained.

The engine temperature sensor is known as an NTC (negative temperature coefficient) resistor. In automotive technology, many temperature sensors fitted around the vehicle are equipped with an NTC resistor.

The core of an NTC temperature sensor is a temperature-dependent, non-linear measuring resistor in the form of a semiconductor.

The resistance of the NTC component decreases as the temperature increases. Therefore, *the higher the temperature, the lower the resistance.*

NTC resistors are also known as thermistors (from 'thermal' and 'resistor').

NTC temperature sensors form part of a voltage-divider circuit, usually supplied with a reference voltage of 5 V in the case of an EMS. The voltage drop across the NTC resistor depends on the prevailing temperature. This voltage value is used by the connected control unit as a measure of the sensor temperature. As the engine temperature rises, the resistance lowers, so the supplied voltage to the sensor increases on its return from the sensor to the EMS. The control unit will then use this voltage reference to identify the related temperature of the engine. The EMS will use this voltage reference to work out how much fuel to use and what the ignition timing should be, along with other adjustments.

When looking at this type of sensor to control a simple temperature gauge (Figure 5.79) the thermistor is part of the gauge circuit on the earth return side.

The thermistor is usually located in the upper part of the engine, such as the cylinder head, as this is the hottest area. The temperature gauge circuit has a voltage supplied from the ignition, which is directed through a voltage stabiliser to maintain a steady current flow to the gauge. The circuit then leaves the gauge to the thermistor and then to earth through the engine. When the engine temperature is cool the current flow through the gauge will be low due to the high resistance present at the thermistor. In this situation, the gauge deflection will be also low, as the heat generated at the bimetallic strip will be low. As the engine temperature rises, the resistance

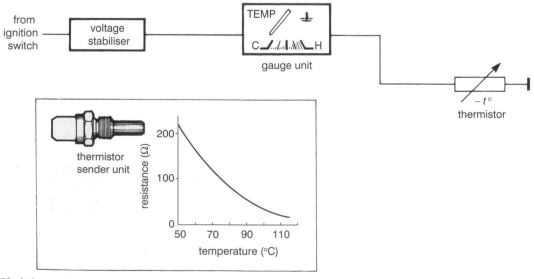

Figure 5.79 A thermal-type engine temperature gauge

at the thermistor will start to fall, which will increase the current flow through the gauge. This increased current flow will cause greater heat to be generated at the bimetallic strip, causing higher deflection of the needle leading to the higher temperature reading.

The source material of this type of sensor comprises different oxides of metals such as iron, cobalt, nickel, copper and zinc. Chemical stabilisers are added to the oxides, which are then pressed into the desired shape.

NTC resistors may be used in engine coolant temperature (ECT) sensors and Intake-air temperature (IAT) sensors.

5.8.3 Electronic gauge systems

Vehicles today are all fitted with ECUs to control the operation of many systems along with the gauges and instrumentation. The ECU tracks information coming in from various sensors located around the vehicle to control the operation of the relevant gauge from the linked sensor input signal.

When a vehicle is moving the fuel in the tank will surge from side to side and forwards and backwards. This movement will constantly alter the float level height of the fuel sender unit. In earlier vehicles, this would lead to the fuel tank gauge also moving erratically, causing the driver to be unclear of the amount of fuel in the fuel tank unless the vehicle was stationary. In a modern gauge assembly, the fuel sender unit is damped so it will not move up and down so quickly, and the voltage is also stabilised to produce a more constant fuel level signal. The ECU will then average out the signal over a short period of time, providing the driver with a steady fuel level signal on the gauge. These electronic control systems also incorporate warning signals to inform the driver when the fuel level is low or the engine temperature is too high.

Many gauges now use a digital display. Although the driver will obviously see the information in a different format from an analogue gauge, the concept of using resistor-type sensors to provide signal voltages is still the same, except that the signal voltages are processed by an ECU many thousands of times a second.

To ensure that the electrical systems operate at their most efficient, they require some general maintenance on a periodic basis. This is generally minimal, especially as modern vehicles have both sealed non-maintenance batteries and ECU-controlled systems, such as engine management and instrumentation. The following section looks at this maintenance in more detail.

5.9 Electrical systems – routine maintenance

5.9.1 Batteries

The maintenance of the battery consists of four key areas:

- Checking external condition
- Checking battery terminals
- Security
- Electrolyte levels

The external condition of the battery is important as it contains the vital components that make up the battery. Dirt building up around the battery will cause it to perform at a reduced rate through blocking of breather holes, reducing cooling and creating high resistances across the terminals. Ensure that the battery is clean and free from water and grease. Wipe the surface of the battery down with a damp cloth to remove general dirt from its surface.

Care should be taken to make sure the dirt around the top of the battery is kept to a minimum, as excess dirt can create a short between the two terminals; this can lead to discharge of the battery over a period. To clean the terminals, use a neutralising agent such as sodium bicarbonate together with a light wire brush. Make sure that the terminals are tight and smear with a light coating of petroleum jelly to protect against corrosion.

Figure 5.80 Battery terminals

The battery needs to be secure in its location to prevent any movement while the vehicle is travelling. Movement of the battery could cause damage to the outer shell of the battery, which could lead to an acid leak and loss of battery power. The battery clamp or fixings should always be fitted securely, but not over-tightened as this could also damage the battery case.

As the battery is constantly charged and discharged, there is a constant chemical reaction within the battery. This chemical reaction generates heat causing some of the battery electrolyte to be lost. The loss of electrolyte increases as ambient air temperature increases, so the battery electrolyte levels need to be checked periodically. Inspection of the electrolyte level is carried out visually with a maintenance-type battery by removing the cell covers and checking the height of the electrolyte. The correct level should be just covering the battery plates. Non-maintenance batteries do not have the facility to top up the electrolyte and these are assessed by checking the light indicator on the top of the battery casing. If the light is green, then the battery is in a good state of charge and requires no attention; no colour or a dark light means that the battery is in a low state of charge and requires charging and retesting; a yellow light equates to the electrolyte level being too low and the battery needs to be replaced. If assessment of the battery's state of charge as a whole needs to be carried out, a heavy discharge test needs to be performed. If the specific gravity (state of charge) of the individual cells needs to be measured, a hydrometer must be used.

Precautions

- Do not use tap water to top up the electrolyte as the impurities within the water will reduce battery performance. Always use distilled water.
- Do not overfill the battery as it may overflow and cause damage to metal parts.
- The battery electrolyte consists of distilled water and sulphuric acid, so if it comes into contact with the skin, rinse with water immediately.
- If the electrolyte comes into contact with the eyes, flush out with water and seek medical advice.
- Check the battery case for cracks or damage while visually checking the electrolyte level.

One of the most effective ways of checking the serviceability of a vehicle battery is through the use of a hydrometer (showing **specific gravity**). A hydrometer is a device that is able to measure the specific gravity of a fluid (Figure 5.81).

Specific gravity: a comparative unit that enables us to gauge the density of a fluid when compared to that of pure water.

A litre of pure water weighs 1 kg. Therefore, if 1 litre of a given fluid weighs 2 kg, then it is twice as dense and therefore has a specific gravity of 2. Battery electrolyte is dilute sulphuric acid; it is therefore a mix of sulphuric acid and distilled water. Concentrated sulphuric acid is considerably more dense than water and therefore its presence increases the density (and specific gravity) of the electrolyte. A fully charged battery in good order will have a specific gravity of 1.27 to 1.28.

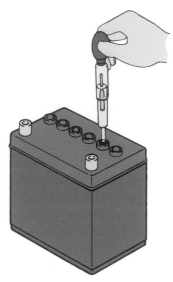

Figure 5.81 Checking the battery state of charge with a hydrometer

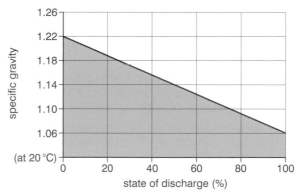

Figure 5.82 Relationship between the state of charge and specific gravity

As the battery discharges, more water is produced. Therefore, the specific gravity will reduce as the battery's charge state reduces. As the hydrometer is capable of drawing electrolyte up from each individual cell, allowing us to read the specific gravity, it is most suited to the inspection of a battery. It also enables us to view the electrolyte. If the electrolyte appears brown (muddy), then the plates are sulphated and the battery should be replaced.

Disconnecting battery terminals

When carrying out work on the vehicle's electrical system or other major units it is sometimes necessary to remove the battery from the vehicle or disconnect the battery leads. To do this correctly, and to avoid any chance of damaging the vehicle's electrical system, the following procedure should be carried out:

1 Check you have the radio codes for the vehicle as these may be lost when disconnecting the battery.
2 Loosen the earth battery lead first and remove from the battery terminal, making sure that it is held away from the battery to avoid accidental reconnection.
3 Loosen and remove the positive battery terminal.
4 Remove the battery securing device and remove the battery.

To refit the battery, ensure that the reverse order is followed by connecting the positive terminal first. The reason for this procedure is to avoid any metallic tools creating an accidental short from the positive battery terminal to an earth point on the vehicle, which could create a large electrical shock and overload the battery.

5.9.2 Starting systems

Generally, the starting system requires very little maintenance to ensure that it is in good working order. The main purpose of the starting system is to ensure that the engine is cranked over at an adequate speed to enable it to start. The main checks to be made include checking battery charge condition, starter motor terminal connections for security and the earth supply to the engine. If the battery charge is low, the engine will not crank at an adequate speed to start the engine. If the earth supply cable or terminals at the starter motor are loose or corroded, this will cause high resistance in the starter circuit and lead to slow cranking speeds. If abnormal noises are heard during cranking, this should be investigated further by the removal of the starter motor. (Ensure all battery terminals are removed in the correct order before attempting this job.) Noises usually indicate a worn pinion or flywheel creating resistance when trying to engage with each other during cranking.

5.9.3 Charging systems

The charging system's purpose is to supply electrical energy to the vehicle's electrical systems while the engine is running. The charging system also supplies electrical energy to charge the battery during the time when the engine is running, which tops up the charge level lost during starting the engine or running any equipment (such as lights and ICE) while the engine is switched off.

Alternator drive belts, like other components on the vehicle, become worn as they become older. These drive belts or auxiliary belts are used to drive many components such as the alternator, power-steering pump, air-conditioning compressor and water pump. Over a period of time, these belts become stretched and cracked, causing a loss in drive to the component. For this reason, they must be changed periodically and visually checked during each service.

Precautions

- Adjust the belt to the correct tension as detailed in the manufacturer's manual.
- If the belt is too tight, then damage may be caused to the bearings within the component and the belt itself.
- If the belt is too loose, then the component will not operate correctly and a whistling or screeching noise will be heard. (This whistling noise can also be caused by the belt becoming old and hard.)
- Check the difference in tension between an old belt and a new belt.
- Check the alignment of the belt to make sure it is running along the pulleys correctly, as misalignment will cause premature wear of the belt.

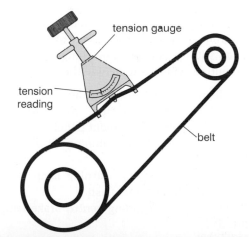

Figure 5.83 Checking drive belt tension using a tension gauge indicator

The auxiliary drive belt needs to be set at the correct tension for the vehicle to avoid damage to the pulley bearings and auxiliary units such as the alternator. To do this, the best practice is to use a drive belt tension indicator gauge (Figure 5.83). Generally, most manufacturers will supply a value for the tension of the belts in their workshop manuals. Check whether the tension value is for a new or used belt as these can sometimes differ.

Check that the alternator fixings are secure as any loose mountings can cause excessive vibration to occur, which will lead to failure of the alternator body or components within the alternator itself.

5.9.4 Additional electrical systems

To check the additional systems fitted to a vehicle, it is usually a case of switching on and visually or aurally assessing the condition of the equipment. While the vehicle is in use, the driver may notice any malfunction through a warning light on the instrument display such as low oil pressure, low washer fluids or loss of charging from the alternator. One of the main areas the driver should check on a regular basis (as part of routine assessment of their vehicle) is the lighting, as it can be very easy for a driver to not notice if a rear light or brake light is not working for some time. The light checks should include an inspection of the functionality of each light unit, along with an assessment of the lens; the technician will check the same things as part of a service routine, which will include the following:

- Headlamps – both 'dipped' and 'main beam', including warning-lamp for main-beam operation on the instrument panel
- Side lamps and daytime running lights (if fitted)
- Rear tail lights
- Indicators – including warning lamp and the rate at which the lights flash
- Brake lamps – including centre brake lamp (if fitted)
- Hazard warning lamps – including warning lamp on instrument panel
- Front and rear fog lamps
- Reversing lamps
- Rear number plate lamp
- Additional driving lamps, such as spotlights

Additional checks to the vehicle's electrical systems include the following:

- Wipers – operation and condition of the wiper blades
- Windscreen and headlamp washers for spray area and level of fluid
- Horn – loudness and tone

Many vehicles now have advanced monitoring systems to constantly check the operation of the electrical equipment fitted. These systems will assess the current draw of the equipment and warn the driver if there is a malfunction via the instrument display. For example, if a rear tail light is faulty, the system will know what the current draw of the rear lights should be when in good working order and will be able to determine if the current draw is lower, and therefore if a bulb is not operational. In some cases where a vehicle's system places a warning on the instrument display, the driver may have to take the vehicle to the garage to have the system checked by a diagnostic scan tool (Figure 5.84). This tool is able to communicate with the vehicle's electrical system to interrogate what the fault is. This then allows the technician to investigate the fault further and carry out a repair.

Figure 5.84 Vehicle scan tool

5.9.5 Headlamp adjustment

The vehicle's headlamp alignment is very important, especially with the latest HID headlamp systems. A misaligned headlamp could cause a dangerous situation for on-coming drivers at night due to dazzling and momentary loss of vision of the road. The headlamp alignment should be checked as part of the main service routine by the technician. To check the alignment, the technician must use special beam-checking equipment (Figure 5.85). This is also used as part of the annual MOT check.

In order to check the headlamp alignment, the vehicle will need to be positioned at the correct height and be totally level. This will include checking the tyre pressures and removing any loads from inside the vehicle. If the vehicle has been raised during service for additional checks, it should be settled back down on its suspension by driving for a short distance. The beam checker is then placed directly in front of the relevant headlight on its parallel track. The headlights are then switched on dip and the beam height is assessed.

The correct beam height can usually be found on the front panel of the vehicle. This is expressed as a

Figure 5.85 Beam setting equipment

percentage, for example 1.2 per cent. The pattern you will see should look similar to Figure 5.86 on a right-hand drive vehicle. You will notice the beam follows the line along corresponding to the percentage of dip (in the case of Figure 5.85, this is at 1.25 per cent). When the dipped beam is correct it will produce a beam pattern with a distinct line rising at 15° (45° in some headlamp types with different designs and beam patterns) on the nearside. The vertical location of the beam centre (hot spot) of the headlamp must be a given distance (recommended by the manufacturer) below the height of the headlamp centre: the horizontal spacing of the hot spots should be equal to the distance between the lamps.

When the special beam-checking equipment is unavailable, the method recommended is to position the vehicle on level ground at a given distance in front of a vertical screen set parallel with the headlamps. Switch the headlamps on and visually check the pattern on the screen to assess the height and adjust to be as equal as possible. Final adjustment should be made using the correct beam setting equipment.

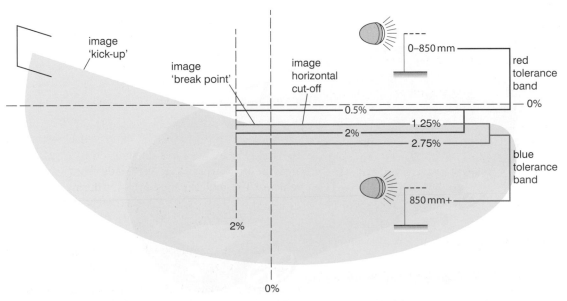

Figure 5.86 Beam pattern seen when checking the headlamp operation and height

5.10 Heating, ventilation and air conditioning

Comfort and convenience are integral parts of vehicle design. Since the time when opening a window was the only source of cold air, the customer's demand for instant hot and cold air to be readily available has greatly increased. This not only keeps the occupants comfortable, but can also aid the driver by supplying constant fresh air to prevent them from falling asleep at the wheel. Over time, heating and ventilation systems have become much more sophisticated and can even be adjusted separately from passenger side to driver side, allowing greater individual or personal settings. The time is long gone when the occupants of a vehicle had to suffer the extremes of temperature and exposure to the elements.

Systems in use today can be divided into three main classes:

- Basic heating and ventilation system
- Full air-conditioning system
- Climate-control system

5.10.1 Basic heating and ventilating system

In the UK, this system was the most common arrangement used on the majority of vehicles, other than the luxury class, but nowadays most manufacturers fit air-conditioning systems as standard. When this is not the case, manufacturers normally offer air conditioning as an optional extra.

The basic arrangement is normally a fresh air system with provision for heating and ducting the air to discharge at foot or face level. Electronic controls allow the occupants to both set the temperature of the air and select the discharge points to suit the conditions. These controls are connected to two or more electrically operated flaps, which direct the air through the appropriate ducts. An electrically driven fan is fitted in the system to speed up the air movement at times when the natural circulation is poor.

System layout

A fresh air circulation system is not effective unless the air can pass through the body compartment and flow out to make more room for fresh air to enter. Figure 5.87 shows the paths taken by the air as it flows towards the various discharge vents in the body. Ideally, these should be situated at points where the external air pressure is low to allow for a natural circulation. In a similar way, the inlet point should be in a region of high pressure; the pressure increase at these points is normally caused by the combination of vehicle movement through the air and change in the airflow direction.

The cut-away drawing (Figure 5.88) shows a typical ducting arrangement for a car. An electronic control system allows the driver to direct the air so that it can be discharged from one or more outlets. These are:

- along the length of the front windscreen (for head-level ventilation and defrost or demist) and two small side outlets (for side window demist)
- at independently controlled central and side vents
- in the footwell region.

The second control switch operates a flap valve, which directs all, or a part of, the intake air through a heat exchanger when warm air is required. Although exhaust gas from the engine has occasionally been used as a heating source, most manufacturers prefer to utilise the engine coolant heat because it is considered to be a safer system.

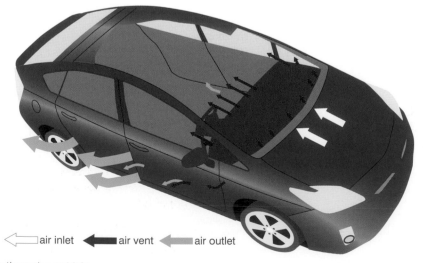

⇦ air inlet ◀ air vent ⬅ air outlet

Figure 5.87 Airflow through a vehicle

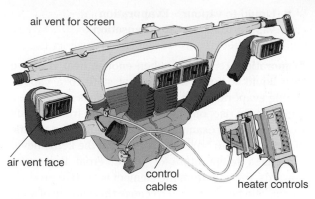

air vent for screen

air vent face

control cables

heater controls

Figure 5.88 Air duct layout

Figure 5.89 shows how the valves control the path taken by the air; in the position shown, part of the airflow is directed through the heater matrix. This provides warm air at the windscreen and from any vent that is opened by the front-seat occupants.

Naturally, the heater will not function until the coolant reaches a sufficient temperature. Assuming the thermostat in the cooling system is serviceable and of the correct type, the heater should soon become effective after a cold-engine start. To meet this requirement, the coolant flow to the heater should be taken from the hottest part of the system – on the engine side of the thermostat.

The multi-point switch that controls the fan enables the speed to be controlled by varying the resistance of the circuit; this alters the voltage applied to the permanent magnetic-type motor.

On some systems, an extra control switch is fitted to allow the outside air to be cut off and the inside air to be used instead. This recirculated air setting is useful when the outside air is heavily polluted. An issue with using this facility can be that if the outside air is

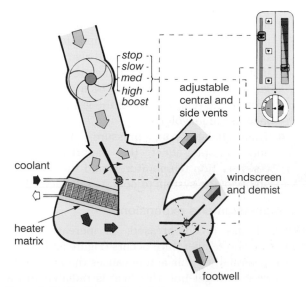

stop
slow
med
high
boost

adjustable central and side vents

coolant

heater matrix

windscreen and demist

footwell

Figure 5.89 Heating and ventilating system

prevented from entering the vehicle for long periods of time, the air in the vehicle can become saturated with humidity and cause the vehicle's windows to mist. A feature on some more modern vehicles is incorporated to prevent this from happening by automatically switching back to allow fresh air to enter the vehicle after approximately 10 minutes.

5.11 Air conditioning

Unlike in the past, many new cars are now being sold with air conditioning as standard in the UK because modern environmental control systems (or climate control systems) offer the following features:

- Cooling in summer to a set temperature
- Dehumidification (removal of moisture) of air in summer
- Dehumidification of air in winter, so preventing misting of windows
- Heating in winter to a set temperature
- Control of the flow of air

These features can be achieved by fitting, in the basic system previously described, an extra heat exchanger. This additional matrix contains a substance that is very cold compared with the hot coolant in the normal heater matrix, so the air passing through it will be cooled. When this cooled air is discharged to the interior of the car, the effect will be similar to the action of the heater except that the air temperature will go down instead of up. Whereas most basic heating and ventilating (non air-conditioning) systems rely on the driver to control the temperature, the sophisticated air-conditioning system used today controls the temperature automatically to suit the setting selected by the driver.

An air-conditioning system is the apparatus needed to maintain a very low temperature in the cooling matrix (evaporator) placed in the ventilating air stream.

5.11.1 Heating and cooling principles

Before considering the layout of an air-conditioning system, it is advisable to consider some fundamentals in order to understand the purpose of the various parts of the system.

Heat transfer

All vehicle air-conditioning systems use these laws or theories of heat transfer to some extent in the way they operate.

There are three ways of transferring heat:

1 Radiation – heat radiation does not require any material to transfer heat.

2 Conduction – heat is transferred directly via contact between different bodies.

3 Convection – heat is transferred (flows) via a liquid or a gas.

Heat transfer often occurs through a combination of ways:

■ Heat from the sun is transferred to a metal rod via radiation.

■ Heat from the metal rod is transferred to the water via conduction.

■ Heat from the water is transferred to the container via convection.

Heat transfer only takes place in one direction. If a beaker of cold water is placed inside a beaker of warm water, heat will be transferred from the warm-water beaker to the cold-water beaker until the temperature in the two beakers is the same. The closer the temperatures in the two beakers, the slower the heat transfer.

Figure 5.90 Example of heat transfer

Heat is always transferred from an object with a higher temperature to an object with a lower temperature. The transfer of heat is faster when the temperature difference is at its greatest.

There are two other rules relating to refrigerant that we also need to bear in mind:

■ When a liquid turns into a gas (boils), it absorbs a great deal of heat.

■ When a gas turns into a liquid (condenses), it releases a great deal of its heat.

Change of state

A change of state is said to have occurred when a solid becomes a liquid, a liquid becomes a vapour, or the reverse of either process has occurred.

A change of state involves a transfer of heat, but is not accompanied by a change in temperature. In air conditioning only two states are required. The refrigerant alternates between its liquid and gaseous state.

■ Liquid to vapour = **Evaporation**
■ Vapour to liquid = **Condensation**

Evaporation: term used when enough heat is added to a liquid to force a change of state to a vapour. During evaporation, the heat added does not cause a temperature rise, only a change in state from a liquid to a vapour. For example, no matter how long a kettle of water is left to boil, the water left in the kettle never exceeds a temperature of 100 °C. From that point onwards, the heat from the element is used to produce steam. The heat required to cause this change of state (vaporisation) is called the 'latent heat'.

Condensation: the reverse of the evaporation process. If enough heat is removed from a vapour, a change of state will occur causing the vapour to revert back to a liquid. When steam from a kettle strikes a cold window, heat is transferred from the steam to the window; water condenses on the window as droplets of water. The heat removed, which causes a change in state, is called the 'latent heat'.

Temperature and pressure

We now need to add to this basic knowledge by looking at what happens to liquids and gases when we change the temperature or pressure acting on them. Here are the important points to remember:

■ The temperature at which a liquid comes to the boil is dependent on the atmospheric pressure as well as the liquid. The higher the pressure, the higher the boiling point. The lower the pressure, the lower the boiling point. Remember what happens in an engine-cooling system where a pressure cap is used to raise the pressure on the coolant, therefore increasing the boiling point.

■ In the case of gases, if the pressure on the gas is increased, there will be a proportional rise in the temperature of the gas and also a decrease in its volume. Conversely, if the pressure on the gas is decreased, there will be a proportional drop in the temperature of the gas and also an increase in its volume.

■ The changes in pressure, temperature and volume affect the vaporisation and condensation temperatures, and therefore the ability of the system to operate satisfactorily.

Compression and expansion

When a gas is compressed, an increase in the pressure and temperature occurs (Figure 5.91a). The heat generated by this action causes the fins on the compressor to get hot; this heat is radiated to the atmosphere.

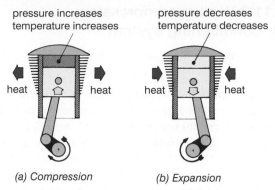

pressure increases
temperature increases

pressure decreases
temperature decreases

heat — heat | heat — heat

(a) Compression | (b) Expansion

Figure 5.91 Heat flow during compression and expansion

Likewise, expansion of a gas decreases the pressure and lowers the temperature (Figure 5.91b). In this case, the fins of the cylinder would feel cold to the touch; this is because the cylinder absorbs the heat from the human hand. A similar expansion effect is produced when the air is released from a tyre valve; the high-pressure air rushing out from the tyre causes a sudden drop in pressure at the end of the valve; on some days, the accompanying drop in temperature may cause frost to form on the metal valve.

In both the compression and expansion actions heat passes from the *hot* to the *cold* substance.

Evaporation

A large quantity of heat, called latent heat, is required to cause a liquid to change its state to a gas. In the case of water, the change to steam requires a large quantity of heat. If this natural evaporation is accompanied by an expansion process, then a large amount of heat from an external source will be needed.

This expansion takes place in the air-conditioning evaporator matrix situated in the duct that supplies air to the interior of the car (Figure 5.92). As the liquid is pumped through the expansion valve, the drop in pressure, together with the heat required to change its state, makes the matrix very cold. This causes heat to be extracted from the air as it is pumped to the car interior.

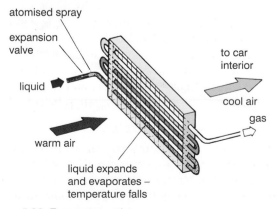

atomised spray

expansion valve

liquid

to car interior

cool air

gas

warm air

liquid expands and evaporates – temperature falls

Figure 5.92 Evaporator action

Refrigerant

A refrigeration system relies on the properties of the refrigerant substance to have both a low boiling point and the ability to change its state readily from a liquid to a vapour, and vice versa.

In the past, this requirement was met by a special chlorofluorocarbon (CFC) substance called Freon-12 or Refrigerant-12 (generally referred to as R-12). Under standard conditions, this substance boils at −30 °C. In other words, at atmospheric pressure and a temperature of −30 °C it evaporates from a liquid to a vapour. R-12 requires only 1/14th of the heat needed by water to change its state, and since it maintains good stability during repeated changes, this comparatively cheap refrigerant was commonly used for the majority of automotive air-conditioning systems.

All refrigerants must be handled with great care in view of the very low temperature at which they are stored.

Note: manufacturer's recommendations should be sought and understood before handling refrigerant or working on any part of an air-conditioning system.

Refrigerant handling legislation

Fluorinated gas (F gas) legislation imposed by the Department for Environment, Food and Rural Affairs (defra) in July 2010 has ensured that any personnel dealing with the recovery or maintenance of mobile air conditioning must hold a valid qualification. This has been introduced to ensure that all air-conditioning systems are recovered and maintained professionally to avoid any discharge of the refrigerant into the atmosphere. This is an important move as during 2005 the mobile air-conditioning sector accounted for 11 per cent of the total emission of F gas in the UK.

Modern refrigerants

CFCs have since been identified as the primary cause of damage to the earth's ozone layer. In view of legislation and various international agreements introduced to combat this environmental damage, CFC-type refrigerants and flushing agents are no longer acceptable for air-conditioning systems.

Since 1993, ozone-friendly chemicals, such as hydrofluorocarbon (HFC) R134a, have been used in all new automotive air-conditioning systems. The refrigerant R134a cannot be used in a system designed to operate with R-12; this is because the properties of R134a are different. As a result, the cost of replacing a system or parts of the system designed to run on R-12 would be very high as many of the components are not transferable between R-12 and R134a.

By 2012, it is planned that all new vehicles will be using a new refrigerant called HFO-1234yf, which has a much lower global warming potential (GWP) compared to that of HFC-R134a.

HFO-1234yf has the following properties:

- Developed and manufactured jointly by DuPont and Honeywell
- GWP of just 4, compared to the maximum allowed of 150
- Operating performance is very similar to HFC-R134a
- Mildly inflammable compared to HFC-R134a, which is not flammable
- Lifespan of HFO-1234yf when released to the atmosphere is only 11 days, compared to 13 years for HFC-R134a
- Costs of HFO-1234yf will be higher than that of HFC-R134

Effect of pressure on refrigerant

As with other liquids, the temperature at the change of state (boiling point) depends on the pressure. The pressure temperature dependence is useful in the operating cycle because, by varying the pressure of the refrigerant as it flows around the system, the temperature can be controlled to suit the need of a particular part. Table 5.8 summarises this pressure and temperature relationship.

Table 5.8 Pressure and temperature relationship

Pressure	Temperature
Low	Low
High	High

5.11.2 Vapour-compression air-conditioning system

The vapour-compression refrigeration system (Figure 5.93) consists of the following:

1 Compressor – driven by the engine, it compresses the refrigerant vapour to raise its pressure and temperature.
2 Condenser – a heat exchanger that uses external airflow to cool the vapour to change its state to a liquid.
3 Receiver-drier – acts as a liquid storage tank and also contains chemicals that remove water from the system.
4 Expansion valve/orifice – meters the refrigerant and lowers its pressure to allow it to expand.
5 Evaporator – a heat exchanger to extract heat from the ventilating airflow as it passes to the car interior.

Basic operation

The refrigeration cycle is a continuous process and is based on the temperature changes as the refrigerant flows around the fluid circuit. These temperature changes are brought about by pressure variations and changes in state of the refrigerant.

When the driver selects the air-conditioning mode, an electromagnetic clutch, contained in the compressor drive pulley, is engaged. Rotation of a compressor

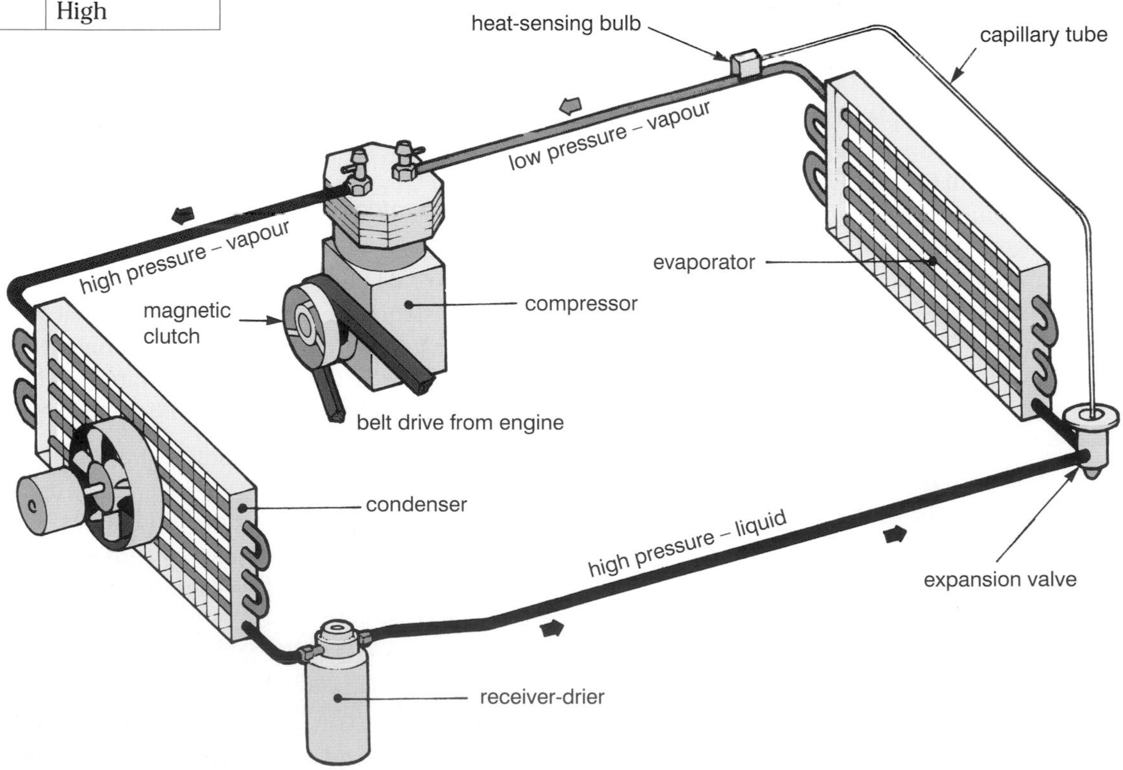

Figure 5.93 An air-conditioning system

(using R134a refrigerant) draws in vapour at a low gauge pressure of 1–2 bar (15–30 lbf in^{-2}) and compresses it to a pressure of 8–18 bar (118–265 lbf in^{-2}); the actual pressure is dependent on the ambient temperature and compressor speed. This pumping action increases the temperature of the vapour to 70–110 °C and causes it to flow to the condenser; this is normally situated in front of the engine-cooling radiator.

As the hot vapour flows through the condenser tubes, its heat is radiated to the air that passes over the condenser fins and tubes. This action cools the refrigerant vapour and causes it to condense (i.e. the refrigerant changes its state from a vapour to a liquid). By making the condenser tube of sufficient length, the refrigerant leaving the condenser is in a totally liquefied state.

Any water in the system chemically reacts with refrigerant to form corrosive acids, so this moisture and other contaminants are removed at this point in the fluid circuit to avoid damage. This duty is performed by passing the liquid refrigerant through silica gel desiccant crystals in the receiver-drier (sometimes called a dehydrator).

In addition to the drying and filtering duty, the receiver-drier also acts as a high-pressure container to store liquid refrigerant in reserve for its supply to the evaporator.

On leaving the receiver-drier, the clean, dry liquid passes to the expansion valve; this meters and atomises the flow of refrigerant at low pressure into the evaporator. The quantity delivered by the valve depends on the temperature at the evaporator outlet. In the system shown (Figure 5.93), a temperature-sensing bulb and capillary tube signal to the expansion valve when the flow should be increased or decreased. A low output temperature indicates that the valve must reduce the flow, and vice versa.

After the flow has been regulated by the expansion valve the atomised refrigerant passes through the evaporator. Here, the heat is extracted from the air that is flowing over the tubes and fins. This cools the air and, as a result of heat transfer from air to refrigerant, the liquid will first change into a vapour and then be heated to a superheated state well above the boiling point of the refrigerant as it passes through the evaporator.

Having completed the cooling function, the low-pressure vapour is returned to the inlet side of the compressor to allow the cycle to be repeated.

5.11.3 Air-conditioning components

Although the basic operation remains the same, the construction of the five basic components needed to perform the refrigeration cycle varies slightly between the different manufacturers of air-conditioning systems.

Compressor

The compressor used in a particular system can be one of two types:

- Reciprocating piston
- Rotary vane

Both types are driven from the engine crankshaft via a single or multi-vee belt. The belt drives a free pulley that is engaged to the compressor by an electromagnetic clutch. When air conditioning is required the driver operates a switch that activates a relay. This energises the clutch windings and connects the vee pulley to the compressor drive shaft until the driver, or an automatic control system, switches off the air-conditioning unit.

On some systems, such as the cycling clutch orifice tube (CCOT), described on page 568, the compressor is cycled (automatically switched on and off) by a thermostatic switch to maintain a nearly constant temperature at the outlet of the evaporator.

For safety purposes, a compressor is fitted with a valve or switch to relieve the pressure if the outlet temperature reaches a given maximum, for example 93 °C; this represents a pressure of 28 bar (400 lbf in^{-2}).

Figure 5.94 shows the construction of a magnetic clutch having a stationary winding around an iron core; this becomes a strong magnet when current is passed through the winding. This action attracts a pressure plate attached to the compressor shaft and causes it to make frictional contact with the driving pulley. Three spring steel straps are fitted; these transmit the drive between the pressure plate and compressor hub, and provide a spring action to release the clutch when the compressor is switched off.

A small quantity (about 175 ml) of special moisture-free refrigerant oil is used in an air-conditioning system to lubricate the seals, gaskets, valves and compressor. Most of the oil circulates around the system and only a small amount (about 20 ml) is retained in the compressor. On most compressors, the refrigerant must be discharged before the oil level can be checked, so the oil check is only carried out when the system fails to operate satisfactorily.

When the refrigerant is exhausted prior to carrying out a repair of a component, the quantity of oil discharged with the gas should be measured. This indicates the amount of oil that must be introduced when the system is recharged.

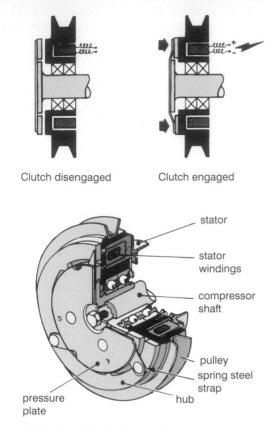

Clutch disengaged   Clutch engaged

Figure 5.94 Magnetic clutch assembly

stator

stator windings

compressor shaft

pulley

spring steel strap

hub

pressure plate

Reciprocating piston compressor

There are three main types;

- Crankshaft
- Swash-plate
- Rotary-vane

Crankshaft type

This is similar to a small engine (Figure 5.95a) and is made as a single, twin or vee-twin two-stroke unit.

Reed valves are used to control the intake and exhaust flow of the gas refrigerant, and lubrication is provided either by a separate built-in oil pump or by utilising the pressure difference between input and output lines.

On this old type of compressor a plug on the side of the compressor is provided for the insertion of an oil-level dipstick. Removal of this plug will allow refrigerant to escape so this should be avoided if possible.

Often, Schrader-type valves are fitted adjacent to the inlet and outlet pipe connectors. These valves are provided for the attachment of special equipment, which allows the technician to check the low- and high-pressure sections of the refrigerant circuit; also the valves allow the system to be topped up or drained.

In the past, these valves were opened to the atmosphere to exhaust the system, but nowadays environmental considerations make it necessary to drain the refrigerant into a sealed container or recharging station (similar to the one seen in Figure 5.96) to allow it to be reclaimed.

Swash-plate type

This compact type (Figure 5.95b) uses either three or five pairs of pistons, positioned radially around the driving shaft. These pistons are moved back and forth in an axial direction by a swash-plate (Figure 5.95c); this is driven by a shaft connected to the electromagnetic clutch.

Reed valves at the end of each cylinder control the vapour flow to and from the low- and high-pressure connectors situated at the rear of the compressor. A small internal oil pump lubricates the compressor.

Rotary-vane type

The rotary-vane type compressor (Figure 5.95d) is becoming popular because of its low-friction, high-pumping output and low noise level.

Construction and operation of the pump is similar to other vane pumps used on vehicles. In the layout shown, two through-vanes, driven by a rotor, form four separate pumping chambers.

Condenser

The condenser shown in Figure 5.93 is a long finned tube that is designed to use the cool air flowing around the tube to change the refrigerant from a superheated vapour to a liquid.

To ensure a good supply of cooling air, the condenser is normally placed in front of the engine cooling radiator. At times when the air speed from the forward motion of the car is insufficient, an extra fan, placed in front of the condenser, is brought into operation. Since this fan is electrically driven, it can be cut out by a thermal switch when extra cooling of the condenser is not desired.

As the refrigerant flows downwards from the compressor connection at the top, the vapour gradually condenses. Generally, two-thirds of the condenser contains vapour; the bottom of the condenser holds warm liquid refrigerant.

Receiver-drier

Although this unit acts as a temporary storage container for the refrigerant, its main duty is to remove moisture and dirt from the liquid. Besides causing corrosion, water in the system allows the formation of ice; this blocks the orifice of the expansion valve and obstructs the flow of refrigerant.

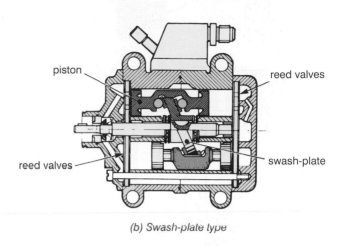

intake   outlet

outlet valve

inlet valve

piston

(a) Crankshaft type

piston

reed valves

reed valves

swash-plate

(b) Swash-plate type

swash-plate

(c) Action of swash-plate

discharge valve stop

discharge valve

rotor

vane

inlet port

(d) Rotary pump

Figure 5.95 Types of compressor

Figure 5.96 Example of an air-conditioning recharging station

Water is removed by passing the refrigerant through either a sieve desiccant or silica gel crystals. Most modern air-conditioning systems have large silica gel driers, because new ozone-friendly refrigerants and associated lubricants are extremely hygroscopic (able to absorb moisture).

Figure 5.97 shows the main details of a typical receiver-drier. Liquid refrigerant from the condenser collects in the aluminium alloy container and then passes through the desiccant and filter on its way to the evaporator.

Often, in earlier systems, the receiver-drier incorporated a sight glass and fusible plug.

Sight glass

This feature allows the condition of the refrigerant to be observed (Table 5.9).

Table 5.9 Main indications of the condition of refrigerant

Condition	Indication
Foamy or containing bubbles	Low in refrigerant and air in system
Streaky	Lack of refrigerant and excess oil is circulating
Cloudy	Circulation of desiccant

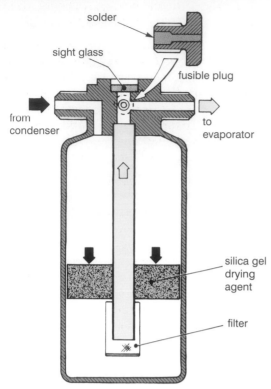

Figure 5.97 Receiver-drier

Fusible plug

Damage to a system by an abnormally high pressure, caused by poor condenser ventilation or a high cooling load, is prevented by this melt-plug.

A special solder filling of a hole in the plug melts when the temperature reaches about 100 °C. At this temperature the fluid pressure is about 29 bar. An issue with this type of safety measure is that the refrigerant is expelled into the atmosphere. As this is undesirable, this type of pressure control system is not used anymore and a more sophisticated process to handle over-pressuring is now used. This system includes pressure sensors and temperature sensors within the air-conditioning circuit. When the pressure rises over a pre-determined pressure the switch will disengage the compressor to prevent pressure building up further and causing damage.

Thermostatic expansion valve

The thermostatic expansion valve (TXV) valve shown in Figure 5.98 is a thermal expansion type. This uses a diaphragm-controlled ball-and-needle valve to regulate the flow of refrigerant into the evaporator. As the liquid refrigerant is forced through the orifice, it becomes atomised. This causes a sudden drop in pressure and the accompanying expansion produces the required low-temperature cooling vapour.

Diaphragm movement adjusts the flow of refrigerant to equal the rate at which the evaporator can vaporise

it. Too much refrigerant causes a severe build-up of ice around the evaporator coil, and too little refrigerant means that the compressor is supplied with vapour that is not in a superheated state.

The control system is a sensing bulb, attached to the evaporator outlet pipe, and a capillary tube. When the cooling load on the evaporator is increased the gas in the bulb senses the rise in temperature. As a result, the gas expands and moves the diaphragm downwards; this increases the valve opening and allows more refrigerant to flow.

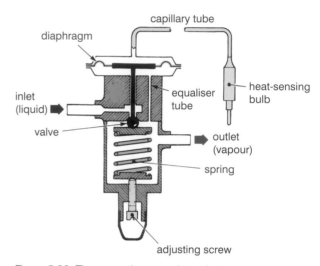

Figure 5.98 Thermostatic expansion valve

Valves-in-receiver type

On some air-conditioning systems, the TXV is fitted in the receiver-drier unit. By mounting the receiver-drier adjacent to the evaporator, this layout overcomes the need for a separate capillary line to the TXV unit.

This type of receiver-drier also incorporates a **pilot-operated** absolute pressure suction throttling valve (POA valve). By means of a capsule, this valve controls the flow of refrigerant from the evaporator to maintain a constant pressure difference across the evaporator of 2 bar (30 lbf in^{-2}).

Pilot-operated: a type of pressure relief valve used to maintain the pressure within the air-conditioning system.

Box-type TXV

The box-type TXV is also used on some vehicle air-conditioning systems. This type uses a heat-sensing rod, similar to the heat-sensing tube of the TXV. With the box-type TXV, the capillary tube and the equaliser pipe are no longer required. In this type of TXV the heat-sensing rod senses the temperature of the evaporator outlet, which is transmitted to the diaphragm, causing the pressure of the gas contained in the diaphragm chamber to vary. This temperature reading is transmitted to the diaphragm and results in movement of the valve. The opening and closing of the valve is regulated as required to control the liquid refrigerant passing through the orifice. This box-type TXV, along with the other types, has three main functions: a metering action, a modulating action and a controlling action.

Restrictor (orifice tube)

The restrictor, or 'orifice tube' as it is sometimes called, serves the same basic function as the TXV. The restrictor is a straight tube of sintered metal or plastic. Some of these tubes have a filter strainer to remove contaminates and a calibrated meter tube is used to meter the refrigerant flow. The orifice opening in the restrictor is fixed and does not affect compressor operation unlike the TXV that cycles the compressor clutch.

The restrictor type has a constant flow of refrigerant flowing through the fixed orifice. This provides a constant pressure drop in the air-conditioning system. As the refrigerant passes through the restrictor orifice the pressure drops rapidly. The refrigerant temperature is cold at low pressure. The restrictor is an interface between the high pressure and low pressure side of the refrigerant circuit. There is a seal fitted to the restrictor to ensure that the refrigerant only passes through the restrictor at the narrowing of the orifice.

The flow of refrigerant through the carefully calibrated orifice limits the pressure in the air-conditioning system. The restrictor ensures that the pressure on the high-pressure side of the refrigerant is kept high. This high pressure acting on the refrigerant ensures that it is maintained in a liquid state when the compressor is running.

When the pressure drops at the restrictor the refrigerant cools down through this lowering in pressure and it then enters the evaporator through partial evaporation. The refrigerant is atomised through the pressure drop and then through a dirt strainer in front of the narrowing orifice. The atomised refrigerant then reaches the evaporator, which is located downstream of the narrowing orifice.

Evaporator

Whereas a condenser gives up the heat of the refrigerant vapour to the air, the duty of an evaporator is just the opposite – it takes the heat of the air that is passing through it and uses the heat to vaporise the refrigerant.

Besides acting as a heat exchanger to cool the air as it enters the car interior, the evaporator also dehumidifies the air. This feature is advantageous at times when excess moisture in the air causes windows to mist up and discomfort for the occupants

in the car. Heating the air after removing the moisture provides a ventilating airflow of excellent quality.

Frosting and icing of the evaporator fins reduces the airflow through the unit; as a result, the effectiveness of the cooling system decreases. This problem is minimised by the incorporation of either an evaporator thermostat switch or evaporator pressure regulator. Fitted to the evaporator outlet, this switch or regulator cuts out the compressor when it senses that the temperature is less than about 4 °C.

Using the air conditioning in humid, ambient conditions causes water to drip from the evaporator. A tray fitted below the evaporator collects this water fall-out and passes it to a drainpipe. An indication of the amount of water passing from this waste pipe is often seen on the ground after the vehicle has been parked for a while. Occasional blockage of this pipe can lead to the footwell filling with water. In some cases, a customer may ask the technician to rectify a water leak filling the footwell, but in fact the problem can often be down to a blocked evaporator drainpipe. Some vehicle owners may also falsely diagnose a water leak from the vehicle when they see the water dripping from below the car. This normal process sometimes needs to be explained to the customer to put their mind at rest.

An evaporator is generally made of aluminium alloy and uses either the tube or film construction. Heat transfer depends on the surface area of the exchanger, so a large number of fins are used to improve the efficiency.

Figure 5.99 shows an evaporator and the fittings that are used to house it in the ventilating air duct.

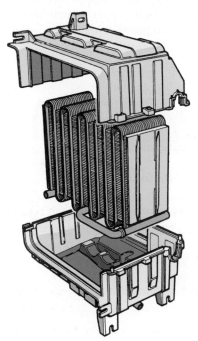

Figure 5.99 An evaporator

Electrical control

Apart from the ventilation control of airflow, the basic air-conditioning system is fitted with a number of electrical switches, sensors and relays to both improve its working efficiency and safeguard the system in the event of overload.

Pressure switches

Most systems have switches in the low- and high-pressure lines that will break the circuit to the magnetic clutch at times when a given pressure is exceeded.

Idle-up control

The air-conditioning system places an extra load on the engine when the compressor is in operation. This would show up when the engine is slow running and would result in a change in speed, or possibly stalling, of the engine. To overcome this problem, an idle-up device is incorporated into the EMS to open the throttle slightly when the magnetic clutch engages the compressor.

Thermostatic switches

An extra switch is often fitted when more than one fan is used to cool the air-conditioning condenser and the engine and oil cooling radiators. For economy reasons, only one fan is in use during normal operation; the other fan is brought into use when the cooling load is high.

Cycling clutch orifice tube system

The cycling clutch orifice tube (CCOT) system (Figure 5.100) differs from the conventional air-conditioning system previously described. It has the orifice tube instead of a TVX unit and an accumulator, containing the desiccant and positioned in the low-pressure line, instead of a receiver-drier.

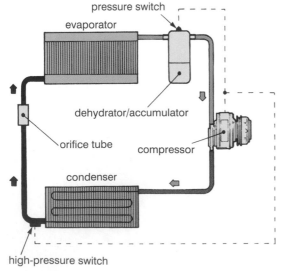

Figure 5.100 Layout of CCOT system

In this design, the flow of refrigerant through the expansion orifice into the evaporator is controlled by a cycling action of the compressor. Magnetic clutch operation for this action is governed by the signals received from two sensors: a pressure switch in the high-pressure line; and a thermostatic switch at the outlet of the evaporator.

5.12 Climate control system

5.12.1 Electronic control of the heating and air-conditioning system

Developments in electronic control have made it possible to use these devices to control the air temperature and quality to the desired needs of the cars occupants. As a result, many cars – particularly those in the luxury category – are now fitted with a sophisticated climate-control system.

Once the driver has selected a given temperature, the ECU automatically maintains that temperature by controlling the path taken by the ventilating air as it flows to the interior of the car. Under hot or humid ambient conditions, the air is cooled or dehumidified respectively by ducting it through an evaporator. At times when the ambient temperature is low, the air is heated.

The control system is sometimes called a heating, ventilation and air conditioning (HVAC) system. The systems fitted to modern vehicles incorporate many sensors and motorised blend flaps to monitor and recirculate the air around the vehicle to maintain the required temperature.

- Ambient air temperature sensor – this sensor monitors the outside air temperature to reference this against the interior temperature. The sensor is located in an area where it is not subjected to **ram air cooling** as the vehicle travels and where it is also away from any heat sink areas that will create false readings.
- Sun light sensor – this sensor monitors the light coming into the passenger area. If there is a great deal of sunlight entering the car, the HVAC system will increase the cooling towards the driver from the higher vents if the temperature rises, and if the driver wishes for warmer air, the system will divert the warmer air towards the lower vents (the system takes into account that the air higher up in the passenger area will be warmer due to heat from the sunlight).
- Interior temperature sensor – this sensor monitors the air temperature of the passenger area. In many cases, more than one sensor will be fitted to reference the rear of the passenger area

with the front and alter the cooling or heating accordingly between the two to maintain the correct overall requested temperature.

■ Pollution sensor – this sensor is situated in the intake area of the ventilation system. When the sensor notices an increase in pollution through vehicle emissions or other external pollutants, the blend motors will redirect the airflow to draw from inside the vehicle instead of drawing air from outside the vehicle. The system will then revert back to drawing air from outside the vehicle after about 10 minutes.

Ram air cooling: the movement of the vehicle is used to force air on to a surface to create cooling; this can be related to the radiator placed at the front of the vehicle, which receives air forced on to it through the forward motion of the vehicle.

Windows misting up on cold, wet and damp days are a constant problem to drivers. The cold glass condenses the moisture in the air in the car and a dangerous loss of visibility often results. A modern climate-control system, which is sometimes called an environmental-control system, overcomes the problem by passing the ventilating air through the evaporator to remove the excess moisture before heating it to the required temperature. This provides 'drier' air, which leads to very rapid demisting.

Filtering the air to remove traffic pollutants before it enters the interior is another feature of all modern climate-control systems. Most systems incorporate an item called a pollen filter. This filters out any particles entering the vehicle to provide cleaner air. This is a serviceable item and is usually replaced at main service intervals.

Figure 5.101 shows the layout of a full air-mix type of system suitable for automatic temperature control. The temperature and airflow pattern are controlled by three flap valves. Movement of the valves is achieved by using either electric motors or vacuum cylinders; the latter arrangement is controlled by small valves opened by electric solenoids or motors.

5.12.2 Control systems

For fascia layout and ease of operation, electrical switches are provided to enable the driver and passengers to select the required temperature and distribution of the air that enters the car interior. After the target temperature, which is often displayed in digital form, has been set by the driver or passenger (both sides of the car can be independently adjusted on most modern vehicles), the computer controls the heating and cooling sections of the system so that the air inside the car is kept at a temperature very close

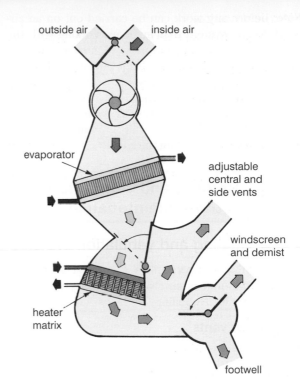

Figure 5.101 Full air-mix climate-control system

to the set value. The in-car temperature is constantly monitored by electrical sensors, and by signalling this information to the computer it is possible for the computer to make the necessary temperature adjustments.

Natural heating of the car is either by the direct rays of the sun or by the heat contained in the incoming air. Since the amount of heat entering the car governs the amount of cooling or heating required, sensors are fitted to measure this input.

Figure 5.102 shows the main items of an automatic electrical control system.

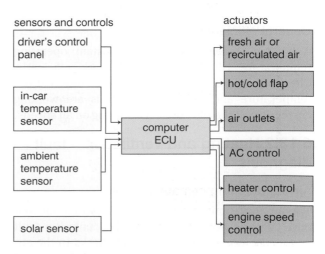

Figure 5.102 Climate-control system inputs and outputs

Note: before any work can be carried out on an air-conditioning system that involves working with the refrigerant, the technician must be qualified by law. This recent legislation has been put forward by the Department for Environment, Food and Rural Affairs (DEFRA). This regulation makes it illegal to recover or recharge any air-conditioning system unless the technician has achieved the minimum required qualifications in handling refrigerant.

5.13 Heating and ventilation – routine maintenance

5.13.1 Heating and ventilation systems

Drivers and passengers alike often adjust the heating and ventilation system to provide a comfortable environment for travelling.

External air vents

Air is forced around the car and enters through the specific vented grilles that direct the air to specific points in the ventilation system. It is vitally important that these points are kept clear and free from debris that could cause blockages.

Pollen filters

Pollen filters are fitted to virtually all cars nowadays to combat against pollution, bacteria and pollen entering the vehicle. These are replaced at regular intervals to stop any restriction of airflow through the vehicle's ventilation system.

Coolant hoses

Coolant passes through the hoses and into the heater matrix, which is usually situated behind the dashboard and is not easily accessible. Hoses should be checked for splits and perishing. Often, a leaking heater matrix can show telltale signs of leakage on the carpets around the footwell areas.

General efficiency

A heating system relies on a constant operating temperature of the engine to work efficiently. Checks should be made regularly to ensure that the temperature and directional controls are working correctly and the blower fan is working on all speeds.

5.13.2 Heating and ventilation – fault diagnosis

Air-conditioning climate control

The air-conditioning system is a closed circuit that once filled is not normally checked unless a fault occurs. However, some additional checks to the air-conditioning components can be carried out.

Filters and air vents

Pollen and particle filters are fitted and should be checked and replaced, and air vents checked for blockages. Blocked pollen filters will restrict the airflow entering the vehicle and possibly cause poor demisting and heating performance.

Compressor

The compressor is usually driven by the auxiliary belt, which should be checked for cracks, damage and correct tension, and the flexi refrigerant pipes should also be checked for damage and serviceability. The compressor clutch can wear over time, so engagement may not take place or it may slip as the drive is taken up by the auxiliary belt.

Condenser

The condenser is positioned at the front of the vehicle and acts like a radiator. It should be checked for damage, security and blockages from road debris such as leaves. A blocked airflow will cause the condenser to operate inefficiently. As the condenser's job is to cool the superheated refrigerant gas as it leaves the compressor, it may not carry this job out as well as it should if the airflow is restricted through the condenser. This would lower the air-conditioning efficiency levels.

Evaporator water drain

Moisture from the air removed by the air-conditioning system is passed out of the vehicle through a pipe under the car. Sometimes a musty smell can be detected after using the air conditioning. If this continues, a suitable disinfectant can be used to kill off any bacteria or microorganisms in the system. Blockages of the water pipe can lead to water building up inside the car. This can sometimes be incorrectly diagnosed as a water leak. Check the pipes leaving the evaporator housing to make sure they exit the vehicle correctly.

Refrigerant

The air-conditioning refrigerant contains a small amount of lubricating oil. This is added when the system is filled with refrigerant and lubricates the internal components, including the compressor. The air conditioning should be used occasionally, even in the winter, to allow the oil to circulate through the circuit and compressor.

General efficiency and servicing

Specialist equipment is used to check and recharge air-conditioning systems and this can only be carried out by a registered specialist. The system is checked by attaching an air-conditioning recharging station to the vehicle. This equipment can measure the pressures within the system to check the operation of the air-conditioning system. The recharging station is also used to evacuate the refrigerant if a repair has

Table 5.10 Heating and ventilation faults

Fault	Possible cause
Coolant leaking from the heater matrix assembly	Possible heater matrix leak or split hose/bad connection
Low air pressure flowing through the heater assembly	Pollen filter blocked or restriction at the intake area
Malfunctioning ventilation fan	Ventilation fan faulty, blown supply fuse or fault on fan circuit
Ventilation fan operates at maximum speed only	Ventilation fan variable resistor pack faulty
Heater only able to produce cool air	Ventilation flaps not moving to required position, engine running temperature too low caused by faulty thermostat, heater coolant input valve seized
Heater only able to produce hot air	Ventilation flaps stuck in hot air position, heater coolant input valve seized in hot position
Unable to alter air distribution through heater assembly	Heater distribution flaps set incorrectly or adjustment mechanism faulty

to take place involving the removal any of the air-conditioning components. The system can then be recharged to the correct capacity after the repair has taken place.

Note: it is now illegal for a technician without formal qualifications to handle refrigerant. All technicians are now required to meet this minimum level of competence before working on the air-conditioning system.

5.14 Passenger safety and restraint systems

5.14.1 Primary restraint using seat belts

The three-point seat belt is considered to be the most important safety feature in a vehicle. When looking at the front seat belt application (and in many cases the rear), the belt has three anchor points mounted into the vehicle body. The anchor points are each side of the seat and above the passenger shoulder (on the B pillar in the front seat and C pillar in the rear seats). The mounting point at the side of the passenger, towards the centre of the vehicle, has a buckle arrangement that securely connects the strap passing over the passenger's lap. This buckle allows quick connection and disconnection of the seat belt for the passenger. The buckle also creates the third point of anchorage of the seat belt by creating the triangle across the lap and then across the chest to the B or C pillar. This creates a very secure harness arrangement for the driver and passengers.

Pioneered in 1959 by Volvo, the three-point seat belt was allowed by Volvo to be fitted to all vehicles. Originally, manual three-point seat belts were used

that could be adjusted to fit individual passengers, but these were replaced by inertia reel (automatic) seat belts that are self-adjusting and lock into position if sudden forces or movements are felt. It became compulsory to wear a seat belt in the UK in 1983 and all manufacturers had to fit seat belts to all seats. The centre rear seat was originally a lap belt before manufacturers started fitting inertia seat belts into the backrests, adding great stresses to the stability of the backrest.

The seat belt anchorage or lock points are usually mounted on the side of the front seats to allow for forward/backward adjustment of the seating position.

Seat belts are required to be checked every year during an MOT test and must comply with strict safety regulations:

- Webbing must be checked for rips/tears in the material.
- Stitching at anchorage points must be checked for damage.
- Attachment fittings must be checked (catch).
- Stalks must be examined for corrosion or weakness (i.e. wiggling stalk to check for clicking noises indicating broken strands of cable).
- Fasten belts and check locking devices also under load.
- Check that each seat that requires a belt has one.

5.14.2 Supplemental restraint systems

In addition to the primary restraint system, other features have been added to protect the driver and passengers. These are known as supplemental restraint systems (SRS) and include items such as safety cages, head restraints, collapsible steering columns, airbags and side curtains.

The SRS is designed to protect the occupants during an accident and will operate depending on the type of accident, whether it is a frontal, side or rear impact.

Airbags

The purpose of the airbag is to protect the driver's or passenger's head from coming into contact with the dashboard, windscreen or steering wheel in an accident. The airbags are only deployed during a head-on or frontal collision and do not go off if the vehicle is hit from the side or rear. There are generally two stages to airbag deployment in modern systems; both stages will always occur but there is a longer time difference between deployment and the full bag state in the event of a minor incident, giving a softer bag. A more severe impact creates a 'harder' bag with shorter time between the two stages. The stages involve the use of two **initiators** and two charges of gas-generating material. The initiator device starts the airbag deployment; when this is detonated by the airbag control module through a high-voltage signal, the initiator ignites the gas-generating material, which can include a substance called sodium azide. This substance has gradually been phased out in pursuit of a less toxic material since the late 1990s.

Initiator: the device that starts the detonation of the airbag module.

When the vehicle is involved in a minor incident the airbag system will deploy one initiator and gas-generating material to provide a softer airbag. If the vehicle is involved in a more severe incident both initiators and gas charges will be deployed, providing a more substantial airbag capable of protecting the driver or passenger in higher speed impacts.

Driver and passenger airbags

The driver's airbag is located in the centre of the steering wheel and the passenger airbag in the dashboard. It is important that nothing is placed over either airbag at any time or correct operation could be jeopardised and the passenger or driver may be injured on airbag deployment.

Figure 5.104 Airbag showing the tear lines after deployment

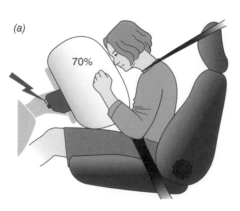

Figure 5.103 Dual-stage airbag

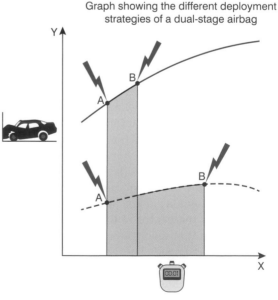

Graph showing the different deployment strategies of a dual-stage airbag

X = time to deploy airbag
Y = severity of impact
A = start of deployment
B = end of deployment

Airbags are designed to rip through the cover of the dashboard area or steering wheel when activated. This is aided by tear lines manufactured into the dashboard and steering wheel material. As the airbag inflates, these tear lines allow the bag to break through the dashboard and steering wheel material, leading to more efficient deployment. On most vehicles, the passenger side airbag can be switched off allowing the safe fitment of a child seat. Under no circumstances should a child seat be fitted to a car with the passenger airbag connected.

Side airbags (SIPS – side inflatable protection system)

The side airbags are fitted into the side of the front seats, and when deployed through a side impact they rip through the vehicle's specially designed seat cover. They are designed to inflate very quickly due to the small space and are usually inflated by a small nitrogen gas canister triggered by a pyrotechnic charge.

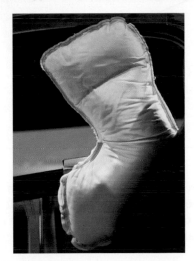

Figure 5.105 Side airbag

Curtain airbags (IC – inflatable curtain)

Curtain airbags are fitted in the roof along the side windows and protect front and rear passengers in the event of a sideways impact. They are deployed at the same time as the side airbags and are designed to deflate slowly to provide protection from head injuries and prevent flailing arms and legs in the event of an accident, until the vehicle has become stationary.

Figure 5.106 Curtain airbag

Rollover bars

These devices are fitted to convertible and soft-top vehicles. The rollover bars operate when the vehicle rollover sensor senses the pitch angle of the car is excessive and triggers the deployment actuators to operate the rollover bars. These bars will extend to a height that will lift the car off the ground sufficiently to prevent the occupants being more seriously injured if the car lands upside down. Side curtains and pre-tensioner seat belts will also activate on these types of vehicles.

Figure 5.107 Rollover bars

Seat belt pre-tensioners

Seat belt pre-tensioners work in conjunction with the airbags to hold occupants in position if an accident occurs. If the SRS ECU detects a collision, it will deploy the airbags along with deploying the seat belt pre-tensioners by triggering the pyrotechnic charge. This action provides a tightening of the seat belt around the occupant, holding them back into the seat to prevent forward movement and contact with the dashboard or steering wheel. This initial tightening of the seat belt happens before the airbag is fully inflated and releases itself so the airbag absorbs the final movement of the occupant in a controlled manner before deflating. A pre-tensioner is designed to operate only once and should always be replaced after activation. Checking whether or not the seat belt pre-tensioners have been deployed requires the following actions:

1 Pull out the belt to its full length and release.
2 Repeat this action a number of times. The belt should roll in and out as normal.

If the belt sticks, jerks or does not roll up properly, this could indicate that the pre-tensioner has deployed and will require further investigation.

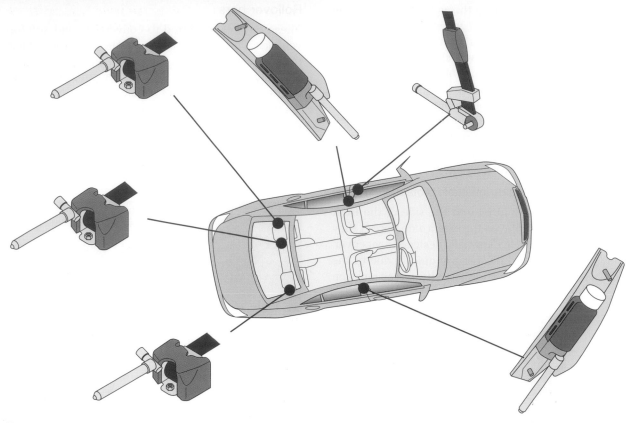

Figure 5.108 Seat belt pre-tensioners

Whips (whiplash protection system) and head restraints

Another area covered under SRS is whiplash protection, or 'whips' as it is commonly known, which works in conjunction with head restraints. In a rear collision, a person's head is thrown back in a whiplash action. This can also happen when a person's head is thrown forward in a frontal collision. The risk of severe head injury is greater on vehicles not equipped with head restraints. For the best protection, the headrest must be as close to the head as possible, as well as being adjusted so the middle of the restraint is at the passenger's eye level. Head restraints must then be locked into position to prevent movement in an accident. Whips is incorporated into the front seat adjuster mechanism and operates when the seat occupant's upper torso is pushed into the seat. This causes the backrest to move backwards, cradling the occupant's head and spine, reducing the possibility of whiplash or spinal injuries. Once activated, whips should be replaced.

Deployment sequence of airbags and pre-tensioner seat belts

The deployment of the SRS system during an accident happens very quickly, as you might expect.

To capture the event, Figure 5.109 shows the WIPS system sequence. Figure 5.110 shows the deployment sequence of the airbags. The following text highlights the general times taken to complete each cycle.

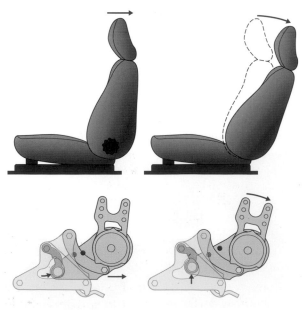

Figure 5.109 Whiplash protection system

Figure 5.110 Deployment of airbags and pre-tensioner seat belts

1 As the vehicle approaches impact, the driver will normally be braking hard and would be initially restrained by the action of the three-point seat belt. This would provide the initial driver and passenger protection.
2 At approximately 15 milliseconds (15 thousandths of a second) after impact, the rapid deceleration of the vehicle is detected by the SRS. The airbag system is therefore triggered, which progressively inflates the airbag using gas under pressure. At this point, the driver will remain in a relatively upright position because of the action of the seat belt pre-tensioning system, which tightens the belt by approximately 10 cm on initial impact.
3 At approximately 30 to 40 milliseconds after impact, the airbag will be fully inflated. The full force of the impact will cause the driver to be thrown forward. The driver's head and chest will make contact with the airbag, which is designed to then progressively deflate, thus cushioning the impact of the driver's body.
4 The passenger or driver returns to their seating position and the airbags have now fully deflated.

Pedestrian protection system

For many years vehicle manufacturers have focused their efforts in designing cars to protect the occupants when the vehicle is involved in an accident. In today's vehicles we now see some of the most advanced safety systems available, which has helped to reduce the number of fatalities on our roads.

A key development is the introduction of pedestrian protection systems. Some manufacturers have started to install electronic systems that help reduce impact damage to the human body if a pedestrian walks out in front of an oncoming car.

This is an area that is not heavily publicised but every manufacturer has to meet very strict governing standards when designing a new vehicle model, not only to high crash standards but also to protect pedestrians. Making the vehicle more aerodynamic and using lighter and more durable materials goes a long way to reduce the impact damage to a human body. In recent years, electronic impact sensing systems have been introduced that activate specially positioned airbags to change the bonnet position and bumpers to absorb a greater amount of the physical impact.

Figure 5.111 shows a vehicle in collision with a pedestrian.

Figure 5.111 Vehicle collision with a pedestrian

The pedestrian protection system works independently from the vehicle supplemental restraints system, but is designed to activate on impact just as fast as some of the driving compartments airbags in a collision situation. Controlled by an ECU and utilising input signals from specially designed movement sensors, the system to designed to operate at 12–28 mph and is disabled when the vehicle is travelling above this parameter. When an impact condition is registered, the system is able to determine if contact has been made with a pedestrian or another object, such as a traffic cone or another vehicle. This is done by the movement sensors located within the front bumper assembly and a number of other input signals from other electronic systems that monitor the vehicle's deceleration or stability movement and the driver's reactions to the situation occurring.

Research found that making the front end of the vehicle more aerodynamic helped reduce lower leg and pelvic injuries. Also a large number of head injuries occurred because the pedestrian was thrown onto the vehicle's bonnet, which is potentially a solid mass as the engine is only millimetres below. Researchers identified that raising the bonnet on impact would reduce some head injuries. Figure 5.112 shows the pedestrian's direction of impact as they hit the front of the vehicle.

Vehicle designers had to incorporate bonnet hinges or latches to mechanically unlock from their locations if the system was deployed. This design feature depended on which way the bonnet opened – from the front-hinged variant to the more common rear-hinged, opening from the from grill area.

With front-hinged bonnets that open from the rear of the bonnet, the activation of opening the bonnet latches is controlled by the pedestrian control module. Because the bonnet's upward movement would be its normal direction, the design and control is much simpler.

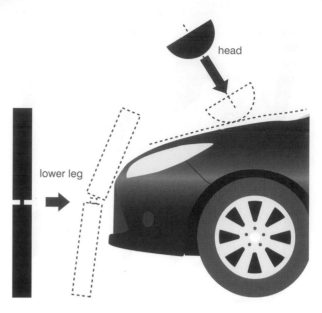

Figure 5.112 Direction of impact of a pedestrian hitting the front of a vehicle

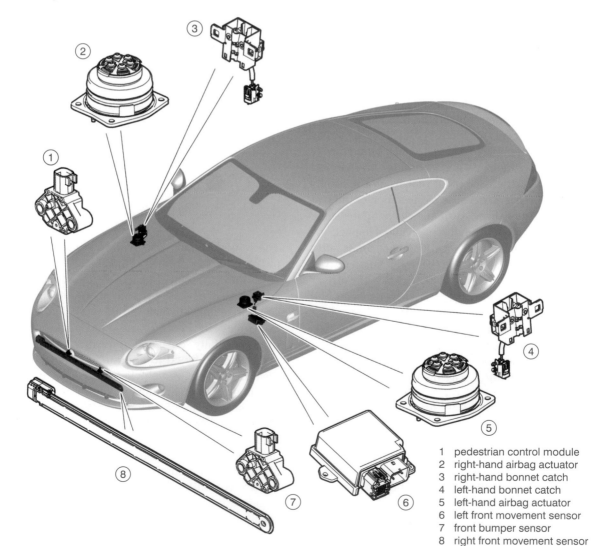

1	pedestrian control module
2	right-hand airbag actuator
3	right-hand bonnet catch
4	left-hand bonnet catch
5	left-hand airbag actuator
6	left front movement sensor
7	front bumper sensor
8	right front movement sensor

Figure 5.113 Vehicle with front-hinged bonnet showing pedestrian protection components

The two specially designed activation airbags are located near to the vehicle's bulkhead area and are mounted on to strengthen inner chassis framework. Deployment is controlled by the control module and its input signals from the two sensors. On activation of the system, the two airbags are deployed within 20 ms (milliseconds) of the impact. The airbag deployment time takes around 30 ms to force the bonnet to raise approximately 170 mm. Research has found that it takes a total of 55 ms before the pedestrian's head impacts onto the bonnet in a frontal collision. Programming and controlling this system to operate within a 50 ms time frame, gives a 5 ms window, which helps reduce the impact forces to the pedestrian by about 10 per cent. This could be the difference that means a pedestrian survives a critical head injury.

Warning light

The SRS system contains a warning light to alert the driver to any faults occurring in the system. When the ignition is turned on, the warning light shows for 10–15 seconds and then goes out. If the light stays on, there is a problem within the system and the SRS will not work until the problem is fixed. The system has an inbuilt fault code system and requires connecting to a diagnostic computer in order to establish the cause of the fault. This should only be carried out by an authorised repairer.

Figure 5.114 SRS warning light

Safety precautions in vehicle

- Once deployed, all SRS systems require replacing.
- **Always** fit genuine manufacturers' new parts when replacing components.
- **Always** refer to the relevant technical data before working on any SRS.
- **Remove** the ignition key and disconnect both battery terminals (earth first) and allow 10 minutes for the ECU back-up power units to discharge before commencing any work on the SRS.
- **Do not** probe SRS components with a test light or multimeter, unless following an approved diagnostic routine.
- **Always** use correct diagnostic equipment.
- **Avoid** working in line with the airbags when disconnecting or connecting them.
- When reconnecting the battery, ensure no one is in the vehicle.

Handling

- **Always** carry airbag modules with the cover facing upwards.
- **Do not** drop SRS components.
- **Do not** carry airbags or pre-tensioners by their wires.
- **Do not** tamper with, dismantle or attempt to repair or cut any SRS components.
- **Do not** immerse SRS components in fluid.
- **Do not** attach anything to the airbag module cover.

Storage

- **Always** keep SRS components dry.
- **Always** store airbag modules with the cover facing upwards.
- **Do not** allow anything to rest on the airbag module.
- **Always** store the airbag module on a flat secure surface and away from electrical equipment or sources of high temperature.
- **Always** place the airbag module or pre-tensioner in the designated storage area.

Warning notice: airbag modules and pyrotechnic seat belt pre-tensioners are classed as explosive articles and must be stored in an approved, secure steel cabinet that is registered with the local authority.

CHAPTER 6 Bearings

6.1 Bearings

6.1.1 Introduction

Throughout the motor vehicle there is a need for components to rotate freely, be supported and handle large amounts of stress for extended periods without creating wear or heat. This requirement is catered for by the various types of **bearings** located in components throughout the different systems of the motor vehicle. Bearings come in many forms but each type plays a specific role in ensuring that units and components can operate efficiently. This chapter deals with these different types of bearing and looks at the design features required to handle specific needs.

Bearing: part of a mechanism or engine that supports and guides a moving part and withstands (bears) friction.

6.2 Plain bearings

By far, the most common type of bearing is that used to support a rotating shaft. Plain bearings are those in which the moving surfaces are in sliding contact with one another, apart from a film of lubricant. Nearly all engine bearings are of this type.

6.2.1 Bushes

The simplest type of bearing consists of a plain hole in the supporting component in which the shaft rotates. In order to provide a suitable combination of materials to minimise friction and wear, and to provide a simple and inexpensive way of repairing a worn or damaged bearing, a sleeve – called a bush – is fitted in the hole. Bushes are usually made using an **interference fit** in the hole of the component so that all movement and wear takes place between the bore of the bush and the shaft.

Interference fit: a fit between two components where the external dimension of one part is slightly greater than the internal dimension of the part it fits into.

There is, however, a type of bush that has a clearance fit in its housing as well as on the shaft. When correctly fitted, this bush rotates at about half the speed of the shaft, thus reducing the rubbing speed of the surfaces. This type is not often used, as there is too much free play for today's suspension systems.

Figure 6.1 shows three types of bush:

- Type (a) is a plain bush and is used to support a shaft where only radial loads (i.e. loads acting at right angles to the shaft) are carried.
- Type (b) is a flanged-blind bush. It has a flange at one end, which, in conjunction with a collar or shoulder on the shaft, will resist an end force (or axial load) on the shaft in one direction. It also has one end closed or blind, to prevent lubricant escaping or dirt getting in.
- Type (c) shows a wrapped bush. This is a popular and inexpensive type of bush made from a metal strip bent into a cylindrical shape.

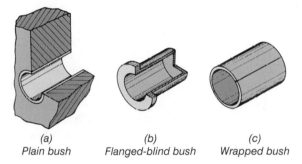

| (a) | (b) | (c) |
| Plain bush | Flanged-blind bush | Wrapped bush |

Figure 6.1 Types of bearing

6.2.2 Split bearings

A bush can only be used when the part of the shaft that runs in it can be inserted from one end. If the shaft is of such a shape that this is not possible, for instance an engine crankshaft, the bearing must be split as illustrated in Figure 6.2. The two halves of the bearing are held together by bolts, screws or studs and nuts. In this case, the equivalent of the bush is known as a pair of bearing shells, or half bearings.

The lower part (4) is the housing in which the bottom shell (3) is fitted. The top shell (2) fits in the cap (1). As in the case of a bush, the shells are prevented from turning in the housing by an interference fit. When a shell is pressed down into its housing, its edges should stand slightly proud of the housing faces, and similarly for the shell fitted in the cap. If the cap is now fitted in place and the two nuts screwed

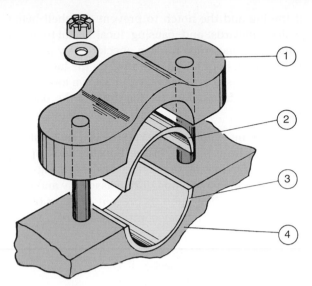

Figure 6.2 Split bearing with detachable shells

down finger-tight, there will be a small clearance between the faces of the cap and housing, although the edges of the shells are touching, as shown (much exaggerated) in Figure 6.3. The gap or nip is actually only a few hundredths of a millimetre, the exact amount depending upon the size of the bearing and the materials of which the housing and cap are made. When the nuts are correctly tightened down, the nip disappears and the shells are tightly held.

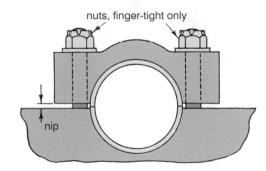

Figure 6.3 Bearing nip (greatly exaggerated)

Location devices

Location devices are provided to ensure correct positioning of the shells during assembly. Two common types are illustrated in Figure 6.4. A dowel (a) is a short peg, one end of which is made a tight fit in a hole in the housing, the other (protruding) end being a clearance fit in a hole in the shell.

Lugs (b) are pressed out at one joint face of each shell and engage with corresponding notches cut in the housing and cap. One lug per shell is used, and the lugs of both shells of a pair are normally arranged at opposite ends of the same joint face (c). It is most important that there is a clearance between the back of the lug and the notch to prevent the shell being pushed inwards and causing local metal-to-metal contact at this point. You can check this by pushing down on the joint face of the shell on the lug side. It should be possible to move it about 1 mm lower than the housing face before the lug touches the back of the notch.

It should be emphasised that the shells must be prevented from moving in the housing and cap by their interference fit alone. The dowels or lugs are purely for correct location during assembly and they must not be relied upon to prevent rotation of the shells, although they may contribute to it.

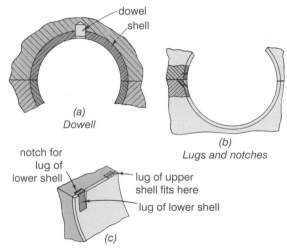

Figure 6.4 Methods of locating shells

Oil holes and grooves

In most bearings, the oil for lubrication is supplied via a hole drilled through the housing, and there must be a corresponding hole in one of the shells. This hole should be placed at the part of the bearing where radial load is least, which is usually the centre of the upper shell. From this hole, oil is carried around by shaft rotation, and pressure causes the oil to spread towards the ends of the bearing. Oil grooves are unnecessary in most pressure-fed bearings and are undesirable in the areas supporting heavy loads, since not only do they reduce the surface area of the bearing but they also let the oil escape easily from the region where it is most important to retain it.

Certain bearings, such as the big-end bearing, are carried on moving parts and cannot conveniently be supplied with oil directly and independently. In such cases, the oil is supplied through a drilling in the shaft, and therefore there is no need for an oil supply hole in the shells. To ensure a continuous supply of oil to the big-ends, a circumferential groove is formed around the main bearing shells into which the oil is fed from the main oil gallery (Figure 6.5). The main

journal end of the hole through the crankshaft runs around this groove, so that the big-end is in constant communication with the main oil gallery. The width and depth of this groove around the main bearing shells should be no more than is necessary to carry enough oil to the big-ends.

Figure 6.5 Bearing shell with transfer channel

6.2.3 Bearing materials

Shafts are almost invariably made of steel or iron, and the surface of the bearing should make a satisfactory combination with the shaft. Some materials used for the housing may be suitable in this respect: for instance both cast iron and aluminium are quite satisfactory for many conditions of operation and could be used without bushes or shells. However, for operation at high speeds, heavy loads or both, some other material is generally preferred. A few are mentioned below.

Bronze

Bronzes are primarily alloys of copper and tin, the exact properties depending upon the proportions and also upon what other elements, if any, are included. A type commonly used contains a small amount of phosphorus and is known as phosphor-bronze.

Bronzes are fairly hard – though softer than steel – and have good load-carrying capacity, but are less suited than some other materials to high rubbing speeds. In cases where the supply of lubricant is difficult, then the plain bearing could be either pre-lubricated or self-lubricated.

Pre-lubricated

Powdered lead bronze can be compressed into a mould and heated to partially fuse the metal particles together; this process is called sintering. The porous structure that results has the ability to absorb and retain a lubricant, which is applied either by soaking the bearing before fitting, or by occasional re-oiling.

Some bushes are made with the bronze sintered to a steel backing and coated with a layer of acetal resin polymer. This surface gives a good bearing performance even when there is only a trace of lubricant. The bearing surface is often indented to give pockets to hold the oil or grease.

Self-lubricated

As the name suggests, this bearing is intended to operate in a dry state. One type in common use is made up of three layers – a steel backing, a sintered bronze interlayer and a coating (called an overlay) of lead mixed with PTFE (polytetrafluoroethylene). This synthetic **polymer** has an exceptionally low frictional resistance and complete immunity to most solvents, including water, so it has many applications for rubbing surfaces on a vehicle.

Polymer: a long-chain chemical compound.

White metal, or Babbitt alloys

First introduced by Babbitt over a century ago, this is an alloy of tin and small amounts of copper and **antimony**. It has very good anti-friction properties and, when used with a comparatively hard shaft, the soft material allows abrasive particles to embed below the surface and so reduce wear.

Softness is good for 'embeddability', but is bad when heavy loads have to be carried. Repeated heavy loads cause **fatigue**, so in order to reduce this problem the thin-wall bearing is used. This type has a steel liner, about 2 mm thick, coated with a thin layer of about 0.1 mm of bearing metal. White metal was used for a number of years for main and big-end bearings, but the large inertia load associated with modern engines is too great for this material. Nowadays, white metal is used for camshaft bearings and thrust washers.

Antimony: a metal element commonly used in alloys.

Fatigue: weakening, break-up or flaking of a metal due to various stresses and strains.

An ideal material for big-end and main bearings should have the following properties:

1 High mechanical strength – to withstand heavy loads and resist fatigue
2 High melting point – to resist damage due to high oil temperature
3 Resistance to corrosion
4 Conformability – the ability to yield easily when slight misalignment occurs
5 Good surface properties – to prevent seizure or pick-up if the oil film breaks down momentarily (this property is also called 'compatibility')

In practice, no material meets the ideal requirements of all of these properties, so the alloy selected must match the properties that are special to the engine type, for example a compression-ignition engine requires a material of high strength, whereas in a spark-ignition engine the material has to withstand high oil temperatures (over 120 °C), extremely thin oil films and high rubbing speeds.

Aluminium-based alloys

A popular alloy used for car crankshaft and big-end bearings is 20 per cent tin-aluminium where the material consists of 20 per cent tin and 80 per cent aluminium. This material, formed in a thin-wall bearing, combines high fatigue strength with good surface properties and can be used without an overlay. When bonded together, the tin and aluminium form a network structure, so this material is sometimes called reticular tin-aluminium.

Where higher loadings prevail, either 6 per cent tin-aluminium or up to 11 per cent aluminium-silicon alloys may be used. The former has a high fatigue strength and the latter even higher with improved resistance to wear and load, but both materials require an overlay to improve compatibility and conformability.

Copper-lead and lead-bronze

These alloys have exceptionally high fatigue strength and are used for heavily loaded bearings. Being harder and less able to embed abrasive particles, they generally require a harder shaft.

The materials have poor corrosion resistance: the lead is dissolved by acidic oil and this destroys the boundary and wear-resisting properties. To overcome this problem, a very thin overlay (0.013–0.038 mm) of lead-tin or lead-indium is used. This overlay is soft, so embeddability and conformability are also improved.

The life of these bearings is linked to the time it takes for abrasive particles in the oil to cut away the overlay. When the overlay is worn off, the wear is extremely rapid, so attention to oil filtration is essential.

6.2.4 Thrust washers

Shafts usually need to be located endways, usually against a certain amount of end thrust. Bushes may be flanged (Figure 6.1a) in conjunction with shoulders or collars on the shaft, and shells may be flanged in a similar manner. In the case of wrapped bushes and thin-wall shells, it is more usual to use separate thrust washers or half-washers. These have steel backs (faced with white metal, copper-lead or lead-bronze) and are located in a recess in the bearing housing (Figure 6.6).

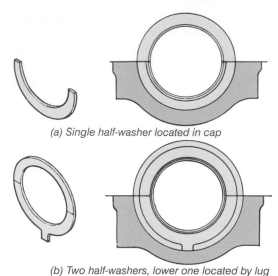

(a) Single half-washer located in cap

(b) Two half-washers, lower one located by lug

Figure 6.6 *Thrust washers*

In many cases only one half-washer is used, and it is prevented from rotating by letting its ends abut the un-recessed edge of the housing half that does not have a half-washer. When a pair of half-washers is used, one has a lug that engages a notch in the housing to prevent rotation.

Shafts are usually located endways by one bearing only, thrust washers being fitted at both ends of this bearing but omitted from all others.

6.3   Ball and roller bearings

In this class of bearing, rolling motion is substituted for sliding by interposing rolling elements between the shaft and its housing. In this way friction is reduced, especially when the speed of rotation is low and no continuous supply of oil under pressure is available.

A complete bearing consists of four components:

1 An inner race, which is fixed on the shaft. (In a few cases, the shaft itself may form the inner race if it is made of suitable material, but replacement may then be more costly when excessively worn.)
2 An outer race, which is fixed in the housing. (As with the inner race, this may sometimes be formed by the housing itself.)
3 A suitable number of balls or rollers.
4 A cage to prevent adjacent balls or rollers from rubbing against one another.

The races and balls or rollers are made from special quality steel, suitably hardened. There may be slight variations in the composition and heat treatment of the steel between different manufacturers and for different types of bearing. Cages may be made of bronze, aluminium or mild steel.

There are four main types of bearing, classified by the shape of the rolling elements as:

- ball
- cylindrical roller
- spherical roller
- taper roller.

6.3.1 Ball bearings

Figure 6.7 shows cross-sections of three examples of ball bearing:

1 Single-row bearing with the balls running in grooves in the races. This type is intended for carrying mainly radial loads, but can also support some axial load in both directions. Double-row bearings of this type are also made and are capable of carrying heavier loads.
2 Self-aligning bearing. The inner race has two ball tracks and both rows of balls run in an outer race whose inner surface forms a section of a sphere having its centre at the shaft centre. This allows the shaft axis to run at a small angle to the axis of the housing. Bearings of this type are used for applications where precise alignment of shaft and housing cannot be maintained.
3 Angular contact ball bearing. This is capable of taking axial loads comparable with the radial loads, but in one direction only. Bearings of this type are generally used in pairs, one at each end of a shaft, and care must be taken when fitting the bearings to ensure that they are placed the correct way round.

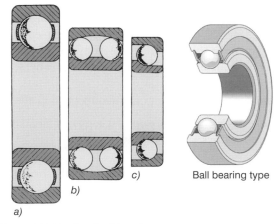

a)   *b)*   *c)*   Ball bearing type

Figure 6.7 *Types of ball bearing*

6.3.2 Cylindrical roller bearings

An example of a cylindrical roller bearing is shown in Figure 6.8. These are capable of carrying greater radial loads than ball bearings, but no axial load. The guiding flanges may be either on the inner or outer races.

Where heavy radial loads have to be carried at low speeds, or where the motion is of an intermittent or oscillating nature, long rollers of small diameter – called needle rollers – may be used.

Figure 6.8 Cylindrical roller bearing

6.3.3 Spherical roller bearings

As shown in Figure 6.9, this is the roller bearing equivalent of the self-aligning ball bearing. It is constructed on similar principles and used for similar applications, but is capable of carrying greater loads.

Figure 6.9 Spherical roller bearing

6.3.4 Taper roller bearings

An example of this important and useful type is shown in Figure 6.10. The working surfaces of both races and rollers are conical, the taper being such that the cones, of which races and rollers form a part, each have their apex at a common point on the axis of the shaft.

Taper roller bearings are always used in pairs facing opposite ways, and are capable of dealing with considerable axial loads as well as radial loads. Different taper angles may be used, depending upon the amount of axial load to be carried. They are provided with some means of axial adjustment to control the amount of end play or preload allowed.

A single-row bearing (as illustrated) can only deal with thrust in one direction (hence the need for using two), but double-row types, each row having its taper facing opposite ways, are also made and are capable of taking thrust in both directions.

Figure 6.10 Taper roller bearing

6.3.5 Fitting bearings

Cleanliness is vitally important. Do not un-wrap new bearings from their packages until the last possible moment. Bearings are coated with preservative by the manufacturer and this need not be removed.

In most cases, the races are an interference fit both in housings and on shafts. The best way to fit the bearings is by pushing them into place with a press, using a mild steel **tubular drift** of correct diameter for each race. Under no circumstances should pressure be applied to one race in order to press the other into place (i.e. the pressure must be applied directly to the race being fitted). Where a press is not available, strike the drifts carefully with a suitable hammer.

Tubular drift: a device used to insert components into an interference fit housing. The drift is usually made from a softer metal than the component to avoid damage.

6.3.6 Removing bearings

Unless the bearing is to be scrapped, the same care must be exercised in removing the bearing as in fitting it. Using a suitable extractor, drift, and press or hammer, force must be applied directly to the race being removed. In many cases, special extractors are available for this purpose.

6.3.7 Bearing adjustment

Where adjustment is provided it may be made by nuts, threaded rings or by distance pieces and **shims**. For many applications, the ideal adjustment is that there should be no end-float and no preload (or over tightening). For certain applications, however, such as rear-axle pinion shafts, correct meshing of the gears demands complete elimination of play, and the bearings are generally preloaded (i.e. they are tightened slightly beyond the point of elimination of play). Specific instructions are given in workshop manuals on this point. Figure 6.11 shows a technician checking for free play in a wheel bearing. Wheel bearings may or may not require preloading, so it is important to find out before trying to take any free movement out of the bearing to avoid damage.

Shim: a thin piece of material, usually metal in automotive applications, used to fill a gap, make a component level or improve the fit of one component with another.

Figure 6.11 Checking wheel bearing adjustment

6.3.8 Lubrication

Bearings are lubricated with oil or grease depending upon the component into which they are fitted. In engines, gearboxes and final-drive gears, oil is used and the design ensures a constant supply to each bearing. In other parts of the vehicle, such as wheel hubs, bearings are grease-lubricated by packing the bearings and the inside of the hub cavity with a suitable grease. Details as to the type of grease to be used and the amount to be put into the housing are given in the service manual for the vehicle. It is very important to use the correct grade of oil or grease, as premature wear or failure may occur if this is incorrect.

Figure 6.12 Oil and grease used to lubricated bearings

7

New vehicle technology and alternative fuels

7.1   Introduction to electric, hybrid and alternative fuels

Increasingly stringent environmental standards and the desire to have less dependency on fossil fuels has stimulated research and development in other areas of fuel technology, the aim being to ensure that we are able to sustain the personal transport needs of present and future customers. A variety of options are currently available to us, which vary in their ability to provide economic forms of transport and to compete with conventionally fuelled production vehicles.

Put simply, alternative fuels need to be able to propel vehicles at speeds we have become accustomed to at costs that are better, or at least no worse, than conventional fuels, and ideally at a reduced

Figure 7.1 Badges of hybrid vehicles

environmental cost. There are five main categories of alternative fuel currently commercially available:

- Liquid petroleum gas
- Electric
- Hybrid – series and parallel
- Fuel-cell

Each type uses a different method of generating power that allows the vehicle to operate in a flexible and convenient manner, without consuming the same levels of fossil fuels as a conventional vehicle.

7.2 Liquid petroleum gas

7.2.1 What is liquid petroleum gas?

Liquid petroleum gas (LPG) is produced during the normal **refining** of crude oil. It is 100 per cent octane (by comparison, four-star petrol is 95–98 per cent and unleaded petrol is 97 per cent). LPG is stored under pressure as a liquid, as this is 250 times denser than as a gas so it needs less space to be stored in the car. Several car manufacturers, including Renault, Citroën and Vauxhall, supply LPG cars direct from the dealership as part of their range. Some other manufacturers without actual LPG vehicles as part of their range will allow conversions to be carried out after manufacture. Cars that run on LPG usually also run on petrol or diesel as well. These types of vehicles are usually referred to as 'dual fuel'.

Refining: the industrial process of distilling crude oil into a series of products including diesel, petroleum, paraffin, LPG and other components that can be used in the production of lubricants, plastics, detergents, solvents and fibres.

7.2.2 How does LPG work?

As described earlier in Chapter 2 on page 29, the internal-combustion engine requires fuel to be ignited to create combustion, which then leads to an expansion of gases that force the piston down the cylinders to create the turning motion of the crankshaft. This rotational movement of the crankshaft provides input torque to the gearbox and then to the vehicle's wheels to provide forward motion of the vehicle.

The internal-combustion engine has fuel either injected into the intake manifold or directly into the engine combustion chamber within the cylinder head. The injectors are normally controlled electronically and consist of solenoid-operated valves with very finely manufactured needles, which open and close to allow the exact amount of fuel the engine requires into the combustion chamber to create power. This amount of fuel and air has to be very carefully metered to ensure that the engine operates efficiently. There is obviously little benefit in injecting too much fuel into an engine if it is not able to burn it completely with the given amount of oxygen, as this will produce more emissions and create an engine that is uneconomical. Figure 7.2 shows the normal process for combustion to take place. The best air/fuel ratio to create the most efficient combustion in a petrol engine is about 14.7 : 1 – this is 14.7 parts of air to 1 part of fuel.

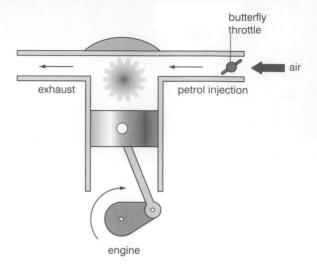

Figure 7.2 The normal process for fuel and air to be mixed for combustion

Cars fitted with fuel injection today also have catalytic converters to lower the harmful emissions produced. Additionally, they have sensors fitted to the exhaust system before and after the catalytic converter to monitor the oxygen content in the exhaust gases – these are often called lambda sensors. These sensors are covered in more detail on page 223. Vehicles fitted with these sensors operate something called a 'closed-loop' engine management system (EMS). 'Closed loop' essentially means that the EMS is able to self-monitor to constantly check the emissions coming out of the engine, check the emission content and then make adjustments if required to ensure that the engine is running efficiently. This loop continues hundreds of times a second.

LPG systems perform two functions:

1 They can switch the engine fuelling from petrol to LPG or LPG to petrol while the engine is running.
2 They can provide the correct ratio of gas at any given engine speed or load to create efficient combustion. This means that the right amount of LPG is injected into the engine's airstream to ensure that all of the fuel is burnt in the available oxygen preventing any unwanted exhaust emissions.

When fitting the LPG system to vehicles as an aftermarket conversion, a 'mixer' is fitted to the intake system just before the throttle valve. The mixer is a tube that allows air to flow through it, and has a specifically designed tapered internal profile. The air enters the mixer at a point where the diameter is at a medium size; as the air continues to flow through the mixer the diameter widens to a maximum point. Due to the air having momentum as it passes through the mixer, it will create a depression or partial vacuum as it reaches the widening point. The depression is directly proportional to the airflow rate as it passes through the mixer. The LPG system uses this depression as the sensing point to introduce the correct amount of gas to the airstream.

At the point where the mixer widens and a depression is created, the mixer has an arrangement of small holes around the internal circumference of the mixer tube. These holes pick up the depression and pass it along a pipe to the vaporiser. Within the vaporiser, there is a large diaphragm that reacts to the pressure differences acting upon it. The depression created in the mixer is sensed on this diaphragm. As the diaphragm is subjected to the depression, it is pulled due to the atmospheric pressure on the reverse side of the diaphragm. The diaphragm is linked to a progression valve that also moves. The movement of the progression valve then allows more or less LPG into the airstream in the mixer and then into the engine. This LPG is burnt with the air to create combustion in the same manner as petrol.

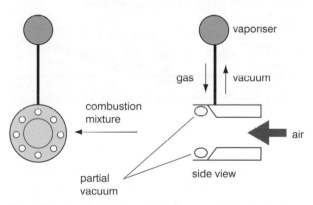

Figure 7.3 A mixer, using radial holes around the intake to create a partial vacuum to influence the vaporiser, and a suspended cone pointing into the airflow as the means of creating the partial vacuum to influence the vaporiser

The LPG systems fitted to vehicles as an aftermarket system are fairly simple in their design. As the system ages, it requires tuning to ensure that it operates at its most efficient. This is due to wear in the LPG components and engine. To overcome this issue, the system will need some alterations to create a closed-loop system.

In these closed-loop systems, the restrictor valve in the pipe between the mixer and the vaporiser (in open-loop systems this is preset by an installer) is controlled dynamically, second to second, by a stepper motor. The stepper motor position is continually monitored by the EMS through the assessment of the exhaust gas by the exhaust lambda or oxygen sensor.

The stepper motor directly alters the amount of vacuum that the vaporiser is faced with, which then controls of the amount of LPG joining the airflow into the engine. These updated types of systems are essentially self-tuning, so are able to offer the best performance and economy. A disadvantage, however, is that the cost is slightly higher, though this can be offset by the saving in the fuel. Additionally, these closed-loop systems require lambda or oxygen sensors; vehicles fitted with catalytic converters will already have these installed but vehicles without catalysts will have to have these fitted to the exhaust system.

Figure 7.4 shows an LPG system fitted to a petrol-injected vehicle. The LPG system has a large heavy-duty gas cylinder fitted to carry the LPG. This is normally fitted to the rear of the vehicle and, in some cases, fits into the spare wheel well. The tank must be able to withstand high stresses from impact if the vehicle is involved in a collision, to avoid any leakage of gas as this could create an explosion. The LPG tank is filled at a service station in the same way as a normal petrol or diesel vehicle, but with a special gas filler fitted to the gas valve fitted to the exterior of the vehicle. Only 80 per cent of the gas tank volume is utilised for gas; the remaining 20 per cent provides space for the gas to expand.

Figure 7.4 demonstrates the gas and air stream mixing together in the inlet manifold; it shows that one injector for each cylinder is used to combine the gas and air. This is not unlike the concept of multi-point fuel injection.

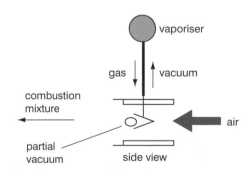

Figure 7.4 LPG system fitted to a petrol-injected vehicle

How does the system stop adding fuel when the LPG system is running?

This depends on the type of system.

Engines using carburettors have a fairly simple method to switch from petrol to LPG. This is done through a valve cutting the petrol feed to the carburettor. Engines fitted with carburettors will continue to run on petrol for a short period of time when the valve is closed, due to the small amount of fuel in the carburettor float chamber continuing to deliver fuel to the engine. The driver will notice that the engine will start to hesitate as the remaining fuel is used up and then it will switch to LPG. At this point, the engine will then start to run purely on LPG.

Engines fitted with petrol fuel injection have a simple system that cuts the signals to the electronic injectors delivering the petrol to the engine. The system intercepts the signal to the injectors and is directed to a relay. Essentially, this isolates the electrical feed to the injectors to stop them injecting petrol. At this point, the circuit is directed to a set of resistors that replicate the injectors and fool the petrol EMS into thinking that the system is still operating the injectors as normal. This type of system is known as an emulator. The emulator allows the injectors to be isolated when the LPG system is in operation to prevent fuel being injected. The emulator can also enable the injectors again later when the engine is to be run on petrol. The switching between the two systems is very quick and virtually seamless, so the driver will not notice whether the engine is running on LPG or petrol.

Table 7.1 shows the difference between using LPG and conventional petrol and diesel fuel.

Table 7.1 Comparison of LPG to petrol and diesel fuel

Compared to petrol	Compared to diesel
75% less carbon monoxide	60% less carbon monoxide
40% less oxides of nitrogen	90% less oxides of nitrogen
87% less ozone-forming potential	70% less ozone-forming potential
85% less hydrocarbons	90% fewer particulates
10% less carbon dioxide	

As the table shows, there are clear benefits from using LPG in terms of reduced emissions. LPG is also considerably cheaper to purchase. More fuel stations are now selling LPG alongside petrol and diesel, enabling more vehicles to run dual-fuel systems.

7.3 Electric

In the past, electric-driven vehicles were something that most of us wouldn't consider buying or even using. However, as concerns about the environment increase and government standards demand that manufacturers look at and use alternative energy sources, things are changing. The electric car market is now something that all manufacturers are investing

a great deal of time and research into, looking for the most cost-effective options.

The basic principle of an electric car is that it is powered by an electric motor rather than a petrol or diesel engine. If we had to try and identify an electric car from looking at the body shape and styling, then you would find it very difficult as most vehicle manufactures use their existing model variants and convert them to the electric concept. It is only when you drive the electric vehicle that you then can confirm its power source. The virtual silence from the powertrain is a major factor, but when you look under the bonnet you will see some major differences between this concept and the conventional fuel-powered vehicles.

Figure 7.5 Tesla Roadster running on pure battery power

Electric cars run purely on electrical energy generated by large battery units. These battery units are often located low down in the centre of the vehicle to improve the balance and centre of gravity of the vehicle, as they can often weigh in excess of 270 kg.

Figure 7.6 Battery unit fitted to an electric vehicle

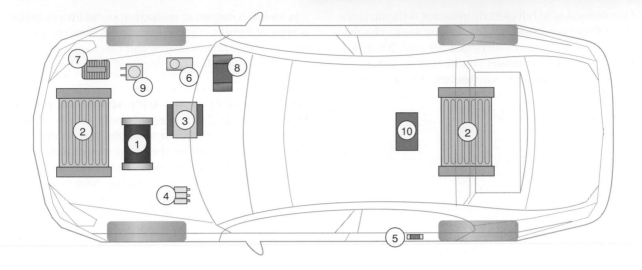

1	electric motor	6	vacuum pump
2	battery pack	7	DC/DC converter
3	motor controller	8	instrumentation
4	contactor	9	power-steering pump
5	fuse	10	battery charger

Figure 7.7 Overview of components fitted to an electric vehicle

The battery units are usually lithium-ion based, as this provides excellent range and recharging capabilities. To provide drive, the electric car has one or sometimes two large AC motors, which are capable of delivering very high torque outputs instantly. An example of this can be seen in the Tesla Roadster (Figure 7.5), which has a motor that produces 288 bhp and up to 295 lb ft (400 Nm) of torque. For this reason, some electric cars are often very quick on acceleration. The Tesla Roadster, for example, accelerates from 0–60 mph in 3.7 seconds and can reach 125 mph.

Electric cars work by taking charge from the large battery packs and passing this through a power electrics module that monitors the requirements of the vehicle's electrical demand, including the drive motor. When the driver presses the accelerator, the module will pass electrical current from the battery pack to the high torque AC motor. (See page 530 to find out how the motors work.) This electrical energy will then power the motor to the required revolutions per minute, passing drive through the single-speed gearbox to the drive wheels.

The motors are intelligent in that they will also *produce* electricity when the vehicle brakes or slows down. They change from being a motor to being a generator, much like the alternator on an engine.

Looking at a conventional car, when the car brakes or slows down the kinetic energy removed from the moving vehicle is absorbed through the braking system in the form of heat generated by the friction linings. This heat is then lost to the atmosphere. In an electric car, this slowing down and braking action is not just handled by the brakes but also by the motor acting as an additional braking element. This energy created by the motor/generator is fed back to the batteries to recharge them. Due to this process, the motor/generator relieves some of the pressure from the braking system so the brake linings will normally last longer than in a conventional car.

Figure 7.8 Motor fitted to an electric-powered vehicle

One downside of full electric vehicles is the distance that they are able to travel between charges. This currently ranges between 50 and 300 miles, depending on the model. If the car is purely for city driving and short commutes, 50–100 miles is probably suitable for most days. However, if the commute is longer and requires motorway speeds, then 300 miles may be required. Electric cars can be recharged completely in about six hours, and if done overnight can utilise lower-priced electricity. For quick top-ups, most electric cars can be fast charged for 30–40 minutes for an 80 per cent charge. Over time, we will see more and more charge points around the country, which will allow quick charges to take place while people go to work or do the shopping. This will gradually build the case for producing more pure electric vehicles.

Figure 7.9 An electric car on charge

7.4   Hybrid

In recent years, car manufacturers have been developing their versions of hybrid vehicles to meet the government's legal requirements and the overall demands of the world markets. The public's understanding for this is that unless we change to this type of technology the world will eventually run out of fossil fuels and our climate conditions will become unmanageable.

Some people will be unaware that hybrid transportation has already been in existence for many years; in fact, most people will have used or owned some form of hybrid vehicle in their day-to-day lives.

In this context, the word 'hybrid' is describing a form of transportation that combines two or more forms of power and converts this into propulsion power in a direct or indirect way. As a simple example, we can look at a moped or motorised pedal bike as being a type of hybrid. This is because it uses the petrol engine as one power source and relies on its rider to operate the pedals when required to aid the second power source.

Looking at other forms of transportation, we can quickly identify that most variants do use forms of hybrid technology. For example, our locomotive trains use a form of diesel-electric power to operate on the railways. Some towns and cities use buses that operate on overhead cables, which provide electricity to power the bus while in the inner-city area and then convert to using the diesel engine to operate in the outer-city areas. Also, vehicles such as massive mining trucks use forms of diesel-electric hybrid energy to operate in the rugged terrain conditions. Another form of transportation that uses hybrid energy is a submarine; these can be powered by diesel-electric or even nuclear-electric systems. For the motor car, the majority of today's cars are petrol-electric, but as technology advances we are now seeing diesel-electric coming to the forefront.

Figure 7.10 A hybrid vehicle

7.4.1 Hybrid core features

A hybrid car utilises the benefits of a conventional fuel engine and an electric-powered system.

Engine

A hybrid car will have the use of a conventional internal-combustion engine. The engine assembly used is normally smaller in its construction and output, but will provide more than sufficient power and meet the emission standards required for today's driving demands. In some hybrid designs, the engine is only used to run a generator to create the electrical power needed. In this concept, you will find that the engine has no link to the transmission driveline.

Fuel tank

A hybrid car will still have a conventional fuel tank to supply the fuel-powered engine. This energy storage assembly is normally smaller in its capacity for a hybrid car than a standard version used. The energy density of petrol is much higher than batteries. To explain this in simple terms, you would need approximately 453.6 kg of batteries to store the same amount of energy as 3.175 kg of fuel.

Electric motors

A hybrid car will use a very sophisticated electric motor to power the drive train. The advanced electronic control system is designed to not only use the electric motor in its true form, but to also adapt it to become a generator when it is required during its drive cycle. An example of this is when the driver demands more power to accelerate; then the motor will draw on the power from the batteries to provide this function but when the driver decelerates it will revert to become a generator to reduce the speed of the car and return the energy back into the battery assembly.

Generator

A generator is very similar to the design of an electric motor. This concept is normally seen on series hybrid variants to provide the electric power to the power the drive train.

Figure 7.11 Generator fitted to hybrid vehicle

Batteries

Battery technology for hybrid vehicles has rapidly progressed in the last few years. The battery assembly in a hybrid car is better known as the energy storage device. The battery assembly that was used on the early hybrid cars was seen to be very large and heavy, which, when located within the vehicle, took up a significant amount of luggage or occupancy space. With the technology advancement of smaller motors, generators and battery units controlled by an advanced electronic control system now maximise the output that these units can produce. Also, lithium ion in the battery cell design has greatly increased its lifespan, reduced the charging times and can take on and give up large amounts of charge depending on the driver's demands and drive cycle conditions.

Transmission

Hybrid cars normally use a conventional transmission assembly to provide the basic gear functionality. However, in recent times, some manufactures now provide the options of a constantly variable transmission (CVT) or they use electric motors to transmit the drive directly to the road wheels.

Figure 7.12 Transmission fitted to a hybrid vehicle

7.4.2 Types of hybrid systems

As previously mentioned, to produce a hybrid car you need to use two power sources. How these two power sources work in conjunction with each other can be achieved in a number of different ways. Parallel hybrid and series hybrid are the most common concepts used in today's hybrid motor cars and other forms of transportation.

Parallel hybrid

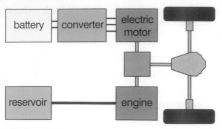

Figure 7.13 Parallel hybrid system

On a parallel hybrid (Figure 7.13) the fuel tank (reservoir) supplies the engine with the required fuel while the battery assembly will provide the energy to power the electric motor. On this system, both the engine and the electric motor can provide the power to drive the transmission at the same time, which in turn will then transmit the drive out to the driving wheels. Also as you can identify from Figure 7.13, the layout of the parallel hybrid system has two independent systems to provide the propulsion power.

Series hybrid

On a series hybrid, the generator is powered by the conventional fuel-powered engine. This then allows the generator to either power the batteries or power an electric motor, which in turn will drive the transmission. So with this layout you will identify that the fuel-powered engine never directly powers the vehicle in a conventional way. Looking at the series hybrid layout shown in Figure 7.14, you can identify that all of the components form a power source linc that is then connected to the transmission and driving wheels. Manufacturers have found that this concept provides the facility of an all-electric drive system, which can produce very low emissions and give the driver the benefit of a longer-range drive cycle than a conventional battery-powered vehicle. Using the latest battery and management technology, some manufacturers are now producing a system that achieves a distance of 50 miles running on pure battery energy, to then having the option of extending the range to approximately 350 miles when using the generator along with the battery power.

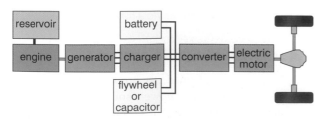

Figure 7.14 A series hybrid system

A recent example of a series hybrid vehicle is the Fisker Karma sports car (Figure 7.15).

Figure 7.15 The Fisker Karma, a series hybrid vehicle

7.4.3 Hybrid performance

Manufacturers who are producing their versions of hybrid cars have identified that the engine used to produce the power needed can be much smaller than in a conventional car and, as a result, more efficient. In a conventional production car, the engine is normally larger in size and output to generate enough power to accelerate the car effectively. Using a smaller engine and lightweight parts can improve the engine's efficiency. Also, manufacturers have found that reducing the number of cylinders and adapting the management system to operate the engine nearer its maximum load can improve the maximum torque and improve the fuel economy. In recent years of vehicle technology and development, it has been found that the smaller engine is more efficient than the much larger engine. Larger engines are much heavier in weight, so the car will have to use more energy to power the car when driving up a hill or when the driver demands to accelerate. The engine's internal components, such as the pistons, will be much larger and heavier and, again, require more energy to operate when moving up and down the cylinders. Larger engines generally have more cylinders operating and the displacement of each cylinder will be much larger, so more fuel will have to be supplied to the cylinders throughout its drive cycle.

Therefore, if we had two identical vehicles with different-sized engines, we would identify that the smaller-sized engine would achieve better mileage efficiencies. If both of the vehicles were travelling along a motorway at the same speed, the vehicle with the smaller engine will use less energy than with the larger engine. In both cases, the engines used will have to output the same amount of power to drive the vehicle, but the smaller engine will use less power to drive itself. A possible issue only arises when the smaller-engine vehicle needs to increase its power to a greater level than the larger engine when driving up an incline. A hybrid vehicle fitted with a smaller engine achieves good results when driving on roads such as motorways, but when the driver demands good acceleration or needs the additional power to drive up an incline, the vehicle needs further support.

This support is achieved by the battery and motor to provide the additional power needed to meet the driver's demands throughout the drive cycle and road conditions.

Fuel efficiency

Hybrid vehicles are designed and suited to provide the average power requirements more than the peak power requirements. As we have identified so far, a smaller engine is more suitable to power a hybrid vehicle, but there are many other factors that can improve the energy efficiency of a hybrid, or even conventional vehicles. As we live in a fast-changing world, manufacturers are always looking at new technology to improve their vehicles to meet tomorrow's environmental requirements.

A key area where significant change has taken place in recent years is to reuse the energy from the braking system. When the vehicle is in motion and you are applying pressure to the brake pedal, you are taking energy from the car. Therefore, the faster you are driving, the more kinetic energy it will generate. On operating the brake pedal, clamping pressure is applied between the linings and discs. This frictional energy will be removed and dissipate as heat. A hybrid vehicle is designed to harness some of this energy and send it to the battery assembly to be used later. This form of recapturing the energy is known as **regenerative braking** and is achieved by using the electric motor as a generator, which then charges the battery when decelerating or under certain braking conditions.

Regenerative braking: the vehicle's ability to use the retardation of the vehicle to produce electrical energy through the use of an engine or transmission-driven generator. This energy is delivered back to the vehicle's battery system to provide electrical power for the vehicle's electrical system.

A major benefit of a hybrid is that the conventional engine is only used when required during a drive cycle. The hybrid system then mainly relies on the battery and motor to be the main power sources. Also, the hybrid vehicle electronic management system can sometimes turn off the conventional powered engine at slow speeds (in traffic) or at a stop light. This key function gives the driver the benefit of running on pure battery power when they are driving in slow traffic and highly populated areas. This then reduces the emission levels and improves the vehicle's overall efficiency.

When the car is required to accelerate up to normal speed from this condition, the engine is then started by the control unit to ensure that there is enough power to bring the vehicle speed up. The starting of the engine is seamless and the driver will barely notice the change due to the engine being started through the electric motor rather than the conventional starter motor arrangement.

Another key factor in improving efficiency is to try and reduce the amount of energy used to move the vehicle through the air, or **aerodynamic drag**. To reduce some of these forces we need to improve the aerodynamics of the vehicle. Styling of the vehicle's body shape is very important if the drag forces are to be minimised. If this can be achieved, then more energy can be used to drive the vehicle more efficiently and economically.

Aerodynamic drag: friction created by the vehicle's body as it passes through the air. If excessive, this frictional drag can slow the vehicle down and create higher fuel consumption and emissions.

When considering a vehicle's design, the manufacturers always try to keep the overall weight to a minimum. This is important to all types of vehicles but especially to the hybrid variants. It is vital that the overall weight of a hybrid vehicle is kept as low as possible to ensure that the efficiency of the hybrid system is not lost in propelling a heavy vehicle. A hybrid vehicle must preserve its energy to use it efficiently throughout its drive cycles. By using composite materials such as carbon fibre, or lightweight metals such as aluminium or magnesium, it is possible to decrease the overall weight while still meeting the crash safety standards.

Another key factor is the type of tyre compound used, which can optimise the efficiency of a hybrid vehicle. The tyres are designed to give a smooth ride, reduce road noise and enable good traction throughout its drive cycle and different road conditions. This, you could say, is the same for any vehicle tyre, but the main difference is that the hybrid tyres are designed to be stiffer in their construction and are inflated to a higher pressure. This helps cut down the drag by about half of what a conventional tyre would produce.

Figure 7.16 Energy-efficient tyres help to reduce drag

Table 7.2 Benefits and limitations of hybrid vehicles

Benefits	Limitations
Lower running costs of the vehicle due to less fuel being used and longer service intervals	Premium price on purchase due to the use of new technologies and materials
More reliability due to less stress on engine and transmission parts and the use of non-service electrical motors	Lifetime on battery unit is around 100,000 miles and batteries are expensive to replace and recycle
No or very little pollution through exhaust emissions	Range of travel can be limiting due to the battery requiring recharging every 50–300 miles dependent on vehicle
Quieter due to the vehicle running on electrical motors improving the impact of noise pollution from current production cars	Performance could be limited on some smaller vehicles due to the size of motors
Overnight charging using lower-rate electricity further improving on the costs of travel and impact on power stations	Weight of the vehicle can be very high due to the weight of the battery and motors
Reduced oil consumption due to low fuel usage and high miles per gallon	Temperature control of the driver and passengers can impact on the range due to running additional electronic systems, such as air-conditioning compressors to keep passengers cool
Lower overall emissions due to the use of electrical drive, high miles per gallon and lower impact on power stations through overnight charging	Recharging time may impact on the use of the vehicle, as most cars need 4–6 hours to fully recharge

All of these efficiency savings enable hybrid vehicles to generally drive much like the conventional fuelled equivalent, but with the savings on fuel and lower emissions. Many manufacturers are now producing sports cars based on hybrid technology. In some cases, power outputs can be over 400 bhp and, due to the instant torque available from electric motors, torque outputs can be over 900 lb ft (1220 Nm).

7.4.4 Hybrid benefits and limitations

A fully powered series hybrid electric car has some key benefits, but it does have its limitations. The choice of whether or not to have a hybrid car comes down to what suits each individual and the drive cycle that is done on a day-to-day basis.

7.5 Fuel cell

Hybrid and electric technology is helping us to find sustainable routes to powering transport into the future. However, these can only be an interim solution to the problem due to the continued requirement for petrol or diesel in the case of the hybrid vehicles, and electricity produced by power stations using fossil fuels in the case of fully electric vehicles.

Scientists are therefore continuing to search for alternative energy sources for automotive applications and there seems to be some hope in the use of fuel-cell

technology. One of the biggest benefits is that fuel cells run purely on hydrogen, so they produce only water as a waste product.

7.5.1 Principles of fuel cells for automotive application

The fuel-cell vehicle (FCV) seems to be the most logical step in developing vehicles that can significantly assist in lowering the amount of fossil fuels the world is consuming to power the vehicles in use today. The fuel-cell vehicle will also help in combating the climatic changes that the petrol and diesel type vehicles are perceived to be causing through CO_2 emissions. The hydrogen fuel-cell engine runs on hydrogen gas instead of regular petrol or diesel and emits only water. This type of vehicle is still in the early phase of development, but one manufacturer has released a small number of vehicles to test the feasibility.

From the look of the FCV, you could be mistaken in thinking that it was merely a modern conventional internal-combustion engine. Underneath the exterior, the vehicle is highly advanced with many components and technologies not seen in any current production vehicle. The main difference is obviously the fuel-cell arrangement called a fuel-cell stack. The fuel-cell stack converts the hydrogen gas stored in a high strength tank, with oxygen to create electricity to power the electric motor, which drives the vehicle. Figure 7.17 shows the main components that comprise a FCV.

Figure 7.17 Fuel-cell vehicle

7.5.2 How do fuel cells work?

The fuel cell is a catalyst for a chemical reaction to take place, combining the hydrogen and oxygen to produce electricity. These are called polymer **electrolyte** membrane (PEM) or proton exchange membrane fuel cells.

Electrolyte: a substance that conducts charged particles.

The fuel cells used in FCVs are able to produce about 1.16 V of electricity; this is obviously not enough to power the vehicle, which requires around 400V for the electric motor. To provide enough electrical power for the vehicle motor, hundreds of cells are packed together to provide a fuel-cell stack. The potential power produced by the fuel-cell stack is dependent on the size and number of individual cells, along with the surface area of the part of the fuel-cell stack called the PEM.

Fuel cells used in FCVs are extremely efficient, especially when compared with conventional combustion engines. The hydrogen used in FCVs is obtained from a variety of sources. When pure hydrogen is used, the fuel cell will emit water and heat alone; this provides one of the cleanest forms of transport that will help alleviate the very real concerns of climate change due to the emission of greenhouse gases such as CO_2.

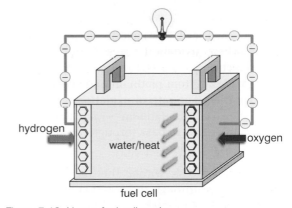

Figure 7.18 How a fuel cell works

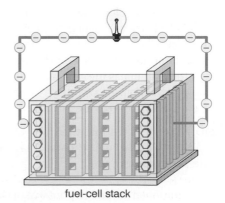

Figure 7.19 Fuel-cell stack showing PEM

PEM fuel cell

The main type of fuel cell used in FCVs is the PEM fuel cell. The construction of the PEM-type fuel cell consists of a electrolyte membrane lodged between an anode, which is a negative electrode, and a cathode, which is the positive electrode. The PEM is an organic compound with a similar consistency to regular clingfilm. The main function of the PEM is to be an electrolyte that attracts the positive protons and not electrons. This provides a means for the fuel cell to conduct electricity. The PEM has to be kept moist in order to allow the protons to conduct through its surface.

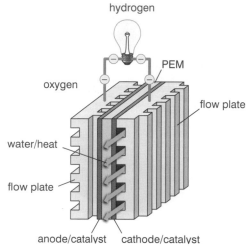

Figure 7.20 Fuel-cell stack showing PEM, anode and cathode

Within the fuel cell, the anode is the negative electrode where **oxidation** takes place. Oxidation is when electrons are lost from the fuel cell. The anode is made up from platinum and supported by carbon particles. The rate of oxidation is increased through the use of platinum – a catalyst. The hydrogen fuel is able to pass through the anode as it is characteristically porous.

Oxidation: a process within the fuel cell when electrons are lost through the reaction between the hydrogen fuel and the anode.

At the cathode (positive electrode), the opposite takes place and the electrons are gained through a process called **reduction**. Like the anode, the cathode is also made up of platinum and supported by carbon particles, and similarly the platinum is the catalyst that speeds up the process of reduction. As per the hydrogen to the anode, oxygen passes through the porous cathode.

Reduction: a process within the fuel cell where electrons are gained through the reaction between the cathode and hydrogen fuel.

Flow plates (positioned around the outside of the PEM, anode and cathode) fulfil several essential functions:

- Provide a channel for hydrogen and oxygen to the electrodes
- Move heat and water away from the fuel cell
- Provide a means for electrodes to be conducted from the anode into the electrical circuit, and then from the electrical circuit back to the cathode

At the anode, the hydrogen fuel (H) is separated by the use of the catalyst: the negatively charged electrons are separated from the positively charged protons. The PEM allows the positively charged protons to pass through to the cathode but prevents the negatively charged electrons from moving through. An electrical current is formed when these negatively charged electrons flow around the PEM by way of an external circuit.

At the cathode stage, the electrons, which are negatively charged, are combined with the protons, which are positively charged, and oxygen to create water (H_2O) and heat. This is the total emission from a FCV.

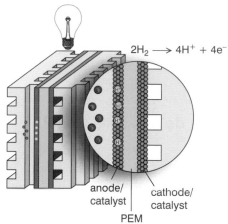

$$2H_2 \longrightarrow 4H^+ + 4e^-$$

Catalyst separates the hydrogen's negatively charged electrons from the positively charged protons

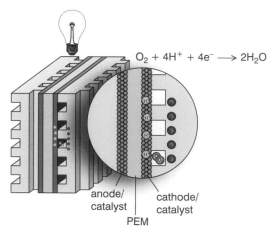

$$O_2 + 4H^+ + 4e^- \longrightarrow 2H_2O$$

Negatively charged electrons must flow around the membrane through an external circuit. This flow of electrons forms the electrical current

Figure 7.21 Image showing the electron flow and current movement

Table 7.3 Summary of fuel-cell technology advantages and disadvantages.
(Reproduced with permission from www.fueleconomy.gov)

Advantages	
Fewer greenhouse gas emissions	Petrol and diesel-powered vehicles emit greenhouse gases, mostly carbon dioxide (CO_2), that contribute to global climate change. FCVs powered by pure hydrogen emit no emissions from their tailpipe, only heat and water. Producing the hydrogen to power FCVs *can* generate emissions, depending on the production method, but much less than that emitted by conventional petrol and diesel vehicles.
Less air pollution	Production vehicles emit a significant share of the air pollutants that contribute to emissions and harmful particulates in the world. FCVs powered by pure hydrogen emit no harmful pollutants. If the hydrogen is produced from fossil fuels, some pollutants are produced, but much less than the amount generated by conventional vehicle tailpipe emissions.
Reduced oil dependence	FCVs could reduce our dependence on oil, since hydrogen can be derived from domestic sources, such as natural gas and coal, as well as renewable resources such as water. This would make our economy less dependent on other countries and less vulnerable to oil price shocks from an increasingly volatile oil market.
Disadvantages	
On-board hydrogen storage	Some FCVs store enough hydrogen to travel as far as petrol and diesel vehicles between fill-ups, this is about 300 miles. However, the storage systems are still too large, heavy and expensive.
Vehicle cost	FCVs are currently too expensive to compete with hybrids and conventional petrol and diesel vehicles. Manufacturers must bring down production costs, especially the costs of the fuel-cell stack and hydrogen storage.
Fuel-cell durability and reliability	Fuel-cell systems are not yet as durable as internal-combustion engines and do not perform as well in extreme environments, such as in sub-freezing temperatures
Getting hydrogen to customers	The extensive system used to deliver petrol and diesel from refineries to local filling stations cannot be used for hydrogen. New facilities and systems must be constructed for producing, transporting and dispensing hydrogen to customers.
Competition with other technologies	Manufacturers are still improving the efficiency of petrol- and diesel-powered engines. Hybrids are gaining popularity and advances in battery technology are making plug-in hybrids and electric vehicles more attractive. FCVs will have to offer customers a viable alternative, especially in terms of performance, durability and cost, to survive in this ultra-competitive automotive market.
Safety	Hydrogen, like any fuel, has safety risks and must be handled with caution. We are familiar with gasoline, but handling compressed hydrogen will be new to most of us. Therefore, developers must optimise new fuel storage and delivery systems for safe everyday use and customers must become familiar with hydrogen's properties and risks.
Public acceptance	Fuel-cell technology must be embraced by customers before its benefits can be realised. Customers may have concerns about the dependability and safety of these vehicles, just as they did with hybrids.

FCVs can obviously provide real benefits to our environment and the way in which we travel in the near future. With many manufacturers already running low numbers of production vehicles testing this technology, it will not be long before we see more of these interesting types of vehicles on our roads.

As can be seen in Table 7.3, there are many challenges in creating FCVs that are both reliable and economical before the FCV is a real option for customers. There is no doubt that the FCV will provide an economical means of transport in the future, achieving the ultimate goal of zero harmful emissions.

Figure 7.22 FCV storage tank

Honda FCX Clarity fuel-cell car operation

The Honda FCX Clarity is the result of a massive investment of resources and money from Honda. This vehicle provides real innovation in its power plant to give excellent and efficient performance across all types of driving conditions. The fuel-cell stack provides the main source of electrical energy and is combined with a powerful lithium-ion battery, which acts to harvest the electrical energy produced by the fuel-cell operation. When the Clarity is started from a standstill or is required to accelerate quickly, the fuel-cell action and the power from the lithium-ion battery will combine to produce enhanced vehicle performance. As we have seen in hybrid vehicles, the drive motor alternates between being a motor and generator. During deceleration, the motor becomes a generator and creates electrical energy that is stored in the lithium-ion battery – that is, brake regeneration. When the FCX Clarity is stationary, the stop system will shut down the fuel-cell stack operation and it will rely on the electrical energy stored in the lithium-ion battery to maintain operation of the vehicle's auxiliary equipment, such as air conditioning. The FCX Clarity continually monitors the power generation to provide highly efficient power generation and storage.

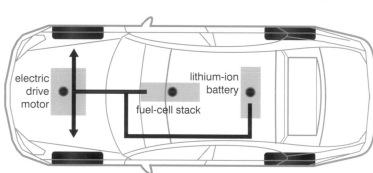

Figure 7.23 Power supplied to the motor from the fuel-cell stack is supplemented with electricity from the battery for powerful acceleration

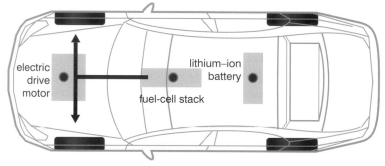

Figure 7.24 Vehicle operates on electricity from the fuel-cell stack alone for fuel-efficient high-speed cruising

Figure 7.25 The motor acts as a generator, converting the kinetic energy normally wasted as heat during braking into electricity for storage into the battery, which also stores excess electricity produced by the fuel-cell stack

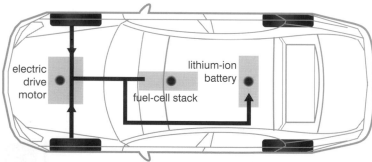

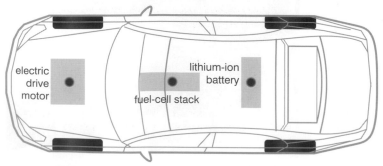

Figure 7.26 The auto idle stop system shuts down electrical generation in the fuel-cell stack. The lithium-ion battery supplies energy for air conditioning and other electrical devices

7.6 Vehicle park assist

Today vehicles carry more and more technology to assist the driver in operating the vehicle both more efficiently and safely. Some manufacturers are now introducing park assist to their vehicles to help the driver manoeuvre their vehicle into suitable parking spaces. This is becoming increasingly popular as vehicle designs alter to be more aerodynamic and aesthetically pleasing, but with a limited rear view and ability to assess vehicle proportions.

The vehicle park assist system works by utilising the following key components to assess the parking space area and then manoeuvres the vehicle into the parking space:

- Electronic power-assisted steering (EPAS) rack
- Rear parking sensors
- Park assist control module
- Park assist switch
- Left-hand park assist sensor
- Front parking sensors
- Right-hand park assist sensor
- ABS
- Audio system
- Display

The park assist system operation is as follows:

1 As the driver travels below 18 mph along a row of parked vehicles and activates the system to 'find' a parking space, the ultrasound parking sensors will scan the spaces for a parking space big enough to park the vehicle. When the park assist system detects a space big enough it will alert the driver through a graphical representation on the instrument panel.

2 If the driver accepts the parking space identified, the driver will stop the vehicle after the space and select reverse gear and also let go of the steering wheel. The park assist system will then inform the driver of the intended path that the vehicle will take during the parking manoeuvre through the graphical display on the instrument panel.

3 The driver will then provide engine power to reverse the vehicle at a set speed monitored by the system. The park assist system will steer the vehicle with the EPAS and manoeuvre it into the parking space by monitoring the front, rear and sides of the vehicle through the ultrasound sensors. The driver will continue to operate the accelerator and clutch if it is a manual vehicle and also apply the brake when the tone from the parking sensors dictates or the message is displayed in the instrument panel. The vehicle

may require up to five manoeuvres to position the vehicle correctly. When the park assist system registers the position of the vehicle is correct, the system will inform the driver that the park assist is finished and select neutral or park position on the transmission.

Figure 7.27 shows the park assist process from start to finish.

a) *Park assist system activated and searching for parking space.*

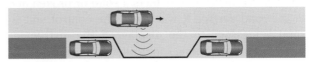

b) *Park assist system detects a space and measures it for size compared to the vehicle.*

c) *The vehicle is positioned at the end of the space to start next stage of parking.*

d) *Driver selects reverse gear and starts reversing the vehicle into the parking space whilst the park assist controls the steering of the vehicle.*

e) *Driver selects forward gear to position the vehicle in the parking space.*

f) *Driver selects reverse gear again to complete the parking manoeuvre.*

Figure 7.27 Park assist process

7.7 Lane departure warning system

The lane departure warning system is designed to prevent drivers from straying from the traffic lane, either into the adjacent lane or off the road in the event that the driver loses concentration.

The lane departure warning system works by utilising a series of infrared sensors mounted in the front of the vehicle, which point down at the road surface. The job of the sensors is to monitor the road surface, especially at both front corners, to detect road markings that depict where the lane boundary finishes. The system will detect the lane boundary to the right and left of the vehicle to avoid veering into oncoming traffic or off the road.

As soon as the system detects a solid or broken line in the road surface it will signal the control unit to send a message to the display on the instrument panel, sound a warning tone and also, in some cases, vibrate the driver seat base to alert the driver that the vehicle is veering off the road lane.

The lane departure warning system does not interact with the vehicle's controls but purely warns and alerts the driver to make corrections to the vehicle's path. This system can be turned off by the driver at any time if it not required, but in many cases will automatically switch on again when the vehicle is started.

Figure 7.28 shows the vehicle travelling along the road with the road sensors monitoring the markings on the road surface.

7.8 Blind spot information system (BLIS)

Blind spot information system (BLIS) is an additional safety system that monitors the area behind the vehicle, which is often out of sight by the driver (their blind spot).

BLIS incorporates camera sensors located in the vehicle's door mirrors, which point towards the rear of the vehicle (Figure 7.29) and a control unit to receive the data from the sensors. This data is calculated by the control unit and will warn the driver through a display message on the instrument panel if there is a vehicle within the blind spot area. This prevents the driver from pulling out into the adjacent lane into the path of a vehicle, such as a motorcycle, which was not seen in the door mirror. The sensors used on the latest systems are small digital cameras that are able to take 25 images per second. The control unit will assess each frame taken and will be able to determine if there is a vehicle in the blind spot area.

Figure 7.29 BLIS in operation

Figure 7.28 Lane departure warning system in operation

The system is programmed so that it does not react to lampposts, parked cars and road barriers, to prevent any unnecessary warnings for the driver. If the visibility behind the vehicle is poor or the camera lens is dirty, the system will warn the driver that the system is not in operation.

7.9 Adaptive cruise control (ACC)

For many years vehicle manufacturers have produced their cars with a cruise control system. They are more commonly found on automatic variants to provide the driver with an additional level of driving comfort throughout the journey by being able to set the speed that they would prefer to drive at when driving along motorways and major road networks.

In recent years, vehicle manufacturers have designed an additional function to the conventional cruise control system. The system is known as adaptive cruise control (ACC) and is designed to use a forward-looking radar sensor that scans the oncoming road ahead, looking for objects that are moving at a different speed to the vehicle. When a target is identified, the ACC system will monitor the time gap between the host and the target vehicle. When that gap falls below a preset driver level, the cruise system will intervene, slowing the vehicle down by backing off the throttle and/or applying the brakes in a controlled manner until the correct gap is attained. The driver has the option to set the speed that they want to travel at and can also programme the system via the vehicle multi-function system and the vehicle instrument pack to set the preferred distance.

The ACC system will detect but will not react to the following:

- Vehicles in the oncoming lane
- Stationary vehicles
- Pedestrians
- Vehicles not in the same lane

The ACC system is active when the vehicle is moving at a minimum speed of around 20 mph (32 km/h) and a maximum speed of around 112 mph (180 km/h). The ACC system is not a collision-warning system and will not override driver inputs of brake or throttle pedal activities. It is very important to remember that this system is designed to provide the driver with additional support during a prolonged journey and in a suitable driving situation, and must not be seen as a system that removes the responsibility of the driver to drive safely at all times.

7.9.1 Radar sensing

The radar sensor is normally located within the front bumper or grill area of the vehicle. The sensor transmits a wide beam forward of the vehicle and covers a range of approximately 130 m (426.5 ft). The radar module monitors the transmitted signal continuously and calculates the changes in the frequency to identify the oncoming objects. This information is then transmitted back to the instrument panel via warning symbols to notify the driver of the oncoming object or possible change in speed.

7.9.2 Cruise 'active'

On activating the ACC system via the steering wheel control buttons, a cruise control 'active' warning symbol will appear in the instrument cluster. This warning symbol will stay on unless the driver deactivates the ACC system.

7.9.3 Follow mode

When the driver has activated the ACC and the preferred speed has been chosen, the vehicle will continue at the selected speed until the radar identifies an oncoming object. On identifying the target object, the ACC module will illuminate the 'follow mode' symbol (Figure 7.30), to notify the driver of a possible oncoming hazard, and monitor the distance between the two vehicles. Depending on the gap setting programmed by the driver, the system will only intervene if the parameters are not met. This is done by throttle intervention and by applying the brakes in a controlled manner to maintain the programmed set gap. If a number of vehicles are within the radar's window then the system will choose the nearest vehicle as its target. Or if the target vehicle changes lane, then the system will continue to monitor and adapt the vehicle's speed and distance accordingly, within a controlled timescale.

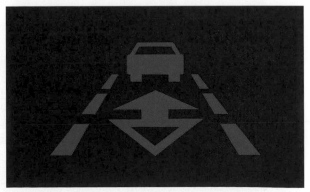

Figure 7.30 Follow mode symbol

7.9.4 Forward alert

Forward alert is an additional support functionality that the driver can have switched on or off during the use of ACC. This secondary support system provides the driver with a warning symbol that appears within the instrument cluster (Figure 7.31) and also transmits an audible sound to warn the driver of the possible oncoming hazard and/or a message is transmitted onto the message centre. The forward alert system uses the radar to track the oncoming object and provides the driver with support by applying the brakes in a controlled manner or throttle intervention.

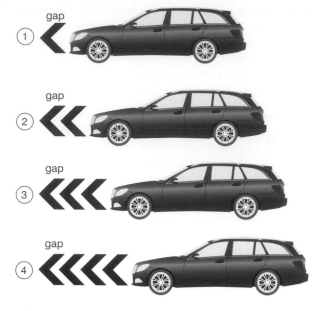

1 gap setting = 1 second
2 gap setting = 1.4 seconds
3 gap setting = 1.8 seconds
4 gap setting = 2.2 seconds

Figure 7.33 Time gap setting display of ACC system

Figure 7.31 Forward alert symbol

Within the instrument cluster (Figure 7.32) the driver has the option to adjust the gap setting to their preferred distance. The setting switch allows the driver to adjust the time gap to one of four preset time gaps. The selected time gap is displayed in the vehicle message centre, as shown in Figure 7.33.

Any driver intervention, by applying the brakes or increasing throttle position, will deactivate the system until the reset button is selected.

System restrictions

The ACC system is only intended to provide the driver with enhanced speed control during the journey, but is subject to monitored conditions. Figure 7.34 shows circumstances where the ACC system may brake late

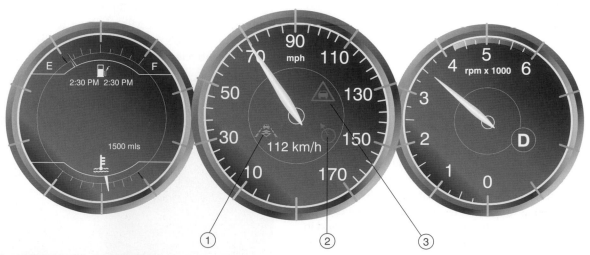

1 adaptive cruise control/follow mode active (amber)
2 cruise control active (green)
3 forward alert active (green)

Figure 7.32 Instrument display showing ACC symbols

or unexpectedly. The driver is required to intervene in these situations:

1 Driving on a different line to the vehicle in front.
2 Vehicles that merge into the same lane are only detected once they have moved fully into the lane and the radar has identified the object's speed and distance.
3 On bends in the road, there can be issues with the direction of the vehicle in front, and when going into and coming out of the bend.

It should be noted that the ACC system is not a collision warning or avoidance system. Driver intervention will be needed if an emergency situation occurs.

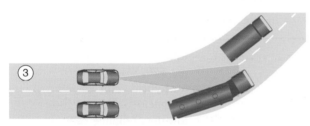

Figure 7.34 Situations that could cause ACC system to brake late or unexpectedly

7.10 Navigation system

The navigation system provides the driver with audible and visual route guidance information to enable the driver to reach a desired destination. The system allows the driver to choose the desired route using minor or major roads or motorways and also gives the driver the options for choosing the quickest or shortest route. In addition to these options, the system also provides the driver with directions to hospitals, fuel stations, hotels and other amenities.

The navigation map software is either stored within an electronic module or on a DVD and inserted into a reader device. Navigation map images are then transmitted onto a visual LCD screen and, in later versions, a touch screen. Map software information gives the driver audible route guidance on the programmed journey, as well as visual images

showing digital two-dimensional or three-dimensional map directions and approaching junctions.

For the navigation system to operate, it needs a network of satellites that transmit signals to receiver equipment on the earth's surface. Known as the global positioning system (GPS), at least 30 satellites are circulating around the earth's orbit. At least 24 satellites will be in operation at any one time, with the reserve satellites ready for activity if called upon. A vehicle's satellite system will receive signals from several satellites at any one time. On average, a moving vehicle will have a minimum of four and possibly six to eight satellites tracking its movement. This information is combined with navigation mapping software to establish the exact position of the vehicle in relation to latitude and longitude, and to calculate the distance travelled and the distance to complete the journey very accurately, often down to several meters.

More recent satellite navigation systems provide the driver with off-road functionalities and traffic message information. By entering map coordinates, the driver is given the option of undertaking more challenging routes across rough terrain, as long as their vehicle is designed for this purpose. More commonly found is the traffic messaging system, which can notify the driver of delays on planned routes and also give them the option of a preferred route to choose.

Figure 7.35 A 2D navigation system (top) and a 3D navigation system (bottom)

Index

Acknowledgements

The author and the publisher would like to thank the following for permission to reproduce material:

Alamy: 1.26 (RJH_RF); 2.371 (David R. Frazier Photolibrary Inc.); **AP Racing**: 4.149; 4.151; 4.154; **Beissbarth (UK) Ltd**: 4.23; 4.61; 4.127; 4.128; 5.96; **Bike It**: 2.231; **BMW**: 2.203; **Calex**: 2.194; 4.123; **Car Bench**: 1.42; **Carbibles.com**: 4.25b; **Chris Newton**: 1.52; 2.236; 3.153; 4.176; 5.36; 5.73; 5.74b; 6.5; **Corbis**: 2.134 and 2.340 (Car Culture); **Cosworth**: 2.24; 2.41; 2.43; 2.53; 2.55; 2.58; 2.62; 2.114; 2.120a; 2.120b; 2.182; **Fisker Automotive**: 7.6; 7.15; **Ford**: 4.107; **Forge Motorsport**: 2.192; 2.193; **Fotolia**: 5.26b; **Fotosearch**: 2.21; 3.105; **Garmin Ltd**: 7.34a; 7.34b; **Greengate Publishing Services**: 5.32; **Honda**: 1.19; 1.47; 1.48; 7.0; 7.1a; 7.1b; 7.10; 7.11; 7.12; 7.17; 7.22; **IStockphoto**: 1.7; 1.8; 1.20; 1.22; 1.23; 1.31; 1.33; 1.34; 2.29; 2.61; 2.91; 2.108; 2.131; 2.133; 2.186b; 2.217; 2.259; 2.278; 2.296; 2.309a; 2.326; 2.370a; 2.370b; 2.373; 2.376; 2.377; 2.386; 3.1; 3.10b; 3.157; 5.0; 5.7b; 5.26a; 5.33; 5.34; 5.80; 5.83b; 5.104; 5.105; 5.106; 5.110; 5.114; 6.0; 6.8; 6.9; 6.10; 6.11; 6.12a; 6.12b; **Jaguar**: 2.1; 3.101a; 5.72; 5.113; **Javad Shadzi/034Motorsport**: 2.219; **Land Rover**: 1.21; 1.24; 1.25; 2.39a; 2.50; 2.208; 2.209; 2.210; 2.339; 3.97; 3.142; 4.49; 4.173; 4.174; 4.175; 5.42; 5.66; 5.74a; 5.75; **NetGain Motors**: 7.8; **Omitec Ltd**: 2.325; 2.330; 2.380; 4.48; 5.84; 5.85a; 5.85b; **Peugeot**: 2.190; 3.15; 4.109; **PRC Racing**: 2.136; 2.178b; **Rex Features**: 2.213; **Sealy Tools**: 4.129; 4.165; **Shutterstock**: 3.48 and 3.100 (Gordon Milic); 5.7 (REDAV); 5.30 (Maksim Toome); 5.35a (Michael Thompson); 5.63 (Petar Ivanov Ishmiriev); **SPAX Racing**: 4.73; **Stobart Group**: 1.29; 1.30; **Tesla Motors**: 7.5; 7.9; **TSX**: 4.15; **Volkswagen**: 2.10; 2.22; 2.181; **Volvo Cars UK Ltd**: 1.0a; 1.0b; 1.4; 1.6; 1.9; 1.15a; 1.15b; 1.17; 1.18; 1.38; 1.39; 1.45; 1.46; 1.49; 1.50; 1.53; 1.54; 1.55; 2.0; 2.71; 2.88; 2.107; 2.169a; 2.169b; 2.179; 2.285; 2.331; 2.338; 3.75; 4.0; 4.7a; 4.7b; 4.10; 4.64; 4.97; 4.106; 4.108; 4.110; 4.113a; 4.113b; 4.114a; 4.114b; 4.116; 4.117a; 4.117b; 4.118; 4.135; 4.153; 4.177; 4.178; 5.107; 5.108; 5.109; 7.16; 7.28; 7.29; **Wikipedia**: 3.102 (Anslaton); 3.103; **Z Cars**: 2.15.

Every effort has been made to contact the copyright holders and we apologise if any have been overlooked. Should copyright have been unwittingly infringed in this publication, the owners should contact the publishers, who will make the correction at reprint.